WORD BIBLICAL COMMENTARY

WORD BIBLICAL COMMENTARY

Volume 24

Isaiah 1–33

(Revised Edition)

JOHN D. W. WATTS

THOMAS NELSON
Since 1798

NASHVILLE DALLAS MEXICO CITY RIO DE JANEIRO

The following have generously given permission to use material from copyrighted works. The Chronological Chart of Reigns 755–700 B.C. is reprinted from *Synchronizing Hebrew Originals from Available Records* by permission of Mervin Stiles, the author. Copyright 1972 by Stiles. Substantial portions of J. D. W. Watts's "Jerusalem: An Example of War in a Walled City (Isaiah 3—4)," from *'Every City Shall Be Forsaken': Urbanism and Prophecy in Ancient Israel and the Near East*, ed. L. L. Grabbe and R. D. Haak, have been reproduced as *Excursus: Jerusalem—An Example of War in a Walled City*. Permission granted by Sheffield Academic Press. Copyright 2001.

Word Biblical Commentary
ISAIAH 1–33

Library of Congress Cataloging-in-Publication Data
Main entry under title:

Word biblical commentary.

Includes bibliographies.
1. Bible—Commentaries—Collected works.
BS491.2.W67 220.7′7 80–71768
ISBN 0–7852–5010–7 (v. 24, rev. edition) AACR2

Printed in Mexico

In the body of the commentary, Scripture quotations marked NRSV are from the New Revised Standard Version of the Bible, copyright 1989 by the Division of Christian Education of the National Council of the Churches of Christ in the USA, and are used by permission. Those marked NIV are from the New International Version of the Bible, copyright © 1973 by New York Bible Society International. The author's own translation of the text appears in italic type under the heading *Translation*.

The Graeca, Hebraica, and TranslitLS fonts used to print this work are available from Linguist's Software, Inc., P.O. Box 580, Edmonds, WA 98020-0580 USA; tel. (206) 775-1130.

ISBN: 978-0-7852-5010-4

To

my colleagues in Isaiah studies, whose names fill these volumes.
Your attention to this prophetic book
has made these decades some of the most productive in scholarly history.

Contents

Essays and Tables

EXCURSUSES

PART I

PART II

STRANDS

PART I

PART II

ILLUSTRATIONS

Editorial Preface

The launching of the Word Biblical Commentary brings to fulfillment an enterprise of several years' planning. The publishers and the members of the editorial board met in 1977 to explore the possibility of a new commentary on the books of the Bible that would incorporate several distinctive features. Prospective readers of these volumes are entitled to know what such features were intended to be; whether the aims of the commentary have been fully achieved time alone will tell.

First, we have tried to cast a wide net to include as contributors a number of scholars from around the world who not only share our aims, but are in the main engaged in the ministry of teaching in university, college, and seminary. They represent a rich diversity of denominational allegiance. The broad stance of our contributors can rightly be called evangelical, and this term is to be understood in its positive, historic sense of a commitment to Scripture as divine revelation and to the truth and power of the Christian gospel.

Then, the commentaries in our series are all commissioned and written for the purpose of inclusion in the Word Biblical Commentary. Unlike several of our distinguished counterparts in the field of commentary writing, there are no translated works, originally written in a non-English language. Also, our commentators were asked to prepare their own rendering of the original biblical text and to use the biblical languages as the basis of their own comments and exegesis. What may be claimed as distinctive with this series is that it is based on the biblical languages, yet it seeks to make the technical and scholarly approach to a theological understanding of Scripture understandable by—and useful to—the fledgling student, the working minister, and colleagues in the guild of professional scholars and teachers as well.

Finally, a word must be said about the format of the series. The layout, in clearly defined sections, has been consciously devised to assist readers at different levels. Those wishing to learn about the textual witnesses on which the translation is offered are invited to consult the section headed *Notes.* If the readers' concern is with the state of modern scholarship on any given portion of Scripture, they should turn to the sections on *Bibliography* and *Form/Structure/Setting.* For a clear exposition of the passage's meaning and its relevance to the ongoing biblical revelation, the *Comment* and concluding *Explanation* are designed expressly to meet that need. There is therefore something for everyone who may pick up and use these volumes.

If these aims come anywhere near realization, the intention of the editors will have been met, and the labor of our team of contributors rewarded.

Author's Preface [to the First Edition]

First, dear reader, a word to you. My often crudely literal translations of this magnificent literature are a poor way to introduce you to the polished literary art, the insightful vision, and penetrating truth of Isaiah's Vision. But it seems the best thing to do. I hope it opens to you the doors of understanding that it has opened to me.

Appreciation is in order for the basic books which make work of this kind possible. BDB and GKC are still indispensable foundations in lexicography and grammar. No one has yet found the way to bring newer insights of Northwest Semitic grammar into handbook form to replace them. The excellent recent texts from which we work, *BHS,* Rahlfs, and Ziegler's LXX, now with the new Jerusalem Bible's text, deserve our acclaim and thanks. To these must be added the dictionaries, atlases, histories, commentaries, and monographs that are cited.

The monumental commentary by Hans Wildberger, to whom this volume is dedicated, has summarized the critical analysis and comment of more than a century of historical critical study. I have made extensive use of its textual notes, and to a lesser degree its form-critical analyses. Because his work takes a very different literary approach to the book, much of the other excellent material in his and other commentaries has not received the notice that it should. The reader is referred to it (hopefully in an English translation soon), to Clements, and to Kaiser for help in tracking the origins and roots of the Isaianic literature which the work of the last century has traced so thoroughly. To my father, J. Wash Watts, to whom the second volume will be dedicated, must go my thanks for an introduction to the study of the Hebrew Scriptures and for the insights that all such study must look for teaching about God. And to my son, James W. Watts, my father's namesake, who has progressed to a point in his studies at which he can share in this enterprise, my thanks for his careful work in preparing the manuscript for the printer. To Professor Leslie C. Allen and President David A. Hubbard, my gratitude is recorded for their careful reading of the full manuscript and the many suggestions which improve the work in many ways.

And to students and colleagues who have shared various stages of the way toward this book, my appreciation and gratitude. Students at Fuller and Southern have endured lectures that "tried out" fledgling ideas for this work and then produced discussion and papers that have added to and corrected much of it. Those who have produced dissertations are recognized in the bibliographies and notes. I have reluctantly passed over such recognition for most others in the interest of limiting references to those that the reader can find and use. I am grateful to my colleague, J. J. Owens, for permission to use the manuscript of his *Maphteah on Isaiah,* which has saved much time in finding words and forms in the lexica, and to all others who spoke encouragingly after hearing papers in SBL and IBR concerning the first steps in this project.

It has been both a surprise and an encouragement to find how many are walking parallel paths to mine in seeking a better understanding of this great book. The work of the late William Brownlee, of Avraham Gileadi, of Roy Melugin, and of W. H. Irwin is only a part of a common movement toward the attempt to establish the wholeness and meaningfulness of the book. It is a privilege to walk with them and hopefully to add a little something to what they have done.

The list of those whose support has made possible this work, the typists, family members, seminary administrations, and librarians, grows far too long to be listed individually. But they are no less important and appreciated.

Most of all, gratitude must be given to God, who has granted life and health, a relatively peaceful time to work, and life-long opportunities to learn among his people. His is the center of this Vision, and he imparts through it a knowledge of himself, of his work, of his counsel, and of the immeasurable patience with which he continues through the generations, even to our own, to work out his will with peoples who are more rebellious than willing, more blind than seeing, more deaf than hearing, more self-willed than understanding. But in his determined strategy he pursues the goal of founding the new city to which the peoples of the earth may come, all who are meek and lowly of mind, to worship the Living God who teaches truth, who gives life, and who upholds justice and righteousness.

If through this work a door is opened to someone to see God in Isaiah's Vision, it will have achieved its goal.

JOHN D. W. WATTS

Louisville, Kentucky
Spring 1984

Author's Preface to the Second Edition

The opportunity to issue a revised edition of this commentary allowed me to make necessary changes and to bring the work up to date by adding recognition of new literature.

The essential recognition of the poetic and dramatic nature of Isaiah remains. But much about the way the commentary structures the material is different. The first edition's use of generations of kings to chronologically arrange all sixty-six chapters went beyond the book's historical references and did not achieve the unity for the book that I had hoped.

Instead, this edition uses insights that have emerged from more recent published studies to present a new literary view of the book. The literary integrity of the different acts (Isa 5:1–12:6; 13:1–27:13; 28:1–33:24; 34:1–49:4; 49:5–54:17*b;* 54:17*c*–61:11) is central to my understanding of the whole book. Chaps. 1–4 and 62–66 are seen as an envelope for the book.

My special thanks go to James W. Watts, who has edited the work, brought order out of chaos, and made my argument much more readable and understandable. Melanie McQuere has done her usual thorough work in copyediting.

JOHN D. W. WATTS

Spring 2004
Penney Farms, Florida

Abbreviations

PERIODICALS, SERIALS, REFERENCE WORKS, AND FESTSCHRIFTEN

AAASH	Acta Antiqua Academicae Scientiarum Hungaricae
AASOR	Annual of the American Schools of Oriental Research
AB	Anchor Bible
ABD	*Anchor Bible Dictionary*. Ed. D. N. Freedman. 6 vols. New York, 1992.
ABR	*Australian Biblical Review*
AbrN	*Abr-Nahrain*
ACEBT	*Amsterdamse Cahiers voor Exegese en Bijbelse Theologie*
ACEBTSup	ACEBT Supplement Series
AcOr	*Acta orientalia*
ACS	*African Christian Studies*
AcT	*Acta theologica* (South Africa)
AfO	*Archiv für Orientforschung*
AfO	Archiv für Orientforschung: Beiheft
AGJU	Arbeiten zur Geschichte des antiken Judentums and des Urchristentums
AIPHOS	*Annuaire de l'Institut de philologie et d'histoire orientales et slaves*
AJBI	*Annual of the Japanese Biblical Institute*
AJSL	*American Journal of Semitic Languages and Literature*
AJT	*Asian Journal of Theology* (Singapore)
AMI	*Archaeologische Mitteilungen aus Iran*
AnBib	Analecta biblica
ANEP	*The Ancient Near East in Pictures Relating to the Old Testament*. Ed. J. B. Pritchard. Princeton, 1954.
ANET	*Ancient Near Eastern Texts Relating to the Old Testament*. Ed. J. B. Pritchard. Princeton, 1950.
ANET[3]	*Ancient Near Eastern Texts Relating to the Old Testament*. 3d ed. Ed. J. B. Pritchard. Princeton, 1969.
AnOr	Analecta orientalia
ANTJ	Arbeiten zum Neuen Testament und Judentum
ANVAO	Avhandlinger utgitt av Det Norske Videnskaps-Akademi i Oslo
AOAT	Alter Orient und Altes Testament
APOT	*The Apocrypha and Pseudepigrapha of the Old Testament*. Ed. R. H. Charles. 2 vols. Oxford, 1913.
AR	*Archiv für Religionswissenschaft*
ARM	Archives royales de Mari
ArOr	*Archiv Orientální*
ASOR	American Schools of Oriental Research
AsSeign	*Assemblées du Seigneur*
ASTI	*Annual of the Swedish Theological Institute*
ATA	Alttestamentliche Abhandlungen
ATANT	Abhandlungen zur Theologie des Alten und Neuen Testaments
ATD	Das Alte Testament Deutsch
ATDan	Acta theologica danica
AThR	*Anglican Theological Review*
Aug	*Augustinianum*
AuOr	*Aula orientalis* (Barcelona, Spain)
Aur	*Aurensia* (Ourense, Spain)
AuS	Dalmon, G. H. *Arbeit und Sitte in Palästina*. 1928. Reprint Hildesheim, 1964.
AUSS	*Andrews University Seminary Studies*
AzTh	Arbeiten zur Theologie
BA	*Biblical Archaeologist*
BAG	Bauer, W., W. J. Arndt, and F. W. Gingrich, *Greek-English Lexicon of the New Testament and Early Christian Literature*. Chicago, 1957.
BAR	*Biblical Archaeology Review*

BASOR	*Bulletin of the American Schools of Oriental Research*
BAT	Die Botschaft des Alten Testaments
Bauer-Leander	Bauer, H., and P. Leander. *Historische Grammatik der hebräischen Sprache des Alten Testaments.* 1922. Reprint, Hildesheim, 1962.
BBB	Bonner biblische Beiträge
BBC	Broadman Bible Commentary
BBET	Beiträge zur biblischen Exegese und Theologie
BBR	*Bulletin for Biblical Research* (Trinity Western University)
BBS	*Bulletin of Biblical Studies* (Athens)
BDB	Brown, F., S. R. Driver, and C. A. Briggs. *A Hebrew and English Lexicon of the Old Testament.* Oxford, 1907.
BEATAJ	Beiträge zur Erforschung des Alten Testaments und des antiken Judentum
BenM	*Benediktionische Monatschrift*
BeO	*Bibbia e oriente*
BETL	Bibiotheca ephemeridum theologicarum lovaniensium
BEvT	Beiträge zur evangelischen Theologie
BFCT	Beiträge zur Förderung christlicher Theologie
BHH	*Biblisch-historisches Handwörterbuch: Landeskunde, Geschichte, Religion, Kultur.* Ed. B. Reicke and L. Rost. 4 vols. Gottingen, 1962–66.
BHK[3]	*Biblia Hebraica.* Ed. R. Kittel. 3d ed. Stuttgart, 1937.
BHS	*Biblia Hebraica Stuttgartensia.* Ed. K. Elliger and W. Rudolph. Stuttgart, 1983.
BHT	Beiträge zur historischen Theologie
Bib	*Biblica*
BiBh	*Bible Bhashyam*
BibInt	*Biblical Interpretation*
BibIntS	Biblical Interpretation Series
BibLeb	*Bibel und Leben*
BibOr	Biblica et orientalia
BibS(N)	Biblische Studien (Neukirchen, 1951–)
Bijdr	*Bijdragen: Tijdschrift voor filosofie en theologie*
BIOSCS	*Bulletin of the International Organization for Septuagint and Cognate Studies*
BJRL	*Bulletin of the John Rylands University Library of Manchester*
BJS	Brown Judaic Studies
BK	*Bibel und Kirche*
BKAT	Biblischer Kommentar, Altes Testament
BLE	*Bulletin de littérature ecclésiastique*
BLex	*Bibel-Lexicon.* Ed. H. Haag. 2d ed. Einsiedeln: Benziger, 1968.
BL	*Bibel und Liturgie*
BMik	*Beth Mikra*
BN	*Biblische Notizen*
BO	*Bibliotheca orientalis*
BOT	*De boeken van het Oude Testament.* Ed. A. van der Born, W. Grossouw, and J. van der Ploeg. 19 vols. Roermond: Romen.
BR	*Biblical Research*
BRev	*Bible Review*
BRL	*Biblisches Reallexikon.* Ed. K. Galling. Tübingen, 1937.
BSac	*Bibliotheca sacra*
BSOAS	*Bulletin of the School of Oriental and African Studies*
BT	*The Bible Translator*
BTB	*Biblical Theology Bulletin*
BTS	Biblisch-theologische Studien
BurH	*Buried History*
BV	*Biblical Viewpoint*
BVC	*Bible et vie chrétienne*
BWANT	Beiträge zur Wissenschaft vom Alten und Neuen Testament
BZ	*Biblische Zeitschrift*
BZAW	Beihefte zur ZAW
CAH	*Cambridge Ancient History.* Cambridge, 1925.
CB	*Cultura bíblica*

CBC	Cambridge Bible Commentary
CBET	Contributions to Biblical Exegesis and Theology
CBib	Cambridge Bible
CBQ	*Catholic Biblical Quarterly*
CBQMS	*CBQ* Monograph Series
CDios	*Ciudad de Dios*
CHAL	*Concise Hebrew and Aramaic Lexicon of the Old Testament.* W. L. Holladay. Grand Rapids, 1971.
CHJ	*Cambridge History of Judaism.* Ed. W. D. Davies and L. Finkelstein. Cambridge, 1984–.
ChSoc	*Church and Society*
ColcTFujen	*Collectenea theologica Universitatis Fujen* (Taipei)
ColT	*Collectanea theologica*
ConBOT	Coniectanea biblica: Old Testament Series
Conc	*Concilium*
COS	*The Context of Scripture.* Vol. 1, *Canonical Compositions.* Vol. 2, *Monumental Inscriptions.* Vol. 3, *Archival Documents.* Ed. W. W. Hallo and K. L. Younger, Jr. Leiden, 1997, 1999, 2002.
CQR	*Church Quarterly Review*
CRTL	Cahiers de la Revue théologique de Louvain
CTM	*Concordia Theological Monthly*
CTom	*Ciencia Tomista* (Salamanca)
CTR	*Criswell Theological Review*
CuadT	*Cuademos teológicos*
CurBS	*Currents in Research: Biblical Studies*
CurTM	*Currents in Theology and Mission*
CV	*Communio viatorum*
CVC	*Communio Verbum Caro*
DBAT	*Dielheimer Blätter zum Alten Testament und seiner Rezeption in der Alten Kirche*
DBSup	*Dictionnaire de La Bible: Supplément.* Ed. L. Pirot and A. Robert. Paris, 1928–.
DCH	*Dictionary of Classical Hebrew.* Ed. D. J. A. Clines. Sheffield, 1993–2001.
DD	*Dor le-Dor*
DDD	*Dictionary of Deities and Demons in the Bible.* 2d ed. Ed. K. van der Toorn, B. Becking, and P. W. van der Horst. Leiden; Grand Rapids, 1999.
Did	*Didaskalia*
DISO	*Dictionnaire des inscriptions sémitiques de l'ouest.* Ed. C. F. Jean and J. Hoftijzer. Leiden, 1965.
DJD	Discoveries in the Judaean Desert
DOTT	*Documents from Old Testament Times.* Ed. D. W. Thomas. London, 1958.
DSD	*Dead Sea Discoveries* (Leiden)
DTT	*Dansk teologisk tidsskrift*
DunRev	*Dunwoodie Review*
EAEHL	*Encyclopedia of Archaeological Excavations in the Holy Land.* Ed. M. Avi-Yonah. 4 vols. Jerusalem, 1975.
EBib	Etudes bibliques
EdF	Erträge der Forschung
EgT	*Église et théologie*
EHAT	Exegetisches Handbuch zum Alten Testament
EncJud	*Encyclopaedia Judaica.* 16 vols. Jerusalem, 1972.
EnsMik	אנצשיקלופדיה מקראית (Jerusalem)
EphMar	*Ephemerides Mariologicae*
ErIsr	*Eretz-Israel*
EstBib	*Estudios bíblicos*
EstEcl	*Estudios eclesiásticos*
EstTeo	*Estudios teológicos*
ETL	*Ephemerides theologicae lovanienses*
ETR	*Etudes théologiques et religieuses*
ETS	Erfurter theologische Studien
ETSMS	Evangelical Theological Society Monograph Series
EuroJTh	*European Journal of Theology*
EVO	*Egitto e Vicino Oriente*
EvQ	*Evangelical Quarterly*
EvRT	*Evangelical Review of Theology*
EvT	*Evangelische Theologie*

ExAud — *Ex Auditu*
ExpTim — *Expository Times*

FAT — Forschungen zum Alten Testament
FB — Forschung zur Bibel
FF — *Forschungen und Fortschritte*
FIOTL — Formation and Interpretation of Old Testament Literature
FM — *Faith and Mission*
FoiVie — *Foi et Vie*
ForumKT — *Forum katholische Theologie*
FOTL — Forms of the Old Testament Literature
FRLANT — Forschungen zur Religion und Literatur des Alten und Neuen Testaments
FT — *Folia theologica* (Budapest)

GB — *Gesenius' Hebräisches und Aramäisches Handwörterbuch.* Ed. F. P. W. Buhl. Berlin, 1915.
GKC — *Gesenius' Hebrew Grammar.* Ed. E. Kautzsch. Trans. A. E. Cowley. 2d ed. Oxford, 1910.
GSAT — Rad, G. von. *Gesammelte Studien zum Alten Testament.* 2 vols. TB 8, 48. Munich, 1958, 1973.
GTJ — *Grace Theological Journal*
GTT — *Gereformeerd theologisch tijdschrift*
GTTOT — *The Geographical and Topographical Texts of the Old Testament.* Ed. J. J. Simons. Leiden, 1959.
GVG — *Grundriss der vergleichenden Grammatik der semitischen Sprachen.* C. Brockelmann. 2 vols. Berlin, 1908–13. Reprint, Hildesheim, 1961.

HAL — Koehler, L., W. Baumgartner, and J. J. Stamm. *Hebräisches und aramäisches Lexikon zum Alten Testament.* Fascicles 1–5. 1967–95 (KBL[3]). ET: *HALOT.*
HAR — *Hebrew Annual Review*
HAT — Handbuch zum Alten Testament
HBT — *Horizons in Biblical Theology*
HCOT — Historical Commentary on the Old Testament
HDR — Harvard Dissertations in Religion
HebSyntax — Brockelmann, C. *Hebräische Syntax.* Neukirchen, 1956.
HeyJ — *Heythrop Journal*
HI — Bright, J. *A History of Israel.* 3d ed. Philadelphia, 1981.
HKAT — Handkommentar zum Alten Testament
HO — Handbuch der Orientalistik
HS — *Hebrew Studies*
HSAT — *Die Heilige Schrift des Alten Testaments.* Ed. E. Kautzsch and A. Bertholet. 4th ed. Tübingen, 1922–23.
HSM — Harvard Semitic Monographs
HSS — Harvard Semitic Studies
HTR — *Harvard Theological Review*
HUCA — *Hebrew Union College Annual*
HumT — *Humanistica e Teologia* (Porto, Portugal)
HvTSt — *Hervormde teologiese studies*

IB — *Interpreter's Bible.* Ed. G. A. Buttrick et al. 12 vols. New York, 1951–57.
IBC — Interpretation: A Bible Commentary for Teaching and Preaching
IBR — Institute for Biblical Research
IBS — *Irish Biblical Studies*
ICC — International Critical Commentary
IDB — *The Interpreter's Dictionary of the Bible.* Ed. G. A. Buttrick. 4 vols. Nashville, 1962.
IDBSup — *IDB: Supplementary Volume.* Ed. K. Crim. Nashville, 1976.
IDS — *In die Skriflig* (Republic of South Africa)
IEJ — *Israel Exploration Journal*
IER — *Irish Ecclesiastical Record*

IJH *Israelite and Judean History.* Ed. J. H. Hayes and J. M. Miller. Philadelphia, 1977.
IJT *Indian Journal of Theology*
Int *Interpretation*
IOFOT International Organization for the Old Testament
IOS *Israel Oriental Studies*
IOTS B. S. Childs. *Introduction to the Old Testament as Scripture.* Philadelphia, 1979.
ISBE *International Standard Bible Encyclopedia.* Ed. G. W. Bromiley. 4 vols. Grand Rapids, 1979–88.
ITC International Theological Commentary

JA *Journal asiatique*
JANESCU *Journal of the Ancient Near Eastern Society of Columbia University*
JAOS *Journal of the American Oriental Society*
JARC *Journal of the American Research Center in Egypt*
JBL *Journal of Biblical Literature*
JBQ *Jewish Bible Quarterly*
JBR *Journal of Bible and Religion*
JBT *Jahrbuch für biblische Theologie* (Neukirchener)
JCS *Journal of Cuneiform Studies*
JE *The Jewish Encyclopedia.* Ed. C. Adler et al. London, 1910.
JEA *Journal of Egyptian Archaeology*
JEOL *Jaarbericht van het Vooraziatisch-Egyptisch Gezelschap (Genootschap) Ex oriente lux*
JETS *Journal of the Evangelical Theological Society*
JJS *Journal of Jewish Studies*
JNES *Journal of Near Eastern Studies*
JNSL *Journal of Northwest Semitic Languages*
Joüon Joüon, P. *Grammaire de l'Hebreu Biblique.* Rome, 1947.
JQR *Jewish Quarterly Review*
JR *Journal of Religion*
JSem *Journal of Semitics*
JSJ *Journal for the Study of Judaism in the Persian, Hellenistic, and Roman Periods*
JSJSup *JSJ* Supplements
JSNT *Journal for the Study of the New Testament*
JSNTSup *JSNT:* Supplement Series
JSOR *Journal of the Society of Oriental Research*
JSOT *Journal for the Study of the Old Testament*
JSOTSup *JSOT:* Supplement Series
JSS *Journal of Semitic Studies*
JTS *Journal of Theological Studies*
JTSA *Journal of Theology for Southern Africa*
Jud *Judaica*

KAT Kommentar zum Alten Testament
KBL Koehler, L., and W. Baumgartner. *Lexicon in Veteris Testamenti libros.* 2d ed. Leiden, 1958.
KD *Kerygma und Dogma*
KHC Kurzer Hand-Commentar zum Alten Testament

LA *Liber Annuus*
LBBC Layman's Bible Book Commentary
LD Lectio divina
Leš *Lešonenu*
Löw Löw, I. *Die Flora der Juden.* 4 vols. Vienna, 1924–34.
LQ *Lutheran Quarterly*
LR *Lutherische Rundschau*
LS *Louvain Studies*
LTP *Laval théologique et philosophique*
LUÅ Lunds universitets årsskrift
LumVie *Lumière et vie*
LW *Living Word*

MBA Aharoni, Y., and M. Avi-Yonah. *Macmillan Bible Atlas.* 2d ed. New York, 1977.

MdB	*Le Monde de la Bible*
MEAH	*Miscelánea de estudios arabes y hebraicos*
MGWJ	*Monatschrift für Geschichte und Wissenschaft des Judentums*
MIOF	*Mitteilungen des Instituts für Orientforschung*
MSJ	*The Master's Seminary Journal*
MTA	*Münsteraner theologische Abhandlungen* (Altenberg)
MTZ	*Münchener theologische Zeitschnft*
Mus	*Muséon: Revue d'études orientales*
MVAG	Mitteilungen der Vorderasiatisch-ägyptischen Gesellschaft
NC	*La Nouvelle Clio*
NCB	New Century Bible
NEchtB	Neue Echter Bibel
NedTT	*Nederlands theologisch tijdschrift*
NGTT	*Nederduitse gereformeerde teologiese tydskrif*
NIBCOT	New International Biblical Commentary on the Old Testament
NICOT	New International Commentary on the Old Testament
NIDNTT	*New International Dictionary of New Testament Theology*. Ed. C. Brown. 4 vols. Grand Rapids, 1975–85.
NIDOTTE	*New International Dictionary of Old Testament Theology and Exegesis*. Ed. W. A. Van Gemeren. 5 vols. Grand Rapids, 1997.
NJBC	*The New Jerome Biblical Commentary*. Ed. R. E. Brown et al. Englewood Cliffs, 1990.
NKZ	*Neue kirchliche Zeitschrift*
NRTh	*La nouvelle revue théologique*
NSK.AT	*Neue Stuttgarter Kommentar: Altes Testament*
NThSt	*Nieuwe theologische Studien*
NTS	*New Testament Studies*
NTT	*Norsk Teologisk Tidsskrift*
Numen	*Numen: International Review for the History of Religions*
OBO	Orbis biblicus et orientalis
ÖBS	Österreichische biblische Studien
OBT	Overtures to Biblical Theology
OIP	Oriental Institute Publications
OLP	*Orientalia lovaniensia periodica*
OLZ	*Orientalistische Literaturzeitung*
Or	*Orientalia* (NS)
OrAnt	*Oriens antiquus*
OTA	*Old Testament Abstracts*
OTE	*Old Testament Essays* (South Africa)
OTFC	*Old Testament Form Criticism*, Ed. J. H. Hayes. San Antonio, 1974.
OTG	Old Testament Guides
OTL	Old Testament Library
OTS	Old Testament Studies
OtSt	Oudtestamentische Studiën
OTT	Rad, G. von. *Old Testament Theology*. Trans. D. M. G. Stalker. New York, 1962–65.
OTWSAP	*Die Ou Testamentiese Werkgemeenskap in Suid-Afrika, Pretoria*
ParLi	*Paroisse et Liturgie*
PEGLMBS	*Proceedings, Eastern Great Lakes and Midwest Biblical Societies*
PEQ	*Palestine Exploration Quarterly*
PG	Patrologia graeca [= Patrologiae cursus completus: Series graeca]. Ed. J.-P. Migne. 162 vols. Paris, 1857–86.
PIBA	Proceedings of the Irish Biblical Association
PJ	*Palästina-Jahrbuch*
PJBR	*Polish Journal of Biblical Research*
POS	Pretoria Oriental Series
POTT	*People of Old Testament Times*. Ed. D. J. Wiseman. Oxford, 1973.
POut	De Prediking van het Oude Testament
PPS	*Pravoslavnyi Palestinskii Sbornik* (Russia)
Proof	*Prooftexts: A Journal of Jewish Literary History*
PRSt	*Perspectives in Religious Studies*

PS	*Philippinana Sacra* (Manila)
PSB	*Princeton Seminary Bulletin*
PSV	*Parota Spirito et Vita*
PTMS	Pittsburgh Theological Monograph Series
PW	Pauly, A. F. *Paulys Real-encyclopädie der classischen Altertumswissenschaft*. New ed. G. Wissowa. 49 vols. Munich, 1980.
PzB	*Protokolle zur Bibel*
QD	Quaestiones disputatae
RB	*Revue biblique*
RBA	*Revista bíblica Augustinum*
RCB	*Revista de cultura bíblica*
REB	*Revista eclesiástica brasileira*
RefR	*Reformed Review*
REJ	*Revue des études juives*
ResQ	*Restoration Quarterly*
RevExp	*Review and Expositor*
RevistB	*Revista bíblica*
RevScRel	*Revue des sciences religieuses*
RGG	*Religion in Geschichte und Gegenwart*. Ed. K. Galling. 7 vols. 3d ed. Tübingen, 1957–65.
RHPR	*Revue d'histoire et de philosophie religieuses*
RHR	*Revue de l'histoire des religions*
RicBR	*Ricerche Bibliche e Religiose*
RivB	*Rivista biblica italiana*
RLC	*Revue de littérature comparée*
RocTKan	*Roczniki Teologiczno-Kanoniczne*
RRef	*La revue réformée*
RSR	*Recherches de science religieuse*
RThom	*Revue thomiste*
RTL	*Revue théologique de Louvain*
RTP	*Revue de théologie et de philosophie*
RTR	*Reformed Theological Review*
Salm	*Salmanticensis*
SANT	Studien zum Alten und Neuen Testaments
SB	Sources bibliques
SBB	Stuttgarter biblische Beiträge
SBeT	Studia Biblica et Theologica
SBFLA	*Studii biblici Franciscani liber annus*
SBL	Society of Biblical Literature
SBLDS	SBL Dissertation Series
SBLEJL	SBL Early Judaism and Its Literature
SBLMS	SBL Monograph Series
SBLSCS	SBL Septuagint and Cognate Studies
SBLSP	*SBL Seminar Papers*
SBLSS	SBL Semeia Studies
SBS	Stuttgarter Bibelstudien
SBT	Studies in Biblical Theology
SBTS	Sources for Biblical and Theological Study
SC	Sources chrétiennes. Paris, 1943–.
ScC	*La scuola cattolica*
ScEs	*Science et esprit*
SCJ	*Stone-Campbell Journal* (Joplin, MO)
Scr	*Scripture*
ScrB	*Scripture Bulletin*
ScrHier	Scripta hierosolymitana
SEÅ	*Svensk exegetisk årsbok*
Sef	*Sefarad*
SeiRon	*Seisho-gaku roushu* (Tokyo)
SEL	*Studi epigrafici e linguistici*
Sem	*Semitica*
SJOT	*Scandinavian Journal of the Old Testament*
SJT	*Scottish Journal of Theology*
SK	*Skrif en kerk*
SMSR	*Studi e materiali di storia delle religioni*
SNTSMS	Society for New Testament Studies Monograph Series
SNVAO	Skrifter utgitt av Det Norske Videnskaps-Akademie i Oslo
SO	Symbolae osloenses
SOTS	Society for Old Testament Studies
SOTSMS	Society for Old Testament Studies Monograph Series
SPCK	Society for the Propagation of Christian Knowledge
Spfd	*The Springfielder*

SSN — Studia semitica neerlandica
ST — *Studia theologica*
STDJ — Studies on the Texts of the Desert of Judah
StG — Studium Generale
STJ — *Stulos Theological Journal*
STU — *Schweizerische theologische Umschau*
StZ — *Stimmen der Zeit*
STZ — *Schweizerische Theologische Zeitschrift*
Stu — *Studia theologica varsaviensia*
SVTQ — *St. Vladimir's Theological Quarterly*
SwJT — *Southwestern Journal of Theology*

TB — Theologische Bücherei: Neudrucke und Berichte aus dem 20. Jahrhundert
TBC — Torch Bible Commentaries
TBT — *The Bible Today*
TD — *Theology Digest*
TDNT — *Theological Dictionary of the New Testament.* Ed. G. Kittel and G. Friedrich. Trans. G. W. Bromiley. 10 vols. Grand Rapids, 1964–76.
TDOT — *Theological Dictionary of the Old Testament.* Ed. G. J. Botterweck and H. Ringgren. Trans. D. E. Green. 8 vols. Grand Rapids, 1974–.
TGI — *Textbuch zur Geschichte Israels.* Ed. K. Galling. 2d ed. Tübingen, 1968.
TGl — *Theologie und Glaube*
THAT — *Theologische Handwörterbuch zum Alten Testament.* Ed. E. Jenni and C. Westermann. 2 vols. Stuttgart, 1971–76.
Theo — *Theologika* (Peru)
Theol — *Theologica* (Braga)
ThSt — Theologische Studiën
ThTo — *Theology Today*
ThViat — *Theologia viatorum*
TK — *Texte und Kontexte*
TLZ — *Theologische Literaturzeitung*
TOTC — Tyndale Old Testament Commentaries
TPQ — *Theologisch-praktische Quartalschrift*
TQ — *Theologische Quartalschrift*
Transeu — *Transeuphratène*
TRE — *Theologische Realenzyklopädie.* Ed. G. Krause and G. Müller. Berlin, 1977–.
TRev — *Theologische Revue*
TRu — *Theologische Rundschau*
TS — Texts and Studies
TS — *Theological Studies*
TSK — *Theologische Studien und Kritiken*
TThSt — Trierer theologische Studien
TTJ — *Trinity Theological Journal*
TTKi — *Tidsskrift for Teologi og Kirke*
TTZ — *Trierer theologische Zeitschrift*
TWAT — *Theologisches Wörterbuch zum Alten Testament,* ed. G. J. Botterweck et al. 4 vols. Stuttgart, 1973–.
TWOT — *Theological Wordbook of the Old Testament.* Ed. R. L. Harris and G. L. Archer, Jr. 2 vols. Chicago, 1980.
TynBul — *Tyndale Bulletin*
TZ — *Theologische Zeitschrift*

UCOP — University of Cambridge Oriental Publications
UF — *Ugarit-Forschungen*
UUÅ — Uppsala Universitetsårskrift

VC — *Vigiliae christianae*
VD — *Verbum domini*
VetChr — *Vetera Christianorum*
VeE — *Verbum et Ecclesia*
VF — *Verkündigung und Forschung*
VH — *Vivens homo*
Vid — *Vidyajyoti* (Delhi, India)
VSpir — *Vie spirituelle*
VT — *Vetus Testamentum*
VTSup — Supplements to *VT*

WC — Westminster Commentaries
WD — *Wort und Dienst*
WF — *Wege der Forschung*
WMANT — Wissenschaftliche Monographien zum Alten und Neuen Testament

WO	*Die Welt des Orients*
WTJ	*Westminster Theological Journal*
WUNT	Wissenschaftliche Untersuchungen zum Neuen Testament
WUS	*Wörterbuch der ugaritischen Sprache.* J. Aistleitner. Berlin, 1963.
WW	*Word and World*
WZ	*Wissenschaftliche Zeitschrift*
WZKM	*Wiener Zeitschrift für die Kunde des Morgenlandes*
ZABR	*Zeitschrift für altorientalische und biblische Rechtgeschichte*
ZAH	*Zeitschrift für Althebräistik*
ZÄS	*Zeitschrift für ägyptische Sprache und Altertumskunde*
ZAW	*Zeitschrift fur die alttestamentliche Wissenschaft*
ZBK	Zürcher Bibelkommentare
ZDMG	*Zeitschrift der deutschen morgenländischen Gesellschaft*
ZDMGSup	ZDMG: Supplementbände
ZDPV	*Zeitschrift der deutschen Palästina-Vereins*
ZKT	*Zeitschrift für katholische Theologie*
ZRGG	*Zeitschrift für Religions- und Geistesgeschichte*
ZS	*Zeitschrift für Semitistik und verwandte Gebiete*
ZTK	*Zeitschrift für Theologie und Kirche*
ZWT	*Zeitschrift für wissenschaftliche Theologie*

TEXTS, VERSIONS, AND ANCIENT WORKS

Akk.	Akkadian
Amor.	Amorite
Arab.	Arabic
Aram.	Aramaic
ASV	American Standard Version
AV	Authorized Version
B	MT MS, ed. Jacob ben Chayim, Venice (1524–25)
C	MT MS, Cairo Codex of the Prophets
CD	Cairo Genizah copy of the *Damascus Document*
Copt.	Coptic
Eg.	Egyptian
Eth.	Ethiopic
Gk.	Greek
Heb.	Hebrew
JB	Jerusalem Bible
K	Kethib
K^{Occ}	Occidental (western) Kethib
K^{Or}	Oriental (eastern) Kethib
L	MT MS, Leningrad Codex
LXX	Septuagint, Greek translation of the OT
LXX^{A}	LXX MS, Alexandrian the prophets
LXX^{B}	LXX MS, Vatican Codex
LXX^{L}	LXX MS(S), Lucianic recension
LXX^{Q}	LXX MS, Marchalian Codex
LXX^{S*}	LXX MS, Sinai Codex, original reading
LXX^{Sc}	LXX MS, Sinai Codex, corrector
$MS(S)^{G}$	Heb. MS(S) ed. C. D. Ginsburg (1908)
$MS(S)^{K}$	Heb. MS(S) ed. B. Kennicott (1776–80)
$MS(S)^{R}$	Heb. MS(S) ed. J. B. De Rossi (1874–88)
MT	Masoretic Text (as published in *BHS*)
NAB	New American Bible
NEB	New English Bible
NIV	New International Version
NJPS	*Tanakh: The Holy Scripture: The New JPS Translation*
NJV	New Jewish Version
NKJV	New King James Version
NLB	New Living Bible
NRSV	New Revised Standard Version
OL	Old Latin
Pesh.	Peshitta
Q	Qere
RSV	Revised Standard Version
Syh.	Syrohexaplaris

Syr.	Syriac (as published in the Peshitta Institute edition, 1980)	1QIsa[a]	St. Mark's Isaiah Scroll from QumranCave 1
Tg(s).	Targum(s)	1QIsa[b]	Hebrew University Isaiah Scroll from Cave 1
Ugar.	Ugaritic	4QpIsa[c]	*Pesher* on Isaiah from Qumran Cave 4
Vg.	Vulgate	α′	Aquila
1QH[a]	*Hodayot*[a] or *Thanksgiving Hymns*[a]	θ′	Theodocian
1QM	*Milḥamah* or *War Scroll* from Qumran Cave 1	σ′	Symmachus

BIBLICAL AND APOCRYPHAL BOOKS

OLD TESTAMENT

Gen	Genesis	Song	Canticles, Song of Solomon
Exod	Exodus	Isa	Isaiah
Lev	Leviticus	Jer	Jeremiah
Num	Numbers	Lam	Lamentations
Deut	Deuteronomy	Ezek	Ezekiel
Josh	Joshua	Dan	Daniel
Judg	Judges	Hos	Hosea
Ruth	Ruth	Joel	Joel
1–2 Sam	1–2 Samuel	Amos	Amos
1–2 Kgs	1–2 Kings	Obad	Obadiah
1–2 Chr	1–2 Chronicles	Jonah	Jonah
Ezra	Ezra	Mic	Micah
Neh	Nehemiah	Nah	Nahum
Esth	Esther	Hab	Habakkuk
Job	Job	Zeph	Zephaniah
Ps(s)	Psalm(s)	Hag	Haggai
Prov	Proverbs	Zech	Zechariah
Eccl	Ecclesiastes	Mal	Malachi

APOCRYPHA

Bar	Baruch	Jdt	Judith
Add Dan	Additions to Daniel	1–2 Macc	1–2 Maccabees
Pr Azar	Prayer of Azariah	3–4 Macc	3–4 Maccabees
Bel	Bel and the Dragon	Pr Man	Prayer of Manasseh
Sg Three	Song of the Three Young Men	Ps 151	Psalm 151
Sus	Susanna	Sir	Sirach/Ecclesiasticus
1–2 Esd	1–2 Esdras	Tob	Tobit
Add Esth	Additions to Esther	Wis	Wisdom of Solomon
Ep Jer	Epistle of Jeremiah		

OLD TESTAMENT PSEUDEPIGRAPHA

2 Bar.	*2 Baruch (Syriac Apocalypse)*

NEW TESTAMENT

Matt	Matthew	1–2 Thess	1–2 Thessalonians
Mark	Mark	1–2 Tim	1–2 Timothy
Luke	Luke	Titus	Titus
John	John	Phlm	Philemon
Acts	Acts	Heb	Hebrews
Rom	Romans	Jas	James
1–2 Cor	1–2 Corinthians	1–2 Pet	1–2 Peter
Gal	Galatians	1–2–3 John	1–2–3 John
Eph	Ephesians	Jude	Jude
Phil	Philippians	Rev	Revelation
Col	Colossians		

HEBREW GRAMMAR

abs.	absolute	impf.	imperfect
acc.	accusative	impv.	imperative
act.	active	indic.	indicative
adj.	adjective, adjectival	inf.	infinitive
adv.	adverb, adverbial	masc., m.	masculine
aor.	aorist	obj.	object, objective
c.	common	pass.	passive
consec.	consecutive	pf.	perfect
const.	construct	pl.	plural
fem., f.	feminine	prep.	preposition
fut.	future	ptc.	participle
gen.	genitive, genitival	sg.	singular
juss.	jussive	suf.	suffix

MISCELLANEOUS

B.C.E.	Before the Common Era	lit.	literally
C.E.	Common Era	MS(S)	manuscripts
chap(s).	chapter(s)	n.	note
col(s).	column(s)	NS	new series
diss.	dissertation	NT	New Testament
DtH	Deuteronomistic History	OT	Old Testament
Dtr	Deuteronomist	p.	page
ed(s).	edition; edited by; editor(s)	pl.	plate
esp.	especially	trans.	translated by; translator
ET	English translation	UP	University Press
EV(V)	English version(s)	v(v)	verse(s)
FS	Festschrift	§	section/paragraph
hap. leg.	*hapax legomenon*		

Commentary Bibliography

Cited in text by author's name only.

Auvray, P. *Isaïe 1–39.* SB. Paris: Gabalda, 1972. **Baltzer, K.** *Deutero-Isaiah: A Commentary on Isaiah 40–55.* Trans. M. Kohl. Ed. P. Machinist. Hermeneia. Minneapolis: Fortress, 2001. **Beuken, W. A. M.** *Jesaja 1–12.* HKAT. Freiburg: Herder, 2003. ———. *Jesaja, Deel II–III* (Isa 40–66). 2 vols. POut. Nijkerk: Callenbach, 1979–89. ———. *Isaiah: Part 2* (Isa 28–39). Trans. B. Doyle. HCOT. Leuven: Peeters, 2000. **Bewer, J. A.** *The Book of Isaiah.* Vols. 3–4 of *Harper's Annotated Bible.* New York: Harper & Bros., 1950. **Blenkinsopp, J.** *Isaiah 1–39.* AB. New York: Doubleday, 2000. ———. *Isaiah 40–55.* AB. New York: Doubleday, 2002. ———. *Isaiah 56–66.* AB. New York: Doubleday, 2003. **Bruno, A.** *Jesaja, eine rhythmische und textkritische Untersuchung.* Stockholm: Almqvist & Wiksell, 1953. **Buhl, F.** *Jesaja.* 2d ed. Copenhagen: Gyldendal, 1912. **Cheyne, T. K.** *The Book of the Prophet Isaiah.* 5th ed. New York: Dodd, Mead, 1904. **Childs, B. S.** *Isaiah.* OTL. Louisville, KY: Westminster John Knox, 2001. **Clements, R. E.** *Isaiah 1–39.* NCB. Grand Rapids, MI: Eerdmans, 1980. **Delitzsch, F. J.** *Biblischer Commentar über den Propheten Jesaia.* Leipzig: Dörffling und Frank, 1869. ———. *Biblical Commentaries on the Prophecies of Isaiah.* Trans. J. Martin. Edinburgh: T & T Clark, 1910. **Dillmann, A.** *Der prophet Jesaja.* Rev. R. Kittel. Leipzig: Hirzel, 1898. **Döderlein, J. C.** *Esaias, ex recensione textus Hebraei.* Altorfi, 1789. **Duhm, B.** *Das Buch Jesaja.* HKAT 3.1. 5th ed. Göttingen: Vandenhoeck & Ruprecht, 1968. **Eichrodt, W.** *Der Heilige in Israel: Jesaja 1–12.* BAT 17.1. Stuttgart: Calwer, 1960. ———. *Der Herr der Geschichte: Jesaja 13–23, 28–39.* BAT 17.2. Stuttgart: Calwer, 1967. **Eusebius Pamphili of Caesaria.** *Der Jesajakommentar* (Gr.). Vol. 9 of *Eusebius Werke.* Ed. J. Ziegler. Berlin: Akademie, 1975. **Feldmann, F.** *Das Buch Isaias.* EHAT. Münster, 1926. **Fohrer, G.** *Das Buch Jesaja.* 3 vols. ZBK. Zurich: Zwingli, 1960–64. **Gesenius, W.** *Der Prophet Jesaia.* Leipzig: Vogel, 1829. **Gray, G. B.** *A Critical and Exegetical Commentary on the Book of Isaiah I–XXVI.* ICC. New York: T & T Clark, 1912. **Guthe, H.** *Jesaja.* Tübingen: Mohr, 1907. **Hertzberg, H. W.** *Der Erste Jesaja.* 3d ed. Leipzig: Schloessmann, 1955. **Hitzig, F.** *Der prophet Jesaja.* Heidelberg: Winter, 1833. **Ibn Ezra** (Abraham ben Meir) (1090–1164). *Commentary of Ibn Ezra on Isaiah.* (Heb.) Trans. M. Friedlander. 2d ed. New York: Feldheim, 1966. **Jensen, J.** *Isaiah 1–39.* OT Message 8. Wilmington: Glazier, 1984. **Kaiser, O.** *Isaiah 1–12.* 2d ed. Trans. R. A. Wilson. OTL. Philadelphia: Westminster, 1983. ———. *Isaiah 13–39.* 2d ed. Trans. R. A. Wilson. OTL. Philadelphia: Westminster, 1983. **Kelley, P. H.** "Isaiah." In *Broadman Bible Commentary.* Vol. 5. Nashville: Broadman, 1971. 149–374. **Kilian, R.** *Jesaja 1–39.* EdF 200. Darmstadt: Wissenschaftliche Buchgesellschaft, 1983. ———. *Jesaja 1–12.* NEchtB 17. Würzburg: Echter, 1986. ———. *Jesaja II: 13–39.* NEchtB 32. Würzburg: Echter, 1994. **Kimchi, D.** (1160–1235). *The Commentary of David Kimchi on Isaiah.* (Heb. with introduction in Eng.) Ed. L. Finkelstein. Columbia University Oriental Studies 19. New York: Columbia UP, 1926. Reprint, New York: AMS Press, 1966. **Kissane, E. J.** *The Book of Isaiah.* Rev. ed. 2 vols. Dublin: Browne and Nolan, 1960. **Koole, J. L.** *Isaiah, Part 3.* Trans. A. P. Runia. 3 vols. HCOT. Kampen: Kok Pharos, 1997–98. **König, E.** *Das Buch Jesaja.* Gütersloh, 1926. **Leslie, E. A.** *Isaiah.* New York: Abingdon, 1963. **Luther, M.** *Der Prophet Jesaia.* Vols. 25, 31.2 of *D. Martin Luthers Werke.* Kritische Gesamtausgabe 25. Weimar, 1883. 87–401. ———. *Lectures on Isaiah Chs. 1–39.* Vol. 16 of *Luther's Works.* Ed. and trans. J. Pelikan and H. C. Oswald. St. Louis: Concordia, 1969. **Luzzatto, S. D.** *Commentary on the Book of Isaiah.* (Heb.) 1855. Reprint, Tel Aviv: Davir, 1970. **Marti, K.** *Das Buch Jesaja.* KHC. Tübingen: Mohr, 1900. **Mauchline, J.** *Isaiah 1–39.* TBC. London: SCM Press, 1962. **Motyer, J. A.** *The Prophecy of Isaiah: An Introduction and Commentary.* Downers Grove, IL: InterVarsity Press, 1993. **Nägelsbach, C. W. E.** *Der Prophet Jesaja.* Leipzig: Klasing, 1877. **Oswalt, J. N.** *The Book of Isaiah, Chapters 1–39.* NICOT. Grand Rapids, MI: Eerdmans, 1986. ———. *The Book of Isaiah, Chapters 40–66.*

NICOT. Grand Rapids, MI: Eerdmans, 1998. **Procksch, O.** *Jesaia I.* (Isa 1–39.) KAT 9.1. Leipzig: Scholl, 1930. **Scott, R. B. Y.** "The Book of Isaiah." *IB.* New York; Nashville: Abingdon, 1956. 5:149–381. **Seitz, C. R.** *Isaiah 1–39.* IBC. Louisville: Westminster John Knox, 1993. **Steinmann, J.** *Le Livre de la Consolation d'Israel.* LD 28. Paris, 1960. **Sweeney, M. A.** *Isaiah 1–39 with an Introduction to Prophetic Literature.* FOTL 16. Grand Rapids, MI: Eerdmans, 1996. **Watts, J. D. W.** *Isaiah 1–33.* WBC 24. Waco, TX: Word, 1985. ———. *Isaiah 34–66.* Waco, TX: Word, 1987. **Whybray, R. N.** *Isaiah 40–66.* NCB. Grand Rapids, MI: Eerdmans, 1975. ———. *The Second Isaiah.* OT Guides. Sheffield: Sheffield Academic Press, 1983. **Wildberger, H.** (1965–82). *Jesaja 1–12.* BKAT 10. Neukirchen-Vluyn: Neukirchener Verlag, 1972. Translated by T. H. Trapp as *Isaiah 1–12.* Minneapolis: Augsburg, 1991. ———. *Jesaja 13–27.* BKAT 10. Neukirchen-Vluyn: Neukirchener Verlag, 1978. Translated by T. H. Trapp as *Isaiah 13–27.* Minneapolis: Augsburg, 1999. ———. *Jesaja 28–39.* BKAT 10. Neukirchen-Vluyn: Neukirchener Verlag, 1982. Translated by T. H. Trapp as *Isaiah 28–39.* Minneapolis: Augsburg, 2002. **Young, E. J.** *The Book of Isaiah.* 3 vols. NICOT. Grand Rapids, MI: Eerdmans, 1965–72. **Ziegler, J.**, ed. *Isaias.* Septuaginta 14. Göttingen: Vandenhoeck & Ruprecht, 1939. ———, ed. *Isaias.* 3d ed. Septuaginta: Vetus Testamentum Graecum Auctoritate Academiae Scientiarium Gottingensis 14. Göttingen: Vandenhoeck & Ruprecht, 1983.

General Bibliography

Cited in text by author's or editor's name and shortened title.

Ackroyd, P. "Isaiah I–XII: Presentation of a Prophet." In *Congress Volume Göttingen 1977.* VTSup 29. Leiden: Brill, 1978. 16–48. **Alt, A.** *Kleine Schriften zur Geschichte des Volkes Israel.* 3 vols. Munich: Beck, 1953–59. **Anderson, B. W.**, and **W. Harrelson,** eds. *Israel's Prophetic Heritage.* FS J. Muilenburg. New York: Harper; London: SCM Press, 1962. **Balentine, S. E.,** and **J. Barton,** eds. *Language, Theology, and the Bible.* FS J. Barr. Oxford: Clarendon, 1994. **Barrick, W. B.,** and **J. R. Spencer,** eds. *In the Shelter of Elyon.* FS G. W. Ahlström. Sheffield: JSOT Press, 1984. **Bartelt, A. H.** *The Book around Immanuel: Style and Structure in Isaiah 2–12.* Biblical and Judaic Studies from the University of California, San Diego 4. Winona Lake, IN: Eisenbrauns, 1995. **Barth, H.** *Die Jesaja-Worte in der Josiazeit: Israel und Asshur als Thema einer Produktiven Neuinterpretation des Jesajaüberlieferung.* WMANT 48. Neukirchen-Vluyn: Neukirchener Verlag, 1977. **Beck, A. B., et al.,** eds. *Fortunate the Eyes That See.* FS D. N. Freedman. Grand Rapids, MI: Eerdmans, 1995. **Becker, J.** *Isaias—Der Prophet und sein Buch.* SBS 30. Stuttgart: Katholisches Bibelwerk, 1968. **Becker, U.** *Jesaja—Von der Botschaft zum Buch.* FRLANT 178. Göttingen: Vandenhoeck & Ruprecht, 1997. **Begrich, J.** *Studien zu Deuterojesaja.* BWANT 4.25. Stuttgart: Kohlhammer, 1938. **Berges, U.** *Das Buch Jesaja: Komposition und Endgestalt.* Herders Biblische Studien 16. Freiburg: Herder, 1998. **Blum, E., et al.,** eds. *Die Hebräische Bibel und ihre zweifache Nachgeschichte.* FS R. Rendtorff. Neukirchen-Vluyn: Neukirchener Verlag, 1990. **Böhnke, M.**, and **H. Heinz,** eds. *Im Gespräch mit dem dreineinen Gott: Elemente einer trinitarischen Theologie.* FS W. Breuning. Düsseldorff: Patmos, 1985. **Bosman, H. J., H. van Grol, et al.,** eds. *Studies in Isaiah 24–27.* OtSt 43. Leiden: Brill, 2000. **Brownlee, W. H.** *The Meaning of the Qumran Scrolls for the Bible.* New York: Oxford UP, 1964. 247–49. **Broyles, C. C.,** and **C. A. Evans,** eds. *Writing and Reading the Scroll of Isaiah: Studies of an Interpretive Tradition.* 2 vols. VTSup 70.1–2; FIOTL 1–2. Leiden: Brill, 1997. **Brunet, G.** *Essai sur l'Isaïe de l'Histoire.* Paris: Picard, 1975. **Budde, K.** *Jesaja's Erleben: Eine gemeinverständliche Auslegung der Denkschrift des Propheten (Kap. 6:1–9:6).* Gotha: Klotz, 1928. **Carrez, M., et al.,** eds. *De la Torah au Messie.* FS H. Cazelles. Paris: Desclée, 1981. **Childs, B. S.** *Isaiah and the Assyrian Crisis.* SBT 2.3. Naperville, IL: Allenson, 1967. **Chilton, B.** *The Glory of Israel: The Theology and Provenience of the Isaiah Targum.* Sheffield: JSOT Press, 1982. ———. *The Isaiah Targum: Introduction, Apparatus and Notes.* Wilmington, DE: Glazier, 1987. **Coggins, R., et al.,** eds. *Israel's Prophetic Tradition.* FS P. Ackroyd. Cambridge: Cambridge UP, 1982. **Conrad, E. W.** "Prophet, Redactor and Audience: Reforming the Notion of Isaiah's Formation." In *New Visions,* ed. R. F. Melugin and M. A. Sweeney. 305–26. ———. *Reading Isaiah.* OBT. Minneapolis: Fortress, 1991. **Conrad E. W.,** and **E. G. Newing,** eds. *Perspective on Language and Text.* FS F. I. Andersen. Winona Lake, IN: Eisenbrauns, 1987. **Darr, K. P.** *Isaiah's Vision and the Family of God.* Louisville: Westminster John Knox, 1994. **Diedrich, F.,** and **B. Willmes,** eds. *Ich bewirke das Heil und erschaffe das Unheil (Jesaja 45,7): Studien zur Botschaft der Propheten.* FS L. Ruppert. FB 88. Würzburg: Echter, 1998. **Dillman, A.** *Der Prophet Jesaja.* Leipzig: Hirzel, 1890. **Donner, H.** *Israel unter den Völkern: Die Stellung der klassischen Propheten des 8. Jahrhunderts v. Chr. zur Aussenpolitik der Könige von Israel and Juda.* VTSup 11. Leiden: Brill, 1964. **Driver, G. R.** "Difficult Words in the Hebrew Prophets." In *Studies in Old Testament Prophecy.* FS T. H. Robinson, ed. H. H. Rowley. Edinburgh: T & T Clark, 1950. 52–72. ———. "Hebrew Notes on Prophets and Proverbs." *JTS* 41 (1940) 162–75. ———. "Hebrew Scrolls." *JTS* 2 (1951) 21–25. ———. "Isaiah I–XXXIX: Textual and Linguistic Problems. "*JSS* 13 (1968) 36–57. ———. "Isaianic

Problems." In *Festschrift für Wilhelm Eilers.* Ed. G. Wiessner. Wiesbaden: Harrassowitz, 1967. 43–57. ———. "Linguistic and Textual Problems: Isaiah I–XXXIX." *JTS* 38 (1937) 36–50. ———. "Studies in the Vocabulary of the Old Testament." *JTS* 34 (1933) 337–381. ———. "Vocabulary of the OT, VI." *JTS* 34 (1933) 375–83. **Driver, S. R.** *Isaiah: His Life and Times and the Writings Which Bear His Name.* New York: Randolph, 1883. **Eaton, J. H.** "The Origin of the Book of Isaiah." *VT* 9 (1959) 138–57. **Ehrlich, A. B.** *Randglossen zur hebräischen Bibel textkritisches, sprachliches und geschichtliches.* Vol. 4, *Jesaia, Jeremia.* Leipzig: Hinrichs, 1912. **Exum, J. C.,** and **H. G. M. Williamson,** eds. *Reading from Right to Left.* FS D. J. A. Clines. JSOTSup 373. Sheffield: Sheffield Academic Press, 2003. **Fey, R.** *Amos und Jesaja: Abhängigkeit und Eigenständigkeit des Jesaja.* WMANT 12. Neukirchen-Vluyn: Neukirchener Verlag, 1963. **Fohrer, G.** "Neue Literatur zur alttestamentlichen Prophetie." *TRu* 45 (1980) 1–39, 108–15. ———. *Studien zur Alttestamentlichen Prophetie (1949–1965).* BZAW 99. Berlin: Töpelmann, 1967. **Goedicke, H.,** ed. *Near Eastern Studies.* FS W. F. Albright. Baltimore: Johns Hopkins UP, 1971. **Gordon, R.,** ed. *"The Place Is Too Small for Us": The Israelite Prophets in Recent Scholarship.* SBTS 5. Winona Lake, IN: Eisenbrauns, 1995. **Gottwald, N. K.** *All the Kingdoms of the Earth.* New York: Harper & Row, 1964. 222–28. **Hardmeier, C.** "Verkündigung und Schrift bei Jesaja: Zu Entstehung der Schriftprophetie als Oppositionsliteratur im alten Israel." *TGl* 73 (1983) 119–34. **Hausmann, J.,** ed. *Alttestamentlicher Glaube und biblische Theologie.* FS H. D. Preuss. Stuttgart: Kohlhammer, 1992. **Hoffmann, H. W.** *Die Intention der Verkündigung Jesajas.* BZAW 136. Berlin: De Gruyter, 1974. **Høgenhaven, J.** *Gott und Volk bei Jesaja: Eine Untersuchung zur biblischen Theologie.* ATDan 24. Leiden: Brill, 1988. **Holladay, W. L.** *Isaiah: Scroll of a Prophetic Heritage.* Grand Rapids, MI: Eerdmans, 1978. **Irwin, W. H.** "Isaiah 28–33: Translation with Philological Notes." Diss., Pontifical Biblical Institute, Rome, 1973. **Jones, D. R.** "The Tradition of the Oracles of Isaiah of Jerusalem." *ZAW* 67 (1955) 226–46. **Kitchen, K. A.** *The Third Intermediate Period in Egypt (1100 to 650 B.C.E.).* Warminster: Aris & Phillips, 1973. **Köhler, L.** *Kleine Lichter.* Zurich: Zwingli, 1945. ———. *Old Testament Theology.* Trans. A. S. Todd. London: Lutterworth, 1957. **Kutscher, E. Y.** *The Language and Linguistic Background of the Isaiah Scroll (1QIsa[a]).* Leiden: Brill, 1974. **Laato, A.** *A Star Is Rising: The Historical Development of the Old Testament Royal Ideology and the Rise of the Jewish Messianic Expectations.* Atlanta: Scholars Press, 1997. **Lack, R.** *La symbolique de livre d'Isaïe: Essai sur l'image littéraire comme élément de structuration.* AnBib 59. Rome: Biblical Institute Press, 1973. **Melugin, R. F.,** and **M. A. Sweeney,** eds. *New Visions of Isaiah.* JSOTSup 214. Sheffield: Sheffield Academic Press, 1996. **Mowinckel, S.** "Die komposition des Jesajabuches Kap. 1–39." *AcOr* 11 (1933) 267–92. **Noth, M.** *Die israelitschen Personennamen.* BWANT 46. Stuttgart: Kohlhammer, 1928. **O'Connell, R. H.** *Concentricity and Continuity: Literary Structure in Isaiah.* JSOTSup 188. Sheffield: Sheffield UP, 1994. **Olyan, S. M.,** and **R. C. Culley,** eds. *"A Wise and Discerning Mind."* FS B. O. Long. BJC 325. Providence, RI: Brown Judaic Studies, 2000. **Postma, F., et al.,** eds. *The New Things: Eschatology in Old Testament Prophecy.* FS H. Leene. Maastricht: Shaker, 2002. **Reid, S. B.,** ed. *Prophets and Paradigms.* FS G. M. Tucker. JSOTSup 229. Sheffield: Sheffield Academic Press, 1996. **Schunck, K.-D.,** and **M. Augustin,** eds. *Goldene Äpfel in silbernen Schalen.* Frankfort am Main: Lang, 1992. **Skilton, J. H.,** ed. *The Law and the Prophets.* FS O. T. Allis. Nutley, NJ: Presbyterian & Reformed P. C., 1974. **Stenning, J. F.,** ed. and trans. *The Targum of Isaiah.* Oxford: Clarendon, 1949. **Sweeney, M. A.** *Isaiah 1–4 and the Post-Exilic Understanding of the Isaianic Tradition.* BZAW 171. Berlin: De Gruyter, 1988. **Talmon, S.** "Observations on Variant Readings in the Isaiah Scroll (1QIsa[a])." In *The World of Qumrân from Within: Collected Studies.* Jerusalem: Magnes; Leiden: Brill, 1989. 117–30. **Tur-Sinai, N. H.** "A Contribution to the Understanding of Isaiah I–XII." In *Studies in the Bible.* Ed. C. Rabin. ScrHier 8. Jerusalem: Magnes; Hebrew Univ., 1961. 154–88. **Van Ruiten, J.,** and **M. Vervenne,** eds. *Studies in the Book of Isaiah.* FS W. A. M. Beuken. BETL 132. Leuven: Peeters, 1997. **Vaux, R. de.** *Ancient Israel: Its Life and Institutions.* Trans. J. McHugh. New York: McGraw-Hill, 1961. **Vermeylen, J.** *Du prophète Isaïe à l'apocalyptique.* 2 vols. Paris: Gabalda, 1977. **Vermeylen, J.,** ed. *The Book of Isaiah = Le livre d'Isaïe: Les oracles et leurs relectures unité et complexité de l'ouvrage.* BETL 81. Leuven: Leuven

UP; Peeters, 1989. **Vincent, J. M.** *Studien zur literarischen Eigenart und zur geistigen Heimat von Jesaja, Kap. 40–55.* BBET 5. Frankfurt am M.: Lang, 1977. **Vollmer, J.** *Geschichtliche Rückblicke und Motive in der Prophetie des Amos, Hosea, und Jesaja.* BZAW 119. Berlin: De Gruyter, 1971. **Waard, J. de.** *A Handbook on Isaiah.* Textual Criticism and the Translator 1. Winona Lake, IN: Eisenbrauns, 1997. **Watts, J. W.,** and **P. R. House,** eds. *Forming Prophetic Literature: Essays on Isaiah and the Twelve.* FS J. D. W. Watts. JSOTSup 235. Sheffield: Sheffield Academic Press, 1996. **Watts, J. Wash.** *A Survey of Syntax in the Hebrew Old Testament.* Grand Rapids, MI: Eerdmans, 1964. **Westermann, C.** *Basic Forms of Prophetic Speech.* Trans. H. C. White. Philadelphia: Westminster, 1967. **Whedbee, J. W.** *Isaiah and Wisdom.* Nashville: Abingdon, 1971. **Wiklander, B.** *Prophecy as Literature: A Text-linguistic and Rhetorical Approach to Isaiah 2–4.* Rev. ed. ConBOT 22. Malmö: Gleerup, 1984. **Williamson, H. G. M.** *The Book Called Isaiah: Deutero-Isaiah's Role in Composition and Redaction.* Oxford: Clarendon, 1994.

Introduction

Summary

The primary goal of this commentary is to interpret the book of Isaiah. Hans Wildberger (vii) notes that it was clear to him from the beginning of his work on Isaiah that what was finally paramount was the interpretation of the book as it now exists. In spite of the invaluable worth of his commentary in summarizing and evaluating all the results of historical-critical research to date, it does not succeed in presenting an understandable interpretation of the whole book. He has used historical exegesis, and his work presents the tremendous results of that method. But it does not make the book come alive for the reader or student.

I think his example demonstrates that it is not possible to mix the two methods. This commentary recognizes the vast literature of research on the prehistory of the traditions and the text in the *Bibliographies,* in the *Introduction,* and, as far as the study of the text itself is concerned, in the *Notes.* Where form criticism's definitions of *genre* can be used in a literature that no longer follows the dictates of oral genres, these, too, have been noted and used. But from that point on the commentary has made no effort to enter discussions of source-, form-, or redaction-criticism. For these the reader is referred to current introductions or commentaries, preeminently Wildberger's great work.

Bibliographies have been assembled to provide the reader access to literature on the passage or subject at hand. They are listed whether or not they have been used by the author or cited in this commentary. The reader will find a more complete review and evaluation of the literature in Wildberger's commentary (the first two volumes now available in English), in Sweeney's commentary on chaps. 1–39, and in the volumes of the Historical Commentary on the Old Testament by Beuken (on chaps. 28–39) and Koole (on chaps. 40–48 and 49–55).

Translations are deliberately literal to give the reader a starting point for understanding the Hebrew idiom. The metrical notation is not, and cannot be, definitive. It is intended to convey the general poetic pattern of parallelism.

Notes deal with textual variations and explain the reasons for translations. In Isaiah there are many *hapax legomena,* words that occur only once in the Bible, so that the need to explain word meanings is immense. Grammatical explanations that will help the student translator are also included.

Form/Structure/Setting sections draw on form-critical and redactional studies where applicable. The analysis in these sections identifies the literary genre and shows other evidence for the shape of the compositions that may aid understanding and exposition. Throughout the discussion, the reader will find more structural analyses showing the use of an arch form than analysis in the form of traditional outlines.

Comment sections deal with the meanings of words or of a verse or two at a time, providing information that may add to the reader's understanding. Sometimes this leads into word studies that relate the use of a word in a verse to its use in the larger work or even in the OT as a whole. Here and elsewhere, *Strands* document the use of particular words or themes through the book. They demonstrate the common vocabulary of the entire book and the dedication to common themes. Occasionally an *Excursus* is used to give a more complete survey of a pertinent subject, discuss ancillary matter, or provide additional information. Some *Excursuses* also provide historical background at intervals to remind the reader what is going on in the world in the time periods portrayed by the Vision and to provide background information helpful for understanding the dialogue and the setting for the action.

Explanation sections attempt to pull together the insights from the earlier sections to show what a passage as a whole is about and what it means in the context of the Vision.

Because the vision genre is like drama, this translation is presented in that form. The larger sections are called "acts" while the smaller ones are "scenes," which in turn contain "episodes." Suggested designations of speakers, found at the left of the *Translation,* serve also to note the limits of the speeches.

I have assumed a date of completion late enough to include all the historical references in the book within the present or past perspective of the "author." This allows the text itself to indicate explicitly the places where the prophet Isaiah is to be identified and heard. My aim is to keep in focus the nature of the book: a vision that dramatically portrays God's view of history rather than a source book from which the historian is to piece together what happened at that time. I hope to recapture the grand view of God's design that the book's sweeping presentation of history was intended to give to a generation badly in need of direction. By looking to the past, like a yachtsman watching the boat's wake in the water, the book points out that God's events have moved in a straight line while succeeding generations have attempted in vain to follow a different course. It argues that God's course continues in a straight line established by Isaiah's messages some two hundred years before, but that current leaders, like those of the past, are insisting on trying to set a different course.

The book of Isaiah explicitly points to datable events (chap. 7, 734 B.C.E.; chap. 20, 714–712 B.C.E.; chaps. 45–46, 540 B.C.E.); these move forward chronologically and accurately. Chaps. 36–39 are quoted from 2 Kings and are an exception to this chronological sequence. The superscription (1:1) announces a time span (the reign of eighth-century Judean kings and the activity of Isaiah) that includes the dates mentioned in 6:1, 7:1–25, 14:28, 20:1–6, 22:14–25, and 36:1–39:8. The chronological movement of the book beyond this period to include the references in chaps. 45–46 indicates a scope broader than Isaiah's lifetime, yet the superscription for the book requires a substantial link to the vision and the words of Isaiah of the eighth century.

I suggest that the book provides exactly that. It establishes the essentials of Isaiah's vision in 7:1–16 and in 20:1–6, including his specific words not found in other quoted accounts or in chaps. 36–39. It then traces the reactions to that message in Judean royal policies of the eighth, seventh, and early sixth centuries, and in the responses of exilic and postexilic generations, including the author's contemporary generation.

The book proclaims that Isaiah in the eighth century revealed YHWH's decisions and strategy concerning Israel, Judah, and the empires. It claims that

YHWH's strategy has not varied throughout that period and that Isaiah's words continue to be valid, i.e., that YHWH has sent the imperial power to serve his purposes and that Israel/Judah's role must be assessed accordingly. That role (from the eighth century onward) no longer includes the Davidic vision of an independent monarchy. Israel and Judah are called to a passive political acceptance of imperial rule (from Assyrian to Persian). Active attempts to reassert Davidic suzerainty had been and would be repelled by YHWH's authority. Israel's/Judah's positive role is to conform to the vision (2:1–4) of Jerusalem as a pilgrimage center for all nations. The book further envisions a role as God's servant for the Jews of the dispersion and for Jerusalem and its inhabitants, and even other peoples (principally in Palestine) who seek YHWH and want to serve him.

Yet the Vision recognizes that the generations that practiced Isaiah's vision of passive political acceptance (those of Ahaz and Manasseh) have in fact been few and despised, and even they showed no inclination to make Jerusalem a pure sanctuary for the worship of YHWH. The Vision presents a melancholy recital of rejection for YHWH's "strategy" and of consequent failure for Israel and Judah. And it expects no change in its own day (chap. 65).

This alternative interpretation of God's relation to history (ca. 750 to 515 or 450 B.C.E.) deserves our attention. Its witness to God's sovereign decision to "change the game plan" in the mid-eighth century, to end the charade of a divided kingdom that purported to serve his purpose, coincides with the prophetic messages of Hosea and Amos. But the book's presentation of God's plan, "his strategy" that replaced the older one, is unique, and it needs to be heard again and again. There are strong reasons for its insistence that the change of political climate in Palestine that brought the entire area under the more or less consistent imperial rule of Assyrians, Babylonians, and Persians (and eventually Hellenists and Romans) was YHWH's doing; that he intended not only to punish his people but to accomplish his own historical goals; and that he had a vital but very different continuing role for his people, a role more in keeping with their Abrahamic election than its Davidic formulation.

Who Was Isaiah?

Isaiah son of Amoz was a prophet who lived and worked in Jerusalem from about 750 to 700 B.C.E. All that is known of him is contained in a few passages of the book that bears his name.

Strand: Isaiah Son of Amoz

Prologue	Act 1	Act 2	Act 3	Act 4	Act 5	Act 6	Epilogue
Isaiah son of Amoz							
1:1 2:1		13:1 20:2		37:2, 21 38:1			
Isaiah							
	7:3	20:3		37:5, 6 38:4, 21 39:3, 5			

The superscriptons (1:1; 2:1; 13:1) name Isaiah son of Amoz and lead a reader to look for things related to him. Isa 1:1 relates the Vision to him and dates his ministry to the reigns of Uzziah, Jotham, Ahaz, and Hezekiah. It names the subject of the Vision as Judah and Jerusalem, which fits the narratives in Isaiah very well. Isa 2:1 stands over the short prophecy in 2:2–4 about the mountain of YHWH's house and calls its genre a "word" related to Isaiah son of Amoz. Isa 13:1 relates directly to chap. 13 or chaps. 13–14 and calls the genre a "burden," which it then relates to Isaiah son of Amoz. It names the subject of the burden Babylon, but it also invokes Isaiah's name over the group of burdens that follow. Isaiah is also concerned with Babylon in chap. 39.

There is a strand of narrative material that runs through chaps. 7–39 concerning him. These are the only prose texts in a book composed otherwise of poetry. Isa 7:1–16 portrays a prophet called to address a king (Ahaz) in a time of crisis. The prophet and his son go out to meet the king outside the city. The troubled young king, having been in office a very short time, faces the challenge of neighboring kingdoms pressuring him to join in a rebellion against Assyria, a foreign power that is trying to get control of all Palestine. They have laid siege to his city and threatened to replace him on the throne. The prophet's message encourages the king to pull himself together with the promise that he will then be confirmed. The prophet offers the king, who is reluctant to ask for one, a sign: a virgin will conceive and bear a son who will never know the tyranny of the threatening kings. The date must be just before the Assyrian invasions of 734 B.C.E.

The second story (chap. 20) occurs some twenty years later, also in Jerusalem. Hezekiah is now king, and again there is a rumor of rebellion in the air. This time the ones involved are the Philistine cities, strongly encouraged by a rejuvenated Egyptian government. Isaiah is instructed to go about the city unclothed, looking like a prisoner or a deportee, proclaiming that this is what the Egyptians will soon look like when they have been overcome by the Assyrians. It is a warning for Hezekiah and Judah to stay well clear of such conspiracy.

The third story (chaps. 36–37) regards Jerusalem under siege by an Assyrian army in 701 B.C.E. The Assyrian general speaks eloquently, urging the city to surrender. Hezekiah and his ministers are distraught. When Isaiah is consulted, he gives them a message that God has heard the enemy's blasphemies. They should not be afraid. God will have the Assyrian receive news from home that will make him return home immediately. There he will be assassinated. When the general sends a second message, Hezekiah prays to God. Isaiah is sent with a second message, an eloquent and powerful response to the Assyrian general (37:22–29). This is followed by a message to Hezekiah promising the survival of a remnant to come out of the crowded city (37:30–32). He summarizes God's determination that the Assyrian not enter the city (37:33–34) and closes with these words:

> I will defend this city and save it,
>   for my sake and for the sake of David my servant.

These words resonate with Isaiah's own name, which means "Yahweh will save." The narrative closes with a note that the angel of Yahweh has come and killed 185,000 Assyrian soldiers in their camp. Sennacherib, king of Assyria, gives up the campaign and returns home. Soon after, he is assassinated by two of his sons.

A fourth narrative (chap. 38) tells of Hezekiah's severe illness, the announcement through Isaiah that he will die from it, Hezekiah's prayer, and Yahweh's response granting him fifteen more years of life. The last story (chap. 39) tells of Isaiah's response to a visit by messengers from Merodach-Baladan, king of Babylon. In answer to Isaiah's queries, Hezekiah admits that he has shown them all his armaments. Isaiah, sensing that this implies Hezekiah's agreement to participate in yet another rebellion against Assyria, denounces the king's actions. He predicts the time to come when all the treasures of the palace and the temple will be carried off to Babylon and some of Hezekiah's descendants will serve as eunuchs in the palace of the king of Babylon. The alert reader recognizes the fulfillment of these predictions in the deportations of 598 and 586 B.C.E. The descendants to which this refers are Jehoiachin and his family, who were "house guests" of Nebuchadnezzar and his son for decades in the sixth century B.C.E.

All of Isaiah's recorded ministry deals with Jerusalem and the Davidic kings Ahaz and Hezekiah. Only in chap. 39 is Isaiah anything but a prophet of salvation.

This is all that the Bible knows about Isaiah son of Amoz, unless the heroes of faith "sawed in two" (Heb 11:37) refer to him. This reflects a later tradition recorded in the apocryphal Ascension of Isaiah (trans. by R. H. Charles, *APOT,* 1:155–62), which reports that Isaiah suffered martyrdom under Manasseh.

The Role of Isaiah Son of Amoz in the Vision

Isaiah's prophecy and prophetic ministry inspired the book and are the heart of its structure. This is acknowledged in the title (1:1) and documented by the inclusion in chaps. 36–39 of the entire Isaiah narrative from 2 Kgs 18–19. Isaiah's active role in the reign of Ahaz is portrayed in chaps. 7–8, in which he provides hope for the monarchy through changing times. The prophet emerges from his retirement in 714 B.C.E. to demonstrate prophetically to the young King Hezekiah the folly of joining an Egyptian coalition of states rebelling against Assyria (chap. 20). Another key element in the Vision concerns Babylon. The initial announcement (chap. 13) is again credited to Isaiah by the title (13:1), just as a later word from the account in 2 Kings credits Isaiah with a strong word about Babylon (chap. 39). Thus the ideas, motifs, and thrust of 2 Kgs 18–19// Isa 36–39 dominate the composition of the entire book. The book presents Isaiah and his words (7:1–16; chap. 20; chaps. 36–39) as the core and inspiration of the Vision that has been composed around them.

It is no wonder, therefore, that first-person accounts throughout the book, from chap. 5 to 64:12, have traditionally been heard as words from the prophet, although the Vision does not identify them as such. In a number of passages, the Vision portrays the self-conscious role of its writer, who knows that the work is inspired, knows that it will not be received well at first, and knows of the need to provide a testimony for the ages:

> So I said: "Here am I! Send me!"
> Then he said: "Go!
>   and you shall say to this people:
> 'Listen constantly! But do not understand!
> Look regularly! But do not know!'

Dull the heart of this people!
Make its ear heavy
and shut its eyes,
lest it see with its eyes,
hear with its ears,
and its heart understand
and it may turn and will have healing." (Isa 6:8–11)

Binding of testimony—sealing of instruction with my disciples (will be there); and I will wait for YHWH, who is hiding his face from the house of Jacob, and I will hope for him. Behold, I and the children that YHWH has given to me (became) signs and symbols in Israel from YHWH of Hosts who dwells in Mount Zion. (Isa 8:16–18)

Now come!
Write it on a tablet near them.
Upon a scroll inscribe it,
that it may become for a later day
a witness forever.
For it is a rebellious people,
lying sons! (Isa 30:8)

My Lord YHWH has assigned me
a student's tongue
to know how to sustain a weary one (with) a word.
He wakes me up morning by morning—
he wakes up my ear
to listen as students do.
My Lord YHWH has opened my ear.
And I, on my part, have not been rebellious.
I have not turned my back (to him).
I gave my back to ones who beat me
and my cheeks to those who pluck them bare.
I did not hide my face
from insult and spitting.
And my Lord YHWH gives me help.
Therefore I have not been insulted.
Therefore I have set my face like a flint,
and I know I shall not be shamed.
My vindicator is near.
Who dares contend with me?
Let us stand up together!
Who wants to be master of my case?
Let him approach me!
See! My Lord YHWH gives me help.
Who would accuse me of wrongdoing?
See! All of them are like a garment that wears out.
A moth can devour them. (Isa 50:4–9)

Seitz suggested that 40:6–7 is the protest of the author of chap. 6 (see Sweeney). This suggestion fits the pattern of the above speeches. In addition, note that in 61:1–3, 10–11, the first-person speaker makes the case for creating a just society in the new order. In 63:7–64:12 he makes one last plea for "all Israel" to be included, although he knows that the entire Vision (from 1:2–4, 2:5–9, and on) argues that history will show otherwise.

So throughout the Vision, the writer depicts his role as extending and applying Isaiah's words and work. The book is properly named "Isaiah" because it applies his prophecies to three centuries of Israel's history with God.

ISAIAH THE PROPHET AND HIS SUCCESSORS

Historical-critical study of Scripture raised questions about the sources behind the canonical book of Isaiah. Assuming authorship by Isaiah son of Amoz in the eighth century, historians noted later accretions or additions to his work. An obvious beginning lay in noting the use in chaps. 36–39 of the relevant material from 2 Kgs 18:13; 18:17–20:19. The differences in the two accounts are very minor. The composer of the Vision has carefully chosen from 2 Kings the material that suited his purpose. The history, of which 2 Kings is a part, continues through the destruction of Jerusalem in 587 B.C.E. and contains a final note on the accession of Amel-Marduk in 562 B.C.E. It was presumably completed soon after that and was known both in the dispersion and in Jerusalem. Writing at or after that time, the composer of the Vision would have had no trouble extracting the relevant material that was useful to him from 2 Kings.

The suggestion of J. C. Döderlein (1775), which was anticipated by Ibn Ezra (ca. 1100), that chaps. 40–66 must have been written in the exile and restoration periods, has found almost unanimous acceptance among critical scholars. Bernhard Duhm (1892) refined the theory by suggesting a third body of material, chaps. 56–66, which he understood to derive from the returned community in Palestine. Opinion on this has been less unified (cf. J. Vermeylen, *Du prophète Isaïe,* 1:451–54). In the first thirty-five chapters of the book, various collections and groups have been isolated, and scholars from Budde to Mowinckel and Fohrer have attempted to show how they were brought together and organized (cf. Vermeylen, *Du prophète Isaïe,* 1:1–31).

Attempts to trace a history of prophetic tradition in the book include those of D. R. Jones (*ZAW* 67 [1955] 226–46) and J. H. Eaton (*VT* 9 [1959] 138–57). They see the book in terms of the gradual growth of material around a core of Isaiah tradition. J. Becker (*Isaias—Der Prophet und sein Buch,* 1968) and H. Barth (*Die Jesaja-Worte in der Josiazeit,* 1977) have used redaction criticism to trace the history and form of the material. W. L. Holladay (*Isaiah: Scroll of a Prophetic Heritage,* 1978) has written a very readable summary of this view. Part of the goal in all this research was to gain a historically verifiable picture of the prophet himself. Gilbert Brunet (*Essai sur l'Isaïe de l'Histoire* [Paris: Picard, 1975]) concentrated his efforts on chaps. 7, 8, and 22. M. A. Sweeney (*Isaiah 1–4,* 1988) continues that research, as does O. H. Steck's dogged tracing of redactional history in his writings and those of his students.

Another part of this monumental effort has been devoted to gaining a clear historical understanding of the nature of Israelite prophecy in the eighth and seventh centuries. Such works have supported studies of the psychology and phenomena of prophecy by Hölscher and Mowinckel. The bibliography on these is enormous. The reader who seeks a more complete bibliography should see the end of Wildberger's third volume, Fohrer (*TRu* 45 [1980] 1–39, 108–15), and Sweeney *(Isaiah 1–39).*

There is a growing discussion of the different roles played by prophets who preach and prophets who write, compose, and edit prophetic literature. Cf. G. B. Gray (liv), Jones (*ZAW* 67 [1955] 226–46), C. Hardmeier (*TGl* 73 [1983] 119–34), J. Jeremias (*Der Prophet Hosea,* ATD 24/1 [Göttingen: Vandenhoeck & Ruprecht, 1983]; "Amos 3–6: Beobachtungen zur Enstehungsgeschichte eines Prophetenbuches," *ZAW* 100 [1988] 119–34), H. Utzschneiter (*Kunder oder Schreiber? Eine These zum Problem der "Schriftprophetie" auf Grund von Maleachi 1,6–2,9,* BEATAJ 19 [Frankfurt: Lang, 1989]), and M. H. Floyd ("Prophecy and Writing in Habakkuk 2:1–5," *ZAW* 105 [1993] 462–81).

Edgar Conrad ("Prophet, Redactor and Audience," 306–26) says that the postexilic community constructed Isaiah the prophet and his world in order to make sense of its own present. Yet many other scholars follow the lead of S. Mowinckel (*AcOr* 11 [1933] 267–97) and other literary-historical critics in trying to identify texts that may be traced back to the historical Isaiah of the eighth century (E. Blum, "Jesajas prophetisches Testament: Beobachtungen zu Jes 1–11 [Teil I]," *ZAW* 108 [1996] 547–68) as well as in tracing the history of the development of the Isaiah tradition in successive layers (H. Barth [*Die Jesaja-Worte in der Josiazeit,* 1977] along with the newer work of O. Kaiser and O. H. Steck and his students).

It is not necessary to agree with Conrad—that the book invented Isaiah the prophet—to conclude that the book's author and the prophet need not be the same person. Without the assumption of Isaianic authorship, the history of research into the composition of this book would look very different.

The Implied Author

Who wrote Isaiah? The text never claims that Isaiah son of Amoz wrote anything. (The reference in 8:16 is ambiguous on this point.) He is mentioned in the titles in 1:1, 2:1, and 13:1. He is the subject of narratives in 7:1–16, 20:1–6, and chaps. 36–39. A prophetic scribe could have recorded his ministry in these narratives. However, early readers took Isaiah son of Amoz as the writer of the entire book. But scholars and readers, especially in the last two centuries, have had difficulties with this assumption because the book deals with some historical events at least two centuries after the time of Isaiah son of Amoz. Since Duhm (1892), interpreters have thought of a writer called "Deutero-Isaiah" for chaps. 40–66, but they continue to think of Isaiah son of Amoz as the writer of "Proto-Isaiah," chaps. 1–39. Now Williamson *(Book Called Isaiah)* has contended that "Deutero-Isaiah" had a major role in editing "First Isaiah." The Vision's implied author, known as "Isaiah" throughout the centuries, is more nearly like the "Deutero-Isaiah" or perhaps the "Trito-Isaiah" of recent scholarship.

Conrad *(Reading Isaiah)* has called attention to the "I" passages in the Vision (5:1–2; 6:1–13; 8:1–8, 11–18; 21:1–17; 22:4; 24:16*b;* 48:16*b;* 49:5–6; 50:4–7; 61:1–3*c;* 62:1, 6–7; 63:7–64:12) and suggested that they represent the "implied author" of the book who gave himself cameo appearances and speeches in the book. (See *Strand: "I" Passages.*)

Whybray (29–30, 38–43) has described the careers of "Deutero-Isaiah" and "Trito-Isaiah" implicit in the book. R. L. Kohn ("The Name of the Second Isaiah," in *Fortunate the Eyes That See,* ed. A. B. Beck et al.) has reminded us of the work of

Strand: "I" Passages

Prologue	Act 1	Act 2	Act 3	Act 4	Act 5	Act 6	Epilogue
	5:1 6:1–13 8:1–18	21:1–16 22:4 24:16*bc*		(42:19–21) 48:16*b*	49:5–6 50:4–7	61:1–3, 10–11	62:1, 6–7 63:7– 64:12

Rabban (*Second Isaiah* [1971]) and Palache (as well as Mowinckel and Schmidt; see *Excursus: Identifying the "Servant of YHWH"* at 41:21 below), who saw in 42:19 the proper name of Meshullam, the eldest son of Zerubbabel, identified as the servant of YHWH, and thus the author of the book. Thus the implied author studied by Conrad, Whybray, and others can be named "Meshullam" on the basis of 42:19. We need no longer use the awkward "Deutero-Isaiah." (Cf. J. D. W. Watts, "Two Studies in Isaiah," in *God's Word for Our World,* FS S. J. De Vries, ed. J. H. Ellens et al. [London; New York: T & T Clark, 2004] 1:135–46; see *Excursus: Meshullam, Son of Zarubbabel* in the *Comment* for 50:4–51:8.)

Combining these studies shows that the book of Isaiah depicts its author as Meshullam son of Zerubbabel, born and raised in Babylon, who went back to Jerusalem when Cyrus entered Babylon (48:16*b*), and was active in Jerusalem after his father's assassination there. He assembled prophetic stories about Isaiah son of Amoz (36:1–39:8; 7:1–14; 20:1–6). Perhaps working with other writers, he created the magnificent Vision of Isaiah. In it, he created a role for himself as a prophet using first-person dialogue through which he claimed particular credit for interpretations that recognized the Assyrian invasions as being YHWH's work of judgment (5:1–7; 6:1–13) against the whole land. He empathized with the sufferings of the peoples (21:1–17; 22:24; 24:16*b*). He identified himself with the Babylonian Golah, the people in exile, in failing to see and hear YHWH's call to be a servant (42:19*b*–21), but he also claimed the presence of YHWH's spirit (48:16*b*). He next appeared in Jerusalem to claim the place as YHWH's servant, but his claim was not well received (50:4–7). He took on the prophetic role of admonishing the people about their place in the new order (61:1–3*c*) and actively promoted the place of the renewed city (62:1, 6). He depicted himself as Israel's spokesman in one last prayer for YHWH to restore the people to the privileged position of children (63:7–64:12). He made cameo appearances in almost every act.

Excursus: Scribal Wisdom and Scribal Prophecy

Wise men and prophets had much in common. Both were counselors to kings. Both based their work on divine revelation. The ambiguity is particularly clear in the person of Daniel. Is he a prophet or a wise man? What about Joseph?

When wisdom and prophecy became literary, the relation became particularly close. Both depended on scribes. The hands and the methods of the scribes are on the Wisdom books as well as the prophetic books. Both interpret old traditions. Both are highly reflective in developing their thought. Their work marks the beginning of "theology" in Israel. Of course, it was also scribes who recorded and arranged the old traditions to create the story of Israel's origins. They recorded and interpreted the law. In this they represented the priests. The singers needed scribes to record their psalms and songs. The scribes produced all the books of literature and created their unity and interactive nature.

When the Vision of Isaiah became a major force in shaping the Jews' view of themselves and their future and when Christians adopted the book as "their own prophet," the prophetic calling of the scribes was amply fulfilled and rewarded. They were in fact the epitome of prophetic vision and service. Anonymous but immensely influential, they, not the historical prophets, are the real "prophets" of the Scripture, the inspired writers of the book.

God is a primary speaker in the book of Isaiah. The place of the book among the sacred writings of Judaism and Christianity has led to the understanding that God inspired the writing of the book and should therefore also be considered its implied author.

What Is Isaiah?

Isaiah is a book called, in the first verse "The Vision of Isaiah the Son of Amoz." It has sixty-six chapters that contain all the information known about the prophet Isaiah woven into a much larger literary complex. It bears witness to YHWH's plan and dialogue with his people through some three centuries of their history, beginning with the decades in which Isaiah lived. The Vision provides a divine perspective on this history of Israel and Judah through speeches by YHWH himself and by his nonhuman representatives. It also records the responses of God's people in each generation. Although prophetic traditions, written and oral, were incorporated into the book, there is no evidence that any part circulated as a book prior to the production of the whole (see B. S. Childs, *IOTS,* 329; W. S. LaSor, D. A. Hubbard, and F. W. Bush, *Old Testament Survey* [Grand Rapids, MI: Eerdmans, 1982] 378).

The Vision portrays Isaiah as a prophet who looked with equanimity upon the violent political changes of his day because YHWH was in charge and was making things work out for good. Isaiah advocated policies that accepted vassalage to Assyria for Kings Ahaz (7:1–8) and Hezekiah (chap. 20), in contrast to the activist politics of independence espoused by the ministers of Kings Uzziah, Jotham, and Hezekiah. He witnessed to God's promises concerning Jerusalem (2:1–4; chaps. 36–37) and urged the kings to give God an opportunity to fulfill these promises without their manipulations.

Then the Vision moves well beyond the specific traditions about the prophet to portray God's plan and policies concerning Israel, Judah, and Jerusalem. It realistically presents Judah's postexilic life under Persian rule as God's plan for his people. It portrays God's judgment over Israel and Jerusalem (chaps. 1–6) and the period 733–721 B.C.E. (chaps. 7–10), but continues to speak about Israel's destiny throughout the book to chap. 64. It pictures Jerusalem's sins in chaps. 1 and 3, but sees a vision of a future Jerusalem free of these faults and open to all peoples who seek the Lord (2:1–4; passim; and 65:17–66:24). It traces the policies of Judean kings and governments (chaps. 7, 22, 28–33), but also describes the vision of God's plan that drew Assyria into Palestine (chaps. 18–19) and that later brought Cyrus from Persia to rebuild Jerusalem and the temple (chaps. 45–46).

The Vision is realistic in portraying the political situation, but it also lifts realism to a higher dimension by claiming that God has a goal beyond "what is" that can be achieved if met by faith (chaps. 11–12, 19, 24–27, 41–48, 49–54, 55–59). The achievement of God's goals was frustrated in each instance by the failure of

God's own people in Israel, Judah, and Jerusalem to see, hear, and believe (chaps. 7, 20–22, 30–33, 48, 50, 63–65). In the Vision the pagans, Assyria and Persia, march at God's command. Only Israel/Jerusalem is recalcitrant, rebellious, and self-willed.

The important point to notice here is Israel's refusal to heed God's call to assume a "servant role." To accept this call would have meant forgoing the claim to political independence and power that had now been delegated to the empires. But Israel was too proud and spirited for that. She had her full share of the natural human drive called *pride,* which is universally applauded. God, however, does not applaud but considers pride grounds for total judgment and destruction (2:5–22). Israel and Jerusalem, "like the nations," prefer to follow human ideals so they, "like the nations," run the risk of God's wrath.

The Vision pictures God's patience and persistence in pursuing his goals for Israel and Jerusalem. He pleads for faith and yielding obedience, for insight and willing attentiveness. But to the very end, leaders in Jerusalem prove unable or unwilling to respond to his call (65:1–16).

ISAIAH IS A TEXT

Bibliography

An exhaustive bibliography is found in Wildberger, 1718–23. See also F. D. James, "A Critical Examination of the Text of Isaiah." Ph.D. diss., Boston University, 1959.

Masoretic Text (MT)—Hebrew
Goshen-Gottstein, M. H., ed. *The Book of Isaiah.* 2 vols. The Hebrew University Bible. Jerusalem: Magnes, 1975. **James, F. D.** "A Critical Examination of the Text of Isaiah." Ph.D. diss. Boston University, 1959. **Kooij, A. van der.** *Die alten Textzeugen des Jesajabuches.* Freiburg: Universitätsverlag; Göttingen: Vandenhoeck & Ruprecht, 1981. **Thomas, D. W.,** ed. *Liber Jesaiae: Biblia Hebraica Stuttgartensia.* Stuttgart: Deutsche Bibelstiftung, 1967.

Septuagint (LXX)—Greek
Baer, D. A. "It's All About Us! Nationalistic Exegesis in the Greek Isaiah 1–12." In *SBLSP 2001.* Atlanta: SBL, 2001. 197–219. ———. "With Due Respect: Speaking about God in LXX Isaiah." *AAR/SBL Abstracts 1998.* Atlanta: Scholars Press, 1998. 326. **Kooij, A. van der.** "Interpretation of the Book of Isaiah in the Septuagint and Other Ancient Versions." In *SBLSP 2001.* Atlanta: SBL, 220–39. ———. "Isaiah in the Septuagint." In *Writing and Reading.* Ed. C. C. Broyles and C. A. Evans. 2:513–29. ———. "The Old Greek of Isaiah in Relation to the Qumran Texts of Isaiah: Some General Comments." In *Septuagint, Scrolls and Cognate Writings.* Ed. G. J. Brooke and B. Lindars. Atlanta: Scholars Press, 1992. 195–213. ———. "The Septuagint of Isaiah: Translation and Interpretation." In *The Book of Isaiah.* Ed. J. Vermeylen. Leuven: Peeters, 1989. 127–33. **Porter, S. L.,** and **B. W. R. Pearson.** "Isaiah through Greek Eyes: The Septuagint of Isaiah." In *Writing and Reading.* Ed. C. C. Broyles and C. A. Evans. 2:531–46. **Rahlfs, A.,** ed. *Septuaginta.* 9th ed. Vol. 2. Stuttgart: Württembergische Bibelanstalt, 1935. **Schweitzer, S. J.** "Mythology in the Old Greek of Isaiah: The Technique of Translation." *CBQ* 66 (2004) 214–30. **Ziegler, J.** "Die Vorlage der Isaias-Septuaginta (LXX) und die erste Isaias-Rolle von Qumran (1QIsa[a])." *JBL* 78 (1959) 34–59. **Ziegler, J.,** ed. *Isaias.* Septuaginta 14. Göttingen: Vandenhoeck & Ruprecht, 1939. ———, ed. *Isaias.* 3d ed. Septuaginta: Vetus Testamentum Graecum Auctoritate Academiae Scientiarium Gottingensis 14. Göttingen: Vandenhoeck & Ruprecht, 1983.

Targum (Tg.)—Aramaic

Chilton, B. *The Glory of Israel: The Theology and Provenience of the Isaiah Targum.* Sheffield: JSOT Press, 1982. ——— *The Isaiah Targum: Introduction, Apparatus and Notes.* Wilmington, DE: Glazier, 1987. **Sperber, A.,** ed. *The Bible in Aramaic.* Vol. 3, *The Latter Prophets according to Targum Jonathan.* Leiden: Brill, 1962. **Stenning, J. F.,** ed. and trans. *The Targum of Isaiah.* Oxford: Clarendon, 1949.

Dead Sea Scrolls—Hebrew

Brownlee, W. H. *The Meaning of the Qumrân Scrolls for the Bible: With Special Attention to the Book of Isaiah.* New York: Oxford UP, 1964. 247–49. **Burrows, M.** "Variant Readings in the Isaiah Manuscript." *BASOR* 111 (1948–49) 16–24; 113 (1949) 24–32. ———, ed. *The Dead Sea Scrolls of St. Mark's Monastery.* Vol. 1, *The Isaiah Manuscript and the Habakkuk Commentary.* New Haven, CT: ASOR, 1950 (hereafter designated 1QIsa[a]). **Cohen, C.** "A Philological Reevaluation of Some Significant DSS Variants of the MT in Isa 1–5." In *Diggers at the Well: Proceedings of a Third International Symposium on the Hebrew of the Dead Sea Scrolls and Ben Sira.* Ed. T. Muraoka, and J. F. Elwolde. Leiden: Brill, 2000. 40–55. **Flint, P. W.** "The Book of Isaiah in the Dead Sea Scrolls." In *The Bible as Book: The Hebrew Bible and the Judaean Desert Discoveries.* Ed. E. D. Herbert and E. Tov. London: British Library, 2002. 229–51. ———. "The Isaiah Scrolls from the Judean Desert." In *Writing and Reading.* Ed. C. C. Broyles and C. A. Evans. 2:481–89. **Flint, P. W., E. Ulrich,** and **M. G. Abegg.** *Edition of the Cave One Isaiah Scrolls.* DJD 37. Oxford: Clarendon, 1999. ———. *Qumran Cave 4: The Prophets.* DJD 15. Oxford: Clarendon, 1997. **García Martínez, F.** "Le Livre d'Isaïe à Qomrân: Les Textes. L'influence. *MdB* 49 (1987) 43–45. **Gonçalves, F. J.** "Isaiah Scroll." *ABD.* 3:470–72. **Goshen-Gottstein, M.** "Die Jesaja Rolle und das Problem der hebräischen Bibelhandschriften." *Bib* 35 (1954) 429–42. **Kutscher, E. Y.** *The Language and Linguistic Background of the Isaiah Scroll (1QIsa[a]).* Leiden: Brill, 1974. **Olley, J. W.** "Hear the Word of JHWH: The Structure of the Book of Isaiah in 1Qsa[a]." *VT* 43 (1993) 19–49. **Parry, D. W.,** and **E. Qimron,** eds. *The Great Isaiah Scroll (1QIsa[a]): A New Edition.* STDJ 32. Leiden: Brill, 1999. **Roberts, B. J.** "The Second Isaiah Scroll from Qumran (1QIsa[a])." *BJRL* 42.1 (1959) 132–44. **Rubinstein, A.** "The Theological Aspect of Some Variant Readings in the Isaiah Scroll." *JJS* 6 (1955) 187–200. **Skehan, P. W.** "The Text of Isaias at Qumrân." *CBQ* 17 (1955) 158–63. **Sukenik, E. L.,** ed. *The Dead Sea Scrolls of the Hebrew University.* Jerusalem: Magnes; Hebrew Univ., 1955 (hereafter designated 1QIsa[b]). **Talmon, S.** "Observations on Variant Readings in the Isaiah Scroll (1QIsa[a])." In *The World of Qumrân from Within: Collected Studies.* Jerusalem: Magnes; Leiden: Brill, 1989. 117–30. **Tov, E.** "The Text of Isaiah at Qumran." In *Writing and Reading.* Ed. C. C. Broyles and C. A. Evans. 2:491–511. **Ulrich, E.** "An Index to the Contents of the Isaiah Manuscripts from the Judean Desert." In *Writing and Reading.* Ed. C. C. Broyles and C. A. Evans. 2:477. ———. *Qumran Cave 4,X: The Prophets.* DJD 15. Oxford: Clarendon, 1997.

The oldest Hebrew text of Isaiah is on a leather scroll found in Qumran (1QIsa[a]) and now kept in Jerusalem. It is thought to have been copied in about 150–125 B.C.E. and is here designated 1QIsa[a]. Important variations from MT are shown in *BHS.* A second scroll from Qumran at the Hebrew University will be cited as 1QIsa[b]. DJD 15 now lists twenty-two scrolls and fragments from Qumran containing parts of Isaiah.

Vulgate (Vg.)—Latin

Weber, O., ed. *Biblia Sacra iuxta vulgatem versionem.* Vol. 2. Stuttgart: Württembergische Bibelanstalt, 1969. For other versions, the most available text is **Field, F.** *Origenis Hexaplorum quae supersunt.* Vol. 2. 1875. Reprint, Oxford: Oxford UP, 1964. **Gryson, R.** "Esaias." In *Vetus Latina Beuron 12.* Freiburg-Br.: Herder, 1987.

Peshitta (Pesh.) = Syriac

Barthélemy, D. *Isaiah.* Vol. 3.1 of *Vetus Testamentum Syriace.* Ed. S. P. Brock. Leiden: Brill, 1987. **Brock, S. P.** "Text History and Text Division in Peshitta Isaiah." In *Peshitta.* Leiden: Brill, 1988. 49–80. **Gelston, A.** "Was the Peshitta of Isaiah of Christian Origin." In *Writing and Reading.* Ed. C. C. Broyles and C. A. Evans. 2:563–82.

Isaiah is read in numerous translations in modern and ancient languages. (See Blenkinsopp, *Isaiah 1–39,* 76–78, for an excellent and succint summary.) The oldest translation is undoubtedly the Greek (G) known as the Septuagint (LXX). Early fourth-century C.E. manuscripts are kept in London and at the Vatican. Excellent critical editions are available.

But Isaiah was written in Hebrew. The best work of editing and transcribing Hebrew manuscripts was done by the Masoretes, scribes of the ben Asher family in Tiberius (MT). A beautiful and accurate manuscript prepared by Moshe ben Asher in 1009 C.E., called the Leningrad Codex, is now in the British Museum. Its text has been published in Kittel's *Biblia Hebraica* (*BHK,* 3d ed. [Stuttgart, 1937]); in the *Biblia Hebraica Stuttgartensia (BHS* [1983]*),* in which D. W. Thomas edited Isaiah (1968); and now in facsimile (D. N. Freedman et al., eds., *The Leningrad Codex: A Facsimile Edition* [Grand Rapids, MI: Eerdmans, 1998]). The *BHS* text is used in this commentary. The so-called Aleppo Codex prepared by Aaron ben Asher in the early tenth century has been published in facsimile as *The Aleppo Codex,* ed. M. H. Goshen-Gottstein (Jerusalem: Magnes, 1976), and as *The Book of Isaiah,* 2 vols. in The Hebrew University Bible (Jerusalem: Magnes, 1975). The British and Foreign Bible Society's Hebrew Bible is based on another ben Asher text kept in Madrid.

The Targumim (Tg.) are early Jewish commentaries on the Hebrew text; these are written in Aramaic. The Vulgate (Vg.) is the official Latin version of the Hebrew Scriptures, translated by Jerome in 406 C.E. It has recently appeared in a new edition by O. Weber. Other early versions of Isaiah are still most accessible to the student in Field's *Origenis Hexaplorum.*

Isaiah, then, is available to us in ancient manuscripts of the second and first century B.C.E. and of the fourth and tenth centuries C.E. In all these it represents one of the books of the Prophets in Holy Scripture. In the Greek version it appears as the first of the major prophetic books after the Minor Prophets. In Hebrew it is the first of the Latter Prophets after the books of history.

ISAIAH'S INFLUENCE IN EARLY JUDAISM AND THE NEW TESTAMENT

Bibliography

Early Judaism

Brooke, G. J. "Isaiah in the Pesharim and Other Qumran Texts." In *Writing and Reading.* Ed. C. C. Broyles and C. A. Evans. 2:609–32. **Chilton, B.** "Salvific Exile in the Isaiah Targum." In *Exile: Old Testament, Jewish, and Christian Perspectives.* Ed. H. M. Scott. JSJSup 56. Leiden: Brill, 1997. 239–47. ———. "Two in One: Renderings of the Book of Isaiah in Targum Jonathan." In *Writing and Reading.* Ed. C. C. Broyles and C. A. Evans. 2:547–62. **Feldman, L. H.** "Josephus' Portrait of Isaiah." In *Writing and Reading.* Ed. C. C. Broyles and C. A. Evans. 2:583–608. **Knibb, M. A.** "Isaianic Traditions in the Apocrypha and Pseudepigrapha." In *Writing and Reading.* Ed. C. C. Broyles and C. A. Evans. 2:633–50. ———. "Isaianic Traditions in the Book of Enoch." In *After the Exile.* FS R. Mason, ed. J. Barton and D. J. Reimer.

Macon, GA: Mercer UP, 1996. 217–29. **Porton, G. G.** "Isaiah and the Kings: The Rabbis on the Prophet Isaiah." In *Writing and Reading.* Ed. C. C. Broyles and C. A. Evans. 2:693–716. **Stern, E. R.** "Beyond *Nahamu:* Stratagies of Consolation in the Jewish Lectionary Cycle for the 9th of Av Season." In *SBLSP 1998.* Atlanta: Scholars Press, 1998. 1:180–204.

New Testament
Evans, C. A. "From Gospel to Gospel: The Function of Isaiah in the New Testament." In *Writing and Reading.* Ed. C. C. Broyles and C. A. Evans. 2:651–91. **Hays, R. B.** "'Who Has Believed Our Report?' Paul's Reading of Isaiah." In *SBLSP 1998.* Atlanta: Scholars Press, 1998. 1:205–25. **Qualls, P.** "Isaiah in Luke." Diss., Southern Baptist Theological Seminary, Louisville, 1996. **Schneck, R.** *Isaiah in the Gospel of Mark, I–VII.* Oakland, CA: Bibal Press, 1994. **Shum, S.-L.** *Paul's Use of Isaiah in Romans.* WUNT 2. Tübingen: Mohr-Sieback, 2002. **Watts, R.** *Isaiah's New Exodus and Mark.* WUNT 2.88. Tübingen: Mohr-Siebeck, 1998. **Wilke, F.** *Die Bedeutung des Jesajabuches für Paulus.* FRLANT 179. Göttingen: Vandenhoeck & Ruprecht, 1998.

Isaiah's position as the first of the prophetic books in the Tanak (the Jewish Bible) and in the Christian Bible indicates something of the esteem accorded it. The frequency with which it is mentioned in ancient literature and with which it appears among the Dead Sea Scrolls is further witness to its popularity and influence.

The Dead Sea Scrolls from Qumran refer to Isaiah and Deuteronomy more than to any other books. The NT quotes from fifty-seven different passages in Isaiah. Philo and the Apostolic Fathers refer to it often. Josephus (*Complete Works,* trans. W. Whiston [Grand Rapids, MI: Kregel, 1960]), in his history, quotes from historical sections of Isaiah. The Mishnah has repeated references that testify to the influence of the prophecy there. An early Christian apocalypse, *The Ascension of Isaiah,* is the only extant witness to an earlier Jewish work called *The Martyrdom of Isaiah,* which develops a legend about the death of Isaiah at the hands of Manasseh. It shows many affinities to the Qumran writings and may date from this time. Heb 11:37 seems to refer to it.

Isaiah's Influence in Judaism, Church History, and Western Literature

The book of Isaiah has been fortunate in its translations. The renderings in Greek, Latin, English, and other languages have to a large extent conveyed a great deal of the literary excellence, the imaginative power, and the theological appeal of the book.

Isaiah has been recognized as "prince of prophets." This reflects his walk with kings, but even more, the title acknowledges the excellence of the book that bears his name. Jews have found in Isaiah a model of the best that Judaism aspires to, in nobility of vision, faith, and life. Christians have found here a book and a person that fit the picture of faith most closely related to Jesus and the NT ideal.

The architecture of the world's cathedrals has repeatedly recognized Isaiah among the saints of old, worthy to stand with Moses and David as a symbolic representation of the work of God. The Vision has left its mark on Western art through paintings like Edward Hicks's "The Peaceable Kingdom," and it has inspired poets like Lord Byron ("When the Assyrian came down like a wolf on the fold / his cohorts all shining in purple and gold") and Matthew Arnold, who arranged its chapters for his pupils to use in learning proper English style. S. Goldman (*The Book of Books, an Introduction* [New York: Harper & Bros., 1948] 8) evaluates its literary worth: "With respect to excellence of style, no page of the *Iliad,* to take one instance of many, need blush before any page of Isaiah." The music of ancient as well as modern times has drawn from Isaiah's sonorous lines. Handel's *Messiah* takes its text from Isaiah rather than from the NT. Countless hymns and anthems repeat its lines. In the liturgies of Western churches, readings from Isa 7, 9, and 11 are prominent at Advent and Christmas, while chap. 53 is prominent on Good Friday. Chap. 1 is a classic text on true and false worship. Chap. 6 is a model of God's call to prophetic ministry; chap. 40 is a moving poem about hope, while chap. 55 is a favorite for evangelistic outreach.

Its interpretation has also been a point of controversy between Jews and Christians. Jewish interpreters have tended to object to the Christian understanding of 7:14 as a prophecy of the virgin birth and chap. 53 as a prophecy of a suffering Messiah (cf. S. R. Driver and A. Neubauer, *The Fifty-third Chapter of Isaiah according to the Jewish Interpreters,* 2 vols. [Oxford; London: Oxford UP, 1876–77]). Isaiah is usually regarded by the Christian as a source of messianic prophecies. It is important to note, however, that the prophecies in chaps. 9 and 11 are acceptably applied to Christ only when they are interpreted in the light of chaps. 51 and 53. Isaiah's Vision showed that the Davidic image was acceptable to the next age only with substantial revision that changed a triumphant king and ruling nation into a humble servant to God acting on God's behalf. The second image is perfectly in keeping with the Gospel's understanding of Jesus the Christ.

John F. A. Sawyer has studied the way the church has used Isaiah in its rhetoric against the Jews. See the following works by Sawyer: *The Fifth Gospel: Isaiah in the History of Christianity* (Cambridge: Cambridge UP, 1996); "The Gospel according to Isaiah," *ExpTim* 113.2 (2001) 40–43; "Isaiah and Zionism," in *Sense and Sensitivity: Essays on Reading the Bible in Memory of Robert Carroll,* ed. A. G. Hunter and P. R. Davies, JSOTSup 348 (Sheffield: Sheffield Academic Press, 2002) 246–60; and "Isaiah and the Jews: Some Reflections on the Church's Use of the Bible," in *Reading from Right to Left,* ed. J. C. Exum and H. G. M. Williamson, 390–401.

Scholarly commentaries (see *Annotated Chronological Bibliography of Commentaries on Isaiah* below) show the continuing theological interest that Isaiah has elicited. Isaiah has held his place among the prophets during the more recent interest in prophets as reformers, although Amos is famed as foremost in that respect. The modern understanding of chaps. 24–27 as belonging to apocalyptic genre has given the book the distinction of containing the first apocalyptic writings.

In all these ways Isaiah, man and book, has been honored as prince of prophets and premier prophetic book in religious and literary circles alike. For example, E. G. H. Kraeling (*The Old Testament Since the Reformation* [New York: Harper & Bros., 1955]) cites Isaiah fifty-four times in discussing the views of theologians and philosophers toward the OT.

Isaiah has always held an honored place in the English Bible. In Protestant Bibles it is the first of the books of prophecy after the books of poetry. It is presented in the excellent translations of the AV, RSV, NIV, and many others. Roman Catholic Bible translations, like the English JB and NAB, also place the book of Isaiah as the first of the Prophets, which compose the last group of books following the poetic books in the OT. In Jewish Bibles, like the NJPS, the order of the books follows that of the Hebrew text. Isaiah is the first of the Latter Prophets, an honored central position in the second most influential group of books of the Scriptures (the most influential being the Pentateuch). It is read as a powerful warning against apostasy as well as a persuasive proclamation of hope for the people of God.

BIBLIOGRAPHIES

Annotated Chronological Bibliography of Commentaries on Isaiah

For *older surveys* of works on Isaiah, see: **Young, E. J.** "The Study of Isaiah Since the Time of Joseph Addison Alexander." In *Studies in Isaiah.* London: Tyndale, 1955. 9–101. ———. "Appendix II." In *The Book of Isaiah.* NICOT. Grand Rapids, MI: Eerdmans, 1972. 1:487–99. **Fohrer, G.** "Neue Literatur zur alttestamentlichen Prophetie." *TRu* 45 (1980) 1–39, 108–15. **Wildberger, H.** *Jesaja 28–39.* BKAT 10. Neukirchen-Vluyn: Neukirchener Verlag, 1982. 1714–38 **Kilian, R.** *Jesaja 1–39.* EdF 200. Darmstadt: Wissenschaftliche Buchgesellschaft, 1983.

Writings on Isaiah have blossomed in the past decade. *Surveys of current work* on Isaiah may be found in the following: **Barstad, H. M.** "No Prophets? Recent Developments in Biblical Research and Ancient Near Eastern Prophecy." *JSOT* 57 (1993) 39–60. **Becker, U.** "Jesajaforschung (Jes 1–39)." *TRu* 64 (1999) 117–52. **Berges, U.** *Das Buch Jesaja: Komposition und Endgestalt.* Herders Biblische Studien 16. Freiburg: Herder, 1998. **Carr, D. M.** "Reaching for Unity in Isaiah." *JSOT* 57 (1993) 61–80. **Darr, K. P.** *Isaiah's Vision and the Family of God.* Louisville: Westminster John Knox, 1994. 1–34. **Deist, F. E.** "The Prophets: Are We Heading for a Paradigm Shift?" In *Prophet und Prophetenbuch.* FS O. Kaiser, ed. V. Fritz et al. BZAW 185. Berlin: De Gruyter, 1989. 1–18. **Hardmeier, C.** "Jesajaforschung im Umbruch." *VF* 31 (1986) 3–31. **Hermisson, H.-J.** "Neue Literatur zu Deuterojesaja." *TRu* 65 (2000) 237–84, 379–430. **Kaiser, O.** *Grundriss der Einleitung in die kanonischen and deuterokanonischen Schriften des Alten Testaments.* Munich: Kaiser, 1994. 2:29–49. ———. "Jesaja/Jesajabuch." *TRE.* 16:636–58. **Sweeney, M. A.** "The Book of Isaiah in Recent Research." *CurBS* 1 (1993) 141–42. ———. *Isaiah 1–39.* FOTL 16. Grand Rapids, MI: Eerdmans, 1996. 1–10. **Tate, M.** "The Book of Isaiah in Recent Study." In *Forming Prophetic Literature.* Ed. P. House and J. W. Watts. 22–56. **Williamson, H. G. M.** *The Book Called Isaiah: Deutero-Isaiah's Role in Composition and Redaction.* Oxford: Clarendon, 1994. 267–87.

The *church fathers* wrote voluminously on Isaiah. (Works are listed chronologically, with the date of the book or a date pertaining to the author in parentheses after the author's name.) **Tertullianus, Q. S. F.** (d. 220). *Libros de Patientia.* Ed. J. W. P. Borleffs. Hagae Comitis: Daamen, 1948. ———. "Of Patience." In *The Ante-Nicene Fathers.* Trans. S. Thelwell. Vol. 4. Buffalo: Christian Literature, 1886. Petitmengin, P. "Recherches sur les citations d'Isaie chez Tertullien." In *Recherches sur l'histoire de la bible latine.* FS H. Frede, ed. R. Gryson and P. M. Bogaert. CRTL 19. Louvain-la-neuve, 1987. 21–41. **Origen** (254). Origen's commentary in thirty books covers the first thirty chapters of Isaiah. ———. *Patrologiae cursus completus.* Series Graeca 13. Lutetiae Parisiorum: Migne, 1864. Fields, F. *Origenis Hexaplarum quae supersunt.* Vol. 2. Oxford: Oxford UP, 1875. Guinot, J.-N. "L'heritage origenien des commentateurs grecs du prophete Isaie." In *Origeniana Quarta.* Ed. L. Lies. Innsbruck; Vienna: Tyrolia, 1987. 379–89. **Cyprianus of Carthage** (258). *Opera Omnia.* 3 vols. Ed. G. Hartel. New York: Johnson Reprint, 1965. ———. *Writings.* Trans. R. E. Wallis. Edinburgh: T & T Clark, 1869–70. **Eusebius Pamphili of Caesaria** (4th cent.). *Der Jesajakommentar* (Gr.). Vol. 9 of *Eusebius Werke.* Ed. J. Ziegler. Berlin: Akademie, 1975.

Hollerich, M. J. *Eusebius of Caesarea's Commentary on Isaiah: Christian Exegesis in the Age of Constantine.* Oxford: Oxford UP, 1999. **Basilius the Great of Caesarea** (379). *Commento al profeta Isaia* (Gr. and Ital. chaps. 1–16 only). Trans. P. Trevisan. Torino: Societa editrice internazionale, 1939. **Tyconius** (ca. 383) "Liber de Septem Regulis." In *Patrologiae Cursus Completus.* Series Latina 18. Lutetiae Parisiorum: Migne, 1864. **Chrysostomus, J.** (407). "Hermeneia" of chaps. 1–8. *Patriologiae Cursus Completus.* Series Graeca 56. Lutetiae Parisiorum: Migne, 1864. ———. *Works.* 6 vols. Buffalo: Christian Literature, 1889–90. Dumortier, J. *Jean Chrysostome, Commentaire sur Isaïe.* Paris: Cerf, 1983. **Hieronymus** (Jerome) (410). *Commentarium in Esiam.* Vols. 1–18. Turnholti: Brepols, 1968. Jay, P. *L'exegese de Saint Jerome d'apres son 'Commentaire sur Isaie.'* Paris: Etudes augustiniennes, 1985. Gryson, R., and P.-A. Deproost, eds. *Commentaires de Jerome sur le Prophete Isaie: Livres I–IV.* Vetus Latina: Aus der Geschichte der lateinischen Bibel 23. Freiburg: Herder, 1993. Gryson, R., and V. Somers, eds. *Commentaires de Jerome sur le Prophete Isaie: Livres VIII–XI.* Vetus Latina: Aus der Geschichte der lateinische Bibel 30. Freiberg: Herder, 1996. **Cyrillus of Alexandria** (441). "Commentarius in Isaiam Prophetam." In *Patrologiae Cursus Completus.* Series Graeca 70. Lutetiae Parisiorum: Migne, 1864. **Theodoretus of Cyrrhus** (457). "Eclogaria Interpretatio in Isaiam." In *Patriologiae Cursus Completus.* Series Graeca 81. Lutetiae Parisiorum: Migne, 1864. ———. *Kommentar zu Jesaia.* Ed. A. Möhle. Berlin: Weidmann, 1932. ———. *The Book of Rules by Tyconius.* Trans. R. C. Burkitt. Cambridge: UP, 1894. Guinot, J.-N., ed. *Theodoret de Cyr, commentaire sur Isaie.* 3 vols. SC 276, 295, 315. Paris: Cerf, 1980–84.

The *Middle Ages* belong to Jewish scholars, who in Europe, Spain, North Africa, and the Middle East wrote voluminously in Hebrew, Arabic, and Latin. Those who made the greatest contribution concerning Isaiah were: **Saadia Gaon** (882–942). Alobaida, J. *The Messiah in Isaiah 53: The Commentaries of Saadia Gaon, Salmon ben Yeruham and Yefet ben Eli on Is 52:13–53:12.* La Bible dans l'histoire 2. Bern: Lang, 1998. Ben-Shammai, H. "Saadia Gaon's Introduction to Isaiah: Arabic Text with Hebrew Translation." *Tarbiz* 60 (1990–91) 371–404. **Ibn Bal'am** (ca. 1070–90). Goshen-Gottstein, M., ed., with the assistance of M. Perez. *R. Judah Ibn Bal'am's Commentary on Isaiah* [Introduction in English. Text in Hebrew]. Bar-Ilan Sources and Studies 5. Ramat Gan: Bar Ilan UP, 1992. **Ibn Ezra** (Abraham ben Meir) (1090–1164). *Commentary of Ibn Ezra on Isaiah.* (Heb.) Trans. M. Friedlander. 2d ed. New York: Feldheim, 1966. **Kimchi, D.** (1160–1235). *The Commentary of David Kimchi on Isaiah.* (Heb. with introduction in Eng.) Ed. L. Finkelstein. Columbia University Oriental Studies 19. New York: Columbia UP, 1926. Reprint, New York: AMS Press, 1966.

The *Reformers* returned the church to an emphasis on the Bible, including Isaiah: **Luther, M.** (1528). *Der Prophet Jesaia.* Vol. 25 of *D. Martin Luthers Werke.* Kritische Gesamtausgabe 25. Weimar, 1883. 87–401. ———. *Lectures on Isaiah Chs. 1–39.* Vol. 16 of *Luther's Works.* Ed. and trans. J. Pelikan and H. C. Oswald. St. Louis: Concordia, 1969. **Zwingli, U.** (1529). *Complanationis Isaiae Prophetae.* Zurich: Froschauer, 1529. ———. *Aus Zwinglis Predigten zu Jesaja und Jeremia.* Ed. O. Farner. Zurich: Berichthaus, 1957. **Calvin, J.** (1551). *Commentarii in Isaiam Prophetam.* In his *Opera quae supersunt omnia.* Brunvigae: Schwetschke et filium, 1863–1900. ———. *Commentary on the Book of the Prophet Isaiah.* 4 vols. Trans. W. Pringle. Grand Rapids, MI: Eerdmans, 1948.

Comments and shorter notices continue through the *eighteenth century* (cf. Young, 1:489–90), but commentaries, as such, are few: **Vitringa, C.** (1714). *Commentarius in Librum Prophetiarum Jesaiae.* 2d ed. Basil: J. R. im Hoff, 1732. **Döderlein, J. C.** (1775). *Esaias, ex recensione textus Hebraei.* Altorfi, 1789.

In the *nineteenth century,* commentaries begin to blossom. Two of the earliest were: **Eichhorn, J. G.** (1819). *Die hebräischen Propheten.* Göttingen, 1816–19. **Gesenius, W.** (1820). *Der Prophet Jesaia.* Leipzig: Vogel, 1829.

In the *middle of the nineteenth century* several excellent conservative commentaries appeared: **Barnes, A.** (1840). *Notes, Critical, Explanatory and Practical on the Book of the Prophet Isaiah.* 2 vols. New and improved ed. New York: Leavitt, 1875. **Alexander, J. A.** (1846). *A Commentary on the Prophecies of Isaiah.* Rev. ed. J. Eadie. Grand Rapids, MI: Zondervan, 1970. **Stier, E. R.** (1850). *Jesaias, Nicht Pseudo-Jesaias.* Barmen: Langewiesche, 1850. Chaps. 40–66. **Drechsler, M.** (1845–57). *Der Prophet Jesaja.* Berlin: Schlawitz, 1865. **Luzzatto, S. D.** (1855). *Commentary on the Book of Isaiah.* (Heb.) Tel Aviv: Davir, 1970. **Delitzsch, F. J.** (1866). *Biblischer Commentar über den Propheten Jesaia.* Leipzig: Dörffling und Frank, 1869. ———. *Biblical Commentaries on the Prophecies of Isaiah.* Trans. J. Martin. Edinburgh: T & T Clark, 1910.

The *last decade of the nineteenth century* inaugurated the age of commentaries written under the discipline of historical criticism and of "first," "second" (and sometimes "third") Isaiah. **Cheyne, T. K.** (1880). *The Book of the Prophet Isaiah.* 5th ed. New York: Dodd, Mead, 1904. **Smith, G. A.** (1890). *The Book of Isaiah.* 2 vols. The Expositor's Bible. New York: Harper, 1928. **Duhm, B.** (1892). *Das Buch Jesaja.* HKAT 3.1. 5th ed. Göttingen: Vandenhoeck & Ruprecht, 1968. **Skinner, J.** (1896–98). *The Book of the Prophet Isaiah in the Revised Version.* CBib. Cambridge: Cambridge UP, 1963. **Marti, K.** (1900). *Das Buch Jesaja.* KHC. Tübingen: Mohr, 1900. **Wade, G. W.** (1911). *The Book of the Prophet Isaiah with Introduction and Notes.* WC. 2d rev. ed. London: Methuen, 1929.

By the end of the first decade of the *twentieth century,* commentators were taking the historical-critical division of the book seriously enough to write of two or three separate and distinct books. Most commentaries used different writers for the two parts. Only a few attempted to cover the whole.

Chapters 1–39: **Whitehouse, O. C.** *Isaiah I–XXXIX.* NCB. Edinburgh: T & T Clark, 1905. **Gray, G. B.** *A Critical and Exegetical Commentary on the Book of Isaiah I–XXVI.* ICC. New York: T & T Clark, 1912. **Boutflower, C.** *The Book of Isaiah (Chapters I–XXXIX): In the Light of the Assyrian Monuments.* London: SPCK, 1930. **Procksch, O.** *Jesaia I.* (Isa 1–39.) KAT 9.1. Leipzig: Scholl, 1930. **Scott, R. B. Y.** "The Book of Isaiah." *IB.* New York; Nashville: Abingdon, 1956. 5:149–381. **Eichrodt, W.** *Der Heilige in Israel: Jesaja 1–12.* BAT 17.1. Stuttgart: Calwer, 1960. ———. *Der Herr der Geschichte: Jesaja 13–23, 28–39.* BAT 17.2. Stuttgart: Calwer, 1967. **Kaiser, O.** *Isaiah 1–12.* Trans. R. A. Wilson. OTL. Philadelphia: Westminster, 1972 (2d ed., 1983). ———. *Isaiah 13–39.* Trans. R. A. Wilson. OTL. Philadelphia: Westminster, 1974 (2d ed., 1983). **Wildberger, H.** *Jesaja 1–12.* BKAT 10. Neukirchen-Vluyn: Neukirchener Verlag, 1972. Translated by T. H. Trapp as *Isaiah 1–12.* Minneapolis: Augsburg, 1991. ———. *Jesaja 13–27.* BKAT 10. Neukirchen-Vluyn: Neukirchener Verlag, 1978. Translated by T. H. Trapp as *Isaiah 13–27.* Minneapolis: Augsburg, 1999.———. *Jesaja 28–39.* BKAT 10. Neukirchen-Vluyn: Neukirchener Verlag, 1982. Translated by Thomas H. Trapp as *Isaiah 28–39.* Minneapolis: Augsburg, 2002. **Auvray, P.** *Isaie 1–39.* SB. Paris: Gabalda, 1972. **Herbert, A. S.** *The Book of the Prophet Isaiah: Chapters 1–39.* CBC. Cambridge: Cambridge UP, 1973. **Clements, R. E.** *Isaiah 1–39.* NCB. Grand Rapids, MI: Eerdmans, 1980. **Kilian, R.** *Jesaja 1–39.* EdF 200. Darmstadt: Wissenschaftliche Buchgesellschaft, 1983. **Jensen, J.** *Isaiah 1–39.* OT Message 8. Wilmington: Glazier, 1984. **Sawyer, J. F.** *Isaiah I.* Louisville: Westminster, 1984. **Wildberger, H.** *Königsherrschaft Gottes, Jesaja 1–39, I–II.* Neukirchen-Vluyn: Neukirchener Verlag, 1984. **Grogan, G. W.** "Isaiah." In *Expositor's Bible Commentary.* Vol. 6. Grand Rapids, MI: Zondervan, 1986. **Kilian, R.** *Jesaja 1–12.* NEchtB 17. Würzburg: Echter, 1986. **Sekine, M.** *Commentary on Isaiah 1–39.* Tokyo: Shinchi Shobo, 1986. **Jacob, E.**

Esaie 1–12. Geneva: Labor et Fides, 1987. **Sheppard, G. T.** "Isaiah 1–39." In *Harper Bible Commentary*. Ed. J. L. Mayes. San Francisco: Harper & Row, 1988. 542–70. **Widyapranawa, S. H.** *The Lord Is Saviour: Isaiah 1–29*. Grand Rapids, MI: Eerdmans, 1990. **Goshen-Gottstein, M. H.** *The Book of Isaiah II: Chapters 22–44* [Introduction in English. Text in Hebrew]. Ramat Gan: Bar Ilan UP, 1992. **Seitz, C. R.** *Isaiah 1–29*. IBC. Louisville: Westminster John Knox, 1993. **Stacy, D.** *Isaiah 1–39*. London: Epworth, 1993. **Kilian, R.** *Jesaja II: 13–39*. NEchtB 32. Würzburg: Echter, 1994. **Sweeney, M. A.** *Isaiah 1–39 with an Introduction to Prophetic Literature*. FOTL 16. Grand Rapids, MI: Eerdmans, 1996. **Beuken, W. A. M.** *Isaiah, Part 2*. (Isa 28–39). Trans. B. Doyle. HCOT. Peeters: Leuven, 1999. **Blenkinsopp, J.** *Isaiah 1–39*. AB. New York: Doubleday, 2000. **Matthews, C.** *Isaiah 1–39*. Berit Olam. Collegeville, MN: Liturgical Press, 2000.

Chapters 40–66: **Budde, K.** *Das Buch Jesaja 40–66*. *HSAT*. 4th ed. Tübingen, 1922. **Levy, R.** *Deutero-Isaiah: A Commentary Together with a Preliminary Essay on Deutero-Isaiah's Influence on Jewish Thought*. London, 1925. **Volz, P.** *Jesaja II: Zweite Hälfte: 40–66*. KAT 10. Leipzig: Scholl, 1932. **Fischer, G.** *Das Buch Jesaja, II*. *HSAT*. Bonn, 1939. **Muilenburg, J.** "The Book of Isaiah." In *IB*. New York; Nashville: Abingdon, 1956. 5:382–773. **Steinmann, J.** *Le Livre de la Consolation d'Israel*. LD 28. Paris, 1960. **North, C.** *The Second Isaiah*. Oxford: Oxford UP, 1964. **Knight, G. A. F.** *Deutero-Isaiah: A Theological Commentary on Isaiah 40–55*. New York; Nashville: Abingdon, 1965. **Smart, J. D.** *History and Theology in Second Isaiah: A Commentary on Is. 35; 40–66*. Philadelphia: Westminster, 1965. **Westermann, C.** *Das Buch Jesaja: Kapitel 40–66*. ATD. Göttingen, 1966. Translated by D. M. G. Stalker as *Isaiah 40–66*. Philadelphia: Westminster, 1969. **McKenzie, J. L.** *Second Isaiah*. AB 20. Garden City, NY: Doubleday, 1968. **Bonnard, P. E.** *Le Second Isaïe, son disciple et leurs éditeurs*. SB. Paris: Gabalda, 1972. **Herbert, A. S.** *The Book of the Prophet Isaiah 40–66*. CBC. Cambridge: Cambridge UP, 1975. **Whybray, R. N.** *Isaiah 40–66*. NCB. Grand Rapids, MI: Eerdmans, 1975. **Elliger, K.** *Jesaja II: 40:1–45:7*. BKAT 11. Neukirchen-Vluyn: Neukirchener Verlag, 1978. **Beuken, W. A. M.** *Jesaja: Deel II–III*. 2 vols. POut. Nijkerk: Callenbach, 1979–89. **Clifford, R. J.** *Fair Spoken and Persuading: An Interpretation of Second Isaiah*. New York: Paulist Press, 1984. **Knight, G. A. F.** *Servant Theology: A Commentary on the Book of Isaiah 40–55*. ITC. Grand Rapids, MI: Eerdmans, 1984. **Hermisson, J. J.** *Deuterojesaja*. BKAT 11.7–9. Neukirchen-Vluyn: Neukirchener, 1987–. **Grimm, W.,** and **K. Dittert.** *Deuterojesaja: Deutung—Wirkung—Gegenwart*. Calwer Bibelkommentare. Stuttgart: Calwer, 1990. **Hanson, P. D.** *Isaiah 40–66*. IBC. Louisville: John Knox, 1995. **Koole, J. L.** *Isaiah, Part 3*. Trans. A. P. Runia. 3 vols. HCOT. Kampen: Kok Pharos, 1997–98. **Baltzer, K.** *Deutero-Jesaja*. KAT 10.2. Gütersloh: Güterloher Verlagshaus, 1999. Translated by M. Kohl as *Deutero-Isaiah: A Commentary*, ed. P. Machinist, Hermeneia (Minneapolis: Fortress, 2000). **Thompson, M. E. W.** *Isaiah 40–66*. Epworth Commentaries. Peterborough: Epworth, 2001. **Zapff, B. M.** *Jesaja 40–55*. NEchtB 36. Würzburg: Echter, 2001. **Blenkinsopp, J.** *Isaiah 40–55*. AB. New York: Doubleday, 2002.

Chapters 55–66: **Glahn, L.,** and **L. Köhler.** *Der Prophet der Heimkehr*. Copenhagen; Giessen: Töpelmann, 1934. **Knight, G. A. F.** *The New Israel: A Commentary on the Book of Isaiah 55–66*. Grand Rapids, MI: Eerdmans, 1985. **Blenkinsopp, J.** *Isaiah 56–66*. AB. New York: Doubleday, 2003.

Chapters 1–66: Only a few in this period have written on the entire book of Isaiah: **Duhm, B.** *Das Buch Jesaja*. 4th ed. HKAT 3.1. Göttingen: Vandenhoeck & Ruprecht, 1922. **Feldmann, F.** *Das Buch Isaias*. EHAT. Münster, 1926. **König, E.** *Das Buch Jesaja*. Gütersloh, 1926. **Ridderbos, J.** *De profeet Jesaja*. Kampen: Kok, 1926. **Wade, G. W.** *The Book of the Prophet Isaiah*. 2d ed. WC. London, 1929. **Kissane, E. J.** *The Book of Isaiah* (1941–1943). Rev. ed. 2 vols. Dublin: Browne and Nolan, 1960. **Slotki, I. W.** *Isaiah*. Soncino Books of the Bible.

London: Soncino, 1949. **Steinmann, J.** *Le Prophéte Isaïe.* Paris: Cerf, 1949–55. **Ridderbos, J.** *Isaiah* (1955). Trans. J. Vriend. Grand Rapids, MI: Eerdmans, 1985. **Penna, A.** *Isaia.* La Sacra Bibbia. Torino: Marietti, 1958. **Fohrer, G.** *Das Buch Jesaja.* 3 vols. ZBK. Zurich: Zwingli, 1960–64. **Leslie, E. A.** *Isaiah.* New York: Abingdon, 1963. **Leupold, H.** *Exposition of Isaiah.* 2 vols. Grand Rapids, MI: Baker, 1963–71. **Young, E. J.** *The Book of Isaiah.* 3 vols. NICOT. Grand Rapids, MI: Eerdmans, 1965–72. **Kelley, P. H.** "Isaiah." In *Broadman Bible Commentary.* Vol. 5. Nashville: Broadman, 1971. 149–374. **Schoors, A.** *Jesaja.* BOT. Roermond: Romen, 1972. **Butler, T. C.** *Isaiah.* LBBC 10. Nashville: Broadman, 1982. **Sawyer, J. F. A.** *Isaiah.* 2 vols. Daily Study Bible. Philadelphia; Louisville: Westminster, 1984–86. **Watts, J. D. W.** *Isaiah 1–33.* WBC 24. Waco, TX: Word Books, 1985. ———. *Isaiah 34–66.* WBC 25. Waco, TX: Word Books, 1988. **Oswalt, J. N.** *The Book of Isaiah, Chapters 1–39.* NICOT. Grand Rapids, MI: Eerdmans, 1986. ———. *The Book of Isaiah, Chapters 40–66.* NICOT. Grand Rapids, MI: Eerdmans, 1998. **Schneider, D.** *Der Prophet Jesaja.* Vol. 1, *Kapitel 1 bis 39.* Wuppertaler Studienbibel. Wuppertal; Zurich: Brockhaus, 1990. ———. *Der Prophet Jesaja.* Vol. 2, *Kapitel 40 bis 66.* Wuppertaler Studienbibel. Wuppertal; Zurich: Brockhaus, 1990. **Höffken, P. von.** *Das Buch Jesaja.* 2 vols. Neue Stuttgarter Kommentar, Altes Testament 18. Stuttgart: Katholisches Bibelwerk, 1993–98. **Miscall, P. D.** *Isaiah: Readings.* Sheffield: JSOT Press, 1993. **Motyer, J. A.** *The Prophecy of Isaiah: An Introduction and Commentary.* Downers Grove, IL: InterVarsity Press, 1993. **Watts, J. D. W.** "Isaiah." In *Mercer Bible Commentary.* Macon, GA: Mercer UP, 1994. 565–613. **Brueggemann, W.** *Isaiah I (1–39).* Westminster Bible Companion. Louisville: Westminster John Knox, 1998. ———. *Isaiah II (40–66).* Westminster Bible Companion. Louisville: Westminster John Knox, 1998. **Childs, B. S.** *Isaiah.* OTL. Louisville: Westminster John Knox, 2001.

Selected Articles and Monographs on Isaiah

This list of articles and monographs on the whole of or large parts of Isaiah appears in chronological order from *1884 to 1980.* The following section lists articles and monographs since 1980 in alphabetical order. Monographs on specific passages or portions are noted in the chapter bibliographies. Those mentioned elsewhere in the *Introduction* are not repeated here.

Cornill, C. H. "Die Composition des Buches Jesajas." *ZAW* 4 (1884) 83–105. **Dillmann, A.** *Der Prophet Jesaja.* Leipzig: Hirzel, 1890. **Condamin, A.** *Le Livre d'Isaïe: Traduction critique avec notes et commentaires.* EBib. Paris: Lecoffre, 1905. **Wilke, F.** *Jesaja und Assur: Eine exegetisch-historische Untersuchung zur Politik des Propheten Jesaja.* Leipzig: Weicher, 1905. **Kenneth, R. H.** *The Composition of the Book of Isaiah in History and Archaeology.* London: British Academy, 1910. **Ehrlich, A. B.** *Randglossen zur hebräischen Bibel textkritisches, sprachliches und geschichtliches.* Vol. 4, *Jesaia, Jeremia.* Leipzig: Hinrichs, 1912. **Fullerton, K.** "The Book of Isaiah: Critical Problems and a New Commentary." *HTR* 6 (1913) 478–20. **Beer, G.** "Zur Zukunftserwartung Jesajas." In *Studien zur semitischen Philologie und Religionsgeschichte.* FS J. Wellhausen, ed. K. Marti. BZAW 27. Giessen: Töpelmann, 1914. 13–35. **Smith, L. P.** "The Messianic Ideal of Isaiah." *JBL* 36 (1917) 158–212. **Mitchell, H. G.** "Isaiah on the Fate of His People and Their Capital." *JBL* 37 (1918) 149–62. **Fullerton, K.** "Viewpoints in the Discussion of Isaiah's Hopes for the Future." *JBL* 41 (1922) 1–101. **Coorley, D. H.** "Messianic Prophecy in First Isaiah." *AJSL* 39 (1922–23) 220–24. **Budde, K.** "Über die Schranken die Jesajas prophetischer Botschaft zu setzen sind." *ZAW* 41 (1923) 154–203. **Köhler, L.** *Deuterojesaja stilkritisch untersucht.* BZAW 37. Giessen: Töpelmann, 1923. **Smith, J. M. P.** "Isaiah and the Future." *AJSL* 40 (1923–24) 252–58. **Feldman, F.** *Das Buch Isaias.* EHAT 14.1. Münster: Aschendorff, 1925. **Mowinckel, S.** *Jesaja-Disciplene: Profetien fra Jesaja til Jeremia.* Oslo: Dybwad, 1926. **Budde, K.** *Jesaja's Erleben: Eine gemeinverständliche Auslegung der Denkschrift des Propheten (Kap. 6:1–9:6).* Gotha: Klotz, 1928. **Torrey, C. C.** *The Second Isaiah.*

Edinburgh: T & T Clark, 1928. **Mowinckel, S.** "Die komposition des Jesajabuches Kap. 1–39." *AcOr* 11 (1933) 267–92. Reprinted from *ZAW* 49 (1931) 87–112, 242–60. **Ziegler, J.** "Zum literarischen Aufbau verschiedener Stücke im Buche des Propheten Isaias." *BZ* 21 (1933) 131–49. **Behr, J. W.** *The Writings of Deutero-Isaiah and the Neo-Babylonian Royal Inscriptions.* Pretoria: Rubinstein, 1937. **Driver, G. R.** "Linguistic and Textual Problems: Isaiah I–XXXIX." *JTS* 38 (1937) 36–50. **Fichtner, J.** "Die 'Umkehrung' in der prophetischen Botschaft: Eine Studie zu dem Verhältnis von Schuld und Gericht in der Verkündigung Jesajas." *TLZ* 78 (1937) 459–66. **Eitan, I.** "A Contribution to Isaiah Exegesis." *HUCA* 12–13 (1937–38) 55–88. **Birkeland, H.** *Zum hebräischen Traditionswesen: Die komposition der prophetischen Bücher des Alten Testament.* Oslo: Dybwad, 1938. **Wordsworth, W. A.** *En-Roeh: The Prophecies of Isaiah the Seer.* Edinburgh: T & T Clark, 1939. **Condamin, A.** *Le Livre d'Isaïe: Introduction.* EBib. Paris: Gabalda, 1940. **Skehan, P.** "Isaias and the Teaching of the Book of Wisdom." *CBQ* 2 (1941) 289–99. **Feuillet, A.** "Isaie (Le Livre d')." *DBSup* 4 (1947) 647–720. **Fichtner, J.** "Jesaja unter den Weisen." *TLZ* 74 (1949) 75–80. **Allis, O. T.** *The Unity of Isaiah.* Philadelphia: Presbyterian and Reformed, 1950. **Halas, R.** "The Universalism of Isaias." *CBQ* 12 (1950) 162–70. **Scott, R. B. Y.** "The Literary Structure of Isaiah's Oracles." In *Studies in Old Testament Prophecy.* FS T. H. Robinson, ed. H. H. Rowley. Edinburgh: T & T Clark, 1950. 175–86. **Steinmann, J.** *Le prophete Isaïe, sa vie, son oeuvre et son temps.* LD 5. Paris: Cerf, 1950. **Hölscher, G.** "Jesaja." *TLZ* 77 (1952) 683–94. **Jones, D. R.** "The Tradition of the Oracles of Isaiah of Jerusalem." *ZAW* 67 (1955) 226–46. **Keller, C. A.** "Das quietistische Element in der Botschaft des Jesaja." *TZ* 11 (1955) 81–97. **Blank, S.** "Traces of Prophetic Agony in Isaiah." *HUCA* 27 (1956) 81–92. **Boer, P. A. H. de.** *Second Isaiah's Message.* OTS 40. Leiden: Brill, 1956. **Klausner, J.** *The Messianic Idea in Israel.* Trans. W. F. Stinespring. London: Allen and Unwin, 1956. **Rignell, L. G.** *A Study of Isaiah, Ch. 40–55.* Lund: Gleerup, 1956. **Tannert, W.** "Jeremia und Deuterojesaja: Eine Untersuchung zur Frage ihren literarische und theologischen Zusammenhanges." Ph.D. diss., Karl Marx University, Leipzig, 1956. **Junker, H.** "Ursprung und Grundzüge des Messiasbildes bei Isajas." In *Volume du Congrès, Strasbourg 1956.* Leiden: Brill, 1957. 181–96. **LeFèvre, A.** "L'expression 'en ce jour-là' dans le livre d'Isaïe." In *Mélanges Bibliques.* FS A. Robert. Paris: Bloud & Gay, 1957. 174–79. **Feuillet, A.** "La communauté messianique dans la prédication d'Isaïe." *Bible et Vie Chretienne* 20 (1957–58) 38–52. **Blank, S. H.** *Prophetic Faith in Isaiah.* New York: Harper Brothers, 1958. **Eaton, J. H.** "The Origin of the Book of Isaiah." *VT* 9 (1959) 138–57. **Anderson, R. T.** "Was Isaiah a Scribe?" *JBL* 79 (1960) 57–58. **Brayley, I. F. M.** "YHWH Is the Guardian of His Plantation." *Bib* 41 (1960) 275–86. **Loretz, O.** "Der Glaube des Propheten Isaias an das Gottesreich." *ZKT* 82 (1960) 40–73. **Martin-Achard, R.** "Sagesse de Dieu et sagesse humaine chez Ésaïe." In *La Branche d'Amandier.* FS W. Fischer. Montpellier: Causse, Graille, Castelnau, 1960. 137–44. **Vriesen, T. C.** "Essentials of the Theology of Isaiah." In *Israel's Prophetic Heritage.* Ed. B. W. Anderson and W. Harrelson. 128–46. **Fey, R.** *Amos und Jesaja: Abängigkeit und Eigenständigkwit des Jesaja.* WMANT 12. Neukirchen-Vluyn: Neukirchener Verlag, 1963. **Haran, M.** "The Literary Structure and Chronological Framework of the Prophecies in Is. XL–XLVIII." In *Congress Volume, Bonn 1962.* VTSup 9. Leiden: Brill, 1963. 127–55. **Schreiner, J.** *Sion-Jerusalem, JHWHs Königssitz.* Munich: Kösel, 1963. **Wildberger, H.** "Jesajas Verständnis der Geschichte." In *Congress Volume, Bonn 1962.* VTSup 9. Leiden: Brill, 1963. 83–117. **Banwell, B. O.** "A Suggested Analysis of Isaiah 40–66." *EvT* 76 (1964–65) 166. **Brownlee, W. H.** *The Meaning of the Qumran Scrolls for the Bible.* New York: Oxford UP, 1964. 247–49. **Margalioth, R.** *The Individible Isaiah: Evidence for the Single Authorship of the Prophetic Book.* New York: Yeshiva Univ., 1964. **Milgrom, J.** "Did Isaiah Prophesy during the Reign of Uzziah?" *VT* 14 (1964) 164–82. **Seierstad, I. P.** *Die Offenbarungserlebnisse der Propheten Amos, Jesaja und Jeremia.* 2d ed. Oslo: Universitetsforlaget, 1965. **Calderone, P. J.** *Dynastic Oracle and Suzerainty Treaty.* Manila: Ateneo University, 1966. **Koch, R.** "Die Theologie des Deutero-Isaias." *TGl* 9 (1966) 20–30. **Morgenstern, J.** "Further Light from the Book of Isaiah upon the Catastrophe of 485 B.C.E." *HUCA* 37 (1966) 1–28. **Napier, B.**

D. "Isaiah and the Isain." In *Volume du Congrès, Genève 1965.* VTSup 15. Leiden: Brill, 1966. 240–51. **Vogt, E.** "Sennacherib und die letzte Tätigkeit Jesajas." *Bib* 47 (1966) 427–37. **Fohrer, G.** "Entstehung, Komposition, und Überlieferung von Jes 1–39." In *Studien zur Alttestamentlichen Prophetie (1949–1965).* BZAW 99. Berlin: Tõpelmann, 1967. 113–47. ———. "Wandelungen Jesajas." In *Festschrift für Wilhelm Eilers.* Ed. G. Wiessner. Wiesbaden: Harrassowitz, 1967. 58–71. Reprinted in *Studien alttestametlichen Texten und Themen (1966–72).* BZAW 155. Berlin: De Gruyter, 1981. 11–23. **Ginsburg, H. L.** "Isaiah in the Light of History." *Conservative Judaism* 22.1 (1967) 1–18. **Hill, W.** "Book of Isaiah." *New Catholic Encyclopedia* (1967) 7:666–71. **Lescow, T.** "Das Geburtsmotiv in den messianischen Weissagungen bei Jesaja und Micha." *ZAW* 79 (1967) 172–207. **Martin-Achard, R.** "Esaïe et Jéremie aux prises avec les problèmes politiques: Contribution à l'étude du thème: Prophétie et Politique." *RHPR* 47 (1967) 208–24. **Petitjean, A.** "Représentations littéraires de Dieu chez Isaïe: Introduction à la théologie isaïenne." *Revue Diacésaine de Namur* 21 (1967) 143–62. **Schreiner, J.** "Das Buch jesajanischer Schule." In *Wort und Botschaft: Eine theologische and kritische Einführung in die Probleme des Alten Testaments.* Würzburg: Echter, 1967. 143–62. **Becker, J.** *Isaias—Der Prophet und sein Buch.* SBS 30. Stuttgart: Katholisches Bibelwerk, 1968. **Coppens, J.** "Les espérances messianiques du Proto-Isaïe et leurs prétendues relectures." *ETL* 44 (1968) 491–97. **Driver, G. R.** "Isaiah I–XXXIX: Textual and Linguistic Problems." *JSS* 13 (1968) 36–57. **Gamper, A.** "Der Verkündigungsauftrag Israels nach Deutero-Jesaja." *ZKT* 91 (1969) 411–29. **Steck, O. H.** *Deuterojesaja als theologischer Denker (1969) = Wahrnehmungen Gottes im Alten Testament: Gesammelten Studien.* TB 70. Munich: Kaiser, 1982. 204–20. **Ward, J. M.** *Amos and Isaiah: Prophets of the Word of God.* Nashville: Abingdon, 1969. **Eichrodt, W.** "Prophet and Covenant: Observations on the Exegesis of Isaiah." In *Proclamation and Presence.* FS G. H. Davies, ed. J. I. Durham and J. R. Porter. London: SCM Press, 1970. 167–88. **Nielsen, E.** "Deuterojesaja: Erwägungen zur Formkritik, Traditions und Redaktionsgeschichte." *VT* 20 (1970) 190–205. **Baltzer, D.** *Ezechiel und Deuterojesaja.* BZAW 121. Berlin: De Gruyter, 1971. **Melugin, R. F.** "DeuteroIsaiah and Form Criticism." *VT* 21 (1971) 326–37. **Müller, H.-P.** "Zur Funktion des Mythischen in der Prophetie des Jesaja." *Kairos* 13 (1971) 266–81. **Odendaal, D. H.** "The 'Former' and the 'New Things' in Isaiah 40–48." *OTWSAP* 1967 (1971) 64–75. **Paul, S.** "Literary and Ideological Echoes of Jeremiah in Deutero Isaiah." In *Proceedings of the Fifth World Congress of Jewish Studies, 1969.* Jerusalem: Magnes, 1971. 102–20. **Rabban, N.** *Second Isaiah: His Prophecy, His Personality, and His Name.* (Hebrew.) Tel Aviv: Kiriath Sepher, 1971. **Vollmer, J.** *Geschichteliche Rückblicke und Motive in der Prophetie des Amos, Hosea, und Jesaja.* BZAW 119. Berlin: De Gruyter, 1971. **Whedbee, J. W.** *Isaiah and Wisdom.* Nashville: Abingdon, 1971. **Ginsburg, H. L.** "Isaiah, First Isaiah." *EncJud* 9:44–60. **Steck, O. H.** *Friedensvorstellungen im alten Jerusalem: Psalmen—Jesaja—Deuterojesaja.* ThSt 111. Zurich: Theologisches Verlag, 1972. **Radai, Y. T.** "Identity of the Second Isaiah according to Y. D. Brach." (Heb. with Eng. summary.) *BMik* 52 (1972). **Scheiber, A.** "Der Zeitpunkt des Auftretens von Deuterojesaja." *ZAW* 84 (1972) 242–43. **Vogt, E.** "Jesaja und die drohende eroberung Palästinas durch Tiglathpileser." In *Wort, Lied, und Gottesspruch.* Vol. 2, *Beiträge zu Psalmen und Propheten.* FS J. Ziegler, ed. J. Schreiner. FB 2. Würzburg: Echter, 1972. 249–55. **Holmgren, F.** *With Wings of Eagles: An Interpretation.* Chappaqua, NY: Biblical Scholars Press, 1973. **Jensen, J.** *The Use of tôrâ by Isaiah: His Debate with the Wisdom Tradition.* CBQMS 3. Washington: Catholic Bibical Association, 1973. **Lack, R.** *La Symbolique de Livre d'Isaïe: Essai sur l'image litéraire comme élément de structuration.* AnBib 59. Rome: Biblical Institute Press, 1973. **Radday, Y. T.** *The Unity of Isaiah in the Light of Statistical Linguistics.* Hildesheim, 1973. **Wildberger, H.** "Gottesnamen und Gottesepitheta bei Jesaja." In *JHWH und sein Volk.* TB 66. Munich: Kaiser, 1973. 219–48. **Hoffmann, H. W.** *Die Intention der Verkündigung Jesajas.* BZAW 136. Berlin: De Gruyter, 1974. **Melugin, R.** "The Conventional and the Creative in Isaiah's Judgment Oracles." *CBQ* 36 (1974) 301–11. **Zimmerli, W.** "Verkündigung und Sprache der Botschaft Jesajas." In *Gesammelte Aufsätze.* Vol. 2, *Studien zur alttestamentlichen Theologie und Prophetie.* TB 51.

Munich: Kaiser, 1974. 73–87. **Bonnard, P. E.** "Relire Isaïe 40–66." *ETR* 50 (1975) 351–59. **Feuillet, A.** "Bibliographie choisie sur le livre d'Isaïe." In *Études d'exégèse et de la théologie biblique A.T.* Paris: Gabalda, 1975. 501–8. ———. "Le messianisme du livre Isaïe: Ses rapports avec la histoire et le traditions d'Israel." In *Études d'exégèse et de la théologie biblique A.T.* Paris: Gabalda, 1975. 223–59. Originally printed in *RSR* 36 [1949] 182–228. ———. "Introduction au livre d'Isaïe." In *Études d'exégèse et de la théologie biblique A.T.* Paris: Gabalda, 1975. 19–21. **Dietrich, W.** *Jesaja und die Politik.* BEvT 74. Munich: Kaiser, 1976. **Huber, F.** *Jahwe, Juda und die anderen Völkern beim Propheten Jesaja.* BZAW 137. Berlin: De Gruyter, 1976. **Melugin, R. F.** *The Formation of Isaiah 40–55.* BZAW 141. Berlin: De Gruyter, 1976. **Spykerboer, H. C.** *The Structure and Composition of Deutero-Isaiah, with Special Reference to the Polemics against Idolatry.* Meppel: Krips Repro, 1976. **Barth, H.** *Die Jesaja-Worte in der Josiazeit: Israel und Assur als Thema einer produktiven Neuinterpretation des Jesajaüberlieferung.* WMANT 48. Neukirchen-Vluyn: Neukirchener Verlag, 1977. **Keel, O.** "Rechtun oder Annahme des drohenden Gerichts?" *BZ* 21 (1977) 200–218. **Schoors, A.** "Isaiah, the Minister of Royal Anointment." *OtSt* 20 (1977) 85–107. **Vermeylen, J.** *Du prophetie Isaïe à l'apocalyptic.* 2 vols. Paris: Gabalda, 1977–78. **Canellas, G.** "El universalismo en el Deuteroisaias." *CB* 35 (1978) 3–20. **Carroll, R. A.** "Inner Shifts in Meaning in Isaiah 1–11." *ExpTim* 89 (1978) 301–4. **Hardmeier, C.** *Texttheorie und biblische Exegese: Zur rhetorischen Funktion der Trauermetaphorik in der Prophetie.* BEvT 79. Munich: Kaiser, 1978. **Holladay, W. L.** *Isaiah: Scroll of a Prophetic Heritage.* Grand Rapids, MI: Eerdmans, 1978. **Ginsburg, H. L.** *The Supernatural in the Prophets, with Special Reference to Isaiah.* Cinncinati: Hebrew Union College Press, 1979. **Kiesow, K.** *Exodustexte im Jesajabuch: Literarkritische und motivgeschichtliche Analysen.* OBO 24. Göttingen: Vandenhoeck & Ruprecht, 1979. **Schmitt, H.-C.** "Prophetie und Schultheologie im Deuterojesajabuch: Beobachtungen zur Redactionsgeschichte von Jes. 40–55." *ZAW* 91 (1979) 43–61. **Vermeylen, J.** "Le Proto-Isaïe et la sagesse d'Israël." In *La Sagesse de l'Ancien Testament.* Ed. M. Gilbert. BETL 51. Leuven: Peeters, 1979. 39–58.

Since 1980, the publication of monographs and articles on large parts or the whole of Isaiah has been prodigous. These are listed here alphabetically, and include articles from several major collections: **Broyles, C. C.**, and **C. A. Evans,** eds. *Writing and Reading the Scroll of Isaiah: Studies of an Interpretive Tradition.* 2 vols. VTSup 70; FIOTL 1–2. Leiden; New York: Brill, 1997. **Melugin, R. F.**, and **M. A. Sweeney,** eds. *New Visions of Isaiah.* JSOTSup 214. Sheffield: Sheffield Academic Press, 1996. **Van Ruiten, J.**, and **M. Vervenne,** eds. *Studies in the Book of Isaiah.* FS W. A. M. Beuken. BETL 132. Louvain: Leuven UP; Peeters, 1997. **Vermeylen, J.**, ed. *The Book of Isaiah = Le Livre d'Isaïe: Les oracles et leurs relectures unité et complexité de l'ouvrage.* BETL 81. Leuven: Leuven UP; Peeters, 1989.

Ackerman, S. "Isaiah." In *The Women's Bible Commentary.* Ed. C. A. Newsom and S. H. Ringe. Louisville: Westminster, 1992. 161–68. **Alonso Schökel, L.** "Isaiah." In *The Literary Guide to the Bible.* Ed. F. Kermode and R. Alter. Cambridge: Harvard UP, 1987. 165–83. **Altmann, T. F.** "Yom, 'Time' and Some Texts in Isaiah." *JNSL* 11 (1983) 3–8. **Anderson, B. W.** "The Apocalyptic Rendering of the Isaiah Tradition." In *The Social World of Formative Christianity and Judaism.* FS H. C. Kee, ed. J. Neusner et al. Philadelphia: Augsberg; Fortress, 1988. 17–38. ———. "The Holy One of Israel." In *Justice and the Holy.* FS W. Harrelson, ed. D. A. Knight and P. J. Paris. Atlanta: Scholars Press, 1989. 3–19. **Asurmendi, J.** "Isaïe, un citadin de haut rang . . . la politique . . . le temple, Sion." *MdB* 49 (1987) 36–40. **Auld, A. G.** "Poetry, Prophecy, Hermeneutic: Recent Studies in Isaiah." *JTS* 33 (1980) 567–81.

Bäckersten, O. "The Morality of the Woe Oracles and the Ethics of Isaiah." Diss., Lund, 1999. **Barton, J.** "Begründungsversuche der prophetischen Unheilankündigung im Alten Testament." *EvT* 47 (1987) 427–35. ———. "Ethics in Isaiah of Jerusalem." *JTS* 32 (1981) 1–18. ———. "Ethics in the Book of Isaiah." In *Writing and Reading.* Ed. C. C. Broyles and C. A. Evans. 1:67–77. ———. *Isaiah 1–39.* OTG 19. Sheffield: Sheffield Academic Press, 1999. **Beauchamp, E.** "D'Isaïe à son livre: A propos d'un ouvrage récent." *LA* 33 (1983) 75–98. **Becker, U.** *Jesaja—Von der Botschaft zum Buch.* FRLANT 178. Göttingen: Vandenhoeck & Ruprecht, 1997. **Beentjes, P. C.** "Wisdom of Solomon 3:1–4:19 and the Book of Isaiah." In *Studies.* Ed. J. Van Ruiten and M. Vervenne. 413–20. **Berger, D.** "Towards the clarification of a difficult passage in R. Joseph Kara's commentary to Isaiah." *Zion* 52 (1987) 114–16. **Berlin, A.** *The Dynamics of Biblical Parallelism.* Bloomington: Indiana UP, 1985. ———. "Motif and Creativity in Biblical Poetry." *Proof* 3 (1983) 231–41. **Beuken, W. A. M.** "Jesaja: gerechtigheid en vrede." In *De mens: Verrader of hoeder van de schepping?* Ed. J. De Tavernier and M. Vervenne. Leuven, 1991. 93–101. ———. "The Unity of the Book of Isaiah." In *Reading from Right to Left.* Ed. J. C. Exum and H. G. M. Williamson. 50–62. **Blenkinsopp, J.** "Cityscape to Landscape: The 'Back to Nature' Theme in Isaiah 1–35." In *'Every City Shall Be Forsaken': Urbanism and Prophecy in Ancient Israel and the Near East.* Ed. L. L. Grabbe and R. D. Haak. JSOTSup 330. Sheffield: Sheffield Academic Press, 2001. 35–44. **Boadt, L.** "Re-Examining a Preexilic Redaction of Isaiah 1–39." In *Imagery and Imagination in Biblical Literature.* FS A. Fitzgerald, ed. L. Boadt and M. S. Smith. CBQMS 32. Washington, DC: Catholic Biblical Association of America, 2001. 169–90. **Bodecki, B.** "Jerusalem-Zion in the Texts of Proto-Isaiah." *The Polish Journal of Biblical Research* 1 (2000). **Bogaert, P.-M.** "L'organisation des grands receuils prophétíques." In *Book of Isaiah.* Ed. J. Vermeylen. 147–53. **Boogaart, T. A.** "The World of the Prophets Revisited." *RefR* 46 (1992) 5–19. **Bosshard-Nepustil, E.** *Rezeption von Jesaja 1–39 im Zwölfprophetenbuch: Untersuchungen zur literarischen Verbindung von Prophetenbücher im babylonischer and persischer Zeit.* Göttingen: Vandenhoeck & Ruprecht, 1997. **Bourguet, D.** "Pourqoui à-t-on rassemblé des oracles si divers sous le titre d'Esaïe?" *ETR* 58 (1983) 171–79. **Bovati, P.** "Le langage juridique du prophète Isaïe." In *Book of Isaiah.* Ed. J. Vermeylen. 177–96. **Brangenberg, J. H.** "A Reexamination of the Date, Authorship, Unity and Function of Isaiah 13–23." Diss., Golden Gate Theological Seminary, 1989. **Brekelmans, C. H. W.** "Deuteronomistic Influence in Isaiah 1–12." In *Book of Isaiah.* Ed. J. Vermeylen. 167–76. **Brueggemann, W.** "Unity and Dynamic in the Isaiah Tradition." *JSOT* 29 (1984) 89–95. ———. *Using God's Resources Wisely: Isaiah and Urban Possibility.* Louisville: Westminster John Knox, 1993.

Carr, D. M. "What Can We Say about the Tradition History of Isaiah? A Response to Christopher Seitz's *Zion's Final Destiny.*" In *SBLSP.* Atlanta: Scholars Press, 1992. 583–97. **Clements, R. E.** "A Light to the Nations: A Central Theme of the Book of Isaiah." In *Forming Prophetic Literature.* Ed. P. House and J. W. Watts. 57–69. **Clements, R. H.** "Beyond Tradition-History: Deutero-Isianic Development of First Isaiah's Themes." *JSOT* 31 (1985) 95–113. **Clifford, R. F.** "The Unity of the Book of Isaiah and Its Cosmogonic Language." *CBQ* 55 (1993) 1–17. **Coggins, R. et al.**, eds. *Israel's Prophetic Tradition.* FS P. Ackroyd. Cambridge: Cambridge UP, 1982. **Collins, T.** "A Book Called Isaiah." In *The Mantle of Elijah: The Redaction Criticism of the Prophetical Books.* Sheffield: JSOT Press, 1993. 37–58. **Conrad, E. W.** "Isaiah and the Assyrian Connection." *AJT* 2 (1988) 382–93. ———. "Prophet, Redactor and Audience: Reforming the Notion of Isaiah's Formation." In *New Visions.* Ed. R. F. Melugin and M. A. Sweeney. 305–26. ———. *Reading Isaiah.* OBT. Minneapolis: Fortress, 1991. ———. "Reading Isaiah and the Twelve as Prophetic Books." In *Writing and Reading.* Ed. C. C. Broyles and C. A. Evans. 1:3–17. ———. "The Royal Narratives and the Structure of the Book of Isaiah." *JSOT* 41 (1988) 129–47. ———. "Second Isaiah and the Priestly Oracle of Salvation." *ZAW* 93 (1981) 234–46. **Conroy, C.** "The Case of the Disappearing Redactor in Second Isaiah." *SOTS Bulletin* (2002) 10. **Craigen, T.** "Isaiah 40–48: A Sermonic Challenge to Open Theism." *MSJ* 12 (2001) 167–77.

Darr, K. P. *Isaiah's Vision and the Family of God.* Louisville: Westminster, 1994. ———. "Isaiah's Vision and the Rhetoric of Rebellion." In *SBLSP.* Atlanta: Scholars Press, 1994.

847–82. ———. "Two Unifying Female Images in the Book of Isaiah." In *Uncovering Ancient Stones.* FS H. N. Richardson, ed. L. M. Hopfe. Winona Lake, IN: Eisenbrauns, 1994. 17–30. **Davis, G.** "The Destiny of the Nations in the Book of Isaiah." In *Book of Isaiah.* Ed. J. Vermeylen. 93–120. **Deck, S.** *Die Gerichtsbotschaft Jesajas: Charakter und Begrundung.* FB 67. Wurzburg: Echter, 1991. **De Vries, S. J.** *From Old Revelation to New: A Tradition Historical & Redaction Critical Study of Temporal Tansitions in Prophetic Prediction.* Grand Rapids, MI: Eerdmans, 1995. 110–29. **Dick, M.** "Prophetic *Poiesis* and the Verbal Icon." *CBQ* 46 (1984) 226–46. **Dobbs-Allsopp, F. W.** *Weep, O Daughter of Zion: A Study of the City-Lament Genre in the Hebrew Bible.* BibOr 44. Rome: Pontifical Biblical Institute, 1993. **Doorly, W. J.** *Isaiah of Jerusalem: An Introduction.* New York: Paulist, 1992. **Dumbrell, W. J.** "The Purpose of the Book of Isaiah." *TynBul* 36 (1985) 111–28.

Eaton, J. H. "The Isaiah Tradition." In *Israel's Prophetic Tradition.* Ed. R. Coggins et al. 58–76. **Erlandsson, S.** "The Unity of Isaiah: A New Solution?" In *A Lively Legacy.* FS R. Preus, ed. K. E. Marquart et al. Lake Mills, IA: Graphic, 1985. 33–39. **Evans, C. A.** "On Isaiah's Use of Israel's Sacred Tradition." *BZ* 30 (1986) 92–99. ———. "On the Unity and Parallel Structure of the Book of Isaiah." *VT* 38 (1988) 129–47. **Exum, J. C.** "Of Broken Pots, Fluttering Birds and Visions in the Night: Extended Simile and Poetic Technique in Isaiah." *CBQ* 43 (1981) 331–52.

Fekkes, J. *Isaiah and the Prophetic Traditions in the Book of Revelation: Visionary Antecedents and Their Development.* JSNTSup 93. Sheffield: JSOT, 1994. **Fischer, I.** *Tora für Israel—Tora für die Völker: Das Konzept des Jesajabuches.* SBS 164. Stuttgart: Katholisches Bibelwerk, 1995. **Fishelov, D.** "The Prophet as Satirist." *Proof* 9 (1989) 195–211. **Forbes, A. D.** "A Critique of Statistical Approaches to the Isaiah Authorship Problem." In *Proceedings of the Third International Colloquium: Bible and the Computer—Interpretation, Hermeneutics, Expertise.* Paris: Champion; Geneva: Slatkin, 1992. 531–45.

Gammie, J. C. *Holiness in Israel.* OBT. Minneapolis: Fortress, 1989. **Geller, S. A.** "Were the Prophets Poets?" *Proof* 3 (1983) 211–21. **Gevaryahu, H. M. I.** "Isaiah: How the Book Entered Holy Writ." *JBQ* 18 (1989–90) 205–12. ———. "The School of Isaiah: Biography and Transmission of the Book of Isaiah." *JBQ* 18 (1989) 62–68. ———. "The School of Isaiah's Biography and Transmission of the Book of Isaiah." *DD* 18 (1989–90) 62–68. **Gileadi, A.** "A Holistic Structure of the Book of Isaiah." Diss., Brigham Young University, 1981. **Gitay, H.** "Back to Historical Isaiah: Reflections on the Act of Reading." In *Studies.* Ed. J. Van Ruiten and M. Vervenne. 63–75. ———. "Isaiah and His Audience." *Proof* 3 (1983) 223–30. ———. "Oratorical Rhetoric: The Question of Prophetic Language with Special Attention to Isaiah." *ACEBT* 10 (1989) 72–78. **Gitay, Y.** "Deutero-Isaiah: Oral or Written?" *JBL* 99 (1980) 185–97. ———. "The Effectiveness of Isaiah's Speech." *JQR* 75 (1984) 162–72. ———. *Isaiah and His Audience: The Structure and Meaning of Isaiah 1–12.* Assen: Van Gorcum, 1991. ———. "Isaiah—The Impractical Prophet." *BR* 4 (1988) 10–15. ———. *Prophecy and Persuasion: A Study of Isaiah 40–48.* Forum Theologiae Linguisticae 14. Bonn: Linguistica Biblica, 1981. **Gordon, R. P.** "Where Have All the Prophets Gone? The 'Disappearing' Israelite Prophet against the Background of Ancient Near Eastern Prophecy." *BBS* 5 (1995) 67–86, esp 70. **Gosse, B.** "Deuteronome 32:1–43 et les redactions des livres d'Ezechiel et d'Isaïe." *ZAW* 107 (1995) 110–17. ———. "L'emploi des *'s'ym* dans le livre d'Isaïe." *BN* 56 (1991) 22–24. ———. "Isaïe 52:13–53:12 et Isaïe 6." *RB* 98 (1991) 537–43. ———. "Isaïe dans le redaction du livre d'Isaïe." *ZAW* 104 (1992) 52–66. ———. "La nouvelle alliance et les promesses d'avenir se référent à David dans les livres de Jérémie, Ezéchiel, et Isaïe." *VT* 41 (1991) 419–28. ———. *Structuration des grands ensembles bibliques et intertextualité à l'époque perse: De la rédaction sacerdotale du livre d'Isaïe à la contestation de la Sagesse.* BZAW 264. Berlin; New York: De Gruyter, 1997. **Gross, W.** "Israel und die Völker: Die Krise des YHWH Volk

Konzepts im Jesajabuch." In *Der Neue Bund im Alten: Studien zur Bundestheologie der beiden Testamente.* Ed. E. Zenger. Freiburg; Basel; Vienna: Herder, 1993. 149–67. **Gruber, M. I.** "The Motherhood of God in Second Isaiah." *RB* 90 (1983) 351–59.

Haag, H. "Der Weg zum Baum des Lebens: Ein paradiesmotive im Buch Jesajas." In *Künder des Wortes.* FS J. Schreiner, ed. L. Ruppert et al. Würzburg: Echter, 1982. 35–52. **Hagelia, H.** *Corum Deo: Spirituality in the Book of Isaiah, with Particular Attention to Faith in Yahweh.* ConBOT 49. Stockholm: Almqvist & Wiksal, 2001. **Hardmeier, C.** "Jesajaforschung im Umbruch." *VF* 31.1 (1986) 3–31. ———. *Prophetie im Streit vor dem Untergang Judas.* BZAW 187. Berlin: De Gruyter, 1990. ———. "Verkündigung und Schrift bei Jesaja: Zu Entstehung der Schriftprophetie als Oppositionsliteratur im alten Israel." *TGl* 73 (1983) 119–34. **Hayes, J.**, and **S. Irvine.** *Isaiah, the Eighth Century Prophet: His Times and His Preaching.* Nashville: Abingdon, 1987. **Helfmeyer, F. J.** *Licht der Volker: Das Buch Jesaja.* Stuttgart: Katholische Bibelwerke, 1987. **Hermisson, J. J.** "'Deuterojesaja' und 'Eschatologie.'" In *New Things.* Ed. F. Postma et al. 89–105. **Höffken, P.** "Der Prophet Jesaja beim Chronistin." *BN* 81 (1996) 82–90. **Høgenhaven, J.** *Gott und Volk bei Jesaja.* **Holt, E. K.** *Prophesying the Past: The Use of Israel's History in Isaiah.* Sheffield: Sheffield Academic Press, 1995. **Hunter, A. V.** *Seek the Lord! A Study of the Meaning and Function of the Exhortations in Amos, Hosea, Isaiah, Micah, and Zephaniah.* Baltimore: St. Mary's Seminary & University, 1982.

Irsigler, H. *Ein Weg aus der Gewalt? Gottesknecht kontra Kyros im Deuterojesajabuch.* Beiträge zur Friedensethik 28. Stuttgart: Kohlhammer, 1998. **Irvine, S. A.** "King and Prophet: Isaiah's Relationship with Ahaz during the Syro-Ephraimite War." Diss., Emory, 1989.

Jensen, J. "Weal and Woe in Isaiah: Consistency and Continuity." *CBQ* 43 (1981) 167–87. ———. "YHWH's Plan in Isaiah and in the Rest of the Old Testament." *CBQ* 48 (1986) 443–55. **Jeppesen, K.** "From 'You, My Servant' to 'The Hand of the Lord Is with My Servants'': A Discussion of Is. 40–66." *SJOT* 1 (1990) 113–29. ———. "Mother Zion, Father Servant: A Reading of Isaiah 49–55." In *Of Prophets' Visions and the Wisdom of Sages.* FS R. N. Whybray, ed. H. A. McKay and D. J. A. Clines. JSOTSup 162. Sheffield: JSOT Press, 1993. 109–25. **Jerger, G.** *Evangelium des ATs: Die Grundbotschaft des Propheten Deuterojesaja in ihrer Bedeutung fur den Religions-Unterricht.* SBB 14. Stuttgart: Katholische Bibelwerk, 1986. **Johnson, A.** "The Concept of Waiting in the Isaianic Corpus: A Rhetorical Critical Study of Selected Texts." Diss., Boston University, 1986. ———. "A Prophetic Vision of an Alternative Community." In *Uncovering Ancient Stones.* FS H. N. Richardson, ed. L. M. Hopfe. Winona Lake, IN: Eisenbrauns, 1994. 31–40. **Jones, R. C.** "YHWH's Judgment and Kingship in the Oracles of Isaiah ben Amoz." Diss., Union Theological Seminary, VA, 1990.

Kaiser, O. "Geschichtliche Erfahrung und eschatologische Erwartung: Ein Beitrag zur Geschichte der alttestamentliche Eschatologie im Jesajabuch." In *Gegenwartsbedeutung des Altes Testament.* Göttingen: Vandenhoeck & Ruprecht, 1984. 167–80. ———. "Jesaja[buch]." *TRE* 16:636–58. ———. "Literaturkritik und Tendenzkritik: Überlegungen zur Methode des Jesajaexegese." In *Book of Isaiah.* Ed. J. Vermeylen. 55–71. **Kaminsky, J. S.** "The Concept of Election and Second Isaiah: Recent Literature." *BTB* 31 (2001) 125–34. **Kapelrud, A. S.** "The Main Concern of Second Isaiah." *VT* 32 (1982) 50–58. **Klein, H.** "Beweis der Einzigkeit Gottes bei Deuterojesaja." *VT* 35 (1985) 267–73. **Klein, R. W.** "Going Home—A Theology of Second Isaiah." *CurTM* 5 (1978) 198–210. **Knohl, I.** "Isaiah and the Holiness School." In *The Sanctuary of Silence: The Priestly Torah and the Holiness School.* Minneapolis: Fortress, 1995. 212–14. **Koch, K.** "Damnation and Salvation: Prophetic Metahistory and the Rise of Eschatology in the Book of Isaiah." *ExAud* 6 (1990) 5–13. **Kohn, R. L.**, and **W. H. C. Propp.** "The Name of 'Second Isaiah': Forgotten Theory of Nehemiah Rabban." In *Fortunate the Eyes That See.* Ed.

A. B. Beck et al. 223–35. **Kooij, A. van der.** "Accident or Method? On 'Analogical' Interpretation in the Old Greek of Isaiah and in 1QIs[a]." *BO* 43 (1986) 366–76. ———. "The Old Greek of Isaiah in Relation to the Qumran Texts of Isaiah: Some General Comments." In *Septuagint, Scrolls and Cognate Writings.* Ed. G. J. Brooke and B. Lindars. SBLSCS 33. Atlanta: Scholars Press, 1992. 195–213. **Kratz, R. G.** "Der Anfang des Zweiten Jesaja in Jes 40,1 f. und das Jeremiabuch." *ZAW* 106 (1994) 243–61. ———. "Der Anfang des Zweiten Jesaja in Jes 40,1 f. und siene literarische Horizonte." *ZAW* 105 (1993) 400–419. ———. *Kyros im Deuterojesaja-Buch: Redaktionsgeschichtliche Untersuchungen zu Entstehung und Theologie von Jes 40–55.* FAT 1 Tübingen: Mohr, 1991. **Kraus, H.-J.** *Das Evangelium der unbekannten Propheten: Jesaja 40–66.* Kleine biblische Bibliotek. Neukirchen-Vluyn: Neukirchener Verlag, 1991. **Kunz, J. K.** "The Form, Location, and Function of Rhetorical Questiones in Deutero-Isaiah." *Writing and Reading.* Ed. C. C. Broyles and C. A. Evans. 1:121–41.

Laato, A. *"About Zion I Will Not Be Silent": The Book of Isaiah as an Ideological Unity.* ConBOT 44. Stockholm: Almqvist & Wiksell, 1988. ———. "The Composition of Isaiah 40–55." *JBL* 109 (1990) 207–28. ———. *The Servant of Jhwh and Cyrus: A Reinterpretation of the Exilic Messianic Programme in Isaiah 40–55.* ConBOT 35. Stockholm: Almqvist & Wiksell, 1992. ———. *Who Is Immanuel? The Rise and Foundering of Isaiah's Messianic Expectations.* Åbo: Åbo Academic Press, 1988. **Labahn, A.** "The Delay of Salvation within Deutero-Isaiah." *JSOT* 85 (1999) 71–84. ———. *Wort Gottes und Schuld Israels: Untersuchungen zi Motiven deuteronomistischer Theologie im Deuterojesajabuch mit einem Ausblick auf dem Verhältniz von Jes 40–55 zum Deuteronomismus.* BWANT 143. Stuttgart: Kohlhammer, 1999. **Leclerc, T. L.** *Yahweh Is Exalted in Justice: Solidarity and Conflict in Isaiah.* Minneapolis: Fortress, 2001. **Leene, H.** "Auf der Suche nach einem redaktionskritischen Modell für Jesaja 40–55." *TLZ* 121 (1996) 803–18. ———. "History and Eschatology in Deutero-Isaiah." In *Studies.* Ed. J. Van Ruiten and M. Vervenne. 223–47. ———. "De vroegere en de nieuwe dingen bij Deuterojesaja." Diss., Vrije Univ., Amsterdam, 1987. **Lenssen, J.** *Jesaja—Predigten.* Wurzburg: Echter, 1986. **Leske, A. M.** "The Influence of Isaiah 40–66 on Christology in Matthew and Luke: A Comparison." In *SBLSP.* Atlanta: SBL, 1994. 897–916. **Levin, C.** *Die Verheissung des neuen Bundes.* FRLANT 137. Göttingen: Vandenhoeck & Ruprecht, 1985. **Light, G. W.** *Isaiah.* Interpretation Bible Studies 12. Louisville, KY: Westminster John Knox Press, 2001. **Lindars, B.** "Good Tidings to Zion: Interpreting Deutero-Isaiah Today." *BJRL* 68 (1985) 473–97.

Ma, W. "The Spirit *(ruah)* of God in Isaiah 1–39." *AJT* 3 (1989) 582–96. ———. *Until the Spirit Comes: The Spirit of God in the Book of Isaiah.* JSOTSup 271. Sheffield: Sheffield Academic Press, 1999. **Machinist, P.** "Assyria and Its Image in the First Isaiah." *JAOS* 103 (1983) 719–37. **Magonet, J.** "Isaiah's Mountain or the Shape of Things to Come." *Proof* 11 (1991) 175–81. **Marböck, J.** "Exodus zum Zion: Zum Glaubensweg der Gemeinde nach einigen Texten des Jesajabuches." In *Die alttestamentliche Botschaft als Wegwesung.* FS H. Reinelt, ed. J. Zmijewski. Stuttgart: Katholische Bibelwerk, 1990. 163–79. ———. "Der Gott des Neuen and das neue Lied (Isa 40–55)." *Ein Gott—Eine Offenbarung.* FS N. Füglister, ed. F. Reiterer. Würzburg: Echter, 1991. 357–71. **Matheus, F.** *Singt dem Herrn ein neues Lied: Die Hymnen Deuterojesajas.* SBS 141. Stuttgart: Katholisches Bibelwerk, 1990. **McCready, W. O.** "'The Day of Small Things' vs. the Latter Days: Historical Fulfillment or Eschatological Hope?" In *Israel's Apostasy and Restoration.* FS R. K. Harrison, ed. A. Gileadi. Grand Rapids, MI: Baker, 1988. 223–36. **McEvenue, S.** "Who Was Second Isaiah?" In *Studies.* Ed. J. Van Ruiten and M. Vervenne. 213–22. **Meade, D. G. A.** *Pseudonymity and Canon: An Investigation into the Relationship of Authorship and Authority in Jewish and Early Christian Tradition.* WUNT 39. Tübingen: Mohr-Siebeck, 1986. **Melugin, R.** "The Book of Isaiah and the Construct of Meaning." In *Writing and Reading.* Ed. C. C. Broyles and C. A. Evans. 1:39–55. ———. "Reading the Book of Isaiah as Christian Scripture." In *SBLSP.*

Atlanta: Scholars Press, 1996. 188–203. ———. "Texts to Transform Life: Reading Isaiah as Christians." *WW* 19 (1999) 109–16. **Merrill, E. H.** "Isaiah 40–55 as Anti-Babylonian Polemic." *GTJ* 8 (1987) 3–18. ———. "Pilgrimage and Procession: Motifs of Israel's Return." In *Israel's Apostasy and Restoration.* FS R. K. Harrison, ed. A. Gileadi. Grand Rapids, MI: Baker, 1988. 261–72. ———. "Survey of a Century of Studies on Isaiah 40–55, Literary Character 1.2." *BSac* 144 (1987) 24–43, 144–56. **Mettinger, T. N. D.** "In Search of the Hidden Structure: Yhwh as King in Isaiah 40–55." *SEÅ* 51 (1986) 148–57. Reprinted in *Writing and Reading,* ed. C. C. Broyles and C. A. Evans. 1:143–54. **Miscall, P. D.** *Isaiah 34–35: A Nightmare/A Dream.* JSOT 281. Sheffield: Sheffield Academic Press, 1999. ———. "Isaiah: New Heavens, Hearth, New Book." In *Reading between Texts: Intertextuality and the Hebrew Bible.* Ed. D. N. Fewell. Literary Currents in Biblical Interpretation. Louisville: Westminster John Knox, 1992. 41–56. ———. "Isaiah: The Labyrinth of Images." *Semeia* 54 (1991) 103–21. **Moor, J. C. de.** *The Structure of Classical Hebrew Poetry: Isaiah 40–55.* OTS 41. Leiden: Brill, 1998. **Mulzer, M.** "Döderlein und Deuterojesaja." *BN* 66 (1993) 15–22. **Murray, D. F.** "The Rhetoric of Disputation: Re-examination of a Prophetic Genre." *JSOT* 38 (1987) 95–121.

Newsom, C. "Response to Norman Gottwald, "Social Class and Idealogy in Isaiah 40–55: An Eageltonian Reading.'" *Semeia* 59 (1992) 73–78. **Niehr, H.** "Bedeutung und Funktion kanaanäischer Traditions-elements in der Sozialkritik Jesajas." *BZ* 28 (1984) 69–81. **Nielsen, K.** "Reinterpretation of Metaphors: Tree Metaphors in Isaiah 1–39." In *Wünschet Jerusalem Frieden: IOSOT Congress Jerusalem 1986.* Ed. M. Augustin and K.-D. Schunck. Frankfurt am Main: Lang, 1988. 425–29. ———. *There Is Hope for a Tree: The Tree as Metaphor in Isaiah.* JSOTSup 65. Sheffield: JSOT, 1989. **Nurmela, R.** "The Growth of the Book of Isaiah Illustrated by Allusions in Zechariah." In *Bringing Out the Treasure: Inner Biblical Allusion in Zechariah 9-14.* Ed. M. J. Boda and M. H. Floyd. JSOTSup 370. London: Sheffield Academic Press, 2003. 245–59.

O'Connell, R. H. *Concentricity and Continuity: Literary Structure in Isaiah.* JSOTSup 188. Sheffield: Sheffield UP, 1994. **O'Connor, K. M.** "'Speak Tenderly to Jerusalem': Second Isaiah's Reception and Use of Daughter Zion." *PSB* 20 (1999) 281–94. **O'Kane, M.** "Isaiah: A Prophet in the Footsteps of Moses." *JSOT* 69 (1996) 29–51. **Oorschot, J. van.** *Von Babel zum Zion: Eine literarkritische und redaktionsgeschichtliche Untersuchung.* BZAW 206. Berlin; New York: De Gruyter, 1993. (A redactional history of Isa 40–51.) **Oswald, J. N.** "The Kerugmatic Structure of the Book of Isaiah." In *Go to the Land that I Will Show You.* Ed. J. P. Coleson and V. H. Matthews. Winona Lake, IN: Eisenbrauns, 1996. 143–58.

Pagan, S. "Apocalyptic Poetry: Isaiah 24–27." *BT* 43 (1992) 314–25. **Partain, J.** *A Guide to Isaiah 1–39.* London: SPCK, 1986. **Patrick, D. A.** "Epiphanic Imagery in Second Isaiah's Portrayal of a New Exodus." *HAR* 8 (1984) 125–41. **Pelletier, A.-M.** "Le livre Isaïe et le temps de l'histoire." *NRTh* 112 (1990) 30–43. **Perez, C. F.** *El códice de profetas de El Cairo: IV. Isaias, edicion de su texto y masoras.* Madrid: Instituto Arias Montano, 1986. **Perlitt, L.** "Jesaja und die Deuteronomisten." In *Deuteronomium Studien.* Tübingen: Mohr, 1994. 157–71. **Plamondon, P.-H.** "Le Deutero-Isaïe: Do la multiplicite de genres littéraires a l'unite d'un discours." *LTP* 39 (1983) 171–93. **Porath, R.** "Die Sozialkritik im Jesajabuch: Redaktions-geschichtliche Analyse." Diss., Munich, 1986. **Porton, G. G.** "Isaiah and the Kings: The Rabbis on the Prophet Isaiah." In *Writing and Reading.* Ed. C. C. Broyles and C. A. Evans. 2:693–716.

Raja, R. T. J. "'Cry' in the Old Testament: A Study of *qara'* with special reference to Isaiah 43–64." *LW* 93 (1987) 43–64. **Rendtorff, R.** "The Book of Isaiah: A Complex Unity. Synchronic and Diachronic Reading." In *SBLSP.* Atlanta: Scholars Press, 1991. 8–20. ———.

"Zur Komposition des Buches Jesaja." *VT* 34 (1984) 295–320. Reprinted as "The Composition of the Book of Isaiah," *Canon and Theology* (Minneapolis: Fortress, 1993) 146–69. **Richter, W.**, ed. *Biblia Hebraica transcripta.* Arbeiten zu Text und Sprache im Alten Testament 33.7. St. Ottilien: Eos, 1993. **Rix, D. S.** "Milton: Blake's Reading of Second Isaiah." In *Poetic Prophecy in Western Literature.* Ed. J. Wojcik and R.-J. Frontain. Rutherford, NJ: Fairleigh Dickinson UP, 1984. 106–18. **Roberts, J. J. M.** "Double Entendre in First Isaiah." *CBQ* 54 (1992) 39–48. ———. "Isaiah in Old Testament Theology." *Int* 36 (1982) 130–43. **Rooker, M. F.** "Dating Isaiah 40–66: What Does the Linguistic Evidence Say?" *WTJ* 58 (1996) 303–12. **Rosenbaum, M.** *Word-Order Variation in Isaiah 40–55: A Functional Perspective.* Assen: Van Gorcum, 1997. **Ruppert, L.** "Critica a los dioses en el libra de Isaias." *RivB* 63 (1996) 129–59. ———. "Die Disputationsworte bei Deuterojesaja in neuen religionsgeschichtlichen Licht." In *Prophetie und geschichtliche Wirklichkeit im alten Israel.* FS S. Herrmann, ed. R. Liwak et al. Stuttgart: Kohlhammer, 1991. 317–25. **Ruterswörden, U.** "Erwagungen zur Metaphorik des Wassers in Jes 40ff." *SJOT* 2 (1989) 1–22.

Sawyer, J. F. A. "Daughter of Zion and Servant of the Lord in Isaiah: A Comparison." *JSOT* 44 (1989) 89–107. ———. "The Gospel in Isaiah." *ExpTim* 113 (2001) 39–43. **Scheiber, A.** "Der Zeitpunkt des Auftretens von Deuterojesaja." *ZAW* 84 (1972) 242–43. **Schibler, D.** "Messianism and Messianic Prophecy in Isaiah 1–12 and 28–33." In *The Lord's Anointed: Interpretation of Old Testament Messianic Texts.* Ed. P. E. Satterwaite et al. Grand Rapids, MI: Baker, 1995. 87–104. **Schmitt, H.-C.** "Prophetie und Schultheologie im Deuterojesajabuch: Beobachtungen zur Redactionsgeschichte von Jes. 40–55." *ZAW* 91 (1979) 43–61. **Schmitt, J. J.** "The City as Woman in Isaiah 1–39." In *Writing and Reading.* Ed. C. C. Broyles and C. A. Evans. 1:95–119. ———. *Isaiah and His Interpreters.* New York: Paulist, 1986. **Schoenstene, R.** "An Image of the Promised Land: Jerusalem in Isaiah." *TBT* 29 (1991) 9–13. **Schoors, A.** "Die Anklagen verurteilt." *Schrift* 34 (1974) 123–58. ———. "Historical Information in Isaiah 1–39." In *Studies.* Ed. J. Van Ruiten and M. Vervenne. 1:75–94. **Schreiner, J.** "Zum Stellenwert von Menschenreden im prophetischen Gotteswort bei Jesaja 40–55." In *Ich bewirke das Heil und erschaffe das Unheil (Jesaja 45,7): Studien zur Botschaft der Propheten.* FS L. Ruppert, ed. F. Diedrich and B. Willmes. FB 88. Würzburg: Echter, 1998. 135–56. **Schroeder, C. O.** *History, Justice, and the Agency of God: A Hermeneutical and Exegetical Investigation on Isaiah and the Psalms.* BibIntS 52. Leiden: Brill, 2001. **Schultz, R.** "The King in the Book of Isaiah." In *The Lord's Anointed: Interpretation of Old Testament Messianic Texts.* Grand Rapids, MI: Baker, 1995. 141–66. **Seitz, C. R.** "The Divine Council: Temporal Transition and New Prophecy in the Book of Isaiah." *JBL* 109 (1990) 229–46. ———. "How Is the Prophet Isaiah Present in the Latter Half of the Book? The Logic of Chapters 40–66 within the Book of Isaiah." *JBL* 115 (1996) 219–40. ———. "Isaiah 1–66: Making Sense of the Whole." In *Reading and Preaching the Book of Isaiah.* Philadelphia: Fortress, 1988. 105–26. ———. "Isaiah, Book of (First Isaiah)." *ABD.* 3:472–88. ———. "The One Isaiah//The Three Isaiahs." In *Reading and Preaching the Book of Isaiah.* Philadelphia: Fortress Press, 1988. 13–22. ———. "On the Question of Divisions Internal to the Book of Isaiah." In *SBLSP.* Atlanta: Scholars Press, 1993. 260–66. ———. *Zion's Final Destiny: The Development of the Book of Isaiah. A Reassessment of Isaiah 36–39.* Minneapolis: Fortress, 1991. **Selms, A. van.** "The Expression 'The Holy One of Israel.'" In *Von Kanaan bis Kerala.* FS J. P. M. van der Ploeg, ed. W. C. Delsman et al. AOAT 211. Neukirchen-Vluyn: Neukirchener Verlag, 1982. **Seybold, K.** "Akrostichie bei Deuterojesaja." In *Die Sprache der Propheten.* Zurich: Pano, 1999. 200–209. ———. "Der Name Deuterojesajas." In *Die Sprache der Propheten.* Zurich: Pano, 1999. 211–15. **Sheppard, G. T.** "The Anti-Assyrian Redaction and the Canonical Context of Isaiah 1–39." *JBL* 104 (1985) 193–216. ———. "The Book of Isaiah as Human Witness to Revelation in the Religions of Judaism and Christianity." In *SBLSP.* Atlanta: Scholars Press, 1993. 274–80. ———. "The Book of Isaiah: Competing Structures according to a Late Modern Description of Its Shape and Scope." In *SBLSP.* Atlanta: Scholars Press, 1992. 549–82. ———. "Isaiah as a Scroll or Codex within Jewish and Christian Scripture." In *SBLSP.* Atlanta: Scholars Press, 1996. 204–24. **Simian-Yofre, H.** *Testi isiani dell'Avento: Esegesi e liturgia.* Studi Biblici 29. Bologna: EBD, 1996. **Sommer, B. D.** "Allusions and Illusions: The Unity of the Book of Isaiah in Light of Deutero-Isaiah's use of Prophetic Tradition." In *New Visions.* Ed. R. F. Melugin and M. A. Sweeney. 156–86. ———. *A Prophet Reads Scripture: Allusion in Isaiah 40–66.* Contraversions. Stanford: Stanford UP, 1998. ———. "The Scroll of Isaiah as Jewish Scripture, or Why Jews Don't Read Books." In *SBLSP.* Atlanta: Scholars Press, 1996. 225–42. **Spradlin, M. R.** "An Investigation of Conditional Sentences in the Hebrew Text of Isaiah." Diss., Southwestern Baptist Theological Seminary, 1991. **Stansell, G.** *Micah and Isaiah: A Form and Tradition Historical Comparison.* SBLDS 85. Atlanta: Scholars Press, 1988. **Stassen, S. L.** "The Plot in Isaiah 40–55." *AcT* 17 (1997) 128–42. **Steck, O. H.** *Gottesknecht und Zion: Gesammelte Aufsätze zu Deuterojesaja.* FAT 4. Tübingen: Mohr-Siebeck, 1992. **Stein, J. W.** "Isaiah and Statesmanship." *Journal of Church and State* 27 (1985) 83–97. **Strauss, H.** *Messianisch ohne Messiah: Zur Überlieferungsgeschichte und interpretation des sogenannten messianischen Texte im Alten Testament.* European University Studies ser. 23, Theology 232. Bern: Lang, 1984. **Streibert, C.** *Schöpfung bei Deuterojesaja und in der Priesterschrift: Eine vergleichender Untersuchung zu Inhalt und Funktion schöpungstheologischer Aussagen in exilisch-nachexilischer Zeit.* BEATAJ 8. Frankfurt; Bern: Lang, 1993. **Stuhlmueller, C.** "Deutero-Isaiah and Trito-Isaiah." In *NJBC.* 329–48. ———. "Deutero-Isaiah: Major Transitions in the Prophet's Theology and in Contemporary Scholarship." *CBQ* 42 (1980) 1–29. **Sweeney, M. A.** "The Book of Isaiah as Prophetic Torah." In *New Visions.* Ed. R. F. Melugin and M. A. Sweeney. 50–67. ———. *Isaiah 1–4 and the Post Exilic Understanding of the Isaianic Tradition.* BZAW 171. Berlin: De Gruyter, 1988. ———. "On Multiple Settings in the Book of Isaiah." In *SBLSP.* Atlanta: Scholars Press, 1992. 267–73. ———. "The Road to Duhm and Isaiah: Selected Nineteenth Century Studies." In *SBLSP.* Atlanta: Scholars Press, 2002. 191–211.

Talstra, E. "Second Isaiah and Qohelet: Could One Get Them on Speaking Terms?" In *New Things.* Ed. F. Postma et al. 225–36. **Talstra, E.,** and **A. L. H. M. van Wieringen.** *A Prophet on the Screen: Computerized Description and Literary Interpretation of Isaian Texts.* Applicateo 9. Amsterdam: VU UP, 1992. **Trever, J. C.** "The Contributions of Second Isaiah to the Semantic Development of Hebrew Words." Diss., Yale Univ., 1991. **Troxel, R. L.** "Eschatology in the Septuagint of Isaiah." Diss., Wisconsin, 1989. **Turner, E. A.** "The Foreign Idols of Deutero-Isaiah." *OTE* 9 (1996) 111–28.

Vaaholz, R. "Isaiah versus 'the Gods': A Case for Unity" (48–49). *WTJ* 42 (1980) 389–94. **Van Ruiten, J.** "'His Master's Voice'? The Supposed Influence of the Book of Isaiah on the Book of Habakkuk." In *Studies.* Ed. J. Van Ruiten and M. Vervenne. 397–412. **Vermeylen, J.** "Le Motif de la creation dans le Deutero-Isaie." In *La création dans l'Orient ancien: Congrès de l'ACFEB.* Paris: Cerf, 1987. 183–240. ———. "Le Proto-Isaïe et la sagesse d'Israël." In *La Sagesse de l'Ancien Testament.* Ed. M. Gilbert. BETL 51. Leuven: Peeters, 1979. 39–58. ———. "L'unité du livre d'Isaïe." In *Book of Isaiah.* Ed. J. Vermeylen. 11–53. **Vermeylen, J.,** ed. *The Book of Isaiah.* Leuven: Leuven UP; Peeters, 1989. **Vincent, J. M.** *Studien zur literarischen Eigenart und zur geistigen Heimat von Jesaja, Kap. 40–55.* BBET 5. Frankfurt am M.: Lang, 1977.

Watson, W. G. E. "Further Examples of Semantic-Sonant Chiasmus." *CBQ* 46 (1984) 21–33. ———. "Gender-Matched Synonymous Parallelism in the Old Testament." *JBL* 99 (1980) 321–41. **Watts, J. D. W.** "The Characterization of YHWH in the Vision of Isaiah." *RevExp* 83 (1986) 439–50. **Webb, B. G.** *The Message of Isaiah: On Eagles' Wings.* Downers Grove, IL: InterVarsity Press, 1996. ———. "Zion in Transformation: A Literary Approach to Isaiah." In *The Bible in Three Dimensions.* Ed. D. J. A. Clines, S. E. Fowl, and S. E. Porter. JSOTSup 87. Sheffield: JSOT Press, 1990. 65–84. **Wegner, P.** *An Examination of Kingship and Messianic Expectation in Isaiah 1–35.* Lewiston, NY: Mellen, 1992. **Weinberg, Z.** "Notes of Jakob Barth to the Consolation Passages of Isaiah, to Song of Songs and to Qohelet." *BMik* 31.104 (1985) 78–87. **Weinfeld, M.** "Zion and Jerusalem as Religious and Political Capital: Ideology and Utopia." In *The Poet and the Historian: Essays in Literary and Historical Biblical Criticsm.* Ed. R. Friedman. HSS 26. Chico, CA: Scholars Press, 1983. **Weippert, M.** "Die 'Konfessionen' Deuterojesajas." In *Schöpfung und Befreiung.* FS C. Westermann, ed. R. Alberz, F. W. Golka, and J. Kegler. Stuttgart: Calwer, 1989. **Werner, W.** *Eschatologische Texte in Jesaja 1–39: Messias, Heliger Rest, Völker.* FB 46. Würzburg: Echter, 1982. ———. *Studien zur alttestamentlichen Vorstellung vom Plan Yahves.* BZAW 173. Berlin: De Gruyter, 1988. **Westermann, C.** *Sprache und Struktur der Prophetie Deuterojesajas.* Calwer theologische Monographien 11. Stuttgart: Calwer, 1981. **Westermeyer, P.** "Exegesis of Isaiah in Choral Music." *WW* 19 (1999) 171–80. **Whybray, R. N.** *The Second Isaiah.* OT Guides. Sheffield: Sheffield Academic Press, 1983. ———. "Two Recent Studies on Second Isaiah." *JSOT* 34 (1986) 109–17. **Wiklander, B.** *Prophecy as Literature: A Text-linguistic and Rhetorical Approach to Isaiah 2–4.* Rev. ed. ConBOT 22. Uppsala: Gleerup, 1984. **Wilcox, P.,** and **D. Paton-Williams.** "The Servant Songs in Deutero Isaiah." *JSOT* 42 (1988) 79–102. **Willey, P. T.** *Remember the Former Things: The Recollection of Previous Texts in Second Isaiah.* SBLDS 161. Atlanta: Scholars Press, 1997. **Willi, T.** *Juda—Jehud—Israel: Studien zum Selbstverständnis des Judentums in persischer Zeit.* FAT 12. Tübingen: Mohr-Siebeck, 1995. **Williamson, H. G. M.** *The Book Called Isaiah: Deutero-Isaiah's Role in Composition and Redaction.* Oxford: Clarendon, 1994. ———. "First and Last in Isaiah." In *Of Prophets' Visions and the Wisdom of Sages.* FS R. N. Whybray, ed. H. A. McKay and D. J. A. Clines. JSOTSup 162. Sheffield: Sheffield Academic Press, 1993. 95–109. ———. *Variations on a Theme: King, Messiah and Servant in the Book of Isaiah.* Carlisle: Paternoster, 1998. **Wodeki, B.** "Synonymic Designation of Jerusalem in Is. 1–39." In *Wünschet Jerusalem Frieden: IOSOT Congress Jerusalem 1986.* Ed. M. Augustin and K.-D. Schunck. Frankfurt am Main: Lang, 1988. **Wojcik, Jan.** "The Uncertain Success of Isaiah's Prophecy: A Poetical Reading." In *Poetic Prophecy in Western Literature.* Ed. J. Wojcik and R.-J. Frontain. Rutherford, NJ: Fairleigh Dickinson UP, 1984. 31–39. **Worgul, J. E.** "Parallelism in the Poetry of Isaiah 1–18." Ph.D. Diss., Dropsie College, 1987. ———. "The Quatrain in Isaianic Poetry." *GTJ* 11 (1990) 187–204.

Young, I. "The Dipthong **ay* in Edomite [clues in Isa.]." *JSS* 37 (1992) 27–30.

Zimmerli, W. "Gottesrecht bei den propheten Amos, Hosea und Jesaja." In *Werden und Wirken des Alten Testaments.* FS C. Westermann, ed. R. Albertz et al. Göttingen: Vandenhoeck & Ruprecht, 1980. 216–35.

DEUTERO-ISAIAH (CHAPS. 40–66)

Bibliography

Begrich, J. *Studien zu Deuterojesaja.* BWANT 77. Stuttgart: Kohlhammer, 1938. Reprinted as *Studien zu Deuterojesaja,* TB 20 (Munich: Kaiser, 1969[2]). **Brettler, M. Z.** "Incompatible Metaphors for YHWH in Isaiah 40–66." *JSOT* 78 (1998) 97–120. **Clark, K. C.** "An Analysis of Is 40 (:1)–44:23 Utilizing the Creation-Redemption of the Creator King and Process Theology." Diss., Claremont, 1977. **Elliger, K.** *Deuterojesaja in seinem Verhältnis zu Tritojesaja.* BWANT 11. Stuttgart: Kohlhammer, 1933. **Gileadi, A.** "A Holistic Structure of the Book of Isaiah." Diss., Brigham Young, 1981. **Goldingay, J.** "The Arrangement of Isaiah xl–xlv." *VT* 29 (1979) 289–99. **Gressmann, H.** "Die literarische Analyse Deuterojasaja." *ZAW* 34 (1914) 254–97. **Haran, M.** "The Literary Structure and Chronological Framework of the Prophecies in Isaiah xl–

xiviii." In *Congress Volume, Bonn, 1962.* VTSup 9. Leiden: Brill, 1963. 127–55. **Hessler, E.** "Gott der Schöpfer: Ein Beitrag zur Komposition und Theologie Deuterojesajas." Diss., Greifswald, 1961. **Hudson, M. H.** "Creation Theology in Isa 40–66: An Expression of Confidence in the Sovreignty of God." Diss., Southwestern Baptist Theological Seminary, Fort Worth, 1995. **Kim, K. C. P.** *Ambiguity, Tension and Multiplicity in Deutero-Isaiah.* New York: Lang, 2004. **Köhler, L.** *Deuterojesaja (Jes 40–55) stilkritisch untersucht.* BZAW 37. Giessen: Töpelmann, 1923. **Lack, R.** "La strutturazione de Isaia 40–55." *La Scuola Cattolica* 101 (1975) 43–58. **Liebreich, L. J.** "The Compilation of the Book of Isaiah." *JQR* 46 (1955–56) 259–77; 47 (1956–57) 114–38. **Melugin, R.** *The Formation of Isaiah 40–55.* BZAW 141. Berlin: De Gruyter, 1976. **Mowinckel, S.** "Die Komposition des deuterojesajanischen Buches." *ZAW* 49 (1931) 87–112, 242–60. ———. "Neuere Forschung zu Deuterojesaja, Tritojesaja, und dem 'Ebad-Jahwe-Problem." *AcOr* 16 (1937) 1–40. **Spykerboer, H. C.** *The Structure and Composition of Deutero-Isaiah.* Meppel: Kripps, 1976. **Waldow, H. E. von.** "Anlass und Hintergrund der Verkündigung des Deuterojesajas." Diss., Bonn, 1953. **Westermann, C.** "Sprache und Structur des Prophetie Deuterojesajas." In *Forschung am Altentestament.* TB 24. Munich: Kaiser, 1964. 92–170.

Ibn Ezra (A.D. 1167) questioned the eighth-century Isaiah's authorship of chaps. 40–66. But Eichhorn (*Einleitung in das Alte Testament* [Leipzig, 1783] 3:76–97) and Döderlein (*Esaias* [1775] xii–xv) first developed the question into a suggestion that the chapters should be treated as a separate literary work (see O. Eissfeldt, *The Old Testament: An Introduction*, trans. P. R. Ackroyd [New York: Harper and Row, 1965] 304). Since the mid-nineteenth century, critical scholarship has referred to chaps. 40–66 as Second Isaiah. Later many interpreters would restrict this work to chaps. 40–55, treating the rest as a third unit (see *Trito-Isaiah [Chaps. 56–66]*).

The date suggested for these chapters was based on references to Cyrus, the first Persian emperor, in chaps. 44–45. He rose to power in the decade before 540 B.C.E. and entered Babylon in 539 B.C.E. A second basis for thinking of the material as having been written within this time frame was the presentation of Babylon, not Assyria, as Israel's principal enemy. Assyria was destroyed as a power between 617 and 609 B.C.E. Babylon was responsible for the final destruction of Jerusalem in 598 and 587 B.C.E.

Chaps. 40–55 have usually been interpreted as a compositional unit written by one author who lived in Babylon as a part of the Babylonian exilic community. He is sometimes called "the great prophet of the Exile." However, some think of the "servant poems" (42:1–4; 49:1–6; 50:4–9; 52:13–53:12) as separate compositions that were inserted into the larger text. (See *Excursus: Identifying the "Servant of YHWH"* in *Isaiah 34–66.*)

Some conservative scholars have opposed the division, maintaining the unity of the entire book, the authorship by Isaiah in the eighth century B.C.E., and these chapters as predictive prophecy (see O. T. Allis, *The Unity of Isaiah* [Philadelphia: Reformed, 1950]; E. J. Young, *Studies in Isaiah* [London: Tyndale, 1955] and *Who Wrote Isaiah?* [Grand Rapids, MI: Eerdmans, 1958]; J. A. Motyer, *The Prophecy of Isaiah: An Introduction and Commentary* [Downers Grove, IL: InterVarsity Press, 1993]; and Oswalt, *Book of Isaiah*, 40–66).

But the arguments for a sixth-century date have proved decisive for most interpreters. These chapters have thus become the major source for understanding the attitudes of exilic and postexilic Jews (J. Blenkinsopp, *A History of Prophecy in Israel* [Philadelphia: Westminster, 1983] 207–24). R. N. Whybray (*Isaiah 40–66,*

20–30) even provides a biography and analysis of the supposed sixth-century prophet who wrote these chapters. Of course, the only evidence for the existence of such a person and all data for the biography had to be extrapolated from these chapters. There are no external data about him.

The isolation of these chapters has proved extraordinarily fruitful. The message to the exiles contains some of the best theological thinking and writing in the OT. Its insistence on pure monotheism ("I alone am God"), its development of the exodus and creation paradigms theologically (see *Excursus: Exodus Typology* and *Excursus: "Create"/"Creator"* [ברא]), and the presentation of the Servant of Yahweh passages (see *Excursus: Identifying the "Servant of Yahweh"*) have proved to be theological mines well worth excavating repeatedly.

This commentary agrees that the unique quality of chaps. 40–54 sets them apart from those before and after. But it also notes many features that relate them closely to chaps. 55–66 and others that bind them to chapters 34–39 that precede them. It views these connections as compositional features rather than as clues to a separate authorship and a different date. It thinks of these chapters, like the rest of the book, as being a product of the late fifth century. Their extraordinary ability to evoke the mood and situation of the exile is a tribute to the creative power that fashioned them.

TRITO-ISAIAH (CHAPS. 56–66)

Abramowski, R. "Zum literarischen Problem des Tritojesaja." *TSK* 96–97 (1925) 90–143. **Achtemeier, E.** *The Community and Message of Isaiah 56–66.* Minneapolis: Augsburg, 1982. **Bastiaens, J., W. Beuken, and F. Postma.** *Trito-Isaiah: An Exhaustive Concordance of Isa. 56–66, Especially with Reference to Deutero-Isaiah: An Example of Computer Assisted Research.* Amsterdam: Free University Press, 1984. **Beuken, W. A. M.** "An Example of the Isaianic Legacy of Trito-Isaiah." In *Tradition and Re-Interpretation in Jewish and Early Christian Literature.* FS J. C. H. Lebram, ed. J. W. van Henton et al. Leiden: Brill, 1986. 48–64. ———. *Jesaja.* Vol. 3A (56:1–63:6). POut. Nijkerk: Callenbach, 1989. ———. "The Main Theme of Trito Isaiah: 'The Servants of YHWH.'" *JSOT* 47 (1990) 67–87. ———. "Trito-Jesaja: Profetie en schriftgeleerdheid." In *Profeten en profetische geschriften.* FS A. S. van der Woude, ed. F. García Martínez, C. H. J. de Geus, and A. F. J. Klijn. Kampen: Kok, 1987. 71–86. **Berquist, J. L.** "Isaiah 56–66." In *Judaism in Persia's Shadow: A Social and Historical Approach.* Minneapolis: Fortress, 1995. 73–78. **Blenkinsopp, J.** *A History of Prophecy in Israel.* Philadelphia: Westminster, 1983. 242–51. ———. "The 'Servants of the Lord' in Third Isaiah: Profile of a Pietistic Group in the Persian Epoch." PIBA 7 (1983) 1–23. Reprinted in *The Place Is Too Small For Us,* ed. R. P. Gordon, SBTS 5 (Winona Lake, IN: Eisenbrauns, 1965) 392–414. **Bonnard, P.-E.** *Le Second Isaïe, son disciple et leurs éditeurs.* SB. Paris: Gabalda, 1972. **Carroll, R. P.** *When Prophecy Failed.* New York: Seabury, 1979. 150–56. **Cramer, K.** *Der geschichtliche Hintergrund der c. 56–66 im Buche Jes.* Dorpat, 1905. **Elliger, K.** *Deuterojesaja in seinem Verhältnis zu Tritojesaja.* BWANT 63. Stuttgart: Kohlhammer, 1933. ———. *Die Einheit des Tritojesaja.* BWANT 45. Stuttgart: Kohlhammer, 1928. ———. "Der Prophet Tritojesaja." *ZAW* 49 (1931) 112–40. **Emmerson, G. L.** *Isaiah 56-66.* OT Guides. Sheffield: Sheffield Academic Press, 1992. **Gressmann, H.** *Ueber die in Jes lvi–lxvi vorausgesetzten zeitgeschichtlichen Verhältnisse.* Göttingen, 1898. **Hanson, P. D.** *The Dawn of Apocalyptic.* Philadelphia: Fortress, 1975. 32–208. **Jones, D. R.** "The Cessation of Sacrifice after the Destruction of the Temple in 586 B.C." *JTS* 14 (1963) 12–31. **Höffken, P.** "Tritojesaja in redaktionsgeschichtlicher Sicht." *BO* 48 (1991) 736–43. **Holladay, W. L.** "Was Trito-Isaiah Deutero-Isaiah After All?" In *Writing and Reading.* Ed. C. C. Broyles and

C. A. Evans. 1:193–217. **Kessler, K.** *Gott geht es um das Ganze: Jesaja 56–66 und Jesaja 24–27 übersetzt und ausgelegt.* Stuttgart: Calwer, 1960. ———. "Studien zur religiösen Situation im ersten nachexilischen Jahrhundert und sur Auslegung von Jes 56–66." *WZ* 6 (1956–57) 41–74. ———. "Zur Auslegung von Jesaja lvi–lxvi." *TLZ* 81 (1956) 335–58. **Könen, K.** *Ethik und Eschatologie im Tritojesajabuch: Eine literarkritische und redaktionsgeschichtliche Studie.* WMANT 62. Neukirchen-Vluyn: Neukirchener Verlag, 1990. ———. "Textkritische Anmerkungen su schwierigen Stellen im Tritojesajabuch." *Bib* 69 (1988) 564–73. **Kraus, H.-J.** "Die ausgebliebene Endtheophanie: Eine Studie zu Jes 56–66." *ZAW* 78 (1966) 317–32. **Lau, W.** *Schriftgelehrte Prophetie in Jes 55-66: Eine Untersuchung in den literarischen Bezügen in den letzen elf Kapiteln des Jesajabuches.* BZAW 225. Berlin; New York: De Gruyter, 1994. **Liebreich, L. J.** "The Compilation of the Book of Isaiah." *JQR* 46 (1955–56) 259–77; 47 (1956–57) 114–38. **Lindblom, J.** *Prophecy in Ancient Israel.* Philadelphia: Muhlenberg, 1962. 403–22. **Littmann, E.** *Über die Abfassungszeit des Trito-jesaja.* Freiburg i. Br., 1899. **Maass, F.** "Tritojesaja." In *Das ferne und nahe Wort.* FS L. Rost, ed. F. Maass. BZAW 105. Berlin: Töpelmann, 1967. 151–63. **Marty, J.** *Les chapitres 56–66 du livre d'Esaïe, étude critique.* Paris, 1924. **McCullough, W. S.** "A Re-Examination of Isaiah 56–66." *JBL* 67 (1948) 27–36. **Michel, D.** "Zur Eigenart Tritojesajas." *ThViat* 10 (1966) 213–30. **Murtonen, A.** "Third Isaiah—Yes or No?" *AbrN* 19 (1980–81) 20–42. **Odeberg, H.** *Trito-Isaiah (Isaiah lvi–lxvi): A Literary and Linguistic Analysis.* Uppsala, 1931. **Oswalt, J. N.** "Righteousness in Isaiah: A Study of the Function of Chapters 56–66 in the Present Structure of the Book." In *Writing and Reading.* Ed. C. C. Broyles and C. A. Evans. 1:177–91. **Pauritsch, K.** *Die Neue Gemeinde: Gott Sammelt Ausgestossene und Arme.* AB 47. Rome: Biblical Institute Press, 1971. **Polan, G. J.** *In the Ways of Justice toward Salvation: A Rhetorical Analysis of Isaiah 56–59.* American University Studies 7.13. New York: Lang, 1986. ———. "Zum Text des Tritojesaia." *ZAW* 33 (1913) 89–91. **Rofé, A.** "Nevertheless 'Trito-Isaiah.'" *'al hePereq* 2 (1986) 7–15 (Hebrew). **Ruszkowski, L.** *Volk und Gemeinde im Wandel: Eine Untersuchung zu Jesaja 56–66.* FRLANT 191. Göttingen: Vandenhoeck & Ruprecht, 2000. **Schmitt, H. C.** "Prophetie und Schultheologie im Deuterojesajabuch." *ZAW* 91 (1979) 43–61. **Schramm, B.** *The Opponents of Third Isaiah: Reconstructing the Cultic History of the Restoration.* Sheffield: Sheffield Academic Press, 1995. **Scullion, J. J.** "Some Difficult Texts in Isa cc. 56–66 in the Light of Modern Scholarship." *UF* 4 (1973) 105–28. **Sehmsdorf, E.** "Studien zur Redaktionsgeschichte von Jesaja 56–66." *ZAW* 84 (1972) 517–76. **Sekine, S.** *Die Tritojesajanische Sammlung (Jes 56–66) redaktionsgeschichtlich untersucht.* BZAW 175. Berlin: De Gruyter, 1989. **Smith, P. A.** *Rhetoric and Redaction in Trito-Isaiah: The Structure, Growth and Authorship of Isaiah 56–66.* VTSup 62. Leiden: Brill, 1995. **Steck, O. H.** *Der Abschluss der Prophetie im Alten Testament: Ein Versuch zur Frage der Vorgeschichte des Kanons.* BTS 17. Neukirchen-Vluyn: Neukirchener Verlag, 1991. ———. "Anschlussprobleme einer redaktionellen Entstehung von Tritojesaja." In *Studien zu Tritojesaja.* BZAW 203. Berlin: De Gruyter, 1991. 269–79. ———. "Tritojesaja im Jesajabuch." In *Book of Isaiah.* Ed. J. Vermeylen. Louvain: Leuven UP, 1989. 361–406. ———. "Tritojesaja im Jesajabuch." In *Studien zu Tritojesaja.* BZAW 203. Berlin: De Gruyter, 1991. 2–48. ———. "Zu jüngsten Untersuchungen von Jes 56,1–8; 63:7–66,24." In *Studien zu Tritojesaja.* BZAW 203. Berlin: De Gruyter, 1991. 229–68. **Wallis, G.** "Gott und seine Gemeinde: Eine Betrachtung zum Trito-jesaja-Buch." *TZ* 27 (1971) 182–200. **Wodecki, B.** "Der Heilsuniversalismus bei Trito-Jesaja." *VT* 32 (1982) 248–52. **Zimmerli, W.** "Zur Sprache Tritojesajas." In *Gottes Offenbarung: Gesammelte Aufsetze zum Alten Testament.* TB 19. Munich: Kaiser, 1963. 217–33. Reprinted from *STU* 20 (1950) 110–22.

The same book that established the separation of the Servant Poems in Deutero-Isaiah (B. Duhm, *Das Buch Jesaja,* HKAT [Göttingen: Vandenhoeck & Ruprecht, 1892]) also suggested that chaps. 56–66 should be treated as a separate unit written by a prophet, to be called Trito-Isaiah, who lived in Jerusalem before the time of Nehemiah (about 450 B.C.E.). Duhm thought the chapters to be a unity, roughly contemporary with the time of Malachi. The idea of their literary independence has found general acceptance, but questions of date, provenience, and unity have been contested throughout the intervening period.

Duhm's idea about the authorship of Trito-Isaiah and his view of its unity were furthered by Elliger's books and article (1928–33) and were followed by Odeberg (*Trito-Isaiah* [1931]), K. Kessler (*WZ* 6 [1956–57] 41–74; *TLZ* 81 [1956] 335–38), H. J. Kraus (*ZAW* 78 [1966] 317–32), and P.-E. Bonnard (*Le Second Isaïa,* 1972). But note that Elliger followed Könen's suggestion to begin Trito-Isaiah with chap. 54. He was followed by Schmitt and currently by Rofé. Note that Lau uses the limits of chaps. 55–66.

T. K. Cheyne (*Introduction to the Book of Isaiah* [London: Black, 1895]) contested the unity of Trito-Isaiah. He was followed by K. Budde (*HSAT* [1922]), R. Abramowski (*TSK* 96–97 [1925] 90–143), and P. Volz (*Jesaia II,* KAT 9 [Leipzig: Deichert, 1932] 198ff.). They think of several authors working on this material in different times. Koole (*Isaiah, Part 3,* 1:20) lists several followers of this position, including Fohrer (*Das Buch Jesaja* [1964]), McKenzie (*Second Isaiah* [1968]), Pauritsch (*Die Neue Gemeinde* [1971]), Whybray (*Isaiah 40–66* [1975]), Hanson (*Dawn of Apocalyptic* [1975]), and Achtemeier (*Community and Message of Isaiah 56–66* [1982]). Redaction critics think of Trito-Isaiah as a *Grundschicht,* or basic layer, only (Vermeylen, Könen, and Steck).

A growing number of commentators who use literary methods have pointed out similarities between chaps. 56–66 and chaps. 1–39. Liebreich (*JQR* 46 [1955–56] 259–277; 47 [256–57] 114–38) made an early study of the relationship. Lack (*La Symbolique* [1973]) found a similar way of thinking *(l'imaginaire)* throughout the book. Vermeylen (*Du Prophète Isaïa* [1977–78] 504–8) pointed to similarities between 1:2–2:5 and what he called the first edition of Trito-Isaiah. Beuken ("Example of the Isaianic Legacy of Trito-Isaiah," 48–64; "Trito-Jesaja: Profetie en schriftgeleerdheid," 71–85; *Jesaja,* vol. 3A) found many connections. Koole (*Isaiah, Part 3,* 1:21–23) notes parallels and similarities between Trito-Isaiah and the early chapters, especially chaps. 6 and 34–35. He cites the lists of words in Odeberg (*Trito-Isaiah* [1931]) and J. B. Payne (*WTJ* 30 [1968] 185–203) to show the similarities in the vocabularies of the two parts. M. Fishbane (*Biblical Interpretation in Ancient Israel* [Oxford: Clarendon, 1985] 498) can refer to chap. 60 as a "skilful interweaving of a cluster of old Isaianic oracles." Koole (*Isaiah, Part 3,* 1:23–28) also deals at some length with the relationship of Trito- and Deutero-Isaiah. Lists of such texts had already been gathered in Glahn's commentary (L. Glahn and L. Köhler, *Der Prophet der Heimkehr* [1934] 118ff.) and in Zimmerli's article ("Zur Sprache Tritojesajas," 217–33).

Most interpreters place the chapters either around 520 B.C.E. or about 450 B.C.E. They see a tumultuous period reflected in the chapters in which the issue of building (or rebuilding) the temple is prominent. See current introductions to the OT and the commentaries for details.

Excursus: Form-Critical Categories in Chaps. 40–66

Bibliography

Alonso Schökel, L. "Genera litteraria prophetica (ad librum recentum C. Westermann)." *VD* 39 (1961) 185–92. **Begrich, J.** "Das priesterliche Heilsorakel." *ZAW* 52 (1934) 81–92.

Reprinted in *Gesammelte Studien zum Alten Testament,* TB 21 (Munich: Kaiser, 1964) 217–31. **Bonnard, P.-E.** *Le Second Isaïe, son disciple et leurs éditeurs.* SB. Paris: Gabalda, 1972. 28–36. **Caspari, W.** *Lieder und Gottessprüche der Rückwanderer* (Jes 40–55). BZAW 65. Giessen: Töpelmann, 1934. **Gressmann, H.** "Die literarische Analyse Deuterojesajas." *ZAW* 34 (1914) 254–97. **Harner, P. B.** "The Salvation Oracle in Second Isaiah." *JBL* 88 (1969) 418–34. **Hermisson, H. J.** "Discussionsworte bei Deuterojesaja." *EvT* 31 (1971) 665–80. **Irons, L.** "A Form-Critical Study of the Trial Speeches in Deutero-Isaiah." Diss., Vanderbilt, 1976. **Köhler, L.** *Deuterojesaja stilkritisch untersucht.* BZAW 37. Giessen: Töpelmann, 1923. **Melugin, R. F.** "Deutero-Isaiah and Form Criticism." *VT* 21 (1971) 326–37. **Schoors, A.** *I Am God Your Saviour: A Form-Critical Study of the Main Genres in Isaiah xl–lv.* VTSup 24. Leiden: Brill, 1973. ———. "The *Riv* Pattern in Is 40–55." *Bijdr* 30 (1969) 25–31. **Schüpphaus, J.** "Stellung und Funktion der sogenannten Heilsankündigung bei Deuterojesaja." *TZ* 27 (1971) 161–81. **Stuhlmueller, C.** *Creative Redemption in Deutero-Isaiah.* AnBib 43. Rome: Biblical Institute Press, 1970. 264–67. **Waldow, H. E. von.** "Anlass und Hintergrund der Verkündigung des Deuterojesajas." Diss., Bonn, 1933. Especially "Die Gattungen bei Dtjes," 11–61. **Westermann, C.** "Das Heilswort bei Deuterojesaja." *EvT* 24 (1964) 355–73.

See also **J. Muilenburg,** "The Book of Isaiah," in *IB* (New York; Nashville: Abingdon, 1956) 5:382–773; **C. Westermann,** *Das Buch Jesaja: Kapitel 40–66,* ATD (Göttingen, 1966), translated by D. M. G. Stalker as *Isaiah 40–66* (Philadelphia: Westminster, 1969); and **R. P. Merendino,** *Der Erste und der Letzte: Eine Untersuchung von Jes 40–48,* VTSup 31 (Leiden: Brill, 1981).

Gressmann began the form-critical analysis of speeches in Deutero-Isaiah when he called for abandonment of analyses that viewed the book as an essential unit in favor of analyses of small units. Köhler, Mowinckel, Caspari, Elliger, Begrich, von Waldow, and Westermann have led the parade of those who accepted his challenge.

Schoors summarized the stand of form-critical studies in 1973 by grouping genres in two types: words of salvation, including oracles and proclamations, and polemic genres, including trial speeches and disputations. Studies since that time have hardly moved beyond this point.

While this commentary acknowledges the great advances in recognition of form and style that this movement has achieved, its essential stance has moved back to a position *ante quo* Gressmann. It looks at the book of Isaiah's Vision as a whole, searching for the signs of composition and unity that define it, and seeing the smaller units as elements of that whole single composition. The book is seen not as a collection of preexisting small units but as a single great drama built up of speeches that are created for their own place within the book. The unit excerpted from prophetic tradition or from prophetic history (chaps. 36–39) is the exception, not the rule.

This approach preserves the gains made by form criticism while remaining free of its limitations. The work of isolating separate speeches and identifying their genres is essential to understanding the Vision as drama, but the dramatic form allows the speeches to be read within the larger context of the book without endangering their individual distinctiveness. As in form criticism, the question of setting is crucial, although it is posed differently: instead of determining the life setting of each speech, this commentary tries to identify its stage setting.

Some Recent Work on Isaiah as a Unity

Ackroyd, P. "Isaiah 36–39: Structure and Function." In *Von Canaan bis Kerala.* FS J. P. M. van der Ploeg, ed. W. C. Deisman et al. AOAT 211. Neukirchen-Vluyn: Neukirchener Verlag, 1982. 3–21. **Beuken, W. A. M.** "The Unity of the Book of Isaiah." In *Reading from Right to Left.* Ed. J. C. Exum and H. G. M. Williamson. 50–62. **Brueggemann, W.** "Unity and Dynamic in the Isaiah Tradition." *JSOT* 29 (1984) 89–107. **Carr, D. M.** "Reaching for Unity." *JSOT* 57 (1993) 61–80. **Childs, B. S.** *Introduction to the Old Testament as Scripture.* Philadelphia: Fortress, 1979. 325–38. **Clements, R. E.** "Beyond Tradition-History: Deutero-Isianic Development of First Isaiah's Themes." *JSOT* 31 (1985) 95–113. ———. "Light to the Nations: A Central Theme of the Book of Isaiah." In *Forming Prophetic Literature.* Ed. J. W. Watts and P. R. House. 57–69. ———. "The Unity of the Book of Isaiah." *Int* 36 (1982) 117–29. **Clifford, R. J.** "The Unity of the Book of Isaiah and Its Cosmogonic Language." *CBQ* 55 (1993) 1–17. **Conrad, E. W.** *Reading Isaiah.* OBT. Minneapolis: Fortress, 1991. **Darr, K. P.** *Isaiah's Vision and the Family of God.* Louisville: Westminster, 1994. **Evans, C. A.** "On the Unity and Parallel Structure of the Book of Isaiah." *VT* 38 (1988) 129–47. **Gileadi, A.** "A Holistic Structure of the Book of Isaiah." Diss., Brigham Young University, 1981. **O'Connell, R. H.** *Concentricity and Continuity: Literary Structure in Isaiah.* JSOT 188. Sheffield: Sheffield UP, 1994. **Rendtorff, R.** "Zur Komposition des Buches Jesaja." *VT* 34 (1984) 295–320. **Seitz, C. R.** *Zion's Final Destiny: The Development of the Book of Isaiah. A Reassessment of Isaiah 36–39.* Minneapolis: Fortress, 1991. **Steck, O. H.** *Friedensvorstellungen im alten Jerusalem: Psalmen—Jesaja—Deuterojesaja.* ThSt 111. Zurich: Theologisches Verlag, 1972. **Sweeney, M. A.** *Isaiah 1–4 and the Post Exilic Understanding of the Isaianic Tradition.* BZAW 171. Berlin: De Gruyter, 1988. ———. *Isaiah 1–39 with an Introduction to Prophetic Literature.* FOTL 16. Grand Rapids, MI: Eerdmans, 1996. **Vermeylen, J.** "L'unité du livre d'Isaïe." In *Book of Isaiah.* Ed. J. Vermeylen. 11–53. **Williamson, H. G. M.** *The Book Called Isaiah: Deutero-Isaiah's Role in Composition and Redaction.* Oxford: Clarendon, 1994. ———. "The Book of Isaiah in Light of Current Discussion." In *Synchronic or Diachronic? A Debate on Method in Old Testament Exegesis.* Ed. Moor, J. C. de. OTS 34. Leiden: Brill, 1995. ———. "The Concept of Israel in Transition." In *The World of Ancient Israel: Sociological, Political and Anthropological Perspectives.* Ed. R. E. Clements. Cambridge: Cambridge UP, 1989. 141–61. ———. *Variations on a Theme: King, Messiah and Servant in the Book of Isaiah.* Carlisle: Paternoster, 1998.

The book of Isaiah has had an honored and influential position in Hebrew and Christian Scripture for two millenia and more. Isaiah, the eighth-century B.C.E. prophet, was recognized as the implied earthly author, while belief in divine inspiration looked to God as the ultimate implied author. Many believers still read the book in this way and interpret the book to have meaning for their own time. Christian messianic hermeneutic is an example. Expositors like Alec Motyer still write commentaries (1993) in this mode.

Some medieval writers, notably Ibn Ezra (twelfth century), doubted Isaian authorship. But it was J. C. Döderlein (1779) who began the modern critical view that portions of the book were written later (see Vincent, *Studien,* 17–21; Young, 9–38). For the next century, however, the literary unity of Isaiah remained a strongly defended option. In 1870–71, K. F. Keil's introduction (*Manual of Historico-Critical Introduction to the Canonical Scriptures of the Old Testament,* trans. C. M. Douglas, 2d ed., 2 vols. [Edinburgh: T & T Clark, 1870–71] 286–87; cf. C. R. Seitz, *Isaiah 1–29,* 7) reflects a literary view prior to the acceptance of the division of the book of Isaiah on historical-critical lines. He deals with sections composed of chaps. 1–12, 13–27, and 28–66.

B. Duhm's 1892 commentary enunciated the pattern of "first" (chaps. 1–39), "second" (chaps. 40–55), and "third" (chaps. 56–66) Isaiah dated to the eighth, sixth, and fifth centuries, which historical-critical scholarship would reflect for the next century and more. When such stalwarts as Franz Delitzsch and S. R. Driver (*Isaiah: His Life and Times*) accepted these views, the trend was set. These critics, while thinking in terms of authors, recognized the role of later editors or redactors and the addition of later materials. Duhm's separation of the so-called Servant Poems (42:1–9; 49:1–6; 50:4–9; 52:13–53:12) is an example. Thus the recognition of many writers and editors addressing different historical situations has become a central assumption for critical studies of the book of Isaiah. In 1965 Otto Eissfeldt's massive introduction to the Old Testament (*The Old Testament: An Introduction. The History of the Formation of the Old Testament,* trans. P. R. Ackroyd, 3d ed. [New York: Harper and Row, 1965] 303–46) presented the "assured results of historical criticism" in dividing the book of Isaiah in three parts: chaps. 1–39 as preexilic prophecy (with the exception of chaps. 24–27, which are viewed as late second century B.C.E.), chaps. 40–55 as exilic prophecy, and chaps. 56–66 as postexilic work. These divisions still exert substantial influence, especially in the division of the book into two parts. Many commentaries divide the work and assign the two parts to different authors.

A thorough review of current work on Isaiah has been made by M. E. Tate ("The Book of Isaiah in Recent Research," in *Forming Prophetic Literature,* FS J. D. W. Watts, ed. J. W. Watts and P. R. House, JSOTSup 235 [Sheffield: Sheffield UP, 1996] 22–56). The revision of my commentary has tried to take into account some of his criticisms and suggestions. Tate considers modern writings on Isaiah under three interpretive categories: the one-prophet interpretation, the three-book interpretation, and the one book of Isaiah interpretation. My commentary fits the latter category.

In 1979 I began work on my commentary on Isaiah for the Word Biblical Commentary. I wanted to treat the book as a whole composition, being less concerned with origins and stages of development of the book than in determining its final design and purpose. I found very little supporting literature for that task and had largely to cut my own path.

I viewed the book as a literary drama and followed the lead of the superscription in seeing it divided according to the generations of the Hebrew kings, Uzziah, Ahaz, Hezekiah, and those who followed them, including the Persian kings of the sixth and fifth centuries B.C.E. I treated these collected speeches by several persons as drama and divided the book into acts and scenes as it might have been presented orally. I dated the book according to its latest identifiable background setting to the fifth century B.C.E. On these bases I projected a series of acts that moved through twelve generations of rulers from Uzziah through the earlier Persian kings.

I. Like a Booth in a Vineyard, 1:1–6:13 (Uzziah and Jotham, ca. 750–735 B.C.E.)
II. The Gently Flowing Waters, 7:1–14:32 (Ahaz, ca. 734–716 B.C.E.)
III. Opportunity and Disappointment, 15:1–22:25 (Hezekiah, ca. 715–701 B.C.E.)
IV. The Impact of Tyre's Fall, 23:1–27:13 (the vassal years of Hezekiah and Manasseh, ca. 700–640 B.C.E.)
V. Requiem for the Kingdom of Judah, 28:1–33:24 (Josiah, ca. 640–605 B.C.E.)
VI. From Curse to Blessing, 34:1–39:8 (Jehoiakim and Zedekiah, ca. 605–586 B.C.E.)
VII. Good News for Jerusalem, 40:1–44:23 (Jehoiachin, 586–540 B.C.E.)
VIII. Cyrus, the Lord's Anointed, 44:24–48:22 (Cyrus/Cambysus, 539–523 B.C.E.)
IX. The Servant of Rulers, 49:1–52:12 (Cambysus/Darius, 522–ca. 518 B.C.E.)
X. Restoration Pains in Jerusalem, 52:13–57:21 (Darius/Xerxes, 518–465 B.C.E.)
XI. Zion's Light Shines, 58:1–61:11 (Artaxerxes, 465–458 B.C.E.)
XII. For Zion's Sake: New Heavens and New Earth, 62:1–66:24 (Artaxerxes, 457–438 B.C.E.)

I now think that the idea of a chronological progression of reigns is not a sufficient key to the structure of the book as a whole. O'Connell is right: other than in the superscriptions and the narratives, "the architecture of Isaiah reflects little concern for temporal sequencing" (*Concentricity and Continuity,* 23). The overall structure will not allow that. There are two historical poles: the age of Isaiah son of Amoz, reflected in the narratives in chaps. 7, 20, and 36–39, and the clear references to Cyrus in chaps. 40–48. There are no other identifiable specific historical points of reference. The Assyrian and Babylonian invasions are a standard part of the work, of course. The attempts to rebuild the temple are there too. But the structure of the book is less historical than I had thought.

However, I have found no reason to change my view of the book as sixty-six chapters of dramatic speeches composing a literary whole. I still see it as a great drama in which YHWH is the principal character and speaker. I do find attractive the dating of later chapters in the time of Haggai/Zechariah instead of in the time of Ezra.

Parallel to my work, and beginning well before its publication, there began an interpretive movement that has produced significant rethinking of the structure of the book of Isaiah. Brownlee (*Meaning of the Qumran,* 247–49) took his lead from the gap between chap. 33 and chaps. 34 in 1QIsa^{a} to produce the following outline:

I. The Ruin and Restoration of Judah (chaps. 1–5)	I. Paradise Lost and Regained (chaps. 34–35)
II. Biography (chaps. 6–8)	II. Biography (chaps. 36–39)
III. Agents of Divine Blessing and Judgment (chaps. 9–12)	III. Agents of Deliverance and Judgment (chaps. 36–40)
IV. Anti-Foreign Oracles (chaps. 13–23)	IV. Anti-Babylonian Oracles (chaps. 46–48)
V. Universal Judgment and Deliverance of God's People (chaps. 24–27)	V. Universal Redemption through YHWH's Servant; Glorification of Israel (chaps 49–54 [55])
VI. Ethical Sermons, Indicating Israel and Judah (chaps. 28–31)	VI. Ethical Sermons; the Ethical Conditions for Israel's Redemption (chaps. 56–59)
VII. The Restoration of Judah and the Davidic Kingdom (chaps. 32–33)	VII. Paradise Regained: The Glories of the New Jerusalem and the New Heavens and the New Earth (chaps. 60–66)

Gileadi ("Holistic Structure") produced another "bi-fid model":

I. Ruin and Renascence	1–5	34–35
II. Biographical Material	6–8	36–39
III. Agents of Divine Deliverance and Judgment	9–12	41–46
IV. Oracles against Foreign Nations	13–23	47
V. Suffering and Salvation	24–27	48–54
VI. Sermons on Loyalty and Disloyalty	28–31	55–59
VII. Dispossession of the Wicked, Inheritance by the Righteous	32–33	60–66

O'Connell *(Concentricity and Continuity)* notes that such bifid schemes were endorsed by J. A. Callaway (*RevExp* 65 [1968]) 403–7), R. K. Harrison (*Introduc-*

tion to the Old Testament [Grand Rapids, MI: Eerdmans, 1969] 787–89), and C. A. Evans (*VT* 38 [1988] 129–47). I used this reasoning to justify dividing my commentary's two volumes between chap. 33 and chap. 34. There has been a great deal of research and writing in the intervening years about the overall structure of Isaiah, which I have followed carefully and from which I have learned much. As a result of that and my own studies, I am revising the basic structure and approach of the commentary.

Recent studies have shifted from questions of "authorship" to theories of creative redaction. The editors are seen as readers of earlier drafts who freely adapted and added to them in stages until the present book emerged. One may trace distinctive lines of research in England and in Germany with scholars from other countries making contributions. In England, D. R. Jones (*ZAW* 67 [1955] 226–46) and J. H. Eaton (*VT* 9 [1959] 138–57) taught that this process should be seen in terms of an "Isaiah school." Peter Ackroyd ("Isaiah 36–39: Structure and Function") and R. E. Clements (*Int* 36 [1982] 117–29) developed this idea to find a "unity" in the finished book. In Germany, J. Becker (*Isaias* [1968]) and H. Barth (*Die Jesaja-Worte in der Josiazeit* [1977]) developed the theory of multiple editions of the book from the eighth through the fifth centuries B.C.E. The second edition of Otto Kaiser's commentary on chaps. 1–12 (1983) incorporated these views. O. H. Steck and Jörg Jeremias, and their students B. Gosse and R. G. Kratz, have applied them, particularly in chaps. 40–55 and 56–66.

Thus a new understanding of the book of Isaiah as a redactional unity was developing. A conference on Isaiah in Leuven, Belgium, in 1988 brought together the leading writers on the subject (published as *The Book of Isaiah,* ed. J. Vermeylen [1989]). There the name of W. A. M. Beuken from Holland stands out as another major contributor to the research. In the United States, a Society of Biblical Literature seminar, The Formation of the Book of Isaiah, has provided a forum for the ongoing discussion since 1990. Melugin, Sweeney, Seitz, Rendtorff, Clements, and many others have contributed to the research and discussion.

Out of this there grew the understanding that no part of Isaiah can be understood without considering its relation to other parts and the whole. The first chapters and the last chapters must be read together. Each of the parts develops with interrelations to the other parts. The roles of authors and editors overlap, and there can be no clear distinction between them. While some still try to date each layer of redaction (Steck sees continuing redaction down into the second century B.C.E.), most find this unproductive. They generally see the focus of the book falling in the fifth century (as did Ibn Ezra in the Middle Ages).

Six recent monographs are particularly instructive for the attempt to deal with the book's structure.

M. A. Sweeney's *Isaiah 1–4* successfully presents the position that the opening chapters of the book of Isaiah along with the closing chapters (65 and 66) form an envelope around the entire book, thus separating them from any consideration of an eighth-century "first Isaiah."

E. W. Conrad's chapter that supports his literary treatment of Isaiah ("Choosing Reading Strategies," in *Reading Isaiah,* 3–33) presents the argument with documentation and supports the position I have taken. He continues with excellent treatments of the role of the royal narratives (34–51), "the Lord's military strategy" (52–82), and "Who Are the "We" in Isaiah?" (83–116).

C. R. Seitz's treatment of the central narratives in Isa 36–39 *(Zion's Final Destiny)* is important because it gives them their due as a part of the book of Isaiah instead of simply seeing them as an intrusion into the text. His commentary *(Isaiah 1–39)* continues this approach and divides chaps. 1–39 into three units: chaps. 1–12, 13–27, and 28–39.

K. P. Darr *(Isaiah's Vision)* analyzes a number of the book's features that show feminine characteristics. But in the process, she establishes a refinement of Sweeney's position: she shows that chap. 1 stands alone in presenting the issue of "rebellious children" to be matched by the concluding chap. 65. Her treatment of the role of cities, called "daughters," in Isaiah shows their importance to its structure.

H. G. M. Williamson *(Book Called Isaiah)* gives an excellent review of recent research in Isaiah and continues the trend toward redaction-critical study.

Robert H. O'Connell *(Concentricity and Continuity)* makes a comprehensive and detailed study of the inner structures of the entire book. He finds a substantial use of concentric structures and finds a macrostructure of seven blocks:

1:1–2:5	A Cameo of a Covenant Disputation
2:6:–22	Threat of Judgment on Idolaters
3:1–4:1	Threat of Judgment on the Unjust
4:2–12:6	The Syro-Ephraimite-Assyrian Scheme for Zion's Judgment and Restoration
13:1–39:8	The Assyrian-Babylonian Scheme for Zion's Judgment and Restoration
40:1–54:17	YHWH's Exoneraton
55:1–66:24	Final Ultimatum

O'Connell looks at Isaiah as rhetoric, intended to persuade. He is particularly interested in repetitions of words or themes that indicate concentric structures and frames. Many excellent insights have been gained from the study. In the process, however, he has not given enough attention to literary signals of structure, particularly superscriptions, headings like "burden" and "woe," and groups of smaller units like those beginning "in that day." These also make decisive contributions to the structure of the book and its parts. A recognition of the particular role of third-person narrative is needed, and also of the convention of using first-person passages. O'Connell's work has been immensely useful to me as I try to fill in these gaps in research and correct his outline accordingly. His analyses of chaps. 4–12, 40–54, and 55–66 are particularly convincing. That of chaps. 13–39 is less so, in my view. However, I agree with O'Connell's summary: "The Book of Isaiah comprises an architectural scheme whereby corresponding blocks of prophetic material have been . . . arranged, with transitional materials . . . into a continuous development of the themes and elements that make up the book's rhetoric" (*Concentricity and Continuity,* 20).

These works show some common tendencies that require attention. One of these is the tendency to view the literature in blocks based on literary structures. A second is openness to recognizing themes that run through the entire book (Darr, Williamson, and others). A third is the recognition of certain literary conventions and their use in structuring the book. These include the use of narrative sections (Conrad and Seitz), the use of "heavenly courtroom scenes" (Conrad), the view of YHWH as warrior, and the use of first-person narrative accounts. The studies undertaken in this commentary will deal with several of these topics, including (1) the definition of literary "blocks" and "books" ("acts") in the Vision, (2) the use of themes (distinctive words) that run through the Vision, and (3) the literary conventions that give this work its flavor and power.

This commentary treats the book (all sixty-six chapters) as a single literary whole. The book is presented as a kind of drama, divided into acts and scenes relating to Israel's life from the mid-eighth century to the mid-fifth century B.C.E.

It dates the final chapters to near 520 B.C.E. Instead of dividing the latter half into two collections (chaps. 40–55 and 56–66), it finds three acts (34:1–49:4; 49:5–54:17*b*; 54:17*c*–61:11) and an epilogue (chaps. 62–66). It views the entire book of Isaiah, including chaps. 1–33, as a single composition intended to depict YHWH's relationship to Israel from the reign of Uzziah in Judah to that of Darius of Persia. Many themes in the final chapters hark back to parallels in the first chapters.

This view accounts for the similarities throughout the book on the basis of a single composition and purpose. It explains the differences in terms of the complex historical changes depicted from one generation to the next, and it accounts for the major change between chaps. 1–33 and 34–66 in terms of a new age in which God offers blessings to his chosen who seek him, replacing those who had fallen under judgment and curse.

Chaps. 34–66 contain several signs that mark the breaks. Chaps. 36–39 are an insertion from 2 Kings. Their narrative prose style sets them off from material on both sides. They stand with chaps. 34–35 and 40:1–11 to form the transition to the last three parts of the Vision of Isaiah.

Isa 40:12 begins a distinctive style of lengthy YHWH speeches that continues to the end of chap. 66. Three times within these chapters a strange theme breaks the flow. Twice it appears in identical words: "There is no peace, says YHWH, for the adversaries" (48:22; 57:21; 66:24).

Changes in the addresses of YHWH's speeches mark the internal structure of these chapters. Isa 40:12–49:4 speaks to Israel (in Babylon) and the nations. Isa 49:5–54:17*b* speaks to Jerusalem. Isa 54:17*c*–59:21 addresses a mixed group called "the servants of Yahweh." Chaps. 62–66 form the epilogue that draws together the themes of the entire Vision. Internal consistency and relevance to the historical setting support this division (see the historical introduction to each act).

The first three acts of the Vision (chaps. 5–33) are dominated by the curse (see chap. 6). The last three (chaps. 40–61) stand under the gracious promise of comfort and blessing (40:1–9). The first three acts (chaps. 5–33) are set against the background of Assyria's rise and rule and Babylon's accession to power. The fourth (chaps. 34–49:4) is set in the last years of Babylon's rule, already under the influence of Cyrus's approach. The fifth and sixth acts are set against a Persian background to which the books of Ezra-Nehemiah provide a welcome aid to understanding.

In a remarkable way, chaps. 62–66 echo themes of chaps. 1–4 to tie the entire Vision into one whole. The promise in 2:1–4 of Zion being raised to the top of the mountains with peoples streaming to it is fulfilled in 66:1–24 as restored Zion becomes the centerpiece of YHWH's new heavens and new earth. On the basis of all these features, I outline the Vision of Isaiah as follows (see the commentary for supporting details):

Prologue	1:1–4:6
Act 1	5:1–12:6
Act 2	13:1–27:13
Act 3	28:1–33:24
Act 4	34:1–49:4
Act 5	49:5–54:17*b*
Act 6	54:17*c*–61:11
Epilogue	62:1–66:24

THE MESSIANIC INTERPRETATION OF ISAIAH

Alec Motyers' 1993 commentary on Isaiah revives a classic Christian interpretation of the book of Isaiah. He adopts a messianic approach to the book, finding in it support for the Christology of the Gospels and the rest of the NT. In doing this he mixes what in modern interpretation is usually kept separate: an interpretation of the text and a hermeneutic with a clearly defined goal and its own set of defining rules.

That this hermeneutic is employed in the NT most effectively is without doubt. Writers there chose selected verses and passages from the OT to make sense out of the experience of the life of Jesus and the emergence of the Christian church. The evidence that they used selected texts from Isaiah to shape their and our view of Jesus and his role is unquestioned. The NT reading of the book of Isaiah is clearly messianic.

But the NT writers made no attempt to read passages from Isaiah in context. Nor did they insist that their reading was the original understanding of the book. And there is no evidence that anyone understood the book or those passages in that way before Jesus came to form the model.

Messianism was a movement and a way of thinking that developed within the last two centuries B.C.E. It focused on a person who would come to be the savior of the Jews. It found many different models and was applied to many potential persons before the Christian model found a lasting acceptance and belief. The Dead Sea Scrolls have brought renewed evidence of the expectation of a messiah in that time. But similar evidence that people expected a supernatural messiah in any of those models during the centuries before that are missing.

Motyer identifies "the main Messianic passages" (13 n. 1) and groups them as (1) 7:10–15; 9:1–7 (Heb. 8:23–9:6); 11:1–16; 14:28–32; 24:21–23; 32:1–8; 33:17–24 (on the king); (2) 42:1–4; 49:1–6; 50:4–9; 52:13–53:12 (on the Servant); and (3) 59:21; 61:1–3; 61:10–62:7; 63:1–7 (on the anointed conqueror). He then organizes his interpretation of the book under those three themes. The choice of the passages is traditonal. The grouping and interpretation of the groups are original to Motyer.

But Motyer does not simply use these groupings to interpret the chosen passages. He uses them to interpret the sections of the book in which they appear. One has to ask whether the context of these passages bears out this interpretation as that which the book intended and in which the book was originally read.

Motyer's scheme turns on a few basic concepts. Word studies on those concepts for the whole book may be instructive in evaluating his method.

First, the word *Messiah* or *messianic* (משיח) occurs in Isaiah only as "his messiah" (45:1), who is clearly identified as Cyrus. The root verb משח, "to anoint," occurs only in 21:5, where swords are anointed, and in 61:1, where the speaker claims to be "anointed" to "preach good news to the poor." This is far from the picture of a conqueror that Motyer's category "anointed conqueror" requires. Isa 61:1 is the passage that Jesus chose to read about himself in the synagogue (Luke 4:17–21); in it he found a prototype for his own preaching and teaching message—hardly that of the conqueror. Isaiah is not "messianic" in using the words for "anointing" or the idea as a controlling metaphor.

The second word is מלך, "king." In the verb for "reign" it occurs five times: 7:6; 24:23 (YHWH reigns); 32:1; 37:38; and 52:7 (God reigns!). In two of these the reference is to God's reign. The noun occurs eighty times, usually describing a king of Israel or Judah or a foreign king. These show that the book of Isaiah was written in and was intended to be read in a time when kings, their status, and their actions were basic to life. The uses with kings other than those of Judah and Israel are by far the most numerous. There is the intermittent reminder that ultimately YHWH is king over all.

Judah's kings are dealt with. They are rescued in chap. 7 and chaps. 36–37. They are shown to be mortal in chap. 38. And the end of the Davidic dynasty in Babylonian exile is predicted in chap. 39. Only one passage using the word מלך, "king," is clearly ideal, futuristic, and "eschatological." That is 32:1–8.

Other passages with a "royal" flavor must also be noted, although they do not use the term. Isa 7:14–17 predicts a remarkable birth, probably royal; the child's growth will mark the time until relief from the pressures of Aram and Israel is experienced. In Isa 9:1–7 a future time of victory and prosperity is marked first by military victory (9:1–5) and then by the birth of a marvelous child who will reign on David's throne and over his kingdom. Isa 11:1–5 refers to Jesse and a branch, clearly implying a royal Davidic heir, spiritually endowed to be a succesful ruler. Isa 11:10 portrays this "root of Jesse" as an international military leader. Chaps. 7–11 do portray the answer to Judah's and Israel's problems as lying in the continuation and strengthening of the Davidic monarchy. To that end the Davidic dynasty is idealized and given its strongest theological base in Scripture.

These passages fit a Christian messianic model. They would have supported the idea of the rise of a Davidic king in any following period. The writer of this section is well aware that the dominant power of the late eighth century is Assyria. The very fact that Judah and Jerusalem could survive at all was a mighty sign of YHWH's favor and power. However, chap. 39 stands as a counterprophecy in the book of Isaiah, warning against seeing long-term salvation in the house of David. They would end up as "eunuchs" in the court of the king of Babylon. Israel's salvation for the readers of Isaiah's vision does not lie in revival of Davidic kingship. The rest of the book of Isaiah ignores the potential of having a Davidide rise to save Judah or the exiles from Babylon or Persia.

Isa 32:1–8 envisions a day in which "a king" and "rulers" will bring order to the land and reverse the subversive work entrusted to the prophet in 6:10–12. But the king is not identified, nor is his "house" identified. Isa 33:17–24 has a parallel picture in which a king will play a role. He too is unidentified. But 33:22 notes that YHWH is the savior and the real "king."

A third word to be investigated is עבד, "servant." The word occurs forty times in Isaiah. Our particular interest is its use as "YHWH's servant" and its singular and plural uses. (See *Strand: Servant/Servants.*)

Strand: Servant/Servants

SERVANT	YHWH'S SERVANT	YHWH'S SERVANTS
14:2 ("menservants")	20:3 (Isaiah)	54:17
House of Israel	22:20 (Eliakim)	56:6
24:2	37:35 (David)	63:17
36:9, 11	41:8 (Israel)	65:8, 9, 13 (2x), 14, 15
37:5, 24	42:1–7	66:14
	42:19 (2x)	
	43:10	
	44:1, 2, 21, 26 (Jacob)	
	45:4 (Israel)	
	48:20 (Jacob)	
	49:3 (Israel)	
49:7	49:5, 6	
	50:10	
	52:13; 53:11	

The idea of YHWH's servant is much broader in the book of Isaiah than the so-called "servant poems" and also than Deutero-Isaiah. And there is a deliberate progression from speaking of these servants one at a time in the singular to speaking only of "servants" as a group. There is an earlier progression from kings, prophets, and government officials as YHWH's servants, to the people of Israel as his servant, to the worshiping congregation as his servants.

Before Isaiah deals with royal figures and kings, the plot of the Vision is spelled out in chaps. 1–5. The protagonists are YHWH and his people. They appear in various metaphorical terms: father and children, king and people, temple patron and worshipers, Lord and servants. The issue for the book is defined in chap 1: YHWH's rebellious children.

The middle sections of the book turn aside to other issues. Chap. 6 tells the reader that the author is aware of this diversion from the issue of helping Israel and Jerusalem to repent and change. But the prophet brings the excuse that YHWH himself had placed a prohibition on him that should last until the destruction of the land was complete.

Motyer's theme of the king corresponds well with the unit of chaps. 7–12. His treatment of the Anointed Conquerer is strained for chaps. 59–63 but covers the material dealing with Divine Warrior and the Day of YHWH in 2:10–22 and chaps. 13–27 (or even through chaps. 34–35). His treatment of the Servant covers the range of chaps. 40–55. The so-called "messianic passages" are scattered through the book. They do not form a consistent whole anywhere here.

NEWER COMMENTARIES

A number of other important commentaries have appeared within the last decade. They represent a variety of approaches and methods. This commentary shares many things with them, but differs from all of them in one way or another. Full references may be found above.

John N. Oswalt has written the current standard conservative commentary. It treats the book as written by Isaiah in the eighth century B.C.E. but recognizes some redactional additions. It reviews current research and presents conservative reactions. Like Oswalt, I hold a high view of Scripture. Unlike Oswalt, I do not think that the book requires the reader to consider Isaiah son of Amoz to be its author. Like Oswalt, I think the writers of the entire book developed the text we have to communicate their message. Unlike Oswalt, I think their work was directed to their own generation and should be interpreted in that way. Its application to later generations should be treated as just that, the reinterpretation of an ancient text for a later time.

Brevard S. Childs reads Isaiah as a modern Christian, who thinks of it as a part of his Bible. This commentary does for the book of Isaiah what Childs's earlier commentary on Exodus had done. He is very attentive to the theological significance of the book. I have also recognized the need for canonical location in two ways: on the one hand I look for the ways that this prophetic work is related to Torah and on the other I have presented in excursuses the ways that distinctive passages like Isa 7:14 and chap. 53 have functioned in the New Testament and in Christian preaching.

Joseph Blenkinsopp has written a commentary, with a new translation and a new introduction on the whole of Isaiah. He uses the standard source-critical method and views Isaiah as three separate books. His is a competent and excellent commentary, but he differs from me in not viewing Isaiah as "artistic literature." I find Isaiah to be an exquisite and carefully crafted dramatic poem. He has examined the literary units with less attention to their overall message. He spends less time on the supposed authors of the units than earlier literary critic have done but still dates "the basic substratum" of chaps. 1–39 to the eighth century B.C.E. and chaps. 40–55 to a time shortly after the exile; he thinks work continued on chaps. 56–66 as late as the third century.

Klaus Baltzer thinks of Isa 40–55 as a liturgical drama to be performed in the temple court. He finds the Psalter's comparable themes particularly helpful in defining this location for Isa 40–66. His introduction provides a survey of liturgical drama in the ancient Near East (pp. 7–14) and of the theological contribution of the book (pp. 33–44.) He provides an original translation and commentary, including detailed notes and bibliography. I have much in common with Baltzer in his approach to the book as drama, but I have tried to deal with the entire book, all sixty-six chapters, as a drama in six acts, and have seen the work as a mirror of contemporary history to a far greater extent than he has.

Marvin A. Sweeney has provided a thorough treatment of First Isaiah with particular attention to form-critical considerations. He considers this work complete by the time of Ezra-Nehemiah.

The commentary by *J. L. Koole* provides the most complete survey of work on Isaiah that exists. He is concerned with the historical background but still deals with the work as divided between three eras for its composition. I have treated the work as a literary composition put together at one time (late sixth or early fifth centuries B.C.E.). I understand that the composition itself wants the reading audience to see the different parts of the drama against the background of historical events of the eighth to the late sixth centuries B.C.E, so I have presented *Excursuses* with historical background treatments throughout the commentary.

Childs (xii) speaks approvingly of *W. A. M. Beuken* as having "opened the way to a new era in interpreting the book of Isaiah." Beuken is more aware of the literary studies of the Dutch school than are any of the other commentaries, and he works for a balance between the older critical methods and the newer forms. My approach to the literature and its relation to history is probably closer to Beuken's than to any other. We both try to picture each part of the book as it would have been understood by its first readers in the fifth century B.C.E. as well as in the way the work wants them to picture their immediate past (eighth to sixth centuries B.C.E.). We both look for literary integrity and purpose.

Isaiah Is a Literary Drama

Isaiah is found in the collection of books in the canon called "the Prophets." It was written by a prophet. It is about God and his prophet. D. E. Gowen (*Theology of the Prophetic Books: The Death and Resurrection of Israel* [Louisville: Westminster John Knox, 1998]) has correctly seen that the unifying theme in the collection of books called the Latter Prophets deals with the interpretation of three moments in history: 722 B.C.E., when Samaria fell to Assyrian armies; 587 B.C.E., when Jerusalem capitulated to Babylonian forces; and 539 B.C.E., when Babylon succumbed to Persian armies, opening a new era for the ancient Near East and for Israel. Isaiah's work turns on the first and third of these events.

Isaiah deals with changes brought about through these events. The nations of Israel and Judah are replaced by the Jews, the people of YHWH. There is continuity, for many characteristic features of preexilic Israel and Jerusalem remain. The later application of rules of Torah to the administration of the temple guarantee that. But other things do not continue. The kingdoms become provinces. No king is in the new scene. Jerusalem is no longer a national capital but is a temple city. Jews are a people scattered through the countries of the Middle East and beyond.

What is the specific kind, or genre, of literature before us? The prophetic books of the OT are a literary form *sui generis.* There is nothing else in literature exactly like them, although many of the smaller forms of prophetic speech are kin to those in other cultures. Among the prophetic books, Isaiah and the Book of the Twelve (Minor) Prophets are different from Jeremiah and Ezekiel, but a thorough analysis of these literary differences remains to be done.

Isaiah's title calls the book a חזון, "vision," a term that also occurs in the superscriptions of Obadiah and Nahum. The verb חזה, "to envision," also occurs in Isaiah's title, but it is used with other genre designations in 2:1 and other books. חזה thus appears to be a unifying term related to the prophetic literature of Isaiah and the Twelve, which used the terms חזון, "vision," דבר, "word(s)," and משא, "burden," for these prophetic genres. All three of the terms appear in superscriptions in Isaiah. חזון must be defined by what is actually found in the literature to which it is attached. As the superscription applies to the book of Isaiah, the content and character of the book will define "vision" as a genre.

In vision literature, the person of the prophet falls into the background. YHWH becomes the dominant speaker, and the dominant subform is that of the YHWH speech. His speeches are supported and amplified by others, but the speakers are seldom identified. They are understood to be YHWH's aides, whether these are taken as members of his heavenly court or as prophets.

The Vision, because it consists of successive speeches by different persons (specifically some by YHWH and some by someone else), is more dramatic and less realistic in setting than other books. While Jeremiah usually places the prophet in a historical setting for his speech, Isaiah seldom does. The Vision is much more suited to the artificial setting of a stage. Is it conceivable that such a work was actually presented by a group of speakers, representing the characters in the drama? Before one dismisses this prospect too quickly, one should be reminded that Greek drama was reaching its height at about the time this was written.

Excursus: Drama in Israel and Early Judaism?

The student of the Hebrew Scriptures who questions the existence of drama in Israel and early Judaism receives confusing and contradictory signals from the handbooks.

There comes an almost unanimous "no!" from dictionaries and encyclopedias, which usually indicate that the earliest Hebrew drama comes from Moses Zacuto of Amsterdam in 1715 C.E. However, one article quotes Eusebius in saying that the earliest known play on a biblical theme by a Jew was on "The Exodus," by Ezekielos, an Alexandrian (so presumably performed in Greek), in the second century B.C.E.

The Encyclopedia of Jewish Knowledge (ed. Jacob de Haas [New York: Behrman, 1946] 126) quotes Josephus to the effect that Jews were opposed to dramatic representations and to all the artistic culture of the Greeks and the Romans. *The Encyclopedia Judaica* (6:193) quotes several explanations: A. J. Paperna (1868) notes "the inherent contradiction between the monotheistic spirit of the Jewish religion and the dualism implicit in drama."

I. Zinburg and others have stressed the objection of the sages to the ritualistic and "heretical aspects" of drama. The latter phrase apparently refers to Christian mystery plays of the Middle Ages. J. H. Shirman (*Gilyonoth* 22 [1948] 217–67) writes: "Jewish tradition undoubtedly inhibited the development of the drama since the art of the theater was incompatible with the traditional way of life."

Bible dictionaries generally have no entry under "drama." Yet an entire genre of critical writing assumes that virtually all ancient cults (including Israel's) consisted of dramatic representations in some form of the basic story (or myth) on which the religion was based. The works of Mowinckel (*Psalmenstudien,* 6 vols. [Kristiania: Dybwad, 1921–24]; *Religion and Cult,* trans. J. Sheehan [Milwaukee: Marquette UP, 1981]; *The Psalms in Israel's Worship,* trans. D. R. Ap-Thomas, 2 vols. [Nashville: Abingdon, 1962]; and many others), of H. J. Kraus (*Worship in Israel,* trans. G. Buswell [Richmond: John Knox, 1966]; *Die Psalmen,* 2 vols. BKAT 15 [Neukirchen-Vluyn: Neukirchener Verlag, 1958–60]), of the British Myth and Ritual School (cf. S. H. Hooke, ed., *Myth, Ritual and Kingship* [Oxford: Clarendon, 1958]), and of the Scandinavian schools regularly assume the pervasive influence of cult drama in shaping the literature of the OT. Recently, J. R. Wood (*Amos in Song and Book Culture,* JSOT 337 [Sheffield: Sheffield Academic Press, 2002] 214) again described Hebrew prophecy as performed art and Hosea as the first prophet to use religious drama for his presentation.

In addition, there have been those who found that some parts of the OT were best understood as drama. H. H. Rowley, in his typically thorough fashion, has documented the view that the Song of Songs is drama ("The Interpretation of the Song of Songs," in *The Servant of the Lord,* 2d ed. [Oxford: Blackwell, 1965] 212–14, 223–42). See Duane Garrett, *Song of Songs,* WBC 23B (Nashville: Nelson, 2004) 76–80, for a survey of interpretations of Song of Songs as drama.

The *Encyclopedia Britannica* (15th ed., 10:199) summarizes the ambiguous situation: "Although there is biblical evidence in the Song of Songs and the Book of Job of Hebraic awareness of drama, Jewish religious traditions prohibited theatricals except for song, dance, and processionals."

These articles help to account for the lack of (or opposition to) drama and theater in Judaism from the Hellenistic period through the Middle Ages. The seat of this opposition lay in the orthodox determination to maintain its distinctive way of life, which was felt to be in peril through contact with the non-Jewish world. In medieval Europe this included Christian culture as well as pagan (or secular) populations. In the Greco-Roman world it included the spectacles of the games, the gladiatorial contests, as well as the drama contests at religious festivals. But there is nothing here to account for the lack of drama in internal Jewish festivals. There is nothing in the Torah to prohibit drama. The Mishnah also contains no such prohibition, only the restriction against contact with foreigners. Proscription of participation in foreign (i.e., Greek) drama is understandable. Even an attitude that restricts imitation of foreign forms may be fitting. But there is nothing here to prohibit specifically Hebrew forms of drama. Thus, let the record show that the evidence against drama in Judaism applies (however appropriately) to later Judaism and is not necessarily applicable to OT times.

Baltzer, in the introduction of his commentary on Isa 40–55, presents an extended survey of liturgical drama in ancient Mesopotamia and Egypt (*Deutero-Isaiah,* 7–13) and concludes that Isaiah "was initially a 'festival scroll' for the master of ceremony" at one of Israel's festivals (*Deutero-Isaiah,* 14). He gives a careful analysis of the various scenes in the work showing their dramatic potential.

While there is no evidence of theater in ancient Israel, there is ample evidence of public dramatic activity in the temple court, the home, and village streets. Jeremiah had a collection of his prophecies read in the temple court by his scribe, Baruch (Jer 36). Josiah held a great public reading of the book of the covenant found in the temple (2 Kgs 23). Both of these qualify as public monologues. Ezra and Nehemiah had the Torah read publicly before the great assembly of the people (Neh 8:1–17; 13:1). Jews celebrate the Festival of Booths by building booths and acting out the experience of living in temporary shelters through the time of the Exodus. They celebrate Passover by acting out around the family table the experience of the last of the plagues in Egypt. The book of Esther tells how the Festival of Purim came to be celebrated by Jews as the victory over Haman the Agagite and how the celebration in the villages led to the giving of presents on that day of joy. Purim has also been a time to dramatize the story of Esther. Job and Isaiah are much more elaborate scripts than these. Unlike Deuteronomy and Jeremiah, which are scripted for one speaker, Job and Isaiah assume multiple voices.

Anyone who questions the viability of these works for presentation on a modern stage should be made aware of the presentation of Job at a large outdoor festival in Kentucky that has had well-attended seasons for several decades.

Excursus: Literary Drama in the Old Testament?

Drama has two faces. One is that of literature: literary drama. The other is acted theater. Although these may be separated (there is theater, even good theater, that is not literature; there is dramatic literature that is never acted), the usual practice combines the two forms, whether this be Sophocles or Shakespeare or Arthur Miller. Literary dramatic form usually presumes a developed arena where it is presented to a live audience.

Several pieces of OT literature have been considered possible dramatic literature. These include the Song of Songs, Job, and Jonah. Other smaller units have been thought to demonstrate a true dramatic character; for example, one might speak of the speeches of Deuteronomy as monologues.

J. Hempel (*Die Althebräische Literatur und ihr Hellenistisch-Jüdisches Nachleben* [Potsdam: Athenaion, 1930]) uses words like *drama* and *dramatic* to describe Canaanite ritual (28), which was not unknown in Israel; the royal songs of Jerusalem (35); prophetic speeches (61); portions of historical narrative (121); and Deutero-Isaiah (171), and notes the resistance to continual reinterpretation into drama of Hellenistic style (183). Yet he never gives a description of Israel's dramatic tradition. Explicit evidence for such is lacking. But what would such a history show, if we should construct one from the materials that we do have in comparison with what was happening in neighboring peoples?

Drama in most cultures begins with cultic observances. Israel was no different. The earliest forms were shaped by the pilgrimage sacrifices referred to in Israel's request to Pharaoh (Exod 7:16) or Melchizedek's communion meal with Abraham (Gen 14:18–21). In Canaan, much more complex forms developed in the three annual festivals that were adaptations of Canaanite festivals. The most clearly dramatic form was that of Passover (Exod 12), but highly developed royal festivals also grew in Jerusalem (1 Kgs 8; Psalms). Each of these had dramatic elements with explanations or narrative to match. Cultic drama was bound to the specific purposes of the cult. It taught, inculcated, and purportedly brought to pass the conditions that the cult fostered. It supported the institutions and the society that the cult was designed to nourish.

Sporadic dramatic acts can also be an effective way to emphasize an oral message. Israel's prophets frequently engaged in such behavior to illustrate their messages more vividly. See, for example, Elijah's contest with the prophet's of Baal (1 Kgs 18), Jeremiah's ox-yoke (Jer 27–28), Ezekiel's "paralysis" (Ezek 4), and Isaiah's nakedness (Isa 20). For a comparative analysis of such prophetic dramatic acts, see David Stacy, *Prophetic Drama in the Old Testament* (London: Epworth, 1990).

The exile brought sharp changes—a secularizing influence and a vacuum where temple and priesthood had been. The ancient traditions could be studied at arm's length, critically, and with an eye toward a different future. Religion was no longer under the patronage of Israel's king. Persian patronage was suspect.

Not bound to either cult or king, literature (including drama) could look critically at life and history and could ask questions beyond those allowed in the cult. Prophecy, having already established a vehicle of protest and of change, now moved beyond the individual figure to literary (and dramatic) forums. The Deuteronomic History, Jeremiah, and Ezekiel belong here. Wisdom (the schools) also moved in to fill the vacuum in the center of the people's consciousness, as did village festival lore (the Festal Scrolls).

This era also produced a second wave of prophetic drama and literature to help gain perspective on the exile. This included Isaiah and the Book of the Twelve (Minor) Prophets. It brought wisdom to the fore in Proverbs and Job, which probed the meaning of guilt and spoke of the way ahead.

A third wave belonged to Ezra and was dominated by the Pentateuch. Moses was invoked. The Torah was applied to the life of Jerusalem, the temple, and the Diaspora through the synagogue. All else was pushed into a second and subordinate position.

A fourth wave sought to reverse the trend, presenting the royal story in Chronicles and leading the people in singing the songs of Zion (the Psalms). It stormed the centers of Judaism but was pushed into a third position in authority (after the Prophets). It succeeded in drawing the literature of village festivals (the scrolls) into its orbit, but it did not shake the trend. Ezra-Nehemiah recounts the new establishment. The Torah is secure, and the tradition of Jewish life that Ezra instituted would remain its flagship.

So, was there drama in ancient Israel? *Yes,* in the cult drama of the confederacy and the royal cult drama of Jerusalem, and in the village festivals throughout its history. *Probably,* in the literature, whose most natural understanding is to be found in the production of oral, multivoiced theater, in which one or more actors, a narrator, and a chorus spoke its measured lines, challenged old ideas, and suggested new ones in Jerusalem under the Persians.

Several scholars have recently expounded the dramatic nature of parts of the Book of the Twelve, which is so similar in literary style to Isaiah. P. R. House (*Zephaniah: A Prophetic Drama,* JSOTSup 69 [Sheffield: Sheffield Academic Press, 1989]; idem, "Dramatic Coherence in Nahum, Habakkuk, and Zephaniah," in *Forming Prophetic Literature,* ed. J. W. Watts and P. R. House, 195–208) has described the dramatic form and function not just of some of the books but also of their interconnections. H. Utzschneider (*Michas Reise in die Zeit: Studien zum Drama als Genre der prophetischen Literatur des Alten Testaments,* SBS 180 [Stuttgart: Katholisches Bibelwerk, 1999]) shows that Micah is "dramatic poetry" and arranges the text of Mic 1:1–4:7 as a dramatic text, pointing out the interaction of multiple voices in these chapters. J. R. Wood ("Speech and Action in Micah's Prophecy," *CBQ* 62 [2000] 645–62) argues that the whole book of Micah is a literary drama intended for perfomance before a live audience. Within a more restricted scope, W. Doan and T. Giles ("Prophecy and Theater," *Journal of Religion and Society* 2 [2000], online: http://moses.creighton.edu/JRS/2000/2000-2.html) apply drama theory to the analysis of the vision reports in Amos.

Since the publication of the first edition of this commentary, other signs of recognition of drama in the OT and specifically in Isa 40–55 have appeared. Baltzer has understood Isa 40–55 in terms of liturgical dramatic poetry. He follows the suggestion of J. H. Eaton (*Festal Drama in Deutero-Isaiah* [London: SPCK, 1979]) and H. Ringgren ("Zur Komposition von Jesaja 49–55," in *Beiträge zur alttestamentlichen Theologie,* ed. H. von Donner [Göttingen: Vandenhoeck & Ruprecht, 1977] 370–76) that we should look to the liturgical use of Scripture in the temple for an understanding of its use. Hendrik Leene (*De vroegere en de nieuwe dingen bij Deuterojesaja* [Amsterdam: Vrije UP, 1987]) thought of Deutero-Isaiah as drama. For a summary in English, see S. J. De Vries, *From Old Revelation to New: A Tradition-Historical and Redaction-Critical Study of Temporal Tansitions in Prophetic Prediction* (Grand Rapids, MI: Eerdmans, 1995) 127–28. John G. F. Wilks ("The Prophet as Incompetent Dramatist," *VT* 53 [2003] 530–43) examines all of our contributions and does not agree, thinking that either this is not drama at all or the prophet is an incompetent dramatist. He works with an overly strict idea of what constitutes "drama" without recognizing the elements I have traced above.

In Athens, Socrates accused the theater of having destroyed his credibility, but a reforming and moralistic city put the philosopher to death instead of judging the theater. In Jerusalem, at close to the same time, Ezra was incensed at the profligacy of the city and ordered reforms that sealed the people off from surrounding cultures and effectively suppressed the thriving literary (and dramatic) movement. Some of the best of its products have survived, shorn of almost all signs of their dramatic presentation. In stodgy literary clothes they have lost some of their power and brilliance and have often been subjected to misinterpretation or to prooftext quotations that ignored their contextual intent. Nonetheless, their influence has been enormous.

This commentary understands the Vision to be a sort of drama in which YHWH and his aides (Heavens and Earth, 1:2) are the principal characters. The superscription names Judah and Jerusalem as the main subjects of the Vision, but this must be revised in light of the actual contents of the book to include Israel and all of humankind.

The basic characteristics of drama have remained remarkably similar throughout history. Drama theory has been discussed ever since Aristotle wrote his *Poetics* (fourth century B.C.E.). Horace (*The Art of Poetry,* ca. 24 B.C.E.), Sir Philip Sidney (*Apologie for Poetry,* 1595), Lope de Vega (*The New Art of Writing Plays,* 1609), and Ben Jonson (*Timber,* 1640) are only a few of those who preceded modern critics like Kenneth Burke with his dramatic theory of literature (cf. W. H. Rueckert, *Kenneth Burke and the Drama of Human Relations,* 2d ed. [Berkeley: Univ. of California Press, 1982]). Some of the following points have been drawn from articles in the *Encyclopedia Britannica,* 15th ed. (3:655–56; 5:980–85; 10:1091; 18:213–20, 588).

Drama mirrors life *(mimesis),* touching on themes familiar to the audience. The Vision of Isaiah does this by tracing familiar eras in Israel's history and presenting familiar personalities: Ahaz, Isaiah, and Hezekiah. The nearness of the subject to its audience, even across the time-distance of centuries, is emphasized by keeping essential issues to the fore, like the fate of Jerusalem and the identity of the true Israel. The audience may sympathize or be in awe, but it is unlikely to laugh. The Vision reveals a thread of alienation and another of empathy to God's purpose, with which the audience is invited to identify.

Drama uses scenes, relating characters in a limited time frame, and uses a chorus to interpret its meaning. Confrontation is a major device. Greek drama used all these, and it typically had all its action occur within one day. In comparison, the Vision of Isaiah has a large time frame from the mid-eighth century to the mid-fifth century B.C.E., which is broken down into a sequence of acts reflecting steps along that route. Some characters sustain the unity of the entire drama: YHWH, his aides, Israel, Jerusalem. Human individuals are, of course, limited to one or two of the acts or scenes. The Vision portrays a continuing confrontation between YHWH and his people. The relationship is tense in 1:2, and it is still strained in 66:24.

Drama uses style to signal the mode or spirit of the scene, the degree of fantasy or reality, and the liturgy or illusion that are to be portrayed. The Vision does this systematically. There are straightforward historical recitals in 7:1–14, 20:1–6, and 36:1–39:8. There is the continual portrayal of God as chief spokesman and actor. History is also portrayed in poetry, and utopian scenes are presented at intervals.

Drama, especially Greek drama, used a chorus to communicate the author's intention. It was a commentary on the action "to guide the moral and religious thought and emotion of the audience through the play." For Aeschylus (525–456 B.C.E.), Sophocles (496–406 B.C.E.), and Euripides (480–406 B.C.E.), it is said that the chorus *was* the play. Similarly, the Vision occasionally uses a chorus to respond to God. The genre of vision requires an implied "stage setting" from which YHWH and his aides can see and relate to mundane events in Jerusalem, Babylon, and other places.

Aristotle taught that a tragic drama should carry an audience through a catharsis of feeling. Horace (ca. 24 B.C.E.) thought it should offer pleasure. The Vision has its audience relive the change and heartbreak of three centuries of Israel's history only to place before it anew the alternatives posed by God's plan for the ages. It leads in typical Hebrew form to a renewed opportunity for faith and commitment that is seen to be offered once again despite Israel's earlier rejections.

Ideally, drama should arise out of contemporary society and should deal with the very foundations of belief. The Vision addresses issues current in fifth-century Jerusalem and traces their roots back to eighth-century Judah. It is polemical in arguing one side of the debate. The Vision portrays this historical era from a perspective that no modern historian can share. It purports to show YHWH's view of the happenings and YHWH's relation to these happenings. YHWH keeps the far nations in view, even as he addresses and exhorts his people in Jerusalem or in Babylon. A play depends on the character of its audience to determine how it is received and what it will mean to them. Some plays tend to unify the audience; some divide it. The Vision will divide those who identify with the minority believers who follow God's lead from those who identify with the majority who reject it. In any case, the Vision leaves no doubt about God's position on the issue.

THE ἀγῶν, "PROBLEM"

A drama is usually composed around a great problem. The Greeks spoke of this as the ἀγῶν. Its description and its solution formed the plot of the drama.

The great problem in Isaiah, as with the other prophets, is the experience of continual warfare in Palestine during the Assyrian and Babylonian periods (ca. 740–540 B.C.E.). These conflicts resulted in the deportation of much of the population of Israel in the eighth century and the destruction of Jerusalem in the sixth century, while those who remained in Babylon and Palestine in the early Persian period (ca. 540–450 B.C.E.) struggled to survive.

Isaiah treats the "troubles" not as threats against God and his people but as judgments inspired and led by God himself against his people and the nations. They are therefore not victims but the punished. As has been true with the "troubles," so with the solution. Israel, Jerusalem, and the nations can only hope in God's work on their behalf to rebuild Jerusalem, reassemble Israelites, and bring worshipers from the nations to the temple.

SPEAKERS/CHARACTERS

YHWH: Protagonist. The primary speaker and character throughout the drama is YHWH, God of Israel, who makes his home in Heaven and in Zion. (See *Strand: "YHWH"* [יהוה] *and "God"* [אלוהים].)

The word אלוהים, "God," appears often. The theme is that YHWH is the God of Israel. The theme is defined by the phrases אל ישראל, "God of Israel" (21:10, 17; 37:16, 21; 41:17; 52:12); אלוהנו, "our God" (1:10; 25:9; 26:13; 29:23; 35:4; 36:7; 37:20; 40:8; 42:17; 52:10; 55:6; 59:13); אלוהי, "your God" (7:11; 35:4; 37:4; 40:1, 9; 41:10, 13; 43:3; 48:17; 51:15, 20, 22; 52:7; 54:6; 55:5; 59:2; 60:9, 19; 62:3, 5; 66:9 [fem.]); and אלוהי, "my God" (7:13; 25:1; 40:27; 49:4, 5; 57:21; 61:10). God's personal role is expounded in the constant use of first-person "I" speeches. The Greeks call such a character the protagonist. He supports the argument of the plot, which finds its major movement and power in him. (See *Strand: God's First-Person Speeches.*) As the strands show, the Vision's depiction of God becomes most intense in act 4 (chaps. 34–49:4), where God addresses the nations and pleads with exilic Israel, and in act 5, where he comforts Jerusalem.

The Vision of Isaiah develops its characterization of YHWH/God by showing him in a number of roles and costumes. He is father to Israelites, his children (11:2–3). He is vineyard builder, owner, and keeper to the land of Palestine (5:1–7; 27:2–6). As a military leader for heavenly forces and the nations he has the title YHWH of Hosts (יהוה צבאות; 1:12–21; 5:26–30; 13:1–16; 63:1–6). He is shepherd to his returning people (40:11). He is patron for the temple in Jerusalem (1:10–20; 66:1–24).

Strand: "YHWH" (יהוה) and "God" (אלוהים)

Bibliography

Toorn, K. van der. "Yahweh יהוה." *DDD,* 910–19.

Prologue	Act 1	Act 2	Act 3	Act 4	Act 5	Act 6	Epilogue
YHWH							
1:2, 4, 10, 28 2:2, 3, 5, 10, 17, 19, 21 3:8, 13, 14, 16, 17 4:2, 5	5:12, 25 6:12 7:3, 10, 11, 12, 17, 18 8:1, 3, 5, 11, 17, 18 9:8, 11, 14 10:20 11:2, 3, 9, 15 12:1, 2, 4, 5	13:4, 5, 6, 9 14:1, 2, 3, 5, 22, 32 16:13, 14 17:6 18:4 19:1, 14, 19, 20, 21, 22 20:3, 17 22:17, 25 23:11, 17, 18 24:1, 8, 10 26:4, 8, 10, 11, 12 27:1, 3, 12, 13	28:13, 14, 21 29:10, 15, 19, 22 30:1, 9, 18, 27, 30, 31, 32, 33 31:1, 3, 4, 9 32:6 33:2, 5, 6, 10, 21, 22	34:2, 6, 8, 15 35:2, 10 36:7, 10, 15, 18, 20 37:1, 4, 6, 14, 15, 16, 17, 18, 20, 21, 22, 34, 36 38:1, 2, 3, 4, 5, 7, 20, 22 39:6, 8 40:2, 5, 7, 13, 27, 28, 31 41:4, 13, 14, 16, 17, 20, 21 42:2, 6, 8, 10, 12, 13, 19, 21, 22 43:1, 3, 10, 11, 12, 14, 15, 16 44:2, 5, 6, 23, 24 45:1, 3, 5, 6, 7, 8, 11, 14, 17, 18, 19, 21 48:1, 14, 17, 20, 22 49:1, 4	49:5, 7, 8, 13, 14, 18, 22, 25, 26 50:1, 10 51:1, 2, 3, 9, 11, 13, 15, 17, 20 52:3, 5, 8, 9, 10, 11, 12 53:1, 6, 10 54:1, 6, 8, 10, 13, 17	55:5, 6, 7, 8 56:1, 3, 4, 6 57:19 58:5, 9, 11, 14 59:1, 13, 15, 19, 20, 21 60:1, 2, 6, 9, 19, 20, 21 61:1, 2, 3, 6, 8, 10	62:2, 3, 4, 6, 8, 9, 11, 12 63:7, 14, 16, 17 64:1, 8, 9, 12 65:7, 8, 11, 23, 25 66:1, 2, 5, 6, 9, 12, 14, 15, 16, 17, 20, 21, 22, 23

Strand: God's First-Person Speeches

PROLOGUE	ACT 1	ACT 2	ACT 3	ACT 4	ACT 5	ACT 6	EPILOGUE
"I" (YHWH)							
1:2*b*–3, 11–20, 24–26, 3:3–4, 14*b*–15	5:3–6 6:8 10:3–6, 12, 24–25	13:3, 11– 13, 17 14:22–23, 24–25 15:9 16:9–11 18:4 19:2–4 22:19, 20–24 27:3, 4	28:16–17 29:1–3, 13–14 30:1 33:10	34:5 27:26–29, 35 40:1, 25 41:4, 8–16, 17–29 42:1–4, 6–9, 14–17, 18–22 43:1*b*–28 44:1–8, 21–22, 24–28 45:1–8, 11–13, 18–19, 21–24 46:3–5, 9–13 47:2, 6 48:3–11, 12–13, 15–16, 17–19	49:6, 8, 11, 13, 15–18, 22–26 50:1–3 51:1–2, 4–8, 12, 16, 22–23 52:13	54:17*c*– 59:21 55:3–4, 8–11 56:4–5, 7–8 57:11–13, 15–19 58:6, 9, 14 59:21 61:8	62:8 65:1-2, 6-12, 13-14, 17-19, 24 66:1–2, 4, 9, 12–13, 18–19, 21–23

Jack Miles (*God: A Biography* [New York: Random House, 1995] 195–337) treats the book of Isaiah as a chapter in the biography of God. Miles says: "It is Isaiah, not Jeremiah, who brings out the eloquence in the Lord God. It is when the Lord is speaking to Isaiah that he goes most deeply and recklessly into himself, providing the most searching inventory of his own responses to the agony occasioned in his own life by the agony he has inflicted on his chosen people. To read these responses is to pass through this crisis in the life of God in the company of the God who is suffering it" (*God*, 202). Miles goes on, "'Like a father' proves just the beginning. He is also like a lover, a husband, a mother, a shepherd, a gardener, a king, and—categories never heard before—a redeemer and 'the Holy One of Israel'" (*God*, 203). YHWH is king in heaven and on earth (6:1). Neither Israel nor Judah is any longer a kingdom with its own king and land, no longer a twelve-tribe confederation in intimate covenant with God, its father. Jerusalem is a city for pilgrims, for a humbled, scattered people. But Isaiah proclaims that YHWH is the king (המלך) in the temple at Uzziah's death (6:1); king over the Assyrian emperor and his armies (chaps. 10, 36–37); king over the kings, the land, the world, and Leviathan (chaps. 24–27); king over death (chap. 25); king over his people (32:21–22); king over "servant" Israel (chaps. 41–44;

cf. 41:21; 43:15; 44:6); king over "servant" Cyrus, Babylon, and "all the land" (chaps. 45–48); king over the "suffering servant" (chaps. 49–54); king over the "servants of YHWH" (54:17*b*–59:21; 63:7–65:16); king over the temple on his mountain (2:2–4; chap. 66); and king over the new heavens and the new land (65:17–25).

Note how the concepts of "king" and "servant" imply each other. What had been implicit with a Davidic king leading worship in the temple is now proclaimed as explicit fact proved by historical events. The turn from emphasis on the Davidic king to YHWH as king parallels the situation in Psalms and Proverbs. Isaiah emphasizes this change through its treatment of the term בטח, "trust." The key passage is found in the narrative in chaps. 36–37 (see Seitz, *Zion's Final Destiny;* see Olley [*VT* 43 (1993) 19–49] for chap. 36). The Assyrian general introduces the idea of false trust to support his offer to allow Jerusalem to trust in him. Ironically, the Vision will agree with four of the five instances of wrong trust: trust in military strategy (36:4) or alliance with Egypt (36:5) or in YHWH (36:7) or in horses and chariots (36:8) or in King Hezekiah himself (36:14–18). The Assyrian overplays his hand only in claiming that YHWH is no more than the other gods whose cities the Assyrian has destroyed (36:18–20). He states the issue: "Do not let the god you trust deceive you" (36:10). Hezekiah's prayer links the idea of "trust" to YHWH's incomparable greatness as "God over all the kingdoms. You have made the heavens and the earth" (37:16). If it was thought before that trust should be lodged in the Davidic king or in Zion itself, this narrative makes clear that trust must be in YHWH alone. The entire book of Isaiah (cf. 7:9) builds on that. There are other speakers who support and fill out YHWH's role but who remain unidentified (I call them Heavens and Earth 1:2).

The second most frequent speaker also speaks in the first person. He remains unidentified, but readers have automatically assumed that he is the implied author, the prophet's "alter ego," and have called him "Isaiah," even if the text does not so specify.

Excursus: Genre in First-Person Passages

Bibliography

Behler, G. M. *Les Confessions de Jéremie.* Bible et Vie Chretienne. Tournai: Casterman, 1959. **Blank, S.** "The Confessions of Jeremiah and the Meaning of Prayer." *HUCA* 21 (1950) 331–54; **Dion, H.-M.** "Le genre littéraire sumérien de 1' 'Hymne à soi-mê me' et quelques passages du Deutérei-Isaïe." *RB* 74 (1967) 215–34. **Elliger, K.** "Ich bin der Herr—Euer Gott." In *Kleine Schriften zum Alten Testament.* TB 32. Munich: Kaiser, 1966. **Harner, P. B.** *Grace and Law in Second Isaiah: "I am the Lord."* Lewiston, NY: Mellen, 1988. **Ittmann, N.** *Die Konfessionen Jeremias: Ihre Bedeutung für die Verkündigung des Propheten.* WMANT 54. Neukirchen-Vluyn: Neukirchener Verlag, 1981. **O'Connor, K. M.** *The Confessions of Jeremiah: Their Interpretation and Role in Chapters 1–25.* SBLDS 94. Atlanta: Scholars Press, 1988. **Zimmerli, W.** "Erkenntnis Gottes nach dem Buche Ezekiel." In *Gottes Offenbarung: Gesammelte Aufsätze.* TB 19. Munich: Kaiser, 1963. 41–119. ———. "Ich bin Jahwe." In *Gottes Offenbarung: Gesammelte Aufsätze.* TB 19. Munich: Kaiser, 1963. 19–40.

First-person passages in the Prophets use several genres. Some are narratives telling of visions or experiences: Jer 1, 2, and passim; Ezekiel (almost all); Hos 3, Amos 7:1–9, Zech 1–6 (inside a third-person narrative frame); Isa 6, 8, 21, and 22. Others are poems or psalms: Jeremiah's confessions (11:18–12:6; 15:10–21; 17:14–18; 18:18–2; 20:7–13 [18]). Others are speeches addressed to an audience or to readers: Isa 50:4–9 and chaps. 61 and 62.

YHWH speeches are also often in the first person. See *Strand: God's First-Person Speeches* on previous page. A particular feature of these speeches is the use of phrases of divine self-predication. The phrase is not unique to Isaiah. Five times in Isaiah there is the variation "I am the Lord YHWH," and five times the phrase occurs with the longer form of the pronoun (Harner, *Grace and Law,* 11; cf. 170–71 n. 20). אני יהוה, "I am YHWH," occurs in Isa 41:1–4, 8–13; 42:8; 43:1–3, 8–13, 14–21; 44:6–8, 24–28; 45:5–7, 18–19; 49:19–23; and 51:9–52:2. Sometimes the words are prefaced by "you shall know that אני אל, "I am God" (Isa 41:10; 43:12; 45:22; 46:9), or אני הוא, "I am He" (Isa 41:4; 43:10, 13; 46:4; 48:12; 52:6). Isaiah thus joins Hosea and Ezekiel in the concern for the knowledge of YHWH, as Zimmerli ("Erkenntnis Gotes" and "Ich ben Jahwe") has shown.

The Prophet/Implied Author. Sometimes first-person direct and indirect quotations come from other identified speakers: Isa 40:27 (Israel); 49:1–4 (Israel); 49:14 (Zion). But the speaker is not identified in a series of first-person accounts that seem to derive from the "implied author." The reader assumes that they represent "the prophet." The thesis followed here is that they consistently reflect a means for the "implied author-prophet" to communicate directly to the reader, giving the opportunity for the reader to form an opinion of the personal attitude and relation of the "implied author" to the things that are being presented.

The first-person account is a literary device, as distinctive in the Vision as are the third-person narrative accounts. They set up a contrast between the prophet written about and the prophet that is writing. They are usually presented in close proximity to each other. The Ahaz narrative (7:1–16) is enclosed within the first-person accounts in chaps. 6 and 8. The Hezekiah narrative in chap. 20 is followed by the first-person accounts of chap. 21. The Hezekiah narratives in chaps. 36–39 are followed by the introduction of servants Israel and Cyrus and the speeches in 49:5–9 and 50:4–8. In the final book there is no narrative, and the first-person accounts in 61 and 62 take center stage. In 63:8–64:12 a first-person prayer to God brings the central issue of the book back to God's attention.

The prophet named in the Vision of Isaiah is Isaiah son of Amoz, the eighth-century champion of Jerusalem and confidant of kings Ahaz and Hezekiah in the narratives (7:1–16; chap. 20; chaps. 36–39) and in the superscriptions (1:1; 2:1; 13:1). However, the "prophet" who makes the Vision a major prophetic book symbolizes all the scribes that composed the classic. This "prophet" reveals himself not only through the consistent message of the book in the speeches of YHWH but also in a series of first-person accounts where the reader is allowed intimate access to the inner working of the mind(s) that shaped the Vision. In chap. 6, this prophet is made the instrument of God's judgment, hardening the hearts of the people prior to the destruction of the land. In chap. 8 he announces the coming of the Assyrian but is unable to stand the pressure of his position and resigns, leaving only the legacy of his message and his children. In chaps. 21 and following, Darius reports the agonizing events that mirror the reasons for anxiety in chap. 20. The small nations are falling before the power of the imperial forces. Finally, the land stands empty, dead, destroyed (chap. 24). The prophet greets the miraculous actions of God with praise and thanks (chap. 25). When God's chosen servant (Israel) resigns (49:1–4), the prophet reports being chosen to fill the vacant place (49:5–9). It is a position that draws persecution (50:4–9). In the new order, which the servants of YHWH inherit, the prophet takes a central role, enunciating the prophetic principles (chap. 61) and standing up for the place of Jerusalem (chap. 62). The prophet makes a final appeal for YHWH to reestablish his relation to Israel as father to children (cf. 1:2–3; 63:8–64:12), an appeal that is denied (65:1–16). The new order will belong to "servants," not "children."

Israel: Antagonist. In the book of Isaiah, opposite YHWH God is Israel: antagonist to his protagonist. Not Judah or Jerusalem, as the title might suggest, and not the prophet, but Israel. The name appears in every part of the book. The term used to describe her in relation to YHWH is עם, "people." It occurs 130 times and is also in every part of the book. The relational character of the term is shown by the possessive pronouns: "my people" (58 times), "your people" (21 times), and "his people" (11 times). (See *Strand: "People"* [עם].)

The people (Israel) are also called the children of YHWH, rebellious children (1:2, 3–7, 8–20, 28–31; 30:1–18; 31:6–7; 33:13–16). In chaps. 63–64 a prayer to YHWH pleads for him to again be their father. Israel is called YHWH's servant in 40:1–49:4.

Choral Speakers and Groups Addressed. Groups as well as individuals fill the stage of Isaiah. They may be spoken about as "they," spoken to as "you," or speak as "we."

Excursus: First-Person-Plural Speeches

Bibliography

Conrad, E. W. "Who Are 'We' in Isaiah?" In *Reading Isaiah.* 83–116. **Hanson, P. D.** *The Dawn of Apocalyptic.* Rev. ed. Philadelphia: Fortress, 1979. **Schramm, B.** *The Opponents of Third Isaiah.* JSOTSup 193. Sheffield: Sheffield Academic Press, 1995.

"You" as a personal pronoun in English covers a large territory that is distinctly differentiated in Hebrew. In Hebrew the second-person pronoun can be distinctly singular or plural, feminine or masculine. The masculine singular form can address a man or a people, like Israel. Or it may address God. The feminine singular can address a woman or a city, like Jerusalem. The plural can address a group, just as the "we" sections speak for a group. The nations are not given general speaking parts. They are quoted second-hand in 24:14–16 and 49:14. One speech belongs to Israel (49:1–4). Among the speakers are choral groups from Zion and Jerusalem. Throughout the Vision there are, however, first-person speakers that cannot be identified so easily.

Thus the book of Isaiah is very much "I/thou" speech in the sense that Martin Buber used in developing his distinctive philosophy. Sometimes the address is "onstage"; that is, it addresses someone within the play. But sometimes the

Strand: "People" (עם)

In addition, the Vision uses inserted poetic pieces exclaimed or sung in chorus. They include 12:1–6, 25:1–5, and 26:1–18. (The places where the Lord speaks in first person plural [6:8; 41:22–23; 43:9] do not belong with the rest of the first-person speeches and have been treated separately above.)

The *Strand: "We, Us, Our"* shows how the dialogical nature of the literature reaches into every part of the book of Isaiah.

Prologue	Act 1	Act 2	Act 3	Act 4	Act 5	Act 6	Epilogue
עם, "people" (130x)							
1:3, 4, 10 2:3, 4, 6 3:5, 7, 12, 13, 14, 15	5:13, 25 6:9, 10 7:2, 8, 17 8:6, 9, 11, 12, 19 9:1, 8, 12, 15, 18 10:2, 6, 13 14, 22, 24 11:10, 11, 16 12:4	13:4, 14 14:2, 6, 20, 32 17:12 18:2, 7 19:25 22:4 23:13 24:2, 4, 13 25:3, 6, 7, 8 26:11, 20 27:11	28:5, 11, 14 29:13 30:5, 6, 9, 19, 26, 28 32:13, 18 33:3, 12, 19, 24	34:5 36:11 40:1, 7 42:5, 6, 22 43:8, 20, 22 44:7 47:6	49:8, 13, 22 51:4, 5, 7, 16, 22 52:4, 5, 6, 9 53:8	56:3, 7, 14 58:1 60:21 61:9	62:10, 12 63:3, 6, 8, 11, 14, 18 64:8 65:2, 3, 10, 18, 19, 22
עמי, "my people" (58x)							
1:3 3:12–15	5:13 10:2, 24	19:25 (Egypt) 26:20	32:13, 18	40:1, 6	52:4, 5, 6 53:8	57:14 58:1 61:7, 10	63:8 65:10, 19, 22
עמך, "your people" (21x)							
2:6	7:17 10:22	14:20		41:10			63:14 64:8
עמו, "his people"							
3:14	5:25 7:2 11:11, 16	13:14 14:32 25:8	28:5 30:26		49:13 51:22 52:9	56:3	63:11
עמים, "peoples"							
2:3–4 3:13	8:9 10:13, 14 11:10 12:4	14:2, 6 17:12 24:13 25:7	30:28 33:3, 12		49:22 51:4, 5	56:7 61:9	62:10 63:3, 6

address, particularly of the plural pronoun, may be addressed to the audience/ the readers. Who is the implied audience (that is, the audience/readers that the book seems to anticipate)? This audience is a community of survivors, an inclusive community, but also a community divided. It is a community that feels cut off from the past, a community "waiting" for justice and God's future to take shape.

Sometimes this audience is identified: people of Judah and Jerusalem (5:3); rulers of Jerusalem (1:10, 22, 23); house of Jacob (2:5); exilic (Babylon) Israel/ Jacob (14:3 masc. sg.). Those directly addressed are: Heavens and Land/Earth

Strand: "We, Us, Our"

Prologue	Act 1	Act 2	Act 3	Act 4	Act 5	Act 6	Epilogue
We							
1:9 2:3	5:19 9:10	16:6 20:6 (3x) 25:9 (3x) 26:1, 8, 13, 17, 18 (3x)	30:16 33:2	36:5, 7, 11 38:20 41:22, 23, 26 42:24 46:5	51:23 53:1, 2, 3, 4, 5, 6 54:16–17	55:10 57:7, 10 (3x), 15, 17 58:2, 3, 9, 12 59:2, 5, 6, 9, 10 (4x), 11 (3x), 12, 19 60:5, 11 61:6, 10	63:17, 19 64:3, 5, 6, 9 65:12, 16, 19, 24 66:4, 5, 6
Us							
1:9, 18 2:3 (2x), 5 4:1	7:6 8:10 9:6	14:10 17:14 25:9, 12 26:12, 13	30:15, 18 32:15 33:2, 14	36:15, 18 41:22 (3x) 44:7	53:5–6	59:9, 11, 12	64:7, 12
Our							
1:10 4:1	7:6	25:9 26:8, 12, 13	28:15 33:2, 20, 22	35:2, 7 37:20 38:20 40:3 42:17 47:4		55:7 56:12 58:3 59:12, 13 61:2, 6	63:16, 17, 18 64:5, 6, 7, 8, 11

(1:2; 44:23; 49:13); Israel/ Israelites (2:5; 35:3–4; 40:27–28; 41:8–16; 42:16–20; 43:1–7, 14–28; 44:1–8, 21–22, 24–28; 46:3–4; 48:1–11, 12–20; 52:11–12); Jerusalem/Zion/Jerusalemites (1:25–31; 5:3–7; 8:19–22; 10:24–25; 22:1–11, 14; 29:9–12; 30:19–26; [women] 32:9–13; 33:12–24; 36:12–20; 40:9; 45:14; 49:15–26; 50:1–3, 10–11; 51:12, 17–23; 52:1–10; 54:1–17*b;* 60:1–22; 62:2–9, 10); rulers in Jerusalem (1:10–20; 3:14*b;* 7:7–9, 13–17); the Judean official, Shebna (22:15–19); King Hezekiah of Judah (36:4–10; 37:5–7, 10–13; 38:5–8; 39:5–7); the Assyrian King Sennacherib (37:21–29); the Babylonian king (33:1); Babylon (33:11; 47:1–3, 5–15); King Cyrus of Persia (42:6–7; 43:8; 45:2–7); the nations and groups from the nations (8:9–10; 34:1; 33:13–14; 34:1 [those who have survived the destruction of the land]; 40:1–2; 40:18, 21, 25–26; 41:1, 21–24; 42:9, 10–12, 23–25; 43:9–13; 45:11–13, 20–25; 46:5–13; 57:14); Philistines (14:29–31); Dedanites (21:13–14); Tyre and Sidon (23:11–7, 10–14); islands/coastlands (41:1; 49:1–4); apostate/rebellious people from Israel (1:4, 5–7; 30:12–19; 31:6; 56:9–12; 57:3–13; 58:3*b*–14; 59:1–3; 65:7, 11–16); believers/obedient people from Israel, Jerusalem, and the nations (51:1–3; 55:1–56:1; 59:21; 66:1–2, 5, 10–14, 22); God (in prayers) (36:15–20; 38:16–19; 25:1–5; 26:3, 8–18; 45:15; 63:14*b*–

Strand: "You"

Prologue	Act 1	Act 2	Act 3	Act 4		Act 5	Act 6	Epilogue
You (masc. sg.)								
3:6, 7, 12 4:1	6:7 7:3, 4, 11, 16, 17, 25 8:8 10:22, 24, 27 12:1	14:3, 4, 11, 16 19:12 20:2 22:16–21 24:17 25:1–5, 12 26:2–20	30:19–22 33:1, 6, 17–20	36:19–22 37:4–30 38:1–7, 16, 18, 19 39:5, 6, 7 40:6, 27, 28 41:6, 8–10, 15 42:6 43:1, 2, 3, 5, 22–27	44:1–3, 8, 21, 22, 24 45:2, 3, 4, 5, 9, 10, 15 48:4–10, 11–13, 17–19 49:3	49:6, 7, 8 51:13–16 52:14	55:5 58:1, 3, 5, 7–14 59:2, 3, 21 61:5, 7	63:2 63:15–64:12 65:5, 15
You (fem. sg.)								
3:25		17:10, 11 22:2–3, 8 23:4, 10, 12, 16	28:3–5 33:23	40:8 41:11, 14–15 45:14 46:1–15 48:8		49:18–26 51:9–10, 12–13, 17, 19–23 52:1, 7, 8 54:1–17*b*	55:5 56:6–13 60:1–21	62:2–6, 8–12
You (masc. pl.)								
1:5–30 3:4, 5	5:5, 8 7:9, 13, 14 8:9, 13, 19 10:3 12:3, 4	16:13, 14 18:2, 3 19:11 21:10, 12, 13 22:9–12, 14 23:2, 6, 7, 14 26:19 27:2	28:14–15, 18–23 29:1, 9–13, 16 30:3, 12–18, 20, 29 31:6, 7 32:11, 13, 20 33:11, 13	34:1 35:4 36:14–18 40:1, 6, 18, 21, 25, 26 41:1, 6, 21–24 42:9, 10, 17, 18, 20, 23	43:10–12, 14–15, 18 44:8, 23 45:8, 11, 19, 20–21, 22 46:3, 5, 8, 9, 12 48:1, 14, 20 49:1, 3	49:13 50:1, 4, 10, 11 51:1–2, 4–7, 12 52:3, 9–12	55:1–12 56:1, 9, 12 57:3, 4, 5, 14 58:3–4, 6 59:2–3 60:2–11 61:6–7	62:6–7, 10–11 65:6–15 66:1, 5, 10–14, 20, 22
You (fem. pl.)								
			32:9–13					

64:12); "my people" (26:19–21; 51:4–8); the apparition from Edom (63:2); "the arm of YHWH" (51:9–10); and the prophet (6:9–13; 7:3; 8:1, 5; 49:6–8; 58:1).

My commentary identifies various groups with these pronouns ad hoc as they appear within the drama. Conrad's study does so as well, but he has also related them to the contentious groups within the restoration community in the way that Hanson (*Dawn of Apocalyptic,* 172 et passim) and Schramm *(Opponents)* have described. Sweeney (*Isaiah 1–4,* 98) thinks the argument of the book is primarily aimed at these groups.

Conrad identifies a number of groups in Isaiah where the second-person plural pronouns are used: The first is that of the readers (like ourselves), the implied audience, who are "divided into a 'we' (the implied community) and a 'they' (a rival faction)" ("Who Are 'We'?" 83; i.e., Isa 1:9–10; 2:5; 16:6; 17:14; 32:15; 33:2, 21–22; 42:23–24; 47:4; 59:9–15; 63:7–64:12). But often this group begins as a united, undifferentiated group that is eventually divided in two. Other groups use first-person plural (Isa 2:3–4; 12:4–6; 9:6; 20:6; 24:16; 25:9; chap. 26; 35:2; 40:3, 8; 53:1–6; 55:7; 61:2, 6). "Some of these quotations have positive connotations and mostly concern what some group will say in the future" (Conrad, "Who Are 'We'?" 87 n. 11). But "future" within the setting of the text may be contemporary to the implied audience. Isa 36:7 and 37:20 are quotations within a narrative belonging to the past. "The other quotations are attributed to groups who tend to be presented negatively" (Isa 4:1; 5:19; 14:8, 10–11; 22:13; 28:15; 29:15; 30:10–11, 16; 33:14; 42:17; 51:23; 56:12; 58:3). Conrad notes the way chaps. 1 and 66 address the "community of survivors" ("Who Are 'We'?" 88; 1:9–10; 66:18–21). This group forms the audience, the first readers, for the Vision and continues to include us.

Hanson, Schramm, and Conrad think of this implied audience as a community of survivors who had experienced the destruction of the land and Jerusalem (13:5). "This community is waiting for the Lord to complete his plan and to create a future world peace for themselves and for all the nations of the earth" (Conrad, "Who Are 'We'?" 87, n. 11; cf. A. Johnson, "The Concept of Waiting in the Isaianic Corpus," Ph.D. diss., Boston Univ., 1986). The survivors include opponents of the prophet and those who stand with him (chaps. 1 and 66). A major goal of the Vision is to define the differences between them and to defend the prophet's program. "The groups are portrayed as having shared a common heritage and a common identity as a social group. The opposition between the survivors and the opponents is internecine" (Johnson, "Concept," 95). But the Vision presents the distinction as being between those who are acceptable to God and those who are not. In both chapters the opponents are associated with idolatrous practices that take place in גנות, "gardens." Compare 1:29 with 65:3 and 55:17 (see Sweeney, *Isaiah 1–4*, 23–24). Finally, both chapters end with the pronouncement of judgment on the opponents as a fire that will not be כבה, "quenched" (Conrad, "Who Are 'We'?" 97; cf. Liebreich, *JQR* 46 [1955–56] 277). Both chaps. 1 and 66 call for the opponents to "hear the word of the Lord" ("Who Are 'We'?" 98; 1:10; 66:5).

Hansen and Schramm are intent on establishing in Trito-Isaiah the historical identities of the groups who opposed the prophet. Conrad, Darr, and I are intent on establishing their identity within the reading experience of the book. We find the references beginning with chap. 1 and moving to the end. As readers, we see ourselves in the book. We stand as the last of a long line of readers reaching back to the very first groups that Hansen and Schramm delineate.

Isaiah is thus a highly interactive drama that draws the readers/hearers into the action and speeches "onstage." We the readers, from the first readers/hearers on, are addressed and are given "lines" to read or sing. They aim to shape our self-identity. They direct our hopes. We are a remnant of the community of survivors. We are struck by the indictments of chaps. 1 and 65–66. We share the short-lived or utopian hopes of 2:1–4, chaps. 11–12, 19:17–25, chaps. 24–27, 32:1–

20, 33:20–24, and 65:17–25. We join the nations to be reminded of the realism of survivors and the challenge that God is still at work (chaps. 34–35) in chaps. 42 and 47. We share the disappointment of 59:9–15. We share the plaintive appeal of 63:7–64:12. We tremble before the judgment of chap. 1 and 65:1–16/66:15–17, 24, which divides the survivors into the judged and the servants of YHWH. We share the challenge to recognize the hand of God in change with the hope of continuity, the Vision of a world in which God is active and real, at work to establish a people for himself, a city where he meets his people.

PLOT

The plot of the book turns on the relation of YHWH and Israel. The complication lies in Israel's חטה, "sin" (1:4, 28; 29:21; 33:14; 38:17; 42:24; 43:27; 64:4; 65:7, 20); פשׁע, "rebellion," and related terms (1:2, 20, 23, 28; 3:8; 24:9, 20; 30:1; 38:17; 43:27; 46:9; 48:8; 50:5; 53:12; 59:13; 63:10; 65:2; 66:24); and the charge that they have עזב, "forsaken," YHWH (1:4, 28; 7:16; 10:3, 14; 17:2, 9; 18:16; 27:10; 32:14; 41:17; 42:16; 54:6, 7; 55:7; 58:2; 60:15; 62:4, 12; 63:10; 65:11) or שׁכח, "forgotten," the God of their Salvation , that is, YHWH (17:10; 23:15, 16; 49:14–15; 51:13; 54:4; 65:16). Because of this they are accounted רעע, "evil" (1:4, 16; 3:1; 8:9; 9:16; 11:9; 14:20; 24:19; 31:2; 41:23; 59:15; 65:15), and רשׁע, "wicked" (13:11; 14:5; 48:22; 50:9; 53:9; 54:17; 57:20, 21).

The book recognizes that rebellious children are condemned to die. But YHWH, the heavenly father, urges them to change their ways (1:15*d*–17) and offers complete absolution for those that do (1:18–19), even as he condemns those who "resist and rebel" (1:20). This sets the line of division between those who become God's enemies who must be purged (1:24–25, 28) and the penitents who will be restored and redeemed (1:26–27). Thus salvation will belong to a remnant only.

The book tries out several alternatives to this radical division between righteous and wicked. First is the possibility that Jerusalem's monarchy might be a basis for salvation of a remnant from Israel (chaps. 7–12), then that YHWH's military actions could lead to an international solution (chaps. 13–19), or that YHWH's life-giving powers could miraculously breathe life back into people and land (chaps. 20–27). The most developed argument is made in chaps. 40–55 (so-called Deutero-Isaiah), where a divine call to the Babylonian exiles promises them a place as special servants in YHWH's economy with Jerusalem as the center. Both exiles and Jerusalemites refuse, leading YHWH to issue an open invitation to any and all who will to come to his banquet (chap. 55). The deep remaining problems are reviewed in chaps. 56–61, and a curtain call of proposed solutions appears in chaps. 62–64. YHWH announces his decision in chaps. 65 and 66. He will separate the wicked from his servants (65:1–16). He will create Jerusalem as a New Heavens and New Earth (65:17–25). And he will follow through with the inauguration of the new temple in Jerusalem, to which worshipers from all the peoples are invited (chap. 66).

The plot is complicated by several factors: by YHWH's determination to raise the house on his mountain high (2:2) and by his desire to have many other peoples, in fact all flesh (22:13; 40:5, 6; 49:26; 65:4; 66:16, 17, 23, 24), join in worship there (2:3–4; 66:23); by his participation in the wars of the period (2:9–

22; 7:17–25; 13:1–22; 63:1–6); by YHWH's decision to delay any real opportunity to repent by blurring the vision and dulling the hearing of the people (6:9–10), with the result that the people are deaf and blind to the warnings from God (1:3; 5:13; 27:11; 29:9–16, 18–19, 29; 32:3–8; 35:5; 42:7, 16, 18, 24; 43:8; 56:10; 59:10); and by YHWH's decision to have Palestine completely destroyed (6:11–13; 10:23; 28:22), which is shown fulfilled in chaps. 24 and 34.

The acts of the drama develop subplots of their own: the eighth-century decree of devastation that continued until the Babylonian period (chaps. 5 and 6); the surprising survival of the Davidic monarchy and Jerusalem in the eighth century (chaps. 7–12; 36–39); the burden of Babylon: destroyed land/the mountain of YHWH and Israel (chaps. 13–27); the woes: survival in a time of chaos (chaps. 28–33); the ריב, "case," of Zion (chaps. 34–59), which includes the offer of redemption to Israel in Babylonian exile (34:1–49:4); the offer of redemption to Jerusalem (49:5–54:17*b*); and the offer of redemption to individual believers (54:17*c*–59). The prologue (chaps. 1–4) and the epilogue (chaps. 62–66) contain independent units that support the main plot lines relating to Israel, Jerusalem, and the temple. All these will be described in more detail in the commentary.

Isaiah is an interpretation of the Assyrian and Babylonian wars in Palestine in terms of God's plan and actions. These centuries effectively destroyed the political infrastructure of the region and much of its economic system.

The actions of the Assyrians reduced the kingdoms of Aram, Israel, and the Philistines to Assyrian provinces. They threatened Egypt and brought Egypt under foreign rule for a short time. They destroyed the coastal ports of Ashdod and Tyre, putting them out of business for a while. Babylonian successors destroyed Jerusalem and devastated Edom, again threatening Egypt, even if only temporarily. Eventually both Assyria and Babylon disappeared from the scene.

Isaiah teaches that YHWH, for reasons of his own, determined to destroy the nations and to devastate the whole land, including his own people in Israel and Judah (5:1–6:13; 10:22–23; 13; 14:22–27; 28:22; 34:1–16). In this way YHWH became God for the nations. They assemble on his command (34:1). They are commanded to "comfort Zion" (40:1) and to support the restoration of Jerusalem. He is called "your God" (35:4), "our God" (36:7).

Settings: Places and Times

Bibliography

Sweeney, M. "On Multiple Settings in the Book of Isaiah." In *SBLSP 1992*. Atlanta: Scholars Press, 1992. 267–73.

The drama sets scenes in the heavenly throne room (e.g., chap. 6), in Jerusalem, in Babylon, and in other unidentified settings. Its temporal settings are equally diverse. It deals with times contemporary with the first readers/hearers in the fifth century, and it specifies dates in the eighth century (6:1; 7:1–16; 14:27; 20:1–6; 22:15–25; chaps. 36–39). It addresses the Babylonian "great king" Nebuchadnezzar of the sixth century (chap. 14). It specifies the beginnings of "the troubles" as well as the completed destruction (chaps. 24 and 34). It addresses Cyrus in the late sixth century. The following list shows identifiable periods of history addressed in the drama.

Late eighth century: 1:1; 2:1; and chaps. 7, 22, and 36–39
Assyrian Period: 14:24–23:18
Between death of Nebuchadnezzar and Persian seizure of Babylon: chaps. 13–14/24–27; 40–48.
After Babylon's fall: chaps. 49–54, 55–62
Unspecified: 2:1–4; 11:6–9; 65:17–25

For the reader to realize that one passage is in a different time from the passage just read can be disorienting. The recognition that chap. 40 addresses a very different time from that of chaps. 36–39 is what began the era of "Deutero-Isaiah." More recently, interpreters have recognized temporal movement in other parts of the book. At first they seemed to be arranged randomly, but now specific patterns are beginning to emerge. For instance, the shift from the Babylonian period in chap. 14 back to the Assyrian period in chap. 15 has bothered interpreters. But the change is clearly marked in 14:23 with the reference to judgment on Babylon and the pronouncement on Assyria in 14:24–27. The material that follows down through chap. 23 is from the Assyrian period. Scholarship has recognized a shift to another era in chaps. 24–27. Chap. 13 fits quite well with chap. 14. The result is a group of scenes in the Assyrian period (14:24–23:18) framed by 13:11–14:23 of the Babylonian period and chaps. 24–27 of an indeterminate period other than the Assyrian.

Chaps. 1–4 are not specifically identified in time. The same is true of chaps. 63–66. They are replete with second-person-plural addresses (especially chaps. 1 and 66), which may be understood to be addressed to the readers of the book. They frame the whole book.

I suggest that the book of Isaiah identifies five focal points in time. One addresses the readers of the book (especially chaps. 1–4 and 63–66), a time when the rebuilt temple is about to be opened to pilgrims. Another pinpoints the late eighth century in Judah (chaps. 5–6; 7–12; 14:24–23:18; 36–39). A third reacts to the Assyrian and Babylonian devastation of the land in the seventh and early sixth centuries (chaps. 24–27, 28–33). A fourth points to a time when the Babylonian Empire is about to fall to the Persians (chaps. 13–14, 34–35, 40–48), or when Persian administration is being installed in Jerusalem (chaps. 49–54) and Judah (chaps. 55–59). A fifth pinpoints the time when Jerusalem is restored (chaps. 60–62). Does this fit the return of Sheshbazzar (Ezra 1) about 530 B.C.E., or the work of Zerubbabel and Joshua (Ezra 3) in 520–15 B.C.E., or the work of Nehemiah (Neh 2) in the middle of the following century? The Vision does not give exact reference points. The prologue and epilogue (chaps. 1–4 and 60–66) use the same time frame. But at other times the Vision moves from the announcement of a divine decree (chaps. 5–6; 13–14; 40:1–11) to the fulfillment of that decree (chaps. 34–35; 24–27; 60–62), which obviously posits movement in time. Yet this promise-fulfillment pattern is not automatic. The descriptions of fulfillment in returning to Jerusalem in chaps. 40–66, which deal with the Babylonian diaspora and the Palestinian and Jerusalemite groups, fall considerably short of the pictures of hoped return in 10:20–22, 11:11–17, 19:16–25, 27:12–13, and 34:16–35:10.

Genre

Bibliography

O'Connell, R. H. *Concentricity and Continuity.* **Rignell, R. G.** "Isaiah Chapter 1." *ST* 2 (1957) 140–58. **Wright, G. E.** "The Lawsuit of God." In *Israel's Prophetic Heritage.* Ed. B. W. Anderson and W. Harrelson. 62–67.

Isaiah is primarily poetry, speeches in poetic meter and style, and first-person narratives (chaps. 6, 8, 21) and speeches. It also contains third-person narratives (chaps. 7, 20, 36–39) and is set in a narrative frame by it superscriptions (1:1; 2:1; 13:1; 54:17*c*). A. L. H. M. Wieringen (*The Implied Reader in Isaiah 6–12* [Leiden; Boston: Brill, 1998]) has correctly differentiated these from the basic discourse sections. The primary form of Isaiah is discourse or dialogue, not narrative. Its genre must be one that employs discourse as its mode of communication.

Isaiah has been called a "covenant disputation" (ריב *rib*). God, his prophet, and his people assess their relation within the covenant and beyond through the "give and take" of courtroom disputation. The dialogue is intended to clarify the issues and arrive at a solution to the problems.

God has problems with his people (Israel), with his city (Jerusalem), and with the nations of the area. The heart of the Vision is the case of Zion (ריב ציון *rib Zion;* 34:8), which begins in 1:21–31, reaches a climax in the destruction of Jerusalem in 586 B.C.E. (34:8–15), and is continued (chaps. 40–54) because a spokesman demands (34:16) that the scroll of YHWH (37:35) be read again. The people are accused of breaking covenant (esp. chaps. 1–4 and 63:7–66; cf. the Song of Moses in Deut 32:1–43, which shows so many similarities to Isaiah, especially to chap. 1 and 63:7–65:16, that one is tempted to see it as a literary forerunner of the great prophetic book). YHWH's case is defensive in later sections (chaps. 40–54), but in the earlier portions of the book it is offensive: a case against Israel, Jerusalem, the land, and the major nations.

The case against Israel opens the book. They are rebellious children (1:2–3). The devastation of their lands is a result of that rebellion (1:4–7). The case continues in 2:6*b*–8; 5:1–7, 8–25; and 9:8–10:4. The land shares the guilt of its peoples, of Israel, Moab, Aram, Philistia, Tyre, and Edom. It is condemned to complete destruction (chaps. 6–24). The larger part of chap. 1 makes the case against Jerusalem (1:8–31). Worship in the temple has been corrupted and is now characterized by violence.

Your princes—rebelling,
    companions of thieves!
Each one a bribe-lover
    and a rewards-chaser!
An orphan they never vindicate!
    A widow's suit never comes before them! (Isa 1:23)

These corrupt elements must be eliminated if the city is to survive (1:27–28). In chap. 3, Jerusalem will have to be purged before redemption is possible (chap. 4). Isa 10:12 identifies the Assyrian invasions with "YHWH's work against Mount Zion and Jerusalem." Chap. 22 presents a realistic picture of corruption in government circles in Jerusalem during Hezekiah's reign. The case against Jerusalem continues in 28:14–15, chap. 29, 30:1–14, chap. 31, and 33:10–14.

The foundation for cases against the nations, who, of course, do not stand under covenant justice, is made in chap. 2. Accusations against them may include superstition and idolatry (2:6*b*–9). But the major charge is one of pride, which YHWH is determined to humble (2:10–22). These nations include Moab (15–16), the Philistines (14:28–32), Damascus (17:1–3, 9), Tyre (23), Edom (21:11; chap. 34), and the Dedanites (Arabs; 21:13–17). Assyria, God's instrument for judgment, also comes under judgment. Although it had done YHWH's work (7:5; 36:10), Assyria never acknowledged the source of its strength, imagining that it depending on its own strength and intelligence, of which it was immensely proud (7:6–11; 13–19; 36:18–20; 37:10–13). So Assyria is judged and punished (7:12; 14:24–27; 30:31–33; 31:8–9). Babylon is not pictured as God's instrument. Merodach-Baladan's Babylon was a temptation for Hezekiah (chap. 39). Nebuchadnezzar's Babylon stands under the judgment of God in 13:17–20 and 14:22–23, and her king's death draws a taunt (14:3–21). The fall of Babylon is heard with great anxiety in 21:1–10. Babylon and her gods stand accused in 46:1–2 and 47:1–15. Egypt was a powerful and fearsome neighbor. The Palestinian kingdoms instinctively turned to Egypt for support and help. But God's support was behind the Mesopotamian powers. The case against Egypt is made in chaps. 18–19. Ethiopia is the ruling element in Egypt at this time. God's judgment is that the entire country will be subdued, eventually to be joined in a peaceful coexistence with Assyria and Israel. Judeans seek an alliance with Egypt in 30:1–7, and the problem persists in 31:1–3.

Some interpreters have suggested that Isaiah is a theodicy, a defense of God for his actions toward Israel and Jerusalem during the Assyrian and Babylonian periods. The book's way of doing this is to have God defend himself. He cites accusations, such as this one from Israel in Babylon (40:27):

> Jacob, why do you say,
>   and Israel, (why) do you declare,
> "My way is hidden from YHWH,
> and my justice is disregarded by my God"?

YHWH answers in 41:28–31 and the following chapters, not by denying the charge but by pointing to a larger work in progress and calling for Israel in Babylon to recognize it and join in it. If Israel were not so blind and deaf, it could see that YHWH has a larger role and task for her in this new age.

But Israel will have no part of it (49:1–4). The complaint from Jerusalem comes in 49:14: "YHWH has forsaken me! / My Lord has forgotten me!" (answer in 49:15–21). The key word in Jerusalem's complaint is עזב, "abandon." This is a word used very frequently in Isaiah to characterize the desolation of the land and the people because God has abandoned them. It appears in every section of the book (see *Strand*).

Jeremiah uses the term frequently of Israel abandoning God, but Isaiah uses it for God forsaking Israel. The charges are at least four: that YHWH has allowed

Strand: "Abandon" (עזב)

Prologue	Act 1	Act 2	Act 3	Act 4	Act 5	Act 6	Epilogue
1:4, 28	7:16	17:2, 9	32:14	41:17	49:14	55:7	62:4, 12
	10:3, 14	18:6		42:16	54:6, 7	58:2	63:10
		27:10				60:15	65:11

(or caused) through the Assyrian/Babylonian invasions the destruction of Canaan; that YHWH has allowed (or caused) the destruction of the kingdoms and made exiles of his people; that Israel's "cause has been disregarded by her God" (40:27); and that YHWH has allowed (or caused) the destruction of Jerusalem and his temple by "forsaking them, or forgetting them" (49:14).

In Isaiah the case against God on behalf of the people begins in 2:6, "You have abandoned your people the house of Jacob," if one follows the conventional translation, or is implied by the sharp reply of 2:6*b* if one follows my reading (see *Translation* and *Comment*). Isa 2:7 goes on to list the pagan abominations that now pollute their land. Here the people and their land are closely associated. This is said to counter an invitation for Israel to "walk in the light of YHWH" in his new temple (2:5). Israel is no longer acceptable in the use of YHWH.

In 6:10 the prophet is commissioned to

Dull the heart of this people!
Make its ears heavy
and shut its eyes,
lest it see with its eyes,
hear with its ears,
and its heart understand
and it may turn and will have healing.

Throughout the book the people's lack of understanding is related to being deaf and blind to the signs and words from God. Its punishment is based on its lack of repentance. This passage reveals that God has ordered the prophet to create the very condition that the people are accused of to prevent them from repenting and thus stopping the devastation of land and people that has now been decreed. It is no wonder that Israel in exile protests God's approach to them with the words "My way is hidden from YHWH. / My justice is disregarded by my God" (40:27*b*). The earlier references show the foundation for such a complaint. Even as it announces YHWH's salvation, 45:15 calls him "a God who hides himself."

The Vision of Isaiah sustains the charge that YHWH decreed that the land should be systematically destroyed. Chap. 6 gives the prophet's report of the decree given from the heavenly throne (6:11–13), and it is repeated twice more (10:22*b*–23; 29:22*b*). Many reports about it culminate in the description of chap. 24, specifically saying "See YHWH destroying the land and laying it waste!" Death covers the land. When the issue is raised and called a conspiracy, YHWH intervenes to demand total obedience and subservience to himself, admitting the problematic situation in the eyes of the people:

You may call YHWH of Hosts "a conspirator"!
He is your fear!
    He is your dread!
He shall become a conspiracy
    and a stone of stumbling;
a rock of offense
    for the two houses of Israel;
a trap and a snare
    for the inhabitants of Jerusalem.
Many shall be offended because of them
    and shall fall and be broken
        and shall be snared and taken captive. (8:13–15)

The prophet, who knows of the decree, decides to resign and withdraw (8:16–17) rather than deal with the problem.

YHWH does not deny the charge. Rather, he details the way this destruction is carried out (for example, chap. 34). He does defend himself by pointing beyond the destruction to the renewal of nature in a land freed of human sin (34:10*b*–35:10). God admits Jerusalem's charge again in 54:7–8 and pleads that the abandonment was temporary. But in 49:15–54:17 begins a more extended response. God protests that even in the troubled times he could not possibly forget Zion (49:15–21), that even in her bereavement she has prospered (49:19–26). He asks for evidence of the intention to divorce her (50:1*ab*) and insists that the separation was caused by her sins and unresponsiveness (50:1*c*–2*a*). He promises comfort and compassion (51:3, 12) and suggests that it was Jerusalem who forgot him (51:13). He protests that it is he who protects his people (51:22). He proclaims his comfort for Jerusalem (52:9). Thus God admits his part in Jerusalem's troubles. Although elsewhere (1:20–27; chaps 3–4) he will argue Jerusalem's guilt made cleansing and retribution necessary, in this section he simply presents himself as prepared to put that behind him and to restore and comfort the city again.

The extended prayer in 63:7–64:12 also levels charges at God. It recognizes that Israel in times past had rebelled against God and that "he turned around (to become) an enemy to them. He himself fought against them" (63:10). It asks: "Why, O YHWH did you make us stray from your ways? (Why) did you harden our hearts so as not to fear you?" (63:17*ab*). This charge that it was God himself that caused Israel to sin is answered directly in 65:1–7. The prayer continues with the charge that God no longer honors his promise of the land for the children of Abraham (63:18). It charges that God has done wonders in other ages for his people, but not this time (63:19–64:3 [64:1–2]). It charges that YHWH's restraint has allowed the destruction of Zion and the temple (64:10–12). While the prayer claims that the people are innocent and worshipful, it charges that, if there is any sin, God caused it. Chap. 1 and 65:1–7 refute this view.

In Isaiah, charges are brought against God in relation to the troubles of the Assyrian and Babylonian eras. The book, however, is not defensive on this charge. Instead, it moves aggressively to show that God was, indeed, active in bringing the armies into the land and in deliberately devastating the land, Israel, Judah, and Jerusalem because of sin on the part of Israel, Jerusalem, and the nations. He does it so that he can begin again to achieve his plans for a city and a people of his own. Thus there are good reasons to view Isaiah as a covenant disputation as well as a theodicy, a defense of God. The work admits the strangeness of God's actions (chap. 8; 28:21; 45:11).

THEMES

Bibliography

Collins, T. "A Book Called Isaiah." In *The Mantle of Elijah: The Redaction Criticism of the Prophetical Books.* Sheffield: JSOT Press, 1993. 52. **Conrad, E. W.** *Reading Isaiah.* **Davies, G. I.** "The Destiny of the Nations in the Book of Isaiah." In *Book of Isaiah.* Ed. J. Vermeylen. 119. **Dumbrell, W. J.** "The Purpose of the Book of Isaiah." *TynBul* 36 (1985) 111–12. **Jensen, J.** "YHWH's Plan in Isaiah and in the Rest of the Old Testament." *CBQ* 48 (1986) 443–55. **Motyer, J. A.** *Prophecy of Isaiah.* 31. **O'Connell, R. H.** *Concentricity and Continuity.* 18, 22. **Rendtorff, R.** "Zur Komposition des Buches Jesaja." *VT* 34 (1984) 32–96. **Roberts, J. J. M.** "Isaiah in Old Testament Theology." *Int* 36 (1982) 130–43. **Watts, J. D. W.** "The Formation of Isaiah Chap. 1: Its Context in Chaps. 1–4." In *SBLSP 1978.* Missoula, MT: Scholars Press, 1978. 1:109–20. **Wiklander, B.** *Prophecy as Literature: A Text-linguistic and Rhetorical Approach to Isaiah 2–4.* ConBOT 22. Malmö: Gleerup, 1984.

Many people have suggested that Isaiah is a book organized around a major theme or issue (see Williamson, *Book Called Isaiah,* 13–15). Oswalt says: "The central theme of the book relates to the nature and destiny of the people of God. . . . The book seeks to answer the question: How can a sinful, corrupt people become the servants of God?" (21). Dumbrell (*TynBul* 36 [1985] 112) suggests that it is "YHWH's interest in and devotion to the city of Jerusalem. . . . If the book is read as a unit there is an overmastering theme which may be said effectively to unite the whole." Roberts (*Int* 36 [1982] 131) writes: "If there is any one concept central to the whole book of Isaiah, it is the vision of YHWH as the Holy One of Israel." Jensen (*CBQ* 48 [1986] 455) observes: "In general there is little that resembles Isaiah's use of this terminology (YHWH's plan) to designate YHWH's control of history, except in Deutero-Isaiah and some other later sections of the Isaiah collection." Davies ("Destiny of the Nations," 119) writes of an overarching redactional activity by compilers "and that means above all the Jerusalem cult tradition with its cosmic and universal perspective."

There are similar paragraphs on a number of themes scattered through the Vision of Isaiah. They permeate and interact with the structures of the blocks and the books of the Vision. They may be distinguished by distinctive words *(Leitwörter)* that make up the shared vocabulary of the Vision's books.

Collins summarizes the recognition of these ideas or words: "The language of the book is dominated by a recurring set of opposing images which interact with one another: heaven and earth, light and darkness, vision and blindness, listening and deafness, service and rebellion, destruction and rebuilding, decultivation and recultivation, depopulation and repopulation, deprivation and prosperity, despondency and joy" (*Mantle of Elijah,* 52). Collins has let his rhetoric move beyond the actual listing of words or, better, word pairs. But his basic idea is correct. Conrad argues that the use of repeated words or phrases is a conscious linking of parts of the book. Rendtorff finds that words in chap. 4, such as "comfort," "the glory of the Lord," and "iniquity," are repeated in key passages in First and Third Isaiah. He surmises that the repetition of these words is used to consciously join the three parts of the book. He also traces the repetition of words like "Zion-Jerusalem," "the Holy One of Israel," and "righteousness" to show these relations between different parts of the book.

O'Connell has noted repetition of many kinds and studies its significance for the structure of various blocks as well as for the book as whole:

> The recognition of patterns of repetition among the tiers was based upon information concerning the presence and structure function of: (1) "structural delineators" such as superscriptions, formulaic introductions and conclusions, and changes of person, addressee, point of view, subject matter, referent, disposition, or discourse mode; (2) "corresponding devices" such as internal allusions, cross referencing, repetitions (of key terms, subject matter, themes, imagery, modes, type-scenes, or recognized form-critical sub genres), collocation, inclusio, paneling, frameworking, or concentric patterning; (3) "developmental devices" such as the development of *Leitwörter,* varied restatements of subject matter, theme, mode or scenarios, and permutations of recognizable formal structures. (*Concentricity and Continuity,* 22)

I have not found as much possibility of discerning structure through the patterns of repetition in corresponding devices as O'Connell has. I think his concentricity study for chaps. 4–12 is credible but would argue that chaps. 2 and 3 should be included. I do not find his work on chaps. 13–39 credible or useful. His work on chaps. 55–66 is very credible and useful, more so than that on chaps. 40–54. My study is more concerned simply to show that the composition of the various acts (or blocks) proceeded simultaneously, with a view of creating the larger Vision. Although they are independent and can be studied that way, they are intentionally linked through the repetition of themes and vocabulary to show that they belong to the same larger work. I have tended to give greater significance to the structural delineators in determining the boundaries of books (blocks) and the internal structure (i.e., the "in that day" endings, the superscriptions, the changes from first to third person in the narrative [esp. between chaps. 7 and 6/8]).

This study will recognize the way distinctive vocabulary is spread through the book and the strands of passages that build on that vocabulary. Sometimes a reading of Isaiah seems like observing a mosaic made up of many little units, each of its own color, design, and character. These can be classified and grouped, but they do not carry a continuous message. Motyer (31) writes:

> Would he [Isaiah] search for a unifying principle and use all this God-given material to elucidate it? . . . His [Isaiah's] method is described as that of a "mosaic" in which stones from differing points of origin and with individual prehistories are brought into a new integration so that it is now not the prehistory but the new design that is significant. The whole book is a huge mosaic in which totally pre-exilic material is made to serve pre-exilic, post-exilic and eschatological purposes. . . . Our task is to take this mosaic-editing seriously.

There are some composed blocks of material (chaps. 7–12; 13–27; 28–33; 36–39; 41–48; 49–54; 55–59). There are some strands of material that follow on in succeeding blocks. But there are also small units that appear in the text without connection to others. They make their contribution on their own. They fit the mosaic description as the small colored stones: 1:2–3; 1:27–28; 1–29–31; 4:2–6; 8:19–22; and so on. To show these designs I will isolate some of the words that designate the platelets or threads and group them in ways that will show the grand picture.

The major themes of the plot are developed around central motifs. A sketch of these was given in my 1978 paper ("Formation of Isaiah Chap. 1"), which is partially reproduced here.

The first motif is represented by an interesting group of words in 1:3, *know* and *understand.* The people are accused of lacking these, and the verses imply amazement that this is so. Vv 18–19 use different but related words: *reasoning together, being willing,* and *hearing (being obedient).* In vv 25–27, the word *turn* is used three times. Isa 6:9–10 adds the word *see* but omits the words *be willing* and *reason together.* The appearance of the other words together (*know, understand, hear, see,* and *turn*) seemed reason enough to wonder at their appearance in chap. 1. So the concordance was used by R. L. Lambert to determine their appearance in other parts of Isaiah. The result is interesting. Groups of at least three of these words *(know, understand, hear, see, turn)* together appear in the following locations: 5:20–21; 6:9–10; 28:9; 29:11–18, 21–24; 30:9–10, 15, 19–20, 30; 32:3–4; 33:13–20; 37:3–9, 17–20; 38:5–8; 39:1–5; 40:13–14, 21, 28; 41:20–23, 26, 28–29; 42:16–18, 22–25; 43:9–13; 44:1–2, 8–9; 45:2–6, 20–23; 47:10–11; 48:5–8, 12–20; 49:5–7, 18–26; 50:4, 7, 10; 51:7; 52:6–8, 14–15; 53:1–3, 10–11; 55:2–3, 5, 7, 10; 56:10–11; 57:17–18; 58:2–4; 60:2–5, 16–18; 61:9; 63:15–17; 64:3; 66:4–5, 8, 14–15, 19 (cf. R. L. Lambert, "A Contextual Study of YD' in the Book of Isaiah," diss., Fuller Theological Seminary, 1982). Even this rough list is startling, suggesting (on this point at least) a closer relation of chaps. 1 and 6 to chapters after 28 than to chapters before it.

A second motif relates to Israel/Jacob and punishment; this appears in 1:3–7; 2:6–8; 5:25; 7:7–9; 9:8–21; 17:4–11; 22:3–4; 28:1–8, 9–18; 40:27; 41:8–24; 42:24–25; 43:1–7; 43:22–24; 43:27–28; 45:9; 46:3; 47:6; 48:1; 49:1–4; 58:1–14; 59:1–19; 63:10–13; 65:1–7. The continuation of this motif through the book is noteworthy.

A third motif relates to the purging of Jerusalem's sin and is depicted in 1:8–17; 1:21–31; 3:1; 4:4; 22:8–14; 29:1–10; 30:20; 31:4–9; 32:9–20; 33:14–24; 40:2; 48:9; 49:8–13; 49:14–21; 50:1–3; 52:3–6; 52:7–10; 52:11–12; 62:1–12; 64:11; 65:8; 66:8. The fact that the Jacob/Israel motif and the purging of Jerusalem motif alternate throughout the book of Isaiah just as they do in chap. 1 is worthy of note in any analysis of the book's structure.

A fourth major motif is the picture of an exalted Jerusalem. The motif owes much to royal Zion traditions. It occurs in 2:2–4; 4:5–6; 8:3–7; 10:12, 24–27; 12:6; 14:32; 18:7; 22:22; 25:6–7; 26:1–6; 28:16; 30:19; 31:4–9; 33:5, 20–22; 34:8; 35:10; 37:33–35; 38:6; 40:9–11; 51:11–16; 52:1–3; 59:20; 60:1–14, 15–22; 61:1–11; 65:18–19; 66:10–14. A picture of ideal conditions often accompanies these promises of the exalted Zion.

There are also a number of secondary motifs that are important. The unique invitation of 1:18–20 has counterparts in 2:5, 24:15, and 31:6; a cluster in chaps. 41–44; and strong elements in 55:1–3, 6–7. The announcements of YHWH's exclusive exaltation and of "humankind's" humiliation (linked with references to idolatry) occur at intervals throughout the book. Citing these instances is enough to demonstrate how threads of meaning, apparent in these first chapters, are a distinctive part of the book's tapestry.

Excursus: Parallels between Isaiah and the Psalms

Bibliography

Begrich, J. *Studien zu Deuterojesaja.* BWANT 4.25. Stuttgart: Kohlhammer, 1938. **Berges, U.** "Die Armen im Buch Jesaja: Ein Beitrag zur Literaturgeschichte des AT." *Bib* 80 (1999) 153–77. ———. "Die Knechte im Psalter: Ein Beitrag zu seiner Kompositionsgeschichte." *Bib* 81 (2000) 53–78. **Creach, J.** "The Shape of Book Four of the Psalter and the Shape of Second Isaiah." *JSOT* 80 (1998) 63–76. **Gillingham, S.** "From Liturgy to Prophecy: The Use of Psalmody in Second Temple Judaism." *CBQ* 64 (2002) 470–489. **Lokfink, N., and E. Zenger.** *Der Gott der Völker: Untersuchungen zum Jesajabuch und zu den Psalmen.* SBS 154. Stuttgart: Katholisches Bibelwork, 1994.

Interpreters have long noted that the writer(s) of Isaiah share similar language, themes, and forms with the Psalmists. Isaiah's style and contents are often lyric or psalmlike. The book of Isaiah even contains some complete psalms. Recent works have documented the extent of this convergence.

Similar language appears in many Psalms and verses from Isaiah:

The futility of idols	Isa 2:8//Ps 115:4
God's judgment on Israel his vineyard	Isa 5:5–6//Ps 80:12
Thanksgiving for deliverance	Isa 12:1//Ps 9:1
	Isa 12:2//Ps 118:14
	Isa 12:3//Ps 105:1
	Isa 12:5//Ps 98:1
Hymnic forms	Isa 24:14–16; 25:1–5; 26:1–6
The self-deceit of the wicked	Isa 29:15//Ps 10:11, 13
The just and righteous ruler	Isa 32:1//Ps 72:1–2

Isaiah uses eschatological hymns of praise: 42:10–13; 44:23; 45:8; 49:13. J. Begrich *(Studien zu Deuterojesaja)* compared these to the kingship and enthronement psalms: Pss 93, 95–99. Creach (*JSOT* 80 [1998] 63–76) cites parallels with the enthronement Psalms and Isa 40:10; 44:23; 49:13; 55:12.

U. Berges (*Bib* 80 [1999] 153–77; *Bib* 81 [2000] 53–78) has studied the common use of the phrase "servants of YHWH" in Isaiah and Psalms (see *Excursus: The Servants of YHWH* and strand chart in introduction to 54:17*c*–61:11). Note that the Psalms speak of "the poor" more often than Isaiah does, but both Isa 54:17–66:14 and the Psalms speak of the "servants of YHWH." Berges notes a third common subject: "Zion theology."

Isa 57:15//Ps 34:18	God protector of the contrite and brokenhearted
Isa 58:10//Ps 85:13	"righteousness will go before him"
Isa 59:1–21	a combination of lament and oracle of deliverance
Isa 60:1–62:12	"fuses together hymnic forms with prophetic intercession.
Isa 60:21//Ps 37:11, 22	promise of inheritance of land to the faithful

Isa 60:(9), 11//Ps 72:(10), 11	the bringing of the wealth of nations
Isa 64:1–2//Ps 18:7, 9	mountains quake and God comes
Isa 64:12//Ps 74:10–11	the silence and absence of God
Isa 65:24//Ps 91:15	God answers the call of prayer

Excursus: Day of YHWH/Divine Warrior

Bibliography

Alomía, M. "El Mesías Victorioso: Isaías 63:1–6." *Theo* 14 (1999) 6–37. **Christensen, D. L.** "Transformations of the War Oracle." In *Old Testament Prophecy: Studies in the Oracles against the Nations.* HDR 3. Missoula, MT: Scholars Press, 1975. 127–53. **Conrad, E. W.** "The Lord's Military Strategy." In *Reading Isaiah.* Minneapolis: Fortress, 1991. 52–82. **Craigie, P. C.** *The Problem of War in the Old Testament.* Grand Rapids, MI: Eerdmans, 1978. **Fredriksson, H.** *Jahwe als Krieger: Studien zum alttestamentlichen Gottesbild.* Lund: Gleerup, 1945. **Gottwald, N. K.** "Holy War." *IDBSup.* 942. **Hobbs, T. R.** *A Time for War: A Study of Warfare in the Old Testament.* Wilmington, DE: Glazier, 1989. 219–22. **Kang, S.-M.** *Divine War in the Old Testament and the Ancient Near East.* Berlin: De Gruyter, 1989. **Kegler, J.** "Prophetic Speech about the Future." In *The Meaning of Peace: Biblical Studies.* Ed. P. G. Yoder and W. M. Swartley. Louisville: Westminster John Knox, 1992. 69–109. **Lind, M. C.** *YHWH Is a Warrior: The Theology of Warfare in Ancient Israel.* Scottdale, PA: Herald, 1980 (lacking a section on the prophets). **Longman, T.,** and **D. G. Reid.** *God Is a Warrior.* Grand Rapids, MI: Zondervan, 1995. **Miles, J.** *God: A Biography.* New York: Random House, 1995. **Niditch, S.** *War in the Hebrew Bible: A Study in the Ethics of Violence.* Oxford: Oxford UP, 1993. **Rad, G. von.** *Holy War in Ancient Israel.* Trans. M. J. Dawn. Grand Rapids, MI: Eerdmans, 1991. 101–8. Originally published as *Der Heilige Krieg im alten Israel,* 3d ed. (Göttingen: Vandenhoeck & Ruprecht, 1958). **Schwally, F.** *Der heilige Krieg im alten Testament.* Leipzig: Dietrich, 1901. **Smend, R.** *YHWH War and Tribal Confederation.* Nashville: Abingdon, 1970. **Steck, O.-H.** "The Jerusalem Conceptions of Peace and Their Development in the Prophets of Ancient Israel." In *The Meaning of Peace: Biblical Studies.* Ed. P. G. Yoder and W. M. Swartley. Louisville: Westminster John Knox, 1992. 49–68. **Stuart, D.** "The Sovereign's Day of Conquest." *BASOR* 221 (1976) 159–64. **Weippert, M.** "'Heiligerkrieg in Israel und Assyrien." *ZAW* 84 (1972) 460–93.

The subject of holy war in the Old Testament has received considerable attention since Gerhard von Rad wrote about its appearance in Deuteronomy. In holy war, YHWH fights for his people and leads them in war. The theme applies particularly to Israel's occupation of the Holy Land (Exodus-Joshua) and defense of the land against intruders (Judges-Samuel).

Susan Niditch's book *(War in the Hebrew Bible)* deals with many ideologies of warfare and draws on contemporary cross-disciplinary discussions. But she hardly touches on the Latter Prophets and the particular issues of YHWH's participation in warfare that they present.

Conrad's treatment *(Reading Isaiah)* of YHWH's military strategy deals much more with Isaiah's ideas, as do several other writers. Miles *(God)* has noted that there was a phase in YHWH's career when he is depicted as an active soldier, the military period. Christensen ("Transformations") notes that a biblical writer collected a group of poems under the title "the wars of YHWH" (Num 21:14). Alomía (*Theo* 14 [1999] 637) shows how OT texts (Josh 5:13–15; 2 Sam 5:17–25; 2 Chron 14:9–14; Ps 2) "portray YHWH as a heavenly warrior who intervenes on behalf of his people and overthrows their enemies." Gen 49:8–12, Isa 34:5–8, and Rev 19:11–15 "describe YHWH and Jesus

Christ respectively as trampling their enemies under foot as one treads grapes." In this respect the Scriptures parallel what other ancient Near Eastern texts and iconography say about their gods.

YHWH's appearance as a Divine Warrior is different in Isaiah. The primary image of YHWH is that of the Divine King of Heaven. As king he has various roles to play. In relation to Israel, he is a father with Israelites as his children. In relation to the nations, he is the supreme emperor ruling over all of them. As such he decides their fates. He is also able to muster their armies for wars to suit his purposes.

God assembles the armies of the nations in persistent warfare to demolish "the whole land." This includes the countries of Palestine, Mesopotamia, and Egypt, that is, the Fertile Crescent of which Israel and Judah are so much a part. This warfare is historically dated to the time of the Assyrian, Babylonian, and Persian periods (late eighth century to fifth century B.C.E.). The time boundaries of the period are noted exactly: from the death year of Uzziah, ca. 735 (6:1), to the coming of Cyrus to Babylon in 539 B.C.E. (chaps. 44–45). Isaiah shows God assuming other roles before and after that period. A major part of the Vision's purpose is to interpret that period, or to interpret God in that period.

Duane Christensen (*Deuteronomy,* WBC 5A [Dallas: Nelson, 1999] 449–50), in commenting on holy-war ideology, cites Paul's teaching concerning spiritual warfare (Eph 6:11–17; 2 Cor 10:3–4) and thinks of the passages that speak of God at war as extensions of the holy-war teaching in Deuteronomy. He mentions also a modern version of it in the *Star Wars* movie trilogy, which pictures an ultimate struggle between good and evil. But in the NT and afterward, the picture of the struggle between good and evil is inherently dualistic. God's realm and Satan's realm are different and struggle against each other. This concept already has a strong hold when Paul is writing.

The OT view is different. There is only one divine power. That is YHWH-God. He battles, but not against spiritual superpowers. His battles are against kings and nations. He battles for the soul of his people. In Exodus, Numbers, Deuteronomy, Joshua, and Judges he rallies the people against peoples and nations that threaten them. In Isaiah he rallies the nations in the great battles that bring an end to an era of culture and economy in "the land" of the Middle East. In doing so he brings judgment on Israel, Judah, and the other nations, including Egypt, Assyria, and especially Babylon. But there is no great spiritual power (Satan) opposing him. There is no great heavenly struggle behind the earthly wars. The book uses supernatural and mythical ideas (such as the "Shining One," which LXX translates as Lucifer [14:12] and Leviathan [27:1]) to depict historical realities, such as Babylon and Babylon's king. But YHWH's battle is clearly against Babylon and the system she and Egypt represent. Jeremiah calls Egypt Rahab in the same sense (Jer 30:7; Ps 87:4). In each case the nation is the primary reality, the mythical monsters only secondary.

The actions ending the prevalence of death (Isa 25:7–8; 26:19; Rev 21:4) are very different, involving divine decree rather than struggle and victory. The NT depiction of overcoming death through the resurrection of Christ does involve struggle and victory, and Satan is clearly an adversary.

This major topic of divine warfare is introduced in Isa 2. It is the Day of YHWH against everything that is proud and lifted up: person, city, or nation. This strand of passages gives the book a distinctive part of its flavor, its tone. God's conflict with "his children" and his determination to raise the mountain of his house spill over into a scenario that draws in the great powers of the day in mortal conflict that will go on for generations.

YHWH's military authority begins with his command of the heavenly armies (hosts). He bears the title יהוה צבאות, "YHWH of Armies (Hosts)," which appears often in conjunction with the Day of YHWH and with YHWH's plans for the nations. (See the following *Strands: Divine-Warrior Passages in Isaiah, "YHWH of Hosts"* [יהוה צבאות], *"The Day of YHWH"* [יום יהוה], and *"In That Day"* [ביום ההוא].)

Isa 1:1–4:6. Isa 2:9–22 enumerates a list of Israel's sins, which are seen as examples of the way that humankind is degraded. The passage announces a day that YHWH of Hosts has in store for all the proud and the mighty.

Strand: Divine-Warrior Passages in Isaiah

Prologue	Act 1	Act 2	Act 3	Act 4	Act 5	Act 6	Epilogue
1:24 2:19–11, 21	5:26–29 7:17–20 8:7–8 9:4–5 10:6–12, 17–19, 23, 26–34 12:5	13:2–5, 11–13, 17–22 14:22–23, 24–27 19:1–15 23:9, 11–12 24:1, 15, 21–22 25:6–7, 9–12 26:11, 15–16, 20–21 27:1, 7–9	28:23 29:2–8 30:27–33 31:4–5, 8–9 33:10–12	34:1–35:4 37:29, 35 40:10, 15–17, 23–24 41:2–5, 11–16, 25 42:1–7, 13–15, 24–25 43:3*b*, 6–13, 14–16 44:26*b*– 45:3, 13–14 46:10–13 47:5–15 48:5	49:8–12, 22–26 51:9–10, 13*b*–16, 22–23 52:10, 12*b* 54:11–17	59:15*b*–20	63:1–7 64:1–3, 12 66:14*b*–16

Strand: "YHWH of Hosts" (יהוה צבאות)

Prologue	Act 1	Act 2	Act 3	Act 4	Act 5	Act 6	Epilogue
1:24 2:12 3:1	5:9 8:13, 18 9:13, 19 10:23, 24, 26, 33	13:4, 13 14:22, 23, 24, 27 17:37 18:7 19:4, 16, 17, 18, 20, 25 21:10 22:5, 12, 14, 15, 25 23:9 25:6, 8, 23	28:5, 16, 29 29:6, 15 31:5	37:16, 32 39:5 40:10	50:4, 5, 7, 9 51:15, 22 52:4 54:5	56:8 61:11	65:13, 15

Isa 5:1–12:6. After a passage dealing with Israel's sins and YHWH's consequent anger, Isa 5:25–30 pictures YHWH as a general assembling his armies from many nations for a strike on the land (of Palestine). In 7:17–24, YHWH brings the Assyrians into Israel and Judah in a terrible invasion. Isa 10:5–19 portrays YHWH dealing with Assyria, which has exceeded its mandate for battle on that day. YHWH's triumphant march through Palestine appears in 10:24–34. Within this picture of YHWH as Divine Warrior, 11:11–16 depicts him using his military might to bring back the captives from Assyria and Egypt. The "in that day" formula fits this mode. It appears at the beginning of five passages (10:20; 11:10, 11; 12:1, 4).

Strand: "The Day of YHWH" (יום יהוה)

PROLOGUE	ACT 1	ACT 2	ACT 3	ACT 4	ACT 5	ACT 6	EPILOGUE
2:12		13:6, 9, 13 22:5		34:8	(49:8)	(61:2)	(63:4)

Isa 13:1–19:25. This segment begins with a Divine Warrior passage (13:2–5) that blends into a Day of the Lord passage (13:6–16). This, in turn, introduces a burden against Babylon and other nations. Isa 17:12–14 shows the international tumult of that day. YHWH single-handedly overcomes Egypt (19:1–15), which leads to the results pictured by "in that day" passages (19:16–17; 19:18; 19:19–22; 19:23; 19:24–25).

Strand: "In That Day" (ביום ההוא)

PROLOGUE	ACT 1	ACT 2	ACT 3	ACT 4	ACT 5	ACT 6	EPILOGUE
2:11, 17, 20 3:7, 18 4:1, 2	5:30 7:18, 20, 21, 23 10:20, 27 11:10, 11 12:1, 4	17:4, 7, 9 19:15, 18, 19, 21, 23, 24 20:6 22:5, 8, 12, 20, 25 23:15 24:21 25:9 26:1 27:1, 2, 12, 13	28:5 29:18 29:23 31:7				

Isa 20:1–27:13. These chapters portray reactions to the Day of YHWH. There is no question of who is responsible for the devastation (23:9; 17–18): it is YHWH who is devastating the land (24:1–3). "In that day" passages structure much of the section (24:21–23; 25:9–12; 26:1–19; 27:1; 27:2–11; 27:12; 27:13).

Isa 28:1–33:24. Isa 29:1–8 pictures YHWH's siege of Jerusalem. Isa 30:27–33 shows the Divine Warrior in action against the nations and particularly against Assyria. Isa 31:4–5 pictures the Divine Warrior in battle to protect Jerusalem, and 33:10–13 portrays the Divine Warrior's announcement that he is about to do battle.

Isa 34:1–49:4. The theme does not play a major role here. Isa 34:1–17 is YHWH's campaign against Edom. Isa 40:1–2 pictures the triumphant sovereign taking steps to bring normality to a people who have suffered through his wars.

Isa 49:5–61:11. The theme does not play an explicit role in these chapters. YHWH's work is being carried out through his servant. But the servant (50:4, 5, 7, 9) makes repeated reference to instructions and help from YHWH of Hosts. The appeal for intervention by "the Arm of YHWH" (51:9–11) is answered by assurances that YHWH of Hosts is the one who comforts Jerusalem (51:15, 22; 52:4; 54:5).

Isa 62:1–66:24. Isa 63:1–6 reviews the wars of YHWH, in which he claims that none of the nations helped him. He acted alone. He "trampled the nations." The Warrior returns home from the wars only to face the domestic problems among his own peoples. Chap. 66 speaks of judgment, but not in "day of YHWH" style.

Tremendous changes are taking place in the political life of the Near East as imperial power makes itself felt in every nook and cranny of the region. The lives of the people of Israel and Jerusalem are affected. They can never be the same. Isaiah insists that God has a hand in this and that even the violence moves to achieve his purposes. The Day of YHWH strand both emphasizes the historical setting of the prophecy in the troubled eighth to the sixth centuries when repeated wars and campaigns ravaged Palestine and gives the whole an apocalyptic, end of the world, tone. Not since the Exodus and the occupation of Canaan has YHWH been pictured as directly interfering in the military affairs of nations, and not again until the very "end times."

Effect and Affect

Violence has two effects: First, property is damaged or destroyed, and people are injured or killed. The result may be major changes in social and political institutions. YHWH assembles and leads great armies (5:26–30). He brings the Assyrian hordes on Palestine, including Judah (7:17–25), resulting in the destruction of cities, villages, and farms. He changes the political map of Palestine. These are clear and measurable effects. Second, violence has an effect on the emotions and spirits of the people involved. It may bring anxiety, fear, despair, loss of hope, or other negative emotions. This is the affective result of war. The Day of YHWH is both effective and affective. As Isa 1:5 says, "every head (is) for sores [effect] and every stomach (is) cramped [affect]." But the day is intended to deal with attitudes also: "The eyes of the haughtiness of humankind shall be humbled" (2:11), "and the haughtiness of the human shall be brought down, and the exaltation of persons shall be abased, and YHWH alone shall be exalted in that day" (2:17). In 8:19–22, the demoralized population grasps at straws. This interplay between effect and affect is a major issue in 9:8–21.

Chap. 13 begins with the announcement of YHWH's assembling the armies (vv 2–5). Its effect is destruction (v 6a), but the poetry turns immediately to the affect (vv 6*b*–7): "Therefore, all hands are feeble, and every moral heart is faint." The goal of the effect—"to make the earth a desolation, its sinners to be destroyed from it. For the stars of the heavens and their constellations do not give light. The sun is dark in its rising, and the moon does not produce its light" (vv 9*b*–10)—is to "stop the arrogance of the proud and the haughtiness of the terrible" (11*b*).

Affect and effect continue to alternate through chaps. 13–19, which portray the results of YHWH's rallying the armies against Babylon. These have dealt with the devastating effects of the wars. But they have tended to move toward the effect on morale, the affective result of the wars. Finally they reached a point where the military action was no longer necessary. The fear of YHWH's actions were enough to achieve submission.

In chaps. 20–27 the description of effects, the acts of destruction, disappears altogether. Only the affects, the fears, anxieties, and terrors, remain. The nervous prophet of chap. 20 gives way to ominous "burdens" in chaps. 21–23. The sense of devastation reaches its culmination in chap. 24: "YHWH (is) destroying the land and laying it waste" (v 1). That is the effect. It affects everyone: priest and people, master and servant, mistress and maid, seller and buyer, lender and borrower, creditor and debtor (v 2). Affectively, the land is dead. There is no hope. What can be said? What can be done?

The Day of YHWH also has a positive goal. These results, effective and affective, are presented in ten "in that day" units. The contrast between YHWH's announcement of good news and the totally demoralized population is found in 24:14–22. The signs of a positive turn are noted by the people of the west and the east and the coastlands (24:14–16*a*). The prophet ("I") cannot accept it (24:16–22). But the positive turn will not be stilled: "May even the moon be ashamed and the sun be abashed! For YHWH of Hosts reigns on Mount Zion and in Jerusalem before his elders in glory" (24:23). This brings a change of heart from the prophet ("I"; 25:1–5). YHWH's actions will be to destroy "the death (which) endures forever" (25:6–8) and bring exiles from Assyria and Egypt to come and worship on the holy mountain in Jerusalem (27:13). Fear and death will be replaced with joy, trust, and life.

Excursus: Isaiah's Worldview

Bibliography

Barker, M. "Beyond the Veil of the Temple: The High Priestly Origins of the Apocalypses." *SJT* 51 (1998) 1–21. ———. *The Older Testament.* London: SPCK, 1987. **Mettinger, T. N. D.** *In Search of God: The Meaning and Message of the Everlasting Names.* Trans. F. H. Cryer. Philadelphia: Fortress, 1988. **Murray, R.** *The Cosmic Covenant: Biblical Themes of Justice, Peace and the Integrity of Creation.* London: Sheed & Ward, 1992. **Ollenburger, B. C. E.** *Zion, the City of the Great King.* Sheffield: Sheffield Academic Press, 1987.

The Latter Prophets share with many psalms a distinctive view of reality in which YHWH is king of heavens and earth. His throne is in heaven, but he also reigns in Zion's temple. As king, he controls history, using the Davidic king as his instrument and surrogate ruler. He is responsible for creation, for the world's stability and order (Ps 93:1). In times of chaos the earth shakes and the nations rebel (Ps 110:4, 8, 10–14).

This is the concept of reality that supports Isaiah. YHWH is the king of heaven. He is pictured on his throne in chaps. 6 and 40. From there he makes decrees that apply to Israel and to the world. The king plays other roles as well. He is "father" to Israel

(1:2–3), a role that evolves into a "lord/servant" relation (42–54; 63:7–65:16). He is a military commander over the armies of the nations (13:1–5; 63:1–6).

When this arrangement, what Murray calls "the cosmic covenant," is in place, peace, prosperity, justice, and righteousness prevail in an ordered society in countries, cities, villages, and cultivated fields. The righteous king reigns supreme. All nature and history, in heaven and on earth, are in order. But when the arrangement is dislocated by rebellion and sin or by God's judgments in reaction to them, all chaos breaks loose. The earth shakes, the heavens rain fire, rains cease or floods prevail, and the political order falls apart, resulting in wars. In Isaiah and the Psalms these events occur, not on the initiative of "the enemy" but in answer to God's decree that all become desolate. When sin and rebellion reach a certain point, God withdraws the controlling powers and allows chaos to have its way (cf. Gen. 6).

When the poets/dramatists of Isaiah composed this epic work, they drew on all the resources of Zion theology and mythological pictures of chaos. They understood that YHWH is in control of the period of wars and devastation that occurred in Palestine during the Assyrian and Babylonian periods (ca. 840–540 B.C.E.). This is not a picture of YHWH being pressed by his enemies. It is a picture of YHWH's responses to a situation in which Israel, Jerusalem, and the peoples of "the land" had pressed their own sins, violence, and rebellion against YHWH and his rule to the point that demanded a response.

That response was a divine decree (6:11–12; 10:23; 13:5*b;* 28:22*b*) calling for the destruction/devastation of the entire land, its peoples, its institutions, its economic and political structures, its cities, and its villages. It marked the end of an era, an age (עולם), as surely and as definitely as that marked by the Flood (Gen 6). Israel's entire history, from Abraham through the reign of Zedekiah, had been within that age in which Egypt and the Mesopotamian powers (Assyria or Babylon) were the "great powers" under whom the Palestinian kingdoms came into being and flourished. This was being brought to an end. Judaism would replace the Israelite kingdoms. The Persian powers were beginning a new age with a totally different kind of orientation. Isaiah's point is that this new world is as much under the rule of God (YHWH) as the old one had been and that YHWH willed Israel and Jerusalem to have significant places in it. The Apostle Paul makes the same point about Rome (Rom 13:1–6).

But the "worldview" remains the same. God rules from heaven. This beneficent rule makes possible nature's ordered ways and society's structures. When humanity's ways diverge from God's requirements of justice and righteousness too much, this arrangement may well be annulled. God makes a clean sweep of things and starts anew. He did this in Noah's time. Isaiah shows that he did this again during the Assyrian/Babylonian period. The Persian period, and Judaism's place in it, is a new start, a new age. Like Noah's new beginning (Gen 9:20–28; 11:1–9), Jerusalem's new beginning has its problems (Isa 66).

M. Barker (in her presidential address to The Society for Old Testament Study in its 1998 Winter Meeting; *JTS* [1998] 1–21) spoke of the veil of the temple that separated the "Holy of Holies" from the "the Holy Place" (Exod 26:33). "It separated eternity from the visible, material world. When the high priest entered the the Holy of Holies, he entered eternity and was able to know all history, past and future." She went on to say: "This accounts for the characteristic subject matter of apocalypses: the throne, overviews of history and the secrets of creation. . . . Consideration of style and vocabulary shows that these ideas underlie Isaiah 40 and also Plato's *Timaeus.*"

This sense of being between God's eternal realm and the earthly realities of time and history permeates all of the book of Isaiah, even if the exact imagery of the prophet being taken into the very throne room of God during his vision in the temple (chap. 6) only occurs in that one place. The book presents YHWH speaking with his aids, Heavens and Earth, concerning his relations with Israel, his children *(1:2–3).*

And then it goes on from there. Barker spoke of this understanding originating in "the high priestly knowledge" of the first temple. Isaiah contains a prophetic adaptation of the concept. Isa 2:2–4 shows the close connection that the temple had to the idea of connecting heaven (eternity) with earth. YHWH makes his earthy dwelling there. He rules from there and makes decisions there (24:23*bc;* 25:6–8).

The book of Isaiah exists on the boundary that separates eternity from the visible, material, and historical world. The book of Isaiah allows the reader to share this particular perspective that the high priest and the prophet enjoyed: to stand between eternity and time, between heaven and earth, between God's knowledge and word and the bitter realities of historical existence.

PURPOSE

The Vision of Isaiah is written for Jews of the early postexilic community. It is intended to orient them to their past and prepare them for the changes that are inherent in their position within the new Persian Empire. It thinks of this new time as a new age, very different from the previous age ("the former times") and calls for a different understanding of the relation of YHWH to his people and to his city.

Other literary models for this age are in circulation. They include Deuteronomy and the Deuteronomic History (Former Prophets of the Hebrew Bible). The prophetic books of Jeremiah and Ezekiel are already in existence. Another work with a similar perspective to Isaiah, the Book of the Twelve (Minor) Prophets, is contemporary with Isaiah. The promulgation of the Torah in its full priestly form by Ezra is still some years off. These visions of what this age should be like for the Jews compete for attention and support. Eventually all of them will play significant parts in the development of Jewish Scripture, thought, and life, even though the results may tend to fragment the Jewish community. The acceptance of all of them into the new Scriptures provides the basis for acceptance and participation by the varied constituencies that they each represent.

Isaiah works to redefine the terms *Israel* and *Jacob* for an age of dispersion and change. The new people of YHWH will not be defined by ethnic origin or geographical location but by their devotion, their adherence to YHWH and his temple. Jerusalem/Zion can no longer be the capital of a country. It is understood as the "mountain of YHWH," the temple city where YHWH dwells on earth, where pilgrims can approach and worship him. It is to be the source for authoritative teaching about him and concerning his will for the lives of his people (2:3). The temple is no longer the royal chapel of the king; it has become the gathering place of YHWH-worshipers from everywhere. It is the unifying symbol (along with the Torah) of the new people of YHWH.

The Vision of Isaiah as Theology

Bibliography

Baltzer, K. "Deutero-Isaiah's Theology." In *Deutero-Isaiah: A Commentary.* Trans. M. Kohl. Ed. P. Machinist. Hermeneia. Minneapolis: Fortress, 2001. 33–46. **Steck, O. H.** *Die Prophetenbücher und ihr theologischen Zeugnis: Wege der Nachfrage und Fährten zur Antwort.* Tübingen: Mohr (Siebeck), 1996. **Vriezen, T. V.** "Essentials of the Theology of Isaiah."

In *Israel's Prophetic Heritage.* Ed. B. W. Anderson and W. Harrelson. New York: Harper Bros., 1962. 128–46.

The Vision identifies YHWH as Israel's former covenant partner. But it goes on to show that the covenant has come under judgment and no longer applies, and it recognizes his continued will to deal with Israel in his new age. Emphasizing YHWH's position as patron of Jerusalem, it teaches that he will continue to use Zion and make it his residence, the place where he will meet the peoples.

YHWH is seen as the true God of humankind. As in Gen 1–11, he stands in judgment over human pride and ambition (cf. Isa 2:9–22 and passim). He also is master of life and death for all the people of the land (cf. especially chaps. 24–26).

The core of the Vision's theological message, however, is that YHWH is the Lord of History. He calls and dismisses the nations. He determines their destinies. He divides the ages and determines the eventual courses of humanity. When the people of Israel in exile doubt God's ability to help them, he cites his role in creation. He contrasts his own immense capacities with the minuscule size of planets and stars, which are but dust. He reduces time by citing his control of all time. And he insists that he, the Creator, the Lord of History, and Israel's God who calls to it, are one and the same (chaps. 40–44).

YHWH's Strategy

Bibliography

Boer, P. A. H. de. "The Counselor." In *Wisdom in Israel and the Ancient Near East.* VTSup 3. Leiden: Brill, 1955. **Brueggemann, W.** "Planned People/Planned Book." In *Writing and Reading.* Ed. C. C. Broyles and C. A. Evans. 1:19–37. **Conrad, E.** *Reading Isaiah.* 52–82. **Fichtner, J.** "Jahwes Plan in der Botschaft des Jesaja." *ZAW* 63 (1951) 16–33. Reprinted in *Gottes Weisheit: Gesammelte Studien zum Alten Testament,* Arbeiten zur Theologie 2.3 (Stuttgart: Calwer, 1965) 27–43. **Vriezen, T.** "Essentials of the Theology of Isaiah." In *Israel's Prophetic Heritage.* Ed. B. W. Anderson and W. Harrelson. 128–46, esp. 142–46. **Werner, W.** *Studien zur alttestamentlichen Vorstellung von Plan YHWHs.* BZAW 173. Berlin: De Gruyter, 1988. **Wildberger, H.** "Jesajas Verstandnis der Geschichte" In *Congress Volume: Bonn.* VTSup 9. Leiden: Brill, 1963. 83–117.

The Vision purports to reveal the עצה, "strategy," that has determined God's actions and relationships for some three centuries prior to the writing of the drama. עצה/יעץ can be used in the sense of advice given (cf. De Boer, "Counselor") like that of Ahithophel to Absalom (2 Sam 15–17) or of the elders to Rehoboam (1 Kgs 12:6–28). The words are used in Isa 40–48 to deny YHWH's need for such a counselor (40:13, 14; 41:28; 44:26; 45:21; 47:13). A similar meaning can be found in chaps. 1–39.

Beyond that, there is throughout the Vision of Isaiah an argument that YHWH has a plan (a strategy) that he is following, which is being fulfilled, and which Israel should recognize and accept. Three times this is explicitly expounded. Each time עצה/יעץ is used to define the strategy: 14:24–27 speaks of the Assyrian; 19:12–17 relates to the defeat of Egypt and Tyre; 46:10–11 speaks of the role of Cyrus. The Assyrian conquests (and fall) and the Persian rise to power under Cyrus are the historical pillars of YHWH's strategy in Isaiah's Vision. But it is

Zion and Israel that are called to play the key roles in the plan. How can it be that Assyria and Persia possess the political might and authority while Israel and Zion are called to be the more important elements in the age to come? That is the theme of the entire Vision.

The idea of God's control over events is common in the prophets and the OT. The use of עצה to describe God's plan occurs elsewhere (cf. Fichtner, *Gottes Weishheit,* 28–29). This conviction expresses a basic prophetic axiom, as Fichtner (*Gottes Weisheit,* 27) describes:

> It is the mark of all genuine prophetic proclamation that they see and interpret the present in relation to the past and the approaching march of time, that they more or less clearly follow and extend the lines, which for the eyes of the prophets become visible from the origins of the people with its God through the now into the immediately imminent to come. God stands in the center of his view of history as the one who is acting. He has a goal in what he does. He is following a plan. Knowledge of these facts stands basically behind the entire prophetic message of the Old Testament.

Yet apparently Isaiah is the classic and perhaps the first book (and prophet) to speak of YHWH's plan on so universal a scale (Fichtner, *Gottes Weisheit,* 28; M. Schmidt, *Prophet und Tempel* [Zurich: Evangelischen Verlag, 1948] 19–54). Vriezen describes it: "He (Isaiah) sees his time in the light of the living God. . . . For Isaiah all sins are rooted in failure to recognize God (his work and his plan), failure to believe, and the willful rejection of him (his plan and his work)" ("Essentials," 131, 135).

The idea of a plan and its execution lies at the very heart of the conception of the entire book as O'Connell (*Concentricity and Continuity,* 244) has shown. The problem outlined in chap. 1, that of Israel as rebellious children, required a response. The first response or plan dealt with the threat to Jerusalem from Israel and Ephraim. In Isa 5:11–17, 18 ff., the plan called for the introduction of Assyrian might into Palestine; here the words God's מַעֲשֵׂהוּ, "work," and עצת קדוש ישׂראל, "the plan of the Holy One of Israel," appear (Werner, *Studien,* 11–32; Conrad, *Reading Isaiah,* 55–57). The concept appears again in 14:24–27, where YHWH's plan for the end of Assyian power is described, and in chap. 19, in an oracle concerning Egypt (Werner, *Studien,* 33–51; Conrad, *Reading Isaiah,* 57–58). Isa 23:1–14 shows YHWH's plan for Tyre (Werner, *Studien,* 54–60; Conrad, *Reading Isaiah,* 58–59). Werner (*Studien,* 61–95) deals with the more general teachings in 28:23–29 and 30:1–5, while Conrad (*Reading Isaiah,* 53–54, 59–61) notes the military nature of YHWH's plan against the proud of all the earth (cf. 2:12–18), which is applied in 36:4–10 and specifically attributed to YHWH's plan in 37:26. Conrad (*Reading Isaiah,* 61–82) describes YHWH's plan for Jerusalem's future (24:21–23; 25:1–2, 6–8), which he regards as a plan against Babylon (chaps. 40–47). Werner (*Studien,* 101–34) also analyzes YHWH's plan in 40:12–17, 44:24–28, and 46:9–11.

This plan cannot be turned aside (14:27). The prophet and his audience live in the middle of the accomplishment of it. Thus the coming of the Assyrian is accomplished history (14:25*a*), while the judgment of the Assyrian still remains to be accomplished (14:25*b*). For the reader of the Vision this, too, has become accomplished history. The Vision confronts the events of history with the reality of the living God whose acts and whose plan are becoming visible in the events of the day. In that light the times reveal "an old world perishing" and a "new about to be born" (Vriezen, "Essentials," 146). Most recent writers have worked within the limits of their discipline in interpreting what the historical prophet saw and said on these issues. To look at the same issues from the vantage point of the complete Vision of the book of Isaiah only strengthens and completes the picture. In this, YHWH's plan/strategy is consistently related to his work. Together they build the basis for a theology of history. "History is the work of YHWH of Hosts, who is enthroned on Zion. It unfolds according to a plan which he has determined" (Wildberger, "Jesajas Verstandnis," 89).

So the Vision's whole plot can be understood in terms of YHWH's plans. The first plan deals with the crisis for Judah and Jerusalem posed by the Aramaean/Israelite invasion of 734 B.C.E. (chap. 7). The answer to this crisis is YHWH's bringing the Assyrian into the land (chaps. 2–12). The second plan deals with the Assyrian and Babylonian invasion (chaps. 13–27). The third plan deals with the issues of the exile and return (38:1–54:17*a;* see Conrad, *Reading Isaiah,* 63–82). The fourth plan (54:17*b*–66:24) deals with issues related to the returning exiles under the title "This is the inheritance of the servants of YHWH" (54:17*b*).

The Deuteronomic History, Jeremiah, and Ezekiel had focused narrowly on the Babylonian destruction of Jerusalem of 587 B.C.E. in trying to interpret God's will for the people in the exile and beyond. The Vision chooses a broader arena (as does the Book of the Twelve).

The Vision says that YHWH in mid-eighth century B.C.E. had already determined a strategy or plan that would make changes far greater than simply bringing about the punishment of Israel. This meant nothing less than the inauguration of a new age. For a millennium or more, Palestine had been a land of small city-states under the fairly tolerant and benign wing of Egypt. Egypt did not lean heavily on the Palestinian states but expected them to serve as a loose buffer against aggression from that quarter. Under this system the Canaanite and Phoenician civilizations had bloomed, David and Solomon had developed an admirable little mini-empire, and trade had flourished. Rivalries between the small states had remained within bounds, and all concerned had prospered.

In the ninth century B.C.E. this situation began to change. Assyrian invasions were prevented only by massive coalitions of armies from the Palestinian states. By the middle of the eighth century B.C.E., Assyria could no longer be withstood. At about the same time, the small Palestinian states experienced growing instability that would soon lead to their extinction. For a hundred years, to the middle of the seventh century B.C.E., Assyrian power worked to overcome every symbol of local autonomy. The last to fall were the Phoenician cities with their considerable commercial sea routes. At that point "the whole land" lay prostrate before the conquerors.

The Vision chronicles these events. It recognizes that Israel's sins as well as the pride of humankind had played a role in determining what happened. But it also says that YHWH, who dwelled in Zion and who had been understood to administer his rule over the world from Jerusalem through its Davidic king, would no longer do so. YHWH still dwelled in Zion and could be approached there for worship or instruction in his law. But the control of history had been transferred from David's throne to the hand of the empire. And Assyria would be only the first in a series of empires.

The prophets, especially Isaiah, as the Vision portrays him, were given the task of revealing this change in strategy to Israel. YHWH would not necessarily be on Israel's side in battle. Indeed, it was he who brought the Assyrians. If a king truly understood this, it behooved him to come to terms with YHWH's chosen vessel, the emperor. Ahaz did this. Hezekiah did not. Manasseh did this. Josiah did not.

The Vision goes on to insist that this was no temporary arrangement waiting for the day when the rule would be returned to David's heir in Jerusalem. On the contrary, Israel and Jerusalem of the postexilic period were called to come to terms with a permanent Persian hegemony. YHWH still had important roles for Israel and Jerusalem to play in his new strategy; but they were "servant" roles, not "ruler" roles.

These ideas were rejected by most of Israel and those in Jerusalem who still dreamed of reconquering the land, as Joshua had done, or of establishing a kingdom, as David had done. The Vision insists that they are out of step with God's new order and that they can only be rejected. There is nothing here to support rebellion against Persia or nationalistic aspirations at any time. God's new era makes Jerusalem a place of pilgrimage for believers from all the nations.

If Isaiah's division between the ages is taken seriously, the biblical theologian must ask whether the proper biblical division of the ages should not be "before 587 B.C.E." and "after 587 B.C.E." rather than our present B.C.E./C.E. formula. This would, for the Christian, put the incarnation at the climax of the new age rather than at the beginning of it.

YHWH'S PROBLEM

YHWH's strategy assigns to the world empires the task of managing and policing the world and invites his elect, saved, and called people to be his servants in worship, witness, and mission. In Isaiah, God seems to have no difficulty persuading the nations to play their part. He had the usual problems of pride, arrogance, and cruelty that regularly made a change necessary, but there was no problem in finding aspirants for the position.

God did have a problem, as the Vision sees it, in getting Israel and Jerusalem to listen, to see, to understand, and to agree to the new role he had for them. Even the centuries of pain, distress, and death that preceded the exile had not stilled their thirst for power and glory, for autonomy and self-determination, and for the imagined prosperity that would go with these.

Israel's complaint is best stated in 49:1–4, while she insists in chaps. 63 and 64 that God has no right to change his plans from those that motivated Joshua and David. The scenes of covenant judgment near the beginning of the Vision (chaps. 1, 3, 5, 10, and so on) have made little impression. The unyielding determination for Israel to regain its old glory remains. That is YHWH's problem. His frustration with a stubborn people is shown repeatedly in the book but is particularly acute in chap. 65.

The practical side of this for the author and his implied audience lies in the tendency of Judah to rebel against its overlords, only to be put down in bloody reprisals. This apparently was still true under the Persians. Half a millennium later it would still be true under the Romans. The book of Isaiah is a major exponent of the view that the people of God be separate from the state, a spiritual gathering of those who would serve God in spirit and in truth. It teaches that God's power can more appropriately be shown in and through such a group than through national power. It teaches that God's ultimate goals are more in the sanctuary than in the palace, more in the heart than in military strength. The Vision has been a prime support for those among Jews and among Christians, including Jesus and Paul, who held to such a view of God and his kingdom.

Isaiah's work leads to a major restatement of the doctrine of election. The children of Abraham/Jacob have been promised a position as the sons of YHWH, possessors of the land of Palestine. But their rebellious behavior has led to a major incompatibility with God. Even after judgment many remain rebellious, even pagan in their worship. Yet there are pleas, even demands, that YHWH honor his pledge to Abraham and recognize all of Jacob's people as his people, worthy of a place in his land. This God refuses to do. Instead, the doctrine is made both more inclusive and more exclusive than that applied by Ezra's priests. It is more inclusive in that people from all nations and peoples are eligible. This takes care of the problem raised by having had many absorbed into other cultures because of exile. It is more exclusive in that only those who are totally devoted to YHWH as his servants may come to worship in the new temple. They, "the servants of YHWH," and they only, are the new people of YHWH.

The structures and forms of society and religion change. It is foolish to presume that any one of these is eternal. But God's promises and the goals that they presuppose are as unchanging as God's own character. They include God's search for a people capable of blessing humanity (Abraham), a covenant people committed to the worship of God and to holy life (Moses; cf. Exodus, Numbers, Deuteronomy), and a kingdom in which God is King (David; cf. 2 Sam 7; Ps 110). The Vision shows God's actions in the life of his people and in the world of the eighth to the fifth centuries B.C.E. to be consistent with these goals.

But the failure of the elect and the called to see God's vision, to hear God's voice, and to rise above human goals of pride, striving, and independence adds a tragic dimension to the Vision. To the bitter end a large proportion of the people cling to their version of the past as the only acceptable pattern for their present and their future. They demand that God conform to their concept of what his plans ought to be (chaps. 62–64) and thus preclude themselves from participation in God's new creation (chap. 65). The parallel to Jonah is unmistakable.

When the NT records that most people of that day refused to accept Jesus as God's Son or the Cross as their oblation, it adds one more chapter to the history traced by the Vision of Isaiah. The Vision also had its predecessors in the books of Kings, Judges, and Numbers. One wonders at the patience of God and the stubbornness of humanity and prays "O God, be merciful to me, a sinner!"

THE VISION
of Isaiah Son of Amoz concerning Judah and Jerusalem in the Days of Uzziah, Jotham, Ahaz, and Hezekiah, Kings of Judah

A Drama
Prologue, Six Acts, Epilogue

Translation and Commentary

Prologue (1:1–4:6)

Bibliography

Carr, D. M. "Reading Isaiah from Beginning (Isaiah 1) to end (Isaiah 65–66): Multiple Modern Possibilities." In *New Visions.* Ed. R. F. Melugin and M. A. Sweeney. 188–219. **Darr, K. P.** *Isaiah's Vision and the Family of God.* Louisville: Westminster John Knox, 1994. **Fohrer, G.** "Jesaja 1 als Zusammenfassung der Verkündigung Jesajas." In *Studien zur alttestamentlichen Prophetie (1949–65).* BZAW 99. Berlin: Töpelmann, 1967. 148–66. First published in *ZAW* 74 (1962) 251–68. **Gosse, B.** "Isaïe 1 dans la rédaction du livre d'Isaïe." *ZAW* 104 (1992) 52–66. **Loretz, O.** *Der Prolog des Jesaja-Buches (1,1–2,5): Ugaritologische und kolometrische Studien zum Jesaja-Buch.* Altenberge: Akademische Bibliothek; Soest: Bestellungen an CIS-Verlag, 1984. **Magonet, J.** "Isaiah 2:1–4:6, Some Poetic Structures and Tactics." *ACEBT* 3 (1982) 71–85. **Sweeney, M. A.** *Isaiah 1–4.* 146–58. ———. "Structure and Redaction in Isaiah 2–4." *HAR* 11 (1987) 407–22. **Watts, J. D. W.** "The Formation of Isaiah 1: Its Context in 1–4." In *SBLSP.* Missoula, MT: Scholars Press, 1978. 109–20. **Wiklander, B.** *Prophecy as Literature.*

Chap. 1 is an introduction to themes for the Vision of Isaiah. Chaps. 2–4 introduce other themes that are necessary for an understanding of the book. Despite the superscription's notice of eighth-century reigns, the prologue makes no historical references or identifications. Its time viewpoint is much nearer that of the epilogue (chaps. 62–66). It reflects the "former times/later times" dichotomy in 1:21–31 and in 2:1–4. Thus it serves the reader as an introduction to the entire book of Isaiah and assumes that this reader lives at or after the time of its completion.

In a paper read before the Society for Old Testament Study in Cambridge, 2000, R. E. Clements spoke of chap. 1 as an introduction and chaps. 2–4 as a prologue to the book. This arrangement solves many problems and makes a coherent whole of the parts. Magonet (*ACEBT* 3 [1982] 71–85), Sweeney *(Isaiah, 1–4),* and Wiklander *(Prophecy as Literature)* have also found this a congenial unit. But there is a stronger sense in which the chapters form an introduction or prologue to the whole, albeit in three parts: chaps. 1, 2, and 3–4.

Chap. 1 stands alone and contains three parts. Each in its own way requires judgment: Isa 1:2–7 about rebellious Israel, which influences various parts of the Vision but is particularly replicated in 63:7–65:12; Isa 1:8–20 about violence on Jerusalem's temple, which is replicated in 66:3–9, 15–18, 24; and Isa 1:21–31 about the unfaithful city of Zion, which is replicated in the reference to the ריב, "legal dispute," of Zion in 34:8.

Chap. 2 stands alone with a separate title (2:1) and contains three parts: (1) Isa 2:2–4 is about the mountain of YHWH's house to which the nations will come. This paragraph introduces the theme of YHWH's relation to the nations and thus to "all flesh." Isa 34:1–49:4 shows YHWH teaching and informing the nations about his ways. (2) Isa 2:5–9 warns that Israel/Jacob is not welcome. She has become too much like the peoples. Isa 40:27–49:4 pictures YHWH wishing to maintain Israel's special status despite her present position as one among the nations. In the end (49:1–4) Israel declines the offer. (3) Isa 2:10–22 announces the day of YHWH against all humankind. Chaps. 13–27 depict it in progress, while 34:2–4 will view the day as having already happened. See also 63:1–6.

Chaps. 3–4 form a discrete and self-contained unit. They have a distinct ending with a series of ביום ההוא, "in that day," units. Like the introduction (chap. 1), they introduce themes for the book and also look to a corresponding unit (chaps. 63–65) in the epilogue at the end of the Vision. Their depiction of Jerusalem's ordeal consists of four sections: 3:1–12, Jerusalem shall totter; 3:13–15, YHWH stands for judgment; 3:16–4:1, the women of Jerusalem; and 4:2–6, the branch of YHWH and the restored city. Isa 49:5–54:17*a* picks up these themes, as do chaps. 60–62.

There is no continuation from chap. 1 to chap. 2 There is also no continuation between chap. 2 and chaps. 3–4. They are fresh, self-contained units. Chap. 2 even has its own title.

Chaps. 1–4 introduce themes that will be important in the rest of the Vision. They are: (1) Israel's problem as "rebellious children" (see especially 63:7–65:16); (2) the temple's problem of violence in the place of worship (see chap. 66); (3) Zion's problem as an "unfaithful" city (see 34:8); (4) YHWH's reign in his temple on the mountain (Zion) with the nations in attendance (2:2–4), also pictured in 34:1–49:4 and in chaps. 55–56; (5) the end of the nation of Israel and debate over whether Israel can continue as the people of God (negative responses [2:5–11; 63:8–65:16] bracket the idea that a remnant will be saved [10:20–22; 11:11–16]); (6) YHWH as the Divine Warrior in the wars that move through the land on this "day of YHWH" (2:12–22), a theme that universalized all humankind in chaps. 13–27 and in 34:2–8; and (7) the judgment and purge of Zion to produce a purified city (chaps. 3–4; also 49:5–54:17 and chaps. 60–62).

Excursus: Isaiah 1–12

Bibliography: Commentaries on Chaps. 1–12

Eichrodt, W. *Der Heilige Israel.* **Jacob, E.** *Esaïe 1–12.* **Kaiser, O.** *Isaiah 1–12.* **Kilian, R.** *Jesaja 1–12.* **Wildberger, H.** *Jesaja 1–12.*

Bibliography: Monographs and Articles on Chaps. 1–12

Ackroyd, P. "Isaiah I–XII: Presentation of a Prophet." In *Congress Volume Göttingen 1977.* VTSup 29. Leiden: Brill, 1978. 16–48. **Bartelt, A. H.** *Book around Immanuel.* **Blum, E.** "Jesajas prophetisches Testament: Beobachtungen zu Jes 1–11." *ZAW* 108 (1996) 547–68; *ZAW* 109 (1997) 12–29. **Brekelmans, C.** "Deuteronomic Influence in Isaiah 1–12." In *Book of Isaiah.* Ed. J. Vermeylen. 167–76. **Brodie, L.** "The Children and the Prince: The Structure, Nature, and Date of Isaiah 6–12." *BTB* 9 (1979) 27–31. **Carroll, R. P.** "Ancient Israelite Prophecy and Dissonance Theory." *Numen* 24 (1977) 135–51. ———. "Inner Tradition Shifts in Meaning in Isaiah 1–11." *ExpTim* 89 (1977–78) 301–4. **Freiesen, I. D.** "Composition and Continuity in Isaiah 1–12." Diss., St. Michael, Toronto, 1990. **Gitay, Y.** *Isaiah and His Audience: The Structure and Meaning of Isaiah 1–12.* Assen; Maastricht: Van Gorcum, 1991. **Johnson, A.** "Sculpted Beauty: The Hand of God in Isaiah 1–12." In *AAR/SBL Abstracts.* Atlanta: Scholars Press, 1994. 290. **Marshall, R. J.**

"The Structure of Isaiah 1–12." *BR* 7 (1962) 19–32. ———. "The Unity of Isaiah 1–12." *LQ* 14 (1962) 21–38. **Nielsen, K.** "Das Bild des Gerichts (*Rib* Pattern) in Jes. I–XII." *VT* 29 (1979) 309–24. **Schedl, R.** *Rufer des Heils in heiloser Zeit: Der prophet Jesajah Kapitel I–XII.* Paderborn: Schöningh, 1973. **Tur Sinai, N. H.** "A Contribution to the Understanding of Isaiah I–XII." In *Studies in the Bible.* Ed. C. Rabin. ScrHier 8. Jerusalem: Magnes; Hebrew Univ., 1961. 154–88.

Contrary to this commentary's interpretation, many interpreters think the first literary unit comprises chaps. 1–12. The beginning of the section as understood by some interpreters is marked by the title/superscription in 1:1. The end is marked by the two hymns in chap. 12, which set the unit apart from what follows. Ackroyd ("Isaiah I–XII") and Blum (*ZAW* 108 [1996] 547–68; *ZAW* 109 [1997] 12–29) have looked at the unit as comprising chaps. 1–12, but Blum also found an inner structure from 1:21–11:5, which was supplemented by what preceded and followed. Bartelt *(Book around Immanuel)* and Williamson, on the other hand, view the unit as chaps. 2–12, the title in 2:1 signaling a new beginning. Williamson (*Book Called Isaiah,* 144–54) even argues that chap. 2 is the beginning of one form of the book of Isaiah that was edited by Deutero-Isaiah (154). But note that 2:2–4 belongs to a series of texts related to the mountain of YHWH (Isa 2:3; 10:12; 11:9; 16:1; 18:7; 25:7, 10; 27:13; 56:7; 57:7, 13; 65:11, 25; 66:20, but not in chaps. 28–55). The arguments relating 2:1–4 to Deutero-Isaiah ignore this connection. The inner development has led writers to different conclusions about the limits of the section. Chaps. 1–6 give the appearance of a series of introductions to themes followed throughout the Vision. Chap. 1 has been viewed by many as an introduction for the book (see commentary on chap. 1). O'Connell expanded that prologue to include 2:1–5. He identified additional introductory elements found in 2:6–22 and 3:1–4:1. For O'Connell, the main unit is 4:2–12:6, which displays an asymmetrical concentric structure and focuses attention on "the Syro-Ephraimite-Assyrian Scheme for Zion's judgment and restoration" (O'Connell, *Concentricity and Continuity,* 81–106).

The central structure of chaps. 6–8 is recognized by many researchers. At the core of chaps. 6–8, the narrative in 7:1–16 and the announcement of the Assyrian invasions in 7:17 provide the twin centers for the "book." The expansion of the Assyrian announcement in 7:18–25 and the expanded envelope of first-person units (5:1–7; 6:1–13; 8:1–18) complete the inner structure. D. Jones ("The Tradition of the Oracles of Isaiah of Jerusalem," *ZAW* 67 [1955] 225–46) follows Duhm in suggesting that chaps. 6–8 formed a *Denkschrift* or *mémoire* for the chapter. A. L. H. M. van Wieringen (*The Implied Reader in Isaiah 6–12* [Leiden; Boston: Brill, 1998]) deals with a unit composed of chaps. 6–12. Bartelt *(Book around Immanuel)* thinks the entire unit forms a concentric structure around chap. 7. Blum (*ZAW* 108 [1996] 547–68) sees 1:21–11:5 as concentric around chaps. 6–8. See similar arguments in Sweeney (134 n. 87) and Wildberger (77).

The end of the unit is marked in chap. 12 by two hymns for "that day," which serve as literary conclusions. "In that day" passages are used again in chap. 19 to conclude the unit of chaps. 13–19, and in chaps. 24–27 for the unit of chaps. 21–27. They give evidence of being conscious literary closing devices in Isaiah that depend on prior "day of YHWH" announcements, such as are first introduced in 2:10–20.

For my analysis of the structure of these chapters, see introductions to part I (5:1–33:24) and act 1 (7:1–12:6) below.

Title (1:1)

Bibliography

Freedman, D. N. "Headings in the Books of the Eighth Century Prophets." In *Divine Commitment and Human Obligation: Selected Writings of David Noel Freedman*. Vol. 1, *History and Religion*. Ed. J. R. Huddleston. Grand Rapids, MI: Eerdmans, 1997. 367–82. **Goldingay, J.** "Isaiah i and ii." *VT* 48 (1998) 326–33. **Tucker, G. M.** "Prophetic Superscriptions and the Growth of the Canon." In *Canon and Authority*. Ed. G. M. Coats and B. O. Long. Philadelphia: Fortress, 1977. 56–70.

Translation

1 THE VISION OF ISAIAH[a] SON OF AMOZ
Which he envisioned concerning Judah and Jerusalem in the days of Uzziah, Jotham, Ahaz, and Hezekiah,[b] *kings of Judah.*

Notes

1.a. ישעיהו, "Isaiah," here and elsewhere in the text. But ישעיה in the title.

1.b. MT records variants among different passages in the forms of personal names of kings (cf. M. Noth, *Personennamen*). The Qumran scribes used frequent *matres lectionis* (vowel letters) to transmit their understanding of the names' pronunciations.

Form/Structure/Setting

A heading like Isa 1:1 is common in prophetic literature. It normally includes a designation of the nature of the book, a prophet's name, perhaps the intended reading audience, and a reference to the period from which it comes. In the context of chap. 1, 1:1 credits the vision of Isaiah with the heavenly accusations against "the rebellious children" who are the people of YHWH, against the temple worshipers for their violence, and against the corrupted city of Jerusalem. This vision not only describes chap. 1 but also accounts for key elements in the concluding chapters of the book as well as the idea of the whole work.

Goldingay (*VT* 48 [1998] 326–33) suggests that 1:1 and 2:1 frame the first chapter. He maintains that this heading applies only to chap. 1 and that the term חזון, "vision," applies only to a single visionary experience or account (but cf. 2 Chr 32:32), not a book. He also maintains that 2:1 is a colophon closing the chapter. The great majority of commentators, however, follow the understanding offered here. To interpret Isa 1:1 and and 2:1 as superscription and colophon respectively for chap. 1 only would be great overkill. The chapter is not weighty enough to deserve all that. Furthermore, the chapter does not fulfill the expectations raised by its first verse. The list of kings in v 1 has no echo in the rest of chap. 1, nor does its identification of the prophet Isaiah.

חזון, "vision," occurs in other superscriptions and in smaller books to be sure. Does it refer to the entire book of sixty-six chapters? Conrad (*Reading Isaiah,* 118) says that "the vision of Isaiah is not to be equated with the whole book." He sees the vision as a book within the larger book and traces the theme of the "vision," which he equates with chaps. 6–39, through the rest of Isaiah. He has a point. This title does not equate the book with the "vision." Rather, Isaiah is a book about the "Vision of Isaiah." The substance of the Vision, however, may be narrower than Conrad suggests. The Vision of Isaiah may be limited to chaps. 6–8 and chaps. 36–39, around which the great poetic drama has been composed.

Perhaps "the vision" does not refer to the book, or even any of its literary units, but rather to the imparted message, the vision of the present and future that Isaiah son of Amoz envisioned and that has now become the central focus of this much larger literary work. That is, the book of Isaiah is about "the vision which Isaiah son of Amoz saw in the days of the kings of Judah."

Then the term in the superscription would point to what Isaiah received from God and passed on in the narratives of chaps. 36–39. The דבר, "word," that he envisioned is that seen in 7:1–16. And the משא, "burden," that he envisioned is particularly that found in 20:1–6. These superscriptions are saying that the literary materials that follow are indebted to Isaiah's "vision," "word," and "burden" for their inspiration and direction. The debt was real. The idea of Isaianic authorship for the whole was a mistaken product of a tradition that sought to give authority to the work and respect to the prophet by ascribing the whole work to him.

In fact his position in prophecy is secure on the basis of the narratives in Kings that are repeated in Isa 36–39. The larger work, which expands on those thoughts and insights, builds the prophet's legacy into something much greater that is particularly applicable to later generations. Isa 1:1 is the heading, title, for this larger work, which encompasses six acts, a prologue, and an epilogue (chaps. 62–66).

Comment

Vision is an appropriate subject for a work in which God is the primary character and the setting is often in his heavenly courts. חזון, "vision," is a term that describes the subject of the entire work of sixty-six chapters. It must encompass other categories of literature like דברי, "words," or משא, "burden," that appear in other headings. The book contains an account of one vision (chap. 6), but the title here is much broader, and its definition must fit the entire book.

Miscall (*Isaiah 34–35* [1999]) has described chaps. 34–35 as "a nightmare and a dream." The same terms could also be used of the Vision. It pictures the nightmare of the destructive Assyrian and Babylonian wars. It keeps alive the dream of Jerusalem as the seat of God's throne on earth (2:2–4; 65:17–25). And it traces the restoration of the city and the rebirth of pilgrimages in the Persian period (chaps. 35–66). This "vision" is arranged in acts and scenes like a play (see the *Introduction—Isaiah Is a Literary Drama*). Isaiah son of Amoz is not named here as the author. His name is a part of the title, and his "vision" is the subject of the book. He appears in passages where he is identified by name in 7:1–16 and in chaps. 20, 37, 38, and 39. His name appears in other superscriptions in 2:1 and 13:1. (On the meaning of the name *Isaiah*, see *Excursus: Symbolic Names for Isaiah and His Sons* at 7:3 below.) First-person accounts in chaps. 6 and 8 are properly referred to him. These are the portions of the Vision that justify his name in the title. They, and the title, imply that the Vision conveys his ideas.

All that is known of Isaiah son of Amoz is contained in this book. He is only mentioned elsewhere in 2 Kgs 18–20 = Isa 36–39 and in 2 Chr 32:20. One book in the Pseudepigrapha is ascribed to him. (For further discussion, see *Introduction—Who Was Isaiah?*)

על־יהודה וירושלם, "concerning Judah and Jerusalem," is clearly intended to direct attention to the subject of the book. A superscription must not necessarily indicate a subject. Those over Jeremiah, Ezekiel, Hosea, Joel, Obadiah, Jonah, Habakkuk, and Zephaniah have none. Constructions like Isaiah's appear in Amos 1:1, על־ישראל, "concerning Israel"; Mic 1:1, על־שמרון וירושלם, "concerning Samaria and Jerusalem"; and Zech 12:1, על־ישראל, "concerning Israel," while Mal 1:1 reads אל־ישראל, "to Israel." Superscriptions for burdens often indicate the subject, sometimes using a construct, sometimes using ־ב, "against."

Isaiah's "concerning Judah and Jerusalem" (1:1; 2:1) is unique in superscriptions, but the pairing of the two proper names appears frequently in other contexts. Judah is a personal name of a son of Jacob. It is the name of a tribe. It is a territory in Palestine. It is a kingdom. And it is a Babylonian and Persian province. In each of the last three cases, Jerusalem is its capital and only significant city.

Jerusalem is a central topic throughout. But its corresponding term inside the book is Israel, not Judah. Judah is seldom singled out for judgment (Amos 2:4–5 is an exception), and it does not come up for separate treatment in Isaiah.

Excursus: Judah

Judah was the eldest son of Jacob (Gen 29:35 and passim). The tribe that bears his name settled in the south of Palestine (Josh 14–15). It played no major role during the time of the judges, but Israel's second king, David, came from Judah. He made his first capital in Hebron and his final capital in Jerusalem on Judah's northern boundary. Under David and Solomon, Judah's significance and power grew (2 Samuel; 1 Kgs 1–11). But the division of the kingdom on Solomon's death isolated Judah, making it the smaller of the resulting kingdoms. The dynasty of David continued on its throne in Jerusalem.

The eighth-century wars between the Palestinian nations threatened Judah's independence. But surprisingly, the Assyrian invasions that reduced the other small nations of Palestine to the status of Assyrian provinces allowed Judah to retain its own identity and Davidic dynasty. This continued until the Babylonian invasion in 587 B.C.E. The Judean exile that followed brought an end to Davidic rule and to national existence. Chaps. 1–33 of Isaiah are set within that period.

Judah was a province of the Persian Empire after 540 B.C.E. It was administered by a governor appointed by the Persian king. Its capital was Jerusalem. The city and the temple were rebuilt by Persian authorities and finances.<16a>*Excursus: Jerusalem*

Excursus: Jerusalem

Bibliography

Berges, U. "Sion als thema in het boek Jesaja: Nieuwe exegetische benadering en theologische gevolgen." *ThTo* 39 (1999) 118–38. **Biddle, M. E.** "The Figure of Lady Jerusalem: Identification, Deification and Personification of Cities in the ANE." In *The Biblical Canon in Comparative Perspective.* Ed. K. L. Younger, Jr., et al. Lewiston, NY: Mellen, 1991. 173–94. **Clifford, R. J.** *The Cosmic Mountain in Canaan and the Old Testament.* HSM

4. Cambridge: Harvard UP, 1972. ———. "The Unity of the Book of Isaiah and Its Cosmogonic Language." *CBQ* 55 (1993) 1–17. **Darr, K. P.** "The Ladies' Lots." In *Isaiah's Vision and the Family of God.* Louisville: Westminster John Knox, 1994. 85–224. **Hess, R. S.,** and **G. J. Wenham,** eds. *Zion, City of Our God.* Grand Rapids, MI: Eerdmans, 1999. **Japhet, S.** "From the King's Sanctuary to the Chosen City." In *Jerusalem: Its Sanctity and Centrality to Judaism, Christianity, and Islam.* Ed. L. I. Levine. New York: Continuum, 1999. 3–15. **Levine, L. I.** "Second Temple Jerusalem: A Jewish City in the Greco-Roman Orbit." In *Jerusalem: Its Sanctity and Centrality to Judaism, Christiany, and Islam.* Ed. L. I. Levine. New York: Continuum, 1999. 53–68. **Webb, B. G.** "Zion in Transformation: A Literary Approach to Isaiah." In *The Bible in Three Dimensions.* Ed. D. J. A. Clines et al. JSOTSup 87. Sheffield: JSOT Press, 1990. 65–84.

Jerusalem was an old Jebusite city, built perhaps as early as 1800 B.C.E. and largely under Egyptian control. It was the city of Melchizedek in Abraham's day (Gen 14:18–20), letters from its king to the Egyptian court appear in the Amarna correspondence of the fifteenth century B.C.E., and the king of Jerusalem was among the Amorite kings that resisted the invasion of Joshua (Josh 10, 15; Judg 1). David and his men took the city (2 Sam 5–6), which he made into his capital. There Solomon built the temple that became the worship center for all Israel (1 Kgs 5–8). Its fortifications were strengthened, and it grew in size and importance.

The city has suffered military attack a number of times throughout history:

ca. 922 B.C.E. attacked by Shishak (Shishonk I) of Egypt (1 Kgs14:25–26)
ca. 850 B.C.E. attacked by the Philistines and Arabs
in 786 B.C.E. attacked by Joash of Israel
in 701 B.C.E. besieged by Sennacherib
in 610 B.C.E. taken by Pharoah Necho
in 598 B.C.E. plundered by Nebuchadnezzar
in 586 B.C.E. temple burned by Nebuchadnezzar
in 538 B.C.E. rebuilt at the encouragement of Cyrus
in 515 B.C.E. the temple rededicated
in 445 B.C.E. the walls rebuilt by Nehemiah
in 333 B.C.E. visited by Alexander the Great
in 320 B.C.E. captured by Ptolemy Soter
in 302 B.C.E. annexed to Egypt
in 198 B.C.E. transferred to the Seleucid Empire
in 170 B.C.E. walls razed by Antiochus Epiphanes
in 167 B.C.E. liberated by the Hasmonians (Maccabees)
in 63 B.C.E. taken by the Romans under Pompey
in 44 B.C.E. walls rebuilt by Antipater, father of Herod the Great
on Sept. 8, 70 C.E., destroyed by the Romans
in 130 C.E. rebuilt by Hadrian
in 335 C.E. Church of the Holy Sepulchre founded by Constantine
in 614 C.E. taken by the Persians
in 637 C.E. taken by the Saracens
in 1076 C.E. taken by the Turks
in 1098 C.E. assigned to Egypt
in 1099 C.E. taken by Crusaders
in 1187 C.E. taken by Saladin
in 1228 C.E. assigned to the Christians
in 1243 C.E. taken by Carizmians
in 1247 C.E. fell to Egypt's Mamluk rulers

in 1517 C.E. taken by the Ottomans
in 1917 C.E. conquered by General Allenby of Great Britan
in 1948 C.E. fought over by Jews and Jordan, leading to a divided city
in 1967 C.E. conquered by the state of Israel
currently in dispute between Israelis and Palestinians

Wars in Palestine have been familiar throughout Jerusalem's history. They were especially notable in the eighth to sixth centuries B.C.E. with Assyria, Babylon, and Egypt; the third to second centuries B.C.E. with the Ptolemaic and Seleucid kingdoms; the first century B.C.E. to second century C.E., the Roman wars with Jewish zealots; the tenth to thirteenth centuries, the Muslims versus Christians (the Crusades); and the twentieth-century Israeli and Arab wars. Longer periods of stability have been few: under David, 40 years; under the Persians, 200 years; under Egypt's Mamluk kingdom, 270 years; under the Turkish Ottoman Empire, 200 years.

The Jerusalem of the Vision of Isaiah is the city of the last quarter of the eighth century down to the rebuilt city of approximately the time of Nehemiah. The Vision portrays the trials of the city during the Assyrian and Babylonian periods and the potential the city has in the Persian period. (See also *Excursus: Jerusalem—An Example of War in a Walled City* at 3:1 below.)

Strand: Jerusalem/Zion

PROLOGUE	ACT 1	ACT 2	ACT 3	ACT 4	ACT 5	ACT 6	EPILOGUE
JERUSALEM (49X)							
1:1 2:1, 3 3:1, 8 4:3, 4	5:3 7:1 8:14 10:10, 11, 12, 32	22:14 24:23 27:13	28:14 30:19 31:5, 9 33:20	36:2, 7, 20 37:10, 22, 32 40:2, 9 41:27 44:26, 28	(ch. 50) 51:1, 2, 9	59:20 (ch. 60)	62:7 64:10 65:18 66:10, 20
ZION (47X)							
1:8, 27 2:3 3:16, 17 4:3, 4, 5	8:18 10:12, 24, 32 12:6	14:32 16:1 18:7 24:23	28:16 29:8 30:19 31:9 33:5, 14, 20 34:8 35:10	37:10, 22, 32 40:9 41:27 46:13	49:14 51:3, 11, 16 52:1, 2, 7, 8	59:20	62:1,11 64:10 (65:17–25) 66:8
MOUNT ZION							
2:2–4 4:5	8:18 10:12, 32 11:6, 9	16:1 18:7 24:21–23 25:6, 7, 10 27:13	29:8 30:29 31:4 35:8–10	37:32		56:7 57:13	65:11, 25 66:20

Jerusalem is a major theme for the Vision. It is dealt with in several ways. The superscription lists the usual political title in the Persian period: יהודה וירושלם, "Judah and Jerusalem." But the city has much more meaning in the Vision than that. Some of that is dealt with under the title Zion. Zion tradition is rich in imagery. It designates the mountain of YHWH, the seat of YHWH's throne, the temple where worshipers come to worship. Jerusalem is called Daughter Zion in 4:3, 4; 5:3; and passim (see the *Excursus: Mountain of YHWH* under 2:1–4).

In chaps. 1–4, ירושלם, "Jerusalem," ציון, "Zion," הר בית־יהוה, "the mountain of YHWH's house," all appear (see *Strand: Jerusalem/Zion*). Passages devoted to Jerusalem are 1:8–21, 2:2–4, 3:1–4:1, and 4:2–4. In 1:8–9, Zion is recognized as a "remnant" of what had once been a large nation. She is compared with Sodom, and even called Sodom (1:10). The integrity of her sacrifices is belied by the violence and sin in her midst. She is called to reform and to repentance. Isa 2:2–4 introduces the theme of the mountain as a gathering place, a place from which torah and the word of YHWH will go out for all peoples. Isa 3:1–4:1 pictures a Jerusalem abandoned and judged by YHWH. Isa 4:2–6 foresees a day beyond judgment when Jerusalem will be cleansed from her guilt and Mount Zion will bask in YHWH's shelter.

The situation in chaps. 6–12 is the realistic historical moment of siege by armies from neighboring countries and the approaching invasion by the Assyrians that devastated the countryside. But Jerusalem is spared. Jerusalem is urged not to be afraid (10:24) for YHWH has the powers under control. Under his inspired ruler (11:1–5), the "mountain of YHWH's holiness" will enjoy perfect peace and prosperity and, with God present among them, the inhabitants of the city will sing his praises (12:1–6).

In chaps. 13–19, the word ירושלם, "Jerusalem," is missing. However, 14:32 brings the assurance that "YHWH has established Zion" and it will be a place of refuge for his people. Isa 18:7 calls "Mount Zion, the place of the name of YHWH of Hosts."

In chaps. 20–27, all three designations appear; passages devoted to Jerusalem are 22:1–13 and 26:1–7. Although the name is not expressed, 22:1–13 pictures Jerusalem in a sad state of disrepair and unprepared for defense, with blame laid squarely on Shebna and Hilkiah. Isa 24:23 pictures Jerusalem/Zion as the seat of YHWH's reign. "This mountain" is the scene of a divine banquet with a significant announcement of the end of death for all peoples (25:6–8). The city will stand when neighboring nations are being destroyed (25:10). Without naming Jerusalem, 26:1 speaks of a "strong city" with salvation for its walls and its ramparts. Isa 27:13 portrays the great day of the return from exile as one of worship on the holy mountain in Jerusalem.

In the remainder of the Vision, passages devoted to Jerusalem are 28:16–19; 29:1–10; 30:19–30; 31:4–5; 33:5–6, 20–24; chaps. 36–37; 40:2–11; 44:26*b*–28; 45:13; 49:14–26; 51:3, 11, 16, 17–23; 52:1–3, 7–10; 54:1–17; 59:20; chap. 60; 62:1–12; 64:10–12; 65:19–25; 66:7–11, 12, 18–21.

Darr, Biddle ("Figure of Lady Jerusalem"), and others have studied the theme of the city (as a woman) and her rivals. Darr ("Ladies' Lots," 124) describes the city's roles in YHWH's unfolding plan. Jerusalem is called עיר יהוה, "the city of YHWH," in 60:14. It is called קריה, "a city," in 1:21. In 1:26 both terms are used in "city of righteousness, faithful city." She is the "holy city" in 48:2 and 52:1. In 33:20 she is the "city of our festivals." In 29:1 she is "the city where David camped."

יהודה וירושלם, "Judah and Jerusalem," should be considered a word pair. The phrase may refer to the southern kingdom of preexilic times, like Micah's "Samaria and Jerusalem," but it is also used consistently in the exile and afterward, where it is most at home. *Judah* and *Jerusalem* are thus terms that have meaning in relation to the kingdom or province throughout the period dealt with in Isaiah. The Vision connects the work of YHWH to Judah and Jerusalem. Isaiah son of Amoz and the kings belong only to the early portion of it (see *Comment* on 2:1).

Judah and Jerusalem were located in Palestine, an unlikely area to be home to a major civilization/religion. It marks a borderland between the two major civilizations of the ancient world. The one to the northeast was Mesopotamia, with its ancient Sumerian civilization and younger embodiments in Assyria and Babylonia. On the south was Egypt, that civilization on the Nile that drew to itself groups from the Mediterranean coast to the west and the upper Nile to the south and southwest. The dividing line between these ran through Palestine, that narrow corridor between the Mediterranean Sea and the desert with its north-south mountain ranges and the defining river valley (also running north-south) of the Jordan.

The actual lines of defense moved from time to time depending on the relative strength and interest of the opposing forces. The line was drawn initially in the south and included the fortress cities of Palestine, of which Jerusalem was one. It was drawn at some times with Megiddo and the mountain spur of Mount Carmel. There was also a more northerly line that included Haran and Damascus. The defense lines included buffer nations. Virtually all the inland nations of Palestine belonged in this category, as did the coastal cities of Sidon, Tyre, and Ashdod. Cities also served as way stations for trade.

Times when the hegemony of one of the powers was uncontested provided periods of relative stability for Palestine. The period when Israelite tribes (and others) made their way into Palestine and established their homes there saw the rather benign overlordship of Egypt secure in this region. Struggles in that period were between the small groups trying to gain a foothold in the land. The united monarchy was under the oversight of Egypt and fitted into its grand design by providing a secure border regime facing the nations to the north.

In times when the rivalry between the big powers was intense, such as the eighth to the sixth centuries, the borderlands were subjected to constant raids and warfare as the boundary of authority and influence was moved back and forth. The ninth and eighth centuries B.C.E. witnessed increased strength for small nations and rivalry between them at a time when Mesopotamian powers were again interested in gaining control in Palestine. This tempted various kings in Palestine to conspire with Mesopotamian interests to undercut Egypt and her allies in the region. The ensuing struggles are documented in the Bible. They reached a climax in the eighth to the sixth centuries and resulted in complete domination of the region by Assyria (A. Malamat, "Caught between the Great Powers," *BARev* 25 [1999] 34–41, 64).

The next relatively stable period occurred under the Achaemenid Empire of the Medes/Persians (540–330 B.C.E.), which conquered Egypt and threatened Greece. Jews under Ezra and Nehemiah completed the rebuilding of Jerusalem and stabilized the position of Judea in the Persian Empire.

The periods of relative stability, as far as big power position was concerned, were not necessarily times of peaceful prosperity for the small powers. They often fought among themselves or with the great powers. But they had relative success at this only when the great-power hegemony was also contested and they could count on the opposing force to counteract the application of one great nation's total power.

"Concerning Judah and Jerusalem" therefore defines a major theme of the Vision. Jerusalem appears in every part of the work and Judah in much of it. It will be a concern of this commentary to trace this treatment in all the various parts.

בימי עזיהו יותם אחז יחזקיהו מלכי יהודה, "in the days of Uzziah, Jotham, Ahaz, and Hezekiah, kings of Judah." This superscription and the stories involving Isaiah and these kings establish a *terminus a quo* for the Vision in the later third of the eighth century B.C.E.

עזיהו, "Uzziah," is called עזריה, "Azariah," in 2 Kgs 15:1 and 2 Chr 26. The latter portion of his reign overlapped that of Jotham because of Uzziah's leprosy (2 Kgs 15:5; 2 Chr 26:19–21).

Jotham reigned sixteen years (2 Kgs 15:32–8//2 Chr 27), as did his son, Ahaz. Both Kings and Chronicles list Ahaz as one of the worst kings and blame him for bringing Tiglath-Pileser into the land. They both say the Lord brought Israel and Aram against Ahaz. The Vision sets aside chaps. 7–14 for the reign of Ahaz and clearly has a view of him and his reign different from that in Kings and Chronicles.

Hezekiah succeeded Ahaz (2 Kgs 18–20; 2 Chr 29–32). He is lauded as one of the greatest kings in both Kings and Chronicles. The Vision repeats a selection of the Kings account (chaps. 36–39). Chaps. 15–21 are set in Hezekiah's reign. But the Vision also has an independent evaluation of Hezekiah and his reign.

Excursus: Chronology of Eighth-Century Reigns

Bibliography

Bright, J. "Chronological Chart: Mid-Eighth to Mid-Sixth Centuries." In *HI.* 470–71. **Jepson, A.,** and **R. Hanhart.** *Untersuchungen zur israelitisch-jüdischen Chronologie.* BZAW 88. Berlin: Töpelmann, 1964. **Stiles, M.** *Synchronizing Hebrew Originals from Available Records.* 12 vols. Aptos, CA: private printing, 1972–77. **Thiele, E. R.** *The Mysterious Numbers of the Hebrew Kings.* 3d ed. Grand Rapids, MI: Eerdmans, 1983. 139–92.

(The references to relative chronology of reigns in 2 Kgs 15–18 are unusually frequent, but are not clearly compatible with themselves or with external data.)

Eighth-Century Reigns and Events as Recorded in Scripture

Reference	King	Year Reign Begun	Place	Length
2 Kgs 15:17	Menahem	39th year of Azariah's reign	Samaria	10 years
2 Kgs 15:23	Pekahiah	50th year of Azariah's reign	Samaria	2 years
2 Kgs 15:17	Pekah	52d year of Azariah's reign	Samaria	20 years
2 Kgs 15:29	*Tiglath-Pileser attacked Samaria and departed.*			
2 Kgs 15:30	Hoshea	20th year of Jotham's reign		
2 Kgs 15:32, 2 Chr 27:1	Jotham	2d year of Pekah's reign	Jerusalem	16 years
2 Kgs 15:37	*Rezin and Pekah came against Judah.*			
2 Kgs 16:1	Ahaz	17th year of Pekah's reign	Jerusalem	16 years
2 Kgs 16:5–9, 2 Chr 28:1, 16, 20	*With Rezin and Pekah against Judah, Ahaz sent for Tiglath-Pileser*			

2 Kgs 17:1	Hoshea	*12th year of Ahaz's reign	Samaria	9 years
2 Kgs 17:3	*Shalmaneser punished Hoshea.*			
2 Kgs 17:5	*Shalmaneser marched against Hoshea in the *9th year of his reign. Shalmaneser captured Samaria and departed.*			
2 Kgs 18:1	Hezekiah	*3d year of Hoshea's reign	Jerusalem	29 years
2 Kgs 18:7	*Hezekiah rebelled against Assyria.*			
2 Kgs 18:9	*Shalmaneser besieged Samaria in Hoshea's *7th = Hezekiah's 4th year of reign.*			
2 Kgs 18:10	*Samaria was destroyed in Hoshea's *9th-Hezekiah's 6th year of reign.*			
2 Kgs 18:13	*Sennacherib attacked and laid siege to Jerusalem in Hezekiah's 14th year of reign.*			
2 Kgs 19:36–37	*Death of Sennacherib.*			
2 Kgs 21	Manasseh		Jerusalem	55 years

This list presents several problems when one is trying to arrive at absolute dates for the reigns and the events. There appear to be errors in synchronization in some of the dates, while others are factual but were presented in terms that were misunderstood by the historians. Such discrepancies relating to the synchronization of the dates for Hoshea and Hezekiah are noted on the above list by an asterisk. Hoshea must have come to the throne at the death of Pekah when Tiglath-Pileser invaded Israel in 733 B.C.E., a date that can be verified by Assyrian annals. If he reigned nine years, the end of his reign would be 724–23 B.C.E., which accords with 2 Kgs 17:3. But Samaria fell two years later in 722–21 B.C.E.

Dating Hezekiah's reign has several problems, especially in its correlation with Hoshea's reign and the fall of Samaria. The key is 2 Kgs 18:13, which equates Hezekiah's fourteenth year with Sennacherib's attack on Jerusalem. It is known that Sennacherib began his reign in 705 B.C.E. If Hezekiah's reign began in Hoshea's third year, 729 or 727 B.C.E., his fourteenth year would fall in Sargon's reign, 715 or 713 B.C.E. (Sargon, mentioned only once in Scripture, appears to have been virtually unknown or ignored by biblical historians.)

But if one takes 2 Kgs 18:13 at face value, knowing that Sennacherib besieged Jerusalem in 701 B.C.E., it follows logically that Hezekiah's reign must have begun in 715 B.C.E. If the other references are to be correctly synchronized, one must assume that Judean kings sometimes had overlapping reigns and that Israel was actually two kingdoms during part of this time: Ephraim/Samaria, west of Jordan, and Israel, east of Jordan. If these factors are reckoned with, the absolute dates of Assyrian conquests can be correlated with the relative dates of 2 Kings. It will also be possible to recognize when kingdoms were subject to Assyrian vassalage and when they were not. In the accompanying Chronological Chart of Reigns (see below), periods of vassalage are marked with shading. Relevant reigns in Babylon, Aram, and Egypt important for the study of Isaiah are also noted. A separate column relates the placement of chapters from the Vision of Isaiah with the reigns of the rulers included in the chart. This arrangement depends principally on the work of M. Stiles. The customary tolerance for dates in this period of plus (+) or minus (-) one year applies.

CHRONOLOGICAL CHART OF REIGNS
755–700 B.C.E.

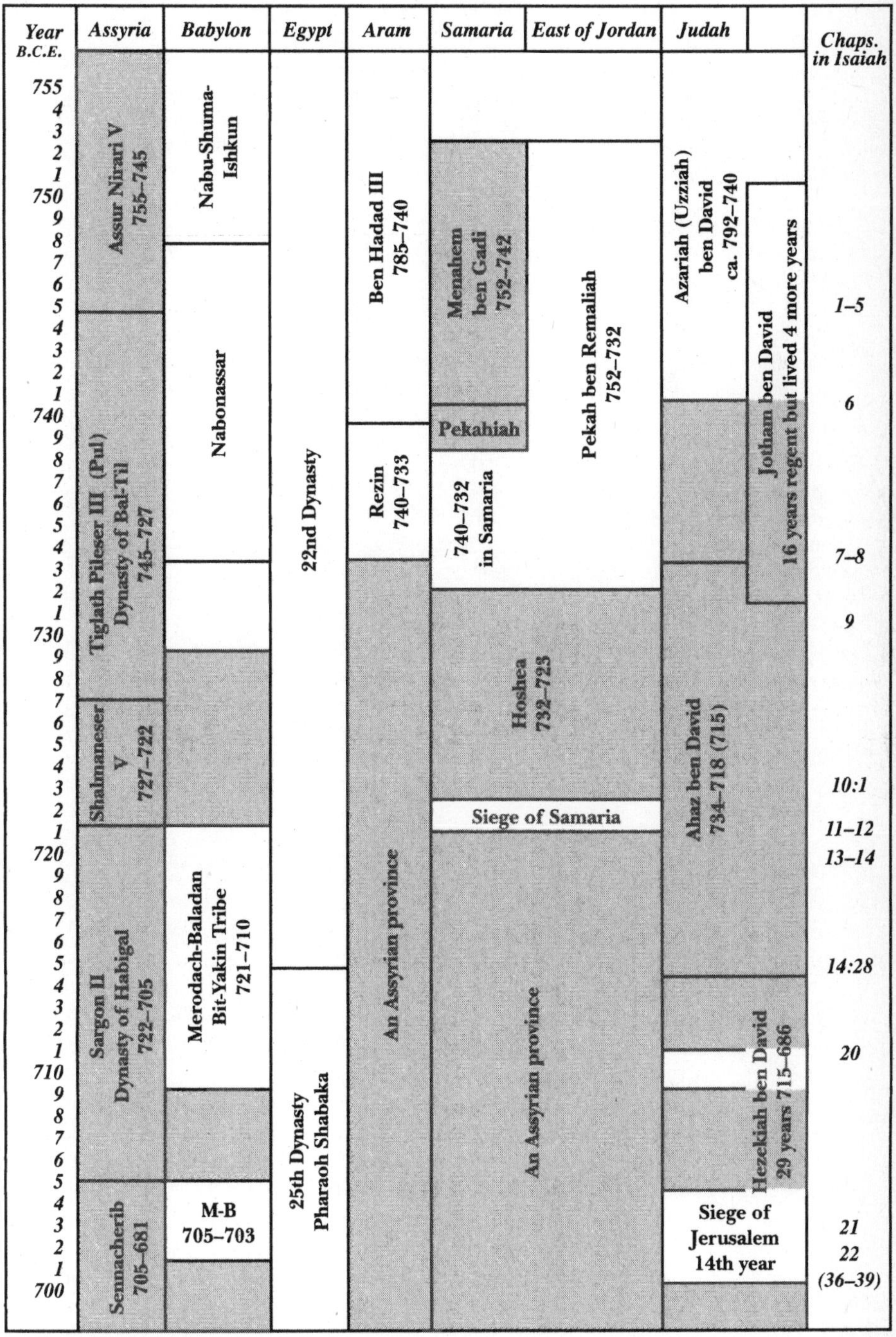
Year B.C.E.
Assyria
Babylon
Egypt
Aram
Samaria
East of Jordan
Judah
Chaps. in Isaiah
755 4 3 2 1 750 9 8 7 6 5 4 3 2 1 740 9 8 7 6 5 4 3 2 1 730 9 8 7 6 5 4 3 2 1 720 9 8 7 6 5 4 3 2 1 710 9 8 7 6 5 4 3 2 1 700
Assur Nirari V 755–745
Tiglath Pileser III (Pul) Dynasty of Bal-Til 745–727
Shalmaneser V 727–722
Sargon II Dynasty of Habigal 722–705
Sennacherib 705–681
Nabu-Shuma-Ishkun
Nabonassar
Merodach-Baladan Bit-Yakin Tribe 721–710
M-B 705–703
22nd Dynasty
25th Dynasty Pharaoh Shabaka
Ben Hadad III 785–740
Rezin 740–733
An Assyrian province
Menahem ben Gadi 752–742
Pekahiah
740–732 in Samaria
Pekah ben Remaliah 752–732
Hoshea 732–723
Siege of Samaria
An Assyrian province
Azariah (Uzziah) ben David ca. 792–740
Jotham ben David 16 years regent but lived 4 more years
Ahaz ben David 734–718 (715)
Hezekiah ben David 29 years 715–686
Siege of Jerusalem 14th year
1–5
6
7–8
9
10:1
11–12
13–14
14:28
20
21
22
(36–39)

Note: Shaded areas indicate years of Assyrian sovereignty.
Unshaded areas indicate years of independence from Assyria.

The issue of independence or vassalage to Assyria is of major importance to the Vision. In the eighth century the kings divided over that issue as follows:

A Policy of Independence	*A Policy of Vassalage*
Pekah (Israel)	Menahem (Israel)
Rezin (Aram)	Hoshea (most of his reign)
Hezekiah, 705–701 B.C.E.	Ahaz
Merodach Baladan (Babylon)	Hezekiah 715–706 B.C.E. 700–686 B.C.E.
Philistine cities (intermittently)	Tyre and Sidon (usually)

Hezekiah's last years were spent in abject subjection to Assyria, and his son, Manasseh, inherited and continued this relation. He obviously had no choice in the matter. (See *Excursus: The Vassal Years of Hezekiah and Manasseh [ca. 700–640 B.C.E.]* at *Burden: Tyre and the Desolate Land [23:1–27:13]* for more details.)

Assyria's relaxation of its hand on Palestine during the last decades of its imperial existence allowed Josiah a measure of choice and freedom unknown to his predecessors. However, this was not without its problems (see the introduction to act 3, chaps. 28–33). Ultimately his freedom led to his death and to the fateful events that followed. Egypt became an active participant in Palestinian affairs during that period and for a short time exercised authority over Palestine.

Babylon inherited Assyria's mantle. By 605 B.C.E. it was prepared to reassert Mesopotamian dominance of the area and push Egypt out (Isa 34–39). Babylon finally brought Judah's monarchy to an end and carried out deportations, scattering Jewish exiles throughout the Near East, where they joined the thousands of Israelites who had preceded them over more than a century (2 Kgs 25). Jehoiachin enjoyed a certain recognition as king in exile under Babylonian patronage.

In the sixth century B.C.E. and afterward, the issue was important to Jews. The sources record a line of leaders who counseled loyal service to the Babylonian and Persian Empires. These included Jehoiachin, Sheshbazzar, Zerubbabel (at least in the beginning), Ezra, and Nehemiah. There are indications that throughout the period there existed factions who counseled rebellion at every opportunity. The following centuries record the rebellions of the Maccabees against the Seleucid rulers and the Zealots against the Romans.

The Vision takes a clear stand on the issue.

Explanation

The Vision takes its name from the prophet. It is firmly rooted in his time, reflecting the belief that God began in the latter eighth century to do an epochal thing that was still in progress almost three centuries later. The Vision refers to the earlier period as "the former times" (41:22 + 5x in chaps. 40–48; 61:4 + 3x in chaps. 61–66). History, it says, will never quite be the same. Not since Noah's flood had a period and its events so divided the ages.

The Vision insists that God's own strategy is behind it all. The coming of the empires is part of that strategy. The scattering of Israel and the restoration of Jerusalem fit the pattern. But his people do not "know," cannot "see" or "hear" or "understand." To the very last, only a small minority are willing to take part in his "new world."

The book gives an account of the role that Isaiah's Vision of God's presence and word played in the life of Israel. It was written in a book, but sealed (8:16), which made the people "blind" because it could not be read and "deaf" because it was not heard (29:11–12). It was then read aloud as the "word of God" (40:6ff.), allowing those who believed to see and hear. But there were others who persisted in being blind and deaf.

In the Hall of the King of Heaven and Earth, Rebellious Children, Violent Worshipers, Polluted City (1:2–31)

Bibliography

Barbiero, G. "'Venite discutiamo!' Lettrua militaria di Is 1,2–20." *Salesiamun* 51 (1989) 11–21, 89–100. **Begrich, J.** "Der Satzstil in Fünfer." *ZS* 9 (1933–34) 204–9. Reprinted in *GSAT.* 1:162–67. **Condamin, A.** "Les Chaptres I et II du livre d'Isaïe." *RB* 13 (1904) 7–26. **Davies, E. W.** *Prophecy and Ethics: Isaiah and the Ethical Traditions of Israel.* JSOTSup 16. Sheffield: JSOT Press, 1981. 40–64. **Gitay, T.** "Reflections on the Study of Prophetic Discourse: The Question of Isaiah 1:2–20." *VT* 33 (1983) 207–21. **Jensen, J.** *The Use of Torah by Isaiah: His Debate with the Wisdom Traditions of Israel.* CBQMS 3. Washington: Catholic Biblical Association, 1973. 68–81. **Jones, D. R.** "Expositions of Isaiah 1." *SJT* 17 (1964) 463–77; 18 (1965) 457–71; 19 (1966) 319–27. **Luc, A.** "Isaiah I as Structural Introduction." *ZAW* 101 (1989) 115. **Mattioli, A.** "Due schemi letterari negli oracoli d'interoduzione al libro di Isaia." *RivB* 14 (1966) 345–64. **Melugin R. F.** "Figurative Speech and the Reading of Isaiah 1 as Scripture." In *New Visions.* Ed. R. F. Melugin and M. A. Sweeney. 282–305. **Milgrom, J.** "Did Isaiah Prophesy during the Reign of Uzziah?" *VT* 14 (1964) 164–82. **Niditch, S.** "The Composition of Isaiah 1." *Bib* 61 (1980) 509–29. **Rignell, L. G.** "Isaiah Chapter 1." *ST* 2 (1957) 140–58. **Roberts, J. J. M.** "Form, Syntax, and Redaction in Isaiah 1:2–20." *PSB* 3 (1982) 293–306. **Robertson, E.** "Isaiah, Chapter 1." *ZAW* 52 (1934) 231–36. **Seitz, C.** "'The Divine Council': Temporal Transition and New Prophecy in the Book of Isaiah." *JBL* 109 (1990) 229–47. **Sweeney, M. A.** *Isaiah 1–4 and the Post-Exilic Understanding of the Isianic Tradition.* Berlin: De Gruyter, 1988. 101–31. **Tucker, G. M.** "Sin and 'Judgment' in the Prophets." In *Problems in Biblical Theology.* FS R. Knierim, ed. H. T. C. Sun et al. Grand Rapids, MI: Eerdmans, 1997. 373–88. **Watts, J. Wash.** *Survey of Syntax.* **Werner, W.** *Eschatalogischer Texte in Jesaja 1–39: Messias, Heiliger Rest, Völker.* 2d ed. FB 46. Würzburg: Echter, 1986. 118–33. **Willis, J. T.** "The First Pericope in the Book of Isaiah." *VT* 34 (1984) 63–77.

Form/Structure/Setting

This first chapter of Isaiah is often treated as a part of chaps. 1–12 (Ackroyd, "Isaiah I–XII"), though others treat it as an integral part of chaps. 1–4 (Sweeney), in introducing principal themes of the book. An increasing number of analysts see it as a separate unit, however, especially in its close relation to chaps. 55–66 (Darr, *Isaiah's Vision*). This commentary, while recognizing that chaps. 2–4 are also introductory in character (O'Connell, *Concentricity and Continuity*), views the second title in 2:1 as a marker for the beginning of a new section consisting of chaps. 2–4. Unlike the superscriptions around it, there is nothing even faintly historical about the prologue. It does refer to the desolation of the countryside (v 7) but does not date the disaster. It is distinctive for its treatment of individual Israelites and worshipers.

The chapter uses a number of key words that run through the entire Vision (see below). It starts the reader thinking about the issues treated in the book from the perspective of Israel's and Jerusalem's commitments to YHWH and their covenant relationship.

Chap. 1 has the following structure:

1:2–3 Announcement of the problem, the issue
1:4–7 Woe on Israel
1:8–31 Against Jerusalem:
  1:8–15 Complaint
  1:16–20 Offer and conditions
  1:21–23 Complaint renewed
  1:24–31 Announcement of purging judgment and redemption

As the opening scene, the chapter provides the setting and introduces the principal speakers for the Vision. It publicizes YHWH's dispute with Israel and the judgment to come on them. The chapter is open-ended, looking for a response and asking the reader to interpret the whole of the Vision in light of Israel's estrangement and Jerusalem's violence. It does not assume a historical setting. It serves as the first half of the outer frame of the Vision corresponding to chaps. 63–66 at the end of the book.

Israel's Disappointed Father and the Outraged Patron of Jerusalem's Temple (1:2–20)

Bibliography for 1:2–9

Ben Zvi, E. "Isaiah 1:4–9: Isaiah and the Events of 701 B.C.E. in Judah. A Question of Premise and Evidence." *JSOT* 9 (1991) 95–111. **Björndalen, A. J.** *Untersuchungen zur allegorischen Rede der propheten Amos und Jesaja.* BZAW 165. Berlin: De Gruyter, 1986. 177–85. ———. "Zur Frage der Echtheit von Jesaja 1,2–3; 1,4–7." *NTT* 83 (1982) 89–100. **Darr, K. P.** "Child Imagery and the Rhetoric of Rebellion." In *Isaiah's Vision.* 46–84. **Delcor, M.** "Les Attaches littéraires, l'origine et la signification de l'expression biblique 'prendre á temoin le ciel de la terre.'" *VT* 16 (1966) 8–25. **Holladay, W. L.** "A New Suggestion for the the Crux in Isaiah 1:4b." *VT* 33 (1983) 235–37. **Koch, K.** "Damnation and Salvation: Prophetic Metahistory and the Rise of Eschatology in the Book of Isaiah." *ExAud* 6 (1990) 5–13. **Loewenclau, I. von.** "Zur Auslegung von Jesaja 1,2–3." *EvT* 26 (1966) 294–308. **Stachowiak, L.** "Grzech Naradu Wybranego i Mozliowasc Rutunku wedlug Iz 1:2–17." *RocTKan* 24.1 (1977) 5–19. **Uchelen, N. van.** "Isaiah 1:9—Text and Context." *OtSt* 21 (1981) 155–63. **Werner, W.** "Israel in der Entscheidung: Ueberlegungen zur Datierung und zur theologischen Aussage von Jes 1:4–9." In *Eschatologie.* FS E. Neuhäusler, ed. R. Kilian, K. Funk, and P. Fassl. St. Ottilien: Eos, 1981. 59–72. **Willis, J. T.** "An Important Passage for Determining the Historical Setting of a Prophetic Oracle—Isaiah 1:7–8." *ST* 39 (1985) 151–69.

Bibliography for 1:10–20

Fuhs, H. F. "Der Reichtum der Armen: Eine Betrachtung im Anschluss as Jes 1,10–17." *TGl* 77 (1987) 218–24. **Fullerton, K.** "The Rythmical Analysis of 1:10–20." *JBL* 38 (1919) 53–63. **Gitay, Y.** "Reflections on the Study of the Prophetic Discourse: The Question of

Isaiah 1:2–20." *VT* 33 (1983) 207–21. **Goldingay, J.** "If Your Sins Are Like Scarlet . . . (Isaiah 1:18)." *ST* 35 (1981) 137–44. **Haag, F.** "Sündenvergebung und neuer Anfang: Zur Übersetzung und Auslegunt von Jes 1:18." In *Die Freude an Gott—unsere Kraft.* FS O. B. Knoch, ed. J. J. Degenhardt. Stuttgart: Katholisches Bibelwerk, 1991. 68–80. **Hasel, G. F.** "'New Moon and Sabbath' in Eighth Century Israelite Prophetic Writings (Isa 1:13, Hos 2:13, Am 8:5)." *IOFOT Summaries, 1986.* 55. **Hoffman, H. W.** *Die Intention der Verkündigung Jesajas.* 82–85; 92–104. **Schoneveld, J.** "Jesaia 1:18–20." *VT* 13 (1963) 342–44. **Willis, J. T.** "The First Pericope in the Book of Isaiah." *VT* 34 (1984) 63–77. ———. "Lament Reversed—Isaiah 1,21ff." *ZAW* 98 (1986) 236–48. ———. "On the Interpretation of Isa 1:18." *JSOT* 25 (1983) 35–54.

Translation

Herald:	2 *Hear, Heavens!* [a]	2+2+3
(to Heavens and Earth)	*And give ear, Earth!*	
	For YHWH speaks!	
YHWH:	*Children I have reared* [b] *and raised up,*	3+3
(to Heavens and Earth)	*but even they have rebelled against me.*	
	3 *An ox knows its owner*	3+3
	and an ass its master's crib.	
	Israel does not know! [a]	3+3
	My people [b] *make no distinction!*	
Heavens and Earth:	4 *Woe! Sinning nation!*	3+3
	People heavy with iniquity!	
	Evil-doing seed!	2+2
	Destroying children!	
	They have forsaken YHWH!	2+3+2
	They have despised the Holy One of Israel!	
	[a] *They have slid backward!* [a]	
(to the people of Israel)	5 *Upon what will you [pl.] be beaten more?*	4+2
	Will you add rebellion?	
	Every head (is) for sores [a]	3+3
	and every stomach (is) cramped!	
	6 *From the sole of foot*	2+2+2
	to the head—	
	no sound spot! [a]	
	A wound or bruise,	2+2
	or bleeding stripe,	
	they have not been closed.	2+2+3
	Nor have they been bound up.	
	And they have not been softened with oil.	
	7 *Your [pl.] country is desolate,*	2+3
	your cities burned with fire.	
	Your farmland, in your presence	2+3
	strangers are devouring it.	
Herald:	*Yea, desolation* [a] *like overthrow of strangers.*	3
(to Heavens and Earth)	8 *And daughter Zion is left*	2+2
	like a watchman's booth in a vineyard,	

	like a hut in a cucumber field,	2+2
	like a fortified [a] *city.*	
People of Jerusalem:	9 *If YHWH of Hosts*	3+3
(to Heavens and Earth)	*had not left to us a remnant,*	
	almost [a] *like Sodom* [b] *we would have become;*	3+2
	Gomorrah [b] *we would resemble.*	
Herald:	10 *Hear (ye) the word of YHWH,*	3+2
(to people of Jerusalem)	*rulers of Sodom.*	
	Give ear to the Instruction of our God,	3+2
	people of Gomorrah.	
YHWH:	11 *For what purpose (do you bring) to me*	2+2+2
	the great number of your sacrifices?	
Herald:	*says YHWH.*	
YHWH:	*I have had enough burnt offerings of rams*	3+2
	and the fat of fed-beasts.	
	Yea, blood of bulls	2+2+2
	and lambs [a] *and he-goats*	
	I do not desire.	
	12 *Whenever you come*	2+2
	to appear [a] *before me,*	
	who has requested this from your hand,	3+2
	(this) trampling of my courts? [b]	
	13 *Do not bring a meaningless offering anymore.*	3+2
	It is an incense of abomination to me.	
	New moon and sabbath,	2+2
	calling of convocation,	
	I cannot bear iniquity	2+2
	with solemn assembly.	
	14 *Your new moons and your set seasons*	2+2
	my soul hates.	
	They are to me a burden.	3+2
	I am tired of bearing them.	
	15 *When you spread your hands [in prayer],*	2+3
	I will hide my eyes from you,	
	and also, when you multiply prayers,	2+3
	I am not listening.	
	Your hands are full of blood!	3
	(Your fingers with iniquity!) [a]	
	16 *Wash yourselves! Be pure!*	2
	Remove the evil of your doings	3+2
	from before my eyes!	
	Cease doing evil!	2+2
	17 *Learn doing good!*	
	Seek justice!	2+2
	Remedy oppression!	
	Bring justice to the orphan!	2+2
	Plead the cause of the widow!	
	18 *Come now! Let us test each other,*	2+2

Herald: *says YHWH.*
YHWH: *If your sins*[a] *are like the scarlet robes,* 3+2
like the snow they may[a] *become white.*
If they are a red like crimson, 2+2
like wool they may become.
[19]*If you become willing*[a] *and shall obey,*[a] 2+3
the good of the land you may eat.
[20]*But if you refuse*[a] *and shall continue obstinate,* 2+2
(by a) sword you may be devoured,[a]
Herald: *For the mouth of YHWH has spoken.* 4

Notes

2.a. The pl. address שמים, "heavens," is maintained in MT but has become sg. in some LXX MSS.

2.b. MT has virtually no variants. LXX translates גדלתי, "reared," with ἐγέννησα, "begot," while σ´and θ´ have ἐζέθρεφα, "reared," and Vg. *enutrivi,* "brought up." LXX probably presumes ילדתי as a Heb. original, which would fit the use with "father" and "son." But the OT usually avoids using that verb with God as subject and very seldom speaks of God producing offspring (exceptions: Deut 32:18; Ps 2:7). MT should be preferred.

3.a. LXX adds με, so "Israel does not know me." This should be viewed as interpretation in translation. MT's concise form, reproduced in the *Translation,* is better style and has a more pungent meaning.

3.b. Several MSS, as well as LXX, Syr., and Vg., add "and," but it is unnecessary. The subject remains the same, and parallelism is complete.

4.a-a. Omitted in LXX. A. Guillaume ("Hebrew Notes," *PEQ* 79 [1947] 40) argues for retaining the phrase. He notes a play on different meanings of words using the syllable זר: v 4 נזרו, "gone, slidden"; v 6 זרו, "pressed out"; v 7 זרים, "strangers"; v 8 נצורה, "besieged"; and v 9 שריד, "remnant." Budde ("Zu Jesaja 1–5," *ZAW* 49 [1931] 21) emended to read מְאַחֲרָיו, "his tarrying." G. R. Driver (*JTS* 38 [1937] 36) connects נזר with an Arab. root *zarra,* meaning "express, drive back." Neither of these is a satisfactory solution. Vg. *(abalienati sunt retrorsum)* and Tg. (אסתחרו והוו לאחרא) appear to support MT (*BHK* to the contrary; so Wildberger). N. H. Tur-Sinai ("A Contribution to the Understanding of Isaiah I–XII," 155) suggests emending אחור to יחד or כאחד and translating "they have become estranged together." This makes sense, but the change is unnecessary. W. L. Holladay ("The Crux in Isaiah 1:4–6," *VT* 33 [1983] 235–37) reads נָזְרוּ אַחֵר, "they have dedicated themselves to another (god)." The two words appear to exceed the metric form and the compact composition and probably should be judged a gloss (with Wildberger).

5.a. MT לחלי. G. R. Driver (*JSS* 13 [1968] 36) suggests the meaning of "sores, pustules, gangrene" from the root חלע. He also notes that לבב is from a root that suggests "something twisted," thus "stomach" or "intestine."

6.a. H. D. Hummel ("Enclitic *Mem* in Early NW Semitic," *JBL* 76 [1957] 105) suggests that אין־בו מתם, "no sound spot," is a scribal error for אין במו תם, "nothing with integrity." But אין מתם also occurs in Ps 38:4, 8. The LXX omits the phrase, but the meter requires it. MT should be kept.

7.a. 1QIsa[a] reads שממו עליה, "they will be upset over it." Marti, Gray, Duhm, and Fohrer consider the entire line a gloss on שממה, "desolate," above. S. Speier ("Zu drei Jesajastellen," *TZ* 21 [1965] 310) follows 1QIsa[a], compares it to Lev 26:32, and considers it a scribal comment.

This entire stich has been challenged on numerous grounds. But the duplication of words is fitting, even necessary, within the larger composition. Both שממה and זרים, "strangers," pick up words from the previous lines to connect the two speeches, as is customary in this chapter (Fohrer). Wildberger notes that מהפכה, "overthrow," is used in the OT without exception with "Sodom and Gommorah" (cf. Deut 29:22; Isa 13:19; Jer 49:18; 50:40; Amos 4:11) and suggests emending זרים to read סדם, "Sodom." However, since the line is a deliberate connection between v 7, with which MT's reading fits, and v 9, where סדם fits, the very tension in the phrase should be seen as intentional and MT's reading sustained.

8.a נצורה has presented difficulties to translators and interpreters alike. LXX πολιορκουμένη (like Syr. Tg. Vg.) gives the word an active meaning and seems to think of "a besieged city." A. Dillmann pointed it נְצוּרָה (*nipʿal* ptc. from צור). F. X. Wutz (*BZ* 21 [1933] 11) suggested emending to read כְּעִיר בְּצִירָה and translating "like a flock on one perch." Wildberger (19) follows the emendation but translates "like a donkey-colt in a bird house." Something like this would preserve the kind of comparison of the previous line but seems most unlikely. Hitzig and Duhm suggested a translation of "watchtower." Dillmann may have been right to reject this literally, but the tendency deserves attention. נצר means to watch or guard. Judean kings did build up fortified border cities throughout their history. Such a city would in fact be an outpost to watch or guard the border and could easily be overrun or bypassed in an attack.

9.a. MT places the verse divider (*ʾatnakh*) after כמעט, "almost, little." This makes an uneven meter and an awkward sense. LXX, Syr., OL, and Tg. have divided the verse one word earlier, giving a balanced meter and a better sense (contra Wildberger).

9.b. 1QIsa[a] has סודם and עומרה for MT's סדם and עמרה. Cf. the Gk. Σοδομα and Γομορρα. Apparently the heavy second syllable has affected the pronunciation of the short first syllable (cf. W. Baumgartner, "Beiträge zum hebräischen Lexikon," in *Von Ugarit nach Qumran*, FS O. Eissfeldt, ed. J. Hempel et al., BZAW 77 [Giessen: Töpelmann, 1958] 29). The meaning is the same.

11.a. וכבשים, "and lambs," is missing in LXX. But the meter requires the word (Procksch), and making the list full adds to the effect. It should be kept.

12.a. LXX ὀφθῆναι μοι and Syr. *lᵉmḫzâ ʾappaj* suggest the reading of one MS: לִרְאוֹת, i.e., an act. *qal* meaning "to see my face." Perhaps the change to *nipʿal*, "to appear before me," was intended to avoid speaking of seeing God. Whoever sees him will die (cf. Exod 23:15; 34:23; Deut 16:16; 31:11; 1 Sam 1:22; Ps 42:3).

Numerous emendations have been suggested (cf. Wildberger) to smooth out the abrupt expressions here. Even that of 1QIsa[a] לרמוס, "to trample," for רמס, "trampling," should be thought of in this way. MT should be kept and the abruptness attributed to conscious style.

12.b. LXX has τὴν αὐλήν μου for חצרי, "courts," making a sg. for MT's pl. But Wildberger notes that 2 Kgs 21:5; 23:12 write about two courts of the temple. Ezekiel distinguishes between an inner and an outer court (Ezek 8:16; 10:5).

15.a. 1QIsa[a] adds אצבעותיכם בעאון, "your fingers with iniquity." The addition is parallel to the previous stich and would be a metrical improvement on MT. Cf. 59:3 and Kutscher, *Language and Linguistic Background*, 536.

18.a., 19.a., 20.a. Four conditional sentences use the impf. tense in both the protasis and the apodosis. The last two add a second verb using a pf. tense with *vav*. This sequence of tenses is the simplest form of condition in Heb. It may be considered indic., stating facts. Or it may be considered subjunctive, stating hypothetical situations (cf. J. Wash Watts, *Survey of Syntax*, 134). The context places these sentences early in the dialogue, thus favoring the understanding that they sketch possibilities, a view that the translation attempts to reflect.

Form/Structure/Setting

Isa 1 is a virtual catalog of words, ideas, and teachings about Israel and Jerusalem as they will be presented in the following Vision. The most important of these strands will be noted in the *Comment* below.

Throughout the Vision of Isaiah certain passages show a marked structural resemblance to the arch in architecture, in which a wall opening is spanned by means of stone blocks assembled into an upward curve that maintains its shape and stability through mutual pressure of the separate pieces. The blocks usually have a wedge shape, with the block at the crown of the arch being called the keystone since it conveys balancing lateral pressures to the two sides of the structure. In the following example, the parallel thoughts of the verses marked A-A´, B-B´, C-C´, and D-D´ serve as the blocks of the two sides of the arch held in balance by the keystone, vv 7*c*–9. (Because of typographical considerations, the textual arch appears on its side, but the resemblance should be readily apparent to the reader.)

A "I reared my children—but they rebelled against me." (1:2)
  B "An ox knows. . . . Israel does not know." (1:3)
    C "Woe! Sinning nation!" Why more? (1:4–5)
      D Only wounds left—countryside desolate (1:6–7*b*)
KEYSTONE Daughter Zion isolated, like a city under siege—except for the remnant left by YHWH, would be like Sodom (1:7*c*–9)
      D′ Empty, useless worship (1:10–15*a*)
    C′ "Hands full of blood! Wash yourselves." (1:15*b*–17)
  B′ "Come, . . . let us test each other." (1:18–20)
A′ How has the faithful city become a harlot? (1:21–23)

The formation ends here, but an overlapping structure balances vv 21–23 with vv 24–26, which follow. The commentary will break at v 20 but will note the overlapping structure in the next pericope.

The passage is in the form of the beginning of a covenant lawsuit (*OTFC,* 164–66; G. E. Mendenhall, "Ancient Oriental and Biblical Law," *BA* 17.2 [1952] 26–46; H. B. Huffmon, "The Covenant Lawsuit," *JBL* 78 [1959] 285–95; J. Harvey, "Le 'Rib-pattern,'" *Bib* 43 [1962] 172–96). Witnesses are summoned (v 2*a*). The witnesses are the same as those found in Deut 32 (cf. Rignell, *ST* 2 [1957] 140–58). In both Deut 32 and this passage the genre is incomplete. G. E. Wright has called this a "broken riv" ("The Lawsuit of God," in *Israel's Prophetic Heritage,* ed. B. W. Anderson and W. Harrelson, 62–67). The chief litigant is announced (v 2*b*). His charges are given in brief (vv 2*c*–3). The accused is named (v 3*c*). Vv 2–7*b* speak of Israel. Vv 7*c*–23 describe and address Zion. Israel is spoken of as "children." Zion is viewed as a daughter. Both are badly alienated.

Vv 4–7*b* and 7*c*–9 are speeches by others than YHWH, perhaps the witnesses already named. The change of speeches is marked by a change of subject and by repetition of a phrase (cf. Fohrer, *Studien,* 149). V 4 is a short woe speech (cf. Hayes, *OTFC,* 164; C. Westermann, *Basic Forms,* 190–94; R. J. Clifford, "The use of HOY in the prophets," *CBQ* 28 [1966] 458–64; E. Gerstenberger, "The Woe-Oracles of the Prophets," *JBL* 81 [1962] 249–63; G. Wanke, "Mitteilungen הוי und אוי," *ZAW* 78 [1966] 215–18; J. G. Williams, "The Alas-Oracles," *HUCA* 38 [1967] 75–91). The meter is irregular, intentionally so. It is artfully composed (Wildberger). There is always a funereal aspect to a woe speech. This is no exception. The "woes" against Israel will be continued in chaps. 5 and 10 and will culminate in confirmation of total destruction decreed against her (10:25). Vv 5–7*b* are a chiding speech of warning instead of the more usual threat following a "woe."

The second speech (vv 7*c*–9) changes the subject from Israel to Zion. It is characterized by six uses of כ, "like," for comparisons in parabolic style. V 9 has a chorus continue the theme. (See *Strand: "We, Us, Our"* and *Strand: "You"* in the *Introduction.*)

Vv 10–17 have YHWH speak in the style of a teacher giving instruction. He is announced by a herald who uses catchwords to join his speech to the preceding chorus. Such instruction may be given by a priest concerning proper forms of worship (Duhm; Begrich, *Studien*). But here the critique of worship is more than usual for a teacher (J. Jensen). A call for attention (v 10) and rhetorical questions (vv 11*a*, 12) fit the style of the Wisdom teachers. The essence of the lesson is presented in a series of statements of God's attitude interspersed with imperative instructions. Vv 16–17 state the terms on which God will deal with his people.

These are not negotiable. The sequence of tenses is instructive. Imperatives dominate the "torah." YHWH's position is stated in emphatic perfects. Zion's habits are pictured in imperfects.

Vv 18–20 are the closing appeal that defines the attitudes that would make negotiation possible. In the context of *riv,* these verses constitute what J. Harvey (*Bib* 43 [1962] 172–96) has called the fourth element (cf. also Hayes, *OTFC,* 166), so I divide this commentary's discussion after v 20. Cultic procedures, like sacrifice, had already been eliminated from consideration. The conditional sentences use imperfect tenses in both protasis and apodosis. They state simple indicative, more probable conditions (J. Wash Watts, *Survey of Syntax,* 134, 139).

Comment

2 The summons introduces two of the *dramatis personae,* "Heavens" and "Earth," which appear without the article. It is normally omitted in the vocative case (Joüon §137*g*). Heavens and Earth are personalized here as members of the divine council, who are called as witnesses to YHWH's indictment against his people (cf. Deut 32:1). They are addressed again in 44:23, 45:8, and 49:13, but they may be thought of as attending YHWH throughout the Vision.

כי יהוה דבר, "for YHWH speaks," demonstrates a reversed word order appropriate to the introduction of YHWH as principal speaker in the Vision. The same reasoning accounts for the emphatic position of other words in the speech. The accused are presented: children, Israel, my people. The emphatic pronoun והם, "they," is put before פשעו, "rebelled": "precisely these [children] have rebelled against me."

פשע, "rebelled," is a particularly appropriate word for the theology of apostasy expounded in the Vision. It fits the parent-child analogy as well as the king-subject pattern. It reflects the deep emotion of the problem and its effects on relationship. It shows the deliberately willed nature of the issue: the unwillingness to recognize the nature of the relationship to God as parent or king and to draw the consequences of that relation and the dependence that it implies. The entire Vision will show the effects and the results of this rebellion from the reign of Ahaz (734 B.C.E.) to conditions that were still current for readers generations later.

YHWH issues a blanket indictment of Israel for rebellion. The OT demands honor and obedience toward parents (Exod 20:12*a;* Prov 1:8–9; 23:22) and defines clear punishments for disobedience and incorrigible attitudes (Prov 30:17; 20:30; 3:11–12). Deut 21:18–21 tells parents what to do with such a child: brought before the elders, he is to be denounced publicly before they stone him to death (see K. P. Darr, "Child Imagery and the Rhetoric of Rebellion," in *Isaiah's Vision and the Family of God* [Louisville, KY: Westminster John Knox, 1994] 46–84). YHWH's denouncement of Israel follows this procedure before the heavenly council.

Strand: Rebellious Children (Individuals)

The term פשע, "rebel," occurs in 1:2; 24:20; 43:25; 44:22; 50:1; 53:5, 8; 57:4; 58:1; and 59:12, 20. A cognate term סרר occurs in 30:1 with בנים, "children" and in 65:2 with עם, "people." The word בנים, "children," occurs in 1:2 and 30:1. אבינו, "our father," addressed to God occurs in 63:16 (2x) and 64:7, 10.

Despite the announcement in the superscription that the topic will be Jerusalem and Judah, the first topic discussed in the book is YHWH's domestic problem with rebellious children (1:2–3). The plural form is distinctive, dealing with persons as individuals. This is the indictment not of Israel or Jerusalem as a whole but of persons in both of them. Possible solutions will also deal with individual decisions (1:18–20; 27–28). The plural indictment continues in 2:5–8. The plural form opens the possibility of separating the people into penitents and stubborn rebels (1:18–20; 27–28; 3:10–11). The indictments of 5:9–25 continue to be plural, as do the woes of 9:8–10:4.

Isa 6:9–10 recognizes a change in the message in the following sections. Only in 30:1–5 does the plural address appear again. The accusation of being rebellious children reappears in 30:9. A call to repentance comes in 31:6–7.

After fruitless appeals to Israel and Jerusalem in chaps. 40–54, Isa 54:17*b* addresses "the servants of YHWH," and chap. 55 brings an appeal in the plural to "all who are thirsty." Isa 55:6 calls upon all to seek YHWH and turn to him to receive pardon. Chaps. 56–59 continue to address the issues in terms of plural persons, some of whom can be saved and some of whom will be lost.

Isa 65:1–7 addresses persons who have failed to answer the call to repentance. Isa 65:8–12 speaks of a division, while 65:13–16 defines the "servants" who have found YHWH and enjoy the status of his servants. It is clear that these chapters pick up the theme of rebellious children from chap. 1. But they do not dare move back to the use of the term בנים, "children," despite the pleas of chap. 64. They are content to be called "servants." This is balanced with the increased use of the title אדני, "Lord," for YHWH. Note the parallel use of language in the parable of the Lost Son in Luke 15:11–32. In the far country the son comes to himself and rehearses a speech to his father when he returns: "I have sinned against heaven and against you. I am no longer worthy to be called your son; make me like one of your hired men [servants]" (Luke 15:18 NIV).

The rebellious-children strand of chaps. 1–5, 30–31, 55, 56–59, and 65 highlights the responsibilities and the possibilities of individuals. They may be separately judged and killed. Or they may repent and share life with God. Those who continue in rebellion are הרשעים, "the adversaries." The separation between the pious and the wicked is complete.

The language of rebellion appears in other prophetic books to stress individual responsibility and the possibility of repentance (see Jer 2:8, 29; 3:13; 5:23; 6:28; 33:8; 52:3; Ezek 2:3; 2:3; 5:6; 17:15; 18:31, 20:8, 13, 21; 38; ; Hos 7:13; 8:1; 14:10; Amos 4:4). Ezek 18 separates the guilt of different generations, freeing children from fathers' guilt and fathers from children's guilt. Isaiah places blame directly on individuals who choose to sin, to rebel, and refuse to change. Isaiah opens the door to repentance, change, and new birth. And if the result does not produce new "children" for God, it does produce acceptable "servants."

The problem is defined in 1:3: "Israel does not know [ידע]. My people make no distinction [do not understand (התבונן)]." These two words continue throughout the book (see *Strand:* דעת*, "knowledge," and* בינה*, "understanding"* below).

There are differences within the book in the way the rebellion is defined and in what change is called for. Social and cultic sins are emphasized in chap. 1 and following. People are called to reform and change their lives in 1:18–20 and in chaps. 27–28, and again in chap. 61. Heavy emphasis on the problems of an unrepentant people comes in chaps. 28–33 for the preexilic period. It is picked up in chaps. 56–59 for the postexilic period to show that the basic issue of an unrepentant and sinful people has not changed.

A final plea from this people comes in 63:8–64:12 on the basis of God's merciful choice and care of his people from Moses to the present. But 65:1–12 again makes the case indicting the people for sins ranging from unresponsiveness to pagan worship. As in chap. 1, YHWH shows that the only hope lies in separating the responsive, repentant servants from the rest. Only the servants will be saved and used (65:9–10, 13–16). To these, willing seekers from the peoples will be added (66:18–23). But the fate of the rebellious wicked must be death and destruction (66:24). There is a shift of emphasis in some intervening chapters. As chaps. 40–55 emphasize the call of God to his people, the ultimate sin becomes failure to answer that call. The words "I called but no one answered" echo through these chapters (41:28; 43:22; 48:14; 50:2; 59:15*b*–16; 63:5; 65:1–2, 12*b*; 66:4*b*). Failure to respond to the good news and to God's call receives a more damning and final indictment than do other sins.

3 After the accusation of rebellion (v 2), Israel is said to have neither knowledge nor discernment. The presumption that these are necessary for a healthy life in covenant with God runs through the Vision. It is one of the strands that bind the work together.

Household animals learn and remember to whom they belong. They recognize their owners, their lords. שור, "ox," was used in myth to symbolize El, but that has no meaning here. One cannot think of the ass as having insight without being reminded of Balaam's patient animal (Num 22:21–30), which recognized what Balaam could not see. Only humankind rebels, refusing the most elementary recognition of god's ownership. Pseudo-Matthew 14 tells of the ox and the ass worshiping Jesus in Bethlehem's cradle and calls them a fulfillment of this part of Isaiah's prophecy. (Cf. E. Nielsen, "Ass and Ox in the OT," in *Studia Orientalia Ioanni Pedersen dicata* [Copenhagen: Munksgaard, 1953] 263–74; J. Ziegler, "Ochs and Esel an der Krippe," *MTZ* 3 [1952] 385–402.) The apocryphal gospel has correctly seen the meaning of the parable in Isaiah. Ox and ass are credited with recognition and discernment that human beings do not display.

The plural קנהו, "its masters," is unusual. It could be a plural of majesty implying a superior being, as in Exod 21:29, 22:10, or Job 31:39 (Wildberger). But this seems unnecessarily complex. Even if the ass has several owners, they keep him in one stall. He has only to find his way to the one place, which he does.

After the two imperative forms that introduce the speech, all the verbs are in the perfect tense. The first, דבר, "speaks," has been translated as an emphatic present (J. Wash Watts, *Survey of Syntax*, 38). The three in the second line are translated as present perfects indicating past actions with present effect (*Survey of Syntax*, 45). The tenses in v 3 are also perfects, but they speak of actions which are typical of their subjects. They are thus characteristic perfects (*Survey of Syntax*, 46).

4–5 The addressee in vv 4–7 continues to be Israel, and the distinction drawn between Israel and Zion in v 8 suggests the northern kingdom. The accusation of vv 2–3 is sustained. Israel is found guilty. The woe speech develops the full range of Israel's guilt with seven words to broaden the picture of rebellious (פשע) children who neither know (ידע) nor understand (בין). The words appear in three pairs with one word finally to summarize the effect.

גוי חטא עם כבד עון, "Sinning nation! People heavy with iniquity!" חטא and עון are the common words for "sin" (R. Knierim, *Die Hauptbegriffe für Sünde im Alten Testament*, 2d ed. [Gutersloh: Mohn, 1967]). They characterize the entire nation (גוי) and the people (עם). This leaves no doubt that the nation is the ten-tribe northern kingdom, which could properly be thought of as living "in sin" since the schism from the Davidic dynasty. The people are the covenant people, sealed to be God's own in covenant ceremonies from Sinai and Shechem on.

Strand: "Knowledge" (דעת) *and "Understanding"* (בינה)

Bibliography

Schmidt, W. H. "Einsicht als Ziel prophetischer Verkündigung." In *Ich bewirke das Heil und erschaffe das Unheil (Jesaja 45,7): Studien zur Botschaft der Propheten.* FS L. Ruppert, ed. F. Diedrich and B. Willmes. FzB 88. Würzburg: Echter, 1998. 371–96.

In Isaiah, not having "knowledge" or "understanding" is a sin or the result of sin. Knowledge and understanding belong to the redeemed. Isa 6:9–10 instructs the prophet to close the people's ears so that they cannot repent or respond. Isa 40:1–2 reverses this decree. But the results of the earlier decree (1:3*b;* 28:19*b;* 29:9–12; 32:3–8; 35:5) continue to be a problem in the new era (42:18–19; 43:8; 53:13*b*). God's call, which makes response possible, must be heard in the period in which it is available, as 55:6 shows: "Seek the Lord while he may be found. Call upon him while he is near." So the problem of hearing, seeing, knowing, and understanding spreads throughout the book.

Prologue	Act 1	Act 2	Act 3	Act 4	Act 5	Act 6	Epilogue
ידע, "KNOW"; דעה דעת, "KNOWLEDGE"							
1:3	5:13, 19 7:15, 16 9:8 (9) 11:2, 9 12:4–5	19:12, 21	28:9 29:11, 12, 15, 24 32:4 33:6	37:20, 28 38:19 40:14, 21, 28 41:20, 22, 23, 26 42:16, 25 43:10 44:8, 9, 18, 19, 25 45:3, 4, 5, 6 47:8, 10 11 48:4, 6, 7, 8	49:23, 26 50:4, 7 51:7 52:6 53:3, 11	55:5 56:10–11 58:2 59:8 59:8, 12 60:16 61:9	63:15 64:1 66:14
בין, "UNDERSTAND"; בינה, "UNDERSTANDING"							
1:3	5:22 6:9, 10 10:12 11:2	14:6, 16 27:11	28:9, 19 29:14, 16, 24 32:4 33:19	40:14, 21, 28 43:10, 18 44:18, 19	52:15	56:11 57:1	

The basic idea of חטא is "to go astray, miss the mark." It means that one has missed the norm required by law, whether that be in society or in relation to God. The parallel word עון has a basic meaning of being "crooked," which leads to a life or deed that is wrong. This word suggests that the subject has an attitude that is not in line with God's will (L. Köhler, *OT Theology*, 172–75). עון seems to always include the sense of guilt. By using the two words together, Israel's position is clearly defined. The people continually fail to do the right thing (note the participial meaning of continuing action), resulting in a condition of guilt. Recent studies (e.g., Koch, *ExAud* 6 [1990] 5–13) have stressed the way in which action, status, and fate are thought to interact and overlap. So here Israel's sin, guilt, and judgment are pictured together.

זרע מרעים בנים משחיתים, "Evil-doing seed! Destroying children!" The second pair of words returns to the idea of children and continues to parallel Deut 21:18–21. זרע, "seed," may be used as a synonym for בנים, "children," but here "seed" takes on a denigrating meaning. Juxtaposition with the word מרעים, "evildoers," places them in bad company, doing bad things. While חטא and עון picture the subject as a citizen or worshiper who has failed and incurred guilt, רעה, "evil," and שחת, "broken," put the sinners in the ranks of criminals and outlaws. Deut 32:4 speaks of God's faithfulness in contrast to the broken (שחת) loyalty of Israel. זרע מרעים is "a seed composed of evildoers" (cf. GKC §128*k–q*). Israel, God's children, has become God's opposite.

עזבו את־יהוה נאצו את־קדוש ישראל, "They have forsaken YHWH! They have despised the Holy One of Israel!" The third pair of words stresses the distance between YHWH and Israel, between what God stands for and what the people of Israel represent. עזב, "forsake," occurs some twenty-five times in Isaiah (see *Strand: "Abandon"* [עזב] in the *Introduction*). In the first half of the Vision, it describes abandoned cities and countryside. In the second half, it is the key word in a continuing debate about God's responsibility for Israel and Zion after 587 B.C.E. (see *Comment* on 41:17 and passim, esp. 54:6–7). Three times in the book עזב, "abandon," is an accusation of breach of covenant in the claim that God's people have abandoned him. In 1:28 the accusation turns against the people of Jerusalem, while 65:11 uses it as one of the summary terms of judgment against those that are rejected in the new order. נאץ, "despise," is a term at home in covenant literature (cf. Deut 31:20; 32:19; also Jer 14:21). It means "to despise" in the sense of "think lightly of" or actually to ignore the covenant. The two terms עזב, "abandon," and נאץ, "despise," are used in the Deuteronomic literature to speak of breaking covenant and turning to other gods (Judg 2:12; 10:6, 10, 13; 1 Sam 8:8; 12:10). Israel's forsaking the covenant implies that YHWH also abandons his covenant obligations (cf. Deut 31:19; Jer 14:21). In Deut 31:16 "forsake" is parallel to "break my covenant," while Num 14:11 uses "despise" as the opposite of faith.

In v 4 a distinctive name for God appears for the first time: קדוש ישראל, "the Holy One of Israel." It appears repeatedly in every part of Isaiah except the epilogue.

6 F. Buhl ("Zu Jesaja 1:5," *ZAW* 36 [1916] 117) cites the Annals of Tabari (3:164) where a police officer is ordered to beat the scribe of the former mayor. Since the scribe's body appeared to be one continuous sore from the top of his head to the sole of his feet, the officer asked, "Where do you want to be beaten?" The scribe replied, "By Allah, there is no place on my body for a beating. But if you wish, then the palm of my hand."

Strand: "The Holy One of Israel" (קדוש ישראל)

Prologue	Act 1	Act 2	Act 3	Act 4	Act 5	Act 6	Epilogue
1:4	5:19, 24 10:20 12:6	17:7	29:19 30:11, 12, 15 31:1	37:23 41:14, 16, 20 43:3, 14 45:11 47:4 48:17	49:7 54:5	55:5	

The figurative flogging has left wound over festered wound until there seems no spot on the bruised, bleeding body where the whip can be applied. The horrible figure then turns toward an equally revolting historical reality: the ravages of war across a countryside, scarring the fields with fire and the cities with destruction.

7 ארצכם שממה עריכם שרפות אש, "Your country is desolate, your cities burned with fire." The verses picture the repeated Assyrian invasions that led to the destruction and exile of the tribes. Interpreters have made intensive efforts to identify the historical references in this chapter (W. T. Claassen, *JNSL* 3 [1974] 1–18). Some have dated material to 734 B.C.E., making the invaders Syria and Israel, while others insist on a picture of Assyria's siege of Jerusalem in 701 B.C.E. (Wildberger). The pericope, like the entire chapter, evades dating and historical identification, apparently deliberately. A fifth-century reader would have little concern to distinguish 734 from 701 B.C.E. He would also have been aware that the description had had multiple applications between the eighth century and his own time. The literary impact is far more important here than historical identification.

This picture of the desolation in the land is the first in the book of Isaiah, but the theme and the idea will reappear frequently. (See *Excursus: "Desolation"* [שממה] *in Isaiah* at chap. 5.) The recognition of the terrible effects in Palestine and the Near East of the wars of the Assyrian and Babylonian eras is everywhere. The theme will be dealt with throughout part I (chaps. 5–33), especially in chaps. 5–6. The book of Isaiah is an interpretation of that era and an exhortation to the people who survive to recognize God's purposes in the restoration.

8 נותרה, "is left." This is the first appearance in Isaiah of a word linked to the doctrine of the remnant. It is repeated (in *hipʿil*) in v 9 with the noun שׂריד, "remnant." (See *Excursus: The "Remnant"* [שאר/שארית] *in Isaiah* at 7:3–9.)

The watchman's booth is a familiar Near Eastern sight. Ripening fruit cannot be left unguarded against human theft or the invasion of animals or birds. The guard needs protection from the sun. So a booth of branches is made for him, elevated to enhance his field of vision. It will only last a season but often remains long after the watchman is no longer needed.

The עיר נצורה, "fort-city" or "watch-city," was a fortified border town built to protect the frontiers. Solomon built these fort cities as did every effective king. The direction from which danger was expected can be seen in the places where such cities are built. But these were invariably as far from the capital and the center of the nation as possible. Now the country has been overrun, and Jerusalem itself is like one of those isolated watch-cities. The enemy has swept past, conquering the countryside and leaving only the walled fortress intact.

The only thing remaining of Israel is Jerusalem, called here בת־ציון, "daughter Zion."

Excursus: "Daughter Zion" (בת־ציון): Cities in Isaiah

Bibliography

Biddle, M. "The City of Chaos and the New Jerusalem.: Isaiah 24–27 in Context." *PRS* 22 (1995) 5–12. ———. "The Figure of Lady Jerusalem: Identification, Deification and Personification of Cities in the Ancient Near East." In *The Biblical Canon in Comparative Perspective.* Ed. K. L. Younger, Jr., W. W. Hallo, and B. F. Batto. Scripture in Context 4. Lewiston, NY: Mellen, 1991. 173–94. **Darr, K. P.** "The Ladies' Lots." In *Isaiah's Vision.* 85–224. **Fitzgerald, A.** "BLWLT and BT as Titles for Capital Cities." *CBQ* 37 (1975) 170–80. ———. "The Mythological Background for the Presentation of Jerusalem as a Queen and False Worship as Adultery in the Old Testament." *CBQ* 34 (1972) 403–16. **Follis, E. R.** "The Holy City as Daughter." In *Directions in Biblical Poetry.* Ed. E. R. Follis. JSOTSup 40. Sheffield: Sheffield Academic Press, 1987. 173–84. ———. "Zion, Daughter of." *ABD.* 6:1103. **Galambush, J.** *Jerusalem in the Book of Ezekiel: The City as Yahweh's Wife.* SBLDS 130. Atlanta: Scholars Press, 1992. **Haag, F.** "Sündenvergebung und neuer Anfang: Zur Übersetzung und Auslegung von Jes. 1:18." In *Die Freude an Gott—unsere Kraft.* FS O. B. Knoch, ed. J. J. Degenhardt. Stuttgart: Katholisches Bibelwerk, 1991. 68–80. **Kaiser, B. B.** "Poet as Female Impersonator: The Image of Daughter Zion as Speaker in Biblical Poems of Suffering." *JR* 67 (1987) 164–82. **Sawyer, J. F. A.** "Daughter of Zion and Servant of the Lord in Isaiah: A Comparison." *JSOT* 44 (1989) 89–107. **Schmitt, J.** "The Gender of Ancient Israel." *JSOT* 6 (1983) 115–25. ———. "The Motherhood of God and Zion as Mother." *RB* 92 (1985) 557–69. **Sheppard, G.** "The Book of Isaiah: Competing Structures according to a Late Modern Description of Its Shape and Scope." In *SBLSP.* Atlanta: Scholars Press, 1992. 549–82. **Steck, O. H.** "Zion als Gelände und Gestalt: Überlegungen zur Wahrnehmung Jerusalem als Stadt und Frau im Alten Testament." *ZTK* 86 (1989) 251–81. **Steinspring, W. F.** "No Daughter of Zion: A Study of the Appositional Genitive in Hebrew Grammar." *Encounter* 26 (1965) 133–41. **Willis, J.** "An Important Passage for Determining the Historical Setting of a Prophetic Oracle." *ST* 39 (1985) 151–69. **Wischnowsky, M.** *Tochter Zion: Aufnahme und Überwindung der Stadtklage in der Prophetenschriften des Alten Testaments.* WMANT 89. Neukirchen-Vluyn: Neukirchener Verlag, 2001.

It was Steinspring who first insisted that בת ציון is properly translated "daughter Zion," not "daughter of Zion." Recently a good deal of attention has been paid to this issue. Cities are usually feminine in Hebrew. Israel's poetic imagery plays on this to the full. Both Jerusalem and Babylon are depicted this way. It is not their beauty or glory that is described, however, but their desolation and pitiable condition. In Isaiah, leading cities (Babylon, Damascus, Tyre, Zion/Jerusalem, Bozrah/Edom) are described as lying in desolation and ruins, the habitation of wild animals (24:12; 25:2; 13:19–22; 14:23; 17:1–3, 9; 23:13; 27:10–11; 32:14; 34:10–15).

Biddle lists other motifs found in chaps. 13–33 (*PRS* 22 [1995] 7–8). He also notes the use of city images in chaps. 50–66. But the city images begin much earlier in 1:8–22, 2:1–4, and chaps. 3–4 (see *Excursus: Jerusalem—An Example of War in a Walled City* at 3:1 below).

9 The choral response accepts the evaluation of their condition, but changes the metaphor.

לולי, "if not," followed by the perfect tense introduces a condition-contrary-to-fact clause (Watts, *Survey of Syntax,* 136). The conditional sentence climaxes a series of comparisons. The comparison to Sodom and Gomorrah does not quite fit. Sodom and Gomorrah were ancient cities near the southern end of the Dead Sea, cities that were reputed to have been destroyed by fire from heaven (Gen 19:24) and that lived only in memory. All the words in this group carry a potential double intention. By stressing that only this fragment is left, there is an implied accusation that God has abandoned the larger element that was destroyed or imprisoned. This negative suggestion appears in v 8. But the Vision will repeatedly stress a positive meaning of providential care, which prevented complete genocide. V 9 is the first such contribution to Isaiah's doctrine of the remnant.

Intensive efforts have been made to identify the historical period to which vv 7*c*–9 apply (W. T. Claassen, "Linguistic Arguments and the Dating of Isaiah 1:4–9," *JNSL* 3 [1974] 1–18). The major problems have turned on the interpretation of "an overthrow of strangers" and the description of Jerusalem's isolation or siege. The latter issue turned on the phrase כעיר נצורה, "like a fortified city," which was usually translated "like a besieged city." If the suggestion in *Note* 8.a. is accepted, the reference is much less specific and the issue of whether this refers to an event in 734 B.C.E. or 701 B.C.E. cannot be determined by a few words.

In view of the description of Israel's problems given in vv 4–7*b,* the period under discussion must come during one of Assyria's incursions into the land before the final fall of Samaria in 721 B.C.E. The language of this verse describes Jerusalem's isolation when the emperor's marauding armies were in the neighborhood. The specific horror of siege will be described later.

Assyria's incursions into west Asia began with Tiglath-Pileser's campaigns of 743 B.C.E. Opposition to him at that time was led by "Azriau of Yaudi" (*ANET,* 282). Bright (*HI,* 270) thinks this refers to Uzziah of Judah. This would mean that Judah was involved in opposition to Assyria at a very early date. Assyria's campaigns wore down the defenses of the smaller western states so that by 738 B.C.E. most of them, including Damascus and Israel, were paying tribute. It is worth noting that Uzziah died about this time.

Tiglath-Pileser was the founder of the Neo-Assyrian Empire. His armies fought for permanent conquest instead of simply seeking booty and prisoners as before. He punished rebellion by transporting leaders to other areas. However, this did not prevent intrigue and struggles for power within the subject states.

Israel's history in this period reflects exactly such fluctuations, with intrigues and assassinations the order of the day (2 Kgs 15–16). Uzziah of Judah and Jeroboam of Israel may have stood together against Assyria in 750 B.C.E. or the years that followed. But neither unity nor stability could be found in the states by 738 B.C.E. Assyria made repeated incursions as punitive expeditions against Israel and Syria in the following years before Samaria's destruction in 721 B.C.E. In all these campaigns, Jerusalem and Judah remained isolated from the earlier coalition. War swirled so close about the city that she must have been strongly affected by it. But she survived, if only barely.

This passage has sketched the effects of this time but has deliberately avoided more specific identifications. The interpreter does well to follow suit.

11–18 Sacrifice is recorded as a part of worship from Abraham onward and is firmly anchored in the Mosaic Torah. (See J. Milgrom, "Sacrifice and Offerings, OT," *IDBSup,* 763–71.) With the tendency toward centralization of worship in Jerusalem, sacrifice became increasingly important for the temple and the city. But prophets stood in succession to Samuel (1 Sam 15:22) in insisting that sacrifice be considered secondary to obedience and faith. The Vision portrays the new Zion devoid of blood sacrifice (66:3). Yet only in that picture of the coming city is sacrifice forbidden.

The term here is שבעתי, "I am satisfied, I have had enough." That which brings displeasure to God is not the sacrifice per se; the "trampling of his courts" (v 12) is revolting to him. The failure to accompany sacrificial and festal worship with a lifestyle of justice and righteousness is the problem. The latter invalidates the former.

The vocabulary of worship in vv 11–16 is comprehensive. Worship occasions vary. In v 12, בוא לראות פני, "come to appear before me," may describe any worship. The phrase should ordinarily have לפני, "before me," for this translation. One Hebrew manuscript and Syriac read לְרְאוֹת פני *(qal),* "to see my face." But this would be very unusual, for the OT teaches that one may not see the face of God and live. In vv 13, 14 the phrase חדש ושבת, "new moon and sabbath," is one of the earliest designations for the lunar worship calendar and indicates worship at designated places at new and full moons, i.e., every fourteen days. קרא מקרא, "a convened assembly," meets in response to some special occasion. עצרה, "solemn assembly" (v 13), is a meeting at which attendance is required. מועדים, "set seasons" (v 14), are the annual festivals that are fixed in the Israelite calendar.

Worship actions include: (v 11) זבחים, "sacrifices," the general word; עלות אילים, "whole burnt offerings of rams"; חלב מריאים, "fat of fed beasts"; and דם פרים וכבשים ועתודים, "blood of bulls, of lambs and he goats." This is a comprehensive list of the types of blood sacrifice. Leviticus speaks of them in terms of function, "sin offering," "guilt offering," and so on, but the same sacrifices are intended. מנחה (v 13) is a cereal offering; קטרת is incense; מנחת שוא, "a vain offering." פרש כפיכם, "spread your hands" (v 15a), describes prayer. תפלה (v 15*b*) is "prayer" in the particular sense of intercession.

The rejection of sacrificial worship is not only a result of the abrogation of covenant but also belongs to the vision of the new Jerusalem (66:3–4) and is stated in much the same language. Sacrificial worship is characterized as something the people have chosen (66:3*b*) rather than responded to as the genuine call of God. God seeks those who will do what he requires and who seek that which delights him, those who are "willing and obedient" (v 19) and who "tremble at his word" (66:2, 5; cf. R. D. Culver, "Isaiah 1:18—Declaration, Exclamation or Interrogation?" *JETS* 12 [1969] 133–41).

Two passages in Isaiah state a policy opposed to sacrifice, indeed to much of formal worship: 1:11–14 and 66:3. However, positive pictures of prayer and pilgrimage appear in various places, including 1:15–17. The goal of blood sacrifice, dealing with the consequences of guilt, is achievable without the sacrifice itself (1:18–19) if one is "willing and obedient."

19 אם תאבו ושמעתם, "if you become willing and obey." The requisites of grace are the milder attitudes of submission and pliable attention: the humble willingness (אבה) simply to be God's own and do his will; the attentive listening (שמע) that heeds God's words and carefully does them. Those of God's people who do this "shall eat the good of the land." The entire book of Deuteronomy expounds this theme.

20 אם תמאנו ומריתם, "if you refuse and continue obstinate." The alternative echoes covenant theology (cf. Deut 27:1–28), which calls upon the people of God to repent and accept God's terms.

Explanation

The Vision of Isaiah portrays a legal dispute, ריב (cf. also 3:12–15 and 5:1–7). The adversaries have been summoned in the title verse. They are Judah and Jerusalem. The witnesses have been called. YHWH is the plaintiff; his children are in rebellion against him. Neither the witnesses nor the readers are asked to judge them. God does that. They are called to observe and understand the ways of Israel and the ways of God.

The estranged children are first indicted for not knowing who they are or to whom they belong. "Not knowing," that is God's complaint! And, of course, action follows failure to know. Israel is called first. This is Israel of covenant and sacred history, as well as the northern kingdom, which claimed to perpetuate them. The people have already been severely chastised, but there is no response from them or sign of repentance. That amazes the witness (vv 5–7*b*). The references to Israel will be continued in 2:5–9 and many times in the Vision. Then attention is drawn to "daughter Zion," isolated and in dire straits. A chorus responds for Jerusalem (v 9). It is a pitiful and inadequate response, but it acknowledges a debt to YHWH for his forbearance.

YHWH takes the opportunity to address the daughter who has at least spoken a word and recognized some benefit from him. He lectures her about the inadequacy of sacrifice and prayer to deal with her problems. When one's hands are bloody, one needs to wash, clean up, and change one's way of life. It is not lack of worship but lack of justice that has produced the bloody hands and God's outrage. Then YHWH signals a willingness to negotiate. Guilt can be forgiven, former insults forgotten. But proper attitude is not negotiable in the covenant. The basic alternatives that Deuteronomy recorded for the covenant still apply. When the daughter is "willing" and attentive to the father's will, the promise of good things is still valid. But for the consistently negative and obstinate there is no room for grace.

V 19 contains the distilled essence of the "knowledge" that Israel lacks (v 3). It teaches a doctrine that runs like a scarlet thread through the Vision. Ahaz will refuse it. Ephraim turns aside from it. Those called to be servants will deny it. For each of them the way of "willingness and obedience" is open, but they cannot find it in themselves to walk that way.

Paul (Rom 9:29) quotes v 9 as proof that God had not abandoned Israel. Although the Vision's primary concern at this point is to show Israel's and Jerusalem's filial sins, there is also deep concern for the future of the people of God.

This first chapter changes the focus of the Vision from the "Judah and Jerusalem" of the title (1:1) to the people themselves, the temple worship, and the city. The title uses a political term used in the eighth century as well as in the postexilic period. The prologue along with the final "book" (chaps. 55–65) turns the attention toward the religious "people of God," the temple, and the city as God's dwelling.

Virtually every reader of the Vision of Isaiah considers himself/herself to be a child of God. We feel able to address him as "Father." We are part of the family of God. It is shocking news to hear God say to his advisers that his children, his family, have become rebels against him. The accusation is not limited to a particular generation or historical period. It involves us all. And we are addressed directly (cf. "you" in 1:5, 7, 10, 11, 12, 13, 15, 16, 18, 19, 20, 22, 23, 25, 26, 29, and 30). Whether the reader identifies himself or herself with the Israel of the covenant, the northern kingdom, Judah, the city of Jerusalem, or the temple congregation, the accusation is still direct and penetrating.

This is the kind of thing Jesus deals with in the parable of the Prodigal Son (Luke 15:11–32) and in the parable of the Rebellious Steward and Workers in Mark 12:1–9. These are not the kinds of sin that one slips into. They represent a chosen path contrary to the will of the Father. Deuteronomy deals with the case of a rebellious son who must be handed over to the community for trial and for execution by stoning. It is a serious offense, a capital offense. The Vision will not take this charge lightly, and finally it, too, must consider this a capital offense (cf. 66:24). Even the impassioned appeal of the prayer in 63:7–64:12 must be denied. Mercy is available, but only for those of us that will repent and becomes "servants of YHWH" (65:13–16).

Isaiah calls Israel "rebellious children" who need to repent. Jesus (Matt 10:6) called his people "the lost sheep of the house of Israel" and instructed the apostles to go to every town to preach to them. Israel's rebellion was not just a fact in the eighth century. It continued in postexilic Judaism and indeed among the Christians who claimed to be heirs of all that the Torah and the Prophets had taught about the people of YHWH.

How Has She Become a Harlot? Let Me Smelt Your Dross Like Lye (1:21–31)

Bibliography

Blum, E. "Jesajas prophetisches Testament: Beobachtungen zu Jes 1–11." *ZAW* 108 (1996) 562–68. **Hardmeier, C.** "Jesajaforschung im Umbruch." *VF* 31 (1986) 3–31. **Haymann, L.** "Note on Isaiah 1:25." *JNES* 9 (1950) 217. **Hermisson, H. J.** "Zukunftserwartung und Gegenwartskritik in der Verkündigung Jesajas." *EvT* 33 (1973) 54–77. **Jones, D. R.** "Exposition of Isaiah Chapter One Verses Twenty-One to the End." *SJT* 21 (1968) 320–27. **Lack, R.** *La Symbolique.* 164–71. **Melugin, R. F.** "The Typical Versus the Unique among the Hebrew Prophets." In *SBLSP.* Ed. Lane C. McGaughy. Missoula, MT: Scholars Press, 1972. 2:331–42. **Tsevat, M.** "Isaiah I 31." *VT* 19 (1969) 261–63. **Williamson, H. G. M.** "Isaiah 6:13 and 1:29–31." In *Studies.* Ed. J. Van Ruiten and M. Vervenne. 119–28. ———. "Judgment and Hope in Isaiah 1:21–26." In *Reading from Right to Left.* Ed. J. C. Exum and H. G. M. Williamson. 423–34. **Willis, J. T.** "Lament Reversed—Isaiah 1:21 ff." *ZAW* 98 (1986) 236–48.

Translation

Heavens and Earth:	21 *How has she become a harlot?*	3
(to YHWH)	*(Zion[a] was) a community of faithfulness,*	3+2+3
	full of justice.	
	Righteousness lodged in her.	
	But now—assassins?	2
Heavens and Earth:	22 *Your silver has become dross!*	3+3
(to Zion)	*Your wine—mixed with water!*	
	23 *Your princes—rebelling*	2+2
	and companions of thieves!	
	Each one a bribe-lover	3+2
	and a rewards-chaser!	
	An orphan they never vindicate!	3+4
	A widow's suit never comes before them!	
Herald:	24 *Therefore—*	1+2+2+2
	Expression of the Lord	
	(YHWH of Hosts),	
	Hero of Israel!	
YHWH:	*Woe!*	1+2+2
(to Zion)	*Let me ease myself on my adversaries!*	
	Let me avenge myself on my enemies!	
	25 *Let me turn my hand upon you!*	3+3+3
	Let me smelt your dross like the lye!	
	Let me remove all your alloy!	
	26 *Let me return your judges as at the first*	3+2
	and your counselors as in the beginning.	
	After this you will be called	3+2+2
	City of the righteous,	
	Community of faithfulness.	
Heavens:	27 *Zion will be redeemed with justice*	3+2
	and her captivity[a] with righteousness!	
	28 *But a crushing[a] of rebels and sinners together—*	4+3
	and those forsaking YHWH will be finished.	
Earth:	29 *For they will be undone because of their groves,*	3+2
(to the people of Jerusalem)	*which you [pl.] have taken pleasure in.*	
	And you will be confounded because of the gardens	2+2
	which you have chosen.	
	30 *For you [pl.] will be like an oak*	3+2
	withered of foliage	
	and like a garden lacking water.	4
	31 *And it shall be that the strong[a] will become lint*	3+2
	and his product[b] a spark.	
	And they shall burn—the two together	3+2
	unextinguishable.	

Notes

21.a. LXX adds "Zion." The addition gives clarity to the sentence and is appropriate.

27.a. וְשָׁבֶיהָ, "her captivity." LXX ἡ αἰχμαλωσία αὐτῆς (and Syr.), "the captivity" = *BHS* (ו)שְׁבִיָה. The emendation וישביה, "her inhabitants," is interesting but unnecessary, especially since ישב usually appears in a fem. pl. (cf. BDB, 442).

28.a. ושבר, "a breaking." BDB (991) suggests a const., but the pointing of abs. is the same. Accents favor abs. LXX translates with a finite pass. verb and the two nouns as subjects as in the second stich: καί συντριβήσονται οἱ ἄνομοι καί οἱ ἁμαρτωλοί ἅμα = ושברו, "and they shall be broken." Vg. *conteret* = ושברו act., "and he will break," with nouns as objs. MT, though unusual, is possible and should be kept.

31.a. MT החסן, "the strong," is infrequent, and as a noun is a *hap. leg.* 1QIsa[a] החסנכם (elsewhere from חסן, "wealth or treasure") is a strange form (the article on a noun with 2 masc. pl. pronominal suf.), "your strong one" *(DCH)* or "your wealth." LXX ἡ ἰσχύς αὐτῶν, "his strength," implies חסנו, parallel to פעלו in the second stich. Vg. follows LXX.

31.b. MT פעלו, "and his product or work." 1QIsa[a] ופעלכם, "your works (also Syr. and Tg.), implies Heb. ופעלו, inf. const. from פעל, "do or make."

The paragraph has varied from 3d to 2d person. 1QIsa[a] has chosen the 2d person. LXX has turned to the 3d person. MT has an impersonal reading for the first and a 3d person for the second. MT should be sustained as the "more difficult reading." The others show signs of attempts to harmonize.

Form/Structure/Setting

This section (1:21–28) is different from 1:2–20 in many respects. Its judgment against Jerusalem and its leaders is more like chaps. 3–4, and it echoes both the message and the setting of chaps. 34–66. The feeling of a period of destruction and chaos that is being replaced with YHWH's new order dominates the passage. The horrors of the chaos in the destroyed and abandoned city are to be replaced with the order and peace of YHWH's new day. But there will be no respite for those who continue in their sin of pagan and rebellious worship forms.

The arch structure that bound vv 1–23 (see *Form/Structure/Setting* to 1:2–20) leads up to the strong "therefore" with which this section begins. The artistic intricacy of the chapter is shown by the overlapping arches that begin in v 21 and continue through v 26 (cf. Lack, *La Symbolique,* 164–71; L. Alonso Schökel, "Poesie hebraique," *DBSup,* vol. 7 [1967] cols. 47–90, esp. 59). The first part (vv 21–23) is a speech of reproach *(Scheltwort).* V 24 begins the announcement of judgment.

A Faithful city has become a harlot (v 21*a*).
B The city was full of justice and righteousness (v 21*b*).
C Silver has become dross (v 22).
D Rulers have become rebels; there is no justice (v 23).
KEYSTONE YHWH intervenes (v 24*a*).
D′ I will take vengeance on my foes (v 24*b*).
C′ I will purge your dross (v 25).
B′ Let me return your judges as before (v 26*a*).
A′ A community of faithfulness will result (v 26*b*).

Alonso Schökel and Lack have shown the careful use of assonance and word choice within the passage.

The reproach speech (vv 21–23*a*) uses metaphors. The accusation (vv 23*b–c*) is direct and realistic. It mourns the state of the city that was once God's pride. It begins with איכה, "how?" The perfect tense in vv 21 and 23 stresses the resultant condition. Imperfects in vv 21 and 23 contrast a characteristic condition with later characteristic results. Participles continue the characterization. V 23*bc* changes to an accusation against the people or leaders of the city and prepares for the announcement of judgment to follow.

"Therefore" in v 24 leads into God's announcement that he will intervene directly to destroy his enemies, purify the city, and restore it. The three actions are bound together by the skillful weaving together of the ideas of justice and righteousness in vv 21, 23, and 26 and by the ideas of change for the worse in v 21 and change back for the better in v 26 (cf. the chiastic structures demonstrated above).

One may also notice the overlapping arch in vv 24–31:

A I will get relief for myself (v 24).
B I will purge you (v 25).
C I will restore you (v 26*a*).
KEYSTONE Afterwards a city of righteousness (v 26*b*).
C´ Zion will be redeemed (v 27).
B´ Rebels and sinners will die together (v 28).
A´ You will be ashamed (vv 29–31).

The use of imperfect tenses throughout the passage is instructive, particularly in vv 27 and 28, which form a kind of summary: "Zion will be redeemed with justice" (v 27); rebels (those who abandon YHWH) will be completely destroyed (v 28). These are continued by similar statements in imperfect in 2:2, 3*d*.

Excursus: Rhetorical Questions in Isaiah

Rhetorical questions play a major role in parts of Isaiah. They and imperatives enliven the dialogue, especially in public speeches seeking to persuade (cf. Deut. 32:6, 34). They provoke questions: Who is the speaker? Who is addressed?

In 1:5 (5–7) Heavens and Earth speak to Israel: "Upon what will you be beaten more? Will you add rebellion?" In 1:11, YHWH speaks to the worshiping congregation: "For what purpose (do you bring) to me the great number of your sacrifices?" In 1:12, YHWH asks: "Who has requested this from your hand, (this) trampling of my courts?" And in 1:21, Heavens and Earth ask YHWH "How has she become a harlot? (Zion was) a community of faithfulness, full of justice. Righteousness lodged in her. But now—assassins?"

The rabshakah's speeches in chaps. 36–37 show that questions were a staple of Assyrian diplomatic oratorical style (36:4, 5, 7, 9, 10, 12, 18*b*, 19, 20; 37:11, 12, 13, 23, 26). So they also dominate a speech attributed to the Assyrian king (10:8, 9, 11, 13, 27–28, 32).

Chap. 40 is composed around a series of rhetorical questions in YHWH's speech to persuade Israel (40:6, 12, 14, 18, 21, 25, 26, 27, 28). They also punctuate later speeches (41:2, 4; 43:9*b*, 13*c*; 44:8, 20*c*; 49:14, 15; 50:10; 51:12*b*, 13; 63:1 [2x], 2; 63:11*b* [2x], 12, 13; 64:5*e*, 12 [2x]; 66:8 [3x], 9 [2x]).

Comment

21 משפט, "justice," and צדקה, "righteousness," are key concepts here as they are throughout the Vision.

Strand: "Justice" (משפט)

Bibliography

Leclerc, T. L. "Mishpat (Justice) in the Book of Isaiah." Diss., Harvard, 1998. **Rendtorff, R.** "Zur Komposition des Buches Jesaja." *VT* 34 (1964) 295–320.

A distinctive prophetic voice uses משפט וצדקה, "justice and righteousness." The word pair occurs in exactly that form in Amos 7, 24; Jer 9:23; 22:3, 15; 23:15; 33:15; Ezek 18:5, 19, 21, 27; 33:14, 16, 19; 45:9; and Isa 32:16; 33:5; 59:14. The two terms are found in close relation to each other in many other texts as the underlined numbers on the table show for Isaiah.

PROLOGUE	ACT 1	ACT 2	ACT 3	ACT 4	ACT 5	ACT 6	EPILOGUE
שפט, "JUDGE"							
1:17, 23, 26 2:4 3:2	5:3 11:3, 4	16:5	33:22	40:23 43:26	51:5	59:4	66:16
משפט, "JUDGMENT, JUSTICE"							
1:17, 21, 27 3:14 4:4	5:7, 16 9:6 10:2	26:8, 9	28:4, 17, 26 30:18 33:5	34:5 40:14, 27 41:1 42:4	49:4 54:17 50:8 51:4, 6, 8 53:8 54:17	56:1 58:2 59:8, 9, 11, 14, 15 61:8	

(For *Excursus: "Righteous"* [צדק] *and "Righteousness"* [צדקה] see *Comment* on 42:13–43:21.)

משפט is found in Isaiah forty-two times. It is also found in Jeremiah forty-two times, in Ezekiel thirty-two times, in Hosea six times, in Amos four times, in Micah five times, in Habakkuk four times, in Zechariah two times (7:9 and 8:16), and in Malachi three times. There are other prophetic modes without these words. They do not appear in Joel, Obadiah, Jonah, Nahum, and Haggai. And, of course, they do not appear in many chapters of Jeremiah and Ezekial.

As the table above shows, the word pair appears in certain texts of Isaiah, but not in the narrative sections. Isaiah son of Amoz who consorted with kings was not a prophet preaching justice and righteousness. But the Vision of Isaiah is such a prophecy, or contains such prophecy.

The point here is that the city is in chaos and these necessary qualities are turned upside down. They are not just missing; the reverse negative qualities are present—not just the milder form of reversal, but the shocking change now to מרצחים, "assassins." Isa 34:9–15 pictures a physical chaos in the city. These verses picture the social chaos.

22 כספך היה לסיגים, "your silver has become dross" (v 22), represents the value of the city's character, her justice and righteousness, as does the parallel figure of watered wine. Both relate to the primary image of the harlot, for whom silver represents her hire and wine her debauchery. The figure carries double significance: corruption of the silver and corruption for silver (Lack, *La Symbolique*, 165). The money itself is worthless, and the product bought with money is devalued.

23 The chaos breeds corruption in the rulers, who are now identified with the very elements of society they are sworn to restrain. Of course they cannot do their duty in relation to the weakest members of society.

24 לכן, "therefore," is a major structural signal. This speech is the culmination of what has gone before. The elaborate introduction of YHWH suggests the importance of the word to follow. Thus far the introductions have used simply "YHWH" (vv 2, 10, 11, 18, 20). The speeches have contained the broader title: "Holy One of Israel" (v 4) "YHWH of Hosts" (v 9). Here to יהוה צבאות, "YHWH of Hosts," is added האדון, "the Lord," and אביר ישראל, "Hero of Israel."

הוי, "woe," shows the dire nature of the announcement. It brings the note of a funeral dirge to God's announcement of his intentions. Six verbs follow (having seven objects) in the first person. Four are clearly marked as cohortative imperfects. They could be translated as expressing determination: "I am determined to ease myself." Or they can be expressions in which the speaker rouses himself to action. They do not ask permission to act. Note the way "avenge" is parallel to 34:8.

The "adversaries" and "enemies" appear to be the apostate leaders of the city cited above.

25 "Turn my hand" means to change from supporting to chastising.

Excursus: "The Hand of God" (יד יהוה)

Bibliography

Johnson, A. "Sculpted Beauty: The Hand of God in Isaiah 1–12." In *AAR/SBL Abstracts*. Atlanta: Scholars Press, 1994. 290.

God's involvement with Israel and in history is pictured as "hands on" in Isa 1–12. In 1:25 he says "Let me turn my hand upon you. . . . Let me smelt. . . . Let me remove all your alloy." And in 4:4 he says "the Lord shall have washed away the filth." In Isa 5:11–12 "the work of his hands they do not see," and in 5:25 "his hand was extended against them, and he chastised them." The prophet feels "his hand strong upon me" ("as though someone took [me] by the hand"; 8:11) in words similar to those used by Ezekiel.

God's continued anger is called "his hand still outstretched" (9:11 [12], 16 [17], 20 [21]). Assyria, the rod of his anger, becomes the hand of God reaching the kingdom of idols, finding the wealth of the peoples (10:5, 10, 14). But God protests that the Assyrian has failed to recognize God's hand in all this. God's hand raises the ax (10:15), lashes with a whip (10:26), lifts a yoke (10:27), cuts down trees (10:33–34). He extends his hand to reclaim exiles (11:11) and waves his hand to create a highway for his people (11:15). The "hand of YHWH" appears later in Isaiah, but never again in such profusion as in these first eleven chapters.

The references to "smelt your dross" and "remove your alloy" pick up the figures of v 22.

26 "Returning your judges and your counselors" returns to the references of v 23. אחרי־כן, "after this": The Vision sees God's action as clearly dividing history into the "before" and the "after." Isa 2:2 speaks of the "latter days." Chaps. 40–48 speak of the "former times." צדקה, "righteousness," and נאמנה, "faithfulness" return to the references of v 21, completing the arch.

27 משפט, "justice, and צדקה, "righteousness," characterize all God's actions. The redemption of Zion will be no exception. The redemption of Zion and her captivity is the heart of the message in chaps. 34–66. There, too, the concern with demonstrating YHWH's righteousness is evident.

28 For rebels and sinners and apostates there can only await a total defeat ("be undone") because of their false worship, their addiction to the pagan pleasures and promises of the fertility worship of Baal, which promised satisfaction and success to its devotees. The message here is parallel to that found in 65:1–15 and to the recurrent phrase "there is no peace for the adversaries" (48:22; 57:21).

29 אילים, "groves," refer to pagan open-air places of worship. They worshiped fruitful nature and sought to participate in its bounty through fertility rites. "They" refers to the pagans. "You" (pl.) is addressed to people in Jerusalem (cf. 65:3–5) and implies that their practices are identical to those of the pagans.

31 החסן, "the strong," is an unusual word with implications of wealth. It implies the apparently prosperous, self-assured follower of the pagan philosophy. פעליו, "his product," speaks of the results of his labor, his apparently successful attempts to build up wealth and power apart from God. The "strong" and successful pagan is like "lint," dry tinder. The product of his thought and labor becomes "a spark" that ignites the conflagration—the dreaded fires of the dry summer which no one can extinguish. Neither the pagan nor his work survives. The Jerusalemites have deliberately chosen that kind of life and will share that end.

Explanation

The passage contains a crucial speech by YHWH with echoes from two other speakers. They are addressed in large measure to the people of Jerusalem.

Having noted the sad state of the city (vv 8–23) and having invited its people and leaders to discuss a change (vv 18–20), apparently without response, the Lord determines to take unilateral action. He will act directly against his enemies in the city and outside. He will purge the city of its evils. He will restore leaders who will administer justice and rule with wisdom. Only then can the city's former character be restored.

Righteousness, faithfulness, and justice are the key qualities that the city of YHWH must exemplify. All else is derivative and secondary. This can only come in Zion when "rebels," "sinners," and apostates are crushed and removed. The end for the pagans will also overtake the apostates who joined in their festivity. This process is pictured in the very appropriate figure of the "gardens." The dry summer has left the gardens and trees dry, lifeless, and easy to burn. The central motif is smelting away dross and removing alloys, a figure for Zion's corrupt leaders (v 23). These leaders have been urged to wash themselves and make themselves clean (v 16). They have shown themselves not willing, not obedient (v 19). Now YHWH proposes to take over the job of cleaning out the city.

The themes are carefully developed in superb poetry, but the importance of the theme is greater. A basic theme for the entire book is introduced here. Since

Zion's place in God's plan is secure, the issue will turn on a people for God's city. This people will have to be pure—in righteousness, justice, and loyalty to YHWH. All other elements—all those not "willing" and obedient—will be purged out. If they will not "wash" themselves, YHWH will remove them. Williamson ("Isaiah 6:13 and 1:29–31," 127) notes the influence of 6:13 and the way it is interpreted here "for his post-exilic contemporaries in a way that challenges them in a manner which the final chapters of the book show to have been very much to the point." The fire that destroys God's enemies will purge the city, making redemption and restoration possible.

Title (2:1)

Bibliography

Ackroyd, P. R. "Isaiah I–XII: Presentation of a Prophet." In *Congress Volume Göttingen 1977.* VTSup 29. Leiden: Brill, 1978. 16–48. ———. "A Note on Isaiah 2:1." *ZAW* 75 (1963) 320–21. **Freedman, D. N.** "Headings in the Books of the Eighth-Century Prophets." *AUSS* 25 (1987) 9–26. **Goldingay, J.** "Isaiah I 1 and II 1." *VT* 48 (1998) 325–32. **Sweeney, M.** *Isaiah 1–4.* 30–32. **Tucker, G. M.** "Prophetic Superscriptions and the Growth of the Canon." In *Canon and Authority.* Ed. G. M. Coats and B. O. Long. Philadelphia: Fortress, 1977. 56–70.

Translation

1 *The word that Isaiah son of Amoz envisioned concerning Judah and Jerusalem.*

Form/Structure/Setting

The title uses a common form and basic vocabulary. Isa 2:1 has usually been understood as a superscription for a separate section, parallel to 1:1. It is superficially similar, but also distinctly different. דבר, "word," should normally be understood to refer to one speech or oracle, not a collection. The function of the verse is parallel to that of 1:24. There the long ascription "Expression of the Lord, YHWH of Hosts, Hero of Israel" lends authenticity and force to the judgment announced in God's name. But rather than ascribing divine origin to the words, 2:1 claims them for Isaiah ben Amoz (Ackroyd, *ZAW* 75 [1963] 320; idem, "Isaiah I–XII," 32–33, n. 44). This may be intended to counter the claim that these words belong to Micah (Mic 4:1–3). But what is more important in the book of Isaiah is the claim that this view of Zion's future without nationalistic goals actually belongs to Isaiah of eighth-century Jerusalem.

This verse has often been read as a title over an extended portion of text, such as chaps. 2–12 (e.g., Bartelt, *Book around Immanuel;* Blenkinsopp). Williamson views chap. 2 as a part of the Deutero-Isaianic redaction, the initial chapter of one form of the book that was edited by Deutero-Isaiah (*Book Called Isaiah,* 144–45, 154; in n. 84 he deals with arguments that 1:1–2:4 belong together and decides that they do not). Goldingay (*VT* 48 [1998] 325–32) suggests instead that this is a colophon closing chap. 1. Whether it is read in this fashion or as introducing the following unit (2:2–4) or all of chap. 2, the view that it does not introduce a longer passage changes its interpretation.

But when it is read as the title of chaps. 2–4, the problem of the verse's relationship to chap. 1 falls away. It claims Isaiah's inspiration for the theme of the future temple (2:2–4) and the theme of the dire results of the Day of YHWH on Israel (2:5–8), on humankind, and over "the land" (2:9–22). It portrays a vision of YHWH's dealing with Jerusalem beginning with a trial and ending with a thorough cleansing of the city (chaps. 3–4).

Comment

דבר, "a word," belongs to an entire class of titles in the OT, especially in prophetic literature. It may designate a sentence or an oral presentation, but it may appropriately refer to a written message. It is often listed as belonging to YHWH, but here it mentions only a prophet and a topic.

Naming the prophet—ישעיהו בן־אמוץ, "Isaiah son of Amoz"—relates the following chapters to the sphere of prophetic literature shown in the title to the larger work, which is called the Vision (1:1). Traditionally, interpreters have understood the title to claim authorship for Isaiah son of Amoz. But a careful reading notes that it says nothing about writing. Isaiah son of Amoz is nowhere pictured as a writing prophet. The words instead claim that the ideas in the book are related to Isaiah of Jerusalem of the eighth century B.C.E.

חזה, "envisioned," is a verb from the same root as חזון, "vision," in 1:1. It is frequently used in titles of prophetic works. It asserts the inspiration of the work. Note that here it is a "word" that is envisioned, not a vision.

על־יהודה וירושלם, "concerning Judah and Jerusalem," is repeated, following 1:1. But the time frame is different. Isa 1:1 referred to the period of the kings in the eighth century B.C.E. This usage is qualified here by the words "after these days" (2:2). This is the Judah and Jerusalem of chaps. 40 and following. The Vision has chosen words appropriate to the period of kingdoms and to the exilic and postexilic periods. Ezra and Nehemiah use the names of Judah and Jerusalem repeatedly, as do Zechariah and Malachi.

Explanation

The title places the unit chaps. 2–4 squarely in the realm of Isaiah's Vision. There is no continuation from chap. 1. This is a fresh, self-contained unit with its own title.

Chaps. 2–4 introduce four themes that will be important in this "book" and in the rest of the Vision. They are (1) YHWH's reign in his temple on Mount Zion (2:1–4) and (2) the end of the nation of Judah and the struggle over whether Israel/Judah continue as the people of God or not. The first responses are negative (2:5–11), but the idea that a remnant will be saved occurs later in 10:20–22 and 11:11–16. The final themes are (3) YHWH as the Divine Warrior involved in the wars that move through the land on this Day of YHWH (2:12–22), bringing the nations into relation with YHWH, and (4) the judgment and purging of Zion, which will produce a purified city (chaps. 3–4).

The Mountain of YHWH's House (2:2–4)

Bibliography

Andersen, F. I., and **D. N. Freedman.** "Excursus: The Relationship between Micah 4:1–5 and Isaiah 2:1–5." In *Micah.* AB 24E. New York: Doubleday, 2000. 413–27. **Barth, H.** *Die Jesaja-Worte in der Josiazeit.* 191–92. **Budde, K.** "Verfasser und Stelle von Mi. 4:1–4 (Jes 2:2–4)." *ZDMG* 81 (1927) 152–58. **Cannawurf, E.** "Authenticity of Micah 4:1–4 (cf. to Isa 2:2–4)." *VT* 13 (1963) 26–33. **Cazelles, H.** "Qui aurait visé, à l'origine, Isaïe ii 2–5." *VT* 30 (1980) 409–20. **Clifford R.** *The Cosmic Mountain in Canaan and the Old Testament.* Cambridge: Harvard UP, 1972. **Delcor, M.** "Sion, centre universel, Is. 2:1–5." *AsSeign* 2.5 (1969) 6–11. **Gosse, B.** "Michée 4,1–5 et Isaïe 2,1–5 et les rédacteurs finaux du livre d'Isaïe." *ZAW* 105 (1993) 98–102. **Holmgren, F. C.** "Isaiah 2:1–5." *Int* 51 (1997) 61–65. **Jensen, J.** *The Use of* tôrâ *by Isaiah.* Washington: Catholic Biblical Association, 1973. **Junker, H.** "Sancta Civitas Jerusalem Nova: Eine formkritische und überlieferungsgeschichtliche Studie zu Jes. 2." *Ekklesia.* FS B. M. Wehr, ed. H. Gross. TThSt 15. Trier: Paulinus, 1962. 17–33. **Kosmala, H.** "Form and Structure in Ancient Hebrew Poetry [includes 2:2–3]." *VT* 14 (1964) 423–45. **Kselman, J. S.** "A Note on Isaiah II 2." *VT* 25 (1975) 225–27. **Limburg, J.** "Swords to Ploughshares: Texts and Contexts." In *Writing and Reading.* Ed. C. C. Broyles and C. A. Evans. 2:279–93. **Lipiński, E.** "*B'hrjt hjmjm* dans les textes préexiliques." *VT* 20 (1970) 445–50. **Lohfink, G.** "'Schwerter zu Pflugscharen': Die Rezeption von Jes 2,1–5 par Mi 4,1–5 in der Alten Kirche und im neuen Testament." *TQ* 166 (1986) 184–209. **Loretz, O.** *Der Prolog des Jesaja-Buches (1,1–2,5).* Altenberge: Akademische Bibliothek, 1984. 63–83. **Magonet, J.** "Isaiah's Mountain or the Shape of Things to Come." *Proof* 11 (1991) 175–81. **Martin-Achard, R.** "Israel, peuple sacerdotal." *CVC* 18 (1964) 11–28. **Navarra, L.** "[Is 2,2s; 60,1] In margine a due citazioni di Isaia nell'Homilia in laudem Ecclesiae di Leandro di Siviglia." *SMSR* 53 (1987) 199–204. **Ollenburger, B. C.** *Zion, City of the Great King: A Theological Symbol of the Jerusalem Cult.* JSOTSup 41. Sheffield: JSOT Press, 1987. 110–12. **Pakozdy, L. M. von.** "Jes. 2:2ff.: Geschichte-Utopie-Verkündigung." In *Vom Herrengeheimnis der Wahrheit.* FS H. Vogel. Berlin: De Gruyter, 1962. 416–26. **Rad, G. von.** "The City on a Hill." In *The Problem of the Hexateuch and Other Essays.* Trans. E. W. Trueman Dicken. New York: McGraw-Hill, 1966. 232–42. **Roberts, J. J. M.** "Double Entendre in First Isaiah." *CBQ* 54 (1992) 39–48. **Rudman, D.** "Zechariah 8:20–22 & Isaiah 2:2–4//Micah 4:2–3: A Study in Intertextuality." *BN* 107/108 (2001) 50–54. **Schottroff, L.**, and **W. Schottroff.** "Die Friedensfeier: Das Prophetenwort von der Umwandlung von Schwerten zu Pflugscharen (Jes 2:2–5/ Mic 4:1–5)." In *Die Parteilichkeit Gottes.* Munich: Kaiser, 1984. 78–102. **Stampfer, J.** "On Translating Biblical Poetry: Isa. chs. 1 and 2:2–4." *Judaism* 14 (1965) 501–10. **Steck, O. H.** "Jerusalemer Vorstellungen vom Frieden und ihre Abwandlungen in der Prophetie des Alten Israel." In *Frieden—Bibel—Kirche.* Ed. G. Liedke. Munich: Kaiser, 1972. 75–95. **Sweeney, M. A.** *Isaiah 1–4.* 134–39. ———. "Micah's Debate with Isaiah." *JSOT* 93 (2001) 111–24. **Wildberger, H.** "Die Völkerwallfahrt zum Zion: Jes. 2:1–5." *VT* 7 (1957) 62–81. **Willis, J. T.** "Isaiah 2:2–5 and the Psalms of Zion." In *Writing and Reading.* Ed. C. C. Broyles and C. A. Evans. 1:295–316. **Wolff, H. W.** "[Is 2,4] Use of the Bible in Theology, a Case Study." *EvRT* 11 (1987) 37–52. ———. "Schwerter zu Pflugscharen—Missbrauch eines prophetenwortes? Praktische Fragen und exegetische Klärungen zu Joel 4,9–12, Jes 2,2–5 und Mic 4,1–5." *EvT* 44 (1984) 280–92. **Zimmerli, W.** "Jesaja 2,2–5." In *FS L. Klein.* Jerusalem: Dormition Abbey, 1986. 49–54.

Translation

Prophet: 2 *And it shall be after these days* 3
(to Heavens and Earth) *that the mountain of the house of YHWH* 2+2
will be established [a]
by the head of the mountains 2+2
and lifted up above the hills,
and unto it [b] *all nations* [c] *will flow,* 2+2
3 *and many peoples* [a] *will go.*
And they will say, "Come, let us ascend 3+2+3
to the mountain of YHWH,
to the house of the God of Jacob,
and he will instruct us from his ways, 2+2
and we shall walk in his paths."
For from Zion Torah issues, 2+2
and the word of YHWH from Jerusalem.
4 *And he will judge between the nations,* 3+3
and he will decide for many peoples. [a]
And they shall beat their weapons into ploughs, 3+3
and their curved swords into pruning hooks.
Nation will not lift a sword against nation. 4+3
Nor will they learn war anymore.

Notes

2.a. Syr. and Mic 4:1 have a different word order and different meter. נכון, "established," is placed at the beginning of the next line. The second stich of that line adds הוא, "it," to gain two smooth 3+3 lines. MT should be supported here.

2.b. MT אליו, "unto it." Mic 4:1 עליו, "upon it."

2.c., 3.a. In Mic 4:1–2 the order of הגוים, "nations," and עמים, "peoples," is reversed and כל, "all," is omitted.

4.a. Syr. adds עד רחוק, "even to a distance." Mic 4:3 also contains the additional words. As in v 2, Micah reverses "nations" and "peoples."

The use of impf. tenses predominates, as in the latter sections of 1:29 and 30. So now the dominant statements in vv 2*b*, 3*d*, and 4*c* use impf. tenses. Consec. pf. tenses are used to bind together the supporting clauses in vv 2–3*a* and v 4.

Form/Structure/Setting

Andersen and Freedman ("Excursus," 416) in their discussion of the relation of Isa 2:1–4 to Mic 4:1–5 consider the possibilities that both texts continue the work of the previous chapters. Williamson (*Book Called Isaiah,* 154 n. 80) reviews arguments on the relation of 2:1–4 to chap. 1. He considers 2:1–4 to be a part of the "Deutero-Isaiah redaction." Though the utter lack of references to the mountain of YHWH in chaps. 38–55 raises serious question about that (see Sweeney, 134 n. 87; Wildberger, 77), both sections' heavy emphasis on the nations before YHWH overrides this argument. See the commentary on Isa 34:1–49:4.

Excursus: A Comparison with Micah 4:1–3

Isa 2:1–4 and Mic 4:1–3 are almost identical. (See Andersen and Freedman, "Excursus," 413–27, for a similar viewpoint.)

והיה באחרית הימים נכון יהיה הר בית־יהוה (Isa 2:2*a*) והיה באחרית הימים יהיה הר בית־יהוה (Mic 4:1*ab*)	And it shall be after these days that the mountain of the house of YHWH will be established
בראש ההרים ונשא מגבעות (Isa 2:2*b*) נכון בראש ההרים ונשא הוא מגבעות (Mic 4:1*cd*)	by the head of the mountains and lifted above the hills,
ונהרו אליו כל־הגוים (Isa 2:2*c*) ונהרו עליו עמים (Mic 4:1*e*)	and unto it all nations will flow,
והלכו עמים רבים ואמרו (Isa 2:3*a*) והלכו גוים רבים ואמרו (Mic 4:2*ab*)	and many peoples will go. And they will say
לכו ונעלה אל־הר־יהוה (Isa 2:3*b*) לכו ונעלה אל־הר־יהוה (Mic 4:2*c*)	"Come, let us ascend to the mountain of YHWH,
אל־בית אלהי יעקב (Isa 2:3*c*) ואל־בית אלהי יעקב (Mic 4:2*d*)	to the house of the God of Jacob,
וירנו מדרכיו ונלכה בארחתיו (Isa 2:3*d*) ויורנו מדרכיו ונלכה בארחתיו (Mic 4:2*ef*)	and he will instruct us from his ways, and we shall walk in his paths.
כי מציון תצא תורה ודבר־יהוה מירושלם (Isa 2:3*e*) כי מציון תצא תורה ודבר־יהוה מירושלם (Mic 4:2*gh*)	For from Zion Torah issues, and the word of YHWH from Jerusalem.
ושפט בין הגוים והוכיח לעמים רבים (Isa 2:4*a*) ושפט בין עמים רבים והוכיח לגוים עצמים עד־רחוק (Mic 4:3*ab*)	And he will judge between the nations, and he will decide for many peoples.
וכתתו חרבותם לאתים וחניתותיהם למזמרות (Isa 2:4*b*) וכתתו חרבתיהם לאתים וחניתתיהם למזמרות (Mic 4:3*cd*)	And they shall beat their weapons into ploughs, and their curved swords into pruning hooks.
לא־ישא גוי אל־גוי חרב ולא־ילמדו עוד מלחמה (Isa 2:4*c*) לא־ישאו גוי אל־גוי חרב ולא־ילמדון עוד מלחמה (Mic 4:3*ef*)	Nation will not lift up sword against nation. Nor will they learn war anymore.

At this point Isaiah breaks off. But Micah continues (4:4–5):

Every man will sit under his own vine
and under his own fig tree,
and no one will make them afraid,
for YHWH of Hosts has spoken.
All the peoples may walk
in the name of their gods;

we will walk in the name of YHWH
our God for ever and ever. (NIV adapted)

The passages are virtually identical. They reverse their uses of עמים, "peoples," and הגוים, "nations." They place the word נכון, "established," differently but with no change in meaning. They use different tenses of a verb in one place. Micah has the longer text: "strong nations unto a distance" (Mic 4:3). But there can be no doubt that we are looking at the same text in two places.

In Isaiah the text prepares for a dialogue on Israel (sinful, rebellious Israel) and her place among the peoples in that future temple. It therefore does not complete the poem.

Comment

2 הימים, "these days," are those of war and desolation that judgment demands. הר בית יהוה, "the mountain of the house of YHWH," refers to Zion and the temple. But there is a strand of passages in Isaiah that refers only to YHWH's mountain or Mount Zion, opening the possibility of referring to the place, that is, the mountain, without the temple.

Excursus: The Mountain of YHWH

Prologue	Act 1	Act 2	Act 3	Act 4	Act 5	Act 6	Epilogue
My Holy Mountain							
2:2, 3	10:12 11:6, 9	24:23 25:6, 7, 10 27:13	30:29	35:8–10		56:7 57:13	65:11, 25 66:20
Mount Zion							
4:5	8:18 10:12, 32	16:1 18:7	29:8 31:4	37:32			

Isa 2:2–4 introduces a motif that runs through most of the book. This stratum takes a number of different forms, but it consistently refers to Zion as YHWH's mountain. Note that this motif is missing from chaps. 38–55.

Isa 2:2–4 pictures the situation of the mountain of YHWH's house, i.e., Zion's Temple Mount, באחרית הימים, "in the aftertime of the days" or "in the latter days." In contrast to the instability shown in eighth-century stories, the mountain will be נכון, "established," as the most important and respected pilgrimage destination for כל־הגוים, "all nations." Zion is the cult center for a huge international fellowship of believers in an era of peace for everyone. (Another picture of a peace overseen by YHWH is found in 19:24–25.) Isa 25:6–8 places the turning point for human history on the mountain of God: "YHWH of Hosts will make for all peoples on this mountain a feast. . . . He will swallow up on this mountain the shroud that enshrouds all the peoples, the shadow that overshadows all nations. He will swallow up the death (that) endures forever." In 27:13 a trumpet calls "those perishing in the land of Assyria" and in Egypt to "bow down to YHWH in the holy mountain in Jerusalem." This vision is fulfilled in 34:1–49:4, chaps. 55–56, and 66:18–24. The people do come from the nations to worship YHWH in Zion. But the hindrances that sinners in Israel put in the path of that great inauguration are substantial, and YHWH deals with their insurrection in a bloody and violent way. Isa 56:7–8 climaxes the call for converts to worship on Mount Zion: "I will bring them to my holy mountain and make them rejoice in my house of prayer. Their burnt offerings and their sacrifices (are) acceptable on my altar. For my house is to be called a house of prayer for all peoples. Oracle of my Lord YHWH who is gathering Israel's outcasts: I gather more to him than those already gathered to him." The mountain will belong to them, according to 57:13. The theme of Israel and the nations gathering in worship at Zion returns in the last chapter: "And I . . . am coming to gather all nations and language groups . . . and they will bring all your brothers from all the nations as an offering to YHWH . . . upon my holy mountain, Jerusalem" (66:18–20).

Isa 4:5–6 describes the effect of YHWH's judgment ביום ההוא, "in that day" (Isa 4:2). The mountain will be covered by "a cloud by day and smoke and glow of fire for a flame by night." like the protection given the Israelites in the desert (Exod 40:34–38; Num 9:15–23; Deut 11:33). But now the protection is permanent and fixed. MT of Isa 10:32 reads "the mountain of daughter Zion." Interpreters have had trouble with this reading and tried to emend the text (see my commentary on the verse). In MT's reading it forms the climax of YHWH's march up the mountains until he stands at Nob opposite Jerusalem and waves his hand toward the mountain. The dull gloom of chap. 24 is broken by the reminder that Mount Zion is the throne room of YHWH (24:23). In 25:10 YHWH's hand rests on this mountain. Isa 30:29 pictures a festival march to Zion "in approaching the mountain of YHWH, to the Rock of Israel."

The theme of YHWH's mountain affects the stories of other nations. A promise of action against Assyria in 10:12 is conditioned on completion of YHWH's "work against Mount Zion and against Jerusalem." The wonderful picture of the mountain's role at the end of days does not obscure the need for purification in chap. 1. Moab recognizes the rule of Jerusalem's king in 16:1 by sending a lamb "of the land's ruler" to "the mountain of daughter Zion." The wording is like that in 10:32. A gift is sent by messengers from Cush to YHWH of Hosts "to the place of the Name, YHWH of Hosts, (to) Mount Zion" (18:7*b*). Jerusalem functions as the recognized cult center for the name of YHWH. God attacks the mountain in some scenes and defends it in others: YHWH uses the nations to fight against Mount Zion in 29:8 while 31:4 pictures YHWH fighting against Jerusalem's enemies "upon Mount Zion and on its hill."

Isa 11:5–10 presents a beautiful picture of the peace that will exist when the Davidic heir is spirit-endowed with every gift and embodies the righteousness and faithfulness required for the health of the city. The picture of peace in "all the mount of my holiness" relates the Davidic ideal with that of the Mount of YHWH. Isa 65:25 makes the newly created New Heavens and New Earth (65:17) the setting for the scene in 11:5–9, culminating in the words: "They will do no harm—they will not destroy in all the mount of my holiness."

The theme of the mountain of YHWH establishes the place of Zion in each of the ways in which the future of Israel and of Jerusalem has been portrayed. For the book of Isaiah, it is a terrible sin "to forget the mount of my holiness" (65:11).

נכון, "established," is a key word. The pictures of the Day of YHWH and of judgment often show the earth quaking and shaking. The established order of nature and of political/social forms is being turned upside down. The first move toward restoring order and confidence will be the temple fixed firmly in its place on Zion. Its position is to be at the very top of the mountains and all things that mountains stand for. Just as the devastation will apply to "all the land," so "all nations and all peoples" will be drawn to the temple. The use of the term נהרו, "flow," is unique. It usually applies to water flowing downhill. This movement up the mountain defies gravity. כל־הגוים, "all nations," appears only in the Latter Prophets. עמים רבים, "many peoples," appears fifty-nine times in the Hebrew Bible, ten of these in Isaiah, none in Micah (see Andersen and Freedman, "Excursus,"

420). The notice that all nations and many peoples are involved introduces the theme of YHWH and the nations, which is of particular importance for the Vision. Isa 34:1 fulfills this picture in calling for an assembly of all the nations and the peoples and the frequent address to the peoples or to elements of them, like the coastlands in chaps. 40–49. In these chapters YHWH does "instruct" the nations about "his ways."

3 The function of the new temple centers on תורה, "torah." There is no reference to sacrifice in 1:13–14 and 66:3, but 56:7 pictures the acceptance of burnt offering and sacrifice along with prayers. Jerusalem is to be known primarily for the temple where YHWH is found. And the temple is to serve as a gathering place for learning YHWH's ways. This relationship of Torah to the temple is a characteristic feature of postexilic Judaism.

Excursus: Torah in Isaiah

Bibliography

Fischer, I. *Tora für Israel—Tora für die Völker: Das Konzept des Jesajabuches.* SBS 164. Stuttgart: Kohlhammer, 1995. **Jensen, J.** *The Use of Torah by Isaiah: His Debate with the Wisdom Tradition.* CBQMS 3. Washington: Catholic Biblical Association, 1973. **Sheppard, G. T.** "The 'Scope' of Isaiah as a Book of Jewish and Christian Scriptures." In *New Visions.* Ed. R. F. Melugin and M. A. Sweeney. 257–81. **Sweeney, M. A.** "The Book of Isaiah as Prophetic Torah." In *New Visions.* Ed. R. F. Melugin and M. A. Sweeney. 50–67.

The discussion of Isaiah and Torah begins with how Isaiah's references to Torah understand and treat it. But recent studies also look at indications that the book of Isaiah was itself regarded as sacred Scripture, as a kind of new Torah.

Sheppard's work treats Torah as the principal subject matter of Isaiah as a book of Jewish Scripture. Passages like 2:3; 8:20; 24:5; 42:4, 21, 24; and 51:4, 7 may originally have had Mosaic Torah in mind. In exilic passages, like 8:16, 20, תורה, "torah," designates the book of Isaiah itself but likewise implies a Scripture and a subject matter larger than merely this book, i.e., Mosaic Torah.

Sweeney looks at the book of Isaiah, when it reached its final form in the fifth century B.C.E., as designed to support the reform program of Ezra-Nehemiah. He is right. In Isa 2:3 Torah refers to YHWH's instruction concerning the proper way to conduct international relations so as to bring about worldwide order. In its broader context, Torah refers to the Mosaic Law. The purpose of that law is to establish the norms of life for the people of Israel (Isa 2:5) and to realize YHWH's worldwide sovereignty (Isa 2:2–4). Chaps. 34–66 suggest that this will come to pass through Cyrus and his new empire.

4 YHWH will decide issues that concern the peoples. The verse assumes the sovereignty of YHWH over the nations and people, a point that chap. 41 will develop. The functions that he has carried out in relation to Israel now will be applied universally. Armaments and wars will be unnecessary because his decisions will settle all disputes. Wars, like those so familiar in Isa 5–33, will no longer occur.

Explanation

This central pericope in the prologue deals with Zion from the perspective of God's purpose and brings the chapters into line with the book's full message (developed most fully in 34:1–49:4 and chaps. 55–56, 66). Zion's ultimate purpose has nothing to do with either Israel's or Judah's nationalistic dreams. Their wish to be "nations like other nations" (1 Sam 8:5) has led to centuries of bloodshed and warfare. Nothing faintly resembling justice or righteousness has come from it, as 2:5–10 makes plain. Parties in fifth-century Jerusalem were prepared to claim God's promises and blessing for new forms of nationalistic efforts. Some were Zionists (cf. chaps. 60–62); some were Israelites (cf. 63:7–64:12). The purpose of the book is to deny both their claims (cf. 65:1–16) and put forward an entirely different view of Zion's destiny.

This pericope is the first clear statement of the promise that the city will be redeemed. The kingdoms will perish, but Jerusalem has an abiding place in God's future. The absolute requirements of justice and righteousness will be achieved. Thus the city will be equipped to be God's instrument. It will be ready to have his presence, to be his dwelling place. In this city he will receive the nations and the peoples (34:1) and teach them his ways (34:2–49:4 and chaps. 55–56).

This irenic picture of Zion reflects neither the ambitions of Joshua nor those of David as depicted in the Psalms. There YHWH (and the Davidic king) rules the world from Jerusalem. The rulers of the nations are forced to come there to acknowledge the sovereignty of YHWH and the Davidic king and bring tribute. The Vision presents the immediate future in terms of turmoil and violence. YHWH instigates and takes a primary part in it. However, this view (vv 2–4) looks at Jerusalem beyond the battles.

The message of 2:2–4 is very practical and realistic. There is little here of the idealistic perfection pictured in 11:6–9 or 35:1–10. It nonetheless describes a sharp reversal of policy and goal. There is nothing here of political dominance or of nationalism. Zion's appeal will be religious and universal. The progress of the Vision will mark the steps toward this goal, especially in 4:2–6; 12:1–6; 24:21–23; 40:1–11; 49:5–54:17 (especially chaps. 52–53); and 65:17–66:24. This beautiful picture defines the form that the restoration of the city, announced in 1:26–27, will assume. In it the first of the dominant themes of the Vision begins to take shape.

The important thing about Zion will be her reputation as YHWH's dwelling. It is YHWH's house, the temple, that stands out because he is present and active there. This will attract the nations to Jerusalem. YHWH's actions are those of "torah" and "word," that is, judging and making wise. As a result, the nations will turn to peaceful pursuits.

It is important to note that YHWH's purpose has been a part of Israel's revealed tradition throughout. Abraham was called to be a blessing to all the families of the earth (Gen 12:3*b*). Israel was called to be a "kingdom of priests" (Exod 19:6). But the people had not succeeded. In Isaiah's Vision, God moves to take things into his own hands. He will do what is necessary to establish the city and judge the nations. He will remove from the population all the elements that do not fit this new mode of operation.

The Vision of Isaiah pictures God's search for a people for his city. The Vision will depict successive generations of the people of God—Israelites, Judeans, and Jerusalemites—who refuse roles in YHWH's new city and its program.

What is this new city and its program? Vv 2–4 show a city centered in YHWH himself. The city is simply the place where he lives. His attraction for nations and peoples is so great that they "flow" uphill to the summit of the mountains to learn from "the God of Jacob" the lessons to which Israel and Judah turned deaf ears. What they learn from YHWH will eliminate war among them. The age of peace will come. Note what is not mentioned: priestly sacrifice. This does not happen by chance (cf. 1:12–14; 66:3). But 56:7 suggests that there will be a place for that, too.

God's new people will include only those who are dedicated to YHWH, "servants of YHWH," from the remnants of Israel, Jerusalem, and the nations. What will be the role of God's people in this city? The rest of the book will speak to that question. Righteousness and justice have already been shown to be nonnegotiable requirements. Willingness and obedience have been named as needed qualities. Faith, patience, and humility will be among the virtues taught to the servants of the King of Zion, YHWH, the God of Israel.

This little gem seems to hang suspended between the domestic court scene in chap. 1 and the "Day of YHWH" scene in 2:5–22. In a very real sense it expresses the condensed and controlling theme of the entire Vision. Accented by the claim that this is an authentic word from Isaiah himself (v 1), it looks to "the end" and the role of Zion in that time. Zion is portrayed as a temple city, the greatest and most popular pilgrimage city in the world. It holds this distinction because it is the place of YHWH's dwelling. Zion will be identified with YHWH as "the God of Jacob." He will be sought out as a teacher of individuals and as a judge who brings peace and order among nations.

Israel Not Welcome/The Day of YHWH (2:5–22)

Bibliography

Alonsa Fontela, C. "Una breve nota marginal de Alphonsa de Samora sobre lahpor perot (Is 2,20)." *Sefarad* 52 (1992) 29–32. **Baker, D. W.** "Tarshish (Place)." *ABD.* 6:331–33. **Barré, M. L.** "A Rhetorical-Critical Study of Isaiah 2:12–17." *CBQ* 65 (2003) 503–21. **Becker, J.** *Isaias—Der Prophet und sein Buch.* 46. **Bertram, G.** "'Hochmut' und verwandte Begriffe im griechischen und hebräischen Alten Testament." *WO* 3 (1964) 32–43. **Blenkinsopp, J.** "Fragments of Ancient Exegesis in an Isaian Poem (Jes 2,6–22)." *ZAW* 93 (1981) 51–62. **Davidson, R.** "The Interpretation of Isaiah 2:6ff." *VT* 16 (1966) 1–7. **De Bruin, W. M.** "De afbakening van Jesaja 2:5 in het licht van de oude tekstgestuigzen (The Delimitation of Isa. 2:5 in Light of Ancient Witnesses)." *NedTT* 56 (2002) 280–98. **Deist, F. E.** "Notes on the Structure of Isa. 2:2–22." *Theologia Evangelica* 10.2–3 (1977) 1–6. **Hoffman, H. W.** *Die Intention der Verkündigung Jesajas.* 107. **Høgenhaven, J.** *Gott und Volk bei Jesaja.* 109–11. **Lack, R.** *La Symbolique.* 38–39. **Marx, A.** "Esaïe ii 20, une signature karaïte?" *VT* 40 (1990) 132–27. **Milgrom, J.** "Did Isaiah Prophesy during the Reign of Uzziah?" (Excursus b: 2:10ff. and the Earthquake). *VT* 14 (1964) 178–82. **Napier, B. D.** "Isaiah and the Isaian." In *Volume du congrès: Genève, 1965.* VTSup 15. Leiden: Brill, 1966. 240–51. **Neveu, L.** "Isaie 2,6–22: Le jour de Yhwh." In *La vie de la Parole: De l'Ancien au Nouveau Testament.* FS P. Grelot. Paris: Desclée, 1987. 129–38. **Roberts, J. J. M.** "Isaiah 2 and the Prophet's Message to the North." *JQR* 75 (1984–85) 290–308. **Rogers, J. S.** "An Allusion to Coronation in Isaiah 2:6." *CBQ* 51 (1989) 232–36. **Seybold, K.** "Die anthropologischen Beiträge aus Jesaja 2." *ZTK* 74 (1977) 401–15. **Sweeney, M.** *Isaiah 1–4.* 139–46, 174–77.

Bibliography on "The Day of YHWH"

Cathcart, K. J. "Day of Yahweh." *ABD.* 2:84–85. ———. "Kingship and the 'Day of Yahweh' in Isaiah 2:6–22." *Hermathena* 125 (1978) 48–59. **Cerny, L.** *The Day of Yahweh and Some Relevant Problems.* Prague: Univ. of Karlovy, 1948. **Everson, A. J.** "The Day of the Lord." *IDBSup.* 209–10. **Gelin, A.** "Jours de Yahvé et jour de Yahvé." *LumVie* 2 (1953) 39–52. **Jenni, E.** "The Day of the Lord." *IDB.* 1:784–85. **Mowinckel, S.** "Jahves Dag." *NTT* 59 (1958) 1–56, 209–29. **Rad, G. von.** "The Origin of the Concept of the Day of Yahweh." *JSS* 4 (1959) 97–108. **Schunck, K. D.** "Strukturlinien in der Entwicklung der Vorstellung von 'Tag Jahwes.'" *VT* 14 (1964) 319–30.

Bibliography on the Phrase ביום ההוא, "in that day"

De Vries, S. *Yesterday, Today, and Tomorrow.* Grand Rapids, MI: Eerdmans, 1975. Chap. 2. **Lefèvre, A.** "L'expression 'En ce jour-là dans le livre d'Isaïe." In *Mélanges Bibliques.* FS A. Robert. Paris: Bloud & Gay, 1957. 174–79. **Munch, P. H.** *The Expression 'bajjom hahu'—Is It an Eschatological Terminus Technicus?* ANVAO 2. Oslo, 1936.

Translation

A Speaker:	5 *House of Jacob,*	2+2+2
(to Israel)	*come and let us walk*	
	in the light of YHWH.	
	6 *For it applies*[a] *to his people,*	3+2
	the House of Jacob.	
Second Speaker:	*But they are full*[b] *from the East*	3+2+3
(to the court)	*and are telling fortunes like Philistines,*	
	and they do business with strangers' sons.	
Chorus:	7 *So that his land became full*	3+2+3
	of silver and gold—	
	no end to his[a] *treasures.*	
	So that his land filled with horses—	3+3
	no end to his chariots.	
	8 *So that his land became full of idols:*	3+3+3
	to the product of his hands they bowed down,	
	to that which his fingers had made.	
	9 *So that humankind became degraded*	2+2
	and a person became humiliated.	
Heavens and Earth:	*Do not release [sg.] them!*	2+2+2
(to the jailer)	10 *Come [sg.] into the rock!*	
	And hide yourself in the dust!	
	From the face of YHWH's dread	3+2
	and from the brilliance of his majesty.[a]	
Heavens:	11 *The eyes of the haughtiness of humankind*	
	shall be humbled,[a]	4+3+3
	and exaltation of persons shall be brought down,	
	and YHWH alone shall be exalted	
	in that day.	2

Earth: 12 *For there is a day belonging to YHWH of Hosts* 4
upon everything high and raised 4
and [a]*upon everything lifted up—and it shall fall,*[a] 4
13 *and upon all the cedars of Lebanon,* 4
which are high and lifted up, 2
and upon all the oaks of Bashan 4
14 *and upon all the high mountains* 4
and upon all the raised hills 4
15 *and upon every high tower* 4
and upon every impenetrable wall 4
16 *and upon all the ships of Tarshish* 4
and upon all boats [a] *of exotic lands.*[b] 4

Heavens: 17 *And the haughtiness of humankind shall be brought down,* 3+3+3
and the exaltation of persons shall be abased,
and YHWH alone shall be exalted
in that day. 2

Prophet: 18 *And as for the idols—they will completely disappear,*[a] 3

Earth: 19 *and they shall go into the caves of the rocks* 3+2
and into the holes of the dust
from the face of the dread of YHWH 3+2+3
and from the splendor of his majesty
when he rises to make the earth tremble.[a]

Heavens: 20 *In that day* 2+2
humankind will abandon
his [a] *silver idols* 3+3+4
and his golden idols,
which he [b]*had made for himself*[b] *to worship,*
for the digging of moles [c] *and bats—* 3+3+2
21 *for the going into the crevices of the rock*
and into the clefts of the crags,
from the face of the dread of YHWH 3+2+3
and from the splendor of his majesty
when he rises to make the earth tremble.

YHWH: 22 [a]*Stop your (talk) about humankind,* 3+3+3
who has (only) breath in his nostrils!
For, in what [b] *(way) can he be evaluated?*

Notes

6.a. Duhm (39) thought the beginning of this section was mutilated. He judged v 5 to be a late addition. Then he read v 6 as the beginning of the new section. He accepted LXX's reading as 3d person but felt the need for an expressed subject and suggested emending to read נטש יה עמו, "Yah has abandoned his people." He is right in noting that the 2d person here is *auffällig* or "strange." He has followed some of the form of the LXX but not its meaning. Ἀνῆκω means "to approach, pertain to," not "to abandon." Wildberger (92) takes a different approach. He accepts v 5 as "applicatio" for Israel, which may have been added for use in worship services (77). He then makes the break between v 5 and v 6. He suggests the assumption that an original relation between vv 6 and 7 existed (92) and works on that basis in a fairly lengthy discussion of the problem, raised by the LXX, reading a 3d person (instead of 2d), and by Tg. using a 2d-person pl. to address the people. Syr. and OL versions follow MT. If, however, v 6*a* is read with v 5, as do 1QIsa[a] and Tg., the next section begins with 6*b*. With this in mind, let us take another look at the relation of MT and LXX.

The Masoretic rendering of this verse seems clear. Only the addition on the verb might draw comment: כי נטשתה עמך בית יעקב, "For you have neglected your people, the house of Jacob." However, the setting in context is rough, to say the least. After the picture of the exaltation of YHWH's house in the last days, when the peoples from the nations will flow toward it, the house of Jacob is invited to join the procession and "walk in the light of YHWH" (v 5). The verb is cohortative, 1st person pl. The tone and the address (2d masc. sg.) of the following, "for you have abandoned your people, the house of Jacob," take a shocking turn. V 6 is in tune with the following verses, which reproach Israel for its sins. But one cannot avoid a sense of shock at the turn from v 5 to v 6.

It is therefore of interest to note a completely different rendering of the verb in LXX (which incidentally is not mentioned in *BHS*): ἀνῆκεν γὰρ τὸν λαὸν αὐτοῦ τὸν οἶκον τοῦ Ισραηλ, "for it applies to his people the house of Israel." The exchange of "his" for "your" requires reading ו as ך. "Israel" for "Jacob" is a frequent variant without change of meaning. So the real difference turns on the verb ἀνῆκε, "it applies," for נטשתה, "you neglected." If the LXX were retranslated into Heb., it should read something like כי נטה את העמו. Cf. the MT: כי נטשתה עמ. The suggestion that the LXX is a witness to a superior text, while the MT records the corruption of הא into שׁ and the evolution of ו to ך to fit the change of person, commends itself strongly. Or can it be a deliberate change with theological motivations? V 5 is undeniably a call to Israel (בית יעקב, "house of Jacob") to go up to worship the God of Jacob at Zion. The *textus receptus* of MT negates that with the announcement that they have now been abandoned, while LXX (consistent with vv 2–4 and 5) confirms that the invitation is valid. This could be interpreted as an open door to Samaritans in later times.

The emended text should then read כי נטה את־העמו בית יעקב and should be translated "for it applies to his people, the house of Jacob." The line is then an explanation of the invitation in v 5. And the next should be translated "but" to begin the explanation of Israel's rejection of YHWH's invitation.

6.b. An obj. appears to be lacking for מלאו. "Full" of what? D. W. Thomas ("A Lost Hebrew Word in Isa 2:6," *JTS* 13 [1962] 323–24) suggests emending מקדם, "from the East," to מעקדים, "enchanters." The suggestion provides a parallel to עננים: "enchanters and soothsayers like the Philistines." It is a possible rendering. MT gives a parallel to Philistines in "from the East," stressing foreign influence. MT is possible and should be kept.

7.a. ו as a sg. suf. is consistently used here with verbs in the pl. until the end of v 9, where the pl. suf. appears. It must be judged a deliberate stylistic usage that cannot be reproduced in English.

10.a. LXX adds ὅταν ἀναστῇ θραῦσαι τὴν γῆν = בקומו לערץ הארץ, "when he takes his place to make the earth tremble." The clause makes the earthquake imagery explicit. The addition adds a stich but would otherwise fit the meter. However, MT seems sufficient as it is.

11.a. שָׁפֵל, "shall be humbled" (sg.), follows a pl. subject. 1QIsa[a] has תשפלנה (pl.), which eliminates the problem. J. Huesman ("Finite Uses of the Infinitive Absolute," *Bib* 37 [1956] 287) emended to inf. abs. שָׁפֹל, but this does not solve the problem.

12.a-a. LXX καὶ ἐπὶ πάντα ὑψηλὸν καὶ μετέωρον, καὶ ταπεινωθήσονται, "and upon everything exalted and lifted up, and it will be made low." This apparently adds ונבה, "and exalted," and may well indicate that this originally stood here instead of (not in addition to, as LXX) ושפל, "and it shall fall."

16.a. שכיות has traditionally been derived from שכה and understood as an "art object." The context calls for a parallel to אניות, "ships." LXX had trouble with both תרשיש, "Tarshish," which it translates θαλάσσης, "sea," and with שכיות, which it translates θέαν πλοίων, "goddess of ships." Modern studies (K. Budde, "Zu Jesaja 1–5," *ZAW* 49 [1931] 198; G. R. Driver, "Difficult Words in the Hebrew Prophets," 52) suggest an Eg. background in the word *šk.tj,* meaning "ship." The same word may explain the Ugar. word *ṯkt* (W. F. Albright, in *Festschrif Alfred Bertholet,* ed. W. Baumgartner [Tübingen: Mohr, 1950] 4 n. 3; J. Aistleitner, *WUS*[2] §2862).

16.b. G. R. Driver ("Difficult Words in the Hebrew Prophets, in *Studies in Old Testament Prophecy,* 52) suggests that החמדה means "the desirable land" and thinks of Arabia. Hence NEB "dhows of Arabia."

18.a. MT has a discrepancy in number between subject and verb. 1QIsa[a] corrects it with יחלופו (pl.), which is also supported by the versions.

19.a. Note the assonance of לערץ הארץ *la'ārôṣ hâ'âreṣ,* "to make the earth tremble."

20.a. The afformative in אלילי כספו applies to the entire construction (cf. J. Weingreen, "The Construct-Genitive Relation in Hebrew Syntax," *VT* 4 [1954] 50–59).

20.b-b. There is a discrepancy of number. LXX reads עשו, "they made," as a sg. It should be emended to עשה.

20.c. לחפר פרות has no meaning as it stands. LXX translates τοῖς ματαίοις, which means "useless" or "powerless" and refers to the idols. θ´ has φαρφαρωθ, transliterating the two words as one. BDB says this is a *hap. leg.* for "a mole" and is parallel to the next word.

22.a. LXX leaves this verse out altogether. Perhaps this is a recognition that it is a break in the context.

22.b. במה, "in what?" Vg. translates *excelsus reputatus est ipse* and seems to have read it as רמה, "height," which is adopted by S. Talmon ("Aspects of the Textual Transmission of the Bible in Light of Qumran Manuscripts," *Textus* 4 [1964] 1270). Syr. *'ajk* and Tg. וכלמא השיב הוא seem to have read כמה, "how much? how long?" M. Dahood ("Hebrew-Ugaritic Lexicography I," *Bib* 44 [1963] 302) proposed to vocalize this as בָּמָה and translate "animal": "Turn away from man in whose nostrils is divine breath, but who must be considered a beast." Dahood bases this on the Ugar. *bmt,* but Wildberger protests that this means "back" not "animal." MT's question makes sense and should be kept.

Form/Structure/Setting

The end of the previous paragraph is clearly marked. V 5 begins with a different address (Israel) and a different subject. The passage is complex. Documentation of Israel's sin and judgment digresses into a treatment of humanity's sin of pride, which YHWH cannot tolerate.

The entire section, from v 6 through v 22, which has an arch structure, responds to the invitation to the House of Jacob in v 5 by identifying the fate of Jacob with that of humankind, and both with the Day of YHWH.

A Come, House of Jacob—the invitation applies to his people (vv 5–6*a*).
  B But they are full of paganism, in which humankind (אדם) is degraded; do not forgive them (vv 6*b*–9).
    C Hide in the rocks from the dread of YHWH (v 10).
      D Arrogant humankind (אדם) will be humbled; YHWH alone will be exalted (v 11).
KEYSTONE The Day of YHWH shall be upon proud and lofty humanity (vv 12–16).
      D´ The pride of humanity (אדם) will be humbled; YHWH alone will be exalted (vv 17–18).
    C´ Flee to the rocks from the dread of YHWH (v 19).
  B´ Humanity (אדם) will throw away idols and riches (v 20).
    C´ They will flee to the rocks from the dread of YHWH (v 21).
A´ Stop your (talk) about humanity (אדם): for how can they be evaluated? (v 22).

The "your" of v 22 refers back to the speakers of v 5, commanding them to respect the ban YHWH has placed on his people, the house of Jacob, that prevents them from joining the peoples ascending the Temple Mount.

The unity of the passage, as well as the identity of the "house of Jacob," has been thoroughly discussed. H. Junker ("Sancta Civitas Jerusalem Nova," 33) defended the intimate connection of vv 2–4 with vv 6–21 on the grounds of Isaiah's view of the high and invulnerable holiness of Zion as the throne of YHWH. The cultic reforms of Hezekiah are seen as the background of the passage in which the introduction of an Assyrian altar into the temple by Ahaz (2 Kgs 16:10–20) was the high point of paganization of the "house of Jacob," which he understands to include Judah. Davidson (*VT* 16 [1966] 1–7) understands "the house of Jacob" to refer to the northern kingdom and places the time in the Syro-Ephraimite war. Kaiser in his first edition (33) understands this as a speech in the temple during a festival occasion in which the prophet may address the people and God. In his second edition (66) he finds the entire composition belongs to the final redaction of the book.

If the search for an original setting be put aside in favor of an attempt to see the passage in its setting in the book, it may be noted that: (1) With the description of the Day of YHWH all the major themes of the book have been touched in these two chapters. They are a most fitting prologue (or overture) for the Vision. (2) The setting of vv 5–9 in the book favors an understanding of references to Israel/Jacob in the eighth-century scenes referring to the northern kingdom. This commentary has so understood this chapter and 1:2–8 before it. (3) The three parts of this chapter—the nations at the mountain of YHWH, problems with Israel's attendance, and the wars of "the day of YHWH"—exactly represent the issues dealt with in 34:1–49:4. The nations are called together (34:1). They are reminded of the destructive wars that YHWH claims as his own (34:2–8). They are instructed in the ways of YHWH by reading from his scroll (34:16; 36–39) and by a series of lessons given by YHWH (40:12–48). Israel is among the gathered nations. She is addressed repeatedly with assurances about God's intention toward her, but she finally declines to participate (49:1–4).

Comment

5 The verse responds to the picture of a new day for the temple with a call for Israel to "walk in the light of YHWH." The metaphor has changed, and the verse introduces the contrast between light and darkness that runs through the entire Vision of Isaiah.

Strand: "Light" (אור) and "Darkness" (חשך)

Bibliography

Clements, R. "A Light to the Nations." In *Forming Prophetic Literature.* Ed. J. W. Watts and P. R. House. 57–64. **Collins, T.** *The Mantle of Elijah.* Sheffield: JSOT Press, 1993. 52–53. **Miscall, P.** "Isaiah: The Labyrinth of Images." *Semeia* 54 (1991) 103.

Walking in light or darkness is a theme that is touched lightly in every part of Isaiah. Darkness describes idols and their worship while light relates to the ways of YHWH.

In context, "Come and let us walk in the light of YHWH" (2:5) is an invitation for Jacob (northern Israel) to join in pilgrimage to the mountain of YHWH at Zion. The contrast between light and dark portrays moral choices (5:20) while the transition from light to darkness portrays the results of wars (5:30). Isa 13:10 speaks of dimming the light of heavenly bodies. The opposite transition depicts a change from bad times to good (8:22–9:2), illustrated by the brightening of sun and moon (30:26). The figure shows a turning from great distress to joy. Chap. 40 calls on the exiles and YHWH's servants "to be a light (for) nations" (42:7; 49:6*b*) in fulfilling the task of redemption for Israel's exiles. (Cf. "the Light of Israel" whose task would be to punish the Assyrian leader in 10:17.)

Light and darkness come to characterize God's work in creation ("I am YHWH. There is no one else. Former of light. Creator of darkness" [45:6*b*–7*a*]) and in history (45:7*b*; 47:5; 51:6). Jerusalem is summoned to pay attention to YHWH's work, "For law goes out from me, and I make my justice flash for light (over) peoples" (51:4).

PROLOGUE	ACT 1	ACT 2	ACT 3	ACT 4	ACT 5	ACT 6	EPILOGUE
אור, "LIGHT" (27x)							
2:5	5:20, 30 9:1 10:17	13:10	30:26	42:6, 16 45:7	49:6 51:4	58:8, 10 59:9 60:1, 3, 19, 20	
חשך, "DARKNESS" (14x)							
	5:20, 30 8:22 9:1		29:18	42:7 45:3, 7, 19 47:5	49:9	58:10 59:9 60:2	
אפלות, "GLOOM" (3x)							
	8:22					58:10 59:9	

Chaps. 58, 59, and 60 use the metaphors extensively. When the people worship as God would have them (58:6–7), they are promised that "your light will break out like the dawn . . . your light will rise in the darkness and your gloom (will become) as noonday" (58:8, 10*b*). But, sadly, this has not come about:

Because of such (sins), justice is far from us,
legitimacy does not come to us.
We wait for light.
But see! There is only darkness.
And for brightness, but we walk in gloom.
We grope like blind persons by a wall.
and as those without eyes we grope.
We stumble at noon as though it were twilight,
and at full vigor as though we were corpses. (59:9–10)

Isa 60:1 exhorts them to "Rise! Shine! for your light comes" and depicts God's light of salvation replacing the sun and the moon for Jerusalem (vv 19–20). So throughout Isaiah, the figures of light and dark are used as symbols of Israel's salvation and her troubles. They often parallel the figures of blindness and sight.

6*a* The proposed emendation (see *Notes*), following LXX, reverses the meaning of the first line from MT and most translations. It emphasizes Israel's role as YHWH's people, that is, her covenant and elect status. The tension between election and conduct that required God to reject God's people is a theme pursued throughout the book. Indeed, Paul is still at it in Rom 5–7.

The ark of YHWH was brought to Jerusalem as an act of "all Israel" (2 Sam 6:1–5). All Israel was accustomed to go up to Jerusalem to worship. Jeroboam had to take measures to discourage this activity when the northern tribes withdrew from the united monarchy (1 Kgs 12:26–33). It is a natural assumption that the restoration of the city should make it accessible to "all Israel."

6*b* It is a sad commentary on two centuries of separation and the resulting religious infidelity that this was not to be. The separation had been politically and economically successful, as the wry comment "they are full" shows. But it had also been spiritually disastrous. "From the East" is apparently a general statement, not intended to imply specific imports.

7–8 V 7 echoes the description of Solomon's wealth (1 Kgs 10:19–29), while v 8 summarizes consequences like those in 1 Kgs 11:4–10. The dehumanizing effect of the conditions of new wealth and the relation of greed and idolatry are nowhere stated more eloquently.

Israel's position astride the major trade routes gave her a very advantageous position for trade and commerce. It also brought her contact with the cultures, religions, and cults of the entire Near East. This was true in Solomon's time, and in Ahab's time, and also in Jeroboam's time. This passage refers to the eighth century of Jeroboam, but continued to be applicable after the fall of Samaria as the area was "filled" with people from other areas. Fifth-century Judah would have understood and seen continued application in the land that came to be that of "the Samaritans."

9 Israel's lifestyle has become indistinguishable from that of humanity in general. אדם, "humankind," becomes the theme that will continue to the end of the chapter. The term evokes thoughts and images from Gen 1–11. Israel is judged to have relived the experiences of the "sons of Adam" and thus to share the same degradation, humiliation, and eventual judgment.

Strand: "Humankind" (אדם), *"All Flesh"* (כל בשר), *"A Human"* (אנוש)

The universal scope of Isaiah begins here and continues through the book in the use of these words.

PROLOGUE	ACT 1	ACT 2	ACT 3	ACT 4	ACT 5	ACT 6	EPILOGUE
אדם, "HUMANKIND"							
2:9, 11, 17, 20, 22	5:15 6:11, 12	13:12 17:7 22:6	29:19, 21 31:38	(34:5) 37:19 38:11 43:4 44:11, 13, 15 45:12 47:3	51:12 52:14	56:2 58:5	
כל בשר, "ALL FLESH"							
				40:5, 6	49:26		66:16, 23, 24
אנוש, "A HUMAN"							
	8:1	13:7, 12 24:6	33:8		51:7, 12	56:2	

9c אל־תשא להם means literally something like "Do not lift up for them!" This has sometimes been understood as forgiveness. However, the context points more to the meaning "Do not allow them to go up in the pilgrimage!" Instead they are to prepare for the cataclysmic events to come. V 6*a* has missed the important point that Zion's elevation and peaceful accessibility were to come in "the last days" after the judgment. The terrible "day" must come first.

A major motif in OT theology appears here (and in vv 11–22): pride and ambition are humanity's besetting and most devastating sins. Idolatry is seen as an expression of this drive by which human beings seek to exalt themselves. The key word is אדם, "humankind." The counterpoint is between words for exaltation and for humiliation. In this passage (v 9) humanity is degraded and humbled by idolatry. The following passage (vv 11–22) views the sin in opposite terms. Idolatry is seen as a symbol of human ambition and pride (v 18), which will be judged. For YHWH alone can be exalted. This, too, is a major theme for the book of Isaiah. Israel, Judah, and the inhabitants of Jerusalem cannot accept the servant role. This determination to avoid the humble role prevents them from participation in God's new city.

10 This verse may be linked with v 19 in reflecting a threat of earthquake. Canaan was earthquake-prone, but a monstrous earthquake during Uzziah's reign made a particular impression on Amos (1:1; 9:1) and on Zechariah (14:4). Milgrom (*VT* 14 [1964] 179) suggests that Isaiah "experienced the earthquake and drew upon it for his description" here.

11, 17 The entire passage relates to its context in terms that contrast the genuine and correct exaltation of YHWH with the temporary and contemptible self-exaltation of humanity. It is a theme reflected in the building of the Tower of Babel (Gen 11) and is a recurrent theme in Isaiah. It speaks of the general day of humiliation for humankind within which Israel's special sin (vv 6–9) will be punished. Israel has not only sinned against covenant but also participates in humanity's attempt at self-exaltation against God. So one writes here of "humankind" and "persons."

12–16 This is a description of YHWH's action against everything high and "exalted." The contents are reminiscent of Ps 29, where the power of YHWH is pictured in terms like those used in Ugarit for Baal (cf. AB, 7:27*a*–41; H. L. Ginsburg, "A Phoenician Hymn in the Psalter," in *Atti del XIX Congresso internazionale degli Orientalisti, Roma 23–29 settembre 1935—XIII* [Roma: Bardi, 1938] 472–76; T. H. Gaster, "Psalm 29," *JQR* 37 [1946–47] 55–65; F. M. Cross, "A Canaanite Psalm in the OT," *BASOR* 117 [1950] 19–21).

The name יהוה צבאות, "YHWH of Hosts," is fitting for the description of the day reflecting the holy-war concepts of early Israel. The words גאה, "high," רָם, "raised," and נשׂא, "lifted up," describe divine characteristics that humanity has tried to appropriate to itself. This is humankind's persistent and pervasive sin, the attempt to be like God (Gen 3:5), which has prevented the achievement of a genuine humanity and led to repeated conflict with God.

The figures that follow illustrate the superlatives of Israelite experience from the "cedars of Lebanon," the "oaks of Bashan," to the "ships of Tarshish." The giant trees were wonders for the Palestinian, who knew only small and warped trees on the hills. The ships were symbols of wonder for the Israelites, who feared the seas. But also included are figures of things nearer home: "mountains" and "hills," "towers" and "walls." These were symbols of pride and power in Canaan. The מגדל, "tower," may be in an open field (Isa 5:2), but it is more likely a fortress tower that may be part of a wall or may stand in the middle of a city (cf. Judg 9:46; E. F. Campbell and J. F. Ross, "Shechem and the Biblical Tradition," *BA* 26 [1963] 16; G. E. Wright, *Shechem* [New York: McGraw-Hill, 1964] 94, 124).

Tarshish was a distant port frequented by Phoenician ships. The phrase אניות תרשׁישׁ, "ships of Tarshish," referred to the strong commercial ships that were used for the longest routes, flagships of the fleets.

18–21 The day of terror will lead to the end of idols, which have proved useless in preventing danger. ביום ההוא, "in that day," at the end of v 17 ties the picture to the יום ליהוה, "day belonging to YHWH," of v 12. The passage blends the motifs of YHWH's day with those of judgment on pride and on idols. The Day of YHWH motif occurs in the OT from the time of Amos (5:18) when he speaks of a day that is already well known. It is a day on which YHWH acts in a special way. He intervenes in the course of history. (See *Excursus: Day of YHWH/Divine Warrior* in the *Introduction.*)

The idea of this "day" was not yet that of a ἡμέρα θεοῦ/κυρίου, which in the NT pictures the end of the world, the last judgment, and the return of Christ (*TDNT,* 2:954). The idea here is much more varied and flexible. Jer 46:10 speaks of "a day of vengeance" against Egypt. Ezek 30:1–9 prophesies a day of judgment against the nations. But in Ezek 7 it is a day of judgment against Israel. In Zephaniah the day brings judgment on Israel and the nations. The motif occurs also in Joel, Obad 15, and Zech 14:1 (cf. Wolff, *Joel und Amos,* BKAT 14.2 [Neukirchen-Vluyn: Neukirchener Verlag, 1969] 38–39). But it has nothing to do with the breach of covenant (1:2–3) or Israel's status here. So the witnesses are called back to deal with the business at hand (v 22).

Milgrom (*VT* 14 [1964] 178–82) notes that judgment on humankind's pride and grab for power runs like a scarlet thread through Isaiah's prophesies (cf. 3:16; 13:11*b;* 14:11–14; 25:11*b*–2; 26:5; 28:1, 3; 30:25; 33:18). The Day of YHWH motif often includes ideas from the holy war (von Rad, *JSS* 4 [1959] 97–108), and some interpreters think it related to a particular festival day.

Explanation

A speaker presumes that the announcement of Zion's future destiny means that Israel is now free. But this mistake is set straight. Israel's guilt has been proved. The jailer is instructed not to release her. Instead all should hide from YHWH's awesome appearance.

Israel's materialism and paganism have caused her to lose her elect and privileged status. She reverts to the status of depraved humanity, exhibiting the characteristics of pride and arrogance that condemned the builders of Babel's tower (Gen 11), earning the reaction from God that idolators deserve. Note the irony: "all nations . . . many peoples" (Isa 2:2–3), but Israel is excluded with unrepentant humanity (האדם). Israel's sentence is not to be set aside. She must await YHWH's appearance and judgment (3:13–15).

The passage is a statement of the main theme of the book (cf. 65:1–16). It shows how and why traditional Israel does not and will not participate in God's new city. The basic tension is stated in v 6. On the one side is the recognized election of "the House of Jacob." On the other is the extent to which the promised "land" has been "filled" with things that are not acceptable to YHWH. Commerce leads to an influx of fortune-tellers and idols that would degrade any part of humankind. It is certainly intolerable for the people of God. The passage puts the judgment of God's people into a perspective of world judgment. It is a reminder that belief in YHWH's universal sovereignty necessarily implies that it must be revealed and justified. Wisdom's teaching concerning the need for humanity is cast within a judgment frame that is truly prophetic. But the teaching is the same. YHWH is Lord, and he is unique. He alone is ruler with the status and right to rule. Every attempt to displace him or to appropriate his prerogatives is treason and will not be tolerated. The day of his judgment applies to all humanity.

Chaps. 5–33 will develop this theme of judgment on the whole land. Isa 41:1–49:4 and 63:7–65:16 deal with Israel's problems continuing in the new era.

Jerusalem's Ordeal (3:1–4:6)

Here attention focuses on Jerusalem. YHWH's extreme displeasure over Jerusalem's corruption and idolatry is ameliorated by his determination eventually to redeem the city.

Episode A: Jerusalem Shall Totter (3:1–12). The setting in the court of YHWH provides opportunity to discuss the worsening conditions in Jerusalem. Only in the last two lines are the people of the city addressed.

Episode B: YHWH Stands for Judgment (3:13–15). When the sentence is pronounced, it falls on the elders of the people for their failure to maintain justice for the poor.

Episode C: Haughty Daughters of Zion (3:16–4:1). The luxury of Jerusalem's society calls for special judgment on the day of reckoning.

Episode D: YHWH's Branch (4:2–6). Through and beyond judgment God has a purpose for Jerusalem's purified remnant.

כי הנה, "for behold" (3:1), connects the material of chaps. 3–4 to the preceding "day of YHWH" in Isa 2:5–22, which describes the collapse of Jerusalem and Judah, an example of the deterioration of a city's social and political infrastructure when adequate leadership is missing. YHWH judges (3:13–15) the problem to lie with the elders and leaders who have been corrupted by greedy pursuit of gain at any cost. The evidence is found in the obscene luxury flaunted by the women of Zion (3:16–17). The "day" will reverse their position vis-à-vis the poor (3:18–4:1)

The "day" brings reversal in other ways as well (4:2–6): YHWH's Branch will thrive for the "survivors in Israel" (4:2; cf. 11:11–16); Jerusalem's survivors will be called "holy" (4:3); Jerusalem, including its women, will be cleansed (4:4); YHWH will create a shield ("a canopy") for Jerusalem (4:5–6). Can this shield, which is likened to "the cloud of smoke by day and a glow of flaming fire by night" of the wilderness journey (Exod 14:24), be a metaphorical reference to the Persian Empire, which under Cyrus allowed the rebuilding of the city and the temple? In return for the loyalty of Jerusalem's leaders, the empire provided military and legal protection for the city.

The prologue (chaps. 1–4) and act 1 (chaps. 5–12) anticipate the continuation of the Davidic dynasty (4:2; 11:1–4, 10). Chap. 39 puts that in doubt, and chaps. 13–27 (exception 16:5?) and 40–66 do not include the Davidides in the new order. Chaps. 28–35 contain only oblique, ambiguous reference to a monarch (32:1). So hope for the restoration of the dynasty fades as the Vision progresses.

Excursus: Jerusalem—An Example of War in a Walled City

Bibliography

Ahlström, G. W. *The History of Ancient Palestine.* Minneapolis: Fortress, 1993. **Seavers, R.** "The Practice of Ancient Warfare with Comparisons to the Biblical Accounts of Warfare from the Conquest to the End of the United Monarchy." Ph.D. diss., Trinity Evangelical Divinity School, 1998. **Watts, J. D. W.** "Jerusalem: An Example of War in a Walled City (Isaiah 3–4)." In *'Every City Shall Be Forsaken': Urbanism and Prophecy in Ancient Israel and the Near East.* Ed. L. L. Grabbe and R. D. Haak. JSOTSup 330. Sheffield: Sheffield Academic Press, 2001. 210–15.

Jerusalem (and other Palestinian cities, such as Beth Shean) was different from the much earlier cities of the Mesopotamian basin and the Nile Valley, which were cities to live in, urban centers of commerce, created by burgeoning populations. The cities of Palestine were smaller and more like fortresses. When populations expanded, they did so outside the walls. But for the most part the larger population lived in villages and towns in the surrounding countryside. The villages were there first, and they maintained their independence until circumstances made them dependent on the protection of the cities and their kings.

The history of walled cities in Palestine begins very early. There were plenty of rocks to build with, and the geography of the land tended to invite invading bands to move on the north-south routes: Jericho/Beth Shan/Jerusalem/Haran/Tyre/Biblos. The biblical story of the Israelites' movement toward Palestine pictures the wanderers being well aware of the presence and might of the walled cities. The architectural feature paralleled the political growth of kingdoms. Tribes tended to move about, and when they settled, it was in villages and towns. The walled city created the role of מלך, "king," one who extended the power and influence gained from his fortified position to rule over surrounding villages and towns and thereby incurred the responsibility for protecting them. This system of small city-states built around walled capital cities sometimes functioned under the benign oversight of far-off empires.

But, when the imperial powers began to install their own administrations and when they assumed the responsibility for protection, the days of the independent walled cities were over. The walled (fortified) cities of Palestine, built over the centuries with Egyptian encouragement as defense establishments against attack from the north, presented Assyrian and Babylonian commanders obstacles that had to be overcome in their campaigns. While some could be bypassed, no commander likes to have such fortresses still intact on their flanks or to their rear, so sieges of walled cities were common elements of warfare (e.g., Sennacherib's siege of Jerusalem in 701 [Isa 36] and Nebuchadnezzar's thirteen-year siege of Tyre, which ended in 571 B.C.E. [Isa 23; Ezek 26–28; 29:17–20]). But some of the walled cities continued to play military roles when they existed near imperial borders or in districts where opposition thrived. They became fortresses for the empire, now much reduced in their importance, pomp, and grandeur.

This is very much the story of Jerusalem. It was built well before Israelite tribes came into the land, was occupied by David, and played a central role in his consolidation of the tribes and in his building a mini-empire to include his neighboring small states in Palestine. Under the benign blessing of Egypt, the united monarchy thrived, and Jerusalem became famous. Even within the much smaller kingdom of Judah, Jerusalem continued its role. But then came the Assyrian invasions of the eighth and seventh centuries. The small states with their walled cities were viewed as threats to the empire, and many were destroyed (Samaria, Damascus, even Tyre, and many others). Jerusalem was threatened repeatedly (834 B.C.E. by Samaria and Damascus [Isa 7]; 701 by the Assyrian armies of Sennacherib [Isa 36–37 = 2 Kgs 18–19]). The toughness of the walled city in such a strategic location proved itself, even against the siege techniques of much superior armies. Jerusalem was allowed to survive. Perhaps it played a different role in imperial plans for the protection of the border against Egypt.

But Babylon found that the walls provided too much protection for rebellious units, and Jerusalem's walls came down in 586 B.C.E. at the time of the exile of her upper classes. Persia apparently had a different view of Jerusalem's role. Ostensibly because it was a temple city, but probably also because it occupied a strategic military position near the border with Egypt, it was gradually rebuilt between 515 and 465 B.C.E. Even its walls stood high.

The role of the city of Jerusalem in the book of Isaiah is large (see *Excursus: Jerusalem* at 1:1 above). Isa 3–4 is a literary unit within the larger book. It provides a summary, even a foreshadowing of the treatment of Jerusalem through the rest of the book.

This metaphorical picture of God at work over Jerusalem uses a figure from the wilderness journey—fire by night and a cloud of smoke by day—but the role is different. In Exodus these signs served to lead the traveling people. In Isaiah they serve to protect the city. They also provide a metaphor for the experiences of Jerusalem with the trials of a walled city during the powerful changes (political, social, and economic) of the eighth to the sixth centuries. Cities such as Jerusalem could only survive and prosper under the protection and patronage of powerful empires.

Jerusalem Shall Totter (3:1–12)

Bibliography

Bahbout, S. "Sull' interpretazione dei vv. 10–11 del cap. III di Isaia." *Annuario di Studi Ebraici* 1 (1963) 23–26. **Borowski, W.** "Ciemiezcy zostana ukarani (Iz. 3:1–15)" (The oppressors will be punished). *Ruch Biblijny i Liburgiezny* 25 (1972) 242–48. **Chaney, M. L.** "Class, Gender, and Age in the Composition and Textual Transmission of Isaiah 3:12–15." In *SBL Abstracts.* Atlanta: SBL, 1994. 227. **Greger, B.** "פתיגיל in Isa. 3:24." *BN* 61 (1992) 15–16. **Holladay, W. L.** "Isaiah 3:10–11: An Archaic Wisdom Passage." *VT* 18 (1968) 481–87. **McKenzie, J. L.** "The Elders in the Old Testament." *Bib* 40 (1959) 522–40. **Platt, E. E.** "Jewelry in Bible Times and the Catalog of Isa 3:18–23." *AUSS* 17 (1979) 71–81, 189–201. **Ploeg, J. van der.** "Les anciens dans l'Ancien Testament." *Lex tua veritas.* FS H. Junker, ed. H. Gross and F. Musser. Trier: Paulinus, 1961. 175–91. **Shedl, C.** "Rufer des Hefts in heiloser Zeit (Is. 3:1–12)." *Theologie der Gegenwart in Auswahl* 16 (1972) 92–98. **Stade, B.** "Zu Jes 3:1,17,24. 5:1,8,1f.,12–14,16. 9:7–20. 10:26." *ZAW* 26 (1906) 129–41. **Vaux, R. de.** *Ancient Israel.* 155–57. **Weil, H. M.** "Exegese d'Isaie 3:1–15." *RB* 49 (1940) 76–85.

Translation

Prophet: 1*For behold the Lord,* 3+2+3
YHWH of Hosts
is removing from Jerusalem and from Judah
support and supply: 2+3+3
every support of bread
and every support of water;

	2 *soldier and man of war,*	3+2+2
	judge and prophet,	
	diviner and elder;	
	3 *company*[a] *commander*	2+2
	and honorable man,	
	counselor and diviner[b]	3+2
	and one skilled in magic.	
YHWH:	4 *And I will make boys their princes,*	3+3
(to Heavens and Earth)	*and the capricious will rule over them.*	
	5 *The people will oppress each other,*	2+2+3
	person against person	
	and a person against his neighbor.	
	They will act boisterously: the boy against the elder,	3+2
	the commoner against the gentleman.	
Prophet:	6 *If a man lay hold of his brother*	3+2
(to the court)	*in his father's house,*	
	"You have a cloak—	2+3
	be a dictator for us!	
	This ruin[a]	2+2
	(be) under your hand."	
	7 *He will refuse in that day, saying,*	4
	"I cannot be a healer	3+3+2
	when there is no bread in my house	
	and no cloak.[a]	
	You cannot make[b] *me*	2+2
	a people's dictator!"	
Heavens and Earth:	8 *For Jerusalem shall totter*	3+2
(to the court)	*and Judah shall fall*	
	because their tongue and their deed toward YHWH	4+3
	(are) to provoke[a] *the eyes*[b] *of his glory.*	
	9 *Their favoritism*[a] *in judgment witnesses against them,*	4+3
	and their sin[b] *they reveal like Sodom.*[c]	
	They do not conceal (it)!	2
	Woe to their souls!	2+3
	For they have dealt out evil to themselves.	
Chorus:	10 *Say ye:*[a] *(as for) the righteous—it will surely be good.*[b]	3+3
	For they will eat the fruit of their deeds.	
	11 *Woe to a wicked one!*[a] *Evil!*	3+4
	For the dealings[b] *of his hand will return*[c] *to him.*	
YHWH:	12 *My people—boys*[a] *(are) his taskmasters.*	3+3
(aside to Jerusalem)	*Women*[b] *rule over him.*	
	My people—your directors are erring,	3+3
	and your way of life they pervert!	

Notes

3.a. The suggestion to emend חֲמִשִּׁים, "fifty," to read חֲמֻשִׁים, "armed" (cf. H. Graetz, "Emendations . . . ," *TLZ* 19 [1894] 68; cf. Exod 13:18; Josh 1:14; 4:12, Judg 7:11), should be rejected with Wildberger. The MT pointing fits the Assyrian military title *rab-ḫanšā*.

3.b. חכם חרשים has been understood to mean "skilled craftsmen" (cf. LXX σοφὸν ἀρχιτέκτονα and Vg. *sapientem de architectis*), taking חרשים from חרש, "to engrave." Wildberger traces its root to Aram. חֲרָשָׁא (Syr. *ḥeršê*), meaning "magic," but suggests that it is a gloss, leaving only יועץ and חכם. The meaning "magic" is probably correct, but the word need not be eliminated.

6.a. המכשלה הזאת, "this ruin." LXX translates καὶ τὸ βρῶμα τὸ ἐμόν (i.e., מאכלתי, "my food"). This must be a translator's misreading of his text, influenced by 3:7 and 4:1 (cf. J. Ziegler, *Untersuchungen zur Septuaginta des Buches Isaias*, ATA 12.3 [Münster: Aschendorff, 1934] 136).

7.a. אין שמלה, "no cloak," denies what v 6 has affirmed, that he possesses a cloak. Wildberger suggests dropping it, and the meter supports him.

7.b. תשימני, "you make." LXX ἔσομαι, "I will be" (אהיה). MT is the more difficult reading and to be preferred.

8.a. לַמְרוֹת, "to provoke," is *hipʿil* inf. with ל. Fully written, it would be להמרות (cf. Ps 78:17; Job 17:2).

8.b. עֵנֵי may be a defective writing of עיני, "eyes," as many MSS have it, but עני is certainly older. The form seems to be an error. Suggestions for emendation include פְּנֵי, "face." LXX διότι νῦν ἐταπεινώθη ἡ δόξα αὐτῶν seems to have read it as ענה, "humble," a verb (cf. Dillmann, *Der Prophet Jesaja*; J. Ziegler, *Untersuchungen zur Septuaginta des Buches Isaias*, ATA 12.3 [Münster: Aschendorff, 1934] 137). Wildberger considers it a corruption of עַם, "people." The early MSS appear to have chosen the best course.

9.a. הכרת. ה as a preformative is rare. But this form is apparently derived from the *hipʿil*. LXX has paraphrased the meaning: καὶ ἡ αἰσχύνη τοῦ προσώπου αὐτῶν, "and the shame of their face." Syr. and Vg. *(agnitio)* understand הכיר to mean "investigate," "recognize," or "know." F. Zimmerman ("OT Passages," *JBL* 55 [1936] 307) suggested on the basis of Arab. the meaning "deceit." The phrase הכיר פנים means "show favoritism" (Wildberger; cf. Deut 1:17; 16:19; Prov 24:23; 28:21). So the noun means "favoritism." Tg. understood the text in this way: מודעות אפיהון אשת, "their respecting of persons" (Stenning, *Targum*). The pronominal suf. refers to the entire const. phrase (cf. J. Weingreen, "The Construct-Genitive Relation in Hebrew Syntax," *VT* 4 [1954] 50–59).

9.b. LXX and Tg. change חטאתם, "their sin," to a pl. But Isaiah consistently uses a sg. (6:7; 27:9; 30:1; and so on); cf. Wildberger.

9.c. כסודם, "like Sodom." Cf. 1:9, 10.

10.a. אמרו, "say ye," has been widely challenged. Dillmann (*Der Prophet Jesaja*) suggested that אַשְׁרֵי, "happy," be substituted for it. This emendation is based on the LXX δήσωμεν, "we declare," which seems to presuppose the verb אסר, "to bind" (= אשר), which in turn was a misunderstood form of אשרי, "happy." It is difficult to bring the LXX and MT into agreement, but LXX also begins with εἰπόντες, "saying," which suggests MT's form (contra J. Ziegler, *Untersuchungen zur Septuaginta des Buches Isaias*, ATA 12.3 [Münster: Aschendorff, 1934] 61). The received form of MT should stand as it is.

10.b. The suggested insertion of לו, "to him," is unnecessary. Cf. Wildberger.

11.a. The suggested insertion of כי, "for," is unnecessary.

11.b. Procksch and Eichrodt suggested emending כי־גמול, "for dealings," to כגמול, "like dealings," like the LXX κατὰ τὰ ἔργα, "according to the deed," but this is also not necessary (cf. Wildberger).

11.c. 1QIsa[a] ישוב, "will return," is a better reading than MT יעשה, "will do." Wildberger notes that עשה, "do, make," never means to do retribution, while גמול and שוב often appear together (Joel 4:4, 7; Obad 15; Pss 28:4; 94:2; Lam 3:64 and especially Prov 12:14*b* וגמול ידי אדם ישיב לו, "and the dealings of a person's hands will return to him").

12.a. נגשיו מעולל, "his taskmasters a boy," is a problem because of the mix of sg. and pl. forms. The early versions have various forms. The best solution is to read מעוללl; as a pl. עול means "to be a child," although G. R. Driver (*JTS* 38 [1937] 38) suggested it meant "incline to one side, deviate from justice," like Arab. *ʿâla*.

12.b. The versions seem to have read נשיו, "his creditors or usurers." This is not necessary if עולל is read as "children" or "boys."

Form/Structure/Setting

The passage opens with כי הנה, "for behold," explaining the previous verse (2:21) and calling attention to the subject at hand: YHWH's decisions and actions toward Jerusalem and Judah on "the day" (2:12). The subject remains the same through v 12: YHWH's decision to remove stable leadership from Jerusalem. V 13 clearly begins a new paragraph.

Comment

1 האדון יהוה צבאות, "the Lord, YWWH of Hosts," is God's full military title. The picture of judgment is directed not toward Israel as in 1:2–9 but specifically toward Jerusalem and Judah, as in 1:1.

משען ומשענה, "support and supply": Judgment is measured in lack of support, in terms of provisions and personnel. The city, strong as it was, depended on supplies of water and food from the hinterlands. Without its supporting area and population, a city is destitute and helpless. That is why a sustained siege over a considerable period of time could bring a city down without ever breaching its walls.

The book of Isaiah pictures two sieges of the city. In chap. 7 Ahaz is under a loose siege by the kings of Aram and Israel while their armies ravage Judah (cf. 2 Chr 28:5–21). By neutralizing the walled capital at the beginning of the young king's reign, they are free to steal whatever they want from the rest of the country. The second is a close siege by the Assyrians intended to neutralize Hezekiah's forces while the Assyrian king attacks Egypt (Isa 36–37 = 2 Kgs 18:17–19:36). Both these sieges were unsuccessful. Ahaz escaped because of the approach of the Assyrian armies. Hezekiah escaped because of the miraculous events of disease among his troops, or bad news from home for the commander. Isaiah does not narrate the successful siege of Jerusalem by the Babylonians in 587/586 (see 2 Kgs 25), though the text does meditate on the consequences of this siege for Jerusalem and Judea.

2–3 גבור ואיש מלחמה שופט ונביא וקסם וזקן: שר־חמשים ונשוא פנים ויועץ וחכם חרשים ונבון לחש:, "soldier and man of war, judge and prophet, diviner and elder, company commander and honorable man, counselor and diviner and one skilled in magic." Cities cannot resupply themselves with enough persons to staff their military or their political positions. Here, too, they are dependent on outside support and supply. Over years of war (the wars of the Assyrian and Babylonian period lasted from 740 B.C.E. to 586 B.C.E., 154 years), the country and the city lose military and civil leadership and personnel. The loss of leadership results in loss of control over the population. Sweeney (112) suggests that v 2 refers to Sennacherib's removal of officials and leading citizens from Judah and Jerusalem in his campaign in 701 B.C.E. (described in Assyrian records; see *ANET,* 288).

4–5 The result is that "boys became their leaders and incompetents their rulers." Violence and oppression become the order of the day. There is no longer respect for the elderly or for the cultured. Their judicial system becomes a sham and a disgrace. (See also vv 12, 13–15; cf. chap. 22.)

6–7 Desperate for leadership and order, people are willing to accept a tyrant for the sake of order. But no one wants the post, even on those conditions. No capable person will accept the role of leader in such a time.

8 Jerusalem's and Judah's sins are ones of speech and deeds toward YHWH, which provoke the עני כבודו, "eyes of his glory." YHWH's presence in his temple implies his awareness of everything that is going on. Acts and words in Jerusalem ignore this presence and the glory that it implies. References of the glory of YHWH continue throughout the book (4:5; 6:3; 24:3; 35:2; 40:5; 42:8; 43:7; 48:11; 49:13; 51:3, 12, 19; 52:9; 54:11), usually in settings that relate to the temple.

9 "Favoritism in judgment" in the very shadow of the temple is their sin. The people and their leaders are responsible for the conditions that have come upon them.

10 A chorus agrees with YHWH's statement but hopes for a favorable judgment on the righteous. Only the wicked will be judged.

11 The chorus alludes to a proverb (Prov 12:14). All of the people, whether righteous or wicked, suffer the effects of the breakdown in the justice system.

12 YHWH's concern is with עמי, "my people." He echoes their laments: "Boys are their taskmasters. Women rule over them." In a patriarchal society, the lack of mature male leadership is considered a sign of the total breakdown of social order and decency in the face of the devastations of war. No matter how strong the walls, if over a period of time one loses this many soldiers and leaders, the city will fall from within. "Their directors err and pervert their way of life." The stronger of the survivors use the occasion to enrich themselves at the expense of the weakened, widowed, bereaved, and poor (vv 14–15).

Explanation

Attention is drawn back to the subject of the day: the announcement that YHWH is removing the support of strong leadership from Jerusalem. Heavens and Earth acknowledge that the step is justified as YHWH laments over the people and their condition.

The judgment against Jerusalem deprives her of "support and supply." Food and water are in short supply, a basic problem of any siege or natural catastrophe. But this is expanded to speak of her leaders. Chap. 1 had placed Jerusalem's guilt on her leaders. Inspired leaders are one of God's gifts to his people throughout history. Leaders of every sort are mentioned: military champions, wise administrators, skillful counselors. Now these will be withdrawn. Immaturity and weakness will characterize rulers. Discipline and courtesy will vanish. No one will want to lead, which is the result of apostasy and injustice. The proverb (vv 10–11) emphasizes the moral basis for the disaster. YHWH's echo to the lament closes the section.

All society is held together by invisible bonds—common concerns that have a moral base. When these disappear, the body politic disintegrates. Judgment on a people may be passive. It does not have to come by external invasion. It may, and often does, come through internal atrophy. The passage suggests that God is responsible for this deterioration. It is his judgment on those who forget that they are all ultimately dependent on him.

YHWH Stands for Judgment (3:13–15)

Bibliography

Chaney, M. L. "Class, Gender, and Age in the Composition and Textual Transmission of Isaiah 3:12–25." In *SBL Abstracts.* Atlanta: SBL, 1994. 227. **McKenzie, J. L.** "The Elders in the Old Testament." *Bib* 40 (1959) 522–40. **Nielsen, K.** "An Investigation of the Prophetic Lawsuit (Rib-Pattern)." In *Yahweh as Prosecutor and Judge.* JSOTSup 9. Sheffield: Univ. of Sheffield Press, 1978. 29–32.

Translation

Herald:	[13] *Taking his position to contend (is) YHWH—*	3+3
	standing to judge peoples.[a]	
	[14] *YHWH comes in judgment*	3+3
	with the elders of my people and its princes.	
YHWH:	*And you—you have devoured the vineyard!*	3+3
(to Leaders)	*The plunder of the poor is in your houses.*	
	[15] *What (right) do you have that you crush my people?*	3+3
	And that you grind the faces of the poor?	
Herald:	*Expression of the Lord YHWH of Hosts.*	3

Notes

13.a. Instead of עמים, "peoples," LXX has τὸν λαὸν αὐτοῦ, "his peoples," and Syr. *le-ʿammeh.* H. D. Hummel ("Enclitic *Mem* in Early NW Semitic," *JBL* 76 [1957] 100) suggests that the final letter is an "enclitic *Mem*" and that this should be read עמו־ם. This is a possibility. Tur-Sinai ("A Contribution to the Understanding of Isaiah I–XII," 162) suggests reading it as עמם, but this leaves the pronoun without antecedent. F. Hesse ("Wurzelt die prophetische Gerichtsrede im israelitischen Kult?" *ZAW* 65 [1953] 48) suggests that Isaiah is speaking like a cult prophet, introducing YHWH as judge over the nations. Wildberger follows LXX and Syr. to read עמו, "his people." Judgment over the nations is the setting for judgment over Israel elsewhere (cf. Amos 1–2). MT may be followed here.

Form/Structure/Setting

The passage is framed by the formal announcement in vv 13–14 and the ascription of v 16. The importance of the words in vv 14*b*–15 is thus highlighted. This is the third time such a solemn introduction has preceded a statement. First, in 1:24–26, YHWH speaks of his determination to purge Zion. In 2:1–4, Isaiah's word about Zion is formally introduced. And now there is the formal indictment of Jerusalem's elders and princes.

The pericope is formulated as a prosecution speech before a court, continuing the judgment setting of 1:2–3. The words ריב, "contend," דין, "judge" (only here in Isaiah), and משפט, "judgment," make this clear. These words occur repeatedly in Isaiah (see *Strand: "Justice"* [משׁפט] at 1:21 above). The formulas testify to a fixed tradition for such speeches in Israel, a tradition that may have been cultivated in covenant festival celebrations (Kaiser).

Comment

13 ועמד לדין עמים, "Standing to judge peoples": The members of the court would be seated. But when one spoke he would stand up (cf. L. Köhler, *Hebrew Man,* trans. P. R. Ackroyd [Nashville: Abingdon, 1956] 155). So it is in Ps 82:1 and in the frequent calls for God to stand up and exercise judgment (Pss 74:22; 82:8; and others).

14 "Elders and princes": The role of the זקנים, "elders," in Israel was central and ancient in matters of law, politics, and business (cf. de Vaux, *Ancient Israel,* 137–38, 152–53; McKenzie, *Bib* 40 [1959] 522–40). שׂרים, "princes," could include everyone from army commanders to kings.

The speech takes the form of a rebuttal through the stress on ואתם, "but you." The meaning of בער, "devoured," in *pi'el* (also 4:8, 5:5, 6:13) is debated. The root in *pi'el* can mean to "burn," "destroy," "clear," or "graze." BDB translates "for destruction," and *HAL* "left for grazing," while *DCH* renders "pillage" here and in 5:5 and 6:13. The Greek translators were divided: LXX ἐνεπυρίσατε, "you set fire" (in 5:5 εἰς διαρπαγήν, "for plunder"); α´ κατενεμήσασθε, "you wasted"; σ´ κατεβοσκήσατε, "you grazed upon." Modern interpreters are no different. Gray translates "departure," as do Hertzberg, Herntrich (*Jesaja 1–12,* ATD 17 [Göttingen: Vandenhoeck & Ruprecht, 1950]), Kaiser, Eichrodt, and Wildberger. Fohrer chooses "burn down." Leslie translates "devour," while Steinmann has "devastate." Procksch speaks of picking every single grape, so that the plants have been robbed and ruined.

This disaster is called the גזלת העני, "plunder of the poor." Whatever is meant by בער, it is understood as a crime against the poor, who are viewed as virtually identical with God's people. The accusation of exploiting the poor finds parallels in Mic 3:2, as well as Hosea and Amos. Robbing one's neighbors is forbidden in the Law (Lev 19:13; cf. Ezek 18:7). Wildberger draws a parallel to Prov 22:22 and suggests an even closer background in ancient Near Eastern Wisdom (cf. Amenemope, 4.4f., 18).

15 Oppression is considered crushing and grinding. No one has found stronger language. Duhm paraphrases this, "You grind the helpless, as being millstones, with your power and your legal maneuvers." The king's responsibility "to help the poor and punish the oppressor" (Ps 72:4) also belonged to the elders and princes.

Explanation

The spotlight falls on YHWH through his formal introduction and signature. His role as judge is announced. The accused are named—the elders and princes of his people—and are indicted on two counts. That they "devour the vineyard" means that they have exploited the agrarian economy for their own gain. No agriculture continues to prosper unless something is put back into the soil, unless care and substance are given to the plants. To fail to do so is to "devour the vineyard." The other charge is that of extortion. The leaders have forced the poor to relinquish their small share of the harvest. This exploitation of land and oppression of the poor arouses YHWH's indignation. The Lord identifies himself with the poor. They are "my people." He demands to know by what right the leaders treat the people in this way. The economic oppression of the eighth century was notorious. Isaiah, like Amos, spoke on the Lord's behalf against it. The conditions of the times were blamed on economic or political circumstances. But God forces blame on the leaders.

The judgment speech of 1:10, 17 is continued in this accusation. The fact that the accuser is also the judge, which was possible in Israelite jurisprudence, leaves no doubt about the result. The fact that the goods of the poor were actually to be found in the homes of the elders could not be refuted. The basis for judgment lies in the law and its place in covenant structure. The crime in God's eyes goes beyond the act against the poor. It is a breach of God's own claim on the people. The elders and princes are judged for crimes against God (cf. Fey, *Amos und Jesaja,* 63).

"In That Day": Haughty Daughters of Zion (3:16–4:1)

Bibliography

Branden, A. van den. "I gioielli delle donne di Gerusalemme secondo Is. 3:18–21." *BeO* 5 (1963) 87–94. **Chaney, M. L.** "Class, Gender, and Age in the Composition and Textual Transmission of Isaiah 3:12–15." In *SBL Abstracts.* Atlanta: SBL, 1994. 227. **Compston, H. F. B.** "Ladies' Finery in Isaiah III 18–23." *CQR* 103 (1926–27) 316–30. **Daiches, S.** "Der Schmuch der Töchter Zions und die Tracht Istars." *OLZ* 14 (1911) 390–91. **Edwards, D. R.** "Dress and Ornamentation." *ABD.* 2:232–38. **Greger, B.** "פתיגיל in Isa. 3:24." *BN* 61 (1992) 15–16. **Hoffman, H. W.** *Die Intention.* **Hönig, H. W.** "Die Bekleidung des Hebräers." Diss., Zurich, 1957. **Myers, J. M.** "Dress and Ornaments." *IDB.* 1:869–71. **Platt, E. E.** "Jewelry in Bible Times and the Catalog of Isa 3:18–23." *AUSS* 17 (1979) 71–81, 189–201. **Stade, B.** "Zu Jes. 3:1.17.24. 5:1. 8:1f.12–14.16. 9:7–20. 10:26." *ZAW* 26 (1906) 129–41. **Zeron, A.** "Das Wort *niqpa,* zum Sturz der Zionstöchter (Is iii 24)." *VT* 31 (1981) 95–97.

Translation

Prophet:	[16]*And then YHWH said,*	2
(to Heavens and Earth)	*"Because the daughters of Zion are haughty,*	4
	they walk—neck extended[a]	3+2
	and eyes ogling[b]	
	(walking and skipping they walk	3+2
	and tinkling with their feet).	
	[17]*The Lord*[a] *shall make bald*	2+3+3
	the heads of the daughters of Zion	
	and YHWH will lay bare their foreheads."	
Heavens and Earth:	[18]*In that day—*	2
(to the court)	*the Lord*[a] *will remove the beauty of*	3
	the anklets, the brow bands,[b] *and the crescents;*	3
	[19]*the eardrops, the bracelets, and the veils;*	3
	[20]*the diadems, the step-chains, and the sashes;*	3
	the vials of perfume and the charms;	3
	[21]*the signet rings and the nose rings;*	3
	[22]*the robes, the over-tunics, the cloaks, and the purses;*	4
	[23]*the mirrors, the linens, the turbans, and the shawls.*	4
Prophet:	[24]*And there shall be—*	1
	instead of sweet odor, rottenness,	4
	instead of a girdle, a rope,	3
	instead of coiffured hair, baldness,	4
	instead of a robe,[a] *a girding of sack-cloth.*	4
	[b]*Indeed shame instead of beauty.*[b]	4
Heavens and Earth:	[25]*Your men will fall by the sword*	3+2
(to Jerusalem)	*and your strength in battle.*	
	[26]*And her entrances shall lament and mourn.*	3+3
	And, having been emptied, she will (have to)	
	sit on the ground.	

(to the court) [4:1] *And seven women will lay hold* 3+2+2
on one man
in that day
to say: "Our (own) bread we will eat 3+2
and our clothes we will wear.
Only let us be called by your name, 4+2
taking away our reproach."

Notes

16.a. The Q form נשויות apparently tries to put the original into a form that is acceptable to Masoretic grammar. There is no change in meaning.

16.b. The reading of some MSS, ומשקרות (*shin* [שׁ] for *sin* [שׂ]), is to be judged wrong.

17.a. A number of MSS read יהוה, "YHWH," for MT אדני, "Lord." 1QIsa[a] places יהוה over אדני as a correction.

18.a. Many MSS have יהוה. 1QIsa[a] places אדני over יהוה.

18.b. 1QIsa[a] והשבישים simply substitutes one sibilant for another. The word is the same.

24.a. פְּתִיגִיל is a word not known in Heb. The context suggests a meaning like "embroidered girdle." Tur-Sinai ("Unverstandene Bibelworte I," *VT* 1 [1951] 307) emended it to תֻּפֵּי גיל, meaning "joyful drums," but this adds nothing to the context.

24.b-b. כי תחת יפי, "indeed, instead of beauty," is lacking in LXX. Many translations have understood כי as a noun like כויה, "branding" (BDB, 465). But this changes the form established in the verse. 1QIsa[a] כי תחת יפי בשת is a better text: "Indeed, instead of beauty shame" (J. T. Milik, "Note sui manoscritti di *'Ain Fešḫa*," *Bib* 31 [1950] 216; F. Nötscher, "Entbehrliche Hapaxlegomena in Jesaja," *VT* 1 [1951] 300). G. R. Driver ("Hebrew Scrolls," *JTS* 2 [1951] 25) takes an opposite view.

Form/Structure/Setting

The pericope is defined by its subject, the women of Jerusalem. It begins with the threat of judgment because of their pride and concludes with the humiliation of women requesting marriage at a cost to avoid the greater threats.

This is a prophecy of disaster (*OTFC*, 159; K. Koch, *The Growth of the Biblical Tradition*, trans. S. M. Cupitt [New York: Scribner's, 1969] 192–94). It is related to the Day of YHWH section by ביום ההוא, "in that day." The outline describes the situation (v 16), brings the threat of judgment (vv 17–26), and describes the conditions that follow (4:1).

This passage contains two "in that day" units (3:18–26 and 4:1). A third follows in 4:2–6. The very form ties them into the "day of YHWH" pattern that was obvious in 2:12–22.

Comment

16 יען כי, "because," introduces a causal clause. It is a stronger construction than כי and thus provides the reason for the judgment. It is typical of the prophets that they support their oracles of judgment by citing the occasion for God's anger. God does not act arbitrarily. בנות ציון, "daughters of Zion," occurs only here in v 16 and 17, in 4:4, and Song 3:11. It can hardly refer to girls; the description fits the dowagers of Jerusalem's society better. Zion is an echo of the term "daughter Zion" as a term for the city, with all its theological implications (1:8; see there: *Excursus: "Daughter Zion" [בת־ציון]: Cities in Isaiah*). Zion is the place where YHWH dwells and reveals himself. The inhabitants of the city, including the women, must be persons fit for that privilege and responsibility. The entire book reflects God's search for a people fit to live in his city in meekness and humility.

Instead the Jerusalem women are נבהו, "haughty" (cf. 2:11). They show it in their manner of walking (נטוות גרון). This is not so much the sense of "with head high" (LXX ὑφηλῷ τραχήλῳ) as it means "with head stretched sideways." Wildberger correctly understands it to mean that the women glance coyly to see whether their elegance is noticed.

17 שפח is another difficult word that appears only here in the Bible. BDB and *HAL* identify it with the postbiblical Hebrew noun ספחת, "psoriasis," or more loosely, an "eruption" or a "scab"—thus as a verb "smite with a scab." G. R. Driver ("Hebrew Notes," *VT* 1 [1951] 241) links it to Akkadian *suppuḫu/šuppuḫu*, meaning "to open" or "to loosen" and to Arabic *ʿasfạu*, "bald on the forehead." The Vg. translated *decalvabit*, "will lay bare." פת has been translated "openings" or "secret parts." B. Stade ("Die Dreizahl," *ZAW* 26 [1906] 1930–33) suggested a relation to Akkadian *puṭu*, "forehead," while G. R. Driver (*JTS* 38 [1937] 38) refers to the Akkadian phrase *muttutam gullubu*, "to shave the hair of the forehead," a humiliating punishment in Babylon. The Vg. follows this line with *Dominus crinem earum nudabit.* The verse has parallel stichs that describe not a disease but humiliations imposed by a conqueror.

18–23 The threat is interrupted by a catalog of the beauty that the Lord will "remove" from Jerusalem. The idea of removal picks up the theme of "purge" from 1:16, 26, which had been continued in 3:1, applying the same word to the basic supports of the city, its leadership. It will appear again in 5:5. Now another essential obstacle to the unhindered presence and work of YHWH is denounced. The list begins with jewelry, includes fine clothes, but also represents everything that human pride can hang on to (cf. Isa 10:2; 28:1, 4, 5). The list suggests that by this time Jerusalem was well aware of fashion in the world's capitals and was able to avail itself of expensive luxuries (cf. Ezek 16:10–13, 17, 39; 23:26, 42). It is impossible now to gain a clear picture of the articles named (but see *ISBE*, 2:406). Fashion then as now changed rapidly and tended to name its articles in ways that defy rational definition. The list has intrigued scholars. In 1745, W. Schroeder wrote "Commentarius philologo-criticus de vestitu mulierum Hebraearum ad Jesai III vs. 16–24," and in 1809–10 a three-volume work by A. Th. Hartmann (*Die Hebräerin am Putztisch und als Braut* [Amsterdam: Ziegler] 203) showed that LXX simply made up a list of such articles from the time of its writing to serve as a translation, which many a translator has done since.

The term סור, "remove," is used elsewhere to speak of the removal of idols (Gen 35:2; Josh 24:14, 23; Judg 10:16; 1 Sam 7:3, 4; and others). A direct connection is drawn here between such luxury in ornament and dress and idolatry. Indeed many items listed originated in cult and in magic rituals.

24 The threat is picked up again with "and there shall be." It contains its own list of cosmetics and ornaments. בשם is the oil of the balsam tree. It was an expensive import from Saba and Ragma (Ezek 27:22; 2 Chr 9:1) to be stored in the royal treasure house (Isa 39:2). It was used in worship (Exod 25:6) and also as a cosmetic (Esth 2:12; Song 4:10, 14). It is to be replaced by מק, which in Ps 39:6 is the smell of a festering wound. The items that follow continue a list that contrasts the abject poverty of prisoners of war or the survivors of destroyed cities with the previously listed luxuries of the well-to-do.

25 The verse pictures deaths by warfare. The second-person singular addresses Jerusalem, however, not the "daughters of Zion." מתים, "men," is an infrequent word (cf. also 5:13), but it is used regularly where the law of the ban is applied (Deut 2:34; 3:6) or in the traditions of the conquest of Canaan (Deut 4:27; 28:62). This stands parallel to גבורה, "strength." The plural would simply mean "soldiers" or "heroes." The singular usage is unusual. Fohrer thinks it represents the generation of unmarried men, while מתים are the married men. Wildberger disagrees, considering the two virtually synonymous.

26 The address changes, but the subject remains the same. The judgment of God levels the city. פתחים means "entrances." It is used instead of the usual שערים, "gates," to emphasize the destruction. There are no "gates" left, only "openings" or "entrances." אנה is "lament" for the dead, paralleled by אבל, "to mourn." The "entrances," no longer proud gates, can mourn as the land is said to mourn (Hos 4:3; Isa 24:4; 33:9; Joel 1:10) or as the fields of the shepherds do (Amos 1:2). The walls and forts can mourn (Lam 2:5), and also the ways of Zion (Lam 1:4). נקה means "be empty," and in *nipʿal* "be emptied." The city has been "emptied," "cleaned out," "purged" of everything of value, of everything that one could be proud of: its children, its youth, its leadership, its furniture, its gates, and its walls. Wildberger cites a parallel in Lam 1:1. Sitting on the ground belongs to mourning customs, but it is also necessary when there is nothing else to sit on.

4:1 Of course this verse presumes the possibility of multiple wives, allowing a married man to add other wives to his household. Polygamy was not the rule in Israel even if it was not forbidden (de Vaux, *Ancient Israel,* 24–26; W. Plautz, "Monogamie und Polygamie im Alten Testament," *ZAW* 75 [1963] 3–27). In normal times the larger household was a financial burden. According to Deut 22:29, a bride price (מהר) of fifty shekels of silver must be paid. The husband must provide food and clothes for his wives and not withhold their marital rights (Exod 21:10). The precarious and extraordinary conditions following the war mean that such rules will gladly be set aside. A bride price is out of the question. Women will even waive their rights to food and clothing, if only they can have the man's name called out over them. This does not simply mean "to bear the man's name." ——— על——— קרא שם, "call the name of ——— over ———," is a legal phrase concerning a change of ownership (K. Galling, "Die Ausrufung des Namens als Rechtsakt in Israel," *TLZ* 81 [1956] 65–70; L. Köhler, *OT Theology,* 15). When it was used in marriage, it confirmed the marriage contract. This would "take away her shame" (חרפה) from rape as well as childlessness, widowhood, or being single. To be taken into a large household meant being freed from these symbols of feminine shame in a patriarchal society. The devastation of war had made survival in economic as well as social terms precarious in a time and place in which opportunities and protection for single women were virtually nonexistent.

Explanation

The entire passage speaks of things that must be removed from Jerusalem. Because of the women's pride (v 16), the symbols of their pride must be removed (vv 17–24). The casualties of battle (v 25) and the destruction of the occupation (v 26) leave surviving women in a humiliated and humiliating state (4:1). The precarious situation makes it especially difficult for the woman who has no man to protect her, be he father, brother, or husband, and the war has significantly reduced the number of men. The women of Jerusalem are depicted as an example of the pride that makes destruction necessary and of the sad result of the judgment. The context will show that God can build his city with people in the latter condition, but not with those in the former.

YHWH's Branch (4:2–6)

Bibliography

Baldwin, J. G. "*Semah* as a Technical Term in the Prophets." *VT* 14 (1964) 93–97. **Buda, J.** "*Semah Jahweh.*" *Bib* 20 (1939) 10–26. **Cazelles, H.** "Qui aurait visé, à l'orgine, Isaïe II 2–5." *VT* 30 (1980) 409–20. **Fohrer, G.** "Σιών." *TDNT.* 7:292–319. **Lipiński, E.** "De la reforme d'Esdros au regne eschatalogique de Dieu (Is. 4:35a)." *Bib* 51 (1970) 533–37. **Mauchline, J.** "Implicit Signs of a Persistent Belief in the Davidic Empire." *VT* 20 (1970) 287–303. **Roberts, J. J. M.** "The Meaning of צמח יהוה in Isaiah 4:2." In *Haim M. I. Gevaryahu Memorial Volume.* Ed. J. J. Adler. Jerusalem: World Jewish Bible Center, 1990. 110–18. **Yalon, H.** "א.בלע לשון כיסוי מקראות בישעיהו (Is 4,6) ב.כבוד חופה. חופת כבוד." *BMik* 12.30 (1967) 3–5 (Lectures in Isaiah).

Translation

Heavens: 2*In that day* 2+3+2
the branch of YHWH will become
a beauty and an honor,
and the fruit of the land 2+2+2
a majesty and a glory
for the surviving remnant of Israel.[a]
Earth: 3*And it shall be that the remainder in Zion* 3+2+3
and the separated in Jerusalem
will be called holy:
everyone written for life in Jerusalem. 4
Prophet: 4*When the Lord*[a] *shall have washed away* 3+3
the filth of the daughters[b] *of Zion,*
he will wash from her midst the bloodguilt of Jerusalem, 4+4
with a spirit of judgment and a spirit of burning.[c]
Heavens: 5*And YHWH shall create*[a] 2+3+2
over all the establishment of Mount Zion
and over her assembly
a cloud by day 2+3+2
[b]*and smoke and glow of fire*
for a flame by night.
Indeed, over all glory 3+3
6 [a]*it will be a canopy and a booth*

for a shade from heat by day,[b] 3+2+2
for a shelter and concealment
from thundershower and from rain.

Notes

2.a. 1QIsa[a] adds ויהודה, "and Judah." Wildberger (150) thinks it is unnecessary, which may be true. But the reason he gives is that Judah is included in Israel. On the contrary, these chapters have carefully separated Israel's fate from that of Judah and Jerusalem. If it is "unnecessary," it would be because צמח, "branch," carries messianic-royal significance and thus includes Judah.

4.a. Tg. has יהוה, "YHWH," for אדני, "Lord," thus taking note of the unique combination of the two terms in the larger passage 3:1–4:6.

4.b. LXX τῶν υἱῶν καὶ τῶν θυγατέρων, "of the sons and the daughters," expands the application of the passage. בנות ציון, "daughters of Zion," occurs only here, in 3:16, and in Song 3:11 (and the phrase בנות ירושלים, "daughters of Jerusalem," in 1:5). Procksch and Fohrer suggest that this was originally בת ציון, "daughter Zion." Wildberger is nearer right in suggesting that 4:2–6 is a conscious continuation of 3:16.

4.c. LXX translates ברוח בער with πνεύματι καύσεως, "spirit of burning." 1QIsa[a] has סער, "stormwind," instead of בער (cf. Exod 1:4; 13:11, 13; Pss 107:25; 148:8, where רוח סערה occurs). Tur-Sinai ("Unverstandene Bibelworte I," *VT* 1 [1951] 164) emends both רוח, "spirit," to דּוּחַ, "to purge," and משפט, "judgment" to מִשְׁטָף, "ablution." Wildberger suggests using the second meaning of בער: "sweep away," "remove" *(HAL)*, or "consume," "utterly remove" (BDB, 129).

5.a. For וברא, "and he shall create," LXX translates καὶ ἥξει, "he will come" (= ובא). The idea that YHWH "comes" in cloud and fire occurs frequently in the OT (cf. F. Schnutenhaus, "Das Kommen und Erscheinen Gottes im Alten Testament," *ZAW* 76 [1964] 1–22). But the subject here is not a theophany, but protection. Ps 105:39 also speaks of the use of clouds and fire to protect Israel. Keep MT.

5.b.-6.b. Lacking in 1QIsa[a], probably due to a scribal lapse. The last word copied is יומם, "by day," and the last word of the omitted portion is also יומם.

6.a. The verse is divided at an unfortunate place, ignoring both metrical and syntactical connections. A better break point would be earlier, after לילה, "by night."

Form/Structure/Setting

The passage is the third "day of the Lord" passage in the chapter, and the only positive one. The other two speak of destruction. The beginning is marked by ביום ההוא, "in that day." Isa 5:1 changes style, subject, and speaker.

The structure of the passage is clearly depicted by its syntax. The latter-day announcement uses an imperfect verb (v 2). The two major sections are introduced with perfects with *vav* (vv 3 and 5). The sequence of tenses is a textbook example of imperfect, perfect with *vav,* and substantive clauses. The time view is future, set by the opening phrase. The resulting outline is as follows:

I. In that day, YHWH's plants will flourish in Israel (4:2).
II. Jerusalem's remnant will be holy since she will have been purged (4:3–4).
III. YHWH will create a shelter and sign of his presence in Zion (4:5–6).

The meter of the passage supports the recognition that vv 2 and 5 belong together. Both have dominant tristich patterns, and both announce the future of Israel and Zion on the great day. Vv 3–4 are in a heavy distich meter. V 3 deals with the remnant and its place in that day, while v 4 picks up the theme of 1:15 and 3:24.

Williamson (*Book Called Isaiah,* 143) ascribes 4:2–4 to Deutero-Isaiah as redactor because of the wilderness wandering themes in vv 5–6. Sweeney (179–80) notes the use of ברא, "create," and other priestly themes to suggest later composition. This commentary does not dispute such evidence but argues that the book is a more unified composition from the postexilic period than they have suggested.

Isa 4:2–6 forms an appropriate "end passage," the first of several in Isaiah. It closes the unit of chaps. 1–4, as chap. 12 closes the next unit and chaps. 24–27 the one after that.

Comment

2 The interpretation of the passage has traditionally turned on understanding the צמח יהוה, "branch of YHWH." LXX translated it ἐπιλάμψει ὁ θεός, "God will shine forth," apparently reading צחח or צמח in the sense of Aramaic צמחא, meaning "brightness" (J. Ziegler, *Das Buch Isaias* [Würzburg: Echter, 1948] 107; Gray). α´ σ´ and θ´ read ανατολη κυριος, "Lord (will be) rising." Vg. has *germen Domini,* "sprout of the Lord"; Syr. *denḥeh dᵉmārjâ,* "appearance or glory of the Lord." Tg. translates משיחא דיהוה, "the Lord's Messiah," and this messianic interpretation of the passage continued in the Middle Ages (Kimchi) and is also represented in later exegetes (Delitzsch; P. A. de Lagarde, *Kritische Anmerkungen zum Buche Isaias* [Göttingen: Kaestner, 1878]; E. Sellin, *Serubbabel* [Leipzig: A. Deichert, 1898]). Young also follows this interpretation (173).

The word צמח, "branch," is used in several OT passages for the king of the time to come. Jeremiah has צמח צדיק, "righteous branch" (Jer 23:5), and צמח צדקה, "branch of righteousness" (Jer 33:15). Zechariah has עבדי צמח, "my servant branch" (Zech 3:8), and איש צמח שמו, "a man branch his name" (Zech 6:12). Wildberger notes correctly that none of these demonstrates a fixed messianic title. Jeremiah adds לדוד, "to David," each time. Zechariah seems only concerned to show that Zerubbabel is a descendant of David. But here the צמח is of יהוה, "YHWH," not David, and parallels פרי הארץ, "the fruit of the land." The words in context refer to YHWH's plans and purpose in their entirety.

The grandeur of that time is pictured in the words גאון, "majesty," and תפארת, "glory." צבי, "beauty," is used again by Isaiah in 28:1, 4, 5. Jeremiah describes God's land as נחלת צבי, "the inheritance of beauty" (Jer 3:19). Ezekiel speaks of Canaan as distinguished from the nations by its צבי (Ezek 20:6, 15). Daniel calls Israel's land ארץ־הצבי, "the beautiful land" (Dan 11:16, 41), and Zion הר־צבי־קדש, "mountain of holy beauty" (Dan 11:45). The word is thus characteristic of the Holy Land and here describes the future fulfillment of God's purpose for Israel in the land. כבוד has a basic meaning of "weight," "importance," and "respect." All these are things that Israel lacked in the later kingdom and in the exile.

The land of Israel can be called her "majesty" as well as her "beauty" (Ps 47:5 [4]; Nah 2:3). The prophets spoke of YHWH alone as Israel's גאון, "majesty" (Amos 6:8; Hos 5:5; 7:10). Both words are used of Babylon as the pride and majesty of the Chaldeans (Isa 13:19). Other places call YHWH, alone, Israel's תפארת, "glory" (Isa 60:19; 63:15). That here the fruit of the land should be the subject of such praise is a contrast to the long, lean years of war and famine that Israel experienced.

The promise is for פליטת ישראל, "the surviving remnant of Israel." The concern of the book for the fate of the people from the northern kingdom that was noted in 1:3 and 2:5 is immensely strengthened in this verse. It will be observed at various intervals throughout the book. The theology of the book certainly builds on the understanding of Israel's election as well as that of Canaan, and struggles to put it into proper perspective in light of her experiences from the eighth to the fifth centuries.

3 The concept of the remnant is expanded to include the הנשאר בציון, "remainder in Zion," and the הנותר בירושלם, "separated portion in Jerusalem." For them the term קדוש, "holy," is applied directly, whereas the exalted phrases of v 2 are applied to the fruit of the land, not the people. For all its interest in Israel, the overriding concern of the book has to do with the people who will inhabit God's city.

This remaining group is described in v 3 as כל הכתוב לחיים בירושלם, "everyone written for life in Jerusalem." The phrase touches a theme with many variations in Scripture. Wildberger gives a survey of the possibilities. The OT speaks of a ספר חיים (Ps 69:28), "book of life," which is cited in Phil 4:3 and seven times in Acts. Dan 12:1 also speaks of a book containing the names of those to be saved. If a name is removed, that person must die. But the meaning is more than simply being alive. It implies God's protection and blessing. The remnant is the group chosen to participate in the life of God's city.

4 The basis for calling Jerusalem's new people קדוש, "holy," is expanded here. The necessary purge envisioned in chaps. 1 and 3 will have already taken place. The idea of being a "holy nation" was a part of Israel's heritage (Exod 19:6). Now it could finally become reality. It was a quality necessary for living in close proximity to the Divine Presence in Zion. This group may be called "holy" because it will have been cleansed by the "spirit of judgment" and the "spirit of burning." The remnant would recognize the work of God in the wars and desolations of 701 and 587 B.C.E.

5–6 The passage closes with the pictures of divine protection over the city: "cloud" and "fire" that will be both a "canopy" and a "booth" to protect from heat and storm. The canopy is of cloth. The booth is a brush-arbor made of palm branches. The pictures of cloud and fire over Jerusalem are reminiscent of the priestly narrative of the presence accompanying the desert pilgrimage toward the promised land (Exod 13:21; cf. also 1 Kgs 8:10). But this verse is not describing a theophany. The cloud and fire are created to protect Zion just as they are in Ps 105:39. The contrast of God's protection with the earlier purge is marked.

Explanation

The passage, parallel to 2:2–4, completes the cycle of speeches by viewing God's goal for Mount Zion. It speaks of the future of Israel in plant language, but of Zion in remnant language. The remnant will be purged (cf. 1:25) of the sins pictured in chaps. 1 and 3 and may therefore be termed "holy." Zion's population will be fit for God's presence in the city. The undisturbed enjoyment of God's presence is reserved for the purged remnant.

God's purpose points the fifth-century Jews to potential fulfillment in their own time, if and when the basic requirements of purge from false pride and the establishment of justice are fulfilled on their part. The preexilic situation should not be an object for nostalgic wishes for a return to the past.

The passage builds on the assurance in 2:2–4 that God intends to dwell in Zion and judge the nations from his throne there. The role of his people in the city, be it only a remnant, is secure. This passage stresses God's action to ensure the safety and permanence of the city and its people.

Part One: The Decreed Destruction of the Whole Land (5:1–33:24)

Chaps. 1–4 belong together as an introductory frame for the entire book of Isaiah parallel to chaps. 62–66 as the closing frame. Isa 34:1–40:11, including the Isaiah son of Amoz narrative in the middle of the book, opens part II (34:1–61:11). It is also a bridge between part I and part II. What remains are the intervening chapters (5–33), constituting a block deserving recognition as part I, or First Isaiah if one prefers.

Historical-critical exegesis has long recognized a section called "First Isaiah" in an attempt to recognize and isolate what could be attributed to Isaiah of Jerusalem as author. This commentary is less concerned with authorship than with literary structure and coherence. But this concern produces similar results to historical-critical analysis for understanding the subject of this section. It recognizes that chaps. 5–33 pay attention to the Assyrian/Babylonian wars that devastated Palestine in the eighth through sixth centuries. Most of this section is devoted to that period and the devastation that was wrought. Chaps. 5–6 form an introduction to make the reader understand that the events of this period are under the rule and decree of YHWH and that he decided that the whole land should be destroyed, a theme first introduced in 2:6–22. Chap. 34 reaffirms this perspective in part II.

Part I is composed of three "acts" that develop the theme. They are each complete in themselves. They are not consecutive, nor is there a continuous time line (contra my position in the first edition of this commentary). Each has a plot of its own that contributes to the larger theme. Act 1 (chaps. 7–12) describes Judah's troubles, which actually preceded the Assyrian invasions and which threatened the continuity of the Davidic dynasty during the early reign of Ahaz. The plot portrays God's assurance through the prophet Isaiah that such intrigue will not succeed. God will assure the dynasty an heir (7:14; 9:6–7) who will accede to the throne (11:1–4) despite the Assyrian invasions. The act (parallel to the narratives in chaps. 36–39) deals with the remarkable historical truth that Judah and Jerusalem did in fact survive the first waves of Assyrian wars of the eighth and seventh centuries, before finally falling to the Babylonian armies in 598 and 587 B.C.E. Act 2 (chaps. 13–27) deals with the destruction of the whole land, finally completed in the Babylonian incursions of Nebuchadnezer in 605–586 B.C.E. It treats the Babylonian period in a frame composed of 13:1–14:23 and chaps. 24–27 and the Assyrian wars in 14:24–23:18. Act 3 (chaps. 28–33) returns to the theme of Judah's troubles with a series of "woe" chapters.

Each act is a whole, complete in itself. Together, they provide three different solutions to the problem of Israel's troubles. In chaps. 7–12, the solution is the Davidic king (chap. 11), who will be Spirit-endowed, will lead the nations, and will bring back Israel's exiles from Assyria and Egypt. In chaps. 13–19, it is the Day of the Lord that will bring about an international coalition of Assyria, Israel, and Egypt and peace and prosperity to the region (19:16–25). In chaps. 20–27, it is the supernatural actions of God that will quiet the anxieties and terrors of the population and give them life instead of death (chaps. 25–27). The title (13:1) marks act 2 as part of the expanded corpus of "Isaiah son of Amoz" (7:1–16; 20:1–6, units around which the book is built).

Introduction to Part I (5:1–6:13)

Chaps. 5–6 introduce a theme that will dominate chaps. 7–33: the Assyrian and Babylonian wars in Palestine (ca. 734–540 B.C.E.). This was a period of constant warfare accompanied by indescribable destruction for all the nations of Palestine and eventually for the great nations on either side of them, from Egypt to Mesopotamia, including Babylon and Assyria. Chaps. 5–6 set the stage for three smaller works (chaps. 7–12, 13–27, and 28–33) by beginning with YHWH's divine decree that the land be completely destroyed (5:1–5; 6:11–13; cf. 2:6–22). This theme is echoed in the woes speeches of 5:8–25 and 9:8–10:4, as well as in 10:22*b*–23, 13:5 (really, all of the unit 13–27, especially chap. 24), and 28:22*b*. Isa 34:1–15 summarizes this picture of divinely decreed destruction to begin part II.

Excursus: "Desolation" (שממה) in Isaiah

Bibliography

Geyer, J. B., "Desolation and Cosmos." *VT* 49 (1999) 49–64. ———. "Mythology and Culture in the Oracles against the Nations." *VT* 36 (1986) 129–45. **McEntire, M.** *The Blood of Abel: The Violent Plot in the Hebrew Bible.* Macon, GA: Mercer UP, 1999. **Watts, R. E.** "The Meaning of *ʿalaw viqasu malakim pihem* in Isa lii 15." *VT* 40 (1990) 327–335.

The words שממה, "desolation" (2x), and אכל, "being devoured," in Isa 6:11–13 emphasize a theme that will run through the entire book of Isaiah. שממה, "desolation," was first introduced in 1:7–8. This desolation is accomplished on orders from God. It is done by the rampaging armies of the nations, but also by relaxing the ordered forms of creation and society that hold back the chaotic forces. Rains are withheld and the earth shakes. The results are hunger, flight of entire populations, devastated cities, and vacant villages.

Destructions of a population or an area are also depicted in the flood narrative (Gen 6) and in the destruction of Sodom and Gomorrah (Gen 18–19). In Gen 6:17 the flood מחה, "wiped out," everyone—האדם, "the human" (6:1, 2, 3, 4, 5–7 [9x in seven verses]). Those who died are further defined as בארץ, "in the land" (3x in vv 1–7; 6x in vv 11–17), in האדמה, "the cultivated land" (2x). שחת, "destroy," is also used in Gen 6:13, 17 (the flood) and 18:28, 31, 32; 19:13, 14, 29 (Sodom and Gomorrah) with the meaning "go to ruin," "cause to go to ruin."

In Isaiah the vocabulary of destruction is more extensive. In 6:11–13 alone it includes שאה, "ruin"; שמה, "desolate"; רחק, "be far"; עזב, "abandon"; בער, "burn"; ערים, "cities"; בתים, "houses"; יושב, "an inhabitant"; אדם, "a human, humanity"; הארץ, "the land." The means of destruction are more varied and include war and the forces of nature, such as earthquake and drought. The results are "desolation"—empty houses, cities, and countryside. The signs of civilization and culture are gone or in ruins. See the table below for vocabulary of desolation in Isaiah.

Desolation Language

שׁמם, "DEVASTATE"	שׁמה, "A WASTE, DESOLATION"	שׁאה, "CRASH TO RUINS"	שׁדד, "DESTROY"	שׁמד, "BE DESTROYED"
1:7 (1:5–9)	5:9	5:14	15:1	13:9
6:11	13:9	6:11	16:4	14:23
17:9	24:12	10:3	21:2	23:11
24:5		17:12	22:4	26:14
33:8		24:8, 12	23:14	
42:14		30:28	33:1	
49:3, 8, 19		37:26, 29		
50:10		47:11		
52:14			**בדד, "STAND" ALONE**	**בדל, "DIVIDE, SEPARATE"**
54:1			5:8	56:3
61:4			16:8	
62:4			26:12	
64:10			27:10	

עזב, "LEAVE, ABANDON"	חרב, "DRY, WASTE, DESOLATION"	יבשׁ, "BE DRY"	דלל, "BROUGHT LOW"	רחק, "BE DISTANT, FAR"
6:12	4:6	15:6	14:30	5:26
7:16	5:17	19:5, 7	17:4	6:12
10:14	19:8	27:11	19:6	22:3
17:2, 9	25:1, 5	40:7, 8, 24	38:14	23:7
18:6	34:10	42:15		29:13
27:10	37:18	44:3, 27		33:13
32:14	42:15			39:3
41:17	44:16			40:12
49:14	49:17, 19			43:6
54:6, 7	50:2			46:12, 13
55:7	51:3, 10			49:1, 19
60:15	52:9			54:14
62:4, 12	58:12			57:19
60:12			59:9, 12	
61:4			60:4, 9	
64:10			66:19	

Note how the desolation language is spread throughout the book. The dominant tone in Isaiah is one of "the blues," despite the efforts of chaps. 12, 35, 40, and 55 to lift their spirits.

Geyer (*VT* 36 [1986] 129–45; *VT* 49 [1999] 49–64) has found the elements of Isaiah's treatment also in the oracles against the nations in other prophetic books (see also D. J. Reimer, *The Oracle against Babylon in Jeremiah 50–51* [San Francisco: Mellen, 1993] 180–85). They are found in the foreign prophecies in Isaiah as well, but they are pervasive in all the parts of the Isaiah vision, not just in oracles against nations.

Geyer (*VT* 36 [1986] 129–45) cataloged mythological vocabulary and images used in these sections of Isaiah. Chaos works against the created order in two ways. One way involves the sea or ocean, which threatens the dry land. The figures that symbolize this threat are the floods and the sea creatures, including Leviathan. The other way involves the desert and its threat to vegetation and the אדמה, "cultivated fields." It is symbolized by the creatures of the desert (Isa 13:21; 34:13–15). It also involves the threat of death. Both of these threaten cosmos; its geographic symbol הארץ, "the land"; its fields, villages, towns, and cities; and its historical symbol העולם, "the age or era," with its economic, cultural, and political configurations.

Geyer (*VT* 49 [1999] 63–64) points out that in Isaiah, judgment on Israel/Jerusalem is part of a larger judgment involving nature, geography (Palestine and its bordering areas in Egypt and Mesopotamia), civilization (the nations), and their economies (trade, etc.). God will "make a clean sweep" (63), "destroying high and low, good and bad alike." Geyer calls this "the hyperbole of poetry drawn from the tradition of mythology." Desolation is intended "to purge the world of evil so that there can be a firm foundation on which to build the future" (63). This demonstrates "humanity's proper place within the cosmos." The "final end (is) his (Yahweh's) unchallenged supremacy." His will is "to establish justice, righteousness and prosperity in all the world."

Chaps. 5–6 introduce a part of the Vision (chaps. 7–35) and a period of time (the Assyrian and Babylonian periods) when there is little evidence of these positive goals and much evidence of destruction and desolation. There are moments of elation and joy (2:2–4; 9:6–7; chaps. 11–12; 24:14–16; chap. 35; 40:1–11; 55:1–56:8; chap. 60; 65:17–25), but even the positive moments are set against the background of past and present problems of unbelief and violence (see esp. chap. 66, which ends in the bitter notice of 66:24; here even the inauguration of the new temple takes place in an atmosphere of the repression of continuing disorder and violence.)

Chaps. 5–6 contain two parts, a funereal requiem for Israel (chap. 5) and the prophet's first-person account of his commission (chap. 6). Chap. 5 has more unity than is apparent at first. The sixfold הוי, "woe," is the signal that this is a giant funeral. Woven into the woe speeches are other themes that tie the scene to the larger judgment scene that preceded. The imagery of the vineyard was anticipated in 3:14 with the charge against the elders, and in 4:2 plant imagery was used in the phrases "branch of YHWH" and "the fruit of the land" for the surviving, purged remnant. The opening "song" is an explanation of the tragic event. The heart of 5:1–7 are the stark words "And now, please let me announce to you what I am going to do for my vineyard!" (v 5). What follows in vv 5*b*–6 is the statement that the vineyard is going to be left unprotected until it becomes an arid waste. This announcement provides the theme for the rest of part I. Isa 5:8–25 builds on this announcement with a series of "woes" ending with the words "the anger of YHWH blazed against his people." The series will be continued in 9:8–10:4 to tie chaps. 5–6 and the rest of act 1 together. Isa 5:26–30 speaks of YHWH raising a signal for the armies of distant peoples to come in to the land.

In 6:1–13 the prophet tells how he was given the task to announce and explain all this. His task is to dull the senses of the people so that they will not repent and thus not stop the effect of the decree. The prophet seems to know that the decree has already been given. He only asks "How long?" To which the Lord replies that it must continue until the devastation is complete. However the task was carried out in life, the narrated chapter defines for the reader YHWH's responsibility for the wars and his determination to carry them through.

Chaps. 5–6 stand alone without introduction in the previous chapters or continuation in those that follow. They use a distinctive literary device, the first-person words of the writing prophet (5:1–2) that introduce the words of Yahweh, also spoken in the first person. (See *Strand: God's First-Person Speeches* in the *Introduction.*) However, two literary devices that appear here are repeated in act 1. The woe speeches of 5:6–25, along with the distinctive "Yet his anger is not turned, his hand is still upraised," are continued in 9:8–10:4. And the use of the first-person report (chap. 6) occurs again in chap. 8.

Requiem for Israel (5:1–30)

My Friend's Song for His Vineyard (5:1–7)

Bibliography

Anderson, B. W. "'God with Us'—In Judgement and in Mercy: The Editorial Structure of Isaiah 5–10(11)." In *Canon, Theology and Old Testament Interpretation.* FS B. S. Childs, ed. G. M. Tucker, D. L. Petersen, and R. R. Wilson. Philadelphia: Fortress, 1988. 230–45. **Bartelmus, R.** "Beobachtungen zur literarischer Struktur des sog. Weinberglieds (Jes. 5:1–7)." *ZAW* 110 (1998) 50–66. **Baumgarten, J. M.** "4Q500 and the Ancient Conception of the Lord's Vineyard." *JJS* 40 (1989) 1–6. **Bentzen, A.** "Zur Erlauterung von Jes. 5:1–7." *AfO* 4 (1927) 209–10. **Boadt, L.** "The Poetry of Prophetic Persuasion: Preserving the Prophet's Persona." *CBQ* 59 (1987) 12–16. **Brooke, G. J.** "4Q500 1 and the Use of Scripture in the Parable of the Vineyard." *DSD* 2 (1995) 268–94. **Emerton, J. A.** "The Translation of Isaiah 5:1." In *The Scriptures and the Scrolls.* FS A. S. van der Woude, ed. F. Garcia et al. Leiden: Brill, 1992. 18–30. **Fang Chih-Yung, M.** "I shou hav i shen chau ti ku shih" (An Ancient Hebrew Poem). *Collectanea theologica Universitatis Fugen* 6 (1970) 541–55. **Graffy, A.** "The Literary Genre of Isaiah 5:1–7." *Bib* 60 (1979) 400–409 **Graham, W. C.** "Notes on the Interpretation of Isaiah 5:1–14." *AJSL* 45 (1928–29) 167–78. **Haelewyck, J.-C.** "Le cantique de la vigne: Histoire du texte vieux latin d'Is 5,1–7(9*a*)." *ETL* 65 (1989) 257–79. **Hannes, O.** "God as Friendly Patron: Reflections on Isaiah 5:1–7." *IDS* 30 (1996) 293–304. Reprinted in *"Feet on Level Ground,"* FS G. Hassel (Berrien Center, MI: Hester, 1996) 301–28. **Höffken, P.** "Probleme in Jesaja 5,1–7." *ZTK* 79 (1982) 394–410. **Huber, K.** "Vom 'Weinberglied' zum 'Winzergleichnis': Zu einem Beispiel innerbiblischer *relecture.*" *PzB* 5 (1996) 71–94. **Irsigler, H.** "Speech Acts and Intention in 'The Song of the Vineyard' Isaiah 5:1–7." *OTE* 10 (1997) 39–68. **Junker, H.** "Die literarische Art von Is. 5:1–7." *Bib* 40 (1959) 259–66. **Kellermann, D.** "Fevelstricke und Wagenseil: Bemerkungen zu Jesaja V 18." *VT* 37 (1987) 90–97. **Korpel, M. C. A.** "The Literary Genre of the Song of the Vineyard (Isa 5:1–7)." In *The Structural Analysis of Biblical and Canaanite Poetry.* Ed. W. van der Meer and J. C. de Moor. JSOTSup 74. Sheffield: JSOT Press, 1988. 119–55. ———. "Structural Analysis as a Tool for Redaction Criticism: The Example of Isaiah 5 and 10.1–6." *JSOT* 69 (1996) 53–71. **Kosmala, H.** "Form and Structure in Ancient Hebrew Poetry." *VT* 16 (1966) 152–80. **L'Heureux, C. E.** "The Redactional History of Isaiah 5:1–10:4." In *In the Shelter of Elyon: Essays in Ancient Palestinian Life and Literature.* FS G .W. Ahlström, ed. W. B. Barrick and J. R. Spencer. JSOT 31. Sheffield: JSOT Press, 1984. 99–119. **Loretz,**

O. "Weinberglied und prophetische Deutung im Protest-Song Jes. 5:1–7." *UF* 7 (1975) 573–76. ———. "Zitat der ersten Hälfte einer Weinberg-Parabel in Jes 5,1–7." *UF* 29 (1997) 489–510. **Luria, B. Z.** "What Is the Vineyard in Isaiah's Proverb ?" *BMik* 31.107 (1985) 289–92. **Lys, D.** "La vigne et la double je: Exercise de style sur Esaia 5:1–7." In *Studies in Prophecy.* VTSup 26. Leiden: Brill, 1974. 1–16. **Margaretha, L.** "A Literary Analysis of the 'Song of the Vineyard' (Is. 5:1–7)." *JEOL* 29 (1985) 106–23. **Marmorstein, A.** "A Greek Lyric Poet and a Hebrew Prophet (Isaiah)." *JQR* 37 (1946–47) 169–73. **Neveu, L.** "Le chant de la vigne (Is. 5)." *AsSeign* 58 (1974) 4–10. **Niehr, H.** "Zur Gattung von Jes 5,1–7." *BZ* 30 (1986) 99–104. **Olivier, J. P. J.** "Rendering *dydy* as Benevolent Patron in Isaiah 5:1." *JNSL* 22.2 (1996) 59–65. **Orbiso, T. de.** "El cantico a la viña del amado (Is. 5:1–7)." *EstEcl* 34 (1960) 715–31. **Premnath, D. N.** "Latifundialization and Isaiah 5:8–10." *JSOT* 40 (1988) 49–60. **Ross, J. F.** "Vine, Vineyard." *IDB.* 4:784–86. **Sanmartín-Ascaso, J.** "*dôdh.*" *TDOT.* 3:143–46. **Schottroff, W.** "Das Weinberglied Jesajas, Jes. 5:1–7: Ein Beitrag zur Geschichte der Parabel." *ZAW* 82 (1970) 68–91. **Scippa, V.** "Il canto alla vigna (Is 5,1–7): Studio esegetco secondo il metodo dell'analisi strutturale." In *Oltre il racconto.* Ed. C. Marcheselli-Casale. Naples: D'Auria, 1994. 49–68. **Sheppard, G. T.** "More on Isaiah 5:1–7 as a Juridical Parable." *CBQ* 44 (1982) 45–47. **Walsh, C. E.** "God's Vineyard: Isaiah's Prophecy as Vintner's Textbook." *BRev* 14.4 (1998) 42–49, 52–53. **Weren, M. C.** "The Use of Isaiah 5,1–7 in the Parable of the Tenants (Mark 12,1–12; Matthew 21,33–46)." *Bib* 79 (1998) 1–26. **Whedbee, J. W.** *Isaiah and Wisdom.* 43–51. **Williams, G. R.** "Frustrated Expectations in Isaiah V 1–7: A Literary Interpretation." *VT* 35 (1985) 459–65. **Willis, J.** Genre of Isaiah 5:1–7." *JBL* 96 (1977) 337–62. **Yee, G. A.** "The Form Critical Study of Isaiah 5:1–7 as a Song and as a Juridical Parable." *CBQ* 43 (1981) 30–40. **Zobel, H.-J.** "*yadid.*" *TDOT.* 5:444–48.

Translation

Troubadour:	1 *Now let me sing for my friend,*	3+3
(to the assembled group)	*a song of my friend for his vineyard,*	
	a vineyard belonging to my friend	3+3
	in a very fruitful hill.	
	2 *He proceeded to dig it, then to clear it (of stones),*	2+2
	then to plant it (with) choice vines.	
	Then to build a watchtower in it,	3+4
	and even a winepress he hewed out in it.	
	He waited for (it) to produce[a] *grapes,*	3+2
	but then it made stinking things.	
YHWH:	3 *And now inhabitant*[a] *of Jerusalem*	3+2
(to Judeans and	*and man of Judah,*	
Jerusalemites)	*judge, I pray, between me*	3+2
	and my vineyard!	
	4 *What (was there) more to do*[a] *for my vineyard*	4+3
	that I did not do with it?[b]	
	Why did I wait	2+2+2
	for (it) to produce grapes	
	but then it bore[c] *stinking things?*	
YHWH:	5 *And now, please let me announce to you*	4+4
(to Heavens and Earth)	*what I am going to do for my vineyard!*	
	Its hedge removed—	2+2
	it shall be (open to) grazing.	

	Its wall broken down—	2+2
	it shall be (open to) trampling.	
	6 a *So I will make it a waste.*[a]	2+4+3
	It will not be pruned, not be hoed.	
	It shall surely grow up (as) thorns and bushes.	
	And upon the clouds I will lay a command	3+3
	not[b] *to rain on it.*	
Prophet:	7 *For the vineyard of YHWH of Hosts*	4+2
(to Heavens and Earth)	*(is) the house of Israel.*	
	And the man of Judah,	2+2
	the planting of his delight.	
	When he waited for justice,	2+2
	behold bloodshed!	
	For righteousness,	1+2
	behold a cry of distress!	

Notes

2.a. G. R. Driver ("Difficult Words in the Hebrew Prophets," 53) suggests that עשׂה, "produce," be understood like the parallel Arab. word "to press out." Wildberger correctly thinks this unnecessary and notes the use of עשׂה פרי, "bear fruit," in 2 Kgs 19:30.

3.a. 1QIsa[a] יושבי for the sg. of MT, but איש is sg. like MT. Both are meant to be collective.

4.a. ל + inf. const. to express necessary action (cf. *HebSyntax* §47).

4.b. Several MSS have לו, "to it," instead of בו, "in it" or "with it": LXX αὐτῷ, Tg. להון, Syr. *leh,* Vg. *ei;* 1QIsa[a] follows MT but also has בכרמי, "in my vineyard," for לכרמי, "for my vineyard," in the first stichs. Wildberger suggests that both changes are due to a copyist who failed to understand that "vineyard" is a metaphor for a woman.

4.c. MT's ויעשׂ, "and it makes," appears in 1QIsa[a] as וישה. Wildberger suggests that it comes from the root נשׂא, "bear" (cf. Ezek 17:8 נשׂא פרי about a vine, as well as Ezek 36:8; Ps 72:3).

6.a-a. Various interpreters have trouble with ואשׁיתהו, "so I will make it." F. Perles ("Übersehenes Akkad. Sprachgut," *JSOR* 9 [1925] 126) amended it to ואשביתהו, "I will cause them to return." But the main problem lies in בתה. G. R. Driver (*JTS* 38 [1937] 38) follows the Akk. *batu,* "destroy," and suggests the meaning "ruin," as did apparently Tg. רטישיך, Syr. *neḥrab,* and Vg. *desertam.*

6.b. מן is used to negate the verb.

Form/Structure/Setting

The song is a self-contained unit with clearly marked beginning and end. Its unity is unchallenged (cf. Whedbee, *Isaiah and Wisdom,* 44–45). The superb literary quality of the passage has drawn much comment. The very creative form is unique and has defied analysis that all interpreters can accept. It calls itself שׁירת דודי, "song of my friend," often translated "song of my beloved." But the דוד in both word and implication is a male friend. It is a song sung by the male friend of the male lover, perhaps the bridegroom. M. Schmidt (*Prophet und Tempel* [Zurich: Evangelischen Verlag, 1948]) and Fohrer think this must be the bride's song about her groom. But this hardly explains the direction the song takes. Junker (*Bib* 40 [1959] 259–66), refers to ὁ φίλος τοῦ νυμφίου, "the friend of the bridegroom" (John 3:29), the intermediary who negotiates the marriage contract, the שׁוֹשְׁבִין of the rabbis. Ancient custom allowed no contact between the couple before marriage. This same intermediary must represent the groom in any complaint against the prospective bride. Wildberger suggests that the song represents this kind of intervention by the "friend" of the groom.

In that case, the vineyard is symbolic of the bride in the song, who in turn is a symbol for Israel as the bride of YHWH. Bentzen (*AfO* 4 [1927] 209–10) suggests that the song was intended to be understood first as a lyric complaint presented on behalf of a bridegroom who felt that he had been cheated by his beloved. Thus v 6 should mean that the marriage will produce no children. Bentzen speaks of a double pseudonymity: the singer speaks of a friend who is really YHWH, and of a vineyard, a bride, who is really Israel.

The discussion concerning the genre of the song has been intense. Various suggestions have been posed (Willis, *JBL* 96 [1977] 337–62, lists twelve). But recently a number of writers have settled on the term "juridical parable" (H. Niehr, *BZ* 30 [1986] 99–104; Graffy, *Bib* 60 [1979] 400–409; Yee, *CBQ* 43 [1981] 30–40; Sheppard, *CBQ* 44 [1982] 45–47; and Weren, *Bib* 79 [1998] 1–26) and C. A. Evans (*Jesus and His Contemporaries:Comparative Studies*, AGJU 25 [Leiden: Brill, 1995] 396) even claims a consensus in its favor. But Bartelmus (*ZAW* 110 [1998] 50–66) finds no such consensus and holds that the song is "a freely formulated, metaphorically defamiliarizing judgment speech." He is right that the original genre is a complaint or, better, an accusation. The setting is that of a court of justice dealing with family matters. Fohrer notes the elements of an accusing speech: the proof that a legal relation and responsibility exist between the parties involved, the description of the fulfillment of responsibilities by the plaintiff, the accusation that the accused has failed to fulfill responsibilities, and the appeal to the court for a judgment. All these appear in vv 1–4. In v 5 the spokesperson for plaintiff becomes the judge, thereby moving beyond the genre, and it becomes apparent that YHWH is the speaker. The last verses support Lawrence Boadt's view of the text as an example of prophetic persuasion. He sees unity and a distinct effort to achieve a rhetorical effect in "the delay in the true protagonist's and antagonist's identification until the final strophe" resulting in the realization of "God's judgment upon the audience itself" (*CBQ* 59 [1987] 16).

The poem is complex. It uses first-person forms in vv 1–6. Vv 1–2 are by the singer or troubadour. Vv 3–4 begin ועתה, "and now," and the speaker is the owner (or husband). While vv 5–6 do not wait for the judgment by Judeans and Jerusalemites called for in v 3, v 7 implies that YHWH himself speaks the judgment because Judah is the accused and cannot stand in judgment of itself. There are therefore three speakers who use first person, and their speeches structure the passage: The Song of the Bridegroom's Friend, vv 1–2; The Demand for Judgment by the Husband/Owner (YHWH), vv 3–4; The Announcement of Divorce by YHWH, vv 5–6; and The Explanation by the Prophet, identifying YHWH as the owner-husband and the House of Israel/Man of Judah as the accused, v 7.

As in chap. 1 and 2:5–22, this unit begins with a statement of judgment on בת ישראל, "the house of Israel." The generation of Uzziah sealed the fate of Israel and left it defenseless before the onslaught of Assyria and its marauding neighbors. Two decades later Samaria would fall and symbolize for all history the collapse. Judeans are included in the judgment, but, significantly, neither Jerusalem nor the house of Judah is included. Their judgment is different. It is proper that YHWH's relation to Israel is dealt with in these terms (cf. Hosea).

Comment

1 ידיד or דוד, "friend," is the bridegroom, husband, owner in this song. Wildberger (167) has shown that the word is used almost exclusively in OT for the "beloved" or "friend" of God (Deut 33:12; Jer 11:15; Pss 60:5; 108:5; 127:2). The term is used in Ugaritic and Akkadian names of gods. The perceptive hearer might well guess that this "friend" of the singer is YHWH himself. Olivier (*JNSL* 22.2 [1996] 56–65) argues that attention to the social situation shows that the song represents God as the patron who takes care of his clients but who also expects loyalty and allegiance from them. He suggests the proper meaning of the word is "patron."

שׁירה, "song," is an unlikely description for the real form and intention of the passage. That is intentional. It begins as a harmless piece of entertainment which becomes a strong accusation of the hearers.

קרן, "hill," normally means a "horn." Only here in the OT does it describe a piece of land. It can hardly mean a mountain peak. KBL suggests "a hillside" (as does A. W. Schwarzenbach, "Die geographische Terminologie in Hebräischen des Alten Testaments," diss., University of Zurich, 1954, p. 19). *HAL* and Wildberger follow Budde (*Jesaja's Erleben*) in suggesting a mountain spur extending out from the range.

כרם, "vineyard," is a designation that brings to mind the land of Canaan, "flowing with milk and honey," a startling contrast to the desert or the fields frequented by herdsmen. The highly cultivated land, like the walled cities, represented Canaan to Israel.

2 עזק, "dig," appears only here in OT. Arabic *'azaqa* means "dig up," and later Hebrew uses the word for "a most thorough working of a field" (Dalman, *AuS,* 14:323; cf. עֲזִיקָה, "ploughed ground"). Neither LXX φραγμὸν περιέθηκα, "put around it a fence," nor Vg. *saepivit,* "enclose," have caught the meaning. This is the first deep breaking of the hard ground that is necessary to prepare it to receive the young and tender plants. The next step in rocky Palestine was to סקל, "clear the ground of stones." These were thrown in the road or piled up to form a wall. With the ground prepared, the first stage is complete with the planting of the שׂרק, "choice vines," apparently ones that will produce bright red grapes (Wildberger). The term is used in names of places (Judg 16:4; Gen 36:36; 1 Chr 1:47) whose owners were proud of their vineyards. The owner went on to build first-class installations. He installed a מגדל, "watchtower." Some kind of shelter for the necessary watchman was needed, usually an elevated shelter covered with palm branches like that mentioned in 1:8 (סכה or מלון). A tower is built of stone, stands higher, and is, of course, much better. Then, as the final touch, he dug out a יקב, "winepress." G. E. Wright (*Biblical Archaeology* [Philadelphia: Westminster, 1958] 133) portrays a press in two parts. The upper part can be insulated with plaster or wood and is the place for trampling the grapes. A lower container collects the juice.

Having done all that can be done, the builder/owner "waited" (יקו) for the vines to produce their famous "grapes" (ענבים). They did produce. But the first fruit was a shocking disappointment. באשׁים is another *hapax legomenon* and unclear in meaning. LXX translates ἀκάνθας, "thorn-plants, thistles." Vg. has *labruscas,* "wild vines." BDB, KBL, and *DCH* relate it to באשׁ, "have a bad smell, stink." *HAL* notes a Coptic word *bees,* "unripe fruit," and conjectures with Vg.

"grapes with a bitter, sour taste." G. R. Driver ("Difficult Words," 53 n. 6) suggests "spoiled by anthracnosa" following α´ σαπριας, "decayed, rotten."

3 In seven terse clauses (all but one using consecutive imperfects) the ballad is sung. The owner turns to the audience for support. The setting is in Jerusalem. The hearers are Judeans, perhaps having vineyards of their own. What went wrong? In what was the owner at fault?

ועתה, "and now" (vv 3, 5), marks turning points in the account (cf. H. A. Brongers, "Bemerkungen zum Gebrauch des adverbialen *we'attah* im Alten Testament," *VT* 15 [1965] 289–99).

5 This is the key verse, not only for the song, but the theme for all of part I. The plan to destroy the vineyard thinly disguises the decree for the destruction of the land. All divine powers to protect the land and to cultivate the land are to be removed. The chaotic forces of invaders and relentless nature will wreak their havoc. (See *Excursus: The Destruction of the Land* at 13:2–6 below.)

7 God expected from Israel משפט, "justice," and צדקה, "righteousness." The same words are used for Jerusalem in 1:21–26 (see *Strand: "Justice"* [משפט]). YHWH's demand for justice and righteousness is consistent throughout Scripture. The bitter fruit that resulted from their absence is described in wordplays on the virtues: instead of משפט *mishpat,* "justice," there was משפח *mispach,* "bloodshed"; instead of צדקה *tsedekah,* "righteousness," there was צעקה *tse'akah,* "a distress cry." משפח is another *hapax legomenon* and thus not easy to interpret. LXX translates ἀνομία, "lawlessness"; Vg. *iniquitas,* "iniquity." But these general meanings are of little help. BDB, Marti, Gray, Procksch, and Wildberger suggest a root ספח (here rendered שׂפח), which can be related to the Arabic *safaha,* "shed blood." (Cf. Qur'an 6:146.) *HAL* suggests "legal infringement" (following LXX) so that the pun on משפט, "legal pronouncement," extends to the meaning of the words as well as their sound. צעקה is the distress cry of those who suffer from political or social violence, as in Gen 27:34; Exod 3:7, 9; 11:6 (Wildberger). Ps 9:13 (12) says YHWH will not forget their "cry."

Explanation

The Song of the Vineyard (5:1–7) combines in one passage the first-person speech of the writing prophet and that of YHWH. It addresses the central issue of the Vision, the disturbed relationship between YHWH and his people.

The poem, like chaps. 3–4, is a *mise en abyme* (a phrase used in heraldry to describe the small unit on a shield that contains all the elements of the larger unit in miniature). It summarizes the message of this part of the Vision. It is a well-defined unit in itself. However, it is an essential element in the connective material that forms the introduction for part I (chaps. 7–33) of the Vision.

For the fourth time in the Vision (cf. 1:2–3; 2:6–8; 3:13–14), judgment on Israel (the northern kingdom) is described and justified. The clear tones of the indictment in each case are mixed with a question: Why have things gone so terribly wrong?

The song for a friend evokes expectations of a wedding song for the bridegroom about his bride. But the theme turns to a vineyard. It is not unusual to describe a bride in terms of a choice vineyard (cf. Song 8:12). One might still imagine that the vineyard speaks of a bride through v 2 with its shocking ending.

But the figure remains a vineyard. The listeners from Jerusalem and Judah have no inkling about its real target. The owner announces his decision to dismantle the protective tower and walls and abandon all care of the plants. It will grow weeds and thistles. It will be eaten and trampled by cattle. It will even be burnt and dried for lack of rain. The owner is finally unmasked as YHWH. If the listeners had missed the point, two figures in the story are identified in v 7 as "the house of Israel" and YHWH of Hosts. Wildberger notes that these words are related to the oldest traditions of Israel. The vineyard is also identified as Israel and the Judeans. The contrast between wine-quality grapes and "stinkers" is now spelled out: instead of justice, bloodshed; instead of righteousness, a cry.

The "song" with its application opens the woe speeches of chap. 5. It gives a setting for the funeral of a nation and its people who had once held such great promise as the chosen and nurtured people of God. But their fruit was a bitter disappointment, which finally necessitated God's withdrawing his protection and support. Now they are mourned—but also seen as the exploiters and ravagers that they had become. The disappointing and shocking "stinking things" of the vineyard are apt symbols of Israel's fruit.

Three times (vv 2, 4, 7) the word "wait" appears. God's patience is stressed. Like Nathan before David (2 Sam 12), the singer asks the hearers first to render judgment and then to accept the judgment as applicable to themselves. The figure here fits the Vision's stress on God's careful and patient planning for Israel and the world (cf. von Rad, *OTT,* 2:187). Planting a vineyard takes time and patient endurance, as does the raising of a son (1:2–3) and the cultivation of a people (2:5–8). God's disappointment in the failure of the enterprise is clear in each case. The "woes" of mourning that follow are fitting and understandable.

An exegesis of Isa 5:1–7 has been found in a document from Qumran (M. Baillet, *Qumran Grotte 4III [4Q482–4Q520],* DJD 7 [Oxford: Oxford UP, 1982] 78–79; Baumgarten, *JJS* 40 [1989] 1–6; Brooke, *DSD* 2 [1995] 268–94). Weren (*Bib* 79 [1998] 1–26) uses this discovery to help understand the relation of the song to Jesus' parable of the Tenants in Mark 12:1–12 and Matt 21:33–46.

Therefore My People Are Exiled (5:8–25)

Bibliography

Anderson, B. W. "'God with Us'—In Judgement and in Mercy: The Editorial Structure of Isaiah 5–10(11)." In *Canon, Theology and Old Testament Interpretation.* FS B. S. Childs, ed. G. M. Tucker, D. L. Petersen, and R. R. Wilson. Philadelphia: Fortress, 1988. 230–45. **Bartelt, A. H**. *Book around Immanuel.* ———. "Isaiah 5 and 9: In or Interdependence?" In *Fortunate the Eyes.* Ed. A. B. Beck et al. 157–74. **Blum, E.** "Jesajas prophetisches Testament: Beobachtungen zu Jes 1–11." *ZAW* 108 (1996) 547–68; *ZAW* 109 (1997) 12–29. ———. "Jesaja und der DBR des Amos: Unzeitgemässe. Überlegungen zu Jes 5,25; 9,7–20; 10:1–4." *DBAT* 28 (1992–93) 75–95. **Brown, W. P.** "The So-Called Refrain in Isaiah 5:25–30 and 9:7–10:4." *CBQ* 62 (1990) 432–43. **Chisolm, R. B.** "Structure, Style and the Prophetic Message, An Analysis of Isaiah 5:8–30." *BSac* 143 (1986) 6–60. **Dobberahn, F.**

E. "O texto nos envia para a rua: sobre o papel da arquelogia na hermeneutica da America Latina [Isa 5:8–10]." *EstTeo* 32 (1992) 138–54. **Emerton, J. A.** "A Phrase in a Phoenecian Papyrus and a Problem in Isaiah 5.14." In *Reading from Right to Left.* Ed. J. C. Exum and H. G. M. Williamson. 121–27. ———. "The Textual Problems of Isaiah V 14." *VT* 17 (1967) 135–42. **Fichtner, J.** "Jahwes Plan in der botschaft des Jesaja." *ZAW* 63 (1951) 16–33. Reprinted in *Gottes Weisheit: Gesammelte Studien zum AT* (Stuttgart: Calwer Verlag, 1965) 27–43. **Fröhlich, I.** "CD2:2–3:12; 4Q252; and the *Genesis Apocryphon.*" In *Biblical Perspectives: The Early Use and Interpretation of the Bible in Light of the Dead Sea Scrolls.* Ed. M. E. Stone and E. G. Chazon. STDJ 28. Leiden: Brill, 1998. 98–99. **Horst, P. W. van der.** "A Classical Parallel to Isaiah 5,8." *ExpTim* 89 (1978) 119–20. **Kellermann, D.** "Frevelsticke und Wagenseil: Bemerkungen zu Jesaja V 18." *VT* 37 (1987) 90–97. **Korpel, M. C. A.** "Structural Analysis as a Tool in Redaction Criticism: The Example of Isaiah 5 and 10:1–6." *JSOT* 69 (1996) 53–71. **L'Heureux, C. E.** "The Redactional History of Isaiah 5:1–10:4." In *In the Shelter of Elyon: Essays in Ancient Palestinian Life and Literature.* FS G .W. Ahlström, ed. W. B. Barrick and J. R. Spencer. JSOT 31. Sheffield: JSOT Press, 1984. 99–119. **Marshall, R. J.** "The Unity of Isaiah 1–12." *LQ* 14 (1962) 21–38. **Okoye, J.** Review of *Exile: Old Testament, Jewish, and Christian Conceptions,* edited by J. M. Scott. *CBQ* 61 (1999) 410–11. **Premnath, D. N.** "Latifundialization and Isaiah 5:8–10." *JSOT* 40 (1988) 49–60. **Rad, G. von.** "Das Werk Yahwehs." In *Studia Biblica et Semitica.* FS T. C. Vriezen. Wageningen: Veenman, 1966. 290–98. **Sheppard, G. T.** "More on Isaiah 5:1–7 as a Juridical Parable." *CBQ* 44 (1982) 45–47. **Speier, S.** "Zu drei Jesajastellen: Jes 1,7; 5,24; 10:7." *TZ* 16 (1960) 439–55. **Zobel, H.-J.** "*hôy.*" *TDOT.* 3:359–64.

Bibliography for the Woe Oracles

Clifford, R. J. "The Use of HOY in the Prophets." *CBQ* 28 (1966) 458–64. **Gerstenberger, E.** "The Woe-Oracles of the Prophets." *JBL* 81 (1962) 249–65. **Janzen, W.** *Mourning Cry and Woe Oracle.* BZAW 125. New York: De Gruyter, 1972. **Kraus, H. J.** "*Hoj* als prophetische Leichenklag uber das eigene Volk im 8. Jahrhundert." *ZAW* 85 (1973) 15–46. **March, W. E.** "Basic Types of Prophetic Speech." In *OTFC.* 164–65. **Wanke, G.** "'אוי' and 'הוי.'" *ZAW* 78 (1966) 215–17. **Westerman, C.** *Basic Forms of Prophetic Speech.* Trans. H. C. White. Philadelphia: Westminster, 1967. 139–41. **Williams, J. G.** "The Alas-oracles of the Eighth Century Prophets." *HUCA* 38 (1967) 75–91.

Translation

Mourner:	8 *Woe! for those touching house with house.*	3+3
	Field on field they joined	
	until there was no place	2+2+2
	and you had to dwell[a] *by yourselves*	
	in the open country.	
Prophet:	9 *In my hearing YHWH of Hosts (swore):*[a]	3
	"Many houses will become a waste,	4+4
	Great and good ones—with no tenant.	
	10 *For ten measures of vineyard*	4+3
	will produce one[a] *bath.*	
	Seed of a homer will produce an ephah."	2+2
Mourner:	11 *Woe!*	1
	Those rising early in the morning,	2+2
	they pursued strong drink.	

Those staying back in the twilight, 2+2
wine inflamed them.
Prophet: 12 *And a harp and a flute,* 3+3+2
a drum and a pipe,
and wine (are in) their banquets.
But of the doing of YHWH 2+2
they take no notice,
and the work of his hands 2+2
they do not see.
YHWH: 13 *Therefore my people are exiled* 3+2
for lack of knowledge,
and their glory was emaciated by famine. [a] 3+3
And their multitude parched by thirst.
Heavens: 14 *Therefore Sheol has enlarged her appetite* 4+4
and has opened her mouth without limit.
And her [a] *splendor, her* [a] *growl, and her* [a] *din* 3+3
have descended with jubilation into her.[a]
Earth: 15 *Thus humankind is humbled,* 2+2+3
and a person falls.
And the eyes of the haughty are humbled.
16 *Thus YHWH of Hosts is exalted in judgment,* 4+4
and the Holy God is sanctified [a] *in righteousness.*
17 *And lambs graze as (in)* [a] *their pasture,* 3+4
and sojourners [b] *eat wasted hulks* [b] *of fattings.*
Mourner: 18 *Woe!* 1
Those dragging "the iniquity" 2+2+3
with the cords [a] *of nothingness,*
and sin [b] *like the cart* [c]*-ropes.*
19 *Those saying "let it hurry!"* 2+2+2
"Let his work come quickly,[a]
so that we may see!"
"Let the counsel of the Holy One of Israel 2+3+1
draw near and come,
that we may know!"
Mourners: 20 *Woe!* 1
Those saying: 1+2+2
"Good" for evil
and "evil" for good.
Those putting 1+2+2
"darkness" for light
and "light" for darkness.
Those putting 1+2+2
"bitter" for sweet
and "sweet" for bitter.
Mourner: 21 *Woe!* 1+2+3
Those wise in their own eyes.
Those prudent before their own faces.
Mourners: 22 *Woe!* 1+3+4

Heroes for drinking wine.
Men of valor for mixing liquors.
Mourner: [23]*Those justifying a criminal for a bribe.* 4+4
Who deprive the innocent[a] *of his rights.*
Heavens: [24]*Therefore,* 1+4+3
Like a tongue of fire consuming stubble,
[a]*a flame (that) makes hay*[a] *sink down.*
Their root was like rot.[b] 3+3
Their sprout rose like dust.
Prophet: *For they had rejected the instruction of YHWH of Hosts.* 6
They had spurned the saying of the Holy One of Israel. 5
Earth: [25]*Because of this,* 2+4+4
the anger of YHWH blazed against his people.
So his hand was extended against them,
and he chastised them.
Then the mountains shook, 2+2+3
so that their droppings became
like refuse in the streets.
In all this, 2+3+3
his anger did not turn.
His hand was stretched out still.

Notes

8.a. הושבתם is a *hopʿal* pf., "you were made to dwell." The versions (LXX, Vg., Tg., Syr.) have given an act. translation without the causative sense. MT is the better reading.

9.a. LXX adds ἠκούσθη γάρ = כִּי נִשְׁמַע, "for he was heard," supported by Vg., Tg., and Syr. *BHS* proposes לָכֵן נִשְׁבַּע, "therefore he swore." This may be implied, but MT can stand as it is.

10.a. 1QIsa[a] reads אחד, "one," a masc. form. But the fem. form is well attested and makes no difference in meaning.

13.a. מְתֵי רָעָב, "men of hunger," is a possible rendering, as Wildberger has observed. But the versions suggest a different pointing: מֵתֵי רָעָב, "died of hunger" (see *DCH*). Another suggestion (BDB; *HAL*) emends to read מזי רעב, "empty from hunger" (cf. Deut 32:24), which is a better parallel to the following "parched by thirst."

14.a. The fem. sufs. have been challenged as not consistent with v 13. (See *Comment* on this verse.) There is no textual reason to change them.

16.a. C and other MSS vocalize נִקְדַּשׁ, "I sanctified," a pf., while L, the Aleppo Codex, and B have נִקְדָּשׁ, "sanctifying," a ptc.

17.a. Syr. *bzdqhwn* = בְּדָבְרָם, "in their pastures," for MT's "as (in) their pastures." MT should be sustained.

17.b. Many attempts at emendation (see Wildberger) have failed to produce an improvement on MT.

18.a. MT בחבלי, "with the cords." LXX σ´ (Syr.) ὡς σχοινίῳ = כחבלי.

18.b. LXX α´ σ´ θ´ all add the article to match the first stich.

18.c. LXX δαμάλεως, "of a heifer." The MT is to be retained throughout v 18. The attempts to create an absolute parallelism are fruitless. Cf. Wildberger.

19.a. יחישה, "come quickly," has a cohortative ending (GKC §48*c*). Syr. *nsrhb mr'* = יחיש יהוה, "let YHWH hasten," has taken the ה as an abbreviation for YHWH. But the parallel stitch does not have YHWH as subject. MT correctly has מעשהו, "his work," as the subject.

23.a. LXX and Vg. are sg., paralleling רשע, "criminal."

24.a-a. 1QIsa[a] ואש לוהבת, "and fire to flame." α´ σ´ θ´ render MT חשש, "hay," by θέρμη, "heat," as does Vg. *cator*. Speier (*TZ* 21 [1965] 311) cites Jewish commentaries that understand חשש as "fire."

But Wildberger cites Isa 33:11 as proof that it means "dry grass" (Arab. *ḥašša*, "dry out"), the emendations of H. L. Ginsburg (in *Hebrew and Semitic Studies,* FS G. R. Driver, ed. D. W. Thomas and W. D. McHardy [Oxford: Clarendon, 1963] 72) and others to the contrary.

24.b. LXX χνοῦς, "dust" or "chaff" = Heb. מוץ.

Form/Structure/Setting

The use of הוי, "woe," places this series of statements in a funeral setting as words of lament over the dead. This observation is important to translation and exegesis because these sentences are *not* threats concerning future judgment. Instead they mourn the present dead and their past deeds (cf. Wanke, *ZAW* 78 [1966] 217). They mourn the announced death of the northern kingdom and its people and the men of Judah (5:7; not just "Judah and Jerusalem," contra Clements [60] and others). The woe speeches single out groups among the people who experience the punishment and travail of the invasion and exile.

The "therefore" speeches (vv 13, 14–17, 24, 25) are comments from those standing outside the ranks of mourners and thus may fittingly be ascribed to the speakers of chaps. 1–2. In v 9 one reports hearing YHWH's oath of judgment. The אם־לא, "if not," formula presumes the full form "May YHWH do so to me and more also" that prefaces a human's oath. God's oath presumably had a different introductory imprecation.

A number of studies have dealt with chap. 5 as a part of the concentric ring involving 9:7–10:4 (Marshall, *LQ* 14 [1962] 21–38; L'Heureux, "Redactional History"; Sheppard, *CBQ* 44 (1982) 45–47; Anderson, "God with Us," 230–45; Brown, *CBQ* 62 [1990] 432–43; Bartelt, *Book around Immanuel,* 20–22; Blum, *ZAW* 108 [1996] 555–57). The presence of the two "woe" sections does tie chap. 5 to the following chapters. However, in act 1 as in chap. 1, the subject immediately turns to Jerusalem. The "woe" units are not decisive for the structure of the act.

Comment

8 The subject of Israelite land-tenure has been widely discussed. Cf. G. von Rad, "Verheissenes Land und Jahwes Land im Hexateuch," *ZDPV* 66 (1943) 191–204 (= *GSAT,* 87–100); A. Alt, "Der Anteil des Königtums an der sozialen Entwicklung in den Reichen Israel und Juda," in *Kleine Schriften,* 3:348–72; H. Wildberger, "Israel und sein Land," *EvT* 16 (1956) 404–22; F. Horst "Das Eigentum nach dem Alten Testament," *Gottes Recht* (Munich: Kaiser, 1961) 203–21; H. Donner, "Die soziale Botschaft der Propheten im Lichte der Gesellschaftsordnung in Israel," *OrAnt* 2 (1963) 229–45; J. Dybdahl, "Village Land Tenure in Ancient Israel," diss., Fuller Theological Seminary, 1981. Ancient Israel was taught that the tribe's inheritance was a sacred right that guaranteed its members land to work and fruit to harvest. 1 Kgs 21 speaks of these rights, as does Lev 25:33 with its prohibition against selling these rights. When these ordinances gave way to the greed of speculators, it created a class of landless unemployed without home, livelihood, or civil rights (L. Köhler, *Hebrew Man,* trans. P. R. Ackroyd [Nashville: Abingdon, 1956] 147). This explains what is meant by "to dwell by yourselves in the open country."

9–10 YHWH's judgment oath against those who violated covenant ordinances in this way calls down economic chaos on the land: vacant villages, fruitless fields. A צמד, "measure," is the land that one span of oxen can plough in one day (*IDB*, 4:838) or about two thousand square meters. A בת, "bath," is a liquid measure of twenty-one to twenty-three liters or five and a half gallons, which equals an איפה, "ephah," of three-eighths to two-thirds of a bushel (*IDB*, 4:834). This suggests that six and one-fourth acres of land would produce two-thirds of a bushel of grapes.

11–12 The הוי, "woe," identifies some of those who are dead. The exploitation of the land occasioned the economic and social chaos that preceded invasion. Amos (2:6–7; 4:6; 5:11) and Micah (2:1–2) speak of similar circumstances.

Morning and twilight are the cool times of the day when leisure can be pleasant. Musical instruments provide entertainment. (For a description of them see *IDB*, 3:470–76.) The concentration on drink and pleasure precludes any notice of פעל יהוה or מעשה ידיו, "the doing of YHWH" or "the work of his hands." Wildberger ("Jesajas Geschichtsverständnis," *Congress Volume: Bonn*, VTSup 9 [Leiden: Brill, 1963] 95) points out the unique contribution that Isaiah makes in combining these references to God's work with his plan (עצה) for history. Israel's inability to recognize these is judged her greatest failure (1:3; 6:9–10; and so on). The Vision contends that the historical events from Uzziah's reign to the postexilic era were "God's work," that they all conform to "his plan" and thus move toward his goal for his people.

13–17 Two results of this lifestyle are noted while two other observations are drawn from it.

YHWH's word sees exile as a direct result deriving ultimately from this "lack of knowledge." Young's comment (1:212) is fitting for the reversal of lifestyle that awaits this people: "By means of a pagan manner of living the nation has profaned the holy and promised land. . . . Eating and drinking had been made to serve their evil purposes; they would therefore face hunger and thirst."

The word גלה, "exile," occurs here for the first time. The word covers forced exile as well as voluntary movement to another place. James Okoye in a review of the book *Exile: Old Testament, Jewish, and Christian Conceptions* (*CBQ* 61 [1999] 410–11) notes: "Since the Babylonian debacle, diaspora has been the normal and normative experience of the majority of Jews who ever lived. The Hebrew Bible is the book of exile (p. 64) and Judaism has preserved an 'exilic self-understanding' (p. 218)." Isaiah fits into that literary understanding. Other references to exile occur in 22:14; 23:1; 20:4; 26:21; 38:12. The idea of exile permeates chaps. 40–54 (specifically 40:5; 47:2, 3; 49:9, 21; 53:1; 56:1).

This verse is the first in Isaiah to specifically attempt an explanation of why the exile came to be. It is instructive to note that the *hipʿil* of עלה, "to carry away into exile," which is frequent in 2 Kings and in Jeremiah, is absent in Isaiah. Isaiah is more concerned about what in Israel sent them into exile. Ida Fröhlich notes that keeping the commandments is the biblical understanding of the condition for possession of the land and keeping it, according to the Bible. In the DSS relating to Genesis, "one finds several (traditions) connected with disobedience resulting in expulsion from and loss of land." This becomes important in the theology of expulsion and exile. "The inhabitants of land consider themselves blessed in a special way, whereas those who live outside the land are in some ways at a disadvantage" ("CD2:2–3:12; 4Q252; and the *Genesis Apocryphon,*" 98–99).

14 הרחיבה שאול נפשה, "Sheol has enlarged her appetite." The funeral setting is supported by reference to large numbers of dead. שאול, "Sheol," the traditional place of the dead, is here animated in a mythological way to emphasize the devastation. (On the idea of death in Isaiah, see *Excursus:YHWH and Death* at chap. 26 below.)

The feminine reference in the second half verse ("her splendor," and so on) must refer to the city or the people. עם (v 13), "people," is usually masculine, but at least once it is understood as feminine (Exod 5:16 וחטאת עמך). Israel (ישראל) is usually masculine, but in 1 Sam 17:21 and 2 Sam 24:9 it is feminine. Here the best understanding is the people. Israel's best and finest are in the grave. They have gone to their death with a mistaken sense of "jubilation" and bravado.

15 This verse resumes the comment of 2:9 that אדם, "humankind," is disgraced by Israel's behavior.

16 The verse notes that the events of judgment, while they humble humankind, actually "exalt" YHWH of Hosts. They prove the integrity of his justice and righteousness. The Holy God is "sanctified" by it. The second line repeats קדש, "holy," to make the point: "the Holy God shows himself to be holy [*nip'al* perfect (BDB, 873)] in righteousness [צדקה]." The semantic spheres of "holiness" and "righteousness" are very different (see the theological dictionaries). The Vision insists on merging them to define YHWH's character and to understand how his acts of "righteousness" relate to his "holy" nature. צדקה, "righteousness," in Isaiah usually refers to rewarding actions. But Wildberger is correct (contra K. Koch, "Vergeltungsdogma im Alten Testament?" *ZTK* 52 [1955] 29; G. von Rad *OTT,* 1:395; F. Horst, "Gerechtigkeit Gottes," *RGG,* 2:1404) that the breach of the positive ordinances that give evidence of צדקה demands God's intervention. This, too, is צדקה, "righteousness."

17 The "lambs" and "sojourners" give a sense of tranquillity that belies the wasted and emptied land.

18 The use of the definite article on העון, "the iniquity," and עבות העגלה, "ropes of the cart," calls for explanation. Can it be that these are references to a diabolical deity or an idol that cannot be named, whose cult, like that of India's Juggernaut, pulls its decorated cart through the streets? Or is the verse to be taken at face value to picture figuratively those who strain to further the cause of evil and tirelessly work to promote sin? Or is the phrase חבלי השוא, "the cords of nothingness," a reference to knotted cords used in magic to effect curses on enemies (cf. S. Mowinckel, *Psalmenstudien* [Kristiania: Dybwad, 1921] 1:51; M. Jastrow, *The Religion of Babylonia and Assyria* [Boston: Ginn, 1905] 285, 288)? The woe hints at much more than it says.

19 Prophetic announcements like these in the first chapters or those of Hosea and Amos have always brought derisive rejoinders from the onlookers. The references here are very relevant to the Vision's announcement of the "work of YHWH" and "the plan of YHWH." They, too, are counted with the "dead" mourned in this chapter.

20 The devaluation of words is a mark of civilization's corruption and has often been a tool for false propaganda in any age. Truth, accuracy, and integrity are moral terms that are necessary ingredients of a society's health. The ones mourned include those who reversed such meanings, who "stood things on their heads."

21 חכם, "wise," and נבון, "prudent," are qualities expected in the greatest of men from Joseph (Gen 41:38–39) to David (1 Sam 16:18) and to the Davidic king (Isa 11:2). They are gifts from God that are recognized as needed for the good of all. For these to be used for self-aggrandizement is a perversion of values. (Cf. Prov 26:12, "Do you see a man wise in his own eyes? There is more hope for a fool than for him" (NIV); cf. Prov 26:5, 16; 28:11.)

22 Others who present themselves as heroes prove only their "heroism" in their capacity to handle liquor.

23 Those who were available for false witness if the price were right are among the dead. The word צדיק, "righteousness," occurs three times in these two lines: מצדיקי, "those who justify a criminal," and צדקת צדיקים, "the rights of the ones in the right," or "the innocent of his rights." The versions were having some trouble in translating this and ended with "the right of the one in the right." (see *Excursus: "Righteous" [צדק] and "Righteousness" [צדקה]* at 42:13 below). The verse should be contrasted with the description of God in v 16 and shows how far the standards of God are from "this people."

24 Again the mourners are interrupted by statements that relate the characteristics cited by the mourners to the events of the times. The figure describes the awesome judgment that was like fire. But it also notes how vulnerable the people had become. They were like stubble, hay. Even their roots were dried like rot, and sprouts that should have been green were dry as dust.

The second half turns from the figure to a sober appraisal: They had lost contact with the source of life and strength. By spurning the word of God (here not the Scriptures, but the words of the prophets and the tradition taught by the priests), they had cut themselves off from his vitality and strength.

So God, like the vineyard owner of "the song," took action to eliminate the vines that produced only "stinking things." His upraised hand signaled the removal of the protective fences and the guard tower, the beginning of the trampling of the vineyard (5:5–6).

This refrain (v 25*c*) is repeated four times more in chaps. 9–10 (9:12, 17, 21; 10:4) while one further woe speech occurs there (10:1). The events of chap. 5 (supposedly, prior to the death of Uzziah, 6:1) are continued in 9:8–10:23 (in the reign of Ahaz) until Israel and most of Judah have indeed become a "trampling place" (5:5–6).

Explanation

The fourfold woes with interspersed conclusions drawn from them continue the funeral scene over Israel and much of Judah that was begun by the Song of the Vineyard (5:1–7). They depict the generation who died or were exiled as "stinking grapes" (vv 2 and 4), who are identified by the mourners as the unscrupulous exploiters of the land (v 8); the drunkards (vv 11–12); the deceivers and scornful (vv 18–19); those who deliberately confuse the issues (v 20); the conceited (v 21); and those whose heroics are only found in alcohol and who have no honor (v 22). The entire passage supports God's decisions announced in chap. 1 and 2:6–8 and confirmed again in 10:4, 22*b*–23. The Assyrian invasion is only a coup de grâce to the self-inflicted agonies that marked the last years of Israel.

Social crimes and degradation are symbols of their "lack of knowledge" (v 13) and their "rejection of the instruction of YHWH of Hosts" (v 24). Ultimately this spiritual insensitivity and moral rebellion account for God's "anger" (v 25). This anger and rejection in turn account for the loss of political, social, and economic cohesion and stability that marked the last three decades of the kingdom of Israel. This passage in the Vision precedes the announcement of the death of Uzziah (6:1) and describes conditions in the decade before 740 B.C.E. It will be continued ("his hand was stretched out still," 5:25) with the use of that refrain in the reign of Ahaz (9:8–10:23) for the last decade of Samaria's existence.

Signal to a Distant Nation (5:26–30)

Bibliography

Crenshaw, J. "A Liturgy of Wasted Opportunity (Am 4:6–12; Isa. 9:7–10:4; 5:25–29)." *Semitics* 1 (1970) 27–37. **Troxel, R.** "Exegesis and Theology in the LXX: Isaiah V 26–30." *VT* 43 (1993) 102–11. **Vargon, S.** "The Description of the Coming of the Enemy in Isaiah 5:26–30." (Heb.) *BMik* 159 (1999) 289–305.

Translation

Heavens: 26 *When he raised a signal to distant nations* [a] 4+4+4
and whistled for him from the ends of the earth,
behold, with swift haste, he came.
Earth: 27 *None weary,* 2+3
none stumbling in it,
not drowsy 2+2
nor asleep,
waistband not loose, 4+4
sandal-thong not torn,
28 *whose arrows (were) sharp.* 3+3
All his bows (were) bent.
His horses' hoofs 2+2+2
were thought (to be) like flint, [a]
his wheels like the very wind.
29 *He had a growl like a lion,* 3+2
a roar [a] *like a young lion.*
He growled and seized prey. 3+3
He dragged it off safely. (There was) no deliverer.
Heavens: 30 *He growled over it* 2+2+2
in that day
like the sea's growl.
When he looked to the land, 2+3+3
behold: darkness, [a] *a distress,*
and light (became) darkness in her spray.

Notes

26.a. The first reference is pl., גוים, "nations," while the second and third—לו, "to him," and יבוא, "he comes"—are sg. A suggested emendation follows Jer 5:15, dividing the letters differently to read לְגוֹי מִמֶּרְחָק, "to a nation from afar."

28.a. 1QIsa[a] כצור, "like rock." Cf. LXX στερεά πέτρα, "solid rock." MT כַּצָּר, "like flint," may be pointed כְּצֹר to make it conform. G. R. Driver (*JTS* 45 [1944] 13; "Difficult Words," 55) suggested the צר meant "a meteor." Tur-Sinai ("A Contribution to the Understanding of Isaiah I–XII," 168) suggests reading כְּצִנּוֹר, "God's lightning." MT or the emended pointing should be kept.

29.a. Q יִשְׁאַג; K וְשָׁאַג. *BHS* presents the consonants of K and the vowels of Q in this text. If the verbs in the second line are a clue, it should be וְיִשְׁאַג.

30.a. MT has accent marks over the first חשך, "darkness," and over ואור, "and light," requiring a reading "and behold darkness; distress and light; darkness in her clouds." *BHS* suggests one accent, *zakef katon,* over צר, "distress," permitting a division like the translation.

Form/Structure/Setting

At regular intervals the Vision reminds its readers (hearers) of God's "work" during this period. Isa 3:1 identified his removal of responsible leaders in Jerusalem. Here "his anger" takes concrete form in an invader, "a distant nation from the end of the earth." The nation will be identified in 7:16 as Assyria. The description of Assyrian military discipline and tactics is accurate. The notice of King Uzziah's death in 6:1 suggests that a time before that is intended here. Tiglath-Pileser III was already known in Palestine. Menahem and possibly Uzziah were involved in stopping his invasion of the west in 738 B.C.E.

V 26 identifies YHWH as the initiator of the invasion. Vv 27–29 is a graphic poetic description of the army. V 30 returns to YHWH as subject in documenting the dark day ahead.

Crenshaw has identified this section as a "Liturgy of Wasted Opportunity" (*OTFC,* 262). This may fit the frame of vv 25 and 30, but hardly does justice to the strong military description of vv 27–29. Williamson (*Book Called Isaiah,* 142) relates vv 25–30 (and 8:22 and 11:11–16) to a Deutero-Isaianic redaction of the earlier material. I think this observation simply supports crediting the whole book to the postexilic period.

Comment

26 The verse pictures a military event in terms of God's direct intervention in the historical process. The subject of נשא, "raise," is understood to be YHWH. His visual and audible signals direct the foreign armies. נס is a flag or ensign to which the troops may rally or reorient themselves (11:10; 18:3). The Assyrians carried elaborate symbols on poles, as their inscriptions show. These were placed on raised ground with high visibility (13:2; 30:17). The emphasis here is on God's participation and direction. The armies respond promptly and with alacrity.

"The enemy from afar" is a theme that fits the historical reality of that period, but it is also a theme that continues in prophecy (cf. Jer 4:16; 5:15). לגוים מרחוק, "distant nation," and מקצה הארץ, "from the ends of the earth," are parallel phrases in much of Hebrew poetry (cf. Deut 28:49; Ps 72:8; Zech 9:10; Sir 44:21). The great distance is matched by the speed with which the army responds. The Assyrians prided themselves on their maneuverability and quickness.

Isa 11:12 and 49:22 also emphasize God raising the signal to the nations (Williamson, *Book Called Isaiah*, 62–67). The word נס, "flag, signal," occurs in 5:26; 11:10, 12; 13:2; 18:3; 30:17; 31:9; 33:23; 49:22; 62:10. Cf. Jer 4:6, 21; 50:2; 51:12, 27.

27–28 The physical condition of the troops is good in spite of the forced marches over great distances. Their equipment is in excellent condition and chosen for the kind of warfare that is needed. The arrow points, made of horn, bone, flint, bronze, or iron, are sharpened and ready. The bow, when not in use, would have the string fastened on only one end. Before use the bow must be bent (דרך) by placing a foot on it to bend it so that the other end of the string may be attached. The bows are ready for combat. The condition of horses and wagons/chariots is excellent, belying the reported distance they have traveled.

29 The picture closes with an analogy to a לביא, "lion," and כפיר, "young lion." Lions were still known in Palestine, and they made a great impact at least on the imagination of the inhabitants. In addition to these words two others, אריה and ליש, were used in the OT. *IDB* (3:136–37) recognizes אריה as the common word, while others are poetic designations. KBL distinguishes לביא, the Asiatic lion of Persia, from אריה, the African lion. כפיר is a young lion old enough to hunt alone. The metaphor emphasizes the terror inspired by the determined successes of the army.

30 In a manner familiar from chap. 1, the metaphorical theme is continued with a very different meaning. The "growl" of the lion/enemy becomes the growl of YHWH, the Divine Warrior, whose appearance on that fearful day brings gloom to all.

Explanation

The Vision contends that God's strategy controls and directs historical events. His signals start the army's advance. His movements keep the action moving or bring it to an end. His upraised hand signals his continued displeasure with Israel (v 25). He will not protect her. He has disavowed her. It is the counterpart of the vineyard owner's removal of fences and guard tower in v 5. In v 26 he raises a banner and sounds a signal for invading armies. (Similar actions occur in 13:2; 30:17.) Such a signal may have a positive purpose (cf. 11:10, 12; 18:3). God's judgment is more than a word. Actions follow. In all of them God is in control.

Neither YHWH nor the invading enemy is named in this section (vv 26–30). But the implication is clear. What is here implicit will be made explicit in 7:17. The light of God's countenance is denied Israel in this time; 2:6 had already confirmed that. No amount of optimism can conceal it. The theme is confirmed in the vision of chap. 6 and continued in 9:7 (8)–10:20 after a section dealing with Jerusalem (7:1–9:6 [7]).

Kaiser (116 = ET 112) calls the author here "a theologian of history from the fifth century, in the guise of a prophet, speaking of the annihilating blow of the Babylonians against the Kingdom of Judah." Whether this refers to the Babylonian or the Assyrian invasions, this passage forms an integral part of the larger picture, which interprets the events of the eighth to the sixth centuries in Palestine and Judah.

YHWH, creator of Heavens and Earth, could have used many means to carry out his judgment. He chose to exercise the military option. That is his "plan."

(See *Excursus: Day of YHWH/Divine Warrior* and the discussion under *YHWH's Strategy*, both in the *Introduction*.)

In God's Heavenly Courtroom (6:1–13)

Bibliography

Ambrose, A. A. "(Is. 6,9) 'Hore, ohne zu horen' zu Koran 4,46(48)." *ZDMG* 136 (1986) 15–22. **Auret, A.** "Jesaja 6:1aa meer as 'n historiese nota?" *NGTT* 32 (1991) 368–77. **Bakon, S.** "Kedusha—Holiness." *DD* 16 (1987) 2–9. **Baltzer, K.** "Considerations regarding the Office and Calling of the Prophet." *HTR* 61 (1968) 567–81. **Barker, M.** "Beyond the Veil of the Temple: The High Priestly Origins of the Apocalypses." *SJT* 51 (1998) 1–21. **Barthel, J.** *Prophetenwort und Geschichte: Die Jesajaüberlieferung in Jes 6–8 und 28–31.* FAT 19. Tübingen: Mohr Siebeck, 1998. **Beale, G. K.** "Isaiah VI 9–13: A Retributive Taunt against Idolatry." *VT* 41 (1991) 257–78. **Béguerie, P.** "La vocation d'Isaïe." In *Études sur les prophètes d'Israël.* Ed. P. Béguerie et al. Paris: Cerf, 1954. 11–51. **Brettler, M.** *God Is King: Understanding an Israelite Metaphor.* JSOTSup 76. Sheffield: Sheffield Academic Press, 1989. **Brodie, T. L.** "The Children and the Prince: The Structure, Nature and Date of Isaiah 6–12." *BTB* 9 (1979) 27–31. **Budde, K.** *Jesaja's Erleben: Eine gemeinverständliche Auslegung der Denkschrift des Propheten (Kap. 6–9:6).* Gotha: Klotz, 1928. **Cazelles, H.** "La vocation d'Isaie (ch 6) et les rites royaux." In *Homenaje a Juan Prado.* Madrid: Consejo Superior de Investigaciones Cientificios, 1975. 89–108. **Chilton, B.** "The Temple in the Targum of Isaiah." In *Targumic Approaches to the Gospels: Essays in the Mutual Definition of Judaism and Christianity.* Lanham, MD: Univ. Press of America, 1986. 51–61. **Clements, R. E.** *Beyond Tradition History: Deutero-Isianic Davelopment of First Isaiah's Themes.* JSOT 31. Sheffield: Sheffield Academic Press, 1985. **Driver, G. R.** "His Train Filled the Temple." In *Near Eastern Studies.* FS W. F. Albright, ed. H. Goedicke. Baltimore: Johns Hopkins UP, 1971. 87–96. **Dumbrell, W. J.** "Worship and Isaiah 6." *RTR* 43 (1984) 1–8. **Eaton, J. H.** *Vision in Worship.* London: SPCK, 1981. **Emerton, J. A.** "The Translation of Isaiah 5,1." In *The Scriptures and the Scrolls.* FS A. S. van der Woude, ed. F. García Martínez and C. J. Labuschagne. VTSup 49. Leiden: Brill, 1992. 18–30. **Engnell, I.** *The Call of Isaiah.* UUÅ 11.4. Uppsala: Lundequistska, 1949. **Eslinger, L.** "The Infinite in a Finite Organical Perception (Isaiah vi 1–5)." *VT* 60 (1990) 145–73. **Evans, C. A.** "Isa 6:9–13 in the Context of Isaiah's Theology." *JETS* 29 (1986) 139–40. ———. "The Text of Isaiah 6:9–10." *ZAW* 94 (1982) 415–18. ———. *To See and Not Perceive: Isaiah 6:9–10 in Early Jewish and Christion Interpretation.* JSOTSup 64. Sheffield: Sheffield Academic Press, 1989. **Gnilka, J.** *Die Verstockung Israels: Isaias 6,9–10 in der Theologie des Synoptiker.* SANT 3. Munich: Kösel, 1961. **Görg, Y.** "Die Funktion der Serafen bei Jesaja." *BN* 5 (1978) 28–39. **Gosse, B.** "Isaïe vi et la tradition isaïenne." *VT* 42 (1992) 340–49. ———. "Isaïe 52:13–53:12 et Isaïe 6." *RB* 98 (1991) 537–43. **Gowan, D. E.** "Isaiah 6:1–5." *Int* 45 (1991) 172–76. **Habel, N.** "The Form and the Significance of the Call Narratives." *ZAW* 77 (1965) 297–323. **Hardmeier, C.** "Jesajas Verkündigungabsicht und Jahwes Verstockungsauftrag in Jes 6." *Die Botschaft und die Boten.* FS H. W. Wolff, ed. J. Jeremias and L. Perlitt. Neukirchen-Vluyn: Neukirchener Verlag, 1981. 235–51. **Hartenstein, F.** *Die Unzugänglichkeit Gottes im Heiligtum: Jesaja 6 und der Wohnort JHWHs in der Jerusalemer Kulttradition.* WMANT 75. Neukirchen-Vluyn: Neukirchener Verlag, 1997. **Hayward, R.** "The Chant of the Seraphim and the Worship of the Second Temple." PIBA 20 (1997) 62–80. **Hesse, F.** *Das Verstockungsproblem im alten*

Testament. BZAW 74. Berlin: De Gruyter. **Hirth, T.** "Überlegungen zu den Seraphim." *BN* 77 (1995) 17–19. **Hollenbach, B.** "Lest They Should Turn and Be Forgiven: Irony." *BT* 34 (1983) 312–21. **House, P. R.** "Isaiah's Call and Its Context in Isaiah 1–6." *CTR* 62 (1993) 207–22. **Hubmann, F. D.** "Der Bote des Heiligen Geistes: Jesaja 6,1–13 im Kontext von Berufung." *TPQ* 135 (1987) 328–39. **Hurley, R.** "Le Seigneur endurcit le coeur d'Israel? L'ironie d'Isaïe 6,9–10." *Theoforum* 32 (2001) 23–43. **Hurowitz, V. A.** "Isaiah's Impure Lips and Their Purification in Light of Mouth Purification and Mouth Purity in Akkadian sources." *HUCA* 60 (1989) 39–89. **Jenni, E.** "Jesajas Berufung in der neueren Forschung." *TZ* 15 (1959) 321–39. **Joines, K. R.** "Winged Serpents in Isaiah's Inaugural Vision." *JBL* 86 (1967) 410–15. **Joosten, J.** "La prosopopée, les pseudo-citations et la vocation d'Isaïe (Is 6:9–10)." *Bib* 82 (2001) 232–43. **Kaplan, M.** "Isaiah 6:1–11." *JBL* 45 (1926) 251–59. **Keel, O.** *Jahwe-Visionen und Siegelkunst: Eine neue Deutung der Majestätsschilderungen in Jes 6, Ez 1 und 10 und Sach 4.* SBS 84–85. Stuttgart: Katholisches Bibelwerk, 1977. **Kellenberger, E.** "Heil und Verstockung: Zu Jes 6,9f bei Jesaja und im Neuen Testament." *TZ* 48 (1992) 268–75. **Key, A. F.** "The Magical Background of Isaiah 6:9–13." *JBL* 86 (1967) 198–204. **Kilian, R.** "Der Vedrstockungsauftrag Jesajas." In *Bausteiner biblischer Theologie.* FS G. J. Botterweck, ed. H.-J. Fabry. BBB 50. Bonn: Hanstein, 1977. 209–25. **Kingsbury, J. R.** "The Prophets and the Council of Yahweh." *JBL* 83 (1964) 279–86. **Klijn, A. F. J.** "Jerome, Isaie 6 et l'Evangile des Nazareens." *VC* 40 (1986) 245–50. **Knierim, R.** "The Vocation of Isaiah." *VT* 18 (1968) 47–68. **Landy, F.** "Strategies of Concentration and Diffusion in Isaiah 6." *BibInt* 7 (1999) 58–86. **Lehnert, V. A.** *Die Provokation Israels: Die paradoxe Funktion von Jes 6,9–10 bei Markus und Lukas: Ein textpragmatischer Versuch im Kontext gegenwärtiger Rezeptionsästhetik und Lesetheorie.* Neuekirchen-Vluyn: Neukirchener Verlag, 1999. **Liebreich, L. J.** "The Position of Chapter Six in the Book of Isaiah." *HUCA* 25 (1954) 37–40. **Lind, M. C.** "Political Implications of Isaiah 6." In *Writing and Reading.* Ed. C. C. Broyles and C. A. Evans. 1:317–38. **Long, B. O.** "Reports of Visions among the Prophets." *JBL* 95 (1976) 353–65. **Love, J. P.** "The Call of Isaiah." *Int* 11 (1957) 282–96. **Magonet, J.** "The Structure of Isaiah 6." In *Proceedings of the Ninth World Congress of Jewish Studies: Jerusalem, August 4–12, 1985.* Jerusalem: Hebrew University, 1986. 91–97. **McLaughlin, J. L.** "Their Hearts Were Hardened: The Use of Isaiah 6,9–10 in the Book of Isaiah." *Bib* 75 (1994) 1–25. **Metzger, W.** "Der Horizont der Gnade in der Berufungsvision Jesajas." *ZAW* 93 (1981) 281–84. **Milgrom, J.** "Did Isaiah Prophesy during the Reign of Uzziah?" *VT* 14 (1964) 164–82. **Montagnini, F.** "La vocazione di Isaia." *BeO* 6 (1964) 163–72. **Moore, C. A.** " Mark 4:12: More Like the Irony of Micaiah than Isaiah." In *My Path.* FS J. M. Myers, ed. H. N. Bream, R. D. Heim, and C. A. Moore. Philadelphia: Temple, 1974. 335–44. **Müller, H. P.** "Glauben und Bleiben: Zur Denkschrift Jesajas 6:1–8:16." In *Studies on Prophecy.* VTSup 26. Leiden: Brill, 1974. 25–54. **Niehr, H.** "Zur Intention von Jes 6,1–9." *BN* 21 (1983) 59–65. **Nielsen, K.** "Is 6:1–8:18 as Dramatic Writing." *ST* 40 (1986) 1–16. ———. "I skal høre eg høre, men intet fatte; I skal se og se, men intet forstå. Jesajas kaldelsesberetning set I lyset af de senere års profetforskning." In *Studier i Jesajabogen.* Ed. B. Rosendal. Åarhus: Universitetsforlag, 1989. 9–29. **Nobile, M.** "Jes 6 und Ezek 1,1–3,15: Vergleich und Funktion im Jeweiligen Redaktionellen Kontext." In *Book of Isaiah.* Ed. J. Vermeylen. 211–16. **Peterson, E. H.** "The Holy Stump." *Crux* 32.3 (1996) 2–11. **Rendtorff, R.** "Isaiah 6 in the Framework of the Composition of the Book of Isaiah." In *Book of Isaiah.* Ed. J. Vermeylen. 73–83. Reprinted in *Canon and Theology* (Minneapolis: Fortress, 1993) 170–80. **Robinson, G. D.** "The Motif of Deafness and Blindness in Isaiah 6:9–10: A Contextual, Literary, and Theological Analysis." *BBR* 8 (1998) 167–86. **Sacchi, P.** "Isaia 6 e la concezione di impurità nel medio giudaismo." *VH* 13 (2002) 55–77. **Savignac, J. de.** *"Les 'Seraphim.'"* *VT* 22 (1972) 320–25. **Sawyer, J.** "The Qumran Reading of Isaiah 6:13." *ASTI* 3 (1964) 111–13. **Schmidt, J. M.** "Gedanken zum Verstockungsauftrag Jesajas (Jes 6)." *VT* 21 (1971) 68–90. **Schreiner, J.** "Zur Textgestalt von Jes 6 und 7,1–17." *BZ* 22 (1978) 92–97. **Sonnet, J.-P.** "Le Motif de l'endurcissement

(Is 6,9–10) et las lecture d' Isaïe." *Bib* 73 (1992) 208–39. **Steck, O. H.** "Bemerkungen zu Jesaja 6." *BZ* 16 (1972) 188–206. **Steinmetz, D. C.** "John Calvin on Isaiah 6: A Problem in the History of Exegesis." *Int* 36 (1982) 156–70. **Tsevat, M.** "ישעיהו (Isa 6)." *FS Z. Shazar.* Ed. B. A. Luria. Jerusalem: Kirjath Sepher, 1973. 161–72. **Van Wieringen, A. L. H. M.** *The Implied Reader in Isaiah 6–12.* Leiden: Brill, 1999. ———. "Jes 6,13: Een structuuronderzoek." *Bijdr* 48 (1987) 32–39. ———. "Jesaja 6: aankondiging van noodlot of oproep tot heil? Een communicatieve lezing." In *Het lot in eigen hand? Reflecties op de betekenis van het (noodlot) in once cultuur.* Ed. P. van Tongeren. Baarn: Gooi & Sticht, 1994. 109–25. **Wagner, R.** *Textexegese als Strukturanalyse: Sprachwissenschaftliche Methode zur Erschliessung althebraischer Texte am Beispiel des Visionsberichtes Jes 6, 1–11.* St. Ottilien: EOS, 1989. **Werner, W.** "Von Prophetenwort zu Prophetentheologie: Ein redationskritischer Versuch zu Jes 6:1–8:18." *BZ* 29 (1985) 1–30. **Whitley, C. F.** "The Call and Mission of Isaiah." *JNES* 18 (1959) 38–48. **Williamson, H. G. M.** "Isaiah 6:13 and 1:29–31." In *Studies.* Ed. J. Van Ruiten and M. Vervenne. 119–28. **Worschech, U.** "The Problem of Isaiah 6:13." *AUSS* 12 (1974) 126–38. **Zeron A.** "Die Anmassung des Königs Usia im Lichte von Jesajas Berufung: Zu 2 Chr. 26:16–22 und Jes. 6:1ff." *TZ* 33 (1977) 65–68.

Bibliography for Prophetic Call Narratives

Crabtree, T. T. "The Prophet's Call—A Dialogue with God." *SwJT* 4 (1961) 33–35. **Habel, N.** "The Form and Significance of Call Narratives." *ZAW* 77 (1965) 297–323. **Tidwell, N. L. A.** "*wāʾōmār* (Zech 3:5) and the Genre of Zechariah's Fourth Vision." *JBL* 94 (1975) 343–55.

Bibliography for the Text of 6:13

Ahlstrom, G. W. "Isaiah VI 13." *JSS* 19 (1974) 169–72. **Brownlee, W. H.** "The Text of Isaiah 6:13 in the Light of DSIa." *VT* 1 (1951) 296–98. **Emerton, J. A.** "The Translation and Interpretation of Isaiah vi. 13." In *Interpreting the Hebrew Bible.* FS E. I. J. Rosenthal, ed. J. A. Emerton and S. C. Reif. Cambridge: Cambridge UP, 1982. 85–118. **Hvidberg, F.** "The Masseba and the Holy Seed." *NTT* 56 (1955) 97–99. **Iwry, S.** "Massebah and Bamah in 1Q. Isaiah A 6:13." *JBL* 76 (1957) 225–32. **Sawyer, J.** "The Qumran Reading of Isaiah 6:13." *ASTI* 3 (1964) 111–13.

Translation

Prophet: [1] *(It was) in the year of King Uzziah's death* 4+2
that [a] *I saw my Lord:* [b]
sitting on a throne, 2+2
high and raised,
his robes [c] *filling the hall;* 3
[2] *seraphim standing above him:* [a] 4
six wings— 2+3
six wings [b] *to each.*
With two he covered [c] *his face.* 3+3+2
With two he covered [c] *his feet.*
With two he flew. [c]
[3] *And one called* [a] *to another and said:* [a] 4
"Holy! Holy! Holy! [b] 3+2
YHWH of Hosts!
The fullness [c] *of all the earth (is) his glory!"* 4

[4]The foundations[a] of the threshold shook 3+2+3
from the sound of the calling
as[b] the hall began to be filled with smoke.
[5][a]So I said: "Woe is me, 2+2
that[b] I was silent,[c]
that[b] I (am) a man of unclean lips, 5
and I dwell in the midst of people of unclean lips, 4+2
that my eyes have seen the King, YHWH of Hosts!" 4+2
[6]Then one of the seraphim flew to me. 4+2+4
In his hand (was) a smooth stone[a]
[b]he had taken with tongs from on the altar.
[7]Then he made it touch my lips and said: 3+4
"Behold this has touched your lips!
Your guilt has departed! 2+2
Your sin has been atoned!"
[8]Then I heard the voice of my Lord[a] saying: 4
"Whom shall I send? 2+3
Who will go for us?"[b]
So I said: "Here I am! Send me!" 3
[9]Then he said: "Go! 2+3
and you shall say to this people:
'Listen constantly![a] But do not understand! 2+2
Look regularly![a] But do not know!' 2+2
[10][a]Dull the heart of this people! 3+3+2
Make its ears heavy
and shut its eyes,[a]
lest it see with its eyes, 3+2
hear with its ears,
and its heart[b] understand 3+2
and it may turn and will have healing."
[11]Then I said: "How long, my Lord?" 3
Then he said: 1
"Until there be desolation: 4
Cities without inhabitant, 3+3+3
buildings without a person,
and the fields are ruined[a]—a desolation."
[12]When[a] YHWH shall have removed humankind 3+4
and the abandoned area[b] in the land's core (shall have become) great,
[13]if (perchance there be) yet in it a tenth part, 3+3
if it turn, will it be for burning?[a]
YHWH: Like the terebinth or like the oak of an Asherah,[b] 3+3+3
cast down,[c] (becomes) a monument of a high place[d]—
the seed of the holy[e] (will be) its monument.

Notes

1.a. 1QIsa[a] omits ו, but the use of *vav* consec. after a temporal phrase is sound Masoretic grammar (*HebSyntax* §123).

1.b. Many MSS read יהוה, "YHWH," for אדני, "Lord." Wildberger thinks a tendency to substitute אדני for יהוה can be found in many places in Isaiah. However, note Amos's distinctive use of אדני combined with יהוה (Amos 7:1, 2, 4, 5; 8:1, 3, 11; 9:5, 8) and alone (7:3; 9:1) in vision texts. The use of אדני appears to have a special intention in these visions.

1.c. LXX καὶ πλήρης ὁ οἶκος τῆς δόξης αὐτοῦ, "The house (was) full of his glory," avoids reference to שוליו, "his robes." This is usually seen as the tendency of the LXX translator to correct what he considers flagrant anthropomorphism and can hardly be considered witness to a different original text. The LXX translator had a special love for δόξα (cf. L. H. Brockington, "The Greek Translator of Isaiah and His Interest in ΔΟΞΑ," *VT* 1 (1951) 23–32). שוליו means "his lower extremities," i.e., from waist to feet. They were undoubtedly thought of as clothed or covered by a robe except the feet (G. R. Driver, "His Train Filled the Temple," 90).

2.a. LXX κύκλῳ αὐτοῦ, "around him," for ממעל לו, "from above him." The translator appears to object to the seraphim standing above the Lord. But MT is consistent. See יעופף, "he flew," at the end of the verse. They are pictured as flying above the throne.

2.b. 1QIsa[a] does not repeat שש כנפים, "six wings," probably due to haplography. Repetition emphasizes the distributive expression (*HebSyntax* §87).

2.c. Each of these impfs. speaks of characteristic or customary action (J. Wash Watts, *Survey of Syntax*, 60).

3.a. 1QIsa[a] reads וקראים, "and they were calling," for וקרא, "and one called," and omits ואמר, "and said." MT sustains the line of verbs in sg. and is correct. 1QIsa[a] clearly thinks of several seraphim. MT might be understood to think of only two. (Cf. Engnell, *Call of Isaiah*, 34, 246.)

3.b. 1QIsa[a] has קדוש, "holy," only two times, which has occasioned a debate (cf. N. Walker, "Origin of the Thrice-Holy," *NTS* 5 [1958/59] 132–33; idem, "Disagion Versus Trisagion," *NTS* 7 [1960–61] 170–71; B. M. Leiser, "The Trisagion," *NTS* 6 [1959–60] 261–63). Wildberger correctly notes that the thrice-holy formula is consistent with liturgical usage in Ps 99; Jer 7:4; 22:29; Ezek 21:32.

3.c. LXX πλήρης, "fullness," appears to have translated מלאה (i.e., an abs. fem. form rather than MT's masc. const.). Vg. follows LXX with *plena*, Tg. מליא, Syr. *d[e]maljâ*, which are all in line with Pss 33:5; 72:19; 104:24. But Wildberger has correctly noted Ps 24:1, ארץ ומלואה, and Deut 33:16; Pss 50:12; 89:12. The Vision uses מלא, "fullness," in 8:8 and 31:4. LXX makes כל־הארץ, "all the earth," the subject. MT makes מלא כל־הארץ the subject (cf. *HebSyntax* §14).

4.a. אמה usually refers to the "forearm" or a "cubit" measure. אמות הספים has been variously translated here: "door spigot" *(HAL)*; "post, pivot, . . . foundation of the door" (*DCH;* cf. R. B. Y. Scott, "The Hebrew Cubit," *JBL* 77 [1958] 205–14). LXX ὑπέρθυρον refers to the upper part of the door. But the term here applies to the entire door structure, hence "foundations of the threshhold" (Leslie; Engnell, *Call of Isaiah*).

4.b. The use of impf. and an inverted word order suggest a circumstantial clause.

5.a. The translation of this verse turns on the meaning of **כי** (3x) and נדמיתי.

5.b. כי may mean "because," or "that," or an emphatic particle "indeed" or "but," or "if, or when." LXX translates two times with ὅτι and once with καί. The second כי clearly introduces a reason clause. The first and third are not so bound.

5.c. נדמיתי is usually translated "I am undone" or something similar (*HAL*, "am destroyed"). LXX κατανένυγμαι, "I am stupefied" or "stunned." Syr. *tawr ʾnâ*, "I am overthrown." But α´ σ´ θ´ have εσιωπησα, aor. "I am silent," and Vg. *tacui*. Jewish exegesis agrees and relates this to Isaiah's silence relating to Uzziah's wrongs (2 Chr 26:16–22); Tg. חבית, "I have transgressed" (Stenning, *Targum of Isaiah*). The meaning "be silent" has now been adopted very widely (cf. L. Köhler, *Kleine Lichter*, 32–34; Jenni, *TZ* 15 [1959] 322; Eichrodt, Fohrer, Kaiser, and Wildberger; *DCH*).

6.a. רצפה apparently means "a smooth stone" used for paving or used as a heated stone for cooking (BDB, 954). LXX translates ἄνθραξ, "glowing charcoal," apparently depending on Lev 16:12. But there the Heb. is גחלי. MT is to be preferred (contra Wildberger and *HAL*).

6.b. Word order and tense structure indicate that the last clause is circumstantial (cf. Engnell, *Call of Isaiah;* Wildberger).

8.a. Many MSS read יהוה, "YHWH." See *Note* 1.b.

8.b. MT לנו, "for us." LXX πρὸς τὸν λαὸν τοῦτον, "for this people," appears to have been drawn in from v 9 (לעם הזה), although some suggest LXX read an original לגוי, "for a nation," for MT's לנו.

9.a. The inf. abs. following its cognate finite verb indicates continuation of the action (cf. GKC §113*r*).

10.a-a. LXX reads ἐπαχύνθη γὰρ ἡ καρδία τοῦ λαοῦ τούτου καὶ τοῖς ὠσὶν αὐτῶν βαρέως ἤκουσαν καὶ τοὺς ὀφθαλμοὺς αὐτῶν ἐκάμμυσαν, "for the heart of this people became dull, and their ears heard with disgust [lit., heavily], and their eyes closed"; i.e., instead of the prophet's receiving an order to dull the hearts, the people have made themselves stubborn and unwilling. The theological problem that the MT presents is eliminated by the change (cf. Wildberger).

10.b. 1QIsa[a] בלבבו, "with its heart," to conform with the other nouns. The versions appear to follow the same pattern (cf. Eichrodt). However, MT makes sense and is the "hard reading."

11.a. LXX reads καὶ ἡ γῆ καταλειφθήσεται ἔρημος, "and the ground will be left desolate," apparently seeing תשאר, "are left," instead of MT תשאה, "are ruined." The appearance of שאו, "desolation," in the previous line has caused some commentators to favor the LXX here.

12.a. The *vav* continues the question. A pf. tense in the protasis of a conditional clause describes a condition taken for granted (J. Wash Watts, *Survey of Syntax*, 134).

12.b. עזובה, "desolation" (BDB, 737). *HAL* identifies it as a pass. ptc. fem. from עזב, "abandon." It also occurs as a proper name. LXX translates the verse καὶ μετὰ ταῦτα μακρυνεῖ ὁ θεὸς τοὺς ἀνθρώπους καὶ οἱ καταλειφθέντες πληθυνθήσονται ἐπὶ τῆς γῆς, "and by this God will remove humankind, and those left in the land will be multiplied." Engnell (*Call of Isaiah*, 14) suggests that LXX has reinterpreted this harsh word of judgment to indicate salvation.

13.a. בער in the *pi'el* stem may mean to burn, destroy, graze, ruin, sweep away, or pillage. BDB (129) sticks with "destroy," while *DCH* opts for "pillage." Wildberger holds that Isa 3:14 and 5:5 have shown that the word means "grazed over," as when goats have eaten every blade and twig to the point that nothing is left (so also Hertzberg; Kaiser; and Budde, "Schranken, die Jesajas prophetischer Botschaft zu setzen sind," *ZAW* 41 [1923] 167). KBL, Eichrodt, Fohrer, and *HAL* contend for the meaning "burn," as with fire.

13.b. MT אשר, "which." Iwry (*JBL* 76 [1957] 230) accepts the next three changes in 1QIsa[a] and emends here to read אשרה, turning the relative particle into a noun, "Asherah." This restores the meters and continues the trend found in 1QIsa[a] of giving meaning to an otherwise obscure passage.

13.c. MT בשלכת, "in falling," a prep. with an obscure noun (BDB, 1021). 1QIsa[a] משלכת, by the change of one letter, becomes a *hop'al* ptc., "being cast down." LXX ὅταν ἐκπέσῃ, "when it falls," seems to support MT in form. But it adds ἀπὸ τῆς θήκης αὐτῆς, "from its funeral vault," thus supporting the broader implications of 1QIsa[a]. Read with 1QIsa[a].

13.d. MT בם, "in them." 1QIsa[a] במה, "high place." One hundred MSS read בה, "in her." Vg. reads *quae expandit ramos suos*, "which spread its branches."

13.e. MT קדש, "holy," an adj. 1QIsa[a] הקדוש, "the holy ones." This *Translation* has adopted the reading of 1QIsa[a] and Iwry's emendation (*JBL* 76 [1957] 230), judging them to make good sense of an otherwise obscure passage (see *Comment*).

Form/Structure/Setting

Chaps. 5–6 form a structural bridge between chaps. 1–4 (especially chap. 1) and chaps. 7–35. The chapter is marked by a monologue, first-person narrative, and a chronological notice. The next chapter changes to a third-person account. This chapter contains the writing prophet's second claim for divine authority to announce the decree of desolation, this time against the entire land, not just against Israel. The devastating wars will continue until the decreed destruction is complete.

Chap. 6 has unity and movement. Wildberger (234) calls it a "kerygmatic unity." It is composed of five parts: (1) vv 1–4: the Hall of the Lord, Heavenly King; (2) vv 5–7: the purging of the prophet's sin; (3) vv 8–10: the task for "this people"; (4) v 11: how long?; and (5) vv 12–13: if some survive and return, what of them? Each builds on what precedes and moves the thoughts along. The combination of the parts is unique. The nearest parallel is the account of Micaiah's prophecy (1 Kgs 22), which involves kings of Israel and Judah and which also deals with the fate of Israel's king. That passage also deals with prophecy that manipulates the one God intends to execute.

The chapter has often been named a "call narrative" (H. G. Reventlow, *Das Amt der Propheten bei Amos,* FRLANT 80 [Göttingen: Vandenhoeck & Ruprecht, 1962]), and interpreters wonder why it does not come at the beginning of the book as in Ezekiel (chap. 1). The chapter is *not* a "call narrative" (cf. K. Koch, *The Prophets* [Philadelphia: Fortress, 1983] 1:113; M. M. Kaplan, *JBL* 45 [1926] 251–59; Y. Kaufmann, *Toledot ha-Emunah ha-Yisraelit* [Tel Aviv: DVIR, 1947] 3:206–7; J. Milgrom, *VT* 14 [1964] 164–82; C. P. Caspari, *Commentar til de tolv foste Capitler af Propheten Jesaja* [Christiania: Mailing, 1867] 240–45; S. Mowinckel, *Profeten Jesaja* [Oslo: Aschehoug, 1925] 16–20; I. P. Seierstad, *Die Offenbarungserlebnisse der Propheten Amos, Jesaja, und Jeremia* [Oslo: Norske Videnskaps-Akademie, 1946] 43; note Wildberger's remark [240]: שלח, "send," is never used of a "call"—always of a particular task and message). Its position in the book marks the *end* of Uzziah's reign, as the opening words clearly indicate. Its purpose is to show that the nature of God's actions toward Israel and Judah that had emerged in Uzziah's reign would remain the same until a complete destruction would come about (i.e., over Samaria in 721 B.C.E.). The time clause "in the year of Uzziah's death" points backward, making this a closing scene. There is no indication that this is the prophet's first vision or first prophetic experience.

Unlike typical prophetic call narratives (such as for Moses, Gideon, Saul, and Jeremiah, where reluctance and excuses must be overcome), a vision plays a much greater role here and in a few other passages (see W. Zimmerli, *Ezekiel,* trans. R. E. Clements, Hermeneia [Philadelphia: Fortress, 1979] 1:97–100). The account of Micaiah in 1 Kgs 22:19 begins ראיתי את יהוה, "I saw YHWH," and Isa 6 begins ואראה, "I saw." The person is drawn into the midst of the Divine Council and observes the glory of the King. He, like the serving spirits about the King, is prepared to do the King's will (cf. Ps 103:20–21). He becomes a part of God's plan and his work. The telling of the vision authenticates him as God's genuine messenger. Zimmerli goes on to draw a parallel with Paul's vision (Acts 9:3–6; 22:6–11; 26:12–18). F. Horst ("Die Visionsschilderungen der alttestamentlichen Propheten," *EvT* 20 [1960] 198) has summarized well: "In all these cases in which the prophet is allowed to be present through visionary experience during discussions or decisions in the throne room of God, and thus know the 'knowledge of God,' and thus know the 'knowledge of the Almighty,' . . . he is claimed and empowered to make an unusual and overwhelming proclamation—unusual in its shocking harshness or in its great expectation."

Such accounts of prophetic vision are often told in the first person (see Micaiah's vision in 1 Kgs 22:17, 19–23; Amos 7:1–9 , cf. J. D. W. Watts, *Vision and Prophecy in Amos* [Leiden: Brill; Grand Rapids, MI: Eerdmans, 1958] 28; Zech 1:8–6:8). Ezekiel's visions are also told in the first person, as are Jeremiah's. A number of these speeches do not use the prophet's name in the immediate context. First-person speeches are frequent in Isaiah. The majority present YHWH speaking for himself (see *Strand: God's First-Person Speeches* in the *Introduction*). Some are choral passages using the first-person plural (see *Strand: "We, Us, Our"* in the *Introduction*). The form fits the dramatic character of the book. It should be a warning against too hasty identification of either the genre, its meaning, or the identity of the speaker. Traditionally the speaker has been identified with Isaiah, whose name is called in the following chapters. But if Isaiah is the subject of the Vision rather than its author (see *The Implied Author* and *Strand: "I" Pas-*

sages in the *Introduction*), one must note that he has not so far been introduced in person (only in the superscriptions of 1:1 and 2:1). Thus the unsuspecting readers/hearers have no way to identify this speaker. In afterthought they may wonder if the mysterious and anonymous speaker was indeed identical with Isaiah the prophet who appears in the following scene.

The setting in the Hall of the Heavenly Council is also a notable feature of these vision narratives and several other OT passages (1 Kgs 22:17–23; Job 1:6–12; 2:1–6; Zech 3:1–5). These may well be related to the prophetic claim to have "stood before YHWH" and "shared his council" (סוד). The subject has been discussed widely (see the lengthy discussion of the tradition in Wildberger, 234–38, and E. C. Kingsbury, "The Prophets and the Council of Yahweh," *JBL* 83 [1964] 279–86). Wildberger (237) notes that the pictures of Isaiah and Ezekiel are carried over into the Vision of the Seer of Patmos (Rev 4–5; cf. H. P. Müller "Formgeschichtliche Untersuchungen zu Apc. 4f," diss. Heidelberg, 1963.)

Discussion concerning the genre of this chapter has been lively. The consensus is that the chapter is a unique combination of forms. The frame of the chapter is composed of a heavenly throne-room scene (vv 1–2) which in turn is a subcategory of narratives of meetings with God (theophanies). As in 1 Kgs 22:19; Job 1:6 and 2:1; and Zech 1:8; 3:1; and 6:1–3, the scene is described in detail. The names and descriptions of the King's servants vary, but they are always there. The reader of the book of Isaiah will find the scene familiar. No such description is found in chaps. 1–5, but YHWH is central in every scene while speakers mill around his room in much the same way they do here.

A second element (vv 3–4) describes the speech in the room. There is no discussion leading to a decision. This decision has already been made (cf. Knierim, *VT* 18 [1968] 58), as described in chap. 1. The seraphim support the decision with a chorus of praises for the holiness and glory of God.

A third element is the cry of woe reflecting the narrator's response. Tidwell (*JBL* 94 [1975] 343–55) sees this as a parallel to the protests of the "call narratives." But v 7 takes the cry to be a confession of sin that is promptly purged. The call for a messenger and the commission are elements in other descriptions, such as 1 Kgs 22:2 or 22 and Job 1:12 and 2:6–7. Only in Isaiah is any other than one of the heavenly court sent on such a mission. The commission is not directed so much toward a message as toward a task, a very unusual assignment (like those in 2 Kgs 19:20; Job 1:12; 2:6). The narrator intervenes for the third time—after his "woe" cry (v 5) and his volunteer's cry (v 8*b*). But this time, his voice contains a tone of protest like that of Abraham (Gen 18:23–25), Moses (Exod 32:11–19), or Amos (7:2, 5). This is an element from another genre altogether. The question elicits a confirmation of the judgment decision (cf. Steck, *BZ* 16 [1972] 195). The narrator persists with his question (see *Note* 12.a.) probing the fate of the surviving and returning remnant in the land. The parallel to Gen 18:23–25 is very close. It tests the continuing effect of the ban on future generations.

The chapter has drawn upon several types of theophanic narratives to create a unique literary piece that has inner consistency and contextual integrity. Vv 12–13 have often been judged extraneous to the core of the chapter. That makes sense only if the chapter is seen as simply an eighth-century composition. Within the larger unity of the fifth-century Vision (see *Introduction*), the verses continue the logical development to answer the inevitable "audience" question: How does that affect us?

Comment

1*a* בשנת־מות המלך עזיהו, "In the year of King Uzziah's death." The coregencies of Judean kings in this period make the precise date difficult to determine. Bright *(HI)* places it in 742 B.C.E. Donner puts it in 736 B.C.E. ("The Separate States of Israel and Judah," *IJH*, 395). In the Vision of Isaiah, it marks the date when God's fateful decision was made to destroy Israel and send its people in exile.

ארא את־אדני, "I saw my Lord." The Vision presents the speaker without identification. It is usually presumed that Isaiah the prophet speaks here. The assumption is based on the view that Isaiah wrote the book (or at least this part) or that the succeeding narrative and autobiographical sections (7:1–8:18) form a unity with this (Duhm calls it a *Denkschrift*, "memoir") and are to be dated from the eighth century. If the Vision is seen essentially as a fifth-century composition and as a unity, this may be questioned. If the reader is intended to read these as Isaiah's words, why is he not introduced at the beginning? Also the unidentified first-person speech must be studied in light of other such speeches in Isaiah (such as 5:1–6; 21:3–4, 10; 22:4; 49:1–6; 50:4–9; 61:3; 62:1–6). One does well to reserve judgment on the issue.

Whether the account is spoken by the historical prophet or (on behalf of him) by the literary prophet, its purpose is clear. It is a claim for divine authority in the task at hand. It claims to place this work with other reports from those who "stood before the Lord," who saw God and lived.

1*b* The throne-room description is the first and only one in the entire Vision. It may well serve to give the background for all the other scenes where God is the center of discussion and drama (such as chaps. 1–5 and 40–59). God is clearly the Heavenly King, exalted on his throne. YHWH is called "king" in 6:5, 24:23, 32:1, 33:17, 41:21, 44:6, and 52:7. His glorious presence dominates the scene, "his robes filling" the room. ההיכל, "the hall," may refer to the temple in Jerusalem or the great heavenly hall. The word cannot settle the question, but the context favors a heavenly setting.

2 The שׂרפים, "seraphim," minister to God's every need. Such throne-room scenes regularly describe the heavenly "host" but use different words. Gen 3:24 calls them כרבים, "cherubs." They are often referred to as מלאכים, "messengers." 1 Kgs 22:21 calls them רוחים, "spirits." Job 1:6 calls them בני האלהים, "sons of God," and identifies one as השטן, "the adversary." Ezekiel's vision (1:5–21) sees them integrated into God's portable throne. They, like the cherubs, reflect ancient Near Eastern ideas. In the Bible they are a part of descriptions of what are more generally called מלאכים, "angels or messengers." These six-winged creatures (*IDB*, 1:131) occur only here in the OT. Only two wings are used to fly. Two more cover each seraph's eyes in deference to God's glory. The remaining two cover his feet. Perhaps רגליו, "feet" is here a euphemism for the genital area as in Exod 4:25 and Isa 7:20. Kaiser connects this to the very ancient experience of relating sexuality and feelings of guilt. One may also note a prevailing oriental custom that forbids showing the soles of the feet in polite society.

3 The threefold sanctus praises the Lord for the revelation of his essential being. God is by definition קדוש, "holy." But he reveals his holiness by his decisions and his acts. The praise is directed to him as "YHWH of Hosts." This is the cult name used in the Jerusalem temple (see *Excursus: Day of YHWH/Divine Warrior* in the *Introduction*). יהוה, "YHWH," had been used with worship around the ark from the beginning of Israel's existence. Exod 3:14 and 6:2 tell of the revelation of the name to Moses. But the seraphim claim "his glory" to be "the fullness" of the entire earth. The "holiness" of God seems opposite to physical nature. Procksch noted that קדוש, "holy," denotes God's innermost nature, while כבודו, "his glory," describes the appearance of his being. God is known through his work.

The theme of "holiness" and "glory" runs through the Vision.

Strand: "Holy" (קדש)

Bibliography

Parekh, S. C. "The Lexical and Theological Significance of the root QDS in the Book of Isaiah." Ph.D. diss., Dallas Theological Seminary, 1998. **Ringgren, H.** *The Prophetical Conception of Holiness.* UUÅ 12. Uppsala: Lundequistska, 1948. 19.

קדש is usually used of God or of things or people dedicated to God. It designates the survivors in Jerusalem (4:3) and of Israel (6:13), and the paths that pilgrims will use to make their way to the new Jerusalem (35:8). (See the table indicating the uses of "holy.")

Prologue	Act 1	Act 2	Act 3	Act 4	Act 5	Act 6	Epilogue
קדש							
	5:16 6:3, 13 10:17 11:9	23:18	30:29	35:8 40:25 43:28 48:2, 13	53:1, 10	57:15, 19 58:13	62:12 63:15, 18 64:10 65:5 66:17
קדוש ישראל							
1:4	5:19, 24 10:20 12:6	17:7	29:19 30:11, 12, 15	37:23 (= 2 Kgs 19:22) 41:14, 16, 20 43:3, 13 14, 15 45:11 47:4 48:17	49:7 54:3, 5	55:3, 5 60:9, 14	

Strand: "Glory, Honor of YHWH" (כבוד יהוה)

Bibliography

Rendtorff, R. "Isaiah 6 in the Framework of the Composition of the Book of Isaiah." In *Book of Isaiah.* Ed. J. Vermeylen. 73–83. Reprinted in *Canon and Theology* (Minneapolis: Fortress, 1993) 170–80.

כבד is a word that indicates weight. Isa 1:4 speaks of the weight of iniquity or guilt. It may speak of honor or riches as in Is 10:6; 61:6; and 66:11, 12. It usually describes God's glory, and it plays an important role in Isaiah indicating God's presence and his commanding appearance.

PROLOGUE	ACT 1	ACT 2	ACT 3	ACT 4	ACT 5	ACT 6	EPILOGUE
3:8 4:5	6:3 11:19	24:3		35:2 40:5 42:8, 12 43:7 48:11	49:13 51:3, 12, 19 52:9 54:11	58:8 59:19 60:1, 2	

4–5 The praise would be fitting at any time, but the dating of the passage suggests a timely meaning here as does the shaking of the threshhold and the smoke of incense. It suggests approval of God's decision to destroy Israel and to purge Jerusalem that was reached in chaps. 1–5 (cf. Knierim's thesis of a decision already made, *VT* 18 [1968] 47–68). Wildberger correctly notes that the "woe" recognizes that the very existence of the speaker is threatened. A funeral cry may already be spoken over him.

נדמיתי has often been translated "I am lost." This fits the context, but the word properly means "be silent." (Zeron, *TZ* 33 [1977] 65–68, relates the silence to Uzziah's leprosy.) The prophet is constrained to join the praise, but dares not. His own nature ("unclean lips") as well as that of his people does not allow him to speak in the assembly. It is astonishing enough that he has been allowed to see "the King, YHWH of Hosts," and still be alive. Hebrew tradition held that to be impossible (Exod 24:10). The prophet's protest parallels those of Moses and Jeremiah (Tidwell, *JBL* 94 [1975] 343–55).

6–7 A seraph performs the purging rite that gives the prophet his right to speak. It parallels the sacrifices that were needed to enter the temple.

8 With the decision fixed, the Lord calls for a messenger to put it into effect (cf. 1 Kgs 22:20). The usual messenger would be one of the heavenly host, called a spirit, or a messenger (angel), or in one case the adversary. Here the prophet volunteers to go at God's command. Such eagerness would be unique to call narratives but is normal in heavenly throne-room descriptions.

9–10 "Go! and you shall say to this people." God accepts the offer and sends the volunteer. לעם, "to this people," picks up the references in 1:3; 2:6; 3:12, 15; 5:13, 25. It will be continued exactly in 8:6 and 11. The references appear without exception to refer to Israel. It is a correct term to use for the covenant people.

"Hearing"—"seeing"—"understanding"—"knowing." The words are part of a motif that runs through the length of the Vision from 1:3 through 42:16–20.

The usual accusation is that Israel *is* "blind" and "deaf." The LXX reflects this understanding of these verses as well: "You shall indeed hear, but not understand . . . the heart of this people became dull." The messenger's task is to testify to an existing tradition which prevents repentance.

The MT, however, sees the messenger playing an active part in hardening and dulling so that repentance will not take place, now that the decision to destroy has been taken. This parallels the spirit's task in 1 Kgs 22:20–23. It is even closer to the "hardening of Pharaoh's heart" (Exod 8:11, 28 [15, 32]; 9:7, 34). Wildberger is right in saying that this is not a one-sided action. That Israel's heart is "hard" and that YHWH has made it so must be spoken in dialectical balance. The message remains the same: there is no turning back. The decision has been made and will be carried out. The commission addresses the question of prophetic success or effectiveness. As evangelists to bring the nations to repentance, the eighth-century prophets, indeed the great seventh-century prophets, were remarkably unsuccessful. This commission insists that this was not their task.

The closing line in a backhanded way provides a lucid description of revelation's normal purpose: Seeing and hearing (the vision and word of God) should lead to understanding (of their perverted and evil ways), which should cause rational beings to change and be healed. שׁוב, "turn," is the usual word for repentance (cf. H. W. Wolff, "Das Thema 'umkehr' in der alttestamentlichen Propheten," in *Gesammelte Studien zum Alten Testament,* TB 22 [Munich: Kaiser, 1964] 139; and G. Saner, "Die Umkehrforderung in der Verkündigung Jesajas," in *Wort-Gebot-Glaube,* FS W. Eichrodt, ATANT 59 [Zurich: Zwingli, 1970] 279–84). The concern for repentence is much more prominent in Jeremiah than it is here.

11 The prophet asks for more precise definition. "How long, my Lord?" The judgment is an effective curse or ban on Israel in which YHWH has "abandoned his people" (2:6) and is "hiding his face from the house of Jacob" (8:17). The inevitable question is whether this is temporary or permanent. Is it a chastisement that is intended to eventually bring about the turning and "healing"? Or does this exclude Israel forever?

The answer is equivocal. It speaks of a total destruction of cities, houses, and fields. This may be understood to include social and political institutions that leave the land of Israel vacant and abandoned. But it does not answer the question about the people or about the possible future rehabilitation of the land. These are relevant questions to postexilic readers or hearers.

12–13 The prophet's second question (see *Note* 12.a. and *Translation*) asks for clarification, assumes the fulfillment of God's judgment, but also (it is hoped) assumes the survival of a tiny remnant. It then poses the question of the future: Will the ban apply to all future generations? Will they too be banned from repentance and summarily condemned to "burn"? The word שׁוב, "turn" or "return," carries a double meaning in this context. It may mean "repent" but may also mean "return." The latter would specifically apply to the exiles who return to Palestine.

The question has certainly raised a fundamental issue. Can the future remnant (the postexilic *Golah,* "exile community") hope to return to the land and faith of their forebears and thus reclaim their inheritance in blessing? Or will they forever be under the "ban"? This answer also is equivocal, the parable of the trees. When the hardwoods are cut down, they play a continuing role as funeral monuments in the burial grounds of the worship areas; that is, the remnant will continue to have a significant role. זרע קדש, "seed of the holy" (see *Note* 13.e.), joins the use of the term in 4:3 and eschews the returning exiles' use of "holy ones" to refer to themselves as God's remnant. But the concluding מצבתה, "its monument," suggests for them a role they would not enjoy. They would be a continuing reminder of the nation that was now dead and of the reason that it was destroyed. The final verse of the Vision (66:24) suggests the same gruesome role.

Explanation

Vv 1–4 give us a formal description of the stage setting for most of the Vision. It functions for the Vision of Isaiah in the same way that Rev 4 and 5:8–14 do for the Apocalypse of John. The Lord, YHWH of Hosts, is the center around whom all else moves. Seraphim serve him and act as his messengers, as the spirits do in 1 Kgs 22:21 and Zech 6:5. Gathered around are the "host of Heaven" in 1 Kgs 22:19. In Job 1:6 the "sons of God" gathered on a certain day. A historical milestone is reached with the death of Uzziah. This first historical reference in the Vision implies that chaps. 1–4 fall outside the historically defined boundaries. Chaps. 5–6 introduce an interpretation of the Assyrian and Babylonian periods beginning with the year Uzziah died (ca. 740 B.C.E.). Chaps. 7–8 will expand the historical identification given in 6:1.

The chapter is intended to authenticate the entire Vision. This is true whether one identifies the spokesman as the historical prophet or the "literary" prophet. It supports the claim that he "stood before YHWH" in his council. It recognizes the uniqueness and strangeness of God's acts toward Israel in this period (cf. 28:21). Its claim to integrity is only that it reflects what God actually said and did. It supports the message of these chapters that the Lord decided in the eighth century to destroy Israel (cf. 7:8b; 10:22*b*–23). Every effort to minimize the judgment is turned back. A basic faith that salvation lies beyond judgment (Jenni, *TZ* 15 [1959] 339), while not totally denied, is not allowed to come to the fore. The message is doom.

Having arrived at the decision (5:5–6), God commissions the prophet to aid in carrying it out. The prophet's two questions only strengthen the gravity and the long-term effect of the judgment. The future role of a "remnant" is narrowly defined in terms that are not hopeful. The Vision will support this view by picturing postexilic Israel as recalcitrant and unwilling (40:12–49:4) and the community in Jerusalem as insisting on forcing God to return to ancient forms (chaps. 62–64). Such peoples are only funeral monuments, reminders of the ill-fated history of Israel during the divided kingdom (6:13).

The question raised by these instructions is, Why does the Lord decide to wait so long before offering Israel and Jerusalem relief? The theological issue parallels the issue raised by the "hardening of Pharoah's heart" in Exod 4:21–11:10. It involves the historical reality of extremely harsh conditions for Israel and Judah during the Assyrian invasions from 734 to 612 B.C.E. These troubles become the problem to be solved in the following chapters, changing from the problem of "the rebellious children," which chap. 1 has set out as the real issue and problem. Only in chaps. 28–33, 56–59, and 65–66 will the text return to that subject. The effect of the instructions given in vv 9–10 is thus to change the subject and to introduce the suspicion of unreliability into the text. It means that the reader of Isaiah knows that the material between chap. 6 and the picture of Zion's devastation in chaps. 34–35 must be suspected of diverting Israel and Judah from anything that would increase self-knowledge (as in chap. 1) or would lead to wholesale repentence and change of life. With chaps. 5–6 the book changes course, no longer following up on the indictment and conditions laid down in chap. 1. The following chapters (7:1–34:15) may speak many truths, but they will not be of the kind that will lead to recognition of sin and repentance.

Act 1. Jerusalem's Royal Heir (7:1–12:6)

Chaps. 7–12 exhibit a distinct plot: Davidic succession to the throne is threatened by a coalition involving Israel and Syria, who want to force Jerusalem to join them in opposing Assyrian forces. The prophet is sent with assurance this will not happen and the further assurance of a royal heir (7:14) who will be a great king, evidence that God is in fact with Jerusalem and the king. This is affirmed in the face of anticipated Assyrian incursions. The royal heir is born amid great acclamation (9:6) and eventually assumes the throne with all the grandeur and accolades that only a Davidic king in Jerusalem could receive (11:1–5). The act ends with a hymn of thanks that Jerusalem and the king have survived safely under God. The basic theme portrays the period accurately, as does the parallel story for one generation later that is found in chaps. 36–37. They both celebrate the remarkable survival of Jerusalem and the monarchy in the eighth and seventh centuries B.C.E. when all around other countries are losing their independence and their thrones.

Within the larger theme of God's judgment on Israel in part I of Isaiah, this is the exception that proves the rule. The entire land of Palestine was being systematically devastated. Jerusalem suffered during the period in many ways, but did survive intact. However, her turn would finally come in the opening decades of the sixth century. The devastation foreseen in chap. 6 would be complete. Neither Israel nor Judah with their kings would exist again in the eras that would follow.

The period that followed the death of Jeroboam II (752 B.C.E.) in Israel was turbulent. The kingdom was apparently divided. Menahem ruled over Samaria and the territory west of the Jordan river and as a faithful vassal followed a policy of paying tribute to Assyria. Pekah ben Remaliah ruled east of the river and followed a policy of independence from Assyria. Menahem was succeeded by his son, Pekahiah, who reigned a brief two years before he was assassinated. He was succeeded by Pekah, who then reigned over a kingdom uniting Samaria and Gilead for eight years. Throughout his reign, Pekah was more influenced by events in and relations to Aram (Syria) than by the more distant Assyria. Israel had competed with Aram in the area since the reign of Ahab more than a century before. Pekah stood first with Ben Hadad III and then with Rezin, who usurped the Syrian throne in 740 B.C.E. Pekah's policy toward Assyria undoubtedly reflected that of his northern neighbor. Social and economic conditions in this period were greatly disturbed. The political chaos must certainly have been reflected in the breakdown of justice and righteousness that Amos and Hosea describe.

In Judah, Azariah's (Uzziah's) longevity combined with the orderly coregency with Jotham to provide much more stability for the tiny kingdom. These Judean kings recognized the futility of resisting Assyria and paid tribute from 742 B.C.E. onward, in spite of their active participation in earlier military coalitions that had repelled Assyrian armies. There were no more Assyrian campaigns in Palestine during the reigns of Azariah and Jotham.

All that changed under the next king, Ahaz. This act of the drama takes place for the most part in periods of crisis during his reign. The primary issue deals with the question of Jerusalem's and the dynasty's survival during the critical period when Israel was losing both. Scene 1, "Of Sons and Signs" (7:1–9:6 [7]), tells of the Syro-Ephraimite war (734 B.C.E.) and the Assyrian intervention. Scene 2, "A Word against Jacob" (9:7 [8]–10:23), describes the siege and fall of Samaria to the Assyrians (724–721 B.C.E.). In scene 3, "A Word for Jerusalem" (10:24–12:6), YHWH guarantees Zion's future (720 B.C.E.). The scenes balance Isaiah's call for reliance on YHWH alone in speeches reminding readers that judgment has been determined and contrasting speeches that are idealistically optimistic. Throughout, the pressure of Assyrian expansion makes itself felt. While the promise of Assyrian invasion relieves pressure on Jerusalem in scene 1, the coming of the armies reduces Israel and Aram to the status of provinces in scene 2. Scene 3 looks hopefully to the possibility that tiny Judah may survive with a modicum of self-government as her neighbors are being subjugated. The major political changes that YHWH is accomplishing through the Assyrians have begun to take shape. Judgment falls on the entire past age in which Israel has had its existence. Small nations collapse before the imperial might. Yet YHWH has preserved Jerusalem as he promised (2:1–4). With change—God-willed change—all about, some things remain firm. Jerusalem as the place where people can go to worship YHWH is intact.

The conditions for the survival of Jerusalem, of Judah, and of the Davidic house are exemplified in Ahaz. The Assyrian, not the Davidic king, has been called to political rule. Ahaz understood the political realities. He was called to adapt himself to the changing times. He submits to be Assyria's loyal vassal. But in this he is also called to remain true in faith to YHWH and his purposes. He is not perfect in these respects, as the account in 2 Kings makes clear. But his conduct is such that his son can be crowned king in Jerusalem with great ceremony and high hope (scene 3). Jeroboam's throne and Ben-Hadad's throne had not survived, but Ahaz was able to pass on his royal status to Hezekiah.

The Vision thus takes a distinctive view of the reign of Ahaz. For all his timidity in response to a call for bold faith (7:10–13), Ahaz did obey the command to be calm and not give in to Rezin (7:4–6). He calmly maintained his status as an Assyrian vassal through the following rebellions and invasions. Although his kingdom did not go unscathed, he, his throne, and his kingdom survived. That in itself is the reason for the optimism of the last scene (10:24–12:6). With God being the activist, Jerusalem's (and Israel's) role was a passive one. This Ahaz accepted and he was rewarded.

A fifth-century reader/hearer could hardly help drawing a parallel to the reign of Manasseh. He also was a loyal Assyrian vassal throughout his reign. His policies also drew the ire of patriots within his realm and among the historians. However, he, too, saved Jerusalem from invasion or plundering. He, too, preserved his kingdom and his throne for his son and grandson.

Excursus: Types of Political Organizations

Political and military power was exercised and experienced at several levels in the ancient Near East. The highest was that of the big power (empire). At this level Egypt, Assyria, Babylonia, and Persia—and, later, the Hellenistic empires and Rome—worked. They all established forms of administration to keep contact with and control over their dominions. Then there were the smaller states who functioned as mini-empires when they were strong, or who banded with (or struggled against) similar states. Judah, Israel, Aram, Moab, Edom, the Philistines, and Phoenicia were such units. And throughout the period there were the cities that preceded the states in existence and importance and usually continued to exist with various states or after the states were gone. Babylon, Damascus, Tyre, and Jerusalem were some of these. (See *Excursus: Jerusalem—An Example of War in a Walled City* at 3:1 above.)

Israel had first existed as a people made up of loosely related tribes. As such they had displaced most of the small city-states of the Canaanites. Then came the united kingdom, followed by the divided kingdoms, north and south.

The Vision of Isaiah spans the following period when the major empires reasserted themselves. The small kingdoms were doomed. One after another they were conquered and reorganized as Assyrian districts. By the time of Tiglath-Pileser III (740–727 B.C.E.), only the Phoenicians, a reduced Israel, Judah, the Philistines, Ammon, Moab, and Edom remained. Hamath, Damascus, Dor, Megiddo, and Gilead were already incorporated into the Assyrian system. Under Sargon II (722–705 B.C.E.), Samaria and Ashdod were added to that group. The other small states were vassals paying tribute. These included Jerusalem, the Philistine cities, Tyre, Edom, and Moab.

Isaiah's Vision is fully aware of these things. Aram and Israel maneuver in preparation to meet the Assyrians in chap. 7, but not after that. Aram was subdued and deported in 734 B.C.E., and Israel and Ashdod in 721 B.C.E. The list of the nations (chaps. 13–23) includes those areas still occasionally capable of some autonomous action but threatened by Assyrian power. Tyre (chap. 23) was attacked in 701 B.C.E., as were the cities of the west, including Ashkelon, Lachish, and Jerusalem. Only Jerusalem escaped destruction. Ammon, Moab, and Edom paid tribute.

Esarhaddon invaded Egypt in 669 B.C.E. When his son Ashurbanipal put down an insurrection there two years later, the empire controlled everything from Egypt to the Persian Gulf and Elam, though during the eighth to seventh centuries Assyria had considerable trouble with rebellions in Babylon (chaps. 13–14, 21), with Elam (21:2) and, with the Medes (21:2; 13:17).

Isa 1–39 mentions only those states or cities that were still participating in intrigue against Assyria: Babylon (13:17–22; Israel is already in exile [cf. 14:1–3]), Babylon again (14:4–23), Assyria (14:24–25), the Philistines (14:29–32), Moab (15:1–16:14), Damascus (with Israel, 17:1–3), Egypt (19:1–20:6), Desert by the Sea (Babylon, 21:1–10), Dumah (Edom, 21:11–12), Arabia (21:13–16), Valley of Vision (Jerusalem, 22:1–25), and Tyre (23:1–18). Though the editorial compilation of the book came after the exile, the editor's perception of eighth- to seventh-century events is clear and accurate.

Scene 1: Of Sons and Signs (7:1–9:6 [7])

The scene is composed of a narrative continued by first-person accounts from the prophet and closes with the announcement of a royal birth.

Narrative: A Word for the King and a Sign (7:1–16)

The setting is Jerusalem. The time stretches from the threat of the Syro-Ephraimite war (734 B.C.E.) in 7:1–2 to the birth of the child announced in 7:14. Following a narrative account of the setting (7:1–2), the scene is presented in nine episodes.

Episode A: Keep Calm and Steady (7:3–9). The prophet brings a word from God to the new king in his time of crisis. His advice is be calm, remain steady, and do nothing.

Episode B: Within Three Years (7:10–16). Ahaz makes a shaky start by refusing the offer of a sign. But Isaiah assures him that he will have a son and that this son will succeed him on the throne in Jerusalem.

Episode C: Critical Times—the Assyrian Era (7:17–25). The episode makes an announcement: God is bringing the Assyrians to Palestine to inaugurate a new age for Judah and her dynasty. The Assyrians' coming will end the alliance of Aram and Israel.

Episode D: Swift Plunder, Hastening Booty (8:1–4). The Assyrian crisis is rushing down on Israel and Judah.

Episode E: Waters of Shiloah Refused (8:5–10). Israel's refusal to accept gradual processes has led to violent measures and strange alliances. No hope remains for the survival of the state.

Episode F: YHWH Is Your Fear (8:11–15). The episode discusses the problem inherent in having God present among the people and in their capital. They depend upon his presence for security while also trying to act autonomously.

Episode G: Sealing the Prophet's Testimony (8:16–18). The prophet determines to withdraw from public life, but his very existence and that of his children will be continuing reminders of the truth that has been spoken in God's name.

Episode H: To Instruction and to Testimony (8:19–22). This episode carries a warning not to be misled by the occult and bizarre. Only genuine revelation, instruction, and testimony should be heeded.

Episode I: To Us a Son Is Born (8:23–9:6 [9:1–7]). This passage heralds a glorious event in Jerusalem. In the gloomy times of the Assyrian wars, which destroy Israel and Aram, the promised sign of 7:14, the birth of an heir for David's throne, is fulfilled.

This scene portrays the essential problem of the house of David (and of Israel, for that matter): their stability depends upon "God being with them." This in turn demands from them a high quality of piety and faithfulness to YHWH. Thus God's holy presence *(Immanuel)* is a "stone of stumbling" for both houses. The scene continues to recognize that "God is hiding his face from Israel." But it closes with the cheerful hope generated by the birth of a royal heir.

Isa 7:1–9:6 (7) is a virtual tapestry of interwoven motifs. The entire section deals with "sons" and "signs." בנים, "sons," appear in 7:1, 3, 6, 14; 8:3–4, 18; 9:5–6 [6–7]. אותות, "signs," and symbols are found in the name of Isaiah's son (7:3), in the reference to the other kings as "smoldering firebrands" (7:4), and in the narrative and prophecies of 7:8–9*a*, 11, 14; 8:1–4, 18, 19, 23; 9:5–6 [6–7]. In addition, the descriptions of the Assyrian as a barber (7:20), the gentle water contrasted with the floods (8:6–8), and "the stone of stumbling" (8:14) may be mentioned as signs.

The section forms an arch whose keystone returns to the subject of "the day." The sounds of battle break through with the brave assertion that the "plans" of the nations will not stand up (8:9–10). The "plan" in 7:6 proposes a coup d'état that would place a usurper on Jerusalem's throne. The entire section deals with that theme, ending with the assurance that the legitimate heir will succeed to the throne in due time.

The arch may be plotted as follows:

A God sends Isaiah and his *son* to confront the *son* of Jotham about the *son* of Tabeel (7:1–6).
  B A *sign* for Ahaz: "It will not happen! . . . If you will not believe, certainly you cannot be confirmed!" (7:7–9).
    C The Lord's *sign:* a virgin and a son, Immanuel; the Lord is sending the king of Assyria (7:10–25).
      D A *son—sign* of approaching disaster for Aram and Israel (8:1–4).
        E This people—the wrong sign. *O Immanuel!* Assyria—a flood over Israel and Judah (8:5–8).
KEYSTONE Do your worst, nations; *Immanuel!* (God with us) (8:9–10).
        E´ *God in your midst*—a stone of stumbling for Israel and Judah (8:11–15).
      D´ Isaiah and his *sons/signs* wait/hope for the Lord (8:16–18).
    C´ Warning of false signs; to the Law and the Testimony; God humbles and *he* exalts (8:19–22).
  B´ Light will come; God will act, as at Midian (8:23–9:4 [9:1–5]).
A God's action, God's gift, God's presence, God's *sign;* to us a *son*—Wonder-Counselor, God-Warrior (9:5–6 [6–7]).

Excursus: Kings in Isaiah

Bibliography

Mettinger, T. N. D. *King and Messiah: The Civil and Sacral Legitimation of the Israelite Kings.* Lund: Gleerup, 1976. **Schultz, R.** "The King in the Book of Isaiah." In *The Lord's Anointed.* Ed. P. E. Satterthwaite, R. S. Hess, and G. J. Wenham. Grand Rapids, MI: Baker, 1995. 141–65. **Williamson, H. G. M.** *Variations on a Theme.* Cumbria: Paternoster, 1998. 113–66.

מלך, "king," designates the head of state in the political systems that surround Israel and Judah in the eighth century. By the time Persia dominates the Near East in the fifth century, kings have been replaced by פחה, "governors." Only the emperor could carry the title of king. Isaiah stresses the title for YHWH, insisting that he alone is in position to put anyone in that position or to eliminate him from it. (See *Strand: "King"* [מלך].)

Davidic kings appear only in the superscription (Uzziah, Jotham, Ahaz, and Hezekiah, 1:1), in the introductory phrase for chap. 6 (Uzziah, 6:1), in the Isaiah narratives in chap. 7 (Ahaz, 7:11), and in chaps. 36–39 (Hezekiah, 36:1, 2; 37:1, 5, 6, 10; 38:9; 39:3).

Foreign kings appear more frequently:

Strand: "King" (מלך)

Prologue	Act 1	Act 2	Act 3	Act 4	Act 5	Act 6	Epilogue
1:1	6:1, 5 7:1, 6, 16, 17, 20 8:4, 7, 21 10:8, 12	14:4, 9, 18, 28 19:4, 11 20:1, 4, 6 23:15 24:21	30:33 32:1 33:17, 22	36:1, 2, 4, 6, 8, 13, 14, 15, 16, 18, 21 37:1, 4, 5, 6, 8, 9, 10, 11, 13, 18, 21, 33, 37 38:6, 9 39:1, 3, 7 41:2, 21 43:15 44:6 45:1	49:7, 23 52:15	57:9 60:3, 10, 11, 16	62:2

"King Resin of Aram and King Pekah son of Remaliah of Israel"	7:1
"make the son of Tabeel king"	7:6
"the king of Assyria"	8:4, 7; 10:12
"the king of Babylon"	14:4
"kings of the nations"	14:9, 18
King Ahaz	14:28
"a fierce king"	19:4
"Pharoah"	19:11
"Sargon, king of Assyria," "king of Assyria	20:1, 4, 6
"a king"	23:15
"the king" (of Assyria)	30:33
"Sennacherib, king of Assyria," "king of Assyria"	36:1, 2, 4, 8, 13, 14, 15, 16, 18, 21; 37:4, 8, 10, 11, 18, 21, 33, 37; 38:6
"Pharoah, king of Egypt"	36:6, 37:8
Tirhaka, the Cushite king of Egypt	37:9
"king of Hamath, the king of Arpad, the king of the city of Sepharvaim, the king of Hena, or the king of Ivvah"	37:13
"Esarhaddon," "the king of Assyria"	37:38; 38:6
"Merodach-baladan," "king of Babylon"	39:1, 7
unnamed "kings"	7:16, 17, 20; 8:4, 7; 8:21; 10:8; 24:21; 41:2; 45:1; 49:7, 23; 52:15; 60:3, 10, 11, 16; 62:2

YHWH as king	6:5; 32:1; 33:17, 22; 41:21; 43:15; 44:6

Note that Cyrus is named in 44:28 and 45:13 but never called "king," only "the servant of YHWH."

The book of Isaiah is interested in the theme of the death of kings. Uzziah's death is noted in 6:1. Assassination is threatened for Ahaz in 7:6; Hezekiah's mortality is the theme of chaps. 38 and 39. Nebuchadnezzar's death is the theme of the taunt in chap. 14; Sennacherib's death is reported in chap. 37.

The future of Ahaz's throne forms a kind of plot in chaps. 7–12. The promise of an heir (7:14) is followed by a birth announcement in 9:6 and an account of the enthronement of a new king in 11:1–5. His future influence and power are celebrated in 11:10. The purpose seems to be to describe the wonderful events that led to Judah's survival as a monarchy during the early invasions of Palestine in the eighth century when all the other little nations were going out of business.

Chaps. 36–39 consist of a series of three stories about Hezekiah and Isaiah. The first tells of the wonderful survival of Jerusalem during the siege by Sennacherib's forces in 701 B.C.E. The second story illustrates Hezekiah's mortality. His life is extended, but only by fifteen years. Kings do die. The third story actually predicts a day when the heirs to Jerusalem's throne would become hostages of a Babylonian king in Babylon.

The rest of the book says little about kings or kingship. It is not at all clear what king Isa 32:1, refers to: "See! A king will reign." There is no hint that the royal house of David would have any role at all in the restoration after the Babylonian exile. Rather, power is wielded by the Persian emperors (Cyrus being called by name in chaps. 44–45). This accords with historical reality. Although members of the Davidide family (Sheshbazzar, Zerubbabel) were appointed governors during the first decades of Persian rule, in the fifth century B.C.E. that appointment went to a Jewish bureaucrat in the Persian court, Nehemiah. The royal house of David played no further role in the political fortunes of Judah, either in the book of Isaiah or in history.

However, there is a consistent picture of leadership, as Williamson (*Variations on a Theme,* 113–66) and J. H. Walton ("Isa 7:14: What's in a Name?" *JETS* 30 (1987) 289–306) have pointed out, that is parallel to the characteristics that YHWH exercises as king:

Spirit on him	11:2	42:1		61:1
Brings justice	11:3–4	42:1		61:1–3
Impact on the nations	11:10	42:6	49:6	61:9–11
Sets prisoner free		42:7		61:1
Reward with him			49:4 (40:2, 9, 10)	62:11
Splendor to Israel	11:10		49:5–6	61:3
Restores Israel	11:11–12		49:5–8	61:3–4

The Vision portrays the appearance of YHWH as king, sitting on a throne. It gives the assurance of the sight of Yahweh as king in 32:1; 33:17, 22; the reality of YHWH's kingship in the temple in 6:1–13 and in chaps. 40–48 and 66; and the transfer with divine approval of kingly authority and responsibility to Cyrus and the Achaemenid dynasty in chaps. 44 and 49.

The Setting (7:1–2)

Bibliography

Ackroyd, P. R. "The Biblical Interpretation of the Reigns of Ahaz and Hezekiah." In *In the Shelter of Elyon.* FS G. W. Ahlström, ed. W. B. Barrick and J. R. Spencer. Sheffield: JSOT Press, 1984. 247–59. Reprinted in *Studies in the Religious Tradition of the Old Testament* (London: SCM Press, 1987) 181–92. **Brunet, G.** *Essai sur l'Isaïe de l'Histoire.* 101–39. **Dietrich, W.** *Jesaja und die Politik.* BEvT 74. Munich: Kaiser, 1976. **Wurthwein, W.** "Jesaja 7:1–9." In *Wort und Existenz.* Göttingen: Vandenhoeck & Ruprecht, 1970. 127–43.

Translation

Narrator: 1 *In the days of Ahaz son of Jotham, son of Uzziah, king of Judah, Rezin.*[a] *king of Aram, went up with Pekah, the son of Remaliah,*[b] *king of Israel, (against) Jerusalem to fight against it.*[c] *But he*[d] *was not able to overcome it.* 2 *When it was announced to the house of David, "Aram has rested*[a] *upon Ephraim," his heart trembled with the heart of his people like the trembling of the trees of the forest before the wind.*

Notes

1.a. רְצִין means something like "a spring." But the LXX has Ραασσων, and Assyrian sources suggest a reading of רְצוֹן or רְצִין, meaning "well-pleasing" (cf. Landsberger, *Sam'al* [Ankara: Türkischen Historischen, 1948] 66 n. 169; W. von Soden, *Das akkadische Syllabar,* AnOr 27 [Rome: Pontifical Biblical Institute, 1948] 108; M. Noth, *Personennamen,* 224).

1.b. MT רמליהו, "Remaliah." 1QIsa[a] רומליה; also in vv 5 and 9, but in v 4 רמליה. LXX Ρομελιου in vv 1, 5, and 9.

1.c. למלחמה עליה, "to fight against her," has often been judged a dittography for להלחם עליה, "to overcome it." But 2 Kgs 16:5 also contains both verbs. It should be kept as it is in MT.

1.d. 2 Kgs 16:5 is pl. But the sg. meaning is clear and accurate. Rezin was the driving force in the campaign (H. M. Orlinsky, "St. Mark's Isaiah Scroll, IV," *JQR* 43 [1952–53] 331–33).

2.a. נחה has usually been translated "rest," "light upon." But this has brought suggestions for correction. Cf. G. R. Driver, *JTS* 34 (1933) 377; KBL נחה II, "support"; O. Eissfeldt, "*nûaḥ* 'sich vertragen,'" in *FS L. Köhler,* STU 20 (Bern: Büchler, 1950) 23–26, "make a contract with"; *HAL* נחה II, "to stand by." These fit the translations of LXX συνεφώνησεν and Syr. *ʾesteʿwî,* "to conspire together." Wildberger (265) suggests that the use of על does not fit this meaning. He correctly notes that Judah's panic must have been caused by more than an agreement. It could be understood if an Aramaean army were already encamped in Israel. נוח should be understood here in the sense of "occupied," "overrun," as it is in v 19 and in Exod 10:14; 2 Sam 17:12; 21:10.

Form/Structure/Setting

These verses are the first direct historical narrative in the Vision. The use of imperfects with *vav*-consecutive in the third person marks the change in syntax. The Vision thus emphasizes its intention to deal with historical situations and realities. However, the reader should note that this kind of historical reference in the book is much rarer than ordinarily recognized.

Note the parallel references in 2 Kgs 16:5–9 and the full account in 2 Chr 28:5–21. The evaluations of Ahaz's reign in these books are significantly different. The

Kings account is brief; only v 5 is quoted in Isaiah. This is preceded by the negative evaluation of Ahaz by the editor. But the account of Israel's and Aram's invasion is without rancor or criticism. The new altar that Ahaz built on the model of an Aramaean altar is described in vv 10–18. Other changes in the temple were made מפני מלך אשור, "in deference to the king of Assyria" (2 Kgs 16:18, NIV). His deference to the king of Assyria is noted, but not criticized. 2 Chr 28:5–21 is much more critical of Ahaz. It describes in much greater detail his humiliation by the armies of his neighbors (vv 5–15). At the same time the Chronicler writes appreciatively of the leaders and people of Israel (vv 9–15). He implies that Ahaz summoned help from Assyria because of the raids by Edomites and the Philistines.

Isaiah's account is clearly dependent on 2 Kings or on the same sources that the writer of Kings used. Isaiah, however, depicts Ahaz more positively as acting, with the prophet's help, in accord with YHWH's plan for the nations. The evaluation of Ahaz in the three stories is thus significantly different.

Comment

1 בִּימֵי אָחָז בֶּן־יוֹתָם, "in the days of Ahaz son of Jotham." The chronology of this reign is notoriously difficult to fix. Bright *(HI)* dates Ahaz's reign 735–15 B.C.E., while Aharoni *(MBA)* dates it 742–26 B.C.E. E. R. Thiele (*The Mysterious Numbers of the Hebrew Kings,* 3d ed. [Grand Rapids, MI: Eerdmans, 1983] 139–92) uses the years 735–16 B.C.E., while Jepson (A. Jepson and R. Hanhart, *Untersuchungen zur israelitisch-jüdischen Chronologie,* BZAW 88 [Berlin: Töpelmann, 1964]) has 741–725 B.C.E. The problems lie in the conflicting testimony of Kings and Chronicles. We will use Bright's dating adjusted to Stiles's table (see Chronological Chart of Reigns at 1:1 above) since that fits the Vision's plan best. It is highly likely that Ahaz's reign overlapped Jotham's, just as Jotham had acted as regent during the last years of his father's reign.

Most of this verse is identical to 2 Kgs 16:5 and undoubtedly depends on that account. However, the attempt to form a perfect correlation is useless (Wildberger).

Rezin was king of Aram from 740 to 733 B.C.E. Early in his reign he is listed among kings paying tribute to Tiglath-Pileser III. But by 735 B.C.E. he is leader of a plot to overthrow Assyrian suzerainty.

Pekah, son of Remaliah, came to power in Samaria in 740 B.C.E. by murdering Pekahiah, son of Menahem (2 Kgs 15:25). He is credited in 2 Kings with reigning twenty years, but a reconstructed chronology must make this five or six years. He was soon caught up in Rezin's scheme. He and the Philistines were Rezin's unquestioning followers.

2 Chr 28:5–7 records Rezin's invasion of Judah (*MBA,* 144). He attacked through Moab, freeing the Edomites and continuing on to Elath and Eziongeber on the Gulf of Akiba. The Edomites then turned on Judah (2 Kgs 16:6; 2 Chr 28:17). The Philistines used the opportunity to take cities in the Negev and Shefelah of Judah (2 Chr 28:18). Rezin's coalition, joined by Pekah, then turned to take Jerusalem, but the fortified city was too much for them. Their momentum came to a halt.

2 וַיֻּגַּד, "when it was announced." The consecutive verb picks up from וַיְהִי, "and it proceeded to be," at the beginning of v 1 and sets the scene near the beginning of the invasion. Ahaz has just been informed of the alliance between Aram and Israel. He is understandably alarmed.

Explanation

These verses introduce act 1, indicating its setting in the reign of Ahaz. Ahaz succeeded Jotham in 734 B.C.E. He inherited a difficult situation. Assyria under Tiglath-Pileser III (745–727 B.C.E.) moved vigorously to establish its authority over its neighbors, including Babylon, Urartu, and Media. In 743 B.C.E. Tiglath-Pileser III began a series of campaigns westward into Palestine. His first campaign was stopped by a coalition led by a certain "Azriau of Yaudi," who may have been Uzziah of Judah. But the results were not permanent. By 738 B.C.E. Israel and the other northern Palestinian and Aramaean states were paying tribute to Assyria.

The death of Jeroboam II (753 B.C.E.) brought to Israel a period of instability that the state would not survive. His son, Zechariah, was murdered, to be replaced by a usurper, Menahem (752–42 B.C.E.), who apparently bought a period of respite by paying heavy tribute to Tiglath-Pileser (2 Kgs 15:19). Menahem's son reigned scarcely a year before being assassinated by an army officer, Pekah ben Remaliah, who assumed the throne (740–32 B.C.E.). Pekah's determination to throw off the Assyrian yoke may have inspired the coup d'état as did his prompt alignment with Rezin of Damascus, some Philistines, and perhaps some Edomites to form a coalition against Assyria. Passages in Hosea and Amos describe that period.

This coalition tried to force Judah to join them. This military pressure was a difficult beginning for the young king's reign, but Ahaz refused to join with the conspiracy. Up to this time Judah had apparently escaped subjection to Assyria and the payment of tribute that weighed so heavily on Israel (2 Kgs 15:19 and the Assyrian inscription, *ANET,* 283). Ahaz abandoned the militaristic policy of Uzziah to accept Assyria's rule.

Assyria's attention was concentrated elsewhere in those years, so Aram and Israel felt secure on their northern borders. They launched an extended campaign against Judah (cf. *MBA,* 144). Rezin marched down the eastern side of Jordan, stripping Judah of its dependencies in Ammon, Moab, and Edom. Pekah joined an Aramaean force in a siege of Jerusalem to force a change of rulers and a more militaristic and nationalistic policy. These moves encouraged Edomites to rise up against their Judean neighbors and take back towns in southern Judah (2 Kgs 16:6; 2 Chr 28:17). The Philistines used the opportunity to seize a piece of Judah on their border (cf. *MBA,* 145), as 2 Chr 28:18 records.

The situation was serious. Ahaz followed protocol as a loyal vassal of the Assyrians. He apparently sent word of his plight and expected them to fulfill their pledge to help him.V 1 describes the stalemate in the campaign. V 2 gives the specific setting for Isaiah's meeting with Ahaz: early in the war, when he had just received word that a Syrian army was encamped on Israelite soil. Succeeding events proved that he had good reason for his anxiety.

Keep Calm and Steady (7:3–9)

Bibliography

Ackroyd, P. R. "The Biblical Interpretation of the Reigns of Ahaz and Hezekiah." In *In the Shelter of Elyon.* FS G. W. Ahlström, ed. W. B. Barrick and J. R. Spencer. Sheffield: JSOT Press, 1984. 247–59. **Albright, W. F.** "The Son of Tabel (Isaiah 7:6)." *BASOR* 140 (1955) 34–35. **Auret, A.** "Hiskia—Die oorspronklike Immanuel en messias von Jesaja 7:14: 'n Bron van heil en onheil." *NGTT* 32 (1991) 5–18. ———. "Die Immanuelperikoop en die Messias vraagstuk (The Immanuel-Pericope and the Messiah Problem: A Literary-Critical and Redaction-historical investigation into the Memoir of Isaiah)." Diss., Pretoria, 1989. **Barr, J.** "Did Isaiah Know about Hebrew 'Root Meanings'?" *ExpTim* 75 (1964) 242. **Bartelmus, R.** "Jes 7:1–17 und das Stilprincip des Kontrastes: Syntaktisch-stilkrytische und traditionsgeschichtliche Anmerkungen zur 'Immanuel Pericope.'" *ZAW* (1984) 50–66. **Begrich, J.** "Der Syrisch-Ephraimitische Krieg und seine weltpolitischen Zusammenhänge." *ZDMG* 83 (1920) 213–37. **Bickert, R.** "König Ahas und der Prophet Jesaja: Ein Beitrag zum Problem des syrisch-ephraimitischen Krieges." *ZAW* 99 (1987) 361–84. **Bjorndalen, A. J.** "Zur Einordnung und Funktion von Jes 7,5f." *ZAW* 95 (1983) 260–63. **Blank, S. H.** "Traces of Prophetic Agony in Isaiah." *HUCA* 27 (1956) 81–92. **Bouzon, E.** "A Mesagem Triologico do Immanuel." *REB* 32 (1972) 826–41. **Brunet, G.** *Essai sur l'Isaïe de l'Histoire.* Paris: Picard, 1975. **Buchsenbaum, J.** "[Is 7:1] Shear-Yashub." *BMik* 33.112 (1987) 35–51. **Budde, K.** "Das Immanuelzeichen und die Ahaz-Begegnung Jesaja 7." *JBL* 52 (1933) 22–54. ———. "Jesaja und Ahaz." *ZDMG* 84 (1930) 125–38. **Christensen, D. L.** *Prophecy and War in Ancient Israel: Studies in the Oracles against the Nations in Old Testament Prophecy.* Berkeley: BIBAL, 1989. 127–29. **Clements, R.** "The Immanuel Prophecy of Isa. 7:10–17 and Its Messianic Interpretation." In *Hebräische Bibel.* Ed. E. Blum et al. 225–40. **Conrad, E. W.** "The Royal Narratives and the Structure of the Book of Isaiah." *JSOT* 41 (1988) 67–81. **Croatto, J. S.** "El 'Enmanuel' (-nm- muchas veces en el texto) de Isaias 7:14 como signo de juicio; Analisis de Isaias 7:1–25." *RBA* (1988) 135–42. **Day, J.** "Shear-jashub (Isaiah VII 3) and the Remnant of Wrath (Ps 76:11)." *VT* 31 (1981) 76–78. **Dearman, J. A.** "'The son of Tabeel' in Isaiah 7:6." In *Prophets and Paradigms.* FS G. M. Tucker, ed. S. B. Reid. JSOTSup 229. Sheffield: Academic Press, 1996. **Drohmen, C.** "Das Immanuelzeichen: Ein jesianisches Drohwort und seine inneraltestamentliche Rezeption." *Bib* 68 (1987) 305–29. ———. "Verstockungsvollzug und prophetische Legitimation: Literarkitische Beobachtungen zu Jes 7,1–17." *BN* 31 (1986) 37–56. **Fensham, F. C.** "A Fresh Look at Isaiah 7:7–9." In Anderson FS. 11–17. **Fichtner, J.** "Zu Jes. 7:5–9." *ZAW* 56 (1938) 176. **Fohrer, G.** "Zu Jes 7,14 im Zusammenhang von Jes 7,10–22." *ZAW* 68 (1956) 54–56. **Gaehr, T. J.** "Shear-jashub: or the Remnant Sections in Isaiah." *BSac* 79 (1922) 363–71. **Gelin, R.** "L'enigma dei 65 anni in Is. 7,8b." *Lateranum* 59 (1993) 49–70. **Gitay, Y.** "Isaiah and the Syro-Ephraimite War." In *Book of Isaiah.* Ed. J. Vermeylen. 217–30 **Görg, M.** "Hiskija als Immanuel: Plädoyer für eine typologische Identifikation." *BN* 22 (1983) 17–25. **Graham, W. C.** "Isaiah's Part in the Syro-Ephraimite Crisis." *AJSL* 50 (1933–34) 201–16. **Gunneweg, A. H. J.** "Heils- und unheilsverkundigung in Jes. VII." *VT* 15 (1965) 27–34. **Haag, F.** "Das Immanuelzeichen in Jesaja 7." *TTZ* 100 (1991) 3–22. **Hammershaimb, E.** "The Immanuel Sign." *ST* 4 (1949) 124–42. **Hardmeier, C.** "Geschtspunkte pragmatischer Erzähltextanalyze: 'Glaubt ihr nicht, so bleibt ihr night'—ein Glaubensappell an schwankender Anhänger Jesajas." *WD* 15 (1979) 33–54. ———. "Verkündigung und Schrift bei Jesaja: Zur Entstehung der Schriftptophetie als Oppositionsliteratur im alten Israel." *TGl* 73 (1983) 119–54. **Höffken, P.** "Grundfragen von Jesaja 7,1–17 im Spiegell neuerer Literatur." *BZ* 33 (1989) 25–42.

———. "Notizen zum Textcharakter von Jes. 7:1–17." *TZ* 36 (1980) 321–37. **Høgenhaven, J.** "The Prophet Isaiah and Judaean Foreign Policy under Ahaz and Hezekiah." *JNES* 49 (1990) 351–54. ———. "Die symbolischen Namen in Jesajas 7 und 8 im Rahmen der sogenannten 'Denkschrift' des Propheten." In *Book of Isaiah.* Ed. J. Vermeylen. 231–35. **Hubman, F. D.** "Randbemerkungen zu Jes 7,1–17." *BN* 26 (1985) 27–46. **Irsigler, H.** "Zeichen und Bezeichnetes in Jes 7:1–17: Notizen zum Immanueltext." *BN* 29 (1985) 75–114. **Irvine, S. A.** *Isaiah, Ahaz, and the Syro-Ephraimite Crisis.* SBLDS 133. Atlanta: Scholars Press, 1990. ———. "Isaiah's *She'ar-Yashub* and the Davidic House." *BZ* 37 (1993) 78–88. ———. "The Isaian *Denkschrift:* Reconsideration of an Old Hypothesis." *ZAW* 104 (1992) 216–31. **Jensen, J.** "The Age of Immanuel." *CBQ* 41 (1979) 220–39. **Keller, C. A.** "Das quietistische Element in der Botschaft des Jesaja." *TZ* 11 (1955) 81–97. **Kronholm, T.** "Den kommande Hiskia: Ett försök att förstå den messianska interpretationen (Matt 1,18–25) av Immanuelsprofetian (Jes 7,14) i ljuset an några rabbinska texter." *SEÅ* 54 (1989) 109–17. **Kruse, H.** "Alma Redemptoris: Eine Auslegung der Immanuel-Weissagung." *TTZ* 74 (1965) 15–46. **Laato, A.** "Immanuel: Who Is God with Us? Hezekiah or Messiah!" IOFOT Summaries (1986) 74. **Lescow, T.** "Jesajas Denkschrift aus der Zeit des syrisch-ephraimitischen Kriege." *ZAW* 85 (1973) 315–31. **Menzies, G. W.** "To What Does Faith Lead? The Two-Stranded Textual Tradition of Isaiah 7.9b." *JSOT 80* (1998) 111–28. **Oded, B.** "The Historical Background of the Syro-Ephraimite War Reconsidered." *CBQ* 34 (1971) 153–65. **Pitard, W. T.** "Aram-Damascus from the Rise of Hazael to the Fall of the City in 732 B.C.E." In *Ancient Damascus.* Winona Lake, IN: Eisenbrauns, 1987. 145–89. **Rehm, M.** *Der königliche Messias im Licht der Immanuel-Weissagungen des Buches Jesaja.* Kevelaer: Butzon & Bereker, 1968. **Reventloh, H. G.** "Das Ende der sog: 'Denkschrift Jesajas.'" *BN* 38–39 (1987) 62–67. **Rice, G.** "A Neglected Interpretation of the Immanuel Prophecy." *ZAW* 90 (1978) 220–27. **Roberts, J. J. M.** "Isaiah and His Children." In *Biblical and Related Studies.* FS S. Iwry, ed. A. Kort and S. Morsehauser. Winona Lake, IN: Eisenbrauns, 1985. 193–203. **Rösel, M.** "Die Jungfrauengeburt des endzeitlichen Immanuel Jesaja 7 in der Übersetzung der Septuaginta." *JBT* 6 (1991) 135–51. **Sæbø, M.** "Formgeschichtliche Erwagungen zu Jes. 7:3–9." *ST* 14 (1960) 54–69. ———. "Isa 7:3–9." In *On the Way to Canon: Creative Tradition History in the Old Testament.* JSOTSup 191. Sheffield: Sheffield Academic Press, 1998. **Seybold, K.** *Das davidische Königtum im Zeugnis der Propheten.* FRLANT 107. Göttingen: Vandenhoeck & Ruprecht, 1972. 66–79. **Shoors, A.** "Isaiah, the Minister of Royal Anointment?" In *Instruction and Interpretation.* OTS 20. Ed. A. S. van der Woude. Leiden: Brill, 1977. 85–107. **Stacey, W. D.** *Prophetic Drama in the Old Testament.* London: Epworth, 1990. 113–20. **Stahl, R.** "'Immanuel' Gott mit uns?" *Forschungen Judentum, Theologische Fakultät, Leipzug. Mitteilungen und Beiträge* 8 (1994) 18–36. **Steck, O. H.** "Beiträge zum Verständnis von Jes 7:10–17 und 8:1–4." *TZ* 29 (1973) 161–78. ———. "Rettung und Verstockung: Exegetische Bemerkung zu Jes. 7:3–9." *EvT* 33 (1973) 77–90. **Tängberg, K. A.** *Die prophetische Mahrede: Form- und traditionsgeschichliche Studien zum Prophetischen Unkehrruf.* FRLANT 143. Göttingen: Vandenhoeck & Ruprecht, 1987. 66–75. **Thompson, M. E. W.** "Isaiah's Sign of Immanuel." *ExpTim* 95 (1983) 67–71. **Vanel, A.** "Tâbe'él en Is. VII 6 et le roi Tubail de Tyr." In *Studies in Prophecy.* VTSup 26. Leiden: Brill, 1974. 17–24. **Van Wieringen, A. L. H. M.** "Wie is de Immanu-el? Een Domain-Analyse van Jesaja 7:1–17 en Mattheüs 1:18b–24." In *Is Het Grote Verhaal verloren? Het schappen van bijbelse verhalen.* (Is the Big Story Lost? The Creation of Biblical Stories.) Ed. P. C Counet et al. Theologie in discussie 3. Kampen: Kok Pharos, 1997. 76–88. **Van Zwieten, J. W. M.** "Jewish Exegesis within Christian Bounds: Richard of St. Victor's De Emmanuele and Victorine Hermeneutics." *Bijdr* 48 (1987) 327–35. **Wagner, N. E.** "Note on Isaiah 7:4." *VT* 8 (1958) 438. **Walton, J. H.** "Isa 7:14: What's in a Name?" *JETS* 30 (1987) 289–306. **Weiss, M.** "The Contribution of Literary Theory to Biblical Research Illustrated by the Problem of She'ar-Yashub." In *Studies in the Bible, 1986.* Ed. S. Japhet. ScrHier 31. Jerusalem: Magnes;

Hebrew Univ. 1986. 373–86. **Wenham, G. J.** "*betulah*: A Girl of Marriageable Age." *VT* 26 (1976) 326–48. **Werlitz, J.** "Noch einmal Immanuel—gleich zweimal!" *BZ* 40 (1996) 254–62. ———. *Studien zur literkritischen Methode: Gericht und Heil in Jesaja 7, 1–17 und 29, 1–8.* BZAW 204. Berlin; New York: De Gruyter, 1992. **Wolff, H. W.** *Frieden ohne Ende: Eine Auslegung von Jes. 7:1–7 und 9:1–6.* BibS(N) 35. Neukirchen-Vluyn: Neukirchener Verlag, 1962. **Wong, G. C. I.** "A Cuckoo in the Textual Nest at Isaiah 7:9*b*?" *JTS* 47 (1996) 123–24. ———. "The Nature of Faith in Isaiah of Jerusalem." Diss., Cambridge, 1995. **Würthwein, E.** "Jesaja 7,1–9." In *Wort und Existenz: Sudien zum Alten Testament.* Göttingen: Vandenhoeck & Ruprecht, 1970. 127–43.

Bibliography on אמונה אמן*, "confirmation, faith, belief"*

Buber, M. *Zwei Glaubensweisen: Two Types of Faith.* Trans. N. P. Goldhawk. London: Routledge & Paul, 1951. 27–29. **Wildberger, H.** "'Glauben': Erwagungen zu האמין." In *Hebräische Wortforschung.* VTSup 16. Leiden: Brill, 1967. 372–86. ———. "'Glauben' im AT." *ZTK* 65 (1968) 129–59.

Translation

Herald:	3 *Then* [a] *YHWH said to Isaiah:*	
YHWH:	*Go out now to meet Ahaz,*	3+4
	You and Shear-yashub, your son,	
	to the end of the conduit of the upper pool,	4+3
	to the highway of the Washermen's Field.	
	4 *And you shall say to him:*	
	"Take hold of yourself and be calm. Do not be afraid.	3
	As for your heart, do not soften (it)	2+3+2
	because of two stumps,	
	these smoking [a] *firebrands,*	
	[b] *because of the burning anger* [bc] *of Rezin*	3+3
	and Aram and the son of Remallah.	
	5 *Because Aram has counseled evil against you*	5+2
	[a] *(with) Ephraim and the son of Reinallah:* [a]	
	6 *'Let us go up against Judah, terrorize* [a] *her and*	3+2
	split it open for ourselves.	
	And let us set up a king in its midst:	3+3
	the son of Tabeel.'" [b]	
Herald:	7 *Thus says the Lord* [a] *YHWH:*	
YHWH:	*It will not stand! It will not happen!*	4
Heavens:	8 *For the head* [a] *of Aram is Damascus.*	4+3
	And the head [a] *of Damascus is Rezin.*	
Earth:	[b] *Within sixty-five years*	4+3
	Ephraim will be too shattered to be a people. [b]	
Heavens:	9 *The head of Ephraim is Samaria,*	3+3
	and the head of Samaria is the son of Remaliah.	
Earth:	*If you [pl.] will not believe,*	3+3
	certainly [a] *you [pl.] cannot be confirmed!* [b]	

Notes

3.a. The *vav* consec. places the narrative in the setting and time just described.

4.a. 1QIsaᵃ העושנים, "smoking," a ptc., for MT העשנים, an adj. The 1QIsaᵃ form is also found in Exod 20:18.

4.b-b. LXX ὅταν γαρ ὀργὴ τοῦ θυμοῦ μου γένηται, πάλιν ἰάσομαι, "in case I restore again the offspring (from the punishment) of the fury of my anger." MT is to be preferred. It explains "smoking firebrands."

4.c. MT בחרי, "because of the burning"; Syr. *men ḥemtâ,* "from the burning." 1QIsaᵃ בחורי: Wagner (*VT* 8 [1958] 438) suggests 1QIsaᵃ is const. ptc., but Wildberger correctly finds it only an orthographic variant of MT.

5.a-a. LXX omits. The words may well be a gloss. They correctly interpret the previous line.

6.a. In place of ונקיצנה, "and let us terrorize her," Gesenius suggested ונציקנה, "and let us oppress her." P. de Lagarde (*Semitica* [Göttingen: Dieterich, 1878] 1:14) suggested וְנִתְצֵנָּה, "and want to burn it." G. R. Driver (*JSS* 13 [1968] 39) follows LXX συλλαλήσαντες and the Arab. *qāṣa*, translating "let us negotiate with him." Orlinsky ("Hebrew and Greek Texts of Job 14:12," *JQR* 28 [1937–38] 65–68) assumes a root קוץ II (= Arab. *qāṣa*) meaning "tear apart," which Speier ("*Unesiqennah:* Isa 7:6a," *JBL* 72 [1953] xiv) applies to Isa 7:6. The form may come from קיץ and mean "let us awaken her," i.e., make her see the error of her ways and change her mind.

6.b. MT טָבְאַל means "Good-for-nothing." But the original may well have intended טָבְאֵל, "God is good," as LXX Ταβεηλ suggests. Ezra 4:7 records such a name, and Zech 6:10, 14 has a parallel טוֹבִיָּה. The form of the name is Aram. Albright (*BASOR* 140 [1955] 34–35) cites a text that indicates that *Bêt Ṭāb'el* was a strip of land north of Gilead. The son of Tabeel was undoubtedly someone who would be friendly to Aram and its policies.

7.a. LXX reads κύριος σαβαωθ, "Lord of hosts," for MT אדני יהוה, "Lord YHWH."

8.a. ראש, "head," has appeared wrong to some commentators. M. Scott ("Isaiah 7:8," *ExpTim* 38 [1926–27] 525–26) suggested emending to ידוש, "will tread upon" or "will thresh." E. Baumann ("Zwei Einzelbemerkungen," *ZAW* 21 [1901] 268–70) suggests that it is a play on words that can mean "capital," but also "poison" (cf. BDB, II, 912; *HAL* II). Wildberger correctly notes the possibility that the double meaning was not lost on Heb. listeners. The form and meaning "head" will, of course, be sustained.

8.b-b. The clause has often been considered a secondary addition. It changes the time reference to the rather distant future, but the prediction is not easily related to an event sixty-five years hence. The next verse follows directly on the first line of v 8. However, the line is firmly anchored in LXX's text tradition.

9.a. כי, "certainly," an emphatic particle. Cf. GKC §159*ee.*

9.b. For MT תאמנו, "confirmed," LXX has συνῆτε, Vg. *intelligetis,* which would translate תָּבִינוּ, "you will (not) understand." The reading of the translations makes sense, picking up the theme of chap. 6. However, the wordplay in Heb. is too artistic and meaningful to be put aside.

Form/Structure/Setting

The limits of the little episode are marked by the narrative imperfect in v 3, which begins the episode within the larger narrative. A similar imperfect with *vav*-consecutive begins v 10, marking a new unit.

The episode is a thematic unit as well. It narrates God's instructions to Isaiah and Isaiah's word given in obedience to the instruction. It fits the genre of prophetic narrative with several characteristics: *(a)* the imperative to go (v 3); *(b)* the mission to be fulfilled (vv 3–6); *(c)* the "word" of YHWH (v 7); *(d)* an explanatory expansion (vv 8–9*a*); and *(e)* an exhortation to faith (v 9*b*). The "word" in v 3 is introduced by the formula "thus says the Lord YHWH" (cf. Westermann, *Basic Forms,* 100; Hayes, *OTFC,* 154–55).

The use of prophetic narrative in chap. 7 of the Vision gives the work its first specific historical foundation. By naming the prophet, his son, and the king;

giving the exact location of the meeting; and describing the historical circumstances, the earthly historical setting is unequivocally presented. God's decisions communicated to "heavens and earth" in chap. 1 and experienced in the heavenly king's court by the prophet in chap. 6 are conveyed to historical earthly rulers to influence political decisions at a very specific time.

Comment

3 This is the first appearance of the prophet by name, except in the superscriptions, 1:1 and 2:1. Isaiah receives divine instruction to confront Ahaz with a personal message from YHWH in the classic tradition of prophetic narrative in the OT.

שׁאר ישׁוב *Shear-yashub,* "a remnant shall return," is the name of Isaiah's son. The practice of naming a child as a prophetic symbol is also documented in Hos 1:6, 9 and Isa 8:3. He is already old enough to accompany his father and has been a witness to Isaiah's participation in prophecy for some time. The name may be viewed positively or negatively: "*only* a remnant shall return" or "*at least* a remnant shall return." It may assure a physical return from battle or captivity, or it may be understood to imply "repentance" as in "turning to God."

Excursus: The "Remnant" (שׁארת/שׁאר) *in Isaiah*

Bibliography

Brunet, G. *Essai sur l'Isaïe de l'Histoire.* 123–39. **Hasel, G. F.** *The Remnant.* Berrien Springs, MI: Andrews UP, 1972. **Müller, W. E.** *Die Vorstellung von Rest im Alten Testament.* Leipzig, 1939. **Stegemann, U.** "Der Restgedanke bei Isaias." *BZ* 13 (1969) 161–86.

The theme of the שׁארת/שׁאר, "remnant," is important in the Vision of Isaiah. It appears in 6:12–13 and again in 10:20–23, and is a fundamental presupposition for chaps. 40–66. It is grounded in the experience of forced exile. Tiglath-Pileser of Assyria had reestablished the practice of mass deportation. 2 Kgs 15:29 records a deportation from Israel while Pekah was still king; this deportation must have taken place within two years of the incident narrated in Isa 7.

PROLOGUE	ACT 1	ACT 2	ACT 3	ACT 4	ACT 5	ACT 6	EPILOGUE
3:8	7:3 10:20–22*a* 11:11–16	14:1–3 27:12–13	28:5 29:9–16, 18–19 32:3–8	35:5 42:7, 16, 18, 19 43:8 45:13 46:3		56:10 59:10	

The use of the term שׁאר, "remnant," implies an acceptance that whoever remains of Israel, Judah, or Jerusalem (or the nations, for that matter) will be much fewer than those who lived before the bad times. This fits the Vision's portrayal of the destruction of "the land" and all its political and economic structures. Peoples would be scattered.

The vocabulary used to describe survivors of that ordeal is varied: בריח, "fugitives" (15:5); פלט, "ones who escape" (4:2; 10:20; 20:6; 37:38; 45:20; 66:19); אבדים, "perishing ones" (27:13); גלה, "exile" (5:13; 11:12; 49:21); and נדח, "banished" (11:12; 13:14; 16:3,4; 27:13; 56:8). But most distinctive are שאר/שארת, "remnant." (See *Strand: "Remnant"* [שאר/שארת].)

These terms become redundant when in 54:17*c*–66:24 the people of God who are returning to worship in the new temple are called "the servants of YHWH." They are the "remnant," reduced through troubles but also through eliminating all but those who voluntarily seek to serve YHWH (chaps. 55 and 65).

Excursus: Symbolic Names for Isaiah and His Sons

Isaiah and his sons have magnificantly meaningful names. And they relate closely to the book in which they appear. Isa 7–8 introduces the reader to the three of them.

ישעיה, "Isaiah," means "YHWH will save." It reflects an unconditional belief in salvation. Isaiah son of Amoz represents this in two stories relating to kings of Judah and the city of Jerusalem. In 7:1–16, Isaiah appears with a divine mandate to assure the king that the conquest of Jerusalem by the kings of Israel and Aram "will not happen" (7:7). Ahaz is urged to stand firm in face of the threat: "If you will not believe, certainly you cannot be confirmed" (7:9*b*). The positive message for the throne is reinforced with the promise of a sign: "Behold, the woman shall conceive and bearing a son—she shall call his name Immanuel" (7:14). This prophecy reflects Isaiah's name: salvation for the king and for the city.

A second narrative fits his name. Chaps. 36–37 tell of another crisis for the city and the king. This time, the king is Hezekiah and the besieging army is Assyrian. The Assyrian general's terms had already been presented before the crowded walls of Jerusalem (chap. 36). Hezekiah sends messengers to Isaiah, who responds with this oracle: "Do not be afraid of the words that you have heard with which the boys of the king of Assyria rediculed me. See me setting a spirit against him. He will hear a rumor (of it) and return to his own country. I will fell him by a sword in his own country" (37:6–7). When the Assyrian increased his pressure on Hezekiah, Isaiah sent him a second message, the essence of which is contained in 37:35: "I shall put a cover over this city to deliver it, for my sake and for the sake of David, my servant." His prophecy was fulfilled. The Assyrian king did withdraw and was subsequently killed at home (37:36–38). Isaiah's reputation was confirmed. This commitment to Jerusalem's well-being and to the monarchy was clearly typical of Isaiah son of Amoz. His name was consistent with his message.

Other narratives show that Isaiah had his own doubts about the sureness of that salvation for the city and for the monarchy. Chap. 20 warns of "a sign and a portent" (20:3) that will shame Judah and its allies for their faith in their ability to overthrow the Assyrians. Chap. 38 relates Hezekiah's deliverance from life-threatening illness and implies that the end of the monarchy is also postponed for over a century. YHWH's salvation, however, is not automatic. When Hezekiah plots another rebellion in collusion with Babylon (chap. 39), Isaiah makes the threat explicit: "See! Days are coming when all your house and whatever your fathers have stored up until this day will be transported to Babylon. Nothing will be left over, says YHWH. And some of your children that will be descended from you, whom you beget, will be taken. And they will become eunuchs in the palace of the king of Babylon" (39:6–7). Here Isaiah's fears for the future of the monarchy find clear expression. Salvation cannot be presumed to apply everywhere and all the time.

שאר ישוב *Shear-yashub* means "a remnant will turn/return." The boy is only mentioned in 7:3, but the name echoes in various parts of the book of Isaiah. The message is very different from that implied by his father's name. ישעיהו, "Isaiah," suggests unlimited salvation. A "remnant" already points to something less: "only a remnant" or, when following a message of complete destruction, "at least a remnant," as in 1:9;

6:13; 10:20–22; 11:11, 16; 28:5; and 37:30–32. Chap. 40 and the following assume that there is hope only for a remnant.

The name Shear-yashub also uses the word שוב, "turn, return." If the exile is in view, the word refers to a return to their homeland. But if rebellion and sin are in view, it speaks of repentence, a turning from evil toward God. It may even imply turning away from God. For the chapters following chap. 40, the word contains the hope of reversing the exile. For the chapters following chap. 1, with its announcement that Israel's poeple are "rebels" whose only hope is change and repentence, it spells a hope that at least some of them will turn and be saved. This strand runs through the book culminating in chaps. 65–66.

Isaiah's second son is named מחר שלל חש בז, "Swift-Plunder, Hastening-Booty" (8:3), which is interpreted: "before the lad knows how to say 'my father, my mother,' one will carry away the wealth of Damascus and the plunder of Samaria before the king of Assyria" (8:4). The name is not mentioned again in the book, but the theme of Assyria's rampaging, plundering armies occurs repeatedly. The destruction of Israel is particularly important.

Chap. 8, along with chap. 6, is told in the first person. In these two chapters, the speakers are very much aware that the commission of chap. 1 to declare Israel's sins and call for repentence and change is not being carried out in the chapters that follow. Chap. 6 is an apology for having to present another message, albeit under the compulsion of divine injunction. Chap. 8 continues to show this discomfort with the message of salvation, when in fact the events of the day call for a much harsher and starker recognition that very bad times lie ahead. The message here is much more in tune with the strand of warning expressed in 7:17–25, 5:9–30, and 9:8–10:19. It also is compatible with the book's Day of the Lord warnings of YHWH's military activities.

The implications of the three symbolic names confirm the view that the book of Isaiah is a complex pattern of interrelating messages. They are all to be heeded: "Behold, I and the children that YHWH has given me (became) signs and symbols in Israel from YHWH of Hosts who dwells in Mount Zion" (8:18). The historical prophet and succeeding generations of prophetic scribes have served as these "signs and symbols" in Israel, and in Judaism and Christianity, pointing to the continuing work of God to save at least a remnant of his people through times of terrible stress and danger.

The reason for the chosen place is not given. "The highway of the Washermen's Field" is the same place mentioned in Isa 36:2//2 Kgs 18:17 outside the walls where the Assyrian officer stood to shout his message to the city. It may be that Isaiah is sent to a place where his confrontation will not be as public as it would have been in the court. Apparently the king is inspecting the construction of the waterworks.

Excursus: "Highway" (מסלה)

Bibliography

Dorsey, D. *The Roads and Highways of Ancient Israel.* Baltimore: Johns Hopkins UP, 1991.
Tidwell, N. L. "A Highway for Our God." Thesis, Oxford, 1982. ———. "No Highway! The Outline of a Semantic Description of *MeSILLA*." *VT* 45 (1995) 251–69.

Building and maintaining an empire required much travel for armies and officials. This paralleled the needs of commerce. All the great empires of the Near East were road builders from the Assyrians to the Romans. Undoubtedly, the Egyptians also fit this role. Camel caravans could move along trails. Chariots, wagons, and larger bodies of troops and people required wider, better, all-weather roads. סלל means "to lift up or cast up." A מסלה is a built-up road, very different from the trails made by the passing of many feet.

The book of Isaiah belongs to the age of empires. Consequently, the idea of roads, of highways, occurs repeatedly though the book. מסלה, "highway," is found ten times in all parts of the book (cf. S. Smith, *Isaiah xl–lv,* Schweich Lectures [London, 1940]). Judah and Israel had become a people that knew the need of travel, not just great migrations as in that from Egypt to Canaan or travels around Palestine as David and his band had done. The picture of an ideal international relation between Assyria, Israel, and Egypt turns on the building of a highway that runs from Assyria to Egypt (19:23).

The first use of the word מסלה, "highway," in Isaiah is in 7:3, which implies that even Jerusalem can boast of a highway along the Washermen's Field. The highway not only brought commerce to the city; it also made it easier for enemy armies to approach (see also 36:2). In 11:3, a highway gives promise of a means of return for exiles. This idea is expanded on repeatedly, in 35:8, 40:3, 49:11, 57:14, 62:10, and 66:20.

The growth and strength of Judaism and later Christianity was made possible by the network of highways built by the Persians and the Romans.

There is no agreement on the location of the "upper pool." It may have been near the spring of Gihon in the Kidron Valley east of the northern part of the city. An aqueduct carried water from it to a pool inside the south wall. This is probably the aqueduct mentioned in 7:3, which would then refer to the southern end of that aqueduct at a point apparently outside the wall. (See *Excursus: Hezekiah's Pools and Waterworks* in chap. 22.) The place is called שׂדה כובס, "a field (for) washing" (cf. G. Brunet, "Le Terrain aux Foulons," *RB* 71 [1964] 230–39), or in older English parlance "a fullers' field."

Excursus: The Ancient Craft of Washing Clothes

Fulling, or washing, in the ancient world was a special craft with learned skills and special equipment (J. R. Forbes, *Studies in Ancient Technology* [Leiden: Brill, 1956] 4:87). There are ancient references to fullers and laundrymen. By Hellenistic times there were guilds of fullers in Syria, Egypt, and North Africa. In the Sudan and in India today there are places outside cities with holes in the ground where men work on a variety of textiles and animal skins. They work in that place because it has a source of clean water and avoids polluting city water with still active catalysts used in the work (Brunet, *RB* 71 [1964] 231).

Ancient Egyptians used several "detergents" such as natron (natural soap), potash, soapwort *(Saponaria officinalis),* asphodel, and other alkaline plants. They knew that these agents absorbed grease and removed dirt. They also used "fuller's earth"—a natural, fine, hydrated aluminum silicate, the *creta fullonica* mentioned by Pliny the Elder (*Natural History* 16.146). The OT refers to such detergents in Jer 2:22, Mal 3:2, Job 9:30, and Isa 1:25. The Hebrews also used depressions in rocks as washing tubs, as did the Homeric Greeks (*Iliad* 6.86). Excavations in the Kidron Valley south of Jerusalem found such depressions near the spring En-Rogel, which Vincent called "the fullers' workplace" (R. Weill, *La Cité de David,* 2:118, quoted in L. H. Vincent, *Jerusalem de l'Ancien Testament* [Paris: Librairie Lecoffre, J. Gabalda, 1959] 290–91). עין רגל, "En-Rogel," probably comes from רגל, "foot" and "to tread." It may well be traced to a place where fullers worked the cloth or leather with their feet. (I am indebted to my student Daniel Bodi for the basis of this material.)

3 (cont'd.) The building of the "conduit of the upper pool" was undoubtedly part of military preparations to maintain supplies of water for the siege that was expected. (Cf. *Comment,* chap. 22.) The king's presence there reflected his concern for the city's military posture at that critical juncture.

4 The message is one of encouragement, of support for the king and his policy of resisting the pressure of his northern neighbors to join them in rebellion against their common liege-lord, Assyria.

Donner ("Separate States," *IJH,* 419) has described Assyrian policy relating to neighboring lands as having three stages. First, they established a dependent (or "vassal") relation by showing Assyrian military power. This meant that the dependent nation cooperated with Assyria and made periodic "gifts" of tribute or taxes to Assyria for the protection that she provided for the state. Second, on suspicion of conspiracy, Assyria intervened to remove the disloyal vassal and install a new king who could be counted on to be dependent on Assyria and therefore loyal to it. This was often accompanied by a sharp reduction in territory with the remainder becoming an Assyrian province. Third, upon suspected disloyalty, further military intervention followed, effecting the "liquidation of political independence . . . and establishment of an Assyrian province with an Assyrian governor."

By paying tribute Syria, Israel, and Judah were already in the first stage of vassalage as a result of Assyria's invasion in 742 and 738 B.C.E. Soon afterward Pekah led a successful rebellion against Menahem's son (Assyria's vassal) in a revolt probably inspired and supported by Rezin, king of Aram. This set the stage for their attempt to organize a movement among the Palestinian states to expel the Assyrians from the region. They tried to force Ahaz to join them in the revolt. 2 Kgs 16:6 says that Rezin's forces captured Elath on the Gulf of Akabah and turned the region over to the Edomites, who had been subject to Judah. 2 Chr 28:5–15 tells of much larger military operations with disastrous defeats in the field for Ahaz.

It is at this point that the two kings approach Jerusalem with plans for a coup d'état that would replace Ahaz with a king more amenable to their plans. It is plain that Ahaz maintained a policy of loyalty to Assyria. God's message through Isaiah urges him to remain firm in this resolve. The kings of Assyria needed no invitation from Ahaz to attack Syria and Israel, although he would have been well within his rights as a vassal to demand that Assyria protect him. The Vision of Isaiah nowhere blames Ahaz for the Assyrian invasion or even implies his participation in the matter, although he will definitely be affected by the military operations that follow (cf. 7:17–8:8). The kings are called "smoking firebrands" because there is more smoke than fire in their conspiracy.

5–6 Isaiah is informed of the detailed purpose of the invasion. This includes the name of the person they hope to make king, the son of Tabeel, who is otherwise unknown.

7–9*a* The specific message of encouragement is simple: "it will not happen." The kings will not succeed. Ahaz need have no fear in resisting his neighbor's forces and policies. They are no stronger than the particular persons who lead them and inhabit their capitals. When they are replaced, the countries will be no threat to Ahaz.

The message is often interpreted as an attempt to dissuade Ahaz from calling for the Assyrians, because 2 Kings and 2 Chronicles accuse Ahaz of asking Assyria for help. But there is no reference to this possibility in Isaiah. Here the issue is, Shall Ahaz give in to Rezin's planned conspiracy against Assyria or remain firm in his policy of cooperation with the Assyrians? Isaiah's word urges him not to fear the invaders. The conspiracy will not succeed. They will not survive.

Vv 8*a* and 9*a* imply that only the policies of the current kings in Damascus and Samaria dictate the actions of these countries. When they are removed, the threat will vanish. That is the point of the riddle using ראש, "head," as the key. The double meaning of ראש as either "head" or "poison" may explain its use here (see *Note* 8.a.). The statement that "within sixty-five years Ephraim will be too shattered to be a people" expresses the applied judgment of chap. 1, which is all the more reason for Ahaz to keep his distance from their adventures.

9*b* Whereas the address in v 4 was singular, here it is plural. Perhaps "you" includes the court and the government that make the policy. Perhaps it only is used in deference to royalty. Or perhaps it is a general maxim that applies to everyone.

The message turns on Hebrew wordplay. The same verb, אמן *'amen,* meaning "to be firm," appears twice in different forms. The first usage is causative, meaning "make yourself firm," i.e., "believe." The second is pointed as a passive by the Masoretes, meaning "you will be confirmed." The sentence is a classic example of a simple conditional sentence (cf. J. Wash Watts, *Survey of Syntax,* 134). LXX has emended the second verb to συνῆτε, which keeps an active sense and means "understand," so that the sentence speaks to the relation of faith to understanding. The translation is suggestive and meaningful—especially in the light of 6:9–10. However, it can hardly be original. A very literal translation of the Hebrew would be: "If you [pl.] do not firm up, you [pl.] will not be confirmed." Another form of the word, אמונה, means "faith" or "faithfulness," providing connotations of "believe." The issue before the king is that his throne is endangered. He has only been king for a short time and might well fear that he does not yet have things fully under control. The prophet calls for the king to "pull himself together," to strengthen his faith, as a necessary condition to being confirmed in office by the Lord and by his people.

Explanation

YHWH sent Isaiah to Ahaz with a message to encourage him to continue his policy of refusing to join Aram and Israel in rebellion against their Assyrian liegelord. This policy was undoubtedly unpopular with the militaristic superpatriots of the realm. The attack by Aram's armies had already broken Judah's authority over Edom and threatened Jerusalem itself. The Aramaeans and Israelites could hardly expect to storm the walls of Jerusalem. But they did hope to force Ahaz to abdicate, making way for a ruler more amenable to collaborations in their resistance to Assyria. The prophet's message is concise and to the point: "Be calm. Do not be afraid." This encouragement from the Lord indicated approval and support from God. The second part brought the content: "It will not come to pass!" Their plan will not succeed. Isaiah shows that YHWH supports Ahaz and his policy of peaceful acceptance of imperial hegemony. This is the meaning of the entire Vision. From the time of YHWH's decisions made in the reign of Uzziah (cf. 1:2–2:4), the Davidic king was no longer destined to be YHWH's means of ruling the nations. Ahaz's policy is the realistic application of this insight.

V 9*b* brings a word of encouragement in one of the most meaningful couplets in Scripture. The verbs shift to second-person masculine plural address, although the king has been addressed in the singular. The words are meant for the entire government, the king and his advisers. The key verb is from the root אמן (our word "amen"), so familiar from liturgical usage. An entire doctrine of the role of faith is in this verse.

The exercise of faith involves risk; without risk—no reward. When David gives his charge to Solomon (1 Kgs 2:4), he couches the promise in terms conditioned on Solomon's walking "faithfully before (God)" (NIV). באמת may also be translated "in truth" and is from the same root אמן that is highlighted here in 9*b*. When the prophet Ahijah presents God's challenge for Jeroboam to be king over ten tribes, it is again couched in conditions of obedience. If the conditions are fulfilled, God will build for Jeroboam בית־נאמן, "a sure house" (1 Kgs 11:38).

At this point Isaiah's message is nearer to the Deuteronomist's understanding of God's promises than to the usual Jerusalemite terms, which view the throne as נכון, "firm, established." The young King Ahaz is clearly uncertain and frightened, as well he might be. He is reminded of God's faithfulness and of God's assurance. But in v 9*b* he is reminded that he has a task to fulfill, like that outlined for Solomon and Jeroboam, before he can be confirmed on his throne. This is his "risk." God tests Ahaz through the offer, just as he tested Abraham (Gen 22:1). When Abraham obeyed the bizarre command, he clearly tested God in return. Every encounter in faith consists of a mutual testing. God's actions toward his people constitute a test and a risk as well (cf. Exod 15:25; 20:20; Deut 4:34; 8:2). So in v 10*a* YHWH offers a sign. Test and countertest are the very stuff of personal encounter and growth in faith.

But this encounter can go wrong. Deut 6:16 speaks of a bitter experience at Massah when Israel "tested" God and warns against "testing" God. Apparently the right encounter begins with God's initiative, with God's offer of a test. In Isaiah, this is the case. God offers a sign (v 11). This will clearly become a "test" both of Ahaz's faith and of God's faithfulness. There is a risk. But without risk there is no reward.

The Sign: "Within Three Years" (7:10–16)

Bibliography

Bergey, R. "La Prophétie d'Esaïe 7:14–16: Accomplissement unique ou double?" *RRef* 46 (1995) 9–14. **Buchanan, G. W.** "The Old Testament Meaning of the Knowledge of Good and Evil." *JBL* 75 (1956) 114–20. **Clements, R. E.** "The Immanuel Prophecy of Isa. 7:10–17 and Its Messianic Interpretation." In *Hebräische Bibel.* Ed. E. Blum et al. 225–40. **Coppens, J.** "Un nouvel essai d'interpretation d'Is. 7:14–17." *Salm* 23 (1976) 85–88. **Feuillet, A.** "Le signe propose à Achaz el l'Emmanuel (Isaie 7:10–25)." *RevScRel* 30 (1940) 129–51. **Fohrer, G.** "Zu Jes. 7:14 im Zusammenhang von Jes. 7:10–22." *ZAW* 68 (1956) 54–56. **Jensen, J.** "The Age of Immanuel." *CBQ* 41 (1979) 220–39. **Kida, T.** "Immanuel-yogen (Immanuel Prophecy—A Study of Is. 7:1–16)." In *FS I. Takayanagi*. Ed. by N. Tajima. Tokyo: Sobunsha, 1967. 275–93. **Kissane, E. J.** "Butter and Honey Shall He Eat (Isaiah 7:15)." *Orientalia et Biblica Louvaniensia* 1 (1957) 169–73. **Kosmala, H.** "Form and Structure in Ancient Hebrew Poetry." *VT* 14 (1964) 423–45. **Lindblom, J.** *A Study on the Immanuel Section in Isaiah* (Is 7:1–9:6). Studien utgiv, au. Kungl. Humanistika Vetenskapssamfunde i Lund 4. Lund: Gleerup, 1957–58. **Manzi, F.** "Il discernimento profetico dei segni di Dio: Spunti teologico-biblici alla luce di Isaia 7,1–17 e del Vangelo secondo Luca." *ScC* 29 (2001) 213–71. **McKane, W.** "Interpretation of Isaiah 7:14–25." *VT* 17 (1967) 208–19. **McNamara, M.** "The Emmanuel Prophecy and Its Context." *Scr* 14 (1962) 118–25; 15 (1963) 19–23. **Olmo Lete, G. del.** "La profecia del Emmanuel (Is. 7:10–17): Estado actual de la interpretacion." *EphMar* 22 (1972) 357–85. **Rice, G.** "The Interpretation of Isaiah 7:15–17." *JBL* 96 (1977) 363–69. **Scullion, J. J.** "Approach to the Understanding of Isaiah 7:10–17." *JBL* 87 (1968) 288–300. **Steck, O. H.** "Beiträge zum Verständnis von Jesaja 7:10–17 und 8:1–4." *TZ* 29 (1973) 161–78. **Wolf, H. M.** "A Solution to the Immanuel Prophecy in Is. 7:14–8:22." *JBL* 91 (1972) 449–56.

Translation

Herald:	[10]*Then YHWH*[a] *spoke again to Ahaz:*	
YHWH:	[11]*Ask for yourself a sign from YHWH your God,*	3+3
	making it deep as Sheol[a] *or raising it to a height!*	
Herald:	[12]*Then Ahaz said:*	2+2
Ahaz:	*I shall not ask, for I shall not test YHWH.*	
Herald:	[13]*Then he said:*	2
Prophet:	*Hear ye now, House of David!*	3+4+4
	Is (it) too small (for) you [pl.]—the wearying of humans	
	that you also weary my God?	
	[14]*Therefore my Lord himself will give you [pl.] a sign.*	
	Behold, the woman[a] *shall conceive*	3+2+4
	and bearing a son—	
	she shall call[b] *his name Immanuel.*	
	[15]*Curdled milk and honey will he eat until he knows to refuse the evil and to choose the good.* [16]*For before the lad knows refusing the evil and choosing the good, the ground will be forsaken by those of whom you are standing in dread, by the presence of her two kings.*	

Notes

10.a. Tg. ישעיהו, "Isaiah." The change makes sense, but the unanimous testimony of MT and versions demands respect.

11.a. α´ σ´ θ´ εἰς ᾅδην, "to Hades." LXX εἰς βάθος, "to depth." MT reads שְׁאָלָה, "please ask it." The versions read another vowel: שְׁאֹלָה, meaning "Sheol," with a ה directive. This reading is universally accepted since it fits the contrast with "heights" to follow.

14.a. LXX ἡ παρθένος, "the virgin." α´ σ´ θ´ ἡ νεᾶνις, "the young woman." The article of MT is attested in all MSS.

14.b. 1QIsa[a] and LXX[s] have a 2 masc. pl.: καλέσετε, "you will call." But other versions, including most LXX manuscripts, support MT.

Form/Structure/Setting

The passage begins like the last one with a narrative imperfect that both relates it to the context of vv 1–2, 3–9 and also sets it off. It is a second episode and has the genre of a sign narrative. In biblical stories, it is usual for a sign to be offered without being requested (cf. 1 Sam 10:7, 9; 1 Sam 2:34). Hezekiah is given such a sign (Isa 37:30//2 Kgs 19:29). So, giving the sign without having Ahaz request it is not out of character.

The pericope has two parts: first the dialogue about the sign (vv 10–13) and then the actual sign itself. The sign supports the prophecy of vv 7–8. The Hebrew particles structure the sign passage. לכן, "therefore" (v 14), begins the speech, relating it to the earlier offer of a sign. The sign itself is presented with הנה, "behold" (v 14). The explanation is introduced with כי, "for" (v 16).

Comment

10 The narrative expressly indicates a second word and a second occasion. The purpose continues that of the previous episode. Ahaz is being encouraged to remain firm in his policy of loyalty to Assyria and resistance to Aram and Israel.

11 A אות, "sign," is frequently offered by a prophet so that someone may know that God is fulfilling the promises he has made. Samuel offers to Saul signs that will confirm God's choice and endowment as king (1 Sam 10:7, 9). Eli is informed that the death of his sons will be a sign that God has brought judgment on him (1 Sam 2:34).

12 God offers Ahaz such a confirmation that these events are all part of his will. But the use of such aids to faith have always been controversial. Some consider a religion built on signs to be a counterfeit of true faith. It could be a means of "testing" or "trying" (נסה) God. Israel is accused of such in Exod 17:2, 7; Num 14:22; Deut 6:16; Pss 78:18, 41, 56; 95:9; 106:14. (This root, closely akin to נסס, "be conspicuous," is the source of the noun נס, "flag" or "ensign," which appears in Isa 5:26; 11:12, 18:3.) So Ahaz piously refuses the offer.

13 Ahaz had been addressed in the singular (vv 10–12). When the formal address turns to "O House of David" (v 13), the plural is used. The appellation gives the entire passage royal (i.e., messianic) significance related to the destiny of the Davidic House in Jerusalem. The Vision has not until this point dealt with the role of the Davidic ruler in the new order. Judgment on Jerusalem's ruling classes had not been explicitly applied to the king in chap. 1 or chap. 3. Now the prophet's mission to the king indicates God's approval of Ahaz's action and offers support for his policies.

The word לאה, "to weary," "to wear out," is used here about the king. It is a key word in Isaiah. In 1:14, YHWH is "weary" of Jerusalem's vain worship. Wildberger notes that the word belongs to the vocabulary of the ריב, "argument," as Mic 6:3 and Job 4:2, 5 show. It means that someone has had enough of his opponent's argument. He will accept no more. LXX, however, has translated this by παρέχειν ἀγῶνα, "occasion strife." This adds a nuance to the meaning of "weary."

In what sense has Ahaz "wearied" or "occasioned strife" for humans? This meeting occurs early in his reign. He has inherited a crisis for which he is not to blame. Undoubtedly, many of his subjects expected from him a vigorous new policy to rescue the country from its difficulties. This has not happened. He has neither rallied his country to a vigorous counteroffensive nor launched a diplomatic move to join his foes in rebellion against Assyria. It is understandable that this had "wearied" many and "occasioned strife" among his subjects.

Isaiah's role was to strengthen the king's resolve to continue his present policy of neutrality and appeasement toward Assyria. But Ahaz did not make it easy. There is no evidence that Ahaz is a man of faith. He distanced himself from the religious confirmation that would have strengthened his hand. Isaiah's word for Ahaz is "wearying" (לאה). Both Kings and Chronicles find stronger condemnation for the king. But at this stage he is young, inexperienced, and indecisive.

14–16 The sign is revealed anyway. העלמה, "the young woman," not yet married (i.e., a virgin), who is apparently present or contemporary, will in due course bear a child and call his name עמנו אל *Immanuel,* meaning God-(is)-with-us. By the time the child is old enough to make decisions, the land of the two opposing kings will be devastated. The sign is simple. It has to do with a period by which time the present crisis will no longer be acute or relevant. This parallels the statement in v 8*b* but indicates a much shorter period. The shorter period accords with history. Tiglath-Pileser's reactions to Rezin and the son of Remaliah came in 733 B.C.E. when he reduced most of Israel to the status of an Assyrian province.

Explanation

YHWH commissions Isaiah with a further mission to Ahaz. He is authorized to offer Ahaz a sign (אות) to bolster his faith and direct his decision. The story develops along two lines. The first shows that Ahaz is incapable of serious spiritual interaction with God or his prophet. His policy is to avoid religious or spiritual contact because it might lead him to a cultic or religious mistake. Perhaps he is thinking of his grandfather's mistake when he tried to exercise priestly office in the temple (2 Chr 26:16). He knows just enough to know that approaching the Lord risks being accused of manipulating him. He knows the laws about not "testing" (נסה) God and quotes them as a reason to avoid "inquiring" of YHWH.

Isaiah refuses to see it that way. He warns the king about "wearying" (לאה) God with his empty excuses. The records show that within his reign Ahaz actually designed and built an altar of Damascene style specifically to "inquire before." He also was very active in rearranging the temple and its worship. The editors of Kings judge his motivation to have been political and pagan (cf. 2 Kgs 16:10–18). The accumulated testimony suggests that Ahaz was religious enough, but that his gods were idols. This word and picture are typical for the book of Isaiah. The Vision portrays God as vocal and active—but his people at every stage as unresponsive, unwilling, disobedient. "Wearying" fits the picture very well for Israel as well as for Ahaz.

The mass of bibliographic references that deal with 7:14 make it necessary to deal with the verse in a special series of excursuses, each with a selected bibliography. The limits of space prevent a full review of all the research.

Perikope: Eine Nachlese." *TZ* 30 (1974) 11–22. ———. "Die Immanuel-Perikope im Lichte neuerer Veroffentlichungen." ZDMGSup 1 (1969) 281–90. ———. "Die Immanuel Weissagung, ein Gesprach mit E. Hammershaimb." *VT* 4 (1954) 20–33. ———. "Die Immanuel Weissagung und die Eschatologie des Jesaja." *TZ* 16 (1960) 439–55. ———. "Neuere Arbeiten zum Immanuel-Problem." *ZAW* 68 (1956) 44–53. ———. "La Propheties d'Immanuel." *RHPR* 23 (1943) 1–26. **Testa, E.** "L'Emmanuele e la santa Sion." *SBFLA* 25 (1975) 171–92. **Vischer, W.** *Die Immanuel-Botschaft im Rahmen des königlichen Zionfestes.* Zollikon-Zurich: Evangelische Verlag, 1955. Cf. R. Tournay, *RB* 64 (1957) 124; J. Hempel. *ZAW* 68 (1956) 284. ———. "La prophetie d'Emmanuel et la fete royale." *ETR* 29 (1954) 3:55–97. **Wolff, H. W.** *Immanuel: Das Zeichen, dem widersprochen wird.* BibS(N) 23. Neukirchen-Vluyn: Neukirchener Verlag, 1959. **Zimmermann, F.** "Immanuel Prophecy." *JQR* 52 (1961) 154–59.

The very size of the bibliography indicates how intense has been the discussion about this name.

עִמָּנוּ אֵל is a statement with two elements: "God—with us." Hebrew sentences may be formed with no expressed verb. There is always an ambiguity about such statements because the hearer or reader must supply the verb form in both its time and its mood. Therefore, the context is of vital importance. The words appear twice more in the larger context. In 8:8 the threatening context suggests a translation "May God (be) with us." In 8:10 the defiant context requires the meaning "For God (is) with us." The issues involved in the cry are then described in 8:12–15.

Names that express faith in God's nearness are known in many languages of the ancient Near East. Ps 46:8, 12 contains the assuring word "YHWH of Hosts is with us," while the reassurances given leaders in holy war were similar: Deut 20:4; Judg 6:12. Vischer (*Die Immanuel-Botschaft,* 22) refers to 2 Sam 23:5, where David speaks of his house being secure עם־אל, "with God." Wildberger (293) notes that Isaiah usually uses יהוה, "YHWH," while here אל, "God," is used. This may indicate that a well-known formula is being employed. Mowinckel (*Psalmenstudien* [Kristiania: Dybwad, 1921] 2:306 n. 1) assumes that עמנו אל was an ancient cultic cry. Vischer calls it a choral shout in the liturgy of the royal Zion festival. (See the *Comment* on 8:10.)

Wildberger (293) rightly seeks a meaning for the name in connection with the prophecy of vv 4–9 and thus with the traditions of the Davidic dynasty. God promised to be "with" the sons of David in a special way (2 Sam 7:9; 1 Kgs 1:37; Ps 89:22, 25; 1 Kgs 11:38). This larger context, which concentrates on the Davidic tradition and succession, suggests that Immanuel will be the king's son and that the עלמה is Ahaz's wife.

Excursus: Isaiah 7:14 in Context

Bibliography

Carreira das Neves, J. "Is. 7:14: da Exegese a Hermeneutica." *Theol* 4.4 (1969) 399–414. ———. "Isaias 7:14 no Texto Massoretico e no Texto Grego: A obra de Joachim Becker." *Did* 2 (1972) 79–112. **Coppens, J.** "L'interpretation d'Is. 7:14 a la lumiere des etudes les plus recentes" (bibliography). In *Lex Tua Veritas.* FS H. Junker, ed. H. Gross and F. Mussner. Trier: Paulinus, 1961. 31–45. **Criado, R.** "El valor de *laken* (Vg "propter") en Is. 7:14." *EstEcl* 34 (1960) 741–51. **Dequeker, L.** "Isaie 7:14: *wqr't smw 'mnw 'l.*" *VT* 12 (1962) 331–35. **Hartmann, K. C.** "More about the RSV and Isaiah 7:14." *LQ* 7 (1955) 344–47. **Hindson, E. E.** "Development of the Interpretation of Isaiah 7:14: A Tribute to E. J. Young." *Grace Journal* 10 (1969) 19–25. **Koehler, L.** "Zum Verständnis von Jes. 7:14." *ZAW* 67 (1955) 48–50. **Lacheman, E. R.** "A propos of Isaiah

7:14." *JBR* 22 (1954) 43. **Lescow, T.** "Das Geburtsmotiv in den messianischen Weissagungen bei Jesaja und Micha (Is. 7:14, 9:11, Micha 5:1–3)." *ZAW* 79 (1967) 172–207. **Lohfink, N.** "On Interpreting the Old Testament (Is. 7:14)." *TD* 15 (1967) 228–29. Reprinted from *Stimmen der Zeit* 176 (1966) 98–112. **Mejia, J.** "Contribucion a la exegesis de un texto dificil." *EstBib* 24 (1965) 107–21. **Messerschmidt, H.** "Se, jomfruen skal undfange og fode en son (Is. 7:14 . . .)." *Lumen* 6 (1962) 160–69. **Moody, D.** "Isaiah 7:14 in the Revised Standard Version." *RevExp* 50 (1953) 61–68. **Motyer, J. A.** "Content and Context in the Interpretation of Isaiah 7:14." *TynBul* 21 (1970) 118–25. **Porubsan, S.** "The Word *ʾot* in Isaiah 7:14." *CBQ* 22 (1960) 144–59. **Salvoni, F.** "La profezia Isiana sulla 'Vergine' partoriente (Is. 7:14)." *Ricerche Bibliche e Religose* 1 (1966) 19–40. **Surburg, R. F.** "Interpretation of Isaiah 7:14." *Spfd* 38 (1974) 110–18. **Sutcliffe, E. F.** "The Emmanuel Prophecy of Is. 7:14." *EstEcl* 34 (1960) 737–65.

What then is the meaning of the verse and the sign? לכן, "therefore," relates to v 13, in which God shows his impatience with Ahaz's timidity and vacillation. So the Lord himself will give them, the House of David, a sign that the position of the royal house and its succession (vv 4–9) is established.

The announcement is of a birth. The queen (העלמה) is either pregnant or soon will be. She will bear a son, a potential heir to all the promises to David. She will name him Immanuel. The sign is specifically a birth (the assurance of an heir to the throne) and a name (the assurance of God's faithfulness to his promise to be "with" the sons of David).

The announcement continues with the description of the child's well-being in v 15 and the explanation in v 16, which comes full circle to relate the whole to the events of vv 1–2 and the prophecy "It will not happen!" of vv 4–9.

Excursus: Isaiah 7:14 as Messianic Prophecy

Bibliography

Berg, W. "Die Identität der 'jungen Frau' in Jes 7:14, 16." *BN* 13 (1980) 7–13. **Creager, H. L.** "Immanuel Passage as Messianic Prophecy." *LQ* 7 (1955) 339–43. **Rehm, M.** *Der königliche Messias im Lichte der Immanuel-weissagung des Buches Jesaja.* Eichstädter Studien 1. Kevelaer: Butzon & Bereker, 1968. Cf. B. S. Childs, *JBL* 88 (1969) 365; G. Fohrer, *ZAW* 81 (1968) 428; J. Bright, *Int* 20 (1970) 389; P. A. H. de Boer, *VT* 20 (1970) 381; G. M. Landes, *CBQ* 32 (1970) 300; D. R. Jones, *JTS* 22 (1971) 559. **Rice, G.** "The Interpretation of Isaiah 7:15–17." *JBL* 96 (1977) 363–69. **Savoca, G. M.** "L'Emmanuele al centro della storia, segno di salvezze e di rovina." *Palestro del Clero* 33 (1954) 753–61. **Sancho-Gili, J.** "Sobre el sentido mesianico de Is. 7:14: Interpretaciones biblicas y magisteriales." *CB* 27 (1970) 67–89. **Willis, J. T.** "The Meaning of Isaiah 7:14 and Its Application in Matthew 1:23." *ResQ* 21 (1978) 1–18. **Young, E. J.** "The Immanuel Prophecy: Isa 7:14." In *Studies in Isaiah.* Grand Rapids, MI: Eerdmans, 1954. 143–98.

Did the sign have "messianic relevance" as it was originally announced? The passage turns on a threat to the throne and to the "son of David" who occupies it. The prophecy "It will not happen" announces that the threat is empty and that the throne will remain secure. V 9*b* speaks of being "confirmed" and surely refers to confirmation in his position on the throne. So the sign deals with the same issue. And whatever involves the Davidic promise of the throne to his heirs must have relevance to "Messiah."

The entire setting shows a positive attitude toward the House of David. העלמה, "the young woman," must be someone in sight to whom Isaiah points. The most likely woman to have been present with the king would have been the queen. If this is true, the son that is to be born will be the heir apparent to the throne, i.e., the Anointed One.

In this sense, at least, the passage is "messianic." It is related to the fulfillment of God's promises to David and his dynasty. It warns Ahaz that it is in the interest of the throne and his succession to allow his troubles to pass without escalating them by rash acts. In this way he can pass on to his son an independent, even if poor and ravished, kingdom.

It is significant that all the passages that explicitly deal with messianic themes related to the Davidic dynasty occur in the Ahaz section of the Vision (7:1–16; 9:5–6 [6–7]; 11:1–5, 10). The survival of the royal house of Judah in the day when Tiglath-Pileser unleashed his armies in Palestine is nothing short of miraculous. That the very king who eschewed military might and the attempt to save his kingdom from Rezin and the son of Remaliah by force would outlive both of them and place his son on the throne of the still-intact little kingdom was indeed a miracle. What would have been seen as impossible by human measures was well within the power of God, who delighted to exalt the meek and lowly but was at pains to humble the proud and ambitious (2:11–18). The sign implied all of this for the Davidic dynasty under Ahaz.

Excursus: Isaiah 7:14 and the Virgin Birth of Jesus

Bibliography

Abschlag, W. "Jungfrau oder Junge Frau? Zu Is. 7:14." *Anzeiger für die kath. Geistlichkelt* 83 (1974) 200. **Beecher, W. J.** "The Prophecy of the Virgin Mother." In *Classical Evangelical Essays in Old Testament Interpretation.* Ed. W. C. Kaiser. Grand Rapids, MI: Baker, 1973. 1979–85. **Brennan, J. P.** "Virgin and Child in Is. 7:14." *TBT* 1 (1964) 968–74. **Feinberg, C. L.** "The Virgin Birth in the Old Testament and Is. 7:14." *BSac* 119 (1962) 251–58. **Haag, H.** "Is. 7:14 als attest. Grundstelle der Lehre von virginitas Mariae." In *Jungfrauengeburt gestern und heute.* Ed. H. J. Brosch and J. Hasenfuss. Mariologische Studien 4. Essen: Driewer, 1969. 137–43. **Kilian, R.** "Die Geburt des Immanuel aus der Jungfrau, Jes. 7:14." In *Zum Thema Jungfrauengeburt.* Stuttgart: Katholisches Bibelwerk 1970. 9–35. **Kruse, H.** "Alma Redemptoris Mater: Eine Auslegung der Immanuel-Weissagung Is. 7:14." *TTZ* 74 (1965) 15–36. **Loss, N. M.** "Ecce Virgo concipiet: Reflexoes sobre a Relacao entre Sinai e Significacao em Is. 7:14–16." In *Actualidades Biblicas.* Petropolis, 1971. 309–20. **Mueller, W.** "Virgin Shall Conceive." *EvQ* 32 (1960) 203–7. **Prado, J.** "La Madre del Emmanuel: Is. 7:14 (Reseña del estado de las cuestiones)." *Sef* 2 (1961) 85–114. **Stuhlmueller, C.** "The Mother of the Immanuel." *Marian Studies* 12 (1961) 165–204. **Vella, G.** "Is. 7:14 e il parto verginale del Messia." *Atti della Settimana Biblica* 18 (1964) 85–93. **Young, E. J.** "The Immanuel Prophecy: Isa 7:14." In *Studies in Isaiah.* Grand Rapids, MI: Eerdmans, 1954. 143–98.

No record exists of special attention given to 7:14 in pre-Christian Judaism. The ambiguity inherent in the word העלמה is reflected in the divergence of Greek translations. LXX translates ἡ παρθένος, "the virgin." α´, σ´, and θ´use ἡ νεᾶνις, "the young woman." These latter three are all Jewish translations from the era of Christianity, and so may in fact reflect anti-Christian attempts to "tighten" the LXX's translation to more closely match the MT. But no record exists of any debate on these issues in pre-Christian times.

Matthew (1:22–23) finds in the LXX rendition of 7:14 a coincidental convergence of this sentence in Scripture with the events he is recounting and interprets it as prophecy and fulfillment. He quotes the LXX almost verbatim, with only the variation καλέσουσιν, "they will call," for καλέσεις, "you [sg.] will call." The translation ἡ παρθένος, "the virgin," suits Matthew's intention perfectly. If one supposes a divine intention in this connection, part of God's work was done through the Greek translator. The translation of the other Greek versions, while accurate enough in context, does not serve Matthew's purpose. However, even in Matthew only a part of the prophecy was literally fulfilled. The Incarnate Son is named by divine command "Jesus," not Immanuel. And no effort is made to relate his childhood to fulfillment of the prophecy concerning Rezin and Pekah. But with Matthew the verse took on heightened significance and importance, becoming a central issue in Jewish-Christian polemic about Messiah and Jesus.

Later christological interpretation focused on the words "a virgin shall conceive" and the child's name, Immanuel. Both were used to develop the doctrine of the incarnation. The divinity of Jesus was expressed in the name, and the virgin birth became the classical means of explaining "how" the incarnation took place.

Several things contributed to connecting Isa 7:14 with the gospel events. The messianic hope burned particularly bright in the Jewish community of the first century. Distance in time separated them from the issues of the eighth-century prophecy and the fifth-century book. Another factor lay in the special relevance that the Vision of Isaiah had for the Jewish and Christian communities of the first century. It provided the "worldview" of God's plan for that period which supported the synagogue and temple. Its teaching of God's plan for that age was very congenial to the Gospel and the church in details (such as messianic teachings) as well as in general direction (antipathy to sacrifice and monarchy). Jesus' and the church's understandings of the Messiah are directly in line with that of the Vision, although the book does not develop such a view or program.

A second factor facilitated the use of Isa 7:14 in Matthew. A hermeneutical method in general use allowed verses to be separated from their contexts. Verses or individual words were understood to have esoteric meanings whose significance could be revealed to an inspired teacher or writer. Thus the entire Scripture was viewed as a prophecy intended to interpret the moment in which the reader lived. Verses were abstracted from both the historical and the literary setting in which they originally appeared. They were then identified with an event or a doctrine that was altogether extraneous to the original context or intention. This kind of interpretation presumes a view of inspiration and of history in which God moves in all ages mysteriously to plant his secrets so that later ages may put the puzzle together and thus reveal his purposes and the direction of his intention.

In the case of Isa 7:14 the relation to Christology was secret no longer. The verse continued to play an important role in Christian teaching and preaching. However, there were those who protested its translation in the way that this interpretation demanded. Aquila, Symmachus, and Theodotian translated העלמה by ἡ νεᾶνις, "the young woman," in their translations of the OT (cf. J. Ziegler, *Isaias*[3], 147). Justin Martyr met the objection of Trypho (*Dialogue with Trypho,* 67) that the passage should be translated ἰδοὺ ἡ νεᾶνις ἐν γαστρὶ λήψεται καὶ τέξεται υἱόν, "Behold! The young woman shall conceive and bear a son." (Cf. E. J. Young, "Immanuel Prophecy," 144.)

However, the line of Christian interpretation of 7:14 in accordance with Matthew continued through the Fathers (both Greek and Latin), the Reformers, and on to current conservative scholars such as E. J. Young. It presumes a christological interpretation of the OT. העלמה is to be translated "the virgin" and is a prediction of Mary, the Mother of Jesus. Equally, Immanuel is the name for Jesus.

This kind of interpretation is subject to the criticism that it ignores the rightful demands of contextual and historical exegesis, which call for a meaning related to the end of the Syro-Ephraimite War in terms of v 16. Christological implications may more profitably be discussed in the commentary on Matthew than in the one on Isaiah.

But a consideration of christological significance must also note the way the Vision calls to a faith that serves rather than conquers, that is humble rather than triumphal, and that accepts suffering rather than seeking vengeance. This is supported by the demonstration that God is thoroughly capable of achieving his goals by miraculous means (2:2–4; 9:1–6 [2–7]; 11:1–16; 35:1–10; 65:17–66:24) as well as by the manipulation of historical forces (7:17; 10:5–11; 13:1–5; 24:1–3; 45:1–7; 63:1–6). Thus the announcement of God's sign to Ahaz in his hour of despair is a fitting reference to illuminate the birth of a lowly infant in stable straw whom God had destined to save the world not by force of arms but by meek acceptance of humiliation and death. That God chooses to accomplish his primary goals in such ways is as much the message of Isaiah as it is of the Gospels.

Announcement: YHWH Is Bringing Critical Times, the Assyrian Era (7:17–25)

Bibliography

Childs, B. S. *Isaiah and the Assyrian Crisis.* **McKane, W.** "The Interpretation of Isaiah VII 14–25." *VT* 17 (1967) 208–19.

Translation

Isaiah: (to Ahaz)	17 *YHWH* [a] *will bring upon you [sg.] and upon your people and upon your father's house times such as have not come since the day Ephraim revolted against Judah:* [b]*(that is, he will bring) the king of Assyria.*[b]	
An Oracle:	18 *It shall be in that day:*	3
	YHWH will whistle for the fly	3+4
	which (is) at the source of the rivers [a]*of Egypt,*	
	and to the bee	1+3
	which (is) in the land of Assyria.	
	19 *They shall come—all of them shall settle*	3
	in the valleys of precipices,[a]	2
	and in the clefts of rocks	2
	and in all the thornbushes [b]	2
	and in all the watering places.[c]	2
An Oracle:	20 *In that day,*	2
	The Lord will shave with a razor	3+3+2
	that is hired beyond the river,	
	the king of Assyria.	
	The head, the pubic hair,[a]	3+3
	and also the beard it will remove.	
An Oracle:	21 *And it shall be in that day:*	3

A person will keep alive a calf and two goats. 2+2+2
[22]*And it shall be that* 1
from the amount of milk produced 3+2
[a]*he will eat curds.*
For[a] *curds and honey will be the food* 4+4
of everyone left in the heart of the land.
An Oracle: [23]*And it shall be in that day:* 3
Every place which has 3+3
a thousand vines (worth) a thousand
(pieces) of silver 4
will become thorns and briers. 3
[24]*One will (only) go there with bow and arrow* 4+4
for all the land will become thorns and briers.
[25]*And all the mountains* 2+3
which should be for cultivation with a hoe,
no one will go there 3+3
(for) fear of briers and thorns.
They will become open range for cattle 3+2
and pastorage for sheep.

Notes

17.a. LXX ὁ θεός, "God." 1QIsa[a] has ו before יביא; LXX has ἀλλα ἐπάξει. These would require a translation "but YHWH will bring." MT's direct statement is to be preferred. It begins a new pericope.

17.b-b. The phrase is often thought to be a gloss, and it does seem to be tacked on. However, it cannot be eliminated without dropping vv 18–28, which depend upon it for meaning. Its abrupt appearance may well be for dramatic effect and emphasis.

18.a. יאר is a transliterated Eg. word (*jtr[w]* or *jrw*). In forty-nine of fifty-three cases in the OT it means the Nile River. The pl. refers to "the arms of the Nile" in its upper stages.

19.a. בתות is of uncertain meaning (cf. also 5:6). LXX χώρα, "country"; Vg. *vallis*, "valley." From Arab., בתת may mean "cut off." Hence the assumed meaning: "precipice."

19.b. נעצוץ, "thornbush." Löw (2:416) identifies this as *Alhagi Camelotum Fisch,* but it has also been called *Zizyphus spina Christi* or "Christ's thorn" (cf. Wildberger, 301).

19.c. נהלל is a *hap. leg.* BDB and *HAL* derive it from נהל and translate "watering place." Dalman (*AuS*, 2:323) suggests another kind of thorny bush, the *Prospis Stephanica,* which grows only three feet high as opposed to some fifteen feet for the Christ's thorn.

20.a. Lit. "the hair of the feet," a euphemism. Cf. Exod 4:25.

22.a-a. Missing in LXX.

Form/Structure/Setting

The announcement of crisis (v 17) is followed by four independent oracles of doom relating to Assyria. Each pictures the catastrophe of "that day." ביום ההוא, "in that day," is a fixed prophetic formula introducing an oracle concerning the coming judgment. It often is related to the Day of YHWH and is an eschatological formula. (See *Excursus: Day of YHWH/Divine Warrior* in the *Introduction* and the discussion on chap. 2.) Here the oracles are related to a historical event: the invasion of the Assyrians. That event is lifted to a new dimension by being depicted as YHWH's action against the king, his dynasty, and his people. It is *a* day of YHWH's wrath and judgment.

v 17	Announcement: The Lord will bring Assyria against Judah.
vv 18–19	First "in that day" oracle
v 20	Second "in that day" oracle
vv 21–22	Third "in that day" oracle
vv 23–25	Fourth "in that day" oracle

Comment

17 The announcement contains three important elements. First, the source of the event is YHWH. In the announcement, Ahaz is not blamed for bringing the Assyrians (as he is in 2 Kgs 16:7–9; 2 Chr 28:16–26). Rather this is portrayed as part of God's plan guaranteeing the suppression of Aram and Israel (v 7). Second, the events are significant for the young king himself (who will have to carefully balance his vassal status in order to survive), for his people (the people of Judah and Jerusalem who have suffered greatly in the Syro-Ephraimite war and must now adjust to being permanently dependent on the Assyrian), and for the Davidic dynasty (which will need to adjust its theological and liturgical base to accommodate itself to the new realities). Third, the announcement suggests that the Assyrian crisis will be more decisive and bring more change for Jerusalem/Judah than any event since Jeroboam led the civil war that divided the kingdom after Solomon's death.

This is a key verse for understanding the Vision. It calls for fifth-century Jews to recognize the Assyrian invasions of the eighth century, not the Babylonian exile of 587 B.C.E., as the watershed in God's history. (Cf. Donner's description of the Assyrians as "an empire of a completely new type, an incomparable power structure that determined the destinies of the ancient Near East for almost half a millennium" ["Separate States," *IJH*, 416].) God created that watershed. Ahaz had to learn to live with that. Jews of the fifth century also had to adjust their thinking to God's reality.

"The king of Assyria" puts a name on what had until then been a mysterious, unnamed force (cf. 5:26–30). Hosea had named Assyria in prophecies fifteen to twenty years earlier (cf. Hos 7:11; 8:9; 9:3; 10:6; 11:12) while Amos had cited Assyrian victories at Calneh, Hamath, and Gath (6:2). God's use of the Assyrian will be discussed in 10:5–16 and 24–26; assurance of an end to the Assyrians' dominance will come in 14:24–25.

18 The mention of Egypt as well as Assyria takes the meaning beyond the immediate Assyrian invasion. V 17 speaks particularly of a new and different era. V 18 defines it as one characterized by big-power conflict in which Judah will continually be involved (cf. Budde, *Jesaja's Erleben;* Fohrer). In some sense this has always been true (cf. Hos 9:3, 6; Jer 2:36), but Assyria pushes the frontier to the river of Egypt in Isaiah's lifetime and in the next century actually conquers Egypt for a short period. Many battles between the two will be fought in Palestine. Hezekiah becomes an active participant in the struggle (cf. chaps. 29–33).

The Egyptian זבוב, "fly," from the sources of the Nile may refer to the Ethiopian pharaoh Pi (730–716 B.C.E.), who founded the Twenty-Fifth Dynasty and fought a battle with Assyria on Palestinian soil about 720 or 714 B.C.E. (cf. chap. 20; *MBA*, 149). Why he is called a fly is not clear. Upper Egypt has the hieroglyphic sign of a wasp.

Apparently Assyria's mountains were famous for their bees. "Whistling" for the bees is described in about 440 C.E. by Cyrillus of Alexandria (PG, 70:209) as the means by which the beekeeper drives the bees out of their hives to the fields and brings them back again. Ovid and Homer described bee culture in detail. The picture here is of wild bees (cf. Deut 32:13; Ps 81:17 [16]; and others), which are used as a figure for war in Deut 1:44 and Ps 118:12. So the figure fits the warring Assyrian armies.

20 Shaving may mark the end of a Nazarite's vow (Num 6:5), but prisoners and slaves were also shaved. It was a mark of dishonor, a sign of being insulted and despised. The river is the Euphrates. The mercenary troops are hired by Assyria.

21–22 The verses picture a reduction in the standard of living to the minimal nourishment of a herder culture rather than the city life of commerce that Judah has known.

23–25 The verses picture a loss of horticulture. The once carefully terraced slopes of vineyards and flat fields of grain will be lost to the wild. Thorns, weeds, and briers have gained control of land once carefully and fruitfully cultivated. Now only the herders take their cattle, sheep, and goats there. War's devastation will remove all signs of culture and prosperity that once made it a "land of milk and honey."

Explanation

Having called Ahaz to turn his attention away from Aram and Ephraim, Isaiah points to Assyria. The Assyrian is coming. He is being sent by YHWH. And his coming will precipitate the greatest crisis that the people of Judah and the Davidic dynasty have experienced since the division of the kingdom two hundred years before under Rehoboam. So the Assyrian crisis is seen as a personal problem for Ahaz, a constitutional problem for Judah, and an issue of survival for the dynasty. It must be seen as a turning point in history.

The reference to Ephraim's defection in 930 B.C.E. puts the announcement in perspective. The kingdom had received God's blessing reluctantly (1 Sam 12), but it was confirmed on a new basis to David (2 Sam 7). Subsequently, Jeroboam's rebellion tore the fabric of the kingdom's unity as successor to the confederacy, and the kingdoms had been living on borrowed time ever since. They had failed to be reunited, and now God was moving to terminate an era and the form of his people's existence as independent political units. The Assyrian is the means used to bring about this change. This theme will control the book's message from chap. 7 through chap. 33.

As Isaiah speaks, Judah has already been devastated by the raids of Rezin and Pekah. Now he announces that Assyria will come and its presence will postpone restoration of the land for a long time. Assyria's presence will be ubiquitous and pervasive (vv 18–19). It will strip the land (v 20). It will reduce the standard of living to a survival limit (vv 21–22). And it will cause the land to lie fallow, uncultivated, and barren (vv 23–25).

The chapter has called attention away from the petty internecine quarrels and battles among the little states of the ancient Near East that had dominated virtually all of Israel's history from its separation from Judah to this time. A new reality was emerging on a much larger scale. The history of the people of Israel would be dominated from this point on by the great empires. These were genuinely unusual "days": a watershed in history.

The prophetic announcement stresses that this is God's doing. The king and the people are urged to look for God's intention and direction in the troubled times to come. Ahaz, whatever his faults, by his more passive acceptance of his vassal status under Assyria, fit this pattern. Hezekiah in his zeal to put things right for God through reform and rebellion was doomed from the beginning. He was blind to the signals from heaven that the Lord was not in it.

Isaiah presents a different evaluation of Judah's kings than do the books of Kings and Chronicles, who value independence and cultic fidelity above all else. The Vision of Isaiah is much closer to wisdom's verdict: "there is a time for everything . . . a time to plant and a time to uproot" (Eccl 3:1–2 NIV). It suggests a divine historical chronology: a time to rise up and a time to remain still, a time to repent, a time to reform, and a time to be quiet and listen to the challenge of God. It suggests that God's will for his people cannot be achieved by simply "going by the book," not by imitating Joshua or David, or Solomon or Jehoshaphat. One must look and listen, know and understand, to catch the change of signals from God.

The program that called for God's people in his land (even in its adapted monarchical form) had failed by the middle of the eighth century. What remained was to clean up the details and launch a new program. Hezekiah, Josiah, and all who like them insisted on "playing David and Joshua" simply got in the way and hindered God's reform. The Vision suggests that God proposed to use the empires in the revised program: first, Assyria in demolishing the old; then Persia (Cyrus) in building the new.

The Vision sees a continuing but different role for "Israel/Jacob" as God's servant in the new age. But Israel feels she is too old to change jobs and change roles. She feels it is unfair for God to expect her to fit into a new plan of organization. He ought to adapt his plan to her old role. The Vision also sees a central role for Zion, but also a vastly different one. No longer a symbol of rule and power, she is a place of pilgrimage, known for God's presence there. Her experience makes her a fitting "Suffering Servant" to demonstrate God's new plan. But she, too, resists having her role redefined.

Memoirs of the Prophet (8:1–9:6 [7])

There are four accounts of the Lord speaking to "me" in 8:1–9:6 (7). Budde (*Jesaja's Erleben*) thought of the unit 6:1–9:6 as a *Denkschrift*, a written reminder or memoir. Some have described the chapters as "confessions," like those in Jeremiah (K. M. O'Connor, *The Confessions of Jeremiah: Their Interpretation and Role in Chapters 1–25*, SBLDS 94 [Atlanta: Scholars Press, 1998]; G. M. Behler, *Les Confessions de Jéremie*, Bible et vie chrétienne [Tournai: Casterman, 1959]; S. Blank, "The Confessions of Jeremiah and the Meaning of Prayer," *HUCA* 21

[1948] 331–54; N. Ittmann, *Die Konfessionwen Jeremias: Ihre Bedeutung für die Verkündigung des Propheten*, WMANT 54 [Neukirchen-Vluyn: Neukirchener Verlag, 1981]). Like Jeremiah, this prophet is torn between confilicting messages: one to assure the king and people of the protection and care of God (chap. 7) and the other inherent in the vision of chap. 6, the experience of 5:1–7, and the announcements in chap. 1. This inner conflict comes to a climax in chap. 8 and leads to the announcement in 8:16–18 that the prophet is withdrawing to wait for YHWH's salvation. The exhortation of 8:19–22 and the recogniton of a new heir to the throne (9:6–7) close the scene.

Swift-Plunder, Hastening-Booty (8:1–4)

Bibliography

Anderson, R. T. "Was Isaiah a Scribe?" *JBL* 79 (1960) 57–58. **Buchanan, G. W.** "The Old Testament Meaning of the Knowledge of Good and Evil." *JBL* 75 (1956) 114–20. **Gryson, R.** "Barachie et la prophetesse: Exercice de critique textuelle sur Isaïe 8,2–3." *RB* 96 (1989) 321–37. **Humbert, P.** "*Maher Shalal Hash Baz.*" *ZAW* 50 (1932) 90–92. **Jepsen, K.** "Die *Nebiah* in Jes 8,3." *ZAW* 72 (1960) 267–80. **Marin, M.** "Bibbia e filologia patristica: Note di lettura." *VetChr* 23 (1986) 73–79. **Morenz, S.** "Eilbeute." *TLZ* 74 (1949) 697–99. **Rignell, L. G.** "'Das Orakel' *Maher-salal Has-bas.*" *ST* 10 (1956) 40–52. **Roberts, J. J. M.** "Isaiah and His Children." In *Biblical and Related Studies Presented to Samuel Iwry.* Ed. by A. Kort and S. Morsehauser. Winona Lake, IN: Eisenbrauns, 1985. 193–203. **Steck, O. H.** "Beiträge zum verständnis von Jesaja 7,10–17 und 8:1–4." *TZ* 29 (1973) 161–78. **Talmage, F.** "*HRT 'NWSH* in Isaiah 8:1." *HTR* 60 (1967) 465–68. **Vogt, E.** "Einige Hebräische Wortbedeutungen." *Bib* 48 (1967) 57–74. **Williamson, H. G. M.** *Book Called Isaiah,* 96–98.

Translation

The Prophet: [1]*Then YHWH said to me, "Take for yourself a large tablet*[a] *and write on it with a* [b]*stylus of disaster*[b] *'To* [c]*Swift-Plunder, Hastening-Booty.'"*[c] [2]*So I took witnesses*[a] *for myself, faithful witnesses, Uriah the priest and Zechariah son of Jeberechiah.*[b] [3]*When I approached the prophetess, she conceived and bore a son. For YHWH said to me, "Call his name Swift-Plunder, Hastening-Booty,* [4]*for before the lad knows how to say 'my father,' 'my mother,' one will carry away the wealth of Damascus and the plunder of Samaria before the king of Assyria."*

Notes

1.a. גליון גדול. The versions all agree in rendering גדול, "large," but they vary in translating גליון: LXX τόμον καινοῦ, "new volume"; α´ διφθερωμα, "tanned hide"; σ´ τευχος, "book"; θ´ κεφαλιδα, "chapter"; Tg. לוח, "tablet"; Vg. *librum,* "book." Galling *(BRL)* uses the only other appearance of the word, in 3:23, to suggest that it means a piece of cloth, perhaps of papyrus. He thinks of a family record to support a claim to land. Wildberger has correctly rejected the suggestion. Isaiah's purpose is to gain the attention of the city, not to keep a family record. G. R. Driver in *Semitic Writing* (2d ed. [London: Oxford UP, 1954] 80, 229) suggests a large placard. In *JSS* 13 (1968) 40, he describes a wax-covered wooden board that was found in Nineveh. This would fit the description here very well. (Cf. also D. Leibel, *BMik* 15 [1963] 50–55.)

1.b-b. חֶרֶט אֱנוֹשׁ. MT points the words to mean "a man's stylus." This is a strange usage and has occasioned much discussion. It is common to translate "an ordinary stylus" and refer to similar usages in Exod 32:16, מכתב אלהים, "God's writing," or in Deut 3:11 and 2 Sam 7:14, where אמת־איש and שבט אנשים are rendered "a usual elle" and "an ordinary rod." But Wildberger notes that both of these are in contrast to God's judgment. That is not the case here. Other commentators (Procksch, Fohrer, and others) have suggested a form of writing known to the common person. Another direction suggests a different vocalization: אָנוּשׁ. H. Gressmann (*Der Messias,* FRLANT 43 [Göttingen: Vandenhoeck & Ruprecht, 1929] 239 n. 1) translates this as "a hard stylus." K. Galling ("Ein Stück judäischen Bodenrechts in Jesaja 8," *ZDPV* 56 [1933] 209–18) noted that אָנוּשׁ means "incurable" (*qal* pass. ptc. אנשׁ) and suggested it means "a writing that cannot be erased." But Wildberger comments that חרט means a "stylus," not a "writing." F. Talmage ("חרט אנוש in Isaiah 8:1," *HTR* 60 [1967] 465–68) draws on Akk. *enēšu* and Arab. *ʾanuṭa,* both of which mean "to be weak," to explain אָנוּשׁ as a broad, soft pen that should make the writing more legible. Wildberger uses the emendation in its literal meaning, "a stylus of sickness," and cites 1QM 12:3, בחרט חיים, "a stylus of life," as the linguistic opposite. The stylus that writes disaster may well be the intention of the phrase. (Cf. also D. Leibel, *BMik* 15 (1963) 50–55.)

1.c-c. Translations of the name have varied. The two verbs, מהר and חשׁ, may be understood as impvs., as pfs., or as ptcs. מהר has also been read as a foreign term for a soldier (A. Jirku, "Zu 'Eilebeute' in Jes 8:1–3," *TLZ* 75 [1950] 118; S. Morenz, *TLZ* 74 [1949] 697–99; J. Aistleitner, *WUS* §1532; A. F. Rainey, "The Military Personnel of Ugarit," *JNES* 24 [1965] 17–27; idem, "The Soldier-Scribe," *JNES* 26 [1967] 58–60; A. R. Schulmann, "*Mhr* and *Mskb,* Two Egyptian Military Titles of Semitic Origin," *ZÄS* 93 [1966] 123–32). They would translate "Soldier of Booty, Hastening to Plunder." H. Torczyner (*MGWJ* 74 [1930] 257) suggested reading both verbs as perfects and pointing מַהֵר as מִהַר. If the verbs are to be understood as ptcs., then מַהֵר is a short form of מְמַהֵר (cf. GKC §525; Zeph 1:14). E. Vogt (*Bib* 48 [1967] 57–74) notes that מהר is often used as an adv., "quick," "soon," "immediately," and suggests that the verb נשׂא in v 4 is to be understood here. The use of ptcs. is clearly the best with the translation: "Swift-Plunder, Hastening-Booty."

2.a. וְאָעִידָה seems to indicate a juss. meaning, "So let me take witnesses." LXX reads καὶ μάρτυράς μοι ποίησον, "make a witness for me" (2 sg. aor. act. impv.). Tg. has ואַסְהֵיד; Syr. has *washed lî sāhdê.* These have led many to suggest emending the word to read וְהָעִידָה—an impv. meaning "take witnesses." But Wildberger is surely right in taking the lesser emendation, וָאָעִידָה, following the Vg. reading *et adhibui,* which brings the verb into parallel with that in v 3. The verse is narrative: "And so I took witnesses."

2.b. יברכיהו "Jeberechiah." LXX reads βαραχιου, which would require ברכיהו, "Berechiah." Yet MT is to be preferred. LXX is probably comparing it with names in Zech 1:1 and 1:7.

Form/Structure/Setting

The pericope is first-person narrative of the type called prophetic autobiography. The passage is composed of two parts, vv 1–2 and vv 3–4. The first half tells of instruction received from God to write on a large board the words למהר שלל חש בז, "To 'Swift Plunder Hastening Booty.'" The second tells of the birth of a son who is given this name and of the meaning the name carries. Although the explanation is directly related to the son, it explains the entire passage and unifies it. Four narrative imperfects describe a sequence of resulting action following the imperatives of v 1. But the next verb, ויאמר, does not indicate a new step; rather it summarizes the entire sequence with a reference to the imperative beginning and is best translated "for YHWH said." (Cf. J. Wash Watts, *Survey of Syntax,* 127.)

The pericope uses the formulas of narratives of symbolic actions: cf. Hos 1:2; Ezek 4:1; 4:9; 5:1; 1 Kgs 11:31; Jer 13:4; 25:15; 36:2, 28; 43:9; Zech 11:15. The closest parallel is undoubtedly Ezek 37:16. (Cf. Hayes, *OTFC,* 172.) The outline of such a report should contain the command to perform the act, the report of its performance, and a statement of its meaning. This account reports a command to write and a statement of compliance with an expansion concerning witnesses; then it reports further actions that continue the symbolic act: the conception, birth, and naming of a son. It closes with the usual explanation.

Steck (*TZ* 29 [1973] 161–78) recognizes vv 8:6–8*a* as an illustration of "the hardening" of the people and their judgment in 6:9–10. Blenkinsopp (138–39) compares the structure of 7:10–17 and 8:1–4. He finds them to be two "sign-acts," the first addressed to the dynasty, the second to the Judean public. The two "represent different aspects of the divine intervention in human affairs at that critical juncture." Steck's interpretation is the more cogent.

Comment

1 It is unusual to tell of prophets "writing." It is likely that this activity was the exclusive prerogative and skill of scribes. Jeremiah uses an emanuensis in Baruch. But, of all the prophets, Isaiah is the one most likely to have known how to write (R. T. Anderson, *JBL* 79 [1960] 57–58). The exact meaning of גליון, "tablet," remains uncertain (cf. *Note* 1.a.). Such tablets may have been shaped of wood, clay, or leather. Ezekiel speaks of עץ (37:16) in a similar situation, but he seems to mean a carved stick rather than a tablet (cf. W. Zimmerli, *Ezekiel,* trans. R. E. Clements, Hermeneia [Philadelphia: Fortress, 1979]). But in 4:1, Ezekiel scratches letters on a tile. It is also unclear where the tablet was to be shown or on what occasion. Wildberger has noted that Hab 2:2 records a century later in Jerusalem the practice of displaying prophecies in easily read letters.

The name is preceded by ל, like that on seals that indicate the owner. But this does not quite fit here. GKC §119*u* speaks of a meaning like "in relation to" or "of" in the sense of "concerning." This is more likely. (Cf. S. Moscati, *L'epigrafia Ebraica Antica* [Rome: Pontifical Biblical Institute, 1951] 85–89 for a discussion of ל.) The name Maher-shalal-hash-baz is not a usual name in the OT or the ancient Near East. M. Noth (*Personennamen,* 9) speaks of it as a product of literary creativity. Yet P. Humbert (*ZAW* 50 [1932] 90–92) and S. Morenz (*TLZ* 74 [1949] 697–99) have noted an Egyptian name, *ʾis ḥʾḳ,* which appears in the documents of the Eighteenth Dynasty. The name is, grammatically, composed of two imperatives: "Hurry! Plunder!" The Egyptian military usage may well have been known in Jerusalem in that time (cf. H. Wildberger, "Die Thronnamen des Messias," *TZ* 16 [1960] 314–32). The applied meaning, however, comes from contemporary history. שלל, "plunder," and בזז, "booty," occur as a word pair also in Deut 2:35; 3:7; 20:14; Isa 10:6; Ezek 29:19; 38:12–13. The second pair, מהר, "swift," and חוש, "hastening," are also parallel forms. The repetition enhances both the certainty and the nearness of the events.

2 The reason for witnesses undoubtedly lay in confirming the date of the prophecy. Months, even years, would pass before its completion. The political situation would have changed drastically. The written words and the sworn witnesses alone could confirm the prophecy and when it had been prophesied.

The practice of taking witnesses is regulated by law (Deut 17:6; 19:15), which requires two. They are called "faithful witnesses" here because it was important that they be trusted by the public as well as by Isaiah. Wildberger comments that the men's names fit Isaiah's times and demonstrate how well the leaders of his day represent the piety of the Psalms. Both men's names include "YHWH." Uriah probably means "YHWH is light" (cf. Isa 10:17 and Ps 27:1; M. Noth, *Personennamen,* 168). Zechariah means "YHWH has remembered" (cf. Ps 74:2, 18; Lam 3:19; 5:1). Jeberekiah means "May YHWH bless" (cf. Pss 67:6–7; 115:12–15). 2 Kgs 16:10–16 tells of a priest named Uriah who, at the command of King Ahaz, had a new altar built in the temple. He was apparently the chief priest. If Zechariah is the man mentioned in 2 Kgs 18:2//2 Chr 29:1 as the father-in-law of King Ahaz and grandfather of Hezekiah, the witnesses are drawn from the highest levels of Jerusalem's leadership.

3 After the sign was written, Isaiah approached his wife. Although YHWH's specific instructions applied only to the message to be written on the board, the narrative's structure leads the reader to understand that the entire process followed God's instructions and served his purpose. קרב, "draw near," is used often to describe sexual relations (Gen 20:4; Lev 18:6, 14, 19; 20:16; Deut 22:14; Ezek 18:6). There is no need to translate the verb as a pluperfect as Duhm, Marti, Rignell ("Isaiah Chapter 1," *ST* 2 [1957] 140–58), and Kaiser do: "and I had approached." Isaiah must have known the meaning of the name from the beginning (contra T. Vriezen, "Prophecy and Eschatology," in *Congress Volume: Copenhagen,* VTSup 1 [Leiden: Brill, 1953] 209 n. 2), and he must have understood the name on the board to be that for the son yet to come (so also Vogt, *Bib* 48 (1967) 57–74; Wildberger). The people knew Isaiah's stand on current policy. They would also have understood the general direction indicated by the announcement on the board even before the birth occasioned repetition and emphasis of it.

הנביאה, "the prophetess," is used of Miriam (Exod 15:20), Deborah (Judg 4:4), Huldah (2 Kgs 22:14; 2 Chr 34:22), and Noadiah (Neh 6:14). But only here does it refer to a prophet's wife. Though there is no record that she was an active prophet in her own right, Wildberger is right (contra Duhm and Procksch) that the title does not simply mean "a prophet's wife." Rather it is understood that she, like Hulda (2 Kgs 22:14), served as a prophet in the temple and also participated in the sign by birthing a son (cf. the discussion and literature in Wildberger, 318; A. Jepsen, *ZAW* 72 [1960] 267–80; E. Vogt, *Bib* 48 [1967] 57–74; Z. Falk, *BMik* 14 [1969] 28–36). The entire episode and its narration confirm Isaiah's message.

4 The statement of the reason for the strange and meaningful name begins with the same words as in 7:16, כי בטרם ידע הנער, "for before the lad shall know." But the specific ability is different: "to say 'my father,' 'my mother.'" A child can do this at a younger age than one could expect him to turn away from evil and do good.

The implication of the inscription is that booty is to be taken from Damascus and Samaria. The plunderer is the king of Assyria. לפני מלך אשור, "before the king of Assyria," pictures a parade of triumph before the king's throne (cf. *ANET,* 274; *ANEP,* vol. 1, fig. 100*a–b*). The prediction was fulfilled. In 733 B.C.E. Tiglath-Pileser III of Assyria invaded Israel (*MBA,* 147). He reported, "Bit-Ḥumria [= Israel] with all its inhabitants and its goods, I led to Assyria. They overthrew their king Paqaha [= Pekah], and I crowned Ausi [= Hoshea] king over them" (*ANET,* 284). Israel's territories were made Assyrian provinces (cf. *MBA,* 148; 2 Kgs 15:29; Isa 9:1) except for a very small area in the highlands of Ephraim. In 732 B.C.E. Tiglath-Pileser III of Assyria conquered Damascus. That event brought to a close a two-hundred-year period in which the Aramaean kingdom played a leading role.

Explanation

Chap. 7 has brought the shocking announcement (early in 734 B.C.E.) that God is bringing the Assyrian army against the land and that his coming will bring very hard times. The prediction put this at some time into the future. In the meantime, Judah's patience wears thin as Aram and Israel press their attacks through that year and into the next.

The opening episode in chap. 8 speaks to that issue. God through Isaiah promises a speedy military action. The first public showing with the witnesses may well have followed the meeting with Ahaz (chap. 7) by only by a few weeks (i.e., early in 734 B.C.E.). The birth of the child and the full explanation came late in that year, emphasizing that military relief was hastening to lift the siege. The Assyrian campaign against Israel came in 733 B.C.E. (i.e., within two years). This timing fits the prediction exactly. Assyria's campaigns have indeed made "swift plunder and hastening booty" against Judah's foes.

This episode follows the announcement in 7:2 of the alliance between Aram and Israel. Isaiah (and apparently Ahaz) is still convinced that Assyria is the major issue for Judah to face. This episode is set between the time of that announcement (ca. 735–34 B.C.E.) and Assyria's invasion of Israel (733 B.C.E.), which it anticipates. It narrates events covering the better part of a year. Isaiah speaks after the birth of his son, recounting his earlier prophecy before the child was conceived, reiterating and explaining the message that retribution on Judah's neighbors is imminent.

The time between the writing and the birth has been critical for Judah. Rezin and Pekah have invaded Judah (*MBA,* 144). Rezin's forces drove down the east bank of Jordan freeing the Edomites from Judean dominance and continuing as far south as Elath (2 Kgs 16:6//2 Chr 28:17). Another force, joined by Pekah's army, surrounded Jerusalem, wreaking havoc on the countryside (2 Kgs 16:5). The freed Edomites attacked the southern cities (2 Kgs 16:6*b*/2 Chr 28:17), and the Philistines used the occasion to raid border towns (2 Chr 28:18). 2 Kings and 2 Chronicles record a plea from Ahaz to Tiglath-Pileser for help. Both of them pass judgment on Ahaz for unfaithfulness to YHWH (2 Kgs 16:3–4, 5–10; 2 Chr 28:1–4, 22–26) for calling for Assyrian help as well as for allowing cultic changes in the temple and pagan practices. It is important to note that the Vision of Isaiah takes a very different stance in this section (chaps. 7–13).

While Kings and Chronicles view Judah's weakness as a result of the unfaithfulness of kings like Ahaz and Manasseh, Isaiah sees a turning point in God's intention for Judah in Uzziah's time, which makes Ahaz's policies more compatible with God's will than were those of Hezekiah. The times (and God's will for his people in them) demanded an acceptance of the Assyrians as God's chosen rulers. Ahaz, for all his religious infidelity to Yahwistic traditions, fits that time.

Hezekiah, with his burning religious and political zeal, did not. That is the point of the Vision with its implied message for fifth-century Jews: Persia's hegemony is YHWH's will. Accept it! Live with it! Find the will of God for you within it.

This pericope (8:1–4) is an example of Isaiah's ministry in supporting Ahaz's policy of not squandering his dwindling military force to counteract armies that are about to be annihilated anyway. It is a difficult time for Judah. But the prophet calls upon her and her king to recognize the "signs of the times," to see God's great scheme, and to make their decisions and policies in light of it. The punitive action against the neighboring outlaws, Aram and Israel, is imminent. So says the Lord through Isaiah's sign. Hang on!

Waters of Shiloah Refused (8:5–10)

Bibliography

Auret, A. "Another look at *wmshwsh* in Isaiah 8:6." *OTE* 3 (1990) 107–14. **Boehmer, J.** "Dieses Volk." *JBL* 45 (1926) 134–48. **Budde, K.** "Zu Jesaja 8:19–10." *JBL* 49 (1930) 423–28. **Driver, G. R.** "Isa I–XXXIX: Textual and Linguistice Problems." *JSS* 13 (1968) 36–57. **Fullerton, K.** "The Interpretation of Isaiah 8:5–10." *JBL* 43 (1924) 253–89. **Honeyman, A. M.** "Traces of an Early Diakritic Sign in Isa 8:6*b*." *JBL* 63 (1944) 45–50. **Klein, H.** "Freude an Rezin." *VT* 30 (1980) 229–34. **Loretz, O.** "Eine assyhrische Parallele zum Topos 'Adlerflügel' in Jes 8,8b: Philologische und kolometrische Anmerkungen zu Jes 8,5–10." *UF* 29 (1997) 465–87. **Lutz, H. M.** *Jahwe, Jerusalem, und die Völker.* WMANT 27 Neukirchen-Vluyn: Neukirchener Verlag, 1968. 40–47. **May, H. G.** "Some Cosmic Connotations of Imayim Rabbim." *JBL* 74 (1954) 9–29. **Rehm, M.** *Der königliche Messias im Lichte der Immanuel-weissagung des Buches Jesaja.* Eichstädter Studien 1. Kevelaer: Butzon & Bereker, 1968. **Saebø, M.** "Zur Traditionsgeschichte von Jesaja 8:9–10." *ZAW* 76 (1964) 132–44. **Schmidt, H.** "Jesaja 8:9–10." In *Stromata.* Festgabe des Akademisch-Theologischen Vereins Zu Giessen. Trans. G. Bertran. Leipzig, 1930. 3–10. **Schroeder, O.** "ומשוש eine Glosse zu רצון." *ZAW* 32 (1912) 301–02. **Sweeney, M. A.** "On *ûmeshôsh* in Isaiah 8.6." In *Among the Prophets: Language, Image and Structure in the Prophetic Writings.* Ed. D. J. A. Clines and P. R. Davies. JSOTSup 144. Sheffield: JSOT Press, 1993. 42–54. **Wolverton, W. I.** "Judgment in Advent: Isaiah 8:5–15." *AThR* 37 (1955) 284–91. **Wong, G. C. I.** "Is 'God with Us' in Isaiah viii 8?" *VT* 49 (1999) 426–32.

Translation

Isaiah: 5 *Then YHWH spoke to me yet again:* 6 *"Because this people has refused the waters of Shiloah which flow gently—a joy* [a] *to Rezin and Remaliah's son—*7 *therefore behold my Lord (is) bringing up over them*

the waters of the river 3+2
strong and many,
the king of Assyria 2+2
and all his glory.

And it shall rise over all its channels, 3+3+2
and it shall go over all its banks.
[8]*And it shall fly into Judah.*
It shall overflow and pass by; 2+2
unto the neck it will reach.[a]
And there shall be a stretching of its wings, 3+3
filling the breadth of your[b] *land."*
Chorus: *God, be with us! (Immanuel)* 2
[9]*Make an uproar, you peoples, and be broken,* 3+4
and give ear all you lands afar!
Gird yourselves and be broken! 2+2
Gird yourselves and be broken!
[10]*Counsel counsel! Nothing will come of it!* 2+1
Speak a word! It will not stand! 2+2
For God is with us (Immanuel). 3

Notes

6.a. ומשׂוֹשׂ את־רצין, "and a joy to Rezin," is a syntactically awkward phrase. F. Hitzig and F. Giesebrecht (*Die Berufsbegabung der Alttestamentlichen Propheten* [Göttingen: Vandenhoeck & Ruprecht, 1897]) suggested omitting את־רצין ובן־רמליהו, "to Rezin and Remaliah's son," and changing משׂוֹשׂ to מסוֹס (cf. 10:18), meaning "the gently flowing and running water." But Wildberger (321) has correctly called this impossible because the water of Shiloah is a picture of YHWH's protection for Jerusalem, an image that cannot be described as running away. The suggestions to omit רצין, "Rezin" (Schroeder, *ZAW* 32 [1912] 301–2), or to amend משׂוֹשׂ to משׁה, "pull out (of the water)" (Honeyman, *JBL* 63 [1944] 45–50) must also be rejected. Wildberger would change it to הָסוֹס and אֶת to לפני to mean "but melts before the pride of Rezin." With all this, it seems better to work with the received text, awkward as it is. But the vowel pointing must be מָשׂוֹשׂ—an abs. before the prep.

8.a. LXX appears to have another text: καὶ ἀφελεῖ ἀπὸ τῆς 'Ιουδαίας ἄνθρωπον ὅς δυνήσεται κεφαλήν ἆραι ἤ δυνατόν συντέλεσασθαί τι, "and he will cut off from Judah a man who will be able to raise a head or complete something mighty." Other versions follow MT.

8.b. The 2d person seems strange and appears to make the passage address Immanuel. In spite of this unclear address, it should be kept. However, עמנו אל, "God with us/Immanuel," should be read with the following line. See *Form/Structure/Setting*.

Form/Structure/Setting

The prophet relates an oracle received from YHWH in vv 5–8. The first lines (vv 5, 6, 7*a*) are prose. The rest of the oracle is preserved in tight parallel lines of poetry. The prophet is the speaker throughout vv 5–8*b* as he relates what God has said to him in indirect quotation.

The speech is a threat. V 6 gives the reason. V 7*ab* announces the act of God. Vv 7*c*–8*b* interpret the results of God's action. V 8*c* adds a comment that changes the metaphor and is only loosely related to the preceding lines. The last stich of v 8 belongs with the following lines. Its first person plural indicates the beginning of the choral speech that continues through v 10. It opens and closes with עמנו אל *Immanuel,* "God (is) with us." The passage fits the genre of the "challenge to battle" (Saebø, *ZAW* 76 [1964] 132–44; R. Bach, *Die Aufforderung zur Flucht und zum Kampf im alttestamentlichen Prophetenspruch,* WMANT 9 [Neukirchen-Vluyn: Neukirchener Verlag, 1962]). Parallel forms are found in Jer 46:3–6, 9 and Joel 3:9–12. Overtones of the belief that Jerusalem will be kept unharmed may be noted like those in Pss 46, 47, 76 (cf. Kaiser). *Immanuel* has a parallel in Ps 46:8, 12: עמנו יהוה צבאות, "YHWH of Hosts (is) with us." Here elements of holy war thought are mixed with those of Davidic kingship and Zion's sanctity (cf. Wildberger).

Comment

6 העם הזה, "this people," continues to echo the covenant identification (cf. 1:3*b*) of the people without understanding who are destined to destruction and exile (6:9, 10). The earlier passages speak of the whole people, but particularly the claims of the northern kingdom to represent them all. Note that it refers directly to the kingdom of Israel (contra Young). הַשִּׁלֹחַ, "Shiloah," is a noun from the common root שלח, "to send"; cf. Akkad. *šalḫu,* "watering pipe," and *šiliḫtu,* "water course." The verb in *pi'el* means to "send water" (Ps 104:10; Ezek 31:4). A parallel word is הַשֶּׁלַח (Neh 3:15), which means an aqueduct or conduit for water. מֵי הַשִּׁלֹחַ occurs only here in the OT. It is unlikely that the reference is to the tunnel of Shiloah, first built by Hezekiah (2 Kgs 20:20; 2 Chr 32:30). The "waters of the Shiloah" are those diverted from the spring of Sihon southward from the east of the city (M. Burrows, *ZAW* 70 [1958] 226). The waters of the aqueduct flow softly and gently. Isaiah uses the "waters of the Shiloah which flow gently" to characterize the policy of Ahaz (cf. 7:1–9), who accepts the necessity of loyalty to Assyria as being in the will of God for that time. The spirit of rebellion has no time for the slow processes to work but demands action now.

משׂושׂ, "a joy," to Rezin. Israel's willingness to participate in Rezin's uprising was undoubtedly a "joy" to him and his puppet ruler in Samaria. The verse has occasioned comment (see *Note* 6.a.). This interpretation tries to deal with the received MT text.

7 מי הנהר, "the waters of the river," contrasts with "the waters of Shiloah." The simple metaphors relate irrigation ditches with rushing river water. But "the river" inevitably also implies the Euphrates and the nations beyond. This contrasts with the policy of Jerusalem's "waters of Shiloah," which have counseled quiet acceptance of Assyria's sovereignty. Rebellion and refusal to pay taxes will bring the floodwaters of the king of Assyria. כבוד, "glory," is a synonym for "might" or "power."

8 עמנו אל *Immanuel* is the name of the child who is a sign (7:14). It means simply "God—with us." It may imply an indicative "God is with us," like the name of the child or the clause in 8:10*c.* Or it may be an imperative, "God be with us," as here in misguided confidence on the part of a chorus of Jerusalemites voicing their belief that God will not allow Jerusalem's destruction.

9–10 The conviction of these verses is that events follow the determined will of God. He has promised that Jerusalem will survive. No effort of the enemy—even the swirling waters of the Assyrian—can change that. Judah's villages may suffer, but God's city will survive. This confidence, while accurate in the short run, proved in the long run to have fundamentally misunderstood God's plan for Jerusalem, as the Vision of Isaiah will show.

Explanation

The second word spoken "to me" speaks of "this people." In the book of Isaiah YHWH expresses his love and compassion to "my people." When he uses the abrupt impersonal "this people," it indicates his distance from them, his impatience toward them.

The reason for his displeasure is clear. They have "refused the waters of Shiloah which flow gently," a way of peace and acceptance. Instead, they have chosen a policy that pleases the king of Aram and Pekah, whose name the writer cannot bear to pronounce. He calls him "Remaliah's son," as he had in 7:5. They have promoted a policy of active rebellion against Assyria, a rebellion that they wanted Ahaz to join (7:1–2). Because of this rebellion against Assyria and against YHWH's will for them, YHWH is bringing an Assyrian invasion that will flood the land, including Judah.

The people respond with a chant on the name *Immanuel*, the name given by the prophet in 7:14. They do not believe it can happen to them for, after all, "God is with us." They have taken the promise to Ahaz to mean that Zion is invulnerable. It cannot be touched. God will not let it or them be harmed. They ignore the word "Swift-Plunder, Hastening-Booty" (8:1–4).

YHWH Is Your Fear (8:11–15)

Bibliography

Driver, G. R. "Two Misunderstood Passages of the Old Testament." *JTS* 6 (1955) 82–84. **Evans, C. A.** "An Interpretation of Isa 8,11–15 Unemended." *ZAW* 97 (1985) 112–13. **Ford, J. M.** "Jewel of Discernment: A Study of Stone Symbolism." *BZ* 11 (1967) 109–16. **Häusserman, F.** *Wortempfang und Symbol in der alttestamentlichen Prophetie.* BZAW 58. Giessen: Töpelmann, 1932. **Jones, B. C.** "Isaiah 8:11 and Isaiah's Vision of Yahweh." In *History and Interpretation.* FS J. H. Hayes, ed. M. P. Graham et al. JSOTSup 173. Sheffield: Sheffield Academic Press, 1993. 145–57. **Lindblom, J.** *A Study on the Immanuel Section in Isaiah* (Is 7:1–9:6). Studien utgiv, au. Kungl. Humanistika Vetenskapssamfunde i Lund 4. Lund: Gleerup, 1957–58. **Lohfink, N.** "Isaiah 8:12–14." *BZ* 7 (1963) 98–104. **Rignell, L. G.** "Das Orakel 'Maher-salal Hasbas.'" *ST* 10 (1956) 40–52. **Stahlin, G.** *Skandalon.* BFCT 2d ser., vol. 24. Gütersloh: Bertelsmann, 1930. 24. **Terrien, S.** "The Metaphor of the Rock in Biblical Theology." In *God in the Fray.* FS W. Brueggemann, ed. T. Linafelt and T. K. Beal. Minneapolis: Fortress, 1998. 157–71. **Wolverton, W. I.** "Judgment in Advent." *AThR* 37 (1955) 284–91.

Translation

Prophet: 11*For thus YHWH said to me, as*[a] *though someone took* [b]*(me) by the hand so that he might turn me away*[c] *from walking in the way of this people.*

YHWH: 12*Do [pl.] not call "a conspiracy"*[a] *everything that this people calls "a conspiracy." What it fears, you need not fear nor*[b] *dread.*

Prophet: 13*You may call YHWH of Hosts* 2+2
"a conspirator"![a]

He is your [pl.] fear! 2+2
He is your (pl) dread![b]
14 *He shall become a conspiracy*[a] 2+2
and a stone of stumbling;
a rock of offense 2+3
for the two houses of Israel;[b]
a trap and a snare 2+2
for the inhabitant[c] *of Jerusalem.*
15 [a]*Many shall be offended*[a] *because of them* 3+2+2
and shall fall and be broken
and shall be snared and taken captive.

Notes

11.a. *BHK*[3] reads בחזקת, "in . . ." *BHS* reads with L, C, 1QIsa[a], and other MSS כחזקת, "as . . ."

11.b. חזקת, "take," is an inf. const. here. Cf. Bauer-Leander §43*g*.

11.c. MT points וְיִסְּרֵנִי, as impf. from יסר, "to teach." But this does not fit the context. Gesenius (1:132 n. 2) suggested reading it as וַיְסִרֵנִי from סור, "to turn away." This is supported by σ´ και απεστησε με, Syr. *nasṭeni*, and 1QIsa[a] ויסירני, and is to be preferred.

12.a. Although the introduction implies a word for the prophet alone, the oracle is in the 2d person pl. It is obviously addressed to a group. The words of v 12 are repeated in v 13, with one variation: קשר, "conspiracy," in v 12 parallels תקדישר, "you call holy," in v 13. Wildberger is right in holding that both should be קשר and that one of these has been changed. The translation of this word is debated. The root means to "tie in a knot." LXX translates here with σκληρόν, "stubborn." G. R. Driver (*JTS* 6 [1955] 82) translates as "knotty affair," "difficulty." Lindblom (*Study on the Immanuel Section*) and Kaiser follow suit. Wildberger, however, correctly notes that the noun קשר in other places in the OT regularly means "conspiracy."

12.b. Tg. makes the line a complete parallel as if MT read: . . . ואת־מערצו לא, "and what it dreads, you need not dread" (cf. *BHS*). But this is not necessary. Heb. parallelism is seldom complete.

13.a. For the change of תקדישר to תקשירו, cf. *Note* 12.a.

13.b. MT has a ptc. A change of one vowel makes מַעֲרְצְכֶם, "dread," a noun parallel to מוראכם, "fear," as Duhm and Buhl suggested. Cf. also α´ θροησις; σ´ θ´ κραταιωμα; Vg. *terror vester*.

14.a. מקדש, "considered holy," continues the problem of תקדישו in v 13. It is not a good parallel to אבן נגף, "stone of stumbling," and צור מכשול, "rock of offense." Wolverton (*ATR* 37 [1955] 288) translates "taboo-place." LXX translates ἁγίασμα, "holy place," but puts a negative before the following parallels. Tg. has פורען, "recompense." Others omit or have מוקש, "snare." Driver (*JTS* 6 [1955] 83) suggests that מקשיר be translated "cause of difficulty." Wildberger (335) is preferable, reading מקשר, "conspiracy."

14.b. LXX reads ὁ δε οἶκος Ἰακώβ, "the house of Jacob," for לשני בתי ישראל, "for the two houses of Israel." It is unusual for MT to speak of "two houses of Israel," especially parallel to יושב ירושלם, "inhabitant of Jerusalem." But there is no compelling reason to change it.

14.c. Many MSS as well as LXX OL σ´ read a pl. יושבי, "inhabitants," for MT's sg. יושב.

15.a-a. Many commentators (including Duhm and Leslie) suggest omitting the beginning of v 15. But Wildberger correctly sees that כשל, "offend," is necessary to pick up the מכשול, "offense," of v 14.

Form/Structure/Setting

The passage is addressed to a group of intimates. Perhaps these are the "disciples" mentioned in the next pericope. They are cautioned against the general panic of "the times." "This people" is often identified as those of Jerusalem. But in chap. 9 it is used of Israel, and the occurrences in 8:6 can also best be understood of Israel. Here, too, it must describe Israel's attitude toward Assyrian sovereignty and Judah's reluctance to join in the rebellion. So YHWH instructs the prophet and his group concerning their position in that troubled time.

The pericope is marked in the beginning by the particle כי, "for," which connects it to the last verse of the chorus. The end in v 15 closes the discussion of choices and turns to other matters. The passage is introduced by a prophetic first-person narrative in prose (v 11). It reports a warning oracle from YHWH (v 12) and continues with an expansion of the oracle by the prophet in the form of a commentary. Note the wordplay in vv 12–15:

vv 12–14: קשר *qasher,* "conspiracy" (2x); תקשיר *tiqshir,* "call a conspirator"; and מקשיר *maqshir,* "a conspiracy"
v 12: תיראו *tir'u,* "you fear," and מוראו *mora'o,* "it fears"
v 12–13: תעריצו *ta'aritsu,* "you shall (not) dread," and מערצכם *ma'aritskem,* "your dread"
vv 14–15: מכשול *mikshol,* "offense," and כשלו *kashlu,* "be offended"
vv 14–15: מוקש *moqesh,* "a snare," and נוקשו *noqshu,* "be snared"

Also note the numerous alliterations:

מורא *mora',* "fear"; מוקש *moqesh,* "a snare"; and נוקשו *noqshu,* "be snared"
מערץ *ma'arits,* "dread"; מקשיר *maqshir,* "conspiracy"; מכשול *mikshol,* "offense"; and מוקש *moqesh,* "a snare"
ונפלו ונשברו ונוקשו ונלכדו *wenaflu wenishbaru wenoqshu wenilkadu,* "and shall fall and be broken and shall be snared and taken captive"

Comment

11 כי כה אמר יהוה, "for thus Yahweh said to me." V 11 introduces a "hard saying" and thus needs the legitimizing formula.The usual prophetic formula to report a word from God is expanded with a note about the manner and intention of the word (cf. Ezek 1:3*d* and 8:1*d*). העם הזה, "this people," resumes the reference of v 6 and must refer to the kingdom of Israel. דרך העם הזה, "the way of this people," refers to their determination to join in rebellion against Assyria. Isaiah is being taught that YHWH has brought the Assyrian to power. To oppose Assyria at this stage is to oppose God.

12 קשר, "conspiracy," is a word of ambiguous intent here. The verse calls for critical and independent thinking from the prophet and the people of Jerusalem. This is an emotional epithet being used to urge Jerusalem to back Israel and Aram in their rebellion. Policy that is born of panic is not sound. Israel's fear of Aram or of Assyria need not be the motive for Jerusalem's decisions.

13 The focus of Jerusalem's attention should be on YHWH—not on the "scare propaganda" of Israel. תקשירו, "a conspirator" (see *Notes* 12.a. and 13.a.), is a reminder that YHWH—not the Assyrian—is the activator of history.

14 The idea of מקשר, "conspiracy," is developed in this verse. The events of those dark decades are incomprehensible to Israelites or Jerusalemites. No easy theological clichés will explain them. The parallel terms "stone of stumbling" and "rock of offense," "trap" and "snare" develop the implicit idea of conspiracy.

Explanation

This third word "to me" also relates to "this people," but it defines that relation more precisely: "as though someone took (me) by the hand so that he might turn me away from walking in the way of this people." This word resembles chap.

6. Like the others, this word is not one to be passed on to "this people." Instead it helps the author and the reader recognize the tension between YHWH and "the way of this people." The author is warned not to use the language of this people when talking about God (his conspiracy). He need not fear what they fear. But he is allowed to call YHWH of Hosts "a conspirator." Chap. 6 has already alerted him to the "conspiracy." There is a conspiracy here all right, but it is not the one that the people think of when they use the word.

The prophet is warned to fear God alone. He, not the people or the enemy, is the one to be feared. YHWH himself is the "stone of stumbling" for both houses of Israel. They both have a problem with him, not with each other. They cannot accept him and his ways, his plans for them. Thus he is "a trap and a snare" that they cannot elude. And this involves every inhabitant of Jerusalem. The reader is reminded of the basic problem in the book explained in 1:19–20 and 27–28. Because of this "many shall be offended . . . , shall fall and be broken and shall be snared and taken captive." The bright promise of chap. 7 is put aside for a darker figure.

This warning, which shows just how confusing the times were for believer and prophet alike, picks up the theme of 6:9–13. It was a natural reaction for Judah and Israel to stand together against the foreign invader. It would have been natural for the Davidic heir from Zion to lead the allies in the name of YHWH as his grandfather had done. It would have been natural for YHWH to defend "his land" against attack as in the time of the Judges. But the entire Vision of Isaiah has stressed that these were not usual times. YHWH was doing something different. The people are called to look to him and wait for his word. He, in judgment, had already decided to turn Israel over to its enemies to be destroyed (1:1–7) and to have Judah "purged" with only Jerusalem surviving (1:8–2:4). YHWH himself had called the Assyrian to do these things (7:17–8:8). All this was difficult to comprehend or to accept. But to resist it was futile.

Sealing the Prophet's Testimony (8:16–18)

Bibliography

Boehmer, J. B. "'Jahwes Lehrlinge' im Buch Jesaja." *AR* 33 (1936) 171–75. **Driver, G. R.** "Hebrew Notes on Prophets and Proverbs." *JTS* 41 (1940) 162–75. ———. "Isaianic Problems." In *Festschrift für Wilhelm Eilers.* Ed. G. Wiessner. Wiesbaden: Harrassowitz, 1967. 43–57. **Ginsburg, H. L.** "An Unrecognized Allusion to Kings Pekah and Hoshea of Israel." *ErIsr* 5 (1958) 61–65. **Guillaume, A.** "Paronomasia in the Old Testament." *JSS* 9 (1964) 282–90. **Hardmeier, C.** "Verkündigung und Schrift bei Jesaja: Zur Entstehung der Schriftptophetie als Oppositionsliteratur im alten Israel." *TGl* 73 (1983) 119–54. **Lindblom, J.** *A Study on the Immanuel Section in Isaiah* (Is 7:1–9:6). Studien utgiv, au. Kungl. Humanistika Vetenskapssamfunde i Lund 4. Lund: Gleerup, 1957–58. **Rost, L.** "Gruppenbildungen im Alten Testament." *TLZ* 80 (1955) 1–8. **Skehan, P. W.** "Some Textual Problems in Isaiah." *CBQ* 22 (1960) 47–55. **Van Wieringen, A. L. H. M.** "Het Volk dat in het donker wandelt." *Heraut* 124 (1993) 331–34. **Whitley, C. F.** "The Language of Exegesis of Isaiah 8:16–23." *ZAW* 90 (1978) 28–43.

Translation

Prophet: [16]*Binding*[a] *of testimony*[b]*—sealing of instruction with my disciples*[c] *(will be there);* [17]*and I will wait for YHWH, who is hiding his face from the house of Jacob, and I will hope for him.* [18]*Behold, I and the children that YHWH has given to me (became) signs and symbols in Israel from YHWH of Hosts who dwells in Mount Zion.*

Notes

16.a. צור, "binding," may be impv. or inf. abs. Its counterpart, חתום, "sealing," is pointed as an impv. sg. If both verbs are understood as impv., the speaker must be YHWH and the למדים are his disciples (as Boehmer, *AR* 33 [1936] 171–75, suggests). V 17 then introduces a new speaker. Following Wildberger (342) and J. Wash Watts (*A Distinctive Translation of Genesis* [Grand Rapids, MI: Eerdmans,1963] 19), the reading as an inf. abs. is preferred (with the pointing change [cf. *BHK*]). Thus the speaker is the prophet throughout vv 16–18.

16.b. תעודה "testimony." Ginsburg's emendation (*ErIsr* 5 [1958] 62), based on the old Aram. *ʿddw*, "soothsayer," is unnecessary. LXX has a totally different understanding of the line.

16.c. LXX renders בלמדי, "with my disciples," as τοῦ μὴ μαθεῖν (מִלְּמֹד), "of those who do not learn." Syr. connects it to the following sentence. Tur-Sinai ("A Contribution to the Understanding of Isaiah I–XII," 175) emends to למדיה, "her strings," following למדים in the Mishnah. No change is justified.

Form/Structure/Setting

Lindblom (*Study of the Immanuel Section,* 46) has called the genre of vv 16–18 a "prophetic confession," to be compared with the words of Jeremiah and the lamentations among the Psalms. The verses are written in prose. The scene in which Isaiah the prophet and his son have been introduced by name in 7:3 and in which he speaks in the first person (8:1–3; 8:4–8; 8:11–15) is brought to climax in the prophet's withdrawal with his sons. However, the scene that makes so much of signs and sons continues on these themes through 9:6 (7).

Comment

16 The words are clipped and abrupt. Each deserves a comment. תעודה, "testimony," is a rare form found only here, v 20, and Ruth 4:7. The basic meaning of the root is "to give testimony," "to be a witness." The *hipʿil* form means "to warn." Wildberger correctly notes how fitting the use is for the speaker of the covenant festival who confronts the people with the word about the will of God. תורה *torah,* "instruction," also fits the teaching activity of the prophet, as well as priestly teaching of tradition, that is, the Torah of Moses, the Pentateuch.

The meaning of בלמדי, "with my disciples," has occasioned wide discussion along with the צור, "binding," and חתום, "sealing." Use of the word למדים, "disciples," undoubtedly implies that Isaiah has built up a circle of supporters who hang on his words. Wildberger's warning not to suppose a formal "school of prophets" like that of Elisha (1 Kgs 20:35; 2 Kgs 2:3, 5, 7, 15; 4:1–38) or a kind of "spiritual Israel" within the nation is appropriate (cf. L. Rost, *TLZ* 80 [1955] 4). Some interpreters (Duhm; Mauchline) have understood this to mean that Isaiah committed to them a written scroll, but there is no further evidence of this. Others translate "with my disciples" to mean "in their presence" (Dillmann; Kaiser) or have taken it to mean "through my disciples," "with their help" (Hitzig; H. Ewald, *Commentary on the Prophets of the Old Testament,* trans. J. F. Smith [London: Williams & Norgate, 1875–81]). Fohrer would eliminate the word למדים, "my disciples," altogether.

A figurative intention is more meaningful, as Gray, Procksch, Leslie, and Wildberger have noted. O. Eissfeldt (*Der Beutel der Lebendigen* [Leipzig: Akademie der Wissenschaften, 1960] 26) suggests that the figure is that of tying up a purse. As one preserves something precious in a purse, so Isaiah deposits his treasure of warnings and teachings with his disciples. (The word למדים, "disciples," appears again in 50:4 and 54:13 of those who are taught and led of God.)

All the reasons for writing and preserving teachings apply just as much to the literary prophet as to Isaiah son of Amoz. Hardmeier (*TGl* 73 [1983] 119–54) describes this as *Oppositionsliteratur* (Williamson, *Book Called Isaiah,* 102; for full discussion and literature, 97–103). Williamson (111ff., 142) thinks this figure stems from Deutero-Isaiah's redaction, along with 5:25–30 and 11:11–16. Whether one accepts the theory of Deutero-Isaiah's redaction or not, the recognition of these intertextual relations is important.

Excursus: The Sealed Testimony

צור תעודה, "binding of testimony," and חתום תורה, "sealing of instruction," is linked by Conrad (*Reading Isaiah,* 130–43) to the passage about a "sealed book" in 29:11–12 and to the string of references to Israel being blind and deaf.

If we do in fact think of the sealed תורה/תעודה, "testimony/torah," as a "book," what was included in that book? If its contents prove that YHWH foretold the events of chaps. 40–48 long ago, what would need to be included?

Some interpreters have thought about the unit of chaps. 6–8 as the material that was sealed. This material would have included the announcement of the decree for "the destruction of the land," the promise that "a remnant shall return," and the coming of the Assyrian at YHWH's command. Such contents might have been enough to make a difference in the situation of chap. 29 (see the commentary there), but is hardly enough to sustain the claim that YHWH foretold the situation of chaps. 40–48. To meet the needs of those claims, virtually all of chaps. 2–12 with the announcement of the return of the exiles (11:11–10) and chaps. 13–27 with the announcement of the complete devastation of the land and the announcement of the fall of Babylon, as well as the return of the exiles, would be needed (see *Comment* on 41:26).

Conrad thinks that the book, sealed in chap. 29 but read aloud by chap. 40, refers to Isa 6–29 (*Reading Isaiah,* 131). Conrad has made an interesting point. This commentary will pick up his argument in relation to chaps. 29 and 41.

17 Isaiah anticipates a longer period of time before his words are fulfilled. His attitude of waiting is expanded to include hope. קוה, "hope," is a word on the lips of the suppliant in the Psalms of lament (Pss 25:2, 5, 21; 27:14; 130:5): "I will hope in YHWH." חכה, "wait," though found in Pss 33:20 and 106:13 (not laments), also fits the context in Hab 2:3 and Zeph 3:8. Wildberger ("'Glauben' im Alten Testament," *ZTK* 65 [1968] 137–38) has noted their near relation to האמין, "believe," of 7:9*b*. (Cf. C. Westermann, "Das Hoffen im Alten Testament," in *Gesammelte Studien*, TB 24 [Munich: Kaiser, 1964] 219–65.)

המסתיר פניו, "hiding his face," is also a theme of lament psalms (Pss 10:11; 13:2; 44:25 [24]; and others). Thanksgiving psalms look back on a time when God "hid his face" (Pss 30:8 [7]; 22:25 [24]). Isaiah hopes not for a return of a personal relationship but for the fulfillment of God's word. When God's face shines over his people, his grace is abundantly in evidence. If it is hidden, they are left to the frightful sense of being lost and abandoned (Pss 104:29; 143:7; Deut 32:20; Jer 33:5; Mic 3:4). This often means being left to the power of the enemy (Ezek 39:23). The historical period here is that of Pekah's and Hoshea's reigns in Israel with the Assyrian incursions of 732 and 724–21 B.C.E., which marked the end of the northern kingdom.

בית יעקב, "house of Jacob," refers to the northern kingdom as do similar references throughout this section. The distinction made here between "Jacob" and "Judah" or "Jerusalem" has been lost on most interpreters, who have failed to note the oscillation between the two themes, which began in chap. 1 and continues especially through chap. 12. The distinction is important in the Vision, not only because of the different fates of the two nations in the eighth century but also because of the identification of Jacob/Israel with the Jewish dispersion in chaps. 40–48 as distinct from the inhabitants of Jerusalem in chaps. 49–54.

18 This section (7:1–9:7) is filled with references to אתות, "signs," and מופתים, "symbols," many of which consist of children and their names (see C. Keller, "Das Wort OTH," diss., Basel, 1946). This verse reinforces the earlier references. The presence of Isaiah and his children in Jerusalem was a reminder of YHWH's presence and intentions during the "silent years" that follow.

"In Israel—from YHWH of Hosts who dwells in Mount Zion." The juxtaposition is not accidental. The period is crucial for the relation of Israel and Jerusalem. The war posed critical questions concerning YHWH's position. Will he support Israel with its traditions of divine election or Jerusalem with its claim of divine favors for David? The question raised by Jeroboam's rebellion two centuries before has come to a head. Isaiah's intervention (7:1–9) and the Immanuel sign (7:10–16) provided one answer. His second son's birth (8:1–4) and the following oracle (8:5–8) provide a second. They remain as signs of YHWH's decision that dooms the northern kingdom and confirms his support of Jerusalem and its king.

Wildberger notes Isaiah's qualified support of Zion traditions. Zion is "the city of God, most holy of the dwellings of the Highest" (Pss 46:5 [4]; 48:2, 4 [3]; 78:3; 84:2 [1]; 87:1–3). When David brought the ark to Jerusalem and installed it in a permanent resting place (Ps 132:5–13), it symbolized YHWH's taking residence in the city (see Pss 74:2; 135:21; and A. Kuschke, "Die Lagervorstellung der priestlichen Erzählung," *ZAW* 63 [1951] 84–86; G. Fohrer, "Σιών, 'Ιηρουσαλημ, . . ." *TDNT*, 7:307–19; W. Schmidt, "מִשְׁכָּן," *ZAW* 75 [1963] 91–92). In exilic and postexilic prophets from Ezekiel to Joel, Zion was a very important concept, as it is here in Isaiah (2:3; 56:7; 57:13; 65:11, 25; 66:20). See T. C. Vriezen, "Essentials of the Theology of Isaiah," in *Israel's Prophetic Heritage*, FS J. Muilenberg, ed. B. W. Andersona and W. Harrelson (New York: Harper & Bros., 1962) 128–31.

Explanation

Isaiah's brief appearance, which began in 7:1, is brought to an end by his own act and decision. The Vision records his next activity in the year that Ahaz died. In the meantime, Assyria's invasions of 732 and 724–21 B.C.E. will have brought the northern kingdom to an end. Only the submissive policies of Ahaz will have spared Judah a similar fate.

Isaiah speaks of "testimony" and "instruction," descriptions of the word of God revealed. He speaks of "binding" and "sealing," that is, recording and preserving teachings through a difficult time until a time of better hearing and understanding. They are committed to his "disciples" who have listened and learned the precious words.

The times are dark because YHWH is "hiding his face" from the northern kingdom. The decision about the fate of the people of the northern kingdom has already been reached (10:22*b*), and God does not entertain further entreaty on their behalf. The prophet sets an example of the proper attitude for the believer in such a time. He will "wait for YHWH," and he will "hope for him," expecting a day when his countenance will turn toward his people, when his spirit will once again move among them. In the meantime Isaiah is aware that he and his children with their meaningful names are signs and symbols reminding Judah and Jerusalem that God has spoken, warned, and encouraged them before and during those dark hours. For YHWH of Hosts, God of history and of judgment, continues to make his home on Zion's ridge.

To Instruction and to Testimony (8:19–22)

Bibliography

Carroll, R. P. "Translation and Attribution in Isaiah 8:19ff." *BT* 31 (1980) 126–34. **Guillaume, A.** "Paronomasia in the Old Testament." *JSS* 9 (1964) 282–90. **Hoffner, H. A., Jr.** "Second Millennium Antecedents to the Hebrew ʾÔḆ." *JBL* 86 (1967) 385–401. **Jepsen, K.** "Call and Frustration: A New Understanding of Isaiah VIII 21–22." *VT* 32 (1982) 145–57. **Müller, H. P.** "Das Wort von den Totengeistern Jes. 8:19ff." *WO* 8 (1975) 65–76. **Rignell, L. G.** "Das Orakel 'Maher-salal Hasbas.'" *ST* 10 (1956) 40–52. **Schmidtke, F.** "Träume, Orakel und Totengeister als Kunder der Zukunft in Israel und Babylonien." *BZ* 11 (1967) 240–46. **Schwarz, G.** "Zugunsten der Lebenden an die Toten?" *ZAW* 86 (1974) 218–20. **Van der Woude, A. S.** "Jesaja 8:19–23*a* als literarische Einheit." In *Studies.* Ed J. Van Ruiten and M. Vervenne. 129–36.

Translation

Protester (derisively): 19 *If they say to you,* 3+3+2
"Seek out the fathers and the diviners,
who chirp and mutter!
Should not a people 2+2

seek out its God?
On behalf of the living, 2+2
(seek out) the dead?"
[20] *To Instruction and to Testimony!* [a] 2
Second Voice: *If not—* [b] 2+3+3
they speak like this word
which has no thing to prevent disaster. [c]
Third Voice: [21] *If someone* [a] *pass by her,* [b] 2+2
hard-pressed and hungry, [c]
when he is hungry 1+2+1
he will rage. [d]
He will curse by his king and by his God 3+2
and turn his face upward.
Fourth Voice: [22] *But let them look at the land.* [a] 2+3
Behold, distress and darkness,
gloom of anguish, 2+2
and being thrust into darkness. [b]

Notes

20.a. תורה, "instruction," and תעודה, "testimony," are translated in terms of their eighth-century B.C.E. meaning. By later postexilic times, after Ezra's reform, they would have been understood as "Law" and "Revelation" (Wildberger).

20.b. This translation takes the opening two pairs of words as short and abrupt phrases to be read alone. MT's accentuation fully supports this for the first pair and partly supports the second break.

20.c. LXX δῶρα and Syr. *šuḥda* suggest שחד, meaning "give a bribe," instead of שחר, "be black." Driver (*JTS* 41 [1940] 162; idem, "Isaianic Problems," 45) refers to the use of שחר in Isa 47:11 and KBL's translation "magic" as well as the Syr. *šḥr (paʿel)* and Arabic *sḥr*, meaning "tame," or "force." He suggests that שחר be translated "magic" or "power to overcome (disaster)." Perhaps δῶρα, "gift," was also understood as the gift to perform magic or to prophesy.

21.a. The subject is unnamed.

21.b. Rignell (*ST* 10 [1957] 49) suggests translating בה "as a result of it." *BHK* and *BHS* suggest emending to בארץ, "in (the) land," which may catch the intended meaning. But emendation is unnecessary.

21.c. Guillaume (*JSS* 9 [1964] 289) translates רעב "frightened, weak, cowardly," following the Arabic *raʿib*. Wildberger (355) rightly responds that Heb. does not have this word and that repetition here is a matter of style, not tautology.

21.d. 1QIsa[a] has יתקצף, an impf. instead of MT's pf. with *vav*. E. Y. Kutscher *(Language and Linguistic Background)* has shown that consec. pfs. were in decline in Qumran literature.

22.a. 1QIsa[a] adds the definite article: הארץ, "the land."

22.b. Wildberger (355) notes that אפלה מנדח may mean "(he is) pushed into the darkness." LXX reads σκότος ὥστε μὴ βλέπειν, "darkness so that (there is) no seeing," which would imply Heb. אפלה מֵרְאוֹת and is not close to MT. Gray noted long ago a similar vocabulary in Amos 5:20 (ואפל ולא־נֹגַהּ) and suggested emending מנדח to read מִנֹּגַהּ (see *BHS*), meaning "from shining, or brightness." (Cf. Jer 23:12.)

Form/Structure/Setting

The first question must settle the limits of the passage and its place in the book. Wildberger (343) has noted that v 19 is certainly not a continuation of the previous verses, but he has failed to draw the obvious consequences. With Isaiah and his family withdrawn from the scene (v 17), responses to his word and work are in order. For the first time in the Vision the opposition has a voice. The people who have been characterized as unknowing, deaf, and blind can now speak out. Most of chaps. 9–12 will express their response.

The end of this first transitional section is more difficult to mark. The different choices in the Hebrew and the versions show this. Even in the Hebrew, B has divided v 23, putting the second part in chap. 9—a division that Wildberger has adopted (355). LXX follows the same division. The English versions put all of v 23 into the ninth chapter. V 23 responds directly to v 22 using the same word, which ties the closing verse to the introductory section. But the verse also moves to the theme of hope and confirmation that will characterize the next six verses. It is a true bridge between the passages.

So this is a transition episode between the Isaiah scenes of chaps. 7–8 and the traditional expressions of comfort that come in chap. 9. When one recognizes the dialogue in the section, the abrupt changes of person and viewpoint that have disturbed interpreters in the past can be appreciated and understood. The genre of the larger section is like one that pits prophet against prophet (cf. S. De Vries, *Prophet against Prophet* [Grand Rapids, MI: Eerdmans, 1979]; J. L. Crenshaw, *Prophetic Conflict* [New York: De Gruyter, 1971]). Elijah's conflict with the Baal prophets (1 Kgs 18) was an extreme form. Micaiah's conflict with YHWH prophets (1 Kgs 22) is more typical, while Jeremiah's disagreement with Hananiah (Jer 28) shows the issue at its height. In Isa 8, unnamed voices attack the prophet. Except for Ahaz's reply to Isaiah in 7:12, this is the first time representatives of people who are "unknowing, deaf, and blind" have a chance to speak. Two times in the Vision the people find a voice: in 8:19–12:6 and in chaps. 60–63.

The Hebrew presents wordplays (עבר *ʿabar,* "pass by," and רעב *reʿab,* "hungry") and alliteration that cannot be reflected in translation: התקצף *hitqatsaf,* "he will rage"/קלל *qillel,* "he will curse"; מלכו *malko,* "his king"/מעלה *maʿlah,* "upwards"; מעוף *meʿuf,* "gloom"/מנדח *menudach,* "being thrust" (and מועף *muʿaf,* "gloom" in v 23); and צרה *tsarah,* "distress"/צוקה *tsuqah,* "anguish." Also wordplay appears in the similar vowel sounds of חֲשֵׁכָה *chashekah,* "darkness," and אֲפֵלָה *'afelah,* "darkness," and the dark closing words מעוף *meʿuf,* "gloom"; צוקה *tsuqah,* "anguish"; and מנדח *menudach,* "being thrust" (cf. Wildberger, 357).

Comment

19 דרשו, "seek out the fathers," is a reference to the cult of the dead and the practice of receiving oracles from the spirits of those who had gone before. Spiritualist mediums flourished throughout the ancient Near East. (Cf. the experience of Saul with the medium from Endor in 1 Sam 28:7–20.) הידענים המצפצפים, "diviners who chirp and mutter," is a derisive reference to practices of necromancy such as were common in the area. Israel's prophets were undoubtedly put on a level with Canaanite fortune-tellers by the unbelieving. המתים, "the dead," is again a reference to the cult of the dead. Ancient saints are sought out to help the living.

The ancient Near East (including Israel) was as inclined to fortune-tellers as any other people and time. Mosaic legislation forbids such (Deut 18:10–11). But the context suggests that this is directed at Isaiah. As a prophet, he brings a "word from the Lord" that is unmediated. This speech implies that he is no better than the diviners and the spiritualists.

20 The first response ends with a call to turn their attention to תורה, "instruction," and תעודה, "testimony." תורה *torah,* "instruction or law," was the area of the priests. The people sought their instruction on forms of worship and on the interpretation of tradition. In postexilic times it would be understood as "law"—indeed as "law book." The reference here is to the official priestly teaching based on legal precedent. Tradition attributes its source to Moses.

תעודה, "testimony," is as unusual as *torah* is familiar. This form appears here, in 8:16, and in Ruth 4:7 only. In Ruth the reference is to the symbolic removal of a sandal: "this was a תעודה in Israel." Earlier in that verse, the words הגאולה, "the redemption," and התמורה, "the exchange," are parallel in form and setting with התעודה, suggesting the means of recording a transaction. Isa 8:2 makes extraordinary use of this word in another form: אעידה עדים נאמנים, "I called reliable witnesses to witness," the Mahershalal-hash-baz prophecy. In v 16 Isaiah instructs that the witness and the torah should be bound up among his disciples. He considers his message to be vital for the instruction and life of his people.

V 20, however, more likely plays on another connotation of the word, more usually expressed by the form עדות from the same root. In 2 Kgs 11:12 and 2 Chr 23:11, עדות was given to kings at their coronation to represent royal authority (cf. Ps 132:12), and it commonly describes traditions and implements of the covenant (Exod 25:16, 21, 22; 25:22; 26:33; 30:6, 26; 39:35; 40:3, 5, 20, 21; Num 4:5; 7:89; Josh 4:16; and others; see *HAL*). The speaker here repeats the prophet's word, תעודה, "testimony," but uses it to refer instead to the royal and priestly legs on which authority rested: the recited account of God's revelation of covenants to Moses and to Nathan (2 Sam 7) and other teachings about the monarchy and Jerusalem. Together instruction and testimony included all the authority of official traditions, which is here opposed to a prophet who claims to be God's spokesman.

21–22 Vv 20*b*–21 warn of the potential result from Isaiah's words of warning, leading to panic and chaos. V 22 calls attention to the reality already abroad in the land.

Explanation

In derisive comments, the crowd expresses its view of a prophet who purports to have a word directly from God. The protesters make fun of the prophet's words and jeer at his boast that he and his children are signs and symbols.

Conflict between prophets is a common theme in the OT (e.g., 1 Kgs 18; 22; Jer 28). Note that in these stories, the opposing prophets are *not* speaking false doctrine in any of these incidents (except Elijah's). They quote from sound traditional (i.e., scriptural) sources. It is in the application to the present that they differ. They meet a purported "Word from the Lord" through an inspired prophet with a word from Scripture (tradition). The same is true here, where the people as a whole reject Isaiah's word by citing tradition.

The first speech mocks Isaiah, identifying him with the heathen spiritualists and fortune-tellers, ecstatic mutterers, and omen readers. It ends by calling people to return to real law and real testimony—not that claimed by Isaiah's private interpretation (v 16). The second speaker notes the lack of a bright message of hope such as the traditional interpreters of law and testimony customarily brought. The gloomy message of doom from Isaiah is clear. A third voice expresses his fears of the kind of reaction such a word will bring. A fourth finds that the gloomy reaction has already set in. These verses bring the debate between the classical prophets and the populace into full focus. The traditional prophets, the priests, the monarchists, and many others surge forward to denounce the lone figure of Isaiah. Here is the evidence that God was right: the people in Jerusalem are blind and deaf, stiff-necked and stubborn, unwilling to listen and turn.

The rest of this scene will develop the opposition, quoting traditional Zionist liturgies including promises concerning David and Jerusalem. The postexilic audience knows that the house of David lost what was left of its sovereign powers in the humiliations suffered by Hezekiah (chaps. 36–39), the servility of Manasseh, and the disastrous reigns of the puppet kings Jehoiakim, Jehoiachin, and Zedekiah. The arguments of assured political and military success by Zionists and monarchists were echoed by contemporary monarchists who urged Judah to rebel against Persia. The eighth-century message from Isaiah carried a fifth-century relevance—and was probably as unpopular as its original.

To Us a Son Is Born (8:23–9:6 [9:1–7])

Bibliography

Alonso Schökel, L. "Dos poemas a la paz." *EstBib* 18 (1959) 149–69. **Alt, A.** "Jesaja 8:23–9:6: Befreiungsnacht und Krönungstag." In *Festschrift, Alfred Bertholet.* Ed. W. Baumgartner. Tübingen: Mohr, 1950. 29–49. Reprinted in *Kleine Schriften,* 2:206–25. **Auret, A.** "Jesaja 8:23–9:6—propaganda vir 'n ideale koning oor 'n herenigde ryk?" *NGTT* 32 (1992) 440–52. **Barth, H.** *Die Jesajah-Worte.* 141–77. **Becking, B.** "Der Text von Jesaja 9:2a." *ZAW* 92 (1980) 142–45. **Bentzen, A.** *King and Messiah.* 2d ed. Oxford: Blackwell, 1970. **Brandscheidt, R.** "Ein grosses Licht (Jes 9,1–6): Standortsbestimmung zur Stärkung des Glaubens." *TTZ* 105 (1996) 21–38. **Carlson, R. A.** "The Anti-Assyrian Character of the Oracle in Is. ix 1–6." *VT* 24 (1974) 130–35. **Coppens, J.** "Le messianisme royal." *NRT* 90 (1968) in six parts. Also printed in *Le messianisme royal,* LD 54 (Paris: Editions du Cerf, 1968) 77–82, 491–96. ———. "Le roi idéal d'Is. IX 5–6 et XI 1–5, est-il une figure messianique?" In *A la rencontre de Dieu.* FS A. Gélin, ed. A. Barucq. Le Puy: Mappus, 1961. 85–108. **Crook, M. B.** "Did Amos and Micah Know Isaiah 9:2–7 and 11:1–9?" *JBL* 73 (1954) 144–51. ———. "A Suggested Occasion for Isaiah 9:2–7 and 11:1–9." *JBL* 68 (1949) 213–24. **Driver, G. R.** "Isaianic Problems." In *Festschrift für Wilhelm Eilers.* Ed. G. Wiessner. Wiesbaden: Harrassowitz, 1967. 46–49. **Emerton, J. A.** "Some Linguistic and Historical Problems in Isaiah VIII 23." *JSS* 14 (1969) 151–75. **Eschel, H.** "Isaiah viii 23: An Historical-Geographical Analogy." *VT* 40 (1990) 104–9. **Gonçalves, F.** *L'expédition de Sennachérib en Palestine dans la littéraire hébraïque ancienne.* Louvain-la-Neuve: Université catholique de Louvain, 1986. 309–13. **Gosse, B.** "Isaiah 8:23*b* and the Three Parts of the Book of Isaiah." *JSOT* 70 (1996) 57–62. **Grelot, P.** "L'interpretation d'Isaïe IX 5 dans le Targoum des prophètes." In *De la Torah au Messie.* FS H. Cazelles, ed. M. Carrez et al. Paris: Desclée, 1981. 535–43. **Gressmann, H.** *Der messias.* FRLANT 43. Göttingen: Vandenhoeck & Ruprecht, 1929. **Harrelson, W.** "Nonroyal Motifs in the Royal Eschatology." In *Israel's Prophetic Heritage.* Ed. B. W. Anderson and W. Harrelson.

149–53. **Høgenhaven, J.** "On the Structure and Meaning of Isaiah VIII 23b." *VT* 37 (1987) 218–21. **Irvine, S. A.** *Isaiah, Ahaz, and the Syro-Ephraimitic Crisis.* SBLDS 123. Atlanta: Scholars Press, 1990. 179–213. **Jagt, K. A. van der.** "Wonderful Counsellor . . . (Isaiah 9,6)." *BT* 40 (1989) 441–45. **Kennett, R. H.** "The Prophecy in Isaiah IX 1–7." *JTS* 7 (1906) 321–42. **Kloppers, M. H. O.** "Jesaja 8:23–9:1 en advent." *NGTT* 32 (1991) 378–86. **Laato, A.** *Who Is Immanuel? The Rise and Foundering of Isaiah's Messianic Expectations.* Turku, Finland: Åbo Academy Press, 1988. 163–73. **Lescow, T.** "Das Geburtsmotif in den messianischen Weissagungen bei Jesaja und Micha." *ZAW* 79 (1967) 172–207. **Lindblom, J.** *A Study of the Immanuel Section in Isaiah: Isa vii l–ix 6.* Lund: Gleerup, 1958. **Luzzatto, S. D.** *Il Profeta Isaia volgarizzato e commentato ad uso degl'Israeliti.* Padua: Bianchi, 1867. 131–33. **Menken, M. J.-J.** "The Textual Form of the Quotation from Isaiah 8:23–9:1 in Matthew 4:15–16." *RB* 150 (1998) 526–45. **Mowinckel, S.** *He That Cometh.* Trans. G. W. Anderson. Oxford: Blackwell, 1956. 102–10. ———. "Urmensch und 'Königsideology.'" *ST* 2 (1948) 71–89. **Müller, H. P.** "Uns ist ein Kind geboren . . ." *EvT* 21 (1961) 408–19. **Na'aman, N.** " Literary and Topographical Notes on the Battle of Kishon (Judges iv–v)." *VT* 40 (1990) 423–36, esp. 434–36. **Olivier, J. P. J.** "The Day of Midian and Isaiah 9:3b." *JNSL* 9 (1981) 143–49. **Rad, G. von.** "Das judäische Königsritual." *TLZ* 72 (1947) 211–16. Reprinted in *GSAT,* 205–13. **Renaud, B.** "La Forme Poetique d'Is 9,1–6." In *Mélanges biblique et orientaux.* FS M. M. Delcor, ed. A. Caquot et al. Kevelaer: Butzon & Bercher, 1985. 331–48. **Reventloh, H. G.** "A Synchronistic Enthronement Hymn in Is. 9,1–6." *UF* 3 (1971) 321–25. **Rignell, L. G.** "Das Orakel 'Maher-salal Hasbas.'" *ST* 10 (1956) 40–52. ———. "A Study of Isaiah 9:2–7." *LQ* 7 (1955) 31–35. **Ringgren, H.** "König und Messias." *ZAW* 64 (1952) 120–47. ———. *The Messiah in the Old Testament.* SBT 18. Chicago: Allenson, 1956. **Roberts, J. M.** "Whose Child Is This? Reflections on the Speaking Voice in Isa 9:5." *HTR* 90 (1997) 115–29. **Saebø, M.** "Isa 8:9–10." In *On the Way to Canon: Creative Tradition History in the Old Testament.* JSOTSup 191. Sheffield: Sheffield Academic Press, 1998. **Scharbert, J.** *Heilsmittler im Alten Testament und im Alten Orient.* Freiburg: Herbert, 1964. ———. "Der Messias im Alten Testament und im Judentum." In *Die religiöse und theologische Bedeutung des Alten Testaments.* Bayern: Katholischen Akademie, 1967. 47–78. **Schmidt, W. H.** "Die Ohnmacht des Messias." *KD* 15 (1969) 18–34. **Schunck, K.-D.** "Der fünfte Thronname des Messias." *VT* 23 (1973) 108–10. **Seybold, K.** *Das davidische Königtum im Zeugnis der Propheten.* FRLANT 107. Göttingen: Vandenhoeck & Ruprecht, 1972. 82. **Staub, J. J.** "A Review of the History of the Interpretation of Isaiah 8:11–9:6." In *Jewish Civilization: Essays and Studies.* Ed. R. A. Brauner. Philadelphia: Reconstructionist Rabbinical College, 1979. 89–107, esp. 103. **Sweeney, M. A.** "A Philological and Form-Critical Reevaluation of Isaiah 8:16–9:6." *HAR* 14 (1994) 229. **Thompson, M. E. W.** "Isaiah's Ideal King." *JSOT* 24 (1982) 79–88. **Vieweger, W.** "'Das Volk, das durch das Dunkel zieht . . .': Neue Überlegungen zu Jes (8,23ab) 9:1–6." *BZ* 36 (1992) 77–86. **Vermeylen, J.** *Du prophète Isaïe à l'apocalyptique.* 2 vols. Paris: Gabalda, 1977. **Vollmer, J.** "Zur Sprache von Jesaja 9:1–6." *ZAW* 80 (1968) 343–50. **Waschke, E.-J.** "Die Stellung der Königstexte im Jesajabuch im Vergleich zu den Königspsalmen 2, 72 und 89." *ZAW* 110 (1998) 348–55. **Wegner, P. D.** "Another Look at Isaiah viii 23b." *VT* 41 (1991) 481–84. **Wildberger, H.** "Die Thronnamen des Messias, Jes. 9,5b." *TZ* 16 (1960) 314–32. **Wolff, H. W.** *Frieden ohne Ende: Jesaja 7,1–17 und 9, 1–6.* Neukirchen-Vluyn: Neukirchener Verlag, 1962. **Zerafa, A.** "Il vestigo intriso de sangue in Is 9:4." In *Sangue e antropologia nella liturgia.* Ed. F. Vattioni. Rome: Centro studi Sanguis Christi, 1984. 363–95. **Zimmerli, W.** "Vier oder fünf Thronnamen des messianischen Herschers in Jes. IX 5b.6." *VT* 22 (1972) 249–52. **Zorell, F.** "Vaticinium messianicum Isaiae 9:1–6 Hebr. = 9:2–7 Vulg." *Bib* 2 (1921) 215–18.

Translation

The Official: 23 (9:1) *Nevertheless, no gloom* [a] 3+3
for her who had such anguish!

An Aide:	*As the first time*[b] *he treated lightly*[c]	3+2+2
	the land[d] *of Zebulun*	
	and the land[e] *of Naphtali,*	
	the later (time) he oppressed[f]	2
	the Way of the Sea,	2+2+2
	Transjordan,	
	Galilee of the Nations.	
Chorus:	9:1 (2) *The people walking in the dark*	3+3
	see a great light.	
	Residents in the land of shadow[a]*—*	3+3
	light shines on them.	
First Bystander:	2 (3) *You multiply the rejoicing;*[a]	2+2
	you magnify the joy.	
	They rejoice before you	2+2
	like rejoicing[b] *in harvest,*	
	just as they exult	2+2
	when spoil is divided.	
Second Bystander:	3 (4) *Nevertheless,*[a] *the yoke of his burden,*[b]	3+3+3
	the staff[c] *of his shoulder,*	
	the rod of his oppressor	
	you smash, like the day of Midian.[d]	3
Third Bystander:	4 (5) *Nevertheless,*[a] *every boot of trampling in tumult*[b]	3+3
	and garment rolled[c] *in bloody deeds*	
	becomes for burning	2+2
	food for fire.	
Chorus:	5 (6) *Nevertheless,*[a] *a child*	2+2+3
	is born to us,[b]	
	a son is given to us.	
Official:	*When*[c] *the administration*[d] *comes to be*	2+2
	on his shoulders,	
Aide:	*when one begins to proclaim*[e] *his name*	2
Chorus:	[f]*Wonder Counselor,*	2
	God-Hero,	2
	Father of Future	2
	Prince of Peace,[f]	2
Official:	6 (7) *to the increase*[a] *of rule*	2+2
(offering a toast)	*and to peace (may there be) no end*	
	upon the throne of David	3+2
	and upon his kingdom,	
Aide:	*to establish it*	2+1
	and to confirm it	
	with justice and with righteousness	1+1
	from now and to the age.	1+2
Chorus:	*May the Zeal of YHWH of Hosts*	3+2
	do this!	

Notes

23.a. Vg. translates *et non potent avolare de angustia sua,* "and is not able to fly because of his anguish." This takes מועף as a form of עוף in the lexicon, meaning "to fly," but fails to note the connection with the word in v 22.

23.b. The subject of the verbs is not named. Budde (*Jesaja's Erleben,* 99) thought הראשון, "the first," stood for Tiglath-Pileser and was subject of the first verb, while a later oppressor was represented by האחרון, "the later." But surely God is the subject here, although it is not necessary to add יהוה, "YHWH" (as Kaiser and Alt, "Jesaja 8:23–9:6," do), to the text.

23.c. הקל is *hip'il* from קלל. It is literally translated "he made light," or "he treated lightly." It could also be understood as "he made light of" or "treated with contempt."

23.d. 1QIsa[a] reads ארץ, "land," for ארצה, "to the land." MT is hardly an Aramaism (Kaiser) but rather an old acc. or locative as Rignell (*ST* 10 [1956] 51) and Emerton (*JSS* 14 [1969] 152) have noted. See GKC §90*f.*

23.e. 1QIsa[a] reads והארץ instead of וארצה. MT is consistent and correct.

23.f. הכביד means "he made heavy," which could mean "he honored" or "he oppressed." The difference is whether this sentence contrasts with the previous one or parallels it.

9:1.a. צַלְמָוֶת was understood by the versions and the Masoretes to be composed of צל, "shadow," and מות, "death": LXX ἐν χώρᾳ καὶ σκιᾷ θανάτου (which is followed by Matt 4:16 and Luke 1:79); Tg. טולי מותא; Syr. *ṭ*[e]*lālê mawtâ;* Vg. *umbra mortis.* But modern study has established the root to be צלם, "be dark" (*HAL* II), and the proper vocalization to be צַלְמוּת (D. W. Thomas, "צַלְמָוֶת in the OT," *JSS* 7 [1962] 191–200).

2.a. הגוי לא, "the nation not." MT's accent suggests that לא, "not," should be read with the second stich: "you do not magnify joy." Yet there has been a persistent attempt to divide the line after לא. Rignell (*ST* 10 [1956] 33) reads "Thou has made the not-a-people great" (cf. H. W. Wolff, *Frieden ohne Ende,* 22). Some MSS, Qere, Tg., and Syr. read הגוי לו, "the nation that belongs to him." Wildberger follows the conjecture that a false division of the words has occurred in transmission and suggests reading הַגִּילָה, "the rejoicing," for הגוי לא. The emendation fits the meaning, temper, and meter, and it commends itself here.

2.b. שִׂמְחַת, "rejoicing," is a const. form followed by a prep. S. Rin ("ת as an Absolute Plural Ending," *BZ* 5 [1961] 255–58) suggests that this is an old abs. ending. But see GKC §130*a* (1). The form is unusual but not impossible.

3.a. Read כִּי as a conditional particle. Cf. GKC §159*l* and J. Wash Watts, *Survey of Syntax,* 135.

3.b. For the form סֻבֳּלוֹ consult GKC §93*q.*

3.c. Wildberger supports earlier suggestions to change the vowel pointing of מַטֵּה, "staff," to מוֹטָה, "pole" (cf. 58:6, 9). The change seems unnecessary. The parallel is close enough for the purpose here.

3.d. LXX Μαδιαμ; 1QIsa[a] מדים. The Gk. appears to have been the normal pronunciation for Midian, as 1QIsa[a] shows. (Cf. Philo, *De mutatione nominum* 110.)

4.a. Read as a conditional particle.

4.b. LXX δόλῳ, "deceit" or "treachery," supported by Tg., seems to have read this as בְּרֶשַׁע. Tur-Sinai ("A Contribution to the Understanding of Isaiah I–XII") changed the vowels. But Wildberger is correct to reject it.

4.c. Syr. *m*[e]*palpal,* "spotted," has left Zorell (*Bib* 2 [1921] 217) and Procksch to emend מגוללה, "rolled," to מְגֹאָלָה, "defiled, polluted." MT makes sense and should be sustained.

5.a. Read as a conditional particle.

5.b. The alliteration in ילד ילד לנו (*yeled yulad lānû,* "is born to us") is worth notice.

5.c. Note the decisive change of tense. The pfs. that have characterized the verses since 8:23 give way to consec. impfs. and finally to infs. in v 6. The translation reads the consec. impfs. as subordinate introductory clauses. The weight of the "toast" to the king falls on the verbless substantive clause beginning v 6.

5.d. משרה is *hap. leg.,* which LXX translated ἡ ἀρχή, "rule." BDB and *HAL* posit an otherwise unknown root שׂרה to support this meaning. Gray related it to שרר, "to rule," the noun שׂר, "a prince," and Akk. *šarru,* "king," and suggested that it should be pointed מֶשְׂרָה/מִשְׂרָה. 1QIsa[a] משורה has still another pronunciation (cf. F. Nötscher, "Entbehrliche Hapaxlegomena in Jes," *VT* 1 [1951] 302; G. R. Driver, "Three Notes," *VT* 2 [1952] 357).

5.e. ויקרא, "one begins to proclaim," has no named subject, which has caused problems in translation and interpretation. 1QIsa[a] וקרא changes the tense to a consec. pf. Others have used a pass. to convey the meaning: LXX καλεῖται; Syr. *ʾetqᵉrî;* Vg. *vocabitur.* If MT is translated with an impersonal subject, it makes sense, fits the tense pattern, and should be kept.

5.f-f. The versions were at a loss to translate these titles, which by that time were understood as names for Messiah. 1QIsa[a] follows MT except for adding the article before "peace." LXX reads: Μεγάλης βουλής ἄγγελος. ἐγώ γὰρ ἄξω εἰρήνην ἐπὶ τοὺς ἄρξοντας, εἰρηνην καὶ ὑγίειαν αὐτῷ, "Messenger of mighty counsel; for I will keep peace over the rulers, (bring) peace and health to them." α´ σ´ θ´ follow MT more closely than LXX does. None of these, however, renders אל as "God," but some MSS add to LXX θαυμαστος συμβουλος θεος ισχυρος, "a wonder of a counselor, mighty God," probably influenced by Origin's *Hexapla* (cf. Ziegler). Tg. reads גיניא קיים עלמיא משיחא דשלמא יסגי עלנא ביומוהי מפלי עיעא אלהא, "Wonderful counselor, mighty God who lives forever, the Messiah in whose days peace will be great over us." Vg. *Admirabilis, consiliarius. Deus, fortis, pater future saeculie, princeps pacis,* "Wonderful, counselor, God, mighty, father of coming ages, prince of peace," has found six names, reading the first four separately and only joining the last two pairs of words (cf. Zorell, *Bib* 2 [1921] 218).

6.a. לםרבה "to increase." The final *mem* within the word is strange. Many MSS as well as 1QIsa[a] and Qere replace it with the usual מ. LXX μεγάλη ἡ ἀρχὴ αὐτοῦ, followed by the other versions, has led to suggestions for emendations: that לם be understood as dittography and dropped, leaving רבה, "the rule is great." Other suggestions have been to read לָמוֹ רַבָּה or מַרְבָּה לוֹ, "to him is great (rule)." Alt ("Jesaja 8:23–9:6," 219) thought of the customary Eg. number five for throne names. He suggested that the למרבה is a fragment of a fifth name such as המשׂרה מרבה, "one who enlarges the realm." Wildberger (365, 394) has taken this suggestion, emended the text in comparison with the versions (assuming dittography "fore and aft") reading רב המשׂרה, and translating *in (seiner) Herrshaft gross,* "great in his rule." These arguments are cogent and draw the name into close connection with the preceding line. However, MT has seen the phrase in close parallel to the following lines in which three more times key words begin with לְ. As parallels to לשלום, "to peace," להכין, "to establish," and לסעדה, "to confirm it," the more traditional reading and translation (with MT) should prevail. (See the discussion under *Form/Structure/Setting.*)

Form/Structure/Setting

The structure and unity of the passage are shown by its syntax and arrangement. It moves with freedom, no slave of metrical structures, shaping its own forms and meanings. It can suspend parallelism (v 5) for five single statements of two words each then resume parallelism with pairs of prepositional phrases. It is capable of putting three pairs of words opposite a single pair in 8:23 and 9:3.

The whole is dominated by the particle כִּי, which in 8:23 and 9:3, 4, 5 introduced the speeches. To understand its meaning and significance for the passage is to open the door to its treasures. The dominant position of perfect verbs (in vv 8:23; 9:1, 2, 3, 5*a*) is instructive—always in inverted order with substantives first. The strange appearance of a perfect with *vav* in v 4*c* breaks the pattern, as does the imperfect in v 2*c*, while the consecutive imperfects in v 5*b–c* are important. The passage closes with an imperfect.

What is one to do with all this? It is no ordinary prosaic, or even poetic, style. First, let us deal with the כִּי particles. They may be strong assertatives—either negative or positive. Apparently the first (v 23) is such and is rendered "nevertheless." The sentence is an objection to the previous one, negating it word for word—but with no verb. The next line softens the contradiction by ascribing them to two different "times" and uses inverted word order and perfect tenses to achieve the effect. The verbs are strong, but the syntax leaves them suspended and timeless, like the substantive statement that introduced them. The first strophe has halted the confused lament with the assertion that the future can be made good, just as the past has been bad. The contrast may be between "contempt" and "honor" but is more likely parallel: the first attack was light, the second, much heavier in its consequences.

In Isa 9:1the two lines are balanced in meter. They support the theme. The present times of trouble are presented by participles, while hope is expressed in perfect verbs as in the first strophe. The contrast is now between "light" and "dark."

In Isa 9:2 the pattern is broken. Inverted order is abandoned, as are also the impersonal verbs. Second-person singular "you" is addressed. This is often taken to be God. It is more likely that the broken pattern indicates a different speaker, who addresses the one who has just spoken either in v 23 or v 1.

Isa 9:3 is the second of four passages beginning with כִּי, "nevertheless." In each the meaning is a contrast drawn to the "gloom" of 8:22. The statements do not contradict the previous line but rather state reasons to hope in a time of trouble. This one poses the issue of the presence of a powerful oppressor who has subjugated the land. If the speaker, like Gideon, can smash that power . . . The apodosis is understood but not uttered. The inverted order poses the threefold emphasis on that oppressor before the verb of deliverance.

The third כי, in 9:4, introduces a reminder of the forces of violence and chaos that stand in the way of a solution. These, too, must be destroyed. The verse is only half spoken: the first part has no verb—stopping abruptly—while the second has a perfect with *vav,* which normally requires an antecedent. It is as though the lines are to be stammered out, being distorted in delivery. But the meaning is clear. Years of war cannot be put aside in a night. All the weapons and uniforms (not to mention psychic scars) must be eradicated.

The fourth כי, beginning 9:5, introduces a more direct suggestion. It is spoken in chorus and takes its "us" from those seeing the "great light" of v 1. They hear this as hope that a descendant of David may seize the chance apparent in the fall of Samaria to reunite the kingdoms and inaugurate a second era of peace and prosperity like that of David and Solomon. The idea, improbable as it is under the Assyrian (or Persian), evokes a nostalgic burst of patriotic fervor—a reminder of what enthronement hymns sound like. Then the section closes on the prayerful invocation of the Zeal of YHWH.

Comment

23 (9:1) The laments of the doomsayers of 8:19–22 are interrupted by claims of hope. The speech denies that gloom and anguish are the inevitable results of the events. While recognizing the bitterness of the moment, it reminds them of a hope based on God's intervention. Election is viewed as a guarantee of his eventual redemption.

The perfect verbs begin a series that extends through the first line of 9:5. Note that they are used here both for "the first" as well as "the later" time. They are independent of a time context. We have tried to show this by translating with present time throughout (J. Wash Watts, *Survey of Syntax,* 46).

The ראשׁון, "first time," for the lands of Zebulun and Naphtali is not easy to identify. זבלון, "Zebulun," was located in south Galilee astride the valley east of Carmel that is drained by the river Kishon. But its significance as a tribe had been diminishing since the days of the Judges. Solomon's districts have the territory absorbed into that of Asher (1 Kgs 4:16). Whatever of its territory was not seized in Tiglath-Pileser's drive down the coast in 734 B.C.E. was taken the following year in the invasion of Naphtali. The province of Dor was established for the coastal region from Carmel south to Joppa (*MBA*, 148).

נפתלי, "Naphtali," was the northernmost territory of the kingdom of Israel, occupying the northwest of the lake of Galilee on up to the southern slopes of Mount Hermon. It had also not been significant since the period of the Judges, although Solomon did have a district named Naphtali. The "first time" could appropriately refer to a time beginning before the monarchy, or it could refer to Tiglath-Pileser's first attack. It is possible that this reference is simply figurative for the area of the northern kingdom that was occupied by Assyria in 732 B.C.E. The Assyrian campaign of 733 B.C.E. drove across the heart of its territory (*MBA*, 147), attacked its major cities, and reduced it to a province under an Assyrian governor (2 Kgs 15:29). The same campaign subdued Gilead, and it, too, was made an Assyrian province (*Annals of Tiglath Pileser III*). Some of its leaders were taken into exile (1 Chr 5:6).

A. Alt's ("Jesaja 8:23–9:6") suggestion to add a line listing parallel terms such as the Valley of Sharon and the Mountain of Gilead is appropriate as a comment on the geography even if it is judged unnecessary for the strophic structure of the passage.

Being "treated lightly" apparently refers to these invasions and the subsequent oppression under a foreign ruler. Both verbs in this verse lack an explicit subject. Two possibilities are likely. One is that YHWH is the subject. Some commentaries suggest that he should be put into the text. This would fit, especially if the second persons of the verbs in 9:3–4 also are addressed to him. Another possibility is that the subject is "the first time" and "the later" (Budde, *Jesaja's Erleben,* 99; Wildberger). We have chosen this second course. The emphasis is on the hope that a later time can bring a reversal of fortunes for the stricken area. But the subject's ambiguity is deliberate and is intended to let the hearer or reader make the choice.

The האחרון, "later" (time), could refer to a subsequent campaign by Tiglath-Pileser. The דרך הים, "Way of the Sea," עבר הירדן, "Transjordan," and גליל הגוים, "Galilee of the Nations," appear to be Hebrew names for the districts the Assyrians called Dor, Megiddo, and Gilead (cf. *MBA*, 148). The fate of this region was separated from that of Samaria as early as the eighth century. Matthew quotes the verses to support the account of Jesus' ministry in that region (Matt 4:15–16).

In content the message is simply an appeal to hope that the future has got to be better, and that the future will rectify the bad times of the past. The announcement proclaims that the new political realities (i.e., redistricting and renaming territory) need not prevent a new period of glory and honor. (Note: the announcement is not given as a word from the Lord or supported in any way.)

9:1 (2) A pro-Israelite group in the crowd picks up the note just sounded. There is אוֹר, "light," at the end of the tunnel for Israel.

2 (3) The second-person singular of the verbs at the beginning of v 2 (3) and the end of v 3 (4) have usually been understood to refer to God. But this need not be necessary if the passage has a dialogical character. They may refer to the previous speaker and the sudden shift of mood that his speech has made in the people. So it is a bystander who challenges the first speaker, asking what in his speech there is to be happy about. And he scornfully derides the gullible crowd who act as though a great victory has been won just by saying so.

3–6 (4–7) Three further characteristics of that great future salvation are each introduced with כִּי, "nevertheless," which may have various meanings. See *Form/Structure/Setting.*

3 (4) The first characteristic emphasizes freedom from foreign domination. The speaker believes this is possible because God has led Israel to victory in impossible situations like the one Gideon successfully faced (Judg 7): "the day of Midian."

4 (5) The second portrays the end of holy war against the enemy when all the booty, including the war boots and military uniforms, had to be burned.

5–6 (6–7) The third is voiced by monarchists in the crowd who see in the prophecy of future light the restoration of power and glory to the House of David. The future of a new heir to the throne can be full of hope that all the promise of the age of the united kingdom when David and Solomon ruled can now be restored and fulfilled. This passage is one of the most beautiful and expressive passages in the OT, reflecting high monarchical tradition and ideology. The ideas and phrases may well echo those used in enthronement ceremonies. (Cf. *Excursus: Messiah, Son of David* below.) J. M. Roberts suggests that the "us" are members of the Divine Council and that "one may read Isa 9:5 as reflecting the joyous assent of the Divine Council to the new king, YHWH's son." However, since the brunt of the Vision's message weighs against such hopes, the speakers here, like those of the previous verses, should be viewed as opponents of Isaiah's message.

The episode ends with the murmured response of the crowd: "May the Zeal of YHWH of Hosts do this." This effectively represents the theologically inclusive faith that united the divergent elements in the crowd. Those who supported the position of northern Israel (8:22–23 [8:22–9:1]); those with a general faith that God would certainly make things right (9:1–2 [2–3]); the rebellious zealots (v 3 [4]); the holy-war enthusiasts, who said "Let God fight the battles" (v 4 [5]); and the monarchists, who saw hope in a revival of the house of David and the birth of a new David (vv 5–6 [6–7])—all these could intone the prayer for God's zeal to save them.

Explanation

This passage has often been understood as promise. Yet the analysis above does not support this for its original setting. It is not spoken by the prophet or in the name of God. It is an attempt to assemble from the resources of faith and doctrine words to bolster hope. Yet the chorus knows that only a miracle can bring the light, restore the joy, or reestablish the power and authority of David's reign. That is why they sigh, "May the Zeal of YHWH of Hosts do this!" Of course, nothing is impossible with God.

The speaker in 8:23 tries to change the mood of doom and gloom that dominated the previous response (8:19–22) to Isaiah's speeches. The anguish of God's people need not be forever. History belongs to God. He can turn things around. But the speakers carefully avoid being too specific about it. The perfect tenses in the passage give a timeless appearance. The speeches directly contradict the message of Isaiah in 6:11–21, 7:8, and 8:7. They turn against the announced plan of God in 2:6–9 and imply an easy grace for the apostasy spoken of in 1:2–8.

The theme is picked up in 9:1 (2) with an eagerness that reflects the great need of the people to believe. The dark moment will pass. There is hope. V 3 (4) is saying that any true change will need to destroy the oppressor in the land and that this would require a miraculous deliverance like that of Gideon. V 4 (5) continues the skeptical mood, noting that a total disarmament will be required to achieve this goal. But the crowd now breaks into a chant that proclaims the royal hopes for an heir to the throne of David in whom all of the promises to David will be fulfilled, as in 2 Sam 7:12–14 and royal psalms like Pss 2, 72, and 89. The destruction of the government in Samaria opens the door to such a dream, if the foreign oppressor can be dealt with.

The episode draws to a climax with the speeches toasting the idea of such a "messianic" hope and closes with the fervent prayer that the Zeal of YHWH of Hosts may do this. The invocation of the old battle name for God recognizes that this is only possible with the kind of miraculous intervention that brought Israel through the Reed Sea, brought down the walls of Jericho, and devastated the Midianite hosts before Gideon.

This hope is a legitimate part of Israel's heritage. It is not, however, a part of Isaiah's word for Israel or Judah in the eighth century or of the Vision of Isaiah for Jerusalem in the fifth century. The traditionalists opposed the prophet in those days, as they opposed Jesus and John the Baptist in their day. The issue is not that God is unable to fulfill his promises or that God is unfaithful to them. It *is* that the people of Israel were not aligned with God's agenda. He is now in the process of judging and cleansing so that his goals for his people can be achieved.

Two places in the Vision allow for the opposition to be heard: 8:19–9:6 (7); 10:3–12:6 and chaps. 60–64. The sharpest contrast to the Isaiah message is in 8:23–9:6 (7) and in 62:1–12 and 63:11*b*–64:12. These passages have many things in common, especially their presumption. They presume upon God's miraculous power and intervention (like Satan's temptations to Jesus, "tell these stones to become bread," "throw yourself down," in Matt 4:3, 6 NIV).

The responses may accurately reflect the popular elements of eighth-century Jerusalem. But they also found echoes in fifth-century Jerusalem. By then the oppressor was the Persian rather than the Assyrian. For both groups the thrust of Isaiah's message was equally obnoxious.

Traditional Christian interpreters have correctly noted that 9:5–6 (6–7) is part and parcel of royal liturgy and therefore used it as a messianic text, like the royal psalms. This is achieved by lifting the verses out of context and changing the genre of the larger work to match. Waschke (*ZAW* 110 [1998] 348–51) notes that some newer interpretations of the Psalter have found a redactional purpose in positioning royal psalms (2, 72, 89) in strategic places and suggests that the composers/redactors of Isaiah have done the same (see *Excursus: Messiah, Son of David*). This is legitimate. The Vision apparently quotes from other contexts. But it is important to keep in mind that the verses do not function as messianic predictions in this context.

The prophetic task lay in interpreting the fall and destruction of the kingdom and in preparing the people to live as God's people without king or royal dominion. The Vision follows in the path of Jeremiah and Ezekiel in this regard and will later reinterpret royal motifs to fit that situation. One should note that in order for Jesus to be understood to be the Messiah these motifs of kingship and dominion had to be radically reinterpreted to fit the crucified carpenter's son. In this, the NT follows the path laid out in the Vision of Isaiah. Christian interpretation has relegated the more royal aspects of messianic hope to Christ's second coming to reign in glory.

Excursus: Messiah, Son of David

Bibliography

Becker, J. *Messianic Expectation in the Old Testament.* Trans. D. E. Green. Philadelphia: Fortress, 1980. **Coppens, J.** *Le messianisme royal.* LD 54. Paris: Editions du Cerf, 1968. Reprinted from *NRTh* 90 (1968) 30–49, 225–51, 479–512, 622–50, 834–63, 936–75. **Fohrer, G.** "υἱός κτλ." *TDNT.* 8:349–52. **Goldingay, J.** "The Compound Name in Isaiah 9:5(6)." *CBQ* 61 (1999) 239–44. **LaSor, W. S.** "The Messiah: An Evangelical Christian View." In *Evangelicals and Jews in Conversation on Scripture, Theology, and History.* Ed. M. Tannenbaum, M. R. Wilson, and A. J. Rodin. Grand Rapids, MI: Eerdmans, 1973. 76–95. **Luzzatto, S. D.** *Il Profeta Isaia volgarizzato e commentato ad uso degl'Israeliti.* Padua: Bianchi, 1867. 131–33. **McClellan, W. H.** "El Gibbor." *CBQ* 6 (1944) 276–88. **McKenzie, J. L.** "Royal Messianism." *CBQ* 19 (1957) 25–52. **Motyer, J. A.** "Messiah." *IDB.* 3:987–94. **Olmo Lete, G. del.** "Los titulos mesianicos de Is. 9:5." *EstBib* 24 (1965) 239–43. **Rehm, M.** *Der Königliche Messias im Licht der Immanuel-Weissagungen des Buches Jesaja.* Eichstätter Studien 1. Kevelaer: Butzon & Bercker, 1968. 145–66. **Ringgren, H.** *The Messiah in the Old Testament.* SBT 18. Chicago: Allenson, 1956. **Snaith, N. H.** "The Interpretation of El Gibbor in Isaiah ix. 5." *ExpTim* 52 (1940–41) 36–37. **Staub, J. J.** "A Review of the History of the Interpretation of Isaiah 8:11–9:6." In *Jewish Civilization: Essays and Studies.* Ed. R. A. Brauner. Philadelphia: Reconstructionist Rabbinical College, 1979. 89–107, esp. 103. **Sweeney, M. A.** "A Philological and Form-Critical Reevaluation of Isaiah 8:16–9:6." *HAR* 14 (1994) 229. **Waschke, E.-J.** "Die Stellung der Königstexte im Jesajabuch im Vergleich zu den Königspsalmen 2, 72 und 89." *ZAW* 110 (1998) 348–55. **Wegner, P. D.** "A Re-Examination of Isaiah ix 1–6." *VT* 42 (1992) 111. **Wildberger, H.** "Die Thronnamen des Messias, Jes. 9:5b." *TZ* 16 (1960) 314–32.

Christian exegesis of the OT is keenly aware of the elements that the NT understands to be fulfilled in Jesus. Foremost among these are the royal aspects of Messiah. Jesus is understood by the NT to be "the Son of David," heir to divine promise of an everlasting and universal throne.

This understanding of Messiah is founded on 2 Sam 7:11*b*–16 and in the royal psalms (including Pss 2, 45, and 110), which proclaim a very high view of the king and the kingdom and in which God is directly involved with both. Among the OT passages that present such a view, none has been more prominent in Christian interpretation than Isa 9:5–6 (6–7) and 11:1–5. The first lists throne names for the Davidic king of Zion, while the second announces, or prays for, the spirit of the Lord to so fill the king that he achieves the highest aims of the kingdom.

Whether this passage is understood to relate to the birth of a royal heir or to his coronation (see Wildberger, 377, for a review), these names certainly and succinctly present the most elaborate statement of Jerusalem's view of its God-given sovereign, the Son of David. Ps 2 and 2 Sam 7:14 prepare the reader for the view that the king will be understood to be God's son. But passages such as this are a strong reminder of the seriousness with which ancient Israel and early Judaism thought of the Davidic kingdom as an expression, indeed the earthly expression, of the kingdom of God. This represents the most widely held understanding of these verses among Christians.

However, Goldingay has now resurrected a view held by many Jewish scholars of the medieval period, such as Rashi, that the first three pairs of names refer to God. It is he who names the "prince of peace." (See Staub,"Review of the History," 103.) Goldingay (*CBQ* 61 [1999] 243) suggests the translation "One who plans a wonder is the warrior God (cf. 10:21); the father forever is a commander who brings peace." He relates the concept of God planning to other places in Isaiah (14:24, 27; 19:12, 17; 23:9; 25:1; 28:29; 29:14) and to the "warrior God" (10:21and 43:13).

Waschke (*ZAW* 110 [1998] 348 n. 3) cites a number of current interpreters of the book of Psalms who think that at "a particular stage in the process of collecting and arranging the psalms, royal psalms were taken up and inserted into specific collections" (e.g., C. Westermann, "Zur Sammlung der Psalmen," in *Forschung am Alten Testament: Gesammelte Studien,* TB 24 [Munich: Kaiser, 1964] 342). G. Braulik ("Christologisches Verständnis der Psalmen—schon im Alten Testament," in *Christologie der Liturgie: Der Gottesdienst der Kirche—Christusbekenntnis und Sinaibund,* ed. K. Richter and B. Kranemann, QD 159 [Freiburg: Herder, 1995] 57–86) has summarized the work of Lohfink, Hossfeld and Zenger, who note that the first three books of Psalms have royal psalms near their beginnings (2, 72, 89). They turn readers' attention to David's position in God's order and thus point toward a "messianic" interpretation of the Psalter.

Waschke suggests that the same thing happens in Isaiah. Strong royal passages have been inserted in 9:1–6 (the end of the so-called *Denkschrift:* 6:1–8:18); in 11:1–8 with additions; in the hymn in chap. 12 to close a passage; and in 32:1–5, 15–20 to mark the end of the Assyrian Circle (chaps. 28–32), which in turn has been thought by some to mark the end of one edition of a proto-Isaianic collection (chaps. 2–32). He sees the same pattern in the transfer of Davidic promises to Israel in 55:3*b*–5 to mark the end of the Deutero-Isaiah collection. Thus, says Waschke, one group of editors has sought to have the entire book of Isaiah interpreted in a messianic sense.

It seems to me that what Waschke attributes to editors has instead been done by interpreters. The brunt of the Vision's message is actually antimessianic, projecting a future for Jerusalem and God's people, but not for the Davidic dynasty. What the OT, including Isaiah, can only record as promises and ideals that contrast starkly with human reality, the NT invites the Christian to expect to see fulfilled in Jesus Christ, Son of David and Divine King of Heaven and Earth, at the end of the age.

Scene 2: A Word against Jacob (9:7 [8]–10:23)

Scene 2 begins in 9:7 (8)–10:4 with the sharp reminder that the Lord has already spoken a word of judgment against Israel. It continues in 10:5–19 with an interpretation of Assyria's role in this era. The scene ends in 10:20–23 with the confirmation that this judgment is total and certain.

The speeches of the scene form an arch. Note the balance of its themes. The capstone of the arch (10:12) is of a completely different genre and meaning from all the rest.

A A word against Jacob; the people know (9:7–12[8–13]).
B The people have not turned; the Lord will cut off (9:13–17[14–18]).
C The wrath of YHWH will scorch the land (9:18–20[19–21])
(10:1–4: A "woe" outside the structure).
D Assyrian, rod of my anger (10:5–6).
E But he does not intend it so (10:7–11).
KEYSTONE After work is finished on Jerusalem and Judah, YHWH will punish the Assyrian (10:12).
E´ The Assyrian's prideful attitude (10:13–14).
D´ Does the axe raise itself against the woodsman? (10:15–16).
C´ The light of Israel will become a fire (10:17–19).
B´ In that day a remnant will rely on YHWH (10:20–21).
A´ The Lord will carry out the decreed destruction upon the whole land (10:22–23).

A Prophetic Interpretation of History (9:7 [8]–10:4)

Bibliography

Albright, W. F. "The Assyrian March on Jerusalem, Isa. X, 28–32." In *Excavations and Results at Tell el Fûl (Gibeah by Saul).* Ed. B. W. Bacon. AASOR 4. New Haven: ASOR, 1924. 134–40. **Bartelt, A. H.** "Isaiah 5 and 9: In- or Interdependence." In *Fortunate the Eyes.* Ed. A. B. Beck et al. 157–72. **Blum, E.** "Jesaja und der DBR des Amos (Is 9,7–20; 10,1–4)." *DBAT* 28 (1992–93) 75–95. **Brown, W. P.** "The So-Called Refrain in Isaiah 5:25–30 and 9:7–10:4." *CBQ* 52 (1990) 432–43. **Carroll,R. P.** "Eschatological Delay in the Prophetic Tradition." *ZAW* 94 (1982) 47–58. **Crenshaw, J. L.** "A Liturgy of Wasted Opportunity (Isa 9,7–10,4)." *Semitics* 1 (1970) 27–37. **Crüsemann, F.** *Studien zur Formgeschichte vom Hymnus und Danklied in Israel.* WMANT 32. Neukirchen-Vluyn: Neukirchener Verlag, 1969. 50–56, 227–29. **Donner, H.** *Israel unter den Völkern.* 64–75. **Goshen Gottstein, N. H.** "Hebrew Syntax and the History of the Bible Text: A Pesher in the MT of Isaiah." *Textus* 8 (1973) 100–106. **Honeyman, A. M.** "Unnoticed Euphemism in Isaiah 9:19–20?" *VT* 1 (1951) 221–23. **Korpel, M. C. A.** "Structural Analysis as a Tool for Redaction Criticism: The Example of Isaiah 5 and 10.1–6." *JSOT* 69 (1996) 53–71. **Kruger, P. A.** "Another Look at Isaiah 9:7–20." *JNSL* 15 (1989) 127–41. **Ockinga, B.** "*rās wĕzānāb kippah wĕʾagmôn* in Isa 9:13 and 9:15." *BN* 10 (1979) 31–34. **Schroer, S.** "'Aus abgehacktem Baumstumpf neues Leben': Jesajas Vision von Gerechtigkeit, Frieden und Bewahrung der Schöpfung." *BK* 44 (1989) 154–57. **Thomas, D. W.** "A Note on the Meaning of *jada* in Hosea 9:9 and Isaiah 9:8." *JTS* 41 (1940) 43–44. **Vollmer, J.** *Geschichteliche Rückblicke.* 130–44. **Wallenstein, M.** "Unnoticed Euphemism in Isaiah 9:19–20?" *VT* 3 (1952) 179–80.

Translation

Heavens: 7 (8) *A word,*[a] 1
the Lord[b] *sent*[c] *against Jacob,* 3+2
fell in Israel.
Earth: 8 (9) *The people, all of them, acknowledged*[a] *(it):* 3+3+3
Ephraim and the inhabitants of Samaria

	[b]with arrogance and a stout heart.[b]	
Ephraim:	9 (10) *If bricks fall,*	2+2
	let's build with hewn stones!	
	If sycamores are cut down,	2+2
	let's exchange[a] (for) cedars!	
Heavens:	10 (11) *Then[a] YHWH incited[b] Rezin's adversaries[c] against him and armed his enemies.*	
Earth:	11 (12) *With Aram before[a] and the Philistines behind, they proceeded to devour Israel with open mouth.*	
Heavens:	*With all this, his anger has not turned.*	4+3
	His hand (is) stretched out still!	
Earth:	12 (13) *The people have not turned toward the one who strikes them.*	4+4
	YHWH of Hosts[a] they have not sought.	
Heavens:	13 (14) *Then [a]YHWH cut off from Israel[a] head and tail,*	3+2
	Palm branch and swamp-reed in one day.	2+2
	14 (15) *Elder and respected man, (he is the head).*	3+2
	Prophet and teacher of lies,[a] (he is the tail).	3+2
Earth:	15 (16) *So the leaders of this people became "misleaders,"*	4+2
	and their followers (were) confused.[a]	
Heavens:	16 (17) *Because of this,*	1
	the Lord[a] cannot rejoice over their choice youth.	3+3
	Their orphans and widows he cannot comfort.	
Earth:	*For everyone of them is profane and an evildoer.*	4+4
	Every mouth speaks foolishness.	
Heavens:	*With all this, his anger has not turned.*	4+3
	His hand (is) stretched out still.	
Earth:	17 (18) *For wickedness burns like a fire.*	4+3
	It devours briers and thorns	
	when it burns in the forest thickets,	3+3
	when it rolls up[a]—a column of smoke.	
Heavens:	18 (19) *When YHWH of Hosts overflows,*	3+2
	a country is burned up.[a]	
Earth:	*So the people become like fuel for fire.*	4+4
	They have no compassion for each other.	
Heavens:	19 (20) *Then one carves on the right, but is hungry.*	4+4+4
	Another eats on the left, but is not satisfied.	
	They each devour the flesh of his neighbor:[a]	
Earth:	20 (21) *Manasseh on Ephraim*	2+2+3
	and Ephraim on Manasseh.	
	Together on Judah.	
Heavens:	*With all this, his anger has not turned.*	4+3
	His hand (is) stretched out still.	
Mourners:	10:1 *Woe—*	1+3+3
	(you who are) decreeing[a] meaningless decrees,[b]	
	who write[c] burdensome writs[d]	
	2 *to turn the needy from judgment[a]*	3+4
YHWH:	*and to tear away justice (due) the poor of my people.*	

	To let widows be their spoil,	3+2
	and (let them) plunder[b] *orphans.*[c]	
Earth:	[3]*What can you [pl.] do for the day of reckoning?*[a]	4+3
	Or for devastation[b] *that will come from afar?*	
	Upon whom can you depend for help?	3+3
	And where[c] *can you leave your glory*	
	[4 a]*unless one crouch beneath prisoners*[a]	4+3
	or they fall beneath the slain?	
Heavens:	*In all this, his anger has not turned.*	4+3
	His hand is stretched out still.	

Notes

7.a. LXX θάνατον has read דָּבָר, "word," as דֶּבֶר, "plague," which has often been translated with θάνατος, "death" (cf. Exod 5:3; 9:3, 15; Lev 26:25; Num 14:12; Deut 28:21).

7.b. 1QIsa[a] יהוה, "YHWH," instead of MT אדני, "Lord." Wildberger follows 1QIsa[a]. MT is adequate and should be kept.

7.c. The time viewpoint of the passage is determined at this point. The pf. and the inverted order here are different from those in 8:23–9:6. The inversion is for emphasis: דבר, "a word," names the theme of the scene. The verb describes in pf. tense a past action that remains valid in the present (J. Wash Watts, *Survey of Syntax*, 35–36). The "word" is pictured in chap. 1 and emphasized in 2:6–8, 7:7–9, and 8:1–3. So the time viewpoint must be past-present throughout the passage, and tenses are translated accordingly.

8.a. ידע, "know," has been understood by some to mean "be subdued" (D. W. Thomas, *JTS* 41 [1940] 43; G. R. Driver, *JTS* 41 [1940] 162). The use of ידע in Isaiah is significant, and the problem of knowing and understanding is so important that it is doubtful that a variation could be expected. Further, the sense of "know" is vital to this passage. The pf. with *vav* indicated a concomitant fact with the first verb (J. Wash Watts, *Survey of Syntax*, 47–54). God's sending his "word," its "falling" on Jacob, and the people's "knowing" of it are central to the meaning of the passage. Yet here the verb introduces the quotation and needs something more than "know." "Acknowledge" serves both purposes.

8.b-b. Interpreters have found this needs emendation (cf. Wildberger). It is abrupt and concise, but the sense is sound.

9.a. LXX adds καὶ οἰκοδομήσομεν ἑαυτοῖς πύργον, "and let us build for ourselves a tower," like Gen. 11:3–4. There has also been much discussion of חלף. G. R. Driver (*JTS* 34 [1933] 381) uses Syr. and Arab. parallels for a meaning "to cut down." F. X. Wutz (*BZ* 21 [1933] 18) suggests "to fell." The ordinary meaning, "exchange" (BDB, *HAL*) or "to substitute for" (KBL, *DCH*), is satisfactory here.

10.a. The consec. impf. tense shows God's next move. This (and the one in v 13) with the pf. in v 7 form the skeleton of the entire passage.

10.b. סכסך, "prick, incite," is an obscure *pilpel* form. See *Note* 19:2.a.

10.c. Wildberger pontificates "צרי רצין cannot be right" and notes manuscript changes and recent attempts to emend the text. But why not? The words mean "Rezin's enemies." Rezin has been Samaria's patron. Chaps. 7 and 8 have announced Assyria's invasion of Aram. The phrase makes good sense. LXX had trouble with the text and tried to turn צרי רצין into על הר ציון, "on Mount Zion." However, MT makes good and fitting sense as it stands. It also reflects the play on sounds and letters that is typical of the Vision.

11.a. קדם means "in front." אחור means "behind." Because one cites direction as though facing the sunrise, קדם becomes "east," אחור "west." This fits Israel's position with Aram to the east and Philistia to the west.

12.a. צבאות, "hosts," is lacking in LXX. σ´ θ´ and Origen's *Hexapla* support MT. However, את before יהוה is unusual. It is used to avoid misunderstanding in the inverted stich.

13.a-a. The suggestion that יהוה מישראל, "YHWH from Israel," is an addition (Wildberger, Duhm, Fohrer, Kaiser) has missed the polarity that dominates the entire passage, making repetition important.

14.a. מורה, "teacher," in MT appears in opposition to נביא, "prophet." However, three LXX MSS (41, 106, 233) and Cyrill read καὶ διδάσκοντα, which would make this stich have two parts reading "and false teachers." However, this is the easier reading and not well attested.

15.a. מבלעים, "confused." Words from two roots בלע appear in Isaiah (BDB, *HAL, DCH*). בלע, "to swallow," appears in 28:4; בלע, "confound, confuse" *pi'el*, in 3:12 and *nip'al* in 28:7. The parallel to מתעים, "those who cause to err, wander about," suggests the second root.

16.a. A number of emendations have grown up around a misunderstanding of the text (cf. Wildberger). If one eliminates אדוני, "Lord," the parallel seems forced. MT makes sense and should be kept.

17.a. ויתאבכו, "when it rolls up," is a *hap. leg.* It has usually been related to Akk. *abāku*, "to bring or carry away," or to Heb. הפך, "turn" (BDB), or אבק, "intertwine," from which *HAL* suggests "swirl" (also *DCH*).

18.a. נעתם is another *hap. leg.* LXX συγκέκαυται, "was burnt," "consumed"; Tg. הרובה, "is destroyed"; Syr. *zā'at*, "is shaken"; Vg. *conturbata est*, "is distracted, confused." KBL does not translate but suggests emending it to נִתְעָה, "led astray." Others follow LXX and Tg. to emend to נִצְּתָה, "be burned" (Cheyne; Procksch; Donner, *Israel unter den Völkern*). W. L. Moran ("*'tm* in Isa 9:18," *CBQ* 12 [1950] 153–54) sees the word as third-person pl. from נוע with enclitic *mem*. Kaiser, H. D. Hummel ("Enclitic *Mem* in Early NW Semitic," *JBL* 76 [1957] 94), and *HAL* agree: "at the wrath of YHWH the earth reeled." Wildberger considers LXX to be about right, judging from the parallel.

19.a. MT's "the flesh of his own arm" does not make good sense. The Alexandrian group of LXX adds τοῦ ἀδελφοῦ, "of his brother." Tg. has קריביה, which in Heb. is רֵעוֹ (Wildberger), eliminating one letter: "his neighbor" instead of "his arm."

10:1.a. 1QIsa[a] חוקקים, "decreeing," without the article. However, MT is valid.

1.b. חִקְקֵי, "decrees," is derived from the noun חֹק, "a decree," by BDB and *HAL;* from the verb חקק, "engrave, decree," by *DCH*. Joüon §96 *Appendix* derives it from חֵק (cf. also GKC §93*bb*). 1QIsa[a] reads חוקקי (cf. G. R. Driver, "Hebrew Scrolls," *JTS* 2 [1951] 21). The pointing חִקְקֵי is also found in Judg 5:15. L. Köhler, "Bermerkungen zur tiberischen Mss," *HUCA* 23 (1950–51) 155, suggested that the double use of ק might be an ancient form of writing. Wildberger (1979) suggests that the alternative pronunciation of חק is chosen to make alliteration with חקקים, "those decreeing," clearer.

1.c. Tg. וכתב, "write," for מכתבים, "writers." A pl. const. form with enclitic מ (cf. H. L. Ginsberg, "Some Emendations in Isaiah," *JBL* 69 [1950] 54; H. D. Hummel, "Enclitic *Mem* in Early NW Semitic," *JBL* 76 [1957] 94; and Kaiser) is the probable explanation for MT's form: ומכתבים, "the writers of."

1.d. כִּתֵּבוּ, "writs," is the only use of כתב in *pi'el*. It demonstrates the thoroughness of the lawmakers and also completes the alliteration with מכתבי, "write." The clause is construed as a contact relative clause, i.e., without a relative particle.

2.a. מִדִּין has caused comment. Some take it as a noun. Others refuse that possibility (Luzzato). Ginsberg ("Some Emendations in Isaiah," *JBL* 69 [1950] 54) and Kaiser suggest another, enclitic *mem*. However, MT has pointed it as a preposition, מִן, "from," before דין, "judgment." The construction is different from משפט חטה, "pervert justice," in Deut 16:19; 24:17; 27:19.

2.b. The use of an impf. to continue the action of an impf. construction is also unusual. Cf. Joüon §124*g*.

2.c. The use of את with an indefinite object is unusual. Cf. Joüon §125*h*.

3.a פקדה is translated by Delitzsch as "penal visitation."

3.b. שואה BDB, 996, suggests the root שאה, meaning "devastation." Wildberger (179) insists on שוא, "emptiness or vanity" (also *HAL*). The distinction is unimportant here.

3.c. ואנה is the particle אן, "where," with ה directive.

4.a-a. The text here presents problems. כרע, "crouch," lacks a subject. It is sg. while its parallel is pl. This has led to many suggested emendations. P. de Lagarde (*Symmicta* 1 [Göttingen: Dieterich, 1877] 1:105) suggested בֵּלְתִּי כֹּרַעַת חַת אֹסִיר, "Belthis is sinking, Osiris is broken." This required no change in consonantal text and has been used by Steinmann, Eichrodt, Leslie, and Fohrer. Budde ("Zu Jesaja 1–5," *ZAW* 50 [1932] 69) objected that Osiris is never mentioned in the OT. Neither is Beltis, which must mean Isis beside Osiris. H. Zimmern (*Oriental Studies*, FS P. Haupt [Baltimore: Johns Hopkins, 1926] 281–92) suggests that Beltis refers to Sarpanitu, the city-god of Babylon. The versions leave out the second half of the line, but that is no help. Gray suggests reading לְבִלְתִּי כְּרֹעַ (or מִבִּלְתִּי), "to avoid crouching under (?) prisoners and falling under the slain." C. J. Labuschagne ("Ugaritic *bit* and *biltî* in Isa 10:4," *VT* 14 [1964] 99) reads בִּלְתִּ יִכְרַע, "No, he will crouch" (cf. Ugar. *blt*, meaning "no" or "yet"). Wildberger (180) suggests letting בלתי stand alone as "nothing (remains)" and making כרע an inf. abs.: כָּרֹעַ, "one must bow down." He also insists that תחת אסיר means not "among prisoners" but "at the place of prisoners" (cf. Exod 16:29; 2 Sam 7:10; 1 Chr 17:9).

Form/Structure/Setting

Repetition of the refrain "in all this his anger has not turned, his hand is still outstretched" in 9:11*b* (12*b*), 16*d* (17*d*), 20*b* (21*b*), and 10:4*b* demonstrates the unity of the passage as well as the strophes of the poetic unit. The refrain also appears in 5:25, which has led Wildberger (207) and others to try to rearrange the book. Isa 10:1–4 does in fact resume the "woe" forms, but the relationships are complex. Note that 10:5 begins with "woe" but has no refrain.

The entire scene is about the word that the Lord has spoken. Israel's response (or lack of response to it) is reflected in the first two strophes. The last two record no such response. Israel is too far gone. In the last strophe the funeral tone of the lament takes charge. Israel is presumed dead.

The strophes recite God's actions and then allow commentary on the reactions of God and Israel. It is as though the speakers are spectators for this play within a play. The reader learns of it through their reports.

Intro.	Vv 7–9	God's "word"—Israel's response.
I.	Vv 10–12	Against Rezin—they are against Israel.
		God's punishment continues—Israel has not turned.
II.	Vv 13–17	Against the leaders—they become tyrants.
		God's punishment continues—wickedness burns on.
III.	Vv 18–20	Overflowing anger—internal strife.
		God's punishment continues.
IV.	Vv 1–4	Woe—God's punishment continues.

The scene resumes the viewpoint of chaps. 1–5. There is no resistence to God here like that shown in 7:1–9:6 (7). The dialogue shows the detached observation of heavenly observers, the personae that we came to know in 1:2 as Heavens and Earth. Isa 10:1 reintroduces the company of mourners that appeared in chap. 5. This woe oracle returns to the form of the series in 5:8–24 and is often considered misplaced. (See *Comment* to that section.) The positive and hopeful notes of 8:23–9:6 (9:1–7) and of 10:5–19 change nothing in the necessity for God to respond to Israel's flagrant sins.

Comment

7 (8) דבר, "a word," is used here in the sense of "a message." But it is also much more, like a verdict from a court, a decision by a business on a contract. It reports a decision and determines a future. This word involved Jacob/Israel, the elect people, the two-hundred-year-old nation that laid claim to that promise with its capital in Samaria, the rival and sometime enemy of Judah/Jerusalem. YHWH's complaint in 1:2–3 was about Israel. The announcement in 2:6–8 was about Israel. The song of the vineyard applied to Israel (5:7). The woes speeches of chap. 5 applied to Israel. Isaiah's vision and "this people" in God's words were about Israel (6:9–10). Isaiah's word to Ahaz was about Israel (7:7–9). His prophecy of "Maher-Shalal-Hash-Baz" (8:1–3) was about Israel. Indeed, a word had gone out from YHWH against Jacob.

8 (9) וידעו העם כלו: "all the people know" is one possible translation. There is no way for the people to ignore the obvious disaster. Yet they choose not to recognize its deeper meaning. "Arrogance and a stout heart" are those human characteristics that most invite God's retribution (cf. 2:11–17).

9 (10) The determination to "tough it out" is bravado. In some times and against some adversaries, it would have been admirable. Against Assyria's determination to root out potential rebellion and restructure the government of the entire region, it was foolhardy. In the face of God's announcement that the kingdoms were doomed, it was spiritually reprobate.

10 (11) The Son of Remaliah was Rezin's puppet. Rezin effectively controlled Samaria. Thus God's first action is against Rezin. Once his enemies gained power in Damascus, Israel had hostile regimes "before and behind" even before the Assyrian reached her borders.

11–12 (12–13) God's "no" sign was still showing. אף, "anger," is not uncontrolled emotion but rather God's stimulus to provoke a response that he can deal with. But the people of Israel do not respond to God. They only respond (inadequately) to the threatening situation (v 9 [10] above).

13–16 (14–17) The second round of encounter has YHWH remove effective leadership from Israel. A second action has the remaining leaders confuse their followers. God cannot bless this situation.

16*b* (17*b*) The refrain observes that the "no" of God continues to apply.

17 (18) Israel's response is pictured as "wickedness [that] burns like fire."

18 (19) The third round of the encounter speaks of God's judgment as a counterfire that singes the land and turns the people into highly combustible material. The figure changes, becomes more personal. The extreme situation leaves no room for compassion and mutual aid.

19–20 (20–21) The people turn on each other in an orgy of self-destruction. The proud boast of self-reliant rebuilding (v 9) is forgotten, and the inner fabric of social and political relationship succumbs to chaotic violence. Yet God's "no," his decision to abandon (2:6) and hide his face (8:17), continues in force. This time there is no reference to Israel's response.

10:1–4 Mourners take the hint and voice a lament. The helplessness of ineffective crisis government is pictured. The show of decrees and executive orders by the "misleaders" (v 15) only increases injustice and brings no order to those chaotic times. The state is dead, the mourners chant, and the leaders have no option but to share its fate. The final comment notes that "God's anger has not changed." Israel's fate, as a nation, is sealed.

Explanation

The scene acts to stem the tide of patriotic euphoria that had broken out in Jerusalem in the previous scene. The optimism that saw only opportunity, glory, and light beyond the crisis tended to be blind to the dire implications inherent in the approach of the Assyrian. They, and the audience, are called back to the grim implications of God's decision to end the northern kingdom's existence as a nation. But the issue of Israel—election and God's intentions for his people—will be back. It cannot so easily be disposed of.

Isa 10:1–4 responds to the dark picture of Israel's condition by lamenting the bad leadership that had precipitated its current state. Oppressive laws against the weak and helpless for the hope of ill-gotten gain have weakened the fabric of society. It cannot withstand the external pressures. The exploiters will suffer like all others. Thus they experience God's anger, which was aroused by their deeds.

The Assyrian King, Rod of My Anger (10:5–19)

Bibliography

Barth, H. *Die Jesaja-Worte.* 28–34. **Childs, B. S.** *Isaiah and the Assyrian Crisis.* 39–90. **Dafni, E. G.** "מנפש ועד בשר (Jesaja x 18)." *VT* 49 (1999) 301–14. **Driver, G. R.** "Isaiah I–XXXIX: Textual and Linguistic Problems." *JSS* 13 (1968) 36–57. **Fohrer, G.** "Wandlungen Jesajas." In *FS W. Eilers.* Wiesbaden: Harrassowitz, 1967. 67–70. **Fullerton, K.** "The Problem of Isaiah, Chapter 10." *AJSL* 34 (1917–18) 170–84. **Huber, F.** *Jahwe, Juda und die anderer Völker beim Propheten Jesaja.* Berlin: De Gruyter, 1976. 35–76. **Machinist, P.** "Assyria and Its Image in the First Isaiah." *JAOS* 103 (1983) 719–37. **Mittmann, S.** "'Wehe! Assur, Stab maines Zorns' (Jes 10,5–9,13ab–15)." In *Prophet und Prophetenbuch.* FS O. Kaiser, ed. V. Fritz et al. Berlin: De Gruyter, 1989. 111–33. **Robertson, E.** "Some Obscure Passages in Isaiah." *AJSL* 49 (1932–33) 319–22. **Sander, O.** "Leib-Seele-Dualismus im Alten Testament." *ZAW* 77 (1965) 329–32. **Schildenberger, J.** "Das 'Wehe' uber den stolzen Weltherrscher Assur." *Sein und Sendung* 30 (1965) 483–89. **Schwarz, G.** "Das Licht Israels?" *ZAW* 77 (1965) 329–32. ———. ". . . das Licht Israels? Eine Emendation (Isa 10:17a)." *ZAW* 82 (1970) 447–48. **Skehan, P. W.** "A Note on Isaiah 10:11*b*–12*a*." *CBQ* 14 (1952) 236. **Tadmor, H.** "The Campaigns of Sargon II of Assur." *JCS* 12 (1958) 22–40; 77–100. **Weinfeld, M.** "The Protest against Imperialism in Ancient Israelite Prophecy." In *The Origins and Diversity of Axial Age Civilizations.* Ed. S. N. Eisenstadt. New York: SUNY Press, 1986. 169–82.

Translation

Mourner: 5 *Woe—* 1
YHWH: *Assyria!* 1
Rod of my anger! 2+2+2
[a]*Staff of my wrath,*
it is in their hand![a]
6 *I send him against a godless nation;* 3+3
I command him against the people of my wrath.
To take spoil! 2+2
To seize prey!
To make it[a] *a trampling ground,* 2+2
like the mire of the streets!
Heavens: 7 *But what about him?* 1
He does not think that way. 2+3
His heart does not feel like that.
On the contrary— 1
his mind is on destruction 2+2+2
on slaughtering nations,

not a few.[a]
Earth: 8 *He says:* 2+4
"Are each[a] *of my vassals not kings?*
9 *Is not Calno*[a] *like Carchemish?* 3+3+3
Or Hamath like Arpad?[b]
Or Samaria like Damascus?
10 *Just as my hand finds (its way)* 3+2+3
to the idolatrous kingdoms
whose idols surpass Jerusalem's and Samaria's,
11 *as I do to Samaria and her idols* 3+2
shall I not do to Jerusalem and to her images?" 2+2
Heavens: 12 *It will be* 1
when the Lord will finish all his work 4+3
against Mount Zion and against Jerusalem—
YHWH: *I will punish*[a] *the fruit of the king of Assyria's* 4+3
expanded mind
and the glorification of his elevated eyes.
Heavens: 13 *Because he says:* 2
"I act by the strength of my hand 3+3+3
for I decide by my wisdom
when I change people's boundaries.
I plunder[a] *their treasure*[b] 2+3
when I knock down inhabitants like a bull.[c]
14 *Then my hand searches as in a net* 3+2
for the people's wealth.
Like gathering abandoned eggs, 3+4
I myself gather the whole earth.
And no wing flutters 4+3
nor does any mouth open or chirp."
Earth: 15 *Does the ax exalt itself* 2+2
over the one cutting with it?
Or the saw magnify itself 2+1
over the one using it?
As (if) a rod were to wave its bearer, 3+3
as (if) a staff were to lift (the one who is) not wood.[a]
Heavens: 16 *Therefore—* 1
the Lord,[a] *YHWH of Hosts, will send* 4+2
leanness against his fat ones.
Earth: *Under his glory* 2+2+2
he will kindle a kindling
like a kindling of fire.
17 *And the Light of Israel*[a] *will become a fire* 4+2
and his Holiness a flame.
It will burn and devour 2+2+2
his thorns[b] *and his briers*
in one day,
18 *with the glory of his forests and his acreage.* 3

Heavens: [a]*Body and Soul it will consume,*[a] 3+3
and he shall be like a sick man wasting away.[b]
Earth: [19]*What is left of the trees*[a] *of his forest* 3+2+2
will be so few
that a child can count them.

Notes

5.a-a. The second half of the line is a problem, complicated by MT's *maqqef.* Various attempts at emendation have been made (cf. Wildberger), but none is satisfactory.

The problem pair of words is הוא בידם. By itself the phrase means "he (is) in their hand." Joined to מטה, "staff," it may be rendered "which (is) in their hand." However, it divides two words, מטה, "staff," and זעמי, "anger," which the parallelism suggests should be in const. relation.

הוא בידם is best understood as a gloss note added by a scribe, to ameliorate the theological problem of ascribing full identification of the Assyrian as God's instrument. It suggests instead that God's instrument was "in their hand." G. R. Driver (*JTS* 34 [1933] 383) suggested transposing the phrase to achieve the same effect: ומטא זעמי הוא בידם, "and the rod of my wrath—it is in their hand."

6.a. K לשימו, "to make it," but Q לשומו, "to make it." Masoretic Heb. knows both forms. The difference is meaningless.

7.a. Tg. translates לא מעט, "not a few," with לא בחיס, "without protection" (cf. S. Speier, "Zu drei Jesajastellen," *TZ* 21 [1965] 312; Hab 1:17*b*).

8.a. M. D. Goldman ("Lexicographical Notes on Exegesis," *ABR* 1 [1951] 63) shows that יחדו means not only "together" but also "alone, separately."

9.a. כַּלְנוֹ, "Calno," is usually pronounced "Calneh." See LXX, Amos 6:2, and the cuneiform inscriptions.

9.b. אַרְפַּת, "Arpad," is usually written with *qamets.*

12.a. LXX ἐπάξει, "he will bring (punishment)." Many suggest changing MT to 3d person.

13.a. שושתי is apparently a variant writing for שוסיתי since several MSS preserve it: *piʿel* pf. 1 sg. שסה (cf. GKC §6*k*) is שסיתי, "I plunder." The context calls for an act. verb.

13.b. Q ועתודותיהם, "their he-goats," meaning their leaders. K ועתידתיהם, "their supplies." Parallelism is better served by K.

13.c. The versions vary the reading: LXX καὶ σείσω πόλεις κατοικουμένας, "and I will shake inhabited cities"; Tg. בתקוף יתיתבי כרכין תקיפין ואחיתית, "and I subdued with force inhabitants of strong cities." MT suits the basic form, meter, and sense as well as any.

15.a. לא־עץ, "not wood," has appeared cumbersome to some interpreters. E. Robertson (*AJSL* 49 [1932–33] 319) suggests emending to ל(ו)חֵץ, "oppressor." MT should be sustained with Wildberger.

16.a. האדון, "the Lord," is missing in some MSS. LXX only has it once, whereas האדון יהוה, "the Lord YHWH," would require it twice. But MT provides good meter in a tristich line and should be kept. (Contra G. R. Driver, *JSS* 13 [1968] 41.)

17.a. אור־ישראל, "Light of Israel," may also be a name for God. Cf. Pss 27:1 and 36:10.

17.b. שִׁיתוֹ, "his thorns," appears only in the first part of Isaiah (cf. 5:6). The form with suf. would ordinarily be שיתו. Wildberger suggests that the alternative pronunciation is given to match וּשְׁמִירוֹ, "and his briars."

18.a-a. MT has only one verb: יְכַלֶּה, "it will consume." LXX has two verbs: ἀποσβεσθήσεται, "will be extinguished," and καταφάγεται, "it will consume." Wildberger suggests changing וכרמלו, "his cultivated land," to a verb form. G. R. Driver (*JSS* 13 [1968] 42) joins σ´ αναλωθήσεται, Vg. *consumetur,* and *BHS* in suggesting a pass. reading: יְכֻלֶּה. However, MT may well be kept as it is.

18.b. כמסס נסס is a *hap. leg.* נסס has been compared to Syr. *nassîs* or *neesîs,* "sick." T. Nöldeke (*Mandäische Grammatik* [Halle: Waisenhaus, 1875 = 1944] xxx; *ZDMG* 40 [1886] 729 n. 2) pointed to Gk. νόσος, "sickness." G. R. Driver (*JTS* 34 [1933] 375; *JSS* 13 [1968] 42) refers it to Akk. *nasâsu* I, "sway to and fro," II, "wave (of hair), shake," while Wildberger prefers to derive it from נס, "signal" ("as if a flag-bearer falls"). Cf. Robertson, *AJSL* 49 (1932–33) 320–22.

19.a. Wildberger has properly rejected the suggestion of *BHK:* עצי, "trees"; MT is to be kept, but considered a collective noun.

Form/Structure/Setting

A formal similarity ties this new section to the last episode: the use of הוי, "woe." But the subject and orientation turn from Israel to Assyria. The episode comes to grips with the anomaly that God is using the enemy—is claiming to own and control the enemy—against his own people. The problems God faces in doing so are portrayed from the viewpoint of those who believe that God has a special relationship with Jerusalem.

The passage has one theme: Assyria, God's chosen instrument. But the disparity in character and intention between God and his instrument tests the unity of the passage. YHWH speaks twice on the issue. In vv 5–6 he announces the Assyrian's commission. In v 12*b* he promises to punish the Assyrian king's ambition. The rest of the section reacts to these announcements. The Assyrian is not actually present, but he is quoted at such length that his presence is felt (vv 8–11, 13–14). The indignation of the players at the appointment (vv 7 and 15) is supported by these quotations, and mollified by the expanded assurance of God's judgment of the Assyrian (vv 16–17).

The quoted speeches of the Assyrian (vv 8–11, 13–14) are modeled on those of the rabshakah (2 Kgs 18:19–25, 28–35; 19:10–13; Isa 36:4–10, 13–20; 37:10–13). However, the literary function differs. In the narrative, the speeches fit naturally into the psychological warfare of the siege. They are intended to intimidate—to prepare for negotiation. Here they are plucked out of context to illustrate the Assyrian's attitude and character, like the words of Babylon's leaders in Gen 11:3–4, of Babylon's king in Isa 14:13–14, of Tyre in Ezek 27:3 and 28:2, of Egypt in Jer 46:8, or of Edom in Obad 3.

The passage begins as though it would continue the woe speeches that precede. But the YHWH-word breaks in to turn attention to the active perpetrator of the violence instead of to its victim. YHWH's speech begins with strong phrases—no verbs (v 5). It continues (v 6) with inverted sentences—prepositional phrases up front—and imperfect tenses. It closes with three infinitives to emphasize the intent of the appointment. The use of cognate verb-object combinations adds strength to the speech. (Note the emphatic use of first person in vv 5–6, 12*b*, with the counterpoint in the first person from the Assyrian in vv 8–11, 13–14.)

An observer raises an objection (v 7) about the Assyrian, by using "but as for him." Vv 5–6 have spoken of God's intention, but this speaker is concerned about the Assyrian's intentions. Again, inverted word order brings emphasis and passion to the words (v 7*a*) while the decisive statement is made with infinitives—no finite verbs (v 7*b*)—matching the Lord's words in v 6*b*. The rhetorical question of v 7*a–d* marks the sharpness of the dialogical exchange.

The opening lines of the Assyrian's quoted speech (vv 8–9) are strong, assertive statements without verbs. The comparison that follows is deliberately insulting and denigrating in likening the idolatrous nations to Samaria and Jerusalem. The verbs in vv 10 and 11*a*, "my hand finds," "as I do," are in the perfect tense, while that in 11*b*, "shall I not do," returns to the imperfect as in v 7*a*. Again the use of a rhetorical question (11*b*) strengthens the speech.

The objection is met by YHWH's announcement of Assyria's punishment, which is justified by another quotation showing the Assyrian's attitude (vv 13–14). לכן, "therefore," in v 16 corresponds to כי, "because," in v 13 and elaborates on the announcement of YHWH's punishment in two forms. The first decrees a wasting illness to replace his plump good health (vv 16*a,* 18*bc*). The second announces a seering fire that will destroy his forests (vv 16b–18*a,* 19).

The composition is a literary masterpiece in which the choice and balance of the vocabulary and grammar, not to mention the sounds of the words, work together to achieve the effect intended. It is one of the strongest literary pieces in the entire Vision.

Comment

5 אשור, "Assyria," is already familiar from the announcement in 7:17 and the following speeches (cf. 7:18, 20; 8:4, 7; for the history, see the introduction to chaps. 7–12 above). Even the idea that God is sending the king of Assyria has been stated there. אפי, "my anger," and זעמי, "my wrath," are also familiar. The Vision began by explaining YHWH's displeasure in chap. 1 and by citing the day of retribution in chap. 2. The great funeral scene in chap. 5 has the repeated refrain "his anger did not turn" (5:25*b*), which is picked up again in 9:16*c,* 20*c,* and 10:4. This passage is, in a sense, an explanation of that repeated phrase.

שבט, "rod," can refer to a ruler's scepter, as it does in Gen 49:10; Num 24:17; Judg 5:14; Isa 9:3 (4); 11:4; 14:5; and Amos 1:5, 8. Or it may refer to the disciplinarian's rod of punishment as in Job 9:34 and 21:9, referring to God's discipline (cf. also Prov 13:24, etc.; 2 Sam 7:14; 23:21; Isa 14:29). מטה, "staff," may also refer to a scepter, as it does in Jer 48:17; Ezek 19:11–14; Ps 110:2 (מטה־עז, "the staff of power"), but not to an educator's tool. It is more likely a magician's wand (cf. Exod 7:12). Aaron and Moses use such (Exod 4:2–4; 7:9–20; 17:5), and it is once called מטה האלהים, "the staff of God" (Exod 17:9). Together, the words indicate that God's royal authority and awesome power have been delegated to the Assyrian—expressions of God's anger and his wrath.

בידם, "in their hand." That God's work should be placed in the power and authority of Assyria raises a serious issue of faith. How can God use this rampaging empire against God's own people? The dilemma was posed in the shocked question of the prophet in 6:11: "How long?" It is implicit in Ahaz's refusal to put YHWH to the test (7:12). It is there in the admonition concerning "conspiracy" in 8:12 and in the rock that causes human beings to stumble in 8:14.

6 The verse precludes the obvious objection that Israel is elect, the children of Abraham. Not so—they are that no longer. They are "a godless nation" or a profane nation. The use of גוי, "nation," is deliberate. (Cf. 1:2*b*–4; 2:6–8.) They are a people of God's wrath. This implies not only rejection but active measures toward extermination. That is the role of the Assyrian.

7 Attention is drawn to the character and intention of the instrument. He is interested in violence and slaughter for its own sake—to build up his own reputation, to expand his ego.

8 The words שׂרים, "vassals," and מלכים, "kings," apparently recognize the distinction in Akkadian between *malku* or *maliku,* which refers to the king of a city, and *šarru,* the king of a country. The Assyrians allowed the defeated city kings to keep their titles.

9 He recites his victories over the great city-states of Syria. As independent powers in an earlier time, they were a barrier to aggression from the north or east.

כַּלְנוֹ, Calno (apparently the same as כַּלְנֵה, "Calneh," in Amos 6:2), is to be located in northern Syria. Opinions differ on the likely location. It fell to Tiglath-Pileser in 738 B.C.E. כרכמיש, "Carchemish," was a city on the Euphrates near the boundary between modern Turkey and Syria. It was known in the early second millennium, and its history touched that of Egypt in the fifteenth century and that of the Hittites in the fourteenth. The city was sacked by the Assyrians repeatedly in the ninth and eighth centuries. Tiglath-Pileser III received tribute from it. In 717 B.C.E. Sargon finally destroyed the city and deported its inhabitants (*ISBE,* 1:616).

חמת, "Hamath," lies well to the south on the Orontes river in Syria. It was an important independent city. David collaborated with its king. It was subdued by Assyria in 738 B.C.E., and a brief uprising was totally put down in 720 B.C.E. ארפד, "Arpad," is always paired with Hamath (cf. 36:19; 37:1); they are mentioned as cities destroyed by Tiglath-Pileser III (*ISBE* 1:298). It was located about twenty-five miles north of modern Aleppo.

שמרון, "Samaria," was the city built by Omri to be the capital of Israel. It had come under pressure from Tiglath-Pileser as early as the reign of Menahem (745–738 B.C.E.; 2 Kgs 15:19–20). In 733 B.C.E. Tiglath-Pileser invaded the land (2 Kgs 15:29), Pekah was murdered, and the Assyrian put Hoshea on the throne and imposed tribute. When Tiglath-Pileser died (727 B.C.E.), Hoshea rebelled. Shalmaneser threw him in prison and besieged the city, which was finally subdued by his successor Sargon II in 722 B.C.E.

דמשק, "Damascus," was the capital of Aram and one of the oldest cities in the world. In 732 B.C.E. Tiglath-Pileser conquered Damascus and its territory. He made it an Assyrian province with an Assyrian governor.

Jerusalem apparently paid tribute to Assyria under Uzziah, Jotham, and Ahaz. But there is no record of a specific threat during this period. Under Hezekiah the threats became serious (cf. chaps. 20 and 36–37).

10 In worldly terms the Assyrian king recognized the role of religion in each of the countries he captured. Undoubtedly, from his point of view, the idols of northern Syria were much better known and more respected than the religion of Samaria and Jerusalem.

11 The speech indicates a threat to Samaria (i.e., prior to 722 B.C.E.) and an extended threat to Jerusalem. This is exactly the situation envisioned by 8:7–8. The taunt against nations easily slips into a blasphemy of their gods (cf. Wildberger). Childs (*Isaiah and the Assyrian Crisis,* 88) has traced a historical tradition of such taunts in the OT from Goliath and David (1 Sam 17:43) to references in Ezekiel and finally Daniel.

12 The announcement by and on behalf of YHWH contrasts with the boasts of the Assyrian. Throughout this section the Vision has recognized the unity of the Assyrian's task. First the destruction of Samaria, including exile of its people, followed by the chastising purification of Jerusalem. Only after this is complete will YHWH turn his attention to the Assyrian.

An example of the artistic language in this pericope is the play here between פרי *pri,* "fruit," and תפארת *tp'rth,* "glorification."

13 The king's second poem of self-praise supplies the evidence to support YHWH's judgment of him. The king should possess physical power and wise counsel to make plans (cf. פלא יועץ, "a wonder counselor," and אל גבור, "God-Hero," in 9:5 [6]). These the king claims.

14 Changing of boundaries was a fixed part of Assyrian imperial practice along with the exchange of peoples. The king is proud of his ability to extort tribute and raise funds for his campaigns and the empire. He finds it as easy as taking eggs from under a nesting hen. No complaint is raised. No resistence dares raise its head.

15 It is not the violence or the destruction to which protest is directed. It is only that the Assyrian claims full credit, putting himself in the place of God. The parable of the ax and the workman has a flavor of the wisdom schools. The use of metaphor, the question, and comparison make the point.

16–19 The statement of judgment picks up its theme from v 12. The announcement uses YHWH's full title, as it was used in holy war of old. As in the old holy-war themes, the application of power is indirect. A wasting disease appropriately attacks, the result of rich living among Assyria's subjects. A fire will destroy the similar signs of a rich land—Assyria's forests.

Explanation

God is not reacting to events of that time; rather he is initiating them. Assyria is his agent. The Assyrian invasions are identified as God's work to accomplish his destructive judgment. But the protest is raised: the Assyrian does not know that. His drives and ambition are totally selfish. How can one identify God's work in one so ungodly? The answer: God will judge the Assyrian in time. One thing at a time. The limitations that time imposes are accepted, even as they apply to the work of God. With this passage a major thesis of the Vision has been fully stated and defended. God uses the pagan empires to further his purpose (cf. Cyrus in chaps. 45–46). This is a change from the kingdom-of-God theology of the united monarchy and the Psalms. There God ruled the world through the Davidic king in Jerusalem. In Isaiah a part of that rule is delegated to the empires, and Israel's role is radically redefined. R. Kittel (*Geschichte des Volkes Israel,* 6th ed. [Stuttgart: Kohlhammer, 1925] 2:386 n. 1) characterizes this as "one of the strongest of Isaiah's speeches and at the same time the first attempt to enunciate in grand style a philosophy of history which is built on the law of a moral world-order in history. World history is world judgment."

The basic issue of faith as it relates to history is faced directly in this scene. The fact of Assyria's ascendancy, power, and tyranny in the latter eighth century is unchallenged. The question probes the deeper explanation of the factors that made that possible. YHWH claims that Assyria belongs to him: "Rod of my anger! Staff of my wrath!" He claims authority over Assyria: "I send him! I command him!" He accepts responsibility for the king's excesses: "I will punish him!" But the speakers insist that another view be heard. The Assyrian proclaims his own autonomy, integrity, and credit: "my vassals," "my hand," "I do." He will not share credit or responsibility: "I act by the strength of my hand. . . . I decide by my wisdom!" He wants full recognition and credit for his acts: "I change people's boundaries. I plunder their treasures. . . . I knock down inhabitants. . . . I myself gather the whole earth." God's commitment that "the haughtiness of the human shall be brought down, . . . and YHWH alone shall be exalted" (2:17) is challenged by the very one that he has chosen and used to do his work of judgment. The doctrine that God works through human agency faces this *dilemma.*

When God strengthens and guides someone to accomplish God's will, he runs the risk of convincing the person of his own importance and ability, which complicates his usefulness to God or at that point makes him the object of God's judgment.

The stark presentation of the problem here (and in chaps. 2, 14, and 27) forms a background to the argument for the "servant" role that could help Israel and Jerusalem break this vicious cycle.

"In That Day": Only a Remnant of Israel (10:20–23)

Bibliography

Binns, L. E. "Midianite Elements in Hebrew Religion." *JTS* 31 (1930) 337–54. **Stegemann, U.** "Der Restgedanke bei Isaias." *BZ* 13 (1969) 161–86.

Translation

Heavens:	20 *And it shall be in that day:*	1+2
	No longer will	3+2+3
	the remnant of Israel	
	and refugees of the house of Jacob	
	rely on their oppressors	2+2
	but will rely on YHWH,	
	the Holy One of Israel,	2+1
	in truth.[a]	
Chorus of Israelites:	21 *A remnant will return!*	2+2+2
	A remnant of Jacob!	
	To the Mighty God!	
Heavens:	22 *Even if there are*	2+2+2
	(of) your people, Israel,	
	(a number) like the sand of the sea,	
	(only) a remnant in it[a] *will return.*	3
Earth:	*Annihilation has been determined.*	2+2
	Righteous (anger) is overflowing!	
	23 *Indeed, what the Lord,*[a] *YHWH of Hosts,*	3+3+3
	is doing in the whole land	
	is a completed and fixed decree.[b]	

Notes

20.a. באמת, "in truth," has been found to be superfluous by Procksch and H. Schmidt (*Die grossen Propheten,* 2d ed. [Göttingen: Vandenhoeck & Ruprecht, 1923]). Wildberger correctly holds that its position intentionally emphasizes its point. LXX τῇ αληθείᾳ, "to the truth," uses a dative case without prep., which patently changes the meaning. Cf. further H. Wildberger, "אמן," *THAT,* vol. 1, col. 201.

22.a. בו, "in it." G. R. Driver (*JSS* 13 [1968] 42) and *BHS* suggest that this be read with the following phrase. Wildberger correctly insists on a partitive meaning: "In Israel—only a few can agree to repent."

23.a. אדני, "Lord," is standard in Isaiah (see 3:17; 6:8; 7:14; 8:7; 9:7–16). LXX has only ὁ θεός for the entire long title. Most of the other Greek versions have κύριος.

23.b. כלה ונחרצה, lit. "completion and a fixed thing," is probably to be understood as hendiadys, i.e., two words that together express one idea.

Form/Structure/Setting

The scene returns to an "earthly" setting as Israel is addressed in v 22. Traditional words of hope are offered, interrupted by heavenly reminders of God's true intentions. The episode is joined to the one before by the formula "and it shall be in that day" and by the play on the word שאר, "remnant." In v 19, "remnant" referred to trees that survived conflict and exploitation, but the word touches off a discussion of the remnant of Israel in vv 20–22. The consecutive of the perfect verb והיה, "and it shall be," continues the thought of ישלח, "he will send," in v 16. The arrangement of vv 20–22 is dialectical, with different voices and ideas engaged. This entire chapter has looked at the predicament of northern Israel as refugees and friends in Jerusalem might see it and as Heavens and Earth might observe it.

Vv 20–23 expressly speak of Israel/Jacob, i.e., northern Israel, while vv 24–27 speak to Jerusalem. Commentators have often created confusion by ignoring this distinction.

Comment

20 יום ההוא, "that day," refers to the Assyrian invasion that has dominated chaps. 8–10, that is, the incursions from 733 to 721 B.C.E.

שאר, "remnant," is taken here to imply that a small group of those left as exiles will finally exercise genuine faith in YHWH, in contrast to the picture in 9:7 (8)–10:4. The verse assumes the dispersion of the people of northern Israel (cf. 11:11, 16; 2 Kgs 17:6) and refers directly to them. It assumes two prior attitudes among the people, both related to the word שען, "lean on." The word appears in a religious context in Mic 3:11, which condemns the corruption among leaders, priests, and prophets who piously "lean on YHWH," saying, "Is not YHWH in our midst? Nothing can happen to us." In Isa 30:12 the word parallels בטח, "trust," and describes those who reject God's word and then "trust in a perverse tyrant" (see *Note* 30:12.c.). In 31:1 it again is parallel to "trust" and speaks of those who "rely" on horses and Egypt. So in a religious context, the term means a frivolous reliance on God to get through regardless of one's behavior. It also referred to political reliance on arms, alliances, or authoritarian methods.

מכהו, "their oppressors," is literally "those striking it." This could well apply to Pekah's puppet relationship to the Rezin of Aram who defeated Israel in 736 B.C.E. and supported Pekah's coup d'état (cf. Bright, *HI*, 271–72). Or it could apply to Hoshea's ascending the throne in 732 under Assyria's sponsorship after the Assyrian campaign of 733 (cf. 2 Kgs 15:25–16:9, especially 15:25–29, 37; 16:5–9). The bootlicking attitude is contrasted with a genuine dependence on YHWH that makes for a genuinely independent policy.

Because "lean on YHWH" had a negative religious connotation, the באמת, "in truth," is particularly appropriate and necessary. The Vision emphasizes Isaiah's view that faithful and trusting שען, "dependence," on YHWH, is essential for life under God.

21 The chorus picks up the hint of hopeful content and interprets it in their own way. They begin by chanting the name of Isaiah's son: ישוב שאר, "A Remnant Will Return." The words are packed with connotations and meaning, some of which are ambiguous and self-contradictory. It is just the kind of thing that makes a good slogan.

שאר, "remnant" (see *Excursus: The "Remnant"* [שאר/שארית] *in Isaiah* at 7:3 above), can mean the pitiful remainder of a decimated people or the army that survives a battle or a war. But it also apparently had a technical (perhaps cultic) meaning: the authentic and integral core of the people who were the genuinely elect, the genuine Israel. The rest of the nation depended on this core and assumed that they all would be saved, or would prosper because of it. They are "the pious remnant," the "righteous remnant," the "faithful remnant." Many would have felt that this second meaning canceled out the first. (Cf. G. F. Hasel, "Remnant," *IDBSup,* 730–36.)

ישוב, "will return," is equally ambiguous. It means simply "to turn" or "to return." It can mean to physically come back, as from exile, or it can refer to a change of mind or policy. It may become "repent" when related to God. The doctrine of repentance becomes widespread from Jeremiah onward (cf. J. Milgrom, "Repentance in the Old Testament," *IDBSup,* 736–38).

שאר יעקב, "a remnant of Jacob." The slogan is narrowed and applied in the second line specifically to northern Israel as v 20 had done.

The third line adds another ambiguous expression: אל גבור, "God, the heroic warrior." However, the same title is applied in 9:5 (6) as one of the throne names of the heir to David's throne. The hint that the misfortunes of the northern kingdom might open the door to a reunited kingdom under Jerusalem and its king reappears in these pages (cf. *Comments* on 9:5–6 [6–7] and 11:12–14).

22–23 The verses are a reminder of the context. God's decree for the political destruction of Israel has been fixed. It will not change (chaps. 5–6). The Lord himself is at work to accomplish it in the land. No pious platitudes will change that fact. Thus שאר, "remnant," is to be taken literally, as if it were the trees of Lebanon in v 19. The surviving fragment of the population will be frightfully small. There is nothing glorious about it from this viewpoint.

This reminder of God's consistent policy toward Israel in this period continues the line of announcements from 1:2–4; 2:6; 3:13–15; 5:13, 24, 25; 6:11–13; 7:8; 8:2, 5–7; and 9:7–21, esp. v 14. The Vision reveals that God's unalterable decision to end Israel's political existence as a nation had been made as early as Uzziah's time.

Explanation

Hope is still alive, if only for a remnant. But it must be postponed until the agenda of destruction for the kingdom of Israel is fulfilled. The Vision bluntly opposes misguided political or spiritual optimism that would mislead Israel or Judah about God's intentions. But, for the writers, this message of unalterable destruction interprets only the past. In their present (the Persian Empire of the fifth century B.C.E.), warnings of judgment are balanced by a message of hope for those willing to accept God's vision of Jerusalem inhabited by "servants" and open to pilgrims from around the empire (Isa 66:10–22).

Scene 3: A Word for Jerusalem (10:24–12:6)

Scene 3 picks up the theme of Jerusalem from chaps. 3–4 and continues the theme of monarchy from 7:1–14 and 9:5–6. However, it is also marked by a clear change of subject, taking the punishment of Assyria, briefly introduced in 10:12, as its dominant theme.

Again an arch structure may be perceived to shape the scene.

A Very soon my anger will be against the Assyrians (10:24–25).
  B The Lord will lash them in the way of Egypt (10:26–27).
    C He marches on Zion and waves at Jerusalem (10:26–27*c*).
      D The Lord is cutting trees in Lebanon (10:33–34).
        E **A** shoot **will emerge** from Jesse's root (11:1).
          F The Spirit of YHWH rests on him (11:2).
            G The fear of YHWH—his delight (11:3*a*).
KEYSTONE YHWH **is righteous and just** (11:3*b*–4).
            G´ Righteousness **is** his belt (11:5–8).
          F´ Knowledge of YHWH **will fill** the earth (11:9).
        E´ The Root of Jesse **will be** a banner to the nations (11:10).
      D´ The Lord will recover refugees and restore the united kingdom (11:11–14).
    C´ YHWH will dry up the sea (11:15–16).
  B´ You will sing in that day (12:1–2).
A´ And you will drink from the well of salvation (12:3–6).

Three layers may be distinguished in the arch. The outer layers AB and A´B´ are directly addressed to God's people in Zion. CDE and C´D´E´ are about YHWH's work of salvation, with E and E´ mentioning the king indirectly but explicitly. F and F´ speak about God's spiritual gifts and the knowledge of YHWH. G and G´ speak of righteous judgment through the fear of YHWH. The keystone speaks of YHWH's just rule.

Interpreters have had trouble marking the divisions here, but the chiastic chart helps to clarify the situation. Isa 10:24–27*c* begins with לכן, "therefore," a strong connective with a previous assertion, which in this case must be the keystone of the previous chiastic order, 10:12. Vv 26–27*c* expand on this, again using the full name of God and an "in that day" construction in 27*a–c*. Isa 10:27*d*–32 is a masterful poetic construction that is unconnected syntactically to what precedes it—a theophanic vision inserted into the developing scene to prepare for the climactic announcement to follow. Isa 10:33–34 interprets the preceding theophany but, more important, introduces the speeches that follow in chaps. 11 and 12. V 33 begins with הנה, "behold." J. G. Herder (*The Spirit of Hebrew Poetry*

[1782], trans. J. Marsh [Naperville; IL: Aleph Press, 1971], 294) noted this separation between vv 32 and 33, as did A. Bruno (*Jesaja, eine rhythmische und textkritische Untersuchung* [Stockholm: Almqvist & Wiksell, 1953]) and Kaiser, but not Wildberger. The subject is the Lord YHWH. The announcement: as a master forester he is trimming and thinning the forests (cf. 10:17–19). Lebanon (read Assyrian power on the northern border) will fall (v 34).

The results are expressed in a series of picture passages (motifs), each beginning with a verb in perfect tense with *vav:* (1) Isa 11:1–10: A shoot from the stump of Jesse will thrive (vv 1–5). The people will not hurt; the earth will be full of the knowledge of YHWH (vv 6–9). In that day the nations will rally to David's heir (v 10). (2) Isa 11:11–16: In that day YHWH will reach out to recover the scattered people. (3) Isa 12:1–6: In that day the king will sing to YHWH (vv 1–2), and the people of Jerusalem will give thanks (vv 3–6).

The complete mosaic pictures the achievement of God's and Jerusalem's goals: stable continuance of the Davidic dynasty, peace with knowledge of YHWH, leadership over neighboring peoples, return of exiles, and unity in the kingdom. These will all be achieved when YHWH "cuts down the trees" (10:33–34), sends his spirit on the king (11:2), judges in righteousness (11:4–5), and acts to bring back the exiles (11:11–12). The emphasis throughout is on YHWH's initiative and YHWH's action. Jerusalem, the king, and the exiles are to be either "receptive" or "reactive" only. Then they can sing (chap. 12).

YHWH has brought the Assyrian (7:17) as a judgment on Israel and Aram. Israel continued rebellious (9:7 [8]—10:4) and was destroyed (10:22–23). But YHWH's promise to purge Jerusalem (1:24–26) so that it can be his dwelling (2:1–4) is being carried out. An heir is promised to Ahaz (7:14) and is born amid rejoicing (9:6 [7]). YHWH promises that the Assyrian will be punished when he has finished his work with Zion and Jerusalem (10:12). This is fulfilled: "See, he is lopping off branches" (10:12). A promise of a successor (Hezekiah), blessed and successful (11:1–4), and of wonderful peace (11:5–9) seems within reach. The destruction of Samaria is past without Jerusalem being drawn into the rebellion. This is reason for hope (11:11–16) and for rejoicing (chap. 12).

Jerusalemites, Do Not Fear the Assyrian (10:24–27c)

Bibliography

Cogan, M. *Imperialism and Religion: Assyria, Judah and Israel in the Eighth and Seventh Centuries B.C.E.* Missoula, MT: Scholars Press, 1974. **Binns, L. E.** "Midianite Elements in Hebrew Religion." *JTS* 31 (1930) 337–54. **Soggin, J. A.** "*Tablitam* in Isaiah 10:25*b*." *BO* 13 (1971) 232.

Translation

Herald: [24] *Therefore—thus says the* [a] *Lord, YHWH of Hosts:* [a] 1+4

YHWH: *"Do not be afraid* 1+3+1
my people dwelling in Zion,
because of Assyria
when he strikes with the rod, 2+3+2
when he lifts his staff against you
[b]*in the Way of Egypt.*[b]
25 *For in a very short while* 3+2+3
indignation[a] *will be finished,*
and my anger, (will be intent) on their destruction."[b]
Heavens: 26 *YHWH of Hosts*[a] *will lay bare a* 2+2+1
whip against him,
like the one that struck Midian 2+2+3
by the rock of Oreb
or his staff across the sea,
and he will raise it in the Way of Egypt.[b] 3
27 *And it shall be in that day* 1+2
his burden will move from your shoulder 2+2
and his yoke be broken from your neck.[a] 1+2

Notes

24.a-a. LXX translates κύριος σαβαωθ, "Lord of Hosts." Since it usually translates יהוה with κύριος, it has omitted the אדוני, "Lord."

24.b-b. בדרך would be literally translated "in the way of." LXX reads τοῦ ἰδεῖν ὁδὸν Αἰγύπτου, "of knowing the entrance of Egypt." In v 26, LXX paraphrases the same phrase εἰς τῆς ὁδόν, which means "before the entrance," but then continues τὴν κατ' Αἴγυπτον, "the one by (or in the manner of) Egypt." The meaning "in the manner of Egypt" is documented in BDB, 203, and is still used by Wildberger, among others. However, the phrase also has a good geographical connotation referring to the coast highway to Egypt, where important battles were fought in this period. Also, the interest in the Red Sea in 11:15 favors a geographical connotation for the phrase here and in v 26.

25.a. *BHS* proposes adding a 1 sg. pronoun, זַעְמִי, "my indignation," but the meaning is clear without it.

25.b. על־תבליתם has caused considerable discussion; cf. Wildberger and full discussion in *HAL*. Some MSS read תכליתם, deriving the word from כלה, "finish," which appeared earlier in the verse. But 1QIsa[a] supports MT. LXX reads ἐπὶ τὴν βουλὴν αὐτῶν, "upon his purpose." This has virtually transliterated בלי for βουλήν. But MT may best be understood as a noun meaning "destruction," coming from בלה (BDB, 115).

26.a. LXX omits צבאות, "Hosts," but there seems to be no reason to drop it in the Hebrew.

26.b. See *Note* 24.b-b.

27.a. *BHS* reflects current views (cf. discussion under 10:27*d*–33) that the verse should be divided after חבל, "be broken," instead of before it, with MT. The last stich should be joined to the following poetic lines. This and the meter of v 27*bc* should make חבל, the verb for the second stich, parallel to יסור, "will move," in the first. W. R. Smith (*Journal of Philology* 13 [1885] 62) suggested reading יחבל and setting the *ʾatnakh* on its last syllable. LXX translates καὶ καταφθαρήσεται, which supports the meaning, if not the division.

Form/Structure/Setting

The episode (vv 24–27) is set off by לכן, "therefore," as was v 16 above. It relates the following announcement to the fact of God's decree, which affects כל־הארץ, "the whole land" (v 23). It is introduced formally by כה־אמר אדני יהוה צבאות, "Thus says the Lord YHWH of Hosts," which designates what follows as a "YHWH word."

This emphasis on the formal title of God is typical of announcements of judgment in this section; cf. v 16 on sending a destruction on the whole land and v 33 on lopping off limbs of power.

The passage is addressed to עמי, "my people," but to that part ישב ציון, "who inhabit Zion." The message is short, "Do not be afraid because of Assyria," and is a "salvation oracle" (J. Begrich, "Das priesterliche Heilsorakel," *ZAW* 52 [1934] 81–92 = *Gesammelte Studien zum Alten Testament,* TB 21 [Munich: Kaiser, 1964] 217–31). The admonition "do not be afraid" has a fixed place in ancient holy-war tradition (cf. N. Gottwald, "War, Holy," *IDBSup,* 942–44; G. von Rad, *Der Heilige Krieg im Alten Israel* [Zurich: Zwingli, 1951] 70). It was used in 7:4 in the message to Ahaz as well as in Isa 35:4; 40:9; 41:10, 13–14; 43:1, 5; and elsewhere.

The imperative is followed by consecutive perfects in vv 25, 26*a, d,* which form the backbone of the oracle. The outline is:

"Do not fear because of Assyria in the Way of Egypt" (v 24).
Indignation will be finished (v 25).
YHWH will lay bare a whip against him (v 26*a*).
He will raise it in the Way of Egypt (v 26*d*).

Comment

24 The strong and encouraging oracle is addressed to the people "in Zion." In contrast to those in northern Israel, they have no need to fear the Assyrians. *Smiting, rods,* and their synonyms dominate the passage. In keeping with the tone in chaps. 9–10, the passage shows how YHWH's violent acts through the Assyrian are to be distinguished from the Assyrian's own acts, and how both are to be distinguished from God's punishment of the Assyrian when his tasks are complete (cf. 10:12, 16).

בדרך מצרים, "in the way of Egypt," may be understood to refer to the oppression before the Exodus. But the most natural designation is to take it geographically to refer to territory along the sea on the way to Egypt, just as דרך הים, "way of the sea," in 8:23 (9:1) refers to the district of Dor or Sharon. In 733 B.C.E., Tiglath-Pileser's campaign reached as far south as the Brook of Egypt (cf. Annals of Tiglath-Pileser). He paused at Aijalon and Gaza on the borders of Judah and then left a garrison on the Egyptian border (*MBA,* 147). This posed a direct threat to Judah, not least because it interfered with the major trade route to Egypt.

25 The Assyrian role is definitely related to the period of God's anger, the day of wrath (cf. 5:25 and 26; 6:11–13; see *Excursus: Day of YHWH/Divine Warrior* in the *Introduction*). When this time and this task (cf. 10:12 and 10:23) are finished, things will change.

אפי על־תבליתם, "my anger on their destruction," needs some explanation. The first part of the line, כלה זעם, is impersonal: "indignation shall be complete." The second brings in two personal pronouns: *my* anger on *their* destruction. The preposition appears to be best understood as indicating intention. "My" is God speaking. "Their" must refer to Israel alone (vv 22*b* and 23). God's anger is directed to their destruction.

26 The instrument of God's retribution against Assyria is compared to the great victory of Gideon over the Midianites (Judg 8:25). The location must have been near the Jordan River but is otherwise unknown. The "whip" of Gideon was neither arms nor armies but was like the "staff across the sea" (see Exod 14:15–16).

It is important to note that ונשׂאו, "and he shall raise it," continues the line of consecutive perfects from ועורר, "and he will lay bare." It brings attention back to the main thought concerning YHWH and the Assyrians.

בדרך מצרים, "on the way to Egypt," locates the scene of God's action to relieve Jerusalem of the Assyrian's presence as the same place as that mentioned in v 24. When this actually happened is not sure, but it is clear that Tiglath-Pileser and succeeding kings were unable to maintain their presence on the border. And so they were unable to continue to assess levies or taxes on the caravan trade that passed through.

27 With this "burden" and this "yoke," i.e., the military presence on the Egyptian highway, removed, Zion's prosperity is assured.

Explanation

Up to this point in act 1, Jerusalem's involvement has been largely peripheral, though there was an expectation that she will become involved (cf. 8:8, 14). The idea that Israel's problems might open doors for reunion are hinted at in 8:23–9:6 (9:1–7), though the Lord through the Assyrian has business with Jerusalem after that with Israel (v 12). But now he turns directly to the Jerusalemites as they have been reminded that Israel's fate is sealed and that it involves "all the land"—and as they fearfully watch the march of Assyrian armies along the coastal plain toward Egypt. They are reassured that this threat, at least, will pass and their city and monarchy will be saved. But the book will remind them later that Judah's destruction is only postponed (chap. 39). For postexilic and later readers of the whole Vision, the passage illustrates the need to understand God's plan in their own time and to align themselves with it.

"In That Day": The March of Conquest (10:27d–32)

Bibliography

Aharoni, Y. *The Land of the Bible: A Historical Geography.* Philadelphia: Westminster, 1979. 387–94. **Albright, W. F.** "The Assyrian March on Jerusalem, Isa. X 28–32." *AASOR* 4 (1924) 134–40. **Arnold, P. M.** *Gibeah: The Search for a Biblical City.* Sheffield: JSOT Press, 1990. **Childs, B. S.** "The Enemy from the North and the Chaos Tradition." *JBL* 78 (1959) 187–98. ———. *Isaiah and the Assyrian Crisis.* 61–63. **Chilton, B.** "Sennacherib: A Synoptic Relationship among Targumim of Isaiah." In *SBLSP.* Atlanta: Scholars Press, 1986. 544–54. **Christensen, D. L.** "The March of Conquest in Isaiah X 27c–34." *VT* 26 (1966) 395–99. **Donner, H.** "Der Feind aus dem Norden: Topographe und archäologische Erwägungen zu Jes. 10,27b–34." *ZDPV* 84 (1968) 46–54. ———. *Israel unter den Völkern.* 30–38. **Federlin, L.** "A propos d'Isaïe X 29–31." *RB* 3 (1906) 266–73. **Gilead, H.** "*w'-hubbal 'al mi-pene samen*"

(Isa 10,27). *BMik* 31.105 (1985) 134–36. **Grayson, A. K.** "Assyria: Tiglath-pileser III to Sargon II (744–705 B.C.)." In *The Assyrian and Babylonian Empires and Other States of the Near East, from the Eighth to the Sixth Centuries B.C.* Ed. J. Boardman et al. 2d ed. CAH 3.2. Cambridge: Cambridge UP, 1991. 86–102, 762–64. **Grelot, P.** "Le Targoum d'Isaïe X, 32–34 dans ses diverses recensions." *RB* 90 (1983) 202–28. **Irvine, S. A.** *Isaiah, Ahaz, and the Syro-Ephraimite Crisis.* SBLDS 123. Atlanta: Scholars Press, 1990. **Sweeney, M.** "Sargon's Threat against Jerusalem in Isaiah 10,27–32." *Bib* 75 (1994) 457–70. **Tadmor, H.** "The Campaigns of Sargon II of Assur: A Chronological-Historical Study." *JCS* 12 (1958) 22–40, 77–100. **Vargon, S.** "An Admonition Prophecy to the Leaders of Judah (Is. 10, 28–32)." In *Shnaton: An Annual for Biblical and Ancient Near Eastern Studies.* Ed. M. Weinfeld and J. C. Greenfield. Vol. 9. Jerusalem; Tel Aviv: Israel Bible Co., 1985. 95–113.

Translation

Heavens:	27d [a]*He has ascended from Pene-Yeshemon.*[a]	3
	28 *He has come upon Aiath.*	2+2+3
	He has passed through Migron.	
	By Michmash[a] *he stores his baggage.*[b]	
Earth:	29 *They*[a] *have crossed the pass.*	2+3
	At Geba they have made[b] *their lodging.*	
	Rama is terrified;	2+3
	Gibeah of Saul has fled.	
Heavens:	30 *Shriek,*[a] *daughter of Gallim.*	2+2
	Pay attention, Laishah.	2+2
	Answer her,[b] *Anathoth.*	
	31 *Madmenah is a fugitive*	2+3
	Inhabitants of Gebim have sought refuge.	
Earth:	32 *Until*[a] *today*	2+2
	to stand[b] *at Nob.*	
	He waves his hand[c]	2+2+2
	to make Zion large,[d]	
	the Hill of Jerusalem.[e]	

Notes

27*d*.a-a. The stich has been the subject of many attempts to point it in a way that is suitable to its context. MT treats it as a continuation of v 27; points עַל as a parallel to וְעֻלּוֹ, "his yoke," earlier in the line and שָׁמֶן like the Assyrian's מִשְׁמַנָּיו, "opulence," in v 16; and puts the *ʾatnakh* before וחבל to produce "and a yoke shall be broken because of fat." LXX reads καταφθαρήσεται ὁ ζυγὸς ἀπὸ τῶν ὤμων ὑμῶν, "the yoke will be broken from your shoulder."

Modern interpreters have judged MT to have wrongly divided the verse. The indication of parallelism and meter lead them to include וחבל, "be broken," in the previous stich (see above). This leaves על מפני־שמן to parallel the following lines: בא על עית, "he has come upon Aiath," etc. The meter is right. The lack of article fits. This would make על a verb, some form of עלה, "to ascend," "go up," and שמן a place name, as in all the lines that follow. Emendations have been many and free: W. R. Smith (*Journal of Philology* 13 [1885] 62): עלה מצפן שדד, "The Destroyer arises from the north"; Duhm: עלה מפני רמן, "He has come up from Pene Rimmon"; Albright (*AASOR* 4 [1924] 134–40): וחגל לעלם בנשמתי, "And be destroyed forever in my wrath"; Procksch, followed by Kaiser, Fohrer, and Wildberger, reads שֹׁמְרוֹן, "Samaria," for שמן; and Christensen (*VT* 26 [1966] 395–99): מפני ישמן, "from Pene-Yeshemon," pointing to the established usage of shared consonants. This last view has the advantage of requiring no change in the consonantal text and of fitting the setting of the passage.

28.a. MT מִכְמָשׂ, "Michmash," was written מכמשׂ in B, and the same variation occurs in 1 Sam 13:2, 5, 11, 16. Ezra 2:27 and Neh 7:31 write מכמס, supporting MT's pronunciation.

28.b. H. Donner *(Israel unter den Völkern)* translates למכמשׂ with the first stich "he passed over from Migron to Michmash" and the remaining words "he gathered his war-materials." But Wildberger is correct to support MT in the division.

29.a. 1QIsa[a], LXX, Syr., Vg., and Tg. read a sg. here (G. R. Driver, *JTS* 38 [1937] 39). The change of person makes sense and accords with the dynamic style of the passage. MT should be kept.

29.b. מלון לנו, lit. "a lodging for us," or, reading as a pf. 3 c. pl. לון, a cognate of מלון, "they made their lodging." (Cf. Josh 4:3.) GKC §73*d* = Judg 19:13.

30.a. צהלי, "cry shrilly," with קולך, "your voice" (an adv. acc.), means "make your voice shrill" (BDB, *HAL*).

30.b. MT עֲנִיָּה, "poor" = "Anathoth is poor." LXX ἐπακούσεται, "hearken to," is repeated with Anathoth after use with Laishah. Syr. *wa*ʿ*nī* has led to the suggested change in pointing: עֲנִיהָ, "answer her," which is widely accepted. A verb here parallels the previous two stichs.

32.a. עוד may indicate continuance, "still," or addition, "again" or "besides." Note use of כי־עוד in v 25, "for yet a very little while," referring to the end of God's anger. So עוד היום seems to mark that point: "again (or still) today."

32.b. לעמד, "to take a stand," is an inf. with no previous verb to depend upon. The subject has again returned to the approaching one. The place name has a prep. as do those in v 28. The inf. may depend on the previous verbs in v 28: "he came up, came, and passed over" in order "to again stand on Nob today" (GKC §114*g*). This makes it mark the purpose of the march from the Jordan.

32.c. ינפף ידו, "he waves his hand." The understanding of this context as referring to the Assyrian has caused translators to interpret this as brandishing a fist. But the words simply mean "to wave his hand." The impf. tense and normal word order mark an ordinary sentence.

32.d. K הר בית, "mountain of the house of," creates some difficulties. Q, followed by virtually all the versions, reads בת־ציון, "daughter of Zion," a parallel to "the hill of Jerusalem." But the real problem lies in the combination with הַר, reading "the mountain of the daughter of Zion." The only other usage of הר and בת is in Isa 16:1. Another solution would read them as one word הִרְבֵּיתָ/הִרְבֵּית (*hip*ʿ*il* pf. 2 m. or f.) or הַרְבּוֹת (*qal* inf. const.; cf. 2 Sam 14:11 [GKC §75ff.]), from רבה, "to make to grow" or "increase." This change makes the section lead directly into the sense and mood of chap. 11, with which it is joined by *vav* consecutives. (See Isa 11:1.)

32.e. K ירושלם/Q ירושלים documents a frequent disagreement in textual sources about the pronunciation of the city's name. Q insists it is "Yerushalayim." K continues "Yerushalem."

Form/Structure/Setting

The passage is marked in the beginning by a sudden change of subject and setting. As v 26 has the Lord for subject, the Assyrian as the object, and the Way of Egypt for the setting, vv 27*d*–32 have an unnamed subject approaching Jerusalem from the east and north. (The passage continues with the identification of the Lord in vv 33–34 as the Divine Forester and with a chain of consecutive plurals through chaps. 11 and 12.)

The poem has similarities to Isa 63:1–6 and belongs in the tradition of YHWH's march (cf. Judg 5:4–5; Ps 68:8–9; and so on). Christensen (*VT* 26 [1966] 396) has identified the poem in 27*d*–32 as a liturgy from the "Ritual Conquest" tradition. This would fit here as a prelude to the Lord's appearance and its interpretation in the old theophanic traditions of God who comes from Paran or Sinai. A major question turns on the intent of the march. It has usually been understood as malevolent—the approaching "destroyer." The words have been translated accordingly. (The view that this represents the approach of an Assyrian force may be found in Wildberger; H. Donner, *Israel unter den Völkern,* 30–38; idem, *ZDPV* 84 [1968] 46–54.) But there is evidence to the contrary. The immediate context (10:24–27; 11:1–10) is positive to Jerusalem. Although there is awesome terror in the villages, appropriate to the approach of the Almighty God, there is nothing in the words that dictate terror for Jerusalem. V 24 had commanded the opposite (contra Christensen and others). The recognition of the form or genre as a theophany is supported by the use of בא, "come" (v 28), and לעמד, "to stand," "to take a stand" (v 32). It also is supported by the formula of identification הנה, "behold," in v 33. The theophanic vision must be seen beginning in 10:24 with "do not fear."

Delitzsch writes, "Seen aesthetically, the description belongs among the most splendidly picturesque that human poetry has ever produced. . . . Through v 32*a* the speech moves in quick stormy steps, then it becomes hesitant as if shaking for fear."

Wildberger notes the rich use of alliteration and the use of dark *o*-vowels (cf. L. Alonso Schökel, "Is 10, 28–32: Análisis estilístico," *Bib* 40 [1959] 223) to depict the dark and awesome movements of suspense: עברו מעברה, עלה על עית, מלון לנו, הרדה הרמה, צהלי קולך בת גלים, עניה ענתות, נדדה מדמנה, בנב ינפף. This is lost in translation, although Duhm made a valiant effort to recapture it in German: "sie *pass*iren *[sic]* den *Pass, Geba* gibt Her*b*erge uns, e*rr*egt ist Ha*r*ama . . . *M*admena *m*acht sich davon, *an*tworte ihr *An*athoth!"

Comment

The passage is dominated by place names that are easily identifiable as towns and villages only a few miles north and east of Jerusalem, but exact location is much less certain (cf. Wildberger). *MBA*, 154, traces the movement from Aiath to Michmash to Geba and on to Nob, which is just across the valley from Jerusalem. The individual places deserve comment.

27*d* פני־ישמן, "Pene-Yeshemon" (see *Note* 27.d.). Christensen (*VT* 26 [1966] 399) has identified this as a location near Gilgal. The word means "facing the wasteland or wilderness." It appears in Num 21:20 and 23:28, "where it refers to the end-point of the wilderness wandering." In 1 Sam 23:19, 24 and 26:1, 3 it applies to a wilderness territory on the Dead Sea north of Ziph.

Christensen thinks this passage uses a Gilgal tradition of monarchical times that reenacted the march of conquest of Josh 8 over Ai. With Jerusalem as the goal, the procession symbolized the movement of the ark from Gilgal to Jerusalem. It established through ritual that YHWH who sits over the cherubim in Zion's temple was identical with YHWH Sabaoth who comes from Sinai, who led Israel in the conquest of Canaan. The path leads sharply up from the river floor to the towns on the mountain ridge.

28 עית, "Aiath," is the Ai of Josh 7 and 8. Neh 11:31 shows the Aramaic name "Ajja" (*GTTOT* §1588 #2). From here the route turns south. מגרון, "Migron," lies a few miles south of Aiath. This is the scene of the narrative in 1 Sam 14:2–42 (cf. *GTTOT* §1588 #3). מכמש, "Michmash," lies a little to one side. The change of tense implies a subsidiary clause like "while he stores his gear at Michmash" (cf. *GTTOT* §1021).

29 The Pass from Migron to Geba appears also in 1 Sam 13:23 (*GTTOT* §674). גבע, "Geba," is the next stop on the road only a couple of miles southeast of Migron. This marks the end of the first stage of the journey. The names that follow are not on the line of march but close enough to justify fear of foraging soldiers.

31 מדמנה, "Madmenah," and הגבים, "Gebim," are unknown. They do not occur elsewhere in Scripture, unless Madmenah is referred to in Isa 25:10. They would both be near Jerusalem. They mean "place of doing" and "the pits," which might indicate the garbage dumps of the city (*GTTOT* §1588 ##11, 12; §1261).

32 נֹב, "Nob" (cf. 1 Sam 21:2; 22:9, 11, 19), had been a temple city and was called a "city of priests" (1 Sam 21:1 and 22:19). Perhaps 2 Sam 15:32 refers to Nob: "the height where God was worshiped." *GTTOT* §96 suggests a location "on the ridge east and north-east of 'Jerusalem,'" which includes the Mount of Olives. From this vantage point YHWH could look across at Jerusalem.

In the ancient ritual, the gesture of waving the hand may have indicated God's claim to the city. In this setting, it indicates his pleasure, his decision concerning the city. In chap. 36 a conquering general stands at another vantage point to negotiate the surrender of the city. But the awesome one here approaching the city does not negotiate. His imperious gesture seals the fate of the city. The gesture is not threatening—on the contrary, the one who has it in his power to utterly destroy indicates his will for the city to prosper. The gesture continues the message of vv 24–25 to the city: it need not fear. God will first deal with his enemies and then turn his attention to Zion when his anger is past.

The ravages of the war with Samaria and Aram of 736–34 B.C.E. and the backlash of Assyrian invasions of Israel and Philistia in 734–32, 728, and 723–721 B.C.E. had left the city, as it had the country, stripped of virtually all economic assets and probably reduced in population. The divine gesture indicates his pleasure that Zion "grow large."

Explanation

The problem with the Assyrian lies "on the way to Egypt," i.e., southwest of Jerusalem on the coastal highway some distance away. The Lord will deal with that problem in that place in his own time (v 25–26), and at that time Jerusalem will be free (v 27*ab*). In the meantime, attention is called to the theophanic scene of an approach from the other side, according to the ancient cultic forms (vv 27*c*–32). The Lord stands at the ancient cultic site of Nob and gestures toward Jerusalem.

A great divine drama unfolds in the majestic words of the text. A major message of Scripture is that God comes in majesty and power. Christians observe this in Epiphany, which celebrates the coming of Christ. Israel celebrated God's coming in a number of ways. One pervasive theme pictured him coming from Mount Sinai or from Paran. Another recited the conquest narrative of God's leading Israel into Canaan as in the book of Joshua. Here the great description of his awesome approach along the road of conquest turns toward Jerusalem, rather than continuing as in Joshua to the conquest of Judah and Ephraim. It supports the word of encouragement and hope of v 24 and prepares for the identification of YHWH as a great forester who chooses which trees will be cut and which will be allowed to grow.

The Forester before Jerusalem (10:33–34)

Bibliography

See *Bibliography* for 10:27*d*–32.

Dalman, G. "Palästinische Wege und die Bedrohung Jerusalems nach Jesaja 10." *PJ* 12 (1916) 37–57. **Stolz, F.** "Die Bäume des Gottesgartens auf dem Libanon." *ZAW* 84 (1972) 14–56.

Translation

Herald: 33 *Behold—* 1+3+3
The Lord [a] *YHWH of Hosts*
designating [b] *beauty* [c] *with awesome* [d] *(skill),*
(as) the tops of the heights are being cut down 3+2
and exalted ones are laid low.
34 *He strikes* [a] *forest thickets with the iron* 4+3
(as) the Lebanese (forest) falls by a majestic (blow).

Notes

33.a. האדון, "the Lord." The use of this form, sg. abs. with article, occurs only three times outside Isaiah (Exod 23:17; 34:23; Mal 3:1) and but five times in Isaiah, two in this chapter (1:24; 3:1; 10:16, 33; 19:4). Exod 23:17 has "the Lord, YHWH"; Exod 34:23, "the face of the Lord YHWH, God of Israel." Isaiah is consistent: "The Lord, YHWH of Hosts." Mal 3:1 has simply "the Lord." Of course the form אדני occurs many times with and without the other titles.

33.b. מסעף, "designating." The verb occurs only here. BDB and *HAL* judge the root to mean "split," "cleave," "divide." Nouns formed on it mean "clefts," as in rocks, or "branches," as in fruit trees, in Isa 17:6; 27:10; Ezek 31:6, 8. A second root produces a *hap. leg.* adj. in Ps 119:113: "divided, half-hearted." The usual translation "lopping-off" goes beyond the evidence. "To divide" or "to branch out" with causative meaning from the *piʿel* stem demands something more like "separating between two alternatives"—in the case of the forester, "deciding which trees shall be felled and which remain." Hence the term "designating." The ptc. follows הנה, "behold."

33.c. K פארה/Q פוארה is a *hap. leg.* meaning "boughs," a collective noun (BDB, *HAL*). The root פאר means to "beautify," "glorify." Derivations mean "a headdress," "beauty," "glory," and something to do with trees, perhaps a "bough." The famous mountain's name is similar: פארן, Paran. It is wiser to remain with the general meaning "a beauty."

33.d. מערצה, "an awesome thing," another *hap. leg.*, derives from a root meaning "cause to tremble, terrify" (BDB, 791–92). It means "awe-inspiring" or "terrifying power" (*HAL*).

34.a. וְנִקַּף is usually thought to be *piʿel* pf. 3 m. sg. with *vav* const. This should give a pass. meaning. Wildberger makes "the forest thickets" its subject. But the controlling noun "thickets" is pl. NIV notes this and continues the sg. subject of the previous verse but forces an act. meaning on this verb. There are apparently two verbs נקף (BDB, *HAL*, *DCH*). The first means "strike off," "cut off" and has usually been understood here. The second means "go around," "revolve" (cf. Isa 29:1; 15:8) but apparently does not occur in *piʿel* or *nipʿal*, which MT's pointing requires. It should be read as *piʿel* pf. 3 m. sg., "he strikes." The second meaning, however, remains attractive if one may emend to וַיַּקֵּף, *hipʿil* impf. 3 m. sg., "he causes to strike."

Form/Structure/Setting

The verses identify the marcher of the awesome theophany and describe his profession and the result of his mission. הנה, "behold," announces the identification and sets it off from the theophany, as G. E. Wright (*The Book of Isaiah* [Richmond: John Knox, 1964] 49) has noted. The full title, "the Lord YHWH of Hosts," indicates the importance of the announcement, as it does in 10:16, 23, 24, and 26. It is followed by a participle describing action in process. This will set the stage for six pericope statements beginning with verbs (perfect + *vav*), which link them to this action that continues through 12:4, twenty-four times in all. For the significance of this syntactical device, cf. J. Wash Watts, *Survey of Syn-*

tax, 113–17. The basic structure is illustrated by the consecutive perfects with YHWH as subject in 10:34 (ונקף, "he strikes"), 11:11 ("it shall be that the Lord will stretch out his hand a second time"), and 11:15 ("and YHWH shall dry up"). (A similar sequence of הנה, participle, and verbs [perfect + *vav*] will begin the great final theophany of the Vision in 65:17–66:24.)

The presence of the marcher and his gesture thus continue to be interpreted throughout 10:33–12:6. The description of the theophany drops the figure of the forester, but the importance of the hand signal (which picks up the note of 9:11 [12], 20 [21]; 10:4) is continued by 11:10, 12. "Behold" identifies the gesturing figure as "the Lord YHWH of Hosts," surely a title of considerable significance in view of the Assyrian on the coastal plains opposite. It is YHWH who "designs a beautiful (thing) with awesome (skill)." Just as cutting trees in the forest can clear the way for a majestic and beautiful one to flourish, the destruction of powerful forces and great nations opens a door for God's chosen city and dynasty.

Comment

33 The verse identifies the Lord as the one at work here. The title "YHWH of Hosts" fits the theophanic description of his ascent to Zion from the Jordan and connects the description to God's ancient relation to Israel and to Jerusalem. It presents that work as מסעף, "cleaning," "separating," "branching," that is, distinguishing between the things to be cut down and those to be pruned and nurtured. The particular work here relates to פארה, "a thing of glory and beauty," like a person's turban headdress. The heart of God's action is not destruction; it looks beyond destruction to glorious nourishment of his beautiful thing. The work has a breathtaking, "awe-inspiring" quality (במערצה) about it. (The three words are infrequently used and have been much misunderstood. See *Notes* 33b., 33.c., and 33.d.)

The sentence interprets the hand signal toward Jerusalem in v 32. From Isa 5:25 through 10:4 the Vision has pictured an unflinching and unbending signal in the still outstretched hand of God that represented his unchanged determination to destroy the northern kingdom. This gesture foresees the day, very near, when the signal toward Jerusalem will change, calling for growth and nurture of the thing of beauty that it is and can be.

The verse continues in circumstantial clauses to describe the work of destruction against the high and mighty as well as the underbrush. It continues the themes of Isa 2:12–18 and 10:18–19 (17–19). The Divine Forester goes about his work with neither fear nor favor. The רמי הקומה, "tops of the heights," are the highest parts of tall trees, as are the הגבהים, "exalted ones." They are cut and lowered.

34 The phrase סבכי היער, "forest thickets," refers to thick underbrush that must be cleared to allow the fine trees to grow. הלבנון, "the Lebanon," refers not to a country, as today, but to a region on the slopes of Mount Hermon to the north of Israel. It was renowned for the magnificent gigantic trees that grew there.

יד, "hand," and עיד, "yet or still," occur frequently together in chaps. 8–12. They are significant. יד, "hand," refers to deeds and signals. עוד, "still," "yet," indicates continuance and continuity. יד, "hand," is used to show God's signals—like the thumbs up or down of the Roman arena. This begins in 1:25, "I will turn my hand against you," and continues in that series of refrains "his hand is upraised" (5:25; 9:11 [12], 16 [17], 20 [21]; 10:4). It also figures in the Lord's actions toward Zion

(10:32; 11:11, 15). It is used throughout the book (see *Excursus: "The Hand of God"* [יד יהוה] at 1:21 above); it was undoubtedly a common term in Hebrew speech.

עוד, "still," is used in loose conjunction with "hand" in several of these texts. It characterizes a series of statements about Israel's continuing rebellion against the Lord and his continuing anger toward them. Then twice it is used for Zion as it urges patience in the continuing process in which judgment on Israel must precede God's favor to Judah: 10:25, "yet a very little while," and 10:32, literally "still today to stand on Nob." The effect is to stress the continuity of Israel's attitude and God's decree of judgment on Israel on the one side (1:1–10:23) with the continuity of God's elective providence for Zion on the other (10:24–12:6).

Explanation

The verses break the dramatic spell of the liturgical recital. The awesome figure is identified as the Lord YHWH of Hosts. In line with references in chaps. 9 and 10, he is pictured as an Imperial Forester who has authority to cultivate the imperial forests. Trees were highly valued and rulers claimed exclusive rights to them. Forest lands, like those of Lebanon on the slopes of Mount Hermon, were admired. The Bible often uses the oak and the cedar as figures for strong personalities. God decides which trees are cut down. He exercises his authority to decide the fate of the greatest and the mightiest.

But the key message lies in 33*b*, a verse that has baffled translator and interpreter alike because it is composed of three rare Hebrew words. As a result it has usually been translated to accord with a presumed threat to Jerusalem. As shown above, v 32 is not a threat, only a signal. Isa 10:24 and 11:1–9 are positive words. So the words need to be examined again (cf. *Comment* on v 33).

The verse shows YHWH as the Forester whose pruning, thinning, and burning of underbrush are all part of a larger plan—"designating beauty." This plan has Jerusalem as its focus and center. The Forester's decision allows this part of his area to grow, to increase (v 32), in order to become a thing of "beauty" (v 33*b*). It will allow an old stump "to sprout" (11:1) and the sprout to become glorious. The verse reflects the Vision's emphasis that neither the kingdoms of Israel nor even Judah but rather the city of Jerusalem will be the primary beneficiary of God's favor.

A Shoot from the Stump of Jesse (11:1–10)

Bibliography

Alonso Schökel, L. "Dos Poemas a la Paz." *EstBib* 18 (1959) 149–69. **Barrois, G.** "Critical Exegesis and Traditional Hermeneutics: A Methodological Inquiry on the Basis of the Book of Isaiah." *SVTQ* 16 (1972) 107–27. **Bodenheimer, F. S.** *Animal and Man in Bible Lands.* Leiden: Brill, 1960. **Childs, B. S.** *Myth and Reality in the Old Testament.* London:

SCM Press, 1960. 65–69. **Conrad, E. W.** "The Royal Narratives and the Structure of the Book of Isaiah." *JSOT* 41 (1988) 67–81. **Crook, M. B.** "A Suggested Occasion for Isaiah 9:2–7 and 11:1–9." *JBL* 68 (1949) 213–24. **Deist, F.** "Jes 11:3*a:* Eine Gloss?" *ZAW* 85 (1972) 351–55. **Delord, R.** "Les Charismes de l'Ancienne Alliance Commandment: La Paix Du Mond Nouveau, Esaie 11:1–10." *ETR* 52.4 (1977) 555–56. **Ebach, J.** "Ende des Feindes oder Ende der Feindschaft? Der Tierfrieden bei Jesaja und Vergil." In *Ursprung und Ziel: Erinnerte Zukunft und erhoffte Vergangenheit.* Neukirchen-Vluyn: Neukirchener Verlag, 1986. 75–89. **Freedman, D. N.** "Is Justice Blind?" *Bib* 52.4 (1971) 536. **Gray, G. B.** "The Strophic Division of Isaiah 21,1–10 and Isaiah 11,1–8." *ZAW* 32 (1912) 190–98. **Gross, H.** *Die Idee des ewigen und allgemeinen Weltfriedens im Alten Orient und im Alten Testament.* ThTSt 7. Trier: Paulinus, 1967. **Haag, E.** "Der Neue David und die Offenbarung der Liebesfülle Gottes nach Jesaja 11,1–9." In *Im Gespräch mit dem dreineinen Gott: Elemente einer trinitarischen Theologie.* FS W. Breuning, ed. M. Böhnke and H. Heinz. Düsseldorff: Patmos, 1985. 97–114. **Harrelson, W.** "Nonroyal Motifs in the Royal Eschatology." In *Israel's Prophetic Heritage.* Ed. B. W. Anderson and W. Harrelson. 1962. 147–65. **Hermisson, H. J.** "Zukunftserwartung und Gegenwartskritik in der Verkundigung Jesajas." *EvT* 33 (1973) 54–77. **Kock, R.** "Der Gottesgeist und der Messias." *Bib* 27 (1946) 241–68. **Lange, F.** "Exegetische Problems zu Jes. 11." *LR* 23 (1975) 115–27. **Lepore, L.** "Isa 11:3*a* '*wahriho beyr't JHWH'* non è una glossa: Apporto della lettura filologico-semantica e strutturale." *RivB* 47 (1999) 61–75. **Montagnini, F.** "Le roi-Messie attendu, Is 11:1–10." *AsSeign* 2.6 (1969) 6–12. **Mowinckel, S.** *He That Cometh.* Oxford: Blackwell, 1959. 17–20. **Rehm, M.** *Der königliche Messias im Lichte der Immanuel-weissagung des Buches Jesaja.* Eichstätten Studien 1. Kevelaer: Butzon & Bercker, 1968. 185–234. **Ridderbos, J.** *De Messias-Koning in Jesaja's profetie.* Kampen: Theologische School van de Gereformeerde Kerken, 1920. **Ringgren, H.** *The Messiah in the Old Testament.* London: SCM Press, 1956. 30–33. **Roberts, J. J. M.** "The Davidic Origin of the Zion Tradition." *JBL* 92 (1973) 329–44. ———. "The Translation of Isa 11:10 and the Syntax of the Temporal Expression ביום ההוא והיה." In *Near Eastern Studies.* FS Y. Mikasa, ed. M. Mori et al. Bulletin of the Middle Eastern Culture Center in Japan 5. Wiesbaden: Harrassowitz, 1991. 363–70. **Schmid, H. H.** *Shalom: Frieden im Alten Orient und im Alten Testament.* SBS 51. Stuttgart: KBW, 1971. **Schmidt, W. H.** "Die Ohnmacht des Messias: Zur Überlieferungsgeschichte der messianischen Weissagungen im AT." *KD* 15 (1969) 18–34. **Seebass, H.** *Herrscherverheißungen im Alten Testament.* Neukirchen-Vluyn: Neukirchener Verlag, 1992. 18 ff. **Stamm, J. J.,** and **H. Bietenhard.** *Der Weltfriede im Alten und Neuen Testament.* Zurich: Zwingli, 1959. **Steck, O. H.** "'. . . ein kleiner Knabe kann sie leiten': Beobachtungen zum Tierfrieden in Jesaja 11:6–8 und 65:25." In *Alttestamentlicher Glaube und biblische Theologie.* FS H. D. Preuss, ed. J. Hausmann. Stuttgart: Kohlhammer, 1992. 104–13. **Sweeney, M.** "Jesse's New Shoot in Isaiah 11: A Josianic Reading of the Prophet Isaiah." In *A Gift of God in Due Season.* FS J. A. Sanders, ed. R. D. Weis and D. M. Carr. Sheffield: Sheffield Academic Press, 1996. 103–18. **Thompson, M. E. W.** "Isaiah's Ideal King." *JSOT* 24 (1982) 79–88. **Unterman, J.** "The (non)sense of smell in Isaiah 11:3." *HS* 33 (1992) 17–23. **Van Ruiten, J.** "The Intertextual Relationship between Isaiah 65:25 and Isaiah 11,6–9." In *The Scriptures and the Scrolls.* FS A. S. van der Woude, ed. F. García Martínez and C. J. Labuschagne. VTSup 49. Leiden: Brill, 1992. 31–42. **Vermeylen, J.** *Du Prophète Isaïe à l'Apocalyptique.* Vol. 1. Paris: Gabalda, 1977. 269–80. **Vervenne, M.** "The Phraseology of 'Knowing YHWH" in the Hebrew Bible: A Preliminary Study of Its Syntax and Function." In *Studies.* Ed. J. Van Ruiten and M. Vervenne. 467–94. **Waschke, E.-J.** "Die Stellung der Königstexte im Jesajabuch im Vergleich zu den Königspsalmen 2, 72 und 89." *ZAW* 110 (1998) 355–58. **Werner, W.** *Eschatologische Texte in Jesaja 1–39: Messias, Heiliger Rest, Völker.* FB 46. Würzburg: Echter, 1982. **Wildberger, H.** "Die Völkerwallfahrt zum Zion, Jes. 11:1–5." *VT* 7 (1957) 62–81. **Zenger, E.** "Die Verheissung Jesaja 11:1–10: Universal oder Partikular?" In *Studies.* Ed. J. Van Ruiten and M. Vervenne. 137–47.

Translation

Chorus:	1 *And a shoot shall go out from the stump of Jesse.*	4+3
	A Branch from his roots will bear fruit, [a]	
	2 *and the Spirit of YHWH shall rest on him:*	4+3
	a spirit of wisdom and understanding,	
	a spirit of counsel and heroism,	3+4
	a spirit of knowledge, and fear of YHWH.	
Interlocutor:	3 [a] *His delight (will be) in the fear of YHWH:* [a]	3+4+4
	[b] *who does not judge by what his eyes see,*	
	nor makes a decision by what his ears hear,	
	4 *when he judges poor people with righteousness,*	3+4
	or when he gives fair decisions to the afflicted [a] *of the land,*	
	or when he smites a land [b] *with the rod of his mouth,*	4+4
	with the breath of his lips he kills the wicked.	
Chorus:	5 *And it shall be, (when)*	1
	righteousness (is) the girdle [a] *of his loins*	3+3
	and faithfulness (is) the belt [a] *of his waist,*	
	6 *wolf will feed with lamb,*	4+4
	leopard will rest with goat,	
	calf, lion, and yearling [a] *together,*	4+4
	with a little child leading them.	
	7 *Cow and bear feed* [a] *together—*	3+3+4
	together their young relax.	
	A lion will eat straw like an ox.	
	8 *A nursing child will fondle the hole of the cobra.*	4+3+3
	On the viper's young [a]	
	the weaned child will put [b] *his hand.*	
YHWH:	9 *They will do no harm—*	2+2+3
	they will not destroy	
	in all the mount of my holiness!	
Spokesman:	*For the earth shall have become full* [a]	3+3+3
	of the knowledge [b] *of YHWH*	
	as waters (are) coverings for the sea. [c]	
Monarchist:	10 *And it shall be in that day:*	3
	the root of Jesse,	2+2+2
	who is standing	
	as a signal to the peoples,	
	to him nations come seeking,	3+3
	and his resting place will be glory.	

Notes

1.a. יפרה, "will bear fruit," is not a close parallel to ויצא, "will go out," in the first half. LXX translated ἀναβήσεται, Tg. יתרבי, Syr. *nafraʿ,* and Vg. *ascendet,* which suggests that they read יפרח, "will spring up." Wildberger follows the versions. However, MT makes sense and should be followed.

3.a-a. Versions and commentaries have had trouble with this stich, which repeats יראת יהוה, "fear of YHWH." LXX adds ἐμπλήσει αὐτόν, "will fill him"; Tg. ויקרביניה, "will approach him"; Syr. *wᵉnednaḫ,* "and he shines"; and Vg. *et replebit eum,* "and fill him." Others have tried emendations (cf. G. Beer,

"Jes. 11,1–8," *ZAW* 18 [1898] 345; G. R. Driver, "Abbreviations in the MT," *Textus* 1 [1960] 129). Wildberger and others judge it dittography of the previous line. It should be read as a choral refrain that echoes the previous line.

3.b. The ו before לא is omitted by most versions.

4.a. עֱנְוֵי, "the poor, afflicted" (BDB, 776), or "the bowed" (*HAL*). σ´ reads πτωχους, "beggars," while LXX reads ταπεινούς, "humble, depressed" ones. *BHS* suggests לַעֲנִיֵּי, "for the humble." MT makes sense, and the change gains little. However, one may compare the parallel terms in 10:2.

4.b. ארץ, "land," "earth," has been thought a repetition from the previous line. Some recommend reading עָרִץ, "a terrorist," "ruthless one," as a parallel to רשע, "wicked." Yet the versions support MT.

5.a. אזור, "girdle," occurs twice, which has forced translators to seek substitutes to avoid repetition (G. R. Driver, *JTS* 38 [1937] 39). Vg. translates *cingulum* and *cinctorium*—similar but not synonomous words. Wildberger emends the second to חֵגֹר, "belt." None of these is a compelling substitute for MT.

6.a. LXX βοσκηθήσονται, "will be tended in pasture," has apparently combined מריא, "yearling," and יחדו, "together," to get this meaning. Vg. has a similar form. Each of the parallel lines has two subjects. ומריא, "and a fatling, yearling," gives this one three. Wildberger suggests reading יִמְרְאוּ, "will fatten" or "become fat." This verb is not found in Biblical Heb. but does appear in Middle Hebrew and is supported by Ugar.

7.a. MT תִּרְעֶינָה, "will feed," has been challenged. P. de Lagarde (*Semitica* [Göttingen: Dieterich, 1878] 1:21) suggested reading תִּתְרָעֶינָה, matching the reflexive *hitpa'el* with the יחדו, "together," of the previous line (cf. LXX ἅμα = יחדו). But this may be simply understood and MT left as it is.

8.a. MT מאורא, a *hap. leg.* One MS reads מאירת, a ptc. fem. sg. const. (cf. M. Dietrich, *Neue palästinisch punktierte Bibelfragmente* [Leiden: Brill, 1968] 52). LXX τρώγλη, OL *cubile,* Tg. חור, Syr. *ḥôrâ,* and Vg. *caverna* seem to have in mind מְעָרָה, "hole," or מְעוֹנָה, "dwelling" or "camp." F. Perles ("Übersehenes Akkad. Sprachgut," *JSOR* 9 [1925] 126) related the form to Akkad. *mûru,* "young." Wildberger follows Perles.

8.b. ידו הדה has often been translated "stretch out his hand." הדה is another *hap. leg.* Its meaning is unknown. BDB and *HAL* use Arab. and Aram. parallels to get its meaning. J. Reider ("Etymological Studies," *VT* 2 [1952] 115) suggests combining the two words into one, יְדַהְדֶּה, which he translates, according to the Arab. *dahdah,* as "throw stones" or "play pebbles." Wildberger correctly put this aside as too daring.

9.a. 1QIsa[a] תמלאה changes the pf. to impf., which may be supported by Tg. ארי תתקלי and Syr. *d[e]tetm[e]le* (cf. S. Talmon, "Textual Transmission," *Textus* 4 [1964] 117). Wildberger recognizes the possibility but chooses to stay with MT, translating "will have become full."

9.b דֵּעָה, "knowing," is an inf. const. (BDB, *HAL*), which explains the following acc.

9.c. לים מכסים, lit. "for the sea, a covering." Joüon §125*k* explains the לְ as an acc. particle and the lack of an article otherwise, §138*f.* However, the simple and literal meaning makes sense as it is.

Form/Structure/Setting

The choral speech begins with a verb (pf. + *vav*). This continues the chain from 10:34 and is carried through the chapter and into chap. 12. The verbs all depend on the participial announcement of God's act in 10:33. The "lopping off" of branches in northern Palestine reduces the power of the Assyrian Empire in that area (10:33*b*). The poem continues with more perfects with *vav* in vv 2, 5, and 10. Vv 3 and 9 clearly interrupt this pattern. V 4 uses perfects with *vav* to relate the thought to v 5. The meter of the entire section is heavy with bicolons and tricolons using three and four accents. Vv 9–10 continue with tricolons but lighten them to two and three accents.

An outline must recognize that the passage contains the central elements of the arch structure that begins in 10:24 and continues through 12:6 (see the introduction to scene 3 [10:24–12:6]):

E The shoot from Jesse's root (11:1)
F The Spirit of YHWH rests on him (11:2)
G The fear of YHWH—his delight (11:3*a*)
KEYSTONE YHWH's righteousness and justice (11:3*b*–4)
G´ Righteousness and justice his girdle (11:5–8)
F´ Knowledge of YHWH in all the earth (11:9)
E´ The Root of Jesse, a banner to the nations (11:10)

Vv 5–9 are set off and related to the preceding by והיה, "and it shall be." But the lack of ביום ההוא, "in that day," indicates that the section relates to the immediately preceding description of "the Branch." In v 10, a new ביום ההוא, "in that day," sets off this third section relating to "the Branch." It is separate in grammar and in theme. It claims that the Davidic king *is* the "signal to the peoples" that the Vision has announced in 5:26, 7:18, and 10:32 and will announce in 13:2 and thereafter.

There is an interplay throughout this passage between Davidic themes and emphatic recognition of YHWH's direct gifts and action. While David's scion appears in vv 1 and 10, the emphasis is on YHWH's spirit (v 2), the fear of YHWH (v 3), and the knowledge of YHWH (vv 6–9). Vv 4 and 5 are not clearly directed and may be understood to apply to YHWH or to the king. The ambiguity is deliberate. Davidic ideology was structured to think in terms of God's work through the king. This passage deftly keeps attention on God's work.

The genre of the literature is to be found in poems that deal with royal ideology in the Psalms and in some prophets. Parallels may be found in Mic 5:2–5*a* and Ps 72:2, 4, 13. Yet there are also distinctive elements unique to this composition. Wildberger (439) sees vv 1–5 as an "oracle" of a future king, wheras Ps 72 sings of a current monarch. Other differences also show that the genre of royal psalms has been subtly reshaped. The explicit position of the king is minimized (only in 11:1 and 11:10 directly). The passage, in tune with the larger context of 10:24–34 and 11:11–16, keeps its attention on the work of YHWH. Its centerpiece in 11:3*b*–4 picks up the work of YHWH from 10:33–34 in picturing his righteous judgment. He is the subject of these verbs, not the king. In addition, the surrounding sections shift the emphasis from the king to YHWH's endowments that are necessary for peace, prosperity, and success: his Spirit (v 2), his "fear" (v 3*b*), his righteousness and justice (v 5), and his "knowledge" (v 9). The king does have a role, but as in 9:6 (7) the composition carefully subordinates it to the wider view of God's work and makes it contingent on the spirit, fear, righteousness, and knowledge of YHWH that are the essential elements for the fulfillment of God's purpose for his people and the world.

Poems describing "the peaceable kingdom" are virtually unique to Isaiah (see also chap. 35 and 65:17–25). They are used in contrast to the violent pictures of YHWH's warfare in the Vision to convey the sense of YHWH's goals toward which his strategy with the nations and with Israel are moving.

Comment

1 ויצא, "and . . . will go out." The verb form (perfect + *vav*) does not set the time as future (see J. Wash Watts, *Survey of Syntax,* 47–54; contra Wildberger) but relates the passage to the controlling sentence (10:33) and the great mosaic of pictures that follows. הנה, "behold," and the participle in 10:33 portray an act of God that is already apparent. Thus this passage begins to picture the possibilities that derive from that act. יצא, "come out," can refer to being born (Gen 35:11) or to his appearance as king (Zech 5:5). Gen 17:6 uses it for his genealogy (cf. Mic 5:1 [2]).

The prophecy reaches behind David to Jesse (just as Mic 5:1 [2] reaches behind Jerusalem to Bethlehem). גזע, "stump," is descriptive of a broken, cut-off dynasty. It takes up the figure of the Master Forester from 10:33–34 with the trimming and thinning of the forest describing the troubled times of Ahaz's reign. It realistically recognizes the severely reduced status of the throne, a reduction by the division of the kingdom (cf. 7:17) and more recently by the vassal status of Ahaz and the reduced area controlled by Judah. A "stump" indeed!

The shoot (חטר) or the branch (נצר) springs not from fresh new ground (a new dynasty) but from the old stump or roots. Jesse's descendants will take on new life. Job 14:7 uses the same words to picture the revival of an apparently dead tree. The term חטר, "shoot," is used only here in this meaning, while נצר, "branch," appears only here in royal Davidic literature. In 14:19 it refers to the dead king of Babylon and in 60:21 to the returned people of Jerusalem. Dan 11:7 designates a royal heir by it. The "Branch of YHWH" in 4:2 uses a different word.

G. Widengren (*The King and the Tree of Life,* UUÅ [Uppsala: Lundequistska, 1951] 50) has drawn on ancient Near Eastern parallels to suggest a relation between kingship and the tree of life. The verse (with v 10) applies such imagery to the concern in act 1 for the survival of the Davidic dynasty (cf. 7:1–14; 9:5–6 [6–7]).

2 In contrast with the usual royal passages, the king is not named again, nor is he the subject of a verb, until v 10. Instead, the passage turns to the gifts, attributes, and acts of God that make survival and revival possible. The first is רוח יהוה, "the spirit of YHWH." This is a feature not found in the parallels from other books, but it is apparent throughout Isaiah's vision (cf. 4:4; 32:15–20; 34:16; 40:7, 13; 42:1; 44:3; 47:16; 48:16; 59:19, 21; 61:1, 3). Although the term is unusual in other Davidic passages, it is not unknown in psalms that speak of the king's needs. Ps 51:12 (10) pleads for a "firm spirit" and v 14 (12) for a "willing spirit"; v 13 (11) prays for God not to remove his "holy spirit"; and v 19 (17) recognizes God's demand for a "broken spirit" (cf. Isa 57:15; 66:2). See also Pss 104:30, 106:33, 139:7, and 143:10. There is, then, a strand in the Psalms that emphasizes God's spirit, like Isaiah. But it is not original to Davidic genres. Perhaps there is a return here to the charismatic nature of kingship (1 Sam 10:6, 10; 11:6; 16:13, 14; 19:9), which had been replaced by the dynastic principle of Davidic promise (2 Sam 7:14). This teaches that God's spirit speaks and acts through his Anointed One. Anointing (1 Sam 12:13) is intended to impart the gift of the spirit.

The spirit of YHWH gives the king the skills needed to reign. They are listed in three pairs. חכמה ובינה, "wisdom and understanding," are standard qualities required in the king (G. von Rad, *Wisdom in Israel* [Nashville: Abingdon, 1972] 28, 36). The Assyrian king claimed them for himself (10:13). They are demonstrated in David (2 Sam 14:17) and Solomon (1 Kgs 3: 5, 6). Wisdom is the quality that enables the king to make good judgments. Understanding is the deeper intellectual insight into events and persons that is required to establish policy. עצה וגבורה, "counsel and heroism," are the second pair. Prov 8:14 lists them among the "fruits" of the spirit of YHWH. Note also the throne names in Isa 9:5 (6): "Wonder Counselor, God-Hero." Counsel includes the formation of strategy and the planning of battle and policies for the kingdom (2 Kgs 18:20; Isa 36:5). The king is commander-in-chief of the armies and leads in battle (1 Kgs 15:23; 16:5, 27; 22:46 [45]). Wildberger cites Prov 8:14 to show that these also have civil usage, a peaceful application. The third pair consists of דעת ויראת יהוה, "knowledge and fear of YHWH." Both words relate to YHWH and are basic terms for Yahwistic faith. The spirit will inspire the king to a powerful life of faith and worship. The knowledge of YHWH has a very special place in the Vision. Lack of knowledge was grave sin (1:3). The major picture of the new age was one in which "the knowledge of YHWH will cover the earth" (11:9). דעת, "knowledge," refers to a true understanding and relation to God and his will. יראת יהוה, "fear of YHWH," depicts the basic awe and submission of the king to the Holy God who, in mystery beyond understanding, can only be worshiped. The spirit of YHWH makes these possible.

3 יראת יהוה, "the fear of YHWH," is a complex phrase, despite being so common in the OT. The complexity begins with the old question of whether it is a subjective or objective genitive. Does the fear come from YHWH, or is it directed toward YHWH? Hebrew does not distinguish the two. Probably overtones of both should be heard in the phrase. The phrase here echoes v 2 and implies that the spirit's work in the king brings genuine devotion, a real הריח, "delight," to his worship and service, or that such devotion is the Spirit's delight.

Vv 3 and 4 lack an expressed subject. Conjunctions join the sentences, but the antecedents of pronouns and subjects of verbs are not defined. The echo nature of 3*a* makes the king the likely antecedent there, but the others are open. The usual conclusion is that the king or the "messianic king" is the subject. However, the theme of these verses is unbiased justice and rule, which are characteristics that belong to YHWH and should also belong to the king. The chiastic outline above and the failure to return to the king as subject after v 1 suggest that YHWH is the understood subject. The translation has shown this by making v 3b a relative clause. Righteousness and justice are elementary requirements of divine justice and of royal rule (Ps 72).

4 YHWH's commitment to justice for the poor is paramount. No regime that fails on this point can claim to be the work of YHWH. God's own participation in judgment makes this a possibility.

YHWH's power is expressed here through "the rod of his mouth" and "the breath of his lips." The naked power of the Forester lopping off branches is no longer necessary. Genuine authority can be exercised by decree (the rod of his mouth), and execution of the guilty criminal can be effected by orderly judicial process (the breath [or spirit] of his lips).

5 צדק, "righteousness," and האמונה, "faithfulness," were basic characteristics required of a good king and expected from God. The question—whose loins? whose waist?—is the same as in v 3. The ambiguity is undoubtedly deliberate. YHWH, his spirit, and the king are properly indistinguishable when the fear and knowledge of YHWH permeate the realm. The reality of these things in the experience of the people is prerequisite to the order of peace that follows.

6–8 The picture of pastoral tranquillity depends on the custom of having a boy (or girl) who serves as the village herder for domestic animals gather the sheep, the goats, and the calves to lead (or drive) them out to pasture in the morning and bring them back at night. After feeding, they lie down in the pastures, seeking any shade available from the heat. Biblical stories like that of David (1 Sam 17:34–37) reflect the hazards of that occupation, hazards that are banned under these conditions. The innocence of the "child" herder, the suckling or "nursing child," and the toddler or "weaned child" accent a world without harm or danger.

9 "My holy mountain" (RSV) is literally "the mount of my holiness" and is a fixed part of Zion's traditions. But here it parallels "the earth" and implies the totality of God's redeemed and re-created world. The knowledge of YHWH imparted by his spirit has made it possible for all the world to be as God's own sanctuary with no need for separations and barriers. The "knowledge . . . of YHWH" (cf. v 2 above) implies such a relationship and commitment to YHWH and his ways that fellowship with him is possible and easy and that the fulfillment of his pleasure is presumed in all. The translation of הארץ as "the earth" rather than "the land" is justified by the contrast with הים, "the sea."

10 אליו גוים ידרשו, "to him nations come seeking." The verse first identifies the function of the Davidic ruler. His rule signals the presence of God's spirit in Israel, a function that the divided monarchy had virtually nullified in practice. It then asserts that this function will be fulfilled and glory restored to the dynasty. The verse balances the episode (10:5–19) as the third Day of YHWH passage in picturing a restored honor for Jerusalem's king.

Explanation

The passage is one element of the larger "vision" that began with the call not to fear the Assyrian (10:24), gathered momentum in the theophanic approach of God to Zion (10:27*d*–32), and was given definition and direction in the call to "Behold the Lord—designing a beautiful thing" (10:33). The passage is connected to this at its beginning by "and [it] shall go out." A clear and unifying theme is the branch from Jesse's roots. This passage (with 9:5–6 [6–7]) is from the stock of literature belonging to the lore of the Davidic monarchy. Parallels can be found in Pss 2, 21, 45, 72, and 110; 2 Sam 7; 1 Kgs 2–3; Chronicles; and some other prophets like Mic 5:2–6.

The announcement that the Davidic monarchy in that time (i.e., Ahaz's reign, eighth century) is a centerpiece of God's design of "a beautiful" thing (v 1) is followed by the promise that God's spirit on him will guarantee the spiritual characteristics needed in a king (v 2), while the qualities of insight (3*bc*), fairness for all his subjects (v 4*ab*), and powerful authority (v 4*cd*) will follow. It presumes the connection of the king to the two-hundred-year-old dynasty and its ideals, including divine choice, promise, and sustenance (2 Sam 7). It equally presumes God's (and therefore, the king's) priorities of justice for the poor and helpless.

This recognition of the requirements that must be fulfilled for a reign of righteousness and faithfulness (v 5) is followed by a picture of a return to Eden's tranquillity and innocence that is unique in its force and power (vv 6–9*b*). The conclusion explains that these conditions flow from the universal presence of "the knowledge of YHWH" (v 9*cd*), neatly closing the circle by recalling the spirit-imbued "knowledge and fear" of YHWH (v 2). We may remember that the Vision sees Israel's fatal flaw in lack of this knowledge (1:3 and passim).

The pictures of the Davidic king resemble oriental ideals for kingship (Wildberger, 457–62, cites parallels). The king needs wisdom for justice and for peace. This peace is often presented as applying to the natural as well as the social and political world. Yet these pictures are unique in the OT, except for the parallels in chap. 35. They are also consistent with the Divine Gardener and Divine Forester motifs, which show God's concern for nature's welfare blending with his rule of peoples and nations.

The classic view of Zion's king understood that natural order as much as social and political order depended on him (A. R. Johnson, *Sacral Kingship in Ancient Israel,* 2d ed. [Cardiff: Univ. of Wales Press, 1967] 58). The effective reign of God's anointed brought justice to the people and peace (שלום *shalom* in the sense of wholeness and health) to all of God's creation. The conditions for this are noted in beginning and end: a king whose entire being is clothed by righteousness and faithfulness to his God, his calling, and his subjects, and one whose "knowledge and fear of YHWH" are spread to cover the whole earth. Thus the chosen king has effectively fulfilled his destiny as "Prince of Peace" (9:5 [6]).

This ideal is worked out in vv 6–8 in the scene of a village with simple huts, mud floors, and human beings and animals in crowded association. The same may be found in large areas of the world today. The people eke out an existence in sharp and often bitter conflict with a hostile nature. Predators prey on the domestic stock. Snakes keep the rats under control but pose a constant threat, especially to the children who live on the mud floor for lack of furniture. (India loses hundreds of children to snakebite annually.) Such villages were (and are) the economic backbones of their societies. The cities could not exist without them. A regime that brought peace and prosperity to the villages was successful beyond belief. But the villages were most vulnerable to the ravages of war, famine, and drought.

But when "righteousness, faithfulness, and the knowledge of YHWH" control the palace, even predators are tamed (obviously otherwise well fed) and the reptiles are no threat. Under God such a scene is possible.

The nature of the passage requires discussion. Wildberger joins a long line of interpreters in calling this "a promise." Yet it is not put in a "thus says the Lord" speech. The element of promise is much closer, however, in the admonition of 10:23–24 and the clear promise that YHWH "in yet a little while" will whip the Assyrians (10:25–26); promise is also apparent in the call to recognize YHWH's theophany and the attendant designation of Zion as a beautiful thing to be spared and nurtured (10:32–33). But this, too, was qualified by "until the day." The context calls for a near fulfillment of these promises. The Assyrian threats in 734–32, 728, and 724–21 B.C.E. had finally destroyed Samaria and northern Israel. Ahaz is on the throne. This section assures the continuation of the Davidic dynasty beyond the Assyrian crisis. This was later fulfilled: Hezekiah, Manasseh, Josiah, and others were yet to occupy the throne.

The thrust of the passage, however, does not emphasize the role of the king. Consistent with the Vision's perspective, God's role stands out. The passage (vv 1–10) begins and ends with confirmation of the dynasty's renewal (v 1) and its established status (v 10). But the emphasis is on three facets of God's support and blessing. First is the "spirit of YHWH" (v 2), which provides the wisdom necessary for rule. The second is the "fear of YHWH" (vv 2*c* and 3*a*), which makes possible the administration of justice (v 4*a*) and the authority to rule (v 4*b*). The third is "the knowledge of YHWH" (vv 2*d* and v 9), which assures the reign of peace. These are not royal achievements. They are facets of YHWH's evident presence in Jerusalem. When a king rules by "the Spirit of YHWH" in the "fear of YHWH," and with the intent of spreading "the knowledge of YHWH," the ethos of Davidic kingship is at work. Unfortunately, the opposite is also true. When kings rule by the guidelines of their own ambition and power, God's purposes are thwarted and judgment awaits.

The Vision was read (perhaps heard) by a people 250 years removed from the scene. They were well aware of the story recounted in 2 Kgs 18:2–5. While they share the thrill inherent in this scene, they know Hezekiah's weakness, Manasseh's shame, Josiah's death in battle, and Zedekiah's final debacle. They are prepared for the shift in mid-chapter (v 11) in which YHWH alone assumes responsibility for returning the exiles. Yet there is also inherent here a deeper promise that reaches beyond the historical and literary context. It rests on the classic understanding that David and his sons, like Abraham and his children, were chosen with a destiny that God will not deny himself.

The Vision of Isaiah is keenly aware of the potential for faith and hope in this promise. It is also aware of the irreparable harm that repeated and ill-chosen royal revolts against imperial power had brought to Judah under Hezekiah, Josiah, Jehoiakim, and Zedekiah, not to mention the plots against the Persians that are only hinted at in our sources. Therefore it is important to note that these exuberant messianic passages are scarce in the Vision. The tendency of the Vision is to lead readers to see that God's purposes can be fulfilled in other ways than political and military authority and power. Yet for this moment in time, even under the pressure of Assyria's yoke (10:27), assurance is valid: "Do not fear the Assyrians!" The throne will survive the crisis, the throne of YHWH's anointed, David's son.

These verses remain among the most beautiful examples of monarchic ritual and poetry in messianic literature. They shine as a luminous light. The problems come from the generations, including our own, that "do not know, do not understand," who have "eyes but do not see, ears but do not hear," with whom God has to work to reach these goals.

YHWH's Second Deliverance (11:11–16)

Bibliography

Erlandsson, S. "Jes. 11:10–16 och dess historiska bakgrund." *SEÅ* 36 (1971) 24–44. **Luria, B. Z.** "The Prophecy in Isa 11:11–16 on the Gathering of the Exiles." (Heb.) *BMik* 26 (1981) 108–14. **Vajda, G.** "Fragments d'un commentaire judeo-arabe sur le livre d'isaïe (Isaïe 11:10–13:14)." *VT* 13 (1963) 208–24. **Vollmer, J.** *Geschichtliche Rückblicke.* 172–73.

Waschke, E.-J. "Die Stellung der Königstexte im Jesajabuch im Vergleich zu den Königspsalmen 2, 72 und 89." *ZAW* 110 (1998) 355–58. **Wegner, P.** *An Examination of Kingship and Messianic Expectation in Isaiah 1–35.* Lewiston, NY: Mellen, 1992. **Widengran, G.** "Yahweh's Gathering of the Dispersed." In *In the Shelter of Elyon.* FS G. W. Ahlström, ed. W. B. Barrick and J. R. Spencer. Sheffield: JSOT Press, 1984. 227–45. **Williamson, H. G. M.** "Isaiah XI 11–16 and the Redaction of Isaiah I–XII." In *Congress Volume: Paris, 1992.* Ed. J. Emerton. VTSup 61. Leiden: Brill, 1995. 343–47.

Translation

Heavens:	11 *And it shall be in that day*	3
	the Lord[a] *will lift*[b] *his hand a second time*	4+3
	to acquire the remnant of his people	
	that is left, from Assyria and (Lower) Egypt,	4+3
	from Pathros, from Cush, and from Elam,	
	from Shinar and from Hamath,[c]	2+2
	and from the islands of the sea.[d]	
Earth:	12 *And he shall raise a banner for the nations*	3+3
	and gather the banished[a] *of Israel.*	
	And the dispersed of Judah he will assemble	3+3
	from the four quarters of the earth.	
Heavens:	13 *Ephraim's jealousy shall turn aside.*	3+3
	Judah's enmities[a] *will be cut off.*	
	Ephraim will no longer be jealous of Judah,	3+3
	and Judah will no longer vex Ephraim.	
	14 *And they will fly on the shoulder*[a] *of the Philistines westward.*	4+4
	Together they will plunder the easterners.	
	Edom and Moab (will be) the extension[b] *of their power,*	4+3
	and the Ammonites their lackeys.[c]	
Earth:	15 *And YHWH shall dry up*[a]	2+2+2
	the tongue	
	of the Sea of Egypt.	
	And he shall wave his hand	2+2+2
	over the River	
	with the violence of his wind.[b]	
Heavens:	*When he breaks (it) into seven streams,*	3+2
	one will cross with his sandals (on).	
	16 *And there shall be a highway*	2+2+3
	for the remnant of his people	
	who are left from Assyria,	
	as there was for Israel	3+2+2
	in the day they came up	
	from the land of Egypt.	

Notes

11.a. Many MSS read יהוה, "YHWH."

11.b. MT שֵׁנִית, "a second time," is redundant with יוֹסִיף, "again." LXX has δεῖξαι, "to show," "declare," "announce." *BHS* proposes שְׁנוֹת, which is suggested by Arab. *sanija*, "be high." But no use of this verb in Heb. is known. H. Fitzgerald ("Hebrew *yd* = 'love' and 'beloved,'" *CBQ* 29 [1967] 369) suggests that יד means "love": "He will move to double his love." The best solution is to compare with 49:22 and read שְׂאֵת, "lift," *qal* inf. const. from נשׂא.

11.c. מחמת, "from Hamath." Hamath is a city in Syria. There is no record of Jewish exiles being there. Numerous emendations have been suggested, but Wildberger's comment, that it should be seen to represent all of Syria and left as it is, prevails.

11.d. מאיי הים, "islands of the sea," is missing in LXX, although the Hexapla inserts it again.

12.a. נדחי, "banished," is usually thought a *nip'al* ptc. m. pl. const. נדח. The *dagesh forte* in ד has fallen out over the vocal *shewa'* (GKC §20*m*).

13.a. צֹרְרֵי, "enmities," has received considerable attention. Some seek an abstract parallel to קנאת (P. Joüon, *Bib* 10 [1929] 195: צִצְרֵי—an abstract pl. meaning "enmity"; Procksch reads MT as an abstract pl. without change). But the pl. verb that follows is reason enough to reject both.

14.a. בְכָתֵף, "on the shoulder," MT points as an abs. form. In this form one must translate "The Philistines fly on the shoulder to the East." The context calls for another subject. General attempts at emendation have been made (F. Wutz, *BZ* 18 [1929] 27). *BHS* follows the Vg. *humeros Philisthiim* to a const. pointing כֶּתֶף, "the shoulder of the Philistines" (cf. BDB, 509), which *HAL* identifies as the "western slopes of the Judaean hill-country" (similarly *DCH*).

14.b. מִשְׁלוֹח, "extension," L and *BHS*, but many editions, including *BHK*, follow correct Masoretic grammar: מִשְׁלוֹחַ.

14.c. MT משמעתם, lit. "the ones who listen to them," i.e., obediently.

15.a. MT וְהֶחֱרִים, "and he will dry up," is pointed as *hip'il* pf. 3 m. sg. from חרם, "to ban, exterminate" (BDB, 355). LXX καὶ ἐρημώσει, "and he will lay waste," followed by Tg. ויביש, Syr. *w^e^raḥreb*, and Vg *desolabit*, implies והחריב, "and he will make desolate." H. J. Stoebe (*TZ* 18 [1962] 399) and *BHS* argue for MT. G. R. Driver ("Vocabulary of the Old Testament," *JTS* 32 [1931] 251) and *HAL* point to the Akk. root *harâmu*, "to cut off, divide" (similarly *DCH*). Wildberger properly follows the versions.

15.b. Wildberger notes that בעים רוחו has no satisfactory explanation. LXX πνεύματι βιαίῳ, "to a violent spirit"; Tg. במימר נביוהי, "by the word of his prophets"; Syr. *b^e'uḥdānâ d^erûḥeh*, "with the power of his wind"; Vg. *in fortitudine spiritus sui*, "in the strength of his spirit." BDB, 744, lists עְיָם as dubious, possibly "glow." J. Reider ("Contributions to the Scriptural Text," *HUCA* 24 [1952–53] 83) supports a connection with Arab. *ġāma*, "plagued by a burning thirst," and translates "with the violence of his wind." H. Beers ("Hebrew Textual Notes," *AJSL* 34 [1917] 132–33) suggests בעים is an adv. from the root בעה (cf. 30:13; 64:1), meaning "beyond the normal, energetic, strong, powerful." H. D. Hummel ("Enclitic *Mem* in Early NW Semitic," *JBL* 76 [1957] 94) calls it an inf. abs. from בעה followed by enclitic *mem*, to be translated "boiling of water." Tur-Sinai ("A Contribution to the Understanding of Isaiah I–XII," 188) relates it to Akk. *ûmu* and sees in it a Heb. word meaning "storm." There is no convincing suggestion here. Keep MT, but translate like the versions (cf. Wildberger, *HAL*).

Form/Structure/Setting

The passage is united by the single theme of YHWH's gathering the scattered exiles of his people (vv 11, 15). The signal with his hand occurs three times (vv 11, 12, 15). The major concerns are with those in Assyria (vv 11, 15), while two middle sections are concerned that both Israel and Judah be involved (vv 12, 13–14). In v 11 two lines are drawn: one from north (Assyria) to south (Cush), a second from east (Elam) to west (Islands of the Sea). This parallels the four "wings" of the earth (v 12).

In the larger chiastic structure, vv 11–16 balance 10:33–34 and 10:27*c*–32 (see introduction to scene 3 at 10:24 above).

Williamson (*Book Called Isaiah,* 125–43) relates 5:25–30, 8:21–23, and 11:11–16 to a single redactional layer to be attributed to Deutero-Isaiah. This observation points to the pervasive fifth-century editing of the entire Vision.

Comment

11 ביום ההוא, "in that day," picks up the relation to the event announced in 10:33. והיה, "and it shall be," falls in line with the verbs plus *vav* that have marked aspects of that event and its concomitant effects from 10:34 to this point.

שנית, "a second time," concedes the failure of earlier efforts, whether those be understood as the exodus or the restoration of the "Branch" (i.e., Hezekiah). It announces a further effort. The rescue concentrates on the שאר עמו, "remnant of his people," the fragments of the elect, the children of Abraham. This has been used in the Vision to refer to the exiles from northern Israel.

קנה, "to acquire," is noteworthy. The noun קנה, "owner," appears in 1:3: "an ass knows its owner." Eve said, "With the help of God I have acquired a son [קניתי]" (Gen 4:1) and named him Cain (קין). The verb appears in Gen 14:19, 22 and Deut 32:6 as a parallel to "create." It is used in Exod 15:16 and Ps 74:2 of God's redemption of his people. With overtones of redemption and creation, God will act to bring back the exiles in a way parallel to the exodus, a way that is like his creation of a people for himself.

The verse documents the places from which they will be rescued. Assyrian captivity is recorded already in 2 Kgs 15:29 in 733 B.C.E., and 2 Kgs 17:6 (18:11) tells of deportation to Halah on the Habor River during the siege of Samaria (724–721 B.C.E.). The references to Egypt pick up the more likely area for Judean dispersion. People from Israel were in Egypt as early as Solomon's day, when Jeroboam fled there (1 Kgs 11:40). Some suspect that Solomon furnished mercenaries in exchange for chariots, so the military settlements that are documented for cities on the Nile in the sixth century may well have been there much earlier. מצרים, "Egypt," is Lower Egypt, which had groups of Israelites from Solomon's time on. פתרוס, "Pathros," is Upper Egypt from Aswan southward. כוש, "Cush," is still further up the Nile into the Sudan (cf. Gen. 10:6, 8). עילם, "Elam," lies east of Mesopotamia. שנער, "Shinar," is in the Euphrates delta (*MBA,* 15; see Gen 10:10.) חמת, "Hamath," is closer to home in Syria (Gen 10:15), while the איי, "islands," turn to the Mediterranean and the Aegean. Perhaps the list anticipates the "four quarters" (lit., "wings") of v 12. Thus great diagonals are drawn from Assyria (northeast) to Cush (extreme south) and from Elam (due east) to the islands (west and northwest). Cf. the list of places in Obad 20.

12 "Raise a banner" interprets the movement of YHWH's hand in v 11. נס, "banner," occurs in 5:26 and 13:2. In each instance YHWH raises the banner as a signal to the "nations." YHWH's use of the nations to accomplish his will is patent throughout. In other passages the nations' task is one of war and destruction, but here the task is one of gathering and assembling Israelites and Judeans from distant places. The ארבע כנפות, "four quarters," are literally "wings" and are defined in the previous verse.

Waschke (*ZAW* 110 [1998] 357 n. 43) relates this theme to 62:10–12 and suggests that this was written with the composition of the entire book in mind. He argues cogently that the exodus motif of 11:15, 40:3, 49:11, and 62:10 supports the same supposition.

13–14 This prediction of a reunited kingdom returns to a theme hinted at before (cf. *Comment* on 9:5 [6]). The tensions and wars between Ephraim and Judah have dominated their history since the time of Jeroboam's split from Rehoboam. This must be overcome for God's purposes with the kingdom to be achieved. When unity is achieved (v 14), the reestablishment of sovereignty over the former subject peoples is possible.

15 לשון ים־מצרים, "the tongue of the Sea of Egypt." The term has no parallel in the OT but apparently refers to the upper end of the Gulf of Suez, which is referred to simply as הים, "the sea," in Exod 14:2, 9; 15:4, 8, 22; Isa 51:10; and 63:11 and as the ים־סוף, "the Reed Sea," in Exod 13:18, Num 14:25, Deut 1:40, and elsewhere.

הניף ידו, "wave his hand," picks up the chain of references to God's hand signals that began in 5:25. Here, like 10:32, the hand is not rigid but moving. However, the purpose is not to signal troops but to bring the עים רוחו, "power of his Spirit/wind," into play. The parallel to Moses' outstretched arm and staff and the mighty east wind (Exod 14:21) is unmistakable: הנהר, "the River," refers to the Euphrates. The return of captives from Assyria is compared to Israel's exodus from Egypt—a theme that reappears in the Vision (see on v 12 above). The meaning of the שבעה נחלים, "seven streams," is not interpreted here. In this setting it shows the silt building up to a point that the stream has seven channels so small one does not need to remove his sandals in crossing.

16 סלה, "highway," means an artificially built-up road, not simply a "path" or a "way." The Vision returns to this in 19:23, 35:8, 49:11, and 62:10. The Persians are known to have developed an extensive network of such roads (cf. A. T. Olmstead, *History of the Persian Empire* [Chicago: Univ. of Chicago, 1948] 299–301), which were forerunners of the famous Roman roads. The parallel to the exodus moves beyond the facts in suggesting that a similar highway existed for Israel's flight from Egypt. This parallel extends throughout the Vision (cf. W. Zimmerli, "Der 'neue Exodus,'" in *Hommage à Wilhelm Vischer* [Montpellier, 1960] 216–27 = *Gottes Offenbarung,* TB 19 [Munich: Kaiser, 1963] 192–204; B. W. Anderson, "Exodus Typology in Second Isaiah," in *Israel's Prophetic Heritage,* ed. B. W. Anderson and W. Harrelson, 177–95).

Explanation

This passage reverses the picture of God's attititude toward Israel that is found in 2:5–9. The pericope is controlled by the opening verse, which sets it "in that day" and which announces God's purpose to "acquire" his people from distant places. The first part (vv 12–14) announces God's signal to the nations to gather the dispersed of Israel and Judah. The reference to the remnant is careful to include both Israel and Judah (v 12) in accordance with practice throughout the Vision. The result is the unification of the kingdom and the reestablishment of its sovereignty over its neighbors, i.e., the return to the conditions of the united kingdom that David established. This theme is still very pertinent to the growing rift between Jerusalem and Samaria in the fifth century.

The second part (vv 15–16) pictures God's direct intervention to remove the natural barriers to return. His power parallels the crossing of the Red Sea when Israel left Egypt under Moses. The result is a highway on an axis from Assyria through Egypt that crosses Canaan for the remnant's return. God's return of his people from both directions miraculously removes the natural barriers, the gulf and the river, by the power of his Spirit, or wind.

Hymns for "That Day" (12:1–6)

Bibliography

Alonso Schökel, L. "De duabus methodis pericopam explicandi." *VD* 34 (1956) 154–60. **Craigie, P. C.** "Psalm XXIX in the Hebrew Poetic Tradition." *VT* 22 (1972) 143–51. **Crüsemann, F.** *Studien zur Formgeschichte vom Hymnus und Danklied in Israel.* WMANT 32. Neukirchen-Vluyn: Neukirchener Verlag, 1969. 227. **Gottlieb, H.** "Jesaja, Kapitel 12." *DTT* 37 (1974) 29–32. **Loewenstamm, S. E.** "The Lord Is My Strength and My Glory." *VT* 19 (1969) 464–70. **Prinsloo, W. S.** "Isaiah 12: One, Two, or Three Songs?" In *Goldene Äpfel in silbernen Schalen.* Ed. K.-D. Schunck and M. Augustin. Frankfort am Main: Lang, 1992. 25–33. **Vermeylen, J.** *Du Prophète Isaïe à l'Apocalyptique.* Vol. 1. Paris: Gabalda, 1977. 280–82. **Williamson, H. G. M.** *Book Called Isaiah.* 118–25.

Translation

Herald:	1 *And you [sg.] shall say in that day:*	
Zion:	*I will raise my hands*[a] *to you, YHWH.*	2
	Indeed, you have been angry with me.	3
	[b]*May your anger turn*	2+1
	that you may comfort me.[b]	
	2 *Behold God*[a] *(is) my salvation.*	3+3
	I shall trust and I shall not live in fear.	
	Because Yah[b] *YHWH (is) my power*	3+2+3
	and my strength,[c]	
	he becomes my salvation.	
Herald:	3 *And you [pl.] shall draw water with rejoicing*	3+2
	from the wells of salvation.	
	4 *And you [pl.] shall say on that day:*	3
Chorus:	*Lift up your hands*[a] *to YHWH;*	2+2
	call on his name.	
	Make known his acts among the nations.	3
	Bring to remembrance—	1+3
	that his name has been exalted.	
	5 *Sing of YHWH*	2+3
	for he has done a majestic thing,	
	making this known[a]	2+2
	in all the earth.	
	6 *Shrill out and sing,*	2+2
	inhabitant[a] *of Zion,*	
	for great in your midst (is)	3+2
	the Holy One of Israel!	

Notes

1.a. MT אוֹדְךָ "I will praise you." 1QIsa[a] דה . . . א has two letters missing but shows no 2d-person suf. A *hip'il* form from ידה could produce דה(הו)א or the *hitpa'el* דה(תו)א (cf. Dan 9:4). Both mean "let me give thanks" or "praise" by using a verb root that suggests lifting the hands as a gesture. MT may also have this meaning and is translated "let me lift my hands to you." For the relation to "hands" symbolism in these chapters, see the *Form/Structure/Setting* section below. כי may here be a strong assertive particle, "indeed."

1.b-b. MT's two juss. verbs are unexpected in a psalm of thanksgiving (cf. Wildberger, 477). LXX διότι ὠργίσθης μοι καὶ ἀπέστρεψας τὸν θυμόν σου καὶ ἠλέησάς με, "because you were angry with me, and you turned back your wrath and were gracious to me" (also Syr. *w'hpkt rwgzk wbj'tnj;* Vg. *conversus est furor tuus, et consolatus es me*) reads the Heb. as consec. impfs. that restore the normal form of a thanksgiving psalm. Wildberger correctly rejects moves to make the text conform, which might rob the text of its own integrity. Gunkel (H. Gunkel and J. Begrich, *Einleitung in die Psalmen* [Göttingen: Vandenhoeck & Ruprecht, 1933] 275) notes that a thanksgiving psalm may include supplication.

2.a. Syr. inserts על, "upon the God of my salvation"; 1QIsa[a] reads אל אל, "toward the God of my salvation," or a double אל, "God," as a parallel to יה יהוה, "Yah YHWH," in the next line. But MT is sound. I read the stich as a substantive sentence without a verb.

2.b. יה is often omitted with LXX and Vg. (cf. *BHS*). The exact parallels in Exod 15:2 and Ps 118:14 are grounds for keeping it. Wildberger follows R. M. Spence ("Yah, Yahve," *ExpTim* 11 [1899–1900] 94) in omitting יהוה, "YHWH," on grounds of dittography for the following ויהי, "he becomes." Both may be kept to sustain the emphasis.

2.c. זמרת יה is an unusual formula (also in Exod 15:2; Ps 118:14). 1QIsa[a] זמרתיה makes the *yod* a suf., "my," but then writes the ה above the line (cf. S. Talmon, "Double Readings," *VT* 4 [1954] 206; "Double Readings in MT," *Textus* 1 [1960] 163 n. 47). G. R. Driver ("Hebrew Scrolls," *JTS* 2 [1951] 25) notes that in both other instances some MSS also read זמרתי. Perhaps the MT has lost a *yod* in liturgical use (cf. Wildberger, 478; O. Lehman, "Biblical Textual Tradition," *JNES* 26 [1967] 98; Loewenstamm *VT* 19 [1969] 465). זמרה has usually been translated "song" (BDB, *DCH*), but studies (J. Zolli, "Note esegetiche," *Giornale della Societa Asiatica Iraliana* 3 [1935] 290–92; KBL; *HAL*) have sought its meaning in Arab. *ḏamara*, "drive," and *ḏimr(un)*, "strong," and Amor. *zmr*, "protect." Also, comparisons with personal names like זמרי (Noth, *Die israelitschen Personennamen,* 176) have turned to the meaning "strength" or "might" (contra Loewenstamm, 465).

4.a. Cf. *Note* 1.a. above.

5.a. K מידעת (*pu'al* ptc.), "something made known," "a monument." Q מודעת (*hop'al* ptc.), "something caused to be made known." LXX ἀναγγείλατε (impv.), "announce it," suggests a Heb. הודיעו. Tg. and Syr. have ptcs. like MT. 1QIsa[a] מודעות (pl. ptc.). MT should be sustained in either K or Q forms.

6.a. Fem. to indicate a collective sense (cf. Joüon §134*c*).

Form/Structure/Setting

ואמרת, "and you shall say," continues the series of perfect + *vav* that began in 10:34 and 11:1. They each and all hark back to the הנה, "behold," of 10:33 with the following participle. Yet they do not constitute a chain in which each link depends on the one before. Each responds to the theophany in 10:27*d*–32 (cf. J. Wash Watts, *Survey of Syntax,* 47–54). This is emphasized by the conscious use of אודך, "I raise my hands to you" (v 1), and הודו, "lift up your hands" (v 4), to respond to the ינפף ידו, "he waves his hand" (10:32), to create a beautiful dramatic effect. Throughout 5:1–10:23, YHWH's hand has remained unyieldingly "outstretched"—a signal that the battle is to continue. In 10:32 he waves his hand toward Jerusalem. In 11:11 he reaches out his hand toward the exiles. And now in response, worshipers extend their hands toward him.

There are two distinct parts to this passage. In the first, the herald instructs the city (vv 1–2) and uses the singular (cf. Crüsemann, *Studien,* 50–55). In the second, instruction is directed to its inhabitants (plural). It gives a promise (v 3) that completes the admonition of 10:24 not to fear the Assyrian. Then it instructs them in the proper liturgical response for "that day." The setting is unusual for liturgy. The events to which the hymns should respond are viewed as yet to occur (cf. 10:24 and the repeated use of ביום ההוא, "in that day"), though normal liturgical forms respond to events as or after they happen.

The tenses reflect this unusual quality. In v 1 אָנַפְתָּ, "you are angry," is perfect, reflecting the existing situation. The song of thanksgiving, which the introductory אוֹדְךָ, "I raise my hands to you," seems to begin, usually is followed by an explanation in perfect tenses throughout. But here the tenses in the second part turn to jussives: יָשֹׁב, "may it turn," and תְּנַחֲמֵנִי, "may you comfort me." The strict form is broken, but the change fits the context here beautifully. In content, the passage contains what Blenkinsopp (270) calls "a patchwork of biblical citations and allusions" from Pss 118:21, 88:22, 25:5, 118:14, 105:1, 148:13, 9:12, 30:5, and Exod 15:2.

Comment

1 "You" is masculine singular and apparently refers to Zion. אוֹדְךָ, "I will confess you," is built on the verb ידה, which is apparently derived from יד, "hand." In the causative *hipʿil* stem it means something like "throw up (or out) the hands" as one might do in prayer, pleading, or worship. It comes to have the meaning "praise" or "confess." It is hardly accidental that the hymn that responds to a scene in which God's hand and that of the Assyrian have been so important should begin with the same phoneme.

God's "anger" is a direct reference to 10:25. The destruction of Samaria seems inevitable. The appearance of YHWH as of old to defend his city (10:27*d*–32) gives rise to the hope that Jerusalem, by a miracle, will survive. The call to give thanks and praise is based on an admonition (10:24), a promise (10:25, 26–27), and the recall of the great theophanic vision (10:27*d*–32).

In this vision, the people of faith saw the mighty God approaching his land and his city like a great forester (10:33–34). They sang out the old promises of history in God's hands and of God's own king and the peace he brings (11:1–10) and a new promise that scattered exiles will be returned (11:11–16). The hymns respond to the great theophany, daring to hope for an end very soon to God's period of anger.

2 The city confesses its reliance on YHWH-God for its hope and its future. Blenkinsopp (269) thinks the repeated reference to "salvation" (ישועה) is a play on the prophet Isaiah's name (ישעיה) to form an inclusio with the first verse of the book

3 The reference to drawing water has been understood as a liturgical reference to the ceremony during the festival of Sukkoth or Booths. What are the מעיני הישועה, "wells of salvation"? The figure most likely points to the sources of blessing existing in the house of David and in Zion, the salvation that is confirmed in the king's prayer in v 2.

4 הודו is from the root ידה (as in v 1), either *hipʿil* perfect third-person plural or *hipʿil* imperative second-person plural. In this context the latter is called for: "lift your hands."

5 נאות, "a majestic thing," is from נאה, "to be high." In contrast to human attempts to make themselves great or to rise to heights, YHWH's acts to redeem Zion and return Israel are inherently "high" and praiseworthy.

6 The poem closes with reference to the Holy One of Israel who played a role in Isa 1:4, 24; 5:19, 24; 6:3; and 10:20.

Explanation

The song is highly nuanced with the tenses conveying the hints of meaning. Words that usually are clear-cut imperatives and indicatives of hymnic praise in other settings are in v 1 tentative, pleading, wanting to believe, testing the water. A single male is addressed and told that these will be his thoughts "in that day." He begins his worship: "I will raise my hands to you, YHWH."

The theme that dominated chaps. 5 and 9–10 was YHWH's wrath toward Israel. It now asserts itself in the song "You have been angry." The perfect tense in the conditional clause indicates a condition taken for granted (J. Wash Watts, *Survey of Syntax*, 134). The worshiper knows that this condition does occur. His prayer in jussive tenses applies to that: "May your anger turn that you may comfort me!" The prayer turns to a confession of faith (v 2).

The theme here is salvation. The prayer has no hope but in God, in YHWH. The tentative approach of v 1 moves to greater confidence and ardor in v 2. This is the opportunity promised for "that day" beyond the *Dies Irae*, "day of wrath." But who is addressed? Is this the heir of David? The song is like psalmic laments of an individual. Is this addressed to Ahaz or his heir? The address in v 3 turns to a group (priests, inhabitants of the city?) who are promised that they will "draw water with rejoicing from the wells of salvation." So now the people share again in God's blessings through the "anointed one" of the stock of Jesse. They are called to join in the worship, praise, and testimony of that event (vv 4–5). They will give again the joyful cries of worship in Zion to lift the hands to YHWH, exalt his name, make remembrance of his acts before all the nations. The women of the city are exhorted to join their shrill voices to the cacophony of praise (v 6).

The reason for all of this is summarized: "For great in your midst is the Holy One of Israel." The Holy, Awesome, Divine Warrior who approached the city in 10:27–32 has again taken up his residence there and is to be worshiped and praised accordingly. The possibility that the Davidic monarchy may again function as conceived under David and Solomon is allowed to bloom in these chapters. The monarchy united and flourishing: that is the picture and the dream portrayed in this act.

These verses bring act 1 of the Vision (chaps. 7–12) to a conclusion. The whole act has responded to the recognition of God's determination to destroy the whole land (chaps. 5–6). The response takes up the fate of Jerusalem and of the Davidic monarchy (chap. 7) during the first Assyrian invasions of Tiglath-Pileser and Shalmaneser (7:17–25; 10:1–34) when Israel (5:8–25; 9:8–10:4) and other parts of Palestine were overrun and incorporated into the Assyrian Empire. However, Judah, Jerusalem, and the Davidic dynasty of Ahaz/Hezekiah survive intact (9:1–7; 10:24–33; 11:1–10) and even aid the cause of exiled and scattered Israelites (11:11–16). Worship in the temple continues (chap. 12).

20. It plays an important role in various texts and contexts within the Vision, most of which have to do with the fall or destruction of the city and the empire. But it is also clear that more than one destruction is in view, although they are sometimes conflated. In 13:17–22 the fall is due to the Medes; in 21:9 neither the date nor the enemy is named; in 23:13 the destruction came from the Assyrians; chap. 39 deals with Merodach-baladan's Babylon but relates it to the Babylon of Nebuchadnezzar (39:7); and chaps. 47 and 48 picture Babylon on the eve of Cyrus's entry into the city.

Williamson uses the unit of chaps. 13–27 (*Book Called Isaiah,* 156–83). He notes that the unit has a superscription (13:1). It has a distinctive genre designation ("burden") and in chaps. 19 and 24–27 it uses "in that day" passages to conclude portions of the section. It contains an Isaiah narrative (chap. 20; cf. Conrad, "Lord's Military Strategy," 119; C. R. Seitz, "Isaiah 1–66: Making Sense of the Whole," in *Reading and Preaching the Book of Isaiah* [Philadelphia: Fortress, 1988] 118–19). Williamson finds signs of Deutero-Isaiah's editing in chaps. 13–27, particularly in 14:1–2. He concludes that the two long poems on each side (13:2–22 and 14:4*b*–21) also belong to Deutero-Isaiah's redaction, as does the material in chap. 21. He finds no evidence that chaps. 24–27 belong to this redactional layer (*Book Called Isaiah,* 157–83).

Chaps. 24–27 have usually been treated as a unit (see the introduction to chaps. 24–27) and thought of as "out of context." Biddle suggests that a treatment of "the city" shows how chaps. 24–27 fill a mediating role between 13–23 and 28–33. Chaps. 13–23 treat the "bad city," and chaps. 28–33 treat the "good city," while "the city" in chaps. 24–27 has characteristics of both. Others like Brangenberg ("Reexamination") and Jenkins ("Development of the Isaiah Tradition") have limited the section to chaps. 13–23, preserving the independence of chaps. 24–27. Isa 13–23 has traditionally been studied as part of the prophecies against the nations.

Excursus: Oracles against the Nations (OAN)

Bibliography

Beentjes, P. C. "Notitie: Oracles against the Nations: A Central Issue in the 'Latter Prophets.'" *Tijdschrift voor Filosofie en Theologie* 50 (1989) 203–9. **Geyer, J. B.** "Mythology and Culture in the Oracles against the Nations." *VT* 36 (1986) 129–45. **Gosse, B.** "Oracles contre les nations et structures comparées des livres d'Isaïe et d'Ezéchiel." *BN* 54 (1990) 19–21. **Hayes, J. H.** "The Usage of Oracles against Foreign Nations in Ancient Israel." *JBL* 87 (1968) 61–92. **Hoffmann, Y.** *The Prophecies against Foreign Nations in the Bible.* (Hebrew.) Tel Aviv: Univ. of Tel Aviv Press, 1977. **Homberg, G. R.** "Reasons for Judgement in the Oracles against the Nations of the Prophet Isaiah." *VT* 31 (1981) 145–59. **Jenkins, A. K.** "The Development of the Isaiah Tradition in Isaiah 13–23." In *Book of Isaiah.* Ed. J. Vermeylen. 237–51. **Jones, B. C.** "Characteristics of OAN and משׂא Texts." In *Howling over Moab: Irony and Rhetoric in Isaiah 15–16.* SBLDS 157 Atlanta: Scholars Press, 1996. 53–88. **Landy, F.** "Prophetic Burdens in Isaiah 13–23." Unpublished SBL paper. Chicago, 1994. **Margulis, B.** "Studies in the Oracles against the Nations." Ph.D. diss., Brandeis, 1967. **Müller, H.-P.,** ed. *Babylonien und Israel: Historische, religiöse und sprachliche Beziehungen.* WF 633. Darmstadt: Wissenschaftliche Buchgesellschaft, 1991. **Petersen, D. L.** "The Oracles against the Nations: A Form Critical Analysis." In *SBLSP.* Ed. G.

McRae. Missoula, MT: Scholars Press, 1975. 1:39–61. **Raabe, P. R.** "Why Prophetic Oracles against the Nations?" In *Fortunate the Eyes.* Ed. A. B. Beck et al. 236–57. **Reimer, D. J.** *The Oracles against Babylon in Jeremiah 50–51: A Horror among the Nations.* San Francisco: Mellen, 1993. **Vanderhooft, D. S.** "Prophetic Oracles against Babylon and Neo-Babylonian Royal Inscriptions." In *AAR/SBL Abstracts.* Atlanta: Scholars Press, 1994. 331. **Witt, D. A.** "The Houses Plundered and the Women Raped: The Use of Isaiah 13 in Zechariah 14:1–11." *Proceedings Eastern Great Lakes and Midwest Bible Societies* 11 (1991) 66–74.

Oracles against the Nations (OAN) in the Latter Prophets have caught the attention of interpreters for some time. They are found in Isa 13–23, Jer 46–51, Ezek 24–32, Amos 1:3–2:3, Obadiah, Nahum, Habakkuk, and Zech 9. What is their function in context? Why are they there?

The Latter Prophets interpret YHWH's role in the events of the eighth through the sixth centuries B.C.E. These war-torn times demanded an explanation of God's activities in them. These oracles all assume that YHWH has authority over these nations and has the right to demand their allegiance. These nations play different roles in God's economy, but they are definitely a part of his reign. His decision to bring judgment on all the peoples of the land (Palestine) involved the neighboring peoples of Assyria/Babylonia and Egypt. YHWH functions as the military director of the period, arranging armies for battle and determining what each of them is supposed to do. The OAN as well as the war speeches that surround them are the literary means by which this theme is communicated.

The "oracles" in a strict sense are short threats or announcements introduced by "thus says the Lord." A number of these occur in Isaiah: against Babylon, Isa 14:22–23; Assyria, Isa 14:25; Philistines, Isa 14:30*b;* Moab, Isa 16:14; Damascus/Ephraim, Isa 17:1–3; Egypt, Isa 20:3–4; Jerusalem, Isa 22:14; and Tyre, Isa 23:11–12, 15–17. As in the other prophetic books, these oracles have been embellished and expanded to produce the present work. This commentary will not take them out of context but treats them as parts of the larger literary whole.

Structural Analysis

The act has its own title/superscription (13:1), which like 1:1 and 2:1 cites the name of Isaiah son of Amoz. Chap. 28 begins a new literary unit marked by "woe" heading each chapter.

The act (chaps. 13–27) can be viewed as bipartite. Chaps. 13–19 and 21–27 have similar literary structures that parallel each other. They each include five burdens (משא) and contain a series of "in that day" sections near the end. The burdens fall into two distinct groups: those using the names of real nations (14:28–29, Philistia; 15:1, Moab; 17:1, Damascus; 19:1, Egypt; and 23:1, Tyre) and those using symbolic names (21:1, Swampland; 21:11, Silence; 21:13, Wasteland; and 22:1, Valley of Vision). "The Burden of Babylon that Isaiah son of Amoz envisioned" (13:1) is the title covering all of chaps. 13–27. The burdens mainly involve nations other than Israel/Judah. But, as in Amos 1–2, Israel (with Damascus in 17:1–11) and Jerusalem (in chap. 22) are included. References to Jerusalem/Zion occur in 14:32, 16:1; 18:7; 19:11; 22:8, 9; 22:21, 22; 24:23; 25:6, 10; 26:1; and 27:13. Israel/Jacob occurs in 14:1–2; 17:3, 4, 7, 9; 19:24, 15; 24:15*b;* and 27:6, 9, 12. The temple is implied in 23:18.

YHWH is the central character in the act. The name יהוה, "YHWH," occurs sixty times; יהוה צבאות, "YHWH of Hosts," twenty-seven times; and אל ישראל, "God of Israel," twice. The use of הנה, "behold, see," emphasizes YHWH's actions, particularly in the first and last units. It appears at strategic points to mark out distinctive units. (Zewi Tamar has written a perceptive analysis of the uses of הנה ["The Particles *hinneh* and *wehinneh* in Biblical Hebrew," *HS* 37 (1996) 21–38]; his analysis addresses the internal relations of the particle to the clause it introduces, but it does not address the role of the particle in structuring the context.)

13:9 "Behold the day of YHWH . . . to make the earth a desolation."
13:17 "Behold me (YHWH) stirring up the Medes against them (Babylon)."
19:1 "See YHWH, . . . coming (to) Egypt."
24:1 "See YHWH destroying the land."
26:21 "Look! YHWH is going out of his place to punish the guilt of the land."
(27:1) "YHWH with his sword will decide the fate . . . of Leviathan. . . . He will kill the monster."

Units beginning with the particle כי, "for, because," support YHWH's actions by citing doctrinal reasons. Units beginning "in that day" and "on this mountain" tell of situations resulting from these actions.

The alternation between the themes of God's actions, the burdens on the nations, and the effects on Israel and Judah is illustrated by the following table:

Divine Warfare	*Burdens (OAN)*	*Related to Israel/Jerusalem*
13:2–16	Babylon 13:17–22 (14:22–23)	14:1–21
	(Assyria 14:25)	
14:24, 26–27	Philistines 14:28–31	14:32
	Moab 15:1–16:14 (16:13–14)	16:1
17:12–14	Damascus (17:1–3)	17:3, 4, 7–11
18:3–6	Cush 18:1–2	18:7
	Egypt 19:1–15 (20:3–6)	19:16–25
21:2–7	Desert by the Sea 21:8–10	
	Dumah (Edom) 21:11–12	
	Wasteland (Arabia) 21:16–17	22:1–14
	Tyre 23:1–17	23:18
24:1–22		24:23–25:8
26:20–21		26:1–19
27:1		27:2–15

Between the panels appears a narrative chapter (chap. 20). It shows Isaiah, son of Amoz, acting out his oracle predicting the defeat of Egypt. He warns against political or military dependence on Egypt that might bring retribution from the Assyrian conqueror. This narrative forms a hinge between the two panels of burdens.

TEMPORAL ANALYSIS

The act lacks historical progression and movement (contrary to my position in the first edition). Isa 13:1–14:27 reflects the time of Nebuchadnezzar in the sixth century. Isa 14:28 turns back to the days of Ahaz, the eighth century. Other passages are difficult to date, although chap. 22 calls the names of officials in

Hezekiah's government. The arrangement is literary, not historical. The effect is less realistic and historical, more abstract and timeless.

Isa 13:1–14:23 reflects the world of the Babylonian period (612–540 B.C.E.). Isa 14:24–27 draws the reader's attention back to the Assyrian period (ca. 740–612 B.C.E.), and the following chapters, especially 14:28, chap. 20, and chap. 22, point to that period. All of Isa 14:24–23:18 fits the Assyrian perspective.

Chaps. 24–27 are ambiguous, but probably fit better the Babylonian period. Chaps. 24–27 have often been understood to be "apocalyptic." All of chaps. 13–27 (except 20) are more apocalyptic than has usually been recognized. The "eschatological" coloring of the unit points to an "end of the age" theme. I suggest that it is exactly that.

The era in which "Egypt/Babylon ruled the East" is coming to a close. This era had functioned for that part of the world from time immemorial. The Hamite powers (Gen 10:6–20), especially Cush (Nimrod/Babylon and Nineveh), Mizraim (Egypt), and Canaan (Sidon/Tyre) had controlled the region (the known world) throughout the period. Their political, cultural, and economic system formed the frame within which life for all the peoples (including Israel) had existed. The Medean overthrow of Babylon (Isa 13:13–20) would bring that system to an end. The slaying of Leviathan (27:1) serves the same literary function in the second half of the unit.

This analysis of temporal settings divides the act into three parts. The middle section (14:24–22:25) is clearly related to the Assyrian period (ca. 740–612 B.C.E.). The first part (13:2–14:23) may cover the entire Assyrian-Babylonian period (ca. 740–540 B.C.E.), but it is certainly focused (13:17–14:23) on the late Babylonian period. The last part (chaps. 23–27) looks beyond the destruction of Tyre by Assyria and toward the fall of Babylon (Leviathan). It, too, focuses on the closing climax in 26:20–7:1 and on the resulting conditions for Israel in 27:2–13.

An Outline

This outline incorporates the structural indicators into the temporal three-part scheme:

Act 2. THE BURDEN OF BABYLON (13:1–27:13)

- Title: "which Isaiah son of Amoz saw" (13:1)
- Introduction (frame): YHWH's wars and Babylon's fate (13:2–14:23)
  - The Day of YHWH (13:2–16)
    - "**See** the Day of YHWH—to make the land desolate."
  - Babylon's fate—Israel's hope (13:17–14:23)
    - YHWH overwhelms Babylon (13:17–22*a*)
      - "**See** I will stir up against them the Medes."
      - "Babylon will be overthrown by God."
    - (**For**) Jacob's hope (13:22*b*–14:2)
    - Taunt over a fallen tyrant (14:3–21)
    - Oracle against Babylon (14:22–23)
- The Assyrian Period (14:24–23:18)
  - YHWH's plan for Assyria and the whole land (14:24–27)
  - In the death year of King Ahaz (14:28–32)

- No response: Wail—
    - **For** further repressions (14:28–30)
    - **For** a cloud of smoke from the north (14:31*a*)
    - **For** YHWH has established Zion (14:31*b*)
- Burden: Moab (15:1–16:14)
    - Wail **for** destruction (15:1–5*a*)
    - Responses: weep and wail **for** (15:5*b*–9)
    - Seek help from Jerusalem **for** afterward their throne will be established (16:1–5)
    - Response (16:6–9*a*): **For** your joy is ended (16:9*b*–12)
    - Summary (16:13–14)
- Burden: Damascus (17:1–18:7)
    - OAN + three "in that day" passages (17:1–9)
        - **See**! Damascus to be destroyed (17:1–3)
        - "In that day" (17:4–6)
        - "In that day" (17:7–8)
        - "In that day" (17:9)
    - Admonition + two "woe" passages (17:10–18:2)
        - Admonition (17:10–11)
        - "Woe" (17:12–14)
        - "Woe" (18:1–2)
    - Address to "all you people of the world" (18:3–7)
        - You will see and hear (18:3)
        - **For** "I will remain silent" (18:4)
        - **For** "before the harvest" (18:5–6)
        - At that time: gifts to YHWH at Mount Zion (18:7)
- Burden: Egypt (19:1–20:6)
    - **See**! YHWH against Egypt (19:1–15)
    - Worship of YHWH in Egypt (five "in that day" units) (19:16–25)
    - Isaiah demonstrates against an alliance with Egypt (20:1–6)
- Four ambiguous "burdens" (21:1–22:25)
    - Burden: A Swampland (21:1–10)
        - One comes from a wilderness (21:1–2)
        - Response (21:3–4)
        - Preparations (21:5)
        - **For**: This is what YHWH says (21:6–7)
        - **See**! "Babylon has fallen" (21:9)
        - From the God of Israel (21:10)
    - Burden: Silence (21:11–12)
    - Burden: In the Wasteland (21:13–17)
    - Burden: The Valley of Vision (22:1–14)
    - Shebna is dismissed (22:15–25)
        - A message for Shebna (22:15–19)
        - "In that day": Eliakim (22:20–24)
        - "In that day": Eliakim's fall (22:25)
- Burden: Tyre (23:1–18)
    - "Howl, O ships of Tarshish" (23:1–12)
    - "**See**! The land of the Chaldeans." (23:13)
    - "Howl, O ships of Tarshish" (23:14)
    - "At that time" (23:15–16)
    - "At the end of seventy years" (23:17–18)

Conclusion: Land devastated "in that day" "on this mountain": A Liturgy (24:1–27:13)

- "**See**! YHWH devastating the land" (24:1–12)
- "**For** this is how it is" (24:13)

- Response: For so it will be: harvest time (24:14–20)
    - Response: Joy in the east, etc. (24:14–16*a*)
    - "But I said" (24:16*bc*)
    - Warning "people of the land" (24:17–20)
- YHWH's throne in Zion (24:21–26:19)
    - YHWH reigns (24:21–25:5)
        - "In that day": YHWH and the kings (24:21–22)
        - "**For** YHWH of Hosts will reign on Mount Zion" (24:23)
        - Response "I" (25:1–5; four "**for**" units)
    - "On this mountain" (25:6–12)
        - A banquet for all peoples (25:6)
        - YHWH will swallow up death for all peoples (25:7–8)
        - "In that day" response: "We trusted in him" (25:9)
        - Hand of YHWH on this mountain (25:10–12)
    - Song of the Judeans (26:1–19)
        - "We have a strong city" (26:1–4)
        - **For** he lays the lofty city low (26:5–6)
        - A way for the righteous (26:7–9*a*)
        - **Indeed,** when your judgments belong to the land, they teach righteousness (26:9*b*)
        - But your dead will rise (26:19)
        - **For** your dew (26:19*b*)
- The judgment and its results for Israel (26:20–27:13)
    - YHWH emerges to judge the people of the land (26:20–21)
        - Go my people, shut the door for a little while (26:20)
        - **For See**! YHWH coming out of his dwelling to judge the people of the land (26:21)
    - Leviathan's (Tyre's) fate/Israel's hope (27:1–5)
        - "On that day" YHWH will judge and slay Leviathan (27:1)
        - Sing about a fruitful vineyard (27:2–5)
    - "On that day" for Israel (27:6–13)
        - **Indeed** a fortified city stands abandoned (27:6–11*a*)
        - **For** this is a people without understanding (27:11*b*)
        - YHWH will thresh and gather the exiles (27:12)
        - They will come and worship YHWH on the holy mountain in Jerusalem (27:13)

A Literary Approach

Chaps. 13–27 of Isaiah form a discrete literary unit, a separate act. In it YHWH is active most of the time, coming out of his house (26:21), but also passive, remaining in his house (18:4) sometimes. Part of the time he acts to fulfill his plan (עצה; 14:24, 26; 19:12, 16; 23:9), and at other times he makes momentous decisions (פקד; 13:3, 11; 24:21, 22; 26:14; 26:21; 27:1). The primary literary form through this section is that of dialogical speeches. YHWH is the major speaker (see *Introduction—Speakers/Characters—YHWH: Protoganist*) and throughout these chapters is cast as a king/warrior. This picks up the theme of war and the Divine Warrior that was first introduced in 2:10–20 and was continued in several passages in act 1.

Chap. 20 changes from the dominant poetic style to narrative. It speaks of Isaiah son of Amoz by name and introduces a specific historical moment into the work. Only here and in the title (13:1) does the name of Isaiah appear in these chapters. These named references tie chaps. 13–27 into the larger book.

Opposite God as featured character is Babylon: not the victorious, ascendant Babylon who defeated Assyria but the failing, weak Babylon whose great king is dead and whose days are numbered. Israel and Judah are present but in the background through most of the act. The other nations of "the land," including Assyria, Egypt, and Tyre, are integral parts of the act.

THEME

The act is a literary whole with a distinctive theme. The burdens in chaps. 13–23 show that Israel is only a part of a larger tragedy, "the destruction of the whole land." Historically, Palestine was wracked by wars throughout the time Israel lived there. To survive in such a time, Israel had to be able to assert itself and resist the other groups (cf. Judg 3:1–6 for battles with nations in the land), and she needed a god who could function in that environment (Exod 15:3: "YHWH is a warrior"). One of the earliest literary works in Israel was called "The Book of the Wars of YHWH" (Num 21:14). Isa 13–27 fits in that genre and into this idea, which explains YHWH's relationship to the wars that had been so great a part of Israel's experience.

But the wars in Palestine during the Assyrian and Babylonian periods were nightmares of such proportions and wrought such devastation in the land that nothing before could be compared with them. Where was YHWH during that time and in those terrible events? The Book of Burdens (act 2) speaks to that question. It claims that YHWH was not simply caught up in the events. He was the cause, the perpetrator, the organizer, and the one who also ended the wars. They were all part of YHWH's "day." They were all a result of Israel's/Judah's/Jerusalem's apostasy, and of the sins of other nations as well. The land had to be cleaned, and YHWH did it.

YHWH's goals and purposes went well beyond the destruction of the land. Egypt's collapse in chap. 19 is but a step toward a peaceful and prosperous region that will extend from Egypt to Assyria and in which Israel and her worship of YHWH will play a central role. The stench of death in the land (chap. 24) called for a divine decree to remove death from the land and bring new life there. Leviathan would be destroyed (27:1; the Apocalypse of John echoes the two themes: the end of Satan [Rev 20:2, 10] and the end of death [Rev 20:14]). YHWH will plant Jacob/Israel again, and they will flourish (27:2–6). He will dwell on his holy mountain, Jerusalem, and the scattered Israelites will come to worship him there (27:12–13). His sovereignty over the armies of heaven as well as the kings of the earth will be established (24:21–23).

In a very real historical sense, the collapse of the Neo-Babylonian Empire marked the end of an age. For well over a thousand years the Fertile Crescent from Mesopotamia through Palestine to Egypt had been a world to itself, an economic and political system that resisted invasions from without. The biblical story of Israel from Abraham through the exile took place within that sociopolitical system, but this period and system came to an end with the collapse of Babylon in 539 B.C.E.

The terrible wars of the eighth to the sixth centuries B.C.E. in Palestine were no less a source of terror and mourning for the peoples when they are identified as having been sent and directed by YHWH himself. The peoples and Israel are called to fear and to wail the losses. If they are indeed the work of God, one should look for "the plan" that guides them, the goals and results that YHWH wants to gain from them. The people of God, Israel, is called to look beyond the terror and destruction to see the hand of God at work in what emerges from the destruction of war. The sovereign kingship of YHWH of Hosts may be seen in the direction of the battles, but also in the reconstruction afterward. He is well worth waiting for. Thus act 2 interprets the period of wars during the Assyrian and Babylonian periods for Israelites in Palestine near the end of the Babylonian period. It represents a God's-eye view of the events and hopes to inspire in its readers the view that YHWH/God is in control and that, beyond the hostilities and destruction, God has a future place for his people in the new order that is to come.

This act is addressed to Israelites under Babylonian tyranny who are encouraged to expect relief very soon. The "onstage audience" is addressed in the second person twice in passages that reveal the time setting for the act. In 14:3 "you" designates those who endure "trouble, turmoil, and hard labor" under a tyrant "king of Babylon." They are promised a day soon when they can celebrate the downfall and death of the tyrant (14:22–23). (Chaps. 45–47 address the same group at a time when the deliverer is already in sight, that is, just a little later than the scene in 14:3.) Then the attention of the act turns to YHWH's actions during the previous Assyrian period (14:24–27 introduces chaps. 15–23). All YHWH's actions fall under his decision to destroy "all the land" (14:26–27; 13:5; 6:11–13; and 2:10–22). The second instance comes in 26:20–21 when the group is addressed in a plea to hide themselves "for a little while until wrath passes over." The act is also very much involved in these responses to the actions of YHWH and the nations. There is a great deal of lament, terror, and fear. But there is also rejoicing at the end. The work empathizes with the feelings of the period, and draws the reader/hearer into the circle of response.

Chronological Signals

Superscriptions label the subjects and indicate the time periods being discussed, which structure the act in the following manner:

- I. Burden: Babylon that Isaiah son of Amoz envisioned
  - A. Babylonian period (13:1–14:23)
  - B. Assyrian period (14:24–23:18)
    1. The year Ahaz died (14:28)
    2. Philistines, Moab, Damascus, Israel, Cush (14:28–18:24)
       YHWH: "I remain quiet and look on from my dwelling." (18:4)
    3. Egypt (four burdens), Tyre (19:1–23:18)
       Sargon at Ashdod (20:1)
       Shebna and Hilkiah in Jerusalem (22:15–25)
       "Look at the land of Babylon—Assyrians did it." (23:13)
       Tyre will be forgotten for seventy years; she will return (23:17)
  - C. Babylonian period (24:1–27:13)

The book looks at the history from two perspectives. One of them, at the beginning and the end of the act, speaks of Babylon in the Neo-Babylonian period, ca. 605–640 B.C.E. It announces the devastations of that period and also the coming destruction and collapse of Babylon (13:17; 14:22–23). It suggests a taunt song (14:3–21) over a great emperor, probably Nebuchadnezzar, who died in 552 B.C.E. Together these place a date for the addressees of this section between the death of Nebuchadnezzar in 552 B.C.E. and the fall of Babylon in 539 B.C.E. The final chapters (24–27) may well be directed to the same period.

But a second perspective is indicated by mention of the destruction of Assyria in 14:24, indicating that this addresses the Assyrian period (ca. 740 to 612 B.C.E.). The temporal reference is made more precise by the title for the "burden concerning Philistines" (14:28) "in the year King Ahaz died" (ca. 725 or 718 B.C.E.). Another precise date occurs in 20:1: "In the year that the Tartan came to Ashdod, when Sargon king of Assyria sent him, he fought against Ashdod and took it." The year is probably 714 B.C.E. Everything between these two references (14:28–20:6) fits that period, and chaps. 21–23 also seem to fit within the Assyrian period.

So the book has an outer "envelope" of 13:2–14:23//24:1–27:13 about the Babylonian era shortly before Cyrus arrives (parallel to the time frame of chaps. 40–54) and a core (14:24–23:18) about the Assyrian period. This earlier period is also suggested by the title (13:1), which invokes the name of Isaiah son of Amoz, who lived and prophesied in the eighth century B.C.E.

One important literary device used here, as in other parts of the Vision, is the implied author in first-person speech (see *Introduction*). After Isaiah son of Amoz has been described in the narrative of chap. 20, the principal voice in chap. 21 speaks in the first person and may be assumed to be the implied author. This voice has previously responded to the ruin of Moab (16:9–11). Sometimes it is difficult to decide whether YHWH or the implied author is speaking, as in 22:4 (but see also 22:14 and 24:16*b*). Some of the poetry that is set in first person singular may be understood as sung by the implied author: Isa 25:1–5; 26:9*a*. He seems here, like Isaiah in chap. 6, to be an observer and commentator/witness.

Major poems inserted into the dialogue respond to YHWH's actions. The first poem appears in the taunt against the king of Babylon (14:4*b*–21). Others are introduced in 25:1–5; 26:1–19; 27:2–5.

Israel, the people of God, witnesses all this history and desolation, and finally the people are the ones who respond. They are those of the Diaspora in Babylon (14:1–2), in Egypt (19:16–25), in Jerusalem (22:1–14), in Judah (26:1–18), those who return to the land (27:2–11), and finally those who return to the temple from everywhere. Their responses range from distress and terror before the military actions to rejoicing and trust in later pieces (at least thirty times). Whereas the first act (chaps. 2–12) had stressed the admonition "Do not be afraid" (7:4, 9; 8:17; 12:1, 2), the entire second act (chaps. 13–27) is imbued with a sense of anxiety (20:5, "will be afraid and put to shame"). Each unit calls for the nations to wail, be in terror, and so on. The act emphasizes responses to the wars and scripts a number of these (14:4*b*–21; 16:6–8, 9–12; 17:13–14; 25:1–5, 9; 26:1–18; 27:2–5), giving the work the feeling of a liturgy.The act provides scripted responses that instruct the players in the drama about how they are to react to the horrors reported and interpreted at the following points:

13:7–8	During the Day of YHWH
The end of the Babylonian period:	
14:4–21	"On the day the Lord gives you relief" (ca. 539 B.C.E.)
Back to the Assyrian period:	
14:28–32	"In the year King Ahaz died"
15:3–4, 5–9	During Moab's devastation
16:6–12	During Moab's trial
17:7–8	After Damascus has been ruined
17:10–11	More an explanation than a response
18:7–8	"At that time" during YHWH's "quiet," gifts brought to Zion
19:8–10	During Egypt's drought
19:16–17	Terror about Judah and her God
20:5–6	Isaiah encourages doubts on Egypt's example
21:3	The prophet trembles at what he sees
21:10	People "crushed to the floor" about Babylon's fall
21:13–17	Despair for Dedanites
22:1–3	Jerusalemites panic before the approaching enemy
22:4	Prophet weeps for Jerusalem
22:12–13	Called to lament; joy and revelry instead
22:15–19	Shebna (Hezekiah's cabinet member) dismissed (8th–7th centuries)
22:20–25	Hilkiah (Hezekiah's cabinet member) appointed and judged
23:1–7, 12–13	Lamentation for Tyre in Tyre, Sidon, Egypt (probably middle 7th century).
Back to the end of the Babylonian period:	
24:14–16	"They" in the east and west rejoice in response to YHWH's devastations (cf. 13:1–16)
24:16*bc*	Prophetic "I" laments
25:1–5	Prophetic "I" in response to YHWH's reign on Zion
25:9	"They" in response to YHWH's banquet
26:1–18	"In that day" in Judah
27:2–5	"In that day" after Leviathan is killed
27:7–11	A question responds to the announcements about Israel in the land
27:13	"In that day" pilgrimage and worship in Jerusalem in response to being gathered by YHWH.

SUMMARY OF ACT 2

Chaps. 13–27 work on at least two levels. One level pictures "the last day." These instances involve the culminating critical event, YHWH's bringing the Medes against Babylon (13:17–22; 14:22–23) and YHWH's slaying Leviathan (27:1). Both of these events are introduced by calling attention to YHWH's military activity to that end (13:2–3; 26:21). They are culminating events. Isa 13:17–22 points to a particular destruction of Babylon by Medes (5:39 B.C.E.). There is also a call for attention to YHWH's placing and using armies "to destroy the whole land" (13:4–5) and the completion of that process (24:1–13). In contrast to the culminating event, this could cover a long period of time. These events are accomplished within a frame of "day of YHWH" units (13:6–16; see also 22:5–13; the "in that day" units of chaps. 24–27 probably belong here as well).

The other level turns attention back to the Assyrian era (14:24–27) and reminds the reader of YHWH's promise to destroy the Assyrian (10:12–19). Isa 14:28 places the time for the following burdens in the eighth century at the time of the death of Ahaz. The three burdens (Philistines, 14:29–32; Moab, chaps. 15–16; and Damascus, 17:1–3) record no new acts of YHWH but bewail the devastations that have happened in their lands. Three "in that day" passages reflect the effect of the events on Jacob (17:4–6), humankind (17:7–8), and Damascus (17:9). An accusation of forgetting God (17:10–11) and two "woe" passages (17:12–14; 18:1–2) follow. The dwellers of the world and the inhabitants of the land are promised front-row seats for the divine events (18:3) as YHWH confides to the prophet/author that he will not be active in that period. He, too, will be an observer (18:4) as the wars of attrition achieve the devastation of the land (18:4–5). These verses set the entire section of burdens in context. They also apply equally to chap. 20 and to the three burdens of chap. 21. The burden of the Valley of Vision is given a Day of YHWH setting (22:9–13). (Does this reflect 586 B.C.E.?) But it turns its accusation back to an eighth-century setting by accusing Shebna and Eliakim of malfeasance (22:14–25).

Chap. 19, the burden of Egypt, is a discrete unit, complete in itself. It is depicted as the direct action of YHWH. It has no structural connections to its surroundings, though like chap. 20 it is about Egypt. One could wonder if the political picture of three powers in vv 23–25 would fit the scene during the Persian period or the Hasmonian period when Israel exists alongside the Seleucid kingdom (= Assyria) and the Ptolemaic kingdom (= Egypt). These are the only times I can think of when this description might have had some political reality. Also the pictures of cultural and religious infiltration of Egypt would fit the Hellenistic period.

Chap. 23, the burden of Tyre, completes the picture of a devastated land. It refers to the Assyrian period, but later than the eighth century as made clear by its reference to seventy years before Tyre will again be active in commerce. It adds a third reference to a destruction of Babylon, this one by the Assyrians.

The result is a picture of the troubled Assyrian and Babylonian eras with the passages about the end of this period forming an envelope for emphasis (13:17–22 and 27:1). Consequently, act 2 brings the action up to the time reflected in chaps. 40–48. The time for the Medes to bring about the end of the Babylonian period is at hand. The inner chapters from 14:24 to 22:24 (exceptions chaps. 19 and 23) have the period of the Assyrian invasions from the eighth century in mind, with an eye on the "last things" (esp. 22:5–13). Chaps. 24–26 picture the culmination of YHWH's actions to devastate the land and his royal actions to bring an end to these matters. Inserted psalmlike responses provide a liturgical setting (24:14–16*a*, 16*bc;* 25:1–5, 9; 26:1–18). The act concludes with a treatment of the status of Israel in all this. Isa 27:2–6 is YHWH's song of assurance for her future. This builds upon the assurance of 14:1–2 and the grim reminders of 17:4–6 and 10–11. Isa 27:7–11 raises a question about YHWH's treatment of this people "without understanding." Isa 27:12 deals with an Israelite diaspora's place in the culminating events. Isa 27:13 defines that participation as pilgrimage to the renewed temple in Jerusalem.

Title (13:1)

Translation

[1]*The burden*[a] *of Babylon that Isaiah the son of Amoz envisioned.*

Notes

1.a. משא is not easily translated or understood. The versions vary: LXX translates ῥῆμα, "speech," "prophecy," or ὅρασις, "vision," or ὅραμα, "vision" (cf. Ziegler[3], 96). α´ always uses αρμα "vision." σ´ and θ´ use λημμα, an obscure word that in the Similitudes of Hermes means "gain" (cf. BAG, 474). Vg. translates *onus,* "burden." See *Comment* and *Excursus: "Burden"* (משא) *in the Prophets* below.

Form/Structure/Setting

The genre of superscriptions is treated in the commentary on 1:1. משא, "burden," is used in superscriptions in Nah 1:1; Hab 1:1; Zech 9:1; 12:1; and Mal 1:1 as a parallel to דבר, "word," and חזון, "vision."

Gehman ("The 'Burden' of the Prophets," *JQR* 31 [1940–41] 120–21) thinks of משא as an oracle or prophetic speech, especially a severe prophecy to be laid on an individual or a nation. Scott ("The Meaning of *massa* as an Oracle Title," *JBL* 67 [1948] 5) identifies it as a threatening oracle accompanied by lifting the hand as a gesture for an oath or curse. It is a "grim vision" or a "harsh oracle." חזה, "envisioned," may indicate a scene witnessed in the Divine Council (D. G. Reid, "The Burden of Babylon: A Study of Isaiah 13," Ph.D. diss., Fuller Theological Seminary, 1979).

The role of the superscription has frequently been understood as a heading for an older collection of oracles that was ultimately incorporated into the book (Wildberger, 506). However, in 2:1 this commentary has shown that the superscription had a different function. Here, too, in 13:1 it signals a change of form and claims Isaianic responsibility for the prophecy against Babylon (cf. chap. 39), as 2:1 did for the prophecy about Jerusalem and chaps. 7–8 did for the admonitions to Ahaz. The superscription may apply only to 13:2–14:23 or to all of chaps. 13–27. Or it may perform both functions. It designates the first of the burdens, and it notes that chaps. 13–14 as well as chaps. 24–27 define the entire act, although the central section applies to the earlier Assyrian period.

Comment

מַשָּׂא, "burden," appears to derive from the root נָשָׂא, "to raise" or "carry." The noun may mean "a burden" or "a heavy speech." The passages in Isaiah where it occurs fit the meaning "a threat of doom" (14:28; 15:1; 17:1; 19:1; 21:1, 11, 13; 22:1; 23:1). Each of these names the city or country that is the target of the threat.

Wildberger suggests that the term מַשָּׂא derives from נָשָׂא קוֹל, "lift the voice" (cf. Num 14:1; Isa 3:7; 42:2; Job 21:12). 2 Kgs 9:25, "he raised over him this מַשָּׂא," uses it in the sense of a speech. Lam 2:14 speaks of empty מַשְׂאוֹת that have led the daughter of Zion astray. Jer 23:33 makes a wordplay on the meanings "speech" and "burden."

Scott suggests that one relate משא to נשא יד, "raise a hand," as a signal. This parallels נטה יד, "stretch out a hand," and נשא נס, "raise a banner," phrases that occur repeatedly in these chapters of Isaiah. נשא, the root of משא, is used with נס, "banner," in 5:26, 11:12, and 13:2. These are signals for armies to gather and march. In 49:22 Yahweh raises his hand to signal the nations, while ארים נסי in the same verse uses a synonym of נשא with God's banner. The same combination of רום and נס occurs in 63:10. In 10:32 Yahweh waves his hand toward Zion (נפף ידו). The pervasive term in chaps. 5–14 is "stretch out his hand." In 5:25 Yahweh's anger against his people, Israel, causes him to "stretch out his hand against them" (ויט ידו עליו) and the statement ועוד ידו נטויה, "his hand is stretched out still," is repeated like a refrain in 9:11 (12), 16 (17), 20 (21) and 10:4. In 14:27 the words occur again: וידו הנטויה, "(It is) his hand that is stretched out." The hand signals parallel verbal ordinances and commands: "The Lord has sent a word" (9:7[8]) and "Yahweh spoke to me with a strong hand" (8:11).

Thus, in Isaiah, especially chaps. 5–23, the interaction of hand signals and words "raised" by Yahweh in threat, warning, or judgment is pervasive. This makes it likely that משא in Isaiah means that which Yahweh signals (by hand or word) against someone or some group. This usually involves bringing other forces to fulfill God's intention or strategy (עצה). It may also signal God's ban, the removal of this protection from someone or some group.

Excursus: "Burden" (משא) in the Prophets

Bibliography

Boer, P. A. H. de. "An Inquiry into the Meaning of the term משא." *OtSt* 5 (1948). **Gehman, H. S.** "The 'Burden' of the Prophets." *JQR* 31 (1940–41) 107–21. **Jones, B. C.** "Characteristics of OAN and משא Texts." In *Howling over Moab: Irony and Rhetoric in Isaiah 15–16.* SBLDS 157 Atlanta: Scholars Press, 1996. 53–88. **Scott, R. B. Y.** "The Meaning of *massa* as an Oracle Title." *JBL* 67 (1948) 5–6. **Weis, R. D.** "A Definition of the Genre 'Massa' in the Hebrew Bible." Ph.D. diss., Claremont, 1986.

משא, "burden," appears only occasionally outside oracles against the nations. Jehu justifies his actions against Joram with a reference to "how YHWH lifted against him this burden" (נשא עליו את המשא הזה, 2 Kgs 9:25). Here the verb נשא, "raise, lift, carry," and the noun derived from it occur together. As in many of the prophetic "burdens," the words are used with על, "against." Ezek 12:10 introduces a prophecy with "thus says the Lord YHWH: one lifting up (or, the prince) this burden in Jerusalem" (הנשיא המשא הזה). Again there is a play on words: נשיא, "prince," as one lifted up and as a משא, "burden." 2 Chr 24:27 speaks of the multitude of המשא עליו, "the burden against him." In Prov 31:1 משא appears to be a title over a collection of proverbs, but many scholars think it should be emended.

The rest of the occurrences of משא are found in just two prophetic collections. One is Isa 13–30. The other is the Book of the Twelve (Minor) Prophets. In Isaiah, it appears ten times as a simple title (13:1; 15:1; 17:1; 19:1; 21:1, 11, 13; 22:1; 23:1; 30:6) and once in a narrated title (14:28). In the Book of the Twelve Prophets, it appears five times (Nah 1:1; Hab 1:1; Zech 9:1; 12:1; Mal 1:1). Note that the last three list "burden" parallel to "the word of YHWH." Cf. Jeremiah's treatment of the prophets who say משא יהוה, "the burden of Yahweh": Jer 23:33 (two times), 34, 36 (two times), 38 (three times). Notice he also used a wordplay in 23:36*b*. This derisive use in Jeremiah and 2 Kgs 9:25 contrasts with the use in titles in Isaiah and the Twelve.

משא appears before prophecies against the nations in Isa 13:1 (Babylon), 14:1 (Philistia), 15:1 (Moab), 17:1 (Damascus), and 19:1 (Egypt); three times in chap. 21 with regard to Babylon, Edom, and Arabia; and in 23:1 (Tyre). This is also true in Nahum (Assyria), Habakkuk (Chaldeans), and Zech 9:1 (Hadrach). But it is not the case in Isa 22:1; 30:6; Zech 12:1 (Israel); Mal 1:1 (Israel); and 2 Kgs 9:25 (the house of Ahab), nor does the sarcasm in Jer 23 seem to have oracles against nations in mind.

Other collections of prophecies against nations do not use משא (Jer 46–50; Ezek 25–29; 35; Amos 1–2; Obadiah). So the word is not intrinsically connected to oracles against the nations. It is possible to have foreign prophecies with משא, and it is possible to use משא for prophetic words about Judah and Israel. משא passages include references to the wars of YHWH, but there are other war passages that do not use the term. It is not a term that has a definite and exclusive meaning. Perhaps Sweeney's (212–14) "prophetic pronouncement" fits it as well as anything.

It is clear that Isa 13–27 is a work dominated by משא passages. It is equally clear that a group of prophecies in the Twelve has been drawn together by using the משא title. Some of the Isaiah units apply משא over another beginning (17:1 "behold"; 19:1 "behold"). But chap. 18 begins with הוי, "woe, ah," and chap. 24 with הנה, "behold." The משא units in Isaiah belong to "a specific type of prophetic discourse that employs a variety of literary elements to explain how YHWH's intentions are manifested in human affairs" (Sweeney [222], citing R. D. Weiss). In Isaiah, משא is the distinctive feature (along with "in that day") marking the second act to bear the prophet's name (chaps. 13–27).

בבל, "Babylon." The name of the fabled city occurs here for the first time in the Vision. The scene speaks of many other things, but the references to Babylon (13:19; 14:22) and to Babylon's king (14:4) catch the ear and earn the headline. Its appearance is surprising. It is the only city or country in this part of the Vision that is not directly involved in the events of eighth-century Palestine. Its role may be explained by the suggestive influence of chap. 39.

Excursus: Babylon and the King of Babylon in the Vision of Isaiah

Bibliography

Brinkman, J. A. *A Political History of Post-Kassite Babylonia.* AnOr 43. Rome: Pontifical Biblical Institute, 1948. ———. "Merodach Baladan II." In *Studies Presented to A. Leo Oppenheim.* Chicago: The Oriental Institute of the University of Chicago, 1964. 6–53. **Buccellati, G.** "Enthronement of the King." In *Studies Presented to A. Leo Oppenheim.* Chicago: The Oriental Institute of the University of Chicago, 1964. 54–61. **Lambert, W. G.** "The Babylonians and Chaldaeans." *POTT.* 179–96. **Smith, S.** "The Supremacy of Assyria." In *Prolegomena and Prehistory.* Ed. I. E. S. Edwards, C. J. Gadd, and N. G. Hammond. 3d ed. CAH 1.1. London: Cambridge UP, 1971. 39–62. **Suggs, J. F. W.** *The Greatness That Was Babylon.* London: Sedgwick & Jackson, 1962.

The cities of Jerusalem, Babylon, Damascus, and Tyre each play a role in Isaiah's Vision. But Jerusalem and Babylon are the central protagonists. In this large central portion of the Vision, Babylon's fate and history are an important concern. The symbolic role goes well beyond the historic reality. The Assyrian Empire was the major threat and oppressor of the eighth century, but neither Nineveh nor Asshur figures in the Vision. The Persian Empire moved to the fore in the sixth and fifth centuries, but none of her cities appears. Only Babylon, which, of course, was used by both (and which at times opposed both), is presented here.

The name Babylon conjures up for the Israelite and the reader of Scripture memories of the Tower of Babel (Gen 11:1–9). The story is consistent with the city's claim to a prestigious antiquity. The name means "The Gate of God." Its influence through the centuries had a religious base. The great Hammurabi used Babylon as his capital in the eighteenth century B.C.E. Other rulers over Mesopotamia treasured the right to "seize the hands of Bel" in the annual Babylonian enthronement ceremonies, which gave them a legitimacy in the eyes of the citizens that nothing else could effect.

The Assyrian Tiglath-Pileser III was concerned simultaneously with affairs in Babylon and in Israel-Judah in the seventh decade of the century as he strengthened the realm and moved to establish his authority in lower Mesopotamia and in the western states. So he had himself crowned king of Babylon, "taking the hand of Bel," in the ancient cultural and cultic center in 728 and 727 B.C.E., claiming authority thereby over the major religious centers and over the Aramaean tribes of the area. His son, Shalmaneser V, continued the dual monarchy during the five years of his reign (726–22 B.C.E.).

Sargon II was initially unable to establish sovereignty over Babylon. Merodach-Baladan, a powerful prince of the Aramaean tribe Bit Yakin that occupied an area on the Persian Gulf, seized power over Babylon with the help of the four other Aramaean (Chaldean) tribes and the neighboring Elamite king. He held the throne for twelve years. In two campaigns in 710 and 709 B.C.E. Sargon II invaded the south. When Merodach-Baladan heard of initial Assyrian successes, he fled Babylon and retired to a town on the Elamite frontier. Sargon II was crowned king of Babylon in 709 B.C.E. In a later battle at his tribal capital of Deir-Yakin, Merodach-Baladan was beaten again, but escaped capture. Many of the Bit Yakin tribe were deported.

Merodach-Baladan appeared again when Sennacherib assumed the throne (ca. 704 B.C.E.). Merodach-Baladan pushed aside Marduk-Zakirsume II, who reigned in Babylon for one month. Sennacherib moved rapidly against the usurper and ousted him within nine months. Again Merodach-Baladan fled. Sennacherib installed Bel-ibni on Babylon's throne. It is remarkable that Merodach could have gained such wide support so quickly. He was undoubtedly a master diplomat, however bad a soldier. 2 Kgs 20 and Isa 39 are witness to his efforts. Apparently he attempted to coordinate uprisings in Babylon and Palestine but was forced to rush his plans for Babylon when another stepped in before him.

In 700 B.C.E. Sennacherib campaigned again in Babylonia, putting his son Asshurnadin-sumi on the throne and carrying out a punitive campaign against Bit Yakin territory. Again Merodach-Baladan escaped. This is the last we know of him. But Sennacherib's troubles with Babylon continued. After the murder of Asshurnadin-sumi in 689 B.C.E., Sennacherib sacked the city, destroying its fortifications and great buildings. The statue of Marduk was taken to Assyria, and Sennacherib assumed the title of king.

The references to Babylon in Isa 13–39 apparently allude to this period. But much more happened to that city before the rise of Cyrus (539 B.C.E.; Isa 45) and the predicted humiliation in Isa 46 and 47. It was the capital for the Neo-Babylonian Empire under Nabopolassar (625–605) and Nebuchadnezzar II (605–562). It tasted again the sweet fruits of power for a few short years only to let it slip away before opening its doors to the Persian emperor. He, like those before him, "took the hands of Bel" and became king of Babylon.

By the time the Vision was written, three more Persian emperors had included that title among their own. Babylon continued to be a rebellious problem for its rulers. Xerxes was forced to put down a rebellion around 480 B.C.E. The city was severely punished. Fortifications were demolished, temples were destroyed, the golden statue of Marduk was melted down, and confiscated land was given to Persians. Babylon was incorporated into the Persian administration. Xerxes and succeeding kings omitted Babylon from their titulature.

The references to Babylon in the Vision are, therefore, intended to be understood as follows:

Isa 13:17–22; 14:22–23: If this is under Ahaz ca. 720 B.C.E. after the revolt of Merodach-Baladan, the king of Babylon in 14:4*a,* for whom the taunting poem was deemed appropriate, must have been Merodach-Baladan. However, if this refers to the period of the Babylonian Empire as indicated above, the king must be King Nebuchadnezzar.
Isa 21:9: Under Hezekiah ca. 710 B.C.E.
Isa 23:13: Under Hezekiah after 710 (or 689) B.C.E.
Isa 45–48: 540 B.C.E. prior to Cyrus's conquest.

The destructions or falls of Babylon that are predicted in the Vision were fulfilled:

Isa 13:19–22; 14:22–23: Conquest by Cyrus in 539 B.C.E.
Isa 21:9; 23:13: Conquest in ca. 710 B.C.E. by Sargon or in 703 B.C.E. by Sennacherib. (Possibly, Sennacherib's thorough destruction of 689 B.C.E. is intended.)
Isa 46–47: The capitulation of the city to Cyrus in 539 B.C.E. (Perhaps there are overtones of the destruction of the city by Xerxes in 480 B.C.E.)

Long passages on Babylon serve as a kind of "enclosure" around a large central section or sections of the book. The "burden" in chap. 13 includes a description of world judgment and an oracle against Babylon promising defeat and destruction. Chap. 14 begins with hope for Israel and continues (vv 4*b*–21) with a powerful taunt to be sung over the king of Babylon. The chapter then has a closing oracle against Babylon (vv 22–23) before a reconfirmation of God's purpose to remove the Assyrian from his land (vv 24–27).

The last passages about Babylon appear in 44:28–48:20. Cyrus is identified as YHWH's appointed servant to return Israel and rebuild the temple (44:28–45:7), but Babylon is not mentioned. Isa 46:1–2 announces the humiliation and captivity of Babylon's gods, while chap. 47 is a major taunting song against "daughter Babylon." Isa 48:14 announces that YHWH's purposes will be fulfilled through his chosen one and calls on Israelites to leave Babylon (v 20). Between these are notices of Babylon's misfortunes in 21:1–10 and 23:13, and of her continued intrigues and conspiracies in chap. 39.

YHWH's plan (14:26) includes the work of the Assyrian as "rod of his anger" (7:17–25; 10:5–6) and the Persian Cyrus as the shepherd-servant to restore Israel to Canaan (44:28–45:13). But Babylon is the supreme example of those who seek to thwart his purpose. YHWH does not support the rebellions against Assyria. Ahaz is warned against involvement either in the intrigue of Pekah and Rezin or in alliance with Assyria to overcome them. YHWH himself will deal with Assyria in his own good time (10:5–19; 14:24–27). In the meantime his "burdens" lie heavy upon the rebels (chaps. 13–23). Babylon also illustrates the pride of humanity (13:11*b*) that must find judgment under YHWH (2:11–17). In this she is like the Assyrian (10:5–34). These motifs are found in 13:19; 14:11–15; 47:5.

The entire section (chaps. 13–48) is a defense of the divine strategy (14:24) that Isaiah had announced, i.e., that God was sending the Assyrian to do his will in punishing the nations and to bring about a change to a new order. He had counseled a passive attitude, a "waiting on the Lord." Israel (and the other subject nations) were restless, repeatedly conspiring revolt. But it could not succeed. God was not in it. By the fifth century B.C.E. God had "finished all his work against Mount Zion and against Jerusalem" (10:12). He had also "punished the Assyrian" and removed him from Canaan. And he was ready to fulfill his own strategy to bring back the exiles and rebuild Jerusalem (chap. 44–45). The entire Vision is an exposition of that strategy, of Israel's and Judah's resistance to it, and of the continued necessity of judgment in carrying it out.

To the reading or hearing audience, about 435 B.C.E., these echoes of Babylon's involvement with Jerusalem's fate in the eighth century and the sixth century were filtered through their knowledge of the destruction of Babylon in 480 B.C.E. by Xerxes. They could not help but view it as another fulfillment of God's curse of chaps. 13–14. This also sharpened the point of the Vision's warning to Jerusalem against active rebellion (cf. Vermeylen, *Du prophète Isaïe,* 1:288).

Introduction (frame): YHWH's Wars and Babylon's Fate (13:2–14:23)

Bibliography

Erlandsson, S. *The Burden of Babylon: A Study of Isaiah 13:2–14:23.* ConBOT 4. Lund: Gleerup, 1970.

The outer limits of the scene are marked by the superscription in 13:1 and by the oracle against Babylon (14:22–23). The scene is in two parts, each given meaning by use of the particle הנה, "see, behold." The first part relates to the Day of Yahweh and the decree to make the land desolate (13:2–16): "Behold the day of Yahweh . . . to make the earth a desolation" (13:9). This is the central subject of act 2, picking up the theme from chap. 2, chap. 6, and 10:23. The counterpart of 13:2–16 is found in chaps. 24–26.

The second part of the scene is 13:17–14:23. Its theme is also marked by הנה, "see, behold" (13:17): "Behold me stirring the Medes against them." Babylon's reign is about to come to an end, and that end is Israel's hope. The counterpart of this is found in chap. 27 in the death of Leviathan and the treatments of Israel's future.

The second part is read as four episodes:

Yahweh overwhelms Babylon (13:17–22*a*)
(**For**) Jacob's hope (13:22*b*–4:2)
Taunt over a fallen tyrant (14:3–21)
Oracle against Babylon (14:22–23)

One may also note the compositional intricacy that binds this scene with the end of the previous act as well as the beginning of the one that follows, even when a totally new subject is introduced.

A A call to arms (13:2–3).
  B The noise of coming battle that will destroy the whole land (13:4–5).
    C The fear of the Day of the Lord (13:6–8).
      D The events of the Day of the Lord (13:9–16).
        E Yahweh stirring up Medes to destroy Babylon (13:17–22*a*).
          F Yahweh will have compassion on Jacob (13:22*b*–14:2).
            G You (m. sg.) will taunt the king of Babylon (14:3–4*a*).
KEYSTONE Yahweh has broken the scepter of rulers (14:4*b*–7).
            G′ You (m. sg.) will taunt the fallen tyrant (14:8–20*a*).
          F′ Curse on the tyrant's family (14:20*b*–21).
        E′ Yahweh will destroy Babylon (14:22–23).
      D′ Yahweh's plan to destroy Assyria himself (14:24–25).
    C′ Yahweh's plan for the whole world (14:26–27).
  B′ Yahweh will destroy the Philistines (14:28–31).
A′ Jerusalem's establishment by Yahweh's order (14:32).

This opening scene of act 2 does not continue the plot of the previous act. It introduces independent treatments of two subjects. One of them, the decreed desolation of the land (2:10–20; 6:11–13; 10:23), continues a subject introduced in the prologue and developed in act 1. The second subject, the coming destruction of Babylon, is new and different. This subject only makes sense in a much later time frame (contrary to the position I took in the first edition of this commentary). It is set in the time when Israelite and Judean exiles are in Mesopotamia and Babylon and when the Babylonian Empire (ca. 612–540 B.C.E.) is about to collapse under Median/Persian pressure (539 B.C.E.).

The readers are invited to think of that later period, which is about the same as that perceived in chaps. 44–48. The view from the heavenly throne notes that the fall of Babylon (the "burden of Babylon") is full of "baggage" from the past. Its history includes the era of the Assyrian Empire and its relations with Egypt over centuries. Now its end marks the end of an era. All "the land," including Mesopotamia, Egypt, and everything in between, will be influenced by this ending. In preparation for that change the entire land is emptied, desolated, destroyed, so that something new may take its place.

Then the question will be, "What will Israel's and Jerusalem's place in that new era be?" The assurance of Isaiah's Vision is that YHWH of Hosts is in control of the desolation and will equally control the restoration and the new era. Israel can rely on its God.

Excursus: The Babylonian Period ca. 612–540 B.C.E.

Bibliography

Ahlström, G. W. *The History of Ancient Palestine.* Minneapolis: Fortress, 1993. **Bright, J.** *A History of Israel.* 3d ed. Philadelphia: Westminster, 1981. 310–54.

The threat to Babylon in chaps. 13–14 is not the Babylon of the eighth century that chap. 39 portrays, nor that of a later time that chap. 21 or 23 portrays. The Babylon seen here is the great Neo-Babylonian Empire that had succeeded Assyria as the master of Palestine but was now in her last days. The Vision does not deal with that history or with the exile of the Judean house. It does deal with the destruction of

Jerusalem of 586 B.C.E. in a passage that has not generally been recognized as such (see the *Comment* on 34:8–15). But these passages assume a vivid memory of this history and its results in the minds of readers.

Assyrian power and pressure on Palestine declined in the second half of the seventh century, allowing the rise of Judah again in semi-independence under Josiah (2 Kgs 22–23). During this period Babylon was also regaining strength.

The last great Assyrian king was Ashurbanipal, who died in 627 B.C.E. His son, Sin-shar-ishkun, came under attack by internal forces and also by the Medes and the Scythians. The Medes were led by Cyaxeres (626–585 B.C.E.). Babylon was led by Nabopolassar (626–605 B.C.E.), a Chaldean prince who founded the Neo-Babylonian Empire. He regained Babylonian independence with a victory over Assyrian forces near Babylon in 626 B.C.E. The Medes and Babylonians continued the pressure on Assyria, taking Asshur in 614 and Nineveh in 612 B.C.E. The final battles with the retreating Assyrian army came at Haran in 610/609 B.C.E.

Egypt took control of Palestine. Josiah died in this conflict, and Jehoahaz was replaced by Jehoiakim, an Egyptian vassal.

Nabopolassar died in 605 and was succeeded by his son, Nebuchadnezzar, whose vigorous campaign at Carchemesh defeated the Egyptians, forcing them to abandon Palestine to him. He marched unopposed through the coastal area accepting the pledges of loyalty from the rulers. Jehoiakim faithfully paid tribute to Babylon until 600 B.C.E., when, motivated by Babylon's failure in 601/600 to successfully invade Egypt, he rebelled (2 Kgs 24:1). But Nebuchadnezzar had not given up on Palestine, and his armies campaigned there in 599 and again in 598/597. Jehoiakim died at this time and was succeeded by Jehoiachin, his eighteen-year-old son. Under Babylonian pressure Jerusalem surrendered to Nebuchadnezzar. Jehoiachin, his family, and between eight thousand and ten thousand leading persons were taken in Babylonian captivity. The treasures of the temple and the royal establishment were taken as well. Zedekiah, Jehoiachin's uncle, was placed in the throne.

Egypt continued to challenge Babylonian claims to Palestine with campaigns by Psammetiches in 591 B.C.E. Zedekiah switched his tribute to Egypt. But Psammetiches died in 589 B.C.E. His son, Hophra, was less interested in Palestine, and Nebuchadnezzar moved back into the area, determined to subdue Jerusalem. The siege lasted a year and a half, during which the fortress towns of Judah were all destroyed. Finally the walls were breached and the city fell in 586 B.C.E. The destruction of the city was complete: the walls broken and houses plundered. Its inhabitants were exiled, though the actual number sent away was not large.

Nebuchadnezzar campaigned again in Palestine in 582/581 B.C.E. A thirteen-year siege of Tyre ended with a negotiated settlement in 571 B.C.E., but his invasion of Egypt in 569 B.C.E. led to nothing. Nebuchadnezzar died in 562 B.C.E. A period of instability followed. Finally, Nabunaid served as Babylon's last king from 555 to 539 B.C.E. His final years were spent in voluntary retreat, leaving the way clear for the Persian army under Cyrus to march into the open gates of Babylon in 539 B.C.E.

The history of the Neo-Babylonian Empire in Palestine was relatively short (ca. 605–539 B.C.E.), but the destruction it wreaked has been substantiated by archaeology (see Ahlström, *History of Ancient Palestine*, 805). Its effect on Judah was devastating. It ended the kingdom, totally destroyed Jerusalem and other cities, and took a number of its leading families into captivity in Babylonia.

Isa 13–14 presupposes readers' and hearers' knowledge of this history, although the section assumes a point in time when Babylon has not yet been destroyed. The same will be true in chaps. 27 and 46–47.

The Day of YHWH (13:2–16)

Bibliography

Alonso Schökel, L. "Traducción de textos poéticos hebreos I (Isa 13)." *CB* 17 (1960) 170–76. **Bach, R.** *Die Aufforderungen zur Fluch und zum Kampf im alttestamentlichen Prophetenspruch.* WMANT 9. Neukirchen-Vluyn: Neukirchener Verlag, 1962. **Budde, K.** "Jesaja 13." In *Abhandlungen zur semitischen Religionskunde und Sprachwissenschaft.* FS W. W. von Baudissin, ed. W. Frankenberg and F. Küchler. BZAW 33. Giessen: Töpelmann, 1918. 55–70. **Erlandsson, W. J.** *The Burden of Babylon: A Study of Isaiah 13:2–14:23.* Lund: Gleerup, 1970. **Everson, A. J.** "Serving Notice on Babylon: The Canonical Function of Isaiah 13–14." *WW* 19.2 (1999) 133–40. **Fensham, F. C.** "Common Trends in Curses of the Near-Eastern Treaties and *kudurru*-Inscriptions Compared with Maledictions of Amos and Isaiah." *ZAW* 75 (1963) 155–75. **Geyer, J. B.** "Mythology and Culture in the Oracles against the Nations." *VT* 36 (1986), 129–45. ———. "Twisting Tiamat's Tail in Isaiah xiii 5 and 8." *VT* 37 (1987) 164–79. **Gosse, B.** "Convention in Hebrew Literature: The Reaction to Bad News (Includes Isa 13:7–8, 21:3–4)." *ZAW* 77 (1965) 86–90. ———. *Isaïe 13,1–14,23 dans le tradition littéraire du livre d'Isaïi et dans la tradition des oracles contre les nations.* OBO 78. Freiburg: Universitätsverlag; Göttingen: Vandenhoeck & Ruprecht, 1988. ———. "Un Texte pré-apocalyptic du règne de Darius. Isaïe XIII,1–XIV,23." *RB* 92 (1985) 200–222. **Grimme, H.** "Ein übersehenes Orakel gegen Assur (Isaias 13)." *TQ* 85 (1903) 1–11. **Hillers, D. R.** *Treaty-Curses and the Old Testament Prophets.* BibOr 16. Rome: Pontifical Biblical Institute, 1964. **Jeppeson, K.** "The *massa Babel* in Isaiah 13–14." PIBA 9 (1985) 63–80. **Manfred, G.** "'Dämonen' statt 'Eulen' in Jes 13:21." *BN* 62 (1992) 16–17. **Martin-Achard, R.** "Esaïe et Jéremie aux prises avec les problèmes politiques: Contribution à l'étude du thème: Prophétie et Politique." *RHPR* 47 (1967) 208–24. **Miller, P. D.** "The Divine Council and the Prophetic Call to War." *VT* 18 (1968) 100–107. **Reid, D. G.** "The Burden of Babylon: A Study of Isaiah 13." Unpublished research paper, Fuller Theological Seminary, 1979. **Schwarz, G.** "Jesaja 13:7–8a, eine Emendation." *ZAW* 89 (1977) 119. **Williamson, H. G. M.** *Book Called Isaiah.* 158–62. **Zapff, B. M.** *Schriftgelehrte Prophetie—Jes 13 und die Komposition des Jesajabuches: Ein Beitrag zur Erforschung der Redaktionsgeschichte des Jesajabuches.* Würzburg: Echter, 1995.

Translation

YHWH: 2 *Upon a bare*[a] *mountain* — 3+2+3
raise [pl.] a banner!
Raise the voice to them!
Wave a hand — 2+3
[b]*that they enter the gates of nobles;*[b]
3 *I myself give command to my dedicated*
(holy, sanctified) ones. — 3+4+2
Also I call my heroes to my wrath,[a]
those rejoicing in my sovereignty.

First Speaker: 4 *A sound of tumult in the mountains* — 3+3
like many people.
A sound of uproar (from) kingdoms,[a] — 3+2
nations gathering.

Second Speaker:	*YHWH of Hosts*	2+3
	mustering an attack force (for) battle.	
	5 *Coming from a distant land,*	3+2
	from the end of the heavens,[a]	
	YHWH and instruments of his indignation[b]	3+2
	to destroy the whole land.	
Third Speaker:	6 *Wail ye!*	1+4+3
	For the day of YHWH (is) near.	
	It comes like destruction from Shaddai.[a]	
	7 *Therefore, all hands*[a] *are feeble,*	4+4+1
	and every mortal heart[b] *is faint*	
	8 *and they are confounded.*[a]	
	Pangs and anguish seize them.	3+2
	Like a travailing[b] *woman they writhe.*	
	Each at his neighbor[b] *stares aghast;*	3+3
	[b]*their faces*[c] *are faces aflame.*	
First Speaker:	9 *Behold, the day of YHWH (is) coming,*	3+4
	cruel, overflowing, burning anger,	
	to make the earth a desolation,	3+3
	its sinners to be destroyed from it.	
	10 *For the stars of the heavens and their constellations*[a]	4+3
	do not give light,[b]	
	The sun is dark in its rising,	3+4
	and the moon does not produce[c] *its light.*	
YHWH:	11 *And I shall visit upon the world (its)*[a] *evil*	3+2
	and upon the wicked their sins,	
	and I shall stop the arrogance of the proud	3+3
	and the haughtiness of the terrible I will lay low.	
	12 *I will make a mortal rarer than pure gold*[a]	3+3
	and a human than pure gold of Ophir.	
	13 *Because of this I will make the heavens tremble,*[a]	3+3
	and the earth will shake in its place.	
Second Speaker:	*In the overflowing wrath of YHWH of Hosts,*	3+3
(echo)	*in the day of his burning anger.*	
Third Speaker:	14 *And it will be that*	1
	like a hunted gazelle,	2+3
	and like a sheep which no one herds,	
	they will turn each to his own people	3+3
	and each to his own land they will flee.	
	15 *Everyone captured*[a] *is stabbed,*	3+4
	and everyone caught falls by a sword.	
	16 *Their babies are dashed in pieces before their eyes.*	3+2+2
	Their houses are plundered,	
	and their wives raped.[a]	

Notes

2.a. נִשְׁפֶּה *nip'al* ptc. from שׁפה, "make smooth," "sweep bare." LXX πεδινοῦ, "on a plain," implies standing alone on otherwise level ground. LXX apparently reads שׁפלה (cf. 32:19). The versions have more trouble with the word: α´ has γνοφωδους, "misty," "gloomy"; Vg. *caliginosum*, meaning about the same. σ´ ομαλου and Syr. "smooth," "even."

2.b-b. 1QIsa[a] יבוא is sg. α´ = MT. LXX ἀνοίξατε is an impv., making "the nobles" the subject. Vg., Syr. also make נדיבים the subject: "the attackers will enter the gates." MT is to be sustained.

3.a. LXX πληρῶσαι τὸν θυμόν μου, "to fulfill my wrath," is a paraphrase that has caught the meaning, as Dillmann, Gesenius, and others have noted.

4.a. LXX φωνὴ βασιλέων, "sound of kings." Vg. also has *regum,* "kings," instead of *regnorum,* "kingdoms." Later LXX MSS have βασιλειῶν, "kingdoms." Erlandsson (*Burden of Babylon,* 19) suggests that ממלכות may have had both meanings, as Phoenician inscriptions would indicate. 1QIsa[a] and Syr. support MT.

5.a. LXX adds θεμελίου, "foundation of," to imply that they did not come from heaven itself. Cf. J. Ziegler, *Untersuchungen zur Septuaginta des Buches Isaias,* ATA 12.3 (Münster: Aschendorff, 1934).

5.b. LXX οἱ ὁπλομάχοι αὐτοῦ, "his armed men."

6.a. MT כשד משדי (cf. also Joel 1:15) is a play on words that sound alike. The versions did not see the humor in them. שד is used in 16:4 and 22:4 with similar meaning: "devastation" from war. שדי is a name for God in Genesis and Job, but here it is apparently related to the root שדד and means "Devastator" (cf. Erlandsson, *Burden of Babylon,* 20; Gray).

7.a. MT ידים is dual, lit. "every pair of hands."

7.b. LXX translates "heart" with ψυχή, "soul," in the accustomed fashion.

8.a. *BHS* places ונבהלו, "and they are confounded," on a line with v 7, separating it from צירים in v 8. Vg. does the same. Syr. begins v 8 after ונבהלו. LXX πρέσβεις, "elders," "ambassadors," translates צירים (BDB, II; *HAL* II) as the subject for "are confounded." However, the parallel with חבל, "anguish," suggests the ציר should be translated with BDB IV; *HAL* III as "pang." ונבהלו simply remains outside the metric lines.

8.b. LXX separates the verbs with καί, "and."

8.c. LXX reads פְּנוּ, "for the turn," instead of MT פני, "faces of," making it a verb, parallel to those in the previous stichs.

10.a. כסיל in the sg. appears in Amos 5:8; Job 9:9; 38:31, meaning "Orion." The usual suggestion for the pl. is "constellations."

10.b. יהלו, "shine," "give light." 1QIsa[a] יאירו has the same meaning using a cognate of אורים.

10.c. Many MSS correctly add the *mappiq:* יַגִּיהַּ.

11.a. *BHS* suggests reading רעתה, "its evil," parallel to "their sins" in the next stich. Wildberger argues against it that the wicked are responsible for their sins but the world (תבל) is not.

12.a. MT פז, "pure gold," BDB, 808; LXX τὸ χρυσίον τὸ ἄπυρον, "unrefined gold." KBL translated "chrysolite," a green mineral, but this suggestion has been rejected by Wildberger, G. Gerleman (comment on Song 5:11 in *Ruth/Hoheslied,* BKAT 18 [Neukirchen-Vluyn: Neukirchener Verlag, 1965] 173), and now *HAL.*

13.a. MT ארגיז, "I will cause to tremble," is parallel to a verb in the 3d person in the stich. LXX θυμωθήσεται (3d pass. pl.), "be enraged," appears to translate יִרְגְּזוּ, "tremble." However, the 1st-person expostulations by YHWH are not infrequent in Isaiah (cf. 10:12). MT should be sustained. LXX smooths the variant with the pass. verb.

15.a. MT הנמצא, lit. "the one who is found." Wildberger translates "is met or encountered," citing Ugar. *mẓa* (J. Aistleitner, *WUS* §1649). See E. Jenni's discussion in *THAT,* 1:922.

16.a. K תשגלנה, "raped," is changed in Q to תשכבנה, "lie down." The meaning is the same but avoids the "unclean" expression שגל. Cf. R. Gordis, *The Biblical Text in the Making* (Philadelphia: Dropsie, 1937) 30.

Form/Structure/Setting

Jeppeson (*PIBA* 9 [1985] 63–80) thinks this section (13:2–16) dates from the time of Isaiah. Williamson (*Book Called Isaiah,* 160–75) thinks of all of 13:2–14:22 being a part of the exilic Deutero-Isaian redaction. Kaiser thinks of the chapter as postexilic, although parts of chap. 13 may be earlier. Martin-Achard (*RHPR* 47 [1967] 208–24) agrees.

Reid's prosodic analysis ("Burden of Babylon") has shown that the chapter is composed of fifteen units. When speakers are assigned to these, they may be grouped in twelve speeches.

YHWH, vv 2–3	2 bicola + 1 tricola, all interrelated
1st speaker, v 4*ab*	2 bicola, interrelated
2d speaker, vv 4*c*–5	3 bicola, interrelated
3d speaker, vv 6–8	1 tricola + 2 bicola + 1 tricola; interrelated
1st speaker, vv 9–10	4 bicola
YHWH, vv 11–13*a*	3 bicola, interrelated + 1 bicola
2d speaker (echo), v 13*b*	1 bicola
3d speaker, vv 14–16	2 bicola, interrelated + 1 bicola and 1 tricola, interrelated
YHWH, vv 17–18	2 tricola, interrelated
1st speaker, v 19	2 bicola
2d speaker, vv 20–22*a*	2 bicola + 3 bicola, interrelated
3d speaker, v 22*b*	1 bicola

When seen in chiastic parallel to 14:22–32, the outline should be as follows (see outline of chaps. 13–14 above):

A A call to arms (13:2–3).
  B The noise of battle will destroy the whole land (13:4–5).
    C Day of YHWH (13:6–8).
      D Day of YHWH (13:9–16).
        E YHWH stirs up the Medes against Babylon (13:17–22).
        E´ The Lord will destroy Babylon (14:22–23).
      D´ YHWH's plan to destroy Assyria (14:24–25).
    C´ YHWH's plan for the whole world (14:26–27).
  B´ YHWH will destroy the Philistines (14:28–31).
A´ Jerusalem is established (14:32).

The chapter is a complex, carefully balanced composition that builds dramatically from theophanic views of the Divine Warrior preparing for battle (vv 2–16) to an explanation of the events in historical terms (vv 17–22). YHWH is acting to subdue and destroy Babylon by subverting her traditional allies, the Medes, against her.

The dramatic format sets the scene in the Heavenly Council. The speakers may well include Heavens and Earth (cf. 1:2) among the members of the court. Neither Israel nor Jerusalem is addressed in this chapter, nor is any direct reference made to them. Both will appear in chap. 14, the center and the second leg of the chiastic arch.

The smaller units are composed in familiar genres. The call to arms (vv 2–3) is typical in Divine Warrior literature (cf. 5:26–30 and parallels cited in Miller, *VT* 18 [1968] 100–101). The dramatic presentation of the sights and sounds of mobilization (vv 4–5) fits the same category. Two Day of YHWH passages follow (cf. 2:10–11, 12–18, 19–21; 22:5; 24:1–3, 21–23). Vv 6–8 follow the genre summons to a people's lament. H. W. Wolff described the form ("Der Aufruf zur

Volksklage," *ZAW* 76 [1964] 55; *Joel/Amos*, BKAT 16.2 [Neukirchen-Vluyn: Neukirchener Verlag, 1964] 23–24), which has parallels in 14:31; 23:1, 6, 14; Jer 4:8; 25:34; 49:3; Ezek 21:12; Joel 1:5, 11, 13; and Zech 1:11. It may be accompanied by fasting (cf. Joel 1:14; 2:15). The genre usually consists of three parts: an imperative beginning (הילילו, "wail ye"); the name of those summoned, if not already clear from the context; and a clause beginning with כי to list the occasion for the summons from the first part. The second element is missing here. The reason for the call is the threat posed by the approaching Day of YHWH. Jeppeson recognizes 13:2–16 as a "Day of YHWH text."

Comment

2 The call to arms of dedicated and loyal troops is ordered by YHWH. Messengers are sent out to gather the armies for the battle. They are not identified, referred to only as להם, "to them." Whether these are earthly or heavenly armies is not revealed.

"The gates of nobles": נדיבים, "nobles," reflects the Song of Deborah (Judg 5:2, 9), where another form of the root describes "volunteers" for battle (cf. Wildberger, 512). The פתחים, "gates," may well be the entrance to the camp. By entering, the nobles swear allegiance and participation in the campaign. The messengers are to call out the noble volunteers by raising a banner, by calling loudly, and by waving a hand. The שאו־נס, "raising of a banner," appears in 5:26 and 11:10. It marks the meeting place or the direction of march.

3 צוה, "command," may also be a technical term for mobilizing an army (cf. E. A. Speiser, *BASOR* 149 [1958] 21; J. Scharbert, *BZ* 4 [1960] 212).

No names are given for those who are called out. The ancient pattern of holy war would have mentioned the tribes of Israel (Judg 5). Here only descriptive titles are given: מקדשי is literally "my hallowed ones" (cf. Josh 3:5; Jer 51:27; Joel 4:9). To participate in "holy war," soldiers were required to prepare themselves with rituals of holiness (Deut 23:10–15; 1 Sam 21:5; 2 Sam 11:11; F. Stolz, *Jahwes und Israels Kriege,* ATANT 60 [Zurich: Theologische Verlag, 1972] 25, 140). The second title is גבורי, "my heroes." While in Ps 103:20 they may be called "heroes of power, doing my word," they are here "heroes for my wrath" as the Assyrians were "rods of God's anger" (10:5). The third title is עליזי גאותי, "ones rejoicing in my sovereignty," i.e., those who delight to be in his service. The theme of volunteerism appears again. There is still no hint to identify more closely the troops being summoned.

4*ab* A speech reports the voices of mobilization. The sounds are those common to the gathering of armies.

4*c*–5 A second speaker identifies the sounds with YHWH's call of vv 2–3. The armies are identified as those from kingdoms in "distant lands" and "from the end of the heavens." War that is carried out by the heavenly host supporting earthly armies is conceivable within the frame of holy war. They combine as "instruments of his indignation" (כלי זעמו) to "destroy the whole land." The phrase echoes 10:23, though the sense of destruction is rendered with a different word, עשׂא, translated as "doing" in 10:23 (however, cf. 10:25). But "the whole land" is the same. Whether this refers to a limited geographical area (Palestine in 10:23; the lower Euphrates in 13:5) or to the whole world must remain open. Perhaps the ambiguity is deliberate. All the descriptions of the Day of YHWH in Isaiah imply a universal application as well as a specific target area (cf. Miller, *VT* 18 [1968] 100).

6–8 A third response to YHWH's mobilization is more emotional: a call to הילילו, "wail," in mourning because of the expected terror of YHWH's day. Wolff has shown that the summons reacts to a threat by causing such an outcry that God may be influenced to change the order. In the dramatic scene the genre reinforces the impression of the awesome and terrible prospect.

כשד משדי, "like destruction from the Destroyer." "The Destroyer" is the divine name, *Shaddai,* which is common as אל שׁדי, "El Shaddai," in the patriarchal section of Genesis and in Job. The usage here in v 6 would support an understanding of שׁדי, which derives it from the root שׁדד, "to destroy." Discussion of the meaning of the name has been extensive (L. R. Bailey, "Israelite ʾEL SADDAY and Amorite BEL SADE," *JBL* 87 [1968] 434–38; M. Weippert, "Erwagungen zur Etymologie des Gottesnamens Saddaj," *ZDMG* 3 [1961] 42–62; *ZDPV* 82 [1966] 305 n. 172). These suggest that the Akkadian word *šadû,* "mountain," may explain the term. The god Enlil is called *šadû rabû.* The understanding of ancient translators varied. LXX translates with θεός, "God." Vg. translates with *Dominus,* "Lord" (G. Bertram, "Die Wiedergabe von *shadad* und *shaddaj* im Griechischen," *WO* 2 [1954–59] 502–13; "IKANOS in den griechischen Ubersetzungen des AT's als Wiedergabe von *shaddaj,*" *ZAW* 70 [1958] 20–31). In Job LXX translates παντοκράτωρ, "overpowering ones," which includes the idea "Omnipotent One," a word usually reserved to translate צבאות, "of Hosts." α´ and σ´ use ἱκανός, "the sufficient," "self-sufficient," which builds on the rabbinic suggestion that שׁדי is formed from שֶׁה + דַּי, meaning "he who is himself sufficient." Gen 49:25 relates the name to שׁדים, "breasts" (cf. M. A. Canney, "Shaddai," *ExpTim* 34 [1922–23] 332; F. Stolz, *Structuren und Figuren im Kult von Jerusalem,* BZAW 118 [Berlin: De Gruyter, 1970] 158). Ancient interpreters were not of one mind about the meaning of שׁדי despite their agreement concerning the importance of the ideas related to it.

Vv 7–8 portray the panic and impotence of the victims. The theme is common in descriptions of holy war when YHWH goes ahead of the armies terrifying the enemy.

9–16 These speeches pick up the themes of vv 2–5 from which vv 6–8 turned aside. The mobilization of an "attack force" (v 4) is pointedly (הנה, "behold") related to the larger cosmic events of YHWH's day, as in v 17 it will point to the historic stirring of Median warriors.

9 הנה, "behold," draws attention to the verse. It announces that "making the earth a desolation" is the reason for the Day of YHWH (see the second הנה in v 13). This announcement is parallel to that in 24:1, also introduced by הנה.

בָּא, "coming," is a form that may be an active participle or a perfect. Wildberger (516) insists that it is a prophetic perfect, citing Zimmerli on Ezek 7:12 (*Ezekiel,* BKAT 13.1 [Neukirchen-Vluyn: Neukirchener Verlag, 1969] 167). However, the comparison is poor. In Ezek 7:12 בא is the first word of the verse as a finite verb should be. Here it is introduced by הנה, "behold," which in Isaiah is often followed by a participle, and it is placed after its subject as a participle usually is. It is a participle emphasizing the dramatic event that is unfolding in their very sight.

The many adjectives modifying "anger" are emphatic. הארץ, "the earth," may point to the world or to a particular land. The setting seems to lean toward a universal meaning. The destruction of its "sinners" through judgment picks up a theme from the flood (Gen 6:13). Cosmic upheaval accompanies the Day of YHWH (cf. Amos 5:18, 20; 8:9; Zeph 1:15; Jer 4:23; Ezek 32:7; Joel 2:10, 3:4 [2:31]). It is the end of an age that is described, however, not the end of the world.

Williamson (*Book Called Isaiah,* 173) points to the scope of "the whole land" as a sign of a late date. "Before the exile, the prophets applied the negative aspects of the Day of the Lord to Israel, during the exile to the enemies of Israel, and then only later did it move in a more apolyptic direction" (cf. Gosse, *Isaïe 13,1–14,23,* 139).

Excursus: The Destruction of the Land

(See *Excursus: "Desolation"* [שממה] *in Isaiah* in the introduction to 5:1–6:13 above.)

The destruction of the land (13:5, 9) is emphasized in v 9 through הנה, "behold." It is one of the two major themes of the burden of Babylon. The other is the overthrow of Babylon itself (vv 17–19), which is also introduced by הנה, "behold."

The theme was already present in chaps. 2–12. It was introduced in a limited form in 1:7, "your land is desolate," and is described in 6:11–12. Isa 10:22–23 says "Annihilation has been determined! . . . Indeed, what the Lord, YHWH of Hosts, is doing in the land is a completed and fixed decree." It is now resumed as a central theme of chaps. 13–27 and reaches its climax in 24:1–13. A number of different words are used to describe this destruction: שממה, "desolate" (1:7; 6:11); שאה, "there be desolation" (6:11); כליון, "annihilation" (10:22); בוקק, "destroying" (24:1); and בולק, "laying waste" (24:1). Chap. 24 continues with "twists its surface," "scatters its inhabitants," "the land is totally emptied—totally plundered," "it dries up . . . withers . . . languishes," "the land itself is contaminated under its inhabitants," "a curse devours land," "broken," "horror," "ruin."

The act (chaps. 13–27) invokes a setting in the land (see *Excursus: "The Land"* [הארץ] at chap. 24 below) and uses 2:10–20 as a background. The land will be punished/destroyed (13:5, 9, 11), but it will one day again hold Israel/Jacob (14:1). The land is the arena of YHWH's action against Assyria (14:25). YHWH's action has been targeted against the land (14:25–27). God's actions often refer to agricultural phenomena even when the land is not mentioned. The land will be blessed when political amity brings Egypt, Assyria, and Israel together (19:24). The land appears in 23:9, 13 in reference to Tyre. The peak of action aganst the land is noted in chap 24, especially vv 1, 4, 5, 6, 17, 18, 19, 20, 21. The land appears again in 26:21. So "the land" is Palestine, but it also includes Egypt, Mesopotamia, and Tyre. It is synonomous with תבל, "world," and refers not only to geographical location but also to a civilization that was contained within it, including the economic and political aspects. Its destruction marks the end of an age.

The wars of the Assyrian and Babylonian periods (eighth to the sixth centuries) brought devastation and ruin to all of Palestine, but also to Assyria and Babylonia in Mesopotamia and to Egypt. They effectively destroyed not only cities and property but also the delicate fabric of civilization and society that makes for political relations and economic prosperity. For well over a millenium commerce and social intercourse had moved freely through the area, creating a sense that the civilized world and the Fertile Crescent, what we call the ancient Near East, were synonymous terms. Of course there were earlier wars, and there were invasions from outside (the Hyksos, the Hittites, the Mittani, and others), but they had been successfully thrown back. Now that world, thanks to the wars for the ambitions of Assyrian and Babylonian kings, was coming to an end.

The destruction marked the end of an age, an era, for the whole land. It was a dividing mark in history, and things would never be the same again. The Vision portrays these events as part of YHWH's plan (14:26–27) and looks to what he has in mind for his people beyond that "end."

11–13 As in 2:12–17, human arrogance is the particular target of divine retributions. YHWH himself speaks the order.

12 אוקיר, "I will make rare," is a rare word probably chosen in alliteration to אופיר, "Ophir" (cf. L. Alonso Schökel, "El juego fonetico oqir-opir," *Estudios de Poetica Hebrea* [Barcelona: Flors, 1963] 408; I. Eitan, "A Contribution to Isaiah Exegesis," *HUCA* 12 [1937] 61). Ophir has been thought to be southwest Arabia, northeast Africa, or even northwest India, but the concept "gold from Ophir" was a real part of ancient Near Eastern commerce. *HAL* links כתם, "pure gold," to Egyptian *ktmt.*

14–15 These verses describe the horrible consequences as vv 7–8 did. "Each to his own people" presumes a population that has migrated to the great cities in search of jobs or buyers for goods or as mercenaries. They return to their villages in times of trouble. It may also picture exiles from other countries who have been deported to the region.

16 שגל means "sexual intercourse" (cf. Deut 28:30), but in the passive stems "rape" (*HAL;* cf. Zech 13:2; Jer 3:2). Wildberger aptly notes: "The offensive word was consciously chosen by the author, just as it is consciously replaced by the Massoretes" (see *Note* 16.a. above).

Explanation

The heavenly court is abuzz with excitement. Intensive mobilization of military forces is underway. YHWH, the Heavenly King, has given the order to mobilize for a massive action. Its goal is destruction of the whole world, the resumption of the order given in chap. 5 and defined in chap. 6, the order that the Assyrian armies were to carry out in chaps. 7–10. But this is a later day. It is the Babylonian period after Babylon had succeeded Assyria in controlling "all the land." She had continued with enthusiasm to carry out Assyria's mission and had destroyed Jerusalem and taken the royal court of Jerusalem along with many of the most important of her inhabitants into exile in Babylon. Mourning is in order, for YHWH's day of reckoning is at hand. Everyone will quail before it. Now it is Babylon's turn to feel God's destructive power.

The extent of the day's action is again defined. It will desolate the earth (v 9*b*). It will destroy its sinners. Its cosmic dimensions involve the stars, the sun, and the moon. Evil, iniquity, and the wicked will be punished. The arrogant will be humbled. The earth will have its population drastically reduced. To this end the cosmic upheaval that serves YHWH's overflowing wrath will be a time of terrible chaos and of violence.

Babylon's Fate—Israel's Hope (13:17–14:23)

YHWH Overwhelms Babylon (13:17–22a)

Bibliography

Erlandsson, W. J. *The Burden of Babylon: A Study of Isaiah 13:2–14:23.* Lund: Gleerup, 1970. **Fensham, F. C.** "Common Trends in Curses of the Near-Eastern Treaties and *kudurru*-Inscriptions Compared with Maledictions of Amos and Isaiah." *ZAW* 75 (1963) 155–75. **Hillers, D. R.** *Treaty-Curses and the Old Testament Prophets.* BibOr 16. Rome: Pontifical Biblical Institute, 1964. **Manfred, G.** "'Dämonen' statt 'Eulen' in Jes 13:21." *BN* 62 (1992) 16–17.

Translation

YHWH:	17 *Behold me stirring the Medes against them,*	4+4+4
	whom silver does not buy	
	nor gold entice.	
	18 *Bows of youths are dashed in pieces.*[a]	3+4+4
	They will not show mercy to the fruit of the womb;	
	upon children their eyes will not look with compassion.	
First Speaker:	19 *And Babylon, jewel of kingdoms,*	4+3
	the glory of Chaldean pride, will become	
	like God's overthrow	2+2
	(of) Sodom and Gomorrah.	
Second Speaker:	20 *It will never be inhabited again;*	3+4
	it will not be dwelt in generation to generation.	
	No Arab[a] *will camp*[b] *there,*	4+4
	and no shepherd will rest[c] *his flocks there.*	
	21 *Desert creatures*[a] *will rest there,*	3+3
	and jackals[b] *will fill their houses.*	
	Owls will dwell there,	4+3
	and wild goats will run around there.	
	22 *Hyenas*[a] *will echo in its palaces,*[b]	3+3
	and jackals[c] *in its temples of pleasure.*	

Notes

18.a. "Young bowmen dash in pieces" is a literal translation but does not seem to make sense. "Bowmen" do not "dash in pieces." LXX τοξεύματα νεανισκῶν συντρίψουσι, "bows of young men break in pieces," reading קַשְּׁתֹת, a const. for קְשָׁתוֹת, an abs. and a pass. verb, perhaps *pu'al* instead of *pi'el*. Syr. *ḳeštātā da'lajme nettabrān* supports this. E. J. Young and Erlandsson (*Burden of Babylon*) defend MT by referring to a parallel *[gis]kakku [d]ašur tiba dapna mušharmṭa šalamda iddi*, "the weapon of Asshur, it threw down as corpses the aggressors, the fierce, the destroyer" (see W. G. Lambert, "Three Unpublished Fragments of the Tukulti-Ninurta Epic," *AfO* 18 [1957–58] 40). Wildberger notes that *kakku* is a staff or club that is properly understood as "breaking things in pieces." This is not true of a bow. The translation above follows LXX.

20.a. The reference is not ethnic but speaks of the lifestyle of the nomad.

20.b. יַהֵל: BDB, GKC §68*k*, *HAL*, and *DCH* consider this a verbal denominative from אהל, "he will pitch his tent." This is supported by the versions, contra Hitzig, who read it as a *hip'il* from נהל, "to lead to water."

20.c. LXX ἀναπαύσονται, "abide," "dwell"; Tg. ישרון, "dwell"; Vg. *requiescent*, "rest," "repose." Wildberger says 1QIsa[a] has put a י over the ב, but a careful reading shows that it is either a ו (as Burrows transcribed it) or a decorative feature like so many on that page. MT's *hip'il* reading is sustained.

21.a. The animals are difficult to identify. ציים: BDB, 850, "desert dweller," "crier," "yelper"; cf. 23:13; 34:14. Wildberger translates "demons" (*HAL* includes this option) but does not support his translation. NEB translates "marmots."

21.b. אחים, a *hap. leg. HAL* identifies them as "howling desert animals," probably owls or hyenas; BDB suggests jackals. *DCH* translates "owls," citing the word's appearance in lists of desert animals in 4QShir[a] 1:5 and 11QapPs[a] 2:12.

22.a. איים means something like "hyena" or "jackal." LXX ὀνοκένταυροι, "apes."

22.b. MT אלמנותיו, "its widows." Syr., Tg., and Vg. translate "palaces," suggesting Heb. ארמנות.

22.c. תנים are other creatures, perhaps jackals.

Form/Structure/Setting

This announcement of God's action against Babylon is the actual "burden," which calls the nation by name (see *Excursus: "Burden"* [משׂא] *in the Prophets* at 13:1 above). Isa 13:17–22 parallels the similar word against Assyria (10:12) and that against Edom (34:5–7). The curse on the city (vv 20–22) is parallel to that on Edom (34:8–15). On the form of curses against cities and nations, compare Fensham (*ZAW* 75 [1963] 155–75) and Hillers *(Treaty-Curses)*. The Vision will later note the fulfillment of the curse on Babylon (21:9) as it also does the fulfillment of the curse on Edom (63:1–3).

Comment

17–18 As the macabre scene resulting from the cosmic quake (vv 2–16) passes, the finger points to a historical movement. YHWH calls attention to stirrings among the feared Medes, for which he claims responsibility.

מדי, "the Medes." See the excursus below. The fall of Babylon to the Medes can only be that under Cyrus in 539 B.C.E. Cyrus's mother was a Mede. He became king of Media before it united with Persia.

Excursus: The Medes

Bibliography

Briant, P. *From Cyrus to Alexander: A History of the Persian Empire.* Trans. P. T. Daniels. Winona Lake, IN: Eisenbrauns, 2002. **Diakonoff, I. M.** "Media." In *The Cambridge History of Iran.* Vol. 2, *The Median and Achaemenian Periods.* Ed. I. Gershevitch. Cambridge, 1985. 142–48. **Frye, R. N.** *The History of Ancient Iran.* Munich: Beck, 1984. 90–92. **Widengren, G.** "The Persians." In *POTT.* 313–16.

The Medes are attested as an ancient people in Gen 10:2. They inhabited the high country of northwestern Iran bordered by the Elburz Mountains, the Salt Desert, Persia, and the lowlands of Mesopotamia. Their capital was Ecbatana. No written records of their early history have survived. Elam lay to the south and Assyria directly east.

In the eighth century Assyria had to deal with the Medes repeatedly, as indeed Shalmanezer III had done in the ninth. From Sargon's time (722–705 B.C.E.) for about three-quarters of a century, Media was subject to Assyria (*IDB*, 3:319). Some Israelites were deported to "cities of the Medes" (2 Kgs 17:6; 18:11).

Media would normally have been separated from Babylon by Elam, which was Babylon's ally against Assyria (*IDB*, 2:70). Isa 21:2 speaks of both Elam and Media as attackers of Babylon. This implies a situation in which Media and Elam support Assyria's campaign against Babylon. Such a situation could well account for Merodach-Baladan's defeat ca. 710 B.C.E. The threat posed by the Medes is obvious. For independence Babylon had to rely on Elamite support. A threat of Elamite military invasion of Babylon would neutralize that support. Since Media was subject to Assyria throughout this period, it takes little imagination to see how the plans were effectively laid to bring Babylon back under Assyrian power.

Media, allied with Persia, is much better known in the OT for the empire of the sixth and fifth centuries, and for the occupation of Babylon in 539 B.C.E. Wildberger (520) sees the Medes as the "dedicated ones" whom YHWH has "called" (v 3). Yet the chapter has set the isolated event of Media's move against Babylon (vv 17–19) in the larger frame of YHWH's day with its cosmic and historical aspects. The Medes may well be seen as only one aspect of the broader picture. Within that broader setting, attention is focused on stirrings among one people, the Medes. Isaiah shows God using them just as he used the Assyrians and Cyrus. They are impervious to bribes. Their famous bow and arrow will overcome all.

19 The target of the Medes' aggression is finally named (only in the superscription v 1 has it appeared so far): "Babylon, jewel of kingdoms, the glory of Chaldean pride." On Babylon, see the *Excursus: Babylon and the King of Babylon in the Vision of Isaiah* at 13:1 above. The Chaldeans were a group of tribes in the lower delta of the twin rivers below the most southerly Babylonian cities (*IDB*, 1:550). They are called כשדים in Ezra and Daniel, but the *Kaldai* in cunieform writings. About 722 B.C.E. the Chaldean leader of the Bit Yakin tribe, Marduk-apla-iddina (called Merodach-Baladan in Hebrew), conquered Babylon, making it his capital. A century later they would recapture the city and establish the Neo-Babylonian Empire of Nebuchadnezzar. For a people of village tribes, the legendary city was indeed their "pride" and "glory."

The comparison with Sodom and Gomorrah (cf. Gen 19:23–29) matches the fabled glory of the city with the symbols above all others of divine destruction (cf. D. R. Hillers, *Treaty-Curses,* 74–76). Jerusalemites referred to Sodom and Gomorrah in 1:9 to describe a fate they had narrowly escaped. The description goes beyond military plunder to set the stage for the curse of permanent devastation (vv 20–22*b*) that follows.

20–22*a* The depopulated city is a virtual ghost town. The ruins are empty. The cries of desert animals hint at ghosts and demons in the eerie place. ערבי, "Arab," probably speaks of a nomad wanderer.

Explanation

The punishment of Babylon is put into the perspective of the Vision, which sees the events affecting Israel and its neighbors from the eighth century to the fifth as facets of "the great and terrible day of YHWH" that ends the old age and inaugurates the new age. (See the *Comment* on 2:5–22 above.) That Babylon should head the list of nations under judgment in chaps. 13–23 comes as a surprise. The suggestion that it should be Assyria is met in 14:25 with the assurance that in all good time her turn will come. In the meantime Assyria is God's tool, not his enemy. Babylon's significance for Israel in all periods was great (see *Excursus: Babylon and the King of Babylon*). At the end of Ahaz's reign its meaning was unique. The Bit Yakin tribe seized control of the city, and their chief was proclaimed king. He was to occupy the throne for some twelve years (chap. 39).

But the Babylon of 13:17–14:23 belongs to a different time. She is the capital of the Neo-Babylonian Empire that Nebuchadnezzar developed. He had, in coalition with the Medes and Egypt, destroyed Nineveh in 612 B.C.E. and defeated the fleeing Assyrian armies in 609 B.C.E. He invaded Palestine at least three times: in 605 B.C.E. he forced Jehoiakim to cede rule to his son Jehoiachin; in 598 B.C.E. he took captive the royal family and others from Jerusalem into exile in Babylon; and in 586 B.C.E. he executed Zedekiah, destroyed Jerusalem, and took a large number of Judeans into exile.

But the Babylon pictured in 13:22–27 is not successful and ascendant. She is on the defensive and about to be destroyed herself. The mighty general and warrior referred to in 14:4–21 is either dead or about to die. And Babylon will never be great again.

God's weapons for battle are more than the direct intervention of the heavenly armies summoned in vv 2–3. The Medes are summoned from the east to do his bidding. Babylon, whose very name conjures memories of glory and majesty, has become a symbol of destruction like Sodom and Gomorrah.

(For) Jacob's Hope (13:22b–14:2)

Bibliography

Franke, C. A. "Reversals of Fortune in the Ancient Near East: A Study of the Babylonian Oracles in the Book of Isaiah." In *New Visions.* Ed. R. F. Melugin and M. A. Sweeney. 104–23. **Quell, G.** "Jesaja 14:1–23." In *Festschrift Friedrich Baumgärtel.* Ed. J. Herrmann and L. Rost. Erlanger Forschungen A10. Erlangen: Universitätsbund, 1959. 131–57.

Translation

First Speaker: [22b] *And her time (is) near to come;* 3+3
her days will not be prolonged.
[14:1] *But YHWH will have compassion on Jacob* 4+3+2
and again elect Israel

and give them rest on their own ground.

Second Speaker: *The sojourner will join himself to them.* 3+3
They will cleave to the house of Jacob.
[2]*Peoples will take them and bring them to their place.* 4+4
And the house of Jacob will divide YHWH's land among themselves.
For slaves and maidservants (to work) 2+3+2
they will be taking their captives captive.
They shall rule over their oppressors.

Form/Structure/Setting

The passage is set off by the change in mood and content on both sides. It contrasts Babylon's fate with Israel's hope. The contrast is balanced on the other leg of the chiasmus with 14:20*b*–21, which stresses the hopeless future for the Babylonian ruler's family.

Comment

22*b* This statement brings the chapter full circle. קרוב, "near," and לבוא, "to come," resume the very words of v 6 concerning the Day of YHWH. Both announcements are portrayed as predicting the near future.

13:22*b*–14:1 The statements concerning Babylon's fate and Israel's hope are related by the two words קרוב, "near," and עוֹד, "again." עתה, "her time," and ימיה, "her days," refer to the events of the end of Babylon just predicted. The OT teaches that everything has its own time (Eccl 3:1–8; G. von Rad, *Wisdom in Israel* [Nashville: Abingdon, 1972]). Babylon's fate cannot be rushed. One must wait for it (cf. J. G. Heintz, "Aux origines d'une expression biblique: *ūmūšū qerbū* in A. R. M., x/6, 8?" *VT* 21 [1971] 535–40). Babylon's time, like the Day of YHWH (13:6), is near and calls for "wailing" and distress.

Israel's hope is contrasted to Babylon's hopelessness. It is to come "again." It continues the promising tone of 11:11–16 in contrast to the heavy sentence of judgment portrayed in scene 2 of act 1 (9:7 [8]–10:23). This hopeful passage concerns Israel, not Jerusalem. It is cast in the thoughts and vocabulary that are usual to Israel's hope.

The speech reiterates the major elements of Israel's ancient faith and hope. It was YHWH's רחם, "compassion," on Jacob that motivated the exodus (Exod 34:6; Deut 4:31; Joel 2:13; Jonah 4:2; Ps 78:38). Quell calls it "the strongest word for love that biblical language has" ("Jesaja 14:1–23," 140). The root is derived from רֶחֶם, "womb," and describes the almost instinctive inclination of a mother to her child, so dependent on her, yet incapable of offering anything in return (Wildberger, 525). The term is used again in 49:10 and 54:8, 10. The statement draws upon other instances when God declares his continued compassion—even in moments when Israel is apostate, such as after the golden-calf incident (Exod 34:6). It is appropriate as a restatement of God's commitment even after the edict of total destruction (10:23).

The speech is developed further with an assurance that YHWH will "elect (or choose) Israel again" (בחר עוד בישראל). The עוֹד, "again," is needed in the context where such election has been set aside to allow judgment to do its work (chap. 10). The doctrine of election stood in jeopardy from the time Israel was no longer unified (i.e., the beginning of the divided kingdom). Destruction of Samaria and deportation of its people from their own land made it even less tenable. Eventually, Jerusalem and Judah would follow suit. All this made exilic Israel and Jerusalem struggle to find a foundation for their faith (cf. H. Wildberger, "Die Neuinterpretation des Erwählungsglaubens Israel in der Krise der Exilszeit," in *Wort, Gebot, Glaube*, FS W. Eichrodt [Zurich: Zwingli, 1970] 307–24).

The assurance is given that the promise to Abraham will apply again. Chaps. 41–48 will pick up the application of this theme to the exilic diaspora, not that the statement that follows concerning the "land" will be different in those chapters. The meaning of this speech about "the house of Jacob" must be seen in the Vision in the context of those that begin in 1:1–7 and 2:5–9. The debate about Israel's position and future in God's plan ranges throughout the book.

This speech continues by tying election to Israel's place in Canaan: והניחם על־אדמתם, YHWH "will give them rest on their own ground" (cf. Deut 3:20; 12:9; Jer 27:11; Ezek 37:14). This statement will become questionable in later parts of the book, as it did in Judaism. Can election be proved only on possession and prosperity in the Holy Land? The speech foresees such economic prosperity and earned esteem that wandering peoples will volunteer to serve them.

2 The ideas are expanded to include an escort of the peoples returning Israel "to their place" (cf. 60:4–12 applied to Jerusalem, 61:4–7 and 66:19–21 applied to pilgrimages to Jerusalem's temple). The passage envisions a reversal of roles from their present miserable condition of subservient captivity. Jacob will "yet" be respected and served again. It reinforces the appeal of these chapters to "wait on YHWH" rather than attempt to follow Babylon's example of violent rebellion.

Explanation

Isa 13:22*b*–14:2 imparts a sense of God's control over all things, which will be ordered in their own time. God assured Jerusalem (10:12) that he himself would deal with the Assyrian when the assigned task was complete. Now here he refers to Babylon's assigned "time"—yet to come, but sure to come—and calls Israel's attention to the goals God has set for her that are "yet" to come to pass—but also sure. These are goals that provide for "rest," and for "quiet" and "singing" according to chaps. 24–27. They are goals, fixed in God's own strategy for the world (chaps. 24–27), which will come only through his direct intervention when his victory is complete.

Taunt over a Fallen Tyrant (14:3–21)

Bibliography

Alfrink, B. "Der Versammlungsberg im äustersten Norden (Is. 14)." *Bib* 14 (1933) 41–67.
Alonso Schökel, A. "Traducción de textos poéticos hebreos II (Isa 14)." *CB* 17 (1960)

257–65. **Anderson, G. A.** *A Time to Mourn, A Time to Dance.* University Park: Pennsylvania State UP, 1991. 60–82. **Avishur, Y.** "'Atudei eretz' (Is 14,9)." In *Shnaton: An Annual for Biblical and Ancient Near Eastern Studies.* Ed. M. Weinfeld and J. C. Greenfield. Vol. 9. Jerusalem; Tel Aviv: Israel Bible Co., 1985. 159–64. **Begrich, J.** "Jesaja 14,28–32." *ZDMG* 86 (1933) 66–79. Reprinted in *Gesammelte Studien zum alten Testament,* TB 21 (Münich: Kaiser, 1964) 121–31. **Bost, H.** "Le chant sur la chute d'un tyran en Ésaïe." *ETR* 59 (1984) 3–14. **Burns, J. B.** "Does Helel 'go to Hell'? Isaiah 14:12–15." *PEGLMBS* 9 (1989) 89–97. ———. "*Hôlesh ʿal* in Isaiah 14:12: A New Proposal." *ZAH* 2 (1989) 199–204. **Carmignac, J.** "Six passages d'Isaïe eclaires par Qumran." In *Bibel und Qumran.* Ed. S. Wagner. B-Ost: Evang. Haupt. Bibelgesellschaft, 1968. **Clements, R. E.** "Isaiah 14:22–27: A Central Passage Reconsidered." In *Book of Isaiah.* Ed. J. Vermeylen. 253–62. **Clifford, R. J.** *The Cosmic Mountain in Canaan and the Old Testament.* Harvard University Monographs 4. Cambridge, MA: Harvard UP, 1972. 160–68. **Cobb, W. H.** "The Ode in Isaiah xiv." *JBL* 15 (1896) 18–35. **Craigie, P. C.** "Helel, Athtar, and Phaethon (Isa 14:12–15)." *ZAW* 85 (1973) 223–25. **Dupont-Sommer, A.** "Note exégétique sur Isaïe 14:16–21." *RHR* 134 (1948) 72–80. **Erlandsson, S.** *The Burden of Babylon: A Study of Isaiah 13:2–14:23.* ConBOT 4. Lund: Gleerup, 1970. **Etz, D. V.** "Is Isaiah XIV 12–15 a Reference to Comet Halley?" *VT* 36 (1986) 289–301. **Franke, C. A.** "The Function of the Oracles against Babylon in Isaiah 14 and 47." In *SBLSP.* Atlanta: Scholars Press, 1993. 250–59. Reprinted as "Reversals of Fortune in the Ancient Near East: A Study of the Babylonian Oracles in the Book of Isaiah," in *New Visions,* ed. R. F. Melugin and M. A. Sweeney. 104–23. **Gallagher, W.** "On the Identity of *Helel Ben Shaher* in Is. 14:12–15." *UF* 26 (1994) 131–46. **Gorman, F. H.** "A Study of Isaiah 14:4*b*–23." Unpublished research paper, Fuller Theological Seminary, 1979. **Gosse, B.** *Isaïe 13,1–14,23 dans la tradition littéraire du livre d'Isaïe et dans la tradition des oracle contre les nations.* Freiburg: Universitätsverlag, 1988. 200–278. ———. "Oracles contre les nations et structures des livres d'Isaïe et d'Ezékiel." *BN* 54 (1990) 19–21. **Grelot, P.** "Isaïe xiv 12–15 et son arrière-plan mythologique." *RHR* 149 (1956) 18–48. ———. "Sur la vocalisation de הילל (Is. 14:12)." *VT* 6 (1956) 303–4. **Heiser, M. S.** "The Mythological Provenance of Isa xiv 12–15: A Reconsideration of the Ugaritic Material." *VT* 51 (2001) 354–69. **Holladay, W. L.** "Text Structure and Irony in the Poem on the Fall of the Tyrant, Isaiah 14." *CBQ* 61 (1999) 633–45. **Hudson, J. T.** "Isaiah xiv. 19." *ExpTim* 40 (1928–29) 93. **Jahnow, H.** *Das hebräische Leichenlied.* BZAW 36. Giessen: Töpelmann, 1923. 239–53. **Jensen, J.** "Helelben Shahar (Isaiah 14:12–15) in Bible and Tradition." In *Writing and Reading.* Ed. C. C. Broyles and C. A. Evans. 1:339–56. **Keown, G.** "A History of the Interpretation of Isaiah 14:12–15." Diss., Southern Baptist Theological Seminary, 1979. **Khoo, J.** "Isaiah 14:12–14 and Satan: A Canonical Approach." *STJ* 2 (1994) 67–77. **Köhler, L.** "Isaiah xiv. 19." *ExpTim* 40 (1928–29) 236; 41 (1929–30) 142. **Köszegby, M.** "Erwägungen zum Hintergrund von Jesaja xiv 12–15." *VT* 44 (1994) 549–54. **Leeuwen, R. C. van.** "Isa 14:12 *ḥôlēs ʿl goyim* and Gilgamesh XI.6." *JBL* 99 (1980) 173–84. **Lohmann, P.** "Die anonymen Prophetien gegen Babel aus der Zelt des Exils." Diss., Rostock, 1910. ———. "Jes 14:19." *ZAW* 33 (1913) 253–56. **Loretz, O.** "Der Kanaanäisch-biblische Mythos vom Sturz des Sahar-Sohnes Helel (Jes 14,12–15)." *UF* 8 (1976) 133–36. **McKay, J. W.** "Helel and the Dawn-Goddess: A Re-examination of the Myth in Isa 14:12–25." *VT* 20 (1970) 450–64. **O'Connell, R. H.** "Isaiah xiv 4B–23: Ironic Reversal through Concentric Structure and Mythic Allusion." *VT* 38 (1988) 407–18. **Oldenburg, U.** "Above the Stars of El: El in Ancient South African Religion." *ZAW* 82 (1970) 187–208. **Onwurah, E.** "Isaiah 14: Its Bearing on African Life and Thought." *BiBh* 13 (1987) 29–41. **Poirier, J. C.** "An Illuminating Parallel to Isaiah xiv 12." *VT* 49 (1999) 373–89. **Prinsloo, W. S.** "Isaiah 14:12–15: Humiliation, Hubris, Humiliation." *ZAW* 93 (1981) 432–38. **Quell, G.** "Jesaja 14:1–23." In *Festschrift Friedrich Baumgärtel.* Ed. J. Herrmann and L. Rost. Erlanger Forschungen A10. Erlangen: Universitätsbund, 1959. 131–57. **Shipp, M.** *Of Dead Kings and Dirges: Myth and Meaning in Isaiah 14:4B–21.* Atlanta: SBL, 2002. **Smith, M. S.** "Rephaim." *ABD.* 5:675–

76. **Stolz, F.** "Die Bäume des Gottesgartens auf dem Libanon." *ZAW* 84 (1972) 141–56. **Talmon, S.** "Biblical *repaim* and Ugaritic *rpu/i(m)*." *HAR* 7 (1983) 235–49. **Tromp, N. J.** *Primitive Conceptions of Death and the Nether World in the Old Testament.* Rome: Pontifical Biblical Institute, 1969. **Twumara, D. T.** "Tohu in Isaiah xiv 19." *VT* 38 (1988) 361–64. **Vandenburgh, F. A.** "The Ode on the King of Babylon, Isaiah XIV, 4b–21." *AJSL* 29 (1912–13) 111–25. **Yee, G. A.** "The Anatomy of Biblical Parody: The Dirge Form in 2 Samuel 1 and Isaiah 14." *CBQ* 50 (1988) 565–86. **Youngblood, R. F.** "Fallen Star: The Evolution of Lucifer." *BRev* 14 (1998) 547–55.

Translation

First Speaker:
3 *And it shall be:* 1
In the day of YHWH's giving you [m. sg.] rest 4+2+4
from your trouble and your turmoil
and from the hard labor done by you,
4 *you will raise this taunt* 3+2
over the king of Babylon,
when you say: 1
"How oppressing has ceased! 2+2
Onslaught[a] *has ceased!*
5 *YHWH has shattered* 2+2+2
the staff of the evil ones,
the rod of rulers.
6 *In anger it was striking peoples—* 3+3
blows without let-up;
in wrath it was pursuing nations— 3+3
pursuit[a] *without restraint.*
7 *All the land is at rest, is quiet.* 4+2
They break into joyful song."

Court Singer:
8 *Even the juniper trees*[a] *rejoice because of you,* 4+2
the cedars of Lebanon:
"Since you have lain down, 2+2+2
the woodcutter comes no more
against us!"
9 *Sheol below is stirred up because of you,* 4+2
to meet your arrival.
Waking ghosts because of you, 3+3
all "the rams"[a] *of the earth.*
Rousing[b] *from their thrones,* 2+3
all the kings of the nations.
10 *They all respond* 2+2
and say to you:
"Even you— 2+2+2
you have weakened[a] *as we (did).*
You have been made like ourselves."
11 *Your pomp is lowered to Sheol,* 3+2
a groan of your disgrace:[a]
Beneath you a couch[b] *of maggots;* 3+2
your covers[c] *(are) worms.*

12 *How you have fallen from heaven,* 3+2
O Shining One,[a] *Son of Dawn!*
You have been cut down to earth, 2+3
you plunderer[b] *of nations!*
13 *But you: you had said in your heart* 3+2
"I will ascend to heaven;
above the divine stars[a] 3+2
I will raise my throne.
I will sit in the mountain assembly[b] 3+2
in the farthest north.
14 *I will rise over the backs*[a] *of clouds.* 3+2
I will be like the Most High."
15 *How you are brought down to Sheol,* 3+2
to the deepest pit!
16 *Onlookers stare at you.* 3+2
They think about you:
"Is this the man 2+2+2
who terrorized the earth?
Who shook the kingdoms?
17 *Who made the world like a desert* 3+2+3
and laid waste its cities?[a]
Who did not release[b] *his prisoners to their homes?"*
18 *All the kings of the nations—yes, all of them*[a]*—* 3+2+2
lie down in glory,
each in his own house.[b]
19 *But you! You are thrown out of your tomb*[a] 3+2
like an abhorred, aborted fetus![b]
(Like) dead men's clothes 2+2
of those stabbed by a sword.
(Like) those who fall to the stones of a pit. 3+2
Like a corpse (that is) trampled.
20 *You cannot be united with them in burial* 3+2+2
for you have destroyed your own land,
killed your own people.
First Speaker: *Never again will anyone recall* 3+2
(such a) race of scoundrels.[a]
Second Speaker: 21 *Prepare a place of execution for his sons* 3+2
because of the guilt of their fathers![a]
So that they cannot rise and possess the earth 3+3
and fill the world's surface with their cities!

Notes

4.a. MT מַרְהֵבָה is otherwise unknown in Biblical Heb., though it appears three times among the Qumran scrolls with the meaning "distress, calamity" (*DCH;* cf. masc. form מרהב four more times). 1QIsa[a] מרהבה supports the conjectured emendation of scholars from a *hipʿil* ptc. of רהב, "assault" *(HAL)*, although there is no parallel for this form in the OT either. Wildberger (533) suggests pointing it as a *hipʿil*, or *piʿel* ptc., and reading it as masc., as LXX ἐπισπουδαστής, "oppressor," and Syr. *mḥpṭnʾ* do. The issue has been discussed at length (cf. F. Nötscher, "Entbehrliche Hapaxlegomena in Jes," *VT* 1 [1950] 300; G. R. Driver, "Hebrew Scrolls," *JTS* 2 [1951] 25; M. D. Goldman, *ABR* 1 [1951] 10; M. Dahood, "Hebrew-Ugaritic Lexicography," *Bib* 48 [1967] 432). Read מרהבה with 1QIsaᵃ and *BHS* as a fem. noun "onslaught" *(HAL, DCH)* with the likely implication of oppressive taẋ gathering.

6.a. MT מֻרְדָּף (*hopʿal* ptc.), "one caused to be pursued" or "persecution." A parallel to רֹדֶה in the first stich would make one expect an act. meaning. LXX has apparently skipped the word. Syr. reads *wᵉrādef* (an act. form) and Vg. *persequentum*, which suggest reading a *piʿel* ptc. מְרַדֵּף, "pursuit" or "pursuing" (so *BHS*).

8.a. *HAL* defines ברוש as the "Phoenician juniper," *Juniperus Phoenicea* (cf. Löw, 3:33–38).

9.a. עתודי, "bucks," refers to the rams or bucks of the flock. Wildberger (534) calls attention to Zech 10:3, where the word is paired with "shepherds." The metaphorical relation of shepherd (the great king) and the heads of the flock (his vassal kings) is appropriate here.

9.b. הֵקִים is pointed as *hipʿil* pf., "he roused." However, its parallel עוֹרֵר, "waking," is *poʿel* inf. abs., which suggests the parallel pointing as *hipʿil* inf. abs. הָקִים, "rousing."

10.a. חלית is usually derived from חלה, "be sick" or "weak" (BDB, *HAL, DCH*). G. R. Driver (*JSS* 13 [1968] 43) suggests the Ugar. root *ḫly,* "was alone," and the Arab. *ḫalâ,* "was vacant," "disengaged."

11.a. MT נבליך, "your harps," appears in 1QIsaᵃ as נבלתך, which could mean either "your disgrace" or "your corpse."

11.b. MT יֻצָּע. BDB, *HAL,* and *DCH* call this a *hopʿal* impf. (cf. GKC §§193–94). Delitzsch (309) thought it a *puʿal* pf. 3d m. sg. (like יֻלַּד in 9:5), "be laid," "spread." Parallelism to מכסיך, "your covers," leads one to expect a noun form and suggest the *BHS* pointing יֵצַע or יְצוּעַ (Duhm; Jahnow, *Das hebräische Leichenlied*) or יְצוּעַ (Marti), meaning "couch."

11.c. Some MSS and 1QIsaᵃ read a sg. מכסך, "your cover." LXX καὶ τὸ κατακάλυμμά σου, "and his covering." *BHK* simply offers an alternative reading where MT knows two forms.

12.a. MT הילל, "shining one" (cf. Grelot, *VT* 6 [1956] 303). *HAL, BHS,* Vandenburgh (*AJSL* 29 [1912–13] 118) would change the pronunciation to הֵילָל, following Arab. *hilālum,* "new moon." LXX translates ἑωσφόρος, "Morning-star," Vg. *lucifer.*

12.b. MT חוֹלֵשׁ (*qal* ptc. act.), "weaken," "prostrating," usually appears with acc. The use of עַל, "over," is strange. LXX ὁ ἀποστέλλων πρὸς πάντα τὰ ἔθνη, "the one sending forth to all the nations," suggests that we read כל for על (cf. McKay, *VT* 20 [1970] 453 n. 4). H. Guillaume ("The Use of חלש," *JTS* 14 [1963] 91) compares Arab. *ḥalasa* to suggest the meaning "to plunder" for חלש.

13.a. MT אל, "God," is the first of two words for God (cf. עליון in v 14) that are also known for separate gods in the Canaanite pantheon. D. W. Thomas ("A Consideration of Some Unusual Ways of Expressing the Superlative in Hebrew," *VT* 3 [1953] 209–24) suggested that it only meant a superlative (cf. Fohrer, "the highest star"). M. Dahood ("Punic *hkkbm ʾl* and Isa 14:13," *Or* 34 [1965] 170–72) has demonstrated the close connection of El to the stars (cf. Job 22:12; Ps 147:4; Isa 40:26).

13.b. הַר־מוֹעֵד, "the mount of assembly," means "the mountain where the gods assemble." Apparently the phrase is so common that "gods" could be left out (cf. Ugar. *pḫr mʿd;* Akk. *puḫur ilī*).

14.a. במתי, "high places," "hills," or, more likely here, "backs."

17.a. תבל, "world," is fem. Therefore the Eth. version has a fem. suf., עריה, "her cities," instead of MT ועריו, "his/its cities." LXX καὶ τὰς πόλεις (followed by Syr., Arab.) suggests reading an abs., וערים, "cities."

17.b. MT פתח, "open." LXX ἔλυσε and Syr. *sᵉraʾ,* "set free." Wildberger (535) suggests an emendation for the last word of v 17 and the first of v 18: instead of ביתה כל, "their homes all," read בת הכלא "the house which he keeps locked."

18.a. 1QIsaᵃ, LXX, Syr. omit כלם, "all of them."

18.b. Wildberger suggests that איש בביתו, "each in his house," is a gloss. The repetition of "house" suggests an echolike gloss or a deliberate emphatic play on the house of prisoners and the tombs of the kings.

19.a. MT מקברך, "from your grave." LXX ἐν τοῖς ὄρεσιν, "in the mountains." Vg. *de sepulchro tuo,* "from his tomb." Wildberger (535) reads as *mem privativum,* meaning "without your tomb." The text does not require the meaning "thrown out of your tomb" but may be read "thrown out without a tomb."

19.b. MT נצר, "sprout." LXX ὡς νεκρὸς ἐβδελυγμένος, "as a loathsome dead one." σ´ ἐκτρωμα, "an abortion," "aborted fetus," which in Heb. would be נפל. α´ ἰχωρ and Jerome's *sanies* mean "fluid from a running wound" (KBL). Wildberger (536) follows the emendation first suggested by F. Schwally ("Miscellen," *ZAW* 11 [1891] 257) to read נפל, "aborted fetus." It makes a good parallel to

כפגר מובס, "like a trampled corpse," at the end of the verse. Erlandsson (*Burden of Babylon,* 37) cites the Vg. *stirps* and Syr., which both mean "shoot," to support MT. He understands it as a "wild vine, which is felled and left useless" (18:5, 6). Schwally's emendation offers the best solution.

20.a. מרעים, "wicked ones," breaks the direct reference to the king by the pl. LXX σπέρμα πονηρόν and Syr. *zarʿā bišāʾ* are sg. Marti understood the phrase to be related to 1:4. Wildberger (536) interprets both instances to mean "a race composed of evil doers" rather than "descendant of evil doers."

21.a. MT אבותם, "their fathers." LXX τοῦ πατρός σου, "your father," and Syr. suggest a sg. to match the previous line. M. Dahood ("Hebrew-Ugaritic Lexicography I," *Bib* 44 [1963] 291) calls the Heb. a pl. *excellentiae.* G. Rinaldi (*BeO* 10 [1968] 24) translates עון אבותם as "fathers' guilt."

Form/Structure/Setting

Isa 14:3–4*b* announces the משל, "taunt poem," that follows in vv 8–20*a.* It further heightens the contrast between Babylon's fate and Israel's hope (cf. vv 1–2). Vv 4*b*–7 directly precede the משל but say nothing specifically about the king of Babylon. The poem is an extended exclamation of joy and relief that "YHWH has shattered . . . the rod of rulers." This is the center of the chiasmus governing chaps. 13–14. The subject of the poem is YHWH, as in most of the units that constitute the two-chapter scene. The meter sets it off from the *qinah* lines in 3+2 that will follow.

The משל, or taunt, proper, is found in vv 8–20*a.* The taunt is characterized by its direct address to the fallen and disgraced tyrant. It has a common style and content that could have been sung by any of Israel's neighbors about any aspiring world conqueror—in sharp contrast to the YHWH-centered content and form of vv 4*b*–7.

Lohmann *(Die anonymen Prophetien)* and Jahnow *(Das hebräische Leichenlied)* recognized the basic elements of the funeral song like those in David's lament over Saul and Jonathan (2 Sam 1:19–27), "How the mighty are fallen!" The taunting song parodies that cry in vv 12 and 15 to portray the tyrant's plunge from his pretentious heights to his unlamented disgrace. Other elements of the lament are reversed in the taunt.

The term משל, "parable" (see *Comment* on v 4 for further discussion of meaning), normally describes a proverb or story that draws a comparison. This describes the poem well. A normal element in a lament contrasts the "once" with the "now." The Vision has already done this effectively in describing Jerusalem's change (1:21–23). (Because the taunt is understood to be appropriate at a future time [14:3–4*a*], the "once" of the taunt is the real "now" of the scene in which it occurs.) The taunt ridicules the pretensions of divine status and power that the tyrant affected with the bitter reality of his overthrow and assassination (vv 11–15). His ambitions are compared to the gods (vv 13–14*a*). His end is compared unfavorably with that of kings (vv 18–19*a*). His abandoned corpse is likened to those that all too often are simply "thrown away" (v 19*b*–*d*). The frame of the poem contrasts his condition in life with that in death.

Similar passages may be found in 37:22–29 and in Ezek 19:1–4; 27:2–10, 25*b*–36; and 28:12–19, where funeral songs are sung after the event and use the perfect tense. This is equally true here. The poem consists of four parts: vv 8–10, the response of the trees and the kings in Sheol; vv 11–14, "How you have fallen!"; vv 16–17, thoughts of onlookers; and vv 18–20*a,* a contrast to the usual royal funeral. Two responses to the poem are included in this pericope because they refer to the king of Babylon, but they are separate speeches: v 20*b* is a proverb; v 21 is an order for the execution of his sons.

The king of Babylon in 14:4*b*–21 functions as a foil to the idealized messianic king of Isa 11. Terms used in chap. 11 to describe the reign of the messianic king recur in 14:4*b*–21 to portray God's destruction of the king of Babylon. Franke sees many parallels between chaps. 14 and 47 in descriptions of the treatment of Babylon.

Comment

3–4*a* ביום, "in the day," refers to the fulfillment of the words of vv 1–2. הנים, "giving rest," is a term taken from Israel's old traditions. In some contexts it meant to settle down in Canaan after long years of wandering (Deut 3:20; Josh 1:3). In others it referred to peace from surrounding foes (Deut 12:10; 25:19; Josh 23:1; cf. Wildberger, 538; G. von Rad, "Es ist noch eine Ruhe vorhanden dem Volke Gottes," in *Gesammelte Studien zum Alten Testament* [Munich: Kaiser, 1958] 1:101–8). But this setting speaks of rest from "trouble," "turmoil," and "hard labor." עבדה, "labor," means the slave labor imposed by an oppressive government or conqueror. The parallel in Israel's tradition is that of slavery in Egypt. Chap. 40 will pick up that theme again.

4–7 The verses portray a time to come for Israel, like that of chap. 11 for Jerusalem. Then Israel will say, as Jerusalem will say (chap. 12), the things that follow.

ונשאת המשל הזה, "you [masc. sg.] will raise this taunt." מָשָׁל means to "compare." The noun is used for a parable, a synonym, or a proverb, but it can also be used for the ironic comparison of a taunting song. משל appears in Num 21:27 and in Isa 28:14 for those who are taunting. The actual song begins in v 8.

על־מלך בבל, "over the king of Babylon." Most readers expect a taunt over Assyria. That is the nation causing Israel's pain and slavery in the eighth century. But the Vision focuses first on the Neo-Babylonian Empire of Nebuchadnezzar. Vv 3–4 look beyond his fall to a time when his prowess will be well on the way to oblivion in the ruins of his city but when YHWH's "rest" for his people will have only begun.

Vv 4–7 precede the taunting song proper. They say nothing about the king of Babylon. Their theme, instead, speaks of the coming rest (v 7). אֵיךְ, "how," is an element taken from funeral poems (cf. 2 Sam 1:19, 25, 27) but is used here in exultation over an end to tyranny rather than in grief over a hero. In these verses (4–7) it is not the person of the tyrant but the condition of tyranny whose end is celebrated. Thus, appropriately, the impersonal מַרְהֵבָה, "onslaught," determines the translation of נֹגֵשׂ, "oppressing" (rather than "oppressor"), and the word שבת, "ceased," is used rather than the usual נפל, "fell." The poem celebrates YHWH's victory; having "shattered . . . the rod of rulers" and brought "rest" and "quiet," his victory provokes "joyful song." YHWH's triumph is the key element in the chiastic structure of chaps. 13–14 (see the chiastic diagram in the introduction to 13:2–14:23). As such it draws together the themes of the entire section. Oppression has ceased because YHWH himself has broken the power of rulers. "All the land is at rest" because of YHWH's intervention.

8 Mesopotamian kings regularly took working parties to the forests of Lebanon to cut timber to build their palaces and public buildings. Such timber is unavailable in Mesopotamia. See the account of Nebuchadnezzar (*ANET,* 307; for other Mesopotamian references, *ANET,* 275, 291; for Ugarit see *ANET,* 134; for Egypt see *ANET,* 27b, 240b, 243). The fall or weakening of a monarch or empire brought welcome respite to Lebanon's forests.

F. Stolz (*ZAW* 84 [1972] 141–56) and R. J. Clifford *(Cosmic Mountain)* have drawn on texts such as *ANET,* 307, and on OT passages such as Ezek 31 and Isa 14 to depict on Lebanon's mountains a divine garden planted by God. The Vision and Ezekiel have used the concept for serious theological reflection (Wildberger, 546). Thus the verse continues the depiction of YHWH as the Forester of 10:33–34 and of 10:15–19.

9–11 If one follows the view of Stolz, the verses portray the fall into the underworld, the nether regions of the dead, of the intruder into YHWH's garden. (Note the parallel to banishment from Eden for the offense of tampering with YHWH's trees.) שאול, "Sheol," without an article, as usual, is the underworld, the place of the dead (cf. *IDB,* a–d, 787–88). The etymology of the word has been explained variously. W. F. Albright (*Oriental Studies,* FS P. Haupt [Baltimore: Johns Hopkins UP, 1926] 143–54) and W. Baumgartner ("Zur Etymologie von *sch*ᵉ*ʾol,*" *TZ* 2 [1946] 233) used the Akkadian *suʾaru,* the dwelling place of Tammuz in the underworld, to explain it. L. Köhler ("Schᵉʾol," *TZ* 2 [1946] 71–74; KBL) derived it from שאה and compared it with Arabic *sûʾ* and *sûʾa,* "catastrophe." Others have sought to derive it from a root שול, like Arabic *safala,* meaning "be low," or from שאל, "to ask," as a place where one must answer for one's deeds. E. Devaud ("Gefilde der Binsen," *Sphinx* 13 [1910] 120) sought to derive it from an Egyptian word for life beyond this one. *HAL* finds neither the Egyptian nor the Akkadian derivation convincing. LXX has translated sixty-one of the sixty-five appearances of שאול with ᾅδης, "Hades," showing that the two concepts are very close (cf. Wildberger, 548). Vg. uses *infernum* or *inferi.* W. Zimmerli's section on the realm of the dead (*Ezekiel,* BKAT 12.2 [Neukirchen-Vluyn: Neukirchener Verlag, 1969] 784) is very useful here.

The inhabitants of Sheol are the רפאים, "ghosts." They are the "dead" (מתים) who are in Sheol (26:14; Ps 88:11 [10]) or in אבדון, "Abaddon" (Ps 88:12 [11]). The origin of the term is complicated by use of the word to describe a race of giants in very ancient Palestine (cf. Gen 15:20; Deut 3:11), which led LXX to translate the word γίγαντες and Vg. *gigantes,* "giants." The Ugaritic texts have added a new complication. They use *rpum* for seven mythical beings. J. Gray ("The Rephaim," *PEQ* 79 [1949] 127–39) considers the Ugaritic *rpum* to be an ancient royal family whose members were later considered able to guarantee fertility as members of the followers of Baal. Wildberger's judicious advice (549) is sound. The three uses of רפאים (in Ugarit, for giants and for the dead) should be considered separately until we learn a better way to relate them. He adds that *rpum* may be related to Hebrew רפא, "to heal," while רפאים in the sense of inhabitants of the underworld may come from רפה, "to sleep." The latter meaning certainly fits the context of v 10.

The realm of the dead is normally still and silent. But the fall of the tyrant "stirs" it, especially the area reserved for the former great ones of the earth, who "rouse" themselves to greet the newcomer. They even speak (or sing) in chorus: "You have been made like ourselves," weak, silent, and helpless.

12–15 *The Fall of Helel.* As v 8 seems to pick up themes of an ancient myth of God's forest in Lebanon, so this section seems to be based on another such myth. A possible summary of the story would be: Helel son of Shachar (or "Shining One, Son of Dawn") was a great hero who determined to make himself the equal of a god, El Elyon (or "the Most High"). His ambition was to raise himself above the clouds, above all the stars of god, to the very mountain in the farthest north where gods gather, there to reign as king over the universe, including the gods. But the conclusion of this ill-advised ambition was his precipitous fall into Sheol, perhaps after a battle with El Elyon himself. It is generally thought that this story must have come from a culture outside Israel, but as yet no such myth has been found in Canaan or among other peoples. The taunt in vv 12–15 has "historicized the motif and poetically related it to the fallen tyrant" (cf. A. Ohler, *Mythologische Elemente im Alten Testament* [Düsseldorf: Patmos, 1969] 175–77).

The passage begins with the usual *qinah* opening: איך, "How!" But the next phrase, "from heaven," sets the one being addressed apart from ordinary mortals. This is further demonstrated by the comparison with Helel son of Shachar. הילל, "Helel," is unknown in the OT. LXX translates the entire name ἑωσφόρος ὁ πρωὶ ἀνατέλλων, "Eosphoros (Morning Star), who makes the morning rise." Vg. has *Lucifer, qui mane oriebaris,* "Lucifer, you who made the morning rise."

שחר, "Shachar," is known as a god's name. In the OT, Ps 139:9 speaks of his "wings"; Job 3:9; 41:18, "his eyelashes" or "rays." Other references (Song 6:10; Pss 57:9; 108:3; 110:3) show personalized poetic views of the dawn that may reflect such an idea. Phoenician theophoric names carry the name ברשחר, שחרבעל, as does 1 Chr 7:10: אחישחר *Achishachar,* "my brother is Shachar" (cf. R. de Vaux, "Le Textes de Ras Shamra et l'Ancien Testament," *RB* 46 [1937] 547 n. 3). A Ugaritic text ("Shachar and Shalem") portrays El's fathering Shachar and also his birth by one of El's wives. He is seen as parallel to Shalem, the god of twilight. In Ugarit, Shahar is also found in personal names (cf. Stolz, *ZAW* 84 [1972] 182 n. 10). Some interpreters would change שׁ to שׂ because in other Semitic languages שׂחר means the moon god, called "Newmoon, son of (old) moon." Wildberger calls this nonsense when applied to "the son of dawn."

הילל, "Helel," is much more difficult to trace (cf. McKay, *VT* 20 [1970] 450–64; Craigie, *ZAW* 85 [1973] 223–25). Arabic *hilâlun,* "new moon," has led many to translate this Hebrew word as "New Moon" (GB, KBL, *BHS, HAL*). N. A. Koenig thought of it as the waning moon. Wildberger points to the Hebrew root הלל, "to shine" (BDB, 237), and relates it to Akkadian usage to show that it is an epithet for a god, not a name. Grelot ("Isaïe XIV 12–15 et son arriere-plan mythologique," *RHR* 149 [1956] 18–49) and McKay have picked up Duhm's suggestion (1922) of a connection with the Greek myth of Phaethon (Φαέθων). The name was used for one of the horses that pulled the chariot of Eos (Homer, *Odyssey* 23.245). The name in other places may refer to the sun or to the son of Helios since it, like הלל, means "shining." Hesiod (*Theogony* 986) calls Phaethon the son of Eos, the star Venus. In *Theogony* 378, Hesiod reports that Eos gave birth to the morningstar ἑωσφόρος, also called φωσφόρος, or Lucifer. Grelot concludes that Helel, son of Shahar, is the same divinity known as Phaethon, son of Eos. The other Phaethon, son of Helios and Klymene, was reported in his ambitious daring to have tried to drive his father's chariot, the sun, with its horses of fire, through the clouds. This exceeded his abilities so that Zeus was forced to intervene to prevent a universal catastrophe. By a lightning bolt he made Phaethon crash to earth (McKay, *VT* 20 [1970] 450–64; Grelot, *RHR* 149 [1956] 30–32). If this story were transferred to the other Phaethon, the parallel to Isa 14:12–15 would be apparent. McKay pursues a similar suggestion. But Wildberger (552) and Craigie have warned against using the Greek parallels. Too many differences appear between the Greek and Canaanite mythologies. Craigie supports Albright (*Archaelogy and the Religion of Israel* [Baltimore: Johns Hopkins UP, 1942] 84, 86) and Oldenburg ("Above the Stars of El: El in Ancient Arabic Religion," *ZAW* 82 [1970] 199) in noting that *ʿAṯtar* had the epithet "the Luminous" (J. Gray, *The Legacy of Canaan*, 2d ed. [Leiden: Brill, 1965] 66). Thus the Canaanite background is more credible than the Greek.

Whatever the myth might have said, the text in Isaiah tells of a tyrant king who is overcome, not by the resistance of a god but by his own ambition to be as high as a god, to "ascend to heaven," to reign above the stars, to sit in "the mountain assembly," and to be "like the Most High." Three locations for the Most High, or Elyon, are given. In Canaanite mythology El's dwelling was above the stars, in heaven. The OT speaks of אל השמים, "El of the heavens" (Ps 136:26; Lam 3:41). In Jerusalem God is commonly understood to dwell in heaven and look down on earth (Isa 18:4; Ps 14:2). "The mountain assembly" is located "in the farthest north." It appears in this context as a synonym for "heavens." The same combination occurs in Greek thought (E. Oberhummer, PW 18.1 [1939] 277–79). The idea of a mountain assembly for the gods was widespread in the area. It was regularly understood to be "in the farthest north," whether this be spoken in Mesopotamia, in Canaan, or in Greece. Ps 48:3 (2) likens Zion, YHWH's holy mountain, to צפון, "the north."

V 14 speaks of עליון, "Most High." This was an epithet for El (cf. Gen 14:18–22) in Jerusalem from earliest times. It was widely used in Canaanite stories. It is particularly suitable in the poem for the assonance of אעלה, "I will rise," with לעליון, "to the Most High." He is also called the Lord of Heaven. He is the highest, the ruler of all. Wildberger (555) properly notes that the OT knows nothing of attempts to dethrone YHWH but often voices the wish of people and tyrants "to be like [דמה] God" (cf. the fourfold use of the word in Ezek 31). If it was common for funeral songs to praise the "incomparable" person who had died, the taunt satirically points to his wish to be "comparable" to divinity.

Yet his ambitions (v 15) led to being "brought down [not up] to Sheol [not heaven], to the deepest pit [not the farthest north]." The same word, ירכתי, has been rendered "deepest" and "farthest." This is the basic message of the taunt: "You have died and gone to Sheol." On *Sheol,* see *Comment* on v 9 above. בור, "pit," is actually a cistern (an underground room) and is regularly used, parallel to Sheol, to describe the place of the dead (cf. N. J. Tromp, *Primitive Conceptions of Death and the Nether World in the Old Testament,* BibOr 21 [Rome: Pontifical Biblical Institute, 1969] 166).

16–20*a* The observations of those who view the corpse reflect their astonishment and horror. The body has not been buried but has been abandoned like garbage (v 19). He shares the fate of the dead among the poorest people: like the "aborted fetus," like the clothes of one stabbed in a brawl, one killed in a fall, or one trampled by a mob or on a battlefield, he is simply dumped in a pit and left to the birds and animals.

It is hard to believe that this man once ruled the world with tyrannical cruelty and absolute power. Now he is contrasted to kings who rule through orderly processes and are buried with honors (v 18). But this tyrant is in disgrace because he is perceived to have "fouled his own nest": he "destroyed [his] own land" and "killed [his] own people."

20*bc* The tyrant has no hope for the future—not even in memory. Poirier reports a parallel to Isaiah in the third century B.C.E. Callimachus' Epigram 56, which was engraved on a candlestick in a dedicatory phrase: "Looking on my light you will say: 'Hesperus, how art thou fallen'" (*VT* 49 [1999] 379). Poirier suggests that "Isaiah and Callimachus independently attest to a stock expression of mock lament, fashioned from a popular myth." He thinks that there are references to two myths: one in v 12 to the Phaeton myth, which is referred to from Plato/Aristotle to the Latin poets of the early Christian century; the other in vv 13–15 reflects a "more diffuse myth of an attempted *coup* of heaven." The metaphors are used extensively in Revelation (cf. D. Aune, *Revelation 1–5,* WBC 52 [Dallas: Word Books, 1997] 210–11).

21 The verse may also be spoken over his corpse. It puts into effect the curse of 20*bc* by ordering the execution of his sons. But a massive change must be noted: vv 8–20 speak of the results of ambition, a kind of fateful, deserved end. But here people are urged to take matters into their own hands. It was often Near Eastern practice to execute the family of a fallen ruler (cf. 1 Kgs 15:28–30; 2 Kgs 10:17). The use of אבותם, "the fathers," suggests that guilt belongs to the dynasty, not simply to the man. But the idea is broader (cf. Exod 20:5; 34:7).

The second half of the verse bases the execution on prevention: "so they cannot . . . possess the earth" and build cities. It was common practice among Assyrians and Persians (and later Greeks and Romans) to maintain control of conquered lands by building their own fortresses and administrative cities there. They guaranteed their fame and protected their borders in this way. Such cities must have been both feared and hated by the indigenous populations.

Explanation

The opening paragraph sees the end of the Babylonian tyranny in terms of the "rest" it brings to Israel. YHWH's aggressive action has brought the power of the tyrant to an end. Now the people can sing.

This powerful taunt song, which is proposed as appropriate for Israel to sing when the king of Babylon is dead, must be seen for what it is and is not. It is not specifically Israelite or Yahwistic in content or theology. It is not specifically tailored for the king of Babylon. It is a masterful poem to be sung over a tyrant who has fallen victim to his ambition and pride. Its picture of death and the realm of the dead was common to the ancient Near East. Israel, for lack of a specific doctrine of its own, shared it, even if without conviction. The apparent reflection of a "Lucifer myth" in v 12 is just that. It is a simile to picture the fall and disgrace of the tyrant.

The poem has meaning in the Vision and in Scripture only in its context as a poetic embellishment of the promises of vv 1–7, the warnings implied by the judgment on Babylon and its king (vv 20*a*–23), and the assurance of God's control of history (vv 24–27). The fragile and temporary nature of tyrannical power is the theme. It speaks to the human tendency to idolize momentary power, forgetting how fleeting its terror and its glitter can be, forgetting that history's mills "grind slow but wondrous fine." Death is the great leveler. This is a universal truth that requires neither revelatory explanation nor theological reflection—only dramatic reminder. The one who depends on the power of an individual, contrary to the lasting social structures and contracts, will not survive death. This bit of common wisdom also needs only to be spoken to be found true. When the poem has been used in apocryphal and Christian circles to picture the fall of an angelic Satan, the reference must be to the shadowy mythical background of the poem rather than to the poem itself. It is significant that the account of the fall of Satan (Rev 12) makes no reference to Isa 14.

Oracle against Babylon (14:22–23)

Bibliography

See listings under *Excursus: Babylon and the King of Babylon in the Vision of Isaiah* in the *Comment* on Isa 13:1.

Translation

YHWH:	22 *And I shall rise against them.*	2+3
Herald:	*Oracle of YHWH of Hosts.*	
YHWH:	*And I shall cut off for Babylon*	2+2+2
	name and (surviving) remnant,[a]	
	offspring and descendant.	
Herald:	*Oracle of YHWH.*	2
YHWH:	23 *And I shall establish her to (become)*	
	a possession of porcupines and pools of water,	3+2+3
	and I shall sweep it with the broom of destruction.	
Herald:	*Oracle of YHWH of Hosts.*	3

Notes

22.a. MT ושאר, "and remnant." Syr. š^{e}ʾer, "flesh" (cf. *BHK*). Wildberger (536) interprets as "blood relative." 1QIsa[a] ושארית is a variant on MT. In 2 Sam 14:7 שם, "name," and שארית occur together (cf. H. Wildberger, "שאר," *THAT*, 2:844–55).

Form/Structure/Setting

Vv 22–23 with their oracle against Babylon are a natural conclusion to the Babylonian-period material of 13:17–14:21. Vv 22–27 have often been treated together, but there are some basic obstacles to doing that. The two passages (vv 22–23 and vv 24–25) deal with two separate eras in Palestine: the Babylonian is the later (ca. 612–539 B.C.E.) preceded by the Assyrian period (ca. 740–612 B.C.E.). Despite the reference to "king of Babylon" in 14:4, Oswalt (7, 10) supposes that the taunt song (14:4–21) refers to Assyrian kings. O'Connell (*VT* 38 [1988] 417–18; *Concentricity and Continuity*, 114 n. 1) thinks the song was "directed, alternatively, against the king of Babylon (where the ending is provided by 14:22–23) or the king of Assyria (where the ending is provided by 14:24–25)."

It seems more likely that the oracle against Babylon (14:22–23) brings to an end the section that deals with the Babylonian period (chaps. 13:1–14:22), while that against Assyria (14:24–25) opens the section that deals with the Assyrian era (14:24–23:18; for more detailed defense of this temporal analysis, see the outline of chaps. 13–27 in the introduction to these chapters). Vv 26–27 emphasize כל הארץ, "the whole earth," and כל הגוים, "all the nations," and are a fitting introduction for the chapters that follow.

Comment

22 As in Isa 13:1 and 14:19–22, the object of God's wrath is again Babylon itself, not simply her king and dynasty. The verse fulfills and strengthens the curse of 13:19–22. Interpreters (most recently Wildberger, 560) have suggested that Babylon is here much more than the Chaldean capital; rather it represents the contemporary "super power" (as it does in Rev 18:10, 12). Undoubtedly, overtones of the broader symbolism are here (cf. *Excursus: Babylon and the King of Babylon in the Vision of Isaiah* at 13:1 above).

The destruction will be total. שם, "name," includes its reputation, fame, and value. A שאר, "remnant," though it be a very small one, may hope for restoration. Babylon will have none. No נין ונכד, "offspring or descendant," emphasizes the absolute destruction of the city as a people.

23 The city as a geographical location, a place of human habitation, will be equally destroyed, covered with swamps, peopled by wild animals. טאטא, "sweep," and מטאטא, "broom," have the same root in Hebrew and occur only here. The root may be derived from טיט, which means "mud," "dirt," "slime," a fitting connection with the pools of water and mud that have occupied the low-lying areas of a city no longer protected by dikes and levees.

Explanation

This oracle of YHWH's determination to "cut off Babylon" closes the section that began in 13:17 with the announcement that YHWH was stirring up the Medes against Babylon. It emphasizes the certainty of that decision. This assurance is the support for Israel's hope that this dark period may be drawing to an end. Israel's nightmare had lasted almost two hundred years, but the end was in sight with the assured fall of Babylon.

The Assyrian Period (14:24–23:18)

Isa 14:24–25 draws the reader's attention back to the Assyrian period. Chaps. 15 through 23 are set in that period. Assyria's king Tiglath-Pileser made a major move to establish his sovereignty over Palestine in 734 B.C.E. by pushing Egyptian force and authority back into Egypt itself. This began a period of Assyrian dominance of Palestine and threat to Egypt that lasted until Babylon, with the help of Media and Egypt, overthrew Nineveh in 612 and the last of the Assyrian army in 609 B.C.E. Isa 14:24–25 turns the reader's attention back to this Assyrian period. Everything that follows through chap. 23 will fit the period.

The first part of the burden of Babylon (13:2–14:23) addressed the implied readers/audience of the end of the Babylonian period (mid-sixth century). This part and the third part (chaps. 24–27) form an envelope around the burdens of 14:24–23:18, which fit in the Assyrian period (eighth to seventh centuries). Isa 14:24–25 alerts the reader to the shift with a reminder (cf. 10:12) that YHWH is in charge of this process and means to use the Assyrian power only briefly to attain his purpose.

Excursus: King Hezekiah (ca. 715–701 B.C.E.)

Bibliography

Donner, H. "The Separate States of Israel and Judah." In *IJH.* 415–21. **Hall, H. R.** "The Ethiopians and Assyrians in Egypt." *CAH,* 3:270–88. **Kitchen, K. A.** *Third Intermediate Period in Egypt.* 362–80. **Randles, R. J.** "The Interaction of Israel, Judah, and Egypt from Solomon to Josiah." Diss., Southern Baptist Theological Seminary, Louisville, 1980. 168–95. **Spalinger, A.** "The Year 712 B.C. and Its Implications for Egyptian History." *Journal of the American Research Center in Egypt* 10 (1973) 95–101.

Isa 14:24–23:18 is marked temporally by references to the death of Ahaz (14:28), a narrative about Isaiah's activity during Hezekiah's reign (chap. 20), and a notice of the demotion of Hezekiah's chief ministers (22:14–25). The years that followed Ahaz's death (14:28) offered unparalleled opportunity to fulfill the glorious vision of 9:1–6 and chaps. 11–12. Assyria had established a line of political and military control along the southern borders of old Israel, Aram, and the coastal area of Philistia. This left to Judah the opportunity to extend her influence in the Transjordan states (chaps. 15–16). Judah's loyal tribute to Assyria over almost two decades, as well as the elimination of rival powers on her northern border, had removed any threats from that direction (chap. 17).

Changes in Egypt offered promising opportunities. A major shift of influence and power occurred in the last quarter of the eighth century B.C.E. Libyan sovereignty, the Twenty-Second Dynasty, was drawing to a close. Nubian (Ethiopian) power was rising under a king called Pianchi. Between 730 and 720 B.C.E. Pianchi invaded and established his rule as the Twenty-Fifth Dynasty as far north as Memphis. But he did not go on to establish his rule over all Egypt. Until 715 B.C.E. the major cities of the delta were ruled by minor kings under what has been called "the Kingdom of the West" with a capital in Sais (the Twenty-Third Dynasty). Pianchi died in 716 B.C.E. and was succeeded by his brother, Shabaka (716–702 B.C.E.). Shabaka's determination to force all Egypt to recognize his rule, as well as his willingness to cooperate with Assyria, offered an unparalleled opportunity for Judah's participation (chaps. 18–19).

This short period marks the years when the party represented by Shebna and Eliakim controlled Judah's foreign policy. Their ill-conceived adventures spoiled any hope that the prophecies of 9:1–6 and chaps. 11–12 could be fulfilled in Hezekiah.

LITERARY STRUCTURE OF ISA 14:24–22:25

After establishing the setting in 14:24–27, three scenes depict the Assyrian period. The first (chaps. 15–16) portrays the hopes and opportunities that existed for Judah early in Hezekiah's reign, about 715 B.C.E. The second (chaps. 17–19) continues the theme of optimism but ends on a shocking note of reversal (chap. 20). The time is about 715–712 B.C.E. The third (chaps. 21–22) portrays the disastrous results of challenging Assyria's suzerainty in 705 to 701 B.C.E.

Following Ahaz's death about 715 B.C.E. (cf. 14:28), Gilead, Samaria, and Ashdod had become Assyrian provinces. The Vision's attention turns to the small nations to the east of Judah. Moab's problem came not from the Assyrians but from someone out of the desert, or from a revolt of the poor in their own land (chaps. 15–16). She turned to Jerusalem for help, thereby rousing the city to hope for a renewal of David's old authority (16:5) over Moab. The ruin of Damascus and the fate of Israel are balanced by a hint of emissaries from far-off Cush who seek Jerusalem's favor (chaps. 17–18).

The act portrays Egypt as weak and in disarray. Her condition provides an opportunity for the Lord to picture hope for an age of blessing in which Assyria, Egypt (under Ethiopian rule), and Israel will play leading roles. Isaiah's prophecy at the time of the Ashdod rebellion (713–712 B.C.E.) is directed against any idea in Jerusalem that help against Assyria could be expected from the Egyptians. Judah apparently did support the Philistine rebels initially, but then sent tribute to Sargon II before he arrived at the theater of war. Hezekiah's essential tendency toward seeking independence by force presages the tenor and events of his reign. The tendency precluded the fulfillment of the beautiful vision of 19:25.

The destruction of Babylon, the site of the only major rebellion against Sargon to succeed for any length of time, came in 710 B.C.E. and is noted in chap. 21 with the emotional disappointment of Jerusalem. The uneasiness of the region is reflected in the burden on Edom and the picture of the Dedanites from Arabia, which matches the depiction of Moab in chaps. 15–16. Chap. 22 is a bitter scene of Jerusalem in confusion, poorly armed, and poorly prepared for battle. Two high officials, Shebna and Eliakim, are charged with neglect of duty. Chap. 23 describes the approaching fall of Tyre. Assyrian armies had accomplished what God had intended: the devastation of the whole land. But the devastation is not complete. Jerusalem is still standing, Edom has not been mentioned, and readers know that Babylon regained its power and eventually overcame Assyria.

Astonishingly, these chapters avoid the name of Hezekiah altogether. He is not mentioned in the hints of hope, in the warnings concerning royal policy, or in the blame for disaster in 701 B.C.E. (See the following *Excursus*.) Instead, senior officials of his administration are introduced by name (22:15–24): Shebna and Eliakim, who are also known from 2 Kgs 18:18. Throughout, a speaker using the first person represents the attitudes of the government (15:5–9; 16:9, 11;

21:2–4, 6–7, 10, 16; 22:4, 14). Shebna is not identified until the end, but he is probably this spokesman.

Excursus: Silence about Hezekiah

Hezekiah is not mentioned by name in the section that obviously portrays a part of his reign. Why not?

2 Kings and 2 Chronicles make much of Hezekiah's religious reforms. The Vision of Isaiah ignores them. Instead it points to his political policies and military ambitions. The unfortunate way in which religious zeal is often equated with "hawkish" and chauvinistic political and military policies is a major problem that receives too little attention. The Vision faces up to the issues involved.

Hezekiah and Josiah are two cases in point. Both are praised in the histories of Kings and Chronicles for monotheistic reforms in conformity with the old confederacy and with the authority of Moses (2 Kgs 18:4–6; 2 Chr 30:14–15). They are also recognized for their conformity to David's ways (2 Kgs 18:3; 2 Chr 29:2). They, more than any others, strove to reestablish the power and greatness of David's era. Like David, they blended commitment to cultic renewal and glory with efforts to expand their borders and press their military advantages to the limit. This entire program won the approval of the historians in 2 Kings and 2 Chronicles. Both of them succeeded briefly (Hezekiah for about four years; Josiah for some twenty-five to thirty years), but the historians uncritically attribute to them total success (2 Kgs 18:7*a;* 22:2; 23:25; 2 Chr 29:2; 31:20–21; 2 Chr 34:2).

Did they whip up religious enthusiasm and zeal to unify and strengthen the state in its political aims? Or did they see political independence and military strength as necessary for religious loyalty and faithfulness? Or did they see them as two sides of the same coin: prosperous independence and power as rewards for reform and faithfulness to God's law?

The Deuteronomistic History (2 Kings) and 2 Chronicles lean to the last of these possibilities. Isa 22 points to the first. It argues that Judah under Shebna and Eliakim, Hezekiah's ministers, presumed upon God's intentions. They presumed that YHWH wanted independence and power for Judah, that God's will and their policies were identical. On this basis they whipped up support for the war (22:13) and made desperate efforts to arm the city (22:9–11*a*) without asking about YHWH's specific intentions for that moment (22:11*b*).

The Vision has contended that political independence did not necessarily lead to fidelity to YHWH. Political power had not brought justice to the poor. Success was more likely to create hubris than to breed spirituality (cf. G. Brunet, *Essai,* 157–58).

Therefore, YHWH was not necessarily committed to a policy of independence and power for Israel or Judah. God looked for more. The Deuteronomistic History, in attributing total "success" to Hezekiah, failed to see that. The Chronicler also missed that point, as many devout interpreters since that time have done. Both the Chronicler and the Deuteronomist thought of Hezekiah and Josiah as "bright spots" in Judah's history. The Vision sees them rather as two more steps to ultimate doom. God has had enough of blood sacrifices and rituals, which cultic reform proliferated (1:11–17). There is no emphasis in 2 Kings or 2 Chronicles on justice for the poor in the land. God wanted political decisions that were realistic in view of his support of the Assyrians (chaps. 8–10). He wanted recognition that only in repentance and turning to YHWH could salvation be found (30:15). Neither Shebna nor Eliakim was capable of this. They both lost God's support and favor.

The Vision refuses to see hope for Judah in cultic reform or in religious revival, as 2 Kings and 2 Chronicles apparently do. It calls instead for a consistent political and religious policy that accepts God's decisions about Israel's and Judah's roles in history. These had been revealed through Isaiah (chaps. 7–10) and are viewed as still valid in 705–701 B.C.E., in 640–609 B.C.E., and indeed in 435 B.C.E. Nationalistic revival is not a part of God's plan for Israel or Judah in that time. Cultic reform that is seen as a means to nationalistic revival is flawed from the start.

The potential for progress toward peace and prosperity that was open to Hezekiah is pictured in chap. 19. It lay in cooperation with Assyria and Ethiopia. His government, presumably in 715 B.C.E. under Shebna, chose instead to depend on Egypt's illusory promises, i.e., those of the delta kings whose days were numbered anyway. Judah entered briefly into the Ashdod conspiracy. Fourteen years later, their policies unchanged, they came under the condemnation of God and the retribution of Assyria.

The Vision names Shebna and Eliakim, but not Hezekiah, although the act certainly applies to his reign. It names them in order that full judgment may fall upon the policies involved rather than be diverted by personal attacks on the popular king.

YHWH's Plan for Assyria and the Whole Land (14:24–27)

Bibliography

Bailey, L. R. "Isaiah 14:24–27." *Int* 36 (1982) 171–76. **Barth, H.** *Die Jesaja-Worte in der Josiazeit.* 103–19. **Childs, B. S.** *Isaiah and the Assyrian Crisis.* 38–39. **Clements, R. E.** "Isaiah 14.22–27: A Central Passage Reconsidered." In *Book of Isaiah.* Ed. J. Vermeylen. 253–62. **Dietrich, W.** *Jesaja und die Politik.* BEvT 74. Munich: Kaiser, 1976. 120–21. **Donner, H.** *Israel unter den Völkern.* 145–46. **Eareckson, V. O.** "The Originality of Isa 14:27." *VT* 20 (1970) 490–91. **Fichtner, J.** "Jahwes Plan in der Botschaft des Jesaja." *ZAW* 63 (1951) 16–33. **Gonçalves, F.** *L'expédition de Sennachérib en Palestine dans la littéraire hébraïque ancienne.* Louvain-la-Neuve: Université catholique de Louvain, 1986. 33–36, 307–9. **Gosse, B.** "Isaïe 14,24–27 et les oracles contre les nations du livre d'Isaïe." *BN* 56 (1991) 17–21. **Høgenhaven, J.** *Gott und Volk bei Jesaja.* 126–27. **Huber, F.** *Jahwe, Juda und die anderen Völker beim Propheten Jesaja.* 41–50. **Jenkins, A. K.** "The Development of the Isaiah Tradition in Is 13–23." In *Book of Isaiah.* Ed. J. Vermeylen. 249–51. **Jensen, J.** "YHWH's Plan in Isaiah and in the Rest of the Old Testament." *CBQ* 48 (1986) 443–55. **O'Connell, R. H.** "Isaiah xiv 4B–23: Ironic Reversal through Concentric Structure and Mythic Allusion." *VT* 38 (1988) 407–18. **Skehan, P. W.** "Some Textual Problems in Isaiah." *CBQ* 22 (1960) 47–55. **Vermeylen, J.** *Du prophetie Isaïe.* 1:252–62, 296–97. **Werner, W.** *Studien zur alttestamentlichen Vorstellung vom Plan Yahves.* BZAW 173. Berlin: De Gruyter, 1988.

Translation

Herald:	24 *YHWH of Hosts has sworn:* [a]	4
YHWH:	*Just as I thought (it),*	2+2
	so it came to be. [b]	
	Just as I plan (it),	2+2
	will it be established: [b]	
	25 *to shatter Assyria in my land.*	3+3
	On my mountains I shall trample him.	

Herald:	*And his yoke will depart from them.*[a] *His burden*[b] *will leave its*[a] *shoulder.*	3+4
First Speaker:	26 *This is the strategy* *that is planned for the whole land.*	2+2
	This is the hand *that is stretched out over all the nations.*	2+2
Second Speaker:	27 *For YHWH of Hosts has planned (it).* *Who can thwart (it)?*	4+2
	His hand (is) the one stretched out.[a] *Who can turn it back?*	2+2

Notes

24.a. For אם־לא in an oath, see Joüon §165*c;* J. Wash Watts, *Survey of Syntax,* 148–49.

24.b. היתה and תקום are fem.; translate as neuter (cf. Joüon §152*c*). The change of tense is remarkable. 1QIsa[a] uses impf. in both (תהיה for MT's היתה). LXX translates ἔσται and μενεῖ, both fut. ind. Donner (*Israel unter den Völkern,* 145) translates היתה as present pf., "has happened," and תקום as fut., "it shall come to pass." The first refers to Assyria's rise to power, the second to God's judgment over its arrogant pride.

25.a. LXX reads ὤμων for שכמו, a pl. "their" for MT's sg. "his," as do OL, Syh., Syr., Tg., Vg., Eth., and Arab. Wildberger (565) notes that this is an almost verbatim quote from 10:25*b* and that congruence in sufs. would probably not be required. 1QIsa[a] has מעליכמה (2 m. pl.) and שכמכה (2 m. sg.), using 2d person instead of 3d (like 10:25) but also moving from pl. to sg. Perhaps "them" refers to the mountains, while "its" refers to the land.

25.b. MT סבלו, "his burden." LXX τὸ κῦδος αὐτῶν, "their fame." H. S. Gehman ("Errors of Transmission in the LXX," *VT* 3 [1953] 399) suggests that κῦδος is an internal Greek corruption of κῆδος, "their trouble." σ´ and θ´ translate literally: βασταγμα, "suffering."

27.a. MT הנטויה, "(is) the one outstretched." LXX lacks the article (cf. M. Lambert, *REJ* 50 [1905] 261), as does the similar construction in chaps. 5 and 10. However, the emphasis on "YHWH's hand" and question of "who can withdraw it" justify keeping it. See also the use of the article in v 26.

Form/Structure/Setting

Vv 24–25 are cast as an oath spoken by YHWH of Hosts that Assyria will, in time, be eliminated from Palestine. It begins with an assurance that YHWH's plans and his fulfillment are congruent and may be trusted. It closes with an echo of his promise in 10:27. This passage parallels the Day of YHWH passage in 13:9–16. YHWH's oath is a form used frequently in prophetic oracles. The closing couplet of v 25*b* is almost an echo, a reminder of the promise spoken in 10:27.

The third passage (vv 26–27) is the strongest claim for YHWH's strategy in a book in which the idea occurs repeatedly. It parallels the first Day of YHWH passage in 13:6–8. The question-and-answer format imitates wisdom style (see Eareckson, *VT* 20 [1970] 490–91; Childs, *Isaiah and the Assyrian Crisis,* 128, 136). It is spoken in the third person in a kind of concluding summary (see 17:14*b;* 28:29), which Childs sees as drawn from wisdom's pedagogical concern (187). The combination of direct quotation from God with prophetic reflection is common in prophetic books (H. Wildberger, "Jahwewort und prophetischer Rede bei Jeremia," diss., Univ. of Zurich, 1942). Most such reflection has explanatory, causal, or adversative content, but this passage strengthens and confirms what precedes (Wildberger, "Jahwewort," 102).

Vv 24–25 turn attention back to Assyria with an oath to destroy Assyria in Palestine. If 13:17–14:21 has a setting near the end of the Babylonian period, then Assyria is no longer a power in Palestine and has not been for decades. This reference to Assyria takes the reader back to a prior period. It introduces the scene (14:24–23:18) that forms the bulk of the following sections, the parts that deal with burdens, all of which fit within the Assyrian period.

The Assyrian invasions were introduced for the Vision in chap.7, and the following chapters (8–10) dealt with that period when Assyria was still very much a factor in Palestine even as Judah and Jerusalem with their king had survived the first onslaughts. See *Excursus: King Hezekiah (ca. 715–701 B.C.E.)* above.

Comment

24 The oath formula stresses YHWH's firm consistency and faithfulness. The two distich lines speak of the ways that thought (plan) and action (fulfillment) go together with God. The thought of having Assyria serve as his agent in change and punishment has, by this time, actually been largely accomplished. The campaigns of 733–32 and 724–21 B.C.E. had demonstrated that, as had the deportation of Israelites in 720 and 718 B.C.E. The second distich calls for recognition of YHWH's plan to limit the period and extent of Assyria's power (10:12) and trust that the "plan will [in due time] be established."

25*a* The intention to destroy Assyria in Canaan, God's land, is spelled out.

25*b* This is a comment on the assuring oath: that the Assyrian hegemony will end for "them," the mountains of Palestine, and for "it," the land that YHWH claimed as particularly his own.

26–27 The "strategy that is planned" is the one that the entire Vision reveals and discusses (see *YHWH's Strategy* in the *Introduction*). It includes the judgment on his people and the purification of his city (chaps. 1–5). It covers the role of the Assyrian and judgment on those who oppose this role. It will be shown in later chapters to span the time to the exile and the Persian period. But the verses stress again the impossibility of successfully opposing God. Only God himself can end the punishment, can call off the Assyrians, can turn back the judgment. Rebellion or resistance is futile.

Explanation

An oath and a proclamation declare YHWH's strategy and power. The destruction of Babylon for its rebellion and the certain end of Assyrian power over Canaan are fixed in God's plan, assured by his authority and sovereignty. The steady diet of terror and anxiety in the book has been broken a second time (after the promise that YHWH will have compassion on Jacob [14:1–12]) with the reminder that YHWH's intervention has reasons and goals. He is still in control.

The terrible wars of the eighth to the sixth centuries B.C.E. in Palestine were no less a source of terror and mourning for the peoples when they were identified as having been sent and directed by YHWH himself. The peoples and Israel are called to fear and to wail the losses. If they are indeed the work of God, one may expect some reason for them. One may look for "the plan" that guides them, the goals and results that YHWH wants to gain from them. Israel's sin and resistance to God have led to her destruction (733 and 721 B.C.E.) and to her deportation (720 and 718 B.C.E.), but the neutral stance of Ahaz had made it possible for his dynasty to continue and for Jerusalem to survive. Undoubtedly, these points were not missed by the early readers of the Vision. Nor should they be missed by the modern reader.

The people of God, Israel, are called to look beyond the terror and the destruction to see the hand of God in what emerges from the destruction of war. The sovereign kingship of YHWH of Hosts may be seen in the direction of the battles, but also in the reconstruction afterward. He is well worth waiting for.

In the Death Year of King Ahaz (14:28–32)

Bibliography

Beck, B. L. "The International Roles of the Philistines during the Biblical Period." Diss., Southern Baptist Theological Seminary, Lousiville, 1980. 146–50. **Begrich, J.** "Jesaja 14, 28–32: Ein Beitrag zur Chronologie der israelitisch-judäischen Königszeit." *ZDMG* 86 (1932) 66–79. Reprinted in *Gesammelte Studien zum Alten Testament,* TB 21 (Munich: Kaiser, 1964) 121–31. **Brunet, G.** *Essai.* 154–57. **Childs, B. S.** *Isaiah and the Assyrian Crisis.* 59–61. **Donner, H.** *Israel unter den Völkern.* 110–13. **Fullerton, K.** "Isaiah 14:28–32." *AJSL* 42 (1925) 80–109. **Gitin, S.** "The Philistines in the Prophjetic Texts: An Archaeological Perspective." In *Hesed ve-emet.* FS E. S. Frerichs, ed. J. Magnes et al. BJS 320. Atlanta: Scholars Press, 1998. 273–90. **Haak, R.D.** "The Philistines in the Prophetic Texts." In *Hesed ve-emet.* FS E. S. Frerichs, ed. J. Magnes et al. BJS 320. Atlanta: Scholars Press, 1998. 37–51. **Irwin, W. A.** "The Exposition of Isaiah 14:28–32." *AJSL* 44 (1927–28) 73–87. **Kedar-Kopfstein, B. A.** "A Note on Isaiah 14:31." *Textus* 2 (1962) 143–45. **Savignac, J. de.** "Les 'Seraphim.'" *VT* 22 (1972) 320–25. **Tadmor, H.** "The Campaigns of Sargon II of Assur: A Chronological-Historical Study." *JCS* 12 (1958) 22–40, 77–100. ———. "Philistia under Assyrian Rule." *BA* 29 (1966) 86–102. **Vermeylen, J.** *Du prophète Isaïe.* 1:297–303. **Wiseman, D. J.** "Flying serpents?" *TynBul* 23 (1972) 108–10.

Translation

First Speaker:	28 [a]*In the death year of King Ahaz* [b] *this burden came to be:*	4+3
YHWH:	29 *Do not rejoice, you Philistines, all of you,*[a] *that the rod that struck you* [b] *is broken.*	4+4
	For, from the root of a snake *a viper will emerge,* *and his fruit (will be) a flying snake.*	3+2+3
	30 *And the firstborn* [a] *of poor people will find pasture.* *The needy will lie down in safety.*	3+3
	But I shall destroy [b] *your root by famine,* *and your remnant someone will kill.*	3+2
Chorus:	31 *Wail,*[a] *oh gate!* *Howl, oh city!*	2+2+3

Melting away,[b] *O Philistia, all of you.*
For a cloud comes from the north, 4+3
and (there is) no straggler[c] *in its ranks.*[d]
First Speaker: 32 *What can one answer a nation's*[a] *ambassadors?* 4
Second Speaker: *That YHWH has secured Zion,* 4+4
and in her[b] *the afflicted of his people find refuge!*

Notes

28.a. In Syr. *mšḳl' dplšt* = משא פלשת, "burden of Philistia," is placed before the section. It is an obvious editorial addition intended to add clarity of organization like the headings that follow.

28.b. MT אחז היה, "Ahaz, there came." J. A. Bewer ("Critical Notes," in *Old Testament and Semitic Studies*, FS W. R. Harper [Chicago: Chicago UP, 1908] 2:224–26; *AJSL* 54 [1937] 62; *FS A. Bertholet* [Tübingen: Mohr 1950] 65) emended to read וָאֶחֱזֶה, "then I envisioned" (cf. 6:1). Wildberger has aptly noted that this would not make sense without the name of the king to date the passage. It was apparently inspired by Bewer's conviction that the passage could not possibly date from this time. MT is to be kept and respected.

29.a. כֻּלֵּךְ, "all of you," is a unique construction (cf. also v 31) with a slight variation, כֻּלָּךְ, in Song 4:7 (GKC §127*b–c;* Joüon §94*h*).

29.b. MT שבט, "the rod that struck you." LXX ὁ ζυγὸς τοῦ παίοντος ὑμᾶς, "the yoke of striking you," seems to read the Heb. as a const. gen.

30.a. MT בכורי, "firstborn of." Some medieval MSS have בכרי, which appears to imply a pointing בְּכָרַי, "my firstborn." But 1QIsa[a] supports MT. LXX omits the word. While the phrase "firstborn of poor people" may be strange, it should be kept (cf. Donner, *Israel unter den Völkern,* 110 n. 1).

30.b. The 1st person of MT והמתי, "I shall destroy," has been challenged. LXX ἀνελεῖ, "he will kill," followed by Tg. 1QIsa[a] supports 1st person here but changes יהרג, "one will kill," to אהרג, "I will kill," harmonizing the second verb with the first, while LXX does the reverse. It is not uncommon in the dramatic style of the vision to have YHWH speak a line that interrupts another's speech. MT should be sustained. For other suggestions, cf. Wildberger; G. R. Driver ("Hebrew Scrolls," *JTS* 2 [1951] 25).

31.a. הילילי, "wail," is fem. sg. while שער, "gate," is masc. Apparently the word עיר, "city," which is fem., dominates the grammar.

31.b. נָמוֹג, "melting away," is an inf. abs. Brockelmann (*HebSyntax,* 1–2) and others suggest that an inf. abs. may serve as an impv. But it is better to maintain its own grammatical integrity and read it as continuing the mood of the previous impvs.

31.c. MT בודד, "one separating himself." 1QIsa[a] מודד, "one measuring." G. R. Driver holds to the original and translates "deserter" (*JTS* 2 [1951] 26). Donner *(Israel unter den Völkern)* follows the variant and translates "no one counts their hosts."

31.d. מוֹעָד is also difficult. BDB (418) translates the *hap. leg.* with "appointed place," like the noun מוֹעֵד. *HAL* and *DCH* provide this option but also an alternative: "horde" or "multitude." Ziegler cites a late LXX MS with the reading ἐν τοῖς συντεταγμένοις αὐτοῦ, "in his completion." B. Keder-Kopfstein ("Note on Isa 14:31, " *Textus* 2 [1962] 144) suggests that this may derive from Heb. בְּנוֹעָדָיו (*nip'al* ptc. pl.), "in his summoned troop." He suggests with Vg.'s reading of *effugiet* that בודד, "one separating himself," should be emended to נודד and the whole translated "none is fleeing among his summoned troop." MT is at least as good and may be kept. The meaning is the same.

32.a. LXX ἐθνῶν, "nations" (also Syr., Tg.). But MT is correct in context and should be kept.

32.b. MT ובה, "and in her." 1QIsa[a] ובו, "and in him," turns the attention back to YHWH rather than to Zion. Either reading is possible. But MT's reading is consistent with the close relation of YHWH and Zion in Isaiah.

Form/Structure/Setting

The introduction calls vv 29–30 a "burden." Like that over Babylon and those that follow, the phrase is used with so-called foreign prophecies. As noted in 13:1, this can be deceiving. Sweeney calls it a "pronouncement." But the setting is not a Zion festival where nations bow to Zion's king. It is one in which YHWH of hosts moves the nations about to do his will and punishes those, like Philistia, that resist him. All four Assyrian rulers of the period campaigned in Philistia, as did Nebuchadnezzar II in the Neo-Babylonian period.

The whole passage becomes a parable for Judah and Jerusalem to teach them the futility of resisting God's signals. V 31 is a choral "woe" over Philistia, whose funeral is near. The avenging army is in sight. V 32 is a cryptic conclusion which, as Blenkinsopp has noted (292), joins other interpolated Zion passages (2:2–4; 4:2–6; 10:12, 20–27*a;* 11:10; 14:1–2) "to establish a common perspective on the events recorded and therefore a vantage point from which they can be viewed and interpreted" (cf. also Pss 46, 48, 76, and 87). In Isaiah, the Ahaz period began with a question mark over Jerusalem's fate in 734 B.C.E. (chap. 7). As it draws to a close, the city and the throne have survived to have the question raised again. In 7:7 Isaiah answered: "It will not happen." V 32 confirms: "YHWH has secured Zion!"

Comment

28 בשנת־מות המלך אחז, "in the death year of King Ahaz." In the confused chronology of the period, this could be 718 B.C.E. (sixteen years after 735–734, when Ahaz began to reign; 2 Kgs 16:1) or 715 B.C.E. (fourteen years before 701 B.C.E.; 2 Kgs 18:13) or 728 B.C.E. (four years before 724 B.C.E., when Shalmaneser marched on Samaria). The more likely dates are 718 or 715 B.C.E.

For משׂא, "burden," see the *Comment* on 13:1 and also there *Excursus: "Burden" (*משׂא*) in the Prophets.*

29 שׁבט, "the rod that struck you." Does this image refer to King Ahaz or to Shalmaneser? The superscription (v 28) may be construed to imply the former, but it would be strange to use serpent imagery of a Judean king. Yet the two may be related. There was a rebellion against Assyria in Palestine after the death of Shalmaneser. Ahaz followed his earlier practice and remained a loyal vassal. Philistine cities joined in the rebellion. The rod and the snake are best understood as references to Shalmaneser, who laid siege to Samaria for so long and who dominated Palestine. The viper and darting adder are references to Sargon, who broke the Palestinian rebellion in 718 and in 714 B.C.E.

30 The repression of uprisings will restore order so the common people can dwell and work in safety. YHWH himself will put down the uprising and punish the rebels. For this rebellion Philistia will share Babylon's fate.

31 The verse returns to the call to mourning of v 29*a*. The coming of Assyrian armies from the north signals their approaching end.

32 The verse implies that an embassy sits in the antechamber of the palace awaiting an answer. What is the occasion? Have they brought an invitation for Ahaz and Judah to join the uprising? Or do they know of Ahaz's illness that has brought him to his deathbed? Either of these or both may be implied by vv 28–31. In either case the answer is clear. YHWH is the foundation of Zion's security. Not Sargon, not alliances, not armed rebellion—but YHWH! It is significant that no mention is made of the new king (or king to be), Hezekiah. The emphasis remains on YHWH alone. The second stich repeats a basic theme of the Vision. Israel's future lies with Zion. This theme, rather than the messianic theme, dominates the book. עמו, "his people," must refer to the remnant of Israel, as well as to Judean villagers. The city is and will be a secure refuge.

Explanation

The notice of Ahaz's death marks the close of an era. Philistia with Babylon symbolized the implacable rebels against Assyrian power in the ninth decade of the century. So together they are judged. The balance of power still lay with Assyria. The constant warfare was a disaster for the village people, and YHWH's signal still summoned the Assyrian. The other side of the coin showed YHWH's support for a neutral Zion, still following the Ahaz doctrine of passive vassalage with Isaiah's support. Neutral Zion will provide refuge for God's people, which the belligerent Samaria was unable to do.

Burden: Moab (15:1–16:14)

Bibliography

Alonso Schökel, L. *Estudios de poética Hebrea.* Barcelona: Flors, 1963. ———. "Traducción de textos poéticos, III. Isa 15–16." *CB* 18 (1961) 336–46. **Barrick, W. B.** "The *Bamoth* of Moab." *Ma'arav* 7 (1991) 67–89. **Bartlett, J. R.** "Edom." *ABD.* 2:287–95. **Bonnet, C.** "Echos d'un rituel de type adonidien dans l'oracle contre Moab d'Isaïe (15)." *SEL* 4 (1987) 101–19. **Carroll, R. P.** *Jeremiah: A Commentary.* Philadelphia: Westminster, 1986. 778–97. **Christiansen, D.** "Zephaniah 2:4–15: A Theological Basis for Josiah's Program of Political Expansion." *CBQ* 46 (1984) 669–82. **Dearman, J. A.** "The Moabite Sites of Honronaim and Lulith." *PEQ* 122 (1990) 41–46. **Donner, H.** "Neue Quellen zur Geschichte des Staates Moab in der zweiten Hälfte des 8. Jahrh. v. Chr." *MIOF* 5 (1957) 155–84. **Easterly, E.** "Is Mesha's *qrhh* Mentioned in Isaiah xv 2?" *VT* 41 (1991) 215–19. **Hookermann, J.** "[Is 15,5 *horonim*] Etymological theories 5." *BMik* 32.109 (1986) 124–34. **Jones, B. C.** *Howling over Moab: Irony and Rhetoric in Isaiah 15–16.* SBLDS 157. Atlanta: Scholars Press, 1996. ———. "In Search of kir Haresheth: A Case Study in Site Identification." *JSOT* 52 (1991) 3–24. **Knauf, E. A.** "Jeremia xlix 1–5: Ein zweites Moab-Orakel im Jeremia-Buch." *VT* 42 (1992) 124–28. **Landes, G.** "The Fountain at Jazer." *BASOR* 144 (1956) 30–37. **Miller, J. M.** "Moab and the Moabites." In *Studies in the Mesha Inscription and Moab.* Ed. J. A. Dearman. Atlanta: Scholars Press, 1989. **Mittmann, S.** "The Ascent of Luhith." In *Studies in the History and Archaeology of Jordan I.* Ed. A. Hadidi. Amman: Department of Antiquities, 1982. 175–80. **Olivier, H.** "Archaeological Evidence Pertaining to a Possible Identification of Ar-Moab and er-Rabbah." *NedTT* 30 (1989) 179–89. **Power, E.** "The Prophecy of Isaias against Moab." *Bib* 13 (1932) 435–51. **Rendtorff, R.** "Zur Lage von Jaeser." *ZDPV* 82 (1966) 163–208. **Rudolph, W.** "Jesaja XV–XVI." In *Hebrew and Semitic Studies.* FS G. R. Driver, ed. D. W. Thomas and W. D. McHardy. Oxford: Clarendon Press, 1963. 130–43. **Schottroff, W.** "Honoraim, Nimrim, Luhith, und der Westrand des 'Landes Astoreth'; (Jes. 15 . . .)." *ZDPV* 82 (1966) 163–208. **Smothers, T. J.** "Isaiah 15–16." In *Forming Prophetic Literature.* Ed. P. House and J. W. Watts. 70–85. **Worscheck, U.,** and **E. A. Knauf.** "Dimon und Horonaim." *BN* 31 (1986) 70–95. **Zapletal, V.** "Der Spruch über Moab: Is. 15–16." In *Alttestamentliches.* Freiburg: Universitäts-Buchhandlung, 1903. 163–83.

Translation

Herald:	1 *Burden: Moab.*	2
Messenger:	*Indeed! In a night*[a] *it was destroyed;*	3+3
(to Jerusalem's	*Ar (in) Moab*[b] *was silenced.*	
court)	*Indeed! In a night it was destroyed.*	3+3
	Kir of Moab was silenced.[c]	
	2 [a]*The daughter of Dibon has gone up*[a]	3+2
	(to) the High Places to weep.	
	Over[b] *Nebo and over*[b] *Medeba*	4+2
	Moab wails.[c]	
	On all its heads[d] *(is) baldness:*	3+3
	[e]*every chin shaved bare.*[f]	
	3 *In its*[a] *streets they dress in sackcloth.*	3+2
	On their rooftops[b] *and in their open areas*[b]	
	all of them wail,	2+2
	collapsing[c] *with weeping.*	
	4 *Then Heshbon and Elealeh cried out.*	3+4
	Their sound was heard as far away as Yahaz.	
	Therefore the loins[a] *of Moab tremble.*[b]	4+3
	His soul is faint within him.	
The Prophet:	5 *My*[a] *heart cries out for Moab!*	3+2+2
	Its refugees[b]*—far as Zoar,*	
	Eglath Shelishiyah!	
Messenger:	*Indeed, (on) the ascent of Luhith*	3+3
	they climb upon it with weeping.	
	Indeed, (on) the way of Horonaim	3+3
	they raise a cry of destruction.[c]	
	6 *Indeed, the waters of Nimrim*	3+2
	are dried up.	
	Indeed, the grass is withered.	3+2+3
	The shoots are used up.	
	Greenness does not exist.	
	7 *Because of this, the savings*[a] *(which) one had made*	4+4
	and their reserve funds,[b]	
	they carry over the valley of the poplars.	
	8 *Indeed, the outcry pervades*	2+2
	the border of Moab.	
	As far as Eglayim her howling (is heard);	3+3
	to[a] *Beer Elim—her howling.*	
	9 *Indeed, the waters of Dimon*[a]	3+2
	are full of blood.	
YHWH:	*Indeed, I shall put additional things upon Dimon:*	3+3+2
(from heaven)	*for the remnant of Moab—a lion,*[b]	
	and for the remainder—terror.[b]	
Moab's spokesman:	16:1 *Send*[a] *the lamb*[b] *of the land's ruler*	4+2+4
(to Moabites)	*from the rock in the desert*[c]	
	to the mountain of daughter Zion.	

2 *And it shall be:* 1+2+2
like a fluttering bird
pushed from the nest,
the women of Moab will be 3+2
(at) [a] *the fords of the Arnon.*
Moab's spokesman: 3 *Give* [a] *advice!* 2+2
(to Jerusalem) *Make decision!*
Establish your shadow like the night 3+2
between the noons.[b]
Hide refugees! 2+2
Do not expose a fugitive!
4 *Let them sojourn with you:* 2+2
Moab's banished ones.[a]
Become a hiding place for him 3+2
from a destroyer!
Herald: *When* [b] *the oppressor* [c] *shall have come to an end,* 3+2+3
destruction shall have ceased,
trampling [d] *shall be finished from the land,*
5 *a throne shall be established in integrity,* 3+3+2
and one shall sit on it with truth
in the tent of David,
judging and seeking justice 3+2
and expediting [a] *righteousness.*
Chorus: 6 *We have heard of Moab's pride:* 3+2
proud [a] *Moab!*
Its pride and its exaltation and its arrogance! 3+3
Its strength [b] *was not so.*
7 *Therefore it wails:* 2+2+2
Moab for Moab.
The whole of it [a] *wails.*
For the adults [b] *of Kir-Haresheth* 3+3
only the stricken moan.[c]
8 *For the fields of Heshbon* [a] 2+3+4
the vine of Sibmah languishes.
[b] *The lords of nations have broken down her choice vines* [b]
(which) touched Jazer, 2+2
(which) spread out (to the) desert.
Her shoots spread out 2+2
and passed over (to) the sea.
Prophet: 9 *Because of this, I weep,* 2+2+2
with Jazer's weeping,
(for) the vine of Sibmah.
I cover you [a] *(with) my tears,* 2+2
Heshbon and Elealeh,
because over your ripe fruit and over your harvest 3+2
a shout [b] *(of conquest) has fallen.*
YHWH: 10 *Joy and gladness are removed from the fruitful land.* 4+3
No one sings in the vineyards. No one cheers.[a]

	No one treads[b] *wine in the presses.*	4+2
	I[c] *have caused shouting to cease.*	
Prophet:	[11] *Because of this*	1+4+3
	my stomach murmurs for Moab like a lyre	
	and my inward being for Kir Haresbeth.	
Heavens:	[12] *And it shall be:*	1
	When he appears,[a]	2+2+3
	when he wearies himself,	
	Moab, on the high place,	
	when he comes to his sanctuary to pray,	4+2
	he will not be able.	
Herald:	[13] *This is the word that YHWH has spoken to Moab in time past.*	
	[14] *But now YHWH says:*	
YHWH:	*In three years*	2+2
	like the years of a bond-slave,[a]	
	the glory of Moab will be reduced	3+3
	in all the great murmur.	
	The tiny minuscule remnant[b]	3+2
	will not be much.[c]	

Notes

1.a. בְּלֵיל as a const. form before a relative clause (cf. Wildberger; Joüon §§129*q*, 158*d*) would mean "In the night (in which) Ar was destroyed." 1QIsa[a] בלילה and LXX νυτός (followed by Syr., Tg., Vg.) read it as an abs., "by night" or "in a night." The latter reading preserves the parallelism and is preferred. Other ways to the same result are to read ליל as לַיִל or simply to understand לֵיל as an abs. form, as König did (§337*y*).

1.b. LXX reads עָר מוֹאָב as ἡ Μωαβῖτις, "Moab," and קִיר־מוֹאָב as τὸ τεῖχος τῆς Μωαβίτιδος, "the wall of Moab." In both cases LXX has failed to see the names of towns or cities, trying instead to understand them as other Heb. words.

1.c. The second נדמה, "silenced," is omitted by LXX and Tg. but translated by α´ and θ´ as εσιωπησεν (aor.), "was silenced "; by σ´ as εσιωπηθη (aor. pass.), "became silent"; and by Vg. as *conticuit*, "silenced." KBL and L. Köhler (*Kleine Lichter*, 32–34) suggested that one should omit with LXX and Tg. But the stark repetition appears to be intended as emphasis. The *Translation* follows MT and the Greek versions.

2.a-a. Syr. and Tg. read עָלְתָה בַּת דִּיבֹן, "the daughter of Dibon has gone up," like Jer 48:18.

2.b. עַל usually means "upon" and has been so translated by most commentaries. It may also mean "concerning" and was so understood by Kissane, J. A. Bewer (vol. 1, chaps. 1–39), and Hertzberg. This would imply that the two cities in the north were already destroyed. But Wildberger notes that the actual invasion occurred in the south.

2.c. יְיֵלִיל (also in v 3 and 16:7) is different from the "normal" יֵילִיל. *BHS* suggests changing it. However, the special form must have been preserved for a reason (cf. אֲיֵלִיל in Jer 48:31, יְיֵלִילוּ in Hos 7:14, and תְּיֵלִילוּ in Isa 65:14; GKC §70*d*). They preserve the letter of the preformative from assimilation into the first letter of the root.

2.d. MT ראשיו, "its heads." 1QIsa[a] ראושו, "its head." Some MSS read simply ראש, "every head" (cf. Jer 48:37). LXX ἐπὶ πάσης κεφαλῆς, "on every head." However, MT makes sense. The pronoun refers to the country, not the cities.

2.e. 1QIsa[a] and many versions and MSS add ו, "and." MT may be kept.

2.f. MT גרועה appears in several MSS as גדועה, which is a more usual word for "hacked off" or "cut off." MT is an unusual form but certainly not impossible (cf. G. R. Driver, *WO* 1 [1947] 29). Cf. Ezek 5:11.

3.a. The suffixes in the verse vary from masc. to fem. Masc. probably refers to Moab as a people. Fem. refers to it as a country or to its cities.

3.b. Ancient and modern scribes have sensed a verb lacking here. LXX supplies καὶ κόπτεσθε, "and beat their breasts in mourning." G. R. Driver (*JTS* 41 [1940] 163) suggests קָעוּ, meaning "they cry." Rudolph ("Jesaja XV–XVI") suggests יְנֹהוּ or נָהוּ, "they oppress," and is followed by Kaiser. A better course is to keep MT and divide the verse differently. See *Translation.*

3.c. ירד, lit. "go down." KBL suggests "weeping up and down." Wildberger sees only a metaphor, "they flow down in tears."

4.a. חֲלֻצֵי, "prepared for military service." LXX reads ἡ ὀσφὺς, "the loins," which renders חֲלָצֵי. The parallelism to the second stich supports LXX.

4.b. יָרִיעוּ, "raise a war cry," fits MT's reading of חֲלֻצֵי, "warriors." But it does not fit a setting of dismay. LXX γνώσεται, "knows," suggests Heb. ידע, as Gray recognized. A. Guillaume disagrees ("A Note on the Roots ריע, ירע, and רעע in Hebrew," *JTS* 15 [1964] 293–95). Others (Marti, Duhm, Kissane, Ziegler) suggest יָרְעוּ, "they trembled." Kaiser suggests רָעֲדוּ, with the same meaning.

5.a. LXX ἡ καρδία, "the heart." Tg. בליבהון, "their heart." But 1st person should be kept with MT. Cf. 16:9, 11.

5.b. 1QIsa[a] ברוחה; Syr. *brwḥh,* "in his spirit." Cf. LXX ἐν ἑαυτῇ, "in herself." G. R. Driver (*JSS* 13 [1968] 44) suggests that MT בריחה, "her refugees," should be read as בריחו, "his refugees." The word is usually an adj. (cf. BDB, 138), but here it is used as a noun.

5.c. יְעֹעֵרוּ is a unique word. BDB (735) and *HAL* explain it as a *pilpel* form from עור = יערערו, "raise a cry of destruction." The form occurs nowhere else and remains obscure.

7.a. יתרה, "savings," occurs only here and in const. in Jer 48:36; BDB (452) The dictionaries read it as a const. fem. noun related to יתר, "remain over," so "what is laid up" *(HAL)* or "abundance" *(DCH).*

7.b. פְּקֻדָּתָם, "their reserve funds," is used only here in this sense. Usually it refers to a commission, appointment, or office of some kind, but the parallel with יתרה, "savings," requires something like "what has been stored, deposited" *(HAL).* Perhaps it means that for which one is responsible.

8.a. LXX ἕως τοῦ φρέατος, "even to the well." Also Vg. *usque* and Syr. *wlbʾrʾ* presume an implied עַד, "unto."

9.a. MT דִּימוֹן, "Dimon"; 1QIsa[a] דיבון, "Dibon"; Vg. *Dibon;* LXX Ρεμμων; Syr. *rjbwn.* No Moabite city called Ribon or Dimon is known, so it would be easy to follow 1QIsa[a] to substitute the well-known town Dibon. But MSS of LXX read δειμων or δεμμων or δημων while Tg. α´ σ´ θ´ all support MT's דימון. (Cf. H. M. Orlinsky, "Studies in the St. Mark's Scroll-V," *EIJ* 4 [1954] 5–8; *The Bible and the Ancient Near East,* ed. G. E. Wright [Garden City, NY: Doubleday, 1961] 117–18.) Wildberger (592) suggests that Dimon may still be identical to Dibon, noting the identification of Dimona in Judah (Josh 15:22) with Dibon in Neh 11:25.

9.b. LXX καὶ Αριηλ . . . Αδαμα transliterates the Heb. words as names rather than as "lion" and "earth." The text of this half verse has raised many questions. J. Reider ("Contributions to the Scriptural Text," *HUCA* 24 [1952–53] 87) suggests emending שארית, "remainder," to שחל to parallel אריה, with a second word for "lion." G. Hoffman ("Versuche zu Amos," *ZAW* 3 [1883] 104) emends אריה, "lion," to אראה, "I have a vision," and אֲדָמָה, "ground," to אֲדַמֶּה, "I speak a parable." Kissane, Rudolph ("Jesaja XV–XVI"), Eichrodt, and Wildberger keep the MT but change אדמה, "ground," to אֵימָה, "terror" or "dread," which appears to be a good solution to a difficult text.

16:1.a. MT points שִׁלְחוּ as an impv., "send." Some MSS point it שָׁלְחוּ, pf., "They have sent." LXX ἀποστελῶ, 1st person fut. ind., "I will send." Also Syr. *ʾšdr* and Tg. יהון מסקי מסין למשיחא דישראל. Modern interpreters have tried many emendations like שָׁלְחוּ, אֶשְׁלַח, (וְ)שָׁלְחוּ, אֶשְׁלָחָה, but none improves MT.

1.b. MT כר משל־ארץ becomes in LXX ὡς ἑρπετὰ ἐπὶ τὴν γῆν, "like a reptile on the land," which apparently read the Heb. consonants as כְּרֶמֶשׂ לָאָרֶץ. Other emendations do not improve on MT. The Moabite ruler was traditionally known to possess great herds of sheep (2 Kgs 3:4).

1.c מדברה, "in or toward the desert," is a problem since Sela is not in the desert. LXX πέτρα ἔρημος, Syr. *kʾpʾdmdbrʾ,* and Vg. *de Petra deserti* are translations that have suggested the emendation סלע הַמִּדְבָּר, "rock of the wilderness." GKC (§90*d*) suggests that MT may be translated "from the rock in the wilderness."

2.a. One would expect a prep. before מעברת, "fords." The ancient versions have usually supplied one, as have modern translations.

3.a. K הביאו, masc. pl.; Q הביאי, fem. sg. Versions and some MSS have followed Q. 1QIsa[a] הביו (from the root יהב) suggests the reading הבי, "give." Wildberger (593) notes that the use of הביא עצה, "bring advice," is unknown in OT. But יהב עצה, "give advice," appears in Judg 20:7 and 2 Sam 16:20.

3.b. צָהֳרַיִם, "noons," is a dual form, perhaps a colloquial emphatic emphasis like "high noon."

4.a. MT נִדָּחַי is pointed as "my banished," *nipʿal* ptc. and 1st-person suffix. The word is familiar in Isaiah: see 11:12; 27:13; 56:8. The question turns on the suffix "my." LXX οἱ φυγάδες Μωαβ and Syr.

mbdr' dmw'b seem to read נִדְּחֵי, "banished one of Moab," as do two Heb. MSS. Kaiser suggests that the pronoun results from an "eschatological interpretation" of the passage.

4.b. כִּי introduces a dependent clause. The question is whether it relates backward to v 4*ab* or forward to v 5. Dillmann suggests the former and adds עַד, "until." But Wildberger is surely right in choosing the latter, as the *vav* that begins v 5 indicates.

4.c. הַמֵּץ is a *hap. leg.* BDB (568) and *DCH* relate it to מִיץ, "to press" or "to stir." Hence "extortioner" or "oppressor." 1QIsa[a] המוץ, "the chaff" (cf. 17:13), or חָמוֹץ (E. R. Rowlands, "Mistranscriptions in the Isaiah Scroll," *VT* 1 [1951] 228), "a ruthless one" (BDB 330), "an oppressor" (*HAL*).

4.d. תַּמּוּ, "finished," is pl. while רמס, "trampling," is sg. 1QIsa[a] תם is sg. LXX, Syr., and Vg. also read a sg.

5.a. מְהִר inf. const. from מהר, "to hasten." (Cf. E. Ullendorff, "The Contribution of South Semitics to Hebrew Lexicography," *VT* 6 [1956] 195.)

6.a. גֵּא is probably an error for גאה (cf. BDB; *HAL*). 1QIsa[a] has גאה, "proud" as do two Heb. MSS (cf. Jer 48:29).

6.b. בַּדָּיו is usually translated "idle talk" (BDB, 95; *HAL* IV; *DCH* III). It could mean "isolation" (BDB, 96). But Vg. translates here and in Jer 48:30 with *fortitudo* and *virtus*, "strength" or "might." C. Rabin suggests a similar meaning for the Hebrew ("Hebrew *baddim* 'Power,'" *JSS* 18 [1937] 57–58; so also *DCH* VI). לֹא־כֵן, "not so," suggests a contrast.

7.a. כֻּלֹּה is a strange but frequent form indicating entirety.

7.b. אשישי can mean "raisin cakes" (BDB, 84), but *HAL* and *DCH* consider "men, adults" more likely, as in 1QpHab 6:11; 4QRitMar 9:4. Jer 48:31 אַנְשֵׁי and Tg. אנש = "men of." G. R. Driver ("Notes on Isaiah," in *Von Ugarit nach Qumran*, BZAW 77 [Giessen: Töpelmann, 1958] 43) suggests comparing אשישי with Arab. *'atta*, "live comfortably." Thus "you shall moan for the luxurious dwellers of Kir-Hareshetti."

7.c. The pl. תהגו from הגה, "moan," breaks the chain of sg. verbs. Many change to a sg. with Tg. and one MS. However, if נכאים, "the stricken," is the subject, the pl. is correct. The word order is emphatic.

8.a. The pl. subject with sg. verb is a problem. GKC §145*u* explains the pl. as collective, but commentators still try emendations. Cf. G. R. Driver (*JTS* 38 [1937] 40), who suggests reading כי שדמות, "for the fields," as כשדמות, "as the fields of Heshbon, (so) does the vine of Sibmah languish." Tg. has a text that reads "Behold the armies of Heshbon are plundered, the districts of Sibmah beaten." Driver's suggestion provides a smoother text with a minimum of change, in spite of the Masoretic accentuation (contra Wildberger).

8.b-b. What is the subject of this stich? Some have thought בעלי גוים the subject and translated "the lords of the nations have broken down her choicest vines" (so NIV, RSV, following Fohrer, Kaiser, Bewer, and Gesenius). But others read שרוקיה as subject and translate "the choice grapes overcame (even) the lords of nations" (so Wildberger, Eichrodt, Steinmann, Duhm, Marti, Dillmann, Delitzsch, Hitzig). Yet the prominent position of בעלי גוים, "lords of the nations," favors the former reading.

9.a. אריוך has been judged an impossible form (cf. GKC §75*dd;* Bauer-Leander §57*t''*). 1QIsa[a] reads ארזיך, but this in itself is no help. Emendation may deal with the troublesome middle letters to read ארויך from רוה, "to saturate," meaning "drench you" (so NIV, Wildberger, *HAL*, and others).

9.b. NIV translates "been stilled," but see RSV "battle shout."

10.a. Many MSS, 1QIsa[a], Tg., and Vg. (perhaps LXX and Syr.) seem to read ולא, adding "and."

10.b. הדרך is missing in LXX. It is difficult to achieve in any other language the effect of the Heb. repetition.

10.c. The 1st person appears for the only time in this verse. LXX reads πέπαυται, a passive that might indicate reading a *hop'al* הָשְׁבַּת, "was stopped." But this is not reason enough to change MT.

12.a. Wildberger and others suggest omitting "when he appears" as dittography, especially since the use of the verb in this sense is unique. However, it makes sense, providing a rising intensity of meaning, and may be kept.

14.a. May also be "a mercenary" (cf. Jer 46:21).

14.b. LXX καὶ καταλειφθήσεται reads ושאר as a verb like וְנִשְׁאַר, "will be left over." Syr. and Vg. support this. MT makes sense as it is and should be kept.

14.c. 1QIsa[a] reads כבוד, "glory." LXX ἔντιμος, "honored." Both may be influenced by כבוד, "glory," in the previous line.

Form/Structure/Setting

Two chapters, 15 and 16, together fall under the title משׂא מואב, "burden of Moab." They are unified around the single theme of Moab's plight. The setting includes Jerusalem's court, where a messenger brings distressing news from neighboring Moab to Shebna, the principal government figure; YHWH's heavenly court, from which YHWH, Heavens, and a herald speak; and room for Moab's spokesman and Judah's chorus. The time is the beginning of Hezekiah's reign (about 718 B.C.E.).

The burden is composed of two "responses" (15:5*a* and 16:9*b*–12) over the disaster and a series of explanations beginning with כי, "for, because" (15:1, 5*b*–9; 16:4*b*). Six speeches surround the central speech in 16:3–4*a,* in which Moab makes her plea for aid. A final announcement brings an up-to-date word from YHWH concerning Moab.

Title: The Burden of Moab (15:1*a*)
A Announcement of Moab's desperate situation (15:1*b*–4)
  B YHWH's sympathetic, but determined, judgment (15:5–9)
    C Moab's decision to flee to Judah (16:1–2)
KEYSTONE Moab's appeal for refugees and its meaning (16:3–5)
    C´ Judah's choral recognition of Moab's collapse (16:6–8)
  B´ Shebna's lament over YHWH's judgment on Moab (16:9–12)
A´ Announcement that a tiny, weakened remnant will survive (16:13–14)

The reference in 14:28 to the death of Ahaz is a signal that these chapters are to be placed in the following reign, that of Hezekiah. The invasion that befalls Moab is not documented historically. An incursion of groups from the desert that drives the refugees toward the border of Judah fits the description given here. Isa 16:13–14 may be a sign that Moab's newfound allegiance to Judah was short-lived, as indeed the references to her participation with Assyria in the events of 701 B.C.E. imply.

The form of the speeches varies. Isa 15:1*b*–4 relates a straightforward account of the disaster, though told in a very emotional way. Vv 5–9 constitute a lament, although it becomes a threat in v 9. In 16:4*b*–5 is found a hopeful oracle that sees in the appeal from Moab the possibility of a restoration of the Davidic empire.

Note that the משׂא, "burden," here is not a prediction of disaster, not "an oracle." It is a scene noting the invasion and its results as a sign that imperial influence and the authority of the Davidic dynasty begin to reassert themselves at this time.

An almost identical verbal parallel to 15:2*c*–7*a* and 16:6–11 is found in Jer 48:29–37 (see Wildberger, 605–11, for a full treatment and bibliography). Jer 48 is clearly based on quotations from many texts, including Isa 15–16 and Num 21 and 24. The two passages have other parallels in Jer 11, 23, and 46.

The Isaiah parallels occur in the corresponding elements of the chiastic structure B-C and C´-B´ noted above. The composition is clean and straightforward. Whatever may have been their relation to the Jeremiah texts, their use in Isaiah is pristine and meaningful. If dependency exists, it is Jeremiah that is dependent on the Isaiah text, as F. Schwally ("Die Reden des Buches Jeremia gegen die Heiden," *ZAW* 8 [1888] 177–217), Duhm, Rudolph ("Jesaja XV–XVI"),

Schottroff (*ZDPV* 82 [1966] 163–208), Kaiser, and Alonso Schökel (*Estudios,* 420) have noted.

Excursus: Moab

Bibliography

Bartlett, J. R. "The Moabites and Edomites." *POTT.* 229–58. **Grohman, E. D.** "A History of Moab." Ph.D. diss., Johns Hopkins, 1958. **Molin, G.** "Moab." *BHH.* Vol. 2, cols. 1229–32. **Worschech, U.** *Die Beziehungen Moabs zu Israel und Ägypten in der Eisenzeit: Siedlungsarchäologische und siedlungshistorische Untersuchungen im Kernland Moabs (Ard el-Kerak).* Ägypten und Altes Testament 18. Wiesbaden: Harrossowitz, 1990. **Zyl, A. H. van.** *The Moabites.* POS 3. Leiden: Brill, 1960.

Moab is mentioned by name in 5:2, 4, 8, 9 and 16:2, 4, 6, 11, 12, 13, 14. All of the place names in the passage are to be found east of the Dead Sea in the strip of land that extends just north of the sea's north end, eastward to the edge of the wilderness, and southward just beyond the sea's southern tip. This is the territory that Moab inhabited during its thousand-year history.

The OT traces Moab's ancestry to Lot (Gen 19:37; Deut 2:9). The language of Moab is preserved on the Moabite Stone, which was discovered in 1868 and is now in the Louvre in Paris (cf. *ANET,* 320–21). The language is West Semitic, like Hebrew (cf. F. Cross and D. N. Freedman, *Early Hebrew Orthography* [New Haven, CT: American Oriental Society, 1952] 35–42; Van Zyl, *Moabites,* 161–92). They apparently occupied their land before the Israelites arrived (Num 21:25; 22; 23).

Interaction between Moab and Israel is attested by biblical references. Balaam's story in Num 22–24 documents a rivalry for territory at an early time. Apparently Benjamin paid tribute to King Eglon of Moab until Ehud delivered it. 1 Sam 14:47 mentions Saul's war with Moab. 1 Sam 22:3–5 tells of David's seeking refuge in Moab. He later subjugated Moab (2 Sam 8:2–12; 1 Chr 18:11).

The Moabite Stone reports that Omri and Ahab ruled the northern part of Moab for forty years. King Mesha brought tribute to the king of Israel (2 Kgs 3:4). Later he stopped the tribute, leading to an expedition by Joram of Judah and Jehoshaphat (2 Kgs 3:4–27). Amos refers to a continued break between Moab and Edom (Amos 2:1–3). But not much else is known of her history during the following century.

Then Moab was touched, like its neighbors, by Assyrian expansion. In 728 B.C.E. its name appears along with Ammon, Ashkelon, Judah, Edom, and Gaza in the list of those bringing tribute to Tiglath-Pileser III (*APOT,* 348, Text II R 77, line 10). Another text, a letter found in Nimrud (cf. H. Donner, *MIOF* 5 [1957] 159; H. W. F. Saggs, "The Nimrud Letters, Part II," *Iraq* 17 [1955] 134), says that Moab, Mushur, Gaza, Judah, and Ammon brought tribute. It would seem that Moab, like Ahaz, bought the Assyrians off from an invasion of their land. However, during this time Moab was threatened by nomadic elements from the desert, as a letter from that time relates (cf. Donner, *MIOF* 5 [1957] 156; Saggs, *Iraq* 17 [1955] 131). The invaders are reported to have come from the land of Gidir, but nothing more is known of this. The Moabites participated in the Ashdod rebellion against Sargon in 713–711 B.C.E., but like Judah and Edom changed their minds and paid tribute (cf. *ANET,* 287 [c]). In 701 B.C.E. Sennacherib reports that Kammusunabdi of Moab brought tribute and kissed his feet (*ANET,* 287, ii.37–iii.49).

Other references to Moab continue in the following century. They withstood an attack by Arabs in the reign of Ashurbanipal. Later they fought in Nebuchadnezzar's armies (2 Kgs 24:1). Jeremiah (27:3; 40:11) speaks of Moab, while Ezekiel records a threat against Moab (25:8–11). Later references refer to Moabites as persons, but never again as a country.

Comment

Most of my comments refer to the remarkable number of geographical names in these chapters. For locating these, Wildberger's map (610), Simons's study (*GTTOT* §§1245–66, map III*a*), and van Zyl (*Moabites*) have been of the most help. The number and precision of place names in these two chapters require comment, but not all can be precisely located now.

1 ער מואב, "ʿAr (in) Moab," is taken by Simons to refer to a district in Moab, which may also stand for the entire country. Its capital is קיר, "Kir," which is located "in the center of the district of the same name" near the middle of Moab in the upper Wadi el-Kerak, as it is known today. (Cf. also Isa 16:7, 11; 2 Kgs 3:25; Jer 48:3, 13.) Both ער and קיר may be related to Hebrew words meaning "city" and thus could be understood here as synonyms (cf. Wildberger, 611).

2 דיבן, "Dibon," is a town some twenty miles north of Kir. נבו, "Nebo," and מידבא, "Medeba," are villages east of the northern end of the Dead Sea another fifteen to twenty miles north of Dibon.

4 חשבון, "Heshbon," and אלעלה, "Elealeh" are villages northeast of Nebo and Medeba. יהץ, "Yahaṣ," is a village nearer Dibon. (Cf. Isa 16:8, 9.)

The disaster seems to have devastated the northern villages of Nebo and Medeba, Heshbon and Elealeh. Towns farther south, like Yahaṣ and Dibon, mourn and tremble.

5 צער, "Zoar" (Jer 48:4, 34; *GTTOT* §§1254, 404), is one of the five "cities of the plain" (Gen 14). The location of these cities near the Dead Sea is disputed. Deut 34:1–3 seems to locate Zoar near the foot of "Mount Nebo, the top of Pisgah (now located as Gebel en-Neba near the end of the Dead Sea), opposite Jericho" (*GTTOT* §§404–14). Another theory places all the "cities of the plain" near the south end of the sea with Zoar at the tip (cf. *MBA*, 26). עגלת שלשיה, "Eglath Shelishyeh," is not identifiable. *GTTOT* §1255 calls it "wholly unintelligible." לוחית, "Luhith" (Jer 48:5), חורנים, "Horonaim" (Jer 48:3, 5, 34), and נמרים, "Nimrim" (Jer 48:34), cannot be positively identified. They seem to describe a route for flight south to Edom.

8 אגלים, "Eglayim," is modern Rugm el-Gilimeh, southeast of el-Kerak. באר אילים, "Beer-Elim" (cf. Num 21:16), may be located in the Wadi et-Temed, northeast of Dibon.

9 דימון, "Dimon," lies some fifteen miles north of el-Kerak. (Cf. Jer 48:2: מדמן means "waters of Dimon.")

16:1 סלע, "rock" (cf. 42:11), may be a proper name. If so, it is the forerunner of Petra at Wadi Musa. But it is far more likely to be a reference to flight to the rocky heights.

2 מעברת לארנון, "fords of the Arnon," must refer to the point where the highway crosses the Arnon river south of Dibon.

7 קיר־חרשת, "Kir-Hareseth," is equivalent to Kir (15:1).

8–9 שבמה, "Sibmah," is located by *GTTOT* §298 near Heshbon. יעזר, "Jazer," is probably modern Hirbet Gazzir just northeast of the northern tip of the Dead Sea.

Explanation

The burden over Moab continues the call to wail and to mourn that appeared in 13:6–8 and continued in 14:31 for the Philistines. It reports mourning in Moab (15:2–4), records YHWH's joining in the weeping (15:5), and combines the two in 16:11–12. The mood of wailing and mourning fits the theme of devastation for the land, and the reader is invited to join in the funereal exercise.

What happened in Moab to occasion this outcry? Dibon's mourning (15:2) concerns the devastation of, first, the villages of Nebo and Medeba and, soon after, their neighboring villages, Heshbon and Elealeh (15:4). It is a national disaster (15:2). People flee the countryside around the southern end of the Dead Sea (15:5) and around the northern tip toward the Jordan. Jerusalem is to be entreated by gifts to accept the refugees (16:1–2). Moab asks for advice and support (16:3–4*a*). An announcement is heard that aggression will cease when the Davidic dynasty holds sway over the territory again (16:4*b*–5).

A chorus of Judeans proclaims Moab's pride to be the cause of her calamity (16:6–8). YHWH laments Moab's destruction, although he had occasioned it himself as judgment on her false worship (16:9–12). He acknowledges that this is judgment upon Moab (16:13) but relents to grant her a tiny and weak surviving remnant (16:14).

No evidence exists to suggest that Assyria invaded the country at this time or that a large army moved down the Jordan toward Moab or approached her from the south. The Transjordanian states were threatened repeatedly in their history by tribes from the desert. A letter tells of such an attack on Edom at about this time by the Gidiraya, who are presumed to be a tribe from the east (H. Donner, *MIOF* 5 [1957] 173; cf. Wildberger, 597). Van Zyl (*Moabites,* 20) regards 15:1–9*a* and 16:6–11 as originally parts of a taunt song composed by the bedouin to celebrate their victory. The suggestion that a slave revolt within the kingdom accounted for the destruction raises another possible explanation.

Moab's rulers appeal to Jerusalem to receive their refugees. A symbolic lamb is to be sent, reminiscent of the thousands that Mesha once sent in tribute (2 Kgs 3:4) to the king of Israel. Judah's authorities and people are sympathetic to the appeal. Even YHWH is sympathetic.

The implication is that Moab becomes Judah's vassal again. The Lord's judgment drives Moab back into the arms of the Davidic king in Jerusalem (16:5). It may well be that Moab joined Jerusalem and Ashdod in the rebellion against Assyria that was suppressed in 710 by Sargon II in his campaign against the Philistine states. Moab and Jerusalem withdrew from the coalition soon enough to avoid Assyrian wrath by paying tribute. The scene portrays the beginning of that process as Jerusalem is beginning to dream of restored glory. The first step is acceptance of Moab's invitation to Jerusalem to "establish your shadow" (16:3), that is, to cast the cloak of her protection over Moab.

Burdens: Damascus and Egypt, 716–714 B.C.E. *(17:1–20:6)*

Chaps. 17–20 form one symmetrical whole, which climaxes with the bringing of gifts to YHWH in Zion (18:7). Characteristic of the section are the "in that day" passages, with the variations "in that time" (18:7) and "in the year" (20:1). The thematic pattern is again an arch:

A *Behold* Damascus and Ephraim, ruined cities! (17:1–3).
  B *In such a day* the glory of Jacob will be like tiny leftovers (17:4–6).
    C *In such a day* mankind looks to the Creator (17:7–8).
      D *In that day* the cities are a desolation (17:9).
        E You (fem. sg.) forgot God your Savior (17:10–11).
          F *Woe!* The nations rage (17:12–14).
            G *Woe!* Go, swift messengers (18:1–2).
KEYSTONE *At that time:* Gifts will be given to YHWH in Zion (18:3–7).
            G´ *Behold!* YHWH will come to Egypt (19:1–15).
          F´ *In that day* Judah will be a terror to Egypt (19:16–17).
        E´ *In that day* five cities in Egypt will speak the language of Canaan (19:18).
      D´ *In that day* there will be an altar to YHWH in Egypt (19:19–22).
    C´ *In that day,* a highway; Egypt and Assyria worship together (19:23).
  B´ *In that day* Israel will be third to Egypt and Assyria (19:24–25).
A´ *In the year* Sargon came to Ashdod, YHWH spoke through Isaiah: those who trust in Egypt will be put to shame (20:1–6).

The setting for chaps. 17–20 is Jerusalem, who is depicted as still having a choice about her future. Aram and Israel do not. So Judah is the central factor from D to D´ of the outline. Chap. 17 begins with the accusation that Jerusalem failed to respond to the effects of the judgment meted out to Aram and Israel, effects that spilled over onto Jerusalem (17:1–3; chap. 7). This accusation is then focused on the confused and violent international scene (17:12–14), on the arrival and dispatch of Ethiopian messengers (18:1–2), and on the note that Assyria sends gifts to Zion (18:7).

YHWH's action against Egypt (19:1–15) has an immediate effect relating to Judah (19:16–17), but the results of other actions spread out and are no longer identified with Judah or Jerusalem. The language of Canaan (19:18) and the altar in Egypt (19:19–22) complete this part of the cycle. Jerusalem's apostasy (17:10–11) in forgetting YHWH has, in this section at least, forced the abandonment of the view that she is the center of YHWH's world. Cult and worshiping congregation are now pictured in Egypt.

The outer frame of the section uses a broader setting. The desolate cities of Damascus and Ephraim are a witness to God's accomplished judgment (17:1–3). Israel is compared to what is left in a field after the harvesters are gone (17:4–6). But when someone "heed[s] his Maker" (17:7–8) in such a time, the experience can be productive. So Israel's situation, though apparently hopeless, could be changed by God's creative power if the tiny remnant turns to him.

The corresponding paragraphs that close the section with the marvelous view of Egyptian and Assyrian cooperation (19:23) bring Israel, not Judah or Jerusalem, back into the section as their partner in the triad (19:24–25). "Humankind . . . should look to the Holy One of Israel" (17:7–8) corresponds to Egyptian and Assyrian worship of YHWH (19:23). Recognition of Israel's minuscule possibility of destiny (17:4–6) contrasts with her position as third in the triad of superpowers (19:24–25).

But the section closes (20:1–6) as it began (17:1–3) with recognition of gloomy reality. In the last two decades of the eighth century, Israel's ruined cities are no more than a monument to her apostasy and God's retribution. Jerusalem is prevented from serving God's purpose by her perverse political leadership and policies that reduced the vision of chaps. 18–19 to a vision of what might have been, like the magnificent vision of what Hezekiah's reign might have been (chaps. 11–12), which was negated by his admiration of Babylon's rebellion (chaps. 13–14).

These chapters describe a high point in Judah's history as interpreted by the Vision. The spark of hope that appeared in chap. 11 was fanned into flame by the response of Moab in chaps. 15–16, by the Ethiopian messengers in chap. 18, and by the vision of political accommodation in chap. 19. But after 712 B.C.E. it died. Hezekiah's Judah was committed to policies that inevitably led to the disaster of 701 B.C.E., as chaps. 20–22 will show.

Twice the sections are introduced with הנה, "behold." Isa 17:1 points to the devastation in Aram and Israel from the Assyrian invasions of 733 to 718 B.C.E. The second (19:1) points to YHWH's intervention against Egypt, which makes it unwise to expect help for rebel causes from that quarter.

Jerusalem is addressed, especially in 17:9–11 and in the final prophecy (20:1–6). The announcement of Assyria's gifts for YHWH in Zion (18:7) is the centerpiece of the broad vision. Yet, amazingly, the subject is Israel (B 17:4–6; B´ 19:24–25). Jerusalem is mentioned only in the capstone of the arch (18:7).

The vision is the second of the book (after chaps. 11–12) to portray what God had in store for his people. But the hopes were frustrated by political decisions that drew Jerusalem away from the plan YHWH had for them.

The two speeches of YHWH are key elements in the arch. The first (18:4) announces his inaction while the messengers carry out their mission. After the gifts are brought to Jerusalem, signaling Assyria and Ethiopia's invitation for Judah to join their coalition, YHWH's second speech announces his active reentry into history to bring a turning point in Egyptian history (19:1).

Planting and harvest imagery is used at key points. Isa 17:4–5 interprets the situation of Israel after the fall of Samaria like that of a field after the harvesters have finished their work, leaving only "leftovers" for the poor to gather. Isa 17:10–11 pictures Jerusalem's pagan worship, which used little artificial gardens. Isa 18:4–6 pictures YHWH's work in terms of a farmer's methods. Isa 19:5–10 and 15 portray the distress of Egyptian farmers and those who depend on agriculture when the waters of the Nile dry up.

Religious issues dominate other passages. The usually human reaction that turns to God after a disaster (17:7–8) is contrasted with Jerusalem's "forgetting" God (17:9). God's goal of bringing Egypt and Assyria to worship him dominates four of the "in that day" sections (19:18–25).

The outer frame is firmly set in historical realities. Damascus and Ephraim are monumental ruins, lessons from the past (17:1–3). Hezekiah's determination to join the Ashdod rebellion with Egypt's (Twenty-Third Dynasty of delta cities) encouragement (20:1–6) renders moot the vision that precedes.

Reflections on Israel's Position (17:1–9)

Bibliography

Donner, H. *Israel unter den Völkern.* 38–42. **Jenkins, A. K.** "The Development of the Isaiah Tradition in Is 13–23." In *Book of Isaiah.* Ed. J. Vermeylen. 242–43. **Olyan, S. M.** *Asherah and the Cult of Yahweh in Israel.* Missoula, MT: Scholars Press, 1988. **Pitard, W. T.** *Ancient Damascus: A Historical Study of the Syrian City-State from Earliest Times until Its Fall to the Assyrians in 732 B.C.E.* Winona Lake, IN: Eisenbrauns, 1987. **Tadmor, H.** *The Inscriptions of Tiglath-Pileser III, King of Assyria: Critical Edition with Introduction, Translations and Commentary.* Jerusalem: Israel Academy of Sciences and Humanities, 1994. 273–78. **Vermeylen, J.** *Du prophète Isaïe.* 1:308–12. **Vogt, E.** "Jesaja und die drohende Eroberung Palästinas durch Tiglatpilesar." In *Wort, Lied, und Gottesspruch.* FS J. Ziegler, ed. J. Schreiner. Würzburg: Echter; Katholisches Bibelwerk, 1972. 2:249–55.

Translation

Herald:	[1]*A Burden:* [a] *Damascus.*	
YHWH:	*See Damascus!*	2+2
	Changed [b]*from (being) a city,*	
	it has become [c] *a twisted* [d] *ruin:* [e]	3+3
	[2]*her cities, abandoned forever:*[a]	
Chorus:	*They are become (a place) for flocks*	3+3
(echo)	*that lie down with no one terrorizing (them).*	
YHWH:	[3]*Fortification has ceased from* [a] *Ephraim,*	3+2
	and royal rule from Damascus.[b]	
	Aram is a remnant [c]	2+4
	like the "glory" (which) the Israelites have become.[d]	
Herald:	*Expression of YHWH of Hosts.*	
YHWH:	[4]*And it is* [a] *in such* [b] *a day*	3
	that the glory of Jacob is faded.	3+3
	The fat of his flesh is wasted away.	
	[5]*It is*	1+3+3
	like harvesting standing grain; [a]	
	one harvests sheaves with his arm.	
	It is	1+3+2+3
	like gleaning sheaves	
	in the Valley of Raphaim	
	[6]*when some gleanings are left in it.* [a]	
	Like [b]*beating an olive tree:* [b]	2+3+2

two or three olives
in the topmost branches;
four or five 2+2
in the fruit-bearing branches.[c]
Herald: *Expression of YHWH,* 2+2
God of Israel.
YHWH: 7 *In such a day* 2+3+4
a human should heed his Maker!
His eyes should look to the Holy One of Israel.
8 *He should no longer heed* [a]*(the sanctuaries)*[a] 4+2
made by his hands.
What his fingers have fashioned 3+2+2
he should no longer see
[b]*(the asherim and the incense altars).*[b]
Earth: (to Jerusalem) 9 *In such a day* 2+3+3
his[a] *fortified cities became*
[b]*like abandoned cities of the Hivites and the Amorites*[b]
that they abandoned before Israel. 5+2
And they are a desolation.

Notes

1.a. On מַשָּׂא, "burden," see *Note* 13:1.a. and the following *Excursus: "Burden" (*מַשָּׂא*) in the Prophets.*

1.b. מוּסָר, *hopʿal* pass. ptc. from סוּר, "turn," therefore "changed." The masc. form is a problem since Damascus and the following verb are fem. *BHK,* with Duhm, Donner (*Israel unter den Völkern,* 39), Kaiser, and Vogt ("Jesaja," 255), reads מוסרה fem. Donner identifies the form as a *hopʿal* of יסר, meaning "chastised." But Wildberger and Clements correctly reject this for the traditional reading.

1.c. וְהָיְתָה, pf. with *vav* of the verb "to be." The form is unquestioned. The problem lies in the time viewpoint. RSV and NIV translate as fut., with most commentaries making the passage a prediction that must be dated prior to the fall of Damascus in 732 B.C.E. The time viewpoint of a pf. with *vav* is dependent on its antecendent (J. Wash Watts, *Survey of Syntax,* 114), which in this case is a ptc. with no hint of time. This is translated here in a "timeless" or neutral way. The contextual setting in a scene from Hezekiah's reign calls for a past time, which the grammar does not forbid. (Cf. *Form/Structure/Setting* for further discussion.)

1.d. מְעִי is a *hap. leg.*, appearing only here. It can be derived from מעה, "internal organs," "guts," but that meaning seems strained in this context. Some have emended to read מעיר, "from a city" (H. Schmidt, *Die grossen Propheten,* 2d ed. [Göttingen: Vandenhoeck & Ruprecht, 1923]; A. B. Ehrlich, *Randglossen zur hebräischen Bibel* [Leipzig, 1908] 4:64; Procksch). Others follow the LXX and see it as dittography for מעיר, thus eliminating it altogether (P. A. de Lagarde, *Semitica* [Göttingen: Dieterich, 1878] 1:29; Gray; Duhm; Marti; *BHS;* Kaiser; and *HAL*). Wildberger is undoubtedly correct in following Delitzsch, C. W. E. Nägelsbach (*Der Prophet Jesaja* [Leipzig: Klasing, 1877]), A. Knobel (*Der Prophet Jesaja* [Leipzig: Weidmann, 1843]), and Young in considering it an alternative form of עִי, a noun from עוה, "bend or twist."

1.e. מַפָּלָה appears in 23:13 and 25:2 as מַפֵּלָה, a noun built on נפל, "fall," hence "what has fallen," a ruin.

2.a. עֲזֻבוֹת עָרֵי עֲרֹעֵר, "the cities of Aroer are abandoned." LXX καταλελειμμένη εἰς τὸν αἰῶνα, "abandoned to the (end of the) age" (cf. 26:4; 65:18). Tg. renders עֲרֹעֵר as עָרֶיהָ, "her cities." Aroer is the name of three places mentioned in the OT. One is a Moabite town south of Dibon on the Arnon river mentioned in Num 32:34, Deut 2:36, and Jer 48:19 (see Simons, *GTTOT,* III b XI/F), which leads Wildberger (635) to suggest that these verses belong in chap. 15. But none of the towns is near Damascus, which has led most commentators, including Steinmann, Mauchline, Fohrer, Donner *(Israel unter den Völkern),* Eichrodt, Alonso Schökel (*Estudios de poética Hebrea* [Barcelona: Flors, 1963]), Kaiser, and Clements, to follow the emendation עֲזֻבוֹת עָרֶיהָ עֲדֵי עַד, "its cities abandoned forever," which draws upon the LXX and Tg. readings. RSV follows this emendation; NIV renders MT literally. There is an unusual proliferation of combinations of the Heb. letters

ר (ד) and ע in this verse—five times forms with ע, three times with ר, the last with both ר and ד. 1QIsa[a] adds ו, "his," to ערער to pronounce it עֲרֹעֵרוֹ, thus different from MT. LXX has changed the ר to ד. The verb עדר has uses meaning "help" (1 Chr 12:34 [33]), "hoe" (Isa 5:6; 7:25), and "be lacking" (1 Sam 30:19; Isa 34:16; 40:26; 59:15; Zeph 3:5; and others). As a noun it seems to mean "flock or herd." The alliteration has become too subtle for the scribes and interpreters.

3.a. A number of interpreters, including Marti, Duhm, Procksch, Eichrodt, and Vogt ("Jesaja," 250), translate "a fortress *for* Ephraim." Wildberger correctly rejects this as a possibility for מִן, which must be translated "from."

3.b. 1QIsa[a] מדרמשק adds ר to MT's "from Damascus." The expanded name appears in 1 Chr 18:5 and often in the Chronicler's history. (See R. Ruzecka, *Konsonantische Dissimilation in den semitischen Sprachen* [Leipzig: Hinrichs; Baltimore: Johns Hopkins, 1909] 78; F. Rosenthal, *Die aramaistische Forschung* [Leiden: Brill, 1939] 15–18.)

3.c. LXX adds ἀπολεῖται, "be destroyed," which has led Duhm, Marti, F. Feldmann (*Das Buch Isaias* [Münster: Aschendorff, 1925]), and Donner (*Israel unter den Völkern*) to insert יֹאבַד in the text. Wildberger suggests moving the accent *ʾatnakh* to the next word. MT has the better reading.

3.d. 1QIsa[a] יהיה (sg.) instead of MT יהיו (pl.). Wildberger correctly supports MT. The subject of the verb is בני־ישראל.

4.a. והיה here and twice in v 5 is often translated fut. because outdated grammar thought all converted pfs. to be futs. However, the context should decide the issue of time (cf. J. Wash Watts, *Survey of Syntax*, 30, 114). The time of vv 1–3, dominated by participles, was present. That viewpoint is continued in this translation.

4.b. The demonstrative pronoun is definite, referring to the conditions already mentioned (GKC §136*b*), but the context is less specific. Therefore the translation "such a."

5.a. קָצִיר is a noun meaning "harvest." It is seen as a problem because the following word, קָמָה, is a noun meaning "standing grain," making קציר superfluous. It also appears to overburden the stich with four words. Luzzatto, Nägelsbach, and Cheyne read it as showing the time of harvest, which Wildberger includes in parentheses. But he prefers to eliminate it as a gloss. Others suggest emending it to קֹצֵר (*BHS*, Duhm, Buhl, Procksch, Kissane, Steinmann, Donner [*Israel unter den Völkern*, 39], Vogt ["Jesaja," 255 n. 11], Kaiser, Clements, *HAL*). Still others suggest seeing קציר as an abstract sg. representing a group (Gesenius, *Lehrgebäude* §§163[3], 164[2]). In this case it designates the agent (A. Knobel, *Der Prophet Jesaja* [Leipzig: Weidmann, 1843]; C. von Orelli, *The Prophecies of Isaiah*, trans. J. S. Banks [Edinburgh: T & T Clark, 1887]; Dillmann; and, earlier, Kimchi [thirteenth century]). The *Translation* follows Wildberger in omitting it.

6.a. The antecedent for בּוֹ, "in it," needs to be clear. Wildberger correctly relates it to "Jacob" in v 4.

6.b-b. The concern for the antecedent discussed in *Note* 6.a. leads some to relate "it" to זית, "olive tree," and to suggest that this be placed at the end of v 5 (Gray and Procksch) while others (*BHS*) suggest adding אוֹ, "or," following LXX ἤ. None of this is necessary if the suggestion in *Note* 6.a. is followed.

6.c. סְעִפֶיהָ פֹּרִיָּה, "her fruit-bearing limbs." פֹּרִיָּה is a fem. act. ptc. (cf. Ezek 19:10), "bearing fruit." The fem. suf. is difficult to explain. זית, "olive tree," is masc. Hitzig and Driver (*JTS* 2 [1951] 25) have suggested dividing the words to make ה the article for פריה. They would read סְעִפֵי הַפֹּרִיָּה, "the limbs of the fruit tree." 1QIsa[a] reads סעפי but omits the ה.

8.a-a. MT המזבחות, "the altars." Wildberger states the objections to this word well: the phrase "works of his hand" is never used of altars in the OT; rather, it is used of idols.

8.b-b. As in *Note* 8.a-a., the phrase "the asherim and the incense altars" is used of idols rather than altars in the OT (so Wildberger, Kaiser, Fohrer, Kissane, Donner *[Israel unter den Völkern]*, and others) However, it must be noted that 1QIsa[a] and the versions uniformly include these words. Whether in the original writing or in the glossator's version, the idols and their sanctuaries have come to be identified. Clements considers this to be a late addition, in a sense extending the gloss to the entire paragraph.

9.a. LXX αἱ πόλεις σου, "which (were) your cities," implies מָעֻזֵּךְ, as in v 10. The emendation in *Note* 9.b-b. should be adopted, making the entire passage an address to Jerusalem with a contrast between dependence on "fortified cities" and failure to look to God, "Rock, your fortress" (v 10).

9.b-b. MT means something like "thickets and underbrush." LXX οἱ Αμορραῖοι και οἱ Ευαῖοι, "the Amorites and the Hivites." *BHK* suggests adoption of the LXX reading, though Wildberger follows MT, Cheyne, and 1QIsa[a] in keeping the rest of the line. Thus the emended Heb. line is עָרֵי מָעֻזּוֹ כַּעֲזוּבוֹת הַחִוִּי וְהָאֱמֹרִי (see *Translation*).

Form/Structure/Setting

Isa 17:1–9 contains an oracle against a nation and three "in that day" passages. The section is called "a burden." The attempts to define the literary form and intentions of a "burden" and of so-called foreign prophecies are nowhere so thoroughly confused as in dealing with sections like this in Isaiah (see *Excursus: Oracles against the Nations [OAN]* and *Excursus: "Burden"* [משׂא] *in the Prophets* at 13:1 above). The name of Damascus is mentioned, but the content of the pericope as well as the following paragraphs that depend on it turns unmistakably to deal with Israel. So the "Burden: Damascus" is primarily concerned with Israel, and the reference to both Damascus and Israel is probably intended to communicate a truth to Jerusalem. The prophecy calls attention to a condition that is lamentable.

The first element (vv 1–3) is introduced by הנה, "See!" It is continued by a participle, מוסר, "changed," and three verbs (perfect with *vav*): והיתה, "it has become," עזבות ערער, "abandoned forever," and תהיינה, "they lie down." The verb היה, "to be," occurs in each of the three verses. Such a frequent recital of "to be" in a language where it can be implied without being written requires attention. It seems intended to stress the resultant condition that has come to exist, a condition that is present in the setting or context.

The other major signal in the passage is נאם יהוה צבאות, "expression of YHWH of Hosts" (vv 3 and 6), which indicates that God himself is speaking. His speech serves here to interpret Israel's position and status in that time, a continuing point in the Vision.

Vv 5–6 are parabolic in nature, comparing Israel's situation to a field that has been harvested, or an olive tree from which most of the fruit has already been taken. The implication is that some will survive and be sustained, if only the very poor.

Vv 7–8 take the form of an admonition to repentence. It is one of the אדם, "humankind," passages in the Vision like 6:11–13, where the cluster of motifs (destroyed cities, humankind, and "hope" for a remnant) is parallel, and like 2:9–22, where the motifs of humankind, destroyed cities, looking to God, and abandoning idol worship are common. But whereas the coming "day of YHWH" was central in chap. 2 and implied in chap. 6, the reference here is to events that have already taken place.

The section notes in an "in such a day" passage (v 9) that Jerusalem has shared some of Israel's and Damascus's destruction. Her outer ring of fortress cities, apparently those along the upper border with Israel, has been abandoned. The section goes on to accuse Jerusalem of having forgotten her God and of pagan practices in contrast to the kind of behavior one expects of humans in disaster (vv 7–8). Ironically, the motif of harvest is cited, in contrast with the pitiful little "Adonis gardens" of the devotees (vv 11–12).

Comment

1–3 The burden laments the devastation of Syria and its capital. Its continued ruin has removed the threat to Ephraim and the need for fortification on either side of that border. One way to stop an armaments race is to have both territories reduced to rubble. Thus the rivalry on the border between Syria and Israel that had raged for more than a century was ended in 732 B.C.E. by the Assyrian invasions. Now peace reigns because there is nothing more to destroy. Royal rule with its pride and ambition has ceased to be. That situation continues in Hezekiah's reign, to which this passage refers. Both Aram and Israel are "remnants" of their former "glory." God himself notes and describes the situation.

A series of words with *mem* preformative, participles, and nouns with occasional parallel formations shape the passage: מוסר, "changed"; מפלה, "fallen"; עזבות, "abandoned" (participle but no *mem*); מחריד, "terrorizing"; מבצר, "fortification"; and ממלכה, "royal rule." The key phrase is מוסר מעיר, "changed from being a city." Her external physical structure is changed. She is a ruin, a pasture for peaceful flocks. But also the concept and dynamic are changed: fortification and kingly ambition have ceased.

The phrase אין מחריד, "no one terrorizing," is a common phrase in Scripture to picture a peaceful promised land (Lev 26:6) after the exile (Jer 30:10 = 46:27). See also Ezek 34:28; 39:26; Mic 4:4; Zeph 3:13; and Job 11:19. The irony is that ignominious defeat and destruction brought the peace (cf. 11:6–9) that royal might promised but could never deliver. Syria and Israel shared a common demotion, from "glory" to the role of a "remnant."

So far as is known, Damascus did not rise again in the decades after 732 B.C.E., and Samaria's fate was sealed by its destruction in 721 B.C.E. and the subsequent crushing of the Philistine-led rebellion in 720 B.C.E. The scene pictured in vv 1–3 fits their status during the last two decades of the century.

The parallel position of Syria and Ephraim in v 3 convinces Clements that the reference must be to 734–32 B.C.E. That is correct, but it is seen here as past history that has led both of them to a common fate as Assyrian vassals. This obviated Ephraim's intense efforts to fortify the border and removed Damascus's ability to exert royal power over its weaker neighbors.

7–8 אדם, "humankind." A proper attitude is contrasted with reactions to such a devastating catastrophe. People should turn from the false worship that has proved ineffective, from their self-made idols and false sanctuaries. (The *asherim* are pillars used in the sanctuaries; these were often objects of worship.) They should look for the true God. They should respect the fact that YHWH's prophets had foretold and correctly interpreted the Assyrians' coming and would therefore "look to the Holy one of Israel."

9 Jerusalem's "fortified cities" were probably those abandoned during the invasion of Israel and Aram and never reoccupied after the march of the Assyrians to Judah's borders in 734–732 B.C.E. The Hivites and the Amorites were some of those who populated Canaan before the entrance of the Israelites. Their "abandoned cities" were ruins that all Israel would know. The implication of this is that not only Aram and Israel had suffered in the years of Assyrian invasions (cf. 8:7–8). Judah also bore its scars.

Explanation

Devastation and destruction, horrible as they are, do achieve certain desirable goals and present some useful possibilities. Damascus can no longer be either a nation or a city. But it is a place of peace and tranquillity, which is more than could be said of it before. Now the feverish activity of "fortification" and the pride of "royal rule" are gone from both Damascus and Ephraim. Neither is necessary any longer.

In a parable (vv 5–6) Israel is likened to a field of grain and to a tree of ripe olives. The field is harvested, and the tree is beaten to make the olives fall down. These are pictures of the Assyrian invasions and the resultant destructions. The field and the tree look desolate, stripped of the grain or olives. But if one looks carefully, one can see that some grain remains at the corners, or in stalks lying on the ground. On the tree some olives remain in the highest branches. The poor in Israel were accustomed to existing on such leftovers (Deut 24:19–22). Israel as a whole now shares their lot. Idolatry is often a temptation to the rich and ambitious. It bolsters pride and self-esteem. It feeds the dreams of wealth and power. But conditions of humiliation and bare survival should lead a people to search for the true God who can save, for the Maker and Savior of Israel (cf. 2:9, 11, 17–18).

Admonition and Two "Woe" Passages (17:10–14)

Bibliography

Alonso Schökel, L. "Textos poéticos: Analisis y traducción. IV." *CB* 19 (1962) 282–94. **Childs, B. S.** *Isaiah and the Assyrian Crisis.* 50–53. **Clements, R. E.** *Isaiah and the Deliverance of Jerusalem.* Sheffield: JSOT Press, 1980. 46–47. **Day, J.** *God's Conflict with the Dragon and the Sea: Echoes of a Canaanite Myth in the Old Testament.* Cambridge: Cambridge UP, 1985. 101–3. **Delcor, M.** "Le problème des jardins d'Adonis dan Isaïe 17,9–11 à la lumière de la civilization Syro-Phénicienne." *Syria* 55 (1978) 371–94. **Fohrer, G.** "Σιων." *TDNT.* 7:291–319. **Gosse, B.** "Isaïe 17,12–14 dans la redaction du livre d'Isaïe." *BN* 58 (1991) 20–23. **Hayes, J.** "The Tradition of Zion's Inviolability." *JBL* 82 (1963) 419–26. **Jenkins, A. K.** "The Development of the Isaiah Tradition in Is 13–23." In *Book of Isaiah.* Ed. J. Vermeylen. 244–45. **Jirku, A.** "Jes. 17:10c." *VT* 7 (1957) 201. **Kaiser, O.** *Die mythische Bedeutung des Meeres.* 2d ed. Berlin: De Gruyter, 1962. **Kilian, R.** *Jesaja II: 13–39.* 49–51. **Lutz, H.-M.** *Jahwe, Jerusalem und die Völker.* WMANT 27. Neukirchen-Vluyn: Neukirchener Verlag, 1968. 47–51. **Müller, H. P.** *Ursprunge und Strukturen alttestamenticher Eschatologie.* BZAW 109. Berlin: De Gruyter, 1969. 86–101. **Schmidt, H.** "Israel, Zion und die Völker." Diss., Univ. of Zurich, 1966. **Schreiner, J.** *Sion-Jerusalem Jahwes Königssitz.* Munich: Kösel, 1963. 261–63, 278. **Stolz, F.** *Strukturen und Figuren im Kult von Jerusalem.* BZAW 118. Berlin: Töpelmann, 1970. **Vaux, R. de.** "The Cults of Adonis and Osiris: A Comparitive Study." In *The Bible and the Ancient Near East.* Trans. D. McHugh. London: Darton, Longman & Todd, 1966. 210–37. ———. "Jerusalem et les prophètes." *RB* 73 (1966) 481–509. **Wanke, G.** *Die Zionstheologie der Korachiten.* BZAW 97. Berlin: Töpelmann, 1966. 113–17. **Welsby, D. A.** *The Kingdom of Kush: The Nabatan and Meroite Empires.* London: British Museum Press, 1996. **Winkler, H.** "Das Land Kus und Jes 18." In *Alttestamentlicher Untersuchungen.* Leipzig: Pfeiffer, 1892. 146–56.

Translation

Earth:	10 *But you [fem. sg.] have forgotten the God of your salvation!*	4+4

You have not remembered Rock, your fortress.
Because of this, you planted gardens of "the Beloved"[a] 4+3
and set them out: a twig for a foreign (god)!
11 *In the day you plant it, you fence in*[a] *carefully.* 3+3
In the morning that you sow it, you make it bud.
A harvest heaped high[b]*—* 2+2+2
a share[c] *in a day—*
like green shoots[d] *that are wilted.*
Chorus: (people of Jerusalem) 12 *Woe—like the raging of many peoples,* 4+3
they rage like the raging of the sea.
And roaring of people,[a] *like the roaring* 3+3
(which) mighty waters roar.
13 [a]*(To peoples who roar like the roar of many waters:)*[a] 5+2+2
When one rebukes[b] *them,*[c]
they[c] *must flee afar off.*[d]
And they[c] *are driven* 1+2+2
[e]*like chaff of the hills*[e]
before the wind,
or like a tumbleweed before a storm wind. 3
14 *Toward the time of evening,* 2+2
see: sudden terror!
Before morning—no one is there.[a] 3
This is the way of those who loot us, 3+2
[b]*the habit of those who plunder us."*[b]

Notes

10.a. נעמן, "the Beloved," is generally believed to be the name of a fertility god. It is pl. to agree with the preceding word in a const. state (GKC §124*q;* Joüon §1360). Jirku (*VT* 7 [1957] 201) suggests that this is a false vocalization of an original נַעֲמָנְמָה, which is mimicry of endearing sounds, as in Ugar. (cf. J. Aistleitner, *WUS* §1494).

11.a. תשגשגי may derive from שגג (שגא, שגה), "grow," "grow large" (BDB, 960), as Gray, Duhm, Marti, Fohrer, Kaiser, Clements, Wildberger, and *HAL* think; or from שוג, "fence in" (סוג, BDB II 962/691), as in Song 7:3 [2] (similar to שׂוּךְ, BDB, 962), as Hitzig, Procksch, Leslie, Ziegler, and others have thought. Both the meaning of quick growth and fencing in would apply. This is the only use of either root in a *pilpel* form in the OT, but see 1QH viii 9 יתשגשגו, "grow upwards" *(HAL)*, referring to trees.

11.b. נֵד (BDB, 622, "a heap") is found only in Exod 15:8; Josh 3:13, 16; and Pss 33:7; 78:13, all of the piling up of waters in miraculous crossings of the Reed Sea or Jordan (see *DCH*). LXX and Tg. apparently read עד, "until." Vg. *ablata est messis*, "harvest has retreated," implies נָד (from נדד), "flee, escape" *(HAL)*.

11.c. נַחֲלָה ordinarily means "inheritance"; Vg. translates *hereditas* and LXX κληρώσῃ, "obtain a portion." Or it may be a *nip'al* ptc. from חלה, "be weak," "sick," as Ibn Ezra had already shown (so BDB, 317; *HAL;* cf. *DCH*).

11.d. LXX reads כאב, "green shoots," to mean "as a father," and אָנוּשׁ, "wilted, incurable," as אֱנוֹשׁ, "a man." *BHS* records Duhm's unlikely suggestion that LXX τοῖς υἱοῖς σου misread an original לפניך, "before you," as לבניך, "to your sons." A basic question remains: Does the second line of verse 11 *(a)* continue the reference to the "gardens of the beloved" or *(b)* return to application to Israel. If *(a)*, it may be translated "harvest piles up in a day—a share (of the harvest), like fresh greenness, (becomes) wilted." If *(b)*, the translation will read "harvest is past in a day of sickness like incurable pain." Or is it possible that the double meaning is intentional? This possibility should not be ruled out. The *Translation* follows the context and *(a)* above.

12.a. "A roaring of people" is set apart in MT by an accent mark, creating an uneven line. LXX adds a word, πολλῶν, "many" or "great," which has led Schmidt ("Israel, Zion und die Völker"), Procksch, and others to suggest a rearranged word order with כבירים, "great" or "mighty," after לאמים, "to people." Wildberger properly rejects the change, suggesting instead that the division in the line be moved over to provide a balanced line.

13.a-a. A word-for-word repetition of five words of the previous line (with רבים, "many," for כבירים, "mighty"). This is an echo or repetition, probably for effect. It falls out of the metric pattern and is omitted from some MSS and Syr.

13.b. וְגָעַר (pf. 3 m. sg.), "and he will rebuke," is rendered ויגער (impf.) in 1QIsa[a]. But problems remain. A subject is missing in the entire section. To supply this, Duhm inserted והוא, "and he"; Marti ויהוה הוא, "and YHWH, he"; and Procksch ויהוה, "and YHWH." Wildberger suggests that יהוה, YHWH, may have been abbreviated to י and then lost in the 1QIsa[a] form יגער, becoming the ו. The subject is understood to be YHWH in any case.

13.c. All these are sg. in Heb. Reference to the preceding pl. suggests they be translated as collectives.

13.d. מן, "from," is used with ideas of flight to mean "away" (GKC §119*v*).

13.e-e. I. Eitan's suggestion ("A Contribution to Isaiah Exegesis," *HUCA* 12–13 [1937–38] 65) to read כַּמֵּץ, "like the pressing," instead of כְּמֹץ, "like the chaff," and הָרִים like the Arab. *harra* meaning "refuse," is not necessary. Wildberger (665) has correctly noted the MT's figure is fitting and strong as it is.

14.a. Many MSS and versions have added a *vav*.

14.b-b. Syr. reads *wmnt' dbzwzn*. See also LXX[A], MSS of the Lucianic transmission, Vg., and Arab. These suggest the reading וגורל בוזינו, omitting ל from the second word as dittography for the ל before it. The change affects syntax but not meaning.

Form/Structure/Setting

This section relates to Jerusalem, as the pronouns in second feminine singular indicate. She is accused of blatant idolatry (vv 10–11).

A chorus of Jerusalemites bewail their condition with a "woe" passage (vv 12–14). They see themselves as the victims of their times, helpless to defend themselves from looters. Recent studies by Schmidt ("Israel, Zion und die Völker") and Lutz *(Jahwe, Jerusalem und die Völker)* have isolated a genre of speeches in which the peoples gather against Jerusalem. Wanke *(Zionstheologie)* places the genre in the temple theology and service of the Korahites. This theme can and should be traced in the prophetic books.

However, there is also a clear direction shown within the Vision of Isaiah. The theme of nations marching at YHWH's signal begins in 5:26–30. Isa 8:9–10 echoes the sentiments of super-patriots whose bravado challenges the nations to do their worst. Isa 14:27 speaks of YHWH's hand outstretched over the nations. Isa 17:12–14 echoes again the fears of the people. Isa 29:5 repeats the motif with a word of hope. Isa 34:2–3 depicts YHWH's destruction of the nations, but there is no hint that this relates to Jerusalem. Only in 34:8 is Zion's cause credited with the motif.

The theme is complex. Some texts in Isaiah and in other prophets have the nations (or peoples) assembling against Jerusalem, but YHWH saves them. Some have YHWH fighting against the nations with little relation to Jerusalem, while in a few texts YHWH fights against the city. The chorus here (17:12–14) seems to repeat a familiar theme that illustrates the anxieties and fears of the city in a time when the citizens have little reason to be so anxious.

Comment

10 Jerusalem did not have a healthy response of renewed concern with the worship of YHWH who had given her salvation in the past, who was *the foundation of her hope for defense.* Instead she increased her devotion to pagan worship.

נעמן, "the Beloved," is probably the name of a fertility god. The gardens described here fit the picture given by Plato (*Phaedrus* 276*b*) and other Greek and Latin authors. H. Ewald (*Commentary on the Prophets of the Old Testament,* trans. J. F. Smith [London: Williams & Norgate, 1875–81] 2:116) was apparently the first to suggest a connection. Greek vases dated about 400 B.C.E. portray the scene. (Cf. H. Haas, *Bilderatlas zur Religionsgeschichte* [Leipzig: Scholl, 1926] 105.) Others have suggested a relation to the worship of Osiris in Egypt or to Tammuz in Mesopotamia (see Wildberger, 658). However this may be, the nearer and more likely relation of the Beloved was with the Canaanite Baal (*IDB,* 1:48). The custom apparently was for grain to be planted in shallow pots or potsherds, watered, and placed in the sun. The plants grew very rapidly but wilted equally rapidly. This represented the rise and the death of the god, who was then mourned with great passion (cf. Ezek 8:14) until the coming of the natural rains caused all the fields to turn green, a sign of his rebirth.

The term נעמן, "the Beloved," is apparently an epithet and does little to identify the "foreign (god)" worshiped in these rites (cf. L. A. Snijders, in *Oudtestamentische Studiën,* ed. P. A. H. de Boer [Leiden: Brill, 1954] 10:1–21; R. Martin-Achard, *THAT,* 1:520–22). The worship of heathen gods in Jerusalem is denounced by Jeremiah and Ezekiel. This passage attests to its presence a century earlier.

12 These people who engross themselves in idolatry's fantasies reflect their hysteria in fear of anyone who might approach their city. When darkness descends (v 14), they are terrified. Daylight reveals no one is there. It is ironic that the genre of poetry that was once used by the temple singers to portray YHWH's unceasing care for his city would be cited by those whose pagan imaginations have been overcome with nightmarish fears.

Explanation

Attention turns from Israel and humankind to Jerusalem. She, too, has been humiliated by the wars, but no salutary effect follows, no awakening of precious memories of faith. Rather, Jerusalem has forgotten YHWH God who has saved her. She cultivates her pagan passions and wails her hysterical fears to the world.

Or the time may be the end of the Day of YHWH. When all the wars of the period are over, YHWH of Hosts will be recognized, not as field marshal of the armies but as the ruler of all the land. Diplomats will approach with gifts. The seat of his throne will be Mount Zion. The verse effectively takes up the strand of "mountain of YHWH" passages begun in 2:1–4.

Against the background of a glance at the ruins of Damascus and her former fortress towns on the border of Israel, Judah is reminded that despair has led the people to forget YHWH and turn to idolatrous practices (17:10–11). Their anxiety about political disturbances (vv 12–13) leads to a notice that in the midst of terrors a limit is set. The terror vanishes before dawn (v 14).

Isa 18:1 presents another anxious moment as messengers arrive from the new Ethiopian ruler Shabaka, to whom the answer is given correctly that they should seek out the Assyrian overlord. Beginning with Isa 18:3 a picture of the potential inherent in that moment is spread over the next chapter. The Lord promises to "remain quiet," i.e., approving, as the coalition between Ethiopia and Assyria is forged with the ostensible purpose of putting the Egyptian delta under firm Ethiopian rule. Assyria will bring gifts to Zion (18:7) to obtain support in the campaign against Egypt (the delta) and to recognize its loyalty in sending the delegation on to Nineveh (18:2). At this point YHWH abandons his spectator position to enter the conflict, ensuring victory over Egypt by creating internal dissension (19:2–4), by drying up the vitally important river (vv 5–10), and by confusing the vaunted wisdom of the Egyptian counselors (vv 12–15).

The result would be demoralization of Egyptians so that even tiny Judah's forces bring terror to them (19:16–17); colonization of five cities in Egypt by Palestinians, probably as garrison cities (v 18); recognition of YHWH in Egypt, leading to worship and dependence on him (vv 19–22); an open highway for diplomatic and commercial activity between Egypt and Assyria, with relations so cordial that the two worship together (v 23); and finally, Israel, whose position lies astride the highway just mentioned, occupying a position exceeded only by Egypt and Assyria with her influence being "a blessing" for all the land. This beneficent result would be possible because YHWH would call Egypt "my people" (cf. vv 19–22) and Assyria "my handwork" (cf. 10:5–6) and Israel "my inheritance," her historic title.

One must keep in mind that all this is predicated on Judah's having learned her lesson from Damascus (chap. 17) and on her having acted as a loyal vassal (18:3, 7; 19:17). This would apply if Hezekiah followed policies of peace and servitude like his father Ahaz.

These chapters suggest a theology of history in which YHWH is seen as the prime mover in Assyrian expansion in Palestine and in which his hand may be seen in the rise of the Twenty-Fifth Dynasty in Egypt, whose openness to Assyrian alliance could have presaged a period of peace and prosperity for the entire region. As a matter of historical fact, this dream or vision was not fulfilled. Hezekiah did not follow his father's policies but succumbed to the hawkish ideas of his advisers, who never gave up their false hope that Judah's salvation lay in Egypt's reassuming sovereignty over the region. It was an unrealistic hope since the Egyptian delta was torn by dissension. These advisors led Israel to participate in the abortive attempt by Ashdod to be free of Assyria, an event that is reflected in chap. 20. Despite Isaiah's warnings, Israel joined Ashdod. The people were so emotionally tied to the success of Merodach-Baladan's rule in Babylon that they became hysterical at the report of his defeat. And finally in chap. 21 they are shown to be what they are under the condemning eyes of God.

But the hopes for Hezekiah, which seemed so great in the pictures of 7:1–9:6 and in chap. 11 and which were so well prepared by his father's carefully cultivated ties to Assyria, were shattered by the willful, nationalistic ambitions and pride of the period and by the dangerously wrong assessment of the relative strength of the other nations. Most of all, they failed because of their inability to be led by the Lord in seeing and doing what he wanted, in joining with him in bringing blessing, peace, and prosperity to that generation and region.

Address to "All You People of the Land" (18:1–7)

Bibliography

Barth, H. "Israel und das Assyrerreich in den nichtjesajanischen Texten des Protojesajabuches." Diss., Hamburg, 1974. **Donner, H.** *Israel unter den Völkern.* 122–24. **James, T. G. H.** "The Twenty-Fifth and Twenty-Sixth Dynasties." In *CAH.* 3.2:677–747. **Janzen, W.** *Mourning Cry and Woe Oracle.* Berlin: De Gruyter, 1972. 60–61. **Jenkins, A. K.** "The Development of the Isaiah Tradition in Is 13–23." In *Book of Isaiah.* Ed. J. Vermeylen. 244–45. **Kitchen, K. A.** *Third Intermediate Period in Egypt.* 362–80. **Lubetski, M.,** and **C. Gottlieb.** "Isaiah 18 in the Egyptian Nexus." In *Boundaries of the Ancient Near Eastern World.* FS C. H. Gordon, ed. M. Lubetski et al. JSOTSup 273. Sheffield: Academic Press, 1998. 364–83. **Török, L.** *The Kingdom of Kush: Handbook of the Nabatan-Meriotic Civilization.* HO 1: Der Nahe und Mittlere Osten 31. Leiden: Brill, 1977. **Winckler, H.** "Das Land Kus und Jes. 18." In *Alttestamentlicher Untersuchungen.* Leipzig: Pfeiffer, 1892. 146–56.

Translation

Chorus:	1 *Woe! The land of winged boats* [a]	4+4
(People of Jerusalem)	*that is* [b]*in the region of the rivers of Cush* [b]	
	2 *is sending envoys by sea* [a]	3+4
	with vessels of papyrus over the surface of the water.	
(to the messengers)	*Go, swift messengers,*	3+4
	to a nation tall and smooth-skinned,[b]	
	to a people feared near and far,	4+3+4
	a very strong nation [c]	
	whose land is divided [d] *by rivers.*	
Chorus:	3 *All you inhabitants of the world,*	3+2
(to the world)	*and you dwellers in the land,*	
	like a banner raised on the mountains, you will see (it).	4+3
	Like a trumpet, you will hear (it).	
Shebna:	4 *But YHWH said to me, thus:*	5
	"I will remain still [a] *and observe in my place."*	3
Heavens:	*Like heat shimmering* [b] *over the light.*	4+4
	Like a cloud of dew in the heat [c] *of harvest.*	
	5 *For at wheat-harvest* [a] *time, when the blossoms are gone,*	4+4
	when the bud becomes a ripening grape,	
	one cuts off the shoots with a knife	3+3
	and removes the branches. He cuts (them) off.	
	6 *They are left, all of them,*	2+2+2
	to mountain eagles	
	and to the beasts of the land,	
	who will spend the summer on them,	3+3+2
	and all the beasts of the land	
	will spend harvest time on them.	
Earth:	7 *In such a time*	2+4+3
	a gift may be brought to YHWH of Hosts	

from [a] *a people tall and smooth-skinned,*
from a people feared near and far, 4+3+4
a nation of great might [b] *and subjugation,*
whose land is divided by rivers,
to the place of the Name, 3+2+2
YHWH of Hosts,
(to) Mount Zion.

Notes

1.a. צלצל is a word with various meanings and kindred words (BDB, 852–53). Wildberger's exhaustive description (679) sums up the possibilities. "Whirring," "buzzing," in comparison with Deut 28:42 and with Akk. and Arab. parallels, leads to the translation "land of whirring wings." Most modern translations follow this. Jerome translated *umbra,* relating it to צֵל, "darkness." He was followed by Luther, Dillmann, Buhl, and others. The Vg. translates *cymbalum,* following the Heb. צלצלים, "cymbals." Tg. translates ספינן, "ships." Jerome cites θ´ *naves.* LXX in Job 40:31 translates בצלצל דגים: ἐν πλοίοις ἁλιέων, "in ships of fishermen." Wildberger cites parallels in Eth. *ṣalala,* "swim," and Aram. צלצל, "ship," and admits that Arab. *ẓul ẓul* is different (cf. G. R. Driver, "Difficult Words," 56; *JSS* 13 [1968] 45; and Gesenius, *Thesaurus* [Leipzig: Vogel, 1829–53] 1167*f*). Wildberger's defense of "winged boats" is convincing (so *HAL*).

1.b-b. מעבר ל means, literally, "beyond," "on the other side of." Most translations and commentaries follow this without question. Some (Duhm; Marti; Donner, *Israel unter den Völkern,* 122) have treated it as a gloss. Wildberger says the obvious: The reference is to Cush (Ethiopia or Nubia), and it does not lie "beyond the rivers." Procksch points it מַעֲבָר ל, "access to," "corridor to," with reference to 16:2 and Gen 32:23 and translates "an access to the rivers of Cush." E. Vogt ("*ʾeber hayyarden* = Regio Finitima Iordani," *BZ* 34 [1953] 118–19) shows that (מ)עבר הירדן often means "in the region of Jordan." In the same way מעבר לנהרי־כוש, "in regions adjacent to the rivers of Cush."

2.a. Many commentators (including Wildberger, 680) would change this to mean "river" on the grounds that such ships were not seaworthy. But Clements (164) is surely right that it is not impossible that "the sea" means the Mediterranean coast.

2.b. 1QIsa[a] has an additional letter, וממורט, as well as the superimposed *vav.* This is the normal form of a *puʿal* ptc., but the shorter form may also be used (cf. G. R. Driver, *JTS* 2 [1951] 25; GKC §525).

2.c. קו means a measuring line. The reduplicated form appears only here (and v 7) in Heb. In 28:10, 13 it seems to be used as a meaningless sound, which leads Donner (*Israel unter den Völkern,* 122) and others to see in it a designation for a foreign language. J. Fischer (*Das Buch Isaias,* 1–39 [Bonn: Hanstein, 1937]) thinks of the sound of marching feet. G. R. Driver (*JSS* 13 [1968] 46) supports BDB in rendering it as a reduplicated adjective, "very strong." K[Or] and 1QIsa[a] have קוקו (one word), which, following the Arab. *ḳuwwatun,* "strength," "power," and *ḳawija,* "tense," "be strong," would mean "tensile strength." See *HAL.*

2.d. בזא occurs only here and in v 7. BDB (102) translates "divide," "cut through," in dependence on Syr. *bzʾ,* "tear," "cut." The versions had trouble with the word but offer no good solution. L. Köhler ("*Bāzāʾ* = fortschwemmen," *TZ* 6 [1950] 316–17) looks to Arab. *bazza,* "forcefully carried away," and suggests the translation "swim away"; similarly *HAL* "wash away." But the meaning "divided" is better (cf. *DCH*).

4a. K offers a different vocalization, but the received text is stronger (Wildberger, 680).

4.b. For different suggestions on צח cf. Wildberger (680).

4.c. בחם means "in the heat of." LXX, Syr., and Vg. have apparently read ביום, "in the day of." The orthographic variation is slight. Wildberger follows the versions.

5.a. קציר means "grain harvest," which comes in early summer. לִפְנֵי does not mean "before" in a time sense; rather it means "in view of" or "facing" (cf. Wildberger, 681). The harvest of grain occurs at the same time that the work in the vineyards must be done.

7.a. עם, "a people." LXX ἐκ λαοῦ; Vg. *a populo;* 1QIsa[a] מעם, "from a people." Following 1QIsa[a] is supported by the parallel phrase three words later.

7.b. See *Note* 2.c.

Form/Structure/Setting

The chapter presents three movements: the approach of a delegation from "the land of winged boats" brings dismay to Jerusalem (vv 1–2*a*); the delegation is sent to "a nation tall and smooth-skinned" (v 2*bc*); and it is anticipated that "the nation tall and smooth-skinned" will bring gifts to YHWH in Zion (v 7). In between, all the world is called to take notice of the delegation's trip (v 3). YHWH intends to sit back and observe developments (v 4*a*). An enigmatic explanation, which uses the parabolic language of the farmer trimming the grain of shoots before actual harvest time, is offered (vv 4*a*–6).

The "woe" (v 1) is not formally an indication of mourning or a curse on Cush. It is simply a cry of dismay at the thought of more military activity in the region. The parable (vv 4*a*–6) continues the series begun in 17:5–9.

V 7 introduces an "in that day" passage that contrasts with what has gone before and afterward. The desolation and frantic action of war give way to the measured pace of peaceful diplomacy. YHWH of Hosts is the ruler. He resides on Mount Zion and receives the envoys there.

Comment

1 הוי, "woe," does not introduce a curse on Cush (Ethiopia). It is a cry of dismay by Jerusalemites at the news that the delegation is approaching. They assume that military operations in their land will bring renewed disasters. צלצל, "whirring wings" (see *Note* 1.a.), may refer to insects in the upper Nile valley. Or it may be a reference to sail boats.

Cush is the land of Ethiopia or Nubia, which at this time had its capital at Napata above the fourth cataract. A strong new dynasty (the twenty-fifth of Egypt) was building. Pianchi in 728 B.C.E. had handed the Libyan ruler, Tefnakht, a defeat and extended his control as far down river as Memphis. But he had not followed up on that advantage. Kitchen (*Third Intermediate Period in Egypt,* 369) has called the period 728 to 715 B.C.E. a lull between storms in Egypt. In 716 B.C.E., Shabaka succeeded his brother to the Ethiopian throne and began immediately to consolidate Ethiopian control of Lower Egypt. An initial success was achieved by 715 B.C.E. This period, 716–715 B.C.E., was one of feverish political activity as he sought allies for his attempt to gain control of the Nile delta. This activity apparently reached as far as Jerusalem.

2 The messengers are sent on their way again, but commentators are not agreed to whom they are sent. The description is not definitive. ממשך is an obscure word that probably means "lean" or "tall." מורט is equally obscure, relating to something cut off, perhaps implying something shaved: hence "smooth-skinned." The lines "a people feared," "a very strong nation," and "divided by rivers" also leave open several possibilities.

Wildberger (with others) assumes that this describes the Ethiopians themselves and sees this as a rejection of the envoys. W. Janzen (*Mourning Cry and Woe Oracle,* BZAW 125 [Berlin; New York: De Gruyter, 1972] 60–61) and Barth ("Israel und das Assyrerreich," 13) understand this to be a summons to other messengers, perhaps divine messengers, to go to Assyria with news of these developments. The key point is that the country referred to is Assyria. This is correct. Clements (165) assumes that the envoys are conspiring against Assyria. But is this true? If the envoys come from Shabaka in 716 B.C.E., then their mission relates to his attempt to control Egypt. Can it be that he is enlisting aid against the delta kings, not against Assyria? And can it be that Jerusalem here is simply referring them to its overlord, Assyria, as the only one who can make such a decision?

At this time (716 B.C.E.) Cush (Ethiopia) and Egypt are not one and the same. There is evidence that after the Ethiopian dynasty gained control they were on friendly terms with the Assyrians. When in 712 B.C.E. Sargon attacked Ashdod, its ruler Iamani fled to Egypt, now under Ethiopian rule. There Shabaka, "the Pharaoh of Egypt," "which land now belongs to Cush," obligingly extradited the fugitive Iamani to the Assyrian's satisfaction (Kitchen, *Third Intermediate Period in Egypt,* 380). If this is true, the vision of friendly relations between Egypt under an Ethiopian ruler and Assyria (Isa 19:23–25) finds its basis in historical fact. So the best interpretation appears to be that the envoys from Shabaka are sent on to Assyria to try to arrange for support or at least a promise not to interfere, as he presses his claims to authority over all Egypt.

3 Williamson (*Book Called Isaiah,* 179) has called attention to the נס, "banner," "a favorite image of Deutero-Isaiah," found also in 5:26, 11:12, and 49:22.

4 The solo voice that speaks in first person requires identification. Similar passages occur in 21:2–4, 6, 10 and 22:14. The last instance is identified in the succeeding verse to be Shebna, Hezekiah's prime minister, who is undoubtedly the designer of Judah's foreign policy throughout this period. The solo passages in first person, not otherwise identified from 18:4 through chap. 22, are assigned to Shebna.

7 בעת ההיא, "in such a time," most appropriately refers to the events envisioned in vv 3–6 and planned for in vv 1–2 to take place when Ethiopia and Assyria begin their campaign against Lower Egypt.

The gifts to be brought to YHWH of Hosts come from the Assyrians (cf. *Comment* on v 2). They relate to the Assyrians' activities in conjunction with Ethiopia and may be seen as recognition of Jerusalem's loyalty in referring the messengers to Assyria. Or they may be intended to secure Jerusalem's commitment to protect Assyria's flanks as they invade Egypt. In either case, Zion and YHWH (and the royal house in Jerusalem) are accorded a high status and privilege. This continues the tendency of chap. 16 to document a considerable recovery of influence and power for Jerusalem even within its vassal status.

Explanation

YHWH has appeared very active, instigating the movement of troops (13:1–3), stirring up the Medes (13:17), and so on. But here he calls attention to happenings in which he joins the people as a spectator. He sits still in his house to observe the developments.

The period of the wars covered more than two centuries. Not all the years saw active warfare by the great powers. But the continuing conflicts ate away at the fabric of life in Palestine and the larger land around it.

Burden: Egypt (19:1–20:6)

See! YHWH against Egypt (19:1–15)

Bibliography

Calderone, P. J. "The Rivers of Masor." *Bib* 42 (1961) 423–32. **Cheyne, T. K.** "The Nineteenth Chapter of Isaiah." *ZAW* 13 (1893) 125–28. **Condamin, A.** "Interpolations ou transpositions accidentelles? (Michée, II,12,13; Osée, II,1–3,8,9; Isaïe, V,24,25; XIX 21,22)." *RB* 11 (1902) 379–97. **Crocker, P.** "Egypt in Biblical Prophecy." *BurH* 34 (1998) 105–10. **Croughs, M.** "Intertextuality in the Septuagint: The Case of Isaiah 19." *BIOSCS* 34 (2001) 60–80. **Elat, M.** "The Economic Relations of the Neo-Assyrian Empire with Egypt." *JAOS* 98 (1978) 20–34. **Feuillet, A.** "Un sommet religieux de l'ancien testament: L'oracle d'Isaïe XIX (vv. 16–25) sur la conversion de l'Egypte." *RSR* 39 (1951) 65–87. **Fohrer, G.** "Die Gattung der Berichte über symbolische Handlungen der Propheten." In *Studien zur alttestamentlichen Prophetie* (1945–65). BZAW 99. Berlin: Töpelmann, 1967. 65–80. Reprinted from *ZAW* 64 (1952) 101–20. ———. *Die symbolischen Handlungen der Propheten.* 2d ed. ATANT 14. Zurich: Zwingli, 1968. **Gosse, B.** "Isaïe 21,11–12, et Isaïe 60–62." *BN* 53 (1990) 21–22. **Gottwald, N. K.** *All the Kingdoms of the Earth.* 222–28. **Hoonacker, A. van.** "Deux passages obscurs dan le chaptre XIX d'Isaïe (versets 11,18)." *Revue Benedictine* 36 (1924) 297–306. **Israleit-Groll, S.** "The Egyptian Background to Isaiah 19:18." In *Boundaries of the Ancient Near Eastern World.* FS C. H. Gordon, ed. M. Lubetski et al. JSOTSup 273. Sheffield: Sheffield Academic Press, 1998. 300–303. **Kitchen, K. A.** *Third Intermediate Period in Egypt.* 362–80. **Kooij, A. van der.** "The Old Greek of Isaiah 19:15–25: Translation and Interpretation." In *VI Congress of the International Organization for Septuagint and Cognate Studies, Jerusalem 1986.* Ed. C. E. Cox. Atlanta: Scholars Press, 1987. 127–66. **Loretz, O.** "Der ugaritische Topos *b'l rkb* und die 'Sprache Kanaans' in Jes 19,1–25." *UF* 19 (1987) 101–12. **Monsengwo-Pasinya, L.** "Isaïe XIX 16–25 et universalisme dans la lxx." *Congress Volume, Salamanca 1983.* Ed. J. A. Emerton. VTSup 36. Leiden: Brill, 1985. 192–207. **Na'aman, N.** "The Brook of Egypt and Assyrian Policy on the Border of Egypt." *Tel Aviv* 6 (1979) 78–90. **Nicacci, A.** "Isaiah xviii-xx from an Egyptological Perspective." *VT* 48 (1998) 214–38. **Randles, R. J.** "The Interaction of Israel, Judah and Egypt: From Solomon to Josiah." Diss., Southern Baptist Theological Seminary, 1980. 155–208. **Sawyer, J. F. A.** "'Blessed Be My People Egypt' (Isaiah 19.25): The Context and Meaning of a Remarkable Passage. " In *A Word in Season.* FS W. McKane, ed. J. D. Martin and P. R. Davies. JSOTSup 42. Sheffield: JSOT Press, 1986. 57–71. **Spalinger, A.** "The Year 712 B.C.E. and Its Implications for Egyptian History." *JARC* 10 (1973) 95–101.

Translation

Herald:	[1]*Burden:*[a] *Egypt.*	2
	See YHWH,	2+3+2
	riding[b] *on a light cloud*	
	and coming (to) Egypt.	
Earth:	*The nonentities*[c] *of Egypt tremble before him,*	4+4
	and Egypt's heart melts within it.	
YHWH:	[2]*I incite*[a] *Egypt*[b] *against Egypt.*	3+3

A man fights against his brother,
a man against his neighbor, 2+2+2
[c]*city against city,*
[d]*kingdom against kingdom.*[d]
3 *The spirit of the Egyptians is poured out*[a] *within them,* 4+2
and its strategy I swallow up.
They seek out the nonentities[b] *and the spiritualists,*[c] 3+2
the mediums[d] *and familiar spirits.*[e]
4 *I confine Egypt in the hand of cruel masters*[a] 2+4
and a powerful king[b] *who will rule over them.*

Herald: *Expression of the Lord,*[c] *YHWH of Hosts.* 4

Heavens: 5 *The water from the river*[a] *dries up,* 3+3
and the riverbed is desolate and dry.
6 *The canals*[a] *stink.*[b] 2+4+3
They diminish, and the streams of Mazur[c] *dry up.*
The reeds and rushes decay.[d]
7 *Plants*[a] *(are)* [b]*upon the Nile,*[b] 2+2
upon the mouth of the Nile—
every sown place along the Nile 3+3
is dried up,[c] *blown away, nothing left.*[d]
8 *The fishermen*[a] *mourn and lament—* 3+4
all who cast[b] *a hook in the Nile.*
Those who spread a net on the surface of the water languish. 4
9 *Those who work with combed*[a] *flax*[b] *are embarrassed,* 4+2
as are the weavers of linen.[c]
10 *Her weavers*[a] *are crushed.* 3+3
All wage[b] *earners are sick*[c] *at heart.*

Earth: 11 *Yet surely the princes of Zoan (are) fools.* 4+3+2
The [a]*wisest of Pharaoh's counselors*[a]
(gives) stupid advice.

(To the Egyptian wise men) *How can you say to Pharoah* 3+2+2
"I am one of the wise men,
one of the kings of old"?[b]

(To Egypt) 12 *Where are they? Where are your [m.] wise ones?* 3+3+1
Let them declare to you [f.] now
that they know[a]
what YHWH of Hosts 2+2+2
has planned
against Egypt.

Heavens: 13 *The princes of Zoan act foolishly.*[a] 3+3+4
The princes of Noph are deceived.[b]
The chiefs of[c] *her tribes cause Egypt to err.*
14 *YHWH has mixed within her*[a] *a spirit of dizziness,*[b] 5+4+3
which causes Egypt to stagger in all[c] *its doings*
like the staggering of a drunkard in his vomit.
15 *Egypt has nothing* 3+2
it can use
(that has) head or tail 2+2
[a]*sprout or stalk.*[a]

Notes

1.a. Concerning משׂא, "burden," see *Note* 13:1.a. and *Excursus: "Burden" (*משׂא*) in the Prophets.*

1.b. Cf. S. Mowinckel, "Drive and/or Rider in the OT," *VT* 12 (1962) 299.

1.c. אלילי, "worthless things, idols." LXX τὰ χειροποίητα, "things made by hand"; Vg. *simulacra,* "images."

2.a. סכסך is an obscure *pilpel* form (otherwise only at 9:10). Wildberger and *HAL* derive it from סוך I, related to Arab. *šawkun,* "thorn," and meaning to "prick" or "needle," that is, "provoke." BDB (697, 968) relates to שׂכך IV, a root derived from Semitic parallels relating to "thorns."

2.b. מצרים, "Egypt." LXX and θ′ Αἰγύπτιοι, "Egyptians." However, the collective meaning would fit. Also the implication that more than one authority claims to be "Egypt" in that time is true.

2.c. 1QIsa[a] ועיר, "and a city." The ו is missing in the versions.

2.d-d. LXX καὶ νομὸς ἐπί νομόν, "and district against district" (cf. the use of νομός for Egypt's provinces in Herodotus, *Histories* 2.4). The rulers of cities were also called "kings," thus also justifying the Heb. term.

3.a. נבקה is *nip'al* pf. 3 fem. sg. from בקק "empty," so "be emptied," "be poured out." *BHS* suggests ונבקה as the grammatically more correct form, but see GKC §67*dd.* Marti and others follow LXX ταραχθήσεται, "agitated," "troubled," to read נָבֹכָה, *nip'al* pf. from בוך (Esth 3:15), "be perplexed," "confused." However, MT may be kept.

3.b. LXX τοὺς θεοὺς αὐτῶν, "their gods."

3.c. LXX καὶ τὰ ἀγάλματα αὐτῶν, "and their images"; Vg. *divinos suos,* "his gods." Heb. אט is a *hap. leg.* BDB (31) translates "mutterer." Wildberger (700) and *HAL* think it is a loanword from Akk. meaning "spirits of the dead;" similarly *DCH* "ghost."

3.d. אבות, "mediums" (cf. Isa 8:19; 29:4). LXX τοὺς ἐκ τῆς γῆς φωνοῦντας, "ones who speak from the ground" (see *Comment* on 8:19). M. Dietrich, O. Loretz, and J. Sanmartin relate Ugar. *ilib* to Heb. אוב, meaning "spirit of the dead" ("Ugaritisch *ilib* und hebraisch *ʾ(w)b* 'Totengeist,'" *UF* 6 [1974] 450–51).

3.e. ידענים, "fortune-tellers" or "familiar spirits," is usually paired with אוב, "mediums," in the OT.

4.a. The combination of pl. noun and sg. adj. requires explanation. *HebSyntax* §19*c* calls it an emphatic pl. to recognize a higher power. Joüon §48*a* explains the sg. adj. as a frequent occurrence. H. D. Hummel ("Enclitic *Mem* in Early NW Semitic," *JBL* 76 [1957] 101) thinks the final *mem* in אדנים was originally a *mem* enclitic on a sg. form. The pl. may well describe local tyrants who are forced, in turn, to render allegiance to a higher ruler.

4.b. LXX βασιλεῖς σκληροί, "fierce kings."

4.c. האדון, "the Lord," has no counterpart in either LXX or Syr.

5.a. ים, as in 18:2, means not "sea" but the Nile river. Cf. Herodotos, *Histories* 2.97, and Pliny the Elder, *Natural History* 37, *in Nilo cuius est aqua marls similis,* "in the Nile whose waters are like the sea"; Seneca, *Naturales quaestiones* 4a.2, *continuatis aquis in faciem lati ac turbidi marls stagnat,* "an expanse of water, broad in shape, indeed which overflows into a troubled sea" (both cited by Wildberger).

6.a. נהרות may refer to the branches of the Nile or to its network of canals.

6.b. האזניחו. 1QIsa[a] omits א to read a *hip'il* pf. from זנח. GKC §§19*m,* 53*g* explain it as *alef prostheticum.* This *hap. leg.* probably means "they stink."

6.c. מָצוֹר is sg. whereas "Egypt" is usually a dual: מצרים. Delitzsch, Dillmann, and Kittel *(BHK)* thought it referred only to Lower Egypt. None of the versions understood it to mean Egypt. Wildberger (701) suggests it is deliberately chosen because it has a double meaning (also "siege") so that its name would also indicate its fate.

6.d. קָמֵל, "decay." The word occurs only here and in 33:9. Other meanings ("become black," Wildberger; "he afflicted with lice," KBL) have been suggested but are no improvement (so *HAL*).

7.a. ערות, a *hap. leg.* LXX καὶ τὸ ἄχι, "swamp-grass." Vg. *nudabitur,* "be stripped"; BDB (788) "bare places." Wildberger (701) traces its meaning to an Eg. word for the stalk or stem of a plant (followed by *HAL*). He also finds LXX καὶ correct, a *vav* lost through haplography, which puts ערות, "stalks," with קנה, "a reed," and סוף, "a rush."

7.b-b. Missing in LXX. But it may be seen as emphatic repetition.

7.c. 1QIsa[a] יבש (for MT יִיבַשׁ) is a pf. form instead of impf. Both mean "be dried up, withered."

7.d. ואיננו, "nothing of it," is missing in LXX. 1QIsa[a] ואין בו has a meaning similar to MT.

8.a. 1QIsa[a] הדגים, "the fish." Wildberger notes the MT הדיגים, "the fishermen," maintains the parallel meaning to the second half of the verse.

8.b. The const. state before a prep. is unusual. Cf. *HebSyntax* §70.

9.a. שריקות, a *hap. leg.*, may be related to a later Heb. root and a Syr. word meaning "combed." KBL, *BHS*, Wildberger (701), and *HAL* suggest moving the *ʾatnakh* back one word and reading שֹׂרְקוֹת, an act. ptc., following Vg. *pectentes* and Syr. *dsrkjn*, "the combers," thus giving a balanced verse:

The flax workers are dismayed: 3+3
the combers and weavers of linen.

9.b. This pl. of a fem. word פֵּשֶׁת speaks of the stems of flax that must be worked to obtain the hemp fiber needed for spinning.

9.c. 1QIsa[a] חורו, "they bleach." However, MT makes sense as it is.

10.a שתתיה appears to be a pl. of שֵׁת, "foundation," but this is meaningless and does not fit the masc. מדכאים, "crushed," that follows. LXX οἱ διαζόμενοι αὐτὰ ἐν ὀδύνῃ, "which draws the chair of the weaver's loom." This suggests a word שְׁתִי, "woven goods," or "warp" (BDB, 1059–60), which led to comparisons with Akk. *šatū*, Heb. שתה, "weave," the Aram. שְׁתָא, "weave," and שְׁתְיָא, "warp" (Wildberger, 702). I. Eitan ("An Egyptian Loan Word in Isa 19," *JQR* 15 [1924–25] 419–22) added Coptic *štit*, "weaver." These lead to שְׁתִיתֶיהָ, "her weavers" (cf. *BHS*, KBL, Wildberger [702], *HAL*, and NIV).

10.b. LXX ζῦτον, "beer"; Syr. *škr*ʾ = שְׂכַר, "drink." These have led to many emendations. But שֶׂכֶר in Prov 11:18 clearly means "wages."

10.c. אגמי usually means "pools of." Vg. *lacunas ad capiendos pisces*, "places for taking fish" (followed by Ibn Ezra) has led some MSS to read אגמי מים, "pools of water." But T. Nöldeke (*ZDMG* 40 [1886] 727) and M. D. Goldman (*ABR* 2 [1952] 50) identified אגמי with עגמי, "ones grieved," which in Job 30:25 is also used with נפש, "soul" (followed by BDB, *HAL*, *DCH*).

11.a-a. The five words in this half verse lead commentators (Wildberger and others) to suspect that it is too full and to suggest that עצה, "counsel," should be eliminated. The unusual double const. form חכמי יעצי, "wisest couselors of," led G. R. Driver (*JTS* 38 [1937] 40) to emend יֹעֲצֵי, "counselors of," to יָעֲצוּ, "they give counsel." But the double const. is possible, and Masoretic accentuation suggests a three-part line.

11.b. קדם may mean "former times" or "the East." The wisdom of Edom and of Teman (cf. 1 Kgs 5:10; Jer 49:7) was famous. But in Egypt the wisdom of the past, especially of past kings, was highly favored.

12.a. וידעו (*qal* impf.), "and they know" or "that they know." LXX εἰπάτωσαν, "let them say," and Vg. *et indicent*, "and saying" or "and let them say" (ptc. as impv.), led Gray, Duhm, Kissane, Kaiser, and Wildberger to read וְיֹדִיעוּ (*hipʿil* juss.), "and make them to know," to parallel וְיַגִּידוּ, "let them declare." The Masoretes abandon metrical balance to point it as they do. MT should be sustained.

13.a.,b. 1QIsa[a] נאולו and נשואו. Wildberger follows KBL in suggesting the existence of so-far unknown verb roots אול beside יאל and שוא beside נשא.

13.c. פִּנַּת, "chief of." Following Syr. and Tg. and in view of Judg 20:2 and 1 Sam 14:38, many (including Duhm, Marti, Ehrlich *[Randglossen]*, and Kaiser) read a pl. פנות, "chiefs of." Wildberger (702) suggests that the sg. is to be understood as collective (cf. Gray; GKC §145*bc*).

14.a. LXX has a pl. αὐτοῖς.

14.b. עועים (pl.), "a spirit of distortings," "warped judgments" (BDB, 730). 1QIsa[a] עועיים strengthens the view that this is a reduplicated form of עוה, "do wrong, twist" (*HAL*).

14.c. A masc. suf. beside a fem. in v 13*c* parallels the use of masc. and fem. for Egypt in v 12.

15.a-a. LXX translates freely as ἀρχὴν καὶ τέλος, "beginning and end."

Form/Structure/Setting

The "Burden: Egypt" consists of three parts: a vision of YHWH's intervention in Egypt (19:1–15) that reverses his stance in 18:4, a prediction of the fine results that could develop from that move (19:16–25), and the narrative in 20:1–6.

The vision in 19:1–15 portrays YHWH's approach and Egyptian dismay (v 1); YHWH's speech announcing internal conflict and deliverance to a fierce king, the Ethiopian Sabaka (vv 2–4); a drought that brings economic disaster (vv 5–10); and a taunt against the counselors of Pharaoh (vv 11–15).

Vv 1–4 are a threat introduced by הנה, "see." Calling attention to God's own action in such a form is typical for Isaiah (cf. 3:1; 8:7; 10:33; 22:17; 24:1; 26:21;

30:27; 35:4; 40:9, 10; 51:22; 54:11; 60:2; 62:11). In chap. 3 the introduction leads to YHWH's own speech in v 4. It is the same here in chap. 19. YHWH's speech begins in v 2. Wildberger (708) notes the parallel between the chapters. In chap. 3 God turns Judah over to its own self-destruction. The same thing occurs in chap. 19, where Egypt is victimized by its own paranoia and by indecisive leaders (v 11–14). Vv 11–15 begin like a speech of judgment (see Wildberger, 717), but the speech is quickly changed by the recognition (vv 14–15) that YHWH is responsible. It is usual in Isaiah to close such a threat with the formula "expression of the Lord YHWH of Hosts," but that phrase is missing here.

Nicacci (*VT* 48 [1998] 214–38) has made a case for seeing Isa 19 as a description of conditions in the late eighth century B.C.E. He notes that Tiglath-Pileser III captured Gaza in 734/735 B.C.E. and "established a tradition center there" (*VT* 48 [1998] 215). Sargon retook Gaza and defeated an Egyptian army at Rafia in 720. "Having thus secured his borders, he could envisage a large area of trade and friendly relations between Assyrians and Egyptians" (*VT* 48 [1998] 215). For a critique of this position, see Sawyer, "Blessed Be My People Egypt."

Comment

1 The burden of Egypt stands as a counterweight to that of Damascus. Both call attention to contemporary developments. Damascus and Israel stood desolate as monuments to YHWH's completed judgment, which Jerusalem chose to ignore (17:10–11). Now events in Egypt are seen as YHWH's work, suggesting new opportunity, if Judah will only see it and act upon it.

The figure of YHWH "riding on a . . . cloud" fits the background of OT celestial imagery that was taken over from Canaanite pictures of Baal, the weather god (cf. Wildberger's summary, 710). YHWH is pictured as riding the heavens (Deut 33:26), riding the cherubim and the wings of the wind (2 Sam 22:11//Ps 18:11), and riding the skies (Pss 68:5 [4]; 104:3). His freedom of movement, his universal scope of action, and his control of nature are recalled. No wonder the idols and Egyptians tremble.

לבב ימס, "heart melts": cf. 7:2, where similar language speaks of Judah's lack of moral strength before Aram and Syria and urges the king not to weaken in his resolve. The words and ideas come from the formal language of holy war (cf. Deut 20:3). They imply that collapse of the opponent's morale ensures victory.

2 "I will incite Egypt against Egypt" (cf. Judg 7:22; 2 Kgs 3:23; Isa 3:5; Zech 14:13; Ezek 38:21; 1 Sam 14:20) and "city against city, kingdom against kingdom" are apt descriptions of the situation in Egypt of the Twenty-Fifth Dynasty. J. H. Breasted (*History of Egypt* [New York: Scribner's, 1905] 536) wrote, "The power of the dominant house rapidly waned until there was at last an independent lord or petty king in every city of the Delta and up the river as far as Hermopolis. We are acquainted with the names of eighteen of these dynasties, whose struggles among themselves now led to the total dissolution of the Egyptian state."

3 Internal chaos leads to Egypt's impotence as it had to Judah's (cf. chap. 3). God turns them over to a strong tyrant ruler from outside the realm. For Judah that was Assyria (7:17). For Egypt it is Ethiopia's new ruler, Shabaka. Their panic leads them to useless necromancy (cf. 8:19–22).

4 Wildberger (712) notes a return to the language of holy war. The usual phrase is נתן ביד, "put into the hand of" (cf. G. von Rad, *Der Heilige Krieg im Alten Israel,* 3d ed. ATANT 20 [Zurich: Zwingli, 1958] 7). The phrase here is stronger: סכר ביד, "shut up in the hand of."

The identity of the "cruel masters" and "powerful king" has been debated. Bright (*HI,* 281) suggests the Ethiopian Pianchi, who took over Upper Egypt in 730 B.C.E. Kitchen (*Third Intermediate Period in Egypt,* 125) suggests that it is Shabaka, who first established the authority of the Ethiopian dynasty over the cities of the delta in 716–12 B.C.E. This suggestion fits the polarity of Egypt-Ethiopia in chaps. 18–19 and the basic time frame of this section of Isaiah. There has been no lack of other suggestions, depending on the particular fragmentation of the book that the commentator preferred. Wildberger favors Sargon since, in his opinion, this refers to a foreign domination. And Ethiopia is not foreign enough. If one breaks away from the contextual setting, almost any king that ever conquered Egypt will do. And there have been many. Shabaka clearly fits the context best, as Procksch and Eichrodt have agreed.

5–10 These verses pick up the theme of YHWH's control of weather and nature, including planting and harvest, which appeared in 17:4–6 about Israel, in 17:10–11 about Jerusalem, and in 18:4–6 about impending developments.

The failure of the Nile to provide sufficient water is the ultimate nightmare for an Egyptian. "The Prophecy of Nefer-Rohu" (sometimes called Nefertiti) pictures such a scene (*ANET,* 445): "The rivers of Egypt are empty, (so that) the water is crossed on foot. Men seek for water for the ships to sail on. Its course is (become) a sandbank. . . . [D]amaged indeed are those good things, those fish ponds (where there were) those who clean fish, overflowing with fish and fowl." The text is much earlier than Isaiah's time but illustrates Egypt's dependence on the Nile's rise and fall. The Egyptians believed the Nile's timely rise and fall were a gift of the gods (see Wildberger, 714). Herodotus (*Histories* 2.9) could not explain the regular annual ebb and flow of the Nile. Of course, it is now known that the winter rains over central African plateaus, which drain through the Nile, and the summer rains over the Ethiopian highlands, which drain through from the Blue Nile, together account for the phenomena (cf. A. Moret, *The Nile and Egyptian Civilization,* trans. M. R. Dobie [New York: Knopf, 1927]; W. S. LaSor, "Egypt," *ISBE,* 2:31).

The speech is a remarkable description of economic distress that follows the failure of the annual Nile floods. The drought affects farmers, fishers, and the secondary enterprises that depend upon them, in this case the textile workers. The context draws upon the picture of YHWH's reign over the weather and over nature (19:1) to account for the conditions. Egypt's troubles are cumulative and interrelated. The external political pressures (18:4) combine with internal ones (18:2–3) and with natural economic disasters (18:5–10) to bring Egypt to its knees.

11–15 The passage begins like an accusation. The speech asks the counselors of the court to defend themselves (v 11). When they are silent, the speech turns to the Egyptians with the challenge that they make the wise men talk (v 12). It closes by recognizing that YHWH has caused the counsel of the wise to err (vv 14–15).

11 צען, "Zoan," is usually identified as Tanis, the Egyptian delta city nearest Palestine. The counsel that is required is political advice. The wise men of Egypt claimed a direct descent from the most ancient kings, who were also the most wise.

12 But the content of wisdom according to this speech lies in knowing "what YHWH of Hosts has planned against Egypt." This the wise men never claimed to know. But the message, actually addressed to Jerusalem and its leaders rather than Egyptians, insists that this is the only basis for true wisdom and political counsel. Chaps. 18–19 are intended to elucidate exactly this "plan" for that period. (See v 17 and *YHWH's Strategy* in the *Introduction.*)

13 נף, "Noph," is Memphis (or On or Heliopolis), at the head of the delta, a city that often served as Egypt's northern capital. Pianchi conquered Memphis in 728 B.C.E., but then he withdrew to Napata. It remained for his brother Shabaka to control it effectively from 715 B.C.E. onward. פנת שבטיה, "the chiefs of her tribes," emphasizes the splintered nature of Egypt in this time—a far cry from the proud and powerful unity of other days.

Kitchen's descriptions (*Third Intermediate Period in Egypt,* 348–77) of the Twenty-Second, Twenty-Third, Twenty-Fourth, and Twenty-Fifth Dynasties shows that in 715 B.C.E. there were four pharaohs in Egypt claiming the throne. (See table in Wildberger, 720–21.) Osorkon IV ruled in Tanis (the eastern delta), the last of the Bubastide or Twenty-Second Dynasty. Shoshenk VI was presumably in Leontopolis (the central delta), the last of the Twenty-Third Dynasty. Bokchoris ruled in Sais (the western delta) as the last of the Twenty-Fourth Dynasty. J. H. Breasted writes of knowing the names of at least eighteen kings or princes who ruled delta cities in that time (*History of Egypt* [New York: Scribner's, 1905] 536). Shabaka was just assuming the throne in Napata (upper Nile). He would take control of Egypt within the year.

14–15 Egypt (the delta kings) seems to have no discernible policy to meet the Assyrian threat and seems to be blind to the rising power of Ethiopia. The Vision suggests that even "the folly of man may serve the purposes of God" (Clements, 169). God has waited for things to develop (that is, for the harvest to ripen; see Isa 17:5). Now he moves toward his goals.

Explanation

See *Explanation* for 19:16–25.

Worship of YHWH in Egypt: Five "In That Day" Passages (19:16–25)

Bibliography

Abel, F. M. "Les confins de la Palestine et de l'Egypte." *RB* 49 (1940) 224–39. **Beek, M. A.** "Relations entre Jerusalem et la diaspora egyptienne au 2e siecle avant J.-C." *OtSt* 2 (1943) 119–43. **Causse, A.** "Les origines de la diaspora juive." *RHPR* 7 (1927) 97–128. **Cowley, A.** *Aramaic Papyri of the Fifth Century B.C.* 1923. Reprint, Osnabruck: Zeller, 1967. **Deissler, A.** "Der Volk und Land überschreitende Gottesbund der Endzeit nach Jes 19,16–25." In *Zion: Ort der Begegnung.* FS L. Klein, ed. F. Hahn et al. Bodenheim: Athenäum Hain

Hanstein, 1993. 7–18. **Delcor, M.** "Le Problème des jardins d'Adonis dans Isaïe 17,9–11." *Syria* 54 (1977) 371–94. ———. "Le Temple d'Onias en Egypte." *RB* 75 (1968) 188–205. **Feuillet, A.** "Un sommet religieux de l'Ancien Testament: L'oracle d'Isa 19:19–25 sur la conversion de l'Egypte." *RSR* 39 (1951) 65–87. **Harmatta, J.** "Zur Geschichte des frühhellenistischen Judentums in Ägypten." *AAASH* 7 (1959) 337–409. **Hayward, R.** "The Jewish Temple at Leontopolis: A Reconsideration." *JJS* 33 (1982) 429–43. **Hengel, M.** *Judaism and Hellenism.* Trans. J. Bowden. London: SCM Press, 1974. **Jirku, A.** "Die fünf Städte bei Jes 19:18 und die fünf Tore des Jahu-Tempels zu Elephantine." *OLZ* 15 (1912) 247–48. **Kooij, A. van der.** "The Old Greek of Isaiah 19:16–25: Translation and Interpretation." In *VI Congress of the International Organization for Septuagint and Cognate Studies, Jerusalem, 1986.* Ed. E. Cox. Atlanta: Scholars Press, 1986. 127–66. **Porten, B.** "The Jews in Egypt." In *CHJ.* 1:372–400. **Randles, R. J.** "The Interaction of Israel, Judah and Egypt: From Solomon to Josiah." Diss., Southern Baptist Theological Seminary, 1980. 155–208. **Sawyer, J. F. A.** "Blessed Be My People Egypt (Isaiah 19:25): The Context and Meaning of a Remarkable Passage." In *A Word for All Seasons.* FS William McKane, ed. J. D. Martin and P. R. Davies. Sheffield: JSOT Press, 1986. 57–71. **Schürer, E.** *Geschichte des jüdischen Volkes.* 3d ed. Leipzig: Hinrichs, 1902. **Shenker, A.** "La fine dela storia di Israeli recapitolera il suo inizio: Esegesi di Is 19,16–25." *RivB* (1994) 321–29. **Steuernagel, C.** "Bemerkungen fiber die neuentdeckten jüdischen Papyrusurkunden aus Elephantine und ihre Bedeutung für das Alte Testament." *TSK* 22 (1909) 1–12. **Vogels, W.** "Egypte mon Peuple: L'Universalisme d'Isa 19:16–25." *Bib* 57 (1976) 494–515. **Wilson, I.** "In That Day: From Text to Sermon on Isaiah 19:23–25." *Int* 22 (1967) 66–86. **Wodecki, B. S. V. D.** "The Heights of the Religious Universalism in Is XIX: 16–25." In *"Lasset uns Brücken Bauen . . .": Collected Communication of the Xvth Congress of the Organization for the Study of the Old Testament, Cambridge 1995.* BEATAJ 42. Bern: Lang, 1998. 117–91.

Translation

Earth:	16 *In such a day,*	2
	Egypt [a] *is like (the) women.*	3+2
	It [b] *trembles and is in dread*	
	in the face of the waving hand of YHWH of Hosts,	4+3
	which he is waving [c] *against it.* [b]	
Heavens:	17 *(As)* [a] *the soil of Judah becomes*	3+2
	for Egypt a festival, [b]	
	everyone who [c] *remembers*	3+3
	her sign [d] *toward it trembles*	
	in the face of the plan of YHWH of Hosts	4+4
	that he is planning against it.	
Earth:	18 *In such a day, there would be*	3+3
	five cities in the land of Egypt	
	speaking the language of Canaan	3+3
	and swearing [a] *(allegiance) to YHWH of Hosts.*	
	One would be called the city of destruction. [b]	4
Heavens:	19 *In such a day, there would be*	3+2+3
	an altar to YHWH	
	in the middle of the land of Egypt	
	and a pillar dedicated to YHWH at its border,	4
	20 *which would become a sign, a witness* [a] *to YHWH of Hosts*	

in the land of Egypt. When they cry out to YHWH in the face of oppressors, he will send[b] *a savior and judge*[c] *who will deliver them.*

[21]*And YHWH will make himself known to Egypt,* 3+3+2
and Egypt will know YHWH
in such a day.
They will worship (him with) sacrifices and offerings. 3+3+1
They will vow a vow to YHWH.
And they will fulfill (it).
[22]*And (if) YHWH strike Egypt with a plague,* 3+2
striking and healing,[a]
(if) they turn to YHWH 2+3
he will respond to them and heal them.
Earth: [23]*In such a day, there would be* 3+3
a highway from Egypt to Assyria.
Assyria would come to Egypt, 3+2
and Egypt to Assyria.
And they would worship,[a] *Egypt with Assyria.* 3
Heavens: [24]*In such a day,* 3+2+2
Israel would be third
to [a]*Egypt and Assyria:* [a]
a blessing in the midst of the land, 3
[25]*with which YHWH of Hosts is blessing them,* 5
"Blessed[a] *(be) my people, Egypt,*[b] 3+3+2
the work of my hands, Assyria,
and my inheritance, Israel."

Notes

16.a. LXX οἱ Αἰγύπτιοι, "the Egyptians" (pl.), has caught the evident sense. The Heb. uses a collective sense and a sg. verb.

16.b. 1QIsa[a] has pl. forms for MT's sg.

16.c. 1QIsa[a] adds ידו, "his hand." But MT's meaning is clear as it is.

17.a. The expansive prose style raises questions of relation to v 16. והיתה, "and it [fem.] will be," has "the soil of Judah" for its subject, and this is not a continuation of the verbs "tremble" and "be in dread." It is better understood as an expansion of the controlling clause "Egypt becomes like the women." Judah's festival is another comparison.

17.b. חָגָּא is a *hap. leg.* LXX φόβητρον, "a terrifying object." Vg. *erit in festivitatem,* "will be in festival mood" has read it as חגג, "to celebrate a festival." The more usual translation follows LXX. G. R. Driver (*JTS* 34 [1933] 378) is followed by KBL and *HAL* with the meaning "shamed," but (in *JSS* 13 [1968] 46) he added "to be struck" as a possible meaning. The *Translation* follows Vg. with BDB, *DCH.* See *Comment.*

17.c. כל אשר: Wildberger (728) translates "everytime when" and suggests different subjects for the two verbs. The time reference is not impossible, referring to the festival. But the common subject for both verbs is surely the celebrant of the festival.

17.d. אֹתָהּ may be the sign of direct obj. with the 3d fem. sg. pronoun "her." But את may also be read as the "defective" form of אוֹת, "a sign." It appears thus frequently (cf. Exod 4:8 and elsewhere) and is regularly written without ו in pl. and with sufs., and, hence, "her sign." As such it is a strong reminder of the festival of YHWH's "signs and wonders," Passover.

18.a. Wildberger notes that "to swear by" someone in Heb. is נשבע ב (so Syr. *wjmjn bmrjh*). However, the reading with ל appears in 2 Chr 15:14 with the meaning "to enter a relationship by an oath" (BDB, 989; cf. *HAL* and also Josh 6:22; 9:20; Isa 45:23, where both combinations appear).

18.b. הַהֶרֶס, a *hap. leg.*, appears to mean "destruction": City of Destruction. 1QIsa[a], supported by many MSS, and several versions have החרס, "the Sun"; Vg. *civitas Solis*. Wildberger traces the translation on to Jerome, who identifies this with Heliopolis. LXX πόλις ασεδεκ transliterates הצדק, "righteousness," as the city's name (see *HAL;* cf. 1:26). α´ and θ´ simply tranliterate הרס as αρες, confirming MT. Syr. also confirms MT. Tg. combines the two meanings: קרתא בית שמש דעתידא למחרב, "the city Beth-Shemesh (House of the Sun), which is to be destroyed because of that." The consensus of interpreters is that it does refer to Heliopolis in Egypt, which is often called אוֹן or אָן, *On*, in the OT but which in Jer 43:13 is called Beth Shemesh.

20.a. לְעֵד, "a testimony." LXX εἰς τὸν αἰῶνα = לָעַד, reading the same consonants but pronouncing them differently.

20.b. 1QIsa[a] has ושלח for MT's וישלח, "he will send." It is only a change of tense.

20.c. וָרָב, "and ruler." *Qamets* under *vav* is apparently to strengthen pronunciation (GKC §104*g*). 1QIsa[a] ויריד (impf.), "and he will rule." LXX reads a ptc., κρίνων, "judge." Vg. *propugnatorem*, "defender." *BHS* וְרָב changes it to pf. with וּ: "and he will rule" (also Kissane, Feldmann, Wildberger). The question is whether it will pair with "savior" before it, as in MT, or with "and he will deliver" after it. There seems to be no reason to abandon MT's reading.

22.a. Two inf. abs. Cf. Joüon §123*m*. The second action grows out of the first.

23.a. עבד in v 21 had a cultic meaning, "to serve," "worship." LXX translates δουλεύσουσιν, giving it a political meaning: Egypt will serve Assyria. If it has the cultic meaning, one must translate "Egyptians will worship with Assyria(ns)." Cf. Gray and Wildberger. The issue is not easy. The verb ועבדו is pl. Egypt and Assyria are sg., joined not by "and" but by אֵת, "with," or a sign of direct obj. "Worship" certainly fits the context best, but "serve," "be a vassal" fits the historical situation more realistically. The context calls for a cultic meaning (cf. Wildberger, 744).

24.a-a. LXX reverses the order.

25.a. LXX ἣν εὐλόγησε (3d sg. aor.), "which [fem.] he praises," i.e., a verb. *BHS* suggests reading בֵּרְכָהּ, a fem. suf., because the antecedent must refer to "blessing" or "land," both of which are fem. This is not reflected in translation because the personal pronoun is absorbed in the English relative pronoun (cf. G. Wehmeier, *Der Segen im Alten Testament* [Basel: Reinhardt, 1970] 87).

25.b. LXX ὁ λαός μου ὁ ἐν Αἰγύπτῳ, "my people who are in Egypt," loses the force of the concluding statement.

Form/Structure/Setting

The results of YHWH's intervention in the Cushite-Egyptian conflict are pictured with five "in that day" announcements: (1) Judah will terrorize the Egyptians (vv 16–17). (2) Five cities will speak a Canaanite language (v 18). (3) An altar to YHWH will be set up in Egypt, Egyptians will worship YHWH, and he will respond to them (vv 19–22). (4) A highway will be built between Egypt and Assyria, and they will cooperate even in worship (v 23). (5) Israel, Egypt, and Assyria will all be under YHWH's rule (vv 24–25).

References to YHWH's "plan" or "strategy" appear in 19:12 and 17. This theme, which figured prominently in YHWH's bringing of the Assyrian (chaps. 7–10), is now invoked in relation to the rise of the Ethiopian (Twenty-Fifth) Dynasty in Egypt. (See *YHWH's Strategy* in the *Introduction*.) It was suggested in 17:7–8 that the time was ripe for humankind to turn to the worship of YHWH after the judgment on Aram and Israel. Egyptian and Assyrian participation in such worship with Israel is portrayed in 19:18–25. But in 17:10–11 Jerusalem was accused of "forgetting God" and of pagan practices. Chap. 20 will show that the governmental policies of Jerusalem have heeded neither the burden of Damascus nor that of Egypt. It marches to the rhythm of a different drummer, Merodach-Baladan's Babylon (chap. 21), which will lead to its downfall (chap. 22).

Comment

16–17 Against the divided princedoms even Judah's force was a threat. But this is only true as YHWH acts through Judah. And that depends on Judah's cooperation with God's plan, i.e., being willing to work with Assyria and Ethiopia (19:2). ביום ההוא, "in such a day" (lit., "in that day"), points back to 19:1, when YHWH rides the clouds in Egypt, the day when his plan matures (18:4–6). The general comparison to women trembling is unique in the OT. Often a woman in childbirth is so pictured.

תנופת יד, "the waving hand," recalls the cultic waving of sacrifices "before YHWH" to dedicate them to him (cf. Exod 29:24). (See R. J. Thompson, *Penitence and Sacrifice in Early Israel Outside the Levitical Law* [Leiden: Brill, 1963] 206 n 4.) Wildberger (732) interprets this to mean that he brings judgment, but also that he claims the land as his own. The waving hand also is a reminder of the plagues against Egypt and of the open way through the Sea of Reeds. The verses picture the Egyptians' dread when they recognize that YHWH is directing the battle ("waving his hand"; cf. 5:25; 9:12, 17, 21; 10:4) against them. The women are not identified. They seem to be civilian nonparticipants who can only tremble at the thought of the developing battle.

אדמת יהודה, "the soil of Judah," is unique. It calls to mind the promised land inherited by YHWH's chosen people.

Some would translate חגא as "shamed" or "be struck" (see *Note* 17.b.). The Vg. directs its thought to חג, "festival," which fits the context, parallel to "remember" or "makes mention" in the next line. The festival must be Passover. The thought that the event celebrated in Passover might repeat itself in YHWH's plan was awful to Egypt. One remembers the plagues on Egypt (Exod 7–10), especially the death of the firstborn (Exod 11–12).

The reason for fear was the recognition of God's plan. The cognate reduplication (יועץ, "planning" and עצת, "a plan") also occurs in 14:26 and 8:10. It suggests that the plan of YHWH will be fulfilled by events in Egypt. The idea that plans proclaimed long ago may be signs of God's later work is found in Isa 40:21; 41:26; 44:8. The news that YHWH, of Passover fame, has plans for Egypt is reason enough for fear. (See *YHWH's Strategy* in the *Introduction*.) It is worth noting with Randles that "Manasseh of Judah . . . was compelled to participate in the invasion of Egypt led by Ashurbanipal in 667 B.C.E." ("Interaction of Israel, Judah and Egypt," 232; cf. *ANET,* 294).

18 מדברות שפת כנען, "speaking the language of Canaan," means speaking Hebrew, or possibly Aramaic. נשבעות ליהיה צבאות, "swearing allegiance to YHWH of Hosts," apparently means that a ruling majority of Jews or proselytes existed.

חמש ערים, "five cities." Jer 44:1 knows of four cities in Egypt where Jews are living some 130 years later: Migdol (apparently near the Palestinian border), Tahpanhes (probably also near the border), the land of Pathos, and Noph (Memphis). One is to be called ההרס, "city of destruction" (see *Note* 18.b.). Nothing further is known of such cities.

Jews were in Egypt from early times, probably from Solomon's time on (cf. 1 Kgs 14:25–28; 2 Chr 12:1–9, which may imply taking prisoners). Lists of Jews/Israelites to be returned to Israel regularly mention Egypt (cf. Isa 11:11, "from [Lower] Egypt, from Pathros [Upper Egypt], from Cush"; in Obad 20, "Sepharad" is probably located in Libya: see J. D. W. Watts, *Obadiah: A Critical Exegetical Commentary* [Grand Rapids, MI: Eerdmans, 1969] 64; J. Gray, "The Diaspora of Israel and Judah in Obadiah v 20," *ZAW* 65 [1953] 53–59). The letters found in Elephantine (modern Aswan) witness to a strong Jewish community of mercenaries (A. E. Cowley, *Aramaic Papyri of the Fifth Century* B.C. [Oxford: Clarendon, 1932]; *ANET,* 222; *DOTT,* 256–69; R. K. Harrison, "Elephantine Papyri," *ISBE,* 2:58–61). They also testify to the presence of Aramaic in Egypt in the fifth century B.C.E. (See *Excursus: Jewish Colonies and Temples in Egypt* below.) It is clear that readers of the Vision would find familiar data in such a reference to the five cities. They would be told that YHWH planned this as early as the reign of Hezekiah.

19–22 מזבח ליהוה, "an altar to YHWH." The usual movement in God's future is directed toward a return to Palestine or Jerusalem (Isa 10:21; 11:11–16; 14:1–2; and so on), but here in chap. 19 the movement is toward Egypt. The movement of political influence from Judah to Egypt (vv 16–17), the cultural influence through language (v 18), and now the religious effect of submission to YHWH are unmistakable. This is the most positive interpretation of the outward flow of population from Israel in the OT (comparable only to the NT's commissions in Matt 28:19–20; Acts 1:8).

Note the alliteration in מִזְבֵּחַ *mizbeah,* "altar," and מַצֵּבָה *maṣṣebah,* "pillar." An altar implies sacrifice and a priesthood (perhaps, though not necessarily, even a temple). It is a public symbol. A pillar or *maṣṣebah* is a usual sign beside a "high place" in Canaan. Both are to be clearly dedicated *to YHWH.* This is the point: the worship of YHWH in Egypt will be open and official. They are both to be a "sign" and a "witness" to YHWH in Egypt (v 20). YHWH will reveal himself to Egypt, and Egypt will "know YHWH" (v 21). A more complete statement of the full mutual relation of YHWH and Egypt cannot be imagined. That relation includes answered prayers (vv 20–22) and a whole range of worship (v 21). YHWH will do saving acts for them. He will send a savior in times of oppression, as he did for Israel in the judges (v 20). He will respond to repentance and prayers in times of distress (v 22).

Most comment on these verses has sought a historical correspondence (see *Excursus* below), but that misses the point. Historical fulfillment here, like historical fulfillment in each of the five ביום ההוא, "in that day," passages, *did not occur.* The political decisions taken by Jerusalem's government in the years between 716 and 714 B.C.E. prevented that (see chaps. 20–22). This Vision, like that of chaps. 11–12, shows God's view of the potential. The Vision puts God's view side by side with human beings' failure to see, hear, or understand and their determination to have their own way—even when that brought disaster.

The thought of an altar and a pillar to YHWH in Egypt runs directly counter to the movement to concentrate worship, even in Palestine, to Jerusalem (or one place) only (cf. Deuteronomy). Hezekiah participated in such a reform (2 Kgs 18:4; 2 Chr 31:1), to which the rabshakah makes reference (2 Kgs 18:22// Isa 36:7). This culminated in Josiah's reform and destruction of high places throughout the land (2 Kgs 22:4–20; 2 Chr 34:33) almost a century later. Ezra brought the process of concentrating sacrifice and worship exclusively in Jerusalem to completion (Ezra-Nehemiah). Contrary tendencies did exist (see *Excursus* below), although Deut 7:5; 12:3; Exod 23:24; 34:13 prohibit the raising of a *maṣṣebah.*

Excursus: Jewish Colonies and Temples in Egypt

Population flowed from Israel probably from Solomon's time onward, and Egypt was a prime recipient of such movement. Even earlier, Genesis reports movements in that direction by Abraham, Jacob, and Joseph. Jacob's descendants are reported to have lived there for four centuries. But there are no reports of altars or temples being built. Patriarchal worship did not require such, at least not in permanent form.

Solomon is reported to have had extensive commercial (1 Kgs 10:28–29) and diplomatic relations with Egypt (1 Kgs 3:1). These may well have called for exchange of personnel. Refugees from Solomon's kingdom were welcome in Egypt. Hadad of Edom (1 Kgs 11:18–22) and Jeroboam (1 Kgs 11:40) spent their years of exile there. Egypt campaigned against Judah and Israel in Rehoboam's day (1 Kgs 14:25–28; 2 Chr 12:2–12; see *MBA,* 120) and in Asa's time (2 Chr 14:8–14; 16:8; see *MBA,* 122). Such campaigns usually took prisoners for slaves or mercenaries.

At the other end of the kingdom period, Jeremiah records a significant number of Judeans who fled to Egypt (Jer 42–45; 2 Kgs 25:26; see *MBA,* 164). Evidence of a strong community of Jewish mercenaries in Aswan (Elephantine) is provided through the discovery of papyri there from the fifth century B.C.E. (cf. R. K. Harrison, "Elephantine Papyri," *ISBE,* 2:59–61; *ANET,* 222, 491). It contained a temple, a cultus, and a priesthood. The mercenaries may have arrived there with the Assyrian conquest of Egypt in the seventh century.

J. Harmatta ("Irano-Aramaica: Zur Geschichte des frühhellenistischen Judentum in Ägypten," *AAASH* 7 [1959] 337–409) names ten places between Migdol and Syene where Jews settled. The names of two priests are mentioned, one of whom lived at Thmuis. In the Hellenistic period Jewish settlements are known in many locations in Egypt (see *MBA,* 182). Josephus (*Jewish War* 3.102) tells of a temple at Leontopolis built by Onias IV, the son of a deposed high priest (cf. Wildberger, 737–39, for a detailed presentation). Alexander used Jewish mercenaries (Josephus, *Against Apion* 1.192). Ptolemy I brought 100,000 Jews to Egypt to colonize military settlements (*Letter of Aristeas* 12–14). M. Hengel (*Judaism and Hellenism,* 27) suggests that Ptolemy continued a policy that the Persians and even the last pharaohs of the Twenty-Sixth Dynasty had practiced.

There were Israelites and Jews in Egypt from early times onward, but that should not obscure the fact that Isa 19 is speaking not of Jews but of Egyptians who worship YHWH. Statistics on Egyptian proselytes are much more difficult to document.

23 מסלה ממצרים אשורה, "a highway from Egypt to Assyria." Roads serve many purposes. (See *Excursus: "Highway"* [מסלה] at 7:3–9.) They bear the traffic of trade. Soldiers and chariots march on them and send their caravans of matériel on them. Pilgrims use them (cf. Isa 11:16; 40:3; 62:10). International routes that connected Mesopotamia and Egypt already existed (*MBA,* 9). Various kinds of roads existed, from trodden paths that could accommodate caravans of camels from Abraham's time to built-up roads to handle chariots from Solomon's time (cf. I. Mendelsohn, "Travel, etc., in the OT," *IDB,* 4:688–90).

What is meant here goes beyond the physical existence of a road. It speaks of its various uses and functions. Communication of all kinds will be made possible. That includes trade and political interaction. But the context here draws one to a cultic meaning for עבד, "serve," and to the meaning "with" for אֵת: "they would worship, Egypt with Assyria." The highway facilitates a common worship. An illustration of this in modern terms is seen in common participation in worship by representatives from Muslim countries during diplomatic negotiations.

Cf. Isa 18:7, where Assyria (a people tall and fierce) sends gifts to YHWH in Jerusalem, implying recognition of YHWH, to say the least. However, one misses here the concrete ליהוה, "to YHWH," that was emphasized in vv 19–20.

A political interpretation would translate "the Egyptians will serve [i.e., be vassals of] Assyria." This would imply that Egypt bows to the Assyrian hegemony that YHWH sponsors (according to 10:5–7). It would fit the announcement in 19:4 if the "fierce king" is Sargon. However, it was shown above that this must refer to Ethiopia and Shabaka. The Egypt mentioned here is that of the Twenty-Fifth Dynasty under Shabaka, who maintained a formal and generally peaceful understanding with Sargon's Assyria.

24 This verse is the climax of the scene. Israel stands with Egypt and Assyria as a means of blessing in the midst of the earth. The highway runs through Palestine. Worship has its highest expression in Jerusalem.

ברכה בקרב הארץ, "blessing in the land," is a reminder of Gen 12:3 (G. Wehmeier, *Der Segen im AT* [Basel: Reinhardt, 1970] 87). Abraham's call promises that he and his descendants will be a blessing and that those who bless him (and his descendants) will be blessed. Worship of YHWH by Assyria and Egypt implies that they "bless themselves" by the God of Abraham. He owns the entire world and is worshiped accordingly in Jerusalem's temple.

25 YHWH's blessing uses phrases usually reserved for Israel: עמי, "my people, Egypt." If Egypt recognizes YHWH as "its God," then they are his people (Wildberger, 795). This is the corollary of v 21 above (cf. Ps 47:9–10 [8–9], where reference is made to "the people of the God of Abraham"). עמי, "my people," has strong covenant meaning in the OT, where Israel is understood to receive and maintain that relation to God through covenant. The vowing of vows to YHWH (v 11) may have a similar connotation, but the theme is not developed. The LXX translation (see *Note* 25.b.), "my people who are in Egypt and Assyria," limits the application to Jews there. Wildberger (745) notes that MT is nearer to the thought of Isa 40–66 than to Hellenistic Judaism.

מעשׂ ידי אשור, "the work of my hands, Assyria." In Isa 64:8 the claim is made that Israel is "God's people" and "the work of his hand." Israel is seen as God's creation in Isa 43:1, 15, בָּרָא, "creating"; 44:2, עָשָׂה, "making"; and 44:2, 24; 45:11, יָצַר, "forming." Other references are found in Deut 32:6, Isa 41:20, and Ps 100:3. But YHWH has also created the peoples of the earth (Ps 86:9). His relation to Assyria is already clear from his commands to her (7:17, 18, 20) and from the term שבט אפי, "rod of my anger" (10:5). Assyria as a world power in Palestine is a creature of YHWH's plan, according to this passage, but this verse goes beyond that to assure Assyria of YHWH's blessing and to claim Assyria as a means of blessing (à la Abraham) to others.

נחלתי ישראל, "my inheritance, Israel." Deut 32:9 reads "YHWH's portion is his people: Jacob his alloted inheritance" (author's trans.; Deut 4:20; Pss 28:9; 47:5; 94:5; Mic 7:14). Some commentators (Duhm, most recently Fohrer) suggest that Israel's title is the highest and best. It is certainly not less than the others. But that is to miss the significance of the passage. All three titles traditionally belong to Israel. Here they are shared with Assyria and Egypt. YHWH's divine *imperium* is seen to draw within its scope and purpose the entire known world.

Isa 19:25 could appear to have some relevance to the Hasmonian period: Assyria representing the Seleucid Empire, Egypt the Ptolomaic kingdom, and Israel the Hasmonian kingdom. But we will not pursue that here.

Explanation

Chap. 19 pictures the latent possibilities in the moves described in chaps. 15–18, as God would see them. The chapter paints a "scenario," a visionary image. The time is 716–715 B.C.E. Shabaka has just ascended the throne of his brother in Ethiopian Upper Egypt (Nubia, i.e., modern Sudan). He is preparing to assert his rule over Lower Egypt as well. To that end he seeks allies in Assyria and Judah (18:2). YHWH gives tacit approval, and apparently Assyria is willing.

In 18:5 the pruning of the shoots before the harvest is mentioned. What YHWH announces in 19:2–11 is exactly that. Egypt (the delta or Lower Egypt) is condemned (a "burden"). YHWH himself assures the outcome of the internal struggle by instigating civil wars among the city rulers of the delta (vv 2–4) and by causing drought in the land (vv 5–10), which brings economic ruin. The leaders are confused and helpless (vv 11–15).

Five passages beginning with "in such a day" portray the potential results. The Egyptians will be terrified at what YHWH is doing (vv 16–17). Hebrew presence and influence (including religious influence) will be felt in five cities (v 18). Worship of YHWH will be practiced in Egypt and recognized by YHWH (vv 19–22). Cooperation between Egypt and Assyria will open routes to peace, trade, and pilgrimage (v 23; cf. 18:7). Israel will have an important place beside Assyria and Egypt and will account for YHWH's blessings for the whole land. YHWH will claim and bless each member of the troika: Egypt, Assyria, and Israel (vv 23–25). This is one of the most universal statements of YHWH's intentions to be found in Scripture. It builds on Isaiah's view of Assyria as YHWH's tool (chap. 10) and points toward the picture of Cyrus as YHWH's servant (chaps. 45–46).

The chapter speaks of God's will. The language of the Vision is "God's plan" or "God's strategy." Suppose, at any juncture in time, God were to make the world do exactly what he wanted it to do. What would happen? Isa 18–19 asks and answers just such a question. Sargon is hard at work about 716 B.C.E. to consolidate a fractured empire. Judah has a new king. Egypt nears the end of a period of chaos as a strong new pharaoh is crowned in the Ethiopian capital, Napata. Pharaoh Shabaka seeks aid, or at least neutrality, on Egypt's northern border while he subjugates the errant cities of the delta (18:1–2). His messengers are referred by Jerusalem to Assyria, which holds genuine authority in the region. YHWH awaits developments (18:4*a*) but is understood to be prepared to act before the harvest (vv 4*b*–6).

The Vision dramatically portrays two basic developments. Gifts are brought to YHWH on Mount Zion by the Assyrians (18:7). This shows their agreement and commitment to his plan. Then YHWH, himself, moves against the Egyptians of the delta to put them under the suzerainty of a cruel, powerful king, Shabaka of the Ethiopian Twenty-Fifth Dynasty, in 716 B.C.E. (19:1–15).

Such developments would pave the way for five specific results of God's plan: (1) Judah's prestige and influence over Egypt increases dramatically (vv 16–17). (2) Five cities in Egypt speak a Canaanite tongue and swear by YHWH (v 18). (3)

An altar to YHWH is established in Egypt, and a memorial monument to him is set up on its border; he is worshiped, and he will respond to the worshipers (vv 19–22). (4) A highway is completed from Egypt to Assyria (of course, by way of Judah) to serve commerce and mutual worship of YHWH (v 23). (5) Israel, Egypt, and Assyria are proclaimed a triad of blessing under YHWH (vv 24–25).

Can one imagine? Modern Egypt, Israel, and Syria-Iraq becoming a triad of blessing and peace today? Open borders, flowing commerce, mutual worship? Even the possibility that Muslims, Christians, and Jews would worship together in Jerusalem? The dream has too many hindrances for it to become reality for our day. It seems that this was also true in 716 B.C.E., as chaps. 20–22 testify.

God's dreams! Worth thinking about!

Isaiah Demonstrates against an Alliance with Egypt (20:1–6)

Bibliography

Beck, B. L. "The International Roles of the Philistines during the Biblical Period." Diss., Southern Baptist Theological Seminary, 1980. 151–53. **Bright, J.** *HI.* 281–80. **Brunet, G.** *Essai sur l'Isaïe de l'Histoire.* 145–53. **Fohrer, G.** *Die Symbolischen Handlungen der Propheten.* 2d ed. Zurich: Zwingli, 1968. **Gottwald, N. K.** *All the Kingdoms of the Earth.* 167–68. **Haran, M.** "Isaiah the Prophet's Walking 'Naked and Barefoot for Three Years' (Isa 20)." In *Homage to Shmuel: Studies in the World of the Bible.* FS S. Ahituv. Jerusalem: Bialik, 2001. 163–66 (Hebrew). **Jenkins, A. K.** "The Development of the Isaiah Tradition in Is 13–23." In *Book of Isaiah.* Ed. J. Vermeylen. 245–46. **Kitchen, K. A.** *Third Intermediate Period in Egypt.* **Lang, B.** "Prophecy, Symbolic Acts, and Politics: A Review of Recent Studies." In *Monotheism and the Prophetic Minority.* Sheffield: Almond, 1983. 83–91. **Redford, D. W.** "Quest for the Crown Jewel: The Centrality of Egypt in the Foreign Policy of Esarhaddon." Ph.D. diss., Hebrew Union College, Cincinnati, 1998. **Spalinger, A.** "The Year 712 B.C. and Its Implications for Egyptian History." *Journal of the American Research Center in Egypt* 10 (1973) 95–101. **Tadmor, H.** "The Campaigns of Sargon II of Assur: A Chronological-Historical Study." *JCS* 12 (1958) 22–40, 70–100. ———. "Philistia under Assyrian Rule." *BA* 24 (1966) 86–102.

Translation

Narrator: (reading from a scroll)

1 *In the year that the Tartan*[a] *came to Ashdod, when Sargon*[b] *king of Assyria sent him, he fought against Ashdod and took*[c] *it.* 2 *In that period, YHWH spoke through*[a] *Isaiah,*[b] *son of Amoz: "Go and take off the sackcloth from your body and your sandals*[c] *from your feet." He proceeded to do so, walking stripped and barefoot.*

3 *Then YHWH said:*

"Just as my servant has walked 4+2
stripped and barefoot,[a]
three years, 2+2+2

a sign and a portent
against Egypt and against Ethiopia,
[4]*so the king of Assyria will drive away* 4
the captivity of Egypt 2+2
and the exiled group[a] *of Ethiopia,*
youths and elderly, 2+2
naked and barefoot,
with stripped buttocks[b] 2+2
and the nakedness of Egypt."
Heavens: [5]*They will be dismayed and ashamed* 2+2+2
of Ethiopia, their hope,[a]
and of Egypt, their boast.
Earth: [6]*The inhabitants of this coast will say* 4+2
[a]*in that day:*[a]
"See! Thus (it has happened to) our hope 3+3
whither we had fled[b] *for help,*
for deliverance[c] *from before the king of Assyria.* 4
How shall we ourselves escape?" 3

Notes

1.a. תרתן, "tartan," is an Akk. title for the military leader, the king, or crown prince. Cf. 2 Kgs 18:17. For the Akk. meanings, see Wildberger, 748. 1QIsa[a] תורתן, "turtan." (Cf. D. M. Beegle, "Proper Names in the Isaiah Scroll," *BASOR* 123 [1951] 28.)

1.b. The exact pronunciation varies: MT סַרְגוֹן, "Saregon." B סַרְגּוֹן, "Sargon." α´ θ´ σαραγων, σ´ σαργων (also LXX[Q]; Chrysostom quotes α´ θ´ as σαργουν), LXX αρνα or σαρνα (Ziegler reads Σαρναν). Akk. *šarru-kinu* means "the king is steadfast" or later *šarru-ukin,* "he (a god) has elected the king" (cf. PW 1A, 2, col. 2498).

1.c. 1QIsa[a] וילכודה indicates an older pronunciation. The form is undoubtedly the same.

2.a. LXX πρὸς, "by," for MT ביד, "by the hand of."

2.b. 1QIsa[a] ישעיה, "Isaiah" (like v 3), instead of MT ישעיהו, "Isaiahu." Syr. adds *nbj*ʾ, "the prophet."

2.c. 1QIsa[a] and the versions are pl. The same variation in sg. and pl. for "sandals" occurs in Exod 3:5 and Josh 5:15.

3.a. *BHS* moves the ʾ*atnakh* forward two words. It judges that this is the logical center of the verse. MT has chosen the metrical center.

4.a. 1QIsa[a] גולה for MT גלות. Meaning is the same.

4.b. חֲשׂוּפַי is an unusual form. Many emendations and explanations have been proposed. *BHS* (with Gray and Wildberger) is most likely with חֲשׂוּפֵי, "bare of," a const. pl.

5.a. 1QIsa[a] מבטחם, "their trust," from בטח for MT מבטם (BDB, 613) from נבט, "their hope," "expectation" (cf. v 6 and Zech 9:5).

6.a-a. LXX omits "in that day."

6.b. MT נסנו from נוס. Wildberger "we fled." 1QIsa[a] נסמך, "on whom one reckoned," *nip*ʿ*al* from סמך, which is usually followed by על, "upon."

6.c. MT has heavy accents (*zaqef katon*) on successive words: a very unusual accentuation.

Form/Structure/Setting

The chapter is a sober narrative. The opening phrase sets the historical frame (v 1). The second verse narrates a command for a symbolic act by his prophet, Isaiah. Vv 3–6 are a YHWH word with its echo explaining the symbolic action.

Isa 7:1–17 is of the same genre: narrative related to a historical incident. However, the narrower classification of recognizable symbolic action occurs only here, unless Isaiah's withdrawal with his children in chap. 8 should be so classified.

On symbolic actions see G. Fohrer, "Die Gattung der Bericht uber symbolische Handlungen der Propheten," *ZAW* 64 (1952) 101–20; and *Die Symbolischen Handlungen der Propheten,* ATANT 25 (Zurich: Zwingli, 1953).

How is the reader to understand the place of chap. 20 within the Vision of Isaiah? One should note that the narratives are in correct chronological order. From the death year of Uzziah (6:1) about 734 B.C.E. to the early reign of Ahaz (7:1–14), also about 734 B.C.E., to the death year of Ahaz (14:28) 725 or 718 B.C.E., to the Ashdod rebellion in Hezekiah's reign (chap. 20) about 714 B.C.E., to the years near the end of the century still in Hezekiah's reign (chaps. 36–39), 701 and 703 B.C.E., the order is correct. But how is the reader to place chap. 20 in act 2 (chaps. 13–27)? Is the narration loosely placed without relevance to the structure? Or does it serve as the center, the fulcrum, of a concentric structure with five burdens before it and five after it? Or is it to be subsumed under the burden of Egypt? See the discussion in the *Comment* on 19:1–15. To make it the center of the act has the problem of having such weighty "burdens" before it and such light literary structures as those in chaps. 21 and 22 after it—hardly a good balance. To join chap. 20 to chap. 19 leaves chaps. 21–22 to stand alone or also to be joined to the burden of Egypt. This commentary has chosen to read the narrative with chaps. 21–22 under "Burden: Egypt" to illustrate the anxieties of that time.

Comment

1 שנה, "the year," is apparently 712 or 711 B.C.E. Sargon has not been active in Palestine since one year after Samaria's destruction, 721 B.C.E., when a residual rebellion of Israelites and Philistines was put down. Assyrian texts report that Azuri, king of Ashdod, withheld tribute and tried to organize a coalition of states to rebel (*ANET,* 286, 249–62). This could well have taken place over several years and may have included contacts with Hezekiah. This brought Sargon's forces back into the area.

The Assyrian military action was thorough. Ashdod and its allies, including Gath, were defeated. A new king, approved by the Assyrians, was soon deposed by a Greek, Iamani. The Assyrians intervened again, reorganized the government, and deported some of their people, bringing in others from the east. The same report mentions friendly notes from the king of Ethiopia.

Sargon's accounts claim personal credit for the victory. This account, probably more accurately, speaks of an officer sent to represent the king, i.e., the tartan. Not since chap. 7 has the Vision presented an event with such precise dating. Sargon ruled from 722 to 705 B.C.E. He was a strong and effective king.

2 בעת ההיא, "in that period," broadens the time span of "in that year" in v 1 to make room for the "three years" of v 3. It is intentionally locating the following events in the period immediately before the invasion in 711 B.C.E.

The words from God order Isaiah to act out a prophetic sign, like Hosea's marriage (Hos 1–3) and Jeremiah's yoke (Jer 27). The literal translation "spoke by the hand of Isaiah" is most fitting. YHWH's message is delivered by Isaiah's actions: taking off his clothes and sandals. השק, "the sackcloth," is probably the basic undergarment worn by the men. The text reports that Isaiah obeyed.

3–4 A word from God interprets the sign that had now been acted out for some three years (i.e., 714–711 B.C.E.). It is a prediction that Assyria will conquer the peoples of Egypt and Ethiopia, leading many of them captive back to Assyria along the highways of Palestine.

Political changes had occurred in Egypt during this period. Shabaka, the Ethiopian king, consolidated his hold on Egypt's delta. The scheming kings of the delta cities who conspired to keep the Palestinians in revolt against Assyria were gone. No effective help would be forthcoming from Egypt in that period.

4 There is no record of an Assyrian invasion of Egypt until the reign of Esarhaddon. In 671 B.C.E. he defeated Tirhaka, occupied Memphis, and installed Assyrian governors over local Egyptian princes. A second rebellion was crushed by Ashurbanipal in 667 B.C.E. with Manasseh's participation. On this occasion the rebel princes *were* marched to Nineveh, much in the way this verse pictures the march of captives.

5 "They" refers to Palestinian rebels who had counted on the new Ethiopian dynasty to continue the policies of the kings of the Lower Egyptian cities. Shabaka apparently sought a diplomatic accommodation with Assyria to replace the confrontation that had existed (cf. 18:2 and Sargon's report of a message from the Ethiopian king). During this period a refugee ruler from Ashdod who sought political asylum in Egypt was extradited at Assyria's request. This policy effectively stripped Ashdod and Jerusalem of substantial support from that side in 712 B.C.E. During Shabaka's lifetime, Egypt kept peace with Assyria. However, when his successor Shebtako came to the throne in 702 B.C.E., he promptly sent his brother Taharqa to aid Hezekiah against Assyria. He was decisively defeated at Eltekeh in 701 B.C.E. (K. A. Kitchen, *Third Intermediate Period in Egypt*, 383–86). The policy of confrontation was again in force, and it was only a matter of time before Assyria undertook a serious invasion of Egypt.

6 The chorus of the Philistines says it all. If the Egyptian might can be so stripped away, the might that had fed their own hopes and dreams, what hope do they have?

Explanation

The grim narrative of chap. 20 with its disturbing acted-out sign brings the beautiful vision back to stark reality. Jerusalem's leaders have agreed to join the so-called Ashdod rebellion of 714–12 B.C.E. This means that they have cast their lot with the delta kings of Egypt (Twenty-Second, Twenty-Third, and Twenty-Fourth Dynasties) against Ethiopia and Assyria. The prophet's protest underscores a fact well known to the readers of the Vision: this flies in the face of the expressed plan of YHWH. The rebellion by the Philistine cities with Hezekiah's support prevented the prompt implementation of Shabaka's search for support on that northern border or, in a way, made it unnecessary.

Isaiah's sign opposes an actual or potential royal policy of dependence on Egyptian support, that is, from the delta kings, against Assyria. Ashdod's messengers had visited Jerusalem, and Hezekiah was tempted to join the revolt.

Isaiah's protest is thoroughly consistent with his counsel to Ahaz (7:4) and his evaluation of the Assyrian's destiny (7:17; 10:5–6). This is no private advice to the kings and his counselors but a public demonstration intended to catch the attention of the nation. It is not a prediction of a specific event but an evaluation of Egypt's long-term inability and lack of will to counter Assyrian pressure.

But Judah stubbornly leaned toward an anti-Assyrian and pro-Egyptian (i.e., the cities of the delta, not the Ethiopian dynasty) stance that was short-sighted and unrealistic. It involved a fateful miscalculation of Assyria's power and will. Hezekiah's ministers had involved Judah in the Ashdod rebellion from the very beginning of his reign. It broke out fully by 714 B.C.E. and was suppressed by Sargon's forces in 712 B.C.E. (cf. *MBA,* 149). Judah apparently lent its support in the early stages but sought Assyria's amnesty before the fighting started. Of course, hopes for Egyptian support were fruitless. Egypt was being overrun by Ethiopian forces friendly to Assyria.

Through the following years, Shabaka (716–702 B.C.E.) maintained correct, almost friendly relations with Assyria, thus gaining external peace for Egypt during his reign (Kitchen, *Third Intermediate Period in Egypt,* 380)

Four Ambiguous Burdens (21:1–22:25)

A SUMMARY OF THE ACTION

The prophet's warning against rebellious alliances (chap. 20) had gone unheeded in the circles that controlled Judah's foreign policy under Hezekiah. His advisers' admiration for Merodach-Baladan's success in holding power in Babylon from 721 to 710 B.C.E. had undoubtedly influenced their decision to participate in Ashdod's rebellion in 714 to 712 B.C.E. When Sargon took Babylon in 710 B.C.E. Merodach-Baladan escaped. At Sargon's death in 705 B.C.E. he took Babylon a second time, only to be ousted in 703 B.C.E. by Shalmaneser. Either of the periods when Babylon was retaken by Assyria could be the occasion for the scene in chap. 21, but the latter period (703 B.C.E.) fits chap. 22.

Hezekiah's activistic tendencies led him to plan his own rebellion against Assyria on the death of Sargon in 705 B.C.E. (cf. *Excursus: The Vassal Years of Hezekiah and Manasseh [ca. 700–640 B.C.E.]* below and *MBA,* 152). By 701 B.C.E. Babylon had been subdued for a second time, and the approach of Sennacherib's forces revealed how pitifully inadequate Judah's military preparations had been (chap. 22). Responsibility is placed squarely on the shoulders of Hezekiah's advisers, who were undoubtedly leaders in the activist faction.

Chap. 19 portrayed Hezekiah's unparalleled opportunity, which was missed because of opportunistic attempts to play power politics. Chap. 20 foresees the collapse of Egypt. Chap. 21 witnesses the fall of Babylon and small peoples near Judah. Assyria's reign is complete. Judah's commitment to independence and power has not changed, and it must face the debacle of that policy. A historian would lay the blame on miscalculation. The Vision in chap. 22 blames the unwillingness of Judah's leaders to heed God's direction revealed through Isaiah, the prophet.

Chaps. 21 and 22 are tied together into one scene by uncharacteristic headings (משׂא, "burden," followed not by a people or country but by a mysterious descriptive word) and by the first-person speaker who is in such anguish about the reports and vision. Not since Isaiah reported in the first person (chap. 8) have so many first-person passages by others than YHWH been strung together. The speaker has authority to order a lookout (21:6), can speak of "my threshed ones" (v 10) in apparent reference to his suffering people, can speak of "my people" (22:4), and can apparently be addressed in the plural (22:9–14). In the first edition of this commentary, I identified the speaker as Shebna, Judah's highest appointed official, whom the Lord addresses in 22:15–25. However, the unified perspective of intermittent first-person accounts throughout the Vision of Isaiah now make me think this speaker is the implied prophet, the author of the book (see *The Implied Author* and *Speakers/Characters—The Prophet/Implied Author* in the *Introduction*). He speaks here in a specific setting as he had in chap. 8, becoming a character in the drama.

The two chapters pursue a common theme: a series of military disasters involving troops from Elam, Media, and Kit that overcome Babylon (21:9) and Arabian strongholds (21:13–17) and threaten Jerusalem (22:1–8). A setting in the years 703–01 B.C.E. as Sennacherib reasserted Assyrian sovereignty in Babylon (against Merodach-Baladan) and in Palestine (against Hezekiah) provides a credible background.

The prophet reacts to a fearful vision (21:2–5) that was anticipated by the interlocutor's announcement (v 1). He is instructed to post a watch (vv 6–8) and then reacts to the messenger's words (vv 9–10). An enigmatic burden intervenes (vv 11–12) but is followed by an ominous word about Arabia's fate (vv 13–16; cf. a similar form and language in chap. 16) and sealed with an oracle from YHWH.

The prophet responds to the interlocutor's questions to a troubled Jerusalem (22:1–3) with an anguished plea to be left alone (v 4). The interlocutor continues to describe the scene and address Jerusalem (second feminine singular; vv 5–8) before he turns to address the king, the royal house, or the chorus (in second masculine plural) with a scathing accusation that they concentrated attention on armament while ignoring YHWH, his plan, and his will (vv 9–13). The prophet concludes by recognizing that their guilt cannot be expunged (v 14).

The prophetic charge to Shebna is in second masculine singular (vv 15–19), supported by two "in that day" passages (vv 20–25). The connection of the scene with events about 701 B.C.E. is confirmed by parallel references to Shebna and Hilkiah in 2 Kings 18–19.

Burden: A Swampland (21:1–10)

Bibliography

Ackroyd, P. *Exile and Redemption.* Philadelphia: Westminster, 1968. 223. **Barnes, W. E.** "A Fresh Interpretation of Isaiah XXI 1–10." *JTS* 1 (1900) 583–92. **Bosshard-Nepustil, E.** *Rezeption von Jesaja 1–39 im Zwölfprophetenbuch.* Freiburg: Universitätsverlag, 1997. 23–42. **Boutflower, C.** "Isaiah XXI in the Light of Assyrian History." *JTS* 14 (1913) 501–15. **Buhl, F.** "Jesaja 21:6–10." *ZAW* 8 (1888) 157–64. **Carmignac, J.** "Six passages d'Isaie éclairés par Qumran." In *Bibel und Qumran.* FS H. Bardtke, ed. S. Wagner. Berlin: Evangelische Haupt-Bibelgesellschaft, 1968. 37–46, esp. 43. **Cobb, W. H.** "Isaiah XXI 1–10 Reexamined." *JBL*

17 (1898) 40–61. **Dhorme, P.** "Le desert de la mer (Isaïe, XXI)." *RB* 31 (1922) 403–6. **Erlandsson S.** *The Burden of Babylon: A Study of Isaiah 13,2–14,23.* Lund: Gleerup, 1970. 81–92. **Galling, K.** "Jes. 21 im Lichte der neuen Nabonidtexte." In *Tradition und Situation.* FS A. Weiser, ed. E. Würthwein and O. Kaiser. Göttingen: Vandenhoeck & Ruprecht, 1963. 49–62. B. **Gosse, B.** *Isaïe 13,1–14,23 dans la tradition littéraire du livre d'Isaïe et dans la tradition des oracle contre les nations.* Freiburg: Universitätsverlag, 1988. ———. "Isaïe 21,11–12 et Isaïe 60–62." *BN* 53 (1990) 21–22. ———. "Le 'moi' prophetique de l'oracle contre Babylone d'Isaïe XXI, 1–10." *RB* 93 (1986) 70–84. **Hillers, D. R.** "A Convention in Hebrew Literature: The Reaction to Bad News." *ZAW* 77 (1965) 86–90. **Jenkins, A. K.** "The Development of the Isaiah Tradition in Is 13–23." In *Book of Isaiah.* Ed. J. Vermeylen. 246–47. **Kleinert, P.** "Bemerkungen zu Jes. 20–22." *TSK* 1 (1877) 174–79. **Lohmann, P.** "Die anonymen Prophetien gegen Babel aus der Zeit des Exits." Diss., Rostock, 1910. 61. ———. "Zur Strophischen Gliederung von Jes. 21:1–10." *ZAW* 33 (1913) 262–64. **Macintosh, A. A.** *Isaiah XXI: A Palimpsest.* Cambridge: Cambridge UP, 1980. **Obermann, J.** "YHWH's Victory over the Babylonian Pantheon: The Archetype of Is 21 1–10." *JBL* 48 (1929) 301–28. **Scott, R. B. Y.** "Inside of a Prophet's Mind." *VT* 2 (1952) 278–82. **Sievers, E.** "Zu Jesaja 21:1–10." In *Vom Alten Testament.* FS K. Marti, ed K. Budde. BZAW 41. Giessen: Töpelmann, 1925. 262–65. **Uffenheimer, B.** "'The Desert of the Sea' Pronouncement (Isaiah 21:1–10)." In *Pomegranites and Golden Bells.* FS J. Milgrom, ed. D. P. Wright et al. Winona Lake, IN: Eisenbrauns, 1995. 677–88. **Wilhelmi, G.** "Polster in Babel? Eine Überlegung zu Jesaja XXI 5+8." *VT* 25 (1975) 121–23. **Winckler, H.** *Alttestamentliche Untersuchungen.* Leipzig: Pfeiffer, 1892. 120–25. **Wong, G. C. I.** "Isaiah's Opposition to Egypt in Isaiah xxi 1–3." *VT* 46 (1996) 392–401.

Translation

Herald:	1 *Burden: A Swampland.*[a]	3
	Like storm winds that sweep[b]	
	into the south country,	3+2+2
	he comes[c] *from a wilderness,*	
	from a land that is to be feared.	
The Prophet:	2 *A hard vision*	2+2
	has been declared to me:	
Heavens:	*The traitor betrays!*	2+2
	The violent work violence!	
Earth:	*Go up, Elam!*	2+2
	Lay siege, Media!	
YHWH:	*I shall stop all her groaning!*[a]	3
The Prophet:	3 *At this my body is full of pain.*	4
	Pangs seize me	2+2
	like pangs of childbirth!	
	I am overcome by what I hear;[a]	2+2
	I am dismayed by what I see.	
	4 [a]*My heart skips a beat.*[a]	2+2
	A shudder overwhelms me.	
	For me it makes the twilight of my love[b]	3+3
	become a time of anxiety.	
Herald:	5 *Setting the table—*	2+2+2
	spreading the rug[a]*—*	
	eating—drinking.	

	The officers rise.	2+2
	They anoint[b] a shield.	
The Prophet:	6 *For thus my Lord says to me:*	5
YHWH, or king:	*Go. Have a lookout stand guard.*	3+3
	Have him report what he sees.	
	7 *If he sees a rider,*	2+2
	a team of horses,	
	a rider[a] (on) a donkey,	2+2
	a rider[a] (on) a camel,	
	have him pay attention,	2+2
	very close attention.	
Herald:	8 *Then, the watchman[a] cried out:*	2
Watchman:	*Upon a watchtower, my lord,*	3+2+2
	I am standing	
	continually, by day.	
	At my post	2+2+2
	I am keeping my station	
	all night.	
	9 *Look! There! Someone is coming!*	3+2+2
	A chariot with a man!	
	A team of horses!	
	He answers and says:	2+3
	"She has fallen! Babylon has fallen![a]	
	All the images of her gods	3+2
	have been shattered[b] on the ground!"	
The Prophet:	10 *My threshed ones,[a]*	1+1
	and my[b] threshing-floor son,	
	what I have heard	2+3
	from YHWH of Hosts,	
	God of Israel,	2+2
	I announce to you [pl.]!	

Notes

1.a. MT מדבר־ים, "a sea wilderness" or "swampland." The title is apparently taken from the word מִמִּדְבָּר in line 3. The style of titles that listed nations in 13:1, 15:1, 17:1, and 19:1 changes here. In 21:1, 11, 13 and 22:1 obscure words, sometimes taken up from the first lines, are used. Wildberger (763) and Macintosh (*Isaiah XXI,* 407) have full reviews of the suggestions of versions and commentators. The translation "desert" is wrong. מדבר is a wilderness, not a desert (BDB, 184; cf. *HAL*).

1.b. Inf. const. defining more precisely (GKC §114*o*).

1.c. The subject is indefinite "he" or "it." In v 3 the subject is personal 3 m. sg.

2.a. MT אנחתה suffix without *rafe,* "her groanings." An unusual but possible form. The fem. pronoun must refer to the one under attack. The "groaning" may be from pain or from strenuous effort.

3.a. MT מִשְּׁמֹעַ, "from hearing." LXX τὸ μὴ ἀκοῦσαι; Tg. מלמשמע; Syr. *dl' 'šm'*. All these translate מן in a negative or a privative sense, followed by Marti, Kaiser, and others. But a causative sense fits the context better, as Duhm, Fohrer, Eichrodt, and Wildberger have noted.

4.a-a. For MT תעה לבבי, "my heart skips," 1QIsa[a] has תועה ולבבי, which Wildberger calls "not understandable."

4.b. LXX ἡ ψυχή μου, "my soul"; Syr. *šwpr'*. G. R. Driver ("Notes on Isaiah," in *Von Ugarit nach Qumran,* FS O. Eissfeldt, ed. W. F. Albright et al., BZAW 77 [Giessen: Töpelman, 1958] 44) related it to Arab. *nasafa* and translated "my faintest [i.e., scarcely breathed] wish has been turned into anxiety for me." The usual translation, "twilight of my love," is better.

5.a. צפה הצפית, "spreading the rug," has given the versions and commentators trouble. See Wildberger (765) and Macintosh (*Isaiah XXI,* 24–25). The meaning of II צפה (BDB, 860; *HAL*) suggests preparation of a meal, which fits the context.

5.b. MT משחו, "they anoint" or "they oil"; מגן, "a shield." LXX ἑτοιμάσατε θυρεούς, "prepare weapons"; Tg. מריקו וצחצחו זינא, "polish or shine weapons."

7.a. 1QIsa[a] רוכב in the second instance and a superimposed *vav* in the first suggest reading as a ptc., "riding," instead of MT רֶכֶב, a noun, "rider." LXX ἀναβάτην supports reading as a ptc. as do the Tg. and Syr. Wildberger correctly chooses to sustain MT.

8.a. MT "then the אריה [lion] called out" makes no sense. LXX Οὐρίαν reads it as a proper noun. Ibn Ezra, followed by Delitzsch, read כאריה, "like a lion" "with a lion's voice." R. Lowth, as early as 1778 (*Isaiah* [London: Nichols]), suggested הָרֹאֶה, "the seer," "the watchman," which is now supported by 1QIsa[a] and accepted by Fohrer, Eichrodt, Young, Auvray, A. Schoors (*Jesaja* [Roermond, 1972]), Kaiser, Wildberger, and Macintosh *(Isaiah XXI)*.

9.a. LXX, Eth., and Arab. versions omit the second נפלה, "she has fallen." MT's emphatic usage should be kept.

9.b. 1QIsa[a] שברו is pl., allowing the pl. subject that precedes. LXX συνετρίβησαν suggests a pass. parallel with the previous line. Both support Procksch's suggestion to read שֻׁבְּרוּ, "they have been shattered." Wildberger and *BHS* agree.

10.a. The *puʿal* ptc. "my threshed" (one or things) does seem to need a noun. Sievers ("Zu Jesaja 21:1–10," 263) suggested עם־מדשתי, "people of my threshing"; Procksch בן־מדשתי, "son of my threshing" *(BHS)*. With Wildberger, it is better to let MT stand.

10.b. The possessive pronoun relates to the controlling noun בן in the construct form. Cf. J. Weingreen ("The Construct-Genitive Relation in Hebrew Syntax," *VT* 4 [1954] 50–59) and Wildberger (767).

Form/Structure/Setting

The episode shifts from a vision (vv 2, 5) to a cry of personal anguish (vv 3–4) to a dramatic confirmation of the vision (vv 6–9) to a closing address to the audience (v 10).

The chapter can be read as a monologue by an unidentified speaker who is distressed at the news of Babylon's defeat. The commentary has elsewhere recognized this first-person speaker as the implied prophet. This fits here also. The *Translation* recognizes this person who carries the scene (vv 2, 3–4, 6–8*a,* and 10) but reflects the very dynamic lines between speakers by having them speak for themselves rather than be cited by the primary speaker.

Ibn Ezra argued that this speaker could not be the prophet Isaiah "since the prophet's views are known to be joy—not sorrow" (cf. Macintosh, *Isaiah XXI,* 15). Ibn Ezra thought they must come from the king of Babylon. The prophet's expressions of dismay are not so out of place as Ibn Ezra and other interpreters after him have thought. Israel's prophets did not celebrate the fulfillment of their judgment oracles but rather wept with their people over God's destruction of the land. The books of Jeremiah and Hosea present most vividly the prophets' psychological turmoil at seeing their predictions of disaster come true. Here in Isa 21–22, the Vision's implied author reacts with understandable distress at the catastrophes overtaking Jerusalem, notwithstanding the fact that he has predicted this outcome all along.

Jenkins ("Development of the Isaiah Tradition," 245) sees some similarity between this section and Deutero-Isaiah and so places it in a postexilic setting. Williamson (*Book Called Isaiah,* 157) thinks that the entire chapter is part of the Deutero-Isaiah redaction. Such observations rightly point to the postexilic composition of the book, but the chapter may still be set in the late eighth century even if written in the fifth.

Comment

1 מדבר־ים, "swampland," is identified as Babylonia by v 9. That which "comes" is either an invading army or the news of such an invasion.

2 Commentators who have expected Isaiah to be the speaker here have been troubled at the prophet's reaction. Why should Isaiah agonize over the fulfillment of his own prophecies, the confirmation of his teaching? But the prophets of Israel did not stop identifying with their people and wishing them well just because they were bearers of oracles of judgment. They desired peace and prosperity for Israel and Judah even as they predicted their destruction. And they themselves often suffered the fate they anticipated for their nations: Ezekiel was taken into exile in 597 B.C.E.; Jeremiah lived through the destruction of Jerusalem in 587 and survived among its ruins for some years thereafter. Similarly, the Vision here presents the prophet, representing the implied author, in great distress over the troubles of Jerusalem's eighth-century ally, Babylon, because he knows that the Assyrians will attack Judah next (see 22:4).The content of the vision is condensed into three cries. The first simply recognizes a violent scene. The second exhorts Elam and Media (or their soldiers) to attack. The object of the attack is not named. The third, in first person, promises to bring a quick end to the victim's (her) groaning. The victim is identified as Babylon later in the scene (v 9*b*).

The last line may well be understood to be spoken by the enemy commander or, better, by YHWH himself. If the enemy commander, this could be the Assyrian general. Sargon forced Merodach-Baladan (cf. commentary on chap. 13–14) to abandon the city in 710 B.C.E. Sennacherib repeated the maneuver in 703 B.C.E. The close connection of chaps. 21 and 22 favors the latter occasion.

עילם, "Elam," and מדי, "Media," were peoples from the Iranian highlands who were becoming active in Mesopotamian affairs near the end of the eighth century (see *Excursus: Elam* below). Elamite collaboration had made possible Merodach-Baladan's capture of Babylon in 720. Commentators have been very occupied with determining their roles here and in 22:6 (cf. Macintosh, *Isaiah XXI*, 63–75). The outcry of the vision does not define their role, whether for or against Babylon, but it does establish their participation in the struggle.

Excursus: Elam

Bibliography

Millard A. "Elam." *ISBE.* 2:49–52 and bibliography there.

Elamites were an ancient people who inhabited the plain now called Khuzistan in southwest Iran. Their capital city was Susa.

Elam emerged in the late eighth century for a period of importance that lasted from ca. 720 to ca. 645 B.C.E. when Ashurbanipal destroyed Susa. During this period Elamite support made possible Merodach-Baladan's successful capture and rule over Babylon in 720–710 B.C.E. This aid to Babylon against Assyria may well have eventually caused Elam's fall.

Elam's support for Merodach-Baladan was sporadic. In 720 its armies prevented Assyrian intervention. But in 710 it retreated, allowing Sargon to take Babylon. It even denied Merodach-Baladan asylum despite receiving an enormous gift. In 703 Merodach-Baladan persuaded Elam to send a large force with eighty thousand archers (cf. Isa 22:6; Jer 49:35), but the effort failed to stop the Assyrians. Assyria retaliated by taking back two areas on Elam's northwest border. In 700 B.C.E. Elam supported Merodach-Baladan's unsuccessful defense against Assyria's campaign in southern Babylonia. Merodach-Baladan apparently died in his exile on the Elamite coast of the Persian Gulf.

The half century that followed brought numerous encounters between Assyria and Elam, encounters that often involved Babylonia. A final confrontation before Susa in 646 B.C.E. brought defeat and devastation. Elam, as an independent nation, faded from history.

3–4 The emotional reaction to the vision, a premonition of news announced in v 8, is the most prominent feature of the entire scene. The same kind of anxiety or dismay is observed in 22:4. Isaiah had called for such concern when Egypt fell (chap. 20). Merodach-Baladan's successful campaign that captured Babylon and held it for a decade (720–710 B.C.E.) had been the signal to other peoples that Assyria might be resisted. It sustained the hopes of Judah's resistance party and led Hezekiah to move away from his father's policies of loyal vassalage. It encouraged Ashdod in its rebellion of 714–711 B.C.E. Merodach-Baladan's reassertion of his claim to Babylon after Sargon's death (705 B.C.E.) sparked an attempted general uprising throughout the empire (chap. 39). It led to Hezekiah's decisions to arm himself and to build a coalition of Palestinian states for such an uprising (see commentary on chap. 22). The collapse of Babylon in 703 B.C.E., to which this vision refers, presaged the collapse of all opposition to Sennacherib and disaster for those who advised it (as Shebna had) or who led it (as Hezekiah had).

4 נשף חשקי, "the twilight of my love" (cf. the parallel figure in v 12), seems to picture the longed-for future that is now put in jeopardy by the vision: the dream of an independent and prosperous country, free from imperial oppression and taxation.

5 The verse pictures the beginning of a military campaign in the field. The cryptic presentation does not show clearly whether this takes place in faraway Babylon or in Judah. The next orders for placing a guard suggest that the verse pictures Judean preparations for the inevitable Assyrian reprisal, when or if their Babylonian campaign is successful.

6 B. Gosse (*Isaïe 13,1–14,23,* 43–67) notes a similarity with 62:6. But Williamson (*Book Called Isaiah,* 157 n. 4) notes that the single watchman there has become watchmen.

8 The MT's "the lion [אריה] called out" makes no sense (cf. *Note* 8.a.). An emended text reads הראה, "the seer." The term lends the account an added dimension; the watchman is more than a military guard on watch. And the account is parallel to the vision of v 2.

9*c* The shattering of images may be intended to depict the physical destruction of temples, but it also reflects the loss of prestige and respect resulting from the idols' inability to protect the city. The recognition that neither Sargon nor Sennacherib destroyed the city, but only reoccupied it, would support the latter meaning. Ludwig Köhler (*Deuterojesaja (Jesaja 40–55) stilkritisch untersucht*, BZAW 37 [Giessen: Töpelmann , 1923] 99) has noted that the double use of נפלה, "she has fallen," is similar to Deutero-Isaiah's style (cf. Isa 40:1; 51:9, 12, 17; 52:1, 11). The depiction of the overthrow of idols also parallels Deutero-Isaiah's theme. (Cf. Jenkins, "Development of the Isaiah Tradition," 245; Goss, *Isaïe 13,1–14,23*, 43–67.)

10 מדשתי, "threshed ones," and בן־גרני, "threshing-floor son," are literal renderings of words apparently intended to show sympathy for the Judean people who have already suffered so much. What, exactly, has been heard from YHWH? Apparently this harks back to the vision of v 2, although it was not at that point attributed to God. The vision in its third statement revealed that YHWH himself was directing the assault. This confirms the prophet's announcement in 7:17 and the presentation of the Assyrian in 10:5–6 as the "rod of [God's] anger."

Explanation

The burden of the Swampland (Babylon) dramatically recounts the reaction of the prophet to news of Merodach-Baladan's collapse before the Assyrian onslaught that involved Medes and Elamites. Either of two occasions would serve as the historical focus. Merodach-Baladan, after some ten years of ascendancy, fled Babylon before Sargon's forces in ca. 710 B.C.E. After he returned to power on Sargon's death (cf. Isa 39), he was again routed by Sennacherib in 703 B.C.E.

The scene focuses on the almost hysterical reaction in Jerusalem to news of his defeat. Why should the prophet have been so concerned about an event so far away? Babylon had stood for more than a decade as living proof that the Assyrians could be overcome. It was evidence that rebellion could succeed. Some in Jerusalem, probably including Hezekiah, had heeded the siren call of that example rather than the prophet's warnings about the collapse of Egypt (chap. 20). Premonitions of their own fate fueled the emotional reaction to the news about Babylon.

In expressing dismay at the news, the book does not simply present the prophet's personal reaction but also presents it as part of the prophetic Vision. As in Hosea and Jeremiah, the prophet's personal distress at the fulfillment of his judgment oracles reflects God's dismay at the destruction. Neither prophets nor God take the position of outsiders calmly observing passing events. They rather participate at every stage and suffer the calamity along with the people (see 22:14). So the prophets react with understandable concern, and in so doing represent God's presence with the people even in the midst of judgment.

The shorter scenes about Dumah and Arabia reflect the anxiety and despair among neighboring peoples before the anticipated reaction of Sennacherib to Hezekiah's challenge, now that he is relieved of concern about Merodach-Baladan's threat to his southern flank. The final verses announce that these peoples (and presumably Judah) have not long to wait.

Burden: Silence (21:11–12)

Bibliography

Bartlett, J. R. "Edom." *ABD.* 2:287–95. ———. "From Edomites to Nabataeans: A Study in Continuity." *PEQ* 111 (1979) 53–66. **Galling, K. B.** "Jes. 21 im Lichte der neuen Nabonidtexte." In *Tradition und Situation.* FS A. Weiser, ed. E. Würthwein and O. Kaiser. Göttingen: Vandenhoeck & Ruprecht, 1963. 49–62. **Geyer, J. B.** "The Night of Dumah (Isaiah XXI:11–12)." *VT* 42 (1992) 317–39. **Gosse, B.** "Isaïe 21,11–12 et Isaïe 60–62." *BN* 53 (1990) 21–25. **Lindsay, J.** "The Babylonian Kings and Edom 605–550 B.C." *PEQ* 108 (1978) 23–29. **Lohmann, P.** "Das Wächterlied Jes. 21:11–12." *ZAW* 33 (1913) 20–29. **Schlossberg, E.** "Who Is the Subject of the 'Burden of Dumah' Prophecy?" *Studies in Bible and Exegesis* 4 (1997) 273–77.

Translation

Herald:	11 *Burden: Silence (Dumah).*[a]	2+3
Watchman:	*Someone is calling to me from Seir:*[b]	
	"Keeper, what (is left) of the night?[c]	3+3
	Keeper, what (is left) of the night?"	
Herald:	12 *The keeper*[a] *said.*	2+2+2
Watchman:	*Morning is come,*	
	but also[b] *night.*	
	If you [m. pl.] must ask, ask.[c]	3+2
	Turn! Come!	

Notes

11.a. Two MSS and LXX (Ἰδουμαίας) read אֱדוֹם, "Edom." One LXX MS ([534]) reads ιουδαιας, "Judah." α´, according to Jerome, reads *duma,* which is explained as meaning "silence" or "likeness." Wildberger makes a good case for keeping MT and the Arabian place names (787–91).

11.b. α´ σ´ θ´ (according to Eusebius, *Die Jesajakommentar* §80; p. 142) προς εμε καλει τους φευγοντας, "to me he calls the men in flight." *BHS* suggests הַנּוֹדְדִים, "ones fleeing," for מִשֵּׂעִיר, "from Seir." The change is unnecessary.

11.c. 1QIsa[a] מליל makes the first "night" identical in form to the second. ליל may well be a contraction for the abs. form (cf. Joüon §96A*m*).

12.a. Note the change from 1st (v 11) to 3d person. But note the relation in vv 6 and 8.

12.b. The text is clear even if the meaning is ambiguous. But several have sought clarity of meaning through emendation (see Wildberger, 788). The ambiguity is apparently intentional.

12.c. For explanation of the Hebrew forms, cf. GKC §75*h*.

Comment

11 A second burden has an even more ambiguous and mysterious title: "Silence." The sound of the Hebrew word is similar to "Edom," and the reference to Seir in the next line leads the LXX to insert that name here. Wildberger thinks it refers to a place name. (Cf. *MBA,* 115; LaSor, *ISBE* 2:995.) Schlossberg has called attention to medieval rabbinic interpretations of this passage. Rav Saadia Gaon interpreted the text in terms of Dumah, son of Ishmael (Gen 25:14) and a place called Dumat al-Gandel in the northwestern area of modern Saudi Arabia. Other rabbis and Karaite commentaries follow his interpretation in relating this prophecy to Ishmael, though earlier Talmudic literature related the prophecy to Edom. However, the parallel to other ambiguous titles (21:1, 13; 22:1) suggests that it be allowed its mysterious character, especially in view of the ambiguity in the keeper's response (v 12). The theme of a lookout or watchman is continued from vv 6 and 8. The question is broad and common.

12 The answer says nothing specific, only recognizing that it is proper to ask, even when nothing can be given in reply. It reflects the times when people want to know what is happening, anxiously anticipating great and fearful events, yet recognizing that those events have not come into sight. Geyer (*VT* 42 [1992] 317–39) provides a very thorough discussion of possible mythological connections.

Burden: In the Wasteland (21:13–17)

Bibliography

Eph'al, I. *The Ancient Arabs: Nomads on the Borders of the Fertile Crescent 9th–5th Centuries* B.C. Leiden: Brill, 1982. **Graf, G. F.** "Deden." *ABD*. 2:121–23. **Knauf, E. A.** *Ismael: Untersuchungen zur Geschichte Palästinas und Nordarabiens im I. Jahrtausend v. Chr.* 2d. ed. Wiesbaden: Harrassowitz, 1989. ———. "Kedar." *ABD*. 4:9–10. ———. "Tema (Place)." *ABD*. 6:346–47.

Translation

Herald: 13 *Burden: In the wasteland.*[a] 2
Earth: *In the thicket in the wasteland*[b] *they lodge,* 3+2
the Dedanite wanderers.
14 *To meet a thirsty one* 2+2
they bring[a] *water.*
Inhabitants of the land of Tema 3+3
meet[b] *a refugee with his bread.*
15 *For they have fled in the face of swords* 3+3
before a drawn sword,
before a bent bow 3+3
and before the weight[a] *of battle.*
The Prophet: 16 *For thus my Lord*[a] *has said to me:* 4
"In just a year,[b] *like a bond-servant's year,* 4+4
all the glory of Kedar will be finished,
17 *and the remnant of the number of bowmen, heroes*
of the Kedarites,[a] *will be small."* 7
For YHWH, God of Israel, has spoken. 5

Notes

13.a. LXX omits both words of the heading. בערב could mean "in the wasteland, desert" or "against Arabia" or "in the evening." See also the same word in the next line.

13.b. LXX (followed by Syr. Tg. Vg) ἑσπέρας, "of evening." MT בערב, "in the wasteland," is more fitting.

14.a. 1QIsa[a] האתיו is the full form of MT התיו, *hipʿil* pf., "they bring" (GKC §76*d*), or *hipʿil* impv., "bring" (LXX, BDB, *HAL*, *DCH*), from אתה, "come" (cf. Bauer-Leander §59*g*). The pf. קִדְּמוּ, "they meet," in the next line supports reading pf. here (but see *Note* 14.b.).

14.b. LXX (supported by Syr. Tg. Vg.) συναντᾶτε, an impv., "meet, encounter," leads many to vocalize Heb. קַדְּמוּ impv. in place of MT's pf. ind. Apparently the verb is intended to parallel הֵתָיוּ, read as an impv., "bring," in the previous line.

15.a. 1QIsa[a] כבוד, "glory." MT כֹּבֶד, "weight" or "vehemence," is better.

16.a. 1QIsa[a] and many MSS and Tg. יהוה, "YHWH."

16.b. 1QIsa[a] שלוש שנים, "three years" (cf. 16:4).

17.a. 1QIsa[a] has בני, lit. "sons of," inserted above the line, apparently to correct an omission in copying. This brings it in line with MT (cf. S. Talmon, "Observations on Variant Readings," 119).

Comment

13 The third ambiguous title may mean "against Arabia," "in the evening," or "in the wasteland." A tendency to expect the name of a country in such a title, connected with the names Dedan and Tema in vv 13 and 14, supports the first. Parallels to "Swampland" (v 1), "the wasteland" (13*b*), and "Valley of Vision" (22:1) support the last. Parallels to "night" (v 11) and "twilight" (v 4) might suggest the second. The overwhelming impression again is mystery and ambiguity. Dedanites are a people of Arabia (Cohen, *IDB* 1:812; LaSor, *ISBE* 1:909; Graf, *ABD* 2:121–23). In Jer 49:8 and Ezek 25:13 they appear in connection with Edom as they do here in relation to the parallel burden (v 11, "Seir" and "Dumah").

14 תימא, "Tema," modern Teima in Arabia, is an oasis (Cohen, *IDB* 4:533; Knauf, *ABD* 6:346–47; *MBA*, 115). The scene is one of devastation and privation, of hungry and thirsty refugees.

15 An explanation cites military invasion as the cause. There are no specific data on which to attempt historical identification of time or event.

16–17 קדר, "Kedar" (J. A. Thompson, *IDB* 3:3–4; Knauf, *ABD* 4:9–10), appears again in 42:11 and 60:7 (cf. Jer 49:28–32; Ezek 27:21). It is a place east of Palestine, apparently in north Arabia. Assyrian records speak of Kedarites and Arabs in the same breath. They were a considerable force that preoccupied the Assyrians under Sennacherib, Ashurbanipal, and Esarhaddon. Sennacherib writes of defeating Hazail, king of the Arabs/Kedarites.

The announced destruction of Kedar is an explicit and specific word from YHWH. If Dumah (v 11) implies a place name (along with Dedan and Tema, cities in Arabia), the question of that verse is answered by the word from YHWH in vv 16–17. The vision/news of Babylon's fall and the vision of Arabian refugees (vv 13–14) interpreted by the prophecy of vv 16–17 prepare for a very negative evaluation of Judah's position, as Assyria advances.

Burden: The Valley of Vision (22:1–14)

Bibliography

Amiram, R. "The Water Supply of Israelite Jerusalem." In *Jerusalem Revealed: Archaeology of the Holy City, 1968–74.* Ed. Y. Yadin and E. Stern. Trans. R. Grafman. Jerusalem: Israel Exploration Society, 1975. 75–78. **Avigad, N.** "The Epitaph of a Royal Steward from Siloam Village." *IEJ* 3 (1953) 137–52. **Bosshard-Nepustil, E.** *Rezeptionen von Jesaja 1–39 im Zwölfprophetenbuch.* Freiburg: Universitätsverlag, 1997. 42–67. **Box, G. H.** "Some Textual Suggestions on Two Passages in Isaiah." *ExpTim* 19 (1908) 563–64. **Broshi, M.** "The Expansion of Jerusalem in the Reigns of Hazekiah and Manasseh." *IEJ* 24 (1974) 21–26. **Childs, B. S.** *Isaiah and the Assyrian Crisis.* 22–27. **Clements, R. E.** *Isaiah and the Deliverance of Jerusalem: A Study of the Interpretation of Prophecy in the Old Testament.* JSOTSup 13. Sheffield: JSOT Press, 1980. 33–34. ———. "The Prophecies of Isaiah and the Fall of Jerusalem in 587 B.C." *VT* 30 (1980) 421–36. **Dahood, M.** "בֵּין הַחֹמֹתַיִם (Isa 22:11 etc. Nota discussionem sensus accurati)." Bib 42 (1961) 474–75. **Dietrich, W.** *Jesaja und die Politik.* Munich: Kaiser, 1976. 193–95. **Donner, H.** *Israel unter den Völkern.* 126–28. **Emerton, J. A.** "Notes on the Text and Translation of Isaiah xxii 8–11 and lxv 5." *VT* 30 (1980) 437–51. **Gottwald, N.** *All the Kingdoms of the Earth.* 193–96. **Guillaume, A.** "A Note on the Meaning of Isa 22:5." *JTS* 14 (1963) 383–85. **Torczynor, H.** "Dunkle Biblestellen." In *Vom Alten Testament.* FS K. Marti, ed. K. Budde. BZAW 41. Giessen: Töpelmann, 1925. 276. **Weippert, M.** "Mitteilungen zum Text von Ps 19:5 und Jes 22:5." *ZAW* 73 (1961) 97–99. **Wilkinson, J.** "Ancient Jerusalem: Its Water Supply and Population." *PEQ* 106 (1974) 33–51.

Translation

Herald:	1 *Burden:* [a]*Valley of Vision.*[a]	
Heavens:	[b]*What is the matter with you,*[b] *then,*	3+2+2
(to Jerusalem)	*that you have gone up,*[c]	
	all of you,[c] *to the housetops?*	
Earth:	2 *Noise!*	1+3+2
	A city full of roaring!	
	A city jubilant!	
Heavens:	*Your profaned are not those profaned by the sword*	4+3
	and not those dead in battle.	
Earth:	3 *All your chiefs*	2+2+2
	who fled together	
	without bowmen were taken prisoner.[a]	
Heavens:	[b]*All who were found in you*[b]	2+2+2
	have been taken prisoner together	
	even when they had fled far away.	
The Prophet:	4 *Because of this I have said:*	2+2+2
(to Heavens	[a]*Look away from me!*[a]	
and Earth)	*I am bitter in my weeping!*	
	Do not hurry to comfort me	2+2
	because of the destruction of the daughter of my people.	
Earth:	5 *Yea, there is a day of roaring and trampling and terror*	5+3+2

belonging to my Lord, YHWH of Hosts,
in the Valley of Vision.
[a]*(A day of) digging a ditch*[a] 2+2
and crying out toward[b] *the mountain,*
6 *for Elam has lifted a quiver* 3+3+3
with manned[a] *chariot, horsemen,*
and Kir uncovered a shield.
(to Jerusalem) 7 *So it came about that your [fem. sg.] choice*[a] *valleys* 3+2
are filled with chariotry.
And the horsemen[b] *are powerfully arrayed at the gates.* 4+4
8 *So he*[a] *stripped away Judah's screen.*
So[b] *you [fem. sg.] looked in that day* 3+4
toward the armory of the House of the Forest.[c]
Heavens: 9 *The breaches*[a] *in the City of David—* 3+2
(to *you [m. pl.] saw*[b] *that they were many.*
government) *Then you collected water in the Lower Pool.* 4
10 *You [m. pl.] counted*[a] *the houses of Jerusalem.* 3+4
Then you [m. pl.] demolished[b] *the houses to make the wall inaccessible.*[c]
11 *You built a reservoir between the walls*[a] 4+3
for the water of the old pool.
But you [m. pl.] did not look[b] *to her Maker.* 3+4
The one shaping it long ago[c] *you [m. pl.] did not see.*[d]
Earth: 12 *Then my Lord,*[a] 1+3+2
YHWH of Hosts,
called in that day
for weeping and for wailing, 2+3
for shaved heads and for wearing sackcloth.
13 *But see!* 1
Joy and revelry, 2+2+2
slaughtering cattle
and killing sheep.
A Reveler: *Eating meat* 2+2
and drinking wine—
eating and drinking— 2+3
for tomorrow we die.
The Prophet 14 *But YHWH of Hosts has revealed in my ears* 2+2
"I swear this guilt will not be atoned for you [m. pl.][a] 5
before you die," [b]*said my Lord YHWH of Hosts.*[b]

Notes

1.a-a. LXX τῆς φάραγγος Σιων, "about the Zion ravine." This interprets the Hebrew to refer to the Hinnom Valley west of Jerusalem, which leads Schmidt to emend חזיון, "vision," to הנם, "Hinnom," which Wildberger (805) properly calls "too simple." Guillaume suggests (*JTS* 14 [1963] 383–85) that one follow Arab. *ḥaḏwa* to read "the valley opposite."

1.b-b. מה־לך, "what to you [fem. sg.]?" 1QIsa[a] מלכי, "my king." Tg מא לכון, "what to you." MT's fem. pronoun refers to Jerusalem. The phrase may ask "What's the matter with you?" or "What do you want?" among other things.

1.c. MT עָלִית, "that you [fem.] have gone up," is rendered by 1QIsa[a] as עליתי, "I have gone up," by LXX as ἀνέβητε, "you [pl.] go up," and by Tg. as סליקתון "you (pl.) go up." The different persons in the versions have led them to variations on כלך, "all of you," in LXX πάντες, "all," and Tg. כולכון, "all of you."

3.a. MT אֻסְּרוּ, "they were taken prisoner," is the only occurrence of אסר in *puʿal.* 1QIsa[a] אסורה seems to be a *qal* pass. ptc. fem., "bound" or "imprisoned." Tg. גלו, "reveal" or "exile," suggests the reading ס(א)רו, "they turned aside," as followed by Procksch, Bruno "depart," and *BHS,* or הֻסְרוּ (*hopʿal* pf.), "they were removed or taken away" (Wildberger and *BHS*).

3.b-b. LXX οἱ ἰσχύοντες ἐν σοί, "the healthy among you [pl.]." Driver (*JTS* 41 [1940] 164) and *BHS* accordingly emend to נֶאֱמָצַיִךְ, "your bold ones," a *nipʿal* ptc. of אמץ, which does not otherwise appear in *nipʾal.* Others (Duhm, Guthe, Feldmann, Procksch, Kissane, *BHS,* and *HAL*) emend to אַמִּיצַיִךְ, "your mighty ones." Wildberger defends MT, treating מרחוק ברחו as a concessive clause, "although they had fled far off."

4.a-a. 1QIsa[a] שועו ממני, "cry for help from me," from שוע, "cry for help," rather than MT שעו, "look away." MT is better.

5.a-a. מקרקר קר is a term occurring only here. BDB (903) relates it to קִיר, "wall," and later Heb. קִרְקֵר, "tear down a wall." GKC and KBL could find no meaning for it. LXX and Syr. were also mystified by it. But new attempts have been made. Aram., Syr., Arab., and latter Heb. have the root meaning "growl," "roar," "crow," or "cackle," and Ugar. *qr* means "call, shout." So *HAL* translates "noise" and suggests the phrase might mean "shout a shout" or "let out a yell" (*HAL* קרר). But Ugar. *qr* also means "a spring" (*Ras Shamra Parallels,* ed. L. R. Fisher, vol. 1. [Rome: Pontifical Biblical Institute, 1972] §II.495, 496; cf. 497 and Wildberger). The possibility that מקרקר may be a *pilpel* form from קוּר, "bore or dig," and קר a shortened form of מקור, "a spring, fountain," has hardly been explored. The references to the building of the reservoirs (vv 9*b*–11*a*) suggest this translation.

5.b. For MT קר ושוע אל, "a ditch and crying out toward," 1QIsa[a] reads קדשו על, "his holy one against."

6.a. MT אדם, "man or humankind." The parallels before and after name nations. A natural suggestion is ארם, "Aram" or "Syria" (C. F. Houbigant, *Biblica Hebraica* [Paris: Briasson, 1753]; Lowth [*Isaiah* (London: Nichols, 1778)]; *BHK*[3]). Others suggest it is a gloss (Duhm, Marti, Gray, Fohrer, Wildberger). Yet the horses and chariots are the very center of attention in v 7. The intention seems to be something like "with chariots manned by riders" (without regard to nationality).

7.a. B. E. Shafer ("מבחר/מבחור = 'Fortress,'" *CBQ* 33 [1971] 389–94) translates מבחר, "choice," as "fortress": "Your valley fortresses were full of chariots." But if the reference continues the thoughts of v 6, the allusion must be to enemy chariots, not Judean (cf. Wildberger, 807).

7.b. The verse is divided after "chariotry" and before "the horsemen" by the *ʾatnakh* in MT (followed by LXX and Tg.). Wildberger (806) suggests putting the *ʾatnakh* under פרשים, "horsemen," and eliminating the article since chariots and horses are usually mentioned together. MT makes sense as it is and should be kept.

8.a. LXX reads a pl. However, the MT reference is to the subject in v 5, YHWH or his emissary.

8.b. Note a change of subject, returning to the form of address of vv 1–3. LXX missed the change and translated with a pl.

8.c. LXX τοὺς ἐκλεκτοὺς οἴκους τῆς πόλεως, "the choice houses of the city." But MT is to be sustained. Wildberger thinks the longer phrase בית יעל הלבנון, "house of the forest of Lebanon," is understood (cf. 1 Kgs 7:2).

9.a. Ehrlich (*Randglossen,* III, 4:136) noted that בקע as a verb usually refers to "digging wells" (Judg 15:19) and that בקיע means "a natural spring" (IV, 4:77). However, to make sense here he had to assume that a לא, "not," had been lost. His suggestion had the advantage of making vv 9–11*a* have a single topic.

9.b. 1QIsa[a] ראית(מ)ה presents an unusual form (cf. R. Meyer, *Hebraïsche Grammatik* [Berlin: De Gruyter, 1952–55] §64:2*b*) but does not improve the text.

10.a. ספרתם, "you counted," has no counterpart in LXX.

10.b. 1QIsa[a] ותחוצו notes an alternate form of the verb (cf. Deut 7:5; Exod 34:13). וַתִּתְצוּ is generally held to derive from נתץ, "pull down" or "break down" (BDB, *HAL, DCH*). The *dagesh forte* has been dropped in תּ (cf. GKC §20*m*), but is marked by *rafe* (cf. R. Meyer, *Hebraïsche Grammatik* [Berlin: De Gruyter, 1952–53] §14:6).

10.c. 1QIsa[a] לבצור is a *qal* inf. for MT's *piʿel* inf. Wildberger (823) has objected, with reason, to the usual rendering "fortify" or "strengthen" (BDB). The verb should mean "make inaccessible" (*HAL* III, *DCH* I).

11.a. 1QIsa[a] is pl. MT is dual.

11.b. 1QIsa[a] adds a final ה, as in v 9*b*.

11.c. מרחוק, "from far off," is missing in σ´ θ´. Donner *(Israel unter den Völkern)* has suggested omitting it. LXX ἀπ' ἀρχῆς, "from of old," takes it to refer to time instead of space.

11.d. A. Sperber (*Historical Grammar* [Leiden: Brill, 1966] 647) suggests that ראיתם, "you see," should be read as יראתם, "you fear." Wildberger (808) correctly rejects the change.

12.a. Missing in LXX, Eth., and Arab.

14.a. 1QIsa[a] changes the word order, placing לכם, "to you," immediately after יכפר, "be atoned." But this is unnecessary.

14.b-b. The closing formula has frequently been thought to be a later addition (Duhm, Gray, Fisher, Procksch, Donner *[Israel unter den Völkern]*, and Wildberger).

Form/Structure/Setting

This moving and turbulent episode does not fit normal molds. It contains: (1) an accusing question about turbulent behavior (vv 1–3); (2) a defensive rejoinder (v 4); (3) a portrayal of war in Judah as "day of YHWH" (vv 5–8); (4) an accusation against the government for inadequate preparation, but especially for lack of spiritual sensitivity (vv 9–11); (5) an accusation of disobedience to YHWH's instructions (vv 12–13); and (6) a confession that YHWH has withheld absolution (v 14).

The scene builds the tension steadily with probing, accusing questions (v 1) and observations (vv 2–3, 5–8, 9–11, 12–13) before a confession of God's unyielding disapproval. The entire episode involves Jerusalem, which is addressed directly in vv 1 and 7–8. The prophet has received the revelation of royal responsibility and imminent punishment. The accusers are like the speakers in chap. 1 and may well be represented as the covenant witnesses, Heavens and Earth.

Comment

1 גיא חזיון, "Valley of Vision," is vague, deliberately so. It is taken from v 5 below.

2–3 The contrast between consternation at the threat and jubilation at the "macho" feeling of preparation for heroic struggle surfaces here and in vv 12–13. The commentaries generally place parts of this chapter in differing times. When seen as drama, this is unnecessary. The chapter describes 701 B.C.E. The Assyrians, with an international contingent of mercenaries, occupy Judah and threaten Jerusalem. The government calls for unusual military measures for defense. The inhabitants vacillate between attempting to flee (v 3) and displaying nationalistic fervor (vv 2, 13).

חלל, "profaned," should be understood in the sense that a dead body is thought of as profaned. But there are no dead—yet! Rather, the behavior of the city's leadership (or army officers, as Clements suggested) is contemptible. They are responsible for the policies that brought the Assyrians. Some try to flee but are caught.

4 The prophet's anguish expressed in chap. 21 is now extended to Jerusalem's situation. (See *Comment* on 21:2.)

5 The crisis is related to the Day of YHWH. The phrase "valley of vision" is applied to Jerusalem, but the implications remain obscure. מקרקר קר, "digging a ditch," picks up a theme that will be developed in vv 9–11: the extension of the city's water system in view of the siege to come. שוע אל ההר, "crying out toward the mountain," may refer to prayers directed toward Zion.

6 The presence of עילם, "Elam," before Jerusalem is a surprise. At Babylon (chap. 21) it was natural, the only question being "On whose side?" The best explanation seems to be that the entire verse is stressing the international makeup of the attacking troops: bowmen from Elam, chariots with drivers from various nations, and foot soldiers from Kir.

קיר, "Kir," is a land or a city, mentioned by Amos 9:7 as the origin of the Aramaeans. Amos 1:5 and 2 Kgs 16:9 report this as the place to which residents of Damascus will be exiled. No place by this name exists in early records of Mesopotamia. M. C. Astour ("Kir," *IDBSup*, 524) points to its meaning "wall" and thinks it is a translation of *Der*, which also means "wall." Der was a city east of the lower Tigris basin (modern Babrah) between Elam and Babylon.

The chariotry is only identified by אדם, "man" or "humankind." The phrase could be emended to read Aram or Edom, but that is too easy and does not really fit. "Manned chariots" may well be intended as a contrast to the ethnic units in Sennacherib's army: an international troop of chariot drivers representing humankind.

7 The invasion is portrayed. The valley roads approaching Jerusalem are held by chariot-riding brigades. The cavalry has taken up positions opposite the city's gates. The rabshakah's force approached from the south, which made the fortress towns on the north and west useless. עמק, "the valleys," are the access roads to Jerusalem near Timnah (see *MBA*, 154) or those that led from Lachish into the highlands between Hebron and Jerusalem.

8 The enemy (or YHWH?) has penetrated the line of fortress towns that protected the city from invasion along the ridge roads in the north or from the valley roads to the west (2 Kgs 18:13).

בית היער, "The House of the Forest" (see *Note* 8.c.), was a storehouse for arms (1 Kgs 7:2–5), a part of the palace complex. Having lost a major part of the army by desertion (v 3) and abandoning the hope that the ring of armed towns could protect the city (v 8*a*), the citizenry of the city called for arms from the royal armory to protect themselves from the anticipated invaders (cf. W. S. LaSor, "Jerusalem," *ISBE* 2:1008).

Vv 1–3 and 7–8 are all addressed in second feminine singular to the city. Vv 9–11 and 14 are addressed in second masculine plural to the ruling house, the government.

9 The government belatedly recognizes the many deficiencies in the city's defenses. Hezekiah's strategy had been to expand his borders and strengthen his perimeter of fortress towns (cf. 2 Chr 32:29; *MBA*, 152). These verses suggest that the efforts to fortify Jerusalem (2 Chr 32:2–8) came only after Sennacherib's campaign began in 701 B.C.E., which did not bring an attack from the north (cf. *Comment* on 10:32, which is seen to picture YHWH's approach, not the Assyrian's). Instead he drove down the coast, regaining control of Philistia (see *MBA*, 154, and *Comment* on v 7).

Excursus: Hezekiah's Pools and Waterworks

Bibliography

Amiram, R. "The Water Supply of Israelite Jerusalem." In *Jerusalem Revealed: Archaeology in the Holy City, 1968–1974.* Ed. Y. Yadin and E. Stern. Trans. R. Grafman. Jerusalem: Israel Exploration Society, 1975. 75–78. **Avi-Yonah, M.** *EAEHL.* 2:597. **Brunet, G.** *Essai sur l'Isaïe de l'Histoire: Étude de quelques textes notamment dans Isa VII, VIII & XXII.* Paris: Picard, 1975. 293–95 (includes a summary of the work of Lods, Simons, and Vincent). **Burrows, M.** "The Conduit of the Upper Pool." *ZAW* 70 (1958) 221–27. **Kenyon, K. M.** *Digging Up Jerusalem.* London: Benn, 1974. 144–60. ———. *Jerusalem: Excavating 3000 Years of History.* New York: McGraw-Hill, 1967. 69–77. (Cf. the excellent summary by W. LaSor, "Jerusalem," *ISBE,* 2:1008.)

From earliest times Jerusalem's water came from the Gihon Spring, located in the Kidron Valley just east of the northern part of the city of David. R. Amiram ("Water Supply," 75) describes the spring as "a typical karst spring, and its waters gush intermittently (this may be the origin of the Hebrew name: *giha,* 'a gushing forth'). Each gush lasts about 40 minutes, with a break of about 6–8 hours between, according to the season. The discharge is about 1200 cubic meters per day, though in summer it drops considerably."

At about the time of David, cisterns lined with lime began to be built to catch and keep rain water. Pools and aqueducts were also built to use the water of the spring efficiently. (See the illustration below.) Access to water was also a prime military consideration in the defense of the city.

Jebusite Jerusalem had an access shaft cut through the rock; archeologists call this "Warren's shaft" (cf. Kenyon, *Jerusalem,* 19–22), to which reference is apparently made in 2 Sam 5:8. They also built the first aqueduct down to the Kidron Valley.

A small reservoir to hold the waters of the spring had existed from the early Israelite monarchy (2 Kgs 18:17). This is probably the "upper pool" of Isa 7:3//36:2. Two aqueducts have been found that lead from this pool down the valley. One aqueduct is short, extending only some fifty-four yards. The second (II) was used for irrigation of terraced gardens extending to the foot of the Kidron Valley. It drained into the Pool of Shelah (or Sheloah), literally "the aqueduct." This is the modern Birket el-Hamra and is probably to be identified with "the lower pool" of Isa 22:9.

Repeated references in the Bible (2 Kgs 20:20; Isa 22:11; 2 Chr 32:2–4, 30; Sir 48:17) report monumental work related to springs, aqueducts, pools, and tunnels, which brought water into the city walls. The discovery of this tunnel in 1880 with an inscription carved into its rock wall (*ANET,* 321) shows how Hezekiah brought water from Gihon to the pool of Siloam. Avigad's discovery of an eighth-century wall to the west leads to the assumption that it joined the old wall of David's city on the south "encompassing the pool of Siloam" (Avi-Yonah, *EAEHL,* 2:597). This was, then, "the pool between the walls" (Isa 22:11).

The Assyrian was virtually at the door. A major part of the effort to protect the city involved assuring the city of an adequate water supply. An aqueduct begun by Ahaz (7:3) was rushed to completion along with other projects (2 Chr 32:3, 30).

9b The Lower Pool (בְּקִיעֵי) was filled to capacity.

10–11*a* A survey of Jerusalem's houses was done both to arrange housing for those villagers who sought safety in the city and to meet needs for defense. Walled cities usually had two walls with a space between, allowing defenders the open space needed to overcome attackers who had penetrated the outer wall. In

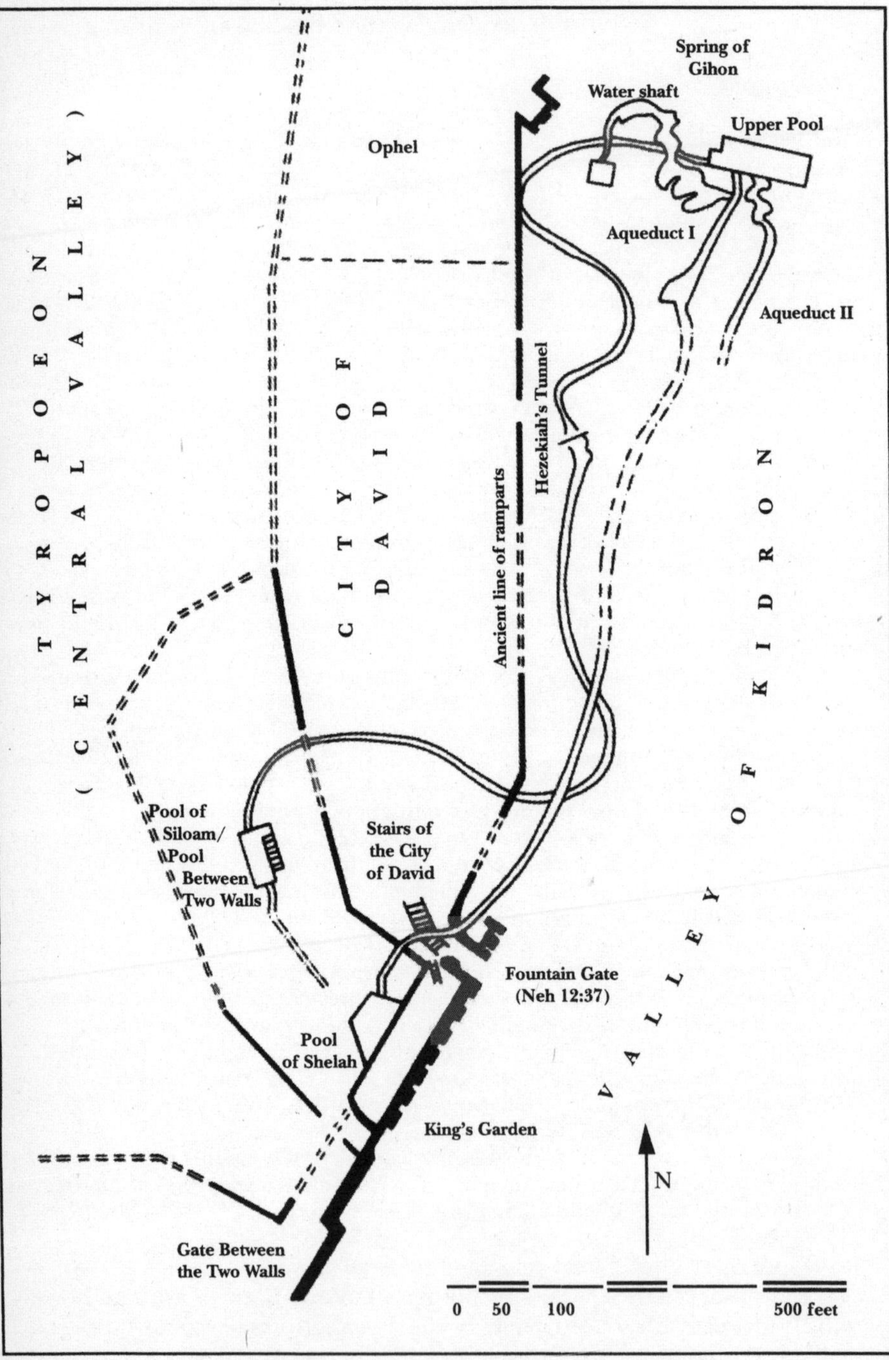
Spring of Gihon
Water shaft
Upper Pool
Ophel
Aqueduct I
Aqueduct II
TYROPOEON (CENTRAL VALLEY)
CITY OF DAVID
Hezekiah's Tunnel
Ancient line of ramparts
VALLEY OF KIDRON
Pool of Siloam/Pool Between Two Walls
Stairs of the City of David
Fountain Gate (Neh 12:37)
Pool of Shelah
King's Garden
Gate Between the Two Walls
N
0 50 100 500 feet

peacetime that space tended to be occupied by squatters who built temporary shacks that soon became permanent dwellings. The government apparently took two steps to address this problem. The houses were demolished to regain the open space between the walls, and part of the space was flooded with water from the old pool. This latter created a flooded moat and also ensured water reserves for the besieged city.

11*b* The government (including the unnamed king) is accused of failure to look to God in its time of peril. It failed to recognize YHWH's stake in the city that he had made and formed long before Israel existed. The Vision's view of Zion emerges here again—a city whose destiny is older than Canaan, the promised land, and one that will survive the collapse of Israel and Judah (2:1–4; 65:17–66:24). The government's failure to reckon with that destiny, even to endanger that destiny as it pursued adventurous nationalistic and personal ambition, is the thrust of this accusation.

The description of this event in 2 Kgs 18:17–19:37//Isa 36–37 contradicts this view. It shows Hezekiah appealing to Isaiah (2 Kgs 19:1–8). In 2 Kgs 19:15–19 Hezekiah prays directly to YHWH about the second threat to the city. He is supported in each instance by divine assurances through Isaiah. How are these two views to be reconciled?

Chap. 22 appears to be set in a time before the final denouement pictured in 2 Kgs 18–19//Isa 36–37. A comparison suggests that Hezekiah's appeal to Isaiah and prayer to YHWH followed a long period in which no such advice or assurance was sought. The Vision maintains that the policies of Shebna and Eliakim during Hezekiah's reign ignored prophetic directions to Ahaz (chap. 7) and warnings to themselves (chap. 20). There is no hint of a mood to seek the Lord's direction now—even with Assyria's cavalry at the gates. Their policy has been one of national independence without regard to God's strategies for them.

12 The Lord (and prudence) called for a reversal of policy, abject humiliation before Sennacherib's authority, penance for their rebellion, promises to rebel no more, payment of tribute due, and penalties for the armies' trouble. Hezekiah did exactly this during the 712 B.C.E. Ashdod rebellion. The city was spared, but it cost virtually everything in the royal treasury.

13 But this time, a nationalistic celebration raises the city's feelings to a fever pitch of bravado—feasting on animals driven into the city, with no thought of needing them to rebuild the country afterward, and drinking an excess of wine, with no thought of saving strength and wit to defend the city. So Jerusalem's rulers have kindled the nationalistic fires in the people's hearts with celebration and feasting (vv 13 and 2a), although they are quite well aware of the city's vulnerability (vv 9–11*a*).

14 Such callous and irresponsible conduct in officials is unforgivable, as YHWH's bitter oath confirms. Not just the leaders but also the people, including the prophet, will suffer the consequences.

The address in vv 9–14 has been consistently in second masculine plural. No names are used. The application would fit the entire government or royal house with its appointed officers, which in this case would be identical. This includes Hezekiah and the officials Eliakim, Shebna, and Joah (2 Kgs 18:18). It is interesting to note that this chapter continues the convention of the Vision and does not mention Hezekiah's name. Only in the superscription (1:1) and in material quoted from 2 Kgs does it appear. This obviously intentional slight, in contrast to the treatment accorded Uzziah (6:1) and Ahaz (7:1–17; 14:28), is significant. The Vision's negative attitude toward Hezekiah's era, as seen in chap. 22, contrasts with the positive views expressed in 2 Kings and 2 Chronicles. Perhaps for this very reason it avoids naming the popular king by name; or, by naming his officials, Shebna and Eliakim, it implies that they must bear responsibility for the policies that they had persuaded the king to follow (cf. prophecies in 3:4, 12).

In any case the chapter does not picture the conclusion of the military confrontation. That was patently known to every Judean who heard (or read) the Vision. Instead, it turns to God's word to Shebna and Eliakim (vv 15, 20).

Explanation

The time approached when the Assyrian armies would be at the gates (cf. chap. 36). Hezekiah's government had been arming to prepare this bid for liberty for some three to four years. But then news came of Babylon's fall in 703 B.C.E. (chap. 21), and the perceptive in Jerusalem simply "waited for the other shoe to drop."

Now the Assyrians with their polyglot armies of mercenaries and impressed troops were in the area. Jerusalem was in an uproar (v 2), but it is difficult to tell whether it was from panic or jubilation. The naive bravado of pumped-up nationalism covered the nervous fears of the city, but the city had no reason to cheer. The first military encounters showed Judean soldiers unwilling to fight (v 2*b*). They were captured in ignominous flight and made prisoners.

The Assyrians made a show of force that promptly stripped Jerusalem of its forward defenses in the armed towns and villages near the border. They all surrendered (vv 5–8*a*). This left the city to fend for itself. The intensive military preparations of the past years had anticipated a very different kind of war, with the enemy kept at a distance from the city by strong outposts of armed towns. Now, feverish preparations were required for the city to withstand a siege, as Jerusalem looked to its internal armaments (v 8*b*).

Whatever the populace may have expected, government ministers were well aware of the weaknesses that their foolish bravado had now laid bare. Jerusalem was in no shape to withstand a siege. The population was undoubtedly swollen with refugees from the countryside. The major concern was for water (vv 9–11*a*). Jerusalem's water supply had always been a problem (see *Excursus: Hezekiah's Pools and Waterworks*). The source for water lay outside the walls, vulnerable to any siege force; so now the government undertook heroic measures to improve the situation. But they showed no sign of understanding how wrongheaded their entire policy had been over some fifteen and more years. They still did not look to God, who made the city and its people long before (v 11*b*).

God was calling for repentance (v 12) as he had through Isaiah (chap. 20) more than a decade before. Nineveh knew what to do when Jonah preached. They wept and wailed, shaved their heads, wore sackcloth, and sat in ashes. That is what God wanted here. This would indicate that the city, beginning with its leaders, had seen the error of its policies and its ways—that it was prepared for radical change. On such a basis they could sue for peace from Sennacherib, pay tribute, and render faithful vassalage as they had in 712 B.C.E.

But just the opposite occurred. There was celebration of temporary liberty—all the more precious because it was unlikely to last (v 13). The drunken show in the streets reflected the irresponsibility of the leaders. They were aware of the precarious nature of their venture. Once again they had counted on Egypt. A new and nationalistic pharaoh promised support, but what came was too little and too late. For the moment Sennacherib's forces could concentrate on Jerusalem, and not even the prophet would be exempt from the troubles of Jerusalem.

Shebna and Eliakim Are Dismissed (22:15–25)

Bibliography

Albright, W. F. "The Seal of Eljakim and the Latest Preexilic History of Judah, with Some Observations on Ezekiel." *JBL* 51 (1932) 77–106. **Auret, A.** "A Different Background for Isaiah 22:15–25 Presents an Alternative Paradigm: Disposing of Political and Religious Opposition." *OTE* 6 (1993) 46–56. **Avigad, N.** "The Epitaph of a Royal Steward from Siloam Village." *IEJ* 3 (1953) 137–52. ———. *Hebrew Bullae from the Time of Jeremiah.* Jerusalem: Israel Exploration Society, 1986. **Brunet, G.** *Essai sur l'Isaïe de l'Histoire: Étude de quelques textes notamment dans Isa VII, VIII & XXII.* Paris: Picard, 1975. **Fullerton, K.** "A New Chapter out of the Life of Isaiah." *AJT* 9 (1905) 621–42. ———. "Shebna and Eliakim: A Reply." *AJT* 11 (1907) 503–9. **Ginsberg, H. L.** "Gleanings in First Isaiah, VI: The Shebna-Eliakim Pericope, 22:15–25." In *Mordecai M. Kaplan: Jubilee Volume.* Ed. M. Davis. New York, 1953. 252–57. **Jenni, E.** *Die Politischen Voraussagen der Propheten.* ATANT 29. Zurich: Zwingli, 1956. 42. **Kamphausen, A.** "Isaiah's Prophecy concerning the Major-Domo of King Hezekiah." *AJT* 5 (1901) 43–74. **Katzenstein, H. J.** "The Royal Steward *(asher 'al ha-bayith).*" *IEJ* 10 (1960) 149–54. **Koenig, E.** "Shebna and Eliakim." *AJT* 10 (1906) 675–86. **Martin-Achard, R.** "L'oracle contre Shebna et le pouvoir des clefs." *TZ* 24 (1968) 241–54. **Mettinger, T. N. D.** *Solomonic State Officials: A Study of the Civil Government Officials of the Israelite Monarchy.* ConBOT 5. Lund: Gleerup, 1971. 70–110. **Ussishkin, D.** "The Necropolis from the Time of the Kingdom of Judah in Silwan, Jerusalem." *BA* 33 (1970) 34–46. **Vaux, R. de.** "Titres et fonctionaires égyptiens à la cour de David et Salomon." *RB* 48 (1939) 394–405. **Wahl, O.** "Woher unsere Festigkeit kommt: Zur Botschaft von Jesaja 22, 20–5 fur uns heute." *ForumKT* 3 (1987) 187–202. **Weis, R. D.** "A Definition of the Genre *Massa'* in the Hebrew Bible." Diss., Claremont Graduate School, 1986. **Wessels, W. J.** "Isaiah of Jerusalem and the Royal Court: Isaiah 22:15–25, a Paradigm for Restoring Just Officials." *OTE* 2.2 (1989) 1–13. **Willis, J. T.** "Historical Issues in Isaiah 22,15–25." *Bib* 74 (1993) 60–70. ———. "Textual and Linguistic Issues in Isa 22:15–25." *ZAW* 106 (1994) 377–99.

Translation

Prophet: 15 *My Lord*[a] *YHWH of Hosts said this:* 5
"Get up and go to this steward 3+3
[b]*against Shebna who is over the house.*[bcd]
16 *What are you doing*[a] *here,* 3+3
and who gave you permission to be here,

that you [m. sg.] have hewed out for yourself a grave here?" 5
Echo Chorus: *Hewing out*[b] *his grave*[c] *on the height,* 3+4
cutting out[b] *a resting place for himself in the rock.*
Prophet: 17 *See! YHWH is hurling you*[a] *[m. sg.]* 3+2+2
a hurling,[b] *O mighty man,*[c]
and grasping you[d] *(with) a grasp.*
18 *Winding up, he will throw*[a] *you [m. sg.] a throw* 3+1+3
like a ball
to a land wide on both sides.[b]
There you shall die. 2+3+3
There the chariots[c] *of your glory*
(will be) a disgrace (to) the house of your master.
King: 19 *I shall dismiss you [m. sg.] from your position!* 2+2
Echo, the Courtiers: *He will*[a] *throw you [m. sg.] out of your office!*
King: 20 *And it will be in that day* 3+2+2
that I shall call to my servant,
to Eliakim, son of Hilkiah.
21 *I shall clothe him in your robe.* 2+2+3
I shall fasten on him your sash,
and I shall place your authority in his hand.
He will become a father 2+2+2
to (every) inhabitant of Jerusalem
(and) to the house of Judah.
22 *I shall place the key of David's house on his shoulder.* 4
When he opens, no one will close. 3+3
When he closes, no one will open.
23 *I shall drive him—a peg in a firm place.* 4
It will become a seat of honor for his father's house. 5
24 *All the weight*[a] *of his father's house will hang on him, the offspring and the offshoot, all the small vessels from the bowls to all the jars.*
Prophet: 25 *In that day,* 2+3
expression[a] *of YHWH of Hosts,*
the peg will be removed 2+3
that was driven in a firm place.
It will be hewn down and will fall, 2+3
and the burden which (hung) on it will be cut off.
For YHWH has spoken. 3

Notes

15.a. Missing in two MSS, LXX, θ´, and Syr., probably because יהוה, YHWH, is also rendered by κύριος.

15.b-b. MT עַל, "upon" or "against," Shebna is parallel to אֶל, "to" or "toward," the steward that precedes. Wildberger (831–32) transposes the entire stich to make it a heading over the paragraph. Others (N. J. Schlögl, *Die heiligen Schriften des Alten Bundes* [Vienna: Burg, 1922]; *BHK*) suggest emending to אֶל, but the changes are unnecessary. "Against" defines the nature of the mission "to" the steward.

15.c. Vg. *praepositus templi qui habitat in tabernaculo,* "the one placed over the temple who dwells in the tabernacle," is explained by Wildberger (840) as mistakenly reading "the house of your master" (v 18) as a reference to the temple of the Lord. But the matter is secular and refers to the royal palace and probably the government.

15.d. Gesenius says two MSS add ואמרת אליו, "and you shall say to him" (v 22), at the end of the verse. LXX, Tg., and Vg. contain the addition. Wildberger (832) considers it original, but it is unnecessary when the arrangement of MT is followed.

16.a. 1QIsa[a] combines the two words מה לך, "what are you (doing)," to make מהלך, presumably a *pi'el* ptc. from הלך, "coming here." This is possible, as the question posed by the second stich shows. However, MT makes the same point with more emphasis.

16.b. Archaic case endings for gen. (cf. GKC §90*m*). Cf. *HebSyntax* §70*f*.

16.c. LXX σεαυτῷ, "for yourself." This smooths out the change of persons. But MT poses the more difficult text, which must be kept and explained (cf. *Form/Structure/Setting*).

17.a. MT טלטל, a *pilpel* form, is unique, usually translated "throw far away, hurl" like the *hip'il* (BDB, 376; *HAL*). I. Eitan ("A Contribution to Isaiah Exegesis," *HUCA* 12–13 [1937–38] 68) suggests that it has an iterative sense, "shake back and forth" (cf. *DCH*). Ehrlich (*Randglossen*, IV, 4:79) says טלטל can mean "stretch out long."

17.b. טלטלה, as a noun or an adj., has been challenged. Duhm expected inf. abs. and suggested removing ה and placing it with גבר, "mighty man," as a vocative. Kaiser (148) follows the emendations of H. L. Ginsberg ("Some Emendations in Isaiah," *JBL* 69 [1950] 51–60), כְּטַלְטֵל הַבֶּגֶד, and G. R. Driver (*JSS* 13 [1968] 48), בְּטַלְטֵלָה בֶּגֶד, in translating "as one shakes out a garment" (see *DCH*). Wildberger (832) is right in rejecting the need for emendation.

17.c. Fohrer, followed by Wildberger, sees this as intended ironically: *du Kerl*, "you fine fellow." For possible emendations, see *Note* 17.b.

17.d. עטה is also a *hap. leg.* (cf. BDB, II, 742). KBL suggests that in Jer 43:12 the root means "rid oneself of lice" (following von Gall, *ZAW* 24 [1905] 105–7). Kaiser (148) uses that meaning here after emending to "garment" in the previous line; similarly *HAL* "delouse." However, the basic meaning of "grasp" or "seize hold of" for this text is supported by BDB, KBL, Wildberger, and others.

18.a. צנף is usually translated "wind up," which led Galling (*BRL*, 239) to think of mummies. LXX καὶ ῥίψει σε, "and he will throw you," and Eitan's suggestion (*HUCA* 12–13 [1937–38] 68) that it be understood like Arab. *ḍafana*, "to kick," provide Wildberger's meaning "throw him with a powerful kick."

18.b. רחבת ידים, lit. "wide of both hands," i.e., to the left hand and to the right hand.

18.c. מרכבות, "chariots," were used as vehicles for persons of rank. Kissane emends to read וְשָׁמְמָה קִבְרֵךְ כְּבוֹדֵךְ, "and thy splendid tomb shall be desolate." LXX reads a singular τὸ ἅρμα. Duhm agreed that "one vehicle is enough." But these emendations are unnecessary; with Wildberger, MT may be sustained.

19.a. Tg., Syr., and Vg. have 1st person followed by many interpreters who point out that י and א were very similar in old Hebrew (cf. *BHK*[3] and *BHS*). It is better to take the change of person as a signal of a change in speaker.

24.a. כבוד in v 23 meant "honor." But here the original meaning of "weight" is called for.

25.a. MT נאם, "expression," is rendered in 1QIsa[a] as נואם, merely a change of form (cf. E. Y. Kutscher, *Language and Linguistic Background*, 498).

Form/Structure/Setting

This highly dramatic chapter consists of five parts. Isa 22:1*b*–8 addresses Jerusalem and its inhabitants in second feminine singular. It chides the city for its ambiguous excitement, mixing despair and revelry (v 2*a*), and for the cowardly behavior of its officers in the field (vv 2*b*–3). It records an official's (is this Shebna?) plea to be left alone with his grief (v 4). A somber reminder that YHWH plans such a day (v 5) is coupled with the military report of troops having overrun Judah's outer defense perimeter (vv 6–8*a*). The final word is a transition to the following section: Jerusalem is forced to look to the royal armory and the defenses of the walled city itself (v 8*b*).

The second part (vv 9–14) addresses the royal house and its ministers in second masculine plural. Vv 9–11 accuse them of following policies of military preparation with no regard to the Lord's intentions in the matter. Vv 12–13 record what the Lord required at such a time—repentance and reversal of policy—and what actually happened—celebration and bravado. V 14 continues this address with YHWH's vow to hold them responsible for this situation.

The third part (vv 15–19) focuses attention on Shebna, the responsible high official, with accusation, threat, and announcement of judgment. The paragraph is clearly marked out from its surroundings and exhibits the characteristics of the "speech of a messenger (Westermann, *Basic Forms,* 98–102). The versions were aware of this: the additions to v 15 in LXX and Tg. fill in what they perceive as gaps in the form (cf. Wildberger, 834).

Note that the first line of the speech parallels that in 22:1.

22:1: מה־לך אפוא כי־עלית
22:16: מה־לך פה . . . כי־חצבת לך

22:1: "What is the matter with you, then, that you have gone up?"
22:16: "What are you doing here . . . that you have hewed out for yourself?"

The same shock with which the question is asked in v 1 reappears in this question to Shebna.

The outline for vv 15–18 is as follows:

v 15*a*	Introductory formula: "Thus says the Lord."
v 15*b*	Instruction to the prophet: "Go to," like instruction to a messenger.
v 15*c*	Additional superscription: "against Shebna."
v 16	Accusation: "What are you doing here?"
vv 17–18	Announcement of YHWH's judgment.

V 19 has the king's measured words that demote Shebna. They, like 8*a,* are transitional, opening the way for the announcement that comes in vv 20–24 of Eliakim's appointment in Shebna's place.

The king's speech continues in vv 20–24, part four, but no longer addresses Shebna directly, as he speaks of his successor, Eliakim. What follows is the fullest description of this position of honor and authority that exists in Scripture.

A prophetic word in heavy prose style closes the chapter in a dark tone of gloomy judgment. The king's change of leadership is seen as more cosmetic than real: the policies remain. God's judgment cuts deeper—Eliakim will also fall.The chapter is a tapestry woven of many colors and styles. It presumes the growing tensions of the Assyrian advance on the city (vv 6–7) and the political demotion of Shebna, the chief architect of Hezekiah's policy of national independence and rebellion (v 19). It sees through the hypocrisy and unrealistic views of the city (v 2), of the government (vv 9–11 and 12–13), of the מֻרְפ-minister (v 16), and of the change of prime ministers (v 25). Judah's ruin, "the destruction of the people" (v 4), is manifest. Hers is a sin that cannot be atoned for (v 14). She, with the government, will collapse (v 25).

The chapter avoids Hezekiah's name, in line with the entire section, but his involvement in every stage is transparent.

Comment

15 This is the first genuinely prophetic word in the chapter. The form is classic (see *Form/Structure/Setting*). As Elijah was sent to Ahab (1 Kgs 21:17–23), now one is sent to Shebna. The messenger (prophet) is unnamed. It may as well be Isaiah as anyone else, but the text does not specify.

שֶׁבְנָא, "Shebna," is written in 2 Kgs 18:18, 26 with ה instead of א. LXX has Σομναν, Vg. *Sobnas*. The name is interesting. R. de Vaux ("Titres et fonctionnaires égyptiens a la cour de David et de Salomon," *RB* 48 [1939] 400) thought it was an Egyptian name, and the idea that Shebna was a foreigner has been carried on by Kaiser (153). But the name appears frequently in its longer form שבניהו/שבניה, "Shebniah" (1 Chr 15:24; Neh 9:4; 10:11, 13 [10, 12]) and must be seen as one indigenous to Judah (M. Noth, *Personennamen*, 258). Inscriptions also bear the name (see Wildberger, 836–37; *HAL*). Shebna's name, along with Hilkiah's, appears in the accounts of the rabshakah's visit in 701 B.C.E. (cf. 2 Kgs 18:18// Isa 36:3; J. M. Ward, "Shebna," *IDB* 4:312).

הסכן, "this steward," appears in the OT otherwise only as a feminine: סֹכֶנֶת, "maidservant, nurse" (1 Kgs 1:2, 4). M. J. Mulder ("Versuch zur Deutung von *sokenet* in I. Kön. I 2, 4," *VT* 22 [1972] 43–54) pleads for the meaning "representative" or "substitute" and thinks of the old queen. Such a meaning in the masculine is supported by inscriptions in several languages (E. Lipiński, "*SKN* et *SGN* dans le sémitique occidental du nord," *UF* 5 [1973] 191–207). Thus the term apparently means the one who represents the king. However, these instructions depreciate the title by adding "this." The tone is unmistakable.

אשר על הבית, "who is over the house," is the title of a ranking member of government under the king (cf. R. de Vaux, *Ancient Israel*, 129–31). It is used first in Solomon's list of officials (1 Kgs 4:6), where it has an unimportant position. Ahishar was apparently only the majordomo. The title is mentioned several times (1 Kgs 16:9; 18:3; 2 Kgs 15:5). By Hezekiah's time the position had grown in importance in much the same way that Joseph's grew under the pharaoh (Gen 40–44; 45:8). Shebna's position must have been very much like that of a vizier in Egypt. "All affairs of the land passed through his hands, all important documents received his seal, all the officials were under his orders. He really governed in Pharaoh's name" (R. de Vaux, *Ancient Israel*, 130). 2 Kgs 15:5 uses the title for Jotham, the heir of the stricken Azariah: "He was over the household, governing the people of the land." (Cf. H. J. Katzenstein, *IEJ* 10 [1960] 149–54; T. N. D. Mettinger, *Solomonic State Officials*, 70–110.)

Eliakim will succeed Shebna in that office. In 2 Kgs 18:18//Isa 36:3 Eliakim leads the delegation and bears the title אשר על הבית, "who is over the house." At this time, presumably shortly before the meeting with the rabshakah, Shebna bears the greater title and the major responsibility.

16 That the instructions say "against Shebna" foretells a message of judgment. The confrontation opens with a challenging question (cf. 1 Kgs 21:19). The word פֹּה, "here," occurs three times in the first half of the verse. The meeting takes place in the royal mausoleum. It is macabre in the extreme. In this episode (a scene that deserves to be remembered beside "Nero fiddled while Rome burned") the prime minister chooses the moment when Jerusalem's citizens are frantically arming for a last-ditch stand against the invaders *to visit the* elaborate mausoleum he was preparing for himself in the royal cemetery. The question conveys the horror at his presumption, along with the irony of this action at this time by this official. Such is the character of the chief administrator of Hezekiah's regime.

The place where the kings from David to Ahaz were buried was inside the walls, in the old city of David (R. de Vaux, *Ancient Israel*, 58; 1 Kgs 2:10; 2 Kgs 16:20). Israelite funeral practices of the period preferred crypts cut into rocky hillsides (cf. *IDBSup*, 119; *ISBE* 2:558). Perhaps Hezekiah's renovations for the city included plans for a new necropolis outside the city "on the height" since the record in Kings omits listing his burial in the city of David. An epitaph on a tomb discovered in Silwan near Jerusalem contains the title "who is over the house," but the name is incomplete. De Vaux (*Ancient Israel*, 129) asks, "Could it be the tomb of Shebna?"

But the bizarre question remains: What is Shebna, Jerusalem's ranking official, doing out there at this time? This may compare with the most scandalous revelations of investigative reporting in another age. Why should he be preoccupied with dignity in death while most people in Jerusalem were still hoping to live?

17–18 YHWH's personal fury exhausts the prophet's language as Isaiah portrays him seizing Shebna and throwing him out, like a ball, into open country (i.e., away from the capital city), to die with his chariot, useless, alone, meaningless without the rank his title symbolized—a disgrace to the royal house he served.

What exactly was Shebna's crime? Kaiser relates it to Isaiah's concern for justice and thinks of exploiting the poor and of pride in office (153–54). Clements emphasizes "the pretensions of a prominent tomb for himself" (187). J. M. Ward (*IDB* 4:312) stresses Shebna's identification with anti-Assyrian policies. Wildberger (841) combines the shock at his pride with recognition of *eine Politik des öffentlichen Ruins,* literally, "a political stand of public ruin."

The context sets the stage: v 4, the recognition of the result of destructive policies; vv 9–11, emphasis on armament and military preparation rather than God's purposes; and v 13, failure to repent and insistence on futile heroics in the face of an overwhelming enemy. These were the faults of the government. Now Shebna's callous attention to preparation of his elaborate mausoleum adds the last straw. Had he been influenced by the Egyptians whom he courted?

"Mighty man" translates גבר *geber,* a man according to his power (Wildberger), but that is as nothing when God takes hold of him. Ps 52:3, 9 (Eng. 1, 7) describes such a hero who is snatched and torn from his tent. M. Klopfenstein (*Die Lüge nach dem Alten Testament* [Zurich: Gotthelf, 1964] n. 319) suggests that Ps 101:7 and Ps 52:4–6 (2–4) were directed at officials of the court who misused their offices. Ps 52:7 (5) is similar to vv 17–18.

ארץ רחבת ידים, "a land wide on both sides," has been taken to refer to Mesopotamia. Fohrer thinks of the Philistine coast. The term is not specific enough for the interpretations laid on it.

19 The tone shifts from having Shebna exiled from the city (perhaps the country) to having him lose his position, standing, or office. This is more in line with his appearance in 2 Kgs 18:18//Isa 36:3, where his title is "the secretary" and he is listed after Hilkiah, who now holds the first position and the title that formerly belonged to Shebna. The indirect speech through the prophet changes to the king's direct speech. In more restrained tones he announces Shebna's demotion from his high position. A spokesman echoes the decree.

20–22 The king's speech continues: Eliakim will be put into Shebna's place with all the symbols of rank. These include a tunic, a sash, and the key to the royal house. His roles, which presumably Shebna had before him, include being "father," for Jerusalemites and Judeans. This probably means being available to help in all affairs—a role somewhere between the Saudi monarch's availability to his subjects and a Chicago ward boss's service to his constituents. He will also serve as chief of ministers in the royal government. He will make decisions that carry royal authority and can not be appealed.

23 The king will establish him in office. The metaphors here appear to be mixed. "A peg in a firm place" seems to picture a tent peg driven in firm ground, while v 24 pictures a fixture to hold pots and pans on a kitchen wall, strong enough to support his broader family ("his father's house"), including direct descendants ("offspring") and related members ("offshoot"). Such an appointment provided economic support and safety for the whole family, as it still does in many countries such as India.

The scene in 2 Kgs 18:18//Isa 36:3, which names both men, appears to reflect the situation after these changes have taken place. Eliakim is the leader over the palace. Shebna has been demoted to a secondary role. But the fact that Shebna is still there is an indication that this was a cosmetic change. Policy remained the same. There is no sign that either of them recognized the error of his ways.

25 ביום ההוא, "in that day," looks beyond the setting of vv 15–24, dealing with Shebna's demotion, to announce YHWH's reversal of Eliakim's promotion. He is no better and must now be removed.

Explanation

The overwhelming accusation of vv 1–14 has its effect. A prophet who is sent to denounce Shebna in YHWH's name (v 15) finds him preparing his own mausoleum (v 16). The prophet passionately announces God's decree of his downfall (vv 17–18). This leads the king to mandate his dismissal (v 19).

But this is not a real change of policy, as the new appointment shows. Eliakim, who has held second position in the government, simply exchanges positions with Shebna (v 20). Eliakim becomes the administrator of the palace, while Shebna is "demoted" to secretary. This game of musical chairs is played out with pomp and circumstance as the new prime minister is installed with all the formality and confidence that the office deserves (vv 21–24).

But all this has an empty ring. Eliakim's policies are identical with those of Shebna. The change will not mislead Sennacherib's representative. The policies that have long characterized Hezekiah's Jerusalem will continue. (See 2 Kgs 18:19–25//Isa 36:4–10.) The rabshakah did not miss the rift that existed between the prophets and the court (2 Kgs 18:26//Isa 36:11).

It is no wonder that the prophet returns to disassociate YHWH from the promises of permanent office for Eliakim that were spoken in the installation ceremony (v 23–24). On the contrary, YHWH declares that Eliakim must also be removed (v 25) so that no part of that wrong policy and wrong administration may remain.

The remainder of Hezekiah's life was apparently a very different one. Manasseh may well have joined him as coregent shortly after this. Manasseh's policy of loyal vassalage, like that of Ahaz his grandfather, marked Judah's behavior over the first half of the following century. From the Vision's point of view, that showed the required change of policy and direction that Shebna's dismissal and Eliakim's appointment did not demonstrate.

Burden: Tyre and the Desolate Land (23:1–27:13)

Bibliography

Ehrlich, E. L. "Der Aufenthalt des Königs Manasse in Babylon." *TZ* 21 (1965) 281–86. **Elat, M.** "The Political Status of the Kingdom of Judah within the Assyrian Empire in the 7th Century B.C.E." *Lachish* 5 (1975) 61–70 (esp. 64). **Ginsburg, H. L.** "Judah and the Transjordan States from 734 to 582 B.C.E." In *Alexander Marx Jubilee Volume*. Philadelphia: Jewish Publication Society of America, 1950. 347–68. **Randles, R. J.** "The Interaction of Israel, Judah, and Egypt from Solomon to Josiah." Diss., Southern Baptist Theological Seminary, Louisville, KY, 1980. 210–38.

One does well to consider chaps. 23–27 as a unit. In these chapters two concepts are intertwined. One has YHWH planning (יעצה 23:9) the course of events and then deciding the fate (יפקד) of Tyre (23:17), the kings (24:21), the land (26:21*a*), and Leviathan (27:1).

But another concept describes processes much less personal by which the land is defiled by the broken covenant (24:5), by a curse that consumes the earth because of bloodguilt (24:6). This concept speaks of the floodgates of heaven opening and the foundation of the earth being shaken (24:18*b*–20) because of guilt. It pictures the royal banquet for all peoples, where it is announced that YHWH of Hosts will swallow up (בלע) the cursed shroud of permanent death—a shroud that has covered all the peoples and nations because of the reproach that lay heavy on the land (25:6–8). It speaks of the land revealing the bloodguilt that it had hidden until that time (26:21). This second concept is like that in Gen 4:10–12, where the ground (אדמה) was under a curse because human blood had been spilled on it. The same view is found in Num 35:33–34: "Bloodshed pollutes the land. . . . Do not pollute the land." 2 Sam 2:21 speaks of land cursed because of a violent crime.

The two concepts are united by the picture of YHWH of Hosts reigning on Mount Zion (24:23). Only under the reigning glory of the Divine King can the two views be reconciled. It is imperative that the entire passage be interpreted as a unit with the two concepts dependent upon each other. In the OT, the consequences of the curse are often pictured, but not the way in which a curse can be lifted or ended. Once unleashed and operative, the damning power of this polluting curse brought on the land by repeated killings seemed to have a demonic life of its own. Temple offerings were designed to effect atonement for such bloodguilt according to Leviticus. The rituals of the Day of Atonement (Lev 16) should have relieved the land and temple of the impurity (= curse) of bloodguilt.

The Vision of Isaiah claims, however, that the people's hypocrisy undermined the effectiveness of the temple rites (chap. 1), so only an extraordinary act by YHWH could relieve the curse. So YHWH of Hosts on Zion decided the fate and swallowed up the curse! Only through such judgment and amnesty could the ominous and pervasive effects of the curse and guilt be counteracted.

Thus this section has a strong element (marked here by "A") relating to that mysterious sphere of blessing/curse or holy/profane. It also has another element (marked here by "B") relating to history. The two are intertwined. In 23:9 YHWH of Hosts planned trouble for Tyre (B). He is also said to defile or pollute (חלל) the pride of their glory (A). In 23:17 YHWH will decide Tyre's fate (B). In 24:5 the land is polluted/profaned (A) by its inhabitants. The eternal covenant is broken (B). A curse consumes the land while the people must bear their contamination (A). In 24:21 YHWH will decide the fate of kings and armies (B). Throughout 25:6–8 the feast of YHWH of Hosts functions in terms of element A, but in 26:21*a* YHWH will settle the fate of the land (B) while 26:21*b* tells of the land's being forced to reveal its bloodguilt (A). In 27:1 YHWH settles the fate of Leviathan, symbol for Tyre (B). In 27:13 Israel will be gathered from far places (B). She will again be sanctified to worship God on the holy mountain in Jerusalem (A).

Just as the specific crime of dumping dangerous chemicals may result in a festering condition that requires a remedy far beyond punishment of the offender, so here the crimes of pride (23:9) and the breaking of laws and covenant (24:5) had brought about a condition in which the curse prevails (24:6) like a shroud over the whole land (25:7) causing destruction, ruin, and death (25:8). The violent crimes have led to bloodguilt and its results so that the entire land is cursed because of the sins of its people. (Cf. J. Pedersen, *Israel III–IV* [Copenhagen: Branner, 1940] 270–76.)

This act is a virtual catalog of the vocabulary of curse: אלה, "curse" (24:6), and חרפה, "disgrace" (25:8), which אכל, "consumes, devours" (24:6), חלל, "profane, defile, dishonor" (23:9), and חנף, "contaminate" (24:5). The people involved are told to דמם, "be silent or mourn" (23:2); they are בוש, "shamed" (23:4), קלל, "humbled, dishonored" (23:9), and אשם, "contaminated, held guilty" (24:6), and they חור, "pale in weakness, disappear" (24:6). The causes of this are עבר, "disregarding instruction, passing over law" (24:5), and חלף, "violating a statute, changing a statute" (24:5); they הפר, "break, making the eternal covenant meaningless" (24:5). In summary, the prophet invokes דמים, "guilt, bloodguilt," and הרוגים, "slain, murder victims" (26:21). The cumulative effect of murders, assassinations, and wars is seen in the curse and its debilitating loss of all vitality. This condition could very properly bear the label המות לנצח, "the death . . . forever" (25:8).

Since the curse was all-consuming, אכלה (24:6), so the remedy had to be able to absorb totally, בלע (25:7, 8), the evil contaminant. The two words share a semantic field. The second often carries the sense of "making to disappear" (*TWAT,* 1:660).

The wonder of YHWH's decree of salvation in 25:8 and his act of salvation in 26:21 can be seen in 27:13 as "those perishing . . . will come . . . and bow down to YHWH in the holy mountain in Jerusalem." The mountain's holiness had been secured or restored, and the people of Israel had been sanctified so that they could enter its sacred walls again.

While the curse that resulted from the breach of covenant had a kind of automatic and autonomous character, the scenes never allow YHWH's judgment to be seen in totally impersonal terms. His sovereign decisions on the throne control the course of events. He planned it (23:9). He determined the fates of the parties involved. He "will swallow up the death (which) endures forever" (25:8), thus taking control of events away from the continuing power of bloodguilt and curse. And he would thresh and gather Israelites from greater Palestine to join those from Assyria and Egypt to worship in Jerusalem.

Excursus: The Vassal Years of Hezekiah and Manasseh (ca. 700–640 B.C.E.)

Bibliography

Ahlström, G. W. *The History of Ancient Palestine.* Minneapolis: Fortress, 1993. **Katzenstein, H. J.** *The History of Tyre.* Jerusalem: Schocken Institute, 1973. **Randles, R. J.** "The Interaction of Israel, Judah, and Egypt from Solomon to Josiah." Diss., Southern Baptist Theological Seminary, Louisville, KY, 1980. 210–38. **Wiseman, D. J.** *Nebuchadnezzar and Babylon.* London: Oxford UP, 1985.

The half century that followed the siege of Jerusalem (700–640 B.C.E.) saw the Assyrian Empire reach the apogee of its power. Sennacherib had even defeated an Egyptian army under Taharqa at Eltekeh (Kitchen, *Third Intermediate Period in Egypt,* 383–85). Judah had no choice other than to submit itself to Assyrian vassalage during the rest of Hezekiah's reign and that of Manasseh, his son.

As in the reign of Ahaz, this put Judah in the spectator's position through most of that period. Twenty years passed quietly, but the accession of Esarhaddon to Assyria's throne (680–669 B.C.E.) brought a more aggressive policy to affairs in West Asia. Between 677 and 663 B.C.E. the Assyrian storm broke over the area with unparalleled fury. Until this time the principal battles had been fought between the superpower Assyria and local coalitions of kingdoms. Egypt, potentially the other superpower, had usually avoided major confrontation. However, in this decade and a half the great powers clashed repeatedly.

The shock waves must have been felt throughout the Near East with apocalyptic intensity. Manasseh had the wisdom to keep to the sidelines as much as possible. Egypt's Phoenician allies caught the brunt of the first assaults. Sidon was attacked in 677 B.C.E. Esarhaddon invaded Egypt in 674 and again in 671 B.C.E. Ashurbanipal (669–627 B.C.E.) drove into Egypt in 667–666 B.C.E. and again with a terrible sack of Thebes in 663 B.C.E. These blows were finally too much for the Twenty-Fifth Dynasty, which withdrew to its Ethiopian home. Esarhaddon's destruction of Sidon and subjugation of Tyre in 677 B.C.E. was a step toward his invasion of Egypt in 674 and 671. Ashurbanipal followed the same procedure in 667. Manasseh was forced to supply forces and participate with Assyria in the invasion of Egypt in that year (*ANET,* 294).

Baal I of Tyre apparently supported Tantamani in Egypt's ill-advised rebellion of 664 B.C.E. Ashurbanipal repaid him by capturing Tyre on his return trip and turning the entire Phoenician area into Assyrian provinces with severe restrictions on their ability to profit from the sea trade that had traditionally been their exclusive province. Perhaps it was at this time that Manasseh, suspected of belonging to the rebellion, was taken to Nineveh, only to be released and returned home (2 Chr 33:9–11; H. J. Katzenstein, *History of Tyre,* 292; Randles, "Interaction," 221).

Once Assyria itself was destroyed, Babylon quickly took its place terrorizing the whole land. Josiah's interesting reign occurs in the interregnum between Assyrian and Babylonian administration in Palestine, but the Vision finds the hope for renewed national independence under Josiah to have lasted so little time as to not be worth mentioning. Babylon's activity in Palestine in 605 and again in 598 B.C.E. put pressure on Jerusalem under Jehoiakim and Jehoiachin, forcing the latter into exile with his family and some other leaders. But it was the siege and overthrow of Jerusalem during Zedekiah's reign in 586 B.C.E. that created the larger group of exiles and brought the reign of David's dynasty to an end.

Sometime near this time Nebuchadenezzar conducted a thirteen-year siege of Tyre (Katzenstein, *History of Tyre,* 319–28; Wiseman, *Nebuchadnezzar and Babylon,* 27–29), which must have ended by 572 B.C.E. (cf. Ahlström, *History of Ancient Palestine,* 802). This put the Babylonians in command of the entire seafront in Palestine. Under the Persians, Tyre, Sidon, Byblos, and Aradus had a semi-independent status with their own kings, at a time when the Persians turned their attention toward the sea (Ahlström, *History of Ancient Palestine,* 828).

This act portrays a depth of oppression unmatched in other eras. The area (הארץ) was totally under the heel of the tyrannical empires. No city (after Tyre) could resist their demands. With the exception of Moab, no nations are mentioned because no organized nation worthy of the name existed. The other nations, including Egypt, had been subdued and kept under Assyria's and then Babylon's discipline.

The depiction of Tyre in chap. 23 seems to fit into the era of Assyrian power that ended the age of small states and cities in Palestine (14:24–22:25). Chaps. 24–27 fit better the following Babylonian period in which Judah (along with Tyre again) met cataclysmic destruction. But the tight thematic links within chaps. 23–24 show that the two periods both demonstrated the extreme helplessness of the peoples of the land. This description of Hezekiah's humiliation (chap. 22) continues to the reign of Manasseh (chap. 23) and reaches its climax in the early sixth century (chaps. 24–27). In terms of sustained humiliation, Judah had never experienced anything like it before. Beyond the range of the Vision, she would again experience such devastation in the days of Antiochus Epiphanes in 167 B.C.E. and under the Romans in 70 C.E. So some scholars' comparison of chaps. 24–27 to Maccabean times is apt. But the literature is prophetic and liturgical in style. Only by stretching the definition and the dating of "apocalyptic" can it be called by that label.

With the fall of Tyre, the last of the great city-states had fallen. After Damascus, Babylon, and Thebes, no city could be found that was strong enough to withstand the imperial invader. Jerusalem was still there, but only because it had capitulated in 701 B.C. and continued to render tribute. And both Jerusalem and Tyre would shortly fall to Babylon, as chaps. 24 and 27 indicate.

The Vision's Interpretation of the Period

Under the repeated onslaughts of Assyrian and Babylonian armies, the last pillar that supported the political, social, and economic system within which Israel had existed collapsed. The Mesopotamian and Egyptian anchors to the east and to the south, which had sheltered and enriched Canaanite civilization and culture, disappeared in the stormy tide that broke over the land. Lacking these, the possibilities of another pax Davidica also vanished. Judah had no chance to survive as a sovereign state. These chapters, with those that follow (chaps. 28–39), mark the end of an age and the civilization it nurtured.

The Vision insists that all this was from God. His judgment over that civilization had deep roots. That judgment had prepared Canaan to receive Israel in the first place, and now Israel is taken into the depths with it. YHWH's larger strategy looked to a different basis for political stability. He was preparing Israel for a better matrix for her mission than Canaan could provide, a better civilization than Canaan's could possibly be. He calls Israel and Judah to see and believe this (chaps. 40–66). He offers them privileged and handcrafted roles in that new age. The future lies not in their old cities and political structures but in a new "planting" (27:2–6). This replanting will be the theme of the last three acts.

In the midst of devastation there is hope because it is God who is acting. On this mountain he who controls life and death sentences tyrants to death (26:14) but promises that the dead of the faithful will rise (26:19). He will punish and slay Leviathan, the dragon (27:1). Israel's new planting will fill all the civilized world (not just Canaan) with fruit (27:6). God will harvest it from the Euphrates to the River of Egypt, David's old boundaries (27:12). Even those beyond, in Assyria and Egypt, can be part of the pilgrim congregation at Zion's festivals (27:13).

The Vision uses the act to pose the question, If national existence for Israel/Judah is no longer possible and if the power of being a fortified city-state is denied Jerusalem, what can the future hold for the people called Israel and for the cult center called Zion? The act establishes a foundation and a direction in answering that question. The foundation that is reiterated is God himself—YHWH of Hosts and his strategy and purpose. The direction looks to the exercise of his great power: The enemy will die, but YHWH will "raise the dead" of Israel; YHWH will kill the dragon, regaining control from the chaotic forces loosed on the region through Assyria. Death poses an ultimate end for the tyrant (as in chap. 14), but it holds no such meaning for Israel, for God reaches beyond death to renewed life. Israel's hope is that ultimately all that the dragon, Leviathan, symbolizes is under the control of God. The key factor in Israel's hope does not really deal with Assyria at all; rather it depends upon the will and strategy (עצה) of God. When the day of his "wrath" is over, all good things are possible again for those who trust and love him.

The chapters fit exactly into the entire Vision's view of God's relation to history. The view is optimistic: the best is yet to be. It is forward looking and sees God's goals staked out in the future. It can relate those to ultimate ends (overcoming death; killing the dragon), but they are not pushed to an ultimate future beyond history. They are drawn into a future that is in God's hands, determined and executed on God's mountain. That mountain is Zion, not heaven, and the means of worship on that golden day is pilgrimage, like that which was possible throughout the Persian and Greco-Roman period to the time of the destruction of Jerusalem in 70 C.E.

These chapters have much more to do with the Vision's perspectives than they do with the apocalyptic outlook of Daniel or Enoch. (See *A Concluding Liturgy: 24–27* below.) To pull them out of their context and treat them from the latter perspective is to do violence to their nature and intention.

THE ANNOUNCEMENT OF YHWH'S ROYAL REIGN

The usual division of these chapters has relegated chap. 23 to the collection of "foreign prophecies" that precede it and has treated chaps. 24–27 as a self-contained unit. However, chap. 22, with its description of Jerusalem in 701 B.C.E., was found to be a natural closing scene for chaps. 15–22. Tyre's fall will be seen to have its natural historical setting in the seventh century. It still belongs to the

Assyrian age, while the following chapters address the Babylonian period (see *Act 2—Burden Babylon: 13–27* above). Yet all of chaps. 23–27 will be shown to present repeated responses to the fall of Tyre, so the chapters are grouped here together. A natural break, universally recognized, occurs after chap. 27.

The internal structure of chaps. 23–27 supports this division. The climactic declaration in 25:6 that YHWH prepares a banquet on Zion is the keystone in a grand arch of announcements in the style of YHWH's royal reign on Zion that begin in 23:1 and continue through 27:13.

Tyre is ordered to respond (23:1–7).
A YHWH planned this against Tyre (23:8–9).
Response from sailors (23:10).
B YHWH stretched his hand over the sea (23:11–12*a*).
Responses from the sailors and prophets (23:12*b*–18).
C See YHWH devastating the land (24:1–3).
Responses (24:1–3).
D YHWH judges armies and kings (24:21).
Responses (24:22).
E YHWH of Hosts reigns (24:23).
Individual responses (25:1–5).
KEYSTONE On Mount Zion, YHWH of Hosts prepares a banquet (25:6).
E´ He destroys death forever (25:7–8).
Response of Jerusalem (25:9).
D´ The hand of YHWH on this mountain: Moab judged (25:10–12).
Response of Judah (26:1–20).
C´ YHWH will come to judge the inhabitants of the land (26:21).
B´ YHWH will judge Leviathan, monster of the sea (27:1).
Response of Israel (27:2–11).
A´ YHWH will thresh and gather Israel (27:12–13).

On the rising steps of the chiastic ladder, Tyre and the land are called to respond. On the descending steps, Jerusalem, Judah, and Israel are called to respond. Note the span of seventy years provided for the act. This skeletal theme of YHWH's royal day is fleshed out in terms that fit the context of the Vision as responses to the fall of Tyre. This destruction (chap. 23) is seen as a symbol of the generation in which the last resistance to imperial tyranny collapses. The entire land, all the cities (city-states), and even the sea, with its channels of commerce and power, come under the rule of the tyrant, "the rod of [YHWH's] anger" (10:5). The land and its cities provide evidence of YHWH's devastation (24:1–13). Response to the devastation varies from jubilation to despair (24:14–16).

The scene is brought under the kingship theme by the announcement that the terror has solid basis, for the ultimates of cosmic judgment are involved (24:17–20). Through these YHWH will judge the powers and will reign gloriously on Zion (24:21–24). A psalm rejoices in this recognition (25:1–5) before the kingship theme is developed through an announcement of the banquet for the peoples when YHWH will "swallow up death . . . forever" (25:6–8). A confessional hymn (25:9) precedes the additional kingship theme of victory over the nations (Moab; 25:10–12). Chap. 26 celebrates and develops the theme's significance for Jerusalem and its people, who are then warned to prepare for a continuation of wrath (26:20).

The closing themes announce YHWH's "going out of his place" to punish the earth/land for its sins (26:21) and his punishment of Leviathan, "the monster which is in the sea" (27:1). The rest of chap. 27 deals with the consequences for Israel.

In its artistry, the chapters communicate on more than one level. The dramatic portrayal of Tyre's historical fall before Assyrian pressure (687 B.C.E.) is used to typify the final subjugation of all the land (see *Excursus: "The Land"* [הארץ] below); it is the last of the great cities (see *Excursus: "The City"* [העיר] below) to fall before the empire. This fall in turn is set in the context of YHWH's rule on Zion, which humbles the proud of the nations and which "visits/punishes"(see *Excursus: Decide One's Fate* below) any dissenting power in heaven or on earth until his rule is complete and acknowledged.

This is not apocalyptic of the type that is characteristic of Judaism of the second century B.C.E. onward (as many have maintained; see *Bibliography* for 24:1–27:13). It is the application of kingship-of-YHWH themes from Solomon's temple on Zion, reborn to new life and meaning in fifth-century Jerusalem, paralleling the development of the themes in Zech 9–14 and in Malachi. A significant difference from the preexilic forms lies in the absence of a role for the Davidic king. Hope lies in the direct intervention of God, who provides a strong city and protects it (26:1) and who preserves his vineyard (27:2–5) in contrast to the ruined land and empty cities all about. The application to the seventh and sixth centuries, when the Judean kings were powerless, is obvious.

Burden: Tyre (23:1–18)

Bibliography

Dahood, M. "Textual Problems in Isaiah." *CBQ* 22 (1960) 400–409. ———. "The Value of Ugaritic for Textual Criticism, Isa 23:9." *Bib* 40 (1959) 160–64. **Erlandsson S.** *The Burden of Babylon: A Study of Isaiah 13,2–14,23.* Lund: Gleerup, 1970. 98–102. **Fischer, T.,** and **U. Rüderswörden.** "Aufruf zur Volksklage in Kanaan (Jesaja 23)." *WO* 13 (1982) 36–49. **Flint, P. W.** "The Septuagint Version of Isaiah 23:1–14 and the Massoretic Text." *BIOSCS* 21 (1988) 35–54. **Grünberg, S.** "Exegetische Beiträge, Jesajah 23:15." *Jeshurun* 13 (1926) 50–56. **Harden, D. M.** *The Phoenicians.* London: Thames and Hudson, 1962. **Høghaven, J.** *Gott und Volk bei Jesaja.* 157–61. **Katzenstein, H. J.** *The History of Tyre.* Jerusalem: Schocken Institute for Jewish Research, 1973. ———. "משא עור—היסטוריה, גיאורגרפיה, ארכיאולוגיה, Onus Tyri—historia, geographia, archaeologia." In *HaMikra' weToledot Yisrael.* Tel Aviv: University of Tel Aviv, 1972. **Kooij, A. van der.** *The Oracle of Tyre: The Septuagint of Isaiah XXVIII as Version and Vision.* VTSup 71. Leiden: Brill, 1998. ———. "A Short Commentary on Some Verses of the Old Greek of Isaiah 23." *BIOSCS* 15 (1982) 36–50. **Lindblom, J.** "Der Ausspruch über Tyrus in Jes. 23." *ASTI* 4 (1965) 56–73. **Linder, J.** "Weissagung über Tyrus, Isaias Kap. 23." *ZKT* 65 (1941) 217–21. **Lipiński, E.** "The Elegy on the Fall of Sidon in Isaiah 23." *ErIsr* 14 (1978) 79–88. **Renz, T.** "Proclaiming the Future: History and Theology in Prophecies against Tyre." *TB* 51 (2000) 17–58. **Reyes, A. Y.** *Archaic Cyprus.* Oxford: Clarendon Press, 1994. **Rudolph, W.** "Jesaja 23:1–14." In *Festschrift Friedrich Baumgärtel.* Ed. J. Herrmann and L. Rost. Erlanger Forschungen A10.

Erlangen: Universitätsbund, 1959. 166–74. **Tsirkin, J. B.** "The Hebrew Bible and the Origin of Tartessian Power." *AuOr* 4 (1986) 179–85. **Tuplin, C.** *Achaemenid Studies.* Stuttgart: Steiner, 1996. **Watson, W. G. E.** "Tribute to Tyre (Isa XXIII 7)." *VT* 26 (1976) 371–74. **Werner, W.** *Studien zur alttestamentlichen Vorstellung vom Plan Yahves.* BZAW 173. Berlin: De Gruyter, 1988. 54–60. **Wolff, H. W.** "Der Aufruf zur Volksklage." *ZAW* 76 (1964) 48–56.

Translation

Herald:	1 *Burden: Tyre.*	2
First Mourner:	*Howl,*[a] *O ships of Tarshish,*[b]	3+3
	for (it) is destroyed without a house[c] *to come home*[d] *to.*	
	From the land of Cyprus	2+2
	it was made known to them.	
Second Mourner:	2 *Mourn,*[a] *inhabitants of the coast,*	3+2
	merchants[b] *of Sidon,*[c]	
	who send[d] *your messengers*[e]	2+2
	3 *on many waters.*[a]	
	The seed of Shihor,	2+3+3
	the harvest of the Nile[b] *(was) her*[c] *revenue.*	
	Thus she became the merchant of nations.	
Third Mourner:	4 *Shame on you, Sidon!*	2+3+3
	For the sea has spoken,	
	the sea's stronghold, saying,[a]	
	"I have not been in labor.	2+2
	I have not given birth.	
	I have not raised boys	3+2
	(nor) brought up girls."	
First Mourner:	5 *As soon as a report*[a] *(is made) to Egypt,*	3+3
	they will writhe in pain at the news about Tyre.	
Second Mourner:	6 *Cross over*[a] *to Tarshish!*	2+3
	Howl, O[b] *inhabitants of the coast!*[b]	
Third Mourner:	7 *Has this been a city of revelry*[a] *for you?*	3+3
	One whose origin[b] *(was) from days of old?*	
	One whose feet took her	2+2
	to sojourn[c] *far away?*	
Heavens:	8 *Who planned this*	3+3
	against Tyre, the giver of crowns,[a]	
	whose merchants[b] *(are) princes,*	3+3
	whose traders[c] *(are) the honored of the land?*[d]	
Earth:	9 *YHWH of Hosts planned it*	3+4+4
	to defile the[a] *pride of all glory,*[a]	
	to dishonor all the honored of the land.	
First Mourner:	10 *Till*[a] *your land,*	2+3+3
	for ships[b] *of Tarshish*[c]	
	no longer have a wharf![d]	
Earth:	11 [a] *When he stretched out his hand over the sea,*	3+2
	he caused kingdoms to tremble!	
	YHWH had issued a command concerning Canaan	3+2

to destroy her fortresses.[b]
12 *Then he said:*[a] 1+3+3
"Do not continue your revels,
oppressed[b] *virgin-daughter Sidon!"*
Second Mourner: *Rise! Cross over (to) Cyprus!*[c] 3+3
Even there you cannot find rest for yourself!
Third Mourner: 13 *See the land of the Chaldeans!*[a] 3+4+3
This was the people who no longer exist!
Assyria assigned her to wild beasts.[b]
They raised their siege towers;[c] 2+2+2
they stripped her citadels,
making her a ruin.
First Mourner: 14 *Howl, O ships of Tarshish,* 3+3
for your stronghold is destroyed.
First Prophet: 15 *And it will be in that*[a] *day* 3
[b]*that Tyre will be forgotten*[c] *for seventy years,* 4+3
like the days of one king.
At the end of seventy years[b] 3+4
it will be for Tyre like the song of the harlot:
16 *Take a harp,* 2+2+2
go about the city,
forgotten harlot.
Make a good melody! 2+2+2
Repeat a song,
so that you will be remembered!
Second Prophet: 17 *And it will be* 1+3
at the end of seventy[a] *years*
YHWH may decide Tyre's fate, 3+2
and it will return to its hire.[b]
It will entice[c] *all the kingdoms of the land* 3+2
upon the face of the ground.
Third Prophet: 18 *And it will be that her merchandise and her profit* 3+2
(will be) dedicated to YHWH.
It will not be hoarded or stored. 4
But to those dwelling before YHWH 4+2+4
will its merchandise belong,
for eating, for satisfaction, and for choice[a] *clothing.*

Notes

1.a. 1QIsa[a] אילילו has exchanged א for ה, which occurs frequently in this text.

1.b. LXX Καρχηδόνος (also in vv 6, 10, 14) and OL *Carthago* have "Carthage"; Vg. *naves maris,* "ships of the sea."

1.c. Note the parallel in v 14, where מָעֻזְּכֶן, "your refuge," stands for מבית, "house."

1.d. MT מִבּוֹא, "from coming" or "when one comes (home)." But see מְבוֹאֹת יָם, "gate of the sea," in Ezek 27:3. If it reads מִמָּבוֹא, it could mean "without a harbor." Wildberger (with *BHS*) suggests simply reading מָבוֹא, "coming home," as an adverbial usage.

2.a. MT דֹּמּוּ, "be silent," an impv. LXX τίνι ὅμοιοι γεγόνασιν, "what have you become like?" has apparently read it as pf. from דמה I, "be similar." Interpreters have made numerous suggestions (cf.

Wildberger). F. Delitzsch (*Prolegomena eines neuen hebräisch-aramäischen Wörterbuch zum Alten Testament* [Leipzig: Hinrichs, 1886] 64 n. 2) suggested a parallel to Akk. *damāmu*, "mourn," and M. Dahood (*CBQ* 22 [1960] 400) has found Ugar. *dmm* to mean "mourn." This makes a good parallel to "howl!" in v 1.

2.b. MT is sg. LXX, Tg., and Vg. are pl., suggesting they read סחרי (cf. BHS, Kaiser, Wildberger).

2.c. LXX Φοινίκης, "Phoenicia."

2.d. MT עבר ים, "crossing sea," is probably a wrong word division of עברים, "crossing, sending" (cf. Procksch, *BHS,* Wildberger).

2.e-3.a. A comparison with Ps 107:23 מְלָאכָה בְּמַיִם רַבִּים, "business on many seas," suggests a different verse division and a similar reading here. 1QIsa^a מלאכיך, "your messengers," adds support to this understanding, so Duhm, Marti, Procksch, Ehrlich *(Randglossen)*, Rudolph ("Jesaja 23:1–14," 168), Auvray, and Wildberger suggest עברים מלאכיו (or ה) במים רבים, "who send his/her messengers on many waters." They are probably correct.

3.b. Omitted in LXX.

3.c. LXX "your."

4.a. Omitted in Syr.

5.a. LXX ἀκουστὸν γένηται, "began to be heard," implies "it is heard," as do Syr. *(d)ʾštmʿ* = נִשְׁמַע and Vg. *cum auditum fuerit.* Wildberger follows the LXX, like Marti, Guthe, Feldmann, Procksch, and Ziegler. However, MT makes sense and may be kept.

6.a. 1QIsa^a עוברי, "(those of Tarshish) passing over." Follow MT.

6.b-b. LXX οἱ ἐνοικοῦντες ἐν τῇ νήσῳ ταύτῃ, "the inhabitants in that island," apparently refers to Tyre itself. אי may mean "island" but is usually "coast," referring to Phoenicia or Philistia.

7.a. 1QIsa^a העליזה adds the article.

7.b. 1QIsa^a has a pl., as does Ezek 36:11.

7.c. Vg. *ad peregrinandum,* "to a stranger." Watson (*VT* 26 [1976] 372) has another translation: "Can this be your joyful city, to whom, since ancient times, her tribute they brought to her feet, obliged to reverence at a respectful distance?" But the plain reference is to successful trade rather than tribute.

8.a. MT is *hipʿil* ptc. 1QIsa^a המעטרה appears to be *piʿel* or *puʿal* ptc. Vg. *coronata,* "crowned." Wildberger correctly supports MT.

8.b. The reading of the Leningrad codex lacks a vowel at the end. With other Heb. MSS, read ־ָהּ, "her," combined with אשר, "whose."

8.c. MT כְּנַעֲנֶיהָ, "her traders," is unusual, but see Bauer-Leander, 564, and *HAL.*

8.d. 1QIsa^a adds the article. Wildberger calls it the *Prosaisierung,* which occurs often in that text.

9.a-a. 1QIsa^a כול גאון צבי, "all the pride of glory," for MT גאון כל צבי, "pride of all glory." *BHS* would make further changes on this example, but MT may be used as it stands, including the tristich accentuation, which *BHS* has ignored (Wildberger, 857).

10.a. MT עִבְרִי, "pass over." 1QIsa^a עבדי, "serve, till," is supported by LXX ἐργάζου, "work."

10.b. MT כַּיְאֹר, "like the Nile," is supported by 1QIsa^a, but LXX has no equivalent for it.

10.c. MT בת־תרשיש, "daughter Tarshish," has been challenged by Kissane, Procksch, and others. Wildberger (857) notes the problems for the first five words of the verse. He solves them by following LXX, reading עבדי, "work," first. Then he divides כיאר בת following LXX to read כי אניות, "for ships," by taking the letters כי א__ת from MT and reading רב as a corruption of ני to get LXX's πλοῖα, "ships": עִבְדִי אַרְצֵךְ כִּי אֳנִיּוֹת תַּרְשִׁישׁ, "till your land, for ships of Tarshish," have no wharf anymore.

10.d. MT מֵזַח, "girdle, waistband" (BDB), makes no sense here. Procksch suggested emending to מַלָּח, "sailors." *BHK, BHS,* and *HAL* suggest מָחוֹז, "harbor" (cf. Ps 107:30), and Kissane מָנֹחַ, "harbor." But KBL draws on Eg. *mdḥ*, "build ships," and *mḥt*, "carpenter shop," and suggests that מזח means "wharf" or "dock"; *DCH* "shipyard."

11.a. *BHS* follows Procksch, Rudolph ("Jesaja 23:1–14,"169), Steinmann, Eichrodt, Kaiser, and Wildberger (857) in reversing the order of the verse halves. They argue that YHWH is presumed as subject in *a-b* while he is only mentioned in *c.* But such anticipation is not infrequent in Hebrew, and MT may be sustained.

11.b. MT מעזניה is difficult to understand. 1QIsa^a מעזיה omits the *nun* and makes good sense: "her fortresses."

12.a. ויאמר, "then he said," falls outside the metrical order.

12.b. 1QIsa^a omits the article of MT and is probably right (see Wildberger, 858).

12.c. כתיים lacks a vowel. K and 1QIsa^a supply it as כִּתִּיִּים. Q reads כִּתִּים. There is no difference in meaning.

13.a. The reference to faraway Chaldea has struck many commentators as irrelevant. H. Ewald (*Commentary on the Prophets of the Old Testament,* trans. J. F. Smith [London: Williams & Norgate, 1875–81]), followed by C. von Orelli (*The Prophecies of Isaiah,* trans. J. S. Banks [Edinburgh: T & T Clark, 1887]) and T. K. Cheyne (*The Book of the Prophet Isaiah,* 5th ed. [New York: Dodd, Mead, 1904]), suggested reading כנענים, "Canaanites," for כשדים, "Chaldeans." Procksch, Kissane, Rudolph ("Jesaja 23:1–14"), and *BHS* suggest eliminating "land of the Chaldeans." Others suggest reading כתיים, "Cyprus," like the previous line (Meier [cited by Duhm], Marti, [*Jesaja* (Tübingen: Mohr, 1907)], Kaiser). Wildberger (858) sees the verse as a gloss on "Cyprus" in the previous verse. But the destruction of Babylon is a major theme in the Vision (chaps. 13 and 21) and may properly be compared to Tyre. MT should be kept.

13.b. צִי, "wild beast" or "demon." Cf. Isa 13:21.

13.c. 1QIsa[a] בחיניה reads "her" for MT "his." KBL calls the meaning of בחין (K) or בחון (Q) uncertain. LXX is no help. But Tg. translates "their watchtowers," followed by Syr. BDB and *HAL* suggest "siegetowers." *DCH* lists both meanings.

15.a. 1QIsa[a] הוא leaves out the article of MT, which the phrase requires. Probably haplography.

15.b-b. Omitted in 1QIsa[a]. Wildberger attributes it to the copyist returning to the second צר, "Tyre," a common copyist's error.

15.c. נִשְׁכַּחַת, "be forgotten," has an old fem. ending for נשכחה (cf. Joüon §42*f*).

17.a. 1QIsa[a] (ש)בעין for MT שבעים, "seventy." This (like ציין in v 13) is probably an old Aramaic pl. ending.

17.b. MT לְאֶתְנַנָּה, "to a prostitute's hire." LXX καὶ πάλιν ἀποκατασταθήσεται εἰς τὸ ἀρχαῖον, "and again be appointed to its former state." Tg. לאתרה, "to its place." Wildberger (859) notes that the ancient translators may have objected to the term "a prostitute's price." He also notes the probable need to add a *mappiq* in the suffix "its."

17.c. Here also LXX refuses to translate the offending words related to prostitution: καὶ ἔσται ἐμπόριον πάσαις ταῖς βασιλείαις τῆς οἰκουμένης, "and will be a traveling merchant to all the kingdoms of the world."

18.a. עָתִיק is a *hapax legomenon.* עַתִּיק, "old," is found in 1 Chr 4:22, and Vg. renders *usque ad vetustatem,* "all the way to old age." Isa 28:9 עַתִּיקֵי מִשָּׁדָיִם, "one taken from the breasts," supports the meaning "removed, set apart" (cf. *HAL* "sacred, magnificent"). But Arab. *ʿtjk,* "noble," suggests that עתיק may also mean "choice" or "eminent" (BDB, 801; see Wildberger, 859).

Form/Structure/Setting

The scene is divided into three parts. Vv 1–7 present mourners regaling Tyre, Sidon, and their dependencies with cries of grief concerning their losses. Vv 8–13 shift to a different setting to reflect on YHWH's involvement and intention in doing this. Vv 14–18 return to the first setting but present three prophecies of Tyre's return to power and influence after an appropriate interval of time.

The chapter stands under the title משא צר, "Burden: Tyre." Its form is clearly a call to lament (Wildberger, 861). הילילו, "howl," occurs in vv 1, 6, 14. But there is a very different tone here from that addressed to Moab (chaps. 15–16). There was a marked sympathy for Moab, but Wildberger (861) correctly detects a kind of sarcasm in this poem. Sidon is called to shame (v 4) and counseled to emigrate to Tarshish (v 6).

The call to lament (vv 1–7) is composed of imperatives: הילילו, "howl" (v 1), דמו, "mourn" (v 2), בושי, "be ashamed" (v 4), עברו, "cross over" (v 6), and הילילו, "howl" (v 6), with the resumption of the theme in הילילו, "howl" (v 14). Yet this is not a lament because of cruel fate but a testimony to YHWH's plan (vv 8–9). His just grounds for these events are brought out in the central reflection in vv 8–13, the heart of the chapter. Moreover, YHWH's action is in accordance with other actions against ambitious, proud countries like Babylon (v 13). See also chap. 2:12–21.

The final portion (vv 14–18) presents three prophecies. Two speak of the length of Tyre's sentence—seventy years. A long generation will pass before she returns to her prosperous trade. V 18 suggests that her return to power and prosperity is predicated on the dedication of her profits to maintaining YHWH's temple and its staff. This prophecy of her return to prosperity stands in contrast to Babylon's permanent destruction (chaps. 14, 21) and Edom's final end (chap. 34).

Interpreters have had difficulty with the identification of Tyre in this chapter; see S. Erlandsson (*Burden of Babylon,* 97–98) for a summary of the varying interpretations. Kaiser (159–68) follows Duhm and Marti in thinking that vv 1–14 refer primarily to Sidon with references to Tyre being glosses. Fohrer (258–60) and others make a threefold division of the chapter with separate oracles referring to Tyre, Sidon, and/or Phoenicia as a whole. A better approach relates the whole chapter to Phoenicia as represented by its most prominent cities, Tyre and Sidon (cf. Erlandsson, *Burden of Babylon,* 98; Hayes, "Oracles against the Nations," Diss., Princeton, 1964, 209; Scott, 294; Rudolph ["Jesaja 23:1–14," 166–74] represents a combination of these views). The chapter is related to Phoenicia under the rich variety of terms that represented the whole area and its principal parts (Kelley, 5:257).

Interpretation of the chapter has also been complicated by trying to distinguish whether this is a prophecy of future destruction or a taunt song recalling a recent destruction (Erlandsson, *Burden of Babylon,* 97; Kaiser, 162). Lindblom (*ASTI* 4 [1965] 56–73) makes a strong plea for the latter approach. From the perspective of drama, this casts the scene as contemporary with the event having just taken place and causing all Tyre's allies to attempt to adjust to the news.

A third problem for interpretation lies in fixing the historical occasion to which this chapter refers. Assyrian kings attacked the region at least four times, each with devastating results—Shalmaneser V (722 B.C.E.) and Sennacherib (705–681 B.C.E.) in the eighth century, and Esarhaddon (677 B.C.E.) and Ashurbanipal (668 B.C.E.) in the seventh. Nebuchadnezzar besieged Tyre for thirteen years before negotiating its surrender in 572 B.C.E. Artaxerxes III put down a rebellion there in 351 B.C.E. But none of these actually destroyed Tyre until Alexander built a causeway to the island in 332 B.C.E.

There are a number of factors in the chapter that help to determine the particular invasion that is pictured. The description of Tyre's political influence (v 8), of its "ships of Tarshish" (v 14), of its control of Cyprus (v 12), and of its commanding commercial position (vv 2–3, 8*b*) do not fit all of these time periods. Although Tarshish is mentioned in a number of biblical texts, it only existed as a colony of Phoenician (or Tyrian) power into the seventh century B.C.E. when it was lost to Phocaean Greeks (cf. Herodotus, *Histories* 1.163 and 4.152), as Wildberger (864) has noted. Cyprus had been colonized by Tyre about 800 B.C.E. or earlier (cf. S. Moscati, *The World of the Phoenicians,* trans. A. Hamilton [London: Weidenfeld and Nicolson, 1968] 103). Later the island became independent before finally falling under Greek dominance.

Arguments for dating the text have often concentrated on the picture of Tyre's destruction (v 1) but have ignored the other considerations. Wildberger (864–65) insists that the chapter pictures the breakdown of Tyrian dominance of the Mediterranean area. This fits the time of Esarhaddon (677 B.C.E.). Such a date also fits the chronological sequence of the parts of the Vision, placing the destruction in the reign of Manasseh.

The sequence of events is described in the Assyrian annals (cf. *ANET,* 291). A rebellion by Tirhaka of Egypt was the occasion for a Phoenician uprising that was brutally put down in 677 B.C.E. (cf. *MBA,* 156). The Assyrian inscriptions go on to speak of the founding of a new port city, called Esarhaddon's Port, and of Assyrian reorganization of the region into three provinces (Moscati, *Phoenicians,* 20–21). At this time Esarhaddon claimed sovereignty over Cyprus and Greece, as far as Tarshish (R. Borger, "Die luschriften Asarhaddons Königs von Assyrien," *AfO* 9 [1956] 86). This action effectively ended Phoenicia's independence, her control of shipping in the eastern Mediterranean, and her control of Cyprus. Having conquered Egypt and taken over Phoenicia's commercial power, Esarhaddon and Ashurbanipal had brought Assyria to the peak of her power and the Palestinian area to the lowest point in its history.

The biblical prophets deal with Tyre (Phoenicia) in three other periods. It is listed with other surrounding peoples as scheduled for judgment by Amos (1:9–10). This relates to the eighth century. It is also listed by Jeremiah as among the nations made to drink YHWH's cup of wrath (25:22) and is one of those to hear YHWH's announcement that he has decided to turn the region over to Babylonian rule (27:3). Ezekiel's great prophecy against Tyre and her king (26:2–29:18) falls in the same early sixth-century period. Zech 9:2–4 and Joel 3:4–8 testify to prophecies against Tyre in the Persian period. Thus the prophets have been concerned with the role of Tyre throughout the period with which the Vision is concerned and continue that interest in the very time in which the Vision is composed.

But the Vision's author has chosen to deal with Tyre's fate in his second act covering the reigns of Hezekiah and Manasseh and the Assyrian kings Esarhaddon and Ashurbanipal in 14:24–22:25, but also the Babylonian period leading to the fall of Jerusalem and exile in 13:1–14:23 and chaps. 24–27. It could have fallen in act 1 (parallel to Amos 1:9–10) or act 4 (parallel to Jeremiah and Ezekiel) or in one of his last two acts (parallel to Joel and Zechariah), but the decision to place it here is deliberate. The fall of Tyre (Phoenicia) before Assyria might mark the climax of Assyria's rise to power over the prostrate bodies of Aram/Israel (chap. 10); of Babylon (21:1–10); of Philistia, Moab, and Egypt (in spite of the hopeful signs of chap. 19); and of Jerusalem under Hezekiah (chap. 22; though spared the destruction of the city and the execution of the king). The depiction of Tyre's fall typifies the period when Palestine lies in abject submission to Assyria's imperial will. Manasseh has no choice but to do his liege lord's will. All chance of resistance or expression of national autonomy is gone, but the promise of restoration after seventy years is parallel historically with the rise of Josiah when Assyria weakened. The later announcement of the destruction of Leviathan (27:1) may apply to Tyre's submission to Babylon in 572 B.C.E. after a thirteen-year siege, fourteen years after the destruction of Jerusalem in 586 B.C.E.

Comment

1 For discussion of משׂא, "burden," see *Excursus: "Burden"* (משׂא) *in the Prophets* and *Comment* at 13:1 above.

Tyre was certainly an ancient city (v 7), known throughout the ancient world. It was built on a rocky island some six hundred yards offshore and some twenty-five miles south of Sidon. The name צר, "Tyre," appropriately means "rock." The name may have a Semitic origin, referring to wanderers from the east who broke through the Lebanese mountain range to establish their homes on the Mediterranean coast.

Tyre was an important city throughout antiquity (cf. A. S. Kapelrud, *IDB* 4:721–23; H. J. Katzenstein, *ABD*). It was closely related to its neighboring Phoenician cities and hinterland, although its position on an island often allowed it to escape degradations that befell its land-based neighbors. The Phoenicians turned the sea into their avenue for trade, commerce, and colonization. Their mighty "ships of Tarshish" were apparently capable of carrying the mineral ores mined in northern Greece, Spain (?), or even on the shores of the Black Sea.

2–6 צידון, Sidon was often Tyre's rival, but here the two city names are used together to represent the Phoenician trading cities as a group. Phoenicia's earliest ties were with Egypt, at least from the sixteenth century B.C.E. Carthage was founded as a colony in north Africa in the ninth century. The Pheonicians put in at ports in Egypt, Cyprus, Rhodes, Sicily, and north Africa. They transported the purple cloth, timber, and glassware for which they were famous, as well as the grain of Egypt (v 3). Tyre's great King Hiram supplied David and Solomon with timber and craftsmen in the tenth century.

7 Phoenicia's mainland merchants in Sidon served as agents for caravans from all Palestine (v 2), helping them trade their products for the exotic imports from overseas. These ports of commerce undoubtedly provided unrestrained recreation for boisterous sailors and caravan drivers in ways known to seaports of all times (v 7). Tyre was indeed the "merchant of nations" of this period (v 3), "one whose feet took her to sojourn far away" (v 7).

8 Phoenicia's strategic importance to all the nations of the region gave pause to any power that threatened to destroy her altogether. Many would have liked to control her power or share her revenues, but all were too dependent upon the network of commercial contacts that she knew and controlled to risk destroying her. She was in fact "the giver of crowns, whose merchants are princes, whose traders are honored of the land."

So the shocked question is justified: "Who planned this against Tyre?" Whose interests are served by this action? The question prepares for the central, most significant section of the chapter.

9 The question is answered directly: "YHWH of Hosts." He has no commercial interests to be served. On the other hand he has two basic reasons for the judgment. The first picks up the Vision's motif concerning judgment against pride and arrogance in the words גאון כל־צבי, "pride of all glory." The very thing that makes humankind admire Tyre (they are נכבדי ארץ, "the honored of the land") makes YHWH determined to להקל, "dishonor," her. In 2:12–21 YHWH announced his intention of bringing judgment on all pride and honor in the land. This verse documents his completion of that announced goal. With the fall of Tyre, the last of "the honored of the land" have fallen.

The word הארץ, "the land," which is brought to prominence in these verses is a key to the interpretation of chaps. 23–27. (See *Excursus: "The Land"* [הארץ].) The reference is to Palestine-Lebanon, extending to the Euphrates in the northeast and to the "River of Eygpt" and beyond to Egypt in the south. All this "land" was served by Tyre's commerce, and, accordingly, it treated Tyre with deference. All the "land" envied Tyre's wealth and imitated her styles.

11 The second reason for YHWH's judgment of Tyre is contained in the term כנען, "Canaan," in v 11*b:* "YHWH issued a command concerning Canaan to destroy her fortresses." This picks up the purposes of YHWH that have deep roots in the biblical culture (cf. H.-J. Zobel, *TWAT* 4:236–43). Israel had an ambiguous relationship to Canaanite culture. Israel adopted Canaan's language, many aspects of its economy and cult, and even its structures of government through David. They took over the Canaanites' fields and their walled cities. Yet a negative attitude also runs through the Bible, from the destruction of Sodom and Gomorrah (Gen 18–19) to the warnings in Deuteronomy and Leviticus against adopting Canaanite customs.

The Vision sees in the Assyrian invasions the destruction of a political and economic way of life that the Canaanites exemplified, a feudalism that centered in walled cities and small kingdoms. YHWH had determined the end of this entire system. Thus the command to dismantle one of the last remnants of that system and that power in the "fortresses of Canaan" is the basis for Tyre's collapse.

To accomplish this, YHWH "stretched out his hand over the sea" (11*a*). The sea, with its synonyms "floods," "streams," is often pictured as YHWH's original archenemy. It is also seen as the one who first fell to YHWH's expression of his cosmic dominion of all things (Pss 93:3–4; 95:5). When YHWH signals to the sea, the kingdoms that depend upon sea power and commerce tremble.

12*b* Even a retreat to Cyprus cannot cure the problem. Phoenicia's strategic position as a mainland port where land and sea merchants and traders could meet has been the basis of her power. Without that she has no foundation; her ships have no home port (v 10).

13–14 Babylon, "land of the Chaldeans," is held up to Tyre as an example of a country that had defied Assyria and felt its wrath. Tyre's fate will be similar. The ships who hear the news when they make port anywhere in the Mediterranean world will have good reason to mourn.

15–18 Three prophecies speak of Tyre's future, for she will have a future. The phrase שבעים שנה, "seventy years," is worth comment. It is used elsewhere to speak of the extent of the exile (Jer 25:12; 29:10; Zech 1:12; Dan 9:2; 2 Chr 36:21). It may also be used of a person's full life span (Ps 90:10). The term was discussed at length some years ago (C. F. Whitley, "The Term Seventy Years Captivity," *VT* 4 [1954] 60–72; A. Orr, "The Seventy Years of Babylon," *VT* 6 [1956] 304–6; O. Plöger, *Festschrift Friedrich Baumgärtel* [Erlangen: Universitätsbund, 1959] 124–30; P. R. Ackroyd, "Two OT Historical Problems," *JNES* 17 [1958] 23–27; R. Borger, "An Additional Remark," *JNES* 18 [1959] 74). The round number is intended to indicate an extended period of time. Tyre did, in fact, recover enough to withstand Nebuchadnezzar's siege for thirteen years—from 585 to 572 B.C.E., just after Jerusalem was besieged and destroyed. But Tyre held out much longer and was not destroyed. Although subject to the Persians, Tyre continued to be active, resisting Alexander for seven months before falling to him in 332 B.C.E.

The prophecies proclaim that Tyre's seductive influence on international trade will again be felt in the Levant after a generation. The distinctive thrust of the prophecy is the claim that her profits will be "dedicated to YHWH," that they will support the temple personnel, presumably in Jerusalem. Tyre's restoration is motivated by the will to make her a contributor to the worship of YHWH in Jerusalem as she was under Hiram in the days of David (1 Kgs 5–7; 1 Chr 14:1). No such contribution is recorded for the rebuilding or maintenance of the second temple.

Explanation

The fall of Tyre with the attendant collapse of the other Phoenician cities of the coast and across the waters had widespread implications. These are noted by the references to Egypt, Canaan, the Chaldeans, and Assyria, as well as to the cities themselves: Tyre, Sidon, Tarshish, and Cyprus. The fall of Tyre marked the completion of the Assyrian conquest of all West Asia. The Vision has recorded the stages by which Assyria has pursued its goal for some eighty years. With the fall of Tyre it has reached its pinnacle. All the land and the trade routes of the sea are in its hands.

On another level the chapter marks the completion of YHWH's plan to use Assyria as the "rod of [his] anger" (10:5), not only against Israel but also, on YHWH's day, against "everything high and raised, . . . everything lifted up, . . . all the cedars of Lebanon . . . all the ships of Tarshish" (2:12–16). With the fall of Phoenician power, this part of God's goal has been achieved.

V 11 implies the achievement of a goal announced much earlier. The verse is reminiscent of the Song of the Sea (Exod 15:12–16*a*), where YHWH "stretched out his right hand; . . . the inhabitants of Canaan melted away" (NRSV). It picks up the memory of the promise of the land of the "kings of Canaan" to Israel (Ps 135:11) and of Israel's early struggles with them (Judg 4:2, 23, 24; 5:19). It echoes the reminder in Judg 3:1–3 that among the nations left in Canaan to test the Israelites were "the Sidonians, and the Hivites, who lived on Mount Lebanon" (NRSV).

The potential for theological associations with the fall of Tyre is fully exploited here. To summarize, they include seeing the defeat and occupation of Phoenicia as the completion of God's conquest of Canaan begun with Joshua, his use of the Assyrian to bring an end to the era of Canaanite city-states, and his judgment against all human pride and arrogance, which Tyre and Lebanon symbolized so well.

The Vision suggests that the fall of Tyre was another sign to Israel's leaders, in this case Manasseh in Jerusalem, to guide them in their political decisions regarding Assyria (cf. chaps. 7 and 20). Seen religiously, the recognition of YHWH's role in the disaster should have led to humble faith in him, to dependence upon him as protector and guide rather than upon any human power. In the larger context the Vision suggests that, although Manasseh did make his policies conform to God's new order by submitting to the empire (chaps. 24–27), succeeding generations did not heed the sign by adjusting their goals politically or religiously. They were still blind and deaf, thus preparing the way for Jerusalem's final collapse before the Babylonians (chaps. 24 and 28–33).

A Concluding Liturgy (24:1–27:13)

Bibliography

Amsler, S. "Des visions de Zacharie à l'apocalypse d'Esaïe 24–27." In *Book of Isaiah.* Ed. J. Vermeylen. 263–73. **Anderson, G. A.** "Isaiah 24–27 Reconsidered." In *Congress Volume: Bonn.* VTSup 9. Leiden: Brill, 1963. 118–26. **Aubert, L.** "Une primiére apocalypse (Esaïe 24–27)." *ETR* (1936) 280–96. **Beek, M. A.** "Ein Erdbeben wird zum prophetischen Erleben." *ArOr* 17 (1949) 31–40. **Biddle, M.** "The City of Chaos and the New Jerusalem: Isaiah 24–27 in Context." *PRSt* 22 (1995) 5–12. **Bosman, H. J.** "Annotated Translation of Isaiah 24–27." In *Studies in Isaiah 24–27: The Isaiah Workshop.* Ed. H. J. Bosman et al. Leiden: Brill, 2000. 3–12. ———. "Syntactic Cohesion in Isaiah 24–27." In *Studies in Isaiah 14–17: The Isaiah Workshop.* Ed. H. J. Bosman et al. Leiden: Brill, 2000. **Brockhaus, G.** "Untersuchungen zu Stil und Form der sogenannten Jesaja-Apokalypse." Master's thesis, Bonn, 1972. **Carroll, R. P.** "City of Chaos, City of Stone, City of Flesh: Urbanscapes in Prophetic Discourse." In *'Every City Shall Be Forsaken': Urbanism and Prophecy in Ancient Israel and the Near East.* Ed. L. L. Grabbe and R. D. Haak. JSOTSup 330. Sheffield: Academic Press, 2001. 45–61. **Coggins, R. J.** "The Problem of Isaiah 24–27." *ExpTim* 90 (1979) 328–33. **Day, J.** *God's Conflict with the Dragon and the Sea: Echoes of a Canaanite Myth in the Old Testament.* Cambridge: Cambridge UP, 1985. **Domínguez, N.** "Vaticinios sobre el fin del mundo." *CTom* 51 (1935) 125–46. **Doyle, B.** *The Apocalypse of Isaiah Metaphorically Speaking: A Study of the Use, Function and Significance of Metaphors in Isaiah 24–27.* BETL 151. Leuven: Peters, 2000. **Elder, W.** "A Theological-Historical Study of Isaiah 24–27." Diss., Baylor University, 1974. **Fohrer, G.** "Der Aufbau der Apokalypse der Jesajabuchs: Jesaja 24–27." *CBQ* 25 (1963) 34–45; *BZAW* 99 (1967) 170–81. **Gilse, J.** "Jesaja XXIV—XXVII." *NedTT* 3 (1914) 167–93. **Grol, H. W. M. van.** "An Analysis of the Verse Structure of Isaiah 24–27." In *Studies in Isaiah 24–27: The Isaiah Workshop.* Ed. H. J. Bosman et al. Leiden: Brill, 2000. 51–80. **Henry, M. L.** *Glaubenskrise und Glaubensbewährung in den Dichtungen der Jesajaapokalypse.* BWANT 86. Stuttgart: Kohlhammer, 1967. **Hilgenfeld, A.** "Das Judentum in dem persischen Zeitalter." *ZWT* 9 (1866) 398–488. **Hylmö, G.** *De s. k. profetishka liturgiernas rytm, stil och komposition.* LUÅ N.F. Avd. 1, 25.5. Lund: Gleerup, 1929. **Jenner, K. D.** "Petucha and Setuma: Tools for Interpretation or Simply a Matter of Lay-Out?" In *Studies in Isaiah 24–27: The Isaiah Workshop.* Ed. H. J. Bosman et al. Leiden: Brill, 2000. 81–117. **Kooij, A. van der.** "The Cities of 24–27 according to the Vulgate, Targum and Septuagint." In *Studies in Isaiah 24–27: The Isaiah Workshop.* Ed. H. J. Bosman et al. Leiden: Brill, 2000. 183–98. ———. "Isaiah 24–27: Text Critical Notes." In *Studies in Isaiah 24–27: The Isaiah Workshop.* Ed. H. J. Bosman et al. Leiden: Brill, 2000. 3–15. **Lagrange, M. J.** "L'apocalypse d'Isaïe (24–27)." *RB* 3 (1894) 200–231. **Liebmann, E.** "Der Text zu Jesaja 24–27." *ZAW* 22 (1902) 285–304; *ZAW* 23 (1903) 209–86. **Lindblom, J.** *Die Jesaja Apokalypse: Jesaja 24–27.* LUÅ N.F. Avd. 1, 34.3. Lund: Gleerup, 1938. ———. "Die Jesaja-Apokalypse (Jes 24–27) in der neuen Jesaja-Handschrift." *K. Humaniska Vetenskapssamsfundets i Lund Arsberattelse* 2 (1950–51) 79–144. **Lohmann, P.** "Die selbständigen lyrischen Abschnitte in Jes 24–27." *ZAW* 37 (1917–18) 1–58. **Ludwig, O.** *Die Stadt in der Jesaja-Apokalypse.* Köln: Kleikamp, 1961. **March, W.** "A Study of Two Prophetic Compositions in Isaiah 24:1–27:1." Diss., Union Theological Seminary, New York, 1966. **Millar, W. R.** *Isaiah 24–27 and the Origin of Apocalyptic.* HSM 11. Missoula, MT: Scholars Press, 1976. **Mulder, E. S.** *Die Teologie von die Jesaja-Apokalypse, Jesaja 24–27.* Djarkarta: Wolters, 1954. **Otzen, B.** "Traditions and Structures of Isaiah 24–27." *VT* 24 (1974) 196–206. **Plöger, O.** *Theocracy and Eschatology.* Trans. S. Rudman. Richmond, VA: John Knox, 1968. **Polaski, D. C.** *Authorizing an End: The Isaiah Apocalypse and Intertextuality.* BibIntS

50. Leiden: Brill, 2001. ———. "Destruction, Construction, Argumentation: A Rhetorical Reading of Isaiah 24–27." In *Vision and Persuasion: Rhetorical Dimensions of Apolyptic Discourse.* Ed. G. Carey and L. G. Bloomquist. St. Louis: Chalice, 1999. 19–39. **Redditt, P.** "Isaiah 24–27: A Form Critical Analysis." Diss., Vanderbilt University, 1972. **Ringgren, H.** "Some Observations on Style and Structure in the Isaiah Apocalypse." *ASTI* 9 (1973) 107–15. **Rochais, G.** "Les origines de l'apocalyptique." *ScEs* 25 (1973) 36–40. **Rudolph, W.** *Jesaja 24–27.* BWANT 4.10. Stuttgart: Kohlhammer, 1933. **Sievers, E.** *Jesaja 24–27.* Verhandlungen der königl. Sächs. Ges. d. Wiss. zu Leipzig, phil.-hist. Kl. B. 56. Leipzig, 1904. **Smend, R.** "Anmerkungen zu Jes 24–27." *ZAW* 4 (1884) 161–224. **Vermeylen, J.** "La composition littéraire de l'apocalypse d'Isaïe." *ETL* 50 (1974) 5–38. **Vriezen, T. C.** "Prophecy and Eschatology." In *Congress Volume: Copenhagen.* VTSup 1. Leiden: Brill, 1953. 199–229. **Zyl, A. H. van.** "Isaiah 24–27: Their Date of Origin." *OTWSAP* 5 (1962) 44–57.

Apocalyptic and Prophecy

Bibliography

Bauckham, R. J. "The Rise of Apocalyptic." *Themelios* 3.2 (1977–78) 10–23. **Fichtner, J.** "Prophetismus und Apokalyptik in Protojesaja." Inaug. Diss., Breslau, 1929. **Hanson, P. D.** *The Dawn of Apocalyptic.* Philadelphia: Fortress, 1975. ———. "Jewish Apocalyptic against Its Near Eastern Environment." *RB* 78 (1971) 31–58. ———. "Old Testament Apocalyptic Reexamined." *Int* 25 (1971) 454–79. **Koch, K.** *The Rediscovery of Apocalyptic.* Trans. M. Kohl. SBT 2d ser. 22. London: SCM Press, 1972. **Schmidt, J. M.** *Die jüdische Apokalyptik: Die Geschichte ihrer Erforschung von den Anfangen bis zu den Textfunden von Qumran.* Neukirchen-Vluyn: Neukirchener Verlag, 1969.

For a long period these chapters have been understood as an independent unit, apocalyptic in nature and genre, as this bibliography demonstrates. Current interpretation tends to treat the chapters as an integral part of the surrounding work. This trend is supported by the fact that the section is a recapitulation of the prophecies in chaps. 13–23, heavily dependent on citations and allusions to prophecies that precede it and to other prophecies, as Sweeney, Williamson *(Book Called Isaiah),* and others have shown. Sweeney finds a high level of "lexical correspondence and thematic correlation" (p. 42) in 24:13 (17:6); 24:16 (21:2 and 33:1); 25:4–5 (4:5*b*–6 and 32:1–2; see J. J. M. Roberts, "The Divine King and the Human Community in Isaiah's Vision of the Future," in *The Quest for the Kingdom of God,* FS G. E. Mendenhall, ed. H.B. Huffmon et al. [Winona Lake, IN: Eisenbrauns, 1983] 127–36, esp. 136 on this verse); 25:11*b*–12 (2:9–17); 26:5 (2:6–21); 26:17–18 (13:8 and 66:7–9); and 27:1–13 (5:1–7 and 11:10–16).

Chaps. 24–27 also seem dependent on other OT passages, as was noted as early as T. K. Cheyne's *Introduction to the Book of Isaiah* ([London, 1985] 147–48). Williamson (*Book Called Isaiah,* 181) lists some of them: 24:2 (Hos 4:9); 24:4 (Hos 4:3); 24:7 (Joel 1:10–12); 24:17–18 (Jer 48:43–44); 24:18 (Gen 7:11); and 24:20 (Amos 5:2). Day (see commentary on chap. 26, in *God's Conflict*) has found eight parallels in 26:13–27:11 that occur in the same order in Hosea 13:4–14: 26:13 LXX (Hos 13:4); 26:17–18 (Hos 13:13); 26:19 (Hos 13:14 LXX); 27:8 (Hos 13:15); 26:19 (Hos 14:6 [5]); 27:2–6 (Hos 14:6–8 [5–9]); 27:9 (Hos 14:9 [8]); and 27:11 (14:10 [9]).

In accord with the general approach of this commentary, this section is interpreted as a literary portrayal of an era of judgment that coincides with Assyrian and Babylonian oppression of Palestine (see *Burden: Tyre and the Desolate Land [23:1–27:13]* above). But the bibliography above shows that many have understood the subject much more broadly, as depicting world destruction in an apocalyptic sense. That is not justified.

The terms ארץ, "land," and הארץ, "the land," occur in chap. 24 thirteen times. The word תבל, "world," occurs once, and the word לעולם, "to the age, forever," which occurred first in 14:20, is repeated here. ארץ appears in chap. 26 six times, תבל twice, and לעולם once. The debated question is, How broadly are these terms meant in these chapters? And that leads to two more questions: What kind of literature is this? With its descriptions of judgment on the Day of the Lord, is it of a genre different from the rest of the Vision?

Gen 6–9 presents the problem of human (אדם) relations with the land (ארץ) in its classic form, just as Gen 2–3 presents humanity's (אדם) relation to the ground (אדמה). Gen 6–9 suggests that humanity's first encounters with the larger problems (social, economic, political) involved in territorial questions (ארץ) were disastrous, leading to judgment and a new beginning with Noah and his family.

The Vision of Isaiah picks up a similar theme dealing with humanity (אדם) and the land (ארץ). The treatment is more focused than in Genesis because its treatment of Israel/Jerusalem involves both territory and people, and parallels the description of God's dealing with the nations, i.e., in history. Three instances (chaps. 2, 6, and 13) are particularly important to the Vision. In chap. 2, אדם, "human," occurs seven times while ארץ, "land," occurs twice. God will come on his day to "shake the land" in such a way that the pride of "humankind" will be humbled. In Isa 6:3 YHWH is praised because his glory fills the whole land. But a judgment is foretold through which the land will be completely desolate (6:11), and even if a tenth remain in the land it will be wasted again. The buildings will stand with no human (אדם) in them, and humankind (אדם) will be banished from the land. In chap. 13, the announcement that armies from distant lands will come to "destroy the whole land" fulfills the prediction of 10:23 of a decreed destruction upon the entire land. The sun, moon, and stars join the battle to make the land desolate (v 10). Humans beings (אדם) will be more scarce than gold (v 12), and the land (ארץ) will be shaken from its place (v 13). This burden then comes to focus upon Babylon (v 19) and upon the king of Babylon (chap. 14). At his death witnesses will ask: "Is this the man who terrorized the earth?" Then the account brings in a synonymous term: "who made the world (תבל) like a desert." It goes on to speak about the destruction of cities.

This is enough to show that the Vision's use of ארץ invokes a meaning of "land" that covers the historical nations of the ancient Near East. Even תבל, "world," is used in this extended meaning. The prophecy of the destruction of the whole land occurred in 10:23 and 13:5. There is no reason to see the meaning in chaps. 24–27 in any other way.

The complete destruction of the land has been anticipated in chaps. 10 and 13. So that is nothing to set it apart. The participation of the cosmic bodies was anticipated in 13:10. Therefore, these chapters should be seen as a climax and culmination of the previous sections and of a piece with them, and it is misleading to give them a distinctively different genre—a position that would lead to the unnecessary fragmentation of the book. Issues raised in and by chaps. 24–27 should be understood in the light of the book itself and as a part of its larger message and meaning. The basic characteristics of apocalyptic are not demonstrated in this section.

"Scatters its inhabitants" (24:1) introduces another element of the destructions. The peoples of the land are scattered. Israel's disapora is created in the scattered communities of Jews in Babylon, Egypt, and other places throughout the Near East. פוץ, "scattered," is found in 18:2, 7; 24:1; 33:3; and 41:10 and is frequent in Jeremiah and Ezekiel. It is also a key element in the Tower of Babel story (Gen 11:4, 8, 9; cf. 49:7). In Gen 11:4 the people's concern for unity and solidarity was judged to be a problem. Even the idea that they should have one culture and language was disapproved, so they were scattered. As for Israel, God had gathered the tribes to Canaan and encouraged one language and culture. In the wars of the Babylonian and Assyrian eras many of her people were scattered. But the book of Isaiah will say that God supported the rise of Persian power, which unified the area as never before and which established one imperial language (Aramaic). The Persian Empire made it possible for Jews to gather in Jerusalem for worship. The ways of God are beyond understanding. He both scatters abroad and gathers together. He destroys and builds again.

The appearance of the word לעולם, "to the age, forever," in 14:20, 24:5, and 26:4 gives a permanence to the message that it might not otherwise have. The parallel to the uses of אדם, "human," and ארץ, "land," in Gen 6–9 as well as the appearance of לעולם in Gen 9:12–16 provides a hint of the direction interpretation should go.

Just as Gen 6–9 describes the end of an age and the beginning of another, so the Vision of Isaiah is doing the same thing. The old order is that into which Abraham came, in which Moses worked, in which Israel occupied Canaan, and in which David built his kingdom. Palestine with its adjacent lands in that age was a territory of tribes and cities, of city-states and small kingdoms. In that age Israel had found its existence as twelve tribes occupying the sparsely settled land alongside others who had migrated thither from other places (Moab, Edom, Philistia). They conquered walled cities and built their own. David and Solomon brought the period to a climax by making the area a mini-empire, but their successors allowed it to disintegrate. In the ninth and early eighth centuries fragmented peoples and cities were in constant warfare with each other.

The Vision of Isaiah takes up the course of events in the reign of Uzziah at mid-eighth century. It announces that YHWH is bringing about drastic changes, not only for Israel and Judah but also for all their neighbors. He is sponsoring the rise of Assyria to establish imperial rule over the entire Near East. Assyria's conquests will destroy not just Israel and Judah but the entire "world" within which they existed: its economy, its political framework, and its social structures.

This destructive goal is reached when Assyria subjugates Phoenicia in 655 B.C.E. (Isa 23) and again in the sixth century along with Judah. Thus YHWH has indeed devastated the whole land from Israel and Damascus (chap. 10), to Babylon (chaps. 13–14 and 21) on one end and Egypt (chaps. 18 and 19) on the other, including Edom, Moab, and Philistia in between. The whole land lies devastated (chap. 24). The cities that had represented the best of that civilization—Babylon, Damascus, Tyre, Memphis, and Jerusalem—have fallen. This is not simply a military tragedy. The economy that had made their prosperity possible has been changed drastically. They would never again have the same power and riches. Truly an age had come to an end!

UNITY

Critical studies of chaps. 24–27 have wrestled with the question of unity. A group of scholars from Duhm on (including Rudolph [*Jesaja 24–27*], Kaiser, Vermeylen [*ETL* 50 (1974) 5–38], and Wildberger) have found that the chapters are best understood as having been formed gradually over a long period of time, with frequent additions along the way. However, a significant counterview has developed with Lindblom (*Jesaja Apokalypse*), Anderson ("Isaiah 24–27"), Ringgren (*ASTI* 9 [1973] 107–15), and Redditt ("Isaiah 24–27"). They see the material as being disparate in genre and style but intentionally put together as a cantata or liturgy. Although Wildberger (904–5) has proposed an analysis in which three or four layers of material are distinguished, he treats the section as a unified prophecy of the eschatological turn of events that he termed a "symphony."

The second view is much closer to the approach of this commentary: these chapters, like the entire Vision, constitute a dramatic literary structure that, on the small scale, includes chap. 23 and, on the large scale, the entire book. For the place of these chapters in these larger structures, see *Burden: Tyre and the Desolate Land (23:1–27:13)* and *Act 2. The Burden of Babylon (13:1–27:13)* above.

LITERARY FORMS

An announcement, introduced by הנה, "behold," opens the section, supported by descriptions of results (24:1–13). This is parallel to such passages as 3:1, 8:7, 10:33, 13:9, and 22:17. It will be continued in 26:21 by a similar announcement, and the entire section builds on it. Contrasting responses follow. A chorus records joyful celebration from afar (24:14–16*a*) while a solo voice cries out in distress and supports this with a picture of the scope of the judgment (24:16*b*–20).

The familiar formula ביום ההוא, "in such a day" or "in that day," introduces several passages (24:21–23; 26:1; 27:1, 2, 12, 13). This manner of presenting the results of YHWH's acts is familiar throughout chaps. 2–31 but appears after that only in 52:6. The seven appearances of the phrase as a compositional device in this section are similar to the frequency of its use in chaps. 2–4 (7x), 7 (4x), 10–12 (6x), 17 (3x), 19 (6x), 22 (4x), and 28–31 (4x). Whether these are understood to be eschatological in nature and intent (with Wildberger and others) depends upon the understanding of the announcement (24:1–13) on which they are based. See *Comment* on 24:1–13. The "in that day" statements parallel passages "on this mountain" or Mount Zion: YHWH of Hosts will reign (24:23), YHWH of Hosts will prepare a banquet (25:6), YHWH of Hosts will destroy death (25:7–8), YHWH's hand will rest on this mountain (against Moab) (25:10–12), and the people will worship on the holy mountain in Jerusalem (27:13).

As in other parts of the Vision, (5:1–7; 12:1–6), songs and hymns are important elements of the section and serve as scripted responses to YHWH's acts. The song in 27:2–4 forms a counterpart to 5:1–7. The hymns in 25:1–5 and 26:1–

6 are very important structural elements of the section. Isa 25:9 is another such poetic piece, a thanksgiving song fragment.

The announcement of the Lord's banquet for the peoples on Zion's mount (25:6–8) stresses the positive results of YHWH's awful acts. Isa 25:10–12 contrasts YHWH's acts "on this mountain" with the destruction of Moab in much the same style that prophecies in chaps. 13–22 have done.

Isa 26:7–21 interacts with events and the announcement in a complex form that consists of "we" sections (vv 8, 12, 18), one "I" response in psalm form (v 9), addresses to YHWH in second person (vv 11–18), and a response to the people in vv 19–20. The passage is begun with an impersonal observation in v 7 and an announcement of God coming to punish (v 21). The latter is one of two summary statements: 26:19–21 and 27:6–11

The whole is an artistic and complex work of response and interpretation based on the announcement in 24:1–13, which is repeated in 26:21.

STRUCTURE

Redditt has proposed a four-part division of the materials ("Isaiah 24–27," 319, 395).

1. The Present World Order is dissolved: 24:1–20.
2. The Place of Jerusalem in the coming order: 24:21–26:6.
3. The necessity of YHWH's judgment: 26:7–21.
4. Conditions for Israel's deliverance: 27:1–13.

Wildberger (904) has followed his own analysis of layers and forms to treat the chapters in the following outline:

I. The basic layer, which is the point of crystallization for all with the theme: world judgment.
   A. 24:1–6 Announcement of the devastation of the whole earth, with additions:
      24:7–9 The drying up of the vines.
      24:10–12 The destruction of the city of Chaos.
      24:13 The harvest among the peoples.
   B. 24:14–20 The premature rejoicing of Israel and the shock of the one seeing the vision.
   C. 26:7–21 YHWH's people in the crisis of the End.
      26:7–18 The lament of the people unable to find salvation.
      26:19 The oracle of salvation: resurrection from the dead.
      26:20–21 Israel during YHWH's approach for world judgment.

II. Eschatological pictures:
   A. 24:21–23 The end of the world's kingdoms and beginning of God's rule.
   B. 25:6–8 The joyous feast on Zion.
   C. 25:9–10*a* An eschatological song of thanksgiving, with additions:
      25:10*b*–11 Moab in the manure pile.
      25:12 Destruction of its fortifications.

III. The City-songs.
   A. 25:1–5 A hymn: the destruction of the strong city (1–3) and protection of the faithful (4–5).

B. 26:1–6 A hymn: YHWH, the protector of Jerusalem (1–4) and the destroyer of the proud city (5–6).

IV. Additions: eschatological impressions.

A. 27:1 The victory over the dragon of Chaos.

B. 27:2–5 The new vineyard.

C. 27:6–11 Israel will bloom as the secure city lies in ruins.

D. 27:12 The gathering of the faithful.

E. 27:13 The return to Zion.

Wildberger's outline is based throughout on the assumption that the section is to be understood in an eschatological sense. Redditt's outline is a much more sober and restrained presentation. This commentary suggests an arrangement in accord with the dramatic or cantata-like form that so many have perceived in it. It contains acts of the king as warrior destroyer and as reigning ruler with responses from various persons and groups: see the outline in *Burden: Tyre and the Desolate Land (23:1–27:13)* above.

THEMES

The final scene of the Act of Burdens (act 2, chaps. 13–27) pulls together the various concerns dealt with in earlier chapters. They all come together in the destruction of the land first revealed in chap. 6 and repeatedly noted to have been decreed (10:23; 13:9; 28:22*b*). The edict of destruction connects with the Day of YHWH (2:10–20; 13:9–16; 22:5–8) and with YHWH's direct action of stirring up the Medes against Babylon (13:17–22; cf. 26:20–21). The mood of extreme anxiety that comes from the narrative in chap 20 and that permeates the "burden" passages is answered by reassuring announcements of divine intervention to end the terror and restore the land and the people.

The scene focuses on YHWH's reign on Mount Zion. In sovereign regalia he "decides the fate" of the powers and kings (24:21) and of Leviathan (27:1). He declares an amnesty from death for the peoples (26:7–8). He restores Jerusalem to dignity as the place of his throne on earth (24:23; 25:10). He struggles with Israel's problem (27:2–11) but will gather the exiles again, and they will come to worship him on the holy mountain in Jerusalem.

The Book of Burdens (act 2) has suggested solutions to the essential problems of the Vision in chap. 19 and here. It is sovereign grace that makes salvation possible even in the face of inadequate response from YHWH's people.

See: YHWH Devastates the Land (24:1–13)

Bibliography

Charles, N. J. "A Prophetic (Fore)Word: 'A Curse Devouring the Earth.' (Isa 24:6)." In *The Earth Story.* Ed. N. C. Habel. Sheffield: Sheffield Academic Press, 2001. 123–28. **De Groot, J.** "Alternatieflezingen in Jesaja 24." *NThSt* 22 (1939) 153–58. **Floss, J. P.** "Die Wortstellung des Konjugationssystem in Jes 24: Ein Beitrag zur Formkritik poetischer Texte im Alten Testament." In *Bausteine biblischer Theologie.* FS G. J. Botterweck, ed. H.-J. Fabry. BBB 50. Cologne: Hanstein, 1977. 227–44. **Hayes, K. M.** "'The Earth Mourns': Earth as Actor in a Prophetic Metaphor." Diss., Catholic University of America, 1997. **Johnson, D. G.** *From Chaos to Restoration: An Integrative Reading of Isaiah 24–27.* JSOTSup 61. Sheffield: JSOT Press, 1988. **Lewis, D. J.** "A Rhetorical Critical Analysis of Isaiah 24–27." Diss., Southern Baptist Theological Seminary, 1985. **Miller, W. R.** "Isaiah, Book of (Isaiah 24–27)." In *ABD.* 3:488–90. **Nevas, J. C. M.** "A Teologia da Traducao Grega dos Setenta no Libro de Isias." Diss., Lisbon, 1973. **Niehaus, J.** "*raz-pešar* in Isaiah XXIV." *VT* 31 (1981) 376–78. **Noegel, S. B.** "Dialect and Politics in Isaiah 24–27." *AcOr* 12 (1994) 177–92. **Pagan, S.** "Apocalyptic Poetry: Isaiah 24–27." *BT* 43 (1992) 314–25. **Polaski, D. C.** "Reflections on a Mosaic Covenant: The Eternal Covenant (Isaiah 24) and Intertextuality." *JSOT* 77 (1998) 55–73. **Redditt, P.** "Once Again, The City in Isaiah 24–27." *HAR* 10 (1986) 317–35. **Sawyer, J.** "Semantic Links between Isa 24–27 and Daniel." In *Understanding Poets and Prophets.* FS G. W. Anderson, ed. A. G. Auld. JSOTSup 152. Sheffield: Sheffield Academic Press, 1993. **Sweeney, M. A.** "Textual Citations in Isaiah 24–27: Toward an Understanding of the Redactional Function of Chapters 24–27 in the Book of Isaiah." *JBL* 107 (1988) 39–52. **Yee, G. A.** "The Anatomy of Biblical Parody: The Dirge Form in 2 Samuel 1 and Isaiah 14." *CBQ* 50 (1988) 565–86.

Translation

Heavens:	1 *See YHWH*	2+3
	destroying[a] *the land*[b] *and laying it waste!*[a]	
	He twists its surface	2+2
	and scatters its inhabitants!	
Earth:	2 *And this happens as much*	1
	to the priest as to the people,	2
	to the master[a] *as to his servant,*	2
	to the mistress as to her maid,	2
	to the seller as to the buyer,	2
	to the lender as to the borrower,	2
	to the creditor as to the debtor.	4
First Mourner:	3 *The land is totally emptied*[a]—	3+2
	totally plundered.	
	For YHWH	2+3
	has spoken this word.	
Second Mourner:	4 *The land dries up. It withers.*[a]	3+3
	The world languishes. It withers.	
	The height of the people of the land languishes.[b]	4
Third Mourner:	5 *The land itself is contaminated under*[a] *its inhabitants.*	4
	For they pass over laws.	2
	They change a statute.	2
	They break a permanent covenant.	3
First Mourner:	6 *Therefore a curse devours the land,*	4+3
	and inhabitants in her are held guilty.	
Second Mourner:	*Therefore inhabitants of a land disappear,*[a]	4+3
	and humankind is left (only) a few.	
Third Mourner:	7 *New wine dries up!*	2+2+2
	A vine withers!	

All who would be light-hearted[a] *groan!*

First Mourner: 8 *Rejoicing with a tambourine is ended!* 3+3+3
The tumult of revelers has ceased!
Rejoicing with a lyre is ended!
9 *No one drinks wine with a song!* 3+3
Beer is bitter to its drinkers!

Second Mourner: 10 *A desolate city*[a] *is broken!* 3+3
Every house is barricaded preventing entry!
11 *A cry for wine (is) in the streets!* 3+3+3
All joy dims.[a]
Revelry is banished (from) the land.[b]

Third Mourner: 12 *Only horror is left in the city!* 3+3
Only ruin (at) a battered gate!

First Mourner: 13 *For this is how it is inside the land,*[a] 5+2
among the peoples:[a]
like an olive tree that has been beaten, 2+3
like gleanings[b] *when the grape harvest is finished.*

Notes

1.a. The verbs בקק and בלק have similar meanings (see Wildberger's survey, 913; *HAL* has "lay waste" for both; *DCH* has "devastate" for both). LXX translates בוקק as καταφθείρει, "destroying," and בולקה as ἐρημώσει αὐτὴν, "will make it desolate." Delitzsch followed Ibn Ezra and Gesenius in interpreting בקק as "emptying." But this is now generally rejected. G. R. Driver (*JTS* 38 [1937] 41–42) posits a bi-radical root בק from which both verbs derive and translates "crack" and "cleave."

1.b. 1QIsa[a] האדמה, "the ground," for MT הארץ, "the land" (cf. E. Y. Kutscher, *Language and Linguistic Background,* 216). ארץ appears twenty-four times in this chapter (see *Excursus: "The Land"* [הארץ]). It may be translated "land" or "earth." The narrower meaning has been used here as more consistent with its use elsewhere in the Vision.

2.a. MT כאדניו, "so his masters," is a plural where parallels are singular; cf. 19:4 and 1:3. However, this may simply be a "plural of majesty" (cf. GKC §124*i; HebSyntax* §19*c*).

3.a. תִּבּוֹק is a unique form of the verb in v 1. It is apparently a *nip'al* impf. form in analogy to the *ayin vav* group (cf. Bauer-Leander §58*p;* followed by Duhm, Marti, Wildberger, *HAL,* and *DCH*). This allows the form to parallel closely the following verbs.

4.a. MT נבלה, "withers," is missing in LXX. Because it is repeated in the second stich, some commentators (Procksch) suggest leaving it out. De Groot (*NThSt* 22 [1939] 156) thinks it is one of the "alternative readings" in the chapter. But Wildberger (914) correctly notes that the style of the chapter is marked by the piling up of synonymous words like בקק/בלק in v 1. Here נבלה supports אבלה, "dries up," in a similar fashion.

4.b. MT אמללו, "languish," is pl. מרום, "height," is sg. 1QIsa[a] אמלל is sg. LXX οἱ ὑψηλοὶ τῆς γῆς, "the heights of the land," and Syr. *dl' rwmh d'r'* lead Talmon ("Aspects of the Textual Transmission," *Textus* 4 [1964] 118–19) to see עם, "people," as a parallel reading to מרום, "height." 1QIsa[a] has עם written in above the line—an apparent correction added after the text was copied. Wildberger prefers to read עִם, "with," and put an article in המרום to read "it has fallen apart—that which is above with the earth." None of these is conclusive, and MT, with a simple correction to sg. following 1QIsa[a], LXX, and others, may be kept.

5.a. LXX διὰ, "through" or "by means of"; σ´ ὑπὸ, "by," but also with an acc. may be "under." However, MT תחת, "under," is correct. Wildberger (914) notes that the earth has to bear the burden of its inhabitants. Notice the alliteration חרו/חפרו/חלפו/עברו/חנפה *ḥru/ḥpru/ḥlpu/'bru/ḥnph* and compare these with חרפה in 25:8.

6.a. MT חרו, "burned," from חרר. 1QIsa[a] חורו from חור, "become white, are bleached white." σ´ ἐκτρυχωθησονται (Eusebius), "are used up." G. R. Driver ("Notes on Isaiah," in *Von Ugarit nach Qumran,* BZAW 77 [Berlin: Töpelmann, 1958] 44) suggested that behind the Gk. lay a Heb. root חור like Arab. *ḫāra(w),* "be weak" or "be limited." KBL and *HAL* suggest a second root חרה comparable to Arab. *ḥarā(j)*, "reduce." Cf. also G. R. Driver, *JTS* 2 (1951) 26, and *DCH* חרה II and חרר. This suggests the translation "they disappear," a good parallel to the following stich.

7.a. MT שִׂמְחֵי, "merry ones." 1QIsa[a] שומחי reads this as an act. ptc. (cf. Kutscher, *Language and Linguistic Background*, 340).

10.a. MT קִרְיַת־תֹהוּ, "city of chaos." LXX πᾶσα πόλις, "every city," reflects a tendency to generalize the judgment.

11.a. MT עָרְבָה. LXX πέπαυται, "restrained, prohibited." Tg. שׁלימת, "is finished, ended." Syr. *bṭlt*, "has ceased." Vg. *deserta est*, "be forsaken." The dictionaries posit a root ערב V, "become evening," based on cognates in Akk., Ugar., Arab., and Mishnaic Hebrew referring to the sun going down, so ערבה here means "has grown dark" (Wildberger, *HAL*). Houbigant (*Biblica Hebraica* [Paris: Briasson, 1753]) and others (including BDB, 788) suggest emending to עברה, "pass away," following the versions, but "grows dark, dims" is more colorful than the bland translation of the versions and emendations.

11.b. הארץ, "the land," is missing in LXX[B].

13.a. De Groot (*NThSt* 22 [1939] 157) thinks "in the midst of the land" and "among the peoples" are alternative readings. Wildberger correctly calls them "parallel concepts."

13.b. *BHS* refers to Jer 6:9 in suggesting that MT כעוללת be doubled to כעולל עוללות, "glean the gleanings." Wildberger (915) agrees, noting in the chapter the tendency to such reduplication and the reformation of 11*b* to a three-stich line, 2+2+2. However, the change is not pressing since MT makes good sense and meter as it stands and is supported by 1QIsa[a].

Form/Structure/Setting

Attention is drawn from Tyre to the hinterland. YHWH is devastating the land. The witnesses converse about the destruction of "the land" and "the city." Tyre's fall has lent a measure of completeness and finality that previous judgment had not had.

The scene concentrates attention on one theme: the devastated land. While always being related to that theme, the dialogue allows variations:

YHWH is the active agent in the devastation (vv 1, 3).
All elements of the population are involved (v 2).
The land is withered because of the people's sin (vv 4–6).
Social life is at a standstill (vv 7–9).
The cities lie abandoned in ruins (vv 10–12).
The land is abandoned and bare (v 13).

The witnesses describe the scene to the audience with animation, with astonishment that it is YHWH who is doing this, and with horror at the thoroughness of what has been done. The narrow attention that chap. 23 had given to Tyre and its clients beyond the sea is now broadened. This survey of the whole land reveals devastation, nothing but devastation.

Comment

1 The recognition that YHWH himself is laying waste the land makes the statement take on a measure of horror. What is to be understood as הארץ, "the land"? The answer one gives determines one's attitude toward the entire section. When one translates it "the earth," that very act predisposes the reader to see this as referring to all the world and thus as apocalyptic in scope and meaning.

However, the Hebrew word is common enough. It is used regularly in Isaiah in the ordinary sense of a defined territory, political unit, or land. It is sometimes defined precisely as "land of Egypt," "land of Judah." (It is interesting to note that the phrase "land of Israel" does not occur in Isaiah.) There seems to be no reason to understand it differently here. It refers to a defined territory.

The land occurs a large number of times in this chapter and deserves special treatment. The sense that is appropriate here takes in the Palestinian-Syrian area, including what, from an Israelite point of view, was embraced in David's kingdom. The Assyrian campaigns have been taking one after another of its constituent elements.

Excursus: "The Land" (הארץ)

Bibliography

Brueggemann, W. *The Land.* Philadelphia: Fortress, 1977. **Habel, N. C.** *The Land is Mine: Six Land Ideologies.* Minneapolis: Fortress, 1995. **Ottoson, M.** "ארץ." *TDOT.* 1:418–36. **Plöger, J. G.** *Literarische, Formgeschichtliche und Stilkritische Untersuchungen zum Deuteronomium.* BBB 26. Bonn: Hanstein, 1967. 60–129. **Rad, G. von.** "Verheissenes Land und Jahwes Land im Hexateuch." *ZDPV* 66 (1943) 191–204. Reprinted in *Gesammelte Studien zum Alten Testament* (Munich: Kaiser, 1958) 1:87–100. **Rost, L.** "Bezeichnungen für Land und Volk im AT." In *Festschrift Otto Procksch.* Ed. A. Alt et al. Leipzig: Deichert, 1934. 125–48. Reprinted in *Das kleine Credo und andere Studien zum Alten Testament* (Heidelberg: Quelle & Meyer, 1965) 76–101. **Stadelmann, L. I. J.** *The Hebrew Conception of the World.* AnBib 39. Rome: Biblical Institute Press, 1970.

הארץ may be paired with "the heavens" and thus properly be translated "the earth" in Isa 1:2. Even this is still in terms of "the land," from horizon to horizon, that is spanned by the sky. The more usual meaning of הארץ in Isaiah is of a particular territory or space in which someone lives or over which someone reigns (see *Excursus: The Destruction of the Land* at chap. 13 above).

The synonyms of אדמה, "ground," and תבל, "world," are helpful but do not change the basic sense. The land is inhabitable, like the ground and unlike the sea. The land, like the world, is unlike תהו, "chaos." It has order and organization. ארץ, "land," is the recognizable territory that one inhabits, visits, knows about. In the Near East, for Israel, "the land" was essentially the territory that faced the eastern Mediterranean Sea. This included Palestine/Syria and the wings in Mesopotamia in the northeast and Egypt/Ethiopia in the south. The edges of Arabia come into view occasionally, as do Libya and distant Tarshish. This was הארץ, "the civilized land," האדמה, "the cultivatable land," or תבל, "the world," to the people of Israel. Its horizons marked the world of their day. Their heavens spanned this land. Their sea, the Mediterranean and perhaps the Reed Sea, was its contrasting member.

In that setting "the land," "the world," and "civilization" were terms that were much nearer to each other than the three terms would be today. They all meant in that time the area of Palestine-Syria and Mesopotamia and Egypt. Therefore, for translations (RSV, NIV, and others) to render הארץ as "the earth" in chaps. 24–27 when they had rendered it "the land" in previous chapters confuses the issue. Brueggemann does not even discuss these instances in his book, presuming that they do not apply. In all these instances the prior judgment that the chapters are apocalyptic in nature and must be treated differently accounts for the change.

This commentary has found reason to doubt that there is a substantial difference in the literary nature of these chapters. הארץ has, therefore, continued to be translated "the land." This means that the devastation, destruction, and shaking described in these chapters involves Palestine, Syria, Mesopotamia, and Egypt. This was the world from Jerusalem's perspective. These are the same territories that have felt the power of Assyrian armies in the previous acts of the Vision.

Yet one should not overlook the deep emotion and meaning that "the land" had for the Israelite. Brueggemann writes (*The Land,* 2), "The land is never simply physical dirt but is always physical dirt freighted with social meaning derived from historical experience." As Brueggemann uses it, this meaning in Exodus and Deuteronomy relates to the promises made to Abraham, the occupation under Joshua, and the consolidation under David. In this sense "the land" was particularly Israel's land. This sense has meaning here.

But the Vision reaches back to a deeper level of meaning like that in Gen 1–11 in its concern with the relation of humankind (אדם) to the land and the issues of the age of Noah. It sees a closer parallel between the issues of the eighth to the fifth centuries and the age of Noah than to the age of Moses and David.

Thus the problem of the ground (אדמה) and of the land (הארץ) lies in the curse upon them because of the blood spilled there. Compare Gen 3:17, in which the ground (האדמה) is cursed because of Adam. In Gen 4:10–12 Cain, who had been so closely related to the ground (האדמה), must flee to a land of homelessness (ארץ נוד) and there build a city (Gen 4:17).

In Gen 6:1–8, although there is repeated reference to the relation of humankind and ground, there is no mention of bloodguilt. But from Gen 6:11 on, the terms change to הארץ, "the land," with constant reference to violent sins. In the story of Noah, God announces the destruction of humankind and the land because of the high level of bloodguilt. But after the flood, God promises that he will never again curse the ground because of humankind.

There is a distinct change in the new age. One might say that the Age of Adam-Ground has become the Age of the Land, of nations, peoples, national boundaries, and wars. Gen 9:6 announces a human's responsibility for his or her own crime: "Whoever sheds the blood of a human, by a human shall that person's blood be shed" (NRSV).

But the blight of curse is not entirely absent. In Gen 9:25 we read of the curse upon Canaan. In chap. 11 people build a city but are cursed because of overweening ambition, so they are scattered over all the land (כל־הארץ). In Gen 12:1–3 Abraham is called to go from his land (ארץ) to the land that God would show him. He was destined to be the decisive reason for blessing or curse.

In the Vision of Isaiah, chap. 2 had emphasized the role of humankind (אדם) related to YHWH's day. The Vision reaches its climax (Isa 65:17) with YHWH creating a "new land" and a new heaven just as he did through and after the flood. Throughout the Vision there is a conscious parallel drawn to the era of the flood with the intention of emphasizing the idea that in the eighth to the fifth centuries B.C.E. YHWH was bringing one age to an end and opening the door to another.

2 The devastation has touched all classes of people.

3 הבוז תבוז, "totally plundered." The completeness of the waste and plunder was achieved by the Assyrian and Babylonian campaigns into Palestine and Egypt in the eighth, seventh, and sixth centuries B.C.E.

4 Hayes ("'The Earth Mourns'") has made a study of earth's (land's) part in this prophetic metaphor in a number of prophetic passages, including Amos 1:2; Hos 4:1–3; Jer 4:23–28; 12:7–13; 13:9–12; Isa 24:1–20; 33:7–9; and Joel 1:5–20.

5–6 The discussion turns to the reasons for the destruction. It is clearly blamed on lawlessness and a breach of covenant by its inhabitants. A moral breakdown lies at the core of the problems. Countries do not have sins, but people do. And countries suffer as a consequence of the guilt of their peoples. So the curse that is normally a part of every covenant obligation (cf. Deut 28:15–68) falls across the land because the covenant was broken.

5 חנפה, "contaminated." The verse describes the result for the land on which blood is spilled (cf. Num 35:33). The violent murders, wars, and executions on this land have brought down the reproach foreseen in the law (see 25:8 for a very similar word).

הפר ברית, "break a covenant." Laws are contained in the covenant, which contains provisions that curses shall fall on those who break them (Lev 26; Deut 28:15–68).

ברית עולם, "a permanent covenant," is more than a political agreement. A comparison with Gen 8:21/9:8–17 is instructive. This also deals with the curse on the land/ground because of human violence. The obvious reference is to the everlasting covenant of Gen 9:12.

6 אלה, "a curse," is the result of a broken covenant and a blood-drenched land (cf. Num 35:33) as v 5 has indicated. The concepts related to the terrible curse, the land, and its inhabitants will be among the major themes of the next two chapters. The curse is understood to have an evil dynamic of its own that, once unleashed, continues without limit. The problem of releasing the land and its people, including Israel and Jerusalem, from this awful ban will occupy the rest of the act.

ויאשמו, "held guilty." The word אשם, "be guilty," does not speak so much of personal responsibility as of being smeared or branded with the dreadful contamination. God's people (Israel) are responsible for a share, at least, of the whole land's guilt, shame, and disgrace. Their violence had spilled blood upon it. Their idolatries contributed to its shame. Their infidelities were a part of its disgrace. They were partly responsible for the shroud of death that had covered the land for centuries.

YHWH's actions make reparation to the land for his people's disgrace and bloodguilt. This is the first step in reversing the curse of the land in 24:6, 17–18.

7–9 Signs of life die out across the country.

10 קרית־תהו, "a desolate city," has occasioned discussion and deserves thorough examination.

Excursus: "The City" (העיר)

Bibliography

Frick, F. S. *The City in Ancient Israel.* SBLDS 36. Chico, CA: Scholars Press, 1977. **Gill, D. W.** "Biblical Theology of the City." *ISBE* 1:713–15. **Grabbe, L. L.,** and **R. D. Haak,** eds. *'Every City Shall Be Forsaken': Urbanism and Prophecy in Ancient Israel and the Near East.* JSOTSup 330. Sheffield: Sheffield Academic Press, 2001. **Ludwig, O.** "Die Stadt in der Jesaja—Apokalypse." Diss., Bonn, 1961. **McCown, C. C.** "City." *IDB.* 1:632–38. **Myers, A. C.** "City." *ISBE.* 1:705–13. **Rad, G. von.** "Die Stadt auf dem Berge." *EvT* 8 (1948–49) 439–47. Reprinted in *Gesammelte Studien zum Alten Testament* (Munich: Kaiser, 1958) 1:214–24.

Studies of העיר, "the city" in these chapters (24:10–12; 25:2–5; 26:1–6; 27:10–11) have usually been carried out under the presupposition that the literature is apocalyptic, giving particular significance to the meaning of "the city." Ludwig's dissertation ("Die Stadt in der Jesaja") is a case in point. His primary concern is to date the apocalypse by use of the city imagery.

The significance of הָעִיר, "the city," is important for the entire Vision, which struggles to uncover the role of Jerusalem from chap. 1 through chap. 66. The song in 25:1–5, a part of that development, stands in dialogue with the views of Psalms and Chronicles.

Other cities are emphasized in the Vision. These include Damascus and Samaria (7:8–9; chap. 17), Babylon (chaps. 13 and 21), and Tyre (chap. 23). It is not the cities themselves that are important here but what they stand for. They have represented an era in which cities dominated the political scene. They were the seats of influence and of wealth, and they were often the real power within the small nations. Sometimes foreigners seized the cities and were thereby able to control the larger countryside for generations.

Such were the "walled cities" of the Canaanites that faced Joshua, the cities of the Philistines, the Phoenician cities, Damascus, Haran, Carchemesh, and even Babylon. Such also was Jerusalem. Each of these was stronger and more important than the territory it dominated—territories that fluctuated in size depending upon the particular strength of the reigning "king" of the city.

The biblical story recognized this. The placement of the narrative of the Tower of Babel (Gen 11) immediately after the genealogies of the sons of Noah indicates the story's evaluation of the importance of both for the age after the flood. The growing importance of the cities in the area can also be sensed in the stories of Abraham. What is not noted in the text is the reason that this was happening. Egypt's previous control of the area had been weakened. Various peoples were beginning to assert their claims by building fortress cities to control trade routes and the surrounding countryside with its villages.

Babylon played the decisive role in Mesopotamia. The Aramaeans moved into Haran and Damascus. The Canaanites controlled the Phoenician plain from their strongholds in Byblos, Ebla, Tyre, and Sidon, but they also spread south into the cities of Palestine. The Israelites infiltrated Palestine and conquered the walled cities wherever they could. Edomites, Moabites, and Ammonites took over the cities across the Jordan. And the Philistines seized the seven cities of the lower coast. For well over a thousand years cities had been the most stable and persistent elements in a political picture that was otherwise very turbulent and changing. But in the period that the Vision pictures, the age of city-states is coming to an end.

This scene (24:1–13) of the Vision presents a picture of a scarred and empty landscape in the area that is dotted with the ruins of these cities—empty and lifeless. The stark reality of the scene conveys a deeper reality. Like the bleached bones of animals of another time, these ruins signify that an age has passed never to return. For the following era (many centuries), cities would not play that role again. In an age of empires they could not.

This is one of the bitter lessons the Vision attempts to convey to postexilic Jerusalem. Jerusalem cannot return to the role she played under David. The Jews, however, did not give up that idea very easily. Jerusalem remained a hotbed of conspiracy and revolt through the Persian, the Greek, and even the Roman periods. The Vision teaches that such hopes will be disappointed. That role for Jerusalem, as also for Babylon, Tyre, Damascus, and Ashdod, is gone forever. This is the desolate and empty city of 24:10.

Of course urban life would continue under imperial rule. Indeed it would flourish with new vigor and meaning in the Persian period, while the Hellenistic city would come to be the measure of a cultured lifestyle unknown to earlier times. Similarly, the

Vision foresees a new role for Jerusalem within the providence of God. It is to be a temple city, drawing pilgrims from the entire empire and beyond (cf. 2:1–4 passim to 66:19–21). The beautiful song in 26:1–4 fits into that strand of the Vision's theme.

13 The common comparison with the barren field stripped of its fruit after harvest, or the bare tree after the olives have been beaten off the trees (it is still done that way), was fitting for the lands and cities that had been plundered of everything of value. The use of the metaphor of olive harvest creates ambiguity. Some may mourn the tree that has been beaten and deprived of leaves and fruit, but others, seeing the gathered fruit, rejoice. There are always those who profit. The tree may look stripped and bare, but the harvest of olives has made someone rich. The destruction of the land of Palestine will please someone.

Explanation

The scene surveys the devastation that the Assyrian campaigns have brought about in the whole country, from the Euphrates to the River of Egypt. YHWH is the prime cause. The effects are universal on all the land's peoples and on all its parts. The fields are barren and unplanted. The cities are ruined and are without life. A curse has bound the land. It looks like a tree after its fruit and leaves have been stripped off.

The passage surveys the terrible effects of God's campaign of judgment through the Assyrian "rod of [his] anger" (10:5). God's judgment is both horrible and thorough. Canaanite civilization had dominated Palestine/Syria for well over a millennium. Now it is about to disappear.

Noah's curse had been on the land for a long time (Gen 9:25–27). Israel's entry into Canaan assumed this curse and capitalized on it, but Israel had not been able to transform the land. It had come to share the Canaanite characteristics that God abhorred, and now Israel shares in the suffering of the land.

Isaiah's Vision sees the land's destruction as the work and will of God. It calls upon those who survive the destruction to be alert to God's will for them, to God's new structures and God's new ways of life within the imperial structures that now dominate the scene. These were destined to exist for a long time. After Assyria came Babylon, Persia, the Hellenistic kingdoms, and the Romans. God was calling for a people to serve him in the new age, just as he had called Abraham, Moses, and David in the old age. Israel and Judah in the old age had been blind, deaf, uncomprehending, and rebellious toward God. The Vision implies that the people of God in the new age tend to be just the same. For those who resist God's plan, there can be no hope (chap. 65). Only those who yield to God and seek to serve him in his new way will share his life and his city.

Responses: They Raise Their Voices (24:14–20)

Bibliography

Ben David, Y. "Ugaritic Parallels to Isa 24:18–19." (Heb.) *Leš* 45 (1980) 56–59. **Irwin, W. H.** "The Punctuation of Isaiah 14–16*a* and 25:4–5." *CBQ* 46 (1984) 215–22. **Loete, J.** "A Premature Hymn of Praise: The Meaning and Function of Isaiah 24:14–16*c* in Its Present Context." In *Studies in Isaiah 24–27: The Isaiah Workshop.* Ed. H. J. Bosman et al. Leiden: Brill, 2000. 226–28. **Niehaus, J.** "*raz-pešar* in Isaiah XXIV." *VT* 31 (1981) 376–78. **Sawyer, J. F. A.** "'My Secret Is with Me" (Isaiah 24:16): Some Semantic Links between Isaiah 24–27 and Daniel." In *Essays in Honour of George Wishart Anderson.* Ed. G. Auld. Sheffield: JSOT Press, 1993. 307–17.

Translation

Heavens:	14 *They raise their voices!*	3+1
	They shout joyously!	
	On account of YHWH's majesty	2+2
	[a]*they cry out from the west!* [ab]	
Earth:	15 *Because of this they glorify YHWH in the east,*[a]	4+2
	in the coastlands of the sea,	
	the name of YHWH,	2+2
	God of Israel!	
First Chorus:	16 *From the extremities of the land*	2+2+2
	we hear songs: [a]	
	"Honor to the Righteous One!"	
Solo Voice:	*But then I say:*	1+2+2
	"I am ruined! [b] *I am ruined!* [b]	
	Woe to me!"	
Second Chorus:	[c]*Traitors betray!*	2+3
	With treachery traitors betray! [c]	
Heavens:	17 *Terror, tomb,*[a] *and trap*	3+3
	(are) upon you, inhabitant of the land!	
Earth:	18 *And it will be that*	1
	whoever flees from the sound [a] *of dread*	3+3
	will fall toward the pit,	
	and whoever climbs from inside the pit	3+2
	will be caught in the snare!	
Heavens:	*For sluices from a height* [b] *have been opened.*	3+3
	So land's foundations quake.	
	19 *The land is thoroughly* [a] *broken up.*	3+3
	[c]*Land* [b] *is split apart.*	
	Land is badly eroded.[c]	3+4
	20 *Land* [a] *trembles much, like the drunkard.*	
Earth:	*It wanders* [b] *like* [c] *the shack!*	2+2+3
	Its guilt be heavy on it!	
	It falls [d] *and does not rise again!*	

Notes

14.a-a. LXX ταραχθήσεται τὸ ὕδωρ τῆς θαλάσσης, "the water of the sea will be troubled," seems to have read a reduplicated מים, "from sea" or "from the west," as מים מים, "water from the sea."

14.b. מִיָּם, "from a sea." Kaiser translates "the shout (louder) than on the sea," referring to GKC §133*e*. Wildberger (932) notes that מים is apparently parallel to בארים, "in the east" (v 15*a;* cf. below). Therefore it probably also indicates a direction "from the west" (cf. *HebSyntax* §111*a;* and M. Dahood, "Hebrew-Ugaritic Lexicography V," *Bib* 48 [1967] 427).

15.a. בארים occurs only here in the pl. אוֹר means to "become light, shine." Wildberger (932) traces the struggle to ascertain its meaning from Kimchi and Ibn Ezra's "valley" and many others to Procksch (באיים) "on the islands" and on to *BHS* באיי הים, "on the islands of the sea." Kaiser refers to a second meaning for אור, "dawn," in M. Jastrow, *Dictionary of the Targum,* vol. 1 (New York: Pardes, 1950), and returns to a suggestion made by H. Ewald (*Commentary on the Prophets of the Old Testament,* trans. J. F. Smith [London: Williams & Norgate, 1875–81]) to translate it "the east" (see *HAL, DCH*).

16.a. For זמרת, "songs," LXX has τέρατα, "miracles," which leads G. R. Driver (*JSS* 13 [1968] 50) to the Syr. word *dmjr,* "astounding, wonderful." He suggests that there was a Heb. word זְמִירוֹת, "strange things." This could be a parallel idea to צבי, "honor." But Wildberger (932) notes that the words are not syntactically parallel.

16.b. רזי has not been definitely identified. KBL writes "meaning unknown." BDB (931) tentatively notes that it is an opposite to צבי, "honor," from רזה, "grow lean." LXX καὶ ἐροῦσιν Οὐαὶ, "and they will say, 'Alas,'" seems to have passed over both occurrences of רזי־לי altogether. σ´ το μυστηριον μου εμοι το μυστηριον μου εμοι (Eusebius), "my secret to myself, my secret to myself." σ´ θ´ το μυστηριον μου εμοι (Syh.), "my secret to myself." θ´ *mysterium meum mihi* (Jerome), "my secret to myself." Vg. *secretum meum,* "my secret." Wildberger (932) notes that all these have apparently thought of the Aram. רז, "secret." However, the following "woe" points, like BDB, to ה, with the meaning "disappear, be overcome." He translates *Aus mit mir!* "Away with me!" (cf. *HAL*).

16.c-c. LXX shortens the lines to τοῖς ἀθετοῦσιν, "they condemn them."

17.a. Literally "pit." To reproduce the alliteration of the Hebrew, I translate "tomb."

18.a. Omitted in LXX.

18.b. ממרום means "from a height." It is not necessary to spell out "in the heavens" (cf. *BHS* and Wildberger's comment [933]).

19.a. MT רעה is missing in 1QIsa[a], but 1QIsa[b] has רוע, leaving out ה. Delitzsch, Duhm, Marti, and Gray (see BDB, *HAL*) had already guessed that ה was a dittograph for the following letter. רֹעַ is a cognate inf. abs.

19.b. The article occurs on only the first us of ארץ, "land." Wildberger (933) follows Gray and Feldmann in calling it a dittograph to be eliminated. For the uses of ארץ in this chapter, see *A Concluding Liturgy (24:1–27:13)* and *Excursus: "The Land"* (הארץ).

19.c-c. LXX ἀπορίᾳ ἀπορηθήσεται, "totally perplexed," shortens and imitates the Heb. form but is a very free rendering.

20.a. 1QIsa[a] הארץ, "the land," adds the article (cf. Kutscher, *Language and Linguistic Background,* 411).

20.b. 1QIsa[a] substitutes a final א for ה (cf. Kutscher, *Language and Linguistic Background,* 163).

20.c. 1QIsa[a] inserts a conjunction: "and (is) like a shack."

20.d. 1QIsa[a] lacks the fem. ending. MT is sustained by noting that this is a quotation of Amos 5:2 and by the consistent fem. subjects in the verse.

Form/Structure/Setting

The dark mood of the last scene is broken by the sound of excited cheers for YHWH from far edges of the land (vv 14–16). But the cheering is not unanimous. A single voice speaks its woe, and a chorus supports him with cries of "Foul!" (v 16). The response of the witnesses is a sharp reprimand, reminding one of the curse recalled in v 6 and of the solemnity of the judgments that mark the end of the age (v 18*c*–20*a*). The renewed curse falls on people (v 18) and on the land (v 20*b*–*d*) This scene, like chap. 23, creates space for a delayed reaction in later scenes ("after sufficient days," v 22).

Comment

14–16 המה ישאו קולם, "They raise their voices." Who are these who shout encouragement to YHWH from the outer edges of the land that forms this stage of action? Are they the Israelites who have been exiled to far places? Are they members of YHWH's heavenly court? Are they admirers from among the nations? Are they allies of the invaders who have done YHWH's work of destruction? They remain unidentified. It is sufficient to note that YHWH's work is known and appreciated. He is recognized as "majestic," as "God of Israel," and as "the Righteous One." The last designation may describe his victories as much as his ethic.

16 There is dissent, both individual and group, from those who would insist that there is no justice in this, only treachery. This cry would come from some who have felt the loss personally but admit no personal guilt to account for it. They think they have been cheated.

אמר, "I say." The familiar voice of the prophet identifies with the sufferers who bear the brunt of the destruction. The anguish is similar to that in chap. 20. He experiences the horrors of such chaotic tragedy.

17 פחד . . . עליך, "terror . . . upon you." The verse implies that the inhabitant of the land deserves everything that happens to him (cf. Jer 48). It reacts to the complaints of v 16 with the first of four curses spoken against the land and its inhabitants. Note the alliteration of פחד *pḥd*, "terror," פחת *pḥt*, "pit or tomb," and פח *pḥ*, "snare or trap."

18*ab* The second curse supports the inevitability of disaster. The words are a quotation from Amos 5:19 (cf. Ps 139:7–12). When the Lord's judgment lies over the land, there is no escape.

18*c*–20 ארבות ממרום, "sluices from a height." This reminder of Gen 7:11 and 8:2 joins the picture of land quaking and moving (v 19) to evoke a sense of a time like that of the flood. As in 2 Kgs 7:2, 19 and Mal 3:10, the picture is of a sky/firmament that keeps out the cosmic ocean beyond. The third curse (v 20*bc*) affirms the quaking disaster and calls for it to be terminal.

Explanation

This scene returns to YHWH, acclaiming his majesty and giving glory to him as God of Israel—glory to the Righteous One. Complaints from inhabitants are met with dire curses that emphasize the judgment on the land, its inhabitants, and its armies. The Vision portrays YHWH's mighty acts relating to the whole land, the sea, and their peoples in chaps. 23–24. The next chapters will keep firmly in view his intentions and acts on behalf of Israel and Jerusalem.

YHWH of Hosts Reigns on Mount Zion (24:21–25:8)

Bibliography

Beuken, W. A. M. "The Prophet Leads the Readers into Praise: Isa 25:1–10 in Connection with Isa. 24:14–23." In *Studies in Isaiah 24–27: The Isaiah Workshop.* Ed. H. J. Bosman et al. Leiden: Brill, 2000. 121–56. **Caquot, A.** "Remarques sur le 'banquet des nations' en Esaïe 25:6–8." *RHPR* 69 (1989) 109–19. **Chilton, R. B.** *Glory of Israel.* 49–50. **Choque, E.** "Canto anticipado por la liberación final: Una exposición escatológica de Isaías 25." *Theo* 14 (1999) 172–87. **Coste, J.** "Le text grec d'Isaïe xxv 1–5." *RB* 61 (1954) 67–86. **Delcor, M.** "La festin d'immortalité sur la montagne de Sion à l'ère eschatologique en Is. 25,6–9." In *Études biblique et orientalis de religions comparées.* Leiden: Brill, 1979. 122–31. **Easterley, E.** "Is Mesha's *qrhh* Mentioned in Isaiah xv 2?" *VT* 41 (1991) 215–19. **Emerton, J. A.** "A Textual Problem in Isaiah 25:2." *ZAW* 89 (1977) 64–73. **Gray, B.** "Critical Discussions: Isaiah 26; 25:1–5; 34:12–14." *ZAW* 31 (1911) 111–27. **Herrmann, W.** "Die Implicationen von Jes 25.8*αα*." *BN* 104 (2000) 26–30. **Kooij, A. van der.** "The Teacher Messiah and Worldwide Peace: Some Comments on Symmachus' Version of Isaiah 25:7–8." *JNSL* 24 (1998) 75–82. **Lobmann, P.** "Die selbstständigen lyrischen Abschnitte in Jes 24–27." *ZAW* 37 (1917–18) 1–58. ———. "Zu Text und Metrum einiger Stellen aus Jesaja: II. Das Lied 25:1–5." *ZAW* 33 (1913) 256–62. **Martin-Achard, R.** *De la mort à la résurrection a'près l'Ancien Testament.* Neuchâtel: Delachaux & Niestlé, 1956. Trans. J. P. Smith under the title *From Death to Life: A Study of the Development of the Doctrine of the Resurrection in the Old Testament* (Edinburgh: Oliver & Boyd, 1960). ———. "'Il engloutit la mort à jamais': Remarques sur Ezaïe 25,8*αα*." In *Mélanges bibliques et orientaux.* FS M. M. Delcor, ed. A. Caquot et al. AOAT 215. Kevelaer: Butzon & Bercker. 283–96. **Vermeylen, J.** *Du prophète Isaïe à l'apocalyptique.* 1:363–69. **Welton, P.** "Die Vernichtung des Todes und ihr traditiongeschichtlicher Ort: Studie zu Jes. 25:6–8, 21–23 und Exod 24:9–11." *TZ* 38 (1982) 129–46. **Wildberger, H.** "Das Freudenmahl auf dem Zion: Erwägungen zu Jes 25,6–8." *TZ* 33 (1977) 373–83. **Willis, T. M.** "Yahweh's Elders (Is 24:23): Senior Officials of the Divine Court." *ZAW* 103 (1991) 375–85. **Wodecki, B.** "The Religious Universalism of the Pericope Is 25:6–9." In *Goldene Äpfel in silbernen Schalen.* Ed. K. D. Schlunk and M. Augustin. BEATAJ 20. Frankfurt am Main: Lang, 1992. 35–47. **Zyl, A. H. van.** *The Moabites.* POS 3. Leiden: Brill, 1960. 158–59.

Translation

Heavens: 21 [a] *In such a day* [a] — 3
when YHWH decides the fate [b] — 2+3+3
of the army of the highlands in the height
and of the kings of the lowlands in the lowlands,
22 *may they be gathered like prisoners* [a] *in a pit,* — 3+2+3
shut up in a locked place,
and after sufficient days have their fate decided.

Herald: 23 *May even the moon* [a] *be ashamed* — 2+2
and the sun [b] *be abashed!*
For YHWH of Hosts reigns — 3+3+3
on Mount Zion and in Jerusalem
before his elders in glory! [c]

A Worshiper: (the Implied Author)	[25:1] *YHWH, you are my God!*	3+3
	I exalt you! I adore your name!	
	For you have done a wonder—	3+2+2
	things planned[a] *long ago—*[b]	
	being faithful (in your) faithfulness!	
	[2]*For you have transformed*[a] *a city*[b] *to a heap of rubble!*[c]	4+3
	A fortified city to a ruin!	
	A foreigners'[d] *stronghold (is) no longer a city!*	3+3
	(It will) never be rebuilt!	
Second Worshiper:	[3]*Because of this a strong people honor you!*	4+4
	A city of ruthless nations fears you!	
Third Worshiper:	[4]*For you continue to be a refuge for the poor,*	4+4
	a refuge for the needy in his distress,	
	a shelter from a storm,	2+2
	a shade from the heat.	
Fourth Worshiper:	*For (there is) a spirit of ruthless persons*	3+2+2
	like a wall of falling rain;	
	[5]*like heat in a drought,*	
	you subdue an uproar of strangers.[a]	3+3+3
	[b]*(Like) heat (subdued) by the shade of a cloud,*[b]	
	a triumph song of ruthless persons becomes subdued.[c]	
Herald:	[6]*YHWH of Hosts will make*	3+2+2
	for all peoples	
	on this mountain	
	[a]*a feast of rich foods,*	2+2
	a feast of treasures,[a]	
	rich foods of marrow	2+2
	of refined treasures.	
	[7]*He will swallow up on this mountain*	3+3+3
	the shroud that enshrouds[a] *all the peoples,*	
	the shadow that overshadows all nations.[b]	
First Elder:	[8] [a]*He will swallow up the death*[a] *(that) endures forever.*[b]	3
Second Elder:	*My Lord YHWH will wipe a tear*	4+2
	from every face.	
Third Elder:	*The disgrace of its*[c] *people he will remove*	3+3
	from all the land.	
Herald:	*For YHWH has spoken.*	3

Notes

21.a-a. Missing in LXX.

21.b. On פקד see G. André, *Determining the Destiny: PQD in the Old Testament* (Lund: Gleerup, 1980).

22.a. *BHS* suggests that ה belongs to the following word: אסף האסיר, "a gathering of prisoners [col.]." However, אסיר, "prisoner," is missing in 1QIsa[a], LXX, and Tg., which leads S. Talmon ("Aspects of the Textual Transmission," *Textus* 4 [1964] 123) and Wildberger to think that אסיר is a later addition, not original. The verse reads well without it, but that is not reason enough to delete it.

23.a. LXX ἡ πλίνθος, "tile, limestone." *BHS* suggests LXX vocalized Heb. הַלְּבֵנָה for this meaning.

23.b. LXX τὸ τεῖχος, "the wall," having read Heb as הַחֹמָה. But cf. 13:10, where different words for sun and moon are found. Wildberger is correct that they are also to be so understood here.

23.c. LXX δοξασθήσεται, "is glorified," assumes יִכָּבֵד a verb (see *BHS*). Although translation is difficult, MT should be sustained.

25:1.a. 1QIsa[a] עצ׳ת (cf. Kutscher, *Language and Linguistic Background*, 221), meaning unknown. *BHS* and Wildberger would move the *ʾatnakh* to this word, but this is unnecessary.

1.b. MT מרחוק, "from afar," is probably to be understood as temporal.

2.a. שמת מן means literally "constitute from," thus "transform."

2.b. מעיר, "from a city." LXX πόλεις, "cities." Tg. קרוי is also pl. Syr. *ḳrjt'* is sg. Vg. *civitas* is sg. With Wildberger and *BHK*[3], keep the sg.

2.c. LXX εἰς χῶμα; Tg. לגלין. Both imply an indefinite form, which leads *BHS* to suggest לְגַל. The difference is minimal.

2.d. LXX τὰ θεμέλια τῶν ἀσεβῶν, "the foundation of the ungodly." Two Gk. MSS read זרים, "insolent ones." But the change is unnecessary.

5.a. LXX ὀλιγόψυχοι, "fainthearted."

5.b-b. Lacking in LXX.

5.c. Tg. ימאכון, "they will be defeated," Syr. *ntmkk*. *BHS* emends the vowels יַעֲנֶה to read a pass. form, but the range of meaning in the act. form is sufficient without change.

6.a-a. Missing in LXX.

7.a. MT לוט is identified in the dictionaries both as a noun meaning "covering" and as an act. ptc. of לוט, "to cover." There is nothing to be gained by changing the vowel with *BHK*[3] and *HAL*. Wildberger (956) reports in detail the attempts at emendation and reordering. The old versions are confused about it. The parallel of לוט with מסכה, "shadow," is the most stabilizing element in the picture. The use of פני, "face," before it raises questions. Long ago Houbigant (*Biblica Hebraica* [Paris: Briasson, 1753]) and Lowth (*Isaiah* [London: Nichols, 1778]) suggested moving it before כל־העמים, "the shroud that covers the face of all the peoples." Delitzsch thought Job 41:5 [41:13] פְּנֵי לְבוּשׁוֹ, "his outer garment," offered a parallel to mean here "the upper (outer) side of the veil." C. W. E. Nägelsbach (*Der Prophet Jesaja* [Leipzig: Klasing, 1877]) describes it as an identical gen.; i.e., לוט and פנים mean the same thing, "the front side." Wildberger judges them all to be signs that no one knows with any certainty.

The form of the second הַלּוֹט has been debated (Wildberger, 959). Kimchi and *HAL* (see also *DCH*) emend to הַלּוּט, a pass. ptc. GKC §72*p* views it as an act. ptc. instead of the usual לָט (supported by Delitzsch, C. von Orelli [*The Prophecies of Isaiah*, trans. J. S. Banks (Edinburgh: T & T Clark, 1887)], Duhm, BDB, and others). Many contemporaries prefer the pass. (cf. *BHS*) in light of 1 Sam 21:10. This translation follows Nägelsbach's suggestion.

7.b. 1QIsa[a] הגואים (Kutscher, *Language and Linguistic Background*, 511), which is explained as the insertion of א to distinguish the similar letters on both sides.

8.a-a. LXX translates κατέπιεν ὁ θάνατος, "death swallows up." α´ καταποντισει τον θανατον, "he will plunge death into the sea"; σ´ καταποθηναι ποιησει τον θανατον, "will make death be swallowed up"; θ´ κατεποθη ο θανατος, "death is swallowed up" (cf. 1 Cor 15:54); Syr. is also pass. Wildberger (960) finds it unlikely that in parallel to ובלע (v 7) a pass. should be read. The Gk. versions have great difficulty with the passage. However, several (with Syr.) suggest reading ובלע, i.e., adding a conjunction.

8.b. לנצח, "(which) endures forever." σ´ (according to Eusebius) correctly translates εις τελος. But α´ (according to Marchalianus) and θ´ (according to Marchalianus and Syh.) as well as 1 Cor 15:54 translate εις νικος, "to victory." נצח means "victory" in Aramaic and Syriac. Jews speaking Aramaic have carried the meaning back for Hebrew (cf. Wildberger, 960), but this leaves the question open concerning the word's relation. Does it modify "he will swallow," or does it modify "the death"? Most translations have chosen the former. Its position in the sentence as well as the parallels suggests the latter.

8.c. LXX τοῦ λαοῦ, "the people." MT is to be confirmed here. But note that the antecedent of the Heb. pronoun is not defined. Most translations have "his," implying YHWH. However the parallelism makes it more likely to be "it," for "all the land."

Form/Structure/Setting

Attention turns to Jerusalem. The vision of chap. 6 is recalled. The dire prediction of an empty and desolate land has been fulfilled. We return to the throne room for matters of great moment.

The throne room of YHWH is portrayed on Mount Zion. This is the second of three such scenes in the Vision. Chap. 6 features the giving of YHWH's word to his messenger. This scene presents a banquet to announce YHWH's great deed. Chap. 66 portrays a tour of his new city, the new heavens and the new earth.

This throne scene has three elements: YHWH's appearance on his throne in glory before his elders (24:23) and the announcement of a banquet for all peoples (25:6), at which a heroic deed will be announced (25:7–8). The mighty deed will effect an end to the long chain of vengeance and curse that has plagued the land and all its peoples—an end to the reign of "the death" in the land.

A song of praise and thanks (25:1–5) adorns the throne scene. It is sung by the implied author and other individuals. Its outline is clear:

Address to YHWH (v 1*a*)
Adoration of YHWH (v 1*b*)
His wonderful acts—the reason for praise (v 1*cd*)
Detail: Destruction of a city (v 2)
Citation of praise from others (v 3; cf. 24:14–16)
Thanks for refuge (v 4*ab*)
Especially, a refuge from violence (v 4*c*–5)

This has been called a "city-song" because it cites a city's destruction and because it is thought to be a link in a chain of such city-songs (24:10–12; 26:5; 27:10). But the worship element of praise is more important here than the incidental reference to "the city." The latter places the song in context; the former demonstrates its form and function in the throne scene.

Comment

21 ביום ההוא, "in such a day." The scene of YHWH's day of judgment over all the powers of the earth (cf. 2:12–17) is recalled to set the stage for the final curse. פקד has sometimes been translated "visit" or "punish" but is probably more accurately understood as "decide the fate of."

Excursus: Decide One's Fate

Bibliography

André, G. *Determining the Destiny: PQD in the Old Testament.* ConBOT. OTS 16. Uppsala: Gleerup, 1980. ———. "פקד." *TWAT.* 6:708–23. **Fürst, H. P.** *Die göttliche Heimsuchung: Semasiologische Untersuchung eines biblichen Begriffes.* Rome, 1965. **Gehman, H. S.** "'Επισκέπομαι, ἐπίσκεψι, ἐπισκοπό, and ἐπισκοπή in the Septuagint in Relation to פקד and Other Hebrew Roots—A Case of Semantic Development Similar to That of Hebrew." *VT* 22 (1972) 197–207. **Grossfeld, B.** "The Translation of Biblical Hebrew פקד in the Targum, Peshitta, Vulgate and Setuagint." *ZAW* 96 (1984) 83–101. **Hooser, J. B. van.** "The Meaning of the Hebrew Root פקד in the Old Testament." Diss., Harvard, 1962. **Scharbert, J.** "Das Verbum PQD in der Theologie des Alten Testaments." *BZ* n.s. 4 (1960) 209–26. Reprinted in *WF* 125 (1972) 278–99. **Schottroff, W.** "פקד *pqd* heimsuchen." *THAT.* 2:466–86. **Spencer, J. R.** "*PQD,* the Levites, and Numbers 1–4." *ZAW* 110 (1998) 535–46.

פקד has defied satisfactory definition. Gesenius, BDB, and *HAL* suggest meanings like "visit, punish, inspect, call to account." But the variety of translations in the versions reflects their uncertainty about its meaning. Gunnel André *(Determining the Destiny)* has demonstrated that its basic meaning is "to determine the destiny, to destine, to assign." He also suggested as a basic meaning "observe exactly" with the conclusion or decision made on its basis (André, *TWAT,* 6:710). This range of meaning is cogent, especially for its use in the prophetic literature.

פקד and its derivatives occur eighteen times in the Vision, eight times in chaps. 23–27. It is the most meaningful word Hebrew possesses to define God's function in determining what will happen to a person or group in a given situation, whether they are under blessing or curse, or placed in battle or rescued from danger. God is pictured as the sovereign making decisions and carrying them out.

The idea is central in the prophets. Jeremiah employs the word repeatedly. The Vision of Isaiah makes use of it in key chapters. In chap. 10 Israel's fate is determined: destruction by the Assyrians. The world's destiny is fixed because of its evil and sin (13:11). YHWH's decision will be accompanied by thunder and earthquake (29:6). In 60:17 the decision is positive to Israel, establishing peace for her. In 62:6 YHWH destines keepers for Jerusalem.

The central and climactic position of chaps. 23–27 is emphasized by the repeated use of פקד. YHWH will determine Tyre's destiny after seventy years (23:17). The armies of the highlands and the kings of the lowlands will have their fate decided after many days (24:21–22). The climax is reached in chap. 26. YHWH's decisions had ruined the tyrants (v 14), and he had been determining Israel's destiny even in her distress (v 16). The great day of destiny is at hand when he will settle the fate of the inhabitants of the land in terms of their sins (v 21). In that day YHWH will determine the destiny of Leviathan (27:1).

פקד means to make a decision, to determine the fate of, the future of, someone or something. This includes judgment as well as providence. It fits God's sovereign activity of moment-by-moment decision making, his control over life and death, blessing and curse, success and failure, his disposition of individuals, peoples, and nations, as well as the heavenly host and the divine powers. It is also an appropriate term to describe his great judgment over the land and its peoples, including Israel and Jerusalem.

The word is parallel to God's work in establishing (שים) a course of action or a fate. That, too, is a sovereign activity of YHWH-King. In this act this sense occurs in 23:13, 25:2, and 27:9. The most prominent uses of שים are found in chaps. 28 (3x), 41–42 (10x), 50–51 (7x), and 57 (4x).

צבא המרום, "the army in the highlands" (v 21), may also be translated "the power in the heights." When the entire section is thought to be apocalyptic, this has been understood to refer to YHWH's overcoming a divine force in heaven; but when the passage is understood to be of the same character as the rest of the Vision, there is no reason to break out of the framework set by that context. In this sense it is far more fitting to understand this to be a reference to armies in the high plateaus and hill country of Syria/Palestine. The antithesis refers to the coastal lands of Phoenicia/Philistia and the lower Jordan Valley. Together they include the entire territory under discussion.

22 מרב ימים, "after sufficient days." Like the "seventy years" that Tyre will need to wait for its final verdict, the final judgment on the kings will come later. In the meantime they will be imprisoned. בור, "pit," is sometimes used as a synonym of שאול, "Sheol." If that were true here, it would be the first hint of the theme of death, which becomes prominent in the following scenes. It would also be the first indication in Scripture of a final judgment after death. But the term is also an indication of a stockade or dungeon, and it should probably not be pressed further.

23 וחפרה הלבנה, "may the moon be ashamed." M. Klopfenstein (*Scham und Schande nach dem Alten Testament,* ATANT 62 [Zurich: Zwingli, 1962] 82) suggests that when something is revealed to have no meaning, its pride is badly damaged and thus "is shamed." In comparison with the glory of YHWH, the sun and moon must recognize their meaninglessness. The phrase may be a formality used in announcing the throne appearance.

יהוה צבאות, "YHWH of Hosts." In this act, the full throne title appears only in this enthronement scene. מלך, "reigns," means that he is holding court. This is a sign that he is in full charge of events (cf. Pss 29:10; 93:2; *Comment* on 6:1).

בהר ציון ובירושלם, "on Mount Zion and in Jerusalem." The Vision has maintained throughout that YHWH's judgments on Israel and the land would preserve the integrity of Jerusalem as his "dwelling" and as the seat of his temple.

ונגד זקניו, "before his elders." In each of the heavenly throne scenes there are other beings surrounding YHWH's throne. Isa 6:2 calls them שׂרפים, "seraphim." 1 Kgs 22:21 calls them רוחות, "spirits." Job 1:6 calls them בני האלהים, "sons of God." Here they are called זקנים, "elders" (cf. Rev 4–19). They all seem to refer to the same beings who have the same functions.

כבוד, "in glory." In Isa 6:3 the whole land was proclaimed to be full of his glory. The phrase means that this is a full-dress royal occasion.

25:1 אלהי, "my God." The singer confesses to being a committed devotee of YHWH.

עשׂית פלא, "you have done a wonder." פלא, "wonder," is the word used in Exod 15:11; Pss 77:15 (14); 78:12 (11) for the exodus. Ps 88:11 (10) speaks of "wonders" God does for his worshipers in judgment and redemption.

עצות מרחוק, "things planned long ago." The phrase picks up the note of 23:9, accepting in faith that all of this is an act of God's faithfulness to his covenants, to his people, and most of all to himself and his strategy.

2 עיר, "a city." The Vision has described the destruction of more than one city. Babylon is outstanding in chaps. 13 and 21. This reference is probably symbolic of the end of the age of city-state culture. (See *Excursus: "The City"* [העיר] at *Comment* on 24:10.)

3 עם עז, "a strong people," respect God's consistent use of power in judgment.

4 דל . . . אביון, "the poor . . . the needy," see in God's actions concern for their plight.

5 שאון זרים, "the uproar of strangers." Palestine had been a prey for foreigners of all types. It was the adopted home of a long list of peoples before Moses took Israel to Canaan (Exod 3:17). The Philistines and others occupied cities in Palestine after Israel entered. More recent developments in Aram, Israel, and other states came about through the usurpation of power by foreigners.

6 משתה, "a feast." The royal invitation is extended to all peoples. It is to be held on Zion so that they can have an audience with YHWH of Hosts. On that occasion he will announce a great royal deed.

Excursus: The Divine Banquet

Bibliography

Davies, E. C. "The Significance of the Shared Meal in Luke-Acts." Ph.D. diss., Louisville, KY, Southern Baptist Theological Seminary, 1967. **Feelley-Harnik, G.** *The Lord's Table: Eucharist and Passover in Early Christianity.* Philadelphia: Univ. of Pennsylvania Press, 1981. **Jenkins, A. W.** "Eating and Drinking in the Old Testament." In *ABD.* 2:250–54. **MacMahon, C. T.** "Meals as Type-Scenes in the Gospel of Luke." Ph.D. diss., Louisvielle, KY: Southern Baptist Theological Seminary, 1987. **Sharon, D.** *Patterns of Destiny: Narrative Structures of Foundation and Doom in the Hebrew Bible.* Winona Lake, IN: Eisenbrauns, 2002.

Royalty and feasts go together in many contexts. Mythology knows of sumptuous feasts of the gods. These feasts celebrate a variety of things, and other gods are the usual guests. YHWH's feast will be for all peoples. He moves beyond the circle of his intimates, the elders, and issues a universal invitation. (Cf. Jesus' parable of the Father's feast in Matt 22:1–14.) This is in line with the Vision's view of all nations coming to worship in the temple (2:2) and all nations gathered to see God's glory (66:18).

God appears as the host of banquets in the Psalms (23:5; 30:9; 63:6; 65:5; 103:5; 132:15; cf. O. Keel, *Die Welt der altorientalischen Bildsymbolik und das Alte Testament* [Zurich: Benziger, 1974] 174).

In Isaiah this scene continues the confrontation with the kings in 24:21–22 and joins the list of heavenly scenes like those in 1:2–31 and 40:1–11.

6–7 בהר הזה, "on this mountain." Identifying YHWH's universal rule with Mount Zion is characteristic of the Vision. The phrase picks up the location from 24:23, stressing both the identical locality of the throne and the banquet, and the timing of the banquet with the throne appearance.

The great deed is announced. The action is described in three ways, all apparently referring to the one great divine-royal deed. It was customary for the king at his banquet to demonstrate his power by a heroic act. Marduk, for example, is pictured as having made a garment disappear and reappear (*Enuma Elish* IV, 28; *ANET,* 66).

YHWH's demonstrative deed was בלע, "to swallow up" (v 7), a garment that was appropriate to his character as Lord of life and to his guest list of all peoples. It was the הלוט, "shroud," one המסכה, "shadow," that lay heavy over all peoples and all nations. It was also appropriate to the time when the land lay so completely under the curse of death. The curse of the broken covenant filled the land (chap. 24) making it uninhabitable (24:6, 13, 17, and so on). בלע, "swallow," is often used of the dragon, Leviathan, or Tiamat, the great demoness of mythology. Note its use with Satan in the NT, "looking for someone to devour" (1 Pet 5:8 NIV). Here the devouring entities that are customarily set against God are themselves devoured. This strange term, used also in v 8, stands in contrast to the phrase "decide the fate." In the latter, YHWH's action is highly personal, the sovereign rationally settling issues, but here the imagery belongs to the curse concept of 24:6. The OT speaks of curses often, illustrating how they were spoken and put into effect. It says little or nothing about how they may be counteracted or terminated, but this is exactly what the "swallowing" by YHWH of Hosts will do. It will bring the awful curse to an end. It will make its baleful results cease. To accomplish this, nothing will do but that the entire contamination be totally eliminated.

8 Two other verbs are used for this act. He will מחה, "wipe," and he will יסיר, "remove." The three verbs together speak of removing or abrogating something or some things. What is to be swallowed, wiped away, or removed is described with five terms (four of the five are specific, with a definite article). Only דמעה, "a tear," is indefinite. The other four apparently refer to the same thing, indeed the same act. "The shroud," "the shadow," "the death," and "the disgrace" share their ominous and sad qualities. Each is qualified: "all the peoples," "all the nations," "that endures forever," "from all the land." But the first two—the shroud and the shadow—are only descriptive, not definitive.

המות, "the death," is the most substantive of them all, while "the disgrace of its people" is the most relevant to this context. The thought that this refers to "death" per se ignores the definite article. A specific death is to be swallowed up. A specific disgrace is to be removed. This death and this disgrace compose the shroud and the shadow over all the peoples, the very ones that had been invited to the feast. They are the peoples whose disgrace he will remove from the land.

Generations of violence had brought bloodguilt on the land. Like the land before the flood (Gen 6), it was destined to devastation and destruction, as the Vision had already described in great detail and summarized in 24:1. Truly this was a curse of perpetual death on all the land and all its inhabitants, a curse that fed on itself as new bloodguilt was incurred for each vengeful and rebellious act.

YHWH of Hosts decrees an end to all this, himself "swallowing" the entire matter: shroud, covering, death warrant, and disgrace. He lifts the burden of each of these from על, "upon," the peoples.

חרפת, "the disgrace" (v 8), or reproach, was the result of actions worthy of such bloodguilt. The word is a synonym for "guilt" and "contamination" in 24:5–6. It picks up the alliteration of the series of words in 25:5. It was understood to continue to influence the life of the perpetrator. The disgrace belonged to the people, but the land had felt the brunt of its terrible ban.

המות לנצח, "the death forever" (v 8). YHWH will completely end the permanent ban of death that had lain on the land (cf. 6:11–12). The curse cannot be reinvoked. It is the counterpart of the violation of ברית עולם, "the permanent covenant" (Isa 24:5; Gen 9:12).

These verses fulfill the same role in the Vision that God's promises to Noah (Gen 8:21) play in the flood narrative. There God promised never to curse the ground again because of humankind's sin. Rather, he will demand an accounting from humans for shed blood (Gen 9:6). Then he speaks of the permanent covenant with the land. In the Vision another age has come to a disastrous end. God avoids putting blame on the land. Its inhabitants (24:5) and its people (25:7) must bear the disgrace. So now he fulfills his covenant with the land. He raises the ban of death "from off" the land, swallowing up its effects forever.

The issue of death has surfaced in the Vision before. In 14:4–20 death and the grave are pictured as appropriate endings for the career of the king of Babylon. Similarly in 26:13–14 tyrants who have ruled Israel are seen as now dead. This stands in sharp contrast to the promise to Israel that "your dead will live." The issue of life and death, of God's gift of life, is the theme of chap. 38 and the illness of Hezekiah.

But the announcement here (v 8) is breathtaking! Surprising! Worthy of the King of kings! The great royal edict is portrayed as final. It is not a temporary reprieve or a delay of sentence. In a section that is so filled with violence and death, the dreadful unspoken fear that the cycle of bloodguilt and vengeance can never be broken has finally been brought into the open. YHWH of Hosts has announced that he will deal with it personally and permanently. He had taken steps to imprison the kings and their armies (24:22) to await their sentences. Now he decrees royal amnesty, removing the shrouded curse that had covered all the peoples, destroying the death-ban on the land.

אדני יהוה, "my Lord YHWH." The title changes; YHWH becomes more personal and is directly related to his subjects. This is fitting as the meaning of the astonishing announcement is made known.

דמעה מעל כל־פנים, "a tear from every face." What face had not felt the tear of grief? The experience of death is universal in every age. How much more in that time of violence and destruction! God's comfort was intended for those of all peoples who mourned, friend and foe alike.

עמו, "its people." This translation sees the land as the antecedent of the pronoun: the land's people. This fits the context and the meaning of all that has led up to this statement. But the antecedent has often been understood to be YHWH himself: YHWH's people. This would refer to Israel's sin, guilt, and disgrace. This interpretation is fitting for the passages that follow, which do refer to Israel and Jerusalem. It would pick up the inferences of 6:5, "people of unclean lips," the people with no comprehension or understanding of 1:2–3 who were capable of the acts recounted in the rest of chap. 1. The empty land predicted in 6:12 has now become a reality, and the people's disgrace is apparent. However, both meanings are fitting since Israel is also one of the peoples of the land. The people's guilt in regard to the land was also removed. Life and happiness would be possible again.

Explanation

The passage is the climax of the entire act. The cataclysmic events for Tyre and the whole land have peaked. In a throne appearance, in the full array and authority of his royal prerogative, YHWH announces that he will turn the course of events around; he will nullify the effect of the curse of death and all its implications. This puts a halt to the momentum of vengeance that has swept the land. It puts the initiative back in YHWH's hands to deal with the outstanding issues. It also gives hope to those whose confidence is in YHWH and who look forward to the restoration of life and hope through him. The NT picture of ultimate renewal borrows Isaiah's language (Rev 21:5).

The recognition here of a need to attack the situation on the level of the curse, as well as on the basis of God's specific decision, parallels a NT understanding that one role of blood-atonement on the cross is to nullify the cursed effects of accrued guilt. Another role, of course, is to implement the specific acts of judgment and forgiveness by God.

Response from a Yahwist (25:9–12)

Bibliography

Doyle, B. "A Literary Analysis of Isaiah 25:10*a*." In *Studies.* Ed. J. Van Ruiten and M. Vervenne. 173–93. **Zyl, A. H. van.** *The Moabites.* POS 3. Leiden: Brill, 1960. 158–59.

Translation

Heavens:	9 *And one will say*[a] *in that day:*	3
First Worshiper:	*See,*[b] *our God,*	3+3
	[c]*for whom*[c] *we waited, and*[d] *he will save us!*	
Second Worshiper:	*This is YHWH! We waited for him!*[d]	4+3
	Let us rejoice, and let us be glad[e] *in his salvation!*	
First Worshiper:	10 *Indeed YHWH's hand rests on this mountain.*	4+3+4
	And Moab will be trampled[a] *in its place*[b]	
	like a strawpile trampled[c] *in*[d] *a dung pit.*[e]	
Second Worshiper:	11 *He will spread his hands in the midst of it*	3+4
	as a swimmer spreads (his hands) to swim.	
	And he (YHWH) will cause his (Moab's) pride to fall	2+3
	along with the skill[a] *of his hands,*	
First Worshiper:	12 *when the fortification*[a]*—the secure height—*	2+2
	of your[b] *walls he has laid low,*[c]	
	has knocked down,[d]	1+3
	and has made them touch the earth—even the dust.	

Notes

9.a. 1QIsa[a] ואמרת, "you [sg.] will say." Also Syr. *wt'mr*. The meaning of an impersonal 3d person is not different.

9.b. 1QIsa[a] adds יהוה, "YHWH."

9.c-c. LXX 'Ἰδοὺ ὁ θεὸς ἡμῶν ἐφ ᾧ ἠλπίζομεν, "This is our God for whom we have waited," has understood זֶה to be a relative pronoun. Cf. *HebSyntax* §105*b;* GKC §138*g(a)*.

9.d-d. Missing in LXX. However, the Hebrew form is correct and meaningful. Cf. Wildberger, 970.

9.e. 1QIsa[a] נשמח, "we will be glad." It lacks MT's cohortative ending, which is parallel to "let us rejoice."

10.a. 1QIsa[a] ונדש, a defective reading for MT's *plene* form of the *nip'al* pf.: "it will be trod upon." σ´ και αλοησομεν understood it as a *qal* form: "and we will thresh" (Wildberger, 970). α´ και αλοηθησεται, "and it will be threshed," and LXX καὶ καταπατηθήσεται, "and it will be trod upon," translate MT.

10.b. MT תחתיו is lit. "under him." It was a problem for the versions. LXX omits it. Tg. באתרהיו. Wildberger (970) suggests a noun "in his place," thus "in the land where he lives" (cf. 2 Sam 7:10).

10.c. 1QIsa[a] כחדוש (i.e., ח for ה) is apparently a scribal error. The form is unusual for a *nip'al* inf. const., הִדּוּשׁ for הִדּוֹשׁ, but see Bauer-Leander §56*u*.

10.d. Q במו stands for the simple ב, "in." K reads במי, "water," but this does not fit the following word.

10.e. מדמנה is apparently derived from דמן, "manure," and thus means "a manure pit." Isa 10:31 lists a town by this name, but not in Moab. Jer 48:2 lists a place מדמן in the land of Moab. Kimchi suggested that this place is meant here, although Wildberger (971) thinks this may be a play on that name (cf. van Zyl, *Moabites,* 80).

11.a. MT ארבות is challenged by many both as to correct form and as to meaning. Cf. *HAL* "holes" or "hatches," *DCH* "windows." See discussion in Wildberger (971), who suggests "skill" as a translation.

12.a. *BHS* suggests eliminating ומבצר, "fortification." Wildberger (971) defends it as part of this fulsome style. Three nouns are followed by three verbs. MT divides them that way: 3+5. A different division here tries to get a better grasp of the awkward sentence. The nouns come first, a reversal of normal Heb. order, suggesting a subordinate clause. The subject must return to YHWH, or his hand, since the 2d-person form indicates that Moab is addressed.

12.b. Note the change of person from 3d to 2d.

12.c. Missing in LXX.

12.d. 1QIsa[a] has יגיע, impf., but keeps the pf. form for השפיל and השח. MT apparently notes the completion of Moab's degradation, whereas 1QIsa[a] expects part of it to still be fulfilled (see Wildberger, 971). However, the syntax puts the temporal factor of all the verbs under the dominant impf. of v 10.

Form/Structure/Setting

The foundation of the scene is a hymn of thanksgiving (v 9). It is closely related to vv 6–8 by "in that day" as a response to the throne announcement. The announcement is greeted as the answer to prayer, which has justified dependence and patience and which calls for rejoicing because YHWH's "hand," his power and his blessing, "rests on this mountain."

The hymn is expanded by application to a nearby problem: Moab. YHWH's assertion of power in Jerusalem calls for the resubjugation of Moab, as in the days of David.

Comment

9 הנה, "see," points to the throne scene that preceded. אלהינו, "our God," lays claim to the great king. The hymn is a common one, like Isa 33:2; Pss 25:5; 40:2; Gen 49:18; Jer 14:22.

10 תנוח יד יהוה, "YHWH's hand rests." The phrase is not used elsewhere but is certainly kin to the "Zion theology" of the Psalms. בהר הזה, "on this mountain," ties the hymn to the previous passages (24:23; 25:6, 7). The verse interprets the throne scene to say that YHWH's presence on Mount Zion means his power will be upon Jerusalem and its government. Moab will be trampled. The speaker will claim his right to a victory over Moab.

11 The verse has a strong tone of irony or satire. The subject has changed from YHWH to Moab. Note the way the word יד, "hand(s)," is used. While YHWH's hand is on Mount Zion, Moab's hands will be working the manure pit. He loses his pride through the skill with which his hands "work" manure. One is reminded of the way that fresh cow dung in India is made into patties and slapped onto walls to dry for fuel.

12 The address turns in second person to Moab. The figure of the dung pit is changed to realistic language.

Explanation

Jerusalem is expected to behave piously in the day of YHWH's throne appearance, but instead the witnesses hear Jerusalem claiming a petty right of sovereignty over its small neighbor, Moab. With childish glee she is demanding, in barnyard terms, the humiliation of Judah's former vassal.

The same littleness that follows so much of her response throughout the Vision is attributed to Jerusalem here. While God is tending to weighty matters that involve the world of that day, the end of an age and the beginning of a new one, Jerusalem's attention is fixed on a spiteful provincial rivalry. The scene pictures God's frustration and elicits the reader's disappointment.

Response: Song of the Judeans (26:1–19)

Bibliography

Beeston, A. F. L. "The Hebrew Verb *SPT.*" *VT* 8 (1958) 216–17. **Birkeland, H.** "The Belief in Resurrection of the Dead in the Old Testament." *ST* 3 (1950–51) 60–78. **Blenkinsopp, J.** "Fragments of Ancient Exegesis in an Isaian Poem." *ZAW* 93 (1981) 51–62. **Day, J.** "A Case of Inner Scriptural Interpretation: The Dependence of Isaiah xxvi.13–xxvii.11 on Hosea xiii.4–vix.10 (Engl. 9) and Its Relevence to Some Theories of the Redaction of the 'Isaiah Apocalypse.'" *JTS* 31 (1980) 309–19. Reprinted in *Writing and Reading.* Ed. C. C. Broyles and C. A. Evans. 1:357–68. ———. "*tal ôrôt* in Isaiah 26,19." *ZAW* 90 (1978) 265–69. **Doyle, B.** "Fertility and Infertility in Isaiah 24–27." In *New Things.* Ed. F. Postma et al. 77–88. **Driver, G. R.** "Mythical Monsters in the Old Testament." In *Studi orientalistici in Honore di G. L. della Vida.* Rome: Pontifical Biblical Institute, 1956. 1:234–49. **Emerton, J. A.** "Notes on Two Verses in Isaiah (26:16 and 66:17)." In *Prophecy.* FS G. Fohrer. BZAW 150. Berlin: De Gruyter, 1980. 12–25. **Fabry, H.-J.** "*nebela.*" *TDOT.* 9:156. **Fouts, D. M.** "A Suggestion for Isaiah xxvi 16." *VT* 41 (1991) 471–75. **Gryson, R.** "'Enfanter un esprit de salut': Histoire du texte d'Isaïe 26:17–18." *RTL* 27 (1996) 25–46. **Helfmeyer, F. J.** "'Deine Toten—Meine Leichen': Heilzusage und Annahme in Jes 29,19." In *Bausteine biblischer Theologie.* FS G. J. Botterweck, ed. H.-J. Fabry. BBB 50. Cologne: Hanstein, 1977. 245–58. **Humbert, P.** "La rosée tombe en Israel." *TZ* 13 (1957) 487–93. **Irwin, W. H.** "Syntax and Style in Isaiah 26." *CBQ* 41 (1979) 240–61. **Johnson, D. G.** *From Chaos to Restoration: An Integrative Reading of Isaiah 24–27.* JSOTSup 61. Sheffield: JSOT Press, 1988. **Kaminka, A.** "Le développement des idées du prophète Isaïe et l'unité de son livre VIII: L'authenticité des chapîtres xxiv à xxvii." *REJ* 81 (1925) 27–36. **Ploeg, R. P. J. van der.** "L'espérance dans l'Ancien Testament." *RB* 61 (1954) 481–507. **Sawyer, J. F. A.** "Hebrew Words for the Resurrection of the Dead." *VT* 23 (1973) 218–34. **Schmitz, P. C.** "The Grammar of Resurrection in Isaiah 26:19*a-c.*" *JBL* 122 (2003) 145–49. **Schwarz, G.** "'. . . Tau der Lichter . . .'?" *ZAW* 88 (1976) 280–81. **Snoek, J.** "Discontinuity between Present and Future in Isaiah 26:7–21." In *New Things.* Ed. F. Postma et al. 211–18. **Sysling, H.** *Tehiyyat Ha-Metim: The Resurrection of the Dead in the Palestinian Targums of the Pentateuch and Parallel Traditions in Classical Rabbinic Literature.* Tübingen: Mohr Siebeck, 1996. 72–73. **Virgulin, S.** "La risurrezione dei Morti in Is. 26,14–19." *BO* 14 (1972) 273–90. **Wahl, O.** "Wir haben eine befestigste Stadt: Botschaft von Jes 26:1–6." In *Ich bewirke das Heil und erschaffe das Unheil (Jesaja 45,7): Studien zur Botschaft der Propheten.* FS L. Ruppert, ed. F. Diedrich and B. Willmes. FB 88. Würzburg: Echter, 1998. 459–81. **Wieringen, A. L. H. M. van.** "'I' and 'We' before 'Your' Face: A Communication Analysis of Isaiah 26:7–21." In *Studies in Isaiah 24–27: The Isaiah Workshop.* Ed. H. J. Bosman et al. Leiden: Brill, 2000. 239–51.

Translation

Narrator:	1 *In that day*	2
	this[a] *song is sung*[b]	3+2
	in the land of Judah:	
Chorus:	*We have a strong*[c] *city!*	3+2+2
	It gives structure[d] *to salvation*	
	(with) walls and bulwarks.	
	2 *Open the gates*[a]	2+3+2
	that a righteous nation may enter,	
	observing faithful deeds.	
	3 [a]*(From) a dependent*[b] *attitude*[a]	2+3+3
	you form[c] *peace, peace,*[d]	
	when one's confidence (is) in you.[e]	
	4 *Trust in YHWH on and on*	3+3+2
	for in Yah,[a] *YHWH,*	
	(there is) a rock (for) ages (to come).	
Speaker:	5 *Indeed, he has humbled*[a] *those living in the height.*	4+3
First Echo:	*He makes a lofty city fall.*[b]	
Second Echo:	*He makes it fall*[b] *to earth.*	2+2
Third Echo:	*He makes it even touch the dust.*	
First Echo:	6 *A foot*[a] *tramples it—*	2+2+2
Second Echo:	*feet of one oppressed,*	
Third Echo:	*steps of poor ones.*	
Speaker:	7 *A way for the righteous (is on) level places.*	3+4
Echoes:	*You smooth*[a] *level*[b] *the path of the righteous.*[c]	
Chorus:	8 *Surely, (in) the way of your judgments,*[a]	3+2
	YHWH, we wait on you.[b]	
	For your name and your memorial[c]	2+2
	(are) [d]*the desire of (our) soul.*[d]	
Solo:	9 *My soul, I wait for you in the night.*	3+3
	Surely, (by) my spirit within me,[a] *I seek you.*	
Speaker:	[b]*Indeed, when your judgments belong to the land,*[b]	4+4
	they teach righteousness to the world's inhabitants.	
First Echo:	10 *A wicked one shown mercy*	2+3
	does not learn righteousness.	
Second Echo:	*In a land*[a] *of honest (persons) he does wrong.*	3+3
	He has no fear of YHWH's majesty.	
Third Echo:	11 *YHWH, your hand is raised,*	3+1
	but he does not envision it.	
First Echo:	[a]*Let them envision (it)!* [b]*And let them be shamed*[b]	2+2
	(by) a people's zeal.[a]	
Second Echo:	*Indeed, let fire (reserved for) your*[c] *adversaries consume them!*	4
Chorus:	12 *YHWH, you provided*[a] *peace*[b] *for us.*	4+4+2
	But also, all[c] *your works*	
	you have performed for us.	
	13 *YHWH, our God,*	2+3
	masters, other than yourself, have owned us.[a]	

	But even (when we were) apart from you,	2+2
	we memorialized your name.	
First Echo:	14 *Dead do not live.*	3+3
Second Echo:	*Ghosts do not rise up.*	
Speaker:	*Truly*[a] *you decide their fate and then you destroy them.*	3+3
	Then you make all memory of them disappear.[b]	
First Echo:	15 *You have brought increase for the nation, O YHWH.*	3+3+3
Second Echo:	*You have brought increase*[a] *for the nation.*	
	You have gained (it) glory.[b]	
Third Echo:	*You have extended all borders of land.*	4
A Tattletale:	16 *YHWH, in the (time of) distress they*	
	(sought to) decide fate (for) you.[a]	3+2+2
	They (sought to) deter[b] *by a whispered charm*	
	your chastening of him.	
Chorus:	17 *As a pregnant woman who draws near to birthing*	4+3+4
	writhes,[a] *cries out because of her birth pangs,*	
	so were we before you, YHWH.	
First Group:	18 *We may have been pregnant. We may have writhed.*	2
	Just the same, we will give birth to wind.	3+3+3
Second Group:	*As for deliverance,*[a] *we will bring the land none.*	
Third Group:	*The world's population will not*[b] *fall.*[c]	
YHWH:	19 *Your dead will live!*	2+2
	My corpses[a] *will rise!*	
Herald:	*Awake*[b] *and sing joyfully,*[c]	2+2
	you that live in dust.	
	For[d] *the dew of lights*[d] *(will be) your dew.*	4+3
	And the land will let fall (the) ghosts.	

Notes

1.a. 1QIsa[a] הזות for MT הזה, a fem. pronoun "this" for the masculine.

1.b. 1QIsa[a] ישיר, "one will sing."

1.c. 1QIsa[a] עוז for MT עֹז, "strong." The meaning is the same.

1.d. MT יָשִׁית, "it gives structure." Tg. יתמם and Vg. *ponetur* both presume a passive form like יוּשַׁת. Wildberger argues that the subject is YHWH, but MT should be kept.

2.a. 1QIsa[a] שעריך, "your gates."

3.a-a. Origen's *Hexapla* transliterated יצר, "shape," as ιεσρο, which apparently implied a reading of יצרו(ו), "his mind" or "form." Ibn Ezra paraphrased מי שיצרו סמוך עליך אתה השם תצרנו בשלום, "the one whose mind is founded on thee, you will keep the name (of that one) in peace."

3.b. סמוך implies "dependence, leaning, being supported," and is passive.

3.c. MT points תִּצֹּר, i.e., from the root נצר, "keep." The same consonants can be pointed תְּצַר from יצר, "shape" or "form," like the first word of the line. These words call to mind the potter shaping his clay.

3.d. LXX and Syr. omit one שלום, "peace." Such repetition is common in these chapters. Both should be kept.

3.e. MT בָּטוּחַ, "being trusted," is a pass. ptc. The same root in different form begins the next verse. LXX translates only the second of the two with ἤλπισαν, "they trusted," suggesting the first was lost to haplography. Vg. *quia in te speravimus*, "because we have trusted in you." *Hexapla* χι βακ βατιου transliterates MT כי בך בטוח. α´ οτι επ αυτω πεποιθασι, "that in him they have trusted." Tg. ארי במימרך אתרחיצו, "for we set our trust in your word." *BHK*[3] suggests emending to בָּטוֹחַ, "trusting," an inf. abs. But Wildberger (976) and *HAL* note that Ps 112:7 uses בָּטֻחַ to mean "confident," supporting Marti's observation that בָּטוּחַ follows סמוך in emphasizing the firmness of trust, the fixed attitude of confidence.

4.a. The presence of both ביה, "in YH," and יהוה, "YHWH," raises questions. LXX translates ὁ θεὸς ὁ μέγας ὁ αἰώνιος, "God, the great, the eternal." This appears to be paraphrase rather than translation. α´ οτι εν τω κυριω κυριος ο στερεωσας τους αιωνας, "for in the Lord, the Lord who has established the eons." *BHS* and *BHK*³ suggest deleting ביה. Wildberger (976) proposes transposing כי and ביה and taking the latter into the first half of the verse, but that simply adds to an already full stich. A. Guillaume ("Psalm LXVIII.5," *JTS* 13 [1962] 322–23) suggests pointing according to an Arabic verb *bāha* as בָּיהּ, meaning "he remembered, he was mindful of," but that is neither likely nor helpful. This, like "peace" in v 3, is an example of the tendency to repeat words in this section.

5.a. 1QIsaª השח is apparently a scribal error.

5.b. The virtual repetition of words again raises questions. The first is missing in LXX, Syr., and 1QIsaª. Tg. translates the first with מאך, "lower, humble," and the second with רמה, "high, be high." So *BHK*³ suggests emending the first to read יַפִּילֶהָ, "he makes it fall." Gray, Ehrlich *(Randglossen)*, Fohrer, Kaiser, Wildberger, and others would shift the *'atnakh*, drawing the first back into the first half of the verse. This is much more helpful and is adopted here.

6.a. רגל, "foot," has no translation in LXX, Syr., or Tg., or equivalent in 1QIsaª. Wildberger (976) defends it as necessary for the style of the passage.

7.a. תפלס, "you smooth," is understood (by Fohrer, Kaiser, Wildberger) to govern a relative clause; so "straight is the path, which you smooth for the righteous." This can only be done by ignoring the Masoretic accents that relate מעגל צדיק, "the path of the righteous," to each other. 1QIsaª has תפלט, "you deliver," perhaps because the scribe did not know the infrequently used word פלס (so Wildberger).

7.b. ישר, "level," is missing in LXX. With Wildberger (982), it is to be kept. NIV "O upright One" and NRSV "O Just One" have taken it as a vocative address to God, but the repetition of the previous word makes this unlikely.

7.c. 1QIsaª צדק for MT צדיק, "righteous," but there is no change in meaning.

8.a. Wildberger (983) correctly takes ארח משפטיך as an adv. acc., "in the way of your judgments."

8.b. 1QIsaª קוינו leaves out the suffix "on you."

8.c. 1QIsaª לתורתך, "for your law."

8.d-d. LXX omits. Syr. and some MSS of Tg. appear to have read נַפְשֵׁנוּ, "our souls." The translation of נפש with "soul" is done with reluctance since it means something very different from the Greek ψυχή.

9.a. *BHK*³, following Guthe, emends to בַּבֹּקֶר, "in the morning," to balance "in the night" of the first stich. However, MT makes sense and is fitting.

9.b-b. LXX διότι φῶς προστάγματά σου ἐπὶ τῆς γῆς, "because your appointments are light upon the earth." This has led Procksch and Rudolph *(Jesaja 24–27)* to suggest emending כי כאשר, "indeed when," to read כָּאֹר, "when it lights up." This translation follows MT.

10.a. LXX, Tg., and Syr. add the definite article, but for a reading in const. state this is unnecessary.

11.a-a. *BHS* suggests deletion. Wildberger (983) complains of such lack of understanding for the text's style.

11.b-b. LXX expands to read γνόντες δὲ αἰσχυνθήσονται· ζῆλος λήμψεται λαὸν ἀπαίδευτον, "but, knowing, they will be ashamed: zeal will seize an ignorant people." Wildberger characterizes it as "full of fantasy but hardly an accurate translation."

11.c. The suffix is missing in LXX, but necessary here.

12.a. The meaning of שפת is agreed. See Wildberger's discussion (984).

12.b. Bruno suggests emending to שִׁלּוּם, "revenge" (cf. *BHS*).

12.c. Bruno suggests emending to כְּגְמֻל, "like recompense," by referring to Syr. But apparently Syr. does not support the changes (cf. Wildberger, 983). Neither is needed.

13.a. LXX adds οὐκ οἴδαμεν, "we did not know," so *BHS* suggests inserting בַּל נֵדַע. The translation follows MT.

14.a. לָכֵן in the sense of "therefore" does not fit well here. Perhaps the meaning of "indeed, surely" (*HAL*, #3, "assuredly") is better.

14.b. 1QIsaª ותאסר, "you imprison." But MT is supported by LXX καὶ ἦρας, "and you remove, destroy," Tg. ותוביד, and Syr. *w'wbdt*. Wildberger (984) notes that אבד, "destroy," is related to זכר, "memory," in Ps 9:7 and to שם, "name," in Ps 41:6.

15.a. The second יספת לגוי, "you have brought increase for the nation," is missing in one MS. Wildberger (984) properly recognizes this as haplography in that MS and notes that the repetition fits the style here.

15.b. LXX has apparently read נִכְבָּדֹת, "glory," for the sense "you have brought increase of glory for the nation." A similar reading occurs in Ps 87:3. Procksch and *BHS* recommend emendation. The change is not necessary.

16.a. Two MSS offer פקדנוך, "we decide your fate." Often the translation "visit" for פקד is given as in Judg 15:1 and Ezek 23:21.

16.b. צָקוּן, "they deter," has been a problem for the translations. LXX ἐν θλιψει, "in affliction," Vg. *in tribulatione,* and Syr. *bḥbwšj'* seem all to have read it as a noun. It can be pointed צְקוֹן in const., meaning "magic power," as Dillmann, Duhm, and Ehrlich *(Randglossen)* have done. Cf. NRSV "they poured out a prayer." Wildberger (984) is correct in looking for a verb form here and suggests צעקנו, "we were chastened" (cf. REB; cf. *HAL*). Gesenius and Delitzsch consider it 3 c. pl. pf. from צוק + *nun* (cf. Deut 8:3, 16). Such a root exists: I *hip'il* "constrain, press upon"; II "pour out, melt." BDB assumes II but emends to צְקוֹן, "constraint of magic"; *HAL* assumes I but emends with Wildberger or the versions. *Translation* here preserves MT צָקוּן and reads with Gesenius as pf. 3 c. pl., "they constrained, deterred."

17.a. LXX lacks the word.

18.a. 1QIsa[a] ישעתך, "your deliverance." Maintain MT.

18.b. C. F. Whitley ("The Positive Force of בל," *ZAW* 84 [1972] 215–16) suggests that בל has a positive meaning here. Wildberger correctly rejects the idea of opposite meanings for בל in the same verse.

18.c. 1QIsa[a] יפולו for MT יפלו. Kutscher (*Language and Linguistic Background,* 331) calls it a pausal form, but Wildberger (985) insists it is an accented penultima form. It is often assumed that this can be an idiom for birth or even for miscarriage because of the context. The meaning is obscure.

19.a. *BHS* follows Syr. *wšldjhwn* in emending to נִבְלֹתָם, "their corpses." Wildberger (985) thinks MT contains a gloss—a note by a reader who wants his own body included in the resurrection. But if the speaker is God himself, the 1st-person suf. lays claim to all the corpses of the righteous as his own.

19.b. 1QIsa[a] יקיצו, "let them awake." LXX translates an ind. fut. ἐγερθήσονται, "they will awake."

19.c. 1QIsa[a] וירננו, "and they shall sing" (pf.). α´ αινεσουσιν, "they will praise." LXX εὐφρανθήσονται, "they will rejoice." Yet MT is consistent in its address to those "who dwell in the dust." The impv. should be maintained.

19.d-d. "The dew of lights." Schwarz (*ZAW* 88 [1976] 280–81) suggests the translation "dew of the spirits of the dead," but this has little to commend it. Cf. Ps 139:12 with "light" in the sg. P. Humbert (*TZ* 13 [1957] 491) suggests the special meaning "luminous particles."

Form/Structure/Setting

The chorus is strong in this scene. Pilgrims from the land of Judah approach the Holy City during the uneasy calm that has settled over the land. The pilgrims try to make this a normal festival occasion such as had been the custom in Jerusalem before the bad times, but the pall of war still hangs heavy in the air. Solo voices represent a teacher, or the prophet/implied author, as well as other pilgrims with different moods. Then YHWH appears with his herald. His announcement picks up the themes of his reaction to the death of his people (25:7–8) and of further judgments (23:17; 24:21).

The opening song (vv 1*b*–4) is a pilgrim's song. The themes of the city, the gates, the righteous, and trust in YHWH are typical. Antiphonal statements develop the themes of their troubled times: "he has humbled those living in the height," v 5; YHWH makes "level the path of the righteous," v 7; "your judgments . . . teach righteousness," v 9. There are responses to each of these. The antiphonal exchange continues with a protest: "A wicked one . . . does not learn," vv 10–11; "YHWH . . . provided peace for us," though foreign lords reigned, vv

12–13. The assembly begins to be unruly with critical observations in vv 14–16 and a despairing chorus in vv 17–18.

This is brought to an abrupt end by an epiphany (vv 19–21). YHWH and his herald appear to the group with an astonishing announcement in line with that of 25:8. They are called to rejoice, then warned to return to their homes, for YHWH is about to emerge from Jerusalem for judgment on the land. Obviously, this is not a fitting time for entertaining pilgrims.

Thus the chapter consists of three formal structures. The pilgrim song (vv 1*b*–4) opens the scene. The dialogue of the pilgrims (5–18) is the body of the scene. The epiphany (vv 19–21) brings it to a close.

Comment

1 ביום ההוא, "in that day," refers to the time of the great throne appearance in 24:23–25:8. עיר עז, "a strong city," is Jerusalem, the goal of the pilgrimage. It stands in contrast to "the ruined city" of 24:10, 12 and 25:2.

2 The שערים, "gates," are those of Jerusalem (cf. Ps 24:7). The צדיק, "righteous," and those שמר אמנים, "observing faithful deeds," are the pilgrims fulfilling their vows.

3 יצר סמוך, "a dependent attitude," refers to the willing and malleable spirit of the worshiper, one not willful or rebellious. The other requirement is that God be trusted. Of such, God does indeed form peace.

5–6 The processional dialogue resumes the theme of the destroyed city (24:10, 12; 25:2). The "lofty city" recalls the picture of the high and mighty ones who will be brought low (2:11–18) and of the mighty king who would be brought down to Sheol (14:11). The verse implies that the city was guilty of oppressing the poor.

7 A theme from the pilgrim psalms stresses that the path of the "righteous" (the pilgrim) will be smooth and level (cf. 40:3).

8 The chorus confesses that "the way of God's judgments" requires patient hope, which a solo voice fervently repeats (v 9).

9 The teacher, or prophet/implied author, reflects that God's judgments are necessary in order for the "world's inhabitants" to learn "righteousness." The implication is that they need something that the faithful pilgrims already know. It also implies that God's judgments are intended for other peoples, not Israel. At this point the discussion begins to get out of hand as it turns their attention to the world's inhabitants.

10–11 The pilgrims see little chance that the wicked can be changed, much less learn righteousness. The wicked are blamed because they do not recognize God's uplifted hand. This is exactly the criticism that the Vision has leveled against Israel/Judah from the beginning. The people are "blind, deaf, and without understanding." Here the pilgrims can see that in the wicked, but not in themselves.

12 The pilgrims get back on track with a confession that YHWH has in fact provided peace for them. In the midst of violence and turmoil they have survived.

13 A second verse notes that it has not been easy under foreign domination, but they have continued to worship YHWH.

14 The reference to other "masters" in v 13 undoubtedly refers to the Assyrian emperors. The ones who brought this up are rebuked for having stirred up the ghosts that had been laid to rest. It is not necessary to mention them, for "ghosts do not rise up." The teacher picks up the point and directs the thought to God, implying praise for his control of them: "You decide their fate and then you destroy them." The teaching recalls 24:21–22, where the kings and armies are imprisoned against the day of their judgment. The teacher then admonishes the speakers that God has made all memory of the masters disappear. It is not necessary to mention them, especially not in God's presence.

15 An objection is raised. גוי, "the nation," would normally be used for someone other than Israel. Here it would properly be related to the other masters and must be the Mesopotamian empires. YHWH did allow the nation (Assyria, then Babylon) to grow, "gain glory," and "extend all borders of land." Note the protests on the same subject in 10:7–11. It is hard to see and understand the workings of God in history from the perspective of only a few years. The Vision calls for us to trace it through the centuries, three centuries.

16 פקדוך, "they (sought to) decide fate (for) you." The literal translation "they judged you," addressed to God, does not fit the context. The references here seem to be to the practice of magic and sorcery. In a time of distress someone tried to take God's place and assume responsibility for determining fate by the use of spells. It is not clear who is accused, whether the foreign masters or some of the Israelites. It is probably the latter.

17 The distress and confusion of the times are compared to a woman in childbirth. Doyle sees four interrelated metaphors in these verses: woman in childbirth, corpses, dew, and the land. They all point to the people's inability to effect their own salvation. He thinks of a historical application, not eschatological.

18 Cynical rejoinders indicate the despair of the times. יפלו, "fall," has sometimes been understood to mean "be born." At this point the mood of the pilgrimage has been turned away from the pious thoughts with which it began.

19 The pilgrims are interrupted by the appearance of YHWH and his herald. One may imagine a scene like that in Acts 9:3. As the pilgrims fall back because of the bright epiphany, God speaks: "Your dead will live! My corpses will rise!" He reasserts the announcement made at the banquet on his mountain (25:7–8). It is significant that the dead are recognized as belonging to Israel and to YHWH. This does not contradict the statement of v 14 that "dead do not live." That was said of foreign masters whom God had condemned to be forgotten. A distinction is made between them and these that belong to Israel and to God. God has decided their fate, too. They will live!

The herald addresses the dead, calling for them to "awake and sing." טל, "dew," is a very important element in Palestine's ecosystem. During the long dry months it is the only moisture the vegetation receives. It became a symbol for life. Light is also an important symbol of life and well-being (cf. 9:1 [2]; 42:6, 16; 58:8, 10; J. Hempel, *Die Lichtsymbolik im Alten Testament,* StG 13 [Heidelberg, 1960] 352–68). Egyptian texts claim a heavenly origin for dew. It is the tears of Horus and Thot and bears the power of resurrection in itself (J. de Savignac, "La rosée solaire de l'ancienne Egypte," *NC* 6 [1954] 345–53). Wildberger (998) suggests the meaning of טל אורת, "dew of lights," to be the "dew that brings life, salvation, and happiness."

Explanation

By using the device of a pilgrimage scene, the Vision has presented the dilemma of Judean faithful worshipers. They want to go to Jerusalem and worship YHWH. They want to believe and repeat the usual rituals of faith in YHWH to bring peace and safety. But they have also experienced the heel of the invader and the tyrant. They have seen what happened to their neighbors and their friends over a long time. They have lived with the constant fact of death all around them for three-quarters of a century. It is not surprising that pious songs are mixed with cynical observations and that despair lies not far beneath the surface of their thoughts.

The epiphany is dramatic and powerful. Once more they are asked to wait a little while. The wrath is not quite finished. But they are assured that God's terrible acts are effectively dealing with the curse of death that has hung over the land so long.

Excursus: YHWH and Death

Bibliography

Bailey, L. R., Sr. *Biblical Perspectives on Death.* Philadelphia: Fortress, 1979. **Birkeland, H.** "The Beliefs in Resurrection of the Dead in the Old Testament." *ST* 3 (1950–51) 60–78. **Boer, M. de.** *The Defeat of Death: Apocalyptic Eschatology in 1 Corinthians 15 and Romans 5.* Sheffield: JSOT Press, 1988. **Botterweck, G. B.** "Marginalien zum alt: Auferstehungsglauben." *WZKM* 54 (1957) 1–8. **Fohrer, G.** "Das Geschick des Menschen nach dem Tode in Alten Testament." *KD* 12 (1968) 249–62. **Haenchen, E.** "Auferstehung im Alten Testament." In *Die Bibel und wir.* Tübingen: Mohr, 1968. 73–90. **König, F.** *Zarathustras Jenseitsvorstellungen und das Alte Testament.* Vienna: Herder, 1964. 214–40. **Krieg, M.** *Todesbilder im Alten Testament: Oder 'Wie die Alten den Tod gebildet.'* Zurich: Theologischer Verlag, 1988. **Martin-Achard, R.** *De la mort à la résurrection.* Neuchâtel: Delachaux & Niestlé, 1956. 101–12. **Nötscher, F.** *Altorientalischer und alttestamentlicher Auferstehungsglauben.* Würzburg: Becker, 1926. 154–59. **Preuss, H. D.** "'Auferstehung' in Texten alttestamentlicher Apokalyptik (Jes 26:7–19, Dan 12:1–4)." *Linguistische Theologie* 3 (1972) 101–72. **Rost, L.** "Alttestamentliche Wurzeln der ersten Auferstehung." In *In memoriam Ernst Lohmeyer.* Ed. W. Schmauch. Stuttgart: Evangelisches Verlagswerk, 1951. 67–72. **Savignac, J. de.** "La rosée solaire de l'ancienne Égypte." *NC* 6 (1954) 345–53. **Sawyer, J. F. A.** "Hebrew Words for the Resurrection of the Dead." *VT* 13 (1973) 218–34. **Stemberger, G.** "Das Problem der Auferstehung im Alten Testament." *Kairos* 14 (1972) 273–90. **Tromp, N. J.** *Primitive Conceptions of Death and the Netherword in the Old Testament.* Rome: Pontifical Biblical Institute, 1969. **Vawter, B.** "Intimations of Immortality and the Old Testament." *JBL* 91 (1972) 158–71. **Virgulin, S.** "La risurrezione dei morti in Isa 26:14–19." *BeO* 14 (1972) 49–60. **Wächter, L.** *Der Tod im Alten Testament.* Stuttgart: Calwer, 1967. **Zolli, E.** "Il canto dei morti risorti e il ms. DSS in Isa 26:18." *Sef* 12 (1952) 375–78.

The size of the bibliography is a sign of the interest that a discussion of the resurrection in the OT awakens. But is the interest due to the content of the OT? Or is it a carry-back of interest from later times, especially the NT?

The issue in this act has more to do with the question of whether YHWH can be trusted with the fate of Israel and the welfare of its people than it does with the doctrine of life after death. The topic of death and the assurance that all matters of life and death are firmly in YHWH's hands are clearly central here.

In a book that is so filled with violence and destruction, it is not surprising that the theme of death would have considerable attention. Words using the roots מות, "die," and הרג, "kill," are spotted at various places in the book to provide a very serious reflection on God's relation to death. Tracing these words will certainly not be a complete study, but they will give us an entrance into it.

Time divisions in the early acts of the Vision are marked by the death years of kings (6:1; 14:28), while 38:1–20 is concerned with Hezekiah's mortal illness. The temptation in times of distress to resort to necromancy and spiritualism is noted in 8:19 and in 26:16.

Serious treatment of the subject begins in chap. 14. Death is here seen as the great leveler of humans. The taunting song is directed to the king of Babylon, who considered himself the greatest of all, perhaps even a god. Now he has been cut down and is dead just like any man. All Sheol prepares to meet him, saying with glee, "You have weakened as we (did)" (v 10). The king's ambition is contrasted with his helplessness in death; he does not even get a proper burial (vv 19–20).

This reminder that death sets limits on the power and ambition of even the most awesome of tyrants recurs in 26:14. The limit to the length of life is part of God's control of events (cf. also Gen 6:3). The Lord reminds the people that the tyrants of which they complain are already dead. Funeral preparations have already been made for Assyria's king (30:33).

In chap. 22 Jerusalem is in crisis. There are dead, but not from battle (v 2). There is a crisis of leadership. Shebna, the prime minister, is found working on his mausoleum in the royal cemetery rather than on the critical problems of the country (v 16). He will have no chance for atonement (v 14) before death finds him in a far country (v 18). Instead of the honored memorial among the royalty he had served so long, he will die alone and unmourned.

In chap. 25 YHWH's throne appearance announces a banquet in which he will totally dissolve the ubiquitous hold of death over all in the land (vv 6–8). Here death is seen as the curse that repeated bloodguilt has brought upon the land and all its inhabitants (24:6). God, and only God, can break the grip of that curse and remove the "reproach" of the people from the land (v 8).

In chap. 26 the people are not comforted by the reference to the death of the tyrants (v 14). They complain of their own unsuccessful efforts even to repopulate the land (v 18), to which YHWH answers that their dead will live, will rise, and will rejoice when the land gives birth to her "ghosts" (v 19). V 20 picks up the theme again. When God judges the people of the land, the dark secrets of previous murders will be secret no longer. "The land will . . . no longer cover up its murder victims" (v 21).

A further reference occurs in chap. 27. The exiles in Assyria and in Egypt are said to have been perishing, but they will be gathered by God to come and worship him on his holy mountain in Jerusalem (v 13). Separation from the temple is equivalent to death. Being allowed to participate again in Jerusalem is like coming back to life.

Rulers in Jerusalem who have made a covenant with death are spoken of in 28:15. "Lie" and "Falsehood" are synonyms. It is as though these are idols, or national deities of foreign powers. God promises that the ruse will not work. The covenant with death will be annulled, and they will be overcome by the scourge that sweeps the land (v 18).

Hezekiah's view of his coming death is presented in detail in 38:1–20. Salvation is seen as preservation of life. And the meaning of life is essentially the ability to participate in Jerusalem's worship.

In chaps. 40–48, the problems are those of life in exile, and death does not play a prominent part. However, the question of whether life is meaningful or has permanent significance is broached.

In chaps. 49–54, the call for Jerusalem to find meaning in her life even through suffering and humiliation leads to the great proclamation that suffering even to death can be vicarious, can be God's will, can have atoning and healing power, justifying many (53:7–12). The people recognized that this was done for them (vv 4–6).

Attention returns to death in 65:15. Death will be the recompense of those who are rejected from a place where long life will be the norm, rather than the exception (v 20). But even in that place to which believers from all peoples may come to worship God, the death of the rebels from among his people will continue to be a bitter memory that cannot be forgotten (66:24).

The Vision is keenly aware of the issues that death brings when the people are called to review ten generations of the most turbulent and disastrous history that Israel ever knew. The major point made is that life and death are clearly in the control of God. Death for the tyrants and for the rebels in Israel is a just retribution for their sins.

Death can become a curse resulting from unbridled violence in the land, but God can and will control that as well. His goal for his people, in fact for all peoples, is life and peace. He is the source of both. Life at its best and most vibrant is that which is lived in his temple, in his presence, and in accord with his teaching. This is his promise for his people, but particularly for the "humble, the contrite, who tremble at his word." These shall have life.

But this survey makes it equally clear that the Vision has no doctrine of a general resurrection. There is no great new hope for life after death that goes beyond the basic Israelite trust in God for all the promises of life. For that, one must wait until apocalyptic thought describes the resurrection as part of God's solution to all the world's problems, as in the Christian gospel.

The Judgment and Its Results for Israel (26:20–27:13)

This unit announces that God is rising to judge the people of the land and Leviathan. Then it deals with Israel's place in the new order that follows. After the delay of seventy years (see 23:15–19), attention returns to Tyre, symbolized as Leviathan the Dragon, whose day of judgment has arrived. This raises the hopes of Israel's exiles. YHWH reminds them that he is watching the vineyard and that the people will be replanted. In the meantime, the land remains desolate for the people, who still do not understand. But Israel will nevertheless be gathered from the lands of her exile to worship before the Lord in Zion.

Three episodes are used here to present the material:

Episode A: YHWH emerges to judge the people of the land (26:20–21).
Episode B: Leviathan's fate/Israel's hope (27:1–6).
Episode C: "That day" for Israel (27:7–13).

The structure of this scene returns to the form dominated by the dialogue between Heavens and Earth. It concerns things that are to occur "in that day" when YHWH goes out from his place (26:21), "after many days" when YHWH decides the fate of kings (24:21–22), and "at the end of seventy years" when YHWH decides the fate of Tyre (23:17). It also includes a vineyard song by YHWH and brief but spirited objections by individual Israelites.

The outline of thought carried by the dialogue is:

Leviathan is to be judged (27:1).
Song of the Vineyard (vv 2–5).
Jacob will take root and flourish (v 6).
The desolation is a witness that this is a people without understanding (vv 10–11).
YHWH will thresh and gather the exiled Israelites (v 12).
They will come and worship YHWH on Zion (v 13).

It is instructive to note what is missing that might have been expected. There is no word about either an Israelite or a Judean government or ruler. There is nothing about Israel's permanent return. Exile is apparently a lasting part of her existence, but Jerusalem will be rebuilt and accessible. As long as the people can make pilgrimage to Zion, they are certainly not dead or nonexistent. YHWH is alive, at work, and in control. Israel can thrive and grow. Jerusalem gains in importance and meaning. Israel's responses and the "in that day" units speak of life beyond the judgment for remaining Israelites in Palestine as well as exiles in Diaspora.

YHWH Emerges to Judge the People of the Land (26:20–21)

Translation

YHWH:	[20] *Go, my people!*	2+2+3
	Go into your rooms	
	and shut your doors [a] *after you.*	
	Hide [b] *yourselves for a little while*	3+3
	until wrath passes over.	
Herald:	[21] *Indeed, look!* [a] *YHWH is going out of his place* [b]	4+4
	to punish the guilt of the land's population.	
	The land will lay bare its violent crimes	3+3
	and will no longer cover up its murder victims.	

Notes

20.a. Q דלתך, a sg. But K with dual "doors" is correct.

20.b. חבי is generally described as an Aramaism. Wildberger notes that Hebrew uses חבא in the *nip'al*. (Cf. G. Bergsträsser, *Hebräische Grammatik,* vol. 2 [Hildesheim: Olms, 1962] §29*c*.)

21.a. 1QIsa[a] lacks הנה, "look!" MT is to be sustained.

21.b. LXX ἀπὸ τοῦ ἁγίου, "from the sanctuary." A good paraphrase, but not a witness to a different text.

Form/Structure/Setting

The dialogue of the pilgrims is interrupted by a brusque imperative to the people to go indoors and hide for a little while.

The verses set the stage for the climax of the act, the moment of truth, the denouement that will turn the tide of events. As at each stage of the action, YHWH's word and act will accomplish the event. Isa 26:21, the first of two parts of this reversal, deals with the land's population. The second in 7:1 will deal with the oppressive tyrant Leviathan.

Comment

20 The next word of the epiphany turns the pilgrims back from Jerusalem to their homes. They are to go inside and close the doors behind them, to "hide . . . until wrath passes over." The horrors of the judgment are not yet finished. For the third time, notice is given that these events stand between the times (cf. 23:17; 24:22).

21 The herald points to YHWH leaving "his place" in Zion to punish (פקד) the guilt of "the land's population." The guilt of the people began to be separated from that of the land itself in 24:5 (cf. 24:6*b,* 17; 25:8*c*). The land will apparently be called as a witness. It will no longer serve to cover up for the people's guilt in all the murders and acts of violence that have transpired. This essential step in moving toward justice is about to take place (cf. 24:5–6, 20).

Explanation

Isa 18:3–4 had assured "the inhabitants of the land" that they would know when the great event was about to occur. The prophet is assured by YHWH that for the moment he would remain quiet in his dwelling and simply observe what was happening. This was said in the context of the Assyrian period.

In 26:20–21 the moment anticipated in 18:3–4 has arrived. YHWH's people are warned to go indoors and hide until "wrath passes over." In contrast to 18:3–4, YHWH is "going out of his place." The climactic moment has arrived toward which the preceding chapters have pointed. The address to "my people" is tender and attentive. The alienation of 1:2–3, of chap. 5 and 9:8–10:4, and even of 17:6–8, 10–11 and 22:5–14 has been overcome. The mood of 25:1–5, 9 and the open dialogue between God and his people of 26:1–19 prevails.

God's action is denoted by the word פקד (see *Excursus: Decide One's Fate* above). Whether it means "punish or decide the fate," its focus here is the guilt (עון) of those who were spectators in 18:3–4. The same word will be used concerning the action against Leviathan in 27:1.

This reminds us that the decisions and actions of God in this period have focused on "the land" and its inhabitants as well as on Israel and Jerusalem. They all stood under judgment. That was the very problem for Israel. They were too *much* like their neighbors in their lifestyle and actions (2:6–9). They had to share the judgment that came on all of them (2:10–20).

Leviathan's Fate/Israel's Hope (27:1–6)

Bibliography

Alonso Schökel, L. "La Canción de la viña: Isa 27:2–5." *EstEcl* 34 (1960) 767–74. **Herrman, J.** "סאסא Jes 27:8 und שאשא Hes 39:2." *ZAW* 36 (1916) 243. **Jacob, E.** "Du primier au deuxième chant de la vigne du prophète Esaïe: Réflexions zur Esaïe 27:2–5." In *Wort, Gebot, Glaube.* FS W. Eichrodt. Zurich: Zwingli, 1970. 325–30. **Robertson, E.** "Isaiah XXVII 2–6." *ZAW* 47 (1929) 197–206.

Translation

Heavens:	1 *In that day*	2
	YHWH with his sword will decide the fate of	3+3
	the hard, great, and strong one,	
	of Leviathan,[a] *a fleeing*[b] *serpent,*	4+4
	Leviathan, a twisting snake.	
Earth:	*And he will kill the monster* [c]*that is in the sea.*[c]	4
Herald:	2 *In that day*[a]	2+2+2
	a fruitful[b] *vineyard (there will be)—*	
	sing to her.[c]	
YHWH:	3 *I, YHWH, am her keeper!*	3+2
	Moment by moment, I watch her!	
	Lest one put her in judgment,[a]	3+3
	night and day I guard her!	
	4 *Wrath*[a]*—I have none.*	3+4
	If one would give me[b] *thorns,*[c] *briers*[d] *in the battle,*[e]	
	I would set out against them.	2+2
	I would burn [f]*them altogether.*[f]	
	5 *Rather let one lay hold on my protection.*	3+3+3
	[a]*Let one make peace with me.*[a]	
	Peace let one make with me.	
Heavens:	6 *In the coming times*[a]	1
	Jacob will take root.[b]	2+3+3
	He will blossom, and Israel will send out shoots.	
	They will fill the world's surface with fruit.	

Notes

1.a. J. A. Emerton, "Leviathan and *ltn:* The Vocalization of the Ugaritic Word for the Dragon," *VT* 32 (1982) 327–33: "The commonly accepted theory that Ugaritic *ltn* was pronounced *lōtān* raises difficulties. It is better to try to relate the word more closely to Hebrew *liwyātān,* and I have suggested the following development: *liwyātānu* > *līyitānu* > *lītānu* (spelled *ltn*)."

1.b. בָּרִחַ, "fleeing," is a unique form in the OT. An adj. from "to flee" would be written בריח, which is apparently what Q intends. 1QIsa[a] בורח is a ptc., "fleeing"; LXX φεύγοντα, "fleeing." α´ μοχλον, "bar, bolt"; Vg. *vectis,* "a lever, a bolt," seem to think of בְּרִיחַ II, "bar" (BDB, 138), but this has no meaning here. Albright ("New Light on the Early History of Phoenician Colonization,"

BASOR 83 [1941] 39 n. 5) suggested "pre-historic serpent." The Ugaritic texts include the same word. The descriptions are clearly very old.

1.c-c. Missing in LXX.

2.a. *BHS*, with Duhm and *BHK*[3], suggests that ביום ההוא, "in that day," is dittography for אשר בים, "which is in the sea," which has been written twice, covering the word ואמר, "and one said" or "and I said." The opening is abrupt, but not enough to justify this change.

2.b. The Leningradensis text reads חֶמֶר, "wine," which is one of the very few consonantal variants from other texts of the Ben Asher group (see *BHK*[3]). Also 1QIsa[a] reads חומר (Kutscher, *Language and Linguistic Background*, 375). Most other MSS, *BHS*, LXX καλός, Tg., and Syr. read חמד, "delight." Cf. Amos 5:11.

2.c. לָהּ, "to her." The antecedent must be כרם, "vineyard," which is usually masc. However, in Lev 25:3 it is fem as it is here. Vg. and LXX ἁλώσεται read a pass. יִפָּקֵד (cf. Num 16:29; Prov 19:23). The same sense is achieved by using an indeterminate subject.

3.a. Vg. and LXX ἁλώσεται read a pass. יִפָּקֵד (cf. Num 16:29; Prov 19:23). The same sense is achieved by using an indeterminate subject.

4.a. LXX τεῖχος and Syr. *šwr'* apparently read חוֹמָה, "wall," instead of MT חֵמָה, "wrath." Robertson (*ZAW* 47 [1929] 200) looks to an Arab. cognate for the meaning "tent" (for a night watchman), while G. R. Driver suggests the meaning "fiery wine" (*TZ* 14 [1958] 133–35). MT should be supported.

4.b. Wildberger (1008) correctly notes that the 1 sg. suf. on יתנני often stands for the dative: "give me." Kimchi already remarked that מי־יתנני stood for מי יתן לי.

4.c. 1QIsa[a] שומיר. Kutscher (*Language and Linguistic Background*, 385) says this should be read שימיר. BDB (1036–39) suggests three roots שמר: I (v) "to keep, guard"; II (n) "dregs"; III (n) "thorns." 1QIsa[a] apparently wants to read it as "a keeper, guardian" from I. MT places it under III, "thorns."

4.d. 1QIsa[a], Syr., Tg., and Vg add the conjunction ושית, "and briers."

4.e. במלחמה, "in the battle," is placed in the first line by MT. Many interpreters, like Wildberger and *BHS*, find the meaning difficult and want to eliminate it altogether or draw it into the second line.

4.f-f. 1QIsa[a] adds a *vav* at both ends of the phrase. *BHS* suggests adding a *dagesh*. The change is of no consequence. It is better to stay with MT, "I burn it altogether."

5.a-a. LXX ποιήσωμεν εἰρήνην αὐτῷ, "let us make peace with him"; Syr. *w'ʿbd lh šlm'*, "and I will make peace for her." MT has the speaker continue to be YHWH and the subject indeterminate.

6.a. הבאים, "the coming ones," has given the commentators and translators trouble. For a survey of suggestions, see Wildberger (1013). The word is a short form for "the coming days" and is used adverbally as an acc. of time (Joüon §126*i*). Cf. Eccl 2:16.

6.b. 1QIsa[a] ישריש, a *plene* writing of the same form. α´ σ´ θ´ ριζώσει, "he will cause to take root." Isa 40:24 vocalizes the word שֹׁרֵשׁ, a *poel*, i.e., pass. BDB and *HAL* see this as a denominative verb dealing with "roots." The meanings in *hipʿil*, and *poel* would apparently differ little.

Form/Structure/Setting

YHWH's acts so far in this scene have been:

to lay waste the land (24:1)
to decide the fate of kings and powers (24:21)
to make a gift of life for all peoples (25:6–8)
to lay his hand on Mount Zion (25:10)

Now it is the time to "decide the fate" of Leviathan (27:1). The decision is foreordained that Leviathan will die. With Leviathan out of the way, the discussion turns back to the character, problem, and future of Israel. Who is Leviathan that his existence had been a barrier to restoration of fellowship between Israel and God?

Excursus: Leviathan = Tyre

Bibliography

Allen, R. B. "The Leviathan-Rahab-Dragon Motif in the Old Testament." Th.M. thesis, Dallas Theological Seminary, 1968. **Anderson, B. W.** "The Slaying of the Fleeing, Twisting Serpent: Isaiah 27:1 in Context." In *Uncovering Ancient Stones.* FS H. N. Richardson, ed. L. M. Hopfe. Winona Lake, IN: Eisenbrauns, 1994. 3–16. **Burney, C. K.** "Old Testament Notes III: The Three Serpents of Isaiah xxvii 1." *JTS* 2 (1909–10) 443–47. **Gorden, C. H.** "Leviathan: Symbol of Evil." In *Biblical Motifs.* Ed. A. Altmann. Cambridge, MA: Harvard UP, 1966. **Kaiser, O.** *Die Mythische Bedeutung des Meeres.* 2d ed. BZAW 78. Berlin: De Gruyter, 1962. **Wakeman, M. K.** *God's Battle with the Monster.* Leiden: Brill, 1973.

לויתן, "Leviathan," probably means "coiled one" from לוה, like Arab. *lwy,* "coil," "wind" (T. H. Gaster, "Leviathan," *IDB* 3:116), and is like Ugar. *ltn* (see *Note* 27:1.a.). It also appears in Pss 74:14; 104:26; Job 41:1; 2 Esd 6:52; *2 Bar.* 29:3–8. Here in Isaiah, Leviathan is described as "the hard, great, and strong one . . . a fleeing serpent . . . a twisting snake . . . the monster that is in the sea."

In another context the word might be explained by the mythical implications of the Baal myth in which Leviathan is killed. But Job's use transparently refers the name to a great sea creature with no mythic or supernatural overtones (cf. T. H. Gaster, *IDB* 3:116). The context here in Isaiah calls for a historical identification. The arch structure for chaps. 23–27 balances the reference to the sea on which Tyre's sailors work (23:11–12*a*) with Leviathan (27:1). The name Rahab, also usually applied to a great mythological dragon, is applied to Egypt by name in 30:7. The same thing is done here. Leviathan is a symbol for Tyre. God's promise to decide the fate of Tyre (23:17) is fulfilled in this passage when God "decides the fate" of Leviathan (27:1).

So, a historical answer based on the outline of the literary context suggests that Leviathan is a symbol for Tyre. Later interpreters thought of someone like Satan. Could the answer be somewhere between these? Tyre (the Phoenicians) was the outstanding example of Canaanite culture, which is recognized repeatedly in the Scriptures as the primary temptation that drew Israel away from God. Should the removal of Tyre (i.e., Canaanite culture) be understood here to make possible the replanting of Israel in the land (27:2–5)?

The song of the vineyard (vv 2–5) is the second time in the Vision that YHWH sings of Israel as his vineyard (cf. 5:1–7). Both songs portray Israel as precious to YHWH. In 5:1 it is laid out on "a very fruitful hill." In 27:2 it is called "a fruitful vineyard." In both, the vineyard is threatened by שמיר, "thorns," and שית, "briers." Wildberger (1009) notes that these words are also paired in 7:23–25, 9:17 [18], and 10:17, but nowhere outside Isaiah. In 27:3 YHWH waters the vineyard "moment by moment." In 5:6 he forbids the clouds to rain on it. In 5:7 he expects justice and righteousness from his people. In 27:5 he offers peace.

This song is a conscious counterpart to the first one. It is part of the announcement that the period of judgment over his people is about to come to an end: "Wrath—I have none" (27:4).

Comment

1 ביום ההוא, "in that day," like the phrase in 25:9 and 26:1, refers to the day at the end of the seventy years (23:17) and after the many days of 24:22 when YHWH comes from his place (26:8). לויתן, "Leviathan," is a symbol for Tyre, its counterpart in this scene (chap. 23). The literature of the ancient Near East thought of animals like the serpent, the lion, and the ram in terms of demonic representations. Isaiah uses the same figures but portrays them as historical persons (see M. G. Klingbeil, "Del Caos al Orden: Temas mitalógicos en el libro de Isaías," *Theo* 14 [1999] 66–85). YHWH will decide Leviathan's fate as promised in 23:17//14:21–22. But that decision, after the reprieve predicted in 23:15–16, will be death for the monster that is in the sea.

Nebuchadnezzar of Babylon besieged Tyre for thirteen years from ca. 585–572 B.C.E., but the city was resupplied from the sea. Finally, a negotiated truce allowed Tyre to survive while its royal family was removed to Babylon under Nebuchadnezzar's control. Ezek 26–29 predicts the city's fall to Nebuchadnezzar, but Ezek 29:18 admits that the city survived. The tension between the destruction announced here in Isa 27:1 and in Ezekial and the city's historical survival, as well as the continuance of its trading activity announced in 23:17–18, lie at the very essence of this oracle's meaning. Tyre will no longer be "Leviathan, a twisting snake." That existence of power and conniving intrigue will be over. She will no longer be a threat to her neighbors, especially Israel/Judah. She can return to the role she played in David's time (cf. 1 Kgs 5; 2 Chr 2:1–16) as announced in 23:18.

2 כרם חמד, "a fruitful vineyard," is a symbol for Israel and is a counterpart to the "vineyard on a very fruitful hill" of 5:1, but there is a substantial difference. In chap. 5 Israel was a people in its land. God's watchful care applied to both the people and the land. Here Israel is a people in exile (cf. v 12). God extols his watchcare over her, and his protection and peace are emphasized (vv 3*b*–5). He promises to plant and cultivate his vineyard, but there is no reference to the land. A return to live in the land of Canaan is not included here. The omission is not an oversight. Rather, they will fill the world's surface (v 6). Israel's destiny, still under God's watchcare, has changed.

3 פן יפקד עליה, "Lest one put her in judgment." The position of the exiles as aliens in a foreign land left them undefended and often without rights before a magistrate or court. YHWH promises his own protection.

4 חמה, "wrath." Earlier acts of the Vision have provided ample descriptions of YHWH's wrath toward Israel in judgment for her sins. But by this time his attitude toward Israel will have "turned the corner": "I have none."

שית, "briers," and שמיר, "thorns," are the symbols of the void in the land left by Israel's evacuation (5:6; 7:23–25; 9:17 [18]; 10:17). Their place and function are now finished. God himself will "burn them altogether."

5 או, "rather," is an emphatic conjunction expressing an alternative. "On the other hand," YHWH is saying, let one seek "my protection. . . . make peace with me." YHWH understands that Israel, as a rebellious people, has been at war with him. He is offering them a peace treaty. He is offering them protection under his sovereignty.

6 ישרש יעקב, "Jacob will take root." Earlier chapters have spoken of being uprooted, a figure of displacement and exile, but also a figure that implies a wilting and dying plant. The figure here is of being transplanted and beginning to prosper in the new ground.

Explanation

The passage picks up the beginning theme of the scene—the destruction of Tyre—affirms it, and then deals with the consequences for Israel. In the vivid description of killing "Leviathan, . . . the monster that is in the sea," generations of readers have seen God's ultimate victory over all evil. Though the Vision of Isaiah does not develop this on the cosmic scale that later apocalyptic literature would, the book does present the destruction of Tyre in mythological language as the paradigm of the end of an era. This leaves room for a new vision of God's intentions for his people.

God affirms his care and protection for Israel, now in exile. The vineyard will be cultivated and protected. Though the people find themselves in new and strange circumstances, they are called to depend on the peace that YHWH offers them.

"That Day" for Israel (27:7–13)

Bibliography

Daiches, S. "An Explanation of Isaiah 27.8." *JQR* 6 (1915–16) 399–404. **Day, J.** "Asherah." *ABD.* 1:483–87. **Galling, K.** "Incense Altars." *IDB.* 2:699–700. **Grol, H. W. M. van.** "Isaiah 27:10–11: God and His Own People." In *Studies.* Ed. J. Van Ruiten and M. Vervenne. 195–209. **Herrman, J.** "סאסא Jes 27:8 und שאשא Hes 39:2." *ZAW* 36 (1916) 243. **Jenner, K. D.** "The Big Shofar (Isaiah 27:13): A Hapax Legomenon." In *Studies in Isaiah 24–27: The Isaiah Workshop.* Ed. H. J. Bosman et al. Leiden: Brill, 2000. 157–82. ———. "The Worship of Yhwh on the Holy Mountain in Light of the Idea of Return: A Short Note on the Confrontation of Theology of the Old Testament and Comparative and Applied Science of Theology." In *New Things.* Ed. F. Postma et al. 129–133. **Kessler, W.** *Gott geht es um das Ganze: Jes. 56–66 und Jes. 24–27.* Stuttgart: Calwer, 1960. 170–72. **Leene, H.** "Isaiah 27:7–9 as a Bridge between Vineyard and City." In *Studies in Isaiah 24–27: The Isaiah Workshop.* Ed. H. J. Bosman et al. Leiden: Brill, 2000. 199–225. **Ploeger, O.** *Theocracy and Eschatology.* Richmond: John Knox, 1968. 71–75. **Rabin, C.** "Bariah." *JTS* 47 (1946) 38–41. **Sweeney, M. A.** "New Gleanings from an Old Vineyard: Isaiah 27 Reconsidered." In *Early Jewish and Christian Exegesis.* FS W. H. Brownlee, ed. C. A. Evans and W. F. Stinespring. Atlanta: Scholars, 1987. 51–66.

Translation

First Israelite: 7 *Has he struck them (with a blow) like the blow of those striking him?* [a] 3+3
Or has he been killed like the killing of those killing him? [b]

Second Israelite: 8 *By driving her away,*[a] *by sending her (away),*[b] *do you contend with her?* 3+5
Or has he removed her[c] *by his fierce wind in a day of east winds?*
Third Israelite: 9 *Therefore, by this will the guilt of Jacob be expiated?* 4+4
And this will be all the fruit of removing this sin?[a]
Heavens: *When he will make all the stones of an altar* 3+3+3
(to be) crushed like stones of chalk,
Asherim and incense altars will no longer stand upright.
Earth: 10 *Indeed, a fortified city stands abandoned by itself alone,* 4+4
a habitation deserted and forsaken like a wilderness.
Heavens: *There a calf grazes.* 3+2+2
There he lies down
and strips away[a] *its branches.*
Earth: 11 *When its twig*[a] *is dry, it is broken.*[b] 3+4
Women come, making a fire of them.
Heavens: *For it was not a discerning people.* 4+3+3
Therefore he had no compassion on them.
His maker did not show him favor.
Earth: 12 *But it will be in that day* 3
YHWH will thresh out grain[a] 3+3
from the River[b] *to the Wadi of Egypt.*[b]
Heavens: *And you, yourselves, will be gathered* 2+2+2
one to another,[c]
O Israelites.
Earth: 13 *And it will be in that day:* 3
A great trumpet will be blown, 3+4+3
and those perishing in the land of Assyria will come,
and those driven away in the land of Egypt.
Heavens: *And they will bow down*[a] *to YHWH* 2+3
in the holy mountain in Jerusalem.

Notes

7.a. LXX πληγήσεται, καὶ, "will he be struck, and" = הֻכָּה וְ is suggested by *BHS,* Gray, and Procksch. The triple use of the same root makes translation difficult, but the LXX is no help.

7.b. 1QIsa[a] הורגיו, "killer," an act. ptc. for MT's pass. ptc., "one being killed." This is seen as a better text by virtually all, including Guthe, Gray, Duhm, Marti, Ehrlich *(Randglossen),* Procksch, Fohrer, Kaiser, Wildberger, *BHK*[3], and *BHS.*

8.a. MT בסאסאה was a problem even for the Masoretes, as the pointing in *BHK*[3] and *BHS* with no vowel under the first א suggests. *BHK*[3] notes that Q in several MSS reads בְּסַסְאָה. α´, σ´, θ´, Tg., and Vg. (but not LXX) understood it as the measure סְאָה used in weighing grain "measure by measure." Gesenius thought the word was contracted from בסאה סאה. Dillmann follows LXX "by warfare" to suggest that it is an inf. with 3d fem. sg. suffix or an action noun בְּאִסְאָה, which has been generally accepted (BDB, *HAL*). But the attempt to find its meaning takes another route. G. R. Driver ("Vocabulary of the OT, II," *JTS* 30 [1928] 371) called it a *pilpel* inf. to be understood from the Arab. *sa'sa'*, "shooing her away," a term used in driving donkeys. F. Schulthess (*ZS* 2 [1923] 15) thought of a verb that was also derived from *ša* or *sa,* sounds used in driving goats. The parallel form שלחה, "sending her," supports this (Wildberger, 1014). In this case the *mappiq* in ה should be inserted and the suffix read.

8.b. *BHK*[3] calls this a gloss, but no explanation is given (see Wildberger, 1014).

8.c. The suffix on הגה needs a *mappiq.*

9.a. 1QIsa[a] חטאו (cf. Kutscher, *Language and Linguistic Background,* 374), "they sinned," turns the last word into a relative clause. MT, reading a noun with suffix, "his sin," is to be preferred. A. C. M. Blommerde ("The Broken Construct Chain," *Bib* 55 [1974] 551) suggests that חטאתו is connected to כל פרי as an example of a "broken construct chain" to be translated "and this is: removing every fruit of his sin." Wildberger (1014) correctly judges this unlikely.

10.a. *BHK*[3] suggests emending to *qal* or a pl. But the form of MT (*piʿel* pf.) makes good sense: "finishes" = "strips" branches.

11.a. Vg. *messes illius,* "its standing grain." MT means "a branch, sprout," understood as a collective.

11.b. *BHK*[3] emends to the "energic form," following the versions. MT makes sense and is followed here.

12.a. The positions of the prepositions מן and עד have raised questions here. *BHK*[3] suggests moving מן from שבלת to the following word, הנהר, "the river." שבל may mean something that flows like a garment or a river (BDB I, *HAL* II) or an ear of grain (BDB II; *HAL* I). MT has apparently chosen the first and understood שבלת to refer to the flowing river. This leaves no object for the verb. The emendation would supply that object, "grain," while keeping the contrast "from the river." The emended form of *BHK*[3] is used here.

12.b-b. LXX ἕως 'Ρινοκορούρων, "to Rinokorouron." A city of this name existed at that time where *el-ʿarīš* is today. The present name of "the river of Egypt" is *wādi el-ʿarīš.*

12.c. לאחד אחד is literally "one to one," i.e., one more added to the one already there.

13.a. 1QIsa[a] והשתחו leaves out a *vav,* a case of haplography.

Form/Structure/Setting

The announcement (v 6) that Jacob will take root again (in the land?) produces a discussion about the fairness of the judgment inflicted on Jacob (vv 7–11*a*), which culminates in the observation that it was, after all, not a discerning people (v 11*b*). This episode closes with two assurances (vv 12 and 13), like those at the end of act 1 (11:11–16), that the people of the Diaspora from Mesopotamia and Egypt will be sought out and returned in order to worship in Jerusalem.

Note the second-person plural pronoun "you yourselves" (27:12*b,* like that in 14:3 except that there it was masculine singular) by which the passage is addressed to the audience, the readers of the book. The episode deals with the issues of a divided Judaism in the restoration period. Some were struggling to hang on to an agricultural existence in Palestine. Others existed on various pursuits in the extended area that surrounded Palestine. God has not forgotten them. Each of the groups is to have a place in the new order.

Recent commentaries (Williamson *[Book Called Isaiah],* Sweeney, and others) have concentrated on the parallel between verses 27:12–13 and 11:11–16. Both passages deal with the return of exiles from Egypt and Assyria, but they differ in the purpose of the return. They are paralleled in other prophecies: הנדחים, "those driven away in the land of Egypt," and האבדים, "those perishing in the land of Assyria," appear together in Jer 23:1; 27:10, 15; Ezek 34:4, 16. Parallel references to Assyria and Egypt are also found in Hos 11:11, Mic 7:12, and Zech 10:10–11. Williamson notes the "extensive use of Hosea in Isaiah 24–27" (*Book Called Isaiah,* 180 n. 41).

Comment

7 "Has he struck them?" This is the first of the skeptical questions, which are addressed not to God himself but to the speaker of v 6. The Israelites want to know whether their adversaries have been dealt a hard retribution similar to their own, or whether they have suffered the brutalities that Israel has suffered.

8 "Do you contend with her?" The question is addressed to YHWH. It asks whether "driving her away," i.e., in the exile, was in fact a form of judicial process. The speaker is skeptical. He thinks it is more likely that God has simply lost patience and let his wrath overflow like a fierce wind. The implication is that justice and a reasoned process had nothing to do with it.

9 "Will the guilt of Jacob be expiated?" The question asks whether this will, in fact, remove the accumulated guilt of Israel's sins. Is it possible that all of this, i.e., the two centuries of almost constant foreign harassment and invasion from the time of Uzziah through the exile, is due to God's removal of the sins of Israel? In answer the witnesses point to the stark evidence left by the desolation. That altars were crushed at least means that idolatry has ceased.

10 Ruins testify to a commercial and militaristic civilization that has now become quietly pastoral.

11 This happened because Israel "was not a discerning people." The Vision has been making this point from 1:2–3 using the figures of blindness and deafness. The questions show that the condition lingers on. God did not show the favor that he has now announced for his people because of that lack of discernment. But now he has come to announce that he will take personal responsibility for his vineyard.

12 ביום ההוא, "in that day," like that in vv 1 and 2, refers to YHWH's actions after the seventy years (23:17) and after the "many days" (24:22) when YHWH goes out of his place (26:21). The other decisions and actions that are entailed, like the judgment of the kings and the destruction of Leviathan, the restoration of a chastened Tyre and the expiation of the guilt of the land, will include gathering the exiled Israelites from Mesopotamia and Egypt. God's nurture of his vineyard includes, to mix the metaphor, "threshing" and "gathering," harvesting like grain, in the dispersion of the Israelites. The election through Abraham of those who seek him and yearn for him is still valid and will be rewarded.

13 האבדים, "those perishing." This act has had a great deal to say about YHWH's acts in regard to the dead in the land. The reference here is to those for whom existence in exile, cut off from contact and relation to the worship of God in Israel, is like a living death. Life for them is unthinkable without a sense of the presence of YHWH and an opportunity to worship him. This was the spiritual "hell" of exile (cf. Ps 137).

ארץ אשור, "the land of Assyria," and ארץ מצרים, "the land of Egypt." These two areas continued to be the major concentrations of Israelites and Jews in the dispersion, although a heavy addition in southern Mesopotamia in 598 and 586 B.C.E. shifted the emphasis to Babylon.

The purpose and the goal of the gathering may come as a surprise or disappointment to many. There is no reference to the reestablishment of the people in Canaan (à la Joshua). Nor are they promised the reestablishment of the kingdom even under a son of David. Instead they are promised the opportunity to make pilgrimage to Jerusalem, to "bow down to YHWH." This should be no surprise to the reader of the Vision. From 2:1–4 on, the future has been promised to a demilitarized "holy mountain in Jerusalem." It will be the place of YHWH's dwelling, and the peoples can come there to worship him and learn of his torah. YHWH here promises exiled Israel that privilege. The people who have the hope of seeing YHWH in his glory in his holy mountain need not consider themselves "dead" or "perishing." To be able to be in his presence is life of the highest order.

Explanation

God's caring words toward his vineyard (27:1–6) are met with skeptical questions. The lessons of the devastation of Israel have not yet been learned. The questions that are asked in vv 7–9 reflect the dissatisfaction in Israel. There is still a petulant spirit reflected here that has neither recognized nor accepted the justice of YHWH's actions. The people are not ready for the new day or participation in it. They are "not a discerning people" (v 11*b;* and also 1:3 passim).

Despite the continuing problems of Israel's character, the grace and commitment of God to Israel is shown. The scene closes with the affirmation that God will make it possible for exiled Israelites to overcome the disabilities of distance and separation to be among the worshipers on his holy mountain in Jerusalem.

He will reach out again to the entire territory of the exiled community to gather all who can be called "fruit." Those who have been scattered will be brought together.

Pilgrims from these exiles will come to worship YHWH in the holy mountain in Jerusalem. The reference to the exiles as "perishing" picks up the theme of "death" earlier in the act. It assures the exiles of meaningful "life" through faithful continuation of their relationship to YHWH, who offers the hope of worship in Jerusalem. The threads are brought together again: chap. 66 will show the restoration of Jerusalem, of the temple, and of the exiles.

Act 3. The Woes of Israel and Jerusalem (28:1–33:24)

Bibliography: Commentaries

Beuken, W. A. M. *Isaiah, Part 2* (Isa 28–39). Trans. B. Doyle. HCOT. Leuven: Peeters, 2000. **Kaiser, O.** *Der Prophet Jesaja: Kapitel 13–39.* ATD 18. Göttingen: Vandenhoeck & Ruprecht, 1973. Trans. R. A. Wilson under the title *Isaiah 13–39: A Commentary,* OTL (Philadelphia: Westminster, 1974). **Kilian, R.** *Jesaja.* Vol. 2 (Isa 13–39). NEchtB 32. Würzburg: Echter, 1994. **Wildberger, H.** *Jesaja.* Vol. 3 (Isa 28–39). BKAT 10.3. Neukirchen-Vluyn: Neukirchener Verlag, 1982.

Bibliography: Books and Articles

Barth, H. "Israel und das Assyrerreich in den nichtjesajanischen Texten des Protojesajabuches." Diss., Hamburg, 1974. **Barthel, J.** *Prophetenwort und Geschichte: Die Jesajaüberlieferung in Jesaja 6–8 und 28–31.* Tübingen: Mohr Siebeck, 1994. **Beuken, W. A. M.** "Women and Spirit, the Ox and the Ass: The First Binders of the Booklet Isaiah 28–32." *ETL* 74 (1968) 5–26. **Dietrich, W.** *Jesaja und die Politik.* BEvT 74. Munich: Kaiser, 1976. **Donner, H.** *Israel unter den Völkern.* **Exum, J. C.** "Isaiah 28–32: A Literary Approach." In *SBLSP.* Ed. P. Achtemeier. Missoula, MT: Scholars Press, 1979. 123–51. **Hardmeier, C.** *Texttheorie und biblische Exegese: Zur rhetorischen Funktion der Trauermetaphorik in der Prophetie.* BEvT 79. Munich: Kaiser, 1978. **Hausmann, J.** *Israels Rest: Studien zum Selbstverständnis der nachexilischen Gemeinde.* BWANT 124. Stuttgart: Kohlhammer, 1987. **Hoffmann, W. H.** *Die Intention der Verkündigung Jesajas.* BZAW 136. Berlin: De Gruyter, 1974. **Huber, F.** *Jahwe, Juda und die andern Völker beim Propheten Jesaja.* BZAW 137. Berlin: De Gruyter, 1976. **Irwin, W. H.** "Isaiah 28–33: Translation with Philological Notes." Diss., Pontifical Biblical Institute, Rome, 1973. **Janzen, W.** *Mourning Cry and Woe Oracle.* BZAW 125. Berlin: De Gruyter, 1972. 49–62. **Jensen, J.** *The Use of torâ by Isaiah: His Debate with the Wisdom Tradition.* CBQMS 3. Washington: Catholic Biblical Association, 1973. **Kraus, H.-J.** "*hôj* als prophetische Leichenklage über das eigene Volk im 8. Jahrhundert." *ZAW* 85 (1973) 15–46. **Laberge, L.** *La Septante d'Isaïe 28–33: Étude de tradition textuelle.* Ottawa: Laberge, 1978. ———. "The Woe-Oracles of Isaiah 28–33." *EgT* 13 (1982) 157–90. **Landy, F.** "Hidden Texts in Isaiah 28–33." Unpublished SBL paper, 1997. **Lutz, H.-M.** *Jahwe, Jerusalem und die Völker.* WMANT 27. Neukirchen-Vluyn: Neukirchener Verlag, 1968. **Pfaff, H.-M.** *Die Entwicklung des Restgedankens in Jesaja 1–39.* European Univ. Studies, ser. 13, theology vol. 561. Frankfurt am Main: Lang, 1996. **Schmidt, H.** "Israel, Zion, und die Völker: Eine motivgeschichtliche Untersuchung zum Verständnis des Universalismus im Alten Testament." Diss., Univ. of Zürich, 1966. **Stansell, G.** "Isaiah 28–33: Blest Be the Tie that Binds (Isaiah Together)." In *New Visions.* Ed. R. F. Melugin and M. A. Sweeney. 68–103. **Vollmer, J.** *Geschichtliche Rückblicke und Motive in der Prophetie des Amos, Hosea, and Jesaja.* BZAW 119. Berlin: De Gruyter, 1971. **Zurro Rodríguez, E.** "Siete hápax en el libra de Isaías (Isa. 3:18; 9:4; 22:15; 30:24; 32:4; 34:15; 56:10)." *EstBib* 53 (1995) 525–35.

Williamson (*Book Called Isaiah,* 184) notes that chap. 28 is commonly treated as the beginning of a new section following the "Isaiah Apocalypse" (Isa 24–27). But he also notes the common understanding that the "woes" are concluded only in chap. 31. Vermeylen *(Book of Isaiah)* believes the section began with the woe oracle in 10:5 and continues through chap. 31. Williamson discusses fully the problem of beginning a new section at 28:1, including the lack of a superscription. He concludes that the edition of Deutero-Isaiah contained a unit that began with chap. 6 and continues through the unit beginning with chap. 28. This commentary views chaps. 1–4 as a prologue before the three acts of chaps. 5–33.

A blank space divides the book after chap. 33 in 1QIsa[a], so I chose to divide the volumes at this point. The same view that a major break occurs at this point has been adopted by Christopher Seitz (*Isaiah 1–39,* 240–42), by W. H. Brownlee (*The Meaning of the Qumran Scrolls for the Bible* [New York: Oxford UP, 1964] 247–59), and by C. A. Evans ("On the Unity and Parallel Structures of Isaiah," *VT* 38 [1988] 129–47). Beuken has made the case that chap. 33 plays a major role in the structure of the book, and Williamson can speak of chap. 33 as rounding off a major section of the book (*Book Called Isaiah,* 228; see p. 238 for those who take chap. 32 as the final chapter of this part of the book).

This commentary will treat chaps. 28–33 as an act within the larger drama. Act 3 has no comprehensive superscription or title like those in 2:1 and 13:1. The title in 1:1 suits it well and should probably be applied. Chaps. 28–33 form a block of six passages beginning with הוי, "woe" (28:1–29; 29:1–14, 15–24; 30:1–5; 31:1–9; 33:1–6); one beginning with משא, "burden" (30:6–7); two with עתה, "and now" (30:8–26; 33:10–24); and three with הנה, "behold" (30:27–33; 32:1–20; 33:7–9). An outline shows the effect of these particles:

הוי "Woe! Crown of the pride of the drunkards of Ephraim" (28:1)
הנה "See! The Lord had someone, mighty and strong" (28:2)
  ביום ההוא "In that day YHWH of Hosts became . . ." (28:5)
    כי "For all the tables were full of vomit" (28:8)
    כי "For '*Tsaw* for *tsaw*'" (28:10)
    כי "For with a stammering lip" (28:11)
  למען "In order that they would balk and stumble" (28:13*d*)
  לכן "Therefore, hear the word of YHWH" (28:14)
    כי "For you have said" (28:15)
    לכן "Therefore, thus says my Lord YHWH" (28:16*a*)
    הנני "See me laying a stone in Zion" (28:16*b*)
    כי "For morning by morning it will pass over" (28:19)
    כי "For the bed is too short to stretch out" (28:20)
    כי "For as Mount Perizim YHWH will rise" (28:21)
  ועתה "And now, do not scoff" (28:22*a*)
    כי "For I have heard annihilation strictly determined" (28:22*b*)
  "Pay attention and heed my voice" (28:23)
    כי "For dill is not threshed with a threshing sled" (28:27*a*)
    כי "For with a stick dill is beaten out" (28:27*b*)
    גם "Also this is from YHWH of Hosts" (28:29)
הוי "Woe! Ariel, Ariel" (29:1)
    כי "For YHWH has poured out over you" (29:10)
הוי "Woe to those who dig too deep" (29:15)
    כי "That the thing made should say to its maker" (29:16*b*)
    כי "For the terrorist shall come to naught" (29:20)
  לכן "Therefore, thus says YHWH, God of the House of Jacob" (29:22)
    כי "For, when he sees his children" (29:23)
הוי "Woe! Rebellious children!" (30:1)
    כי "For his princes are in Zoan" (30:4)

לכן "Therefore, I call this one 'Rahab.'" (30:7*b*)
עתה "Now come! Write on a tablet" (30:8)
כי "For it is a rebellious people" (30:9)
לכן "Therefore, thus says the Holy One of Israel" (30:12*a*)
יען "Because you are rejecting his word" (30:12*b*)
לכן "Therefore, may this guilt be for you" (30:13)
כי "For thus says my Lord, YHWH" (30:15)
לכן "Surely YHWH waits to be gracious to you" (30:18*a*)
כי "For YHWH is a God of justice" (30:18*b*)
כי "For, O people in Zion, you dweller in Jerusalem, you will surely not weep!" (30:19)
הנה "See! The Name of YHWH, coming from afar" (30:27)
כי "For, at the sound of YHWH, Assyria will be broken" (30:31)
כי "For a funeral pyre was being prepared days ago" (30:33)
הוי "Woe! Those going down to Egypt for help" (31:1)
כי "For thus YHWH has said to me" (31:4)
הנה "Suppose a king should reign in righteousness" (32:1)
כי "For a fool speaks folly" (32:6)
כי "For a grape harvest will fail" (32:10*b*)
כי "For over every joyous house" (32:13*b*)
כי "For a palace shall be forsaken" (32:14)
הוי "Woe! You destroyer, who are not yet being destroyed" (33:1)
הנה "See! Their Ariel!" (33:7)
כי "For if there YHWH abides" (33:21)
כי "For YHWH will be our judge, YHWH our commander" (33:22)

Act 3 contains no historical narrative. (A possible exception is 31:8–9: "Assyria will fall.") Egypt's intervention, which occurred throughout the period, is referred to repeatedly (30:2–4; 31:1). The wars of the Assyrian period still rage (30:28), and Assyria is still active (30:31–33; 31:8–9). Beuken (*Isaiah, Part 2,* 8) thinks that the editing of these chapters assumes that the fall of Jerusalem has already taken place. He says that in chaps. 28–32 "the fall of Jerusalem constitutes the background against which the rest of the people, in exile and at home, reflect on the significance of this disaster for their future." He understands that judgment hangs like a sword over the heads of the people (28:17–22; 29:1–4; 30:13–17; 31:1–3; 32:9–14). But Beuken considers this to be viewed as "past history" in light of the promises of salvation (28:5–6; 29:22–23; 30:18–26; 31:8–9; 32:15–20), which "presume the fall of Jerusalem" to the Babylonians, not the Assyrians. Babylon is not mentioned in these chapters. So why does Beuken think this refers to them and their period? He thinks that originally "Chaps. 28–39 thus cover the final years of the activities of the prophet Isaiah" (*Isaiah, Part 2,* 2). Because of chaps. 36–39 still to come, Beuken (5–6) thinks of the last quarter of the eighth century for original background here. In this he takes a different view from that noted above. This leaves the reader in the same problematical situation faced in the past when we juxtaposed First Isaiah (i.e., Isaiah son of Amoz) of the reigns of the four kings of Judah mentioned in 1:1 with Deutero-Isaiah of the exilic or postexilic period. Much of the research in the meantime has found the book relevant to the entire period, not just the beginning and the end (cf. U. Becker, *Jesaja—Von der Botschaft zum Buch*). This commentary will suggest that chaps. 36–39 refer to an earlier period than do the surrounding chapters.

I think chaps. 28–33 are set in the final half century of Judah's existence (ca. 640–605 B.C.E.) in the reigns of Josiah and Jehoiakim. The disintegration of the Assyrian Empire with the concurrent rise of Egypt and Babylon occupied world attention while Judah was acting out the final scenes of the judgment pronounced on her a century earlier. Repeated threats to Jerusalem had come in the reign of Manasseh, and the uncertain rise and fall of optimism about threats of destruction and hopes of salvation fit the period well.

Beuken (*Isaiah, Part 2,* 8) finds that chaps. 28–32 and 36–39 present "conflicting messages." He is right. However, the solution to the changed time sequence is to be found in chap. 34, where a description of the fall of Jerusalem and its desolation (34:8–15) is followed by a command to read from the Scroll of YHWH (34:16). This scroll seems to have contained 2 Kgs 18–20 and is presented in Isa 36–39. The reading before the nations (34:1) gathered after the destructions of Edom (34:5–7) and of Zion (34:8–15) recalls an earlier time, the reign of Hezekiah, in order to hear again YHWH's commitment to defend the city. There is indeed a contradiction here that only the words of 40:1–11 can resolve.

Each of the five scenes in chaps. 28–33 begins with הוי, "woe," a monotonous funeral chant. The "woes" of these scenes forbid seeing renewal, new life, or hope of return to the glory of Judah's past in the extension of Davidic boundaries under Josiah; in the renewed importance of the Holy City, Jerusalem; in the promise of Egyptian patronage; or even in God's promise to judge the tyrant. Clearly, the message is that Judah has no political future. Instead, the act continues to portray true hope as centered in YHWH's support of Zion as a city of worship, YHWH's promise of grace, and the outpouring of his spirit, as previous acts of the Vision have done. Comparison reveals that these five "woe" scenes are parallel to the "woes" for Israel in chaps. 5 and 10, while the Jerusalem scenes are parallel to chaps. 2, 4, and 66. But note the contrast to chap. 11. There is no Davidic heir apparent in these scenes.

Scene 1: Disaster from Expansion (28:1–29)
- Woe, Ephraim's Drunkards (28:1–13)
- Scoffers in Jerusalem (28:14–22)
- YHWH's Strategy: A Parable (28:23–29)

Scene 2: Disaster in Jerusalem's Political Involvement (29:1–24)
- Woe, Ariel (29:1–8)
- Like a Sealed Book (29:9–14)
- Woe, You Schemers (29:15–24)

Scene 3: Disaster from Self-Help in Rebellion (30:1–33)
- Woe, Rebellious Children (30:1–18)
- Hope from the Teachers (30:19–26)
- A Cultic Theophany (30:27–33)

Scene 4: Disaster from False Faith in Egypt (31:1–32:20)
- Woe to Those Who Depend on Egypt (31:1–9)
- Suppose a King . . . (32:1–8)
- Until Spirit Is Poured Out (32:9–20)

Scene 5: God's Promise to Judge the Tyrant (33:1–24)
- Woe, You Destroyer (33:1–6)

Excursus: The Era ca. 640–587 B.C.E.

Bibliography

Breasted, J. H. *A History of Egypt.* New York: Charles Scribner's Sons, 1946. 565–81. **Bright, J.** *A History of Israel.* 3d ed. Philadelphia: Westminster, 1981. 313–17. **Kitchen, K. A.** *Third Intermediate Period in Egypt.* 339–408. **Oded, B.** "Judah and the Exile." In *IJH.* 456–69.

Specific references to Assyria and to Egypt occur in the central chapters of this section. The references to Assyria are preoccupied with its imminent fall (30:31; 31:8). References to Egypt deal with the eagerness of certain parties in Jerusalem to make contacts and alliances with Egypt (30:2; 31:1). These references fit the conditions of the second half of the seventh century B.C.E. and are credible historical innuendos of that time.

It is an age in which Egypt is active and gaining strength while Assyria is weakening and fading away. Psamtik I (Psammetichus I) had first fled to Assyria. Then under the patronage of the Assyrians, he returned to rule Sais and Memphis by the order of Ashurbanipal in 665 B.C.E. Assyria's preoccupation with wars in Mesopotamia left him largely to his own resources, which he used extremely well. By 640 B.C.E., when Ashurbanipal had reestablished his rule over Babylon and Elam and had brought major elements in eastern Palestine to order, Psamtik was firmly in control of all Egypt. He had first seized control of Thebes, over a period of time placing his own men over the major cities. He had shrewdly gained mastery of the priesthood there and brought the mercenary lords under firm control. Egypt was united as it had not been for centuries. He had made an alliance with Gyges of Lydia by 654 B.C.E. and had apparently positioned himself as an ally to Assyria in its final struggles to keep its empire alive. He reestablished close relations to the port cities of the western Mediterranean. His strength may have come partially from his use of Greek mercenaries.

This newfound strength undoubtedly led to renewed claims to Egypt's traditional position of power and privilege in Syria-Palestine, especially along the coast. He invaded Philistia and laid lengthy siege to Ashdod.

Meantime, Assyria had troubles of its own. In 652 B.C.E. Babylon rebelled. There was conflict in Palestine, perhaps fomented by Psamtik (cf. 2 Chr 33:11), and Arab tribes raided Assyrian garrisons on the eastern edges of Palestine. By 640 B.C.E. Ashurbanipal had brought order to that part of his empire and settled down to spend his last years in more peaceful pursuits. He made no effort to reconquer Egypt.

Manasseh died in 642 B.C.E. and was succeeded by his son Amon, but it was apparently a sign of those troubled times that Amon was assassinated two years later by persons in the palace who were in turn killed by outraged citizens (2 Kgs 21:23–24). The violent acts reflected Judah's position as a vulnerable buffer state in the international power struggles of the period. Josiah was crowned king before his eighth birthday. The account in 2 Kings is primarily concerned with his great reforms (2 Kgs 22:1–23:29), and only the cryptic news of his death fighting the Egyptians at Megiddo hints at the political tightrope that he walked in keeping his nation out of trouble in those unsettled times. In some sense he kept both the weakening Assyrian rulers and Psamtik I satisfied with his relations to them for thirty years before that fateful battle.

At exactly the time that Josiah was reforming worship in Judah and consolidating his political hold on a wider territory, Assyria was facing a coalition of forces that

Historical Data Parallel to Isaiah 28:1–33:24

YEAR	EGYPT	JUDAH	ASSYRIA	BABYLON
660 B.C.E.	Psamtik I (663–609)	Manasseh (697–642)	Ashurbanipal (669–633)	
640	Psamtik I controls all Egypt (640).	Amon (642–640) assassinated; Josiah begins rule (640–609).		Ashurbanipal reestablishes rule over Babylon (640); Nabopolassar (633–605)
630	(Scythians drive to the border of Egypt.)			Assyrians defeated at the gates of Babylon (626). Egyptians fight Babylon north of Babylon; no decision (616).
620	[Isa 28–29]		Cyaxares takes Asshur (614).	Babylon rules east of the Euphrates (609–604).
610	Neco (609–593) marches through Judah (609). Egypt rules west of the Euphrates (609–604). Neco defeated at Carchemesh; withdraws from Palestine (605). Neco withstands Babylonian invasion, holding his border (601).	[Isa 30–33] Josiah dies (609). Jehoiakim (609–598); under Egypt (609–604). Jehoiakim tests Babylon's rule (598).	Nineveh falls (612). Haran falls (610).	Nebuchadnezzar (605–562) reestablishes control of Palestine to the River of Egypt (604).
600		Nebuchadnezzar lays siege to Jerusalem, deports leaders to Babylon. Zedekiah (598–587) Babylonian vassal.		
590	Psamtik II (593–588) Apries (Hophra) (588–526)	Nebuchadnezzar puts down Judaean revolt (587). Apries marches to help Jerusalem but backs off without a fight. Destruction of Jerusalem and temple. Deportations begin.		

would destroy it over a fifteen-year period. In 626 B.C.E. the Assyrians were defeated at the gates of Babylon.

At this time apparently a horde of foreigners that Herodotus calls Scythians swept down through Palestine to the borders of Egypt, where they were finally stopped. With the force of their march halted, they retreated from the territory. Their presence may well account for a decade's delay in further developments in Mesopotamia.

By 616 B.C.E. the issues in the struggle were clear. Assyria's fate was sealed. The major contest for succession to its imperial power was joined. The principal claimants were Media, Babylon, and Egypt. Media apparently agreed to support Nabopolassar's claim to Babylonian ascendancy, but Egypt contested his claims. In 616 B.C.E. an Egyptian army fought a battle with Babylonian forces north of Babylon. The result was indecisive. The Egyptians withdrew. Cyaxares led Median forces in the successful assault on Asshur in 614 B.C.E. United Babylonian and Median forces destroyed Nineveh in 612 B.C.E. Assyrian armies retreated to Haran in Syria, which was also captured in 610 B.C.E.

In 609 B.C.E. Neco, who had just succeeded to the Egyptian throne, pressed north to stop the Babylonian armies before they could occupy Palestine. (On this campaign Josiah tried to stop him at Megiddo and died in the process.) Neco apparently intended to help the last Assyrian king retake Haran. This failed, but he did establish the Euphrates as the boundary between Egypt and Babylon. This meant that all Palestine including Judah came under his direct control for a brief period (609–604 B.C.E.). He placed Jehoiakim on the throne and thus made Jerusalem a pawn in the struggle for sovereign power over the Near East.

The tone of the references in chaps. 30–31 reflects a time well before Assyria's fall but with the prospect of that fall already "in the air." It is a time when Egypt's ambitions are known and there are eager supporters in Judah. Almost any point between ca. 650 and 620 B.C.E. might fit. Perhaps a point early in the boy-king Josiah's reign (ca. 640–633 B.C.E.) might serve best.

But the respite from Babylonian pressure was brief. In 605 B.C.E. Nebuchadnezzar, as a general, was pressing a campaign in northern Syria. He defeated Egyptian forces at Carchemesh and again near Hamath, apparently gaining Neco's recognition that West Asia belonged to the Babylonian sphere of influence (cf. 2 Kgs 24:7). When Nabopolassar died, Nebuchadnezzar returned to Babylon to assume the throne. He required only a short time to consolidate the empire before resuming his campaigns in the west. In 604 B.C.E. he asserted sovereignty over Palestine. His armies took Ashkelon and deported its leaders. Jer 36:9 reports a great assembly held in Jerusalem to meet the crisis. Jehoiakim became a Babylonian vassal (2 Kgs 24:1), though apparently an unwilling one.

Meanwhile, Pharaoh Neco turned his attention to domestic issues. With or without royal permission, some from his court continued to encourage border states like Judah to keep Babylon occupied. An indecisive battle at the border in 601 B.C.E. prevented Nebuchadnezzar from moving into Egypt, but this failure apparently encouraged Jehoiakim to rebel against him in 598 B.C.E. The Judean rebellion received no Egyptian support. Jehoiakim died and Jehoiachin was taken off as a hostage. Zedekiah ascended the throne under Babylonian patronage, but continued patriotic agitation under the mirage of Egyptian favor characterized his ten-year reign.

Psamtik II succeeded Neco in 593 B.C.E. and was in turn succeeded by his son Apries (Hophra in Hebrew usage) in 588 B.C.E. Apparently under the active encouragement of Apries, Tyre, Sidon, Moab, and Ammon pressed Zedekiah to join in revolt. The Egyptian lobby in Jerusalem won out, but Apries used the occasion for his own ends, attacking Tyre and Sidon in naval and land battles, and occupying the Phoenician plain. He may also have gained control of Lebanon. These successes meant little to

Jerusalem, for Egypt showed neither the will nor the ability to penetrate inland from the coast. Babylonian forces worked unhindered throughout the siege and destruction of Jerusalem (cf. the account in 2 Kgs 25).

Thus the politics of Judah's last half century were overshadowed by its position as a miniature border state between empires in Mesopotamia and Egypt. When Assyrian power ebbed at mid-seventh century, a great Egyptian wave swept across Palestine to the Euphrates. But when Babylonian power prevailed in 605 B.C.E., the Egyptian tide ebbed. And Judah was drowned in the undertow.

During this period there were those in Jerusalem who saw the extension of Egyptian influence as Judah's opportunity to reassert itself. And well they might, for the great period of Israel's beginnings from Moses to Solomon was made possible by Egypt's benign nominal control of Palestine.

But others in Jerusalem, like Jeremiah, were not impressed. They correctly saw that Egypt's real interests lay in Africa and the Mediterranean basin. This meant only marginal interest in Palestine, which hardly reached beyond the coastal areas. Egypt simply wanted to use states like Judah as a buffer against Mesopotamian invasion.

The pro-Egyptian party was undoubtedly active in Josiah's reign but not dominant. Josiah's policy welcomed Egypt's pressure on Assyria and Babylon but kept them at arm's length. That he should have died fighting an Egyptian army that was only passing through remains an enigma, perhaps understandable only within the impossibly complex politics of that day.

The pro-Egyptian party was dominant during the early part of Jehoiakim's reign and continued to be influential until the very end in 587 B.C.E., with tragic results.

Disaster from Expansion (28:1–29)

This scene comprises three episodes. The first, "Ephraim's Drunkards" (vv 1–13), casts a sad backward look at Ephraim's closing years (as in acts 1 and 2) and at the intervening years in that region. (Josiah was apparently able to reincorporate a substantial part of the area into his kingdom, and, presumably, Jehoiakim continued to have control there until the Babylonian invasions.) The second, "Scoffers in Jerusalem" (vv 14–22), is addressed to the leaders in Jerusalem who claim to be bound by a "covenant with death." The third, "YHWH's Strategy" (vv 23–29), uses a lesson from a farmer's experience to illustrate God's work for Israel.

Woe, Ephraim's Drunkards (28:1–13)

Bibliography

Aitken, K. T. "Hearing and Seeing: Metamorphoses of a Motif in Isaiah 1–39." In *Among the Prophets: Language, Image and Structure in the Prophetic Writings.* Ed. P. R. Davies and D. J. A. Clines. JSOTSup 144. Sheffield: JSOT Press, 1993. 12–41. **Asen, B. A.** "The Glands of Ephraim:

Isaiah 28.1–6 and the *Marzeah.*" *JSOT* 71 (1996) 73–87. **Bailey, K. E.** "'Inverted Parallelism' and 'Encased Parables' in Isaiah and Their Significance for OT and NT Translation and Interpretation." In *Literary Structure and Rhetorical Strategies in the Hebrew Bible.* Ed. L. J. de Regt et al. Assen: Van Gorcum, 1996. 14–30. **Barthel, J.** *Prophetenwort und Geschichte.* Tübingen: Mohr Siebeck, 1997. 280–303. **Betz, O.** "Zungenreden und süsser Wein: Zur eschatologischen Exegese von Jesaja 28 in Qumran und im Neuen Testament." *Bibel und Qumran.* FS H. Bardtke, ed. S. Wagner. Berlin: Evangelische-Haupt-Bibelgesellschaft, 1968. 20–36. **Beuken, W. A. M.** "Isaiah 28: Is It Only Schismatics That Drink Heavily? Beyond the Synchronic Versus Diachronic Controversy." In *Synchronic or Diachronic? A Debate on Method in Old Testament Exegesis.* Ed. J. C. de Moor. OTS 34. Leiden: Brill, 1995. 15–38. **Boehmer, J.** "Der Glaube und Jesaja: Zu Jes 7,9 und 28:16." *ZAW* 41 (1923) 84–93. **Childs, B. S.** *Isaiah and the Assyrian Crisis.* 28–31. **De Vries, S. J.** *From Old Revelation to New: A Tradition-Historical & Redaction-Critical Study of Temporal Transitions in Prophetic Prediction.* Grand Rapids, MI: Eerdmans, 1995. **Driver, G. R.** "'Another Little Drink'—Isaiah 28:1–22." In *Words and Meanings.* FS D. W. Thomas. Cambridge: Cambridge UP, 1968. 47–67. ———. "Hebrew Notes." *ZAW* 52 (1934) 51–56. **Exum, C.** "'Whom Will He Teach Knowledge?' A Literary Approach to Isaiah 28." In *SBLSP.* Ed. P. Achtemeier. Missoula, MT: Scholars Press, 1979. 2:123–51. Reprinted in *Art and Meaning: Rhetoric in Biblical Literature.* Ed. D. J. A. Clines, D. M. Gunn, and A. J. Hauser. JSOTSup 19. Sheffield: JSOT Press, 1982. **Floss, J. P.** "Biblische Theologie als Sprecherin der 'Gefährlichen Erinnerung' dargestellt an Jes 28,7–12." *BN* 54 (1990) 60–80. **Ford, J. M.** "The Jewell of Discernment (A Study of Stone Symbolism)." *BZ* 11 (1967) 109–16. **Gese, H.** "Die Strömmende Geissel des Hadad und Jesaja 28,15 und 18." In *Archäologie und Altes Testament.* FS K. Galling, ed. A. Kuschke and E. Kutsch. Tübingen: Mohr, 1970. 127–34. **Görg, M.** "Die Bidsprache in Jes 28:1." *BN* 3 (1977) 17–23. ———. "Jesaja als 'Kinderlehrer'? Beobachtungen zur Sprache und Samantik in Jes 28,10(13)." *BN* 29 (1985) 12–16. **Graffey, A.** "'The Lord However Says This': The Prophetic Disputation Speech [Is 28:14–19; 49:14–25; Ezek 37:11–13]." *ScrB* 20 (1989) 2–8. **Hallo, W. H.** "Isaiah 28:9–13 and the Ugaritic Abecedaries." *JBL* 77 (1958) 324–38. **Halpern, B.** "'The Excremental Vision': The Doomed Priests of Doom in Isaiah 28." *HAR* 10 (1986) 109–21. **Healey, J. F.** "Ancient Agriculture and the Old Testament (with Special Reference to Isaiah xxciii 23–29)." *OtSt* 23 (1984) 108–19. **Hooke, S. H.** "The Corner Stone of Scripture." In *The Siege Perilous.* London: SCM Press, 1956. 235–49. **Jackson, J. J.** "Style in Isaiah 28 and a Drinking Bout of the Gods (RS 24.258)." In *Rhetorical Criticism.* FS J. Muilenburg, ed. J. J. Jackson and M. Kessler. PTMS 1. Pittsburgh: Pickwick, 1974. 85–98. **Janzen, W.** *Mourning Cry and Woe Oracle.* BZAW 125. New York: De Gruyter, 1972. 54–55. **Landy, F.** "Tracing the Voice of the Other: Isaiah 28 and the Covenant with Death." In *The New Literary Criticism and the Hebrew Bible.* Ed. J. C. Exum and D. J. A. Clines. JSOTSup 143. Sheffield: Academic Press, 1993. 140–62. **Lanier, D. E.** "With Stammering Lips and Another Tongue: 1 Cor 14:20–22 and Is. 28:11–12." *CTR* 5 (1991) 259–85. **Lindblom, J.** "Der Eckstein in Jes.28:16." In *Interpretationes ad Vetus Testamentum pertinentes Sigmundo Mowinckel.* Oslo: Land Ogkirk, 1955. 123–32. **Löhr, M.** "Jesaja-Studien 3. Schlusswort: Zur Komposition der Kapp. 28–31." *ZAW* 37 (1917–18) 59–76. ———. "Zwei Beispiele von Kehrvers in den Prophetenschriften des Alten Testaments." *ZDMG* 61 (1907) 1–6. **Loretz, O.** "Das Prophetenwort über das Ende der Königstadt Samaria (Jes. 28:1–4)." *UF* 9 (1977) 361–63. **Melugin, R. F.** "The Conventional and the Creative in Isaiah's Judgment Oracles." *CBQ* 36 (1974) 305–6. **Möller, H.** "Abwägen zweier Übersetzungen von Jes 28,19b." *ZAW* 96 (1984) 272–74. **Montgomery, J. A.** "Notes on the Old Testament." *JBL* 31 (1912) 140–46. **Mosca, P. G.** "Isaiah 28:12*e:* A Response to J. J. M. Roberts." *HTR* 77 (1984) 113–17. **Oudenrijn, M. A. van den.** "Priesters en profeten by Isaias (Is XXVIII 7–13)." *Studia Catholica* 14 (1938) 299–311. **Peterson, D. L.** "Isaiah 28, a Redaction Critical Study." In *SBLSP.* Ed. P. Achtemeier. Missoula, MT: Scholars Press, 1979. 2:101–22. **Pfeiffer, G.** "Entwöhnung und Entwöhnungsfest im Alten Testament: Der Schlüssel zu Jesaja 28:7–13?" *ZAW* 84 (1972) 341–47. **Prinsloo, W. S.** "Eighth-Century Passages from the Book of Isaiah? Reflection on Isaiah

28:1–6." *OTE* 1 (1988) 11–19. **Qimron, E.** "The Biblical Lexicon in Light of the Dead Sea Scrolls." *DSD* 2 (1995) 294–329. **Roberts, J. J. M.** "A Note on Isaiah 28:12." *HTR* 73 (1980) 49–51. **Rost, L.** "Zu Jesaja 28:1ff." *ZAW* 53 (1935) 292. **Selms, A. van.** "Isaiah 28:9–13: An Attempt to Give a New Interpretation." *ZAW* 85 (1973) 332–39. **Stewart, A. C.** "The Covenant with the Dead in Isaiah 28." *ExpTim* 100 (1988–89) 375–77. **Stolz, F.** "Der Streit um die Wirklichkeit in der Südreichsprophetie des 8. Jahrhunderts." *WD* 12 (1973) 9–30. **Tanghe, V.** "Dichtung und Ekel in Jes xxviii 7–13." *VT* 43 (1993) 235–60. **Terrien, S.** "The Metaphor of the Rock in Biblical Theology." In *God in the Fray.* FS W. Brueggemann, ed. T. Linafelt and T. K. Beal. Minneapolis: Fortress, 1998. 157–71. **Thexton, S. C.** "A Note on Isaiah xxviii 25 and 28." *VT* 2 (1952) 81–83. **Toorn, K. van der.** "Echoes of Judean Necromancy in Isaiah 28:7–22." *ZAW* 100 (1988) 199–216. **Virgulin, S.** "Il significato della pietra de fondazione in Is 28,16." *RivB* 7 (1959) 208–20. **Vogt, E.** "Das Prophetenwort Jes 28:1–4 und das Ende der Königsstadt Samaria." In *Homenaje a Juan Prado.* Ed. L. Alvarez Verdes and E. J. Alonso Hernández. Madrid: Instituto Benito Aries Montano, 1975.

Translation

Heavens: 1 *Woe!* 1
[a]Crown of the pride[b] of the drunkards[c] of Ephraim, 4+4
[d]the beauty of its glory, now a drooping blossom,[da]
who (were)[e] at the head[f] of a fertile valley,[g] 3+2
(are now) those struck down by wine.

Earth: 2 *See! The Lord[a] had someone, [b]mighty and strong.[b]* 4+4
Like a hailstorm, a destructive storm,[c]
like a storm of [d]mighty, overflowing[d] water, 4+3
he threw[e] (them) to the land by hand.[f]

Heavens: 3 *They [fem.] were trampled[a] by feet,* 2+4
crown of the pride of Ephraim's drunkards.
4 *And she became[a] a drooping flower,[b]* 3+2+4
the beauty of its glory,
which (was) at the head of a fertile valley.
Like a firstborn[c] (fig) before summer 3+4+3
which, when one sees it,
no sooner[d] is it in his hand than he swallows it.

Chorus: 5 *In that day* 2+3
[a]YHWH of Hosts became
a crown of glory 2+2+2
and a diadem[b] of beauty
for a remnant of his people
6 *and a spirit of justice[a]* 2+2
for the one who sat on the (seat of) judgment[a]
and strength 1+3
for those who were turning back the battle (at the) gate.[b]

Heavens: 7 *But these too* 2+2+2
reeled[a] with wine
and staggered[b] with strong drink.
[c]Priest and prophet[c] 2+2+2
reeled[a] with liquor,
were swallowed up[d] from wine.[e]

They staggered [b] *from liquor.* 2+2+2
They reeled [a] *with drink.*[f]
They overflowed [g] *(with) booze.*[h]
[8] *For* [a] *all the tables* 2+2+3
were full of vomit,[b]
filth,[c] *with no clean place.*
Earth: [9] *To whom could such a one have taught knowledge?* [a] 3+3
And to whom could he have explained a message?
Ones weaned from milk? 2+2
Or ones just taken from the breast?
[10] [a]*That* [b] *(it should be)* 1
"Tsaw[c] *for* tsaw.[c] 2+2
Tsaw[c] *for* tsaw.[c]
Qaw[d] *for* qaw.[d] 2+2
Qaw[d] *for* qaw.[d]
Little one,[e] *here!* 2+2
Little one,[e] *here!"*
Heavens: [11] *Yet even* [a] 1
by such a stammering [b] *lip* 2+2+3
and with another tongue,
he spoke to this people, 3
[12] *he who had said to them:* 3
"This (is) your [a] *(place of) rest.* 2
Give rest to the weary. 2
This is your (place of) repose." 2
But (there was) no willingness to listen.[b] 3
Earth: [13] *The word of YHWH* [a] *for them was:* 4
"Precept [b] *for precept.*[b] 2+2
Precept [b] *for precept.*[b]
Line [c] *for line.*[c] 2+2
Line [c] *for line.*[c]
A little here. 2+2
A little there."
In order that they would walk and stumble back 4+3
and be broken, be snared, and be captured.

Notes

1.a-a. Irwin ("Isaiah 28–33," 4–5) notes that עטרת . . . תפארתו, "crown . . . drooping blossom," forms a stereotyped phrase (cf. Isa 62:3; Jer 13:18; Ezek 16:12; 23:42; Prov 4:9; 16:31), which is here deliberately broken up.

1.b. 1QIsa[a] נאון is the more usual form for MT נאות, "pride," which also occurs in 9:17.

1.c. LXX μισθωτοὶ, "hirelings," reads the Heb. as שְׂכִיר. α΄ σ΄ θ΄ translate MT correctly: μεθυοντες, "drunkards." (Cf. F. X. Wutz, *BZ* 21 [1933] 12; G. Rinaldi, "Οἱ μισθωτοὶ 'Εφσθωτοὶ 'Εφραὶμ bei Is 28,1," *BeO* 9 [1967] 164.)

1.d-d. Two pairs in gen. relation form a substantive sentence. Cf. M. Gilula, "צְבִי in Isaiah 28:1—A Head Ornament," *Tel Aviv* 1 (1974) 128.

1.e. The past-time viewpoint (cf. J. Wash Watts, *Survey of Syntax*, 30–31) is chosen for vv 1–13. The passage looks back on conditions in Ephraim a century earlier.

1.f. ראש, "head," may describe the hill of Samaria above a fertile valley (cf. Mic 1:5; É. Dhorme, *L'emploi métaphorique des noms de parties du corps en hébreu et en akkadien* [1923; reprinted Paris: Geuthner, 1963] 22). But "head" may also refer to its status as capital of the country.

1.g. 1QIsa[a] נאי, "proud ones of," for MT גֵּיא, "valley." G. Driver ("'Another Little Drink,'" 48) and NEB favor the change. Irwin ("Isaiah 28–33," 6) argues that the parallelism supports MT.

2.a. 1QIsa[a] ליהוה, "to YHWH," for MT לאדני, "to the Lord." But cf. Isa 6:11 and 7:20.

2.b-b. Syr. *ḥjl' w'wšn',* "strength and might"; Vg. *ecce validus et fortis Dominus,* "behold powerful and strong (is) the Lord"; LXX ἰδοὺ ἰσχυρὸν καὶ σκληρουν ὁ θυμὸς κυρίου, "behold robust and fierce (is) the anger of the Lord." All these take חזק ואמץ to be nouns referring to YHWH (cf. *BHS*). Irwin ("Isaiah 28–33," 8) suggests making לְ emphatic, which comes to the same thing. However, MT makes sense as it is and refers to the Assyrian. See the comparison with other usage made by Laberge (*La Septante d'Isaïe 28–33,* 266–70).

2.c. קטב, "destructive." Jews at a later date knew a demon by this name (M. Jastrow, *Dictionary of the Targum* [New York: Pardes, 1950] 2:1346). Irwin ("Isaiah 28–33," 8) sees it as the name of a god Qeteb, who was a companion of Reshep or Deber as agents of Death (cf. A. Caquot, "Sur quelques demons de l'Ancien Testament: *Reshep, Qeṭeb, Deber,*" *Sem* 6 [1956] 53–68) and translates "tempest hell-sent." The intention is to indicate a superlative (cf. 13:6). Irwin cites full literature.

2.d-d. 1QIsa[a] כברים שוטפים does not change the meaning of MT.

2.e. הֵנִּיחַ is the same root as "Noah" and has two families of meaning: I "to give rest to"; II "to lay or set down." This pointing relates it to II (cf. BDB, *HAL*). The figure of a powerful rainstorm (cf. 8:6–8; 14:3) adds to the symbolic implication. Donner *(Israel unter den Völkern)* is concerned that an object for the verb is missing. Wildberger suggests that the "crown of the pride" (v 1) is intended.

2.f. ביד, "by hand," is often understood as "power" or "force." But note the parallel position to ברגלים, "by feet," that follows.

3.a. The fem. pl. form is followed by a sg., עֲטֶרֶת, "crown." *BHS* suggests a change in pointing to make it sg. with an "energetic" ending. *BHK*[3] suggests changing "crown" to עַטְרֹת, "crowns." Other emendations abound. Of these, the singular energic is preferable (cf. Irwin, "Isaiah 28–33," 10). However, the mixture of pl. and sg. has continued from v 1, and the sg. "crown" may also be read as a collective.

4.a. 1QIsa[a] והייתה, but no change in meaning.

4.b. ציצת is a fem. form of ציץ in v 1.

4.c. MT כְּבִכּוּרָהּ, "its firstborn." The versions have, with α´, ως πρωτογενημα, "the firstborn [pl.]," suggesting that one drop the *mappiq* in ה.

4.d. 1QIsa[a] בעודנה adds a seemingly meaningless *nun* epenthetic before the suf.

5.a. Tg. inserts משיחא, "Messiah." Wildberger (1043) comments that they could not conceive that the change announced here could happen except by the appearance of the Messiah.

5.b. צפירה, according to Wildberger and BDB (cf. *HAL*), is like the Arab. *ṣafara,* "to braid." It means here "a braided crown" (cf. Ezek 7:7, 10).

6.a. The *'atnakh* needs to be moved to the second משפט, "judgment" (cf. Delitzsch; Wildberger, 1044).

6.b. Dahood, following Syr. and θ´, translates "from the gate." But this requires elaborate explanations of why the מן, "from," is missing and the *he*-directive has lost its force (cf. Irwin, "Isaiah 28–33," 13–14; GKC §90*e*). 1QIsa[a] שער eliminates the *he*-directive.

7.a. שגו, "reeled," has a basic meaning "go astray, err," but a use for drunkenness occurs in Prov 20:1 and for love in Prov 5:19–20. Driver has challenged this meaning ("'Another Little Drink,'" 51), preferring "was wrapped up in, addicted to." Irwin ("Isaiah 28–33," 14) defends the translation "reel"; *HAL* "stagger."

7.b. תעו, "staggered" (BDB, 1073), has also been challenged by Driver, who prefers meanings like "cackled, croaked, guffawed" ("'Another Little Drink,'" 52). I. Eitan ("Isaiah Exegesis," *HUCA* 12–13 [1937–38] 71) derives the word from תלל and translates in accordance with an Arab. root meaning "be faint, languid." Irwin ("Isaiah 28–33," 15) defends the meaning "stagger"; so also *HAL.*

7.c-c. 1QIsa[a] כוהן ונבי shows the variant spellings for the same words used at Qumran. Tg. has ספר, "scribe," in place of "prophets."

7.d. בלע, "befuddled" (BDB, 118), has as its basic meaning "are swallowed up." G. R. Driver (*ZAW* 52 [1934] 52) points to a Syr. parallel root "was struck down." Wildberger (1053) notes that the meaning "were struck down by wine" is not impossible but prefers "confused." Irwin ("Isaiah 28–33," 16) cites J. Barth's *Beiträge zur Erklärung des Jesaias* (Karlsruhe-Leipzig, 1885) 4, and *HAL* for "confused" (so also BDB, *DCH*) but then makes a strong case with parallels in Isaiah for the meaning "are swallowed up." Both meanings are possible.

7.e. LXX and α´ omit "with wine."

7.f. רֹאֶה is pointed in MT as a ptc., "seeing," i.e., a vision." *HAL* supports this meaning with reference to חָזֶה, "vision," in v 15 (but see *Note* 28:15.b.). Its parallels in this verse suggest an alcoholic drink. It is the only occurrence of this form (BDB, 906). G. R. Driver (*JTS* 36 [1935] 151–53; "'Another Little Drink,'" 52) supported by C. S. Rodd ("Rediscovered Hebrew Meanings," *ExpTim* 71 [1959] 131–34), D. W. Thomas ("Isaiah LIII," *ETL* 44 [1968] 85), and M. Dahood (*Proverbs and Northwest Semitic Philology* [Rome: Pontifical Biblical Institute, 1963] 206; *Psalms*, AB 17 [Garden City, NY: Doubleday, 1968] 2:78), makes רֹאֶה a noun from ראה, "drink one's fill," a by-root of רוה (cf. Irwin, "Isaiah 28–33," 18). M. Pope (*The Use of the Old Testament in the New, and Other Essays*, FS W. F. Stinespring, ed. J. M. Efird [Durham, NC: Duke UP, 1972] 196) thinks the word has been altered to conceal an offensive word. From Ugaritic he suggests an original חרא, meaning "excrement" (see Irwin's comment, "Isaiah 28–33," 18).

7.g. פקו, "they stumble." Driver ("'Another Little Drink,'" 53) and NEB translate "collapse" or "hiccup." Irwin ("Isaiah 28–33," 18–19) suggests reading the root פוק as cognate with פוץ (BDB, II, 807), "flow, overflow," and supports his view with parallels. He reads it in parallel to נבלעו, "were swallowed up." The meaning continues in the next verse.

7.h. פליליה, "making decisions" (BDB, 813; GKC §118*g*), "verdict" (*HAL*). But Irwin ("Isaiah 28–33," 19) suggests "soddenness, moisture," reading פלל = בלל, "mix, confuse." Hence the meaning "booze." There is no prep. here as in the other statements. *BHK*³ and *BHS* supply ב, which Wildberger notes is required in fact or as understood. Irwin ("Isaiah 28–33," 20) deals with the issue by treating the noun as "accusative of material," citing Dahood ("Ugaritic-Hebrew Syntax and Style," *UF* 1 [1969] 19; *Psalms*, AB 17A [Garden City, NY: Doubleday, 1970] 3:397–98).

8.a. כי may also be read as an emphatic particle "indeed" (cf. Irwin, "Isaiah 28–33," 20).

8.b. 1QIsa[a] קיה for MT קיא is probably a careless transcription (cf. Wildberger, 1053).

8.c. צאה, "filth," is put in the second stich by MT. Recent interpreters are virtually unanimous in moving the *'atnakh* back one word and putting it into the third line.

9.a. דעה, "knowledge," is rendered κακα, "evil," in LXX (apparently reading רעה; cf. Wildberger, 1053) and אוריתא, "law," by Tg. Irwin ("Isaiah 28–33," 21) draws on Ugar. parallels to translate "the message" as a parallel to שמועה, "a report." This is helpful but does not adequately deal with the root meaning.

10.a. The verse is made up of repeated sounds: צו, "tsaw," four times; קו, "qaw," four times; and a pair of words repeated once. Wildberger (1053) understands these to be names of letters of the alphabet: *tsade* and *qof*. LXX has paraphrased the verse: θλῖψιν ἐπὶ θλῖψιν προσδέχου, ἐλπίδα ἐπ' ἐλπίδι, ἔτι μικρὸν ἔτι μικρὸν, "accept trial upon trial, hope upon hope: yet a little, yet a little." It has found a single repetition sufficient and supplied a verb for the first two stichs. Only the third corresponds to MT.

10.b. כי is a particle of result following a question.

10.c. צו, "precept," is from צוה, "command." LXX θλῖψιν, "pressure, affliction, trial," apparently read צר, "straits, distress."

10.d. קו, "line," is understood to be the second root meaning of קוה (BDB, *HAL*). LXX follows the first meaning, "hope, wait for." Some interpreters have thought these are intended as nonsense sounds repeated endlessly, i.e., in the same sense as v 11. This translation follows the nonsense explication for v 10 and contrasts the meaningful explanation in the repetition in v 13 (see *Form/Setting/Structure* and *Comment*).

10.e. LXX understands this to be "a little." Wildberger (1053) points to the suggestions that this pictures a drunken schoolteacher who orders his pupils to repeat the alphabet and has come to the letters *tsaw* and *qaw*. They then understand זעיר, "little," to refer to a child being called upon to recite. G. R. Driver (*Semitic Writing* [London: Cumberlege, 1944; Oxford UP, 1954] 90) suggests emending שם, "there," to שִׂים, which could be understood as "pay attention" (cf. Kaiser's "Boy, be careful!"). The main question is whether "little" applies to what is taught or to who is being taught. Driver ("'Another Little Drink,'" 104) thinks it refers to "another little drink."

11.a. See *Note* 10.b. above.

11.b. לעג comes from a root meaning "mock, deride, stammer." It is sometimes used of foreigners (Isa 33:19; 37:22). BDB suggests the noun means "stammerings," and *DCH* refers to parallel uses in Hos 7:16 and 1QH[a] 4:16. KBL thinks this refers to the people of stammering lips. *HAL* refers it to the stammering itself, "with stammering lips."

12.a. המנוחה, lit. "the rest." The definite article is used to imply the possessive pronoun. Cf. Irwin ("Isaiah 28–33," 24), Joüon §137*f* (12), and Dahood (*Psalms*, AB 17A [Garden City, NY: Doubleday, 1970] 3:379).

12.b. Irwin's suggestion ("Isaiah 28–33," 24) to divide MT's בוא שמוע, "not willing to listen," as אשמאע אבו, "they would not let us listen," creates more problems than it solves.
13.a. LXX κυρίου τοῦ θεοῦ, "Lord, the God." MT should be kept.
13.b., c. See *Notes* on v 10 above.

Form/Structure/Setting

The episode is composed of three parts: Vv 1–4 are a mourning cry over Ephraim and the loss of its sanctuary, using the metaphor of drunkards to recall the confused last years of the northern kingdom almost a century before (cf. chaps. 5 and 10). Vv 5–8 recount YHWH's presence with the remnant and their potential for renewed social health, but a series of disasters followed because the leaders continued in a state typified by drunkenness. Vv 9–13 use a parable of teaching children their letters to show how God used even drunken priests and prophets to speak his message to a people doomed to repeated disaster.

The episode's unity lies in the consistent metaphors of "the crown" (28:1, 3, 5), which is destroyed and replaced by YHWH himself, and of the drunkenness for Ephraim (the northern kingdom). It contrasts the bumbling and repulsive ineptness of people, priest, and prophet (vv 1, 3–4, 7–8) with the decisive (v 2), determined compassion (vv 5–6) and patience (vv 9–10) of YHWH as he worked with them. The episode fits the beginning of Josiah's reign when he apparently extended his sovereignty over the territory formerly occupied by northern Israel and thereby may well have aroused dreams in Jerusalem of renewing the days of David's glory.

Comment

1 הוי, "woe." The lament continues that of chap. 10, recalling the dreadful fall of the kingdom of Israel.

עטרת, "crown," may be of gold or silver for a king or of flowers for a party, or it may refer to the crownlike figure of a walled city on a hill. Terrien ("Metaphor of the Rock," 159) notes that this word is used for a shrine idol in 2 Sam 12:30 and can refer to the Jerusalem temple (Jer 13:18; Ezek 16:12) or to Jerusalem and Samaria (Ezek 23:42). He also notes that the phrase צבי תפארת, "beauty of glory" (vv 1, 5), is used for the Jerusalem sanctuary (Ps 96:6) and the heavenly temple (Isa 64:10 [11]). גאות, "pride," and פארה, "glory" (cf. Isa 13:19 of Babylon), are contrasted with ציץ נבל, "a drooping blossom" (cf. 40:7–8), which pictures Ephraim's present state. A similar contrast is made between being "head of a fertile valley" and "those struck down with wine."

The metaphor of drunkenness dominates the episode. It is a figure of Israel's stumbling, bumbling life during the last decades of its existence (ca. 740–21 B.C.). Its relevance a century later lies in Josiah's regained control over that territory. Now one mourns again the circumstances that led to that earlier disaster.

2 חזק ואמץ, "one mighty and strong," is a fixed pair of words (cf. Laberge, *La Septante d'Isaïe 28–33*, 266–700, for a study of its appearance in the OT). Here it refers to the Assyrian emperor Shalmaneser, who laid siege to Samaria (cf. Isa 10:3 and 2 Kgs 17:3–6), or to Sargon II, who actually captured the city and took its people into exile (2 Kgs 17:6). He was the Lord's agent in destruction (Isa 10:5–6).

3–4 The Assyrian attack is seen as an explanation of the faded crown. כבכור, "like a firstborn fig," refers to the first figs to appear on the tree and represents the ease with which the mighty Assyrians swallowed up the city.

5–6 The chorus chants its faith that YHWH used the catastrophe in order that he become a "crown of glory" for the "remnant" who were left (cf. 10:20–23). Although the king and his court were gone, YHWH remained. ביום ההוא, "in that day," recognizes the moment of YHWH's intervention (De Vries, *From Old Revelation to New,* 121). Through his spirit, justice could again be found in the courts and genuine strength for its defenders. Vermeylen (*Du prophetie Isaïe,* 388–89) notes a similarity in language and figure with Isa 9:1–6 and 11:1–5.

7–8 The remaining representatives of God, the priests and the prophets, are accused of being drunkards. The disgusting picture is portrayed in detail.

9–10 One scoffs at what such teachers could possibly teach, even to the youngest children. Interpreters have understood this verse to mean everything from speaking in tongues to being code words for great thoughts (cf. *Notes* for vv 10 and 11). But the picture of the drunken teacher is most simple and appropriate. Like a bumbling schoolmaster, they repeat letters of the alphabet (צ *[tsade]* and ק *[qof]*, using their earlier names *tsaw* and *qaw*) for the children to learn (Wildberger, 1053). זעיר, "little," in this context, seems most likely to refer to the children of v 9*b*. Both verses deal with the issue of teaching knowledge (9*a*) and the incompetency of the drunken teachers, the prophets, and the priests (7*b*).

11 The respondent insists that God continued to speak to his people, even through such a "stammering lip." "With another tongue" is understood (Wildberger, 1060) to refer to the Assyrians. Isa 33:19 speaks of "the people of speech too obscure to hear, a stammering tongue," while 36:11 tells of the Assyrians being asked to use their usual tongue, Aramaic. God spoke to that age even if it had to be through drunken prophets/priests and through the Assyrian invaders.

העם הזה, "this people," is a specific, but impersonal, designation that contrasts with the personal "my people" or "your people" in other places. Wildberger (1061) notes the deep disappointment inherent in its tone (cf. Isa 6:9). Laberge (*La Septante d'Isaïe 28–33,* 271–79) has an extended excursus on the phrase, noting its usage fifty times in the Pentateuch and Deuteronomistic History and thirty-one times in Jeremiah. He concludes that it is not specifically Deuteronomic. It is used in two ways, one with a good, positive sense and the other a shifting, changing sense. The phrase occurs ten times in Isaiah, always (according to Laberge) concerning the population of Jerusalem and always, like Jeremiah, in a bad sense. But Laberge's identification of the people with Jerusalem must be questioned. In Isa 6:9–10 the reference is ambiguous, but this commentary has found its likely reference in the doom pronounced on northern Israel. In Isa 8:6, 11, 12 the references again point to northern Israel following the prophecy in v 4. The reference here (in 28:11) is to Ephraim. In Isa 29:13–14 for the first time the context favors an identification with Jerusalem. Laberge is right in sensing a consistent negative implication in the use.

12 Note the close association of these verses with Exod 33:13–14, where a discussion between Moses and God over which of them should own "this people" leads to God's promise that "I will give you rest." G. von Rad (*Holy War in Ancient Israel,* trans. M. Dawn [Grand Rapids, MI: Eerdmans, 1991 (German, 1958)]) and

C. A. Keller ("Das quietistische Element in der Botschaft Jesajas," *TZ* 11 [1955] 81–97) have both stressed the relation of this vocabulary to the theme of holy war in Deut 12:10; 25:19; 1 Kgs 5:8 (4); 8:56. Note how Mic 2:10 negates this promise for his own time.

המנוחה, "the rest," carries connotations of dwelling and of the secure condition of that residence. It could refer here to YHWH's rest in Zion (e.g., Ps 132:8, 14; 1 Kgs 8:56), but the context refers to Ephraim, not to YHWH or Zion. Hence, the implication "your rest" (cf. *Note* 12.a.). The words are much closer to Deut 12:9, 28:65, and Ps 95:11, referring to Israel's rest (contra Wildberger; see *Notes*). The verse builds a beautiful chiasmus of five lines that portray YHWH's original offer to Israel of rest in Canaan and her responsibility to "give rest to the weary" there. The same sovereign Lord spoke through priest, prophet, and foreigner to interpret his action in the days of Assyria's rise to power. The original offer was conditioned upon Israel's willingness to listen, according to the emphasis in Deuteronomy. That condition was understood still to apply in the eighth century, but Israel failed to fulfill that one condition.

ולא אבוא שמוע, "but (there was) no willingness to listen." Like the condition of God's offer to Jerusalem in 1:19, those in Deuteronomy and here were not fulfilled (cf. Isa 30:9, 15). Laberge (*La Septante d'Isaïe 28–33,* 280) notes a close relation to the Pentateuch (esp. Deut 13:8; 23:5; Lev 26:21). The verse contrasts God's original good news for Israel with the garbled instruction given through drunken prophet and priest.

13 But even the basic lesson by a drunken teacher, teaching the alphabet (v 10), was turned by YHWH into an authentic word to Israel. When צו, "tsaw," is understood to derive from צוה, "command," the name of a letter can mean "precept" or "command" (cf. *Note* 10.c.). The name of the second letter, קו, "qaw," is understood as a noun from קוה, meaning "line" (cf. *Note* 10.d.). In the same vein the reference to "little ones" becomes impersonal, "a little."

What began in v 10 as mumbling incompetence is turned by the Lord to be, in v 13, an instrument of judgment leading to the leaders' destruction. The four verbs in the last two lines, "stumble," "be broken," "be snared," and "be captured," are repeated from 8:15, reinforcing the understanding that this section points back to the events of 734–21 B.C.E. that are pictured in act 1 (chaps. 7–10).

Explanation

The word *crown* is a key to vv 1–5. It is first seen as a reference to Samaria, the pride of Ephraim (28:1, 3), which is trampled by the conquerer that YHWH sent (28:2). Isa 28:5–6 pictures a day of restoration in which YHWH of Hosts becomes "a crown of glory," when judges and defenders return to the city. But then these, too, become drunkards again (28:7–13).

The low circumstances recall the sorry last days of northern Israel. They had become alcoholics, or like alcoholics. The Lord sent a strong power to destroy them (v 2). Even the reminder that YHWH will turn things around in the day of his triumph (vv 5–6) does not prevent the continued description of those sorry days when even priests and prophets in drunken stupor could only repeat nonsense syllables (vv 7–11). Even efforts to get his message through by foreigners brought no better response. So "the word of YHWH" to that generation, which appeared to be only monosyllabic nonsense spoken by drunken prophets and priests (vv 11–13), turns out to have been deliberate reminders of the inexorable processes of judgment that fulfilled the predictions of 8:15.

The passage is not a sign of Isaiah's struggle with priests and prophets, as Wildberger (1061) and others have thought. Priests and prophets joined with all the other leaders of Israel in being caught up in the alcoholic stupor. The passage specifies the result of Israel's failure to recognize Assyria's rise to power (cf. 7:17; 10:5–6) and the ambivalence inherent in the covenantal doctrine of election. For an earlier scene of Israel's drunkenness, cf. Amos 6:6–7.

In the first failure, Israel's leadership continued the petty rivalries and politics of intrigue when it needed to recognize that the extent of Assyria's power marked a fundamental shift in world political balance that demanded corresponding changes in their political philosophy and in their religious understanding of what YHWH was about. Isaiah understood that YHWH had caused the change and thus that their very allegiance to him demanded a changed attitude toward Assyria. He who had promised Israel "rest" in Canaan now called for this recognition. But they were not "willing to listen."

The second failure lay in their deafness to the "ifs" and "if nots" in the covenant formulations (cf. Deut 28:1, 15). Election through Abraham was no guarantee of protection under all circumstances. It promised that God would address them. This address demanded an answer. When they were unwilling to listen, much less to answer, Israel had forfeited her special relationship to YHWH (cf. Wildberger, 1062).

In this situation, the sanctuaries ("crowns") are destroyed. YHWH alone remains as "crown." The theme continues in v 16 when the rock is fixed as a symbol of YHWH's presence.

Scoffers in Jerusalem (28:14–22)

Bibliography

Barthel, J. *Prophetenwort und Geschichte.* Tübingen: Mohr Siebeck, 1997. 306–28. **Blenkinsopp, J.** "Judah's Covenant with Death (Isaiah xxviii 14–22)." *VT* 50 (2000) 472–83. **Boehmer, J.** "Der Glaube und Jesaja: Zu 7,9 und 28:16." *ZAW* 41 (1923) 81–93. **Bronznick, N. M.** "The Semantics of the Biblical Stem *yqr.*" *HS* 22 (1981) 9–12. **Donner, H.** *Israel unter den Völkern.* 146–53. **Driver, G. R.** "'Another Little Drink'—Isaiah 28:1–22." In *Words and Meanings.* FS D. W. Thomas. Cambridge: Cambridge UP, 1968. 47–67. **Fullerton, K.** "The Stone of the Foundation." *AJSL* 37 (1920) 1–50. **Gese, H.** "Die Strömmende Geissel des Hadad und Jesaja 28,15 und 18." In *Archäologie und Altes Testament.* FS K. Galling, ed. A. Kuschke and E. Kutsch. Tübingen: Mohr, 1970. 127–34. **Graffey, A.** "'The Lord, However, Says This': The Prophetic Disputation Speech (Isa 28:14–19; 49:14–25; Ezek 37:11–13)." *ScrB* 20 (1989) 2–8. **Hooke, S. H.** "The Corner-Stone of Scripture." In *The Siege Perilous.* London: SCM Press, 1956. 235–49. **Jeppesen, K.** "The Cornerstone (Isa 28:16) in Deutero-Isaianic Re-Reading of the Message of Isaiah." *ST* 38 (1984) 93–99. **Köhler, L.** "Zu Jes 28:15a und 18b." *ZAW* 48 (1930) 227–28. ———. "Zwei Fachwörter der Bausprache in Jesaja 28:16." *TZ* 3 (1947) 390–93. **Laberge, L.** *La*

Septante d'Isaïe 28–33: Étude de tradition textuelle. Ottawa: Laberge, 1978. **Lindblom, J.** "Der Eckstein in Jes 28:16." *NTT* 56 (1955) 123–32. **Möller, H.** "Abwägen zweier Übersetzungen von Jes 28,19b." *ZAW* 96 (1984) 272–74. **Quiring, H.** "Der Probierstein." *FF* 25 (1949) 238–39. **Roberts, J. J. M.** "Yahweh's Foundation in Zion (Isa 28:16)." *JBL* 106 (1987) 127–45. **Szlaga, J.** "Symbolika kamienia i fundamentu w Ks. Izajasza 28:16–17." *Studia Peplinskie* 2 (1971) 149–57. **Terrien, S.** "The Metaphor of the Rock in Biblical Theology." In *God in the Fray.* FS W. Brueggemann, ed. T. Linafelt and T. K. Beal. Minneapolis: Fortress, 1998. 157–71. **Tromp, N. J.** *Primitive Conceptions of Death and the Nether World in the Old Testament.* Rome: Pontifical Biblical Institute, 1969. **Virgulin, S.** "Il significato della pietra di fondazione in Isa 28:16." *RivB* 7 (1959) 208–20.

Translation

Heavens:	14 *Therefore, hear*[a] *the word of YHWH,*	4+2
	you scoffers,	
	you speech makers[b] *of this people*	3+2
	who (are) in Jerusalem.	
	15 *For you have said:*	2+3
	"We have made a covenant with Death,[a]	
	and with Sheol[a]	2+2
	we have made an agreement.[b]	
	An overwhelming scourge,[c]	2+2+2
	when (it) passes over,[d]	
	will not come upon us.	
	For we are established.	2+2+2
	A Lie (is) our refuge.	
	We have hidden ourselves in the Falsehood."	
Herald:	16 *Therefore, thus says my Lord YHWH:*	5
YHWH:	*See me laying*[a] *a stone in Zion.*[b]	4
Courtier:	*A tested*[c] *stone.*	2
Second Courtier:	*A corner (stone)*[d] *of value.*[e]	2
Third Courtier:	*A foundation (well) founded.*[f]	2
Herald:	*He who believes*[g] *will not be in haste.*[h]	3
YHWH:	17 *And I establish justice as a line*[a]	3+2
	and righteousness as a plumb line.	
Herald:	*Hail will sweep away*[b] *refuge Lie,*	4+3
	and waters will overflow (any) shelter.	
	18 *Your covenant with Death will be annulled,*[a]	3+4
	and your agreement[b] *with Sheol will be invalidated.*	
	When an overwhelming scourge passes over,	4+3
	you shall become a victim of its devastation.	
	19 *As often as it passes over*	2+2
	it will strike you.	
	Indeed, morning by morning it will pass over,	3+2
	by day and by night.	
Earth:	*The understanding of this message*	3+2
	will be sheer terror!	
	20 *For the bed is too short to stretch out,*[a]	3+3
	and the covering (too) narrow to wrap oneself in.[b]	
Heavens:	21 *But*[a] *YHWH will rise as*[b] *(at) Mount Perazim;*[c]	4+3[d]

as (in) a valley in Gibeon, he will quiver
to do his work. 2+2
Chorus: *Strange*[e] *(is) his work!*
Heavens: *And to serve his service.* 2+2
Chorus: *Alien (is) his service!*
Prophet: 22*And now, do not scoff [pl.]* 3+3
lest your bonds[a] *be made strong(er)!*
For I have heard annihilation strictly determined 3+4+3
from my Lord,[b] *YHWH of Hosts,*
upon the whole land.

Notes

14.a. 1QIsa[a] reads a sg. for MT's pl.

14.b. משלים may be understood as LXX ἄρχοντες, "rulers," or, from another use of the root, to mean "speak in parables or proverbs." Wildberger (1064) notes that the other references to politics seem to favor the former, while the parallel to אנשי לצון, "scoffers," favors the latter. He suggests the passage is directed not to the politicians themselves but to the counselors and theoreticians of Jerusalem's policies (cf. Kaiser). Irwin's ("Isaiah 28–33," 25) "reigning wits" keeps one foot in each camp.

15.a. Note that neither מות, "death," nor שאול, "Sheol," has an article. The Canaanite concepts are explained by N. J. Tromp, *Primitive Conceptions of Death,* 99.

15.b. חֹזֶה, "agreement" (BDB, 302 n.), appears again in the pl. in v 18. LXX has συνθήκας, "agreement, common deposit," to parallel διαθήκην, for ברית, "covenant." However, Syr. *ḥzw'*, "vision," takes up another meaning of the Heb. root. Vg. *pactum* agrees with LXX, having its synonym *foedus* for ברית. The issue is being widely discussed (cf. Wildberger, 1065; Irwin, "Isaiah 28–33," 27) and is not yet settled. Until it is, the translation can hold to something like "agreement."

15.c. 1QIsa[a] and Q read שוט (cf. v 18), "scourge, whip" (BDB; *HAL* I). K has שיט, "oar." LXX καταιγίς, "hurricane," and Syr. *šwwt' dgrwpj'*. "flood plain" (see *HAL* II, "outburst, sudden spate of water"), seem to have understood שֶׁטֶף, "flood," as the next word (see *HAL*). But MT reads שׁוֹטֵף, an active ptc., "overwhelming, overflowing." J. Barth ("שוט שטף," *ZAW* 33 [1913] 306–7) referred to the Qur'an (89:12): "God poured out on them the *sawṭ* (the watery flood) of punishment." S. Poznanski ("Zu שוט שטף," *ZAW* 36 [1916] 119–20) noted that Jewish traditions used this meaning of the phrase. Irwin ("Isaiah 28–33," 27–28) translates "the flood lash" and cites H. Gese ("Die strömmende Geissel des Haddad und Jes. 28:15 u. 18," in *Archäologie und Altes Testament,* FS K. Galling [Tübingen: Mohr (Siebeck), 1970] 127–34), who refers to coins and statues of the rain-god Haddad with a lash in his hand.

15.d. K עָבַר (pf.); Q יַעֲבֹר (impf.), "it passes over." Wildberger (1065) chooses Q. Irwin ("Isaiah 28–33," 27) discusses the grammatical issue in light of Ugar. and favors K.

16.a. יִסַּד, "laying," is apparently a 3 m. sg. *pi'el* pf. (cf. BDB, 413; GKC §155*f*). Irwin ("Isaiah 28–33," 30) correctly notes that in this form it must be considered a relative clause without a relative particle to account for the change of person. 1QIsa[a] מיסד is a *pi'el* ptc. 1QIsa[b] יוסד is a *qal* ptc. The versions support the latter reading, suggesting the pointing יֹסֵד (*BHK*). Irwin (31) keeps the *lectio difficilior* of MT. *HAL* and most other interpreters follow Qumran and the versions.

16.b. בציון, "in Zion," is the natural rendering. Irwin ("Isaiah 28–33," 31) understands בּ as *bet essentiae* (GKC §119*i*) and translates "I have founded Zion as a stone." Thus Zion is the stone. He then draws parallels to Isa 29:1–8 and 31:4–9. But one may ask whether it should not also parallel Isa 8:14*b*.

16.c. בחן, "tested, testing" (BDB). The word's meaning has not been clearly established (cf. Wildberger's review of research, 1066–67). L. Koehler (*TZ* 3 [1947] 390–93) compares it with the Eg. *bekhen*-stone. Driver (NEB) calls it granite. *HAL* offers *schist gneiss* as the technical term. With all the confusion, it is best to stay with the traditional meaning.

16.d. פנת, "corner of," is a const. form.

16.e. יקרת, "preciousness of, weight of" (BDB, *DCH;* GKC §130*f*[4]). Wildberger (1067) and *HAL* prefer the sense of value. Irwin ("Isaiah 28–33," 31) insists on the sense of weight.

16.f. מוּסָד מוּסָד (GKC §71). MT places the *zakef qaton* above the second word, causing them to be read together, the first a noun and the second a *hopʿal* ptc., "a founded foundation." Irwin ("Isaiah 28–33," 30–31) moves the accent to the first word, dividing them and making the second govern the remaining words of the stich: "a weighty corner foundation, founded by . . ." Irwin must then find a new meaning for the following word (see *Note* 16.g. below). *BHK* and Wildberger (1067) take the second word to be dittography and recommend deletion, with some LXX MSS. MT's arrangement and understanding seem to have the best of it.

16.g. המאמין, "he who believes." The root means "to support" and could in the *nipʿal* be understood as the one who builds a sure or supported structure. But the form is a *hipʿil* ptc., and *hipʿil* is consistently used in the OT for faith (cf. 7:9). There is a noun אָמָּן, which means "builder, artist," but it occurs only in Song 7:2. Irwin ("Isaiah 28–33," 30–32) translates "the Master Builder" and thus makes the entire verse conform to the imagery of building the wall. But the result is too contrived to be credible. In Deut 1:32 the form (*hipʿil* ptc.) means "none of you (was) a believer in YHWH your God."

16.h. יחיש has several possible identities. If it is derived from חוש I, it means "will be in haste" (BDB, *HAL*) or "give way, be dislodged" (*DCH*). A second meaning of this root, "will worry," is found in Eccl 2:25 (G. R. Driver, "Vocabulary of the Old Testament," *JTS* 32 [1930–31] 253–54; F. Ellermeier, "Das Verbum חוש in Koh 2:25," *ZAW* 75 [1963] 197–217; W. von Soden, "Akkadisch *hâšum* I 'sich sorgen' und hebräisch *ḥūš* II," *UF* 1 [1969] 197). LXX οὐ μὴ καταισχυνθῇ, "never be put to shame," apparently read יבוש. Syr. *lʾ ndḥl*, "not be afraid," followed the second meaning of the root חוש. Vg. *non festinet*, "not be hasty," followed the first meaning. Or the word may be derived from נחש, "practice divination." But the root with that meaning occurs only in *piʿel*. Another root חשה may be considered. It means "be silent, unresponsive, still." M. Tsevat (*TWAT* 1:591) considers this a *hipʿil* form and translates "he who trusts, does not press." While the meaning nearest MT is maintained, the interpreter does well to hear the overtones of other meanings.

17.a. קו, "line"; cf. v 13.

17.b. יעה is a *hap. leg.* יָע is a small shovel used to clean the altar, hence the meaning "sweep away."

18.a. כֻּפַּר would normally mean "be atoned" (BDB; *DCH;* GKC §145*o*). Tg. ויבטיל, "will cause to cease"; LXX μὴ καὶ ἀφέλῃ ὑμῶν τὴν διαθήκην τοῦ θανάτου, "no, and he will take away your covenant of death." Driver ("'Another Little Drink,'" 60–61) defends MT. Irwin ("Isaiah 28–33," 33) thinks the word should be הפר, "break," since this is the usual word with "covenant." But Wildberger (1068) joins Delitzsch (who points to Gen 6:14) and M. Weinfeld ("Covenant Terminology in the Ancient Near East and Its Influence on the West," *JAOS* 93 [1973] 197 n. 101) in defending MT's reading and calling for a broader meaning of כפר in the sense of "annul, cancel" (*HAL*). Perhaps it also means to compensate for any guilt left over from breaking the covenant oath.

18.b. See *Note* 15.b. LXX ἐλπίς, "hope"; OL *spes*, "hope"; but Vg. correctly *pactum*, "pact, agreement."

20.a. 1QIsa[a] משתריים (cf. Kutscher, *Language and Linguistic Background*, 289). Read MT.

20.b. 1QIsa[a] uses ב as the prep. of comparison rather than MT's כ. 1QIsa[a] is probably right. Cf. Irwin ("Isaiah 28–33," 35) and Dahood's list of the uses of מן and ב in comparison (*Psalms*, AB 17A [Garden City, NY: Doubleday, 1970] 3:397–98).

21.a. כִּי, "but." In v 20 the particle was used in explanation of the previous verse. Here it is in contrast (cf. Irwin, "Isaiah 28–33," 34).

21.b. MT כ, "like"; 1QIsa[a] ב, "on"; LXX ὥσπερ ὄρος, "just as a vision." 1QIsa[a] also reads ב in the second half of the verse and is supported by LXX. The changes from MT bring very different understandings of the verse (cf. Irwin, "Isaiah 28–33," 35). Keep MT but note the significance of the others.

21.c. LXX ἀσεβῶν, "ungodly." Laberge (*La Septante d'Isaïe 28–33*, 284) suggests that it represents Heb. רפאים, "Rephaim." Note the appearance of both words in 2 Sam 5:18, 20.

21.d. This meter follows MT. Irwin ("Isaiah 28–33," 35) suggests 3+1+3 with *YHWH* "suspended between parallel cola" and serving as subject of both (cf. M. Dahood, "A New Metrical Pattern in Biblical Hebrew," *CBQ* 19 [1967] 574–79; *Psalms*, AB 17A [Garden City, NY: Doubleday, 1970] 3:439–44).

21.e. MT זר, "strange"; LXX πικρίας, "of bitterness." Wildberger notes that LXX apparently read מר for זר.

22.a. 1QIsa[a] uses a fem. form. Both genders are possible.

22.b. אדני, "Lord," is missing in some MSS, in LXX, Syr., and 1QIsa[a]. יהוה, "YHWH," and אדני appear together frequently in Isaiah and should be kept.

Form/Structure/Setting

The episode begins with "therefore," joining it to the preceding episode. But the setting has changed.

The words are addressed to leaders in Jerusalem (vv 14, 18, 22). They are to turn their attention from old Ephraim to current events in Jerusalem, where YHWH's crucial actions are about to take place (vv 16, 21). The leaders put forward their "covenant with Death" (v 15) as their reason for recalcitrance. YHWH announces his own initiative, continuing his commitment of a "stone" laid in Zion (v 16) to accomplish his continued goals of "justice" and "righteousness." He will insist on breaking the offending treaty (covenant) (vv 18–19). The very idea brings terror (vv 19*c*–20). YHWH's new initiative is formally announced (v 21). The leaders are warned of the decree of full annihilation that had been divinely determined for the whole land (v 22, as in chap. 24 and Isa 6:11–13). The polemical dialogue turns on "the covenant with Death" and "the stone" that YHWH has placed in Zion. The strategic position of this episode in act 3 is clear. It states the terms of tension that will dominate the act as they had the history of Judah during its final decades of existence.

Comment

14 לכן, "therefore," relates the entire episode to the previous review of the attitudes of northern Israel prior to 721 B.C.E. (vv 1–13). God speaks and acts in light of previous experience, and Jerusalem, probably under Jehoiakim, bears a haunting resemblance to those last years of the northern kingdom.

"Scoffers" and "speech makers" are degrading terms applied to the political leaders of Jerusalem. אנשי לצון, "scoffers," lit. "men of scorning," may mean "men worthy of scorn" or "men whose attitude is scornful," i.e., "scoffers." The latter is a better parallel to משלי, "speech makers" or "makers of proverbs." A second meaning of משל could result in "rulers of this people," but that does not fit here. Ehrlich (*Randglossen,* 4:100) translates "wits, epigrammatists, sloganeers." Irwin ("Isaiah 28–33," 25) combines the two meanings in translating "ruler, wit."

העם הזה, "this people." See *Comment* on v 11. Here the reference is to the people of the enlarged Judean kingdom of the Josiah/Jehoiakim era.

15 The verse presents the leaders' statement of Jerusalem's foreign policy and thus of their faith. ברית, "covenant," is to be understood in the sense of "treaty" or "firm agreement." מות, "death," and שאול, "Sheol," are used metaphorically to excuse an action that might otherwise be deemed unacceptable or that jeopardizes their lives. It may imply that they felt they had no choice in the matter. If the setting is in Josiah's reign, this could refer to Judah's long-standing vassal treaty with Assyria and its new relation to Egypt, which under Psamtik I had become Assyria's ally.

כזב, "Lie," and השקר, "the Falsehood," round out the names attributed to the treaty partner, probably Egypt. The speech has parodied the kind of thing that Jehoiakim's ministers might actually have said. But why should the names Death, Sheol, Lie, and Falsehood be used? Duhm (200) and Schmidt ("Israel, Zion, und die Völker," 93) suggested that these refer to the Egyptian god of death, Osiris. This does not mean that they pray to that god; rather they have signed a treaty guaranteed by that god. Thus Osiris would have served as the divine guarantor of this treaty with Egypt. "Death" and "Sheol" come directly from such an identification. "Lie" and "Falsehood" are derisive prophetic characterizations of the idol and its mythical representation, מות *Moth,* "Death," also a Canaanite god. It was easy to draw the comparison to the Egyptian Osiris. Blenkinsopp understands the passage as a parody of the Sinai Covenant, a kind of "black mass." In that case, the covenant is a real agreement with the gods.

מות *Moth* or *Maweth,* "death," and שׁאל *Sheol* (see the Bible dictionaries) are gods of the Phoenician cities and like Osiris, the Egyptian god, chthonic or infernal dieties of the nether world. Terrien ("Metaphor of the Rock") agrees and sees the passage as part of Isaiah's announcement that YHWH will overcome the cult of Death and Sheol. The new temple will be the symbol of that victory. These religious references may compose a second level of meaning, a kind of pun, but the basic complaint against Jerusalem's leaders has to do with their international policies. Overtones of meaning spill over the literal speech. A pact with death had dire connotations, even if it was made under extreme pressure (cf. 2 Kgs 23:33–34). That anyone in Jerusalem could realistically have expected good to come from it, much less genuine security, is hard to believe. The speech implies such incredulity. (But compare Jeremiah's encounters with the supporters of Egypt.) Jehoiakim probably had no choice in the matter.

שׁיט שׁוטף, "an overwhelming scourge," is used to describe great foreign invasions. The overwhelming scourge in this setting might refer to the Assyrian and Babylonian attacks, or perhaps to the Scythian invaders who swept down through the weakening Assyrian defenses. The Vision has pictured such attacks as the work of God in chaps. 10, 13, and other places. This speech interprets Jerusalem's foreign policy in light of the conviction that these invasions are actually inspired by YHWH. This makes the phrase "covenant with Death" take on massive ironic meaning.

שׂמנו, "we are established," מחסנו, "our refuge," and נסתרנו, "we have hidden ourselves," are all phrases with religious meaning and were common to temple usage (Wildberger, 1073). שׂים, "establish," is regularly used of God's assurance concerning the temple and the throne. The others appear in the Psalms (cf. Ps 27:5). The leaders undoubtedly mixed pious religious language (cf. Ps 46:6*a,* 12 [5*a,* 11]) with their political assurances that Jerusalem was secure under their policies. This speech derides their policy as a treaty with "Lie" and "the Falsehood," both referring to idolatrous Egypt or its Pharaoh.

16 YHWH responds to the implication that these policies were necessary for their time. He repudiates the implication that the old values could no longer be held. He affirms again that what he has done and is determined to do in Zion deserves trust and faith.

הנני יסד בציון אבן, "see me laying a stone in Zion." He calls attention to his choice and commitment to Zion. What God is doing in Zion is the key to all this history. Such a cornerstone of Zion could be understood as the Davidic dynasty, but in Isaiah is more likely the temple (so Terrien, "Metaphor of the Rock"; cf. Wildberger, 1076, for a survey of the many meanings that interpreters have found in this verse). In the vision, from 2:1–3 through 65:17–66:24, the future of Zion is secure in its role as a place of worship. The temple, its function and its witness, is the abiding element in Zion. It continued as the symbol of God's presence, his work, and his will.

There is an ancient and continuing tradition of a rock on Zion. The Psalms echo it (Pss 28:1; 61:3 [2]). Isa 30:29 calls it "the Rock of Israel." H.-J. Kraus (*Psalmen,* BKAT 15.1 [Neukirchen-Vluyn: Neukirchener Verlag, 1978] 225) speaks of it as "that mythical, weathered bedrock which the fires of chaos cannot reach." (Cf. also H. Schmidt, *Der heilige Fels in Jerusalem* [Tübingen: Mohr, 1933].) The Muslim Dome of the Rock is built over the stone that tradition says was the surface of Araunah's threshing floor (2 Sam 24), which David bought to be the site of the new temple. The site is also identified as Mount Moriah (2 Chr 3:1), relating it to the place of Isaac's sacrifice (Gen 22:2). These traditions were accepted by Josephus (*Jewish Antiquities* 1.13.224, 226; 6.13.333), *Jubilees* (18:13), ancient rabbis, and Jerome. It is continued in Muslim tradition by the name *maqam el-Khalil,* "Abraham's place," applied to the Dome of the Rock.

Terrien ("Metaphor of the Rock," 160–61) notes that Zion was thought of "as the cosmic mountain, the world center, and thus the navel of the earth. . . . The myth of Zion was at best an ambiguous inheritance from West Semitic cults" (see also S. Terrien, "The Omphalos Myth and Hebrew Religion," *VT* 20 [1970] 315–18; 337–38; D. Bodi, "Jerusalem and Babylon as the Navel of the Earth," in *The Book of Ezekiel and the Poem of Erra,* OBO 104 [Freiburg: Universitätsverlag, 1991] 219–30; S. Talmon, "The 'Navel of the Earth' and Comparative Method," in *Scripture in History and Theology,* FS J. C. Rylaarsdam, ed. A. L. Merrill and T. W. Overholt [Pittsburg: Pickwick, 1977] 243–68; S. Talmon, "The 'Comparative Method' in Biblical Interpretation—Principles and Problems," in *Congress Volume: Göttingen, 1977,* VTSup 29 [Leiden: Brill, 1978] 320–56, esp. 348–49; S. D. Sterling, "Navel of the Earth," *IDBSup* [1976] 621–23). The consequences for heathen practices in the temple in the times of the kings is documented by Terrien. He notes the common idea in New Testament times "that the Rock on which the temple was erected constituted the meeting point not only between heaven and earth but also between earth and Sheol." Isaiah "boldly demythologizes a prehistoric belief inherited from the Canaanites and tenaciously adopts Yahwism. . . . Yahweh builds his own temple with a tested stone; indeed the foundation stone will keep the myth of Sheol and Death from corrupting the people" ("Metaphor of the Rock," 161).

17 God commits himself again to "justice" and "righteousness" as the only fitting standards by which to measure right and wrong. The implication is that the fluctuating reasonings of practical politics or personal advancement (as in Jehoiakim's case) are not to be trusted in that time any more than in the time of Ahaz (7:4–9). The very thing that Jerusalem's rulers had hoped to avoid will sweep over them (v 15*b*), but the military scourge will be aided by cosmic forces of "hail" and "flood waters."

18–19*a* Their self-serving "covenant" will be swept away, and repeated waves of the "scourge" will devastate the land again. The regular incursions by Nebuchadnezzar in 603, 598, and 587 B.C.E., as well as other unrecorded military pressures such as the Scythian invasions, are clearly in view.

19*b* This message could do no other than bring terror, for it shows Jerusalem's policies to be totally and disastrously wrong. They have failed to assess what God is doing in their time. They have misjudged the relative strength and will of the great powers.

20 The figure of bed and covering being too short and too narrow applies to the inadequacies of the treaty alignment that had been made with Egypt. It left Judah no room to accommodate itself to Babylon's resurgence in Palestine or to YHWH's new initiatives.

21 כהר־פרצים יקום יהוה, "YHWH will rise as at Mount Perazim." Mount Perazim is not further identified in the OT, but a place called Baal Perazim turns up in a story (2 Sam 5) in which David routs the Philistines in a battle that also moves past Gibeon. (Some interpreters have seen the latter as a reference to Josh 10.) The Philistines moved to try to crush David's new kingdom and its capital, Jerusalem, but were beaten back in decisive battles (*MBA,* 100). Wildberger (1079) notes that the account in 2 Sam 5 is formulated as a holy war in which YHWH himself enters the battle. It is also interesting to note the reference to floods of water (2 Sam 5:20).

In the Isaiah text the holy-war concept, that YHWH fights for Israel, is turned around. Here the reference, "his work," is to the Assyrian and Babylonian invasions begun in the days of Tiglath-Pileser and continued by Nebuchadnezzar. The implications were clear, though neither name is called. That Jerusalemites should cry out in disbelief זר מעשהו, "His work is strange!" and נכריה עבדתו, "His service is alien!" is understandable. They believed that YHWH's proper work lay in calling, saving, and leading Israel to fulfill his promise to Abraham to establish his people in Canaan and his promise to David to establish Zion in safety and security. The Vision has argued repeatedly that they were blind, uncomprehending, and unbelieving to his "other work" that the prophets had announced, that through the Assyrians and the Babylonians he was bringing total devastation to the land and exile to its peoples. Thus, in their eyes, this message contradicted their understanding of what they considered to be his real "work" in and through Israel. It is no wonder they called it "strange" and "alien." They may well have found that God himself had become strange and alien to Israel.

22 The last speech exhorts Jerusalemites not to התלוצצו, "scoff," at this announcement and not to ignore it.

מוסריכם, "your bonds," are those that political alliances had placed upon them. Prudence and restraint were needed to keep a bad situation from getting worse because the ban, announced in 6:13 and continued at various points in the Vision since that time, is understood still to be in force upon "the whole land" (see the discussion in *Excursus: "The Land"* [הארץ]).

Explanation

Judah's current leadership found itself in a hopeless situation. (The text probably reflects Jehoiakim's position under Egypt.) The irony of a covenant with death, Sheol, a lie that was supposed to provide refuge and safety from the overwhelming scourge, is not lost on the hearers. That was not the first, nor the last, time that politicians lamely portrayed hopeless policies as full of assurance and promise.

But YHWH would not allow himself to be identified with their defeatist and misguided policies. His work in Zion was begun long before and continued through this time. His foundation stone was a standard for judging righteousness and justice. These policies could not survive that test. Not the shifting political treaties but the recognition and acceptance of YHWH's affirmed foundation in Zion deserve faith.

Parallel to that is the recognition of the "work" of YHWH, which is identified with the "overwhelming scourge." This is consistent with the Vision's picture of God's instigation and involvement in the Assyrian invasions from the time of Tiglath-Pileser and in the Babylonian invasions and devastations under Nebuchadnezzar. This message, from that of Isaiah in 734 B.C.E. (Isa 7:17) through the intervening century to this time, had lost none of its shocking quality. It defied understanding for most Israelites. Thus it is accurately called "his strange work," "his alien task." (See *Comment.*) The prophetic faith, which holds that God works not only in the comfortable ways of election, salvation, and protection for his people, but also through the great movements of history for the accomplishments of his purposes for his people and the world, is mind-boggling. Few indeed are those who hold such a faith. The Vision of Isaiah does hold it.

The political machinations by which Judean kings tried to put off the inevitable were doomed from the start, partly because their age already lay under the ban announced in 6:11–13, and repeated since then, that "the whole land" would be completely devastated, but also because they could not find the spiritual insight and humility to come to terms with God's work in their time.

The "stone" (v 16) could be construed to refer to the Davidic dynasty, but this does not conform to the usual line of the Vision's assurance. The place of Zion as God's chosen meeting ground with Israel and the peoples, that is the temple, is promised throughout the Vision as that to which God is committed for the future. It is the place of the word (Torah in 2:3) and of his presence. The reference to the "stone" must be compared to that in 8:14. The language is different. There YHWH "becomes" the stone, the offense, the test. Here he lays it in Zion. In both instances the stone that provides assurance (8:14, MT and LXX "sanctuary"; 28:16, "a foundation well founded") is also a standard by which leaders and their policies are to be tested (of both kingdoms in 8:14; of those who proclaim a "covenant with Death" in 28:18).

This laying of the foundation stone is part of the action deemed so "strange" and "alien" (v 21). That God could at one and the same time affirm the durability and value of Zion with its temple (v 16) and also rise against its government through foreign invaders was incomprehensible to most Israelites. The Vision proclaims that this was in fact God's strategy. The kingdom was doomed. But the values inherent in Zion and the temple, symbols of YHWH's presence and purpose, would remain the foundations of faith (cf. 2:1–3; 65:17–66:24).

The NT sees the stone of v 16 as a reference to Christ. The LXX has already added ἐπ' αὐτῷ, making the last line of v 16 read "one believing on him." So Christians interpreted the verse christologically. 1 Pet 2:6 quotes the verse to support the view that Jesus Christ is the cornerstone of the church into which believers are built as living stones (vv 4–5). Terrien ("Metaphor of the Rock," 165) points to Matt 16:18 and notes that there "temple and underworld are related." The passage goes on to use stone imagery from Ps 118:22 and Isa 8:14–15 to show that the distinction between believers and unbelievers is determined by God's laying the cornerstone. Rom 9:33 mixes references to 8:14 and 28:16 to describe Israel's attempt to gain righteousness through the law. All the NT references follow LXX readings, "not be put to shame" (cf. *Notes* for v 16).

Christians have seen in Christ the successor to that symbol of God's presence and saving work that the temple on Zion represents here. The threat to the continuity of the symbol when the Romans besieged Jerusalem is met in the NT with the meaning of Christ's resurrection (John 2:19–22; Mark 13:2; 14:58; 15:29; Matt 26:61).

YHWH's Strategy: A Parable (28:23–29)

Bibliography

Amsler, S., and **O. Mury.** "Yahweh et la sagesse du paysan: Quelques remarques sur Esaïe 28:23–29." *RHPR* 53 (1973) 1–5. **Auvray, P.** *Isaïe 1–39.* SB. Paris: Gabalda, 1972. 253–56. **Barthel, J.** *Prophetenwort und Geschichte.* Tübingen: Mohr Siebeck, 1997. 329–48. **Childs, B. S.** *Isaiah and the Assyrian Crisis.* **Guthe, H.** "Eggen und Furchen im Alten Testament." In *FS K. Budde.* Ed. K. Marti. BZAW 34. Giessen: Töpelmann, 1920. 75–82. **Jensen, J.** *The Use of* tora *by Isaiah: His Debate with the Wisdom Tradition.* Washington, DC: Catholic Biblical Association of America, 1973. 50–51. **Liebreich, L. J.** "The Parable Taken from the Farmer's Labors in Isaiah 28:23–29." *Tarbiz* 24 (1954–55) 126–28. (Heb. with an English resumé.) **Mury, O.**, and **S. Amsler.** "Yahveh et la sagesse du paysan: Quelques remarques sur Esaïe 28,23–29." *RHPR* 53 (1973) 1–5. **Schuman, N. H.** "Jesaja 28:23–29: Een Boerengelijkenis als politieke profetie. Ook een manier van exegetiseren." *Segmenten* 2 (1981) 83–141. **Thexton, S. C.** "A Note on Isaiah XXVIII 25 and 28." *VT* 2 (1952) 81–83. **Vriezen, T. C.** "Essentials of the Theology of Isaiah." In *Israel's Prophetic Heritage.* Ed. B. W. Anderson and W. Harrelson. 128–46. **Whedbee, W. J.** *Isaiah and Wisdom.* 51–68. **Wilbers, H.** "Étude sur trois textes relatifs à l'agriculture: Is. 28:27,28; Amos 2:13 et 9:9." In *Melanges de l'Université St. Joseph.* Beyrouth, 1911–12. 269–83.

Translation

Prophet: 23 *Pay attention and heed my voice!* 3+3
Hearken and hear (what) I say!
24 *(Is it) all day* 2+3+3[a]
(that) the plowman plows for sowing?[b]
(That) he breaks and harrows his ground?
25 *Does he not, when he has leveled its surface,* 3+2+2
scatter dill[a]
and sow cumin?
(Does he not) set[b] *wheat in rows,*[c] 3+2+2
and barley in its place,[d]
and emmet (on) its border?[e]
Earth: 26 *He instructs one concerning good order.*[a] 2+2
His God[b] *teaches him.*
Heavens: 27 *For dill is not threshed with a threshing sled.* 5+4
Nor[a] *is a cart wheel rolled over*[b] *cumin.*
For with a stick dill is beaten out, 4+2
and cumin with a rod.

[28]*Grain*[a] *is crushed,* 2+3+2
but not forever[b]
does it continue to be threshed.[c]
If[d] *one drive the wheel of his cart (over it),* 3+3
he does not crush it with his horses.[e]
Earth: [29]*Also this (is) from YHWH of Hosts* 4+1+4[a]
(from whom) goes out
wonderful strategy, excellent success.[b]

Notes

24.a. MT's meter is 2+3+3. Kissane and Irwin ("Isaiah 28–33," 38) divide after החרש for 4+4.

24.b. לזרע, "for sowing." *BHS* considers it redundant and suggests deletion. The question concerns the meaning of ל, "for" (cf. Irwin, "Isaiah 28–33," 38). If it is understood as privative, "without sowing" (cf. A. Blommerde, *Northwest Semitic Grammar and Job* [Rome: Pontifical Biblical Institute, 1969] 21), the meaning parallels v 25. Or it can be understood as emphatic: "Indeed the sower breaks and harrows his soil." In Heb. the word falls in the middle of the verse. All three meanings are fitting.

25.a. קצח, "dill," is *nigella satina* or black cumin (cf. H. N. and A. L. Moldenke, *Plants of the Bible* [Waltham, MA: Chronica Botanica, 1952] 152–53).

25.b. שם, "put, set" (BDB, 962). Irwin ("Isaiah 28–33," 39) notes that it means "plant" in Isa 41:19 and Ezek 17:5. For another meaning, cf. S. C. Thexton, *VT* 2 (1952) 81–83.

25.c. שורה, "in rows," from its root שור, "to saw." Irwin ("Isaiah 28–33," 39) suggests "millet" following BDB's (965) hint that it should be some grain and other suggestions depending on Arab. *ḏurratun,* which refers to a kind of grain. LXX omits it.

25.d. נסמן, "in its proper place" (BDB, 702), a *hap. leg.*, is missing in LXX. *CHAL*'s "unexplained" sums it up.

25.e. 1QIsa[a] and LXX make it pl., "its borders." This word (sg. or pl.) is clear. If שורה and נסמן are parallels, they fit the customary meanings "on rows" and "in its place."

26.a. משפט is generally understood here in this way. Cf. Wildberger (1084) and Irwin ("Isaiah 28–33," 40).

26.b. אלהיו, "his God." Irwin ("Isaiah 28–33," 40) calls this "an example of delayed explication."

27.a. The first לא, "not," applies to both verbs.

27.b. יוסב, "rolled over," *hopʿal* impf. 3 m. sg. from סבב (BDB, 686). 1QIsa[a] יסוב is *qal* impf.

28.a. לחם, "grain." For this meaning Wildberger (1084) cites Isa 30:23 and Ps 104:14 while Irwin ("Isaiah 28–33," 42) turns to Ugaritic.

28.b. לנצח, "forever" (BDB, 664). D. W. Thomas ("Further Remarks on Unusual Ways of Expressing the Superlative in Hebrew," *VT* 18 [1968] 124) considers this a superlative, as does NEB "to the uttermost," LLS *hasta lo ultimo.* Irwin ("Isaiah 28–33," 42) pleads for the meaning "forever."

28.c. אדוש, "threshing," *qal* inf. abs. "as if from אדש" (BDB, 190; GKC §113*w*[3]), but this verb does not otherwise exist. J. Barth (*Die Nominalbildung in den semitischen Sprachen,* 2d ed. [1894; reprinted Hildesheim, 1967] §49*b*) suggests that it is like Aram. *apʿel,* a causative form. 1QIsa[a] הדש (*nipʿal* inf.), "being trampled, threshed," is a reasonable substitute.

28.d. Read the parallel clauses as an implied condition with Irwin ("Isaiah 28–33," 42).

28.e. The reference to horses has caused extended discussion. Irwin ("Isaiah 28–33," 43) cites Jerome's comment that "horses" is used here parallel to "wheel" as "sled" is used in v 27.

29.a. With Irwin ("Isaiah 28–33," 43), who reads יצאה, "goes out," as related to both parts of the verse (cf. vv 20–21). He then reads the second as a relative clause.

29.b. תושיה, "wisdom" (BDB, 444), "success" (*CHAL*, 388*b*), cannot be clearly analyzed. Its meaning is largely drawn from being parallel to עצה, "counsel," "strategy" (cf. Job 5:12).

Form/Structure/Setting

The opening formula, "Pay attention and heed my voice!" marks the beginning of the episode and its nature. This is the kind of thing a teacher would say.

It is a wisdom formula (cf. Prov 4:1; 7:24; Job 33:1, 31; 34:2; Ps 49:2 [1]). The closing phrase (v 29) has been appropriately called a "summary-appraisal form" (B. S. Childs, *Isaiah and the Assyrian Crisis,* 128).

The parable of the farmer who must work differently in different seasons and who is careful not to destroy the results of one season's work while doing that of another is applied to YHWH's plans and work. To whom is this spoken (cf. Wildberger, 1088–89)? The "scoffers" and "speech makers" of this people (v 14) are likely candidates, especially if some of "the wise" are among them (cf. Amsler and Mury, *RHPR* 53 [1973] 1–5). They would claim that God's ways are consistent and fixed. The parable in wisdom style defends the prophetic understanding that God acts in history in accordance with the times and conditions as he moves to achieve his goals. This is God's עצה, "strategy" (v 29).

The genre of this passage is called תורה, "instruction" (v 26), and אמרה, "saying" (v 23). These stand in clear contrast to the ordinary prophetic genres but are at home in Wisdom literature. אמרה appears repeatedly in Isaiah; see Isa 5:24, 29:4, and 32:9. In the last two instances it is paralleled by קול, "voice." Wildberger (1090–91) notes that the only other occurrence of these together is in Gen 4:23. The comparison with Lamech's speech in Gen 4:23 leads to the recognition of how the parable of God's instruction to the farmer parallels the tradition that God introduced agriculture to humankind (Gen 3:23; 4:1–16). While this is merely implied in Genesis, it is stated in considerable detail in the literature of the ancient Near East. An ancient Sumerian myth describes the process by which Enlil and Enka taught the farmer (S. N. Kramer, *History Begins at Sumer* [Garden City, NY: Doubleday, 1959] 104–12; "Sumer," *IDB* 4:460). Diodorus of Sicily reports Egyptian teachings that Osiris was interested in agriculture, among other arts and crafts (*Diodorus of Sicily,* trans. C. H. Oldfeather, vol. 1 [New York: G. P. Putnam's Sons, 1933] §15, p. 51). Isis was credited with the discovery of wheat and barley culture (*Diodorus* §14, p. 49). Virgil, the Latin poet (70–19 B.C.E.), wrote a beautiful passage describing how Ceres instructed farmers in their craft (*Georgics* 1.287–310). Ovid, another Latin poet (43 B.C.E.–17 C.E.), wrote a similar passage (*Metamorphoses* 5.341–45).

However, the genre of each of these passages is different from the one here in Isaiah. They tell of the god's instruction with no intention to project meaning beyond the telling. Here, the material becomes a "parable" because it is told as an analogy for another truth: that God's strategy for history, like his strategy for agriculture, is wonderful and achieves success. Thus his instruction should be sought by political leaders, as it is sought and followed by farmers. And his strategy is to be trusted with patient faith by the king's counselors as it is by simple farmers.

Excursus: Wisdom in Isaiah

Bibliography

Anderson, R. T. "Was Isaiah a Scribe?" *JBL* 79 (1960) 57–58. **Fichtner, J.** "Jesaja unter den Weisen." *TLZ* 74 (1949) cols. 75–80. Reprinted in *Gottes Weisheit: Gesammelte Studien zum Alten Testament* (Stuttgart: Calwer, 1965) 18–26. Translated under the title "Isaiah among the Wise," in *Studies in Ancient Israelite Wisdom,* ed. J. L. Crenshaw (New York:

Ktav, 1976). **Hermisson, H.-J.** "Weisheit und Geschichte." In *Probleme biblischer Theologie.* FS G. von Rad, ed. H. W. Wolff. Munich: Kaiser, 1971. 149–52. **Jensen, J.** *The Use of tôrâ by Isaiah: His Debate with the Wisdom Tradition.* Washington: Catholic Biblical Association of America, 1973. **Leeuwen, R. C. van** "The Sage in Prophetic Literature." In *The Sage in Israel and in the Ancient Near East.* Ed. J. G. Gammie and L. G. Perdue. Winona Lake, IN: Eisenbrauns, 1990. 295–309. **McKane, W.** *Prophets and Wise Men.* Naperville, IL: Allenson, 1965. 57–73. **Martin-Achard, R.** "Sagesse de Dieu et sagesse humaine chez Ésaïe." In *maqqél shâqéd.* FS W. Vischer. Montpelier, 1960. 137–44. **Morgan, D. F.** "Wisdom and the Prophets." In *Studia Biblica 1978: 1. Papers on Old Testament and Related Themes.* Ed. E. A. Livingstone. Sheffield, 1979. 209–44. ———. *Wisdom in the Old Testament Traditions.* Oxford: Blackwell, 1981. 76–83. **Vermeylen, J.** "Le Proto-Isaïe et la sagesse d'Israël." In *La Sagesse de l'Ancien Testament.* Ed. M. Gilbert. Leuven, 1979. 39–58. **Whedbee, J. W.** *Isaiah and Wisdom.* Nashville: Abingdon, 1971. **Whybray, R. N.** "Prophecy and Wisdom." In *Israel's Prophetic Tradition.* Ed. R. Coggins et al. 181–99. **Williamson, H. G. M.** "Isaiah and the Wise." In *Wisdom in Ancient Israel.* FS J. A. Emerton, ed. J. Day, R. P. Gordon, and H. G. M. Williamson. Cambridge: Cambridge UP, 1995. 133–41.

Williamson's article is the most up to date and thorough. The issue has been complicated by a debate about the nature of wisdom. Folk wisdom has undoubtedly been a part of all the life of ancient Israel. School wisdom and the wisdom required of counselors to the king were something else.

Isaiah shows the application of folk wisdom in the use of nature parables. He also is interested in the advice to be given to kings as the narratives in chaps. 7, 36–37, and 39 show. This advice is also seen in Isaiah's talk of strategy (see *YHWH's Strategy* in the *Introduction*), both that of YHWH and the military strategy of Judah. He especially warned against dependence on Egypt. Chap. 22 levels heavy criticism against Hezekiah's government for failure to prepare for war.

Comment

23 The call for האזינו, "attention," implies an intimate group of listeners in the style of the wisdom teachers.

24 A plow in OT times consisted of a wooden beam to which the yoke of oxen or asses (1 Kgs 19:19) was attached to pull the plow. At the other end, a second piece of wood was fixed vertically at an angle with the handle on the upper end and a metal point on the lower (1 Sam 13:20) to break the ground. The farmer guided the plow with one hand and goaded the oxen with the other (Luke 9:62; Judg 3:31; 1 Sam 13:31).

"All day" translates the Hebrew (הכל היום) literally. In parallel to v 28 לנצח, "forever," it apparently means "all the time," "continually." Other tasks need to be interspersed with plowing in the process of agriculture.

25 The farmer's work is diverse in what he does and what he plants. His seeds include spices (dill and cumin) as well as a variety of grains. One should note how different this is from the culture of the vineyard in chap. 5.

26 It was commonly believed in the ancient world that God (or the gods) taught the farmer how and when to do the complex things involved in agriculture (see *Form/Structure/Setting*). Undoubtedly the Canaanites taught the same thing. The content of this instruction is therefore generally acknowledged. God teaches the farmer how to do his work in "good order" (משפט). This word is usually translated "justice." Its use in this setting demonstrates a facet of its meaning that is not immediately obvious when used in law.

27 The verse returns to the "good order" of the farmer, which has different work for each season and which is careful that one kind of work does not destroy the work of another kind. חרוץ, "a threshing sled" (*IDB* 4:636), is a device, probably using iron, to be drawn by oxen or an ass. It was dragged over the grain to separate kernels of grain from the husks. Then the mass was thrown into the air to allow the wind to separate the heavy kernels, which fell back on the floor from the husks that were blown away (i.e., winnowed). עגלה, "a cart wheel," was a frame with rollers for the same work. But it would be nonsense to use such massive equipment for the delicate spices of dill and cumin.

28 Even threshing can be overdone. The farmer is careful not to let the cart wheel damage the kernels of grain on the threshing floor.

29 The general observations of the parable and its implications from the culture-myths are now brought to focus. "YHWH of Hosts" is identified as the one who is behind all of this. Every Israelite and Judean knows that. The parable is not told to teach this obvious truth. By analogy, the parable ascribes to YHWH the same skills, knowledge, and strategy in managing political and historical matters. From him "goes out" the design of the times. הפליא עצה, "wonderful strategy," picks up that strand of the Vision that teaches that YHWH's עצה, "strategy," controls the events and movements of the centuries (Isa 8:10; 11:12; 16:3; 30:1; 36:5) and that he advises a strategy to meet such times (יעץ in Isa 7:5; 14:27; 19:12; 23:8; 32:7; 32:8; cf. G. von Rad, *OTT,* 163 n. 21). It is used here to counter the argument of pragmatic political strategy defended by the "scoffers" and "speech makers" of v 14.

פלא, "wonder," is used in the OT to describe God's wonderful acts of deliverance. The telling of God's deeds includes humankind's astonishment and surprise (R. Albertz, *THAT,* 2:418). The Psalms praise God for these acts in extravagant terms.

עצה, "strategy," in the Vision refers to God's decision in the specific historical situation. It is not an ideal plan fixed in eternity (Wildberger, 1095). The royal heir is titled פלא יועץ, "Wonder Counselor" (9:5), and the king to come is promised רוח עצה, "a spirit of counsel" (11:2). Both foresee the ability to master a situation, to plan a way out of or through a problem. Wildberger (1095) notes that the Divine King, YHWH of Hosts, is seen to act the same way. תושיה, "success," is a word with several facets. It implies "prudence," which results in "success" and "salvation."

Explanation

The episode uses a description of how God instructs the farmer in the complex tasks of agriculture. In this, one recognizes that every season demands different tasks and every crop must be treated individually. This example is an analogy for God's "strategy" for the nation and his willingness to teach the leaders how to guide their people through the intricate pressures and problems of their times. The politician needs instruction in "good order" or "justice" just as much as the farmer does. The "scoffers" and "speech makers" of v 14 had made their "covenant with Death" without seeking such instruction.

The episode ends by recommending YHWH of Hosts to the political leaders as one who had proved his "wonderful strategy" in the work of the farmer. This "strategy" sometimes employed miraculous happenings that evoked wonder, as it did for Hezekiah in 701 B.C.E. (Isa 37:36–37). God's strategy is geared to fit the circumstances, but it is not limited or controlled by them.

This is a strategy with "excellent (or great) success." This must be measured by God's own standards, not limited to human expectations. The "speech makers" were wrong in assuming that God had no plan for the changed circumstances (Egypt's seizure of power over Palestine), which they thought forced them to accept "the covenant with Death." God continued to confirm his "cornerstone" in Zion. This was his firm commitment (v 16). To recognize this was a base for firm faith and the patience that grows from such faith (v 16*b*).

The analogy of the farmer who follows God's instructions very carefully but still has to wait in patient faith for the harvest is applicable to the leader and the people. God has a strategy for their times that will achieve the "justice and righteousness" that are always his goals. The analogy pleads for patience and understanding of the ways of God. He had taught the farmer to pace his work to the changing seasons. God seeks to teach Judah's leaders to recognize how he paces himself to the course of history in directing the rise and fall of nations. The three episodes in this scene plead for Judah not to make the mistakes that Israel made in a similar situation a century earlier.

Disaster for Jerusalem's Policies (29:1–24)

The first of three episodes, "Woe, Ariel" (29:1–8), mourns Jerusalem (or the founding patron deity of the city), which will now be attacked and humbled by YHWH himself. The second episode, "Like a Sealed Book" (29:9–14), portrays the fulfillment of the task assigned in 6:11–13 as an incomprehensible vision to the city's inhabitants. The third, "Woe, You Schemers in Jerusalem" (29:15–24), speaks against those who plot in Jerusalem. It foresees a new opportunity for Jacob.

Woe, Ariel (29:1–8)

Bibliography

Albright, W. F. "The Babylonian Temple-Tower and the Altar of Burnt-Offering." *JBL* 39 (1920) 137–42. **Barthel, J.** *Prophetenwort und Geschichte.* Tübingen: Mohr Siebeck, 1997. 349–76. **Feigin, S.** "The Meaning of Ariel." *JBL* 39 (1920) 131–37. **Godbey, A. H.** "Ariel, or David-Cultus." *AJSL* 41 (1924) 253–66. **Jeremias, J.** *Theophanie: Die Geschichte einer alttestamentliche Gattung.* Neukirchen-Vluyn: Neukirchener Verlag, 1965. 123–36. **Mare, W. H.** "Ariel (Place)." *ABD.* 1:377. **Mattingly, G. L.** "Ariel (Person)." *ABD.* 1:377. **May, H.**

G. "Ephod and Ariel." *AJSL* 56 (1939) 44–56. **North, C. R.** "Ariel." *IDB.* 1:218. **Petzold, H.** "Die Bedeutung von Ariel im Alten Testament und auf der Mescha-Stele." *Theol* 40 (1969) 372–415. **Routledge, R. L.** "The Siege and Deliverance of the City of David in Isaiah 29:1–8." *TynBul* 43 (1992) 181–90. **Schreiner, J.** *Sion-Jerusalem—Jahwes Königssitz: Die Theologie der Heiligen Stadt im Alten Testament.* Munich: Kösel, 1963. 255–63. **Tromp, N. J.** *Primitive Conceptions of Death and the Nether World in the Old Testament.* Rome: Pontifical Biblical Institute, 1969. **Werlitz, J.** *Studien zur literarischen Methode: Gericht und Heil in Jesaja 7,1–17 und 29, 1–8.* BZAW 204. Berlin; New York: De Gruyter, 1992. **Wong, G. C. I.** "On 'Visits' and 'Visions' in Isaiah xxix 6–7." *VT* 45 (1995) 370–76. **Youngblood, R.** "Ariel, 'City of God.'" In *Essays on the Occasion of the Seventieth Anniversary of Dropsie University.* Ed. A. I. Katsh and L. Nemoy. Philadelphia: Dropsie UP, 1979.

Translation

Herald:	1 *Woe!*	1
	Ariel,[a] *Ariel,*[a]	2+3
	city [b]*where David camped.*[b]	
YHWH:	*Add* [c] *year to year.*	3+2
(to Jerusalem)	*Let festivals take place on schedule,*	
	2 *when I shall bring distress to Ariel*	2+3+3
	and there will be moaning[a] *and lamentation.*[a]	
	She will be[b] *for me like an ariel.*[c]	
	3 *And I shall encamp encircled*[a] *against you.*	3+3+3
	I shall lay siege against you (with) a tower.[b]	
	I shall raise siegeworks[c] *against you.*	
Heavens:	4 *You will be humbled.* [a]*From a land you will speak.*[a]	3+3
(to Jerusalem)	*From dust your sayings will mumble.*[b]	
Earth:	*And it shall be:*	1
(to Jerusalem)	*Your voice will be like a ghost from a land.*	3+3
	From dust your sayings will whisper.	
Heavens	5 *And it shall be:*	1
(to Jerusalem)	*Your insolent horde*[a] *(will be) like fine dust,*	4+4
	the horde of ruthless ones like chaff blowing away.	
Herald:	*And it will happen with sudden suddenness:*	3+4
	6 *By YHWH of Hosts her fate will be decided!*[a]	
	With thunder, earthquake, and great sound,	4+5
	whirlwind and storm, and flame of devouring fire.	
Earth:	7 *And it shall be:*	1
	Like a dream, a night vision (will be)	3+4+4
	the horde of all the nations mustered[a] *against Ariel,*	
	and everyone fighting[b] *(against) her,*	
	and those causing her distress.[c]	
Heavens:	8 *And it shall be:*	1
	just as a hungry person dreams he is eating	5+3
	but wakes (to find) his throat[a] *empty,*	
	or just as a thirsty one dreams he is drinking	5+5
	but wakes to find he is faint,[b] *his throat dry,*	
	so will be the horde of all nations	4+3
	mustered around Mount Zion.	

Notes

1.a. 1QIsa[a] ארואל, "Aruel," for MT's אריאל, "Ariel." D. M. Beegle (*BASOR* 123 [1951] 29) and Kutscher (*Language and Linguistic Background,* 97) doubt the transcription of *vav* where the difference between *vav* and *yod* is often so tenuous. LXX interprets in support of MT: πόλις Αριηλ, "City Ariel." Tg. has מדבחא, "altar" (M. Jastrow, *Dictionary of the Targum* (New York: Pardes, 1950) 731). Wildberger notes parallels to the personal name in Ezra 8:16 and to an altar in Ezek 43:15–16 (cf. also Gen 46:16; Num 26:17; 2 Sam 23:20; Isa 33:7). See *Comment.*

1.b-b. The sentence follows a noun in construct (cf. GKC §130*d*). Wildberger observes that this construction tends to follow nouns designating time (Gen 1:1) or place (Ezek 39:11). Irwin ("Isaiah 28–33," 47) notes that "camped" can imply both "dwell" and "besiege," and that the latter sense becomes clear in v 3.

1.c. 1QIsa[a] ספי (fem. sg. for MT's masc. pl.) addresses the command to the city, MT to its inhabitants.

2.a. A repetition of virtually the same word. E. König (*Stilistik, Rhetorik, Poetik* [Leipzig: Weicher, 1900] 157) considered the duplication deliberate for effect.

2.b. 1QIsa[a] והייתה, "and you shall be," for MT's "she shall be."

2.c. כאריאל, "like Ariel," is the same as the proper name in v 1. But the setting leads many to translate as "hearth of God" (Wildberger) or "an altar hearth" (NIV; cf. 31:9). NEB translates "my Ariel indeed," and Irwin ("Isaiah 28–33," 47) suggests changing MT's כַּאֲרִיאֵל to כִּי אֲרִיאֵל and parsing כי as emphatic: "Ariel indeed." A further possibility is to read here "as a lioness of God" (Irwin, 48). The potential for double entendre would surely not have been lost on the author.

3.a. MT כדור, "like the circle." LXX ὡς Δαυιδ, "like David," reads *dalet* in place of *resh.* However, Syr. and Vg. support MT.

3.b. MT מצב, "tower," is a *hap. leg.* LXX χάρακα, "a rampart"; BDB "palisade, entrenchment"; *DCH* "siege-mound," *HAL* "an uncertain military technical term."

3.c. MT מצרת, "siegeworks" (BDB) or "fortified cities" *(HAL)*. 1QIsa[a] and some other MSS read מצדת, "stronghold," but this comes to the same thing. For a full discussion, see Wildberger, 1098.

4.a-a. LXX reads "your words shall be made to fall to the ground." Wildberger (1099) properly calls it a free translation.

4.b. MT תשח, "shall mumble" (BDB "shall come low"; *HAL* "utter low, muffled sounds"). G. R. Driver (*JSS* 13 [1968] 51; "Notes on Isaiah," in *Von Ugarit nach Qumran,* FS O. Eissfeldt, BZAW 77 [Giessen: Töpelmann, 1958] 45) suggests "pour out."

5.a. 1QIsa[a] זדיך, "your insolent ones," for MT זריך, "your strangers." LXX has missed it altogether in ὁ πλοῦτος τῶν ἀσεβῶν, "the riches of the ungodly." 1QIsa[a] has the best reading.

6.a. LXX translates ἐπισκοπὴ γὰρ ἔσται, "for there shall be a visitation," i.e., changing the verb to a noun. Note that MT has returned to a 3 fem. sg. *BHS* (and others) suggests emending to 2d person, but variation seems to be consistent with the nature of Isaiah's text.

7.a. 1QIsa[a] הצובאים writes it fully *(plene)* but suggests no different word.

7.b. צביה is *qal* ptc. pl. with a fem. suf.: "fighting against her" (BDB and *HAL*). The gen. is obj.: "(against) her."

7.c. 1QIsa[a] מצרתה, "her siegeworks," as in v 3 above. But MT makes sense and should be kept.

8.a. נפשו, "his throat," usually means "person, breath or soul." Irwin ("Isaiah 28–33," 55) translates "throat," citing Dahood, "Hebrew-Ugaritic Lexicography," *Bib* 49 (1968) 368. So also *HAL* and *DCH.*

8.b. Two MSS leave out הנה עיף, "behold faint." Wildberger, Procksch, Kaiser, and *BHS* suggest omitting them, but the rhythm and sense fit. I have kept MT.

Form/Structure/Setting

The episode begins with "woe" and ends with a kind of concluding "thus it will be," which mark its limits. It is compactly and carefully crafted. The "woe" cry (v 1*a*) is followed by an imperative, functioning as a protasis in a conditional construction: "Add year to year. Let festivals take place," with the meaning "if" or "when" you hold festival. This is followed by twelve sentences beginning with *vav* with perfect tenses (so-called converted perfects). The first eight (vv 2–4) extend the protasis by describing the festival's drama of divine testing for Zion, which leads to her humiliation as unto death. The last four provide the apodosis of the construction, which applies the figure to the besieging "hordes of nations" that surround Jerusalem. Four (vv 2–3) are in the first person with YHWH as speaker. They dominate the first section. Two are in the third feminine singular of היה, "to be" (v 2*bc*), and expand the first of the group. Two are second feminine singular (v 4*ab*) to expound the emphasis of the three first-person verbs. Five occurrences of והיה, "and it shall be" (vv 4*b*–8), introduce ten similes, six of them headed by כְּ, "like," with others implied. This list of similes is capped by a concluding line (v 8*c*) beginning with כֵּן, "so" or "thus," and a repetition of the verb היה, "be." The whole is in the form of an arch that relates the imagery of the royal Zion festival to the realistic siege at the walls of Jerusalem by "the horde of nations." It is further supported by the theme "Ariel" (vv 1, 2, 7), the theme of "siege" (vv 2, 7, 8), and "the horde" (vv 5, 7, 8).

The outline of the arch is as follows:

A Let festivals take place (v 1).
  B I shall bring distress to Ariel (vv 2–3).
    C You shall be humbled (v 4).
KEYSTONE Your hordes shall be like fine dust (v 5).
    C´ YHWH will decide her fate (v 6).
  B´ The horde of nations against Ariel will be like a dream (v 7).
A´ Thus will be the horde of nations (v 8).

The episode deals with the critical siege of Jerusalem by interpreting it in the context of the Zion festival in which YHWH tests the city by ordeal in order to humble her, after the fashion of the king's ordeal. The great drama demonstrates the helplessness of the city in itself; indeed, it is as good as dead. She exists by the decree and power of YHWH God. If that is understood to be true in the festal drama, it is equally true of the historical reality. Once YHWH has decided Zion's fate, the oppressing nations will no longer be a factor. They will appear like a dream, a memory of the festal drama's terrible moment of humiliation. (Note the parallel experience in chaps. 36–37, in which the prophetic oracle serves the same purpose that the reference to the festal drama does here.)

On the place of ritual humiliation in the Jerusalem royal festival, see J. D. W. Watts, *Basic Patterns in Old Testament Religion* (Louisville, KY: Jameson, 1971) 134; A. R. Johnson, *Sacral Kingship in Ancient Israel* (Cardiff: Univ. of Wales Press, 1955) 93–126; J. H. Eaton, *Kingship and the Psalms*, SBT 32 (London: SCM Press, 1976) 199–201; and idem, *Festal Drama in Deutero-Isaiah* (London: SPCK, 1979) 24–26.

If the "horde of nations" around Jerusalem is taken as the central theme, a different focus is brought to view. This is a common theme in Isaiah (5:26–30; 8:9–10; 13:1–5; 31:4–5, to name a few). It has historical roots in the siege of Jerusalem in Ahaz's day (734 B.C.E.; chap. 7), Sennacherib's siege in Hezekiah's day (701 B.C.E.; chaps. 22 and 36–37), and Nebuchadnezzar's sieges in 598 and 587 B.C.E. The theme is picked up in Jeremiah, Ezekiel, and Zechariah. (Cf. R. de Vaux, "Jerusalem et les prophétes," *RB* 73 [1966] 481–509; J. H. Hayes, "The Tradition of Zion's Inviolability," *JBL* 82 [1963] 424; H. J. Hermisson, "Zukunftserwartung und Gegenwartskritik in der Verkündigung Jesajas," *EvT* 33 [1973] 56 n. 8.) The usual form has the nations gathered around the city with YHWH defending it. But here the situation is reversed. YHWH lays siege to the city and is identified with the besieging peoples. This is a literary inversion of the *Völkerkampf* pattern, which derives its meaning as a parallel to the humiliation of the king in ancient festal ritual. In this case it portrays a ritual humiliation that is carried to the very point of death.

Comment

1a הוי, "woe," picks up the feeling of death in Jerusalem that was introduced by the mood of chap. 28, especially by "the covenant with death" (28:15). אריאל, "Ariel," has various possible meanings (cf. *Notes* 1.a. and 2.c. and the dictionary articles by Mare and Mattingly [*ABD* 1:377] and North [*IDB* 1:218]). These include "lioness of God," "God's champion or hero," and "altar-hearth of El." The name identifies Jerusalem. If the reference is to an ancient epithet related to the city, as is probable, it refers to El as the founding patron deity of the city. The meaning here is that although Jerusalem is a city founded by God in Jebusite, pre-Israelite times, and although David himself claims the city, YHWH must fight against it. Cf. v 8 below.

קרית חנה דוד, "city where David camped." The phrase refers to David's troops kept there. It establishes the relation to David but avoids associating "David's city" with the divine promises about the city.

1b ספו שנה על־שנה, "add year to year," is probably a reference to the celebration of New Year's festivals in which YHWH's beneficent patronage for another year is sought. This view is reinforced by the references to festivals. The Vision has noted the emptiness of ritual observance (1:11–15) when it fails to reflect God's attitude and intention. Although the ritual stresses Jerusalem's ties to God and is intended to ensure her safety and prosperity, the verse implies that the celebration will not deter God from his determined path.

2 The first two lines clearly indicate that YHWH will be an enemy to Ariel, with predictable results (cf. Lam 2:5). The third line is cryptic. Does כאריאל, "like an ariel," mean something like the use of the word in 2 Sam 23:20, "a heroic champion"? If so, this is deliberate wordplay that reflects the ambivalence of the message. YHWH's usual stance is that of staunch defender against all enemies, but now his strange or alien stance (cf. 28:21) makes him Jerusalem's enemy.

3 God is laying siege to the city. Two words from the root צרר/צור are used: צרתי, "I shall lay siege," and מצרת, "siegeworks." G. Gerlemann ("Contributions to the Old Testament Terminology of the Chase," in *Miscella Veteris Testamenti* [Lund, 1946] 4:89) found this word used of hunting when a wild animal is surrounded. Irwin ("Isaiah 28–33," 48) thinks this makes the meaning of Ariel as "Lion of God" much more plausible. The Lion of God is surrounded by the Divine Hunter. This is the artistic metaphor that interprets the siege of Jerusalem.

4 ארץ, "a land," must here refer to the world of the dead (cf. N. J. Tromp, *Primitive Conceptions of Death,* 23–46, 85–91, 98; M. Ottoson, "ארץ," *TWAT* 1:430–31). Ariel, after being besieged, descends into the land of the dead, becoming like a ghost.

5 The alternative readings of 1QIsa[a], "your insolent population," and MT, "your foreign horde" (Irwin's translation, "Isaiah 28–33," 52), state the issue. Does this refer to Jerusalem's population or to the besieging enemy? המון, "horde," recurs in v 7 with a clear reference to the enemy. Here, however, the context makes it parallel the "dust" (v 4) of the land of the dead. The "horde" consists of the nations who represent YHWH (vv 2–3) before Jerusalem. They belong to Jerusalem ("your . . . horde") in the sense that they are her problem.

The humiliation (v 4) has five parallel observations:

Jerusalem's voice will be like that of a ghost (v 4*b*).
Her hordes will be like fine dust (v 5).
YHWH will decide her fate (vv 5*c*–6).
These hordes of nations will seem like a dream (v 7).
The experience will prove ephemeral (v 8).

If the experience humbles Jerusalem to the point of deathly helplessness, then the nations around the city are a part of that deathlike unreal experience, "like dust."

6 YHWH is the only reality. He alone has power and can make a decision. After he has acted (vv 7–8), all the threats of the nations will seem as unreal as a dream only partly remembered.

Explanation

The meaning of this passage is similar to that of chap. 7. Attention is called away from the threatening military situation to the underlying reality of God's purpose and action. By referring to the ancient ritual of humiliation through ordeal that preceded the "deciding of fate," the passage interprets Jerusalem's military difficulty as God's humiliation of the city, which must precede his decision about her fate. When the decision has been made, everything else will seem unreal, like a dream. YHWH, his sovereign decisions, and his salvation—these are the only realities to consider, the only decisive factors.

Paul refers to life's trials in a similar vein when they are seen from the perspective of participation in Christ's resurrection (Rom 8:18; Phil 3:7–11).

Like a Sealed Book (29:9–14)

Bibliography

Aitken, K. T. "Hearing and Seeing: Metamorphoses of a Motif in Isaiah 1–39." In *Among the Prophets: Language, Image and Structure in the Prophetic Writings.* Ed. P. R. Davies and D. J. A. Clines. Sheffield: JSOT Press, 1993. 12–41. **Carroll, R. P.** "Blindsight and the Vision Thing." In *Writing and Reading the Scroll of Isaiah.* Leiden: Brill, 1997. 1:79–93. **New, D. S.** "The Confusion of *Taw* with *Waw-Nun* in Reading 1QIsa[a] 29:13." *RevQ* 15 (1992) 609–10. **Schmidt, J. M.** "Gedanken zum Verstockungsauftrag Jesajas (Is. VI)." *VT* 21 (1971) 68–90. **Schmidt, K. L.** "Die Verstockung des Menschen durch Gott." *TZ* 1 (1945) 1–17. **Tromp, N. J.** *Primitive Conceptions of Death and the Nether World in the Old Testament.* Rome: Pontifical Biblical Institute, 1969. **Williamson, H. G. M.** *Book Called Isaiah.* 94–115.

Translation

Earth:	[9]*Tarry*[a] *and be astounded!*[b]	2+2
(to Jerusalemites)	*Delight yourselves*[c] *and gaze intently!*[c]	
	You, who are drunk[d]*—but not from wine,*	2+2
	you, who stagger[e]*—but not from liquor!*	
	[10]*For YHWH has poured out*[a] *over you*[b]	3+2
	a spirit of deep sleep.	
Heavens:	*So he closed your eyes, the prophets,*[c]	3+3
	and your heads, the seers,[c] *he has covered.*	
Earth:	[11]*So the whole vision became for you*	4+3
	like the words of the sealed book,	
	which when they give it to one who knows the book,[a]	4+3
	saying, "Read this, please,"	
	he says, "I cannot,	3+3
	for it is sealed."	
	[12]*But if one had given* [a]*the book to*[a] *one who does not know how to read saying "Read this please," he would have said, "I do not know how to read."*	
Herald:	[13]*So my Lord*[a] *proceeded to say:*	2
YHWH:	*Because this people approaches with its mouth*[b]	6
	and with their lips they[c] *honor me*	2+3
	while its heart is far from me,	
	so that their fear of me is (only)[d]	3+3
	a human command[e] *(that is) memorized,*	
	[14]*therefore, see me*[a] *again*[b]	3+3+2
	doing wonders[c] *for this people,*[d]	
	the wonder[c] *and a wonder!*[c]	
Heavens:	*But the wisdom of the wise shall perish,*	3+3
	and the discernment of the discerning ones will be hidden.[e]	

Notes

9.a. התמהמהו ותמהו, "tarry and be astounded," are considered a *hitpalpel* impv. from מהה and a *qal* impv. from תמה by BDB (554, 1069) and GKC §55*g* (cf. *DCH*). LXX ἐκλύθητε καὶ ἔκστητε and Vg. *obstupescite et admiramini* support this distinction, contra *BHK, BHS,* Wildberger, and *HAL,* who emend in order to derive both from תמה.

9.b. Delitzsch, followed by Irwin, suggests that the use of two forms of the same root here and in the second stich should be understood as hendiadys, "the expression of an idea by the use of two independent words connected by 'and'" (*Webster's New Collegiate Dictionary*). But cf. *Notes* 9.a. and 9.c.

9.c. LXX omits one of these terms. The other versions give varying translations. השתעשעו is usually seen as a *hitpalpel* impv. from שעע, "blind yourselves" (BDB, *HAL*). As such it is the only occurrence with that sense in that stem (cf. 32:9 in *qal*). A second use of this root means "make sport, take delight in" and occurs in *hitpalpel* twice in Ps 119 (vv 16, 47) and several times in *pilpel,* including Isa 11:8 and 66:12. Another possibility is the root שעה, "gaze at" (BDB, 1043), which is also known in Isa 17:7, 22:4, 31:1, and 41:10. This translation, "delight yourselves and gaze intently," uses the second root meaning of שעע for השתעשעו and reads the second word ושעו, from שעה (with J. M. Schmidt, *VT* 21 [1971] 68–90).

9.d. MT שָׁכְרוּ, "they are drunk" (BDB, 1016). 1QIsa[a] שכרון is apparently a noun, "drunkenness" (but Irwin ["Isaiah 28–33," 56] sees the form as *qal* pf. plus *nun paragogicum* [cf. GKC §44*l*] and parallel to the form of the next verb), occurring otherwise in Jer 13:13; Ezek 23:33; 39:19. LXX κραιπαλήσατε, "debauch yourselves," supported by Tg. and Vg., suggests the impv. שִׁכְרוּ (cf. *BHK* and *BHS*). MT may be kept and read as a relative clause.

9.e. MT נָעוּ, "they stagger," *qal* pf. from נוע. Tg. טעו, "go astray" (M. Jastrow, *Dictionary of the Targum* [New York: Pardes, 1950] 542), and Vg. *movemini,* "move about," again suggest that an impv. is indicated (cf. *BHK, BHS,* and Wildberger). However, 1QIsa^a נעוו raises the same question of tense as in *Note* 9.d. It also suggests a different root from MT, a *nip'al* pf. 3 m. sg. from עוה, "be bowed down, twisted." Irwin ("Isaiah 28–33," 56) translates "they are agitated" (cf. Isa 21:3; 24:1). With Irwin, MT should be sustained and read as a relative clause.

10.a. Vg. *miscuit,* "he mixed" or "he confused." There is no other witness to this meaning.

10.b. 1QIsa^a עליכמה. The additional *he* is common in 1QIsa^a. Cf. Kutscher, *Language and Linguistic Background,* 442.

10.c. "The prophets" and "the seers" are often dubbed glosses. There is no textual evidence for this.

11.a. K הַסֵּפֶר, "the book." The usual reading today follows Q ספר *(BHK, BHS),* "to read." Wildberger (1112–13) follows K, translating "the Scripture" as in Dan 1:4, 17. But note that the article is missing in Daniel. The *Translation* follows K. See *Comment.*

12.a-a. 1QIsa^a has a number of insignificant variations.

13.a. Many MSS have יהוה, "YHWH." Wildberger thinks it is original. MT may be kept.

13.b. LXX omits. LXX^B, OL, and Vg. include "his mouth" with the previous phrase; i.e., they move the *zakef qaton* to בְּפִיו.

13.c. MT כבדוני, "they honor me," has concerned interpreters and translators because of the sg. possessive pronouns on "mouth" and "lips." 1QIsa^a כבדתי, "I honor," does not make sense, but see Irwin's note ("Isaiah 28–33," 58) that *BHS* misreads נו for ת. Syr., OL, and Vg. read a sg. כבדני, "it honors me," to correct the problem. But note the return to pl. in יראתם, "their fear." Such changes are frequent in Heb. Keep MT and read sg. as collectives for "this people."

13.d. LXX μάτην δέ, "but in vain" (cf. Matt 15:8–9), which *BHS* retranslates to תֹהוּ, "[their fear of me] is in vain." However, MT makes sense and should be kept.

13.e. 1QIsa^a כמצות, "like a command"; Tg. concurs. Syr. uses the prep. ב, "by commands of." But MT has "command" as the predicate nominative and should be sustained.

14.a. MT's short form הנני is written fully in 1QIsa^a הנה אנוכי, "see me."

14.b. K יוֹסֵף (ptc.), "adding"; Q יֹסִיף (*hip'il* impf. 3 m. sg.), "(who) will multiply." K fits the context; Q strains it through a shift of person. LXX προσθήσω, "I shall add"; Syr. *mwsp,* "adding"; Vg. *addam,* "add." Irwin ("Isaiah 28–33," 59) follows K: "I am he who will again."

14.c. 1QIsa^a reads פלה, "be separate, distinct," in all three instances for MT's פלא, "be wonderful." The ideas are related, but MT's is better.

14.d. את־העם־הזה, "this people," is often thought to be superfluous because it breaks up the metrical form. That is not reason enough to delete it here. If the line is read as a tristich, even that argument is not valid.

14.e. Irwin ("Isaiah 28–33," 59) argues that the verb is denominative, from סתר, "the secret place," which refers to Sheol in Isa 28:18; 45:19; Ps 139:15, as Tromp (*Primitive Conceptions of Death,* 46–47, 97) has shown. If this is true, it adds to the imagery of life after death in this section. The verb is a contrast to "will perish" in the previous line.

Form/Structure/Setting

This episode turns from the political emergency to address the people. It begins, like v 1*b,* with an imperative addressed to the citizens of Jerusalem. The setting continues to be that of festival. But the episode is not concerned with the festival drama, as vv 1–8 were; rather it focuses on the people and their reactions.

The syntactical structure is this:

Imperatives: "Tarry!" "Gaze intently!" "Delight yourselves!" (v 9)
כִּי with perfect tense: "For YHWH has poured . . . sleep." (v 10*a*)
Three clauses begun with *vav*-consecutive and imperfects:

"So he closed [the] eyes [of] the prophets." (v 10*b*)
"So [it] became . . . like words of a sealed book." (v 11*a*)
"So my Lord proceeded to say:
Because this people approaches . . .
so that their fear of me is only . . ." (v 13)
A verbless clause using הִנֵּה, "Therefore, see me . . . doing wonders." (v 14*a*)
Perfect with *vav* followed by inverted order with imperfect:
"But the wisdom of the wise shall perish." (v 14*b*)

The episode picks up the theme of drunken stupor from chap. 28 and that of God-caused blindness from 6:9–10. It also resumes the theme of insincere worship from chap. 1.

Comment

9 The commands are still addressed to the festal throng, moving through Jerusalem to the throbbing carnival sounds. They move in a kind of stupor.

10 But the stupor is from God, as he had predicted in 6:9–11. The prophets, leaders, and seers are affected alike.

11–12 חזות הכל, "the whole vision." This book is called the Vision, but every act has complained that the people of that generation did not "see" and did not respond. Having a sacred tradition, a holy Scripture, or divine vision is of no use if it is sealed.

E. W. Conrad (*Reading Isaiah,* 130–43) has understood "the whole vision" as the "The Vision of Isaiah," specifically chaps. 6–39. It was not understood by Isaiah's opponents (8:11), so Isaiah is instructed to bind it up and seal it (8:16). Because the book is sealed and cannot be read aloud, the people are made "deaf and blind" (6:9–10). There will be a future day in which they can hear and see (29:18). For the moment, however, the word must be written so that in the future it may become a "witness" (30:8–9) against them. This is fulfilled in 40:6 when that generation is called to "read aloud the word of God." Having now the prophecy read aloud, they are no longer "blind and deaf" (35:5) This becomes a testimony against the nations in 45:21–23. The pious of that future generation are distinguished by their relation to "the word" (the prophetic book; 66:2, 5).

13 The Lord's speech specifies his analysis. העם הזה, "this people," is a term that has appeared before (6:10; 8:11) when God wants to distance himself from the people's attitudes and decisions. Their religion is found to be only verbal. It lacks heart, mind, and will. This affects the character of their worship. יראתם, "their fear," means their attitude in worship. It should be founded on a divinely inspired awe, deep respect of the Holy One, but it has become מצות אנשים, "a human command," which can be taught and recited without involving the will.

14*a* For this reason God must intervene with "wondrous acts" to restore the sense of his holy and awesome presence.

14*b* Because God is going to intervene, the ordinary prognoses of wise and discerning persons cannot advise correctly concerning the course of coming events.

Explanation

God does not reveal himself the same way in all seasons. The Vision reveals God's strategy and intentions to its readers, but the generations portrayed in the Vision were blind to the implications just as Isa 6:9–11 predicted that they would be. Even the sacred texts were meaningless to them. God recognizes the sorry state of religion that is only lip worship, the repetition of learned phrases. Truly "the fear of YHWH" is not only the beginning of wisdom but also the foundation of worship that involves the heart. Holy awe leads to genuine devotion. Yet God in his grace determines to do more "wonders" for this people, miracles that defy prediction or explanation. The ways of God can be neither confined nor limited.

Woe, You Schemers (29:15–24)

Bibliography

Beuken, W. A. M. "Isa 29,15–25: Perversion Reverted." In *The Scriptures and the Scrolls.* FS A. S. van der Woude, ed. F. García Martínez, A. Hilhorst, and C. J. Labuschagne. VTSup 49. Leiden: Brill, 1992. 43–64. **Carroll, R. P.** "Blindsight and the Vision Thing." In *Writing and Reading.* Ed. C. C. Broyles and C. A. Evans. 1:79–93. **Clements, R. E.** "Patterns in the Prophetic Canon." In *Canon and Authority.* Ed. G. W. Coates and B. O. Long. Philadelphia: Fortress, 1977. 42–55. **Conrad, E. W.** "Isaiah and the Abraham Connection." *AJT* 2 (1988) 382–93. **Donner, H.** *Israel unter den Völkern.* 155–58. **Laberge, L.** *La Septante d'Isaïe 28–33: Étude de tradition textuelle.* Ottawa: Laberge, 1978. **Payne, J. B.** "The Effect of Sennacherib's Anticipated Destruction in Isaianic Prophecy." *WTJ* 34 (1971–72) 22–38. **Robinson, T. H.** "The Text of Isaiah 29:16." *ZAW* 49 (1931) 322. **Stolz, F.** "Die Bäume des Gottesgartens auf dem Libanon." *ZAW* 84 (1972) 141–56. **Virgulin, S.** "Il significato della pietra di fondazione in Isa 28:16." *RivB* 7 (1959) 208–20. **Werlitz, J.** *Studien zur literarkritischen Methods: Gericht und Heil in Jesaja 7,1–17 und 29,1–8.* BZAW 204. Berlin: De Gruyter, 1992. **Whedbee, W. H.** *Isaiah and Wisdom.* Nashville: Abingdon, 1971. 73–75, 130–31. **Williamson, H. G. M.** *Book Called Isaiah.* 58–63. ———. "Isaiah and the Wise." In *Wisdom in Ancient Israel.* FS J. A. Emerton, ed. J. Day et al. Cambridge: Cambridge UP, 1995. 133–41. **Wong, G. C. I.** "On 'Visits' and 'Visions' in Isaiah xxix 6–7." *VT* 45 (1995) 370–76. **Ziegler, J.** "Zum literarischen Aufbau im Buch des Propheten Isaias." *BZ* 21 (1933) 138–41.

Translation

Heavens:	15 *Woe to those who (try to) dig too deep for YHWH* [a]	3+2
	to hide a strategy.	
	Whose deeds are in the dark.	3
Earth:	*Who say:*	1
	"Who sees us?	2+2
	Who knows (about) us?"	
Heavens:	16 *Oh, your perversity!* [a]	1+3

As if the potter be regarded like clay!
As if the thing made should say to its maker, 3+2
"He did not make me!"
Or a thing formed of clay[b] *to the one who forms it,* 3+2
"He does not understand!"
Earth: 17 *Will not*[a] *very soon now* 3+3+3
Lebanon turn into the orchard[b]
and Carmel be reckoned a forest?
18 *The deaf hear in that day* 4+2
words (read from) a book.
After[a] *gloom and darkness* 2+3
blind eyes will see.
19 *The meek shall increase joy in YHWH.*[a] 4+2+3
The humble of humanity[b]
will exult in the Holy One of Israel.[a]
20 *When the terrorist*[a] *shall come to nought,* 2+2+3
the scoffer[b] *shall be finished,*
all who are intent on evil shall be cut off:
21 *those who by a word make a person to*
be an offender, 3+3+3
who lay a trap[a] *for one who reproves*[b] *in the gate,*
and so turn aside a just case with an empty argument.[c]
Herald: 22 *Therefore, thus says YHWH, God*[a]
of the House of Jacob, 5+3
who redeemed Abraham:
YHWH: *Not now will Jacob be shamed!* 4+4
Not now will his face grow pale!
23 *For when he sees his children,*[a] 3+3
the work of my hands, in his midst,
they will sanctify my name. 2
Heavens: *And they will sanctify the Holy One of Jacob.* 3+3
They will be in awe of the God of Israel.
Earth: 24 *Those errant of spirit will know understanding,* 3+3
and the murmurers[a] *will learn (their) lessons.*

Notes

15.a. מיהוה, "from YHWH." LXX οὐ διὰ κυρίου, "not through the Lord," has interpreted this as a privative מן, building on the basic idea of "separation, apart from, not from." Tg. מן קדם יהוה translates "before YHWH's face," building on another sense of מן. Vg. *a Domino,* "away from the Lord," is a more literal translation of the Heb. The idea of "hiding" suggests that "from" means to keep away from his knowledge and sight. Irwin ("Isaiah 28–33," 61) would combine with the previous word to translate "too deep for YHWH." His argument is cogent.

16.a. MT הפככם appears to be a noun (BDB, 246; GKC §147*c; HAL*) with a pronominal suffix "your perversity." 1QIsa[a] הפך מכם, "he overturns from you." LXX and Syr. omit the term. Vg. *perversa est haec vestra cogitatio,* "wrongheaded is this idea of yours"; Wildberger (1125) correctly calls this a free translation. T. H. Robinson ("The Text of Isaiah 29:16," *ZAW* 49 [1931] 322) suggests reversing two letters to read הַכְּפָכִים, "as flasks" (cf. *BHS*). Wildberger (1126) suggests reading MT as a vocative and points to a parallel meaning in Ezek 16:34.

16.b. 1QIsa[a] חמר, "clay," for MT's אמר, "says." The reading is aesthetic and makes better sense. For an opposing view see M. Held, "The YQTL-QTL (QTL-YQTL) Sequence of Identical Verbs in Biblical Hebrew and Ugaritic," in *Studies and Essays in Honor of Abraham A. Neumann,* ed. M. Ben-Horin et al. (Leiden: Brill, 1962) 281–90.

17.a. הלוא is a particle for a negative question, but many interpreters translate in the same sense as הנה, "see, indeed, look." This translation fails to reflect the aesthetic change of the Heb.

17.b. הכרמל is a "cultivated garden" or "orchard." It is also the name of a mountain in Israel. Wildberger (1133) and Irwin ("Isaiah 28–33," 62–63) translate the first usage in the generic sense and the second as the proper name.

18.a. מן in מאפל and מחשך is literally "from gloom" and "from darkness." The meaning may be "in contrast to gloom" or "away from the time of gloom," i.e., "after."

19.a. Wildberger (1134) joins Procksch in deleting ביהוה, "in YHWH," and בקדוש ישראל, "in the Holy One of Israel," as being pious glosses. There is no textual ground for this, nor does the irregular meter justify it.

19.b. Irwin ("Isaiah 28–33," 64) follows *CHAL* (14) in translating אדם as "land" (cf. M. Dahood, "Hebrew-Ugaritic Lexicography," *Bib* 44 [1963] 292; *Psalms,* AB 17A [Garden City, NY: Doubleday, 1970] 3:39–40) rather than the usual "human." Both meanings are fitting. Wildberger (1134) sees superlative meaning in the phrase: "the poorest of mankind."

20.a. MT עריץ, "terrifying," is sg., as is LXX ἄνομος, "lawless." Both are adjectives used in place of nouns. Perhaps "the terrorist" will fill the place.

20.b. MT לֵץ, "scorner"; LXX ὑπερήφανος, "one who appears great"; Tg. בזוא, "plunderer."

21.a. יקשון is understood by BDB (881) as *qal* impf. from קוש and thus a *hap. leg.,* "lay a snare." Others propose reading it as יָקְשׁוּ, *qal* pf. from יקש, or as יִיקָשׁוּן, *qal* impf. from יקש or נקש *(BHK, BHS, HAL).* Neither changes the meaning. It refers to legal traps, parallel to the "by a word," i.e., slander, of the parallel stich.

21.b. Cf. Amos 5:10. V. Maag, *Text, Wortschatz und Begriffswelt des Buches Amos* (Leiden: Brill, 1951) 153: "the resident lawyer who sees to it that the great scoundrels are publicly called to order."

21.c. תהו, "emptiness," also means "wasteland." Wildberger (1134) thinks of "empty arguments," parallel to "words" of the previous stich. Irwin ("Isaiah 28–33," 65) translates "thrust the innocent into the wasteland" and points to Amos 5:12. The preposition ב favors Wildberger's point. It is used three times here, but never as "into."

22.a. The relative particle obviously has "YHWH" as its antecedent, yet it is followed directly by "to the House of Jacob." *BHK* and *BHS* suggest changing אֶל, "to," to אֵל, "God," reading "God of the House of Jacob" to eliminate the problem. LXX translates ἐπὶ τὸν οἶκον Ιακωβ ὃν ἀφώρισεν ἐξ Αβρααμ, "upon the house of Jacob, whom he selected from Abraham." But Wildberger (1135) curtly notes that פדה does not mean ἀφορίζειν and את does not mean ἐξ. The emendation to read אֵל, "God," is the simplest. The fact that YHWH's speech is 3d person, i.e., not addressed to Israel, strengthens the suggestion.

23.a. ילדיו, "his children," is often thought to be a gloss. The thinking goes: not children but YHWH's great deeds are "the works of his hand." There is no textual evidence for this. Irwin ("Isaiah 28–33," 66) brings metrical data to support MT.

24.a. רוגנים, "murmurers" (BDB, 920) or "grumblers" *(HAL).* But Ehrlich (*Randglossen* 4:105) insists that it means "persons who speak falsehood." G. R. Driver ("Notes on Isaiah," in *Von Ugarit nach Qumran,* FS O. Eissfeldt, BZAW 77 [Giessen: Töpelmann, 1958] 45) uses Syr. and Arab. to derive the meaning "muddled." Wildberger (1135) finds a reference to the wilderness journey of ancient Israel and pleads for the traditional meaning.

Form/Structure/Setting

The episode has three parts and a conclusion (cf. J. Ziegler, *BZ* 21 [1933] 138–41):

Vv 15–16	Woe to planners who exclude God (v 15), who presume to be able to hide (v 15), "as if" (a threefold simile of clay and potter; v 16).
Vv 17–21	God's reversal is near (v 17) when blind and meek will be advantaged (vv 18–19),

	when violent cunning will fail (vv 20–21).
Vv 22–23	YHWH announces a new opportunity for Israel.
V 24	Conclusion—Then even the "errant of spirit" can understand.

Comment

15–16 המעמיקים מ—, "dig too deep." Strategists who think they can elude YHWH's sight or knowledge are ridiculed (cf. Ps 139).

17 In YHWH's plan, things will soon be reversed: the forest turned into an orchard, the orchard into a forest. כרמל, "Carmel," appears also in 16:10; 33:9; 35:2. The word may be a proper noun for a mountain or a common noun for an orchard. לבנון, "Lebanon," is famed for its forests and great trees (cf. S. Virgulin, *RivB* 7 [1959] 343–53).

18–19 The deaf, the blind, the meek, and the humble have suffered much in a world that honors power and cunning, but their day will come when God changes all the rules to work to their advantage.

Conrad (*Reading Isaiah,* 130–34) understands דברי־ספר, "words (read from) a book," to refer to the sealed witness of 8:16 and that this is a promise fulfilled in the command to "read" ("cry") in 40:6. This reading makes the blind see and the deaf hear.

20 Then the cunning and the evildoers will no longer be able to do their work.

22 Note the identification "God of the house of Jacob, who redeemed Abraham." The message is about Israel, who will have her chance again. לא עתה, "not now," may carry the meaning "no longer." Israel has not had an identifiable existence for well over a century. "Redeemed": Laberge (*La Septante d'Isaïe 28–33,* 300) has a study of the uses of פדה, "redeem," in Isaiah. The word occurs in 1:27, 35:10, and 51:11, as well as in this verse. It is frequent in the Psalms, occurring a total of fifty-seven times in the OT. One group of uses refers to redemption from slavery. Only once is it used of a חרם, "banned thing," related to sacrifice. Isa 51:11 has the positive sense of liberation like that in Deuteronomy. Some uses identify God as the one who liberates, but only this verse speaks of God redeeming Abraham. The name Abraham appears in 41:8, 51:2, and 63:16.

23 God expects the sight of surviving children after all the terrible and uncertain times to lead Israel to view them as the "work of God's hands," as products of his miraculous preservation. This should prompt genuine worship and commitment in contrast to that in v 13. מעשׂה ידי, "the work of my hands," may be found in Deuteronomy to mean the people's conduct. In other places it refers to their sins, idols, or the work of an artisan (cf. Laberge, *La Septante d'Isaïe 28–3,* 312). It occurs of God's work especially in the Psalms and in Isaiah (5:12; 19:25; 60:21; 64:8). את־קדושׁ יעקב, "the Holy One of Jacob," is unique. Isaiah usually says "The Holy One of Israel."

24 Recognizing God's work and responding with worship will reverse the conditions of v 14*b*. Understanding will return to the leaders.

Explanation

The reversal of fortunes takes a strange turn. Judgment on those who seek to elude YHWH's scrutiny is understandable. The turn of fate that makes the deaf, blind, meek, and humble have their day is to be expected in the Vision, as is the end of shrewd conniving. But the word about Jacob comes as a surprise. God's continued love for Israel and his undying hope of genuine response are manifestations of his unending grace.

Disaster from Rebellious Self-Help (30:1–33)

The scene builds upon the real struggle between God and the Judean leaders, who are determined to follow their own plans. Episode A, "Woe, Rebellious Children" (30:1–18), draws a contrast between what God is doing and the policies of Judah's leaders, while the second and third episodes portray religious teachers and prophets teaching a blind, euphoric hope that ignores the real rebellion of their leaders. Episode B, "Hope from the Teachers" (30:19–26), calmly repeats the doctrine of hope in God. The teachers, blind to the real issues on which the fate of the nation hung, continue teaching "peace, peace, when there is no peace" (Jer 6:14; 8:11, NIV). Episode C, "A Cultic Theophany" (30:27–33), presents the religious exercise of cultic prophecy. Judah's leaders cultivated the shallow hope that YHWH would appear in a miraculous way to effect their salvation without their having to be concerned about the policies of the nation.

Woe, Rebellious Children (30:1–18)

Bibliography

Barthel, J. *Prophetenwort und Geschichte.* Tübingen: Mohr Siebeck, 1997. 391–427. **Beuken, W. A. M.** "Isaiah 30: Prophetic Oracle Transmitted in Two Successive Paradigms." In *Writing and Reading.* Ed. C. C. Broyles and C. A. Evans. 1:369–97. **Childs, B. S.** *Isaiah and the Assyrian Crisis.* 32–33. **Couroyer, B.** "Le Nes biblique: Signal ou enseigne." *RB* 91 (1984) 5–29. **Dahood, M.** "Accusative *'esah* 'Wood' in Isaiah 30:1*b*." *Bib* 50 (1969) 57–58. ———. "Some Ambiguous Texts in Isaias (30:15; 52:2; 40:5; 45:1.)" *CBQ* 20 (1958) 41–49. **Darr, K. P.** "Isaiah's Vision and the Rhetoric of Rebellion." In *SBLSP.* Atlanta: Scholars Press, 1994. 847–82. **Day, J.** *God's Conflict with the Dragon and the Sea: Echoes of a Canaanite Myth in the Old Testament.* Cambridge: Cambridge UP, 1985. **Donner, H.** *Israel unter den Völkern.* 132–34, 159–62. **Dorsey, D. A.** "On." In *Harper's Bible Dictionary.* Ed. P. Achtemeier. San Francisco: Harper & Row, 1985. 730–31. **Emerton, J. A.** "A Further Note on Isaiah XXX." *JTS* 33 (1982) 16. ———. "A Textual Problem in Isaiah XXX.5." *JTS* 32 (1981) 125–28. **Exum, J. C.** "Of Broken Pots, Fluttering Birds, and Visions in the Night: Extended Simile and Poetic Technique in Isaiah." *CBQ* 43 (1981) 331–52. **Fichtner, J.** "Jahwes Plan in der Botschaft des Jesaja." *ZAW* 63 (1951) 16–33. Reprinted in *Gottes Weisheit,* ed. K. D. Fricke, Gesammelte Studien (Stuttgart: Calwer, 1964), 27–43. **Galling, K.** "Tafel, Buch und Blatt."

In *Near Eastern Studies.* FS W. F. Albright, ed. H. Goedicke. Baltimare: Johns Hopkins UP, 1971. 207–33. **Gerstenberger, E.** "The Woe Oracles of the Prophets." *JBL* 81 (1962) 249–63. **Gray, A. H.** "The Beatitude of 'Them That Wait.'" *ExpTim* 48 (1936) 264–67. **Hertlein, E.** "Rahab." *ZAW* 38 (1919–20) 113–54. **Huber, F.** "Semantische Analyse der Wörter *bitha* und *suba* in Jes 30:15." In *Jahwe, Juda und die andern Völker beim Propheten Jesaja.* BZAW 137. Berlin: De Gruyter, 1976. 140–47. **Jenni, E.** *Die Politischen Voraussagen der Propheten.* ATANT 29. Zurich: Zwingli, 1956. 83. **Kuschke, A.** "Zu Jes 30:1–5." *ZAW* 64 (1952) 194–95. **Melugin, R. F.** "Isa 30:15–17." *CBQ* 36 (1974) 303–4. **Murison, R. G.** "Rahab." *ExpTim* 16 (1904) 190. **Nötscher, F.** "Entbehrliche Hapaxlegomena in Jesaia," *VT* 1 (1951) 300–302. **Reymond, P.** "Un tesson pour 'ramasser' de l'eau à la mare (Esaie xxx, 14)." *VT* 7 (1957) 203–7. **Schunck, K.-D.** "Jesaja 30:6–8 und die Deutung der Rahab im Alten Testament." *ZAW* 78 (1966) 48–56. **Smelik, K. A. D.** "Ostraca: schrijftafel of boekrol? Jeremia 36, Jesaja 30,8 en twee ostraca uit Saqqara." *NedTT* 44 (1990) 198–207. **Werner, W.** *Studien zur alttestamentlichen Vorstellung vom Plan Jahwes.* Berlin: De Gruyter, 1988. 85–94. **Williamson, H. G. M.** *Book Called Isaiah.* 103–6. **Wong, G. C. I.** "Faith and Works in Isaiah xxx 15." *VT* 47 (1997) 236–46. **Ziegler, J.** "Zum literarischen Aufbau im Buch des Propheten Isaias." *BZ* 21 (1933) 131–49.

Translation

YHWH:	1 *Woe, rebellious children!*	3+2
Herald:	*Expression* [a] *of YHWH.*	
YHWH:	*To those executing a plan,*	2+2
	but not one from me!	
	To one making an alliance,[b]	2+2
	but not (by) my spirit!	
	With the result: adding[c]	2+2
	sin upon sin.	
	2 *Those hurrying*[a] *to descend to Egypt,*	3+3
	but who did not ask my advice,	
	to take refuge[b] *in Pharaoh's protection*	3+3
	and to seek shelter in the shadow of Egypt.	
Heavens:	3 *Pharaoh's protection shall become a shame for you*	5+4
	and shelter in the shadow of Egypt a humiliation!	
Earth:	4 *Although his*[a] *princes are in Zoan*	3+3
	and his[a] *envoys reach Hanes,*	
	5 *everyone will be made odious*[a]	2+3
	by (this) people that are useless to them.[b]	
	Not for help, [c]*not for profit,*[c] *(do they live),*	4+4
	but for shame and also disgrace.	
Court Jester:	6 [a]*Burden: animals of the Negev.*[a]	3
	In a land of trouble[b] *and anguish,*	3+3+3
	of lioness and growling[c] *lion,*	
	of viper and flying serpent,	
	they carry[d] *their riches on the backs of asses,*	4+3+3
	on the hump of camels their treasures,	
	on behalf of[e] *a people that are useless.*	
YHWH:	7 *Egypt*[a] *(is) worthless!*	2+2
	They provide empty help!	

	Therefore, I call this one [b]	3+3
	"Rahab: [c] *Roaring (while) Sitting Still."* [c]	
Heavens:	[8] *Now come!*	2+3+2
	Write it on a tablet near them. [a]	
	Upon a scroll inscribe it,	
	that it may become for a later day	3+2
	a witness [b] *forever.*	
Earth:	[9] *For it is a rebellious people,*	4+2
	lying sons!	
	As sons, they are not willing to heed [a]	3+2
	YHWH's instruction,	
	[10] *who say to the seers*	3+2
	"Do not see!" [a]	
	and to the visionaries	1+3
	"Do not envision for us what is right!	
	Speak to us flattering things!	3+2
	Envision praiseworthy things! [b]	
	[11] *Turn* [a] *from* [b] *the way!*	2+2
	Turn aside from [b] *the path.*	
	Stop bringing up before us	2+2
	the Holy One of Israel!"	
Herald:	[12] *Therefore,* [a] [b] *thus says the Holy One of Israel:* [b]	5
YHWH:	*Because of your rejecting this word*	4+3+2
	so that you trust in a perverse [c] *tyrant* [d]	
	and so that you rely on him,	
	[13] *therefore, may this guilt*	3+2
	be for you	
	like a break collapsing,	2+3
	bulging out in a high wall,	
	which suddenly, with suddenness,	3+2
	comes (to) its breakup.	
	[14] *It shall break up* [a]	1+3+3
	like a clay vessel breaking up,	
	smashed—not spared. [b]	
	No shard will be found among its fragments	4+3+3
	(big enough) to take fire from the hearth	
	or to scoop up [bc] *water from a pool.* [bc]	
Herald:	[15] *For* [a] *thus said my Lord,*	3+3
	YHWH, [b] *the Holy One of Israel:*	
YHWH:	*In returning* [c] *and rest you could be saved.*	3+2+2
	In quietness and in trust [d]	
	could your heroism consist.	
	[e] *But you are not willing!* [e]	2
Heavens:	[16] [a] *Then you say: "No!* [b]	2+2+2
	But on a horse [c] *let us flee!"*	
	So you proceed to flee.	
	And "On a speedster let us ride!"	2+3
	So your pursuers were speed(ier).	

Earth:	[17]*One thousand,*	2+3+4
	facing the threat [a] *of one,*	
	facing the threat [a] *of five, you flee,*	
	until you are left	2+3+2
	like a flagstaff on top of the [b] *mountain,*	
	or like a banner on the [b] *hill.*	
Heavens:	[18]*Surely* [a] *YHWH waits to be gracious* [b] *to you.*	4+3+3
	Surely he rises up [c] *to show you mercy,*	
	for YHWH is a God of justice.	
Earth:	*Blessed are* [d]*all who wait for him!* [d]	3

Notes

1.a. 1QIsa[a] נואם is an orthographic variant for MT נְאֻם, "expression." Cf. Kutscher, *Language and Linguistic Background,* 178, 498.

1.b. MT לנסך מסכה is a cognate usage, which has four possible meanings: (1) "pour out a libation" (as in 48:5); (2) "cast a molten image" (30:22; 42:17); (3) "weave a web" (25:7); or (4) "negotiate an alliance." The last fits the parallel with "doing a plan" (BDB, 650–51; *HAL; DCH*). M. Dahood (*Bib* 50 [1969] 57–58) suggests that עצה means "wood" or "idols of wood" and Irwin ("Isaiah 28–33," 71) translates "making a wooden idol without my consent, and casting a molten image without my spirit." But the passage calls for political acts, and the idea that YHWH might have at some other time given consent for idolatry is unimaginable. The usual understanding fits the LXX translation συνθήκας, "understandings, agreements," and the normal meaning of עשות עצה, "execute a plan" (cf. 2 Sam 17:23; Isa 25:1).

1.c. ספות should be understood as *qal* inf. const. from יסף, "to add." So LXX προσθεῖναι, "to add, join," with similar meanings in Syr. Tg. Vg. Then the change that *BHS* recommends is superfluous.

2.a. Cf. NEB; Irwin, "Isaiah 28–33," 71; Gen 37:25.

2.b. לָעוֹז, "to take refuge," would usually be written לְעוּז, but the form as written does occur (cf. GKC §72*q;* Joüon §80*k*).

4.a. LXX omits the pronouns. Vg. includes them.

5.a. K הִבְאִישׁ, *hipʿil* pf. 3 m. sg. from באש, "be odious, stink"; Q הֹבִישׁ, *hipʿil* pf. 3 m. sg. from בוש, "come to shame" (GKC §78*b*). Q seems to be the first of numerous emendations (cf. *BHS,* following Procksch). 1QIsa[a] כלה באש has divided the words differently and omitted *yod.* If this is pointed כָּלָה בָאֵשׁ, it means "destroyed by fire" (cf. Irwin, "Isaiah 28–33," 75; Zeph 1:18; and *Anath* 3.42–43, in C. H. Gordon, *Ugaritic Handbook,* AnOr 25 [Rome: Pontifical Biblical Institute, 1947] 188). If it is pointed כָּלֹה בֹאשׁ, it means "be utterly shamed" (cf. Ps 71:13; Irwin, "Isaiah 28–33," 75). K offers the most interesting variant on the theme of humiliation and deserves acceptance as the "difficult reading."

5.b. This is MT's division of the verse. *BHS,* supported by Wildberger, would move the *ʾatnakh* back, making למו a part of the second line. But MT's division makes sense and is metrically sound with the uses of *maqqef.* The change makes all kinds of emendations seem necessary (cf. Wildberger, 1149).

5.c-c. LXX omits; *BHK* and Wildberger (1149), following Duhm, Marti, and Fohrer, follow LXX. Wildberger's metrical reasoning only applies if the *ʾatnakh* is moved. As it stands, MT is sound.

6.a-a. LXX ἡ ὅρασις τῶν τετραπόδων τῶν ἐν τῇ ἐρήμῳ, "the vision of the four-footed ones of the wilderness." Note the wordplays and ambiguity of the passage (see *Comment*).

6.b. 1QIsa[a] adds between MT's two terms a third, וציה "drought," although S. Talmon ("Aspects of the Textual Transmission," *Textus* 4 [1964] 113) thinks that it is simply a variant of one of the other two.

6.c. MT מֵהֶם, "from them." The meaning is not clear, which has led to numerous attempts at emendation (cf. Wildberger, 1158; Irwin, "Isaiah 28–33," 76–77). 1QIsa[a] reads ואין מים, "and no water." In view of the parallel, the emendation נֹהֵם, "growling," seems to be the best solution.

6.d. 1QIsa[a] reads a sg. "one carries."

6.e. MT על usually means "upon, over." Here the meaning "on behalf of" is more fitting.

7.a. *BHS* suggests omitting מצרים, "Egypt" (see Wildberger, 1158), but the metrical reasons are not valid. Irwin ("Isaiah 28–33," 77) calls this "a good example of delayed explication."

7.b. Irwin ("Isaiah 28–33," 75) ignores the *ʾatnakh* to read "this Rabah," but the order should be reversed for that.

7.c-c. MT הֵם שָׁבֶת seems to be the pl. pronoun "they" and a pausal form of a seldom-used noun שֶׁבֶת, "a sitting still" (BDB, 992). The phrase is strange and has naturally led to many attempts at emendation (cf. *BHS;* Wildberger, 1158–59). Irwin ("Isaiah 28–33," 77) reads הם as a noun, a shortened form of המון, "a roar." This is coupled in this "double–barrelled name" with שבת, which may come from the root שבת, "cease," or from שבב, "burn." As such it may be a deliberate pun. The best possibilities in context would be for שבת to be from שבת, "resting," or an inf. const. from ישב, "sitting down." This translation follows Irwin on הם and the derivation from ישב.

8.a. *BHS* advises deletion. See explanation in Wildberger (1166). No textual evidence supports it.

8.b. MT לָעַד, i.e., the preps. ל, "to," and עד, "unto." Since a second עד follows, it makes no sense. Tg. לסהדו קדמי, "for a testimony before me" or "a previous covenant"; Vg. *in testimonium,* "in witness"; α´ σ´ θ´ εις μαρτυριον, "for a witness." They all suggest reading לְעֵד, "for a witness" (cf. *BHS*).

9.a. MT שמוע inf. const., "to hear." 1QIsa[a] לשמוע inf. const. + prep., "to hear." Both forms are grammatically possible with no difference in meaning.

10.a. LXX adds ἡμῖν= לָנוּ, "to us, at us" (cf. *BHS*). The addition is unnecessary. The prohibition is against exercise of their clairvoyant gift. The parallel forms that follow do not require the addition even if they explain the LXX's insertion.

10.b. 1QIsa[a] מתלות (cf. F. Nötscher, *VT* 1 [1951] 302) for MT מהתלות, "deceptions" (BDB, 251 and corrective note on 1122), a *hap. leg.* related to התל or תלל, "mock, deceive." Both terms remain obscure. Irwin ("Isaiah 28–33," 81) reports a suggestion from M. Dahood that the parallel to חלקות, "smooth or flattering words," indicates a derivation from הלל, "praise." He translates "give visions of glory."

11.a. 1QIsa[a] תסורו impf. for MT's impv., but the impv. form in parallel הטו supports MT.

11.b. מִנִּי is not "from me" but is an older form of מן, "from" (GKC §102*b*).

12.a. Wildberger (1174) correctly distinguishes between לכן here, which joins related sections to each other, and the same word in v 13, in which it follows a complaint with a judgment.

12.b-b. The entire formula is missing in some LXX MSS, making this a part of the previous section. MT is right. The formula introduces a new form.

12.c. 1QIsa[a] ותעלוז, "and you will rejoice," for MT ונלוז, "perversity." Irwin ("Isaiah 28–33," 84) joins the two words to read "perverse tyrant," lit., "tyranny most perverse."

12.d. Many commentators, including Wildberger, have trouble with עֹשֶׁק, "oppression," and emend to עִקֵּשׁ (transposing two letters), "a crooked way."

14.a. *BHS* suggests omitting as dittography. See Irwin's defense ("Isaiah 28–33," 84) of the repetition on the grounds of style.

14.b. 1QIsa[a] records variant spellings, but they seem to be of no textual significance.

14.c. גבא, "cistern," is a *hap. leg.* in this meaning. Ezek 47:11 and the Damascus Scroll 10:12 suggest that this is an open pool used to get salt through evaporation. P. Reymond (*VT* 7 [1957] 203–7) has shown that the word originally meant "collect, gather." That could lead to either of these meanings. He suggests that חשף means "scrape, to lift up"; *HAL* "scoop, skim." So Wildberger (1175) suggests that גבא means something like "puddle" or "pool."

15.a. Missing in LXX.

15.b. Missing in LXX because אדני is also translated κύριος, "Lord."

15.c. The usual translation sees שובה as a noun from שוב, "returning, turning back" (BDB, *HAL*). As such it may mean returning from war or from a warlike diplomacy (Fohrer, Duhm). Wildberger (1181) uses this derivation but translates "conversion." Irwin ("Isaiah 28–33," 86) follows 1QIsa[a] שיבה, "sitting," from ישב. M. Dahood (*CBQ* 20 [1958] 41–45) defended MT but understood שוב to also mean "sit" as a by-root of ישב. G. R. Driver (*JSS* 13 [1968] 51) points to Arab. *rağaʿa* and its development in meaning ("returned, came home, rested, stayed quiet, was reconciled") to suggest that שובה be translated "staying quiet." With *HAL,* the translation stays with the first option.

15.d. 4QIsa ובטח, "security" (cf. J. M. Allegro, *Qumran Cave 4,* vol. 1 [4Q158–4Q186] [Oxford: Clarendon, 1968] 24), although 1QIsa[a] agrees with MT בבטחה, "in trust." Irwin ("Isaiah 28–33," 86) sees the 4QpIsa reading as making the parallel phrase conform exactly, the four words serving as synonyms.

15.e-e. LXX καὶ οὐκ ἐβούλεσθε ἀκούειν, "but you were not willing to hear." Wildberger (1182) notes that this fits 28:12 and 30:9, as well as 1:19, but does not fit here. The point here is not "hearing" but "turning."

16.a. *BHS* put this on the same line with the preceding stich.

16.b. לא־כי is a strange construction. Irwin ("Isaiah 28–33," 86) suggests dropping *maqqef* and joining כי with the following line. Donner (*Israel unter den Völkern,* 161), among others, suggests reading לא־כן as an emphatic "No!" Wildberger (1182) notes that MT's combination also occurs in Gen 18:15*b*, 19:2, 42:12, and elsewhere, meaning "no, but" or simply "no." MT may be kept.

16.c. This may mean in horse-drawn carts or chariots (cf. S. Mowinckel, "Drive and/or Ride in OT," *VT* 12 [1962] 286).

17.a. גערת, "threat" (BDB, *HAL*). Irwin ("Isaiah 28–33," 87) translates "roar," following the suggestion of H. G. May ("Some Cosmic Connotations of *Mayira Rabbîm*," *JBL* 74 [1955] 17) about its use in other passages.

17.b. The definite article may indicate a particular mountain, Mount Zion (cf. Irwin, "Isaiah 28–33," 87).

18.a. לכן usually means "therefore." A. C. M. Blommerde has collected a bibliography on לכן as an emphatic particle (*Northwest Semitic Grammar and Job,* BibOr 22 [Rome: Pontifical Biblical Institute,1969] 31–32), which Irwin ("Isaiah 28–33," 88) uses to support "surely" as the translation here. The distinction changes the entire meaning of the verse (see *Comment*).

18.b. חֲנַנְכֶם, "be gracious to you," is a unique form of a *qal* inf. const. (GKC §67*cc*). 1QIsa[a] חונכם is apparently an inf. of חון (cf. F. Nötscher, *VT* 1 [1951] 299, #4). But Leslie Allen in a private conversation suggests that 1QIsa[a] is simply a *plene* form corresponding to MT-type orthography: חֲנֹכֶם. Wildberger (1190) recommends MT as the "difficult reading" and refers to Bauer-Leander §58*p* on Amos 5:15.

18.c. Some MSS read ידום, "stands still," for MT ירום, "raises himself." G. R. Driver (*JTS* 38 [1937] 44) renders רום, "desire eagerly, wait, tarry," as the Arab. *rāma.* All these serve to gain parallelism with חכה, "waits," in the first stich. However, MT makes good sense as it stands.

18.d-d. The construction כל־חוכי לו, "all who wait for him," has a const. ptc. followed by a prep. when it would ordinarily require a noun. But cf. GKC §130*a* or Joüon §129*m*.

Form/Structure/Setting

The episode displays a succession of genres to contrast the leaders' policies with YHWH's revealed strategies. These genres are arranged in a structure that places YHWH's curse at the crown of an arch.

A A lament over rebellious children who depend on Egypt (vv 1–7).
  B An indictment of a rebellious people who are unwilling to heed YHWH's instruction (vv 8–11).
KEYSTONE Because you reject this word and trust in a tyrant, your guilt becomes a curse (vv 12–14).
  B′ YHWH's word rejected (vv 15–16).
A′ Therefore you are abandoned, helpless; YHWH's grace waits on justice: "blessed be all who wait for him" (vv 17–18).

The historical setting must be placed before the fall of Assyria (cf. 30:31; 31:8) but after Egypt had begun to conspire in Palestinian politics. This was a situation that prevailed through most of Josiah's reign. Blenkinsopp (411) characterizes this passage as "a protracted argument about the wisdom or folly of pursuing the policy of playing off one great power . . . against another."

Comment

1 The complaint about "rebellious children" picks up a theme begun in 1:2. The following sections define the nature of the rebellion. עצה, "a plan": The Vision has consistently avowed that YHWH has a strategy, a plan, for Israel. The political leaders have one, too. But the strategies differ.

2 The leaders plan an alliance with Egypt. In Ashurbanipal's late reign and in those of his successors, Assyria had become less aggressive. But Psamtik I, pharaoh of Egypt, increased in power and ambition. Jerusalem's leaders were determined to play the game of power politics, pitting one superpower against the one they thought would be its successor.

3–4 This prediction is seen as false. In solid fact, it was a misjudgment. Egypt's power in Palestine was short-lived. Babylon, not Egypt, was destined to succeed Assyria—and that for just over a half century.

5 Thus, reliance on Egyptian suzerainty by princes in Egypt as well as by leaders in Jerusalem was "useless," no help, destined to be a "shame," and a "disgrace" (note the repetition from v 3). Those who are not willing to be humble will be humiliated by their willful folly.

6 A derisive משא, "burden," or prophecy of judgment pictures the poor animals of burden, camels or donkeys, that make up Egypt's caravans in the south of Palestine. They are made to travel through the terrors of wild animals in the "land of trouble and anguish." The Negev was wilderness and part desert, a wild and rugged terrain. אפעה is a snake. J. J. Hess ("Beduinisches zum Alten und Neuen Testament," *ZAW* 35 [1915] 126) suggested that this is the Uraeus serpent representing Egyptian royalty. Y. Aharoni (*Osiris* 5 [1938] 474) understood it to be a poisonous snake of that region. Wildberger (1162) remarks that the writer could hardly have cared about the exact definition. As for שרף מעופף, "flying serpent," see also Isa 14:29, and שרפים with wings appear in 6:2 around the throne of God. Wildberger (1163) cites Num 21:4–9, a scene that took place in the Negev. Esarhaddon reported on his campaign to Egypt seeing yellow serpents that could fly (R. Borger, *Die inschriften Asarhaddons,* AfO Beiheft 9 [Graz: Weidner, 1956] 112). Herodotus (*Histories* 2.75; 3.109) reports similar occurrences. J. Feliks (*The Animal World of the Bible* [Tel Aviv: Sinai, 1962] 107) thinks of the cobra, which often climbs trees, but there are very few trees in the Negev. Cf. also O. Keel, *Jahweh-Visionen und Siegelkunst,* SBS 84–85 (Stuttgart: Katholisches Bibelwerk, 1977) 71.

7 רהב, "Rahab," was the name of the mythical monster that ruled chaos (cf. Ps 89:11 [10]). Egypt is called Rahab in Ps 87:4, where she stands beside Babylon (cf. H. J. Kraus, *Psalmen,* BKAT 15.2 [Neukirchen-Vluyn: Neukirchener Verlag, 1978] 604; Wildberger, 1164). But here Egypt is called by the monster's name only to be doomed to inactivity. YHWH's word makes her a harmless monster, a dragon that breathes fire and roars but is in fact innocuous. Ps 89:11 (10) tells of YHWH's victory over Rahab at Creation. She is his opponent now in appearance only. (See J. Day, *God's Conflict with the Dragon,* 88–101; idem, "Rahab [Dragon]," *ABD* 5:610–11.)

8–9 YHWH calls for his accusation against the people to be written down for a "later day." In a sense, this is exactly what the Vision of Isaiah does. It bears witness that Israel and Jerusalem are "not willing to heed YHWH's instruction" through all those twelve generations. The call to write fits the larger genre of covenant judgment against Israel based on YHWH's complaint (1:2). That complaint is repeated for Josiah's generation.

10–11 They tried to still the voices of the prophets so that the will of God would not be presented. Even in Jesus' day, he could say: "Jerusalem, Jerusalem, the city that kills the prophets" (Matt 23:37 NRSV).

12 YHWH's judgment condemns them for rejecting this word. עשק ונלוז, "a perverse tyrant," must refer to the pharaoh of Egypt.

13–14 The judgment curse is pronounced with the metaphor of a high masonry wall that has begun to bulge in the middle. This guilt will be like that wall. When it collapses, as collapse it must, it will leave behind nothing large enough to be useful. The curse is spoken in masculine plural to the people, or more likely, to the ruling party.

15 The judgment is supported by a repetition of God's word and plan. He had called for retreat and quiet patience, for a heroic restraint and waiting, but the activists in the palace could not wait. They saw in the crumbling decadence of Assyria's imperial power an unparalleled opportunity, especially since Egypt was prepared to encourage them. But their plans were shortsighted, fixed on the immediate goal of relative autonomy for a brief generation (Josiah's reign, 640–609 B.C.E.). That slight glory would be bought with the price of Jerusalem's complete destruction by the Babylonians in 598 and 587 B.C.E.

16 The activists refused YHWH's call to patience and acquiescence. Instead they tried to flee (presumably to Egypt), but their pursuers were faster.

17 After all their bravado, they broke and ran before the first show of authority appeared. Thus they became a hollow and lonely symbol without meaning or following.

18 So now, YHWH's mercy for them must wait on justice. The phrase "rises up to show you mercy" contains an inner tension. ירום, "rise up," usually refers to YHWH's rousing himself for war on his enemies. Here it is paired with לרחמכם, "to show you mercy." YHWH is forced to a violent course of action because Israel refused the quiet course that he had planned, for he is "a God of justice." The final line is a sigh over what might have been: "Blessed are all who wait for him!" Judah under Josiah had not been willing to do this.

Explanation

Vv 15 and 18 contain two of the clearest expressions of the Vision's message: YHWH has been calling upon Israel/Judah since the days of Uzziah to accept a passive role in international politics in order to assume a new part as God's spiritual representative, his servant, to the world. This role will be defined in later chapters. He called for a willingness on the nation's part to turn inward to its faith and to rest on God's grace and promises. It would require quietness in the midst of turmoil and trust that God would control the great forces that were devastating the region. That would be a heroism of a very different sort. The final blessing of this episode (v 18) is dedicated to such who wait.

God waits in expectation for Israel (5:2, 4, 7). The prophet Isaiah waited in hope (8:17). In the day of God's salvation, the redeemed will say, "Our God, for whom we waited, and he will save us" (25:9). The righteous say, "We wait for you" (33:2). "Those waiting on YHWH will renew strength" (40:31). "You will know . . . those waiting will never be disappointed" (49:23). "Coastlands . . . hope for (God's) arm" (51:5). Sometimes God does fearful things that are not expected ("waited for") (64:2, [3]). The Vision's presentation of a people who live in hope, waiting for YHWH, often surprised by YHWH, comes to a poignant focus in this passage. There is much more here than a reflection of the forward thrust in faith toward a future goal. (Cf. D. A. Hubbard, "Hope in the Old Testament," *TynBul* 34 [1983] 33–59; J. van der Ploeg, "L'esperance dans L'Ancien Testament," *RB* 61 [1954] 481–507; H. W. Wolff, *Anthropology of the Old Testament,* ed. M. Kohl [Philadelphia: Fortress Press, 1974] 149–55; W. Zimmerli, *Man and His Hope in the Old Testament,* SBT, 2d ser., 20 [Naperville, IL: Allenson, 1971] 1–11.) The emphasis in the Vision lies on those who were willing in faith to listen to God and to leave the fulfillment of his vision to him. Israel and Jerusalem were not willing. They insisted on fashioning their own salvation. In this they failed repeatedly, for God's power and God's plan were not part of their actions. In doing this, they confirmed their "rebellion" against God, which is documented in this episode.

Hope from the Teachers (30:19–26)

Bibliography

Bacher, W. "Isaïe, xxx, 21." *REJ* 40 (1900) 248–49. **Beuken, W. A. M.** "What Does the Vision Hold: Teachers or One Teacher? Punning Repetition in Isa. 30:20." *HeyJ* (FS R. Murray) 36 (1995) 451–56. **Köhler, L.** "בליל חמיץ Jes 30,24." *ZAW* 40 (1922) 15–17. **Laberge, L.** "Is 30:19–26: A Deuteronomic Text?" *EgT* 2 (1971) 35–54.

Translation

First Teacher: 19 *Indeed,*[a] *O people in Zion,* 2+2
you dweller[b] *in Jerusalem,*
you will surely not weep! 2+2
He will certainly be gracious to you![c]
(Responding) to the sound of your cry, 2+2
as soon as he hears it,[d] *he will answer you.*

Second Teacher: 20 *Although*[a] *my Lord has given you* 3+2+2
bread of adversity
and water of affliction,
your Guide[b] *will no longer hide himself.*[c] 3+4
Your eyes will be seeing your Guide.[b]

First Teacher: 21 *And your ears will hear a word* 3+2
from behind you saying,
"This is the way! 2+2
Walk in it!"
when you turn to the right 2+2
or when you turn to the left.

Second Teacher: 22 *You shall defile*[a] *your silver-plated images* 4+3
and your gold-plated idols.
You will scatter them like[b] *a contaminated thing.* 3+3
"Filth!"[c] *you will say of it.*

First Teacher: 23 *He will give the rain for your seed* 3+2
(with) which you seed the ground.

Bread will come (from) the ground, 3+3
rich and nutritious.
Your sheep will graze 2+2+2
in that day
(in) enlarged pasturage.

Second Teacher: 24 *The oxen and the asses,* 2+2+3
that work the ground,
will eat prepared fodder
that is a winnowing[a] 2+2
of shovel and pitchfork.

First Teacher: 25 *On every high mountain* 3+3+3
and on every raised hill
there shall be streams of running water,
in the day[a] *of great slaughter* 3+2
when towers are falling.

Second Teacher: 26 *The light of the moon shall be like the sun.* 4+4+3
And the light of the sun will be sevenfold
[a]*like the light of the seven days,*[a]
in the day of YHWH's binding up 3+2+3
the fracture of his people,
when he heals the wound (from) his blow.

Notes

19.a. כִּי is emphatic. Irwin ("Isaiah 28–33," 88) takes it as a sign of the vocative.

19.b. יֵשֵׁב, "he dwells," *qal* impf. The word must be a relative clause (Irwin, "Isaiah 28–33," 88) or be repointed יֹשֵׁב as a ptc., "dweller," as apparently Syr. *jāteb* and Tg. יתיב have done (cf. *BHS* and Wildberger). The ptc. fits best.

19.c. MT יָחְנְךָ, "be gracious to you," is a remarkable form of the impf. (cf. GKC §67*n*). 1QIsa[a] supplies the more usual form יחונך.

19.d. MT כשמעתו, "according to his hearing," is a fem. inf. const. (GKC §45*d*). 1QIsa[a] שמועה.

20.a. The relation to the previous verse suggests that the clause be read conditionally or as a concession (cf. RSV/NRSV).

20.b. מוריך, "your Guide," comes from ירה, "throw, cast, direct, instruct." Irwin ("Isaiah 28–33," 90) draws on the context and the use in Hos 10:12, "rain down," to translate "Rain-giver." Perhaps it is a double entendre with a play on both meanings. The following lines support the translation "Guide."

20.c. יכנף, "hide himself," is a *hap. leg.* derived from a noun meaning "wing." Irwin ("Isaiah 28–33," 91) draws on a Ugar. text to translate "lift wing," but his interpretation stretches the entire text beyond reason.

22.a. LXX^{BS*} καὶ μιανεῖς, "you will defile" (as well as LXX^{AQSc} καὶ ἐξαρεῖς, "you will drive out"), is sg., as are OL and Vg. But the entire passage moves from a collective sg. back to pl. There is no reason to change MT, in spite of the following sg. pronouns.

22.b. LXX ὡς ὕδωρ, "like water," reads כמי for MT כמו. If one takes the LXX reading, then תזרם should be understood from "pour in a flood." The stich would read "you will pour forth filth like water." But MT makes sense and may be kept.

22.c. צֵא is frequently understood (Fohrer, Kaiser) as *qal* impv. from יצא, "go out" (BDB, *HAL*). The parallel calls for it to be like דוה, "contaminated thing." *BHK*[3] suggests צואה, "excrement," to keep the fem. parallel. *BHS* repoints as צוֹא, which probably has the same meaning. G. R. Driver (*ZAW* 77 [1958] 45) agrees with *BHK* and derives צא from צוא, "filth" or "excrement." This meaning fits the text and context (cf. LXX κόπρον, "dung, manure," and the versions).

24.a. זֹרֶה is a *qal* act. ptc. If it is kept, it may be understood as a const., and one must translate "which is a winnowing of." 1QIsa[a] יזרה turns it into an impf., also active. Most translators point it זֹרָה as a *pu'al* pf., "is winnowed."

25.a. LXX ἐν τῇ ἡμέρᾳ ἐκείνῃ, "in that day," for MT ביום, "in the day." Wildberger (1192) remarks that this emphasizes the eschatological understanding of it.

26.a-a. LXX omits. Commentators have generally viewed it as a gloss (cf. *BHS*). It is a kind of comment, but there is no hint about when it was inserted. It may well have been original. Irwin ("Isaiah 28–33," 96) defends it on metrical grounds.

Form/Structure/Setting

The setting of the episode is a place where teachers are to be found, perhaps a corner of the temple court or a schoolroom. It does not deal with the issues of the previous episode, nor are the teachers aware of the matters that dominated the confrontation between YHWH and the political leaders.

This little homily on assurance and hope is presented in a style not unlike the teaching of the wise or the admonitions of the Deuteronomists. It addresses the pilgrims in Jerusalem. It recognizes that past times have been difficult (v 20) but assures that better times are coming.

The entire mood and tone are mild and calm. The sermon is built in an arch capped by a version of the second commandment (v 22):

A Good news for Jerusalem: your gracious Guide responds to you (vv 19–20).
  B Your Guide teaches: This is the way! Walk in it! (v 21).
KEYSTONE Defile and get rid of your idols (v 22).
  B´ Your Guide provides rain and blessing even through crisis (vv 23–25).
A´ In that beautiful day YHWH heals his people (v 26).

Comment

19 The repeated addresses עם בציון, "people in Zion," and בירושלם, "in Jerusalem" are to be distinguished from "people of Jerusalem," who are those who are gathered in Jerusalem for the festival, not those who live there. לא־תבכה, "not weep," directs the episode away from lament. זעקך, "your cry," is a cry for help such as would come from a people in distress (Wildberger, 1196). In 15:8 it was Moab's cry for help. Ps 22:6 (5) cites the patriarch's cry, which God answered (cf. also Pss 107:13; 142:2, 6). A lament pleads with God to answer. This verse assures the plaintiff of his response.

20*a* Like Ps 107, this verse recalls the trials of Israel in the wilderness when hunger and thirst were major problems. God sent manna to eat (Exod 16:12, 15, and so on) and water from the rock. Wildberger (1189) supplies the word "without" to make the lines conform to this sense of assurance. This is unnecessary and wrong. The verse acknowledges the distress that has been the people's lot (see *Note* 20.a.). "Bread of adversity" and "water of affliction" are provisions for prisoners (cf. 1 Kgs 22:27). The bad times are seen to have been like a prison sentence from God.

20*b* מוֹרֶיךָ, "your Guide," is unique as a name for YHWH (cf. Wildberger, 1197). In Gen 12:6 and Deut 11:30 the phrase "the oak(s) of Moreh" uses the term. But the meaning there is obscure. The verb ירה in *hip'il* is used of God teaching his people in Isa 2:3 and 28:26. His teaching can be called תורה, "torah" or "instruction" (Pss 25:8; 94:12).

לא־יכנף עוד, "no longer hide himself," recognizes periods when God's guiding, instructing presence has not been sensed. It promises that this will no longer be true. The idea of God's withdrawal appears in Exod 19:21 and 20:21–23. This is explained in some places by the brilliance of his glory, which a person could not survive (cf. Isa 6:5). But it is also understood in terms of deliberate withdrawal. YHWH is called "A God who hides himself" (45:15), and psalmists plead for him not to hide his face from them (Pss 27:9; 102:3 [2]; 143:7). Ps 44:25 (24) asks why he hides his face from his people. Job acutely experienced God's absence and silence. The OT understands that God's presence is not simply a fact of existence, presumed to be universal and constant. It is a gracious and deliberate gift offered by God, a gift to be welcomed and recognized as such.

In Judaism from Ezra on, the Torah functioned to teach the people. But in the Vision this is done by the instructing, guiding presence of YHWH with his people (cf. 2:3). "Seeing" God and hearing his voice in instruction are understood to be ways of knowing and experiencing his presence.

21 God's words are like those of a shepherd who speaks "from behind," keeping his flock on the path.

22 The anticipated presence of the Guide makes urgent the need to rid the place of "idols." Such were often plated with "silver" or "gold." The role of idols to represent God's presence is understood here. The true presence of God among his people removes the need for artificial symbols.

23 Palestinian agriculture is totally dependent on rain. YHWH claims to be able to give and to withhold rain (Amos 4:7; Isa 5:6; 2 Kgs 8:1; Deut 11:13; 28:12).

24 בליל חמיץ, "prepared fodder," is a unique and obscure phrase. BDB (330) translates "seasoned." L. Köhler (*ZAW* 40 [1922] 15–17) identified חמיץ as "sorrel," a plant with a sharp taste. The text implies a favored food for cattle. בליל implies a treatment of some kind, so *HAL:* "sorrel-fodder prepared by soaking."

25 "Streams" on the heights suggest abundance of water. "Great slaughter" and "towers . . . falling" set the scene in a time of war when destruction is commonplace and expected.

26 The effect of the sun and the moon is felt for the great day. Moderns would be appalled at the thought of a sevenfold increase in the sun's heat and light. The intention here is symbolic of participation by the cosmos, which is also a part of YHWH's realm, in God's healing work. Isa 24:23 had pictured an opposite reaction, where the sun and moon were ashamed (became pale) before the Lord's glory.

YHWH's healing work will be applied to his people's wounds, even to those that his punishment had caused. The idea that God punishes but also heals is found in Deut 32:39, Job 5:18, and Hos 6:1.

Explanation

The implied hearers within the Vision are despondent pilgrims in Jerusalem. With heightened political tensions, the threat of war, and prophetic teachings that YHWH has sent the wars against them, they tended to despair of YHWH's help and goodness.

The passage is a classic example of an assuring homily in the Wisdom/Deuteronomic style. The gracious, healing, guiding nature of God is certain and dominant. The most prominent name for God is "your Guide" (v 20). Because God is responsive, his people need not weep (v 19). Past afflictions and trials should not cloud the hope that God will again appear to guide his people (v 20). God's presence is a gentle reminder of "the way" whenever they are tempted to stray (v 21) and is a strong admonition against idolatry (v 22). God provides what is needed for the farmer and the herder (vv 24). The basic understanding of YHWH's role in bringing rain to Palestine is dominant here, as it is in Deuteronomy. The blessing of rain will be abundant enough to provide streams on the mountain tops (v 25*a*).

Only v 25*b* gives a hint that the episode is set in a time of turmoil and war. This stressful factor is otherwise ignored, but the distress and wounds are recognized in v 20*a* and in 26*b*. In both instances YHWH's responsibility for the people's hurt is recognized. Yet the positive message of God's grace, his providential guidance, the gift of rain, and the healing of his people's hurt dominates all else. One strong demand is clear: Get rid of the idols (v 22)! (Cf. John's final plea to his fledgling church, 1 John 5:21.)

A Cultic Theophany (30:27–33)

Bibliography

Barth, H. *Die Jesaja-Worte.* 92–103. **Day, J.** *Molech: A God of Human Sacrifice in the Old Testament.* Cambridge: Cambridge UP, 1989. **Ginsberg, H. L.** "An Obscure Hebrew Word." *JQR* 22 (1931) 143–45. **Gordis, R.** "Midrash in the Prophets." *JBL* 49 (1930) 421–22. **Guillaume, A.** "Isaiah's Oracle against Assyria (Isaiah 30:27–33) in the Light of Archaeology." *BSOAS* 17 (1956) 413–15. **Heider, G. C.** *The Cult of Molek: A Reassessment.* Sheffield: JSOT Press, 1985. 319–32. **Huber, F.** *Jahwe, Juda und die anderen Völker beim Propheten Jesaja.* Berlin: De Gruyter, 1976. 50–54. **Irwin, B. P.** "Molek Imagery and the Slaughter of Gog in Ezekiel 38 and 39." *JSOT* 65 (1995) 93–112. **Irwin, W. H.** "Conflicting Parallelism in Job 5,13; Isa. 30,28; 32:7." *Bib* 76 (1995) 72–74. **Kruger, P. A.** "The Obscure Combination כבד משאה in Isaiah 30:27: Another Description of Anger?" *JNSL* 26 (2000) 155–62. **Milgrom, J.** "An Alleged Wave-Offering in Israel and in the Ancient Near East." *IEJ* 22 (1972) 33–38. **Pea, J.** "La 'fiesta solemne y santa' en Isaias 30:27–33 como pascua." *Theo* 14 (1999) 104–20. **Ringgren, H.** "Behold Your King Comes." *VT* 24 (1974) 207–11. **Sabottka, L.** "Is. 30, 27–33: Ein Übersetzungsvorschlag." *BZ* 12 (1968) 241–45. **Sasson, V.** "An Unrecognized 'Smoke Signal' in Isaiah xxx 27." *VT* 33 (1983) 90–95. **Schedl, C.** "Gedanken zu einem 'Übersetzungsvorschlag' Is 30:17–33." *BZ* 13 (1969) 242–43. **Smelik, K. A. D.** "Moloch, Molech, or Molk Sacrifice? A Reassessment of the Evidence Concerning the Hebrew Term Molekh." *SJOT* 9 (1995) 133–42. **Weinfeld, M.** "The Worship of MOLECH and the Queen of Heaven and Its Background." *UF* 4 (1972) 133–54.

Translation

First Prophet: 27 *See! The Name of YHWH,* 2+2
coming from a distance,
his anger burning, 2+2
[a]*his liver raging;*[a]
his lips are full of indignation 3+3+3
and his tongue devouring like fire,
28 *and his breath*[a] *like an overflowing stream,*[b]
(which) reaches[c] *to the neck* 2+2+2
to signal[d] *nations*
with a signal for destruction[e]
and a restricting bridle 2+3
on[f] *the jaws of*[g] *peoples.*
Second Prophet: 29 *This song will be yours* 3+2
like a night (when) one celebrates a festival,
when the heart's gladness starts when a flute (plays), 4+4
in approaching the mountain of YHWH, to the Rock[a]
of Israel.
First Prophet: 30 *When YHWH makes the majesty of his voice heard* 4+3
and his descending[a] *arm seen*
with raging anger 2+3
and a flame of devouring fire,
a cloudburst, a storm, 2+2
and hailstones.
Second Prophet: 31 *For at*[a] *the sound of YHWH* 2+2+2
Assyria will be broken—
the very rod (with which) he strikes.
First Prophet: 32 *When it shall be:* 1
every stroke of the appointed[a] *staff* 4+4
that YHWH lays on it (will be)
(accompanied) by timbrels and by lyres 2+2+2
and a battle wave offering,[b]
(the kind) with which[c] *he sets out to battle.*
Second Prophet: 33 *For a funeral pyre*[a] *(was) being prepared days ago.*[b] 3+3
This particular one has been made ready for the king.[c]
Deep he made (it). Wide he made (it). 2+2+2
Its pyre (for) fire,
and wood aplenty.
First Prophet: *YHWH's breath,* 2+2+2
like a stream of lava,
(will be) kindling it.

Notes

27.a-a. משאה may have a range of meanings from "burden" to "utterance" to "smoke," which might relate to נשא, "lift up." θ´, Syr., Tg., and Vg. related it to the basic meaning of כבד to translate "burdensome is his oracle." Wildberger (1208) recommends staying with "burden." Hummel ("Enclitic *Mem* in Early Northwest Semitic," *JBL* 76 [1957] 100) proposed emending to וּכְבֵדוֹ־ם שָׂאָה (adding a *vav* parallel to אפו, "his anger," separating enclitic *mem* and reading *sin* as *shin*), "his liver raging," which is followed by Irwin ("Isaiah 28–33," 97), saying "27–28 read like an anatomy handbook." The emendation is very attractive since no other form fits the context.

28.a. This entire verse is deliberately ambiguous, beginning with רוחו: "his breath" if seen as a third of the parts of YHWH, "his spirit" if seen as a contrasting picture of God.

28.b. נחל is the second ambiguous term: "stream" or "portion, inheritance" (but the latter is usually fem.).

28.c יחצה is the third ambiguity: "reaches to" if נחל is "stream," "apportioned" if it is "inheritance."

28.d. נפה means "wave, swing back and forth," which may refer to water's action or to the liturgical "wave offering."

28.e. שוא may mean "destruction" (usually fem.) or "emptiness."

28.f. עַל is usually seen as the prep. "upon." However, a change of vowel produces עֹל, "yoke," parallel to "bridle."

28.g. לחיי is usually read as "jaws of." However, if על is read as a noun, the possibility opens for ל to be a preposition and חיי to be "lives (or life) of."

29.a. For צור, "rock," LXX πρὸς τὸν θεὸν, "before God"; θ´ φυλακα, "guard"; α´ στερεον, "firm, steadfast"; σ´ κραταιον, "strong one." But the Heb. is a regular designation for YHWH.

30.a. נחת, "descending." LXX τὸν θυμόν, "the anger"; σ´ την επαναπαυσιν, "rest upon"; Vg. *terrorem*, "dread." The word is a *hap. leg.* meaning "descend, sink down" (BDB, *DCH*), "lowering" *(HAL)*.

31.a. Cf. M. Dahood ("Ugaritic-Hebrew Syntax and Style," *UF* 1 [1969] 19) for an analysis of the syntax, implemented by Irwin ("Isaiah 28–33," 102).

32.a. MT מוסדה, "appointment"; 1QIsa[a] מוסדו, "his appointment." Some MSS *(BHS)* read מוסרה, "his chastisement" from יסר.

32.b. תנופה may mean a "wave offering." Irwin ("Isaiah 28–33," 104) compares this to Isa 19:16 and Exod 20:25 to translate "the slashing stroke." The issue is whether this describes a liturgy or a realistic battle.

32.c. בה, "against her." Assyria was addressed as masc. before. Irwin ("Isaiah 28–33," 104) makes the pronoun refer to תנופה, "wave offering."

33.a. תָּפְתֶּה, "funeral pyre," is an unexplained form. Procksch (cf. *BHS*) proposed reading תָּפְתֹּה, which has a dative force. Thus Irwin ("Isaiah 28–33," 105) translates "Topheth for him."

33.b. אתמול means "yesterday." LXX πρὸ ἡμερῶν and Syr. *mn ḳdm jwmt'* are something like "days ago" (cf. Wildberger, 1210).

33.c. O. Eissfeldt (*MOLK als Opferbegriff im Punischen und im Hebräischen und das Ende des Gottes Moloch* [Halle: Niemeyer, 1935] 45; cf. also M. Weinfeld, *UF* 4 [1972] 133–54) suggested removing the article to read "to Molech," a view rejected by Wildberger (1210) and Irwin ("Isaiah 28–33," 105) but recognized by Kaiser.

Form/Structure/Setting

This episode parodies cultic ceremonies of YHWH's coming in the Zion festival. Vv 27–28 portray the coming of the Name of YHWH from afar, burning with anger against the nations. They employ six anthropomorphic terms:

Name of YHWH	coming from a distance
His anger	burning
His liver	raging
His lips	full of indignation
His tongue	devouring like fire
His breath	like a stream
	a signal to the nations
	a bridle for the peoples

Vv 29–33*b* turn to the people's response and to the historical consequences that are promised. YHWH's coming will occasion a song like festival songs of old when Israel climbed toward Jerusalem to worship YHWH, "the Rock of Israel," and witnessed the drama of YHWH acting in the storm (v 30) and the cultic punishment he meted out, portrayed in v 32 by musical accompaniment. But the real joy of the worshiping people is occasioned by historical events that mirror the festival drama. Assyria will fall (v 31), and her king will be buried (v 33*ab*). V 33*c* returns to the theme of theophany. YHWH's anger lights the funeral pyre of the Assyrian king.

The theophany account is a careful literary construction in two movements. The ten anthropomorphic references (six in vv 27–28, three in vv 30–31, one in v 33) center in the storm figure of vv 30–31. The "voice of YHWH" occurs twice, while reference to "his descending arm" comes between them. This is the keystone of the arch. YHWH's act ("his arm") has descriptions of his emotions before (vv 27–28) and after (v 33). A second element of the structure consists of words related to fire: "burning" (vv 27, 33), "like a devouring fire" (vv 27, 30, 33), "like a stream" (vv 28, 33), and words of similar sound or letters (vv 28, 32). The artistry of the composition lies in the choice and arrangement of words.

Comment

27 שם־יהוה, "the Name of YHWH." Wildberger (1216) and others have argued that the formula must read "see YHWH coming," as in Isa 26:21; 40:10; 66:15; Pss 96:13; 98:9; Deut 33:2; and Hab 3:3. "The Name of YHWH" is usually the object of worship or veneration. This usage is unique. Apparently the Name here is like the "Glory" in Ezek 1:28 and passim, intended to represent YHWH himself.

A theophany usually tells where YHWH is coming from: Seir/Edom (Judg 5:4), Teman/Mountains of Paran (Hab 3:3), Sinai (Deut 33:2), the Heavens (Mic 1:3; Isa 26:21; 63:19; Jer 25:30; Pss 18:10, 144:5), Zion (Amos 1:2; Ps 50:2), stormwind from the north (Ezek 1:4). The phrase ממרחק, "from a distance," is unique. Common to all of these is the recognition that YHWH is not bound to any place. He comes when and where he chooses.

אפו, "anger," speaks of YHWH's motivation. Wildberger (1218) notes that אף also means "nostril," which fits the list of anatomical terms used. Concerning the use of משׂאה, "liver," for the expression of anger, see H. W. Wolff, *Anthropology of the Old Testament* (Philadelphia: Fortress, 1974) 64.

28 The objects of God's anger are the "nations/peoples." In Isa 17:2 and 29:7 the plural was used to describe military actions involving Assyria. Its army was composed of different ethnic units. This may be true here as well. נפה, "signal," is usually used with יד, "hand," as in Isa 11:15 and 13:2. Here it appears in a mixed metaphor with רסן, "bridle." God's intervention will rein in Assyria's power and lead to its destruction (v 31).

29 The theophany is set in a festival. It is to be understood as the festal drama of Zion's New Year. Its purpose is clear from the name used for God: צור ישׂראל, "the Rock of Israel." It stresses assurance that YHWH will defend and care for his people.

30 The theophany turns to the picture of the storm revealing God's voice and act: his arm descending for deliverance. The storm god with raised arm is a familar motif in ancient Near Eastern art (cf. *ANEP,* 481, 484, 486, 490, 531, 532). Storm imagery is frequently used in the Psalms (Pss 18:13; 46:3; 68:3, 7–9; 77:18).

31 The name Assyria gives political focus to the theophany. It anticipates the breakup of the empire. In Isa 10:5 YHWH called Assyria "the rod of my anger." Here Assyria's destruction is announced. ב must be construed as indicating more precisely what will be broken up (BDB, 88, I.7). יכה, "he strikes," follows with no particle. Yet it must be a contact relative clause. Hence the translation "with which he strikes." YHWH is the implied subject. The very passage that acknowledges Assyria to be YHWH's agent had announced that he would, in time, also determine Assyria's fate (10:12). In this episode that day has come.

32 The verse announces the identity of YHWH, celebrated in Jerusalem's worship, with God who controls the giants of history. Every military blow against Assyria will coincide with representations in the temple's worship.

33 The reference to the king's funeral is parallel to chap. 14. The context suggests that תפתה, "funeral pyre," is related to a ceremony for the dead. Cremation was not usual in Palestine nor, as far as is known, in Mesopotamia, although it is documented for military funerals in Greece and is the usual means of dealing with bodies as far east as India. When the OT speaks of burning bodies, it is taken as a sign of vengeance or degradation (cf. 1 Sam 31:12; Amos 6:10; Lev 20:14; 21:9; Josh 7:25; *ISBE,* 1:812; *IDB,* 1:475). The passage eloquently celebrates the fact that the king is dead. The motif of fire is continued in YHWH's fiery breath that ignites the funeral pyre. That is reminiscent of fire from heaven devouring Elijah's altar on Carmel (1 Kgs 18:38).

Explanation

Themes from cultic drama and theophany have been blended to shape a powerful episode (see Jörg Jeremias, *Theophanie: Die Geschichte einer alttestamentlichen Gattung* [Neukirchen-Vluyn: Neukirchener Verlag, 1965] 57). Within the Vision, it, like the second episode (30:19–26), shows religious attempts to counter the message of the first episode (30:1–18). Like the prophets of salvation who opposed Jeremiah, the teachers and the theophanie prophets salve the worries of the people, preventing them from facing up to the hard political decisions. This is how religious assurance can in fact be, as Karl Marx once wrote, "an opiate for the people."

Disaster from False Faith in Egypt (31:1–32:20)

The next scene centers on the criticism of those whose policy calls for dependence upon Egypt to gain independence from Assyria. Political scheming ignores God's determination of events that the drama's previous acts have portrayed.

The first episode of the scene, "Woe to Those Who Go Down to Egypt for Help!" (31:1–9), is a dialogue about political leaders who prefer human dependence on alliances to dependence on an alliance with God. The second episode, "Suppose a King . . ." (32:1–8), is a lesson in civic righteousness from the teachers. In the third episode, "Until Spirit is Poured Out" (32:9–20), a dialogue between a speaker and a group of women contrasts their prosperity with the devastation to come in "less than a year."

"Woe to Those Who Go Down to Egypt for Help!" (31:1–9)

Bibliography

Amsler, S. "Les Prophètes et la politique." *RTP* 23 (1973) 14–31. **Barré, M. L.** "Of Lions and Birds: A Note on Isaiah 31,4–5." In *Among the Prophets.* JSOTSup 144. Sheffield: JSOT Press, 1993. 55–59. **Childs, B.** *Isaiah and the Assyrian Crisis.* 33–35, 57–59. **Davis, M. T.,** and **B. A. Strawn.** "Isaiah 31:4–5 in the Light of Lion Iconography in the Ancient Near East." In *AAR/SBL Abstracts 1996.* Atlanta: Scholars Press, 1996. 293. **Dietrich, W.** *Jesaja und die Politik.* Munich: Kaiser, 1976. 144–52. **Donner, H.** *Israel unter den Völkern.* 135–39. **Driver, G. R.** " Hebrew Notes on Prophets and Proverbs." *JTS* 41 (1940) 162–75. **Eidevall, G.** "Lions and Birds as Literature: Some Notes on Isaiah 31 and Hosea 11." *SJOT* 7 (1993) 78–87. **Exum, J. C.** "Of Broken Pots, Fluttering Birds, and Visions in the Night: Extended Simile and Poetic Technique in Isaiah." *CBQ* 43 (1981) 331–52. **Geers, H.** "Hebrew Textual Notes." *AJSL* 34 (1917) 133–34. **Hempel, J.** "Jahwegleichnisse der israelitischen Propheten." In *Apoxysmata.* BZAW 81. Berlin: Töpelmann, 1961. 1–29. **Höffken, P.** "Bemerkungen zu Jesaja 31:1–3." *ZAW* 112 (2000) 230–38. **Klijn, A. F. J.** "Jerome's Quotations from a Nazoraean Interpretation of Isaiah (Isa 8:14,19–9:1; 29:20–21; 31:6–9)." In *Judéo-Christianisme.* FS J. Daniélou, ed. B. Gerhardsson et al. Paris: Recherches de science religieuse, 1972. 241–55. **Stansell, G.** "Isaiah 32: Creative Redaction in the Isaiah Tradition." In *SBLSP.* Chico, CA: Scholars Press, 1983. 1–12. **Sweeney, M. A.** *Isaiah 1–39.* 401–8. ———. "Parenetic Intent in Isaiah 31." In *Proceedings of the Eleventh World Congress of Jewish Studies: Division A. The Bible and Its World.* Ed. D. 'Assaf. Jerusalem: World Union of Jewish Studies, 1994. 99–106. **Wong, G. C. I.** "Isaiah's Opposition to Egypt in Isaiah XXXI 1–3." *VT* 46 (1996) 392–401.

Translation

Heavens: [1] *Woe! Those going down to Egypt* [a] *for help,* 4+2
(who) rely on [b] *horses.*
They trust [c] *in a chariot that is big* 4+4
and upon horsemen [d] *that are very strong.*
They do not look to the Holy One of Israel, 4+3
nor do they seek YHWH.
Earth: [2] *And indeed he is the Wise One.* 3+2+3
He achieves (his) purpose [a]

	and does not retract his words.	
	He will rise up against the house of the wicked	3+3
	and against those who help evildoers.	
Heavens:	3 *Egypt (is) human,*	2+2
	not God! [a]	
	Their horses (are) flesh,	2+2
	not spirit! [b]	
	When YHWH stretches out his hand,	3+4+3
	the helper will stumble, the one helped will fall.	
	They will all be finished off together.	
Earth:	4 *For YHWH said this to me:*	4
	"Just as the lion growls,	3+2
	or the young lion, over his prey	
	when a band of shepherds	3+2
	is called out against him,	
	he is not terrified by their voice,	3+3
	nor is he daunted by their noises."	
	So YHWH of Hosts will descend	4+4+2
	to fight upon Mount Zion	
	and on its hill.	
Heavens:	5 *Like birds hovering,*	2+4+2
	so [a] *YHWH of Hosts* [a] *will provide cover*	
	over Jerusalem.	
	Protecting, he will deliver! [b]	2+2
	Sparing, he will rescue! [c]	
Earth:	6 *Turn* [a] *to him,*	1+3+2
(to Jerusalem)	*against whom Israel's sons* [b]	
	have rebelled so deeply. [c]	
Heavens:	7 *For in this day*	3+4+2
	they would reject, each his [a] *silver idols,*	
	his [a] *gold idols,*	
(aside to Jerusalem)	*which your sinful* [b] *hands have (also) made for yourselves.*	5
YHWH:	8 *Assyria will fall by a sword, not by a person,* [a]	4+3
	and a sword—not a human being [a]*—will devour it.*	
	Someone may flee to it [b] *from before a sword,*	4+3
	but its choice soldiers will become slaves. [c]	
	9 *Its rock* [a] *will disappear because of terror.*	3+3
	Its officers will desert at sight of a battle flag, [b]	
Herald:	*Expression of YHWH,*	2+3+3
	whose fire (is) in Zion	
	and whose furnace (is) in Jerusalem.	

Notes

1.a. 1QIsa[a] למצרים, "to Egypt," uses a prep. in place of MT's adv. acc.
1.b. LXX πεποιθότες, "depending on."
1.c. LXX omits.
1.d. Or "horses" that pull the chariots.
2.a. Reading with Irwin ("Isaiah 28–33," 111) רֵעַ, "purpose," for MT רָע, "disaster."

3.a. Tg. רב, "noble prince."

3.b. LXX καὶ οὐκ ἔστι βοήθεια, "and it is no help."

5.a-a. LXX omits.

5.b. *BHS* follows Vg. *liberans* to read וְהַצִּיל, *hipʿil* inf. abs., "delivering," for MT וְהִצִּיל, *hipʿil* pf. 3 m. sg., "he will deliver." Follow MT.

5.c. 1QIsa[a] הפליט, "cause to escape, make secure," for MT המליט, "he will rescue." Vg. again suggests inf. abs. Follow MT.

6.a. שובו, "turn," is 2d person while the following clause is 3d person, causing *BHS* to suggest a 3d-person juss. וישובו, "and let them turn." The variation continues through the verse (cf. Joüon §158*n*). This is not unusual. L. Sabottka (*Zephanja* [Rome: Pontifical Biblical Institute, 1972] 66) cites parallels in Zeph 2:3; Mic 3:3, 9; Isa 54:1; Jer 5:21.

6.b. LXX omits. בני, "sons," is sometimes viewed as the ones addressed by "turn." But Irwin ("Isaiah 28–33," 115) is nearer right in seeing it as the subject of the second verb.

6.c. העמיקו (*hipʿil* pf. 3 c. pl.), "they made deep." The word is used for the grave in 30:33, for the plans of the government in 29:15, and for the sign to be proposed in 7:11. The figurative speech here in relation to סרה, "rebellion," refers to their determination.

7.a. LXX omits the pronouns. But MT is in order when the pronouns are related to the dominant word in the const. relation: not "the idols of his silver," but "his silver idols" (cf. J. Weingreen, "The Construct-Genitive Relation in Hebrew Syntax," *VT* 4 [1954] 50–59).

7.b. LXX, Eth., and Arab. versions omit. Various commentators have trouble fitting חֵטְא, "sinful," into the sentence. Wildberger (1237) considers it a gloss. Irwin ("Isaiah 28–33," 116) follows M. Dahood ("Ugaritic-Hebrew Syntax and Style," *UF* 1 [1969] 30–31) in considering ידיכם חטא to be "a construct chain with intervening suffix." He translates "your sinful hands."

8.a. See Joüon §160*k* on contrary statements.

8.b. לו, "to it." 1QIsa[a] ולוא, LXX οὐκ, Vg. *non* all read it as לא, "not." They have missed the contrast. Wildberger (1237) notes that "they all flee the sword, but not that of humans."

8.c. LXX ἥττημα,"defeat." But α´ σ´ θ´ agree on φορον, "gift, tribute," which is an imprecise rendition of MT מס, "slave" (cf. Judg 1:30, 35; Prov 12:24; Lam 1:1) or "subject to forced labor" (BDB, *HAL*). *DCH* adds another possibility, from a second root: "melting."

9.a. The use is ironic and may refer to the Assyrian god (cf. Deut 32:2; Num 14:9).

9.b. LXX ὁ δὲ φεύγων; Vg. *fugientes*, "fleeing one(s), fugitive(s)." They have read נָס from נוס, "flee." But נֵס means "standard, flag" (BDB, 651) and is quite suitable here. G. R. Driver (*JTS* 38 [1937] 45) suggests the meaning "trembling, quivering" (cf. *DCH*), but the usual meaning should be kept. מן may mean "because of," or it may mean "away from." The first meaning suggests "because of a flag (the enemy's)." The second "from the flag (their own)." The parallel supports the first.

Form/Structure/Setting

Höffken (*ZAW* 112 [2000] 230–31) provides a thorough discussion of current critical scholarship on these verses, most of which is devoted to delineation of redactional layers.

The fourth woe speech begins a dialogue about the fate of a city whose political leaders continue to make political decisions without reference to YHWH's decisions concerning the direction history is to take. The speakers cannot believe that they prefer human political alliances when an alliance with YHWH is possible. A parable (or simile) is used in v 4 to describe YHWH's protection of Jerusalem, followed by a parallel simile in v 5. The challenge to repent (v 6) is set against Israel's previous apostasy, which had taken place under very different circumstances (v 7). The climax is reached in YHWH's announcement of the fall of Assyria (vv 8–9).

The setting of the episode is the familiar "balcony of Heaven" from which YHWH and his aides view and discuss Israel and the world.

Comment

1 הוי, "woe," expresses distress over the situation in Jerusalem. In Assyria's declining years, Jerusalem's leaders cast about for political alliances that will help them profit from that collapse. Egypt seems to be the best support for their aims. They have not looked for God's goals, yet only he is dependable and sure. They fail to appreciate the advantage of divine assistance over human promises.

2–3 Egypt is fighting against an Assyrian invasion, which in Isaiah is understood as God's judgment against Judah and the land of Palestine. For Judah to side with Egypt is to act against YHWH's plan (Wong, *VT* 46 [1996] 392–401).

Note the contrast between divine and human plans and powers: "Egypt is human, not God! Their horses are flesh, not spirit!" Egypt is not reliable. It often breaks its promises and fails to reach its goals. Beyond that, Egypt has not been chosen to play the key role in this period of history. But God! He is רוח, "spirit," not בשׂר, "flesh." The words do not define God's essence. But in "flesh" they do summarize the totality of human finitude. God is beyond that. He is constant. He achieves his רֵעַ, "purpose," and his strategy. Yet humankind, like Jerusalem here, prefers its own crutches to dependence upon God. It seals its own doom, for

When YHWH stretches out his hand,
the helper will stumble, the one helped will fall.
They will all be finished together!

4 The lion's self-assured and undeterred attention to his purpose is a parable of YHWH's intention to protect Zion. The noise and disturbance of international upheavals will not deter him.

5 The figure is changed, but the assurance of YHWH's protection is even stronger. This promise fits the period and holds for the immediate future. Yet the reader is aware that Jerusalem is destroyed in the next generation.

6–7 Sentences in second-person plural are apparently addressed to seventh-century Jerusalem. The rest of the verses are in third-person-plural form, referring to eighth-century Israelites. The comparison is intentional. Israel's apostasy in the eighth century (1:2–7; 2:6–8; 5:8–25; 9:8–10:4) had occurred during Assyria's rise to power. Even then their attitude had been inexcusable. But now, Assyria is weak and near collapse. The day that 10:20–21 had foretold is near at hand when Israel will be forced to recognize how useless its idols are. Instead Jerusalem's leaders are determined to adopt an idolatrous political course. They are challenged to repudiate it.

8–9 YHWH's announcement is dramatic: Assyria is about to fall. "A sword—not . . . a person" is explained by what follows. The morale of the army is deteriorating. Its בחוריו, "choice soldiers," are its elite core, the סלעו, "rock," of its military prowess. Its officers will desert and disappear, and the power that Assyria once represented will be gone. YHWH, whose awesome seat of power is in Zion, announces this. The references to אור, "fire," and תנור, "furnace," recall the burning anger of 30:27–33, yet the political leaders are apparently oblivious to him and his announcement.

Suppose a King . . . (32:1–8)

Bibliography

Barth, H. *Die Jesaja-Worte.* 211–15. **Becker, J.** *Messianic Expectation in the Old Testament.* Trans. D. E. Green. Philadelphia: Fortress, 1980. 71. **Fichtner, J.** "Jesaja unter dan Weisen." *TLZ* 74 (1949) 75–80. **Gerleman, G.** "Der Nicht-Mensch: Erwägungen zur hebräischen Wurzel NBL." *VT* 24 (1974) 147–58. **Gosse, B.** "Isaïe 28–32 et la rédaction d'ensemble du livre d'Isaïe." *JSOT* 9 (1995) 75–82. **Hermisson, H. J.** "Zunkunftserwartung und Gegenwartskritik." *EvT* 33 (1973) 54–77. **Hertzberg, H.-W.** "Die Nachgeschichte alttestamentlicher Texte innerhalb des Alten Testaments." In *Beiträge zur Traditionsgeschichte und Theologie des Alten Testaments.* Göttingen: Vandenhoeck & Ruprecht, 1962. 69–80. **מנשה הראל**: (**Hr'l, M.**) "נופי מדבר בנבואת יע״הו." *BMik* 29 (1966) 79–82. **Irwin, W. H.** "Conflicting Parallelism in Job 5:13; Isa 30,28; Isa 32:7." *Bib* 76 (1995) 72–74. **Labuschagne, C. J.** "The Particles הֵן and הִנֵּה." *OtSt* 18 (1973) 1–14. **Olley, J. W.** "Notes on Isaiah xxxii 1, xlv 19,23, and lxiii 1." *VT* 33 (1983) 446–53. **Roberts, J. J. M.** "The Divine King and the Human Community in Isaiah's Vision of the Future." In *The Quest for the Kingdom of God.* FS G. Mendenhall, ed. H. B. Huffmon et al. Winona Lake, IN: Eisenbrauns, 1983. 127–36. **Sklba, R. J.** "Until the Spirit from on High Is Poured Out on Us (Is 32:15): Reflections on the Role of the Spirit in the Exile." *CBQ* 46 (1984) 1–17. **Stade, B.** "Jes. 32, 33." *ZAW* 4 (1884) 256–71. **Stansell, G.** "Isaiah 32: Creative Redaction in the Isaian Traditions." In *SBLSP.* Chico, CA: Scholars Press, 1983. 1–12. ———. *Micah and Isaiah: A Form and Tradition Historical Comparison.* SBLDS 85. Atlanta: Scholars Press, 1988. 62–63. **Thompson, M. E. W.** "Israel's Ideal King." *JSOT* 24 (1982) 79–88. **Waschke, E.-J.** "Die Stellung der Königstexte im Jesajabuch im Vergleich zu den Königspsalmen 2, 72 und 89." *ZAW* 110 (1998) 358–60. **Wegner, P.** *An Examination of Kingship and Messianic Expectation in Isaiah 1–35.* Lewiston, NY: Mellen, 1992. 275–300. **Whedbee, J. W.** *Isaiah and Wisdom.* Nashville: Abingdon, 1971. **Williamson, H. G. M.** "Isaiah and the Wise." In *Wisdom in Ancient Israel.* FS J. A. Emerton, ed. J. Day. Cambridge: Cambridge UP, 1995. 133–41. ———. "The Messianic Texts in Isaiah 1–39." In *King and Messiah in Israel and the Ancient Near East.* Ed. J. Day. Sheffield: Sheffield Academic Press, 1998. 264–70.

Translation

Teacher:	[1] *Suppose* [a] *a king should reign with righteousness*	4+3
	and likewise [b] *princes should rule with justice.*	
First Student:	[2] *Then each would be like a refuge from wind*	4+2
(reciting)	*and a shelter* [a] *from a storm,*	
	like streams of water in a dry place, [b]	3+3+2
	like the shade of a massive rock	
	in a parched land.	
Teacher:	[3] *And if* [a] *the eyes of those who see should look*	4+3
	and the ears of those who hear should hearken	
	[4] *and the mind of the hurried have sense to know*	4+5
	and the tongue of stammerers speak fluently,	
First Student:	[5] *then a fool would no longer be called noble* [a]	4+4
	nor a knave [b] *be called honorable.*	
Second Student:	[6] *For a fool speaks folly,*	3+3

and his mind does[a] *wickedness*
to practice ungodliness 2+3
and to speak error toward YHWH,
leaving the hungry with an empty throat[b] 3+3
and denying the thirsty a drink.
Third Student: [7]*The weapons of a knave*[a] *are evil.* 3+3
He plots evil plans
to ruin the poor[b] *by deceitful words* 4+3
[c]*and by slandering the needy in court.*[c]
Fourth Student: [8]*But a noble one*[a] *plans noble things* 3+3
and takes his stand upon noble things.

Notes

1.a. הֵן is usually translated "behold, see." But Kissane and Scott, followed by Irwin ("Isaiah 28–33," 120), propose reading it as hypothetical. This changes the genre to wisdom instruction and may be compared to Job 34:18–19, where a similar grouping of words occurs.

1.b. LXX καὶ ἄρχοντες, "and rulers," and Syr., Tg., and Vg. leave out ל, which Wildberger (1250), *BHK,* and *BHS* also recommend. F. Nötscher ("Zum emphatischen Lamed," *VT* 3 [1953] 380) suggested that this is an "emphatic ל." Irwin ("Isaiah 28–33," 120) seems to follow Nötscher, translating "likewise."

2.a. 1QIsa[a] סתרם, "their shelter," i.e., adds *mem.* This has led to guesses that *mem* belongs before the next word to produce "from": LXX ὡς ἀφ' ὕδατος, "as from water," and Vg. *a tempestate,* "from a storm" (cf. *BHK, BHS*). "From" is necessary to make sense in English, as indeed in Greek or Latin, but was not necessary in Hebrew.

2.b. בְּצָיוֹן, "in a dry place." Another pointing produces "in Zion" as LXX ἐν Σιων reads it. MT is correct (cf. 25:5).

3.a. MT לא, "not," is difficult to fit here, leading σ´ αμαυρωθησονται and Vg. *caligabunt,* "will become dim," to think of the Heb שעע and *BHK* and *BHS* to vocalize תְּשֹׁעֶינָה *(qal)* or תְּשָׁעֶינָה *(hop'al),* "they were smeared shut, blinded." However, if הֵן in v 1 is read as a conditional particle, then reading לוֹ for לא would produce a parallel hypothetical sentence here, as Irwin ("Isaiah 28–33," 121) proposes, and the problem is solved.

5.a. נדיב, "noble." M. Dahood compares a similar combination of the meanings "noble" and "willing, generous" ("Hebrew-Ugaritic Lexicography," *Bib* 48 [1948] 436–37; also see the discussion in Irwin, "Isaiah 28–33," 122).

5.b. כילי appears only here (and perhaps v 7). Duhm (quoted by Wildberger, 1250) writes that the rabbis derived the word from כול and translated "miser." Hitzig derived it from כָּלָה and translated "waster," while most derive it (BDB, *HAL, DCH*) from נכל, "a swindler, knave." Irwin ("Isaiah 28–33," 123) takes it as masc. pl. from כליות, "kidneys," to get the translation "his mind" to parallel "heart" in the next line. The translation "knave, swindler" remains the best.

6.a. LXX νοήσει and Tg. מחעשתין appear to support 1QIsa[a] חושב, "devise, think." But H. M. Orlinsky ("The St. Mark's Isaiah Scroll," *JBL* 69 [1950] 152–55), Kutscher (*Language and Linguistic Background,* 239), and J. R. Rosenbloom (*The Dead Sea Scroll of Isaiah* [Grand Rapids, MI: Eerdmans, 1970] 40) warn that LXX usually translates חשב with λογίζεσθαι, "to reckon." MT makes sense as it is.

6.b. נפש, "throat," as the seat of appetite *(HAL, DCH);* cf. *Note* 29:8.a.

7.a. כלי כליו, taking Irwin's suggestion discussed in *Note* 5.b.: "his kidney of kidneys," as in the phrase "heart of hearts" (cf. Irwin, "Isaiah 28–33," 125, who translates "his inmost mind"); Wildberger (1249) "the weapons of the knave." It remains a difficult word pair.

7.b. K ענוים is a synonym for Q עניים. Both mean "poor, humble."

7.c-c. ובדבר אביון משפט, lit. "and by a word the needy justice," is difficult. M. Dahood (*Proverbs and North-West Semitic Philology* [Rome: Pontifical Biblical Institute, 1963] 39) suggests "in driving the poor from court," and G. R. Driver (*ZAW* 11 [1934] 56) "by driving (out of court) the poor in judgment" (so *HAL* דבר I; *DCH* דבר IV). Irwin ("Isaiah 28–33," 125) translates "and by slandering the needy in court," referring to BDB, 182*b*.

8.a. LXX εὐσεβεῖς, "pious ones," which Wildberger (1251) discounts as one of its favorite words.

Form/Structure/Setting

The teachers are back on stage with a lesson in civics. They offer a series of definitions. Their scholarly detachment is broken only once: in v 5 with לא עוד, "no longer." In that phrase they imply that their clear definitions are blurred in their own society.

The episode may be analyzed in two ways. One could see the passage as an arch with v 5 as the keystone:

A King/princes = righteousness and justice (v 1)
    B Resultant security and prosperity (v 2)
        C If eyes, ears, minds, and tongues of public function (vv 3–4)
KEYSTONE: Then no more confusion of fools and nobility,
        of knaves and persons of honor (v 5)
        C′ For a fool speaks folly (v 6)
    B′ A knave plots evil plans (v 7)
A′ Nobility plans noble things (v 8)

Or, the passage may be analyzed as a series of definitions:

1. Kings and princes should be associated with righteousness and justice. They should serve like shelters and refreshing streams (vv 1–2).
2. The public should be able to see, to hear, to know, and to speak, so that the character of public officials is known and judged accordingly (vv 3–5).
3. For the character of the fool is marked by folly, wickedness, ungodliness, and error. This feeds no one, provides water to no one (the opposite of v 2*b*) (v 6).
4. The character of the knave is equally transparent: evil, deceitful, and slanderous. This results in a deceitful and oppressive government (the opposite of justice and righteousness, v 1) (v 7).
5. The character of nobility is equally clear. It can be seen in the nature of the plans presented and the stands taken (v 8).

The episode belongs to the teaching of the wise. Its temporal setting is determined by its literary context. Such a teaching in the times of the deceptive politics described in chap. 31, especially in view of that telltale "no longer" in v 5, must be set in the reign of Josiah, for the destruction of Assyria is still ahead.

It may be that this is intended to be presented tongue in cheek. The truisms or platitudes of wisdom are presented with mock seriousness as a satirical comment on a society that has neither justice nor righteousness, in which people do not see, hear, know, or say that they have confused the folly and knavery of their political policies with nobility and honor (cf. chap. 31). At this point the Vision may well be in dialogue with the assessment of Josiah's reign given in 2 Kgs 22–23, just as Isa 22 was concerned with the evaluation of Hezekiah.

The kind of form-critical analysis that feels at liberty to restructure the book may miss these points (cf. most recently, G. Stansell, "Isaiah 32," 4–7). Waschke (*ZAW* 110 [1998] 358–60) suggests that 32:1–5, 15–20 are references to Davidic kingship inserted along with 9:1–6 and 11:1–8 to tilt the interpretation of the book in messianic terms as the insertion of royal psalms 2, 72, and 89 do in Psalms. Interpreters looking for messiah prooftext are likely to find material for their work here, but it does not seem likely that the composers/editors of the book had this in mind.

Comment

1–2 The lesson begins with the definition of rulers, kings and princes. They are to be identified with justice and righteousness. They are to be symbols of security and vital prosperity.

3–4 The second and perhaps key definition of the episode deals with the public. Even in a nondemocratic society, the perception and support of the public are necessary for the government. They were in Israel. The public has eyes, ears, minds, and tongues, but they are not often used, as was apparently the case in that time. If those faculties are used to look, to hearken, to know, and to speak, the public good is served, for the character and motives of public officials (implied are the king and his ministers) can be understood and judged on their merit.

5 The implication of עוד, "no longer," is that this has not been the case. Fools and knaves are being called noble and honorable without challenge. The Vision complains repeatedly that Israel and Jerusalem are blind, deaf, unperceptive, unknowing (1:3; 6:9–10; and so on). Usually their ignorance is of God and his plans. Here the reference is to politics and the character of the leaders. The immediate reference is to the age of Josiah, but the intention of the Vision includes the failure of later ages to correctly assess the mistakes of that earlier period, thereby making false judgments in their own times.

6–8 The remaining verses give definitions that may help to eliminate the confusion.

6 נבל, "a fool." In the wisdom schools the fool was regularly contrasted with "the wise" (cf. Proverbs). He is the one who has failed to master the disciplines of wisdom. But he is also the one who has a weak character, is easily tempted, and is impetuous in his decisions. The fool can be recognized by foolish speech, a mind dedicated to wickedness, an ungodly lifestyle, and the speaking of heresy against YHWH. That should be clear enough for the public to recognize. The results of having a fool in charge of things include neglect of welfare programs and failure to take care of water resources in a dry country. That should be warning enough of the consequences of allowing a fool to rule.

7 כלי, "a knave," is different from the bumbling fool. He knows better. He deliberately chooses means that are evil and hatches evil plots. His victims are the poor and the needy, God's special wards according to the prophets and the Torah. His weapons are slander and false testimony, in the very courts that are intended to protect the rights of the people. The definition is clear. No knowledgeable public should tolerate a knave in government.

8 "A noble one" (נדיב) is here only defined by reusing the same word. The dictionaries relate the word to overtones of motivation and voluntariness. The implication is that this is one who has no ulterior motive, who can deal objectively, thinking in ways that are not dictated by his personal interests. נדיבות, "noble things," are those that such an independent and willing person would support. He would be free of the pressures of party and special interests. The arch structure suggests that nobility be related to the justice and righteousness of v 1.

Explanation

The "civics lesson" gives the hearer/reader the tools to pass judgment on the leaders and their policies described in chap. 31. Are "those going down to Egypt" to be termed fools, knaves, or nobles? Chap. 31 would probably have accepted the designations of both fool and knave as accurate. The episode also serves to place the blame on the public. Any public that fails to recognize the character of its public officials, that fails to speak out in protest and so bring about changes in personnel and policy, shares the blame for the results. The people of God are often blind, unperceptive, and uncommunicative, not only about the ways of God but also about the ways of human beings in leadership and government. When they are so, they stand judged along with the fools and knaves they failed to identify and remove.

Until Spirit Is Poured Out (32:9–20)

Bibliography

Barth, J. "Eine verkannte hebräische Imperativform." *ZDMG* 56 (1902) 247–48. **Beuken, W. A. M.** "De os en de ezel in Jesaja literair (Jes 1:3 en 32:20)." In *Herinnering en hoop.* FS Herman Servotte, ed. R. Michiels. Averbode: Altiora, 1995. 161–83. **Eichrodt, W.** *Die Hoffnung des ewigen Friedens im alten Israel.* BFCT 25. Gütersloh: Bertelsmann, 1920. **Fensham, F. C.** "The Wild Ass in the Aramean Treaty between Bar-Ga'ayah and Mati'el." *JNES* 22 (1963) 185–86. **Fohrer, G.** "Entstehung, Komposition und Überlieferung von Jesaja 1–39." In *Studien zur alttestamentlichen Prophetie (1949–1965).* Berlin: De Gruyter, 1967. 2:122–28. **García Recio, J.** "'La fauna de las ruinas,' un 'topos' literario de Isaías." *EstBib* 53 (1995) 55–96. **Gross, H.** *Die Idee des ewigen und allgemeinen Weltfriedens im Alten Orient und im Alten Testament.* TThSt 7. Trier: Paulinus, 1956. **Humbert, P.** "פֶּרֶא: zèbre ou onagre?" *ZAW* 62 (1949–50) 202–6. **Käser, W.** "Beobachtungen zum alttestmentlichen Makarismus." *ZAW* 82 (1970) 225–50. **Köhler, L** "פֶּרֶא = Equus Grevyi Oustalet." *ZAW* 44 (1926) 59–62. **Lofthouse, W. F.** "The Beatitude of Security." *ExpTim* 48 (1936) 505–9. **Ma, W.** *Until the Spirit Comes: The Spirit of God in the Book of Isaiah.* JSOTSup 271. Sheffield: Sheffield Academic Press, 1999. **Nielsen, E.** "Ass and Ox in the Old Testament." In *Studia Orientalia Ioanni Pedersen septuagenario dicata.* Ed. F. Hvidberg. Hauniae, 1953. 261–74. **Reider, J.** "Contributions to the Scriptural Text." *HUCA* 24 (1952–53) 88. **Schmid, H. H.** *Salôm: 'Frieden' im Alten Orient und im Alten Testament.* SBS 51. Stuttgart: Katholisches Bibelwerk, 1971. **Sklba, R. J.** "Until the Spirit from on High Is Poured Out on Us (Is 32:15): Reflections on the Role of the Spirit in the Exile." *CBQ* 46 (1984) 1–17. **Stade, B.** "Miscellen.2. Jer 3,6–16; 5. Jes. 32.33." *ZAW* 4 (1884) 151–71. **Stansell, G.** "Isaiah 32: Creative Redaction in the Isaiah Traditions." In *SBLSP.* Chico, CA: Scholars Press, 1983. 2–4, 7–11. **Vattioni, F.** "I precedenti letterari di Isaia 32:17: Et erit opus iustitiae pax." *RivB* 6 (1958) 23–32. **Vollers, K.** "Zu Jesajas 32:11." *ZDMG* 57 (1903) 375. **Westermann,**

C. "Der Frieden (Shalom) im Alten Testament." In *Studien zur Friedensforschung.* Vol. 1. Stuttgart: Klett, 1969.

Translation

First Speaker:	[9]*Women*[a] *at ease,*	2+3
	rise up! Heed my voice!	
	Complacent[b] *daughters,*[a]	2+2
	give ear to my speech!	
	[10][a]*(In) just days less than a year*[a]	2+2
	you will shudder, complacent women.	
	For a grape harvest shall fail;	3+3
	a fruit harvest will not[b] *arrive.*	
	[11]*Tremble,*[ab] *you at ease!*	2+2
	Shudder,[b] *you complacent!*	
	Strip[b] *and be bare!*[b]	2+2+2
	Sackcloth on loins,	
	[12]*on mourning breasts!*[a]	
Incredulous Woman:	*Over pleasant fields,*	3+3
	over fruitful vine,	
	[13]*over my people's ground,*	3+3
	briars (and) thorns will grow up?	
Second Speaker:	*Indeed*[a]*—over every joyous house!*	3+2
	Happy city!	
	[14]*For a palace*[a] *shall be forsaken.*	2+3
	A populous city shall be deserted.	
	Ophel[b] *and Bachan*[c] *shall become*[d]	3+3
	caves[e] *for an age,*	
	a joy for zebra,[f]	2+2
	pasture (for) wild asses.[g]	
Chorus of Women:	[15]*Until spirit is poured upon us from above,*	4+3+3
	and a wilderness becomes the fruitful field,	
	and a fruitful field[a]*is considered the forest?*	
	[16]*(As) justice is at home in the wilderness,*	3+3
	(so) righteousness abides in the fruitful field.	
Second Speaker:	[17]*The result of righteousness is peace,*	4+2+3
	and the product of righteousness	
	quietness and trust for an age,	
	[18]*so that people dwell in peaceful homes,*	4+2+2
	in secure dwellings,	
	and in quiet resting places.	
First Speaker:	[19]*The forest descends*[a] *with condescension.*[b]	3+3
	The city is debased[c] *in humiliation.*[d]	
	[20]*The fortunate ones of you*	1+2+3
	are those who sow beside all waters,	
	who send out[a] *the feet of the ox and the ass.*	

Notes

9.a. Tg. מדינן, "provinces," for MT נשים, "women," and כרכין, "cities," for בנות, "daughters." Wildberger (1262) commends Tg. insofar as it has correctly seen that the passage addresses cities or a specific city. But this has robbed readers of arriving at that identification for themselves.

9.b. בֹּטְחוֹת, "complacent, trusting," is a rare case of Masoretes leaving a letter (ט) with no vowel sign or syllable divider on it.

10.a-a. ימים על־שנה, lit. "days upon a year," is unclear. Wildberger (1262) translates "concerning year and day." Irwin ("Isaiah 28–33," 127–28) has an intensive discussion to support his view that "days" and "year" should be viewed as synonymous to "in a year plus a year" and translates "next year." This is the only time reference in the passage, so there is no parallel to measure by. Perhaps Wildberger is nearer right. These do not give a measure of time but state the subject of the warnings that deal with seasonal disasters of nature. The most natural meaning, however, seems to be "in just days less than a year."

10.b. MT בלי, "without" (BDB, 115; GKC §152*t*); 1QIsa[a] בל. Either reading is possible. Irwin ("Isaiah 28–33," 128) explains 1QIsa[a] as "the scribal practice of writing a shared consonant only once."

11.a. Syr. *zwʿjn* (supported by Syh. Eth. Arab.) suggests reading חֲרָדָה (Aramaizing impv. 2 fem. pl.; GKC §48*i*), an ancient attempt to deal with the masc. impvs. (see *BHS*).

11.b. These impvs. are masc. although they are addressed to women. The discussion has been intense (cf. Wildberger, 1263; Irwin, "Isaiah 28–33," 128–29). It is best to let MT stand and translate simply.

12.a. LXX κόπτεσθε, "beat yourself." *BHS* recommends reading impf. 2 fem. for MT's pl. ptc. ספדים, "lamentings." Irwin ("Isaiah 28–33," 128) translates as a relative clause: "at your breasts that mourn." But the על phrases should be parallel. The first two, "on loins, on . . . breasts," are parallel. The next three plus one are parallel. Irwin ("Isaiah 28–33," 130) calls these "על of motive," referring to BDB, 745*a*. But if they are governed by the following "will grow up," of course they refer to place. (See *Note* 14.d.)

13.a. כי is emphatic here.

14.a. ארמון, "palace" is sg., as are עיר, "city," עפל, "Ophel/hill," and בחן, "Bachan/ watchtower."

14.b. עפל, "a hill," an acropolis within a city, perhaps Jerusalem. Irwin ("Isaiah 28–33," 131) transliterates as a proper name, "Ophel."

14.c. בחן, "watchtower" (BDB, *HAL, DCH*), is a *hap. leg.* A. Erman and H. Grapow (*Wörterbuch der aegyptisches Sprache,* 7 vols. [Leipzig: Heinrichs, 1926] 1:47) call it an Egyptian loan word. See Wildberger (1264).

14.d. בְּעַד, "in place of" (BDB, 126). But this does not make good sense. Irwin ("Isaiah 28–33," 131–32) would emend to בָּעַד, "forever," following Fohrer. But Masoretic Hebrew has no other usage like this. Seeking a solution, most scholars omit the word. The particle should be seen as the first of a series in vv 14*b*–15. עד defines the end result for the series of things governed by על in vv 12–13, which are transformed. Exact translation is difficult. For עד(ב) after היה, "will be," read something like "ultimately" or "finally," indicating the resultant condition.

14.e. מערות may be derived from ערה to mean "bare places" (BDB; G. R. Driver, *JSS* 13 [1968] 52; *DCH*) or "cleared field" *(HAL),* or from ערר to mean "caves" (BDB, *DCH*).

14.f. פראים, "zebra," with L. Köhler, *ZAW* 44 (1926) 59; and KBL/*CHAL*, 296, instead of the more usual "wild ass" (cf. P. Humbert, *ZAW* 62 [1949–50] 202–6; *HAL*).

14.g. עדרים, "flocks" (BDB, 727), but note the ambiguity of the root. Kaiser, followed by *HAL*, emends to ערדים, "wild asses" (Job 39:5). The repetition of עד in this passage suggests reading עד רים, "even for wild asses" (BDB, 910, reading רים as ראם with BDB, 937).

15.a. K וכרמל, "and a fruitful field"; Q והכרמל, "and the fruitful field." Wildberger (1273) thinks the Masoretes thought of the mountain near Haifa, though this cannot be the meaning here. K keeps the parallel with the previous stich: the indefinite becomes defined. The use of articles is very carefully done here.

19.a. MT וברד, "it shall hail" (BDB, *HAL, DCH*), is a *hap. leg.* Tg. ויחות ברד, "and hail will descend"; Syr. similarly. *BHS* cites one MS with וירד, "will descend." J. Reider (*HUCA* 24 [1952–53] 88), followed by G. R. Driver (*JSS* 13 [1968] 52), compares Arab. *baruda* to mean "it is cool": "the forest will be cool." Irwin ("Isaiah 28–33," 133–34) derives ברד from a root that usually occurs as רד, "cut, divide," and cites E. Ullendorff ("Ugaritic Marginalia II," *JSS* 7 [1962] 345) and E. Lipiński ("Banquet en l'honneur de Baal, *CTA* 3 [VAB], A, 2–22," *UF* 2 [1970] 78) to support his view that ב and פ are frequently interchanged. Ugar. *brd* has this meaning. *BHS* and Wildberger have the best reading, וירד, "descends."

19.b. ברדת, prep. and inf. const. from ירד, "with descending, condescension." This repetition of the same root is an artistic device, contrasting the following pair. Irwin ("Isaiah 28–33," 134) understands this as a noun and translates "with an ax."

19.c. תשפל, "become low, be abased."

19.d. ובשפלה, "humiliation" (BDB, *HAL*), a *hap. leg.* related to שפל, which follows.

20.a. משלחי, "sending out," may mean, as here, "driving cattle." But it also means "stretch out" a hand or a weapon against a foe. The double entendre is deliberate in contrasting the passive pastorale to the previous history of activist warfare.

Form/Structure/Setting

The episode develops as a dialogue between a speaker and a group of women. They may be pictured as gathered around a well. They are small-town housewives, economically dependent upon the surrounding vineyards and orchards, which witness to generations of skill and labor in planting, tending, and protecting. The dialogue contrasts developed urban and rural society with the devastation to come in "less than a year." There is nothing but the context to hint at the historical setting intended. The first-person speech and the chorus, often found in the Vision, are heard here. There is no evidence that God is the speaker. The prophet's justification for the disaster is also absent. There is only the concession that where justice and righteousness abide peace and stability can be found, which is obviously not the case here.

Comment

9 The "women at ease" would appear to be an ordinary group of Judean women, perhaps lounging around a well while the slowly flowing water fills their jars. They are at ease because the normal patterns of the agricultural year move ahead with promise of harvest. Their homes are secure, their families intact.

10 Yet, the speaker warns, in less than a year disaster will strike. The harvests will fail. That would be a blow to the village.

11 The speaker, with emotion, urges them to extreme responses of mourning. Stripping off normal clothing and wearing underclothes of rough sackcloth were signs of mourning reserved for death or for an extreme disaster.

12–13 An incredulous person cannot believe that the currently fruitful and well-cared-for fields that her people had owned and cultivated for generations could be allowed to lie waste.

14 The speaker affirms his warning and extends it to the village itself, to cities, even to the palace. עפל, "Ophel," the original core of Jerusalem, came to house the temple and the palace (cf. *MBA*, 114), or the word may simply refer to a hilltop, such as was frequently the place of a walled town. בחן, "Bachan," means a watchtower. If *Ophel* is understood as a proper name, then *Bachan* would be likely to be a particular tower on the walls of Jerusalem. If *Ophel* is taken to be "hilltop," then it simply refers to watchtowers in general, i.e., to the defenses of the country at large. "Zebra" and "wild ass" have no significance except to illustrate that the towns are uninhabited by human society.

15 The chorus of women still does not believe the message. The women ask in effect, How long will this last? as they recite the litany of hope that in a future age the spirit of God will make all the world fruitful and productive.

16 They comment that the wilderness has no monopoly on justice. Righteousness can live in developed culture as well as in a primitive wasteland. They seem to assume here the implied accusation of injustice and unrighteousness to account for the disastrous judgment, although the speaker had said nothing to this effect. They also seem to be reading into the announcement of disaster a theology that implied that Israel was righteous in the wilderness but had become corrupted by the culture of the developed land.

17–18 A speaker representing the women lectures the first speaker: righteousness produces peace and stability, which her people now have every right to expect.

19 The היער, "forest," is clearly a metaphor that must refer to the larger political or economic unit, whether the kingdom or the empire. Either could fit here. Assyria is on its last legs, and the kingdom of Judah is experiencing its last real existence or prosperity under Josiah. העיר, "the city," may refer to Jerusalem or simply to the culture that is based on city-states. The villages and their prosperity were dependent on what was happening in the surrounding world, whether they knew it or not.

20 This last verse looks almost with envy at those who have little to lose, who are not bound to houses and fields. They can move to avoid danger, can exist in almost any circumstances, and can simply drive their assets (ox and ass) to another place to start over again. That is difficult for the landowner and planter.

Explanation

The episode warns of a coming disaster that will wipe out a way of life. The women, looking about them at the homes and fields that make up their lives, see only peace, tranquillity, and prosperity. They presume that this implies that justice and righteousness have brought this about and will continue to guarantee their future. They are examples of the blind, deaf, and uncomprehending people that the Vision has complained about throughout. It is hard, in the midst of plenty, to imagine hunger. It is hard, in the setting of economic and social order, to imagine chaos and disruption.

Yet the earlier episodes have pictured wrong-headed political policies and major international upheavals in the making. No interior small town, no matter how isolated, will escape the resulting problems. The relation between justice/righteousness and order/prosperity is not wrong. But the failure to see beneath the surface the things that were anything but just and righteous constituted culpable blindness.

Civilized and developed societies can be comfortable and efficient, but they are also very vulnerable. Loss of some basic services can threaten life itself. Those who had never come to depend on those services or structures survive very nicely without them. They are to be envied in the time of disaster. Although there is no "thus says YHWH" word from a prophet, the whole flow of dialogue reveals the intended meaning.

God's Promise to Judge the Tyrant (33:1–24)

Bibliography

Beuken, W. A. M. "Jesaaja 33 als Spiegeltext im Jesajabuch." *ETL* 67 (1991) 5–35. **Childs, B. S.** *Isaiah and the Assyrian Crisis.* 112–17. **Galling, K.** "Der Beichtspiegel: Eine Gattungsgeschichtliche Studie." *ZAW* 47 (1929) 166–76. **Gunkel, H.** "Jesaja 33, eine prophetische Liturgie." *ZAW* 42 (1924) 177–208. **Murray, R.** "Prophecy and the Cult." In *Israel's Prophetic Tradition.* Ed. R. Coggins et al. 200–216. **Roberts, J. J. M.** "Isaiah 33: An Isaianic Elaboration of the Zion Tradition." In *The Word Shall Go Forth.* FS D. N. Freedman, ed. C. L. Meyers et al. Winona Lake, IN: Eisenbrauns, 1983. 15–25. **Thompson, M. E. W.** "Vision, Reality, and Worship: Isaiah 33." *ExpTim* 113 (2002) 327–33.

In this final scene, Isaiah's vision approaches a major critical point as violence increases and God prepares to intervene. As the first episode opens ("Woe, You Destroyer," 33:1–6), impending violence brings reactions from YHWH's counselors and from a chorus in Jerusalem. In the second episode, "See! Their Valiant One!" (33:7–12), the situation becomes worse. In the third episode, "Who Can Survive the Fire?" (33:13–24), YHWH intervenes. Those near and far are challenged to assess the event and recognize what the results of God's intervention will be.

Woe, You Destroyer! (33:1–6)

Bibliography

Delekat, L. *Asylie und Schutzorakel am Zionheiligtum: Eine Untersuchung zu den privaten Feindpsalmen.* Leiden: Brill, 1967. 166–76. **Gerlach, M.** "Die prophetischen Liturgien des Alten Testaments." Diss., Bonn, 1967. **Ginsburg, H. L.** "Emendations in Isaiah." *JBL* 69 (1950) 57. **Mowinckel, S.** *Psalmenstudien.* 6 vols. Kristiana: Dybwad, 1921. Repr. Amsterdam: Shippers, 1966. 2:235–38. **Poynder, A.** "'Be Thou Their Arm Every Morning': Isaiah 33:2." *ExpTim* 13 (1901–1902) 94. **Schoeps, H. J.** "Ein neuer Engelname in der Bibel? (Zur Übersetzung des Symmachus von Jes 11:3)." *ZRGG* 1 (1948) 86–87. **Stade, B.** "Jes. 32.33." *ZAW* 4 (1884) 256–71. **Weiss, R.** "On Ligatures in the Hebrew Bible (נו = ם)." *JBL* 82 (1963) 188–94. **Williamson, H. G. M.** *Book Called Isaiah.* 238–39. **Ziegler, J.** "Das Heuschreckengleichnis Is. 33,4." *Bib* 14 (1933) 460–64.

Translation

Heavens: 1 *Woe, you destroyer,* 2+3
who are not yet being destroyed!
And you traitor, 1+2
whom[a] *no one betrays!*

When you finish destroying,[b] *you will be destroyed.* 3+4
As you cease[c] *treachery, someone will betray you.*
Chorus: 2 *YHWH, have mercy on us!* 2+2
We wait for you!
Be our arm[a] *in the mornings!* 3+3
Yea! Our salvation in a time of siege.[b]
Earth: 3 *From the roaring sound* 2+2
peoples flee![a]
From your rising up[b] 1+2
nations scatter![a]
4 *Your*[a] *spoil is gathered* 2+2
(as) the caterpillar[b] *gathers,*
like a locust[b] *attacking,*[c] 2+2
leaping on it.
Chorus: 5 *YHWH is exalted!* 2+3
Indeed, he dwells on high![a]
He fills Zion 2+2+2
(with) justice and righteousness
6 *and is*[a] *the*[b] *stability of her times.*[b]
The abundance of salvation, wisdom,[c] *knowledge,* 4+2+2
and fear of YHWH—
that is his treasure.

Notes

1.a. Many MSS read בָּךְ, "you" (cf. *BHS*), probably correctly; cf. *Note* 1.c.

1.b. Irwin ("Isaiah 28–33," 137) calls attention to Zorell's (*Lexicon Hebraicum et Aramaicum* [Rome: Pontifical Biblical Institute, 1947] 822*b*) reading of שׂוֹדֵד as *poel* inf. instead of GKC's (§120*b*) ptc. (cf. R. Meyer, *Hebraïsche Grammatik* [Berlin: De Gruyter, 1960] §108.2*b*). See Irwin for further discussion.

1.c. MT כַּנְּלֹתְךָ. BDB (649) locates as *hipʿil* inf. with prep. and suf. from נלה ("obtain"?) with ה prefix absorbed into the *nun*. 1QIsa[a] supports the emendation suggested by Döderlein, Lowth, Knobel, and Wildberger to read בְּכַלֹּתְךָ *piʿel* inf. from כלה, "when you cease."

2.a. MT זרעם, "their arm." Syr., Tg., and Vg. have the 1st pl. suf. "our," which fits the context.

2.b. צרה is usually "need, distress" *(HAL)*. Irwin ("Isaiah 28–33," 138) translated "siege" on the basis of the description of war that follows. See J. Ziegler, "Die Hilfe Gottes am Morgan," in *Altestamentliche Studien*, FS F. Nötscher (Bonn: Hanstein, 1950) 286–88, and other references cited by Irwin.

3.a. Irwin ("Isaiah 28–33," 140) translates these verbs as precative perfects: "let peoples flee, let nations scatter," citing M. Buttenwieser's and M. Dahood's use in the Psalms. Irwin overlooks the fact that the speaker has changed in v 3 so that the beginning imperatives are not so closely related to these verbs.

3.b. MT מרוממתך, "from your rising up" or "from your exaltation," from the root רום *(HAL);* 1QIsa[a] מדממתך, "from your silencing" (BDB, 199; J. Lust, "A Gentle Breeze or a Roaring Thunderous Sound?" *VT* 25 [1975] 110–15); LXX ἀπὸ τοῦ φόβου σου, "from fear of you." P. Wernburg-Møller ("Defective Spellings in the Isaiah Scroll," *JSS* 3 [1958] 262) sees 1QIsa[a] meaning "be scared stiff" and thus parallel to LXX. G. R. Driver ("Notes on Isaiah," in *Von Ugarit Nach Qumran*, FS O. Eissfeldt, BZAW 77 [Giessen: Töpelmann, 1958] 46) posits a noun רממה for MT, which like Akk. *rimmatu* means "rumbling." Irwin ("Isaiah 28–33," 139) and Dahood divide MT into מרם מתך, "at the sound of your soldiers" (M. Dahood, "Ugaritic and Phoenician or Qumran and the Versions," in *Orient and Occident*, FS C. H. Gordon [Neukirchen-Vluyn: Neukirchener Verlag, 1973] 53–54). *HAL* and this translation stay with MT as a noun from the root רום.

4.a. שללכם, "your spoil." The pl. suffix has raised questions. Does it address the chorus of v 2? Does it mean "the spoil you gather" or "the spoil gathered from you"? Syr. *ʾjk,* Tg. כמא, Vg. *sicut,* followed by *BHK, BHS,* Irwin ("Isaiah 28–33," 141), and *HAL* divide the word in two: שלל כמו, "spoil like," or כמאסף (joining two letters to the following word), with the same results. The context calls for a comparison in any case, but MT does not need to be changed.

4.b. The exact meanings of these words remain obscure, but the best suggestion is that they are different stages of locust development. Cf. Joel 2:1–11 for the figure of locusts for a military invasion.

4.c. משק is a *hap. leg.* BDB, 1055; GKC §§67*g,* 85*h,* "running," derives the noun from the same root as the following שֹׁקֵק, "run, rush." Thus *HAL* and *DCH* "infestation." LXX συναγάγῃ, "gathering," has drawn on the parallel stich for the meaning. H. L. Ginsburg ("Emendations in Isaiah," *JBL* 69 [1950] 57), reversing *shin* and *qof,* reads a *nipʿal* כִּמְקֹשׁ, "like stubble," from קשׁשׁ. But the root only occurs in Heb. as a *poʿlel,* "gather stubble." Irwin ("Isaiah 28–33," 141) reports a suggestion from M. Dahood deriving the word from נשק II, "weapons," as a noun. Irwin translated "attack," and *DCH* renders the same derivation as "swarm." Both maintain the usual meaning "jump" or "rush about" for the following שֹׁקֵק. This suggestion merits attention. So מַשָּׁק is a *hipʿil* ptc. from נשק, meaning "attack."

5.a. LXX ἐν ὑψηλοῖς, "in the heights," has inserted a prep. to express the locative meaning of the Heb. adverbial accusative (BDB, 928–29).

6.a. MT והיה, "and he is," ties the first stich closely with the preceding verse and should be considered a part of it (cf. Irwin, "Isaiah 28–33," 142).

6.b-b. The difficulties of the phrase have led to a plethora of emendations (see Wildberger, 1284). Irwin ("Isaiah 28–33," 142–43) meets the problem of a 2d-person suf., עתיך, "your times," by suggesting the *kaf* be separated and pointed כִּי to begin the next line and that the *yod* ending be understood as a 3d fem. pronominal suffix. See his notes for a bibliography. His suggestions are better than emending the text.

6.c. חכמת, "wisdom of," is a const. form with no following abs. It is usually read as חכמה, "wisdom." However, another possibility should see all four const. nouns, ישועת, "salvation"; חכמת, "wisdom"; ודעת, "and knowledge"; and יראת, "fear," as governed by חסן, "abundance of," at the beginning and "YHWH" at the end: a case of delayed or interrupted const. relation.

Form/Structure/Setting

The division of the chapter into three parts has been recognized ever since Gunkel's article. Yet the elements within this first part do not fit a single pattern.

V 1 is a woe speech directed against someone accustomed to doing violence who had not yet felt the pressure of reprisal. V 2 is a plea for God's mercy in this time of crisis. Vv 3–4 address God, expecting his intervention. Vv 5–6*a* announce YHWH's exaltation on Zion. V 6*b–d* responds with a summary confession of faith in YHWH.

No hint of the setting is given. It assumes the "balcony of heaven" setting, so frequent in the Vision, which can accommodate YHWH and his counselors but also provide direct sight and access to the people of Jerusalem.

Comment

1 The identity of the שודד, "destroyer/traitor," is not revealed. The context suggests a time when Assyrian power is waning and Egypt is maneuvering for a favorable position. The most likely identification is Assyria itself. The verse picks up the prediction of 10:12 in the words "when you finish destroying." The Vision has from the beginning viewed the Assyrian role as one of destruction and judgment. In what sense בגד, "traitor/treachery," is understood is not clear, although Assyria will undoubtedly have shared in both.

2 The plea from the people is parallel to many Psalms. קוה, "wait," is an attitude recommended throughout the Vision. Sometimes it represents God's hopes for his people (5:2, 4, 7). More often it confesses the people's hope in God (25:9;

26:8) as here. Sometimes it is contained in a promise (49:23; 51:5). Sometimes it is used in the bitterness of disappointed hope (59:9, 11; 64:3).

3 The כל המון, "roaring sound," combines the possibilities of battle with indications of YHWH's approach. They are in some sense identical (note the use of the singular "your"). The resulting flight and chaos is real enough, as peoples and nations scramble to escape the violence.

4 "Your" is plural, addressing the people speaking in v 2. It is unclear whether they gain or lose by the plunder. But the chaos is everywhere, allowing the local poor to crawl like "caterpillars" and pounce like "locusts" on the undefended homes and stores.

5–6*a* In the midst of this chaos "YHWH is exalted." What can this mean? He is exalted in Zion, which means that he still deserves worship in the temple. Worship provides Zion with a "stability" in troubled times. Beyond that, the chaotic events are understood to serve YHWH's purposes. He uses them (or introduces them) to promote justice and righteousness, which were not being adequately served in the previous situation.

6*b* This justifies the confession that ישועת, "salvation," חכמת, "wisdom," דעת, "knowledge," and יראת יהוה, "fear of YHWH," are the treasures that he bestows—a treasure no plunderer can touch. All four words are in construct state in Hebrew, genitives dependent on יהוה, "YHWH": salvation acts of YHWH, wisdom of YHWH, knowledge of YHWH, and the fear of YHWH.

Explanation

This fifth woe speech moves toward completion of the requiem. It marks the last period of authentic existence for the kingdom of Judah. Following after laments over elements of the population and over government planners, this episode turns its attention to the first of the great empires, "the rod of [God's] anger" (10:5), which now approaches collapse. It is time. It has served its purpose, and the accumulated guilt of its excesses is about to overwhelm it (cf. Nahum).

But the episode turns from the scene of chaotic defeat and plunder to celebrate YHWH's place in and above it all. God is in history. He determines its critical changes. There is even purpose in apparent chaos. Beyond that, God provides his most precious treasures in the sanctuary where one celebrates "the abundance of salvation, wisdom, knowledge, and fear of YHWH," that is, the total spiritual and worship benefits that faith makes possible for those who know themselves to belong to him.

See! Their Valiant One! (33:7–12)

Bibliography

Johnson, A. R. *The Cultic Prophet in Israel's Psalmody.* Cardiff: University of Wales Press, 1979. **Schwantes, S.** "A Historical Approach to the ʾRʾLM of Is 33:7." *AUSS* 3 (1965) 158–

66. **Weis, R. D.** "Angels, Altars and Angles of Vision: The Case of *ʾrʾlm* in Isaiah 33:7." In *Tradition of the Text.* FS D. Barthélemy, ed. G. J. Norton and S. Pisano. OBO 109. Freiburg: Universitätsverlag, 1991. 285–92.

Translation

Heavens:	7 *See! Their valiant one*[a] *(Ariel)!*	2+2
	Outside they cry out.	
	Messengers of peace (Shalom)	2+2
	weep bitterly.	
	8 *Highways are empty!*	2+3
	Travelers have ceased!	
	A treaty has been broken!	2+2+3
	One despises witnesses![a]	
	One has no regard (for) human beings.	
Earth:	9 *One mourns!*[a]	1+2
	The land languishes!	
	Lebanon is confounded!	2+1
	It is molded![b]	
	Sharon is like the desert.	3+3
	Bashan and Carmel are shaking[c] *(off their leaves).*	
YHWH:	10 *Now, I will rise up!*[a]	2+2
Herald:	*Says YHWH.*	
YHWH:	*Now, I lift myself up!*[b]	2+2
	Now, I shall be exalted!	
	11 *You [pl.] conceive chaff!*	2+2+3
	You [pl.] give birth to stubble!	
	Your [pl.] spirit[a] *(is) a fire (that) will consume you.*	
	12 *Peoples*[a] *shall become burnt lime:*[b]	4+4
	thorns cut down, burned by fire.	

Notes

7.a. MT אראלם; a few MSS have a pl. אראלים. Wildberger (1294) calls it "simply not understandable." He traces the history of attempts to explain it from the root ירא, "fear," as LXX ἐν τῷ φόβῳ ὑμῶν, "in your fear," or from the root ראה, "see," as 1QIsa[a] ארא לם, Syr., Vg. *videntes,* α´ οραθησομαι, and σ´ οφθησομαι have done with variant forms of "I shall be seen by them." Kimchi and Ibn Ezra thought it meant "messenger," parallel to מלאך in the next stich. Delitzsch divided the word ארי אל, "lion of God" (cf. BDB, 72), and thus derived the meaning "their valiant one." RSV follows Delitzsch but points it as a pl. *HAL* and *DCH* suggest emending to אראלים, "heroes," or אריאלים, "priests," or, from the name Ariel, "Jerusalemites." Irwin ("Isaiah 28–33," 144) translates "the leaders." He considers also the possibility that אלם is a divine name parallel to שלום, "Shalom," in the next line and that אר אלם should be translated "kinsmen of El," which would point to the patron God of David's city, which appears in אריאל, "Ariel," and ירושלם, "Jerusalem."

8.a. MT ערים, "cities"; 1QIsa[a] עדים, "witnesses." The context supports 1QIsa[a]. Irwin ("Isaiah 28–33," 145) cites M. Dahood (*Psalms,* AB 16 [Garden City, NY: Doubleday, 1966] 1:56) for the suggestion that ערים are "'Protectors' of the covenant who guarantee its existence." He points to the parallel of עיר and שלם in Job 8:6.

9.a. MT אבל, "mourns," is masc. It is followed by a fem. noun and verb. *BHS* suggests emending to a fem. form as the versions have done. This is superfluous if one maintains an impersonal subject as in the previous verse. Irwin ("Isaiah 28–33," 146) finds a metrical reason to support this.

9.b. MT קמל, "be decayed, mouldy" (BDB, 888), is found only here and in 19:6. KBL and *CHAL* (319) translate "become infested with injurious insects" on the basis of Old Aramaic *qml*, Eth. *quĕmāl*, and Arab. *qaml*, "louse." Wildberger (1295) disagrees vigorously, following GB and F. Zorell (*Lexicon Hebraicum et Aramaicum Veteris Testamenti* [Rome: Pontifical Biblical Institute, 1964]) on the basis of Syr. *qml* and Arab. *qamila*, to maintain "dead plants turning black" (followed by *HAL*).

9.c. MT נֹעֵר, "shake off its leaves." LXX φανερὰ ἔσται, "will be apparent, conspicuous," leads Procksch and *BHS* to read נָעֵר, "are bare," an inf. for MT's ptc. Irwin ("Isaiah 28–33," 147) concurs. But the change is unnecessary (see Wildberger, 1295).

10.a. Tg. אתגלי, "I will reveal myself."

10.b. 1QIsa[a] אתרומם makes explicit that MT ארומם, "I will raise myself," is in fact a *hitpoʿel* form with *tav* assimilated (BDB, 927; GKC §54*c;* Bauer-Leander, 405; *HAL*).

11.a. As in v 4, the 2d pl. suf. on רוחכם, "your [pl.] spirit, breath," has proved difficult. Some expect רוח to belong to YHWH and emend with Gunkel ("Jes 33, eine prophetische Liturgie," *ZAW* 42 [1924] 177–208), Kissane, Fohrer, and *BHK*: רוחי כמו, "my spirit is like fire." Procksch suggests רוח כמו, "spirit-like," followed by Irwin ("Isaiah 28–33," 148). Wildberger (1295) defends MT, saying that the OT sees no contradiction in "the godless digging their own grave."

12.a. Irwin ("Isaiah 28–33," 148) reads the final *mem* as enclitic and translates "my people." But the parallel "thorns" is pl. MT is to be followed.

12.b. שיד, "lime" (BDB, 966). LXX omits. Tg. נור, "clearing, ploughed-over land" (M. Jastrow, *Dictionary of the Targum* [New York: Pardes, 1950] 909). Wildberger (1295) remarks that neither seems to have understood the Heb.

Form/Structure/Setting

Vv 7–8 portray the worsening situation. Efforts at compromise and peace have failed. The challenge for combat has been given. V 9 is the sad reaction. In v 10 YHWH intervenes. The background situation is very near that of episode A but lacks the narrow focus on Jerusalem.

Comment

7 אראל, "valiant one," is a champion put forward in challenge, like Goliath of the Philistines. The Hebrew word is related to "Ariel" (see *Note* 7.a. and cf. the discussion in 29:1). The military figure has taken the place of the diplomats, "messengers of peace," who lament the failure of their efforts.

8 The impending war has emptied the highways of commercial traffic. With a treaty broken and legal procedures being ignored, violent confrontation with no regard for life or limb is the order of the day.

9 The whole land reflects the sorry situation. Commerce, agriculture, and even nature itself stand still. Normal life and growth have ceased, as is usual in war.

10 At this point YHWH determines to intervene.

11 He begins by telling the belligerents how foolish is their action. It is a fire that will consume all of them. A war begun in order to gain an advantage has become a curse of death on the very ones who initiated it. How often that is true!

12 משׂרפות שיד, "burnt lime." It is not clear whether skeletons are burned to extract lime (as in Amos 2:1) or whether lime is poured over the bodies as they are burnt up (see W. E. Staples, "Lime," *IDB* 3:134). The ignominious deaths during such catastrophes cause people to be treated like thorn bushes, to be cut down and burnt up with no respect for human dignity or worth.

Explanation

This description of that ancient crisis in which negotiations gave way to military confrontation with its horrible results has a chillingly modern ring to it. Things have not changed very much. The effects of the war announcement are shown in v 8. The appalled reaction of everyone and everything is pictured in v 9, God's incensed arousal in v 10, his rebuke in v 11, and his prediction in v 12. The emotional spirit of anger in such a situation is like a spark in a powder keg.

Who Can Survive the Fire? (33:13–24)

Bibliography

Holmgren, H. R. III. "Does Isaiah 33:23 Address Israel or Israel's Enemy?" *BS* 152 (1995) 273–78. **Koch, K.** "Tempeleinlassliturgien und Dekaloge." In *Studien zur Theologie der alttestamentlichen Überlieferungen.* FS G. von Rad, ed. K. Rendtorff and K. Koch. Neukirchen-Vluyn: Neukirchener Verlag, 1961. 45–60. **Steingrimsson, S. Ö.** *Tor der Gerechtigkeit: Eine literaturwissenschaftliche Untersuchung der sogenannte Einzugliturgien im AT: Ps 15; 24,3–5 und Jes 33,14–16.* ATS 22. St. Ottilien: EOS-Verlag, 1984.

Translation

YHWH:	13 *You that are far off, hear*[a]	2+2
	what I have done!	
	You that are near, know[b]	2+1
	my might!	
Chorus:	14 *Sinners in Zion are afraid;*[a]	3+3
	a trembling has seized[a] *the godless.*	
	Who among us can dwell indefinitely[b]	3+2
	(with) devouring fire?	
	Who among us can dwell indefinitely	3+2
	(with) everlasting burnings?[c]	
Teacher:	15 *One walking (with) righteous acts,*	2+2
	one speaking upright things,	
	one despising gain from acts of oppression,	3+4,
	one shaking his hands so as not to hold a bribe,	
	one stopping his ears so as not to consent to[a] *bloodshed,*	4+4
	one shutting his eyes so as not to favor[b] *evil—*	
	16 *only that one will dwell in the heights.*	3+3
	Rock fortresses[a] *(will be) his defense.*	
	His bread will be provided.	2+2
	His water will be assured.	
Heavens:	17 *Your [sg.] eyes will envision a king in his beauty.*	4+3+3
	They will see a land[a] *of great distances.*[b]	

18 *Your [sg.] mind*[a] *will muse on terror:*[b]
Where is the counter? 2+2+3
Where is the weigher?
Where is the one who counts the forts?
Earth: 19 *The barbarous*[a] *people* 2+2
you [sg.] will see no more,
the people of speech too obscure to hear, 4+4
a stammering tongue that none could understand.
Heavens: 20 *Envision [sg.] Zion:* 2+2
a city of festival gatherings.[a]
Your [sg.] eyes will see Jerusalem: 3+2
a quiet habitation,
a tent one will never pack up,[b] 2+4+4
whose stakes one will never again pull up,[c]
none of whose cords will be broken.
Earth: 21 *But rather there*[a] 2+3
YHWH abides[b] *in majesty!*
A place of rivers, 2+3
streams broad of span
on which no boat moves with oars,[c] 4+4
through which no majestic ship passes.
Chorus: 22 *Indeed YHWH will be our judge.* 3+2
YHWH, our commander.
YHWH, our king. 2+2
He will be our savior.
Heavens: 23 *Your [f. sg.]*[a] *apportionments*[b] *are released.* 2+2+2
They[c] *cannot reinforce the pedestal of their*[c] *standard;*[d]
they[c] *cannot spread a flag.*[e]
Earth: *At that time it will be divided* 2+2+3
until (there is) spoil aplenty.
(Even) the lame will get their share of plunder.
Heavens: 24 *No inhabitant will complain* 3+1
"I am sick!"
The people dwelling in it [f. sg.] 3+2
will be forgiven (any) guilt.

Notes

13.a. *BHS* suggests 1QIsa[a] has a pf. instead of an impv., only a change of vowel. This only because of *Note* 13.b. below. 1QIsa[a] has no vowels. LXX ἀκούσονται, "they will hear," supports the identification as pf.

13.b. 1QIsa[a] ידעו, "they know," for MT ודעו impv., "know ye." Yet MT makes sense and should be kept in both instances (cf. Wildberger, 1295; Irwin, "Isaiah 28–33," 148).

14.a. Irwin ("Isaiah 28–33," 149) treats both verbs as precative pfs. to be translated as impvs., but the indic. sense is fitting and has been kept here.

14.b. יגור, "dwell indefinitely" (BDB, *DCH* "sojourn"; *HAL* "dwell as alien"), is translated "find protection" by Wildberger (1293) while Irwin ("Isaiah 28–33," 149) falls back on the AV's "abide."

14.c. מוקדי, "burnings," occurs only here, in Ps 102:4 (3), and perhaps in Lev 6:2. BDB and *DCH* "burning masses"; *HAL* and *DCH* "hearths." Wildberger (1295) thinks of the altar for burnt offerings in the temple. Irwin ("Isaiah 28–33," 150) translates "braziers."

15.a. Lit. "from hearing deeds of bloodshed." Irwin ("Isaiah 28–33," 151) points to BDB (1034) to note that שמע also means "consent" and should be translated here "not to consent to bloodshed."

15.b. Irwin ("Isaiah 28–33," 151) remarks that ראה ב may mean "look favorably on" (BDB, 908).

16.a. MT מצדות, "fortresses." LXX σπηλαίῳ, "a cave." Wildberger (1296) correctly notes that מצד is a place that is difficult to get to or attack. Irwin ("Isaiah 28–33," 152) points out Psalm parallels that picture YHWH's abode as both a mountain and a fortress.

17.a. Irwin's translation ("Isaiah 28–33," 153) of ארץ as "city" is pushing a legitimate identification of city and city-state much too far. The Vision has made a sharp distinction between עיר, "city," and ארץ, "land."

17.b. Irwin ("Isaiah 28–33," 154) agrees with Gunkel ("Jes 33, eine prophetische Liturgie," *ZAW* 42 [1924] 179) on the meaning "distant" rather than "broad." That meaning is more likely than Gunkel's emendation to מחמדים, "delightful" *(HAL)*. Irwin lists parallels where ארץ מרחקים always means distant city/land: Isa 13:5; 46:11; Jer 4:16; 6:20; Prov 25:25. He thinks it refers here to the distant heavenly Zion.

18.a. Lit. "heart."

18.b. אימה, "terror." The interpretation of this word determines the meaning of v 18. If it is "terror," it means "the former terror" (NIV), "frightful memories" *(HAL)*. If, however, one translates, with Irwin ("Isaiah 28–33," 155), "awesome sight," it refers to the envisioned Holy City. To get this he reads אֲיֻמָּה from אָיֹם (BDB, 33), which occurs only in Hab 1:7 and Song 6:4, 10 in this meaning. MT's more usual form אֵימָה apparently always means "terror" (BDB, *DCH*). The issue turns on whether one translates v 18 to fit v 17 or v 19. Most translators have done the latter; Irwin and NJPS the former. I do the former here but discuss both in *Comment.*

19.a. נוֹעָז is a *hap. leg.*, which must be a *nip'al* ptc. The dictionaries derive it from יעז, "barbarous" (BDB), "insolent" *(HAL, DCH)*. Wildberger (1310) derives it from עזז, "be strong" (BDB, 738), possibly also meaning "insolent" or "defiant." Irwin ("Isaiah 28–33," 157) compares Ps 114:1 and Isa 25:3 and relates to יעז, which he calls a by-root of עזז (cf. *HAL*). He translates with BDB: "barbarous." *BHS* לועז follows H. Ewald's emendation (*Commentary on the Prophets of the Old Testament,* trans. J. F. Smith [London: Williams & Norgate, 1875–81] 1:476), referring to Ps 114:1, but this is now unnecessary.

20.a. MT מועדנו (sg.), "our appointed festival, assembly," which Irwin ("Isaiah 28–33," 158) defends as referring to the heavenly assembly, in line with his interpretation of previous verses. 1QIsa[a] and the versions read מועדינו pl., "our festivals or assemblies," which fits an understanding of a restored Jerusalem with its annual pilgrimage festivals.

20.b. יצען is a *hap. leg.* BDB translates "wander, travel"; *HAL* "pack up, break off."

20.c. MT יִסַּע, "plucked up." Several versions read a pass., such as יִסָּע. *BHS* suggests יסעו, a pl., to fit the subject. All are possible, but MT is to be kept.

21.a. שם, "there." Irwin ("Isaiah 28–33," 158) identifies it with *šumma* of the El Amarna tablets (cf. W. L. Moran, "Amarna *šumma* in Main Clauses," *JCS* 7 [1953] 78–80) and translates "look upon." For other bibliography, see Irwin and *HAL*, which calls this translation "not at all convincing."

21.b. לָנוּ, "for us." The word can also be a 3 m. pl. pf. from לון, "lodge, abide." This would fit the contrast to v 20. A problem lies in its pl. form. But if the divine subject could be seen as sufficient to account for that, its meaning would be clear. Otherwise one could transfer *vav* to the following word, leaving לן, "he abides."

21.c. אֳנִי־שַׁיִט, "a rowboat." But שיט is found only here and K of 28:15. 1QIsa[a] reads שט, which P. Wernburg-Møller ("Defective Spellings in the Isaiah Scroll," *JSS* 3 [1958] 262) understands to be a ptc. The parallel to צי אדיר, "stately ship," has led to the translation "galley," a big rowboat indeed, even if a bit ridiculous for an inland city like Jerusalem.

23.a. The suf. is fem. sg. This usually refers to Zion, as it does here (cf. v 24*b*). Tg. and *BHS* have missed the point.

23.b. חבל can mean "cord, band" (BDB, 286) and is often connected with the nautical picture in v 21 to read "tackle," but a second word with the same letters means "pain, pang." Another meaning of the first usage is "a measured portion, lot."

23.c. The 3 pl. "they" must refer to the foreign rulers of the city.

23.d. תרן, "standard," means a pole (BDB, 1076). If the nautical imagery is used, it is the "mast" *(HAL)*. For the flag, it is the "flagpole."

23.e. נס, "flag," has been translated "sail" in the nautical image, but it is the symbol of authority.

Form/Structure/Setting

YHWH challenges those near and far to "hear" and "know" (v 13). The rest of the episode responds to that challenge, assessing what the results of God's intervention and rebuke will be. Vv 14–16 reflect on the tension inherent in "dwelling with the devouring fire," that is, in depending on and worshiping YHWH, who in his holiness is understood to devour whole nations. Vv 17–19: Jerusalem is called to imagine what life will be like without the reminders of the distant imperial liege-lord, without the terrors of secret police, tax collectors, or strangers with foreign accents, who for more than a century had ruled over them.

Vv 20–22: In a different frame of mind, Jerusalem is called to think of herself as a city preparing for a festival in honor of YHWH.

Vv 23–24 return to the political and economic results following the withdrawal of the emperor's representatives.

The historical setting is the period that ended effective Assyrian administration of Judah. The last decades of Assyrian suzerainty were chaotic. Babylon turned back an Assyrian army in 626 B.C.E. Scythian invasions of Palestine during the following decade cloud the picture. Historians have had difficulty determining whose side Egypt was on in these struggles between Babylon and Assyria between 626 and 609 B.C.E. If this is true at this distance, how much more confusing must it have been for those living at that time? (See *Excursus: The Era ca. 640–587 B.C.E.* in the introduction to act 3.)

Comment

13 YHWH's challenge sounds like one that would be heard during the celebration of his reign in Zion's temple.

14 חנפים/חטאים, "sinners/godless," point to those who have turned away from YHWH during the times when foreign powers (and gods?) were in charge of things. They include outright idolaters who worshiped Assyrian deities, those who became indifferent to YHWH worship, and those who took advantage of the uncertainty to ignore all laws of justice and decency. They had good reason to tremble at the thought that YHWH and Yahwism would dominate Jerusalem. They see in YHWH only the "devouring fire"/"the everlasting burnings." For the sinner and the rebel it could not be otherwise. They cannot abide in the presence of the deity (cf. 66:24).

That YHWH is אש אוכלה, "a devouring fire," is understood throughout the OT as a symbol of his holiness. The destructive aspect of deity was first faced by Abraham on Moriah (Gen 22). Then Moses wrestled with the issue on Sinai (Exod 19–34). The liturgies used when entering the temple, where one experienced the presence of the holy God, dealt with it (Pss 15; 24:3–6). The answer given here may be compared to the Psalms. The essence of worship is to recognize the gift of his mercy, which makes it possible and even desirable to live in near contact with the Holy One.

15 God has chosen the kind of persons he wants to dwell with him: those doing "righteous acts" and speaking "upright things," those having nothing to do with "oppression" or "a bribe," and those who avoid violence or "evil." What separates a person from God is not finite vulnerability to his holy fire but incompatibility in terms of character and commitment. It is the sinner and the godless who cannot abide God's presence, not the human penitent and worshiper who follows God's principles in life.

16 One so committed and of such character is welcome to "the heights," be they of Zion or of what it represents as God's dwelling place. God will be that person's defense and provide for his or her needs.

17 "Your" is masculine singular, apparently addressing the individual worshiper. The vision set before him deals with anticipated realities in government and society. מלך ביפיו, "a king in his beauty," means one in his official royal regalia. It does not define what (or what kind of) king. It brings to mind a Judean king who can in his own dignity and worth appear before the people as his own person—not simply a vassal puppet of some other power. Judah achieved such a status for a brief period under Josiah. ארץ מרחקים, "a land of great distances," describes an enlarged area under the control of the crown. This, too, was Judah's experience under Josiah.

18 The terror will only be a memory, defined by experiences with "the counter" and "the weigher" in the humiliating routine of collecting taxes and with the military supervisor of forts, who kept a watchful eye to see that Judah's forces were able to join Assyrian expeditions when ordered to do so but were not so strong as to encourage dreams of rebellion. The vision of the new time makes the presence of foreigners, military and civilian officials and observers, with their strange accents and obscure speech, only a memory.

20 The worshiper is challenged to "envision Zion" after the withdrawal of the Assyrians: a city of stability and permanence where the quiet is interrupted only by its festivals.

21 It will be a city known by YHWH's presence celebrated in "majesty." אדיר, "a place of rivers," is a metaphor with no real counterpart in Jerusalem. Rivers are symbols of prosperity, smooth in contrast to the ocean's waves. The absence of boats with oars and majestic ships contrasts it to the Nile and the Euphrates, where imperial naval ships and royal barges are found. Their absence symbolizes the return of Jerusalem to the status of a small, landlocked country with no need of such.

22 Not the emperor but YHWH will be "judge," "commander," "king," and "savior." The city apparently returns to the status of Israel before Saul was made king, when Samuel could protest "YHWH was your king" (1 Sam 12:12*b*).

The Vision has noted the destruction of "all the land," including the kingdoms of Israel and Judah. But chap. 6 had allowed the prophet a view of YHWH as the king over all. Postexilic Israel will have no king and no kingdom, but it will be able to address YHWH as king and acknowledge his beneficent rule over them. That is exactly what they do in this verse.

23 "Your" is feminine singular, referring to the city. "Lot" or "apportionment" is the normal reading of the Hebrew word חבל. Wildberger (1318) follows others in other meanings to fit a presumed Egyptian setting for the previous verse. But boats/ships are not the dominating motif here. Recognizing YHWH as king, judge, commander, and savior in place of the emperor called for a new political and economic order. With tax collectors gone (v 18), new economic arrangements had to be made at all levels. "Apportionments" applies to the fields that are assigned peasants to work for a period. It applies to the assignment of lands that belong to the crown and to permits to do business in the cities. Now that the Assyrian overlord is no longer present, many changes are called for. The Assyrians can no longer enforce their authority or defend their flag. The fact that the military and police officials are already gone means that the civilian apparatus must soon follow. When they are gone, "it" (the apportionments) will be divided up again. There will be jobs and privileges and land, "spoil aplenty" to be divided by the new ruler. Obviously, hometown people will get their share of things that foreigners and their lackeys had enjoyed before. "Even the lame will get their share."

24 None will be sick on that day, or disadvantaged in the division of spoils. There will be a general amnesty for past crimes to celebrate the return of freedom.

Explanation

The episode is an illustration of the close relation between religion and politics in ancient Judah. The event described is political. Assyria must relinquish sovereignty over the city, along with all the privileges that this entailed. But the result is described in terms of YHWH's reoccupation of the city, its defense, and its economic structure.

The episode is also consistent with the Vision's position. The future for Jerusalem and for Israel will not include the reconstitution of the Davidic kingdom. It will bring recognition that YHWH is present in Jerusalem and may be worshiped there. "Indeed YHWH will be . . . our king . . . our savior!" (v 22).